FUNK & WAGNALLS
NEW ENCYCLOPEDIA

fw

VOLUME 12
GREELEY to
HORTHY

FUNK & WAGNALLS NEW ENCYCLOPEDIA

JOSEPH LAFFAN MORSE, Sc.B., LL.B., L.H.D., LL.D.
Editor in Chief, Funk & Wagnalls Encyclopedias, 1946–69
WILLIAM H. HENDELSON, Editorial Director,
and successor Editor in Chief

Funk & Wagnalls, Inc., New York

Funk & Wagnalls
New Encyclopedia
© 1973
By Funk & Wagnalls, Inc.

Library of Congress Catalog
Card Number 72–170933

Copyright Under the Articles of the Copyright Convention
of the Pan-American Republics and the United States

**PRINTED IN THE UNITED STATES OF AMERICA
ALL RIGHTS RESERVED**

mgb

FUNK & WAGNALLS
NEW ENCYCLOPEDIA

LIST OF ABBREVIATIONS USED IN THE TEXT*

abbr.	abbreviated	fr.	from	O.T.	Old Testament
AC; a-c	alternating current	Fr.	French	oz.	ounce
A.D.	anno Domini (Medieval Lat., in the year of the Lord)	ft.	foot	P.M.	*post meridiem* (Lat., after noon)
		g	gram		
		Gael.	Gaelic	Pol.	Polish
		gal.	gallon	pop.	population
alt.	altitude	Ger.	German	Port.	Portuguese
A.M.	*ante meridiem* (Lat., before noon)	Gr.	Greek	prelim.	preliminary
		Heb.	Hebrew	pron.	pronounced
AM	amplitude modulation	Hind.	Hindustani	q.v.	*quod vide* (Lat., which see)**
amu	atomic mass unit	h.p.	horsepower		
anc.	ancient	hr.	hour	r.	reigned
Ar.	Arabic	Hung.	Hungarian	R.	River
AS.	Anglo-Saxon	Hz	hertz or cycles per second	rev.	revised, revision
A.S.S.R.	Autonomous Soviet Socialist Republic			R.R.	railroad
		I.	Island	Rum.	Rumanian
at.no.	atomic number	i.e.	*id est* (Lat., that is)	Russ.	Russian
at.wt.	atomic weight	in.	inch	Ry.	railway
b.	born	Ind.	Indian	S.	south; southern
bbl	barrel	Ir.	Irish	sec.	second
B.C.	before Christ	It.	Italian	S.F.S.R.	Soviet Federated Socialist Republic
bd.ft.	board feet	K.	Kelvin		
bev	billion electron volts	kg	kilogram	Skr.	Sanskrit
		km	kilometer	Sp.	Spanish
b.p.	boiling point	kw	kilowatt	sp.gr.	specific gravity
B.T.U.	British Thermal Unit	kw hour	kilowatt hour	sq.	square
		lat.	latitude	sq.mi.	square mile
bu.	bushel	Lat.	Latin	S.S.R.	Soviet Socialist Republic
Bulg.	Bulgarian	lb.	pound		
C.	centigrade	long.	longitude	St.; Ste.	Saint
cent.	century	m	meter	Sum.	Sumerian
Chin.	Chinese	M.	Middle	Sw.	Swedish
cm	centimeter	mev	million electron volts	temp.	temperature
Co.	County			trans.	translation
colloq.	colloquial	mg	milligram	Turk.	Turkish
cu.	cubic	mi.	mile	U.A.R.	United Arab Republic
Czech.	Czechoslovakian	min.	minute		
d.	died	M.L.	Medieval Latin	U.K.	United Kingdom
Dan.	Danish	mm	millimeter	U.N.	United Nations
DC; d-c	direct current	mod.	modern	U.S.	United States
Du.	Dutch	m.p.	melting point	U.S.A.	United States of America
E.	east; eastern	m.p.h.	miles per hour		
ed.	edition; editor	Mt(s).	Mount, Mountain	U.S.S.R.	Union of Soviet Socialist Republics
Egypt.	Egyptian	N.	north; northern		
Eng.	English	N.T.	New Testament		
est.	estimated	OE.	Old English	var.	variant
ev	electron volt	OF.	Old French	vol.	volume
F.	Fahrenheit	OHG.	Old High German	vs.	versus or against
fl.	flourished	ON.	Old Norse	W.	west; western
FM	frequency modulation	ONF.	Old Norman French	yd.	yard

* For a more extensive listing of abbreviations, widely used by authoritative sources in many fields, see ABBREVIATION. Charts of pertinent abbreviations also accompany the articles BIBLE, CANON OF THE; DEGREE, ACADEMIC; ELEMENTS, CHEMICAL; MATHEMATICAL SYMBOLS; WEIGHTS AND MEASURES. Accent marks and special letters are explained in the article DIACRITIC MARK.

** The abbreviation (q.v.) stands for the Latin words "quod vide," meaning "which see". The placement of this abbreviation after a word—or a name or term—indicates that the word itself is the title of a separate article in the encyclopedia. By looking up the article on this word, or the entries on each word in a series that is followed by the plural form (qq.v.) of the abbreviation, the reader will find specific information about the words used as well as additional data about the main topic of the article he is reading.

FUNK & WAGNALLS NEW ENCYCLOPEDIA

GREELEY, city in Colorado, and county seat of Weld Co., on the Cache la Poudre R., 52 miles N.E. of Denver, at an altitude of 4637 ft. above sea level. It is served by railroads, and is the center and shipping point of a farming and coalmining region. The principal industries in the city are flour milling and the refining of beet sugar. Greeley is the site of the Colorado State College, established in 1889. The city was founded in 1870 by a group of settlers from New England and New York under the leadership of the American colonizer and journalist Nathan Cook Meeker (1817–79). Known as the Union Colonists, the group organized for the purpose of establishing a colony in Colorado, and were sponsored by the American journalist Horace Greeley (q.v.), for whom the city is named. Greeley was incorporated as a city in 1885. Pop. (1960) 26,314; (1970) 38,902.

GREELEY, Horace (1811–72), American journalist and political leader, born in Amherst, N.H. He was apprenticed in 1825 to a printer in East Poultney, Vt., and became an itinerant journeyman printer four years later.

In 1831 Greeley settled in New York City, where he became editor successively of the *New Yorker,* the *Jeffersonian,* and the *Log Cabin,* rapidly gaining a reputation as an influential political writer. He also became associated with the Whig leaders Governor William Seward (q.v.) of New York and the journalist Thurlow Weed (1797–1882), with whom he worked in behalf of progressive governmental policies.

In order to serve the Whig cause with a low-priced newspaper that would avoid the sensationalism of the New York *Herald* and the academic detachment of the New York *Evening Post,* Greeley in 1841 founded the New York *Tribune.* It met with immediate success and Greeley remained its editor for thirty-one years. During this period he opposed unequal distribution of wealth, denounced monopoly, and attacked the preemption of public lands by the railroads and speculators. He advocated a protective tariff, the development of agriculture, and migration to the west; his advice to a Congregational clergyman, who had lost his voice and had to leave the ministry, to build his future in the west, widely popularized the phrase of the Indiana newspaperman John Soule (1815–91), "go west, young man". For a time Greeley was sympathetic to the ideas of such utopian socialists as the French philosopher François Marie Charles Fourier and the British social reformer Robert Owen (qq.v.), and to those of the English Chartists (*see* CHARTISM). For several years, Greeley employed the German revolutionist Karl Marx (q.v.) as a European correspondent, publishing dispatches which later became famous as classics of Marxian socialism.

Although opposed to the abolitionists (q.v.), who denounced him as a conservative, Greeley was unequivocally opposed to slavery. He opposed the Mexican War because he saw it as a plot conceived by slave-owners, and for the same reason, he urged rejection of the Kansas-Nebraska Act (q.v.). His increasing preoccupation with these issues led him, in 1854, to break his ties with Seward and Weed.

In 1856, and again in 1860, Greeley attended the national conventions of the Republican Party; in the latter year, he was influential in bringing about the nomination of Abraham Lincoln (q.v.) for President. Believing at first that the South should be allowed to secede if a majority of its inhabitants voted to do so, Greeley later urged that the Southern States be compelled by force to abide by the decision of the national electorate and its government under Lincoln. He urged vigorous prosecution of the American Civil War and frequently criticized Lincoln's hesitation to free the slaves.

After the war, he urged a general amnesty,

thus antagonizing the Republican Party; and his proposal of unrestricted universal suffrage to form a basis of reconstruction (q.v.) in the South pleased neither side. Greeley provoked great anger in the North and alienated many erstwhile admirers when he signed a bail bond for Jefferson Davis (q.v.), leader of the defeated Confederacy, whose long imprisonment he held to be a violation of constitutional rights.

Later holding that the administration of President Ulysses Simpson Grant (q.v.) was corrupt,

Horace Greeley

Greeley, in 1872, accepted the nomination for President by the dissident Liberal Republican Party. He was subsequently endorsed by the Democrats, but was defeated by Grant in the election. Thereafter his health failed and he took little part in the *Tribune* editorship.

Greeley's published works are chiefly collections of his editorials, speeches, and lectures. They include *Hints toward Reforms* (1850), *A History of the Struggle for Slavery Extension or Restriction* (1856), *The Overland Journey to California* (1860), *The American Conflict* (2 vol., 1864–66), and *Recollections of a Busy Life* (autobiography, 1868).

GREELY, Adolphus Washington (1844–1935), American arctic explorer and army officer, born in Newburyport, Mass. After participating as a volunteer with the Union forces during the American Civil War, he entered the regular army in 1867. He was subsequently appointed to the signal service and from 1876 until 1879 supervised the erection of 2000 mi. of telegraph line in Texas, the Dakotas, and Montana. In 1881 he became commander of a United States expedition to establish one of a chain of thirteen circumpolar meteorological stations recommended by the International Geographical Congress in 1879. His expedition discovered new territories north of Greenland and several members of the group reached 83°24′ N. lat., the northernmost point attained to that date. Relief parties sent out during 1882 and 1883 failed to reach the expedition, and during the winter of 1883 all of the party except Greely and six of his men died. In the spring of 1884 survivors were rescued by Commander Winfield Scott Schley (q.v.) of the United States Navy. For his service in the arctic Greely was awarded the Founder's Medal of the Royal Geographical Society. In 1887 he was made chief signal officer and brigadier general, becoming the first volunteer and enlisted man in the United States Army to attain that rank. During the Spanish-American War he was in charge of constructing telegraph lines and establishing communications in Puerto Rico, China, Cuba, and the Philippines. He was later given a similar commission in Alaska, establishing the first wireless stations in the territory. Greely supervised relief operations in San Francisco after the earthquake of 1906. In that year he was promoted to major general, and in 1908 he retired from the army. He wrote *Three Years of Arctic Service* (2 vol., 1885), *Handbook of Alaska* (1912), and *The Polar Regions in the Twentieth Century* (1928).

GREEN, river of Wyoming and Utah, rising in western Wyoming, and flowing s. and E. through the N.W. corner of Colorado into Utah. There, after a southerly course, it unites with the Colorado R. in San Juan County. One of the principal headstreams of the Colorado R., the Green R. is 730 mi. long. In N.E. Utah and N.W. Colorado the river flows through the Dinosaur National Monument (q.v.). At the site of the monument the river is noted for the scenic beauty of its canyons.

GREEN, Bartholomew (1666–1732), American printer and publisher, born in Cambridge, Mass. He succeeded to the printing business of his father, Samuel Green (1615–1702) in 1692, and moved the business from Cambridge to Boston. He subsequently became the foremost printer in New England. Green printed the first American newspaper, the *Boston News-Letter* (q.v.), from 1704 to 1707, and again from 1711 until his death. In 1723 he also became publisher of the paper, which became known for its independent and original thinking on politics and religion.

GREEN, Julian (1900–), American novelist, born in Paris, France, of American parents. His education at the University of Virginia was interrupted by service with the French army in World War I. He settled in Paris to study painting and music before establishing himself as a writer. His novels, written in French, show a preoccupation with the forces of evil and abnormal psychology. The novels that have been translated into English include *Adrienne Mésurat* (1927; Eng. trans., *The Closed Garden*, 1928); *Léviathan* (1929; Eng. trans., *The Dark Journey*, 1929); and *Partir Avant le Jour* (1963; Eng. trans., *To Leave Before Dawn*, 1967). He also wrote the plays *Sud* (1953; Eng. trans., *South*, 1955) and *L'Ennemi* (1954; Eng. trans., *The Enemy*, 1954). His only work written in English, *Memories of Happy Days* (1942), consists of personal recollections.

In 1971 he became the first non-French member of the French Academy.

GREEN, Paul Eliot (1894–), American playwright, born in Lillington, N.C., and educated at the University of North Carolina and Cornell University. He began his career as a playwright with the Carolina Playmakers, writing a number of one-act plays about conditions among Southern Negroes. In 1927 he was awarded a Pulitzer Prize for his play *In Abraham's Bosom*. His full-length plays about Southern life include *The Field God* (1927), *Tread the Green Grass* (1928), *The House of Connelly* (1931), and those in *Five Plays of the South* (1963). *The Lost Colony* (1937), a pageant concerning the colonial life of Roanoke Island, is produced there annually. His other books include collections of short stories, *Wide Fields* (1928) and *Dog on the Sun* (1949); a novel, *This Body the Earth* (1935); and collections of essays, *The Hawthorn Tree* (1943), and *Drama and the Weather* (1958).

GREEN, Thomas Hill (1836–82), British philosopher and educator, born in Birkin, Yorkshire, England, educated at Rugby and the University of Oxford. He taught at Oxford from 1860 until his death, initially as a fellow and after 1878 as Whyte Professor of Moral Philosophy.

A disciple of the German philosopher George Wilhelm Friedrich Hegel (q.v.), Green led the revolt against empiricism (q.v.), the dominant philosophy in Great Britain during the latter part of the 19th century. The empiricists reasoned that knowledge is impossible to achieve and that conduct has no ethical significance; Green, however, insisted that consciousness provides the necessary basis for both knowledge and morality. He argued that man's highest good is self-realization and that the individual can achieve self-realization only in society. Society has an obligation in turn, he held, to provide for the good of all its members. The political implications of his philosophy laid the basis for sweeping social-reform legislation in Great Britain. In addition to being the most influential British philosopher of his time, Green was a vigorous champion of popular education, temperance, and political liberalism. His writings include *Prolegomena to Ethics* (posthumously published, 1883) and *Lectures on the Principles of Political Obligation* (posthumously published, 1895).

GREEN, William (1873–1952), American labor leader, born in Coshocton, Ohio. After receiving a public-school education, he worked in the bituminous-coal mines of Ohio. He became a

William Green (seated at left) conferring in December, 1932, with President-elect Franklin Delano Roosevelt. Standing are Joseph N. Weber (left) and Matthew Woll, officials of the American Federation of Labor. UPI

GREEN ALGAE

member of the United Mine Workers of America (q.v.) in 1890. From 1900 to 1906 he was president of one of the subdistricts of the U.M.W., and for the following four years was president of the Ohio district. From 1912 to 1924 he was secretary-treasurer of the entire union. In 1913 Green was appointed to the Executive Council of the American Federation of Labor, and in 1924 he succeeded Samuel Gompers (q.v.) as president of the A.F.L., a position he held until his death.

During the struggle in the A.F.L. in 1935–36 over the organization of the unorganized workers in the basic industries of the United States, Green opposed the Committee on Industrial Organization established in the A.F.L. by a number of labor leaders, including John Llewellyn Lewis (q.v.), president of the United Mine Workers; see AMERICAN FEDERATION OF LABOR AND CONGRESS OF INDUSTRIAL ORGANIZATIONS. In the course of the bitter feud which ensued Lewis had Green expelled from the U.M.W.

From 1910 to 1913 Green served two terms as Democrat in the Ohio State senate. As a State senator he secured passage of the Ohio Workmen's Compensation Law, subsequently used as a model in other States, and other measures beneficial to labor. He was a delegate to the Democratic National Conventions of 1912, 1920, and 1924. Green was also a member of several Federal government bodies, including the Labor Advisory Council of the National Recovery Administration, in 1935–37. During those years he was also a member of the governing board of the International Labor Organization (q.v.), at that time an agency of the League of Nations.

GREEN ALGAE. *See* ALGAE; CHLOROPHYCEAE.

GREENAWAY, Kate (1846–1901), British artist, born in London, England, and educated at the Slade School. She exhibited her water-color drawings at the Dudley Gallery, London, in 1868. She drew the illustrations for the children's book, *Little Folks*, in 1873, and began to draw for the *Illustrated London News* in 1877. In the following years she illustrated such commercially successful books as *Mother Goose*, *Under the Window*, *The Birthday Book*, and *Little Ann*. Kate Greenaway's work featured a revival of the fashions in children's clothes dating from the beginning of the 19th century and had great influence on the style of children's clothes in her own day.

GREENBACK, popular name for the paper currency issued by the Federal government during the Civil War (*see* CIVIL WAR, THE AMERICAN) to facilitate the payment of war expenses; it was so called because the reverse side of each note was printed in green ink. This action by the government constituted the first issue of legal-tender notes since the adoption of the Constitution of the United States (q.v.) in 1787. The law authorizing this currency, passed in February, 1862, provided for an issue in the amount of $150,000,000. Further issues totaling $300,000,000 were authorized in July, 1862, and March, 1863.

The greenbacks were not backed by gold reserves and their market value began to depreciate almost immediately after issuance. Thus, they contributed to a sharp inflation of the entire economy. In 1866 an act was passed which provided for the gradual retirement of the greenbacks. It was repealed two years later, however, and the notes continued to circulate without gold-reserve backing until 1879. In that year, when the amount of greenback currency in circulation was about $347,000,000, the greenbacks were made redeemable in gold; thereafter they circulated on the same basis as all other forms of legal tender. *See* GREENBACK-LABOR PARTY; GREENBACK PARTY.

GREENBACK-LABOR PARTY, in United States history, popular name for the National Party, a political party organized in 1878 by workers and farmers as a means of relieving their economic difficulties resulting from the depression of the 1870's. The party was formed by greenbackers, members of the defunct Greenback Party (q.v.), and by the members of a number of labor organizations. The Greenbackers sought labor support for their program, which called for the issuance of the greenback (q.v.), or paper currency not backed by gold, and the initiation of a monetary policy based on bimetallism (q.v.); the labor groups desired greenbacker support for their demands, which included a reduction in working hours, the establishment of a labor bureau in the Federal government, and the curtailment of Chinese immigration, which was viewed as a cause of lowered wages. At its first national convention, held in Toledo, Ohio, in February, 1878, each element within the party pledged to support the demands of the other.

The Congressional elections of 1878 marked the height of power of the Greenback-Labor Party, which polled about 1,000,000 votes and elected fourteen representatives to Congress. In the following year, economic conditions in the nation improved, and interest in politics among the workers and farmers decreased. The 1880 convention of the party, held in Chicago, Ill., nominated Iowa Congressman James Baird Weaver (1833–1912) for the Presidency. In the election he received only 308,578 votes, but eight Greenback-Labor candidates were elected to Congress. In ensuing years the party continued to decline. Its last national campaign was conducted for the elections of 1884, in which its Presidential candidate, the American Civil War general Benjamin Franklin Butler (q.v.) won 175,370 votes. Soon afterward the Greenback-Labor Party passed out of existence; it was succeeded in the 1890's by the Populist Party (see POPULISM).

GREENBACK PARTY, in United States history, a political party formed in 1875, chiefly by middle western and southern farmers. The primary aims of the party were the adoption of a national monetary policy based on bimetallism (q.v.) and Federal issuance of paper currency not backed by gold. The name of the party was derived from the popular name for this currency, greenback (q.v.), and its members were called Greenbackers.

The party was organized as a result of the depression of the early 1870's, when the indebtedness of farmers to merchants and banks was rising and the prices of farm products were declining. The farmers believed that the adoption of the measures they advocated would result in general prosperity for the nation, and would at the same time enable them to pay off their debts and to raise the prices of their products.

The Greenbackers decided on the formation of an independent party late in 1874, after they failed to persuade the Democratic Party to adopt their views. The first national convention of the Greenback Party was held in Indianapolis, Ind., in 1876, and Peter Cooper (q.v.), a manufacturer and philanthropist, was nominated for the Presidency. Cooper received 81,737 popular votes, but no electoral votes in the election held that year. Two years later the Greenback Party dissolved, and its farmer-members united with workers to form the Greenback-Labor Party (q.v.).

GREEN BAY, city and port of entry in Wisconsin, and county seat of Brown Co., at the S. tip of Green Bay, an arm of Lake Michigan, and at the mouth of the Fox R., 114 miles N. of Milwaukee. The surrounding area is noted for lumbering, farming, and dairying. Green Bay is served by railroads and by lake and river steamers; a county airport is on the outskirts of the city. The Green Bay harbor is one of the finest on the Great Lakes (q.v.), with extensive dock facilities for accommodating a large trade in coal and paper pulp. The city ranks second only to Milwaukee in importance as a distributing, wholesale, and jobbing center in Wisconsin, and is the largest United States center for the processing and shipping of cheese. It is also noted for the manufacture of paper, canned foodstuffs, paper-mill machinery, lumber and woodwork, brick and tile, precision machinery, power shovels, cranes, and automobile parts. The city has steel plants, railroad shops, cold-storage plants, warehouses, breweries, fisheries, and a shipyard. It is also the home of the well-known professional football team, the Green Bay Packers of the National Football League. Within Green Bay are eighteen municipal parks covering 400 acres. Among interesting buildings in the city are Tank Cottage (about 1775), said to be the oldest house still standing in the State, and the Neville Museum, which contains historical exhibits pertaining to the region.

Green Bay is the oldest permanent settlement in Wisconsin. Its site was first visited in 1634 by Jean Nicolet (1598–1642), a French explorer, and in 1671 Claude Jean Allouez (1622–89), a Jesuit missionary, built a mission there which was destroyed by fire in 1687. The French commenced the construction of Fort Saint Francis on the site in 1717, and in 1745 the French-Canadian fur trader Augustin de Langlade (about 1695–about 1771) established a permanent settlement near the fort. In 1760 the fort was surrendered to the British, who named it Fort Edward Augustus, and occupied it intermittently until 1816, when it was officially possessed by American troops, and named Fort Howard. The old hospital building of the fort has been preserved. In 1839 the two fur-trading centers, Navarino and Astor, which had been established within the limits of the present city, were united as the town of Green Bay; in 1854 Green Bay was chartered as a city. The city of Fort Howard was consolidated with Green Bay in 1893. Pop. (1960) 62,888; (1970) 87,809.

GREEN BERETS. See SPECIAL FORCES.

GREENBRIER. See SMILAX.

GREENE, Graham (1904–), British novelist, born in Berkhamsted, Hertfordshire, England, and educated at the University of Oxford. He was employed in 1926 by the London *Times*. In 1935 he became motion-picture critic for the *Spectator*, a British newspaper, and in 1940 was named literary editor. In 1942–43 he worked for the British Foreign Office in western Africa. Widely traveled after World War II, Greene based many of his works on his own experiences.

Greene's earliest novels were *The Man Within* (1929), *The Name of Action* (1930), and *Rumour at Nightfall* (1931). His popularity came, however, with *Stamboul Train* (1932), a spy thriller

GREENE, NATHANAEL

published in the United States as *Orient Express*. Subsequent novels of this period, which Greene was later to categorize as "entertainments", were *It's a Battlefield* (1934) and *England Made Me* (1935). His next "entertainment", *A Gun for Sale* (1936), published in the U.S. as *This Gun for Hire*, has as a central theme man's conflict between good and evil. It may be considered a precursor to the type of book that the author specifically labeled as "novels". These writings are seriously concerned with the moral, social, and religious problems of the time. Greene himself had been converted to Roman Catholicism in 1926. The "novels" include *Brighton Rock* (1938); *The Power and the Glory* (1940), published in the U.S. as the *Labyrinthine Ways*; *The Heart of the Matter* (1948); and *The End of the Affair* (1951).

Subsequent major works by Greene include *The Third Man* (1950), *The Quiet American* (1955), *Our Man in Havana* (1958), *The Comedians* (1966), and *Travels with My Aunt* (1969). As an essayist, Green has compiled *Lost Childhood and Other Essays* (1952) and *Collected Essays* (1969), the latter comprising mostly studies of other writers. He has also written children's books. As a playwright, he has contributed *The Living Room* (1953), *The Potting Shed* (1957), and *The Complaisant Lover* (1959). Many of his novels have been adapted for films. All of Greene's works are characterized by vivid detail and by objectivism. His earlier books exhibit several different interest levels, as the political, the sociological, and the psychological. In his later novels he adds a moral conflict factor, shown through the characters' struggle between good and evil.

GREENE, Nathanael (1742–86), American Revolutionary soldier, born in Warwick, R.I., and self-educated. In 1770 he was elected a member of the General Assembly of Rhode Island. In the period before the American Revolution, Greene took part in military exercises to prepare for war, which he regarded as inevitable. In 1775 he was appointed brigadier general of the Rhode Island forces sent to join the Continental Army besieging the British in Boston. Later, after winning the esteem of General George Washington (q.v.) for his service in battles in the vicinity of New York City, Greene was made a major general and was assigned to the command of the revolutionary troops in New Jersey. Subsequently he fought in the battles of Princeton, the Brandywine, and Germantown. In 1778 he was appointed quartermaster general of the revolutionary army, occupying that post until 1780. In the latter year he sat as president of the military court that tried the British major John André, the accomplice of the American traitor Benedict Arnold (qq.v.) for espionage. Greene was then given command of the southern revolutionary army and, in 1781–82, conducted a notably successful campaign against the British in Georgia and the Carolinas, forcing the enemy to retreat to three coastal bases where they were subsequently trapped. North Carolina, South Carolina, and Georgia honored Greene with gifts of valuable estates, including Mulberry Grove on the Savannah R. in Georgia, to which he retired after the war. See AMERICAN REVOLUTION. See also separate articles on the battles mentioned.

GREENE, Robert (1560?–92), English dramatist and prose writer, born in Norwich, and educated at the universities of Oxford and Cambridge. After traveling in Europe between 1578 and 1583 he settled in London, where he spent the rest of his life. Greene was a prolific and popular prose writer. Some of his prose romances were *Mamillia* (1583), written in imitation of *Euphues*, by the English novelist John Lyly (q.v.); *The Myrrour of Modestie* (1584); *Perimedes the Blacke-Smith* (1588); and *Menaphon* (1589), written in imitation of *Arcadia*, by the English writer Sir Philip Sidney (q.v.). Greene's verse and songs are scattered throughout his prose. He wrote many pamphlets, including a series on the London underworld. The autobiographical *Greene's Groatsworth of Wit Bought with a Million of Repentance*, which contains an alleged allusion to William Shakespeare as an "upstart crow"; *The Repentance of Robert Greene, Master of Arts*; and *Greene's Vision* were all written in 1592. His most outstanding dramatic works are *The Honorable History of Friar Bacon and Friar Bungay* (1592) and *The Scottish History of James IV* (1592).

GREENEVILLE, town in Tennessee, and county seat of Greene Co., about 62 miles E. of Knoxville. The town is a marketing center for the area and has varied manufacturing. It is the site of Tusculum College, founded in 1794. Also in Greeneville is the Andrew Johnson National Historic Site, where the home and grave of the seventeenth President can be seen. Pop. (1960) 11,759; (1970) 13,722.

GREENFIELD, city of Wisconsin, in Milwaukee Co., about 7 miles S.W. of central Milwaukee. Greenfield was incorporated in 1957. Pop. (1960) 17,636; (1970) 24,424.

GREENFINCH, common name for any of a number of birds of the Finch family, Fringillidae, often classified as a genus, *Chloris*. The most common species is the European greenfinch,

GREENHOUSE

Chloris chloris. Its plumage is green, mixed with gray and brown. The male, generally yellowish-green in color, is more brightly tinted than the female. The greenfinch is a poor singer in its native state, but readily mimics the songs of other cage birds when confined with them. Its nest is cup-shaped, and four to six eggs are laid in one setting. Greenfinches are found throughout Europe and in western Asia and northern Africa. They are among the commonest birds in England, and are found there in all seasons of the year. Greenfinches are also sometimes called green linnets.

An entirely different bird, the Texas sparrow, *Arremonops rufivirgata,* is sometimes called greenfinch in the United States. Its plumage is olive-green in the upper parts and dull white below. It frequents bushes and thickets from southeastern Texas to the eastern part of Mexico, and is about 6 in. long.

GREENGAGE. *See* PLUM.

GREENHEART, *or* BEBEERU, South American evergreen timber tree, *Nectandra rodioei,* belonging to the Laurel family, Lauraceae, native to Guiana. It has thick, shiny leaves, pale-yellow bisexual flowers borne in clusters, and a bitter, one-seeded fruit. The greenish wood, called greenheart, is extremely strong and hard and takes a high polish. It is very resistant to water-soaking and insect attack, and is extensively used in the building of wharves, docks, and canal locks. The bark, called bebeeru, contains the alkaloid *bebeerine,* a drug formerly used to reduce fever.

GREENHOUSE, glass building used for cultivation and protection of tender plants and of plants grown out of season. Several specialized types of greenhouses are named according to their function. A conservatory is a greenhouse used primarily for displaying plants, particularly cultivated ornamental plants. A hothouse, or stove, is a greenhouse in which the temperature is sufficient to maintain normal growth rates of tropical plants. A dry stove is a greenhouse in which humidity and soil moisture are controlled to aid the growth of plants, such as cactus, which require a dry environment.

Modern greenhouses are adapted to any greenhouse use by suitable control of temperature, moisture, and lighting. Small greenhouses are frequently of the lean-to type. A lean-to house is built against an existing wall, and consists of a glass-paned sloping roof and three supporting glass-paned sides. Larger green-

A general view of a greenhouse in which experimental studies are in progress.   Purdy—U.S. Dept. of Agriculture

The Climatron, a geodesic dome at the Missouri Botanical Garden, Saint Louis. The dome is a fully climate-controlled greenhouse providing native environments for tropical and semi-tropical plants.
Saint Louis Chamber of Commerce

houses have roofs which slope toward two sides; the roof is supported by two sidewalls and two endwalls. When more than one greenhouse is built on the same site, the buildings are arranged in a row so that two adjacent buildings share the same inside wall. Another extensively used type of greenhouse, the ridge-and-furrow house, has no walls between adjacent units, so that a row of structures comprises a single large house. Posts supporting greenhouse walls and roofs are usually steel pipe or structural steel in the form of I-beams. The frames of the walls and roofs are usually made of a combination of wood and steel. A frame must be strong enough to hold panes of glass in severe weather and still be so narrow that a minimum of shade is cast. The upper row of panes on each side of the roof may be opened partially or completely for ventilation. All wooden and metal parts are painted prior to the erection of a greenhouse, and must be repainted frequently to protect them from extremes of moisture and temperature.

Light. Natural sunlight, in temperate regions, is usually sufficient to meet the light requirements of plants during spring and fall. In winter, natural light is sometimes supplemented by artificial light to assist plants which are in active growth. The amount of sunlight is sometimes too great in summer, and so the glass panes of greenhouses are often covered with slat shades or white-washed to reduce the light.

Temperature. Proper temperature conditions in greenhouses are maintained through much of the year by heat derived from the sun's rays. Energy given off by the sun is transmitted by short waves, which pass freely through the atmosphere and glass. Short-wave energy falling on objects in greenhouses is transformed to long-wave energy which cannot pass through glass; *see* FLUORESCENCE AND PHOSPHORESCENCE but is absorbed or reflected by the glass walls and roof. Most of this energy is retained within the greenhouse. During the winter months it is often necessary to supplement natural heat. During the hotter months, greenhouse heat is reduced by whitewashing the panes, by opening ventilators, and sometimes by use of artificial cooling systems.

Moisture. Humidity is primarily controlled by the quantity of water used in the greenhouse. The humidity of houses containing plants which are adapted to arid environments is controlled by watering the plants sparsely. Humidity necessary to plants which are adapted to moderately moist situations is supplied by evaporation from thoroughly-watered soils. When greater

GREENLAND

humidity is required, extra moisture is supplied by watering the floor of the greenhouse. Humidity may also be raised by opening the ventilators when outside air is more humid than greenhouse air, and may be lowered by the same means when outside air is less humid than greenhouse air. Pot-grown plants, such as orchids, are often humidified by setting them on racks above beds of moistened cinders.

The Climatron, a geodesic dome built according to principles set forth by R. Buckminster Fuller (q.v.), houses tropical and subtropical plants. Heated by air warmed in an underground tunnel and injected along one side, it is 70 ft. high and covers ¼ acre. Twenty fans ventilate the structure. Constructed of aluminum tubing arranged in hexagonal patterns, the Climatron is lined with clear plexiglas sheeting.

GREENLAND, largest island in the world, belonging to Denmark and situated between the North Atlantic and Arctic oceans. Greenland lies mostly within the Arctic Circle, and is separated from the Canadian Arctic Archipelago chiefly by Davis Strait and Baffin Bay, and from Iceland, on the E., by the Strait of Denmark. From Cape Morris Jesup (83°39′ N.) to Cape Farewell (59°45′ N.), the extreme N. to S. distance is about 1650 mi. The maximum distance from E. to W. is nearly 800 mi. (near the 70th parallel). The entire coast, lined with fjords, is roughly estimated at 3600 mi. The total area is about 840,000 sq.mi., of which about 710,000 sq.mi. is icecap and 130,000 sq.mi. is ice-free land.

THE LAND

The interior of Greenland is a lofty plateau, 4000 to 9000 ft. or more in altitude, composed chiefly of granite and gneissose rocks, and covered with ice. The icecap is thickest near the center of the island where the maximum depth is estimated at between 7000 and 8000 ft. The greatest heights of land are along the coasts, especially in the E. where the extreme elevation is Mt. Gunnbjørn (12,139 ft.). Drainage is afforded mainly by the so-called ice-fjords, in which thousands of icebergs are formed each year. The climate is extremely cold, but during the short

A steamship arrives at a port on iceberg-strewn Disko Bay, Greenland. Richard Harrington—Pix, Inc.

GREENLAND

summer in the s. the mean temperature is 48° F. The mammals of Greenland are more American than European, and include the musk-ox, wolf, lemming, and reindeer. The varieties of seal and whale, and most of the species of fish and sea birds, are also American rather than European. The polar bear, Arctic fox, polar hare, and stoat are circumpolar animals.

THE PEOPLE

Greenlanders are a mixed people, most of whom have Eskimo and European, especially Danish-Norwegian, blood. The latest census (1966) showed a total population of 42,102. The 1969 United Nations estimate was 47,000.

The capital, Godthaab (pop. in 1967, 6933), on the s.w. coast, is the largest and oldest Danish settlement on the island, having been founded in 1721. Holsteinsborg, on the w. coast just N. of the Arctic Circle, is the second town in population (3782). Other settlements include Julianehaab (3018), Frederikshaab (2323), and Narssaq (2051) on the s. coast, and Angmagssalik (2886) on the E. coast.

Education is free and compulsory for all children between the ages of seven and fourteen. About 100 school centers have been established, and their languages of instruction are both Greenlandic (an Eskimo speech) and Danish. A teachers' training college at Godthaab has the same standard as Danish training colleges on the European mainland.

The national costume of Greenland: beaded jacket, wide sealskin boots, and fur trousers.
Richard Harrington — Pix, Inc.

THE ECONOMY

Whaling, sealing, fishing, and fur trapping are the principal industries. Cattle, sheep, and goats are raised in small numbers in some portions of the s.w. coast; and hardy vegetables are grown. Greenland is the main source of natural cryolite, a mineral used in the manufacture of aluminum. Only a small part of the narrow coastal fringe is inhabited, chiefly the southwestern portion. The trade of Greenland, except in cryolite, is a government monopoly. Exports are cryolite (to Denmark and the United States), fish, hides and skins, whale and fish oil, lead, and zinc.

GOVERNMENT

In 1953 Greenland became an integral part of Denmark. Greenlanders elect two representatives to the Danish parliament. Local government is under the supervision of the Greenland Council, which is elected by the local population.

HISTORY

Greenland was discovered by the Norwegian navigator Eric the Red (fl. 10th cent.), father of Leif Ericson (q.v.), toward the end of the 10th century, and Norse settlements, which later vanished, were established in the extreme southern portions; see NORSEMEN. In the course of the search for the Northwest Passage (q.v.), Greenland was rediscovered. The English navigator John Davis (q.v.) visited the island in 1585, and his explorative work, together with that of the English explorers Henry Hudson and William Baffin (qq.v.), afforded knowledge of the west coast of Greenland. The foundation of Danish Greenland was laid by the establishment of a Danish mission at Godthaab in 1721, by a Norwegian missionary Hans Egede (1686–1758). In the 19th century Greenland was explored and mapped by numerous explorers and navigators. From 1930 to 1931, British and German expeditions made weather observations on the inland ice north of the Arctic Circle. In 1933 an American expedition fostered by the University of Michigan and Pan-American Airways were engaged in meteorological research more than 340 mi. north of the Arctic Circle. See ARCTIC EXPLORATION.

The United States relinquished its claim to land in northern Greenland, based on the discoveries made by the American explorer Robert Edwin Peary (q.v.), when it purchased the Virgin Islands (q.v.) from Denmark in 1916. In May, 1921, Denmark declared the entire island of Greenland to be Danish territory, causing a dispute with Norway over hunting and fishing rights. In 1931 a strip of land on the east coast was claimed by some Norwegian hunters,

Fishing is the principal industry of Greenland, and the catch is a major part of the diet of the island population.
Richard Harrington—Pix, Inc.

whose action was recognized shortly thereafter by the Norwegian government. The occupation was invalidated by the Permanent Court of International Justice (*see* WORLD COURT) at The Hague in 1933. Germany's occupation of Denmark in 1940, during World War II, brought the status of Greenland again into question. Negotiations between the U.S. government and the Danish minister at Washington resulted in an agreement on April 9, 1941, granting the U.S. the right "to construct, maintain and operate such landing fields, seaplane facilities and radio and meteorological installations as may be necessary" to protect the status quo in the Western Hemisphere; at the same time the U.S. assumed protective custody over Greenland for the duration of World War II, although recognizing Danish sovereignty.

Greenland is the source of many of the weather changes in the northern hemisphere, and knowledge of Greenland weather is of prime importance for the prediction of conditions in the North Atlantic Ocean and in western Europe. Weather and radio stations are of inestimable value for Atlantic aerial traffic. In 1944, during World War II, a German radio-weather station on the northeast coast was destroyed by the United States Coast Guard, and various German attempts to establish weather bases on Greenland were dispersed by Coast Guard vessels. Three American bases were established, one above the Arctic Circle on the west coast, one at Julianehaab, and one on the east coast at Angmagssalik. In May, 1947, Denmark requested that the U.S. end the 1941 agreement. The U.S. reply stressed the importance of Greenland "in the defensive system of the . . . Western Hemisphere". Protracted negotiations culminated during April, 1951, in a twenty-year pact providing for Danish control of the chief U.S. naval station in Greenland and for the establishment of jointly operated defense areas. By the terms of other provisions the armed forces of the members of the North Atlantic Treaty Organization (q.v.) were authorized to use all naval, air, and military bases on the island. Later in 1951 the U.S. began construction of a vast strategic air base at Thule, an Eskimo settlement on the northwestern coast, about 930 mi. from the North Pole. The base was completed in 1953.

In June, 1952, the Danish government and private Danish, Swedish, and Canadian interests formed a company to exploit recently discovered deposits of lead, zinc, and tungsten in eastern Greenland. Under the provisions of the new Danish constitution, adopted in May, 1953, Greenland became an integral part of the Danish Commonwealth and obtained representation in the national parliament. Greenland's new political status was formally recognized by the United Nations General Assembly on Nov. 22, 1954.

GREENLET. *See* VIREO.

GREEN MOUNTAIN BOYS

GREEN MOUNTAIN BOYS, name applied to the soldiers of Vermont in the American Revolution (q.v.). They were originally organized in 1775 by the American soldier Ethan Allen (*see under* ALLEN) to oppose the claims of New York to Vermont territory. At the outbreak of the war, the Green Mountain Boys, with reinforcements from Massachusetts and Connecticut, seized British-held Fort Ticonderoga, at the head of Lake Champlain; *see* TICONDEROGA.

GREEN MOUNTAINS, range of the N. section of the Appalachian Mts. (q.v.), extending N. and s., for a distance of about 160 mi., through Vermont. The greater part of Vermont, called the Green Mountain State, is covered by the forested peaks of the Green Mts. Erosion and weathering have worn and rounded the peaks, the average elevation being about 2000 ft. The highest elevations reached exceed 4000 ft. above sea level: Mt. Mansfield, the highest, rises to 4393 ft.; others are Killington Peak (4241 ft.); and Camels Hump (4083 ft.). The valley of the Connecticut R. lies to the E. of the range and on the w. is the Lake Champlain basin. The N. section of the range is indented by the valleys of the Missiquoi, Lamoille, and Winooski rivers. Several streams rising in the mountains furnish waterpower to communities in the region. The mountains are heavily wooded with pine, spruce, and other evergreens, and also contain forests of beech, birch, and sugar maple. The area is rich in desposits of asbestos, granite, marble, and talc. Some farming and dairying are carried out in the fertile valleys, and maple syrup is produced.

The Green Mts. are a popular summer and winter resort area. Smugglers Notch, a rocky, wooded gorge more than 1000 ft. deep, lying just N. of Mt. Mansfield, is frequently visited. The many lakes and streams in the mountains abound in fish, and the mountain slopes afford many miles of ski trails. The Long Trail, a path for hikers built by the Green Mt. Club in Rutland, Vt., extends along the length of the mountains. The Appalachian Trail crosses the s. section of the range. Much of the range is part of the Green Mt. National Forest.

GREENOCK, Great Britain, seaport and parliamentary burgh of Renfrew County, Scotland, on the s. shore of the Firth of Clyde, 23 miles N.W. of Glasgow. Greenock has a fine harbor, which has been continuously enlarged and improved since 1710. Its chief import is raw sugar, and its principal exports are machinery and ships. Greenock has been a shipbuilding and sugar-refining center since 1765; other important industries in the burgh include fishing, distilling, and the manufacture of aluminum, engines, woolens and worsteds, sailcloth, cordage, and paper. The burgh fronts on the firth, or estuary, for a distance of about 4 mi., rising gradually to a series of hills in the s. Among its outstanding buildings are the museum and lecture hall, dating from 1876, and the Watt Institution, founded in 1837 in memory of the noted mechanical engineer and inventor James Watt (q.v.), who was born in Greenock in 1736. The institution contains the public library, a scientific library, and a marble statue of Watt by the British sculptor and painter Sir Francis Chantrey (1781–1841). Also in Greenock is the grave of Mary Campbell (d. 1786), the "Highland Mary" celebrated in the works of the Scottish poet Robert Burns (q.v.), and the subject of his poem "To Mary in Heaven". Greenock became a burgh of barony in 1635 under a charter granted by Charles I (q.v.), King of England. Early in the 18th century, with the increase of trade between Great Britain and its American possessions, Greenock developed from a small fishing village into an important seaport. It became a parliamentary burgh in 1832. Pop. (1969 est.) 70,267.

GREENOUGH, Horatio (1805–52), American sculptor, born in Boston and educated at Harvard University. He executed busts of President John Quincy Adams (q.v.) and other leading citizens in Boston in 1826. He then went to live in Florence, Italy, where he received a commission to sculpture some figures for the American author James Fenimore Cooper (q.v.). A large statue of President George Washington (q.v.), which he executed by commission of the Federal government, was unveiled in 1843 and is now in the Smithsonian Institution in Washington, D.C. "The Rescue" (1837–51), his large group sculpture representing the conflict between the Indians and the white settlers, is on the portico of the capitol in Washington. Among his other works is "Lafayette" (1831), in the gallery of the Boston Athenaeum.

GREENSBORO, city in North Carolina, and county seat of Guilford Co., 80 miles N.W. of Raleigh. It is served by a railroad and maintains a municipal airport. The city is the commercial and manufacturing center of a cotton-growing region. The principal industry in Greensboro is the manufacture of cotton textiles, especially blue denim; the city has a denim mill reputedly the largest of its kind in the world. Other important industries in the city are the manufacture of chemicals, automobile bodies, sheet metal, machine tools, stoves, fertilizer, and cigars. Greensboro is the site of the University of North Carolina at Greensboro, established in 1891;

Greensboro College (Methodist, 1838); the Agricultural and Technical College of North Carolina (1891); and Bennett College for women (Methodist, 1873). Guilford College, founded in 1834 by the Society of Friends, is about 5 miles W. of the city, in a Friends settlement dating from colonial period. William Sydney Porter (q.v.), known as O. Henry, the short-story writer, was born in Greensboro; the Masonic Temple Museum stands on the site of his birthplace. Guilford Courthouse National Military Park, commemorating a battle of the American Revolution (q.v.), fought on March 15, 1781, is 6 miles N.W. of the city.

Greensboro was founded as the county seat in 1808 and named in honor of the American general Nathanael Greene (q.v.), the hero of the Battle of Guilford Courthouse. At the end of the American Civil War, the Confederate general Joseph E. Johnston disbanded his army at Greensboro after his surrender to General William Tecumseh Sherman (qq.v.) on April 26, 1865. Pop. (1960) 119,574; (1970) 144,076.

GREENSBURG, city in Pennsylvania, and county seat of Westmoreland Co., about 26 miles S.E. of central Pittsburgh. The city is in a bituminous coal-mining region and manufactures include metal products, glass, and beverages. It is the site of Seton Hill College, established in 1883. Pop. (1960) 17,383; (1970) 15,870.

GREEN TURTLE, edible sea turtle, *Chelonia mydas,* used in the preparation of such table delicacies as turtle soup and turtle steak. It derives its name from the green color of its fat. The eggs of the green turtle are also valued as food.

Green turtle, Chelonia mydas

The green turtle is common in all warm seas and may sometimes be found, in summertime, along the north Atlantic coasts of the United States and Europe. Adult green turtles reach a shell length of over 3½ ft. The body weight of a turtle this size is over 400 lb. Commercial specimens usually weigh from 50 to 150 lb. The smooth shell on the green turtle's back is olive-green blotched with yellow. The head and the seal-like flippers are dark brown. They are covered with rough, horny plates, each plate bordered with white or brilliant yellow. The shell covering the chest and abdomen of the green turtle is soft and yielding, and cannot long support the weight of the animal out of water; specimens that are to be kept alive and fresh in market are turned on their backs. The male green turtle never leaves the sea; the female leaves it only to lay her eggs. As many as 200 eggs are laid at night, in sand above the reach of the sea. The young are hatched by the sun's heat and soon crawl into the sea in search of food. Green turtles are omnivorous but subsist chiefly on marine vegetation.

GREENVILLE, city in Mississippi, and county seat of Washington Co., on the Mississippi R., 95 miles N. of Vicksburg. It is served by railroads and an airline, and by riverboats and barges. A bridge at Greenville spans the Mississippi R. to Lake Village, Ark. The city is the center and shipping point of an agricultural region producing large quantities of long-staple cotton, and also corn, oats, alfalfa, hogs, and beef cattle. Greenville contains extensive stockyards, warehouses, cotton compresses, cotton-oil mills, woodworking plants, and a pulp mill manufacturing wallboard and insulating material. A yacht harbor at Greenville serves pleasure craft on the river.

The city was established after the American Civil War just north of the site of its first settlement, known as Old Greenville, which was burned by Federal troops following the capture of Memphis. It was incorporated as a town in 1870 and as a city in 1886. Pop. (1960) 41,502; (1970) 39,648.

GREENVILLE, city in North Carolina, and county seat of Pitt Co., on the Tar R., 84 miles S.E. of Raleigh. It is served by railroads, has shipping facilities on the Tar R. and the Atlantic Intracoastal Waterway (*see* INTRACOASTAL WATERWAYS), and has an airport. The city is the commercial center of a rich agricultural area producing bright-leaf tobacco, cotton, corn, potatoes and sweet potatoes, peanuts, cucumbers, livestock, and poultry. Greenville is one of the largest tobacco markets in the United States and contains many tobacco warehouses and processing plants. The city is also a market for cattle and hogs. Among the industrial establishments in the city are lumber mills, a chick hatchery, a feed mill, a hosiery mill, printing plants, sheet-metal works, machine shops, and factories manufacturing fertilizer, soft drinks, plastics, cotton

GREENVILLE

yarns, and drugs. Greenville is the site of East Carolina University (1907). The town was founded as Martinborough in 1774, and renamed Greenville in 1786 in honor of General Nathanael Greene (q.v.), a hero of the American Revolution. Pop. (1960) 22,860; (1970) 29,063.

GREENVILLE, city in Ohio, and county seat of Darke Co., on Greenville Creek, about 33 miles N.W. of Dayton. The city is a marketing center for the area. Manufactures include machinery, clothing, and electrical appliances. Pop. (1960) 10,585; (1970) 12,380.

GREENVILLE, city in South Carolina, and county seat of Greenville Co., on the Reedy R., about 30 miles S.W. of Spartanburg. It is served by railroad and has a municipal airport. The city lies near the foot of the Blue Ridge Mts., at an altitude of 1040 ft. above sea level. It is one of the leading textile centers of the South, and a large cotton market. Among the textile plants in the city are a worsted mill, a yarn-dyeing plant, and two of the largest bleaching, printing, and finishing plants in the South. Other important industries in Greenville are meat packing, the processing of peanuts, and the manufacture of textile equipment. Greenville is the site of Furman University (Baptist), organized in 1826, Bob Jones University (1927), and the Shriners Hospital for Crippled Children. The site was laid out for the county seat in 1797; in 1831 the original name of the town, Pleasantburg, was changed to Greenville. In 1868 Greenville was incorporated as a city. Pop. (1960) 66,188; (1970) 61,208.

GREENVILLE, city in Texas, and county seat of Hunt Co., on the Sabine R., about 45 miles N.E. of Dallas. The city is in a rich agricultural area, and is a trade, processing, and commercial center. The city manufactures clothing, furniture, aircraft, and electrical equipment. Oil-refining and food-processing are other industries. Pop. (1960) 19,087; (1970) 22,043.

GREENWICH, town of Connecticut, in Fairfield Co., on Long Island Sound, 28 miles N.E. of New York City, of which it is a residential suburb. The town is served by a railroad. It occupies an area of 48 sq.mi. and is noted for the beauty of its houses and estates and for its many recreational facilities. Greenwich has about 6 mi. of coastline, containing numerous public and private beaches, beach clubs, and yacht clubs; 330 mi. of bridle paths; and six golf courses. Among the interesting buildings in Greenwich is Putnam Cottage, built in 1731, from which revolutionary general Israel Putnam (q.v.) fled when surprised by a British force in February, 1779. The cottage contains relics of the colonial and revolutionary periods. Greenwich was settled in 1640 by Captain Daniel Patrick and Robert Feaks, agents of the New Haven Colony; see CONNECTICUT: *History*. From 1642 to 1650 it was a part of the Dutch province of New Amsterdam. In 1656 the settlement again became a part of the New Haven Colony and was united with Stamford. Greenwich became a separate town in 1665. Pop. (1960) 53,793; (1970) 59,755.

GREENWICH, Great Britain, borough of Greater London, England, on the S. bank of the Thames R., and including, since 1965, that part of the former Woolwich borough lying S. of the Thames. The main street, extending through the borough from W. to E., is Woolwich Road, part of the old Roman highway through Kent. The Royal Naval College, established in 1873, occupies the famous Greenwich Hospital building opened as a hospital for seamen in 1705. Before the hospital was built the site was occupied by Greenwich House, a royal palace. The National Maritime Museum is attached to the Royal Naval College. Greenwich is perhaps most familiar as the site of meridian longitude 0°, the point of departure for time zones throughout the world; see INTERNATIONAL DATE LINE; TIME. The Woolwich portion of the borough is best known for its Royal Dockyards and ordnance factories. Pop. (1969 est.) 228,030.

GREENWICH OBSERVATORY, astronomical observatory situated at Herstmonceux Castle in East Sussex, England, about 60 miles S.E. of its original site in Greenwich (q.v.). The former location of the observatory was arbitrarily established in 1884 as longitude 0°. A placque in the original structure marks the zero point from which longitude is calculated. Because the London haze had made accurate astronomical observations almost impossible, the observatory equipment was gradually moved, beginning in 1946, from its original site to Herstmonceux Castle. The move was completed late in 1953.

The observatory was founded in 1675 by Charles II (q.v.), King of England, to keep accurate tables of the position of the moon for the calculation of longitude by English ships. In 1750 publication of the tables was begun in the *Astronomical Observations,* which were published annually after 1838. Meridian observations of the sun, stars, and planets were also made at the observatory. Photographs of the sun were taken daily, conditions permitting, and a continuous photographic record of sunspots was kept, starting in 1873. Faint satellites of the planets Neptune and Uranus were discovered by the British astronomer William Lassell (1799–1880) in 1846 and 1851, respectively, using the 24-in. Newtonian reflector telescope. Another discovery made at the observatory was that of the eighth satellite of Jupiter. The observatory, officially known as the Royal Greenwich Observatory, is managed by the Science Research Council. Its director is called the astronomer royal. Famed astronomers royal have included Edmund Halley (q.v.) and Nevil Maskelyne (1732–1811).

See ASTRONOMY; TELESCOPE.

GREENWICH VILLAGE, residential section of the borough of Manhattan, New York City, usually regarded as comprising the area within West 14th Street on the N., Broadway on the E., West Houston Street on the S., and the Hudson R. on the W. The history of Greenwich Village dates from colonial times, when a number of wealthy residents of the city, which was then confined to the region S. of Wall Street, constructed country homes in the area. At the close of the 18th century the village still retained its rural character, but subsequent events, particularly a series of yellow-fever epidemics which caused hundreds of New Yorkers to take refuge beyond the city limits, speeded the growth of the community. By the middle of the 19th century the village, largely inhabited by well-to-do families, had become an integral part of the metropolis. Because the area was developed at a comparatively early date, however, the streets of the village never conformed with the regular street plan of Manhattan; the many short, angled, or crooked streets in the neighborhood give the village a distinctive character.

Shortly after 1900, Greenwich Village became the mecca of artistic, literary, and political rebels from all parts of the United States. They transformed the community into a stronghold of the cultural renaissance then burgeoning in America. The center of the Bohemian movement, as the rebellion against conventionalism was popularly termed, Greenwich Village rapidly and justifiably gained wide renown. Such village publications as *The Seven Arts* and *The Masses* became the focus of liberal-radical thought in art and politics. The "A" Club, led by the sociologist Frances Perkins (q.v.), the writer Mary Heaton Vorse (1881–1966), and other prominent feminists, substantially advanced the struggle for woman suffrage and social reforms. The Washington Square Players, nucleus of the present-day Theater Guild, and the Provincetown Players (q.v.) provided opportunity and scope for the fresh and genuinely creative talents of such distinguished figures of the American theater as the dramatist Eugene Gladstone O'Neill (q.v.), the impresario-playwright George Cram Cook (1873–1924), the novelist and playwright Susan Glaspell, the lyric and dramatic poet Edna St. Vincent Millay, the stage designer Robert Edmond Jones (qq.v.), and a host of others.

The Washington Square Arch in Greenwich Village erected in commemoration of the 100th anniversary of the inauguration (1789) of the first president of the United States. Russell Reif-Pictorial Parade

After the U.S. entered World War I, stringent wartime curbs on radical activity and strong pressure for social conformity tended to disperse the Bohemian community in Greenwich Village. Since that time Greenwich Village has become an increasingly fashionable residential area. Artists, sculptors, writers, and poets, professional as well as neophyte, still gravitate toward the section, however, and periodic open-air exhibits of their paintings, sculptures, and other works are one of the notable features of the neighborhood.

The village has numerous historic landmarks, including the site of the house in which the Anglo-American political philosopher Thomas Paine (q.v.), the pamphleteer of the American Revolution, lived for several years ; Washington Square, the traditional center of the community and the site of a former potter's field; MacDougal Alley, a lane fronted by rows of century-old mews converted into dwellings; and Saint Luke's Chapel, dating from 1822. Many 19th-century town houses also survive in the area.

GREENWOOD

Among the well-known cultural and educational institutions situated in Greenwich Village are the New School for Social Research and several of the schools that compose New York University.

GREENWOOD, city in Mississippi, and county seat of Leflore Co., on the Yazoo R., about 85 miles N. of Jackson. It is served by railroad and bus lines, and is an important market and shipping point for long-staple cotton. Among its industrial establishments are cotton compresses and gins, cottonseed-oil mills, canneries, sawmills, woodworking shops, and factories manufacturing furniture, drugs, agricultural implements, and radio-testing machines. Greenwood was settled in 1834 and incorporated in 1844. It was named for the wealthy cotton planter and Choctaw (q.v.) chieftain Greenwood Leflore (1800–65). His home, Malmaison, built in 1854, is 10 miles E. of the city. Greenwood was chartered as a city in 1915. Pop. (1970) 22,400.

GREENWOOD, city in South Carolina, and county seat of Greenwood Co., about 35 miles S.E. of Anderson. The city is a marketing and shipping center for the area. Manufactures include textiles, synthetic fibers, foundry products, and lumber. It is the site of Lander College, founded in 1872. Pop. (1960) 16,644; (1970) 21,069.

GREGG, John Robert (1867–1948), inventor of a shorthand system of writing, born in Rockcorry, County Monaghan, Ireland. He attended public school and at the age of ten took up the study of "speed writing". After studying existing shorthand methods, Gregg, in 1888, wrote the pamphlet *Light Line Phonography, the Phonetic Hand Writing,* containing a shorthand system of his own invention. He emigrated to the United States in 1893, and his shorthand system became popular soon thereafter. The system was adapted to thirteen languages, and by the time Gregg died 18,000,000 people throughout the world had studied his system. The basic book on Gregg shorthand is *The Gregg Shorthand Manual*; some of Gregg's other books are *The Gregg Phrase Book, Gregg Speed Practice, The Gregg Reporter,* and *The Private Secretary.*
See SHORTHAND.

GREGORIAN CHANT, official liturgical chant used in the Roman Catholic Church. It is also known as plainchant and plainsong. The name "Gregorian" is derived from the name of Pope Gregory I (*see under* GREGORY). *See* CHANT.

GREGORY, name of sixteen popes and two antipopes, of whom the most important were the following.

Saint Gregory I (540?–604), called GREGORY THE GREAT, pope from 590 to 604, born in Rome of a wealthy patrician family. When about thirty years of age he was made prefect of Rome by Emperor Justin II (d. 578). At the death of his father, Gregory inherited considerable wealth, which he used for religious purposes. He founded six monasteries in Sicily and one (Saint Andrew's) in Rome. He resigned his civil office, gave all his money, jewels, robes, and furniture to the poor, and retired to St. Andrew's as an ordinary monk. Soon thereafter he was made a regionary deacon. In 579 Pope Pelagius II (d. 590) appointed Gregory ambassador to the imperial court of Constantinople (now İstanbul, Turkey), where he began what was to become his largest work, the 35-volume *Moralia* (Lat., "Morals"), an exposition of the book of Job (q.v.), and delivered lectures on other books of the Old Testament. During this period, according to the English historian Bede (q.v.), he saw a group of handsome Anglo-Saxon youths in the slave market and, learning that they came from a pagan land, resolved to devote himself to the conversion of England to Christianity. Gregory is said to have set out for England to pursue this purpose, but to have been intercepted by direction of the papacy and ordered to return to Rome; at any rate, he remained in Rome as deacon and served as counselor to the pope.

When Pelagius died of plague, Gregory was unanimously chosen to succeed him and, over his own earnest protest, was consecrated pope in September, 590. His pontificate was marked by zeal in propagating Christianity. His most important missionary endeavor was the conversion of Britain, which was begun in 597, under his direction, by Augustine (q.v.), who later became the first archbishop of Canterbury. Gregory vigorously opposed paganism and the Christian heresies, such as Arianism, Donatism (*see* ARIUS; DONATISTS), and Manichaeism (q.v.), of Italy, Spain, and Gaul, but protected the Jews from persecution and loss of legal privilege. The organization of the medieval papacy was patterned after his administration. He introduced several changes into the liturgy of the Mass (qq.vv.), such as the inclusion of the *Pater Noster* prior to the division of the Host, and of the *Gloria* after the Gradual. Gregorian chant (q.v.) is traditionally considered to have been his revision of the system of church music; *see* RELIGIOUS MUSIC. He exerted great influence in matters of doctrine and in later ages was designated one of the Fathers of the Church (q.v.) and the fourth doctor of the Church. His feast day is Sept. 3.

GREGORY

Saint Gregory II (about 669–731), pope from 715 to 731, born in Rome. He succeeded Constantine (d. 715). During the early part of his pontificate Gregory supported the Eastern Roman Empire in preference to the Lombard invaders of Italy; see BYZANTINE EMPIRE; LOMBARDS. He later broke off with Leo III, Emperor of the East (680?–741), because of Leo's excessive taxation of Italian imperial subjects and his policy of iconoclasm (q.v.). Leo attempted to subdue Gregory by violence, but the pope, with the support of the Lombards and the people of Rome, succeeded in evading the emperor. Gregory supported Saint Boniface (q.v.), an English Benedictine monk, in his missionary work in Bavaria, Thuringia, Hesse, and Friesland. His traditional feast day is Feb. 13.

Saint Gregory III (d. 741), pope from 731 to 741, born in Syria. In the first year of his Pontificate, Gregory excommunicated the iconoclasts (see ICONOCLASM) at a council (q.v.) held in Rome. The retaliations of Emperor Leo III weakened the already tenuous tie between the Eastern Empire and the papacy. The encroachment of the Lombards in Italy during his pontificate became so formidable that Gregory sent three papal missions to Charles Martel (q.v.), the Frankish ruler, offering him a protectorate over Rome in return for assistance against the Lombards. The missions yielded no results during the lifetime of Gregory (and of Charles, who died the same year), but an alliance was later concluded with Charles' son, Pepin the Short, King of the Franks (see under PEPIN), during the pontificate of Stephen III (see under STEPHEN). The feast day of Saint Gregory III is Nov. 28.

Saint Gregory VII (1020?–85), original name HILDEBRAND, pope from 1073 to 1085, born in Siena, Tuscany, and educated at the convent of Saint Mary on the Aventine, in Rome. As a Benedictine monk he became chaplain to Pope Gregory VI (d. 1076) and shared a year of exile with that pontiff at Cologne, where he gained a thorough knowledge of ecclesiastical and political conditions in Germany. He accompanied the succeeding pope, Leo IX (see under LEO), to Rome in 1049. Leo appointed Hildebrand administrator of the patrimony of Saint Peter. Hildebrand was a dominant personality in the papacy not only during the pontificate of Leo, but in the pontificates of Stephen IX (see under STEPHEN), Nicholas II (see under NICHOLAS), and Alexander II (d. 1073), as well. Under Nicholas, Hildebrand was instrumental in bringing about an alliance with the Normans of southern Italy and in instituting legislation for the future election of pontiffs by the College of Cardinals.

Hildebrand was unanimously elected pontiff in Rome three days after the death of Alexander II and was consecrated as Gregory VII on June 30, 1073. He believed that the divine will should be the force governing a unified society comprising all mankind, and his efforts to realize his vision kept him in conflict with civil governments throughout his pontificate.

Controversy over the right of investiture (q.v.) supplied the motive for the battle that Gregory carried on until his death. Henry IV (q.v.), Holy Roman Emperor, in 1076 declared Gregory deposed from the pontificate. Gregory excommunicated Henry the following day. The nobles of Germany threatened to use the excommunication as a pretext for deposing the emperor, and so Henry followed Gregory to Canossa (q.v.) in January, 1077, and submitted himself to a humiliating three-day penance before finally gaining absolution from the pontiff. When his political position had again became secure, however, Henry resumed his attitude of hostility toward Gregory and, in 1080, again declared the pontiff deposed. Under the influence of Henry, the bishops of Germany and northern Italy then elected Guibert, the excommunicated archbishop of Ravenna, as antipope, under the name Clement III (d. 1100).

Henry besieged Rome until 1084, when the city finally fell. Gregory shut himself up in the Roman castle of Sant'Angelo. As he was on the point of falling into imperial hands, he was rescued by Robert Guiscard (q.v.), Duke of Apulia and Calabria, who sacked the city and forced Henry to return to Germany. Guibert was still antipope, however, and Gregory was taken to Monte Cassino by his Norman allies. He sent out appeals for help and held a reforming synod at Salerno, where he uttered his famous dying words: "I have loved justice and hated iniquity, therefore I die an exile". His feast day is May 25.

Gregory XIII (1502–85), original name UGO BUONCOMPAGNI, pope from 1572 to 1585, born in Bologna, Italy. He was one of the prominent theologians at the Council of Trent (see TRENT, COUNCIL OF) in 1562–63 and was created cardinal by Pius IV (see under PIUS) in 1564. He was elected pontiff on the death of Pius V (see under PIUS). The reform of the calendar (q.v.) to the system currently in use and called the Gregorian calendar was carried out under his direction. He issued a new edition of the compilation of canon law (q.v.) *Corpus Juris Canonici* (1582), expended large sums for education and the building of colleges, and constructed many great public works, such as the papal palace, subsequently the residence of Italian Kings and

GREGORY OF ARMENIA

Pope Gregory XIII   Granger Collection

presidents, on the Quirinal hill, in Rome. He was vigorous in anti-Protestant propaganda, attempted to form a coalition against the Protestants, and aided Philip II (q.v.), King of Spain, in an attack on the largely Protestant Netherlands. Gregory's numerous efforts to restore Catholicism or Catholic supremacy in various parts of Europe, though largely unsuccessful, bore fruit not only in the southern portions of the Netherlands, but also in Poland and Austria and in Bavaria and other parts of Germany.

GREGORY OF ARMENIA, Saint, called GREGORY THE ILLUMINATOR (about 257–about 332), first patriarch and patron saint of the Armenian Church (q.v.). Reputedly the son of a Parthian chieftain (see PARTHIA), Gregory is believed to have been born at Valarshapat, in the Armenian province of Ararat. According to legend, his father was killed by soldiers of the Armenian king, and Gregory was taken to Caesarea, in Cappadocia, where he was educated as a Christian. He then entered the service of Tiridates III (238–about 314), King of Armenia, but was persecuted for his refusal to participate in pagan rites. According to tradition, Gregory was confined in a pit for fourteen years and was released as the result of a mystical revelation granted to the king's sister. Historically, Gregory was ordained at Caesarea in 290, converted Tiridates, and was made vicar-general for Armenia. He was consecrated bishop of Armenia about 315. Toward the end of his life, Gregory forsook his position as head of the Armenian Church and became a hermit. Although Gregory is frequently called the founder of the Armenian Church, he did not in fact bring Christianity to Armenia. He is responsible, however, for organizing the church in that country, for stamping out paganism, and for allying the Armenian Christians with the Catholic Church.

GREGORY OF NAZIANZUS, Saint (329?–89?), called GREGORIUS THEOLOGUS (Gr., "Gregory the Theologian"), with Saint Athanasius, Saint Basil (qq.v.), and Saint John Chrysostom (see CHRYSOSTOM, SAINT JOHN), Father of the Church and a doctor of the Church, born near Nazianzus, in Cappadocia, and educated in Alexandria, Egypt, and Athens, Greece. He was baptized in 360 by his father, who was bishop of Nazianzus. Deciding then to pursue a life of devotion, he went to Pontus, where he lived in the desert near the Iris R. (now the Yeşilirmak R., in Turkey) with Saint Basil. The two men compiled an anthology of the writings of the Christian teacher and theologian Origen (q.v.) called the *Philokalia* (Gr., "Love of the Beautiful"). Basil later became bishop of Caesarea and, in 371 or 372, prevailed upon Gregory to accept the see of Sasima, a small village in Cappadocia. Gregory disliked public life, however, and retired until the death of his father in 374. In 378 or 379 he took charge of the Nicene congregation of Constantinople (now İstanbul, Turkey). There he delivered five discourses on the Trinity (q.v.) that earned him his fame as "the Theologian". He was appointed bishop, but retired in the face of resistance from the Arians (see ARIUS) and, in the hope of preventing further schism, returned to Nazianzus, where he remained until his death. His feast day is Jan. 2 in the Roman Catholic Church and Jan. 25 in the Orthodox Church. His surviving works comprise about 45 sermons, 243 letters, and 407 dogmatic and moral poems.

GREGORY OF NYSSA, Saint (335?–94), bishop of Nyssa, in Cappadocia, and an early Father of the Church, born in Neocaesarea (now Niksar, Turkey), younger brother of Saint Basil (q.v.). Gregory married, but on the death of his wife he entered the monastery founded by Basil in Pontus, near the Iris R. About 371 he was ordained by his brother and made bishop of Nyssa. Gregory's religious position was strictly orthodox, and he was particularly zealous in combating the doctrine of Arianism (see ARIUS). The Arians charged Gregory with fraud in his election to the bishopric and with mishandling the funds of his office. Convicted of these charges, he was exiled from Nyssa from 376 to 378. After his return Gregory was a strong supporter of the orthodox position against the Arians at the first Council of Constantinople (see CONSTANTINOPLE, COUNCILS OF), in 381. In the next year he was sent by the Church to reorganize the churches of Arabia.

Gregory's fame is chiefly as a theologian. Among his important theological treatises are *Against Eunomius,* a defense of the Nicene Creed (q.v.); *Great Catechetical Discourse,* a defense of the Christian faith against Jews and pagans; *On Faith,* a treatise against the Arians; and *Ten Syllogisms,* directed against the Apollinarists (*see* APOLLINARIS OF LAODICEA), who in many ways were allied to the Manichaeans (*see* MANICHAEISM). His feast day is March 9.

GREGORY OF TOURS, Saint, original name GEORGIUS FLORENTIUS (538?–94), Frankish bishop and historian, born in Augustonemetum (now Clermont-Ferrand, France). Gregory was educated by an uncle and received instruction in classic literature and religious principles, but made no special study of theology or the writings of the fathers of the Church. He was ordained a deacon in 563. Shortly thereafter he journeyed to the tomb of the 4th-century prelate Saint Martin (q.v.) in Tours, seeking a cure for a serious illness, and became the protégé of Euphronius (d. 573), bishop of Tours. On the death of Euphronius, Gregory was elected by the people of Tours to replace him. During his bishopric Gregory resisted the power of Chilperic I, King of Neustria (r. 561–84), who held the city of Tours from 575 until his death. Gregory was accused of vilifying Chilperic's wife, Fredegund (d. 597), and was tried but acquitted; *see* BRUNHILDE.

Gregory wrote, edited, and translated a number of books, including accounts of the life and miracles of St. Martin. His most important work, however, is his *Historia Francorum,* a ten-volume history of the Frankish people from the creation to the year 591, of which the last six books are the most valuable source of historical information on Merovingian (q.v.) times. His traditional feast day is Nov. 17.

GREGORY, Lady (1852–1932), Irish playwright, born Isabella Augusta Persse in Roxborough, County Galway. In 1881 she married Sir William Gregory (1817–92), a noted member of the British Parliament from Galway and governor of Ceylon. She worked with William Butler Yeats (q.v.), the Irish poet and playwright, to found the Irish National Theatre Society, and became director of the Abbey Theatre (q.v.), Dublin, where many of her plays were produced. Much of her work concerns Irish folklore, and she was instrumental in making popular the dialect of English spoken in the west of Ireland. Many of her own plays were written in this dialect; she also translated into the Anglo-Irish idiom several of the works of the French dramatist Molière (q.v.), collected and published as *The Kiltartan Molière* (1910). She provided help and encouragement to such modern Irish writers as the dramatist John Millington Synge, the novelist and poet George Moore, and the playwright Sean O'Casey (qq.v.), and is said by Moore to have collaborated with Yeats in the writing of *Cathleen ni Houlihan* (1902) and *A Pot of Broth* (1904). In 1911 and in 1913 she visited the United States with the Irish Players.

Lady Gregory also wrote sketches, stories, and translations of Gaelic sagas. Her plays, mostly one-act comedies of modern Irish life, include *The White Cockade* (1912), *Coats* (1913), *The Full Moon* (1913), and *McDonough's Wife* (1913). Her other works include *Poets and Dreamers* (1903), *The Kiltartan History Book* (1909), *Our Irish Theatre* (1914), and *Coole* (1931).

GRENADA, island and British-affiliated state of the West Indies (q.v.), part of the Lesser Antilles, in the Caribbean Sea about 85 miles N. of Port of Spain, Trinidad. The state includes the S. half of the Grenadine Islands, notably Carriacou. Grenada is the most southerly of the Windward Islands (q.v.). It is of volcanic origin and is traversed by a mountain range, the highest point of which is Mt. Saint Catherine, 2749 ft. above sea level. The many mountains of Grenada contain deposits of sulfur and fuller's earth; the valleys lying between are picturesque and fertile, producing important crops. The principal exports of Grenada are cacao, nutmegs, mace, raw cotton, lime oil, and bananas. The island has several streams, many hot springs, two mountain lakes, and excellent beaches along the coast. Saint George's, the capital, is on the S.W. coast and has a landlocked harbor.

Christopher Columbus (q.v.) discovered the island for Spain in 1498, but it remained uncolonized. In 1627 Spain granted it to England, from which France acquired it in 1650. The French settled there and established cacao, coffee, and cotton plantations, eventually exterminating the Caribs, the island's aboriginal inhabitants. After changing hands twice between England and France, Grenada became a permanent British possession in 1783. From 1958 to 1962 Grenada formed part of the Federation of The West Indies. In 1967 it became one of the West Indies Associated States, internally self-governing and in voluntary association with Great Britain, which continues to administer defense and external affairs.

Area, excluding Carriacou, 120 sq.mi.; area of

A steep hill overlooks the harbor of Saint George's, Grenada.   British West Indian Airways

Carriacou, 13 sq.mi. Total pop. (1968 est.) 104,168.

GRENADE, missile filled with an explosive charge, an incendiary, or a smoke-producing, illuminating, or chemical agent. Grenades are used to attack enemy troops, vehicles, or fortified positions at close range, and are categorized as hand or rifle grenades according to the method of delivery; see RIFLE.

High explosive fragmentation grenades are especially effective against personnel in foxholes or behind barricades, and against non-armored transport vehicles. The effectiveness of the grenade depends upon fragmentation of the body of the missile. Incendiary grenades set fire to matériel, and to wooden and other flammable military structures. Smoke grenades are used for area identification, or for signaling, and illuminating grenades produce artificial light that is particularly effective against night infiltration and sabotage attempts. Grenades filled with irritant chemical agents are used to force the withdrawal of the enemy, and being non-lethal, are also used by civilian law-enforcement agencies to quell riots and disperse crowds.

The latest fragmentation grenade used by the United States Army is lemon-shaped, weighs about 17 oz., and can be thrown about 35 to 50 yd. It contains 5 oz. of so-called Component B, the explosive charge, and the ignitor in the center, and these are encased in a shell of serrated-spring steel. The outer shell is smooth-pressed steel, and a curved lever, held in place with a pin, is attached to one end of the outer shell. The pin is pulled before the grenade is thrown, and this causes the lever to fly off, allowing a striker to ignite the primer and this in turn, explodes the grenade 4 or 5 sec. later. Rifle grenades are bullet-shaped and explode on impact; they are about 6-in. long, and can be fired accurately up to 400 yd. from a grenade launcher, which is similar in appearance to a sawed-off shotgun (q.v.).

Origin. The earliest grenade, a round earthenware container filled with powder and ignited by a wick, was made at Casalmaggiore, Italy, in 1427, but did not come into general use until the 16th and 17th centuries. At this time, metal or cardboard balls filled with a fine explosive powder and equipped with a hand lit fuse were thrown by hand or catapult, and were designed to set fires to enemy barricades and ammunition storage areas. Louis XIV (q.v.), King of France, organized elite grenade units called grenadiers, comprising the tallest and most powerful men in the regiments. With the perfection of muskets (see SMALL ARMS), grenade units became obsolete. Grenades were used again to some extent in the Russo-Japanese War (q.v.) in 1904–05, and used extensively in the trench-type battles of World War I.

Many types of grenades such as tin cans or bottles filled with explosives, have been improvised. During the Spanish Civil War (q.v.), bottles filled with gasoline were used effectively against tanks and vehicles. The so-called Molotov cocktails, which are glass bottles filled with paraffin and motor oil and covered with flaming petrol-soaked waste, were used effectively by Soviet Russia in World War II against vehicles and buildings.

Rifle grenades were introduced in World War I. They were equipped with a steel tail rod on the rear of the grenade that was inserted into the barrel of the rifle. The firing of a blank cartridge in the rifle generated sufficient force to propel the grenade about 150 yd. Similar launchers were used in World War II and the Korean War (q.v.), but they have now been replaced by the M–79 grenade launcher and the 40-mm family of grenade ammunition. See WARFARE.

GRENADINES, group of about 600 islets in the West Indies, within the Windward Islands, extending N.E. and S.W. between the islands of Grenada and Saint Vincent (qq.v.) for a distance of 60 mi. Only a few of the islets are inhabited. The N. section of the group is administered from St. Vincent, and the S. portion from Grenada. The largest of the Grenadines, Carriacou (area, 13 sq.mi.; pop., 1968, 8179), is administratively attached to Grenada. Bequia (area, 6 sq.mi.; pop., 1960 est., 3148) is the chief island of the northern group. Cotton and cattle are raised in the Grenadines. Total area, about 30 sq.mi.; pop. (1960 est.) 13,000.

GRENFELL, Sir Wilfred Thomason (1865–1940), British physician and missionary, born in Parkgate (now Neston), England, and educated at the University of Oxford and London Hospital. In 1889 he joined the Royal National Mission for Deep Sea Fishermen, and organized the first hospital ship to serve fishermen in the North Sea. In 1892 he began his famous work as a medical missionary among the fishermen and Eskimo in Labrador, where he established missions, hospitals, and schools, and helped organize industries. Grenfell lectured in Canada, the United States, and England to raise funds for his missions, and, in 1912, his supporters in those countries united to form the International Grenfell Association. In the same year Grenfell organized the Seaman's Institute at Saint John's, Newfoundland. Grenfell was knighted in 1927. He wrote many books about his experiences, including *Adrift on an Icepan* (1909), *Down North on Labrador* (1911), *The Adventure of Life* (1912), and *Forty Years for Labrador* (1932).

GRENOBLE, city in France, and capital of Isère Department, on the Isère R., in a mountainous region, 60 miles S.E. of Lyon. Grenoble is an important hydroelectric center with electrical and

Using an M-79 grenade launcher, an infantryman sights a target during an army exercise.   I. C. Rapaport – U.S. Army

machinery works. The city attracts about 100,000 tourists annually. Other industries include the manufacture of cement, chemicals, gloves, leather goods, paper, textiles, and hydroelectric turbines. A fortified garrison town until the 1850's, old fortresses remain southeast of the city. Grenoble is the seat of a bishopric dating from the 4th century A.D. Among the many old ecclesiastical buildings in the city are the 11th-century Church of Saint Laurent; the Cathedral of Notre Dame, parts of which date from the 11th century; and the 13th-century Church of Saint André. The renowned Carthusian monastery La Grande Chartreuse (see CARTHUSIANS) is nearby. The 15th-century Palais de Justice is the principal public building. The University of Grenoble (q.v.) was founded in 1339.

Grenoble is the ancient Cularo of the Allobroges, a tribe of Gaul. After the 4th century it was known, in honor of the Roman emperor Gratianus (q.v.), as Gratianopolis, the name eventually being transformed to Grenoble. The city was a part of the Kingdom of Provence (q.v.) from the 9th to the 11th century. Later it was made the capital of the former province of Dauphiné (q.v.); it became the capital of Isère upon the formation of that department in 1790. Pop. (1969) 165,902.

GRENOBLE, UNIVERSITY OF, institution of higher learning, located in Grenoble, France, under the jurisdiction of the ministry of education and supported by the National govern-

27

GRENVILLE

ment. The university was founded in 1339 by a papal bull, suppressed during the French Revolution, and reestablished in 1896. The university consists of the faculties of law and economic sciences, sciences, letters and human sciences, and medicine and pharmacy, as well as fifteen affiliated schools and institutes. The *licence,* the approximate equivalent of an American baccalaureate degree, is awarded after a three- to four-year course of study. The *diplôme d'études supérieures,* the approximate equivalent of an American degree of master, is awarded after an additional year of study. The *doctorat du troisième cycle* requires two years of study beyond the *licence* and the completion of a thesis. The highest degree is the *doctorat d'état,* which requires several years of additional study and the completion of a major and minor thesis. This degree qualifies the recipient to teach at a university and is comparable to an American Ph.D. The doctorate is awarded after the graduate diploma upon completion of a thesis, research, or both. The library contains about 430,000 volumes. In 1966–67 students numbered about 19,730 and the faculty, about 250.

GRENVILLE, name of a family of British statesmen. The most important members of the family were the following.

George Grenville (1712–70), born in London, England, and educated at Christ Church College, University of Oxford. In 1741 he became a member of Parliament, where he served for the rest of his life. Except for a brief period in 1757, he held office as treasurer of the navy from 1754 until 1762. Grenville was leader of the House of Commons and a member of the cabinet in 1761. In 1762–63 he occupied the post of first lord of the admiralty. In the following year he was named prime minister, first lord of the treasury, and chancellor of the exchequer. During his administration, libel proceedings were started against John Wilkes (q.v.), the British politician and reformer, and the Stamp Act (q.v.), one of the chief causes of friction between Great Britain and the American colonies, was enacted. He was in disfavor with George III (q.v.), King of England, who dismissed him in 1765. Grenville was known in Parliament as "the Gentle Shepherd" after the British statesman William Pitt the Elder (*see under* PITT) recited the words to a popular song "Gentle Shepherd, tell me where!" in reply to Grenville's querulous request that Parliament direct him where to impose new taxes.

William Wyndham Grenville, Baron Grenville (1759–1834), youngest son of George, educated at the University of Oxford. He became a member of Parliament in 1782, and in 1782–83 he was chief secretary for Ireland. He was made speaker of the House of Commons in 1789 but resigned in the same year to become secretary of state for the home department. In 1790 he was created baron. From 1791 to 1801 he served as secretary of state for foreign affairs during the ministry of William Pitt the Younger (*see under* PITT). In that office he negotiated Jay's Treaty (q.v.), a treaty resolving major differences between Great Britain and the United States. Although not always in accord with Pitt, Grenville resigned with him in protest against the refusal of George III to consent to legislation providing Roman Catholic emancipation. When offered a place in the new Pitt ministry in 1804, Grenville rejected it because his political ally, Charles James Fox (*see under* FOX), was excluded from the cabinet by the king. After the death of Pitt in 1806 Grenville became prime minister of a coalition government, called the Ministry of All-the-Talents, which secured the passage of a law abolishing the slave trade. The ministry, however, handled foreign affairs poorly. Unwilling to comply with the request of George III that no more measures proposing concessions to Roman Catholics be presented to Parliament, the Grenville cabinet resigned in 1807. Grenville did not again serve in an administrative office, although he was asked many times to do so, but he continued to hold a seat in Parliament.

GRENVILLE, Sir Richard *or* **GREYNVILLE, Sir Richard** (1541?–91), English naval officer, born in Cornwall. He headed the fleet of seven ships in which colonists organized by his cousin, the English soldier and explorer Sir Walter Raleigh (q.v.), went to Roanoke Island, N.C., in 1585. In 1591 Grenville sailed to the Azores as second-in-command of an expedition sent to capture a Spanish treasure fleet. His ship, the *Revenge,* was cut off from the rest of the English fleet and captured by the Spanish after a battle in which Grenville was mortally wounded. The battle is described in "The Revenge", a ballad by the British poet Alfred Lord Tennyson (q.v.).

GRESHAM, Sir Thomas (1519?–79), English financier, given credit in the history of economics as the formulator of Gresham's law (q.v.), born in London, and educated at the University of Cambridge. After attending the university, he was apprenticed to his uncle, a merchant, in whose service he displayed unusual business ability. In later years he became one of the wealthiest men in England. In 1551 he was appointed a factor, or royal agent, by Edward VI (q.v.), King of England, and charged with the management of the royal debt abroad, which he virtually liquidated subsequently by adroit financial manipulations on the bourse, or stock exchange, of Antwerp.

He was knighted by Elizabeth 1 (q.v.), Queen of England, in 1559. While serving as her financial agent abroad, Gresham found that his tasks were difficult to execute because of the lower value of English currency in relation to the currencies of other countries; he attributed this situation to the earlier debasement of English currency. In attempting to persuade Elizabeth to restore the currency of England, Gresham observed that "bad money drives out good". Although that principle of economics had been known long before Gresham's observation, it later became known as Gresham's law. He financed the construction of the Royal Exchange, which was opened in 1571; see EXCHANGE; STOCK EXCHANGE. His will made provision for the establishment of an institution of higher learning in London, which became known as Gresham College.

GRESHAM, Walter Quintin (1832–95), American soldier, jurist, and statesman, born near Lanesville, Ind., and educated at Indiana University. In 1854 Gresham was admitted to the bar and in 1860 was elected to the Indiana legislature as a Republican. In 1861, after the outbreak of the American Civil War, he was commissioned a colonel of the 43rd Indiana Infantry and served during the Vicksburg Campaign; see VICKSBURG, CAMPAIGN OF. After Vicksburg, Gresham was made brigadier general in command of the Union forces at Natchez, Miss. In 1864 he received a wound which lamed him for life. The following year he was awarded the honorary rank of major general.

Gresham returned to law practice and Republican politics and was made Federal district judge for Indiana in 1869. He was postmaster general under President Chester Alan Arthur (q.v.) in 1883 and 1884 and was secretary of the treasury briefly in 1884. He resigned that post after a month in order to accept appointment to the Circuit Court of Appeals. Gresham sought the Republican Presidential nomination unsuccessfully in 1884 and 1888, after which, disagreeing with Republican tariff policies, he became a Democrat. In 1892 he supported the campaign of former President Grover Cleveland (q.v.). He became secretary of state in Cleveland's second administration, serving in this post from 1893 until his death.

GRESHAM'S LAW, in economics, the principle that when depreciated or debased currency is in circulation along with coins that have full value in terms of precious metal, the latter tend to disappear. According to Gresham's law, the good coins, those of full value, are either exported or melted down in order to realize their higher market value in foreign exchange (q.v.) or as bullion. After the use of paper money became widespread, Gresham's law was also applied to the similar effect of the circulation of depreciated paper money on metallic money.

The phenomena described by Gresham's law were noted by merchants, financiers, and statesmen long before the 16th century. When the English financier Sir Thomas Gresham (q.v.) expressed the thought that "bad money drives out good", he made no theoretical exposition of the formulation, and not until the latter part of the 19th century did his principle become known as Gresham's law.

See MONEY.

GRETNA, city in Louisiana, and parish seat of Jefferson Parish, on the S. bank of the Mississippi R., opposite New Orleans, with which it is connected by ferry and the Greater New Orleans bridge. Gretna, a rail junction, manufactures petroleum and wood products, chemicals, fertilizer, cottonseed oil, and alcohol. The city was founded early in the 19th century as Mechanicsham. Incorporated in 1884, Gretna ab-

Sir Richard Grenville (1571), by an unknown artist.
National Maritime Museum, Greenwich

sorbed McDonoghville in 1913. Pop. (1960) 21,967; (1970) 24,875.

GRETNA GREEN, Great Britain, village of Dumfries County, Scotland, about 65 miles s. of Edinburgh, and just above the boundary between Scotland and England. Between 1754 and 1856 Gretna Green was the site of runaway marriages of citizens of England. Scottish law required only that a couple assent to marriage vows before witnesses. Anyone could officiate at a wedding ceremony, and the village blacksmith traditionally read the Anglican wedding service at a runaway marriage. The practice of performing such marriages for English couples in Gretna Green ended in 1856 with the passage of a statute requiring that at least one of the contracting parties should be a resident of Scotland for at least twenty-one days. Pop. (1961) 1930.

GRÉTRY, André Ernest Modeste (1741–1813), Belgian composer, born in Liège. He studied in Rome from 1759 to 1767, and settled in Paris in 1768. Grétry was a popular composer of comic opera. Among his most notable works are the comic operas *Zémire et Azor* (1771) and *L'Amant Jaloux* ("The Jealous Lover", 1778), and the serious opera *Richard Cœur de Lion* ("Richard the Lion-Hearted", 1784).

GREUZE, Jean Baptiste (1725–1805), French painter, born in Tournus. He studied in Lyon and Paris and became a leading practitioner of genre painting (q.v.). The subject of the first picture he exhibited, "A Father Explaining the Bible to His Children" (1755), was in marked contrast to the rococo (q.v.) painting then prevailing in France, and attracted wide attention. Greuze went on to paint a great number of moralistic genre works, including "The Village Bride" (1761, Louvre, Paris) and "The Wool Winder" (1759, Frick Collection, New York City). Greuze was also an eminent portraitist; among his portraits are those of Napoleon I (q.v.), Emperor of France (Versailles Museum); Armand Gensonne (1758–93), a French revolutionary politician (Louvre); and Sophie Arnould (1744–1802), a noted French opera singer (Wallace Collection, London).

GREVILLE, Sir Fulke, 1st Baron Brooke (1554–1628), English poet, born in Beauchamp Court, Warwickshire, and educated at Shrewsbury School and Jesus College, University of Cambridge. At Shrewsbury he met the English writer Sir Philip Sidney (q.v.), and the two became and remained close friends until the death of Sidney in 1586. Greville went to the court of Elizabeth I (q.v.), Queen of England, with Sidney in 1577, and soon became a prominent courtier. He was a member of Parliament four times between 1592 and 1620. In 1598 he became treasurer of the navy, and from 1614 to 1621 he was chancellor of the exchequer. He was created Baron Brooke in 1621. His writings include *The Tragedie of Mustapha* (1609), *Humane Learning* (1633), and *The Life of the Renowned Sir Philip Sidney* (1652).

GREVILLEA, large genus of trees and shrubs belonging to the Protea family Proteaceae. The genus, which includes approximately 230 species, is native to Australia and southern Asia and has become naturalized in the waste areas of Florida. The silk oak, *G. robusta*, which is especially valuable because of its resistance to drought, is cultivated in desert areas of Australia; it grows to a height of 150 ft. Its wood, used for barrel staves, is elastic and durable. The silk oak is used as a cultivated shade tree in the warmer parts of the United States, particularly in California. Young silk oaks, which are easily propagated from seed, are used on ornamental plants in greenhouses and on lawns. They bear graceful, orange-yellow flowers and have delicate, fernlike foliage. The wood of *G. striata*, which is harder and closer-grained than that of silk oak, is used extensively in the manufacture of furniture and cabinets. Another grevillea, *G. thelemanniana*, is a spreading shrub, cultivated in the U.S. and growing up to 5 ft. in height. It bears flowers that vary in color from pink to red.

GRÉVY, François Paul Jules (1807–91), French lawyer and statesman, third president of the

"The Wool Winder" (1759), painting by Jean Baptiste Greuze.   Frick Collection

Third French Republic, born in Mont-sous-Vaudrey, near Dôle. He was educated in law in Paris and became an advocate. A strong republican, he was elected to the constituent assembly in 1848. When it became apparent in 1852 that Louis Napoleon, later Napoleon III (q.v.), would become the next president of the republic, Grévy proposed making the president of the council, instead of the president of the republic, the highest public officer in France. (The president of the council was elected by the assembly and subject to removal by it, in contrast to the popularly elected president.) For that act Grévy was compelled to withdraw from politics. He was subsequently made president of the Paris bar. In 1868 he reentered politics and was chosen president of the national assembly in 1871, serving for two years. From 1876 until 1879, he was president of the chamber of deputies. When the distinguished French soldier Comte Marie Edme Patrice Maurice de MacMahon (q.v.) resigned from the presidency of the republic in 1879, Grévy was elected president. On the completion of his first term of office in 1885, he was reelected. In 1887, however, because his son-in-law, Daniel Wilson (1840–1904), was accused of trafficking in decorations of the Legion of Honor (q.v.), Grévy, although in no way implicated in the scandal, was forced to resign.

GREW, Nehemiah (1641–1712), English plant physiologist, born in Warwickshire, and educated at the universities of Cambridge and Leiden. He is known as one of the first investigators of the morphology and physiology of plants, and his books are among the earliest on those subjects. The Swedish botanist Carolus Linnaeus (q.v.), founder of the modern system of classification of organisms, named a genus of trees *Grewia* (q.v.) in his honor. Grew wrote *The Anatomy of Plants* (4 vol., 1682).

GREWIA, genus of Old-World shrubs and trees belonging to the Linden family Tiliaceae, named after the English plant physiologist Nehemiah Grew (q.v.). Plants of the genus have simple, alternate leaves, flowers borne in cymose clusters, and drupaceous fruits. Most grewias are native to tropical or subtropical Africa, Asia, and Australia. Several species which grow in India, such as *G. sapida* and *G. asiatica*, bear cherrylike fruits which are used in the manufacture of beverages. Fibers of the inner bark of *G. oppositifolia* are used by Himalayan tribes to make rope, and leaves of *G. laevigata* are fed to their cattle.

Several shrubby species have been introduced into the United States as cultivated ornamental plants. One hardy example is *G. parviflora,* native to China; it grows 6 to 10 ft. tall and bears large, toothed leaves and small clusters of light-yellow flowers. It is grown in all but the coldest parts of the U.S. A South African shrub or small tree *G. caffra,* bears purple flowers; it can be grown outdoors only in the warmer parts of the U.S.

GREY, name of a distinguished British family of statesmen and military leaders, including the following.

Charles Grey, 1st Earl Grey (1729–1807), military leader, born in Northumberland, England. At the age of nineteen he obtained a commission in the British army. In 1776, during the American Revolution (q.v.), Grey was posted to North America with the rank of major general. He commanded British forces in several successful engagements in New England and Pennsylvania. Upon his return to England in 1782 he was advanced to lieutenant general and named commander in chief of the forces in America; the war, however, was concluded. He retired from the service in 1801. He was named Viscount Horwick and Earl Grey in 1806.

Charles Grey, 2nd Earl Grey (1764–1845), statesman, the son of the 1st Earl, born near Alnwick, England, and educated at the University of Cambridge. In 1786 he became a Whig member of the House of Commons, and soon associated himself with the British statesman Charles James Fox (*see under* Fox). In 1797, when his proposals for electoral reform were rejected, Grey promoted the unsuccessful Whig secession from Parliament. After the deaths of Fox and of Prime Minister William Pitt the Younger (*see under* PITT), in 1806 Grey became foreign secretary in the coalition government of Prime Minister William Wyndham Grenville (*see under* GRENVILLE), and leader of the House of Commons. The government lost power after one year, however. Grey succeeded to the earldom in 1807, and in January, 1808, took his seat in the House of Lords. From 1812 to 1830 he was the leader of the opposition. In 1815 he broke with Grenville, who supported the decision of the ministry to renew the war with France upon the escape of Napoleon I (q.v.), Emperor of France, from Elba. When, in 1830, the agitation for reform had developed into a dangerous crisis, William IV (q.v.), King of England, summoned Grey to form a new government as prime minister. By convincing the king to threaten to create enough new peers to defeat the strong opposition in the House of Lords, Grey was able to pass the Reform Bill through Parliament in 1832; *see* REFORM BILLS. He resigned the prime ministry in July, 1834.

GREY

Albert Henry George Grey, 4th Earl Grey (1851–1917), statesman, the grandson of the 2nd Earl and the nephew of the 3rd Earl, born in London, England, and educated at the University of Cambridge. He entered the House of Commons in 1880 as a member of the Liberal Party but was defeated for reelection in 1886. From 1894, when he succeeded to the earldom, until his death, he was a member of the House of Lords. In addition he served as administrator of Rhodesia (1896–97) and as governor-general of Canada (1904–11); in the latter position he became extremely popular with the Canadian people.

Edward Grey, 1st Viscount Grey of Falladon (1862–1933), statesman, great-grandson of the 1st Earl, born in London, England, and educated at the University of Oxford. In 1885 he entered Parliament. He became undersecretary of state for foreign affairs in 1892, a member of the privy council in 1902, and secretary of state for foreign affairs in 1905. During the troubled years before World War I (q.v.), he conducted the negotiations with France and Russia that led to the formation of the Triple Entente (q.v.). He also warned Germany that Great Britain intended to support the French in Morocco, and he attempted to mediate in the Balkan Wars (q.v.) of 1912 and 1913, presiding over the negotiations of European ambassadors at the 1913 London Peace Conference.

At the outbreak of World War I he made his most famous speech, including the statement, "The lights are going out all over Europe; I doubt if we shall see some of them again in our time". In 1916 he resigned from the ministry and was elevated to the peerage. He was president of the League of Nations Council from its foundation in 1919 until his death and became chancellor of the University of Oxford in 1928. Among his writings are *Twenty-Five Years,*

Greyhound

1892–1916 (2 vol., 1925), and *Fallodon Papers* (1926).

GREY, Lady Jane (1537–54), Queen of England for nine days, born in Bradgate Park, near Leicester, a great-granddaughter of Henry VII (q.v.), King of England, and daughter of Henry Grey, Duke of Suffolk and 3rd Marquis of Dorset (d. 1554). When Lady Jane was fifteen, John Dudley, Duke of Northumberland and Earl of Warwick (*see under* DUDLEY), arranged a marriage for her with his son, Guildford Dudley (d. 1554). The duke's purpose was to change, through Lady Jane, the royal succession upon the death of the ailing young king, Edward VI (q.v.). Edward VI gave his approval of the marriage and through coercion secured the witnessing signatures of all but one of the judges in the council to a deed declaring Lady Jane his successor. Upon the death of the king, on July 6, 1553, Lady Jane was proclaimed queen, but the half-sister of Edward, Mary Tudor, later Mary I (q.v.), contested the succession. When the army of Mary defeated that of Northumberland, Lady Jane agreed to relinquish the throne to Mary. Lady Jane was subsequently imprisoned in the Tower of London (q.v.) with her father, who was soon released. The former queen and her husband were accused of treason, and both beheaded on Feb. 12, 1554.

GREY, Zane (1875–1939), American novelist, born in Zanesville, Ohio. He studied dentistry at the University of Pennsylvania, and practiced in New York City from 1898 to 1904, when he turned to writing. He wrote about sixty books, most of them tales of adventure with a Western setting, including *Riders of the Purple Sage* (1912), *The Lone Star Ranger* (1915), *The Wanderer of the Wasteland* (1923), *The Thundering Herd* (1925), *Code of the West* (1934), and *West of the Pecos* (1937). Most of his novels were best sellers and several were adapted for motion pictures. He also wrote several books on his hobby, fishing, including *Tales of Swordfish and Tuna* (1927) and *Adventures in Fishing* (posthumously published, 1952).

GREYHOUND, breed of hunting dog noted for its speed and keen sight. Carvings on Egyptian tombs prove that the greyhound was known in the third millennium B.C. The first complete description of the dog was written by the Roman poet Ovid (q.v.) in his *Metamorphoses,* about the beginning of the Christian era; the dog was known in England as early as the 9th century A.D. The derivation of its name is not certain; some authorities claim the term greyhound is derived from Graius or Grecian and others that the term came into being because the prevailing color of the breed once was gray. The dog has been used for hunting goat, fox, deer, and other game, particularly the hare. In England for the past 200 years the greyhound has been used in the popular sport of coursing (q.v.). In recent years the greyhound has been used as a racing dog in England and the United States; on race tracks built for the purpose, the dogs pursue an electrically propelled replica of a rabbit.

The greyhound is a large dog; the male weighs from 65 to 70 lb., the bitch from 60 to 65 lb. The breed is characterized by a long and narrow head; small, pointed ears; bright, intelligent eyes; a broad, muscular, and well-arched back; a deep, wide chest; thin, well-muscled loins; and a long tapering tail with a slight upward curve. It has a coat of smooth, short hair which is white, black, gray, or a combination of these colors. The greyhound is slender and graceful in appearance, and gentle in disposition.

GREYHOUND, ITALIAN. See ITALIAN GREYHOUND.

GRIBBLE, small, elongate, marine crustacean (see CRUSTACEA) of the genus *Limnoria* in the order Isapoda. One species, *L. lignorum*, is primarily a cold-water animal, found along European and North American coasts. Along the Pacific coast it occurs as far south as northern California; *L. quadripunctata* and *L. tripunctata* occur along the coats of central and southern California. These animals eat wood and often cause serious destruction to the submerged portions of harbor timber. The gribble is flattened and lacks a hard outer shell. It is about $\frac{1}{8}$ in. long. See BORER.

GRIEG, Edvard Hagerup (1843–1907), Norwegian composer, born in Bergen. He was taught the piano by his mother, a professional pianist, and from 1858 to 1862 studied piano, harmony, and theory at the Leipzig Conservatory. Subsequently Grieg was encouraged to become a composer by the Danish composer Niels Wilhelm Gade (q.v.); his interest in Norwegian folk music was awakened by the Norwegian composer Rikard Nordraak (1842–66). From 1866 to 1876 Grieg lived in Christiania (now Oslo), where he taught music and became conductor of the Philharmonic Society; during that time he also composed a number of his best-known works. In 1867 he married his cousin, Nina Hagerup (1845–1935), a distinguished soprano.

Grieg's advocacy of a school of music based on Norwegian folk music met with opposition from conservative musicians and critics, and his own works were at first slow in gaining recognition. The first musician of international stature to encourage his work was the Hungarian composer Franz Liszt (q.v.), who invited Grieg to visit him in Rome in 1870. In 1874 the Norwegian government granted Grieg an annual stipend that enabled him thenceforth to devote all his time to composition. He became world-famous for the incidental music he composed in 1875 for the poetic drama *Peer Gynt* by the Norwegian dramatist Henrik Ibsen (q.v.); two or-

Edvard Grieg

chestral suites drawn from this music are among the most popular of modern orchestral works. In 1877 Grieg moved to an isolated studio at Lofthus and in 1885 he built the villa "Troldhaugen" near Bergen, where he lived the rest of his life.

Grieg was the most important of Norwegian composers. Although his music was greatly influenced by that of the German Romantic composers, particularly Robert Schumann, and also by the works of the Polish musician Frédéric François Chopin (qq.v.), Grieg fashioned his melodies in the style of Norwegian folk music, and was a master of a harmonic style that has the power to evoke the atmosphere of his native land. Among his compositions are the works for string orchestra "Heart Wounds" and "The Last Spring" (melodies after a Norwegian poem), and Holberg Suite; the works for chorus and orchestra *Landsighting* and *Olaf Trygvason*; chamber music, including three sonatas for violin and piano and a string quartet; and numerous piano pieces, including *Lyric Pieces* (in ten books), Ballade in G minor, and the popular Piano Concerto in A minor. He was particularly distinguished as a writer of songs; among the 150 songs he composed are "I Love Thee", "Solvejg's Song", and "The Odalisque".

GRIFFIN, or GRIFFON or GRYPHON, mythical creature, half bird, half animal, usually represented in literature and art as having the head, beak, and wings of an eagle, and the body and legs of a lion. In variant forms it appears with a horned head, of either a leopard or tiger, or with the head of a cock and all four legs like those of an eagle; occasionally it has a serpent for a tail. The griffin seems to have originated in the East, as it is found in the paintings and sculptures of the ancient Babylonians, Assyrians, and Persians. The Romans used the griffin merely for decorative purposes in friezes and on table legs, altars, and candelabra. The griffin motif appeared in early Christian times in the Bestiaries, or beast allegories, of Saint Basil and Saint Ambrose. Stone replicas of griffins frequently served as gargoyles in the Gothic architcture of the late Middle Ages. The griffin is still a familiar device in heraldry.

GRIFFIN, city in Georgia, and county seat of Spalding Co., 35 miles s.e. of Atlanta. It lies in a region of cotton fields, fruit orchards, and truck farms. Industries include peach and vegetable canning and the manufacture of furniture, textiles ber, industrial equipment, chemicals, and rubber products. A State agricultural experiment station is nearby. Griffin was laid out in 1840 and incorporated a few years later. Pop. (1960) 21,735; (1970) 22,734.

GRIFFITH, Arthur (1872–1922), Irish political leader and journalist, born in Dublin, and educated in local schools. After several years of working as a printer and newspaperman, he founded, in 1899, the weekly *United Irishman*, to which such well-known Irish writers as George William Russell and William Butler Yeats (qq.v.) contributed. Griffith himself wrote eloquent editorials urging the Irish to work for self-government within their own country, rather than to strive for representation in the British Parliament. He founded a group in 1902 which later became the nucleus of the Sinn Féin (q.v.), whose policy was to refuse to pay taxes to the British government, and to form a separate Irish Parliament, the only link with Britain being a formal submission to the crown. Griffith, who was against any partition of Ireland, supported the Irish National Volunteers, a group opposed to the Home Rule Bill of 1912 which excluded Ulster from the future state of Ireland.

Although Griffith took no overt part in the Easter Rebellion (q.v.) of 1916, the British imprisoned him as a Nationalist leader. He was released the following year, but again imprisoned in 1918. After the Armistice of 1918, a general election put the Sinn Féin leaders in power, and the new members of Parliament, meeting as the Dáil Eireann (q.v.), or "Assembly of Ireland", elected Griffith vice-president of an Irish republic, under President Eamon de Valera (q.v.). Months after his election Griffith was still in prison, but after his release, while de Valera was in the United States in 1919–20, he served as head of the new republic, and in 1921 he accepted the responsibility of leading the delegation to Great Britain to negotiate the treaty of recognition for the Irish Free State. Griffith was elected first president of the duly constituted Dáil Eireann in January, 1922, but died the following August, shortly after the outbreak of the Irish civil war. His newspaper, always a powerful force in the Irish Nationalist movement, was several times compelled, by political or economic pressure, to cease publication and to reappear under a different name. *See* IRELAND: *History*; IRELAND, REPUBLIC OF: *History*.

GRIFFITH, David (Lewelyn) Wark (1875–1948), American motion-picture director, born in La Grange, Ky., and educated in local schools. Griffith was an actor in stock and road companies before he became a motion-picture actor for the Biograph Film Company in 1908. He then became a director for the company in New York City and in California, and in 1913 an independent producer. His pictures *Judith of Bethulia* (1913), *Birth of a Nation* (1915), and *Intolerance* (1916) established him as the leading motion-picture producer of the time. With these and other pictures Griffith established a new standard for motion-picture production.

Up to his time motion pictures had been short, rarely exceeding one reel; episodic rather than dramatic; and poorly produced, acted, and edited. Griffith's motion pictures contained powerful dramatic situations and vivid characters, were produced with technical virtuosity, and frequently were several hours in length. He originated some of the best-known devices in motion-picture production, such as the close-up, a close view of a character's face or figure, or of an object, shown for dramatic emphasis; the fade-out, a transition from one scene to another by the gradual disappearance of the first scene from the screen; and the cutback or flashback, the introduction, for purposes of clarification of plot or characterization, of scenes antedating those already shown.

In 1920, with the film actors Douglas Fairbanks, Mary Pickford, and Charles Spencer Chaplin (qq.v.), Griffith formed the United Artists Corporation for the production of feature pictures. Among the motion pictures he directed for that company were *Broken Blossoms* (1919), *Way Down East* (1920), *The Orphans of the Storm* (1921), *Battle of the Sexes* (1928), and *Lady of the Pavement* (1928). All the above-mentioned productions were silent pictures, with the exception of the last, in which there was some singing. Griffith made only two talking pictures, which were not so successful as his silent films. He retired as a motion-picture director in 1932 and as a member of United Artists in 1933.

See MOTION PICTURES: *History: Rise of the American Film.*

GRIFFON, breed of dog named for the griffin (q.v.), a mythological animal, which it supposedly resembles. Two principal types of griffon are found: a hunting dog known as the wire-haired pointing griffon; and a toy dog known as the Brussels griffon.

The wire-haired pointing griffon was first bred in the last quarter of the 19th century by the Dutch breeder E. K. Korthals, near Haarlem, the Netherlands; the breed was subsequently developed, by him and by others, in France, and was imported into England in the late 19th century and into the United States in 1900. The wire-haired pointing griffon has a keen scent and great ability both in pointing and retrieving game. It is a medium-sized, vigorous animal, the male standing 21½ to 23½ in. at the shoulder and the bitch 19½ to 21½. It has a hard, stiff and bristly coat which makes the dog well adapted to swimming and to hunting in marshy country. Its color is steel gray or gray white, with chestnut splashes, or entirely chestnut. The dog has a long head; a square muzzle; brown nose; flat ears set high; and long, sloping shoulders.

The Brussels griffon is a tiny dog valued as a pet. There are two types: the small, which weighs 7 lb. or less; and the large, which weighs no more than 11 lb. (males) or 12 lb. (bitches). The dog has a wiry, dense, reddish-brown coat; a large, round head; a short nose; unusually large and prominent eyes, black in color; and an undershot chin.

GRIGNARD, Victor (1871–1934), French chemist, born at Cherbourg, and educated at the University of Lyon. He taught organic chemistry at Lyon from 1906 until 1909 and then at the University of Nancy, where he was a full professor from 1910. Grignard's fame rests upon his discovery, first disclosed in his doctoral thesis

Brussels griffon

written in 1900, of the so-called Grignard reagents, which are of great value in synthesizing complex organic compounds. For this discovery he shared the 1912 Nobel Prize in chemistry with the French chemist Paul Sabatier (q.v.).

GRILLPARZER, Franz (1791–1872), Austrian playwright, born in Vienna. He studied law at the University of Vienna, but for financial reasons left after two years. Starting in 1813 as a clerk in the government revenue administration, he had a successful career in the civil service until his retirement in 1856, but he regarded his official career merely as a means of income. Grillparzer wrote many plays of dramatic and poetic beauty, particularly notable for their psychological insight into character. He was an influence on later dramatists, including the German playwright Gerhart Hauptmann and the Belgian dramatist Maurice Maeterlinck (qq.v.). Among Grillparzer's works are the dramas *Sappho* (1818), *Das Goldene Vlies* ("The Golden Fleece", 1822), *Das Meeres und der Liebe Wellen* (1831; Eng. trans., *Hero and Leander*, 1938), *Der Traum ein Leben* (1834; Eng. trans., *A Dream Is Life*, 1946), *Die Jüdin von Toledo* (1872; Eng. trans., *The Jewess from Toledo*, 1953); and the novella *Der Arme Spielmann* (1844; Eng. trans., *The Poor Minstrel*, 1915).

GRILSE. See SALMON.

GRIMALDI. See MONACO; RANIER III.

GRIMALDI, Joseph (1779–1837), British clown and pantomimist, born in London, England, the son of an Italian actor. He made his stage debut at the age of two at the Drury Lane Theatre (q.v.), London, and appeared at that theater every season until 1806, when he moved to the Covent Garden Theatre (q.v.). His best-known role was that of the clown in the pantomime *Harlequin and Mother Goose,* first produced in 1806 and frequently revived. Grimaldi was the

35

most famous clown in the history of pantomime (q.v.); his nickname "Joey" came into colloquial use in England as a synonym for clown. He retired in 1828, worn out by hard work. His last appearance was as "Harlequin Hoax" in a benefit given for him in 1828 at the Drury Lane Theatre. His *Memoirs of Joseph Grimaldi* (1838) were edited by the British novelist Charles Dickens (q.v.).

GRIMM, name of two German philologists and mythologists who were brothers: **Jacob Ludwig Karl Grimm** (1785–1863) and **Wilhelm Karl Grimm** (1786–1859). They were frequently referred to as "The Brothers Grimm".

The brothers, both born in Hanau and educated at the University of Marburg, followed similar careers. Jacob was primarily a scientific philologist, having become interested at the university in medieval literature and the scientific investigation of language. Wilhelm was more a textual and literary critic. After several years in diplomatic and library posts in Kassel, the brothers went in 1830 to the University of Göttingen, where Wilhelm became a librarian and Jacob a lecturer on ancient law, literary history, and philosophy. For political reasons the brothers returned to Kassel in 1837. In 1841, at the invitation of Frederick William IV (q.v.), King of Prussia, they settled in Berlin, where they remained for the rest of their lives as teachers at the university.

Jacob Grimm's greatest scientific work is *Deutsche Grammatik* ("German Grammar", 1819), generally considered the foundation of Germanic philology. The 2nd edition (1822) contains his formulation of Grimm's Law (q.v.). His other works include *Über den Altdeutschen Meistergesang* ("On the Old German Meistersinging", 1811), *Deutsche Mythologie* ("German Mythology", 1835), and *Geschichte der Deutschen Sprache* ("History of the German Language", 1848). Some of Wilhelm Grimm's works, which include editions and critical discussions of medieval German literature and folklore, are *Altdänische Heldenlieder* ("Old Danish Hero-Songs", 1811), *Die Deutschen Heldensage* ("The German Heroic Legends", 1829), *Ruolandslied* ("The Song of Roland", 1838), and *Altdeutsche Gespräche* ("Old German Speech", 1851).

Jacob and Wilhelm Grimm were attracted to old German folktales, which they collected from many sources and published as *Kinder- und Hausmärchen* (2 vol., 1812–15; Eng. trans., *Household Tales*, 1884). The collection, which the brothers revised and expanded as late as 1857, is popularly known in English as "Grimm's Fairy Tales". The brothers collaborated on numerous other works. In 1854 they published the first volume of the monumental *Deutsches Wörterbuch*, the standard German dictionary, which was completed by other scholars in 1954.

The brothers Grimm, Jacob (right) and Wilhelm.
German Information Center

GRIMM, Baron (Friedrich) Melchior von (1723–1807), French writer, born in Ratisbon (now Regensburg, West Germany), and educated at Leipzig. In 1748 he traveled to Paris as the tutor of a young German nobleman. He remained in France, becoming friendly with the French writers Jean Jacques Rousseau, Madame Louise Florence Pétronille de la Live d'Épinay, Denis Diderot (qq.v.), and other members of the group known as the Encyclopedists (q.v.). In 1753 Grimm and Diderot, assisted by Mme. d'Épinay, began a newsletter for foreign monarchs, commenting on life in Paris. The letters, written mostly by Grimm and sent every two weeks through diplomatic channels, related, frankly and confidentially, literary and social gossip, political news, and analyses of new books. They dealt extensively with current ideas in Parisian literary and philosophical circles. Among the subscribers were Stanislas II Augustus, King of Poland and Catherine II (qq.v.), Empress of Russia. After 1773 the letters were taken over by Grimm's secretary, the Swiss writer Jakob Heinrich Meister (1744–1826); they were published as *Correspondence Littéraire,*

Philosophique, et Critique ("Literary, Philosophical, and Critical Correspondence", 17 vol., 1812–14).

During most of his career in Paris, Grimm was also engaged in diplomatic work. In 1775 he was made a baron of the Holy Roman Empire. He gained the favor of Catherine II, and lived in Saint Petersburg (now Leningrad) from 1792 to 1795, after the French Revolution had driven him from France. In 1796 Catherine sent him as minister to Hamburg, but upon her death the same year, he retired to Gotha, where he spent his last years.

GRIMMELSHAUSEN, Hans Jakob Christoffel von (about 1620–76), German writer, born reputedly in Gelnhausen. He was a soldier in the Thirty Years' War (q.v.); in the latter part of his life he was converted from Protestantism to Catholicism, entered the employ of the bishop of Strasbourg, and in 1667 became a magistrate at Renchen, Baden-Württemberg. Grimmelshausen was the author of a number of picaresque novels (see PICARESQUE NOVEL), including *Der Abenteuerliche Simplicissimus* (1669; Eng. trans., *The Adventuresome Simplicissimus*, 1912), one of the outstanding German novels of the 17th century. In this work, dealing with the adventures of a naïve youth who is in turn soldier, jester, robber, slave, and hermit, a realistic picture is given of the social and economic conditions created in Germany by the Thirty Years' War. His other novels include *Der Keusche Joseph* ("Innocent Joseph", 1667), *Dietwald und Amelinde* (1670), and *Die Erzbetrügerin und Landstörtzerin Courasche* ("The Female Archimposter and Troublemaker", 1670).

GRIMM'S LAW, phonetic law enunciated by the German philologist Jacob Grimm (see under GRIMM) in the second edition of his *Deutsche Grammatik* published in 1822. It describes the pattern of the two stages of sound changes known respectively as the German consonant shift and the High German consonant shift.

The first stage occurred between 2000 B.C. and 200 A.D., when certain consonants of the Germanic language, one of the family of Indo-European Languages (q.v.), evolved from corresponding consonants in the Indo-European parent language.

The second stage occurred between 500 and 700 A.D. in the High German dialects of southern Germany. Among these dialects, only those of the most southerly regions experienced the full development. Standard Literary German reflects an incomplete stage of the development found in the other High German dialects. The following table shows the regular correspondences of both stages of the consonant shift but does not include aberrant developments. The symbols are those traditionally used in comparative grammar.

STAGE I (2000 B.C.–200 A.D.)		STAGE II (500–700 A.D.)
Indo-European	Germanic	High German
p	f	f
t	th	dh/d
k	x, then h	h
b	p	pf
d	t	tz (written z)
g	k	kh/k
bh	b	p/b
dh	d	t
gh	g	k/g

Examples: Latin *pes*, English *foot*, German *Fusz*; Latin *duo*, English *two*, German *zwei*; Sanskrit *dhati*, English *deed*, German *Tat*.

There are no inscriptions in Indo-European, but the recorded languages evolved from it indicate that at least the corresponding consonant-sounds formulated in Grimm's Law existed in the parent language. The recorded languages suggest also the relation of these Indo-European consonants to each other with respect to the vocal organs that produced them and the manner of their articulation. The exact sounds produced in their pronunciation are unknown.

The Germanic and High German consonant changes did not occur individually but as part of parallel developments. The parallelism was governed by the manner of articulation; for example, the German fricatives /f/, /th/, and /h/ (bars represent phonemic symbols; see PHONETICS) developed from the Indo-European consonants /p/, /t/, and /k/, which were all articulated in the same manner. However, all of the consonants involved in these changes remained as distinct from each other after the shifts had taken place as the corresponding Indo-European consonants had been previously distinct from each other; see PHONETIC LAW.

The changes described in Grimm's Law were so comprehensive that few Indo-European consonants were not affected; those which remained unaltered are /r/, /l/, /m/, /n/, and /s/. However, /s/ joined the shifted consonants in certain additional changes explained by the Danish philologist Karl Adolf Verner; see VERNER'S LAW.

The Danish philologist Rasmus Christian Rask (q.v.), in a work on the origin of Old Norse published in 1818, noted the existence of the consonant shifts. Grimm, however, further perceived that both the Germanic and High German shifts

GRIMSBY

were part of the same phonetic tendency and first formulated the pattern of those changes.

E.S.K.

GRIMSBY, Great Britain seaport and county borough of Lincolnshire, England, on the North Sea, near the mouth of the Humber R., 18 miles S.E. of Hull. Grimsby is the major fishing port of Great Britain, and one of the greatest fishing centers in the world. Trawlers operating out of Grimsby range from the Arctic Ocean to the Mediterranean Sea. In addition to fish docks, the harbor facilities of Grimsby include dry docks, and wharves accommodating ship lines with regular service to the Continent. Other leading industries are shipbuilding, brewing, and the manufacture of chemicals and rope. Large quantities of coal are exported from the port, and timber is a principal import. Among the notable buildings in Grimsby are the Church of Saint James, of Norman and Early English architecture, the Exchange, and the structure containing the town hall and the grammar school (founded in 1547). Grimsby is the traditional site of the landings of the Danish in their invasions of Britain in the 8th century. In 1201 John (q.v.), King of England, granted the town a charter and the right to hold an annual fair. During medieval times Grimsby was a noted seaport, but it declined in importance as its harbor became blocked by silt from the Humber R. In the 19th century the harbor underwent constant improvement and expansion. Pop. (1969 est.) 96,500.

GRINDELIA, genus of herbs belonging to the Composite family Compositae, named after the Russian botanist David Hieronymus Grindel (1776–1836). The genus comprises about 50 species, found in the temperate and tropical regions of North America, mostly west of the Mississippi R. The yellow-flowered plants are coarse biennials or perennials, many of which exude a sticky resin. Leaves and flowers of three species, *G. robusta, G. squarrosa,* and *G. cuneifolia,* commonly called gum plants or tarweeds, are used in preparing fluid extract of grindelia, a medicine that has been administered internally in the treatment of asthma, whooping cough, and bronchitis, and applied externally in cases of ivy poisoning. Grindelias are not usually cultivated, although *G. robusta* is sometimes transplanted to poor garden soils for ornament.

GRINDING AND POLISHING, two abrasive processes for shaping and smoothing hard materials such as metal, glass, and precious and semiprecious gems. Polishing uses extremely fine abrasive substances, such as jeweler's rouge, tripoli, whiting, putty powder, and emery dust to rub or burnish an extremely smooth and brilliant finish on the surface of a material. The polishing materials are coated on the surface of cloth, felt, or leather wheels. One special type of polishing wheel is made of soft rubber with the abrasive grains molded into it.

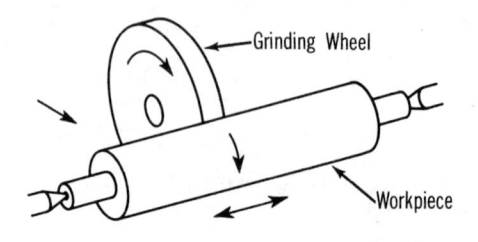

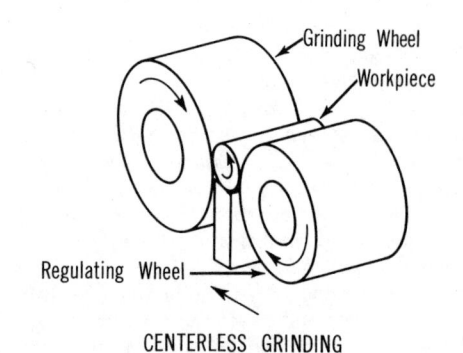

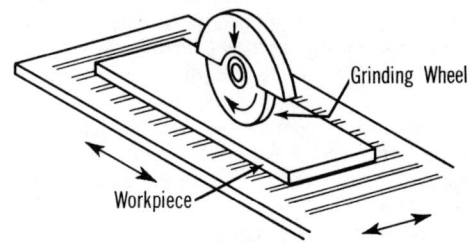

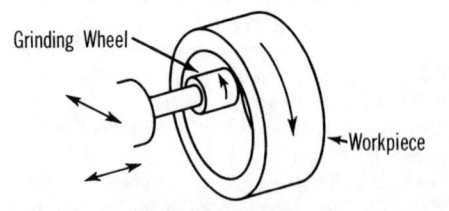

CENTERTYPE GRINDING

CENTERLESS GRINDING

SURFACE GRINDING

INTERNAL GRINDING

Methods of grinding. (Top to bottom): Centertype grinding: A method of producing cylindrical forms. Centerless grinding: An alternate method of producing cylindrical forms, used especially for mass production. Surface grinding: A method of producing flat surfaces. Internal grinding: A method of finishing internal diameters.

Two special finishing operations used in metalworking are honing and lapping. Honing improves the accuracy and finish of automobile cylinder bores, hydraulic cylinders, and similar parts. The honing machine consists of four fine-grain abrasive stones attached to an expandable tool which is then slowly revolved and oscillated inside the cylinder until the desired finish and diameter are obtained. Lapping is done by rubbing a surface with an abrasive lubricated with oil, grease, or alcohol. This operation is usually performed with a tool called a lap that matches the contour of the surface being finished. The lap is spread with a thin layer of the abrasive, and the two parts are then rubbed together with irregular strokes. Less than .001 in. of material is removed during lapping, and both the accuracy and the surface finish of the finished product are improved.

Grinding is actually a cutting operation in which each grit that comes in contact with the material cuts out a minute chip, or swarf. Grinding wheels usually consist of particles of a synthetic abrasive, such as silicon carbide or aluminum oxide, mixed with a vitrified or resinoid bonding material. Grinding can be coarse or fine, depending on the size of the grit used in the grinding wheel. Metal and glass can be ground to a mirror finish and an accuracy of 0.000001 in. On a production basis, hundreds of millions of parts per year are routinely ground to an accuracy of 0.0005 in.

Grinding machines are machine tools equipped with precision grinding wheels and suitable means for holding, positioning, rotating, or traversing the workpiece so that it can be ground to the desired size, shape, and finish. The grinding wheel is mounted on a motor-driven spindle that turns the wheel at about 6500 surface feet per minute. Grinding machines are usually classified according to the shape of the workpiece being ground, the manner in which it is held or supported, and the structure of the machine. Basically, the four types of precision grinding machines are: center-type cylindrical grinders, centerless grinders, internal grinders, and surface grinders.

Center-type grinders accommodate cylindrical workpieces that have been center-drilled at each end, enabling the workpiece to be held between two centers and rotated. Parts ground between centers range from valve spools weighing a few ounces to steel mill rolls more than 5 ft. in diameter and weighing nearly 100 tons.

Centerless grinders eliminate the need for center-drilling the ends of the workpiece. Instead, the workpiece is supported by a rest blade and regulating wheel, the latter also controlling the rotation of the workpiece. Such items as bowling balls, surgical sutures, and tapered roller bearings are ground on centerless grinders.

Internal grinders finish-grind the inside diameters of gears, bearing races, and similar parts. The grinding wheels used are small and rotate at extremely high speeds, from 15,000 to 200,000 revolutions per minute (r.p.m.). The workpiece rotates slowly against the grinding wheel.

Surface grinders grind flat surfaces. The workpiece is laid on a flat table and held in place by magnetism or hold-down devices. The grinding wheel is lowered onto the workpiece, and the table moves back and forth or rotates slowly.

GRIQUA, name applied to descendants of Dutch farmers and Hottentot women, now inhabiting Griqualand West and the Transkeian Territory of Griqualand East, both in Cape of Good Hope Province, Republic of South Africa (see CAPE OF GOOD HOPE, PROVINCE OF THE); they were formerly known as Bastaards. The Griqua, who at one time lived farther south in the present Cape of Good Hope Province, migrated north in the early decades of the 19th century under the leadership of two chiefs, Andries Waterboer (d. 1852) and Adam Kok II (d. about 1835). In 1862 the son of the latter, Adam Kok III (d. 1876), with some 15,000 followers, moved eastward to the region now known as Griqualand East. *See also* HOTTENTOT.

GRIQUALAND WEST. See CAPE OF GOOD HOPE, PROVINCE OF THE: *History.*

GRIS, Juan (1887–1927), Spanish-born French painter, born José Vittoriano Gonzalez in Madrid, and educated there at the Escuela de Artes y Manufacturas (now the Escuela Industrial). He left Madrid in 1906 and went to Paris, making the acquaintance of the Spanish artist Pablo Picasso and the French painter Georges Braque (qq.v.). Gris' first Cubist paintings appeared in 1912; *see* CUBISM. He spent the next summer in Céret, France, with Picasso, and while there adopted the use of papier collé, shapes cut from paper and glued to the canvas. During World War I he worked in Paris; he had his first one-man exhibition in Paris in 1919. From 1922 to 1924 he designed settings for the ballets of the Russian producer Sergei Pavlovich Diaghilev (q.v.), *Les Tentations de la Bergère* ("The Temptations of the Shepherdess") and *La Colombe* ("The Dove"), as well as continuing work upon his own paintings. After 1925 he worked mainly on gouaches, watercolors, and illustrations for books. Typical of his cut-paper technique is "Glasses and Newspaper" (1914; Smith College

GRISSOM

"La Table du Café" by Juan Gris (1912).
Art Institute of Chicago — Gift of Kate L. Brewster

Museum of Art, Northampton, Mass.). Typical of his Cubist paintings are "Guitar and Bottle" (1917; Philadelphia Museum of Art), "The Chessboard" (1917; Museum of Modern Art, New York City), and "Guitar and Fruit Dish" (1919; Albright Art Gallery, Buffalo, N.Y.).

GRISSOM, Virgil Ivan (1926–67), American astronaut, born in Mitchell, Ind. He received a B.S. degree from Purdue University in 1950 and became a pilot in the United States Air Force in 1951. In the Korean War Grissom flew more than one hundred combat missions. After the war he served as a test pilot and flight instructor. He was one of the first seven astronauts selected in 1959 for the space program of the National Aeronautics and Space Administration (NASA). Grissom was the second American in space, following Naval Commander Alan B. Shepard, Jr. (1923–). In the Mercury capsule Liberty Bell VII Grissom spent 15 min. in suborbital flight in July, 1961. In March, 1965, Grissom and Naval Lieutenant Commander John W. Young (1930–) completed three orbits in 5 hr. in Gemini III, the first American two-man space mission. On Jan. 27, 1967, Grissom was killed in a fire during a simulated flght at Cape Kennedy, Fla. Killed with him in the Apollo capsule were Naval Lieutenant Commander Roger B. Chaffee (1935–67) and Air Force Lieutenant Colonel Edward H. White (1930–67). *See* ASTRONAUTICS.

GRODNO, city of the Soviet Union, in the White Russian S.S.R., in Grodno Oblast, on the Niemen R., about 125 miles w. of Minsk and 20 miles E. of the Polish border. An important port, rail, and diversified industrial center, the city produces ball bearings, clothing, construction materials, electric apparatus, foodstuffs, glass, kitchen and plumbing equipment, shoes, and textiles.

Dating from the 10th century, Grodno was part of an independent principality until 1398, after which it was alternately under Lithuanian and Polish rule. It was ceded to Russia in 1795, made part of Poland in 1920, and incorporated into the U.S.S.R. in 1939. During World War II Grodno was occupied by German troops from 1941 until 1945. Pop. (1970) 132,000.

GROETE, Gerhard. See GROOTE, GERHARD.

GROFÉ, Ferde (1892–   ), American composer, orchestral conductor, and orchestrator, born Ferdinand Rudolph von Grofé in New York City. He studied violin, piano, and harmony with his mother, viola with his grandfather, and orchestration with the Italian-American composer Pietro Floridia (1860–1932), and became a member of symphonic, theater, and jazz orchestras. About 1920 he became pianist and orchestrator with the noted band conducted by the American jazz musician Paul Whiteman (q.v.). Grofé is particularly known for his orchestration of *Rhapsody in Blue* (1924) by the American composer George Gershwin (q.v.), a pioneer work in symphonic jazz, or jazz written in large musical form. Subsequently Grofé conducted his own orchestra on radio programs, and wrote a number of compositions in symphonic jazz, including *Mississippi Suite* (1925) and *Grand Canyon Suite* (1931).

GROMWELL, English name for an erect perennial herb, *Lithospermum officinale,* in the Borage family, Boraginaceae, with small, white, funnel-shaped flowers that are borne singly in the axils of the upper leaves. Native to Eurasia, it attains a height of 3 ft. and grows as a weed in waste places in northeastern North America. Species of *Lithospermum* that are native to North America bear larger, bright yellow or orange, trumpet-shaped flowers. Mostly plants of prairies and open woods, these gromwells are known by their Indian name of puccoon; see BLOODROOT. Plants in the closely related genus *Onosmodium* are popularly referred to as false gromwells.

GROMYKO, Andrei Andreevich (1909–), Soviet diplomat, born in Starye Gromyki, near Minsk. He received an M.A. degree from the Institute of Economics in Moscow, in 1936. Gromyko joined the People's Commissariat of Foreign Affairs in 1939 and received increasingly important appointments, including counselor of the Soviet embassy in the United States (1939–43), ambassador to the U.S. (1943–46), and chief of the Soviet delegation to the Dumbarton Oaks Conference (1944). He was also a member of the Soviet delegation to the United Nations Charter conference in San Francisco, Calif., in 1945. In 1949 Gromyko was permanent Soviet representative to the U.N. and a first deputy foreign minister (1949–52), ambassador to Great Britain (1952–53), and chief deputy foreign minister (1953–57). He became foreign minister of the U.S.S.R. in 1957, a position in which he implemented rather than initiated Soviet foreign policy.

GRONCHI, Giovanni (1887–   ), Italian statesman, born in Pontedera, and educated at the University of Pisa. Gronchi became active in the Roman Catholic trade union movement at the age of fifteen and later served with distinction in World War I. In 1919 he was elected to parliament as a candidate of the Popular (Popolare) Party, which he helped to found. As a leader of that group, the forerunner of the Christian Democratic Party, he held an undersecretaryship in the government formed in October, 1922, by the Italian dictator Benito Mussolini (q.v.). Gronchi joined the anti-Fascist opposition in August, 1923, whereupon he was expelled from the government and parliament. He was prominent in the anti-Fascist underground movement during World War II, serving as a representative of the Christian Democratic Party on the leading committee of the National Liberation Front, and held cabinet positions in several postwar governments. Widely respected for his liberalism, militant Roman Catholicism, and oratorical ability, he was elected speaker of the chamber of deputies in 1948 and served until April, 1955. Gronchi was president of Italy from that time until May, 1962. His autobiography was published in the same year.

GRONINGEN, city in the Netherlands, and capital of Groningen Province, on the canalized Hunse R., about 90 miles N.E. of Amsterdam. Groningen, the largest city in the N. region of the country, has a number of canals and is an important port. The principal industries are the production of beet sugar, beer, flax, furniture, bicycles, pianos, and tobacco; a large trade is carried on in cattle, wheat, and oilseed. In addition, many goldsmith, silversmith, and book-printing shops are located in the city. Among

Andrei Gromyko UPI

GROOTE

the places of interest are Saint Martin's Church (13th to 16th centuries), the Aa Church (13th century), and the New Church (17th century). In the library of the University of Groningen, founded in 1614, is a copy of the Latin translation of the New Testament by the Dutch humanist Desiderius Erasmus, annotated by the German religious reformer Martin Luther (qq.v.). Groningen is the site of an ancient Roman camp. In 1040 the settlement was granted to the bishop of Utrecht by Henry III (q.v.), Holy Roman Emperor. The town was fortified in 1255, and prior to 1284 it joined the Hanseatic League (q.v.). By the end of the 14th century, power was wrested from the bishop by the rich burghers. The subsequent history of the city parallels that of the country; see NETHERLANDS, THE: *History.* Pop. (1968) 167,670.

GROOTE, Gerhard or **GROOT, Gerhard** or **GROETE, Gerhard** (Lat. *Gerardus Magnus*) (1340–84), Dutch preacher, born in Deventer, and educated at the University of Paris, where he studied theology, medicine, and astronomy, and in Germany and Poland. Groote, as a traveling deacon, preached against the barriers that Greek and Latin presented to lay people and advocated translation of the Scriptures into the language of the country. He translated the Psalms (q.v.) into Dutch and in 1376 gathered together a group of men to do further translations. These men put their goods into common trust and called themselves the Brethren of the Common Life. Groote taught them the monastic priciples of Saint Augustine (q.v.) of Hippo; after Groote's death, many of them broke with the original order to found (1386) the Augustinian Order of Canons Regular, at Windesheim, near Zwolle, the Netherlands. In the 15th century the order brought about moral reforms in the way of life of clerics in numerous monasteries (*see* AUGUSTINIANS).

GROPIUS, Walter (Adolf) (1883–1969), German-American architect, born in Berlin, and educated at the Technische Hochschule, Munich, and the Technische Hochschule, Berlin. He began to practice as an architect in 1910, interrupting his career for military service during World War I. At Weimar in 1919, he founded the Bauhaus (q.v.), a school of design at which art and architectural training were related to modern technology. In 1925 he designed the new Bauhaus in Dessau; this became the model for a

Walter Gropius   Harvard University News Office

revolutionary type of architecture described as functional and later called the International Style. He continued as director of the school until 1928 and then returned to architectural practice in Berlin. With the apointment of Adolf Hitler (q.v.) as chancellor of Germany in 1933, Gropius, who was opposed to the government restrictions on art, left Berlin. He settled in London, England, in 1934 and in the United States in 1937. From 1938 he was professor and chairman of the School of Architecture at Harvard University, where in 1952 he was named professor emeritus.

Gropius was one of the foremost architects of his time, influencing modern architecture in almost every country of the world. His primary principle of design was that form should follow function, meaning that the design of a building, a product, or even a city should be coordinated with its intended use. Gropius's structures were distinguished by their simplicity of shape, the elimination of all surface decoration, and the use of unusual materials, particularly glass. The most famous of his writings is *The New Architecture and the Bauhaus* (1935).

See also ARCHITECTURE: *Modern Times.*

GROS, Baron Antoine Jean (1771–1835), French painter, born in Paris. He studied art with his father, a painter of miniatures, and with Jacques Louis David (q.v.), the leading figure in the French classical school of painting. Gros painted mainly portraits and historical scenes; his works of the latter category were the foremost in French historical painting during the time of Napoleon I (q.v.), Emperor of France, and the Bourbon restoration (1814–30). In 1811 he decorated the cupola of the Panthéon in Paris by painting the dynasties of France offering homage to Saint Geneviève (q.v.), the patron saint of Paris. In 1816 he became a member of the French Institute and professor at the École des Beaux-Arts.

The paintings of Gros mark the transition from the classicism of David to the Romantic school. Although trained in the methods of the classical school, Gros was the first French historical painter of the period to abandon subjects taken from the history of ancient Greece and Rome for subjects from contemporary history. The rich color, dramatic action, and depth of feeling of his paintings also foreshadowed the Romantic interest in psychology. Among his historical paintings are "Bonaparte at the Bridge of Arcole" (1796), "Plague at Jaffa" (1804), and "Napoleon at Eylau" (1808), all in the Louvre, Paris. Among his best-known portraits are those of the Napoleonic marshal André Masséna (1758–1817) and Eugène de Beauharnais, son of Napoleon's wife Joséphine by her first marriage (*see under* BEAUHARNAIS).

GROSBEAK (Fr. *gros*, "large"; *bec*, "beak"), common name for any of a number of species of large-billed birds, especially of the Finch family, Fringillidae. Among the true grosbeaks is the evening grosbeak, *Hesperiphona vespertina,* so named because of the false belief that it sings only in the evening. The male is more brightly

Evening Grosbeak, Hesperiphona vespertina
Alvin E. Staffan — National Audubon Society

colored than the female, its upper portions being a mixture of yellow and olive-brown. Evening grosbeaks are about 8 in. long. They nest in the summer in Canada, and may winter in the United States.

The strength of the bills of grosbeaks is illustrated by the habits of the pine grosbeak, *Pinicola enucleator,* which breaks open pine cones with its beak and eats the seeds. The North American pine grosbeak measures about 9 in. It breeds in the far northern part of the continent. It is also found in Asia and Europe. Other important species are the cardinal grosbeak or cardinal bird (q.v.), and the rose-breasted grosbeak, *Pheucticus ludovicianus,* a North American bird which measures about 8 in., breeds from Maine to Manitoba and winters in Central and South America. The breast plumage of the male of the later species is rose-red in color.

GROSS

The genus *Geospiza* was studied in the Galápagos Islands by the British naturalist Charles Robert Darwin (*see under* DARWIN) in 1835. The study furnished considerable data for his *Origin of Species.*

GROSS, Chaim (1904–), American artist, born in Kolomea, Austria (now Kolomyya, U.S.S.R.). Gross studied briefly at art schools in Budapest and Vienna before coming to the United States in 1921. Upon his arrival in New York City he began to study painting; within a year he had switched to what would prove to be his major interest, sculpture. From 1926 Gross worked on his own, finally achieving a one-man exhibition in 1932. In 1934 he was naturalized an American citizen. During the 1930's Gross was involved with Federal and State projects, carving many works in wood and stone. In his later work Gross turned to modeling in clay for subsequent casting into bronze. His subjects are people, portrayed with strength and a vital sense of movement. Gross continued to work as a graphic artist, and his exhibitions usually include some of his drawings and watercolors. Examples of his work are found in many American museums.

GROSSE POINTE, city of Michigan, in Wayne Co., on Lake Saint Clair, 9 miles S.E. of Detroit (pop., 1960, 6631; 1970, 6637). Grosse Pointe proper is surrounded by three residential communities: Grosse Pointe Park to the south, about 7 miles N.E. of Detroit (pop., 1960, 15,457; 1970, 15,585); Grosse Pointe Farms to the north, about 10 miles N.E. of Detroit (pop., 1960, 12,172; 1970, 11,701); and farther to the north Grosse Pointe Woods, about 12 miles N.E. of Detroit. Originally called Lochmoor, this city received its present name in 1939. Pop. (1960) 18,580; (1970) 21,878.

GROSSETESTE, Robert (1175?–1253), English prelate, born in Suffolk, probably in Stradbroke, and educated at the universities of Oxford and Paris. He taught theology at Oxford, founding the Franciscan school there in 1224, and was named bishop of Lincoln in 1235. He had a profound effect on the scholastic and religious life of medieval England, and zealously protected the church in England from foreign and secular intrusion. As a scholar, he wrote numerous works in Latin and in French, including treatises on light, sound, heat, angles, and witchcraft, and is considered one of the first modern scientists. He also wrote philosophical works and pastorals.

GROSS NATIONAL PRODUCT, term in economics used to describe in monetary value the total annual flow of goods and services in an economy. The G.N.P., as it is usually referred to, is normally measured by adding together all personal spending, all government spending, and all investment spending made by industry for capital goods, such as machinery and inventory.

A G.N.P. figure can also be obtained by the earnings and cost approach of accounting in which all forms of wages and income, such as corporate profits, net interest returns, rent, indirect business taxes, and unincorporated income are added together. Both methods produce the same result; they differ only in the kinds of data added together.

From the basic G.N.P. figure various other figures are derived that, in turn, are used to describe different aspects of a nation's economy. A Net National Product (N.N.P.) figure, for example, uses only a net investment component after deducting the amount of depreciation which industry normally includes in its gross investment spending figure.

GROSSULARITE. *See* GARNET.

GROSVENOR, Gilbert Hovey (1875–1966), American geographer and editor, born in Constantinople (now İstanbul), Turkey, and educated at Amherst College, Mass. In 1899 he became a director of the National Geographic Society (q.v.) and a member of the staff of the *National Geographic Magazine,* of which he was editor from 1903 to 1954. From 1920 to 1954 Grosvenor served also as president of the National Geographic Society. Under Grosvenor, the society grew into a major organization for scientific research and sponsored extensive work in geography, archeology, and anthropology, especially in the form of field expeditions. He was a regular contributor to the magazine and wrote several books about the expeditions.

His son, Melville Bell Grosvenor (1901–), joined the staff of the *National Geographic Magazine* in 1924, and became editor in 1957. In the same year he was chosen president of the society. He also wrote several books about the field expeditions of the society.

GROS VENTRES (Fr., "great bellies"), name given by early French traders to two unrelated tribes of North American Plains Indians: the Hidatsa, or Minitari, of Siouan stock (q.v.), and the Algonquian (q.v.) Atsina, an offshoot of the Arapaho (q.v.). The home of the Hidatsa is the Missouri R. region of North Dakota; the Atsina, to whom the name Gros Ventres is now generally confined, are settled in Montana. The two tribes are sometimes distinguished from one another by the terms "Gros Ventres of the Missouri" and "Gros Ventres of the Prairie."

GROSZ, George (1893–1959), German-American painter and illustrator, born in Berlin. He studied art at the Royal Academy, Dresden, the Kunstgewerbemuseum, Berlin, and the Académie Colarossi, Paris. His first successful works were expressionist paintings (see EXPRESSIONISM), but later he turned to the fiercely satirical drawings for which he is famous. Collections of these drawings, concerned with conditions in Germany at the end of World War I, appeared in *Ecce Homo* ("Behold, the Man", 1922) and *Geschichte der Herrschenden Klasse* ("History of the Upper Class", 1922). An uncompromising opponent of militarism and National Socialism (q.v.), Grosz was one of the first German artists to attack the future German dictator Adolf Hitler (q.v.). Grosz emigrated to the United States in 1932 and became a U.S. citizen in 1938. Recognized as one of the most brilliant draftsmen of his time, Grosz was also well known as a teacher. His work is represented in many museum collections in the U.S. and Europe. An account of his experiences as an artist appears in his autobiography, *A Little Yes and a Long No* (1946). He was elected to the National Institute of Arts and Letters (q.v.) in 1954.

GROTE, George (1794–1871), British banker, historian of Greece, and politician, born near Beckenham, England, and educated at the Charterhouse School. When he was sixteen he entered the banking business. Between 1826 and 1830 he aided the British economist John Stuart Mill (*see under* MILL) and the British political leader Henry Peter Brougham (1778–1868) in founding the University of London, serving for a time as a member of the council that organized the faculties and curriculum of University College. Between 1832 and 1841 he was a member of the House of Commons. He retired from the banking business in 1843 and devoted much of his time thereafter to the study of Greek history and philosophy and to writing. In 1849, on his reelection to the council of University College, he resumed his activities at the University of London. He was made vice-chancellor of the university in 1862 and six years later president of the University College council. Grote established an endowment for a chair in philosophy of mind and logic in University College. His greatest work is the *History of Greece* (12 vol., 1846–56). Among his other writings are *Plato and Other Companions of Sokrates* (3 vol., 1865) and an unfinished commentary on the ancient Greek philosopher Aristotle (q.v.) posthumously published in 1872.

GROTIUS, Hugo, or HUIG DE GROOT (1583–1645), Dutch jurist, theologian, and statesman, born in Delft, and educated in law at the University of Leiden. He spent his early years editing and writing judicial treatises. In 1613, as chief magistrate of Rotterdam, he became involved in a religious-political controversy with the orthodox Calvinists. He was imprisoned in 1618 for asserting the superiority of state over church, but managed to escape to France in 1621. In 1625 he published *De Jure Belli et Pacis* ("On the Laws of War and Peace"). In this treatise, regarded as one of the foundations of modern international law (q.v.), Grotius asserts that rules of conduct for both individuals and nations are found not in divine revelations, but in social precedents derived from classical societies. War may be used to enforce these commonly accepted rules only in the absence of judgment by an international tribunal; otherwise war is a crime.

Later Grotius returned to Rotterdam, but was again forced to leave the country. He fled to Sweden, and for a short time held the post of Swedish ambassador to France.

GROTON, town of Connecticut, in New London Co., on the E. bank of the Thames R., opposite the city of New London. The town is the site of a United States submarine base and of the United States Coast Guard Academy (q.v.). Among the industrial establishments in Groton are a chemical plant, engine factories, and one of the largest submarine-building yards in the world.

The first settlement of Groton was made from New London in 1649, and in 1705 it was incorporated as a separate town, receiving its present name. From the early days of settlement it has been a shipbuilding center; among the other early industries were whaling and deep-sea fishing. On Sept. 6, 1781, during the American Revolution (q.v), occurred the attack on Fort Griswold at Groton called the "Massacre of Fort Griswold". The fort was garrisoned at the time by a force of 150 colonial militiamen under the command of Lieutenant Colonel William Ledyard (1738–81). The small garrison attempted to beat off an attack by about 800 British soldiers. When the Americans finally surrendered, most of them were massacred, and Ledyard was killed by his own surrendered sword. The site of the massacre is now a State reservation and contains the ruins of Fort Griswold. Near the monument is a memorial library containing the Ledyard sword. Pop. (1960) 29,937; (1970) 38,523.

GROUND, in electricity, connection in an electrical circuit that leads to the earth, or to a large conducting object (such as the metal frame of an airplane) which is at zero potential with respect to the rest of the circuit; *see* ELECTRICITY.

45

GROUND BEETLE

In every type of electrical system or device, accessible metal parts, such as frames, cases, and switches, are usually maintained at ground potential. All such parts are interconnected electrically and provide a ground connection for the whole group. If this precaution is not observed, a failure of insulation or some other accident may put part of the system at a potential different from that of the ground, creating a shock hazard. A man touching such a part will receive a shock, because his body forms a connection between the part and the ground. In electrical-distribution practice, one wire of a set of transmission lines is grounded. Radio and television sets are grounded, not only as a safety measure but also because the earth, when connected electrically to the set, increases the effectiveness of the antenna. In modern household-wiring practice, electrical outlets often have a third hole to match the ground-wire prong of many appliance connections.

Accidental grounds sometimes occur in electrical systems because of the failure of insulation. Grounds of this kind frequently are destructive because they pass a heavy current which burns out or melts equipment.

GROUND BEETLE, common name for any of the swift-running, carnivorous beetles in the family Carabidae. More than 17,000 species are known, of which more than 2000 are found in North America. Ground beetles are world-wide in distribution, and live under rocks, or in moist or sandy soil, from which they get their name. Many ground beetles do not fly. On these forms the hind wings are generally atrophied and the wing covers fused along the midline. The slender legs are well developed for swift running. These beetles are most often unmarked black or brown; several species have wing cases that are striped or bordered with metallic blue, green, or bronze. The head of a ground beetle is narrower than its body; long, thin, threadlike antennae jut out from the sides of the head. The mouth parts are adapted for crushing and eating insects, worms, and snails. Members of *Carabus*, the type genus, are about 1 in. long. The larvae of the ground beetles have well-developed legs and mouth parts, and are also carnivorous. They live underground and pupate within the earth.

Ground bettles are agriculturally important and valuable because they destroy such harmful insects as the potato beetle, brown-tail moth, gypsy moth, cutworm, cankerworm, June beetle, and plum curculio. Few ground beetles are considered harmful; species in the genus *Harpalus* feed on seeds, corn, and strawberries.

For representative members of the ground beetle family, see separate articles on BOMBARDIER BEETLE; CATERPILLAR HUNTER.

GROUND DOVE, common name for several land birds of the Pigeon family Columbidae. Most species differ from typical pigeons in having inferior flying power, because of their short, rounded wings, and in having longer legs. The plumage of most species, except for that of the bronzewings, is dull in color. Among the important North American species is *Columbagallina passerina*, which is common throughout the southern United States. These ground doves are about 7 in. long. They live mostly on the ground, nesting in the trees only at night. Ground doves are generally seen in pairs.

GROUND-EFFECT MACHINE. See AIR-CUSHION VEHICLE.

GROUNDHOG or **WOODCHUCK,** name in the United States for a marmot (q.v.). In South Africa the aardvark (q.v.) is sometimes called groundhog.

GROUNDHOG DAY, February 2 of each year, when, according to rural American tradition, the groundhog (see MARMOT) leaves the burrow where it has been hibernating to discover whether cold winter weather will continue. If the groundhog cannot see its shadow, it remains above ground, ending its hibernation, but if its shadow is visible (that is, if the sun is shining), there will be six more weeks of cold weather and the animal returns to its burrow. Groundhog day falls on Candlemas (q.v.). An old church tradition that a pleasant Candlemas means a cold spring probably inspired the legend.

GROUND IVY, common name of *Nepeta hederacea*, a small creeping perennial herb of the Mint family Labiatae, also known as gill-over-the-ground. Native to Eurasia, the ground ivy was introduced to the United States where it grows near hedges and forests and in waste places. It has kidney-shaped, crenate leaves, and pale purple flowers which are borne in clusters of three. The aromatic leaves were formerly used as a stimulant, usually as an herb tea. The leaves of ground ivy were used also to clarify and flavor ale, but have been supplanted by the flowers of hops. Ground ivy is sometimes used in hanging baskets and window gardens.

GROUND LAUREL. See ARBUTUS.
GROUNDNUT. See PEANUT.
GROUND PINE. See CLUB MOSS.
GROUNDSEL. See SENECIO.
GROUND SQUIRREL, or SPERMOPHILE, any medium-sized, burrowing, terrestrial, western American rodent of the genus *Citellus* in the Squirrel family Sciuridae, characterized by large

cheek pouches opening inside their mouths; they are often erroneously called gophers. Like the true gophers, they are agricultural menaces, destroying grass and grain. The name spermophile (Gr., "seed lover"), is derived from their usual diet. The ground squirrel resembles both the prairie dog and the chipmunk (qq.v.). Most of the ground squirrels have longitudinal stripes along their backs. In the northern part of their range these animals hibernate during the winter; the duration of hibernation varies with the environment. Ground squirrels are found in open country, often in arid regions.

The Great Plains ground squirrel, *C. elegans,* found west of the Rocky Mts., is typical of most of the spermophiles. This rough-haired ground squirrel has a length of 11 in., including a 3-in. bushy tail. Its back is brown and its lower parts yellowish-gray; it has a white chin and a white ring around each eye. The head is stubby, with round, wide ears. The legs are short. These animals seek their food close to their burrows. They mate after they emerge from hibernation in the spring; the female bears five to thirteen offspring at a time. The thirteen-striped spermophile, *C. tridecemlineatus,* found near the Mississippi R., has seven grayish-yellow stripes running down its back, interspersed with six stripes composed of spots. Its lower parts are pale fawn in color. This ground squirrel subsists on mice and small insects as well as grain.

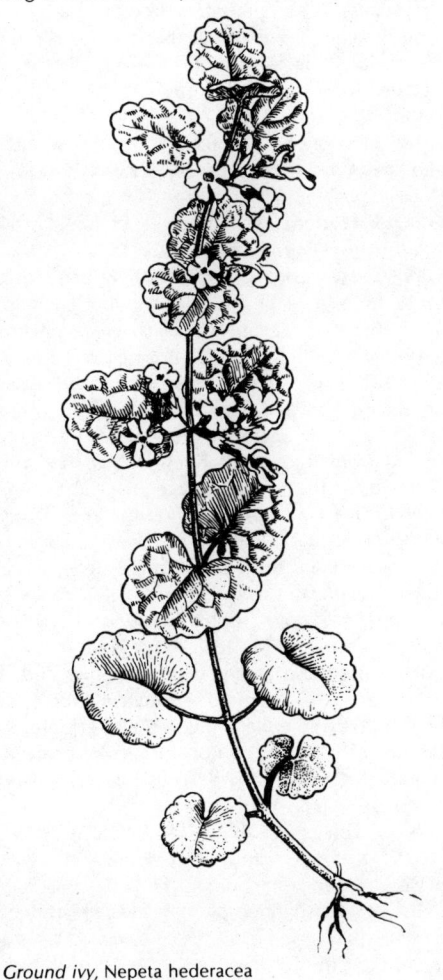

GROUPER, common name for fish of the genus *Epinephelus* and related fish of the family Serranidae, subfamily Epinephelidae. The name has been applied loosely; all species of groupers are not invariably called groupers, and the name is sometimes applied to unrelated fish. The terminal mouth is large, and the conical teeth in the jaws are strong and may be crowded into bands. The front part of the dorsal fin has nine to eleven prominent spines, and the caudal fin is usually rounded or slightly forked.

The various species may be recognized by their coloration, but the recognition may be uncertain; most groupers can bring about specific changes in their coloration. Some can do this instantaneously, as in changing from a dark to a light color phase when feeding or alarmed. Some species are dark red when taken in deep water and are much lighter when caught in shallower waters. Still other species have two or three different color phases in individuals of the same species; these phases may have a genetic basis. Many species have been shown to undergo sex reversal, from female to male.

Groupers, primarily carnivorous, are caught by sport and commercial fishermen. They are common table fish. These fish occur in all coastal, tropical waters. The maximum size of the various species is moderate to very large; western Pacific areas report groupers weighing 1000 lb. and measuring 10 ft. long. The two largest American species are the giant sea bass, *Stereolepis gigas,* of the Pacific coast and the jewfish (q.v.). Species common in the West Indies and around the southeastern United States are the Warsaw grouper, *Epinephelus nigritus*; Nassau grouper, *E. striatus*; red grouper, *E. morio*; rock hind, *E. adscensionis*; red hind, *E. guttatus*; black grouper, *Myctoperca bonaci*; gag, *M. microlepis*; yellowfin, *M. venenosa*; scamp, *M. phenax*; grasby, *Petrometopon cruentatum*; and coney, *Cephalopholis fulva*. Species common along the Pacific coast of California and Mexico are the spotted cabrilla, *E. analogus*; Gulf grouper, *M. jordani*; and broomtail grouper, *M. xenarcha*.

Ground ivy, Nepeta hederacea

GROUP THERAPY

GROUP THERAPY. See PSYCHOTHERAPY.

GROUSE, common name for any of eighteen species of galliform birds of the family Tetraonidae. Grouse resemble small domestic fowl in appearance, but have thick, strong legs which enable the birds to jump quickly into flight when surprised. The plumage of grouse is thick and soft. In most species, the color of the plumage is somber, generally brown, speckled and barred with black. All species have short, thick bills with the upper portion of the bill rounded. The nests, built in slight hollows in the ground, consist of leaves, grasses, and a few feathers of the parent birds. The young are covered with a fine, heavy down. The diet is varied and includes snails, worms, insects, berries, seeds, and buds. Some species frequent woods, and a few species, such as the ptarmigan, which generally inhabit northern regions, are found in open country. All grouse, except ptarmigans, are polygamous. The males of polygamous species fight for possession of the harem, and the males of some species gather at certain fixed "fighting fields" in the spring.

Of the ten species of grouse found in North America, one of the most important is the blue or dusky grouse, *Dendragapus obscurus,* an inhabitant of the western United States, noted as an easy bird to hunt because it has no fear of man. The sage grouse, *Centrocercus urophasianus,* is the largest grouse in North America and is native to the western U.S. The ruffed grouse, *Bonasa umbellus,* sometimes called partridge or pheasant, is well known for the drumming sound produced by the males in spring. The noise is part of the mating behavior, as are the songs of some other birds during the mating season. The mechanism which the ruffed grouse uses to produce this noise has long been a subject of controversy. High-speed photographs have proved that the noise comes from vibrations caused by the quick beating of the wings in the air. The cock often stands on a log during the drumming.

The red grouse, *Lagopus scoticus,* is found only in the British Isles, particularly in Scotland and northern England. The red grouse is bred on the moors of Scotland as a game bird. Extensive regions in Scotland, called grousemoors, are owned and rented for grouse shooting only. Each year the grouse season traditionally opens on August 12, and hunters from all over the world travel to Scotland at that time. The birds are flushed, or frightened into air, either by beaters or by game dogs, such as pointers and setters.

For descriptions of various species of grouse, see BLACKCOCK; CAPERCAILLIE; PRAIRIE CHICKEN; PTARMIGAN.

GROVE, Frederick Philip. See CANADIAN LITERATURE: *English-Canadian Literature.*

GROVE, Sir George (1820–1900), British music critic, born in Clapham, near London, England, and educated at Stockwell (later Clapham) grammar school. As a young boy he was apprenticed to a civil engineer, and he worked as an engineer for several years. Grove was appointed secretary of the Society of Arts in 1849, and resigned from that position in 1852 to become secretary of the Crystal Palace (q.v.) at Sydenham. Grove wrote excellent evaluations of the works performed at the Crystal Palace, particularly of the Beethoven symphonies. He was editor of *Macmillan's Magazine* from 1868 to 1883. Grove is best known for his *Dictionary of Music and Musicians* (4 vol., 1879–89), a work that has been revised and enlarged several times and is still used as a standard reference source in music. In 1883 he was knighted and appointed the first director of the Royal College of Music. Among his other books is *Beethoven's Nine Symphonies* (1884).

GROVE, Lefty, in full ROBERT MOSES GROVE (1900–), American professional baseball player, born in Lonaconing, Md. Grove was one of the best left-handed pitchers in the history of baseball (q.v.). He began his career in 1920, as a member of the Baltimore (Md.) team of the In-

Ruffed grouse, Bonasa umbellus
Hugh M. Halliday — National Audubon Society

GROWTH

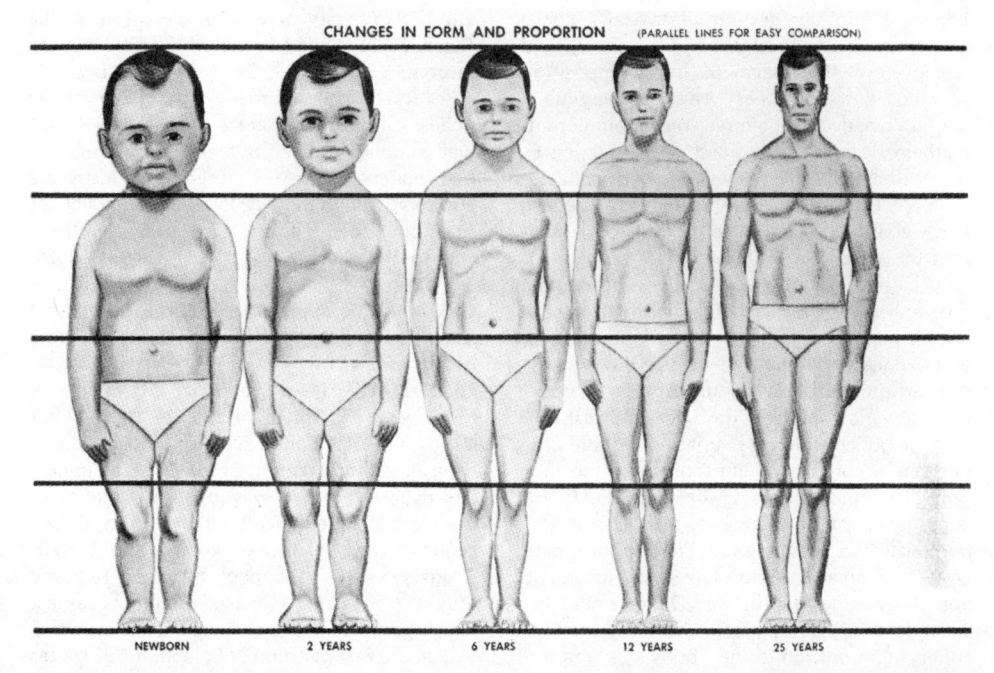

CHANGES IN FORM AND PROPORTION (PARALLEL LINES FOR EASY COMPARISON)

NEWBORN — 2 YEARS — 6 YEARS — 12 YEARS — 25 YEARS

Growth changes in form and proportion from newborn to adult life. TODAY'S HEALTH, published by the AMERICAN MEDICAL ASSOCIATION

ternational League. In five years with the Baltimore team he won 108 games and lost 36, for a percentage of .750. From 1925 to 1934 he was a member of the Philadelphia (Pa.) Athletics of the American League, and from 1935 to 1941 of the Boston (Mass.) Red Sox of the American League. During his American League career he won 300 games and lost 141, a percentage of .680. He was the sixth pitcher in modern baseball to win 300 or more games in a major league. During his career he struck out 2217 batsmen, becoming the eighth pitcher in baseball history to strike out more than 2000. Grove was elected to the Baseball Hall of Fame in 1947. *See* BASEBALL HALL OF FAME AND MUSEUM, NATIONAL.

GROVES, city of Texas, in Jefferson Co., near Sabine Lake, about 4 miles N. of Port Arthur. Pop. (1960) 17,304; (1970) 18,067.

GROWTH, increase in total volume of any animate or inanimate object. Growth is one of the primary characteristics of living things; *see* LIFE. Normal growth is carried on by all living organisms during all or part of their lifetimes. All plants grow until they die. Growth in unicellular life is accomplished by expansion of the protoplasmic content of the cell (*see* AMOEBA) growth in more complex plants usually takes place in definite areas which are known as meristems. In animals, growth may continue throughout life, but most higher animals, such as insects and vertebrates, arrive at a fixed adult size. Many segmented animals, such as tapeworms and earthworms, have special growth zones which periodically produce additional segments. In both animal and plant forms, growth rates may be high during certain seasons and greatly reduced or arrested during the remainder of the year. Both animals and plants are vulnerable to pathological conditions which lead to abnormal rates of entire growth (*see* DWARF; GIGANTISM), or to uncontrolled growth of specific tissues or organs (*see* CANCER).

Differentiation of Matter and Growth Rate. Normal growth in higher organisms is accompanied by differentiation of new organic matter into tissues and organs. This occurs in the early growth of organisms; *see* EMBRYOLOGY. Differentiation is not a necessary concomitant of growth; normal growth in lower organisms, and abnormal growth in most organisms, may proceed without differentiation.

The absolute rate at which growth takes place varies widely between organisms and between parts of a single organism. It is governed by a fundamental mathematical law which states that the rate of growth is proportional to the absolute size, so that an organism, as it increases in size, accelerates its rate of growth in direct proportion. The same law applies to inanimate

GROWTH HORMONE

growth (as in the growth of cyrstals), social growth (as in the growth of populations), and negative growth or decay (as in decomposition of radioactive substances). All such phenomena are governed by a simple but all-important mathematical equation; $y = e^x$; see article on E. (in mathematics). A newly formed cell, for example, undergoes a brief initial "lag" period, followed by a long middle period of accelerated growth, which eventually ceases altogether. This pattern of growth is called the normal growth curve. The accelerated growth of the middle period is slowed down by gradual aging and by inherent limitations on size.

Proportion and Growth Support. The proportions of various parts of the body are relatively uniform but considerable variation in these proportions occurs during the course of the lifetime. The human infant, for example, has a larger head and shorter limbs in proportion to body size than does an adult. The proportionate growth of organs in closely related species is not always uniform. In the Deer family, for example, the smallest species have the smallest antlers in proportion to their body size, and the largest deer have the largest antlers in proportion to their body size. This type of growth is called allometric or heterogonic growth.

The upper and lower limits of effective growth are governed by a mathematical law which states that if growth is symmetrical, the doubling of all linear dimensions increases volume by a factor of eight, but it increases the area by a factor of only four. For example, if a man were to grow to twelve feet in height, he would be eight times as heavy as a normal six-foot man, but the arches of his feet would be only four times as great in area, so that he would have insufficient support for his body. At the other extreme, a tiny mammal such as a shrew (q.v.) has an enormous surface area in proportion to its weight, and must eat an enormous quantity of food to compensate for the loss of heat through its skin. A still smaller mammal could not eat fast enough to keep alive.

Growth must be supported by the accumulation of organic matter necessary to build new protoplasm (q.v.). This process is governed by the effect of two classes of substance, hormones (q.v.) and vitamins (see VITAMIN). The presence of small quantities of vitamins permits considerable growth, but growth is severely restricted or arrested when vitamins are absent. Hormones act on the metabolism (q.v.) of an organism, which in turn determines the rate of growth.

GROWTH HORMONE. See HORMONES: *Hormones in Animals*; PITUITARY GLAND.

GROZNYY, city of the Soviet Union, in the Russian S.F.S.R., and capital of the Chechen-Ingush A.S.S.R., in the N. Caucasus Mts., about 110 miles N.E. of Tbilisi. Groznyy lies in one of the richest oil-producing areas in the U.S.S.R. Oil-well supplies and equipment, chemicals, and by-products of the oil refining industry are also produced in the city. Pipelines and rail lines run from Groznyy to the Caspian Sea on the E. and to the Black Sea on the W. Pop. (1970) 341,000.

GRUB, name applied to certain legless insect larvae, particularly the legless forms of some beetles. See LARVA.

GRUDZIĄDZ (Ger. *Graudenz*), city of Poland, in Bydgoszcz Province, on the Vistula R., about 60 miles S. of Gdánsk. Situated within a low-lying agricultural region, Grudziądz is an important river port and railway junction. Chief manufactures include agricultural machinery, bricks, ceramics, metals, rubber goods, and timber. Grudziądz was founded by the Teutonic Knights (q.v.) in 1291. In 1466 the city became a Polish possession; it was annexed to Prussia in 1772 at the first partition of Poland. In 1920, after World War I, Grudziądz was included in the reconstituted Polish nation. The city was occupied by Germany from 1939 to 1944, during World War II. Pop. (1968 est.) 74,700.

GRUENTHER, Alfred Maximilian (1899–   ), American soldier, born in Platte Center, Nebr. He was graduated (1919) from the United States Military Academy and commissioned a second lieutenant in field artillery. Gruenther rose through ranks until his appointment (1951) as general. Among various military assignments he was chief of staff of the United States Third Army (1941–42), Fifth Army (1943–44), Fifteenth Army Group (1944–45), and at Supreme Headquarters Allied Powers in Europe (1951–53). He was supreme commander of the North Atlantic Treaty Organization (1953–56) and, after his retirement (1956), headed the American National Red Cross (1957–64). He was appointed (1969) to a Presidential commission for an all-volunteer army.

GRÜNEWALD, Matthias, called NEITHARDT (fl. 1500–28), German painter, born Mathis Gothardt probably in Würzburg between 1460 and 1470. He lived first in Aschaffenburg. From about 1490 until after 1500, when he resided in Seligenstadt, no records of his activities exist. During the next few years he painted the "Mocking of Christ" for the cathedral of Aschaffenburg and a small crucifixion now in the museum at Basel, Switzerland. In 1508 he was employed as court painter by the archbishop of

"The Small Crucifixion" (about 1510) by Matthias Grünewald.
National Gallery of Art — Samuel H. Kress Collection

Mainz, Ulrich von Gemmingen. He remained in this position under Gemmingen's successor, Archbishop and Elector of Mainz, known as Albert of Brandenburg (see ALBERT), until 1526, when Albert broke with him because of his support of the Protestant Reformation. Grünewald then went to Halle in Saxony.

Some of his better-known works are the "Heller Altar" panels painted for the Dominican church in Frankfurt (1511–13); his great masterpiece, the altarpiece painted originally for the monastery Church of Saint Anthony in Issenheim, Upper Alsace, now in the museum in Colmar, France (1513–15); the altarpiece for the Maria Schnee Chapel, Aschaffenburg (completed before 1519); and his "Crucifixion" (about 1523) at Karlsruhe, Germany.

Grünewald is regarded as one of the finest painters of the late German Gothic period. Grünewald's life is the subject of the opera *Mathis der Mahler* by the German-American composer Paul Hindemith (q.v.). See GERMAN ART AND ARCHITECTURE: *Painting*. See also CRUCIFIXION IN ART, THE.

GRUNION, small, silvery, marine fish, *Leuresthes tenuis*, closely related to the mullets, and found only on southern and Baja Californian beaches. Male grunions are about 5 to 7 in. long; females are about 6 to 8 in. long. The grunions have gray backs and silver sides with a longitudinal stripe of black along each side. They are the only North American fish which come out of the water to mate and lay their eggs. Their spawning season begins in March and ends in August. The spawning of these fish is strictly regulated by the tides; they always breed on the first four nights after the highest tide of the full moon or the new moon. They are so prompt and predictable in their spawning time that the California State Fisheries Laboratory yearly publishes a timetable indicating when they will appear. Thousands of the fish appear at a time on the long, gently sloping beaches and are netted by sportsmen; they are excellent food fish. The grunions come in on high waves about 15 minutes after the peak of high tide. The females dig holes 2 in. deep in the sand and deposit about 2000 eggs each; the accompanying males fertilize the eggs. The entire process of deposition and fertilization takes about 25 seconds; the fish return to sea on the ebb of the wave after the one which carried them in. The eggs remain in the sand for two weeks, until the next high tide, when the young hatch and are washed out to sea.

GRYPHIUS, Andreas (1616–64), German poet and dramatist, born Andreas Greif, in Glogau, (now in Poland). After three years as tutor in the home of an influential German nobleman, Gryphius spent the period 1637 to 1643 in Leiden, where he lectured at the university. After some years of travel throughout Europe he settled in Fraustadt in 1647. His poetry is marked by morbidness and indignation; many poems in the collection *Kirchhofsgedanken* ("Thoughts of a Cemetery", 1656) deal with the theme of human vanity. Unlike his verse, his plays have much charm and humor; perhaps his best-known play is *Absurda Comica, oder Peter Squenz* (1663), based on the farcical episode of Pyramus and Thisbe in *A Midsummer Night's Dream* by William Shakespeare. Among his other plays are *Die Geliebte Dornrose* ("The Thorny Rose", 1660), a pastoral written in his native Silesian dialect, and the satirical play *Horribilicrifax* (1663). The tragedies of Gryphius are in the bombastic style of the Roman poet Seneca and the Dutch playwright Joost van den Vondel (q.v.), and include *Leo Armenius* (1646); *Carolus Stuardus* (1649), on the life of Charles I (q.v.), King of England; and *Cardenio und Celinde* (1657). Gryphius is considered one of the leading lyric poets and dramatists of the baroque period in Germany.

GUACHARO. See OILBIRD.

GUADALAJARA, city in Mexico, and capital of Jalisco State, near the Río Grande de Santiago, more than 500 ft. above sea level, about 275 miles N.W. of Mexico City. Guadalajara, the second-largest city in Mexico, lies in a rich farming region and is also an important commercial center. Hydroelectric power from the nearby Juanacatlán Falls is used to operate the factories of the city. Among the products manufactured in Guadalajara are textiles, leather goods, furniture, hats, and cordage. The Indians of Guadalajara and its environs fashion high-quality handmade pottery and glassware. The city was founded in 1531 and became an episcopal see in 1549. The cathedral, constructed between 1571 and 1618, is noted for its size and for the magnificence of its decoration. The principal educational and cultural institutions of the city are the University of Guadalajara (founded in 1792), the Autonomous University of Guadalajara (1935), the State museum, a regional museum of anthropology and history, and a museum devoted to the work of the Mexican muralist and painter José Clemente Orozco (q.v.). Pop. (1969 est.) 1,352,100.

GUADALCANAL, island of the S.W. Pacific Ocean, the largest in the British Solomon Islands Protectorate, with an area of 2509 sq.mi.; see SOLOMON ISLANDS. The volcanic Kavo Mts., which reach a maximum height of 8000 ft. above sea level, run lengthwise through the jungled terrain. Copra is the only product of commercial importance.

Guadalcanal was the site of heavy fighting between United States and Japanese forces during World War II, in which the Japanese had occupied the Solomons in January, 1942. On Aug. 7, American Marines landed on Guadalcanal in the first of the amphibious assaults against Japanese-held positions in the Pacific. The Marines obtained and held Henderson Airfield on the island in face of bitter ground, sea, and air attacks by the Japanese. On Oct. 13, United States Army reinforcements began to arrive on Guadalcanal, and on Dec. 9 the command of the area was assumed by the Army under the direction of Major General Alexander McCarrell Patch, Jr. (1889–1945). Fighting continued in the jungles of Guadalcanal until Feb. 9, 1943, when the Army and Marine forces secured the island against Japanese resistance. Continual naval engagements between the Japanese and the Americans were fought off Guadalcanal. American naval forces, under the command of Admiral William Frederick Halsey (q.v.), were dispatched to the battle area and a naval battle was fought on Nov. 13–15, 1942. Japanese losses in the engagement were at least twenty-three naval craft sunk, including one battleship; eight U.S. craft were lost. *See also* WORLD WAR II: *The War Becomes a Global Conflict: Battle of the Solomon Islands.*

GUADALQUIVIR (anc. *Baetis*), river of S. Spain, rising in the E. part of the province of Jaén and flowing 374 mi., generally S.W., to Sanlúcar de Barrameda, where it empties into the Gulf of Cádiz. After coursing through the provinces of

GUADELOUPE

Jaén, Córdoba, and Seville, the Guadalquivir forms the boundary between the provinces of Huelva and Cádiz for the 10 mi. above its mouth. For the 40 mi. between the town of Coria del Río and the mouth of the river, the Guadalquivir traverses a region of tidal marshes called *Las Marismas.* Supplied by rainwater in the winter and by the melting snows of the Sierra Nevada Mts. in the summer, the river maintains a full flow throughout the year, providing essential irrigation water and hydroelectric power. During the Moorish occupation of Spain in the Middle Ages, the river was navigable as far as Córdoba; now, as a result of silt accumulation, it is navigable no farther upstream than the city of Seville, a distance of about 50 mi.

GUADALUPE HIDALGO, former name of a town in Mexico, and now called Gustavo A. Madero, in the Federal District of Mexico, 2½ miles N. of Mexico City. Guadalupe Hidalgo was named for Our Lady of Guadalupe, the patron saint of the Mexican Indians, and for the Mexican priest and revolutionist Miguel Hidalgo y Costilla (q.v.). A shrine to Our Lady of Guadalupe, the princpal Roman Catholic shrine in the Western Hemisphere, now stands on the Hill of Tepeyacac, where an Indian, Juan Diego (b. 1476?) had visions of the Virgin in 1531. In the town the Treaty of Guadalupe Hidalgo was signed on Feb. 3, 1848, ending the Mexican War (q.v.).

GUADALUPE MOUNTAINS, branch of the Rocky Mts. extending from southern New Mexico to western Texas. Guadalupe Peak (8751 ft. above sea level), the highest point in the chain, is in Texas.

GUADALUPE MOUNTAINS NATIONAL PARK, region of geological and archeological interest in Culbertson and Hudspeth counties, Texas. In this region several ranges of the Sacramento Mts. culminate at Guadalupe Peak (8751 ft.), the highest point in Texas. El Capitan (8076 ft.), just south, can be seen for 50 mi. During the Permian Period (q.v.), more than 200,000,000 years ago, the limestone mountains formed the edge of an extensive sea, which is now a desert; consequently, many fossils can be found in the region. The modern fauna and flora in the park are also of interest, as are the prehistoric Indian cave pictographs and pottery remains. The park includes the spectacular McKittrick canyons. The park, covering 81,077.02 acres, was established in 1966. It is administered by the National Park Service (q.v.).

GUADELOUPE, island and overseas department of France, situated in the Lesser Antilles, French West Indies (q.v.). Guadeloupe lies between approximately lat. 15° N. and lat. 16° N. and long. 60° W. and long. 62° W. The department comprises two islands, separated by the Salée R., a narrow arm of the Caribbean Sea. The island on the w. is called Basse-Terre, and that on the E. Grande-Terre. The five smaller islands Marie Galante, Les Saintes, Désirade, St. Barthelemy, and St. Martin, are dependencies of Guadeloupe. The area of the department is 688 sq.mi. The population of Guadeloupe (census 1967) was 312,724; the United Nations estimated (1969) 323,000. The overall population density is 468 per sq.mi. (U.N. est. 1969). The climate of the islands, though hot and humid, is tempered by the surrounding waters; the mean annual temperature is 78° F. The town of Basse-Terre (pop., late 1960's est., 16,000), on the island of the same name, is the capital. The chief town on Grande-Terre, and principal port of the department, is Point-à-Pitre (pop., 28,000).

Guadeloupe is governed by a prefect and a popularly elected general council, and is represented in the French parliament by three deputies and two senators. The population is comprised mainly of Negroes and mulattoes, and a small minority of Europeans. The island dependencies are inhabited by descendants of the original Breton and Norman colonists who settled there three centuries ago. These folk, engaged in shipbuilding, farming, and fishing, maintain a patriarchal family organization, and have little or no contact with the outside world.

More than 30 percent of the total land area is under cultivation; of this figure almost 50 percent is planted with sugarcane. The chief products are sugar, bananas, cocoa, coffee, pineapples, and rum. About 185,000 tons of sugar were exported annually in the late 1960's. In a recent year national budget figures showed in revenues about $45,650,000, and a similar amount in expeditures.

History. The island of Guadeloupe was discovered by the Italian-born navigator Christopher Columbus on Nov. 3, 1493, and named for the monastery of Santa Maria de Guadalupe in Estremadura, Spain. Colonists of the French Company of the Islands of America established settlements in 1635, and inaugurated a policy of extreme cruelty toward the native Carib Indians, resulting in the virtual extinction of the aborigines. After the failure of four chartered companies to colonize the island permanently, it was annexed by France in 1674 and made a dependency of Martinique (q.v.). Durng the latter half of the 17th century the French colonists resisted a series of attacks by the British, who fi-

A mild, tropical climate characterizes the city of Agaña, capital of Guam. UPI

nally captured the island in 1759, retaining it until 1763, when it again passed to France. In 1775 Gaudeloupe and Martinique became separate colonies. The British repossessed Guadeloupe in 1794 and again in 1810, the latter occupation lasting for six years. Slavery was abolished in 1848. Since World War II, an autonomist movement has emerged, which has been involved periodically in conflict with the authorities.

GUADIANA (anc. *Anas*; Ar. *Wadi Ana*), river of Spain and Portugal, rising as the Upper Guadiana, or Guadiana Alto, on La Mancha Plateau in central Cuenca Province. After flowing s. through a series of small lakes, the Upper Guadiana turns N.W. and, 3 mi. from the Zancara R., disappears underground, reemerging when it reaches the Zancara R. At Ciudad Real the combined streams form the Guadiana, which from there flows circuitously s.w. to Badàjoz. From Badàjoz, the river forms the boundary between Spain and Portugal; it enters Portugal near Mourão. The Guadiana again forms the Spanish-Portuguese boundary near Mértola, Portugal, and remains a frontier stream until it empties into the Gulf of Cádiz, through an estuary 25 mi. long. In its total course of 515 mi., the river is navigable for a distance of 42 mi. from its mouth. It drains an area of about 32,000 sq.mi.

GUAM, unincorporated territory of the United States, largest and southernmost of the Mariana Islands (q.v.), in the w. Pacific Ocean, about 1500 miles E. of the Republic of the Philippines. Guam, covering about 209 sq.mi., is 30 mi. long and from 4 to 8.5 mi. wide. Apra Harbor, on the w. coast, is the only good anchorage. One of the chief U.S. defense bastions in the w. Pacific, Guam is the site of extensive naval, military, and air-force installations. Farming and fishing are the principal native occupations and the chief export is copra. In addition, the provision of services to the military establishment is an important aspect of the local economy. The native Guamanians are mainly Chamorros, a mixed-blood people basically of Micronesian origin; *see* MICRONESIA.

Guam is governed according to the provisions of the Organic Act of Guam, legislation enacted by the United States Congress in 1950. The Organic Act conferred U.S. citizenship on the natives of Guam; the Guamanians may not, however, vote in U.S. elections and have no representation in Congress. The Organic Act also placed the island under the jurisdiction of the United States Department of the Interior. Executive power is vested in a governor, who was appointed by the President of the U.S. before November, 1970, but is now elected by the people of Guam. Legislative authority is vested in a unicameral congress consisting of a maximum of twenty-one members and elected every two years by universal adult suffrage. Judicial power is exercised by a Federal district court, an island court, and various minor courts. Agaña is the capital of the territory and the site of the College of Guam, founded in 1952.

GUANTÁNAMO BAY

History. Discovered in 1521 by the Portuguese navigator Ferdinand Magellan, who claimed it for his patron Charles V (qq.v.), Holy Roman Emperor and King of Spain, the island was annexed by Spain in 1565. In 1889, at the end of the Spanish-American War (q.v.), Guam became a U.S. possession. The Japanese captured Guam in December, 1941, during World War II (q.v.), but American forces recaptured the island between July 20 and Aug. 10, 1944. Pop. (1970) 84,996; servicemen and dependents (1969 est.) 38,500.

GUANACO, common name of a species of wild South American ruminant, *Lama guanicoe,* to which the domesticated alpaca and llama (qq.v.) are closely related. The guanaco is one of the two wild, humpless species of the Camel family found in South America, the other being the vicuña (q.v.). It is found on mountains and plains from Peru to Tierra del Fuego. The guanaco takes to water readily and has often been seen swimming from one island to another. A full-grown male stands about 3½ ft. high at the shoulder and is covered with a thick coat of long, soft, reddish-tan hair. The head is small, with pointed ears; the neck is long, with a graceful curve; the legs are long and slender. The fur on the belly is pure white. Guanacos are fast-running animals, but are often destroyed through their curiosity; an entire herd, containing an average of eight animals, will be attracted to the antics of a performing human and will remain in the vicinity after shots are fired, accepting gunfire as part of the performance. This characteristic is utilized by South American natives who value the wool, skin, and flesh. The dung is also used for fuel, and it commonly accumulates in a distinctive ring about areas used repeatedly by the guanacos.

GUANAJUATO, city in Mexico, and capital of Guanajuato State, about 170 miles N.W. of Mexico City. The city lies in a ravine in the heart of a mountain range rich with gold and silver mines, that have been worked by the native Indians for more than 500 years. The city has several colonial buildings, the most important of which is the Alhóndiga de Granaditas, built as a public granary in 1798, and turned into a fortress by the Spanish. Guanajuato was founded in 1554 and was designated as a city in 1741. It served as a center for the Mexican revolt for independence which began in 1810; *see* MEXICO: *History.* Pop. (1966) 32,200.

GUANO (Quechua, *huanu,* "dung"), dried excrement of certain vertebrates, particularly sea birds, valued as fertilizer. The Peruvians have used guano since before the Spanish conquest. One of their sources of supply was the Chincha Islands, off the S. coast of Peru. These islands and the Lobos groups off N. Peru were breeding grounds for sea birds, whose accumulated droppings resulted in piles of guano often more than 100 ft. high. In 1804 a visitor to Peru took some guano to Europe. Its value as a fertilizer soon became widely known and by 1850 the Peruvians had begun to export it in large quantities. Other sources of guano, such as Mexico, Chile, and various Pacific islands, were used as the Peruvian supply dwindled. The dried feces of other creatures also came into use as guano, particularly bat guano, found in caves in New Zealand and the United States. The term "guano" is sometimes applied to other organic fertilizers; for example, the dried and powdered bodies of certain fish are often called fish guano.

GUANTÁNAMO, city of Cuba, in Oriente Province, about 8 mi. inland from Guantánamo Bay, and about 40 miles N.E. of Santiago de Cuba. The city has rail, highway, and air communications with the rest of Cuba, and is connected by railroad with the bay ports of Caimanera and Boquerón. Guantánamo is the trading and processing center of an agricultural region devoted chiefly to sugarcane and coffee. Principal industries include coffee roasting, sugar milling, and salt processing. Originally called Santa Catalina de Saltadero, the city was renamed and experienced rapid growth in the early 19th century, when large numbers of French refugees from the slave rebellion on Hispaniola settled in the area. Pop. (1960) 124,685.

GUANTÁNAMO BAY (Sp. *Bahía de Guantánamo*), sheltered inlet of the Caribbean Sea, on the S.E. coast of Cuba, in Oriente Province. The bay is 8 miles S.E. of the city of Guantánamo (q.v.). The principal port on the bay is Caimanera. The bay, one of the largest in the world, is about 12 mi. long and about 5 mi. wide. Access to the harbor, which can accommodate large vessels, is through a narrow channel at the southernmost section of the bay. The land on either side of this entrance channel, plus about 9000 acres of adjoining waters, is the site of the Guantánamo Bay United States Naval Reserve (total acreage 28,000). Guantánamo Bay with its airfields and extensive supply, repair, and training facilities, is the chief U.S. naval base in the West Indies. The sheltered harbor, its position near the Windward Passage, an important maritime route between the U.S. and Central and South America, and its proximity to the Panama Canal, make it strategically important. During the Spanish-American War the U.S. captured

GUAPORÉ

and fortified much of the outer harbor of Guantánamo Bay and used it as an anchorage for American warships. Through an agreement signed with Cuba in 1903, the U.S. obtained the right to maintain a naval base at Guantánamo Bay. In 1934 the agreement was superseded by a treaty that reaffirmed the U.S right to lease the site of the base from Cuba. The U.S. has continued to hold the base despite harassment by Premier Fidel Castro (q.v.) of Cuba.

GUAPORÉ or **ITÉNEZ,** river of South America, rising in Mato Grosso State, Brazil, and flowing N.W. between Brazil and Bolivia to the Mamoré R., a tributary of the Madeira. The Guaporé is navigable for the greater part of its course of about 950 mi.

GUARANI, group of aboriginal Indian tribes of South America, constituting a linguistic subdivision of the Tupi-Guaranian (q.v.) family of languages. They were once widely diffused through central and southern Brazil, Paraguay, Bolivia, Argentina, and Uruguay. Most present-day Paraguayans have some Guarani blood. Descendants of the Guarani in Brazil dwell in villages surrounded with a double line of palisades; family life is communal. The Indians are industrious, and engage in farming, hunting, and fishing. Their weapons are the bow and arrow and the club. Netted hammocks are made on primitive upright looms. The Guarani are short in stature, their average height not exceeding 5 ft. 4 in. They are long-headed and have a light pigmentation.

GUARANTY or **GUARANTEE,** in law, obligation undertaken by one party to answer for the default of another. It is an agreement by one person to answer to another for the debt, or the performance of some contract or duty in case of default, of a third person who is originally liable for such payment or performance. The party who promises that the obligation of the principal or debtor will be paid or performed is called the guarantor. A guaranty is similar in principle to a suretyship, in which a party known as the surety agrees to answer for the debt or default of another; it differs in that the promise of the guarantor is distinct from and collateral to that of the principal debtor, whereas a surety, although an accessory, is bound with the principal debtor as a copromisor. The contract of the surety is made at the same time and usually jointly with that of its principal, whereas that of a guarantor is a contract distinct from that of his principal. A surety is the insurer of the debt or obligation, whereas a guarantor is an insurer of the ability or solvency of the principal. Consequently, the surety may be joined with the principal as a defendant when the principal is sued for nonpayment of a debt, whereas the guarantor may be sued only after a judgment (q.v.) has been rendered on a suit for nonpayment brought by the creditor against the debtor. In many cases, however, the term surety is defined as including the term guarantor, so that a guaranty may be only one of several types of surety contract. In English common law (q.v.) a guaranty was equally enforceable whether made in writing or orally. Under existing statutes in the United States, a guaranty must be in writing.

GUARDAFUI, CAPE. See CAPE GUARDAFUI.

GUARDI, Francesco (1712–93), Italian painter, born in Venice. He studied with his brother Giovanni Antonio Guardi (1699–1760); the brothers worked together on many religious paintings for churches in and near Venice. In the 1750's Francesco Guardi turned to painting landscapes of Venice in the manner of the older Venetian painter Antonio Canaletto (q.v.). Guardi quickly developed his own brilliant, romantic style and his pictures of Venice, unlike those of Canaletto, usually include processions of figures in brilliant colors and animated groups in brightly hued costumes. Among his most important works are "Allegories" and "Faith and Hope" (both 1747, Ringling Museum, Sarasota, Fla.), "Fantastic Landscape" (about 1760, Metropolitan Museum of Art, New York City), and "The Doges' Palace, Venice" (1770, National Gallery, London).

GUARDIAN, in United States law, individual to whom is entrusted the care of a person, his property, or both, when such person, by statutory definition or judicial finding, is incapable of administering his own affairs, whether because of age, inability to understand, or lack of self-control. The usual form of guardianship is that of infants, individuals considered as minors under State statutes.

Three types of guardianship with respect to infants were distinguished at common law: guardianship by nature; guardianship by nurture; and guardianship by socage. Guardianship by nature was that possessed by a father, or by his widow, with respect to the person of the heir apparent or oldest son. Guardianship by nurture was that exercised by the father or by his widow with respect to the persons of children other than the heir apparent. Guardianship by socage was that vested in the next of kin of a tenant (see TENURE) under fourteen years of age. This guardianship could be claimed only by relatives other than the heirs of the infant.

In the U.S., guardianship by nature is the prevailing form and is the right of the father, mother, and next of kin, in the order named, to the custody of the person of a minor child. Guardianship by nurture does not exist in the U.S. and guardianship by socage is almost unknown, except in the State of New York, where it obtains only when a minor has acquired realty.

In most States the appointment of guardians and their duties to their wards are regulated by statute. In general, such statutes vest jurisdiction over appointment and control of guardians in the courts, usually in courts of probate in the case of the death of the paternal parent. The legal right to guardianship of minor children, as at common law, normally belongs to the surviving parent, since the statutes generally provide that a married woman is, with her husband, a joint guardian of her children, with equal powers, rights, and duties with regard to them. Whether such surviving parent will be appointed guardian, however, depends on the determination of the court as to whether such action will best promote the child's welfare under all circumstances. The laws of most States authorize the surviving parent to designate a guardian for minors by will. Such a guardian is termed a testamentary guardian. A guardian may be appointed by a court when the parents of a minor child are still living if the parents appear unfit for control of the minor or have interests adverse to it.

Guardians appointed by a court or by will have control both of the ward's person and of his entire property. It is the duty of the guardian to take possession and control of his ward's personal property and of the rents and profits of his real estate; to keep, invest, and protect them; and to render a true account when the ward comes of age (see AGE, in law) or at the demand of the court.

When a cause of action exists directly in favor of an infant or when an action or lawsuit is brought against an infant, in some States the court of appropriate jurisdiction will appoint a guardian ad litem to protect the interests of the infant in such action; the guardian ad litem may or may not be the same as the infant's general guardian. In estate-administration proceedings in which a minor is involved, the probate courts appoint special guardians for the purpose of protecting his interests. A special guardian is usually an attorney, rather than the infant's general guardian.

In New York State the natural parent may prosecute an action on behalf of a minor without the necessity of having a guardian ad litem appointed.

GUARINI, Giovanni Battista (1538–1612), Italian poet, born in Ferrara, and educated at Pisa and Padua. After fourteen years in the diplomatic service of Alphonso II d'Este, Duke of Ferrara (1533–97), he became the duke's court poet in 1581. A year later he resigned and withdrew to his family estate, the Villa Guarina, where he wrote his most notable work, *Pastor Fido* (1590; Eng. trans., *The Faithfull Shepheard,* 1647). This play, a pastoral tragicomedy, polished in style, was translated into many languages and became popular during the 17th century. It set the pattern for a code of refinement and gallantry that lasted in Europe until the late 18th century. Guarini's work has been compared to that of his predecessor at the court of d'Este, Torquato Tasso (q.v.), but it lacks the deep feeling and sentiment of Tasso.

GUARNIERI or **GUARNERY,** name of a family of Italian violin makers, all of whom were born in Cremona and whose activities for the most part were carried on in that city. The family is often known by the Latinized form of its name, Guarnerius. The principal members of the family are the following.

Andrea Guarnieri (1626–98). He learned the art of violin making in the Cremona workshop of the noted violin maker Nicolò Amati (*see under* AMATI). The violins made by Andrea Guarnieri were patterned after the Amati violins.

Pietro Giovanni Guarnieri (1655–1728?), elder son of Andrea. He settled in Mantua and consequently is known as "Peter of Mantua". He made a number of technical improvements in the type of violin made by his father; instruments made by him are highly valued today.

Giuseppe Giovanni Battista Guarnieri (1666–1739?), younger son of Andrea. He also made a number of changes in the violin model created by his father; some of Giuseppe's innovations had influence on the work of his son, Giuseppe Antonio.

Pietro Guarnieri (1695–1765?), son of the preceding, and known as "Peter of Venice" because he utilized in his work some of the features of the work of Venetian violin makers.

Giuseppe Antonio Guarnieri (about 1687–1745), son of Giuseppe Giovanni. He was known as Giuseppe del Gesù ("Giuseppe of Jesus") because of the sacred monogram, IHS (the first three letters of the Greek word for Jesus), which he added after his name on the labels that he placed in his violins. Giuseppe del Gesù is regarded as second only to the greatest of all violin makers, Antonio Stradivari (q.v.). The violins made by Giuseppe del Gesù are particularly noted for their rich tone. One of his

GUATEMALA

best instruments was played by the great Italian virtuoso Nicolò Paganini (q.v.); that violin is today in the Municipal Palace, Genoa.

GUATEMALA, republic of Central America, bounded on the N. and W. by Mexico, on the E. by British Honduras and the Gulf of Honduras, on the S.E. by Honduras and El Salvador, and on the S. by the Pacific Ocean. It lies between about lat. 13°45′ N. and lat. 17°40′ N. and long. 88°20′ W. and long. 92°18′ W. The country has an area of 42,042 sq.mi.

THE LAND

Roughly two thirds of the total land area of Guatemala is comprised of mountains, many of which are volcanic. The Sierra Madre system, traversing Guatemala from E. to W. divides the country into two drainage areas of unequal extent. The Pacific slope, relatively narrow, is abundantly watered and fertile in its mid-region, in which the greatest density of population occurs. The Atlantic slope, and notably the broad area around Lake Petén-Itza in the N. ranges from grazing land to forest, and is thinly populated. Most of the volcanoes of Guatemala are extinct; severe eruptions have been recorded, however, for Tacaná on the Mexican border. Earthquakes are frequent in the vicinity of the southern volcanic belt, where many towns have been destroyed.

The largest rivers, all on the Atlantic slope, are the Motagua, the Usumacinta which forms part of the boundary with Mexico, the Chixoy, and the Sarstún, forming the boundary with British Honduras.

Climate. The climate of Guatemala is, for the most part, equable, although temperatures vary considerably according to altitude. Between 3000 and 8000 ft. above sea level, where most of the Guatemalan population is concentrated, the days are warm and the nights cool; the average annual temperature is about 68° F. The weather in the low-lying coastal regions is more tropical in character, with an average annual temperature of around 83° F. The rainy season occurs between May and October, with a corresponding dry season from November to April. Annual rainfall on the Caribbean side averages between 60 and 100 in.; Guatemala City receives about 52 in. annually.

Natural Resources. Exceedingly fertile soil is the most important resource of Guatemala, which is basically an agricultural country. Mineral products include lead, zinc, and chromite; deposits of uranium and mercury have been reported. Extensive forests provide valuable timber and other products for local consumption as well as for export. The short rivers of the steep Pacific slope furnish abundant waterpower

A volcanic mountain rises from the shore of Lake Atitlán.
United Fruit Company

GUATEMALA

which in the late 1960's totaled about 181,000,000 kw hours annually.

Plants and Animals. Most plants typical of the tropical zone are found in the lowlands of Guatemala. In the mountain regions oak forests predominate on the lower slopes, giving way to pine forests above 7000 ft. Orchids and other brilliant flowers grow abundantly in all parts of the country.

Deer, monkeys, and peccaries are common, especially in the sparsely populated lowlands. Other wild animals, including jaguars, tapirs, and pumas, are found in smaller numbers, and crocodiles inhabit the rivers. Birdlife is extremely rich; the brilliantly plumaged quetzal parrot is the national emblem.

THE PEOPLE

Pure-blooded descendants of the Maya Indians make up about 45 percent of the population of Guatemala, and the remainder consists largely of mestizos, that is, persons of mixed American, Indian, and Spanish descent. More than 65 percent of the population is rural.

Population. The population of Guatemala (census 1964) was 4,287,997; the United Nations estimated (1970) 5,189,000. The overall population density is about 125 per sq.mi. and is concentrated mainly in the central highland region. The northern third of the country is virtually uninhabited.

Political Dvisions and Principal Cities. Guatemala is divided into twenty-two administrative departments, each headed by a governor appointed by the president. Guatemala, the capital and largest city, has a population of 768,987 (1970). Other principal cities are Quezaltenango (54,487), the center of a grain-growing region, and Puerto Barrios (29,435), the chief port on the Atlantic coast.

Religion and Language. Roman Catholicism is the faith of the vast majority of the people. The leading Protestant denominations are the Baptist and the Evangelical. Spanish is the official language of Guatemala, but Indian languages are widely spoken.

Education. In the mid-1960's, more than 63 percent of persons over ten years of age were illiterate. Education is theoretically free at all levels, but, because of the grave shortage of public schools, many private schools are in operation. Primary education is compulsory.

ELEMENTARY AND SECONDARY SCHOOLS. In the late 1960's, the school system included about 4700 primary schools, which were attended annually by some 475,000 pupils, and about 360 secondary schools with an annual enrollment of about 63,000 students. About 7 percent of eligible students of secondary-school age were enrolled in that period.

UNIVERSITIES AND COLLEGES. The autonomous University of San Carlos de Borromeo (founded in 1678) in the city of Guatemala is the major institution of higher education. A private Catholic university, the Rafael Landivar University, is also in Guatemala. Three additional universities were opened in the late 1960's. Total university enrollment in 1969 was approximately 13,000.

Culture. The contrast between the modern modes in Guatemala, the capital and center of Guatemalan cultural life, and the customs of the descendants of the highly civilized Maya Indians, whose crafts and traditions still predominate today, gives Guatemala a colorful and dynamic culture. Spanish colonists gave Guatemala its official language and many architectural and art treasures. Magnificent buildings of the colonial period remain at Antigua, the colonial capital, 12 miles w. of Guatemala. Contemporary crafts such as weaving, jewelry making, and ceramics combine Indian design and color patterns with Spanish technical skills.

Among 20th-century Guatemalan artists of international repute, the writers Enrique Gómez Carrillo, Rafael Arévalo Martinez (1884–   ), and Miguel Ángel Asturias (q.v.), winner of the 1967 Nobel Prize in literature, are preeminent. The contemporary painters, Carlos Mérida, Alfredo Gálvez Suárez, and Valentín Abascal have been inspired by the Indian heritage of their nation.

LIBRARIES AND MUSEUMS. About 100 libraries are located throughout the country, of which more than 50 percent are found within Guatemala City. The most noteworthy in the capital are the National Archives, the Library of the Supreme Court of Justice, and the Library of the Government Printers.

Also situated in the capital is the Museum of Archeology and Ethnology, with its excellent collection of Mayan artifacts. The Colonial Museum in Antigua has vast exhibits of colonial art works.

Archeology. The principal archeological sites in Guatemala are Tikal, Uaxactún, and Piedras Negras in the northern lowlands, and Kaminaljuyú in the southern highlands. These sites are generally identified with the Old Mayan Empire that flourished between the 3rd and 10th centuries; see MAYA.

In recent years large-scale excavation and restoration projects have been carried out at Tikal, the largest known Mayan ruin complex. Five of the giant temples at the site rise to heights of more than 200 ft. Some 450 buildings of the total

GUATEMALA

complex, comprising many sq.mi., have been excavated either entirely or in part. The most famous structure is a huge pyramid known as Temple I, or Temple of the Giant Jaguar.

Excavations have also yielded beautiful stone carving, pottery, and jade objects. Late-period finds show cultural elements that archeologists attribute to Teotihuacán, Toltec, and possibly other influences from areas of modern Mexico; see MEXICO: *Archeology.*

THE ECONOMY

Since World War II the government has encouraged the expansion of industry in order to offset an overdependence on coffee and banana production. Despite these efforts, living standards are low and the economy remains at the mercy of foreign market trends and climatic uncertainties. In a recent year the national budget figures showed a balanced budget of about $250,900,000.

Agriculture. In the early 1970's, agriculture continued to be the most important industry of Guatemala. The chief commercial crop is coffee, with about 340,000 acres devoted to its cultivation and a total production of about 145,000 tons annually. Some 12,000 plantations have about 138,000,000 trees; however, 80 percent of the crop is harvested from about 1500 large plantations employing more than 425,000 workers. Bananas are grown principally on the extensive American-owned United Fruit Company plantations along the Pacific coast and in the Motagua R. valley. Annual production of bananas in the late 1960's was about 6,000,000 stems. Other leading crops in order of commercial importance are cotton and sugarcane. Corn, rice, beans, and wheat are raised for local consumption.

Pigs and poultry are raised for domestic use. Cattle raising is being developed, and in the mid-1960's the number of beef cattle on ranges was about 1,400,000.

Forest and Fishing Industries. About 45 percent of the land area is covered with forest, making forestry an important mainstay in the Guatemalan economy. Important forest products are cabinet woods, balsam, chicle, and oils. Guatemala ranks second only to Mexico in world production of chicle, which is used in the manufacture of chewing gum. Commercial fish-

Young girls draw water from a village fountain before a church of the Spanish colonial period. UPI

People of Amatitlán, a typical village of Guatemala. Right: A family at dinner outside their one-room adobe house. Below, left: Two young Indian girls of Mayan descent, as are most Guatemalans. Below, right: A woman grinds corn to make tortillas, a pancake-like staple of the Guatemalan diet.

United Nations

GUATEMALA

ing is on a small scale but is increasing in importance.

Mining. Lead, zinc, silver, and chromite are the only minerals mined in commercial quantities.

Manufacturing. In the mid-1960's manufacturing accounted for about 14 percent of the annual gross national product. Most firms operate on a very small scale. Major products include foodstuffs, beverages, cement, chemicals, hides and skins, and textiles.

Currency and Banking. The unit of currency is the quetzal, which, since 1926, has remained at par with the U.S. dollar. The Bank of Guatemala (established in 1946) is the central bank and bank of issue. The country has several other banks, including the National Agrarian Bank, established in 1953 to make loans to farmers who receive land under the agrarian reform law.

Commerce and Trade. In 1969 Guatemala's imports were about $250,000,000 and exports amounted to about $262,000,000. The United States, West Germany, and members of the Central American Common Market are the chief trading partners. The principal imports, in order of value, are raw materials and intermediate products; consumer goods; machinery, tools, and equipment; petroleum products, and building materials. The chief exports are coffee, cotton, bananas, beef, essential oils, timber, chicle, and shrimps.

Transportation. In the early 1970's the total length of all railroads in Guatemala was 500 mi., owned by the government's Ferrocarriles de Guatemala since 1968. A railroad link between North and South America was established in 1942 with the opening of a railroad bridge across the Suchiate R. from Mexico to Guatemala. The country has about 7400 mi. of highways and secondary roads, of which about 1200 mi. are paved. The Inter-American Highway traverses Guatemala from Mexico to El Salvador. Motor vehicles number about 54,000. The government-owned airline Aviateca provides domestic service, and international traffic is handled by several commercial airlines.

Communications. Most postal, telephone, and telegraph services are government-owned. In the late 1960's about 40,000 telephones were in use. Guatemala is served by about 70 radio and 3 television stations; about 250,000 radios and 72,000 television receivers are in use.

Labor. Of a total labor force of approximately 1,400,000 about 68 percent are employed in agriculture, 11 percent in mining, and 10 percent in services. In the mid-1960's it was estimated that 10 percent of the labor force was unemployed and 33 percent (mostly farm workers) underem-

A keeper leads a cow from its pen at the school of veterinary medicine of San Carlos University of Guatemala. In addition to training veterinarians, the school conducts experiments to improve strains of cattle and sheep.
United Nations

ployed. Trade unions exist but are small.

GOVERNMENT
Guatemala is a republic under the constitution of 1966. Voting is compulsory for all literate citizens of eighteen years and over.

Central Government. Executive power is vested in a president and a vice-president, both of whom are elected by popular vote for terms of four years. The president has a wide range of power, including the authority to preserve public order, propose legislation, and appoint officials. He is advised by the vice-president, who advises the council of state and Congress, as well. The fourteen-member council is an advisory body.

HEALTH AND WELFARE. A social-security program was established by a law of 1946. As amended, the law requires participation by all employers of five or more persons. Accidents, maternity, hospitalization, disability, and old age are covered under the program, and coverage extends to about 20 percent of the total work force. Life expectancy in Guatemala is the lowest in Latin America (49.4 years), a contributing factor being the shortage of physicians (2.5 per 10,000 population).

Legislature. The unicameral Congress is elected by popular vote to four-year terms. Congress imposes taxes, sets the budget, declares war; a two-thirds majority vote is necessary before a presidential treaty or convention may be enacted. The Congress is made up of fifty-five members.

Political Parties. In 1963 a government decree restricted participation in national elections to parties with at least 50,000 members. As a result, only three of the thirty extant groups were allowed to offer candidates in the 1970 elections. The participating parties were the Revolutionary Party, a moderate left-wing group; the Institutional and Democratic Party, a conservative body, and the Movement of National Liberation, a militant right-wing and pro-Catholic faction, which merged in 1970; and the Christian Democrats, a radical, left-wing group. The Guatemalan Labor Party (Communist) is outlawed.

Local Government. Each of the twenty-two departments of the nation is ruled by a governor appointed by the president. Departments are divided into municipalities, the mayors and councils of which are also presidential appointees.

Judiciary. The judicial system consists of a Supreme Court, courts of appeals, and courts of original jurisdiction. Judges of the Supreme Court and appeals courts are appointed by the president, and judges of original jurisdiction are appointed by the Supreme Court.

Defense. All male citizens between the ages of eighteen and fifty are required to serve in the armed forces for two years. The regular army has a total strength of about 8000. The country has a small air force and navy.

HISTORY
Guatemala, site of the ancient civilization of the Maya, was conquered by a Spanish force under Pedro de Alvarado (q.v.) in 1524. After three centuries of Spanish domination, Guatemala, virtually coextensive with all that is now known as Central America, proclaimed its independence on Sept. 15, 1821. Almost at once, Agustín de Iturbide (q.v.), emperor of Mexico, incorporated the territory into the Mexican Empire. Guatemala did not regain its autonomy until 1823, when a revolution in Mexico forced Iturbide to abdicate, and a Mexican republic was proclaimed. In the same year, the Confederation of Central America was established, including present-day Guatemala, Honduras, El Salvador, Nicaragua, and Costa Rica. The confederation was maintained only with the greatest difficulty,

Drill operators at work in the first stages of an irrigation project.
United Nations

A father and son at work in their corn field.
United Nations

however, and finally collapsed upon the secession of Guatemala in 1839.

The government of Guatemala has been in the hands of military men virtually from the beginning of the republican era. These military leaders were often self-appointed and had come up through the ranks in the process of frequent revolutions. In 1854 Rafael Carrera (q.v.), who fourteen years earlier had made himself dictator of Guatemala and a large portion of Central America, became president for life. In 1873, eight years after the death of Carrera, Justo Rufino Barrios (1835?–85), formerly supreme commander of the army, was elected to the presidency. Barrios, seeking to revive the Central American federation by military means, invaded El Salvador, and was killed in the ensuing battle between the two countries. His successor, General Manuel Barillas, reestablished peaceful relations with El Salvador and the other countries of Central America. José María Reina Barrios, elected president in 1892, and reelected five years later, was assassinated in 1898.

Early 1900's. For the next twenty-two years, the politician Manuel Estrada Cabrera (1857–1924) was dictator of Guatemala. In 1906, ex-president Barillas organized a revolt against the Cabrera regime which soon involved all Central America in war, Nicaragua alone excepted. Further hostilities were averted by the intervention of Presidents Theodore Roosevelt (q.v.) of the United States and Porfirio Díaz (q.v.) of Mexico, who arranged an armistice.

Guatemala severed diplomatic relations with Germany on April 27, 1917, during World War I. In 1920 the dictatorship of President Estrada Cabrera came to an end with a revolution of liberal elements which forced Cabrera to resign. Dr. Carlos Herrera was appointed provisional president, taking the oath for the unexpired term (1916–23). On Dec. 7, 1921, Herrera was overthrown and Gen. José María Orellana (1872–1926), Guatemalan chief of staff, succeeded to the presidency, serving until his death in 1926. Unrest resulting from economic depression and charges of corruption leveled against the dictatorship of the new president, former army officer and politician Lázaro Chacón (1873–1931), culminated in a brief revolution and the overthrow of the government.

General Jorge Ubico Castañeda (1878–1946) was elected president in February, 1931. Under his regime Guatemala recovered from the economic depression of the 1930's, and its economy enjoyed some prosperity. Ubico quickly proved, however, to be only the latest in the line of military dictators who had dominated Guatemala for a century. His exercise of power became so repressive that in June, 1944, a general strike forced his resignation.

GUATEMALA

INDEX TO MAP OF GUATEMALA

Cities and Towns

Amatitlán	B2
Antigua	B2
Asunción Mita	C2
Chajul	B2
Champerico	A2
Chichicastenango	B2
Chimaltenango	B2
Chiquimula	C2
Coatepeque	B2
Cobán	B2
Comalapa	B2
Cuilapa	B2
El Progreso	B2
Escuintla	B2
Flores	C1
Gualán	C2
Guatemala (cap.)	B2
Huehuetenango	B2
Ipala	C2
Jacaltenango	B2
Jalapa	B2
Jutiapa	B2
Livingston	C2
Mazatenango	B2
Momostenango	B2
Puerto Barrios	C2
Quezaltenango	B2
Quezaltepeque	C2
Rabinal	B2
Retalhuleu	B2
Salamá	B2
San Felipe	B2
San José	B3
San Luis Jilotepeque	C2
San Marcos	B2
San Martin	B2
San Mateo	B2
San Pedro Carchá	B2
Santa Cruz del Quiché	B2
Sololá	B2
Totonicapán	B2
Zacapa	C2

Physical Features

Atitlán (lake)	B2
Atitlán (vol.)	B2
Chixoy (river)	B1
Izabal (lake)	C2
Minas (mts.)	C2
Motagua (river)	C2
San Pedro (river)	B1
Sarstún (river)	C2
Tacaná (vol.)	A2
Tajumulco (vol.)	B2
Tres Puntas (cape)	C2
Usumacinta (river)	B1

In the more liberal political atmosphere that followed, labor was permitted to organize and political parties were formed.

In December, 1944, after a period of general strife, the Guatemalan educator Juan José Arévalo Bermejo (1904–), who had the support of the National Renovation and Popular Front Liberation parties, was elected president. Arévalo's administration was plagued by recurrent political crises in which the government charged that reactionary forces were plotting its overthrow. In January, 1945, the government severed diplomatic relations with the government of Spain. A new constitution was promulgated in March.

Boundary and United Fruit Company Disputes. In September, 1945, Guatemala renewed its claim, outstanding since the republic was formed, to British Honduras (q.v.). A treaty negotiated with Great Britain in 1859 had laid down the southern boundary between Guatemala and British Honduras; claiming that Great Britain had not complied with all the terms of the boundary agreement, Guatemala reopened the entire dispute in the late 1930's. In January, 1946, Great Britain proposed that the border dispute be submitted for arbitration to the United Nations International Court of Justice. The dispute was aggravated in 1948 when units of the British Caribbean navy were dispatched to the port of Belize City, British Honduras, to avert an alleged Guatemalan move to take over the colony. Guatemala issued a protest to the U.N.,

GUATEMALA

the Pan-American Union, and all American countries. The republic then sealed off its frontier with British Honduras.

Minor rightist uprisings occurred during the first half of 1949, but the principal political development of the year was the intervention by the government in a long-standing dispute between the United Fruit Company and its workers. As a result of official pressure the company capitulated to the demands of the workers. In August, 1949, Guatemala was accused by the Dominican Republic of aiding Dominican revolutionaries. The Council of the Organization of American States (q.v.) confirmed the charge in April, 1950, and threatened Guatemala with sanctions.

General elections were held in November, 1950. Supported by a coalition of left-wing parties, presidential candidate Jacobo Arbenz Guzmán (1913-71), minister of national defense in the Arévalo cabinet, won a decisive victory. The new administration assumed office in March, 1951, and during the remainder of the year President Arbenz generally perpetuated the centrist domestic policies of his predecessor.

The administration moved steadily leftward during 1952. Among numerous indications of the growing influence of Guatemalan Communists were a government order (January) forbidding anti-Communist demonstrations and enactment of a radical social-security bill. During the early part of the year the government intervened in another dispute between the United Fruit Company and its employees. In March, the company again capitulated, making substantial concessions.

In May President Arbenz vetoed the social-security bill, which he termed a threat to the national economy. The national assembly enacted in June an agrarian-reform law providing for the distribution of uncultivated estates of more than 225 acres to landless workers.

The agrarian-reform program went into effect on Feb. 17, and several days later the government approved expropriation of 225,000 acres of United Fruit Company lands on the Guatemalan west coast. By the middle of June expropriated private property, paid for with nonnegotiable government bonds, totaled 300,000 acres; over 400,000 acres of government-owned lands had been distributed to landless workers.

Opposition to the Arbenz regime mounted on both the international and domestic fronts during the first half of 1954. At the 10th Inter-American Conference, held in March, the United States secured approval of the anti-Communist resolution implicitly condemning the Guatemalan government. In April the Roman Catholic archbishop of Guatemala, in a pastoral letter to his charge, appealed for an uprising against Communism. Claiming discovery of a plot aimed at its overthrow, the government began a wholesale roundup of opposition leaders on May 31; on June 8 civil rights were suspended.

Anti-Communist Takeover. On June 18 a so-called liberating army of political exiles, led by Colonel Carlos Castillo Armas (1914?-57), invaded Guatemala from headquarters in Honduras. The rebels' ground forces quickly captured key supply points and their planes bombed the capital and other cities. Troops of the regular army offered only token resistance to the invaders. Arbenz resigned on June 27 and two days later an anti-Communist military junta, accepting the terms laid down by Castillo Armas for a cease-fire, dissolved the legislature, ordered the arrest of prominent Communist leaders, and released 600 political prisoners. Various differences between the rebels and the junta were mediated by foreign diplomats, including the U.S. ambassador to Guatemala, and the civil war was formally ended on July 2. A new junta with representatives of both factions assumed supreme governmental authority.

Castillo Armas was named provisional president on July 8. On Oct. 10 a national plebiscite resulted in an overwhelming victory for Castillo Armas; he was formally installed as president for a five-year term on Nov. 6. Meanwhile a constituent assembly convened to draft a new constitution. In November, 1955, the government authorized the formation of political parties. Elections for a new national assembly were held in December. The government party won all sixty-six seats. President Castillo Armas signed the new constitution on Feb. 2, 1956, and the new assembly took office on March 1.

On July 26, 1957, President Castillo Armas was assassinated in the presidential palace by a palace guard. Two days later the Guatemalan congress named Vice-President Louis A. González López provisional president. González López pledged continuation of the democratic, anti-Communist policies of Castillo Armas and proclaimed a presidential election for Oct. 20, 1957. The election, which was held as scheduled, was won by the lawyer and industrialist Miguel Ortiz Passarelli. The validity of the election was challenged by several minor political parties, and on Oct. 25 a three-member military junta seized the government and forced González López to resign. The junta then elevated the second vice-president, Guillermo Flores Av-

Guatemala. Plate 1. Above: Farm lands in the highlands near Quezaltenango, the second-largest city of Guatemala, in the western part of the country. Right: Women shop for produce in an open-air market at Palín in the foothills of a fertile farm region near the capital. Black Star

Guatemala. Plate 2. *Above: A view of the municipal center of Guatemala City, with modern buildings under construction. Below: A woman artisan weaves a length of cotton textile; most such fabrics made in Guatemala incorporate traditional Indian designs.*

United Nations

endaño, to the presidency. Another presidential election was held on Jan. 19, 1958, but no candidate received the required 51 percent majority of the vote. As a result, on Feb. 12 the congress chose as president the military leader Miguel Ydígoras Fuentes (1895–); he was inaugurated on March 2, 1958. Guatemalan military aircraft on Dec. 29 attacked three Mexican fishing vessels operating in an area claimed by Guatemala as territorial waters. In reprisal, Mexico broke off diplomatic relations on Jan. 17, 1959. Ydígoras announced on Sept. 15 that, following settlement of the dispute, diplomatic relations had been restored.

Cuban Influence. Following the exchange of accusations by Cuba and Guatemala that each country was plotting to overthrow the government of the other, Guatemala, in April, 1960, severed diplomatic relations. Serious revolts occurred in Guatemala in July and again in November. On orders of President Dwight D. Eisenhower (q.v.) of the U.S., surface and air units of the U.S. Navy were stationed off the Caribbean coasts of Guatemala and Nicaragua on Nov. 16 to prevent an attack from Cuba which the two Central-American countries claimed was imminent. The attack did not occur and the naval units were withdrawn on Dec. 7. After the abortive attempt to invade Cuba on April 17, 1961 (*see* CUBA: *History*), it was disclosed in hearings before the U.S. Senate in May that the invasion force had been recruited by U.S. intelligence agents and that many of the men had been trained in Guatemala. Widespread demonstrations preceding the elections scheduled for December, 1963, offered the military an excuse for enacting a coup. In March, 1963, Ydígoras was removed from office by his former defense minister, Enrique Peralta Azurdia (1908–). Peralta declared a state of emergency and canceled the elections.

In December, 1965, the Peralta regime promulgated a new constitution and called for new national elections in March, 1966. Dr. Julio Cesar Méndez Montenegro, a member of the Partido Revolucionario, failed to receive an absolute majority but was officially elected to the presidency by the Congress.

After a campaign marked by violence the rightist candidate, Colonel Carlos Arana Osorio (1918–) was elected to succeed him in March, 1970.

In the early 1970's political instability continued to dominate Guatemalan national life, and violence was common. Numerous persons were slain by guerrillas in 1972, including several political leaders and a member of Congress. Several guerrilla leaders also were reported slain in clashes with Guatemalan troops.

GUATEMALA *or* **GUATEMALA CITY,** city and capital of Guatemala, and largest city of Central America, on a plateau almost 5000 ft. above sea level, 50 miles N.E. of the Pacific Coast port of San José and 150 miles S.W. of the Caribbean port of Puerto Barrios. The capital is also the commercial and cultural center of the country. The principal articles of trade are coffee, lumber, hides, and native handicrafts. The city has international air and rail service and is situated on the Inter-American Highway section of the Pan American Highway (q.v.). Educational institutions include San Carlos de Borreomeo University of Guatemala (founded in 1678), Rafael Landivar University (1961), and the National Academy of Music (1880). The city is the seat of an episcopal see; the great cathedral is an excellent example of Spanish colonial architecture.

The present city is the third capital in the history of Guatemala. The first capital, also called Guatemala and founded in 1527, was destroyed by flood and volcanic action in 1541. The second capital, founded the next year, was almost completely destroyed by an earthquake in 1773; it is located 25 miles W. of the present city and is now known as Antigua. The present capital, founded in 1776, suffered heavy earthquake damage in 1917–18. Most of the modern buildings today are of reinforced concrete. Pop. (1966) 621,044.

GUATEMOTZIN *or* **GUATEMOC** *or* **CUAUHTEMOC** (1495?–1525), last Aztec Emperor of Mexico, nephew of the Aztec emperor Montezuma II (*see under* MONTEZUMA). Guatemotzin was leader of the opposition to Montezuma's policy of appeasing the Spanish invaders. He organized the attack, known as "la Noche Triste", which drove the Spanish commander Hernando Cortes (q.v.) from Mexico City on June 3, 1520. Upon the death of his uncle, Guatemotzin was chosen emperor of the Aztec. As emperor he succeeded in defending the capital city throughout the spring and summer of 1521. When he was finally captured by the Spanish, he refused to reveal the location of the Aztec gold treasury. He was taken as hostage by Cortes and his party on their march through Honduras; *see* HONDURAS: *History*. During this march the emperor was tortured and killed by the Spanish. A commemorative statue of Guatemotzin is in Mexico City.

GUAVA, common name of shrubs or small trees of the genus *Psidium*, belonging to the Myrtle family Myrtaceae, and of the fruits which they produce. Guavas are native to the tropics

GUAYAQUIL

of America but are now cultivated throughout the world. The most common cultivated guava is the fruit of a small tree, *P. guajava*, which bears white or yellow fruit about the size of an orange. The tree, which attains a height of 15 to 20 ft., is native to tropical America and is cultivated in Florida. Red guava, *P. guajava* var. *pomiferum*, bears a globular red fruit with sour red pulp. Strawberry guava, *P. cattleianum*, is a Brazilian species producing a large, spherical, claret-colored fruit with soft white pulp which has a flavor similar to that of strawberry. Strawberry guava has been cultivated in tropical America since the pre-Columbian period; in Florida and southern California, it is occasionally grown as an ornamental. Jellies, preserves, and pastes made from guavas are considered delicacies.

GUAYAQUIL, largest city and chief seaport in Ecuador, and capital of Guayas Province, on the w. bank of the estuary of the Guayas R., at the Gulf of Guayaquil, about 40 mi. from the Pacific coast, and about 170 miles s.w. of Quito. The city is a terminus for river, highway, railroad, and air transportation, with most of the imports and exports of the nation passing through it. Chief exports are bananas, coffee, cacao, so-called Panama hats, and balsa wood. Sugar mills, leather tanneries, and sawmills are among the industrial establishments of the city. Guayaquil is the site of one of the seven universities in Ecuador and of a government aviation school. Pop. (1966 est.) 680,209.

GUAYCURUAN, distinct stock of South American Indians living in the Gran Chaco (q.v.) and comprising about twenty tribes, of which the Guaycuru is the most prominent. *See* AMERICAN INDIAN LANGUAGES.

GUAYULE, common name of a shrubby perennial herb, *Parthenium argentatum,* belonging to the Composite family, Compositae, yielding guayule rubber. Guayule is native to the dry regions of southwestern Texas and northern Mexico. The plant grows about 2 ft. tall, bearing gray, silvery leaves. The dry weight of five-year-old plants is about 20 percent guayule rubber. Crude guayule rubber contains a large amount of resin, which must be removed, at considerable expense, to obtain good-quality rubber. Guayule rubber, in small quantities, was formerly obtained from wild Mexican plants of this species. Because of the shortage of rubber from the most important rubber tree, *Hevea brasiliensis,* during World War II, scientists of the United States Forest Service carried on experimental cultivation of 30,000 acres of guayule in southern California. By the late 1960's, however, guayule rubber was only produced in commercially negligible quantities. *See* RUBBER.

GUELDER-ROSE. *See* VIBURNUM.

GUELPH, city of Canada, in Ontario Province, and county seat of Wellington County on the Speed R., 27 miles N.W. of Hamilton and 45 miles s.w. of Toronto. Guelph is a rail center in an agricultural region. Industries include meat packing, food and dairy processing, woodworking, and the manufacture of chemicals, carpets, hats, tobacco products, rubber and paper products, auto parts, electrical equipment, and machinery. Gypsum and limestone are mined nearby. A hydroelectric station is situated at a 30-ft. waterfall on the river. The city is the site of the University of Guelph and of Ignatius College, a Roman Catholic theological seminary. Guelph was founded in 1827 by John Galt (*see under* GALT), Scottish novelist and pioneer in Canada, and incorporated in 1879. Pop. (1966) 51,337.

GUELPHS and **GHIBELLINES,** names of two great political factions existing in northern and central Italy from about the 12th to the 15th centuries. These factions originated in the early 12th century in Germany as the partisans of a struggle between two princely houses, the Welfs, who were the dukes of Saxony and Bavaria, and the Hohenstaufens, then the ruling house of the Holy Roman Empire (q.v.). (For the most famous Welf ruler, *see* HENRY THE LION.) During the course of the 12th century, the struggle between the German factions was transferred to Italy. The name Guelph was a corruption of Welf; Ghibelline was a corruption of Waiblingen, an estate belonging to the Hohenstaufen emperors.

By the beginning of the 13th century, the names of the two groups had lost their original German significance. The Guelphs became the party opposing the authority of the Holy Roman emperors in Italy and supporting the power of the papacy. The Ghibellines supported the imperial authority, particularly the rule of Frederick I (q.v.), Holy Roman Emperor known as Barbarossa. The Guelph party, moreover, became a nationalist party in a sense, for it enlisted itself in support of the Italian principalities and city republics which were demanding provincial or municipal rights and liberties.

Medieval Italy was disrupted by the violent political and military conflicts between the partisans of the two great factions. In general the great noble families adhered to the Ghibellines and the great cities supported the Guelphs. Eventually the division became more geographical. The nobles in the more northern districts inclined toward the Ghibellines and those in the central district toward the Guelphs. Pisa, Verona, and Arezzo were Ghibelline strongholds; Bologna, Milan, and, particularly, Florence supported the Guelphs. In Florence, struggles between the parties resulted in civil war which raged for more than ten years until, in 1266, the Ghibellines were expelled from the city.

About the 14th century, after the emperors had ceased to be a major power in Italy, the contest degenerated into a struggle of local political factions availing themselves of the prestige of ancient names and traditional or hereditary prejudices. In 1334 Pope Benedict XII (d. 1342) forbade, under pain of the censures of the Church, the further use of the Guelph and Ghibelline names. After the 14th century they were rarely used as the names of existing factions.

GUERCINO (It., "squint-eyed") (1591–1666), Italian painter of the Bolognese school, born Giovanni Francesco Barbieri in Cento, and educated there and in Bologna. He studied with various painters, including Lodovico Carracci (see under CARRACCI). During the reign of his patron, Pope Gregory XV (r. 1621–23), Guercino was in Rome, where he painted several well-known canvases and the "Aurora" fresco on a ceiling of the Villa Ludovisi. He lived in Cento from 1623 until 1642, when he went to Bologna to succeed the painter Guido Reni (q.v.) as head of the Bolognese school. In attempting to imitate Reni's style, Guercino lost much of the force which previously characterized his own.

Guercino is famous for more than 250 paintings and for numerous frescoes. Among his best-known works is the frescoe "Aurora" (1621, Casino Lodovisi, Rome). Other works include "Death of Dido" (1631, Spada Gallery, Rome) and "Saint Petronella" (1621, Museo Capitolino, Rome).

GUERICKE, Otto von (1602–86), German physicist, born in Magdeburg. He studied law at the universities of Leipzig and Jena and mathematics at the University of Leiden. In 1627 he was elected alderman of Magdeburg and in 1646 was elected burgomaster of that city. In 1681 he retired to Hamburg. Von Guericke spent his leisure in the study of natural science, and having heard of the experiments of the French scientist Blaise Pascal and the Italian scientists Galileo Galilei and Evangelista Torricelli (qq.v.) in connection with atmospheric pressure, he began to work on the properties of air and the creation of a vacuum. After various trial experiments he fitted a globe of copper with a stopcock and pump, and found that he could pump the air out of the globe. In the course of these experiments he invented the first air pump in 1650. In 1654 he carried out before the Imperial Diet at Regensburg the famous demonstration of the Magdeburg hemispheres. Two hollow bronze hemispheres were carefully fitted together and the air removed from the resulting sphere by means of a pump. Two eight-horse teams could not pull the halves apart; when the air was readmitted the hemispheres fell apart. Similar evacuated hemispheres are used today in laboratory demonstrations of atmospheric pressure.

Von Guericke investigated fields of natural science other than pneumatics. In 1672 he developed the first machine for producing an electric charge; see ELECTROSTATIC MACHINE. In astronomy he worked on predicting the periodic return of comets.

GUERNICA, or GUERNICA Y LUNO, town of N. Spain in Vizcaya Province, 12 miles N.E. of Bilbao. It has traditionally been a center of Basque culture; see BASQUES. Food processing, metalworking, and furniture manufacturing are principal industries of the town. A stronghold of the Loyalist forces during the 1936 to 1939 Spanish Civil War (see SPAIN: History: Civil War), Guernica was devastated by German air bombardment in April, 1937. The tragedy has been memorialized by the Spanish painter Pablo Picasso (q.v.) in a monumental oil painting, "Guernica" (1937, Museum of Modern Art, New York City). Pop. (1960) 4855.

GUERNSEY, Great Britain, island in the English Channel, one of the Channel Islands, about 75 miles s. of England and 35 miles w. of France. The N. part of the island is flat and low and the s. part rises to a plateau about 300 ft. above sea level. Agriculture and tourism are the principal industries. Flowers, fruits, and tomatoes, the chief crops, are raised for export. Guernsey is particularly noted for its breed of cattle; see GUERNSEY CATTLE. Saint Peter Port is the capital and principal seaport. Steamships and airplane service link the island with England. Area, 24.5 sq.mi.; pop. (1968 est.) 46,182.

GUERNSEY CATTLE, sometimes called Alderney cattle, breed of dairy cattle developed on the island of Guernsey in the Channel Islands (q.v.). Guernsey, like its sister island, Jersey, where Jersey cattle are developed, has for more than 100 years prohibited the introduction of any other breed of live cattle except for slaughter. The purity of the Guernsey breed is thus assured. Guernseys were first brought to the United States in 1833, and after 1874 were imported in considerable numbers. The breed is also common in Great Britain and Canada. Guernseys are famed for the richness of their milk. On the island, the average cow is expected

GUERRILLAS

Guernsey cow

to produce 5000 lb. of milk and 300 lb. of butterfat a year. In the U.S. individual cows have produced over 18,000 lb. of milk and 1000 lb. of butterfat a year. The standard size for mature Guernsey bulls is about 1500 lb.; for cows, about 1000. See CATTLE.

GUERRILLAS *or* **GUERILLAS** (Sp., diminutive of *guerra,* "war"), irregular military groups engaged in warfare against the regular armed forces of a foreign occupying power. Classic examples of guerrilla warfare include the operations of the French *franc-tireurs* against the German forces who invaded France during the Franco-German War (q.v.), the Boers who fought against British forces occupying the Transvaal and the Orange Free State during the South African War (q.v.), and the resistance led by Emilio Aguinaldo (q.v.) against the American forces who occupied the Philippines immediately after the Spanish-American War (q.v.). During World War I the guerrilla operations of the Arabs, under the leadership of Thomas Edward Lawrence (q.v.), against the Turks became famous. During World War II guerrillas known as Maquis fought the German forces occupying France, and in Yugoslavia guerrillas known as Chetniks and Partisans fought German and Italian occupation troops.

Lacking the numerical strength and weapons to oppose a regular army in the field, guerrillas avoid pitched battles. Instead, they operate from bases established in remote and inaccessible terrain, such as forests, mountains, and jungles, and depend on the support of the local inhabitants for recruits, food, shelter, and information. The guerrillas may also receive assistance in the form of arms, ammunition, medical supplies, and military advisors from their own or allied regular armies.

The tactics of guerrillas are those of harassment. Striking swiftly and unexpectedly, they raid enemy supply depots and installations in rear areas, ambush patrols and supply convoys, and cut communications lines, hoping thereby to disrupt enemy activities and to capture equipment and supplies for their own use. Because of their mobility, the dispersal of their forces into small groups, and their ability to disappear among the civilian population, guerrillas are extremely difficult to capture.

The term "guerrilla" originated during the Napoleonic Wars (q.v.) in the engagements of Spanish irregulars against the French armies occupying Spain. In its original sense, the term referred to independent groups of armed men formed into a militarylike organization operating in enemy-held territory in conjunction with their country's regular armed forces.

After World War II, the meaning of the word guerrilla was extended to include the guerrillalike tactics of any insurgency, rebellion, or uprising against an established government. The Hukbalahaps, or Huks, a Communist force that was fighting in the Philippines for several years, are an example of such an underground group.

The struggle in China (q.v.) between the Communist forces led by Mao Tse-tung (q.v.) and the Nationalist government of Chiang Kai-shek (q.v.), which began in 1927, gave a new meaning to guerrilla warfare. The armies led by Mao Tse-tung were not guerrilla forces in the traditional sense, but they used guerrillalike tactics until they were strong enough to engage and defeat the Nationalist armies in pitched battles. In so-called wars of national liberation stress is placed on armed insurgency, especially paramilitary and guerrilla tactics, sometimes at the expense of the political machinery.

This strategy was adopted by the North Vietnamese leader Ho Chi Minh (q.v.) in his fight against the French government in Indochina and is the scheme advocated by the Cuban leader Fidel Castro (q.v.) to those who wish to overthrow existing governments of South and Central America. It is also the strategy followed in South Vietnam by the pro-Communist Vietcong guerrillas fighting against the South Vietnamese government. To counter this strategy, the United States Army has trained the Special Forces (q.v.), including the so-called Green Berets, to organize counterinsurgency forces, to lead these forces against guerrillas, and at the same time to help the local inhabitants to improve their living conditions.

See also FIFTH COLUMN. M.B.

GUESCLIN, Bertrand Du. *See* DU GUESCLIN, BERTRAND.

GUESS, George. *See* SEQUOYA.

GUEST, Edgar Albert (1881–1959), American poet, born in Birmingham, England. He came to the United States in 1891, and attended grammar and high school in Detroit, Mich. He became a U.S. citizen in 1902. Starting in 1895 Guest wrote a column in the Detroit *Free Press*, and his verse and sketches of a simple, colloquial quality won him a wide audience. The verse, "Home", beginning with "It takes a heap o' livin' in a house t' make it home" was one of his earliest successes, and provided the title for his collection of verse, *A Heap o' Livin'* (1916). Some of his other collections are *Over Here* (1918), *When Day Is Done* (1921), *Rhymes of Childhood* (1924), *The Friendly Way* (1931), *All in a Lifetime* (1938), *Today and Tomorrow* (1942), and *Living Years* (1949).

GUEVARA Y DE NORONA, Antonio de (about 1480–1545), Spanish writer, born in Treceño, Santander Province. He became a Franciscan monk, and in 1518 was made court preacher and historiographer by Charles V (q.v.), King of Spain. In 1523 he was appointed inquisitor, in 1527 bishop of Guadix, and in 1537 bishop of Mondoñedo. Most of his writings were didactic in content and artificial in style. His *Relox de Príncipes* (1529; Eng. trans., *The Dial of Princes*, 1557), purported to be a biography of the Roman emperor Marcus Aurelius (q.v.), based on historical documents; actually the documents were nonexistent, and the work was merely an idealized characterization of a perfect prince. Guevara's affected style was developed by the English author John Lyly (q.v.) as euphuism.

GUGGENHEIM, name of a family of American industrialists and philanthropists, the most important of whom are listed below.

Meyer Guggenheim (1828–1905), born in Langnau, Switzerland. He emigrated to the United States at the age of nineteen, and established a flourishing business in Philadelphia, Pa., as a retailer and importer of Swiss embroidery. Guggenheim purchased mining property in Colorado, and believing that processing minerals rather than mining them was the more profitable enterprise, built large smelters in Colorado and Mexico and a refinery in New Jersey. The firm of Guggenheim Brothers was organized in 1881 by Guggenheim and his seven sons. In 1901 the Guggenheims gained control of the American Smelting and Refining Company.

Daniel Guggenheim (1856–1930), son of Meyer, born in Philadelphia, Pa., and educated in Europe. As a member of the firm of Guggenheim Brothers he became a leading figure in the copper industry of the U.S. and extended the activities of the firm to include gold mines in Alaska, rubber plantations in Africa, tin mines in Bolivia, and nitrate deposits in Chile. He negotiated the merger of Guggenheim Brothers with the American Smelting and Refining Company and was president and chairman of the board of directors of the American Smelting and Refining Company from 1901 to 1919. Daniel Guggenheim's philanthropic activities included the establishment of the Daniel and Florence Guggenheim Foundation to promote "through charitable and benevolent activities the wellbeing of mankind throughout the world" in 1924, the school of aeronautics at New York University in 1925, and the Daniel Guggenheim Foundation for the Promotion of Aeronautics in 1926.

Solomon R(obert) Guggenheim (1861–1949), son of Meyer, born in Philadelphia, Pa., and educated at public and private schools there and in Switzerland. He was a member of the firm of Guggenheim Brothers. In the 1920's he began to collect abstract art and in 1937 he established the Solomon R. Guggenheim Foundation to promote public understanding of modern art. In 1939 the foundation opened the Museum of Non-Objective Art, later the Solomon R. Guggenheim Museum, in New York City. The museum, designed by the American architect Frank Lloyd Wright (q.v.), is a major center for the display of abstract art in the U.S. *See also* AMERICAN ARCHITECTURE: *Modern Ameri-*

can Architecture: Frank Lloyd Wright and the Prairie Style.

Simon Guggenheim (1867–1941), son of Meyer, born in Philadelphia, Pa., and educated in Philadelphia public schools and in Europe. He was a member of Guggenheim Brothers, and from 1919 until his death was president of the American Smelting and Refining Company. He was United States Senator from Colorado for the term 1907 to 1913, but declined to be a candidate for reelection. In 1925 he established, with his wife, the John Simon Guggenheim Memorial Foundation in memory of a son; see GUGGENHEIM MEMORIAL FOUNDATION, JOHN SIMON.

Harry F(rank) Guggenheim (1890–1971), son of Daniel, born in West End, N.J., and educated at Yale University and Pembroke College, University of Cambridge. He began his association with the American Smelting and Refining Company in Mexico in 1907, and was a member of Guggenheim Brothers from 1916 to 1923. He was instrumental in the development of the Chile Copper Company, which became the largest low-grade copper producer in the world. Guggenheim was the U.S. delegate on commercial aviation to the Third Pan-American Conference in Washington, D.C., in 1927 and to the International Conference on Civil Aeronautics in Washington in 1928. During World War II he was a naval aviator, advancing to the rank of captain in 1945. He wrote *The Seven Skies* (1930) and *The United States and Cuba* (1934). In 1940 he and his wife, the former Alicia Patterson (1907–63), founded *Newsday*, a daily newspaper published at Garden City, N.Y. He was president of the newspaper until 1970.

Peggy Guggenheim (1898–   ), granddaughter of Meyer, born Marguerite Guggenheim in New York City, where she was educated. In 1920 she went to Paris, where she became friendly with avant-garde writers and artists. In 1938 she opened a gallery for modern art in England and began to collect works of art. She opened a gallery, called Art of This Century, in New York City in 1942; and she became instrumental in advancing the careers of many important modern artists, including the American painter Jackson Pollock, the German-American modernist Hans Hofmann, and Miss Guggenheim's husband, the German-French painter Max Ernst (qq.v.). In 1946 she returned to Europe and eventually established her collection in a Venetian palace, where it became one of the few European collections of modern art to display many works by Americans.

GUGGENHEIM MEMORIAL FOUNDATION, JOHN SIMON, fund established in 1925 by the American industrialist Simon Guggenheim (*see under* GUGGENHEIM) in memory of his son John Simon Guggenheim (1905–1922). The initial endowment was $3,000,000. The purpose of the fund is "the advancement and diffusion of knowledge and understanding and the appreciation of beauty, by aiding without distinction on account of race, color or creed, scholars, scientists, and artists of either sex in the prosecution of their labors". Fellowships are granted to citizens and permanent residents of the United States for work in all fields of knowledge or the fine arts. A limited number of fellowships are also offered to Puerto Ricans and to citizens of other countries. Fellows may go to any part of the world where their work can best be done. The foundation has headquarters in New York City.

See FOUNDATION.

GUIANA, region in the N.E. part of South America, bordering the Atlantic Ocean and extending between the Orinoco, Negro, and Amazon rivers. Its area of 690,000 sq.mi. embraces Guyana (formerly British Guiana), Surinam (Dutch Guiana), French Guiana (qq.v.), and parts of Venezuela and Brazil.

The coast of Guiana was first visited in 1499–1500, by the Italian navigator Amerigo Vespucci, and by the Spanish explorers Vicente Yáñez Pinzón (qq.v.) and Alonso de Ojeda (1465?–1515). During the 16th century, missionaries traveled into the interior of the region. Sir Walter Raleigh (q.v.), inspired by legends of gold (*see* EL DORADO), explored the Orinoco R. in 1595, and in succeeding years his sailing masters carefully explored the coast to the east.

After the formation of the Dutch West India Company (q.v.) in 1621, the Dutch gained a permanent foothold at the head of the Essequibo delta in S.W. Guiana. In 1648, the Peace of Westphalia confirmed the possession of the territory by the Dutch West India Company. Meanwhile, the French had settled in the east and the English near the mouth of the Suriname R. in the north. In 1667, by the Treaty of Breda, England gave its Guiana settlement to the Netherlands in exchange for the Dutch colony of New Netherlands on the Hudson R., including its capital, New Amsterdam (New York). In 1814 the Dutch formally surrendered the colonies of Demerara, Berbice, and Essequibo to the British.

The boundary between British Guiana and Venezuela was still a subject of dispute in the late 1960's. The boundary between French Guiana and Brazil was determined in 1900, between British Guiana and Brazil in 1904, and between French Guiana and Surinam in 1905.

GUIDED MISSILES

GUICCIARDINI, Francesco (1483–1540), Italian historian and statesman, born in Florence, and educated at the universities of Ferrara and Padua. He studied law and in 1506 became professor of law at Florence. Six years later he was sent to the court of Spain as Florentine ambassador. In 1515 he entered the service of Pope Leo X (see under LEO), and became governor of the papal states of Reggio and Modena; Parma was added to his domain in 1521. Pope Clement VII (see under CLEMENT) appointed him vice-regent of Romagna in 1523 and lieutenant general of the papal army in 1526. Guicciardini governed Bologna from 1531 to 1534, when he entered the service of the Medici (q.v.) family in Florence.

A cynical mercenary, Guicciardini is known to have hated bitterly the despotic princes whom he served. He spent his last years writing *La Storia d'Italia* ("The History of Italy", 1561–64), the greatest historical work of the 16th century. This book is remarkable because of its scientific impartiality, and because it treats Italy as a whole rather than as a group of separate sovereignties.

GUIDANCE, EDUCATIONAL AND VOCATIONAL. See EDUCATION, VOCATIONAL; PSYCHOLOGICAL TESTING: *Aptitude and Skills-Testing*.

GUIDED MISSILES, pilotless vehicles and projectiles that can be steered automatically toward a target during flight, either by remote control or by a self-contained mechanism. Although guided missiles are generally used for destructive purposes, they are sometimes also used for constructive scientific research, and are then usually known as rockets; see ROCKET.

The term "guided missile" came into use during World War II, but the concept is much older. In an early form the guided missile consisted of a pilotless airplane loaded with explosives and controlled from a distance by radio signals transmitted from the ground or another aircraft. Experiments with such pilotless planes, called drones, were carried out at the end of World War I, but technology was not sufficiently advanced at that time for the drones to have practical military value. A few war-weary B-17's were used as drones in the bombing of Germany during World War II.

Guided missiles became practical because of the tremendous technological advances that took place during World War II in fields such as aerodynamics, electronics, jet propulsion, radar, servomechanism (qq.v.), inertial guidance and control systems, rockets, and aircraft structures; see AIRPLANE. The simultaneous development of

An Army infantryman fires a Redeye air defense missile from a shoulder launcher. U.S. Army

U.S. Air Force

Raytheon Manufacturing Co., for U.S. Army

Above: The Hound Dog *missile, launched from beneath the wings of a B-52 high-altitude bomber, is designed to strike at ground targets.* Left: *Fired from a mobile launcher, the Hawk missile is equipped with a radar guidance system to seek out low-flying enemy aircraft.*

nuclear warheads justified the enormous expense of developing complex delivery vehicles; see NUCLEAR WEAPONS.

Guided missiles are usually classified as either aerodynamic missiles or ballistic missiles. Aerodynamic missiles are supported in the air and controlled by aerodynamic surfaces, as an aircraft is. The aerodynamic missile usually follows a relatively flat or straight-line trajectory toward the target. Ballistic missiles are powered during flight and are controlled by jet reaction. The trajectory of a ballistic missile resembles that of an artillery (q.v.) projectile.

The first aerodynamic missile to be used on a large scale was the German buzz bomb, or *V-I*, launched against London during World War II. The *V-I* was a pilotless aircraft propelled by a pulse-jet engine and guided to its target by a preset automatic pilot. At a preset distance, which could be as great as 150 mi., the fuel was cut off automatically and the *V-I* would dive at its target.

The first successful ballistic missile was the *V-II*, called the *A-IV* by the Germans. It weighed 12 tons, burned alcohol and liquid oxygen, and could deliver a 1600-lb. warhead a maximum distance of 200 mi. The accuracy of both the *V-I* and *V-II* was poor, because only about half of them would land within an 8-mi. aiming circle; they were suitable only against large targets such as the city of London.

Guided missiles today are generally grouped into four categories: surface-to-air, air-to-air, air-to-surface, and surface-to-surface. "Surface" in each case is intended to mean below as well as on the surface of the sea or the land. Guided missiles are also grouped according to function, such as strategic missiles, tactical missiles, and air-defense missiles.

Surface-to-Air Missiles. This category, also known as SAM, includes missiles used to defend an area against bomber and long-range missile attacks; missiles to protect military units in the field and ships at sea against attack by tactical aircraft and missiles; and missiles to defend individual infantrymen against air attacks.

Air defense missiles protecting the continental United States from attack include the *Nike-Hercules,* which can be launched against attacking bombers. The *Nike-Hercules* replaced the earlier *Nike-Ajax* beginning in 1957, and *Nike-Hercules* batteries are now widely deployed in the U.S. and overseas. The *Nike-Hercules* missile can destroy bombers flying at extremely high altitudes and at a distance greater than 75 mi. from the launching site. For defense against intercontinental ballistic missiles, the Safeguard

The Minuteman intercontinental missile is fired from an underground silo and is capable of delivering nuclear warheads.
U.S. Air Force

antiballistic missile (ABM) system is being deployed, with a low-altitude (15–25 mi.) interception missile, the *Sprint,* and a high-altitude (over 100 mi.) missile, the *Spartan.* Tactical air defense missiles of the U.S. include the United States Navy's *Terrier* and the United States Army's *Hawk.* The first protects ships against attack by enemy aircraft and certain types of tactical missiles; the second performs the same function for tactical land targets. The *Redeye* is a small missile designed to be fired against attacking aircraft from a launcher carried by an infantryman.

Air-to-Air Missiles. These missiles are usually solid-propellent rockets launched from one aircraft against an enemy aircraft. A homing device in the missile enables it to follow the enemy aircraft despite any evasive maneuvers taken. The homing device usually employed depends either on radar reflections or on infrared radiation

GUIDED MISSILES

emitted by the jet engine of the enemy aircraft. Proximity fuzes (see FUZE) in the missile cause the warhead to explode on a near-miss, greatly increasing the effectiveness of the missile. The *Sidewinder* is an air-to-air missile that has been used successfully in combat. The *Sidewinder* homes in on its target from a distance of several miles, attracted by the infrared radiation emitted by the jet engines of the enemy aircraft.

Air-to-Surface Missiles. This category is made up of a great variety of missiles, including those carried by strategic bombers to suppress enemy air defenses in the path to the target and missiles launched from tactical aircraft against ground targets such as bridges or tanks. Missiles carried by bombers to help penetrate enemy defenses must have a range of several hundred miles to provide an adequate defense for the bombers. On the other hand, an antitank missile launched from a helicopter need have a range only as far as the gunner can see the target, perhaps a few thousand meters. Some air-to-surface missiles require little or no propulsion equipment; they depend on gravity and the speed imparted by the aircraft to reach their targets. In addition to missiles that are guided visually by a pilot or gunner, this category includes missiles that can home in on a target following enemy radar signals or by following a television image of the target; or a missile can be preset to land on selected map coordinates. Such U.S. missiles include the *Hound Dog*, carried by B-52 bombers; the *Bullpup*, which is guided visually and manually controlled by radio signals; and the *Walleye*, which finds its target by following a television image.

Surface-to-Surface Missiles. Included in this category are intercontinental and long-range ballistic missiles and shorter range missiles that have augmented artillery projectiles. The *Minuteman* is a solid-fuel, multistage intercontinental ballistic missile that is launched from an underground silo. The *Polaris* and the later, multiwarhead, *Poseidon* are launched underwater from a nuclear-powered submarine. These missiles can carry thermonuclear warheads thousands of miles with great accuracy. The *Atlas* and *Titan* missiles that preceded the *Minuteman* were propelled by liquid fuels. They were the prototypes for the large, liquid-propellent rockets used in the U.S. space program. In the early 1970's both the U.S. and the Soviet Union were simultaneously developing the multiple independently targetable reentry vehicle system (see MIRV) in which each missile would carry a number of warheads aimed at different targets.

The short-range tactical missiles consist of both aerodynamic and ballistic missiles. Some of them are propelled and controlled by jet reactions. An interesting example of the latter is the *Shillelagh*, which is fired from a tank gun and will strike any target the gunner keeps in his gunsight. The missile automatically follows the gunner's line of sight, receiving directional control signals from infrared transmitting equipment. Similar antitank missiles, such as the French *Entac* and the German *Kobra*, receive their control signals through wires trailed from a spool carried by the missile.

Guidance Systems. When the location of a fixed target is known relative to the launching site of a missile, the target can be attacked by presetting the guidance system of the missile so that it flies a proper course. The *V-I* used a system of this type, as do some of the more modern guidance systems described below.

Beam-rider guidance systems cause the missile to follow a radar or infrared signal as already described. The signal is held on the target either automatically, as in the *Terrier* missile, or manually, as in the *Shillelagh* missile.

In command guidance systems, both the missile and its target are tracked either by radar or visually, and the course of the missile can be changed to intercept the target. In the *Nike-*

In the weapon direction equipment employed by the Navy's surface-to-air missiles, a panel of illuminated buttons are used to evaluate targets, assign, and fire appropriate missile batteries, and feed additional information into display scopes. Sperry Gyroscope Co.

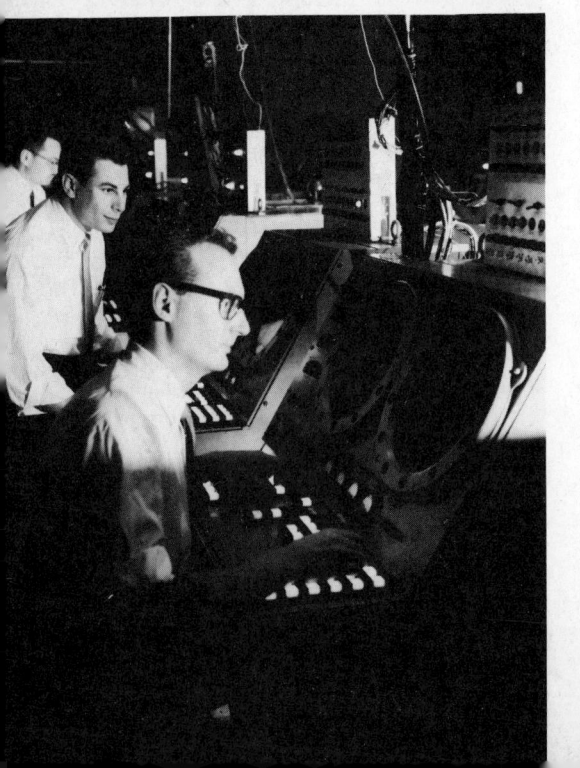

Hercules and *Bullpup* missiles, the control signals are transmitted by radio. In the United States Army heavy assault missile *Tow*, the control signals are transmitted through trailing wires.

In homing guidance systems, the missile automatically seeks out the target by means of signals that emanate from the target itself. These may consist of radar signals, as in the antiradar missile, *Shrike*; reflected radar signals, as in the air-to-air missile, *Sparrow*; or heat from the engine, as in the *Redeye*. Homing is often combined with command or beam-riding guidance systems, the homing system taking over as the missile approaches the target to ensure greater accuracy.

Inertial guidance systems use gyroscopes and accelerometers to sense the course of the missile. Inertial guidance systems are used on long-range ballistic missiles, some of which also use stellar navigation systems to improve accuracy.

See also WARFARE. E.F.S.

GUIDI, Tommaso. *See* MASACCIO.

GUIDO D'AREZZO *or* **GUIDO ARETINO** (about 995–1050), Benedictine monk and reformer of music, born either near Paris or in Arezzo, Italy. He is also called Fra Guittone. As a monk in the monastery of Pomposa, near Ferrara, he made a number of innovations in regard to musical notation (q.v.). About 1030 he went to Rome on the invitation of Pope John XIX (*see under* JOHN). Later he returned to Pomposa and also worked in the monastery of Saint-Maur-des-Fossés near Paris. Guido was the first to use systematically the lines of the staff and the spaces between them, and to give to the notes of the scale (q.v.) the names which are still used today. Among his writings on music is *Micrologus de Disciplina Artis Musicae* ("Aphorisms on the Discipline of Musical Art", about 1025).

GUIDO RENI. *See* RENI, GUIDO.

GUILD *or* **GILD,** association of persons who have similar interests in a craft, business, or profession; the purpose of the association is mutual aid and protection. The term is particularly applied to two types of such association that flourished in continental Europe and England during the Middle Ages: the merchant guild or guild merchant; and the craft guild, sometimes known as the trade guild or trade corporation.

The Merchant Guild These guilds began on the European continent in the 11th century, and in England after the Norman Conquest (1066). The guild arose as a consequence of the growth in that century both of commerce and of urban communities. Merchants traveled from market to market in foreign countries, and, for the sake of mutual protection, a group of merchants from the same city often banded together in a caravan. The members of a caravan elected a leader and made rules which they were pledged to obey. In addition to prescribing duties for defense against physical attack, the rules obliged the members to stand by each other in legal disputes in which any might engage. The name for such a caravan was *Gilde* or *Hansa* in the Germanic countries of Europe; in the countries speaking languages derived from Latin the term was *caritas* or *fraternitas*. Frequently the members of a *hansa* or *fraternitas* remained in close association after they had made the return journey to their city. Such an association then began to assume rights and privileges in regard to the trade of the municipality or community. These rights might have been conferred by a feudal lord or, in later times and in cities free from feudal control, by the city itself. In time the merchant guild gained a monopoly over the entire industry and commerce of the city, supervising the various crafts, and selling, at both wholesale and retail, all the commodities manufactured in the city. Merchants who were not members of such a guild were also permitted to sell goods, but only at wholesale, and were subject, in business transactions, to many special restrictions from which the members of the guild were free; for example, the nonmember was forced to pay special dues to the feudal lord or to the city, but the guild paid the dues annually for all its members, who also enjoyed freedom from other municipal taxes. The merchant guild was usually composed of the richest merchants of the city and acquired considerable political influence, often becoming vested with the power of administration of some of the municipal functions. A merchant guild sometimes admitted to membership merchants of other cities; as a result merchant guilds occasionally developed which monopolized the commerce of several cities. This was particularly true on the Continent.

Decline of the Merchant Guild. The merchant guilds declined and by the 14th century had almost completely disappeared. The principal cause of their elimination from economic life was the rise of craft guilds which included in their membership all those engaged in any particular craft, and which monopolized the making and selling of a particular commodity within the cities in which they were organized. As the various craftsmen of a city organized into craft guilds, the merchant guild of that city was little by little deprived of its power to regulate the commerce of that municipality and in time

79

GUILD

Coat of arms of the coopers' guild (detail from a German 15th-century stained glass window).
Metropolitan Museum of Art – Cloisters Collection

ceased to function altogether. Where the merchant guilds were strongly intrenched in the municipal governments, they also came into conflict with the strong national governments which were coming into being toward the end of the medieval period, and frequently yielded their powers to these governments.

The Craft Guild. An organization known as a craft guild in England and as *corporation de métier* in France, *arte* in Italy, and *Zünft* or *Innung* in Germany, came into existence about the beginning of the 12th century. In general, the craft guild arose when a group of artisans, imitating the example of the merchants of the city, decided to unite for mutual benefit. In some instances a group which had organized originally for religious purposes, and which had drawn its membership entirely from the artisans of one craft, began to stress aid for the economic rather than the religious needs of its members, and in time became a full-fledged craft guild. By the middle of the 12th century, craft guilds had been established in all parts of western Europe. In some cities the individual worker was permitted the right to join or remain out of the guild in his craft. In others, a guild would purchase from the municipality or the royal government the right to control its branch of industry, and in such instances everyone who desired to follow his trade in that particular city was compelled to join the guild. The members of a craft guild were divided into three classes: masters, apprentices, and journeymen. The master, who was a small-scale proprietor, owned the raw material and the tools and sold the goods manufactured in his shop for his own profit. The apprentices and journeymen lived in the master's house. The apprentices, who were beginners in the trade and learned it under the direction of the master, usually received only their board in return for the work they did. After an apprentice had completed his training he became a journeyman and was paid a fixed wage for his labor. In time a journeyman might become a master. Because it was to the advantage of those who were already masters not to increase their own number, the conditions under which a journeyman might become a master were always made difficult. After the 14th century the requirements became so severe that it was virtually impossible for any journeyman to become a master.

In the 14th, 15th, and 16th centuries journeymen organized into associations of their own, the object of which was to obtain better wages and working conditions from the masters. In England such associations were known as journeyman or yeoman guilds, and in France as *compagnonnages*. They succeeded, sometimes by means of strikes, in somewhat improving working conditions and pay, but on the whole they did not greatly improve the economic status of their class. Because of their defense of the rights of labor, their strong control over the members, and the benefits provided, the journeyman guilds are considered the forerunners of the modern trade union.

A Powerful Economic Force. The craft guild was important in the life of the medieval city, closely affecting the economic welfare of both the artisan and the consumer. It sought to aid the artisan in two principal ways: by protecting him against the competition of artisans in the same trade in other cities, and by protecting him from possible competition of fellow citizens working in other shops belonging to the same trade. The guild accomplished the first aim by monopolizing its trade in the city, thus permitting no goods from other cities to be imported for sale. It fulfilled the second by establishing uniform hours for all shops making the same commodity, and uniform wages for workers in the same industry. To prevent any one master from obtaining an advantage over another, the guild decreed how many people were to be employed in each shop, the number of tools to be used, the hours of labor, and the prices the master could charge for his finished goods. The guild enforced its rules by constant and close supervision of the shops. No master was permitted to advertise his goods, lest he attract more business than another master. Any improvement in the technique of production, which might enable one shop to produce goods more quickly and cheaply than another, was likewise prohibited. The aim of the craft guild was to create complete equality among the members of each of the three classes into which it was divided. The consumer benefited from the existence of the craft guild chiefly because of the high standards the guild set up for finished work, although he was deprived of the possibility of lower prices from improved methods of production and from competition in selling.

The craft guilds were a large force in the economic life of Europe from the 12th to the 15th century. In France and Flanders in the 12th and 13th centuries they frequently threatened to seize control of municipal governments. To weaken the guilds, some municipalities deprived them of many privileges, including the right to regulate industries. Nevertheless, in the 14th century the guilds began to compete with the rich merchants of the cities for the right to govern. In some cities the guilds actually succeeded in taking over the municipal government completely. In Liège, in 1384, for example, the municipal council was composed entirely of representatives from the thirty-two craft guilds of that city.

The Rise of Capitalism. In the 15th century, however, the power of the craft guilds began to decline. They became subject to the internal tensions described above, between masters and journeymen. They were also subjected to much criticism and sometimes to action by public authorities because of the restrictions they placed upon industrial activity and freedom of labor. The chief cause, however, of the decline and eventual disappearance of the craft guilds was the rise in the 16th century of a new system for producing and distributing commodities, capitalism. This new economic system stressed large-scale production of goods, competition for markets between producers, and wide distribution of goods. Inasmuch as the craft guild was inclined against all three principles, the capitalist generally established his shops in centers where no craft guilds existed. The latter, unable to produce goods even for their own local markets as quickly or cheaply as did the capitalistic enterprises, were little by little forced out of existence. Anne Robert Jacques Turgot (q.v.), controller general of finance for Louis XVI (q.v.), King of France, in 1776 abolished all but four of the craft guilds in order to permit workers freely to offer their services to employers, and during the French Revolution all guilds were abolished. Prussia and other German states abolished the German craft guilds at the beginning of the 19th century, and those craft guilds that still remained in Great Britain were abolished by acts of Parliament in 1814 and 1835.

The term "guild" is still in considerable use today. It is applied to associations of various kinds, for example, associations for charitable work and organizations formed to promote various cultural activities, such as music and the drama; and to certain labor organizations such as the American Newspaper Guild. It is also applied to a type of modern socialism; *see* GUILD SOCIALISM.

GUILD SOCIALISM, variety of socialism (q.v.), advocated in Great Britain early in the 20th century as a substitute for capitalism (q.v.). The outstanding leader of the short-lived movement organized to propagate guild socialism was the British economist George Douglas Howard Cole (1889–1959).

The social system advocated by the guild socialists centered on the ownership and operation of the means of production, distribution, and exchange by nationwide industrial guilds, which were to differ radically from the guilds of medieval times; *see* GUILD. Each of these modern guilds was to have the following characteristics: it would include all of the workers, managerial and technical as well as clerical and manual, in the industry, trade, or profession over which it had jurisdiction; it would have autonomy within its spheres of production; and it would elect its officers democratically. Even managerial officials were to be elected by the workers whose operations they supervised, and were to be subject to recall by those workers.

The nature of the state under the proposed society was a subject of disagreement among the guild socialists. Some believed that the state should carry out only the functions of preserving public order and conducting foreign relations and national defense. Others, particularly Cole, advocated a system of government by communes, which would comprise organizations representing consumers and producers, and which would be charged with the responsibility for national economic planning, the enactment and interpretation of legislation, the management of finances, and the conduct of foreign relations and national defense.

Most guild socialists believed that the change from capitalism to socialism was basically economic rather than political, and therefore regarded political action solely as a means of propagating their ideas. In preference to political action they put forth the principle of encroaching control, whereby the workers, through trade-union activity, would gradually take over the administration of industrial enterprises and eventually drive out the private owners.

The first organized body to advance the principles of guild socialism was the Guilds Restoration Movement, which was formed in 1906 and was superseded in 1915 by the National Guilds League. The membership of the league began to decline in the mid-1920's, as the Labour Party (q.v.) grew in numbers and influence. By 1930 the league had passed out of existence. See SYNDICALISM.

GUILFORD COURTHOUSE, formerly a small village in Guilford Co., N.C., now a national military park, 5 miles N.W. of Greensboro. It is the site of a five-hour battle during the American Revolution (q.v.), fought on March 15, 1781, between 4400 Americans under General Nathanael Greene, and 2200 British under General Charles Cornwallis, 1st Marquis Cornwallis (qq.v.). The Americans lost 400 soldiers, the British 600, in dead, wounded, and captured. Although neither side gained a decisive advantage, the battle is considered to have been a strategic victory for the Americans, as the depletion of the British troops compelled Cornwallis to abandon the Carolinas, the loss of which contributed materially to the final defeat of the British. Guilford Courthouse National Military Park, covering 233 acres, was established in 1917. It is administered by the National Park Service (q.v.).

GUILLAUME, Charles Édouard (1861–1938), French physicist, born at Fleurier, Switzerland, and educated at the universities of Neuchâtel and Zürich. Most of his research was done in connection with the work of the Bureau of International Weights and Measures at Sèvres, France, where he worked from 1883, becoming director in 1915. Guillaume is best known for his invention of the nickel-steel alloy, invar. For his discovery of anomalies in nickel-steel alloys he was awarded the 1920 Nobel Prize in physics. His writings include *Les Applications des Aciers au Nickel* ("The Uses of Steel and Nickel", 1904), and *Les Récents Progrès du Système Métrique* ("Recent Progress of the Metric System", 1921).

GUILLAUME DE LORRIS (d. about 1235), French poet. He is the author of the first 4000 lines of the 22,000-line verse romance the *Roman de la Rose* (Eng. trans., *Romaunt of the Rose*, late 14th century), the second part of which was written by the French poet Jean de Meung (d. about 1305). Nothing is known of Guillaume's life. His section of the poem is distinguished by the beauty of the imagery and the allegorical setting. See FRENCH LITERATURE: *Medieval French Literature*.

GUILLAUME D'ORANGE (about 750–812), military leader under Charlemagne (q.v.) and the hero of a group of southern French poems called *chansons de geste*. He is also known as Fierabrace, Saint Guillaume de Gellone, and the Marquis au court nez ("Marquis Short Nose"). An able soldier, he was in charge of educating Charlemagne's oldest son Louis, later Louis I (q.v.), Holy Roman Emperor, and he led Charlemagne's forces against the Saracens in 793. Although Guillaume's forces were defeated, he avenged the defeat ten years later when he commanded an army that invaded Spain and captured Barcelona. In 804 he founded a monastery at Gellone (now Saint Guihelm-le-Désert) near Lodève, France, to which he retired in 806, and where he later died.

The *chansons de geste* in which Guillaume d'Orange appears as a principal character often incorporate the exploits of other historical personages in their descriptions of his feats. They include *Fierabras* and *Aliscans*, considered to be among the finest examples of early French epic poetry. See FRENCH LITERATURE: *Medieval French Literature*.

GUILLEMOT, common name for a narrow-billed seabird of the Auk family Alcidae. Guil-

Guillemot, Uria aalge.
Eric Hosking—
National Audubon Society

lemots are swimming and diving birds, found chiefly in the Arctic Region. Their legs are set far back on the body, and are highly efficient for swimming, but cause the birds to waddle awkwardly, with the body upright, when on land. The feet, which are fully webbed, each have three long toes. The bill is straight. Guillemots, like some other birds such as dippers (q.v.), are remarkable for their capacity for subaqueous flight. After diving they appear to fly under water, beating their short wings in the same manner as in flight, instead of paddling with their legs.

A common North American species, the pigeon guillemot, *Cepphus columba,* is found along the Pacific Coast, from Alaska to California. Pigeon guillemots are about 13 in. long. The plumage is black, except for a large white patch on the wings, and the legs are a bright red. Similar in color and size to the pigeon guillemot is the black guillemot, *C. grylle.*

Guillemots of the genus *Uria* are called murres, because of the sound of their guttural note. They are 16 to 18 in. long. The species *U. aalge* is also called foolish guillemot because, during the breeding season, it will stand still and allow a human to capture it by hand. It summers in northern areas and winters as far south as the Mediterranean and off the northeastern and western United States. It is black or dark-brown on the back and whitish underneath, with streaks of these colors on the sides. It lays only one egg and makes no nest. When incubating the egg, murres place their webbed toes beneath the egg and warm it beneath and between their legs and thighs.

The murrelets are similar in appearance to the murres, but are only 9 or 10 in. long. Seven genera and nine species are found on the Pacific Coast of North America. One of the most widely distributed species is the marbled murrelet, *Brachyramphus marmoratus,* found from Alaska to southern California.

GUILLOTINE, decapitating machine, named after a French physician, Joseph Ignace Guillotin (1738–1814), who proposed its use in 1789. It consists of two upright posts, grooved on the inside and connected at the top by a crossbeam. A sharp, oblique blade, placed between the grooves, is held at the top of the machine by a rope. On release of the rope, the blade drops onto the neck of the victim strapped to a board at the base of the machine. Similar devices were used for executions from early times. The Italian *mannaia,* used from the 13th century, the Scottish maiden, used from 1581 to 1685, and the German *dolabra* of the 16th century, were similar to the guillotine, but had horizontal blades. The guillotine was used extensively during the French Revolution (q.v.).

GUINEA FOWL, common name for any fowl of the family Numididae, order Galliformes, native to Africa and the island of Madagascar. The plumage is alike in both sexes, jet black in most species, dotted with small, light-colored spots; the neck is surrounded by a ruff of feathers, and except in the crested guinea fowl of the genus *Guttera* the skin of the head is completely bare. Guinea fowl nest on the ground and roost in trees. Minor differences mark the sexes, such as larger wattles in the males. The call of the female normally has two syllables, and sounds like "buckwheat", although it is occasionally monosyllabic. The call of the male always sounds like "quit". Because of their shrill cries, guinea fowl are rarely raised domestically on small farms;

GUINEA, GULF OF

The common "helmeted" guinea fowl, Numida meleagris UPI

they are sometimes kept in chicken houses on relatively large farms where they raise a clamor when the chickens are endangered.

Of the various species of guinea fowl, the common "helmeted" guinea fowl, *Numida meleagris,* is one of the best known. The head is covered with a bony cap, or casque, rising into a hard crest. A similar species, *N. mitrata,* is noted for its red crown. The best-known species of crested guinea fowl is *Guttera cristata,* which has a large tuft of feathers on its crown. The handsomest species of guinea fowl is *Acryllium vulturinum,* of Somaliland, which has bright blue plumage.

Guinea fowl are cooked and eaten like other poultry, and are considered a delicacy.

GUINEA, GULF OF, arm of the Atlantic Ocean on the w. coast of Africa between Cape Palmas, at the S.E. tip of Liberia, and Cape Lopez, in Gabon Republic. The gulf forms two open bays, the Bight of Benin and the Bight of Biafra.

GUINEA PIG, common name for any rodent of the genus *Cavia;* guinea pigs are domesticated cavies, but in popular usage the term is applied to all species, domesticated or wild. Guinea pigs resemble rabbits, but have short, rounded ears and no tails. They are small, stout-bodied animals, about 6 to 7 in. long. The hair in some species is long, and varies in texture from rough to smooth. Some guinea pigs are solidly white, black, or tawny; others are white, streaked, or blotched with darker colors. In the wild state guinea pigs live in burrows. The diet consists of vegetation. Wild guinea pigs breed only annually and produce litters of one or two young. The young are born in an advanced stage of development, and are able to feed themselves by nibbling foliage the day after birth. Wild guinea pigs are native to South America. Among the most important species are *C. porcellus,* native to Brazil; *C. boliviensis,* found in the higher ranges of the Andes; and *C. cutleri,* a Peruvian species.

Some authorities believe the domestic guinea pig was developed from the Peruvian animal; others believe that it was developed from the Brazilian. Domestic guinea pigs resemble wild guinea pigs in the rapidity of their early maturity. They develop so quickly during gestation that they shed their lacteal teeth in the womb, being born with their definitive teeth already in place. Domesticated guinea pigs begin to breed at the age of two months. They breed five or six times a year, and the litters comprise from four to twelve animals. Because of this breeding ca-

Guinea pig, Cavia porcellus   New York Zoological Society

GUINEA, REPUBLIC OF

pacity, guinea pigs have been valuable as experimental laboratory animals, especially in bacteriology for research on the effects of pathogenic microorganisms. Guinea pigs have been largely replaced in the laboratory by smaller animals, such as mice, rats, and hamsters. They are useful in diagnostic tests for tuberculosis, however, because of their low resistance to the tubercle bacillus, which kills them in from four to eight weeks.

The origin of the term "guinea pig" is an unsolved etymological problem. Some authorities believe the name may come from "Guineamen," who were in the slave trade, and may have been the first to bring the animals from South America to England. Others believe it is a corruption of cony, basing this theory on evidence that guinea pigs were called pig conies in 1607.

GUINEA, PORTUGUESE. See PORTUGUESE GUINEA.

GUINEA, REPUBLIC OF, independent nation of W. Africa, bounded on the N. by Portuguese Guinea, Senegal, and Mali, on the E. and S.E. by the Ivory Coast, on the S. by Liberia and Sierra Leone, and on the W. by the Atlantic Ocean. It is situated between lat. 7°35' N. and lat. 12°30' N. and between long. 8° W. and long. 15° W. The total area of the country is about 95,000 sq.mi., including the Los Islands off Conakry.

THE LAND

Guinea has four chief topographic regions. Lower Guinea, the coastal plain, extends about 30 mi. inland from the shoreline, which is about 170 mi. in length. Beyond the coastal plain is middle Guinea, the Futa Jallon, a mountainous plateau with an average elevation of about 3000 ft. Upper Guinea is gently undulating savanna country broken by occasional rocky outcrops with an average elevation of 1000 ft. In the extreme S.E. are forested highlands of which Mt. Nimba (about 6000 ft.) is the highest point in the country.

The chief rivers are the Senegal and the Gambia (qq.v.), which rise in the mountains of the Futa Jallon and descend to the coastal plain where they divide into many branches, and the Niger (q.v.) and its important tributary the Milo, which have their origins in the Guinea highlands.

Climate. The dominant factor in the considerable climatic variation is altitude. Rainfall is highest and range of temperature lowest in lower Guinea. Conakry, the capital, has an annual rainfall of 168 in. and average temperatures range between 74° F. and 87° F. In the Futa Jallon annual rainfall averages between 60 in. and 80 in. and the average temperatures range between 50° F. and 85° F. In upper Guinea annual rainfall is less than in the Futa Jallon and the annual average temperature is 70° F. In the Guinea highlands annual rainfall averages 110 in. The highest temperatures (100° F.) are also found in this region. The climate in the highlands is equatorial with no clearly distinguishable seasons. The rainy season in the remainder of the country occurs from April or May to October or November. April is the hottest month and July or August the wettest.

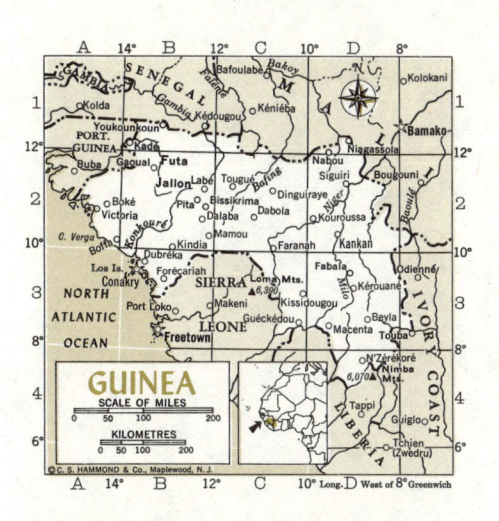

Natural Resources. The mineral wealth of Guinea makes the economy of this country potentially one of the strongest in Africa. More than one third of the known world reserves of high-grade bauxite ore is found in Guinea. Large deposits of iron ore, gold, and diamonds exist. Guinea has great potential for hydroelectric power and a promising agricultural economy.

Plants and Animals. The vegetation of Guinea varies considerably from area to area. Dense

INDEX TO MAP OF GUINEA

Cities and Towns

Beyla	D 3
Bissikrima	C 2
Boffa	A 2
Boké	A 2
Conakry (cap.)	A 3
Dabola	C 2
Dalaba	C 2
Dinguiraye	C 2
Dubréka	B 3
Fabala	D 3
Faranah	C 2
Forécariah	B 3
Gaoual	B 2
Guéckédou	C 3
Kadé	B 1
Kankan	D 2
Kérouané	D 3
Kindia	B 2
Kissidougou	C 3
Kouroussa	D 2
Labé	B 2
Macenta	D 3
Mamou	C 2
Niagassola	D 1
N'Zérékoré	D 4
Pita	B 2
Siguiri	D 2
Tougué	C 2
Victoria	A 2
Youkounkoun	A 1

Physical Features

Bafing (river)	C 2
Futa Jallon (plat.)	B 2
Konkouré (river)	B 2
Loma (mts.)	C 3
Los (isls.)	A 3
Milo (river)	D 3
Niger (river)	D 2
Nimba (mts.)	D 4
Verga (cape)	A 2

85

Modern buildings form a backdrop for metal-roofed shacks, making Conakry, the capital, a study in contrasts.   United Nations

mangrove forests abound along the coast and the river banks. The Futa Jallon, which has been subject to excessive burning, is covered with sedge. The higher plateau areas have dense forests. Upper Guinea is characterized by savanna woodland. Trees include the shea and the tamarind. The Guinea highlands are characterized by dense rain forests.

Animal life is abundant and varied. Snakes and crocodiles are common and numerous species of tropical birds abound, including parrots and touracos. Mammals include the leopard, hippopotamus, wild boar, antelope, and civet cat. Large mammals are confined mainly to the Futa Jallon.

THE PEOPLE

The ethnic makeup of the people of Guinea is diverse. The most numerous of the groups (about 1,000,000) are the Fula (q.v.), a people of Hamitic-Negroid stock. They are concentrated mainly in the Futa Jallon. The principal non-Fula groups comprise people who belong to the Mande group. They include the Mandingo (about 600,000) of N.E. Guinea, and the Susy (about 330,000) who inhabit the coastal area. Nearly 4000 Europeans live in Guinea. About 80 percent of the population lives in rural areas and is engaged in farming. The population of Guinea (census 1955) was 2,570,219; the United Nations estimated (1969) 3,890,400. The overall population density is 16 sq.mi. (U.N. est. 1969).

The capital and principal city is Conakry, a seaport on the Atlantic Ocean (pop., 1969 est., 172,500). Other important cities are the railroad centers Kankan (1964 est., 176,000) and Kindia (1964 est., 152,000).

Religion and Language. Approximately 40 percent of the population is Muslim and most of the remainder adhere to animist beliefs. Christians form a very small portion of the population. French is the official language of Guinea, but the principal languages spoken by the population are Malinke, Kissi, and Poulah.

Education. The government provides free education to all children between the ages of seven and sixteen. Private schools were nationalized by 1962. Higher education is provided by a polytechnical institute, a school of administration, and one university.

THE ECONOMY

The chief economic activity of Guinea is agriculture. Ninety percent of the people are dependent on subsistence farming. The principal food crops are cassava, yams, bananas, pineapples, rice, millet, honey, and peanuts. Cash crops include bananas, citrus fruits, pineapples, coffee, tobacco, palm kernels, and kola nuts. Livestock includes cattle, sheep, goats, horses, pigs, and asses.

In the late 1960's annual exports in order of value were alumina production ($27,000,000), bananas ($4,500,000), iron ore ($3,000,000), palm kernels ($2,500,000), bauxite ($1,000,000), and diamonds ($600,000). Mining operations in Boké, planned to begin in the early 1970's, are ex-

GUINEA, REPUBLIC OF

The People of Guinea. Right: A young Fula woman of a Guinean village. Below: Children, wearing their school uniform, parade on a tree-lined street in Kindia, in the southwestern part of the country. United Nations

GUINEA, REPUBLIC OF

pected to yield more than 5,000,000 to 6,000,000 tons annually, with an estimated value of more than $70,000,000. In a recent year the national budget showed a balance in revenues and expenditures of about $256,000,000. The monetary unit is the Guinea franc which is provisionally valued at 247 per U.S. $1 (1970).

Transportation facilities in Guinea include a state-owned 410-mi. railroad between Conakry and Kankan; a privately owned railroad which transports alumina from Fria to Conakry; and 6525 mi. of road, 125 mi. of which are paved.

GOVERNMENT

The 1958 constitution describes Guinea as a democratic republic based on secular and socialist principles.

Central Government. A president is chief of state and of the government, as well as of the armed forces. Elected by universal suffrage for a seven-year term, the president is assisted by a cabinet responsible to him. Cabinet ministers may not belong to the National Assembly, a body of seventy-five members, having five-year terms, who are chosen by popular vote from a single national slate of candidates presented by the only political party, the Democratic Party of Guinea. Both the assembly and the cabinet are subordinate to the dictates of the party.

HISTORY

Guinea is heir to the empires of Ghana, Mali, and Songhai; see AFRICA, *History: West African Kingdoms*. Parts of northern and eastern Guinea were within Mali and Songhai. A theocratic state was founded in the Futa Jallon about 1725 by the Torobde, a Fula clan which became the missionaries and clerical leaders of the whole of the Fula nation and which believed in conversion by jihads (holy wars). A young cleric from Futa Toro, known as Al-Haji Umar ("The Pilgrim"), made the pilgrimage to Mecca and on his return settled in Futa Jallon to prepare a jihad. He equipped his forces with firearms obtained from the Europeans in coastal countries. When he captured Timbuktu in 1863 his empire stretched from the Niger bend to the upper Senegal. Umar was killed in 1864 and was succeeded by his son Ahmadou (q.v.). In 1881 Ahmadou signed a treaty with the French by which the left bank of the Niger R. as far as Timbuktu was put under French protection. He later repudiated this treaty but was driven from his chieftaincy by the French in 1893.

The leader of resistance to French penetration was Samory Touré (1835–1900), a Mandingo born in the area that is now upper Guinea. Until 1898 he held off the French across much of modern Guinea and the Ivory Coast.

In 1891 Guinea was constituted a French colony separate from Senegal, of which it had formerly been a part. The colony was named French Guinea in 1893. In 1899 the portion of the Sudan containing the upper Niger districts was added to French Guinea. In 1895 the several

Basket weaving is a valuable cottage industry in the Republic of Guinea. United Nations

French territories in western Africa were federated under a governor-general into the Federation of French West Africa.

In September, 1958, the constitution for the Fifth French Republic was overwhelmingly rejected by a referendum held in Guinea. In accordance with a warning which President Charles de Gaulle (q.v.) of France had issued to the French overseas territories in August, 1958, the rejection of the constitution caused an automatic severence of economic and financial trade with France and the withdrawal of French technical and administrative officers. Guinea achieved independence on Oct. 2, 1958, with Sekou Touré (1922–), formerly premier, as president. Guinea came to lean more and more toward the Communist countries, receiving gifts and loans from the East European countries and from China. By 1962 most trade was with the Communist countries.

An embryonic federation of Guinea with Ghana and Mali, the Union of African States, was formally dissolved in August, 1963. In November, 1965, Guinea accused members of the French government of being involved in a plot against the regime and relations with France were broken off. Accusations of involvement in this plot were also made against the governments of the Ivory Coast, Niger, and Upper Volta. In March, 1966, Touré welcomed Kwame Nkrumah (1909–72), the ousted president of Ghana, to his country, where Nkrumah remained until his death. In 1972 President Touré created the office of premier and named to it the former minister of economics and of foreign affairs, Louis Lansana Beavogui (1923–).

GUINEA WORM. See FILARIA.

GUINEVERE (Welsh *Gwenhwyfar*), wife of the semilegendary King Arthur (q.v.) of Britain. She appears in the 12th-century *Historia* cycle of Arthurian romances by the English chronicler Geoffrey of Monmouth (q.v.) as Gwanhumara, a lady of noble Roman family who surpassed all the women of Britain in beauty, and who became a nun after the defeat of King Arthur by Mordred. In the 12th-century romance *Le Chevalier à la Charette* ("The Knight of the Cart"), the French poet Chrétien de Troyes (q.v.) introduced the character of Sir Lancelot du Lac (q.v.), in the first of the Arthurian cycle (q.v.) of romances to relate the tragic love affair between Guinevere and Lancelot. The same story was treated by later English writers, notably by Sir Thomas Malory (q.v.) in *Le Morte d'Arthur* ("The Death of Arthur", 1485) and by Alfred Tennyson (q.v.) in *The Idylls of the King* (1859–85).

GUINNESS, Sir Alec (1914–), British actor, born in London, England. He made his stage debut in 1933. In 1938 he played the title role in *Hamlet* by William Shakespeare at the Old Vic Theatre (q.v.) in London. Following service in the Royal Navy (1941–45), he returned to the Old Vic for another season (1945–46). He later appeared on the New York stage in *The Cocktail Party* (1950) and *Dylan* (1964). During the 1940's and 1950's Guinness achieved international success in a series of film comedies, including *Kind Hearts and Coronets* (1948), in which he played seven roles, *The Lavender Hill Mob* (1951), and *The Captain's Paradise* (1953). For his performance as the heroic, indomitable army officer in *The Bridge on the River Kwai*, he received the 1957 best-actor award of the Academy of Motion Picture Arts and Sciences. His later films include *Tunes of Glory* (1960) and *Cromwell* (1970). He was knighted in 1959.

GUIPURE. See LACE.

GUISCARD, Robert (1015?–85), Norman adventurer, born near Coutances in Normandy. Like many other impoverished Norman knights, Guiscard went to Italy, arriving there about 1046. After serving in the forces of the prince of Capua, he organized an army to secure possessions for himself in Calabria. When Pope Leo IX (*see under* LEO) attempted to expel the Normans from Italy, in 1053, Guiscard played an important role in defeating the papal forces at Civitate, near the modern city of San Severo. After the death of his older brother Humphrey Guiscard (d. 1057), Robert became leader of the Normans in Italy. The pope, seeking independence from the Holy Roman Empire (q.v.), decided to enlist the Normans as allies. In 1059 Pope Nicholas II (*see under* NICHOLAS) created Robert "by the Grace of God and Saint Peter, duke of Apulia and Calabria and, with their help, hereafter of Sicily". Sicily was in Greek hands at the time, and so Robert and his brother Roger I (q.v.) of Sicily embarked on a series of campaigns, capturing Messina in 1061 and Palermo in 1072. In 1081 Robert gained a great victory over the Byzantine emperor Alexius I Comnenus (q.v.) at Durrës. His campaigns at Macedonia and Thessalía were being carried on, meanwhile, by his son Bohemund I (*see under* BOHEMUND). Robert was recalled from his victorious campaigns in 1085 to go to the aid of Pope Gregory VII (*see under* GREGORY), who was besieged in the castle of Sant'Angelo by Henry IV (q.v.), Holy Roman Emperor. Robert drove Henry from Rome, and reduced one third of the city to ashes. Because of the unpopularity of Gregory VII in Rome, Robert took the pope to Monte Cassino. Robert

GUISE

then went to the support of Bohemund in the Greek campaign, but died of fever at Kefallinía a few weeks later.

GUISE, name of a junior branch of the ducal family of Lorraine (q.v.), important as rivals to the power of the French kings, especially in the 16th century. The principal members of the family are the following.

Claude I, Duc d'Aumale, 1st Duc de Guise (1496–1550), son of René II, Duc de Lorraine (1451–1508). In 1513 Claude married Antoinette de Bourbon (1493–1583), daughter of a powerful French noble family. He subsequently entered the service of Francis I (q.v.), King of France, in the French wars in Italy, distinguishing himself in the Battle of Marignano in 1515. As governor of the province of Champagne, beginning in 1523, Claude fought against the army of the Holy Roman Empire (q.v.) in that same year and against the Anabaptists (q.v.) in 1525. In 1527 Francis I transformed the countship of Guise into a duchy, making Claude a duke, a dignity previously reserved for princes of the royal family. Although Francis continued to favor the Guise family, he became increasingly jealous of its growing power and ambition. Mary of Guise (1515–60), daughter of Claude, became the wife of James V (q.v.), King of Scotland, and their daughter was Mary, Queen of Scots (q.v.).

François de Lorraine, 2nd Duc de Guise (1519–63), soldier and statesman, called le Balfré ("the Scarred") because of wounds received at the siege of Boulogne in 1545, the son of Claude I, born in Barcastle, Provence. He participated in the various battles of the wars of France against Charles V (q.v.), Holy Roman Emperor, rendering outstanding service, especially at Metz in 1552. In 1557 he fought against the Spanish in Italy and in the following year took Calais from the English, allies of Spain against France. François and his brother Charles (see below) gained great influence over the youthful Francis II (q.v.), King of France, and in that way almost completely controlled the French government during the short reign of Francis. In that period the Guises directed the persecution of the Huguenots (q.v.), becoming widely disliked for their violent suppression of the Huguenot conspiracy of Amboise (q.v.) in 1560. After the death of Francis II in 1560, Catherine de Médicis (q.v.), mother and regent for Charles IX (q.v.), King of France, ousted François and his brother from their position of influence. François subsequently joined the French marshal Duke Anne de Montmorency (1493–1567) in the leadership of the Catholic party, opposing both the Huguenots and the tolerance of the regency. The massacre of Huguenots at Wassy by the soldiers of François in 1562 caused a civil war to break out in that year between the Catholics and the Protestants. In the following year François was assassinated by a Protestant, Jean de Poltrot, Seigneur

François de Lorraine, 2nd Duc de Guise

de Méré (about 1537–63). Despite allegations of cruelty imputed to François, he was considered by his soldiers to be a generous man and he was respected for his military skill.

Charles de Lorraine (1524–74), Roman Catholic prelate and politician, brother of François. He became archbishop of Reims in 1538 and was made cardinal of Guise in 1547 and three years later cardinal of Lorraine. With his brother François he held control of the French government during the reign of King Francis II. After the exclusion of the Guises from power at court Charles de Lorraine entered into intrigue with Philip II (q.v.), King of Spain, promising at one point to acknowledge Philip as king of France should the French king die without direct heirs. Charles is considered responsible for most of the acts which brought opprobrium upon the name of Guise during his lifetime.

Henri I de Lorraine, 3rd Duc de Guise (1550–88), politician and soldier, leader of the Catholic party, son of François. With a desire to avenge the assassination of his father, in 1567 he entered the struggle against the Huguenots. In 1569 he defeated the forces of the Huguenot leader Gaspard de Coligny (q.v.), then besieging Poitiers. He took a leading part in the Massacre of Saint Bartholomew (*see* SAINT BARTHOLOMEW'S

DAY, MASSACRE OF) in 1572, personally supervising the murder of Coligny, whom he believed to have been one of the chief instigators of his father's assassination. Unwilling to recognize the peace established in 1576, Henri formed in that year an alliance of Catholic nobles, called the Holy League, for the resumption of war against the Huguenots. It is possible that Henri's aim in establishing the league was to secure the French kingship for himself. Henry III (q.v.), King of France, however, assumed nominal leadership of the league and disbanded it on the conclusion of peace in 1577 (see FRANCE: *History: The Valois Dynasty*). The league was revived in 1584, when, on the death of François, Duc d'Alençon (1554–84), the succession to the throne was assigned to the Huguenot Henry of Navarre, later Henry IV (q.v.), King of France. In the ensuing civil war against the government, as champion of the Catholic interest, Henri de Lorraine attained great popularity with the people, at the expense of the king's prestige. On May 12, 1588, leading the people of Paris in an insurrection known as the Day of Barricades, Henri de Lorraine was in a position to seize the kingship, but he allowed the king to escape the mob. About a month later the king made an agreement with the league and appointed Henri lieutenant general of the royal armies. Henri de Lorraine was assassinated a short time later by the king's guard.

Charles de Lorraine, Duc de Mayenne (1554–1611), brother of Henri I. He participated in the Huguenot wars with his brother and after the assassination of the latter, Charles became commander of the forces of the Holy League, renewing war against the combined forces of Henry III and Henry of Navarre. The forces of Charles de Lorraine suffered several defeats at the hands of Henry IV, notably at Arques in 1589 and Ivry in 1590, and in 1596 Charles recognized the kingship of Henry, who became a Catholic convert. For the rest of his life Charles remained loyal to Henry IV.

François Joseph, 7th Duc de Guise (1670–75). After his death and the death of his successor, his great-aunt Marie of Lorraine (1615–88), the titles and lands of the Guise family were absorbed by the Bourbon-Orléans family (see ORLÉANS).

GUITAR, musical instrument of the lute family, with a long fretted neck along which are stretched six strings, three of catgut and three of wire. The strings are tuned upward from E (one line below the bass clef) as follows: E, A, D, G, B, and E (first line of the treble clef); the guitar has a range of three octaves. The instrument is played by plucking the strings with the fingers of the right hand while those of the left hand stop the strings at the various frets to produce the different tones or chords. Its soft tone makes it a particularly suitable instrument for the accompaniment of voices, but it is also used for playing music independently and has been played in solo recitals by such virtuosos as the Spanish musician Andrés Segovia (q.v.).

Forms of the guitar existed in ancient times. In the 12th or 13th century the instrument, then made with four strings, was introduced into Spain by the Moors. A fifth string was later added and in this new form the guitar became the national instrument of Spain (about 17th century) and was known there and elsewhere as the Spanish guitar. The guitar became popular throughout Europe in the 19th century and is in considerable use in Europe, the United States, and Latin America today.

GUITEAU, Charles Jules. See GARFIELD, JAMES ABRAM.

GUITRY, Sacha (1885–1957), French actor, director, and playwright, born in Saint Petersburg (now Leningrad, U.S.S.R.). He wrote and produced nearly one hundred light comedies in his life, and achieved his first success at twenty-one with the play, *Nono* (1905). Guitry generally played the lead in his own plays, usually that of a comic "great lover", but he did write more serious plays for his father, the French actor Lucien Guitry (1860–1925), notably *Pasteur* (1919) and *Béranger* (1920). Later in his career he wrote, directed, and acted in several films. Guitry was arrested in 1945 for allegedly pro-German sympathies and was tried in Paris but acquitted. After his release he remained active in both drama and films until his death.

GUIZOT, François Pierre Guillaume (1787–1874), French historian and statesman, born in Nîmes, and educated in Geneva and Paris. He became professor of modern history at the University of Paris in 1812, and used this post to spread opposition to the extreme royalist tendencies of Charles X, King of France (see under CHARLES) and his followers known as the Ultras. Guizot was spokesman for the Doctrinaires, a bourgeois group that sought a constitutional monarchy based on the British model. The group achieved victory over the aristocratic Ultras when Louis Philippe (q.v.) became monarch after the revolution of 1830. Guizot began his political career in the same year when he was elected to the Chamber of Deputies, but once in office he became increasingly conservative. As minister of the interior, he was a determined foe of democracy, suppressing the liberals who

GUJARAT

were demanding more domestic reforms. He was appointed premier in 1840, and throughout his ministry he strove to maintain cordial relations with Great Britain and the other European powers. His preoccupation with foreign affairs and his failure to grant even the slightest domestic concessions, such as the long overdue extension of the suffrage, made him extremely unpopular. By 1847 the demands for reform became stronger, particularly after the failure of the corn and potato crops had precipitated both an agricultural and an industrial depression. In February, 1848, the government ban on a demonstration so aroused the people that they overwhelmed the ministry. Louis Philippe resigned and the Second Republic was begun. Guizot fled to England but returned to France a year later. He remained active in the French Academy and supported himself chiefly by his writings. His most important works are *Histoire des Origines du Gouvernement Représentatif* ("History of the Origins of Representative Government", 2 vol., 1821–22), *Histoire de la Civilisation en Europe* (6 vol., 1829–32; Eng. trans., *General History of Civilization in Modern Europe*, 3 vol., 1846), and *Memoires pour Servir à l'Histoire de mon Temps* ("Memoirs to Serve as a History of My Time", 8 vol., 1858–67). *See also* FRANCE: *History: Restoration of the Bourbons.*

GUJARAT, State of the Republic of India, bordered on the N.E. by Rajasthan State, on the E. by Madhya Pradesh State, on the S.E. by Maharashtra State, on the S. and S.W. by the Arabian Sea, and on the N.W. by West Pakistan Province of Pakistan. Characterized by a varied topography, Gujarat has a fertile plain in the S. cut by several rivers, low hills in the W., and broad mudflats in the N. which adjoin the Great Indian Desert. The leading crops are rice, jowar, maize, groundnuts, cotton, and tobacco. Among livestock raised are buffalo and other cattle, sheep, and goats. Minerals produced include salt, manganese, limestone, and bauxite. Oil-field production began in 1960, and at Baroda (q.v.) there is an oil refinery. One of India's most industrialized States, Gujarat has a variety of industries, the principal ones being general and electrical engineering and the manufacture of textiles, vegetable oils, chemicals, soda ash, and cement. New industries include fertilizers and petrochemicals. The capital of Gujarat is Ahmadabad (q.v.).

Gujarat State was formed on May 1, 1960, from the northern and western portion of Bombay State, a predominantly Gujarati-speaking area. The remainder of Bombay State became Maharashtra State. *See* BOMBAY; GUJARATI LANGUAGE AND LITERATURE.

Area, 72,245 sq.mi.; pop. (1965 est.) 23,200,000.

GUJARATI LANGUAGE AND LITERATURE, one of the fourteen regional languages recognized under the Indian constitution, spoken by about 25,000,000 people in Gujarat, Baroda, and neighboring regions in N.W. India. Along with Hindi (q.v.), Gujarati is the official language in that State. To the east, the language merges gradually into Rajasthani, to which it is closely related. It belongs in the Sanskritic group of Indo-Iranian languages (q.v.), and is derived from the medieval dialect group called Prakrit. Gujarati contains many words borrowed from Sanskrit (q.v.), Arabic, and Persian; *see* ARABIC LANGUAGE AND LITERATURE; PERSIAN LANGUAGE AND LITERATURE. It is written in a vernacular alphabet of the type of the western group of Nagari alphabets, derived from the ancient Sanskrit script Devanagari. The manner in which the language is pronounced varies among the different religious groups who speak it, and among the educated and the illiterate.

Early Gujarati literature includes many bardic chronicles. Two of the most distinguished poets who wrote in this language are Narsingha Mehta (1413–79) and the poetess Mira Bai (1499–1570?), both of whom composed short religious poems. The Indian nationalist leader, Mohandas Karamchand Gandhi (q.v.), who spoke and wrote Gujarati as his native tongue, influenced modern writers in the language, including the novelist Kanailal M. Munshi (1887–   ).

GUJRANWALA, city of Pakistan, in West Pakistan Province, 40 miles N.W. of Lahore. A commercial center, the city trades in oilseeds, oranges, rice, sugar, and wheat. Gujranwala was once the center of Sikh power (*see* SIKHS), and was the birthplace of Ranjit Singh (1780–1839), founder of the Sikh kingdom. Pop. (1961) 196,154.

GÜLEK BOGAZ. *See* CILICIAN GATES.

GULFPORT, city and port of entry in Mississippi, and county seat of Harrison Co., on Mississippi Sound, an arm of the Gulf of Mexico, 13 miles W. of Biloxi, and about midway between Mobile, Ala., and New Orleans, La. It is served by railroads and oceangoing ships. The city has a fine harbor, with a deepwater channel to the gulf, and excellent dock and storage facilities. It has a frontage of 6 mi. on the gulf, and is protected by a sea wall extending along the shore for a distance of 27 mi. The city has many industrial establishments which include seafood, canning, and the manufacture of naval stores. Gulfport is a popular resort, with bathing beaches, golf courses, yacht clubs, and waterfront bridle paths included among its recreational facilities. It is the site of Gulf Park College, a junior college for women, established in 1921; and of a U.S. veterans hospital. The city was founded in 1898. Pop. (1960) 30,204; (1970) 40,791.

GULF STREAM, warm current of the North Atlantic Ocean flowing in a general N.E. direction from the Strait of Florida to the Grand Bank, E. and S. of Newfoundland. The term is often extended to include the North Atlantic Drift, which flows from the Grand Banks to the shores of W. Europe, Scandinavia, and the islands of the Arctic Ocean as far north as Novaya Zemlya. The Gulf Stream is of great climatological importance because of its effects on the climate of W. Europe. This great moving body of warm water gives France, the Low Countries, and the British Isles a comparatively temperate climate, despite the fact that they lie in latitudes comparable to those of Newfoundland and Labrador in the Western Hemisphere.

The sources of the Gulf Stream are the two west-flowing equatorial currents: the North Equatorial Current, which flows roughly along the Tropic of Cancer; and the South Equatorial Current, which flows from the coasts of S.W. Africa to South America and thence N. along the coasts of N. Brazil, French Guiana, Surinam, and Guyana into the Caribbean. The result of these two currents is a concentration of warm water in the Caribbean Sea and in the Atlantic Ocean N. of Cuba and the Greater Antilles. The fusion of these two currents and a certain amount of water from the Gulf of Mexico forms the Gulf Stream.

In the straits that separate Florida from the Bahamas and Cuba, the stream has a maximum width of about 50 mi. and a depth of about 2100 ft. The surface temperature is about 25° C. (77° F.) and the surface current about 2.7 to 3.8 m.p.h. At a depth of 670 ft. the temperature is 10° to 18° C. (50° to 64° F.), and the current flow between 0.9 and 1.7 m.p.h. Farther N., the stream widens and is approximately 150 mi. wide off the coast of South Carolina, and 300 mi. wide off New York. Between the stream and the E. coast of the United States lies an area of colder water, sometimes called the Cold Wall.

South of the Grand Banks, the stream meets and mixes with the Labrador Current (q.v.), which flows S. from Baffin Bay, forming numerous whirlpools. From this point the stream, or properly the North Atlantic Drift, moves N.E. across the ocean, driven at a rate of about 4 to 5 mi. per day by the prevailing S.W. winds. The drift then splits into several branches, of which the most important are: the central flow, which reaches the coasts of Europe and then turns N.; a northerly tongue, the Irminger Current, which reaches the S. and W. shores of Iceland; and a southerly tongue, which flows past the Azores and then past the Canary Islands.

All the way N. from its source to the region of the Grand Banks, the Gulf Stream has special physical characteristics, including a markedly bright blue color and strong salinity. After mixing with the Labrador Current the characteristic color is lost, but the water of the North Atlantic Drift remains markedly salty. Because of this salt concentration, the water of the drift sinks below the surface as it cools and is found as a warm underwater current when it reaches the arctic regions.

See OCEAN AND OCEANOGRAPHY: *Ocean Currents.*

GULL, common name for any number of water birds in the family Laridae, which also includes the tern (q.v.). Gulls are similar in appearance to

Gulls frequent beaches, where they feed on small fish and insects. UPI

terns, but are larger and have heavier bodies and bills more sharply hooked at the tip. The plumage of most species is white, mixed with gray, black, or brown. The majority nest on cliffs or beaches; some species make their nests in trees. The nests of all species are characteristically lined with grass, moss, and feathers. The diet is varied and includes small fish, insects, shellfish, and garbage. Some species drop shellfish from a height onto rocks, and even on cement and macadam roads, to break the shells. A number of species are migratory. About twenty-three species of gulls are found in the United States.

GULLSTRAND, Allvar (1862–1930), Swedish ophthalmologist, born in Landskrona, and educated at the universities of Uppsala, Vienna, and Stockholm. While professor of ophthalmology (1894–1913) at Uppsala, he formulated a new concept of the formation of optical images. He discovered that the eye accommodates itself to refracted light largely by rearrangement of its internal parts, and only partially by changes in the shape of the lens. Gullstrand presented his findings in 1908 in the paper, *Die optische Abbildung in heterogenen Medien und die Dioptrik der Kristallinse des Menschen* ("The Optic Image in Heterogeneous Media and the Dioptrics of the Human Crystalline Lens"), for which he was awarded the 1911 Nobel Prize for medicine and physiology. He continued his research into the general laws of dioptrics (science of refracted light) as professor of physiological and physical optics (1913–1927) at Uppsala. The slit lamp, which projects intense light into the eye, is his invention. His other important writings include *Allgemeine Theorie der Monochromatischen Aberrationen* ("General Theory of Monochromatic Aberrations", 1900) and *Einführung in die Methoden der Dioptrik des Auges des Menschen* ("Introduction to the Refractive Mechanism of the Human Eye", 1911).

GUM, colloidal substance exuded by plants. Gums are composed of complex organic acids, called gum acids, or the salts of these acids. When hydrolyzed, gum acids such as arabin yield sugars such as arabinose, galactose, and xylose, and simple acids. Gums have a consistency similar to glue when moist, but are hard when dry. They are colorless and odorless and will not dissolve in organic solvents, although they are readily soluble in water. Gums are used as a base for mucilage, in cloth finishing and calico printing, and as emulsifying or soothing constituents of medicines.

Gum arabic, an exudate of several species of acacia (q.v.), is typical of gums that contain arabin. Gum arabic of the finest quality is obtained from *Acacia senegal* and *A. arabica,* found in western and northern Africa. The gum forms a clear, viscid solution in water. When ethyl alcohol is added to an aqueous solution of gum arabic which has been slightly acidified with hydrochloric acid, arabin is precipitated. A similar gum, cherry-tree gum, is exuded from the bark of several species of *Prunus,* such as common cherry and plum trees.

Tragacanth, which is obtained from various Turkish and Iranian species of *Astragalus,* particularly *A. gummifer,* is typical of gums which contain bassorin. Tragacanth, like gelatin, absorbs water readily; it will take up as much as fifty times its weight in water, forming a thick mucilage. Tragacanth, also known as gum dragon, is a type of dragon's blood (q.v.).

Many gum resins and other plant exudates are commonly called gums; see GUM TREE. Gum resins are substances which contain both gum and resin, so that both water and alcohol are required to dissolve them. The principal gum resins are the so-called gums of ammoniac, asafetida, benzoin, galbanum, gamboge, myrrh, and sandarac. Latex (q.v.), from which chicle, rubber, and gutta-percha are derived, is composed of gum resins, waxes, and fats. Chewing gum is usually made from chicle. *See also* RESINS.

GUMBO. *See* OKRA.

GUMTI, river of N. India, rising near Pilibhit in Uttar Pradesh State, and flowing generally S.E. for 500 mi., emptying into the Ganges R. (q.v.) about 20 mi. below Varanasi (Benares). The principal towns on the river are Lucknow and Jaunpur.

GUM TREE, common name of many trees that exude gum or resin. The sapodilla, *Sapota achras,* yields chicle, used as the base for chewing gum. In the United States, the name is infrequently applied to *Liquidambar styraciflua,* the sweet or red gum (*see* LIQUIDAMBAR), and to *Nyssa sylvatica,* the tupelo (q.v.), also called black or sour gum. Species of *Eucalyptus* (q.v.) are called gum trees in Australia, and *Styrax benzoin,* which produces benzoin (q.v.) is called the gum tree in southeast Asia. Many other trees throughout the world that exude gums or resins are called gum trees in their native localities.

GUN. *See* MACHINE GUN; PISTOL; REVOLVER; RIFLE; SMALL ARMS.

GUNNISON, river of Colorado, formed at Gunnison by the confluence of the Tomichi and Taylor rivers, and flowing generally N.W. for about 200 mi., emptying into the Colorado R. at Grand Junction. The Gunnison R. falls a distance of 6477 ft. through a series of deep canyons. It is particularly famous for Black Canyon (see BLACK CANYON OF THE GUNNISON NATIONAL MONUMENT), near which the Gunnison Tunnel (30,582 ft. long) diverts the waters of the Gunnison R. for irrigation.

GUNPOWDER, explosive powder used in ballistics, specifically black powder, an explosive mixture of about 75 percent potassium nitrate (see POTASSIUM), 15 percent charcoal, and 10 percent sulfur. Gunpowder was the first explosive known. The formula for gunpowder appears in the writings of the 13th-century English monk Roger Bacon (q.v.), but it seems to have been discovered by the Chinese, who had used it in firecrackers several hundred years before his time. Gunpowder was probably introduced in Europe from the Middle East. Berthold Schwarz, a German monk of the early 14th century, may have been the first person to employ gunpowder for propelling a projectile. Whatever the precise dates and identities of its first discoverers and users, it is certain that gunpowder was manufactured in England in 1334, and that powder-manufacturing plants existed in Germany in 1340. In the time of Elizabeth I (q.v.), Queen of England, the manufacture of gunpowder was conducted as a monopoly of the crown. Regulations relating to gunpowder in England date from about 1623. It was the only explosive known to man until the discovery of fulminating gold, a powerful explosive first used in 1628 in European wars. For historical and modern uses of gunpowder, see EXPLOSIVES.

GUNPOWDER PLOT, conspiracy to kill James I (q.v.), King of England, as well as the Lords and the Commons at the opening of Parliament on Nov. 5, 1605. The plot was formed by a group of prominent Roman Catholics in retaliation for the oppressive anti-Catholic laws being applied by James I. The originator of the scheme was Robert Catesby (1573–1605), a country gentleman of Warwickshire. First he took his cousin Thomas Winter (1572–1606) and his friends Thomas Percy (1560–1605) and John Wright (1568?–1605) into his confidence, along with Guy Fawkes (q.v.), a soldier of fortune. They in turn drew other Catholic gentlemen into the plot, among them Sir Everard Digby (1578–1606), John Grant, Ambrose Rokewood (1578?–1606), Francis Tresham (1567?–1605), Thomas Winter's brother Robert, and John Wright's brother Christopher (1570?–1605). The conspirators discovered a vault directly beneath the House of Lords. They rented this cellar, and stored in it thirty-six barrels of gunpowder.

In the final arrangement for the execution of their design on November 5, Fawkes was to set fire to the gunpowder in the cellar and then flee to Flanders. Through a letter of warning written by Tresham to a peer, the plot was exposed. Fawkes was arrested early on November 5 as he emerged from the cellar. On his person were found fuses, and in the cellar a lighted lantern and the barrels of gunpowder. Examined under torture on the rack, Fawkes confessed his own guilt and after long obstinacy revealed the names of his associates, nearly all of whom were killed on being taken, or were hanged with Fawkes on Jan. 31, 1606. The Gunpowder Plot is commemorated in Great Britain by an annual celebration on November 5, in which it was the custom to burn Guy Fawkes in a ragged effigy, from which the slang word "guy" is derived.

GUNTER, Edmund (1581–1626), English mathematician, born in Hertfordshire, and educated at Westminster College and at Christ Church College, University of Oxford. He was professor of astronomy at Gresham College (now a part of the University of London) from 1619 until his death. He introduced the words cosine and cotangent into trigonometry (q.v.) and is credited with the discovery of the magnetic variation of the compass; see TERRESTRIAL MAGNETISM. Among his many practical inventions are a portable quadrant (1618); the chain (q.v.), known as Gunter's chain (1620), a linear measuring device or unit consisting of a chain 66 ft. long with 100 links of 7.92 in. each, still used in surveying (q.v.) where the unit of measurement is the acre and great accuracy is not important; and Gunter's scale, a measuring device graduated in trigonometric functions and logarithms. His most important writings are *New Projection of the Sphere* (1623) and *Canon Triangulorum, or Table of Artificial Sines and Tangents* (1620).

GUNTER'S CHAIN. See CHAIN.

GUNTHER, John (1901–70), American writer and journalist, born in Chicago, and educated at the University of Chicago. He became a reporter on the Chicago *Daily News* in 1922, and from 1924 until 1936 was European correspondent for various American newspapers. In 1939 Gunther was a radio commentator on international affairs for the National Broadcasting Company, and during World War II he was a war correspondent in Europe, Africa, and Asia.

Gunther is best known for his books of commentary, based on personal observations and interviews, on the political and cultural life in different parts of the world. The first of these books was *Inside Europe* (1936). Others in the series include *Inside Asia* (1939), *Inside Europe Today* (1949; rev. ed., 1961), *Inside Africa* (1955),

GUNTUR

John Gunther — Bob Brower—NEWSWEEK

and *Inside South America* (1967). These heavily researched, frequently updated volumes contain a wealth of detailed information and have enjoyed international success; some have been translated into more than ninety languages.

Among Gunther's other works are *Death Be Not Proud* (1949), written in memory of his young son who died of cancer; *A Fragment of Autobiography* (1962); and *Twelve Cities* (1969), memoirs of travels in a dozen cities of Europe and Asia. He also wrote five novels, including *The Indian Sign* (1970).

GUNTUR, city of the Republic of India, in Andhra Pradesh State, in the Kistna R. delta, 220 miles N. of Madras. It is in a fertile area growing cotton, rice, tobacco, and cashew nuts; industries in the city include rice, paper, and oilseed milling; tobacco processing; tanning; and the manufacture of textiles, pharmaceuticals, metal products, paint, soap, and ghee. Guntur is the site of Andhra Christian College (1885), a Hindu College, the Government College for Women (1947), a medical college, and Saint Joseph's Training College for Women (1946). Nearby to the W. is Kondavid, a hill fortress of the Golconda kingdom in the 16th and 17th centuries. Founded by the French in the 18th century, the city was ceded to a local ruler in 1766 and to the British in 1788; the cession was confirmed in 1823. The name is sometimes spelled Guntar. Pop. (1965 est.) 213,932.

GUPPY, small, active, carnivorous freshwater fish, *Lebistes reticulatus,* belonging to the Topminnow family Poeciliidae. It is found in the islands of the southern Caribbean Sea and as far south as southern Brazil. It was named after the Trinidadian ichthyologist R. J. Lechmere Guppy. The guppy is often kept in aquariums because of the brilliant coloration of the male, which is about 1 in. long, tinted with combinations of yellow, red, orange, green, blue, and purple, and spotted with black. No two individuals show the same color pattern. The female, which is about 2 in. long, is dull in color. Male guppies go through an elaborate courtship ceremony, spreading their fins before the female much in the manner of certain birds. The female produces a new litter every four weeks, the number of young varying from 2 to 126 at a time: as many as five litters are produced as a result of a single mating. The young, which are frequently devoured by the parents, survive in their native

Male (left) and female guppies, Lebistes reticulatus.

surroundings by staying in the bottom vegetation. In aquariums, separate tanks or thick vegetation must be provided to insure segregation of the young from other guppies. The aquariums must be kept at about 75° to 85° F. for the fish to thrive. Guppies are valued in the West Indies because they destroy the larvae of mosquitoes that carry malaria.

GUPTA DYNASTY. See INDIA: *History: Hindu Dynasties.*

GURKHAS (Skr. *gōraksa*, "cowherd"), Tibeto-Mongolian Hindus of Nepal (q.v.). The Gurkhas first came to Nepal in the 12th century after being driven out of northern India by the Muslims. The Gurkhas claim descent from the warlike Rajputs of northern India in the present State of Rajasthan (q.v.), and they speak a Rajasthani Sanskrit dialect. In physique they are short and stocky. An attempt to extend their power southward resulted in the Gurkha War, lasting from 1814 to 1816, against Great Britain, in which they were defeated. Since then many of the Gurkhas, who are excellent fighters, entered British military service in India and in the British colonies, serving in separate Gurkha regiments that still exist in the British and Indian armies. Many so-called Gurkha soldiers, however, are Nepalese of other tribes. The Gurkha troops carry a short, broad-bladed sword called the kukri, which they use in close combat in preference to the bayonet.

GURNARD (Fr. *grogner*, "to grunt"), common name for any of several species of spiny-rayed marine fish of the family Dactylopteridae. Their name comes from the grunting sound certain species make when taken from the water. Gurnards attain a length, in the largest specimens, of not more than 18 in. Gurnards, like the sculpin, have rough and spiny skull bones; their bodies are covered with bony scales, and their heads are angular and wholly covered with bony plates. The body is elongated, nearly round, and tapering; there are two dorsal fins. The lower three rays of the large pectoral fins are detached and elongated into long feelers, which are used in the search for food, and for locomotion. Gurnards live on the bottom of the sea generally along the coast. They often frequent depths of several hundred fathoms. Several gurnards are called by the name of sea robin (q.v.).

GUSTAVUS I, known as GUSTAVUS VASA or GUSTAVUS ERICKSSON (1496–1560), King of Sweden (1523–60), born in Lindholmen, and educated at the University of Uppsala. As a young man he entered the army, and from 1518 to 1519 fought against Christian II (q.v.), King of Denmark, who had invaded Sweden to regain the throne. Gustavus was taken hostage but managed to escape. He was still a fugitive when he heard of Christian's massacre of his father and other nationalist Swedish nobles in Stockholm in 1520. With an army of peasants, Gustavus led a successful revolt (1521–23) and drove the Danes out of Sweden. His victory resulted in the dissolution of the Union of Kalmar, which in 1397 had placed Sweden and Norway under the Danish crown. Gustavus was administrator of the kingdom from 1521 until 1523, when the Riksdag, or national assembly, elected him king. He strengthened his political hold and restored order by introducing the Reformation (q.v.) into Sweden. The Catholic Church had supported Christian II, and Gustavus used this as an excuse for stripping the Church of political power and confiscating its property. In 1527 he made Swedish bishops subject to royal power, and in 1529 he proclaimed Lutheranism (q.v.) the state religion. He joined with Norway in 1537 to defeat the German city of Lübeck, thereby making Sweden economically independent of the powerful Hanseatic League (q.v.). Gustavus created a strongly united state by introducing a sound financial administration, strengthening manufacturing, trade, and agricultural interests, and increasing the military forces. In 1544 he made the Swedish kingship hereditary through his line, the house of Vasa. He was succeeded by his son, Charles IX (q.v.).

GUSTAVUS II, known as GUSTAVUS ADOLPHUS (1594–1632), King of Sweden (1611–32), son of King Charles IX (q.v.), born in Stockholm. Known as the "Lion of the North", he was a brilliant military leader noted for his direction of the Protestant forces in the Thirty Years' War (q.v.). When he succeeded to the throne in 1611, Sweden was at war with Denmark, Russia, and Poland. Gustavus concluded a peace with Denmark in 1613, but Sweden regained its southern provinces only after agreeing to pay heavy financial indemnities. He waged a successful war against Russia (1613–17), acquiring lands that completely cut off Russian access to the Baltic Sea. From 1621 to 1629, Gustavus waged war against his cousin, Sigismund III, King of Poland (1566–1632), who maintained a claim to the Swedish throne. Poland was forced to cede lands and cities along the southern and eastern Baltic coasts in 1629, and Gustavus' right to the Swedish throne was ensured. A religious interest in the Protestant cause and a belief that an imperialist conquest of northern Germany would be militarily and economically dangerous to Sweden impelled Gustavus to enter the Thirty

GUSTAVUS III

Years' War. After securing an alliance with France, he landed his army on the coast of Pomerania (q.v.) and succeeded in driving the imperial forces back from the Baltic. His victory at the Battle of Breitenfeld in 1631 gave the Protestants the military advantage and they went on to occupy Bavaria and Bohemia (qq.v.). Gustavus turned his army north in 1632. At the Battle of Lützen in Saxony (q.v.), he defeated the imperial forces, but was fatally wounded. Gustavus was noted not only as a great general but as a capable administrator. With the help of his chancellor, Count Axel Gustafsson Oxenstierna (q.v.), who managed internal affairs and diplomacy while the king was involved in military campaigns, Gustavus developed a sound and centralized system of government and did much to develop the natural mineral resources of his country. He was succeeded by his daughter, Christina (1626–89).

GUSTAVUS III (1746–92), King of Sweden (1771–92), son of King Adolphus Frederick (1710–71), born in Stockholm. When Gustavus succeeded his father, the power of the monarchy had been greatly curtailed and the ruling assembly, the Riksdag, was torn by intense party strife. After failing to reconcile the divided factions, Gustavus decided to regain complete control of the government for the monarchy. With the help of the army he staged a mock revolt in 1772 and forced the Riksdag to accept a new constitution that gave him absolute power. He then instituted a series of financial and judicial reforms to correct corruption in high office, granted freedom of the press and complete religious toleration, and enlarged the navy, making it one of the most powerful in Europe. In 1788 he undertook an inconclusive war with Russia which was marked by treason among the nobility at home and mutiny among his troops. A Swedish naval victory in 1790, however, destroyed a third of the Russian fleet and enabled him to end the war on terms favorable to Sweden. While preparing to intervene in the French Revolution (q.v.) in 1792, Gustavus was assassinated in a plot conceived by hostile nobles. He was a devotee of French culture, and throughout his reign was a patron of literature, art, and science. He founded the Swedish Academy in 1786.

GUSTAVUS IV, full name GUSTAVUS ADOLPHUS (1778–1837), King of Sweden (1792–1809), son of King Gustavus III (q.v.), born in Stockholm. He was king under the regency of his uncle from 1792 until 1800, when he was crowned. Gustavus was a reactionary and despotic ruler. His hatred of the French Republic prompted him to join the Third Coalition against Napoleon I (q.v.), Emperor of France, a move that resulted in the loss of Pomerania (q.v.) to France in 1807, and Finland to Russia in 1808. Because he was believed insane, the king was captured by nobles and compelled to abdicate in 1809. He died in exile in Switzerland. He was succeeded by his uncle, Charles XIII (see under CHARLES).

GUSTAVUS V, known as GUSTAF (1858–1950), King of Sweden (1907–50), son of King Oscar II (q.v.), born near Stockholm, and educated at the University of Uppsala. After serving several times as regent for his father when the latter was ill or absent from the kingdom, Gustavus became king in 1907. He insisted on preserving Swedish neutrality in World War I and World War II, and built up a strong system of military defenses. During his reign much progressive social legislation, including extension of the franchise, instigation of an eight-hour workday, state-subsidized housing, and public child welfare, was enacted. He was succeeded by his son, Gustavus VI (q.v.).

GUSTAVUS VI, in full OSCAR FREDRIK WILHELM OLAF GUSTAF ADOLF (1882–   ), King of Sweden (1950–   ), son of King Gustavus V (q.v.), born in Stockholm, and educated at the universities of Uppsala and Oslo. He entered the army in 1902, served with both the Swedish and Norwegian forces, and obtained the rank of general in 1932. Gustavus is known as a patron of the arts, and has won an international reputation as a classical archeologist. The heir apparent is his grandson, Carl Gustavus (1947–   ).

GUSTAVUS ADOLPHUS, or GUSTAF ADOLF. See GUSTAVUS II; GUSTAVUS IV.

GUSTAVUS VASA. See GUSTAVUS I.

GUT. See CATGUT.

GUTENBERG, Johann (1400?–68?), German printer, and pioneer in the use of movable type, born probably in Mainz. His family later settled in Strasbourg, where in 1438 Gutenberg entered into a partnership with three others to conduct experiments in printing. In Mainz, about 1450, Gutenberg formed a partnership with the German money-lender Johann Fust (q.v.), and set up a press on which he may have started printing a large Latin Bible and some smaller books and leaflets. Fust's demands for the repayment of money he had invested led to a lawsuit in 1455, and Gutenberg surrendered his share of the firm. The famous Bible known as the Gutenberg Bible (q.v.) was finished before the middle of 1456, but was actually printed by the German printer Peter Schöffer (about 1425–1502) who was Fust's son-in-law. Following the break with

Johann Gutenberg examining the proofs of his Bible, the first European book known to have been printed from movable type (from a 19th-century engraving).
Bettmann Archive

Fust, Gutenberg continued printing, either at Mainz or the nearby town of Eltville. In 1465 the German statesman, Adolph II, Archbishop of Nassau, Elector of Mainz (d. 1475), became his patron. See also PRINTING: *History of the Printing Trade: Printing in the West.*

GUTENBERG BIBLE, known also as the MAZARIN BIBLE and the BIBLE OF 42 LINES, Latin edition of the Bible (q.v.), printed at Mainz, Germany, sometime between 1450 and 1456. Although German bibliographers claim that it was printed by the German printer Johann Gutenberg (q.v.), the edition probably was the work of the German printers Peter Schöffer (1425–1502?) and Johann Fust (q.v.), both of whom had been associated with Gutenberg. The book is the first volume known to have been printed with movable metal type (q.v.). The first copy that attracted attention was discovered about 1760 among the books of the French statesman Cardinal Jules Mazarin (q.v.). The finest known copy was acquired by the Library of Congress (q.v.), Washington, D.C., in 1930. Only two other perfect copies of the Gutenberg Bible are known to be in existence. See BOOK.

GUTHRIE, Sir (William) Tyrone (1900–71), British stage director and playwright, born in Tunbridge Wells, England, and educated chiefly at the University of Oxford. While at Oxford, Guthrie made his professional debut as an actor and assistant stage manager at the Oxford Playhouse. During the following six years he held various positions, notably as a writer of radio plays with the British Broadcasting Corporation in Belfast, Northern Ireland. In 1929, working with the Festival Theatre in Cambridge, England, Guthrie pioneered in the writing and staging of plays in the expressionist mode. Much of his best work has been done in producing the plays of Shakespeare; he was in charge of productions at the Old Vic Theatre from 1938 to 1945, and was administrator of the Sadler's Wells Theatre from 1939 to 1945 and again from 1951 to 1952. Guthrie's highly praised staging of the English-language production of the opera *Carmen* in London, in 1949, was brought to New York City in 1952. The following year he was named the first director of the Shakespeare Festival Theater in Stratford, Ontario, Canada, a position he retained through the 1955 season. In 1963 he became the director of the Minnesota (Tyrone Guthrie) Theatre Company, which he helped found in Minneapolis, Minn.

Guthrie wrote several plays, among them *Follow Me* (1931) and *Top of the Ladder* (1950). His autobiography, *A Life in the Theater,* was published in the United States in 1960. He was knighted in 1961.

GUTTA-PERCHA. See RUBBER.

GUTTA ROSACEA. See ACNE ROSACEA.

GUYANA

A view of Georgetown, the capital, with Saint George's Cathedral, constructed entirely of wood, in the foreground.
Guyana Information Services

GUYANA, country on the N.E. coast of South America, formerly British Guiana, member of the Commonwealth of Nations (q.v.); bounded on the N. and N.E. by the Atlantic Ocean, on the E. by Surinam, on the S. by Brazil, and on the W. by Brazil and Venezuela. The country (Guyana is an Amerindian word probably meaning "land of waters") achieved independence on May 26, 1966. Guyana has an area of 83,000 sq.mi.; its coastline is 270 mi. long. Large areas in the E. and W. are claimed by Surinam and Venezuela respectively.

THE LAND

The country can be divided into three geographical regions. A belt of alluvial soil, varying in width from 5 to 40 mi. and mostly below sea level, extends along the coast and is protected by a system of dams and dikes. To the S. lies the dense forest area that comprises four fifths of the country. The forests extend into an interior highland region with a maximum elevation (Mt. Roraima) of 9094 ft. Some of the rivers form spectacular waterfalls, notably Kaieteur Falls, 741 ft., one of the highest single-drop waterfalls in the world. Beyond the forest lies a savanna grassland. Several important rivers, the Essequibo, Demerara, and the Berbice, cross the country in a north-to-south direction. The rivers are only navigable by oceangoing freighters from 60 to 100 mi. from the sea; farther inland only small craft can traverse the rapids and falls.

Climate. Guyana has a tropical climate, with little seasonal temperature change. The annual rainfall (60–80 in.) on the coast occurs in two seasons, April to August, and November to January. The S. savanna region receives some 60 in. of rain annually from April to September.

Natural Resources. The economy of Guyana is basically agrarian; the principal crops are sugar and rice. Important mineral deposits include bauxite and manganese; gold and diamonds are also mined. Surveys in the mid-1960's found deposits of copper and indications of deposits of

GUYANA

INDEX TO MAP OF GUYANA

Districts

East Berbice	C 3
East Demerara	C 2
Essequibo	B 2
Essequibo Islands	B 2
Mazaruni-Potaro	B 3
North West	B 2
Rupununi	B 4
West Berbice	C 2
West Demerara	B 2

Cities and Towns

Adventure	B 2
Annai	B 4
Anna Regina	B 2
Apoteri	B 3
Aurora	B 2
Baramanni	B 2
Bartica	B 2
Biloku	B 5
Charity	B 2
Christianburg-Wismar-Mackenzie	B 2
Danielstown	B 2
Enmore	C 2
Epira	C 3
Fort Wellington	C 2
Georgetown (cap.)	C 2
Imbaimadai	A 3
Kamakusa	A 3
Kamarang	A 3
Karasabai	B 4
Kurupukari	B 3
Lethem	B 4
Lumid Pau	B 4
Mabaruma	B 1
Mahaica	C 2
Mahaicony	C 2
Mara	C 2
Morawhanna	B 1
Mount Everard	B 2
New Amsterdam	C 2
Orealla	C 3
Parika	B 2
Pickersgill	B 2
Queenstown	B 2
Rockstone	B 2
Rosignol	C 2
Springlands	C 2
Suddie	B 2
Tumatumari	B 3
Temerere	B 2
Vreed-en-Hoop	B 2
Wichabai	B 4
Yupukari	B 4

Physical Features

Akarai (mts.)	B 5
Amakura (river)	A 2
Ariwa (mt.)	B 3
Barama (river)	A 2
Berbice (river)	B 3
Courantyne (river)	C 3
Cuyuni (river)	B 2
Demerara (river)	B 3
Essequibo (river)	B 3
Great (fall)	B 3
Kaieteur (fall)	B 3
Kanuku (mts.)	B 4
Kwitaro (river)	B 4
Marudi (mts.)	B 5
Mazaruni (river)	A 2
Moruka (river)	B 2
Pakaraima (mts.)	B 3
Playa (point)	B 1
Pomeroon (river)	B 2
Roraima (mt.)	A 3
Rupununi (river)	B 4
Wakenaam (isl.)	B 2

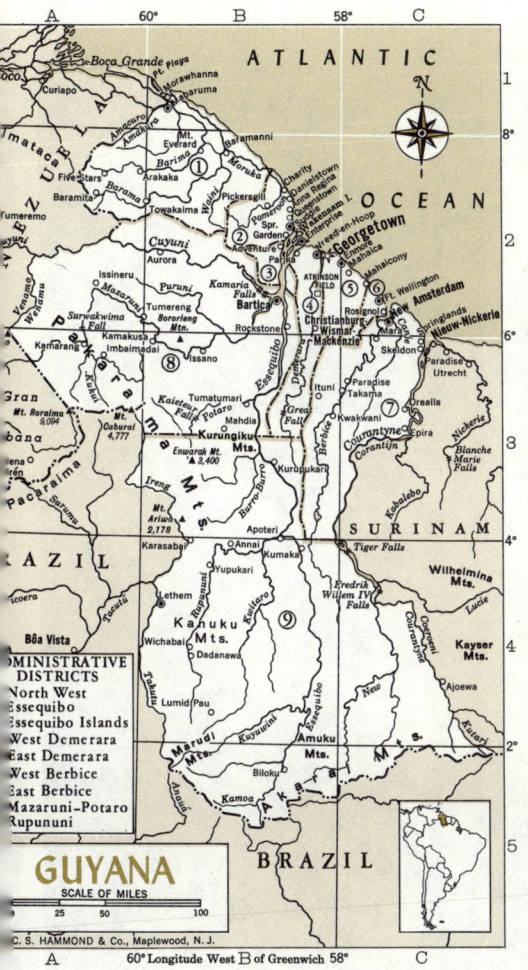

oil, uranium, silver, nickel, molybdenum, and other minerals.

The plants and trees of Guyana are noted for their great size; the giant water lily, *Victoria regina*, is common. The dense forests contain excellent woods, such as greenheart and mora, for use in the lumber industry. The animal life is varied and includes deer, anteaters, and two species of monkeys. Among the birds are manakins, sugarbirds, and cotingas; the diversity of brilliantly colored birds and insects is considerable.

THE PEOPLE

More than 50 percent of the total population is East Indian; 32 percent is African; 12 percent is mixed; the indigenous Amerindians comprise some 4 percent; Portuguese and other Europeans and Chinese are also represented. About 90 percent of the largely rural population live along the coast. More than 50 percent of the people are Christians, most being Anglicans or Roman Catholics. The remainder are mainly Hindus and Muslims.

The official language is English.

Population. The population of Guyana (census 1970) was 714,000. The United Nations estimated the overall population density at 10 persons per sq.mi. in 1970. Georgetown, the capital and principal port, has a population (1970 est.) of 195,250. In the late 1960's New Amsterdam had a population of about 15,000. The mining community of Mackenzie-Wismar-Christianburg had a population of about 20,000.

In the late 1960's about 170,000 pupils were enrolled in some 485 primary and secondary schools. The University of Guyana (opened in 1963) had an enrollment of about 1000.

Culture. Until independence, Guyana was tied culturally more closely with the two other colonial Guianas than with the rest of South America. Guyana was settled by East Indians, who still speak Urdu, Hindi, and Tamil dialects; Africans; and a few Europeans, mostly Britons.

These various ethnic strains have remained fairly distinct, and today each group has its own style of life and culture, although the new ties of nationhood bind them together.

Kaieteur Falls, on the Potaro River, one of the highest single-drop falls in the world. Guyana Information Services

THE ECONOMY

The country is currently operating under a seven-year plan, planned to end in 1972, developed by British, American, and Canadian experts. The resources of the country were in the early stages of development immediately prior to independence. Private investment contributes substantially to the economy of Guyana. Manufacturing industry was on a small scale in the late 1960's but was beginning to expand. The sugar and bauxite industries are mainly financed by British and Canadian capital. In a recent year national budget figures showed about $153,620,000 in revenues, with slightly higher expenditures.

Agriculture. Agriculture, the main economic activity, provides about 60 percent of the total value of exports and a large part of domestic food needs. Sugar and its by-products and rice account for more than half of exports. Coconuts, coffee, cocoa, citrus fruits, corn, manioc, and other tropical fruits and vegetables are grown primarily for home consumption. Large areas of rough pasture exist in the interior savannas.

Cultivation is confined almost entirely to the narrow coastal strip of rich, alluvial soil. Agricultural expansion requires heavy expenditures for protection against flooding and for drainage and irrigation because part of the strip is below the high-tide mark of the sea and rivers and because of the heavy seasonal rainfall. The government is making efforts to increase the available land through reclamation projects. Also, it is continuing research into the possibility of producing new crops and more livestock products.

About 0.5 percent of the land is under cultivation, but it is estimated that an additional 2,500,000 acres may be cultivated.

Forest and Fishing Industries. In the late 1960's the government made plans to increase production and markets for the forest and fishing industries which had been developed to a very small extent. Only 20 percent of the 70,000 sq.mi. of forests were economically exploitable at that time.

Mining. Guyana is a major producer of bauxite, producing about 4,000,000 tons annually in the late 1960's. Other mining output included alumina (299,000 tons), manganese (38,000 tons), gold (2000 oz.), and diamonds (98,000 carats).

Commerce and Trade. The Guyana dollar, consisting of 100 cents, was valued at U.S.$0.5440 (1972). The Bank of Guyana, established in 1965, is the central bank.

The chief exports in the late 1960's were sugar, rum, rice, timber, bauxite, alumina, and diamonds. The principal imports were machinery, diesel oil and other fuel oils, tobacco, cotton fabrics, dairy products, footwear, and alcoholic beverages.

Transportation. Guyana has some 370 mi. of hard-surface roads. The government operates 80 mi. of railway lines. The rivers continue to be an important means of access to the interior. The Guyana Airways Corporation serves domestic needs, and international airlines also provide service to foreign points.

Communications. Guyana had some 13,500 telephones in the late 1960's; radio-telephone links are often the only efficient means of communication with the interior. Each of the two commercial radio stations broadcast some seventeen hours daily; valuable work in the field of adult education is achieved by school broadcasts transmitted by the government station. In the late 1960's Guyana had some 80,000 licensed radio receivers.

Labor. Guyana has a labor force of 184,000 that comprises some 29 percent of the population. In the mid-1960's Guyana had 6 employer associations and 54 worker organizations.

GOVERNMENT

Guyana is a republic with a parliamentary form of government.

Central Government. The head of state is a president, elected to a six-year term of office by the National Assembly. Executive power is exercised by a prime minister, who is leader of the majority party in the assembly.

HEALTH AND WELFARE. The government provides social assistance, including old-age pensions and relief for the aged, the infirm, and destitute

A young girl of mixed African and East Indian parentage.
UPI

children; delinquency services; and community services. Public-health measures have virtually eliminated malaria as a major health problem.

Legislature. The prime minister and cabinet are responsible collectively to the National Assembly, a unicameral legislature that consists of fifty-three members elected by proportional representation and four nonelected members.

Political Parties. Guyana has three major parties. The People's Progressive Party (P.P.P.) was founded in 1950 by Cheddi Jagan (1918–), who is of East Indian descent. A left-wing organization, the P.P.P. is supported by East Indian rice farmers and sugar workers. L.F.S. Burnham (1923–), a Negro who was formerly deputy leader of the P.P.P., formed the socialist People's National Congress (P.N.C.) in 1955 when he left the P.P.P. The P.N.C. comprises mainly citizens of African descent and mixed urban groups. The smallest party, the United Force (U.F.), is a conservative group representing chiefly the Portuguese and Chinese, Indian middle-class business interests, and the Amerindians. Peter D'Aguiar (1912–), who is of Portuguese descent, formed the U.F. in 1960.

Local Government. Guyana is divided into nine districts, each headed by a district commission; Georgetown and New Amsterdam are each administered by a mayor and town council.

GUYANA

Judiciary. The law of Guyana is based on English common and statute law. The Supreme Court, which has unlimited jurisdiction in probate and administrative matters, consists of a chief justice as president and six puisne judges. Jurisdiction is original and appellate.

HISTORY

The territory that is now Guyana was first charted by Spanish explorers in 1499. By the mid-18th century Dutch settlers and traders had prevailed over rival Spanish and British expeditions. Although formal possession fell to the British in 1814, the Dutch system of administration persisted during most of the pre-colonial period (the colony of British Guiana came into being in 1831). During the years of British rule, the native Amerindian population was reduced to a tiny minority by large influxes of African and East Indian peoples. Guyana received its first constitution under the British administration in 1928, but universal suffrage was not granted until 1953.

In 1961 Guyana achieved full internal self-government. In the elections held in August, the People's Progressive Party, under the leadership of Cheddi Jagan, gained a majority in the wholly elected legislative assembly. In January, 1962, Prime Minister Jagan introduced a program of severe economic austerity. Almost immediately the program gave rise to violent riots and a general strike. British troops were called in to restore order in February and again in the spring of 1963.

In April, 1963, the disorders took on racial overtones; persons of African descent clashed with the East Indian supporters of Jagan. When calm was restored in July, the nation was left on the brink of economic chaos.

Following constitutional conferences between Guyana and Great Britain in 1962 and 1963, elections were held in December, 1964. The P.P.P. again received the most votes but failed to gain a majority of seats in the assembly. The British government thereupon called on L.F.S. Burnham, leader of the minority P.N.C., to form a coalition government. The new govern-

Prime Minister L.F.S. Burnham (right) unveils a monument in 1966, marking the independence of Guyana, achieved the previous year. UPI

ment was formed with Burnham as prime minister and Peter D'Aguiar, leader of the United Front, as minister of finance.

Independence for Guyana. In November, 1965, following a period of relative stability, the British Guiana Independence Conference was convened in London, England, where a new constitution providing for independence was approved. On May 26, 1966, Guyana was declared a sovereign and independent nation within the Commonwealth of Nations, and Burnham was made prime minister.

In May, 1968, Guyana was a signatory of the treaty establishing the Caribbean Free Trade Area (CARIFTA). The government of Prime Minister Burnham continued in office following the victory of the P.N.C. in general elections in December of that year. On Feb. 23, 1970, Guyana was proclaimed a republic, and Judge Arthur Chung (1918–   ) was named president.

In the early 1970's Guyana established diplomatic relations with several Communist nations, notably Poland and the People's Republic of China in 1972. Guyana was host in August, 1972, to a conference of some sixty nonaligned countries. These moves were viewed as signaling departure of Guyana from colonial ties.

GUY FAWKES DAY. See FAWKES, GUY.

GUYON, Madame, name used by JEANNE MARIE DE LA MOTTE-GUYON (1648–1717), French mystic, born Jeanne Marie Bouvier in Montargis, and educated in convent schools. Left a rich widow at the age of twenty-eight, she came under the influence of Père François Lacombe (d. 1715), a French Barnabite monk, and with him started spreading her philosophy of mysticism in southeastern France. She introduced into France the doctrine of quietism (q.v.), which stressed the religious value of contemplation. Her ideas aroused the severe criticism of the archbishop of Paris, and in 1688 she was imprisoned; she was released the next year through the influence of Françoise d'Aubigné, Marquise de Maintenon, wife of Louis XIV (qq.v.), King of France. During the next four years, Madame Guyon was often present at the court and formed a friendship with the French writer and prelate François de Salignac de La Mothe-Fénelon (q.v.), to whom she imparted many of her views. Imprisoned again for her quietist writings in 1695, she remained incarcerated until 1703, when she was released on condition that she leave Paris and live in retirement with her son near Blois. She spent her last years performing charitable deeds, and died professing absolute belief in the Roman Catholic Church. Her writings include *Le Cantique des Cantiques Interprété selon le Sens Mystique* ("The Song of Solomon Interpreted According to Its Mystical Sense", 1685), and *Discours Chrétiens et Spirituels* ("Christian and Spiritual Discourses", 1716).

GWALIOR, city of the Republic of India, in Madhya Pradesh State, 50 miles S. of Agra. The new section of the city, called Lashkar, situated a few miles S. of the old city, is the site of factories producing cotton, yarn, paint, ceramics, chemicals, and leather products. The nucleus of Gwalior is a citadel crowning an isolated rock about 300 ft. in height, 2 mi. in length, and 900 yd. in width. The rock is said to have been a stronghold for more than ten centuries. On the E. base of the rock is the old city of Gwalior, which contains a noted white-sandstone mosque, palaces, rock temples, and statues of archeological and architectural interest. Gwalior was the capital of the princely State of Gwalior until 1948 and the summer capital of the Indian State of Madhya Bharat from 1948 to 1956, when Madhya Bharat became part of Madhya Pradesh. Pop. (1961) 300,587.

GWELO, city in Rhodesia, and capital of Midlands Province, near the Gwelo R., in the high veldt area of Matabeleland, 95 miles N.E. of Bulawayo and 135 miles S.W. of Salisbury. Gold, iron, chrome ore, diamonds, tungsten, asbestos, nickel, and limestone are mined in the surrounding district. Cattle are raised in the district and grain and potatoes are grown. Industries in the city include gold and ferrochromium processing, tanning, corn milling, woodworking, and the manufacture of textiles, metal products, shoes, cement, and candles. Founded in 1894, Gwelo was a camp for European settlers during the Matabele Rebellion against the British South Africa Company, in 1896. Pop. (1969) 46,030.

GWINNETT, Button (about 1735–77), American patriot, born in Gloucester, England. As a young man he exported goods to the American colonies. He emigrated to Charleston, S.C., and about 1765 bought a plantation on Saint Catherines Island, Ga. He was politically active early in the revolutionary movement in Georgia, became a member of the Continental Congress (q.v.), and was one of the signers of the Declaration of Independence. From 1776 to 1777 he was a member of the convention that met to frame the Georgia constitution. He was killed in a duel with the American General Lachlan McIntosh (1725–1806), his successful rival for the command of Revolutionary troops from Georgia.

GWYN, Eleanor *or* **GWYNNE, Eleanor,** known as NELL GWYN (1650–87), English actress, and mistress of Charles II (q.v.), King of Eng-

GYMNASIUM

land, born either in London or Hereford. As a child she sold oranges outside the Drury Lane Theatre in London; she became an actress at the age of fifteen. Her first known stage appearance was in *The Indian Emperor* (1665) by the English dramatist John Dryden (q.v.). She was well suited to the gay feminine roles common in Restoration comedies, and Dryden wrote several plays with roles especially for her. She was the mistress of the king from about 1669 until his death in 1685. Although almost completely illiterate, she was a favorite in London society, and the English diarist Samuel Pepys (q.v.) described her as "pretty, witty Nell". She bore the king two sons, Charles Beauclerk, Duke of Saint Albans (1670–1726), and James Beauclerk (1671–80).

GYMNASIUM (Gr. *gymnasion*, from *gymnazein*, "to exercise naked"), in German education, traditionally a high school emphasizing classical languages and literature. The term was derived from the gymnasiums of ancient Greece, where youths met for exercise, conversation, and discussion. (For gymnasium as a place for athletics or sports, see GYMNASTICS.)

German gymnasiums arose during the humanistic movement of the early part of the 16th century; see HUMANISM. Schools existing at that time were either owned by the Roman Catholic Church or staffed by clergy. These schools were devoted to the study, in Latin, of the traditional liberal arts, which consisted of the trivium (grammar, rhetoric, and logic) and the quadrivium (arithmetic, astronomy, geometry, and music). The influence of the humanistic movement resulted in the emancipation of schools from the teaching of the church. Meanwhile the Protestant Reformation which favored secularization and uniformity of education, had begun; see REFORMATION.

The first Protestant school of the humanistic type was established at Magdeburg in 1524. The first general system of schools which provided for gymnasiums was that of Saxony, initiated in 1528. The most influential gymnasium, that of Strasbourg, Germany (now in France), was placed under the leadership of the German educator Johannes Sturm (q.v.) in 1538. In 1540 the Jesuit order established the first of numerous schools that differed from gymnasiums only in being under religious control. Rivalry between the gymnasiums and Jesuit schools, together with a decline in emphasis on humanism, was responsible for a decline in character of the gymnasiums. Instruction became very formal, with little attention given to the meaningful content of the literature studied. Late in the 17th century, however, members of the Pietistic movement (see PIETISM) were largely responsible for the formation of new nonclassical schools, designed for students who did not intend to enter the learned professions. The Prussian monarchy exerted a stimulating influence on education throughout the 18th century, but not until late in the century did a new humanistic spirit become infused into the German gymnasiums, under the influence of such men as the philosophers Johann Gottfried von Herder and Immanuel Kant and the poets and dramatists Gotthold Ephraim Lessing, Johann Wolfgang von Goethe, and Johann Christoph Friedrich von Schiller (qq.v.). During the 19th century, the rapid rise in importance of mathematics and the natural sciences influenced the curriculum of these institutions, but the study of classical antiquity continued to be the chief object of gymnasial teaching.

Just prior to World War I, the curriculum of the gymnasium was extensively modernized. Latin remained the basic subject, but Greek, long compulsory, was put on an elective basis, and a considerable part of the language instruction was devoted to French. The study of German included instruction in mythology, grammar, rhetoric, poetics, and reading of the *Nibelungenlied* (q.v.), a medieval German epic poem, the works of Lessing, Schiller, and Goethe, and German translations of the plays of William Shakespeare. Mathematical subjects included arithmetic, algebra, geometry, trigonometry, and analytical geometry. Instruction in natural sciences included descriptive natural history, botany, zoology, anthropology, mineralogy, physics, astronomy, chemistry, and physical geography. The history curriculum was so organized that each period was covered twice, once in the lower school and again in the upper school. Geography, religion, singing, drawing, and gymnastics comprised the remainder of the curriculum.

After World War I and especially since World War II, the gymnasiums have become less important in the general structure of German education. In East Germany, which follows the Soviet emphasis on technology, they have all but disappeared. In West Germany, the term "gymnasium" is now applied to high schools that concentrate on mathematics and science, with Latin an elective subject, as well as to the classical and modern semiclassical schools. See GERMANY: *Education: West Germany*.

GYMNASTICS, individual physical exercises requiring muscular agility, coordination, and control, designed for improving health and de-

Gymnastics employing fixed gym equipment. Right: Seemingly in flight, a graceful gymnast makes a smooth descent after swinging free of the high horizontal bar. Below: Every body muscle can be brought into play in the physical discipline required by exercise on the flying rings.
UPI

GYMNASTICS

veloping the body. The term, of Greek derivation, originally meant all forms of athletics. In Greek gymnastics, each youth would try to perform whatever feat he could, but soon the games were reduced to formal contests, including running and javelin and discus throwing. Greek youths spent a large part of the day in the gymnasium (q.v.), a public place for athletic training and competition. The Romans adopted the Greek forms of gymnastics, especially as part of military training, but soon abandoned them.

The history of modern gymnastics begins in the 18th century, when physical training was advocated by educational theorists, including the French philosopher Jean Jacques Rousseau and the German educator Johann Bernhard Basedow (qq.v.), who trained gymnastic teachers and established the first modern public gymnasiums. Gymnastics were revived during the 19th century as a result of German and Scandinavian influence. The German educators Friedrich Ludwig Jahn (q.v.) and Guts Muths (1759–1839) were responsible for developing most of the equipment used in modern gymnasiums. Jahn wrote one of the first books on gymnastics and established *Turnvereine* ("tumbling clubs") for young men in Germany. At about the same time other educators, notably the Swedish gymnast Pehr Henrik Ling (1776–1839) and the Spanish gymnast Francisco Amoros (1770–1818), who worked in France, introduced gymnastics into European schools. German emigrants to the United States in the second half of the 19th century were particularly concerned with physical training, and organized *Turnvereine* in the U.S. Gymnastics was quickly adopted by most American schools and colleges. *See also* PHYSICAL EDUCATION.

Modern Gymnastics. Today gymnastics is an integral part of most European educational systems. Gymnastics forms part of U.S. school and college curricula, and is essential to the training of firemen, soldiers, policemen, and others whose occupations demand physical coordination. Gymnastic team meetings are important to indoor sports during the winter. Championships are awarded, notably in the contests sponsored by the Amateur Athletic Union of the U.S., the Young Men's Christian Association, the National Collegiate Athletic Association (qq.v.), the United States Gymnastic Federation, and various colleges and athletic associations. Gymnastics is also an integral part of the Olympic Games (q.v.).

Modern gymnastic exercises can be divided into two main categories: light gymnastics or calisthenics, and heavy gymnastics. The former, usually undertaken by beginners are intended primarily to develop muscle strength. They may involve such movements as knee bends, push-ups, kicks, and headstands. They may also be in the form of exercises that gradually increase stress on the muscles by the use of various devices, including dumbbells, bar bells, and pulley weight machines. Heavy gymnastics, emphasizing muscular control and coordination, involves the use of fixed gymnasium equipment, such as the vaulting horse and mats, designed for vaulting and jumping exercises; side horse, and parallel bars, for support exercises; flying rings, horizontal bar; climbing ropes, horizontal and vertical ladders, and the trapeze, all designed for hanging, swinging, or climbing exercises.

In recent years there has been an upsurge of gymnastics for women in the U.S., consisting primarily of light gymnastics (or gymnastics moderne), and heavy gymnastics. The former is a kind of dance in which balls, hoops, jump ropes, wands or flags, and free calisthenic movements are employed. Heavy gymnastics involves the use of stationary apparatus, such as the balance beam, the vaulting horse (on which the width is vaulted rather than the length), the uneven parallels and floor exercise—a combination of dance and tumbling performed to music.

GYMNOSPERMS. *See* SPERMATOPHYTES.

GYNECOLOGY, branch of medicine dealing with the study, diagnosis, and treatment of disorders and diseases of the female reproductive tract. Care of the woman before, during, and after childbirth is the province of a separate but closely related field, obstetrics (q.v.).

Gynecology was practiced with remarkable understanding by primitive peoples. Later, the Egyptians, East Indians, Hebrews, Greeks, and Romans produced very able practitioners of gynecology, who wrote many treatises that evidence an excellent understanding of many processes and diseases in this area; and in some instances they developed instruments and surgical techniques similar to those in use today. This knowledge was forgotten during the Middle Ages and was reacquired during the Renaissance.

Modern gynecology is considered to have originated in the early 19th century through the work of two American surgeons, Ephraim McDowell (1771–1830), who developed an operation for the removal of ovarian cysts (*see* OVARY), and James Marion Sims (1813–83), who perfected a technique for the repair of vesicovaginal fistula (a connection between the bladder and vagina resulting from tearing of the intervening tissues), formerly a frequent and chronic aftermath of childbirth; see FISTULA. Subsequent advances were rapid as a result of progress in surgery, endocrinology, and control of infection.

Disorders of the Female Reproductive System. Cancer is the most serious disease of the female reproductive tract. After the breast, the most common site of cancer in the female is the uterus (q.v.). About 75 percent of uterine cancers occur in the cervix, or neck of the womb, with the remainder involving the uterine lining. For additional information see the article CANCER, subdivisions on *Uterine Cancer* and *Detection and Diagnosis.*

Benign tumors of the female reproductive tract are common. One of five women develop fibroid tumors of the uterus; such growths usually occur in women in their late twenties and early thirties, particularly among those who are childless. Many fibroid tumors cause no symptoms and are discovered only on routine gynecological examinations. Sometimes they cause abnormally heavy menstrual bleeding or bleeding between periods; see MENSTRUATION. Occasionally they cause discomfort. Rarely they may cause more severe pains, particularly from internal bleeding or degeneration of tissue. They may make it difficult for a woman to carry a pregnancy through to term. They are sometimes treated by X rays or radium; when they cause no symptoms, surgical removal is not always required. Ovarian cysts and benign ovarian tumors, some of which may attain enormous size, also are not uncommon.

The female reproductive tract is a common site of infection. Infections of the internal organs may be caused by disease-causing bacteria or by venereal disease or tuberculosis or may follow childbirth or abortion. External infections result from infestation by parasites of the genus *Trichomonas,* by fungi such as *Monilia,* or by bacteria, sometimes of gastrointestinal origin. The cervix, which often becomes lacerated in childbirth, is a frequent focus of inflammation and infection. The advent of the antibiotic (q.v.) and other drugs has enormously facilitated control of these conditions.

Displacement or dropping of the uterus also is a gynecological problem. The condition may be congenital or, more frequently, the result of stretching, weakening, and laceration of the supporting structures of the uterus during pregnancy and childbirth. It may sometimes be corrected by exercises or temporarily by the use of a pessary, which is a device, usually of hard rubber, applied internally to hold the uterus in position. Surgical repair may be necessary, however, in some cases, and in cases in which the uterus falls below its normal level in the pelvis, a condition known as prolapse, great discomfort might occur. Surgical repair of the supporting structures or removal of the uterus is the most effective treatment in such conditions.

Gynecology includes also the treatment of disorders of menstruation and menopause (q.v.). *See also* EMBRIOLOGY; FERTILIZATION; FETUS; GESTATION; REPRODUCTION. In addition the gynecologist is called upon to deal with problems of frigidity, sexual incompatibility, and sterility, which may be of psychological or physical origin. *See* STERILITY.

GYÖR (Ger. *Raab*), city in Hungary, and capital of Györ-Sopron County, at the confluence of the Rába R. with a tributary of the Danube R., about 65 miles N.W. of Budapest. Györ is a market for the cereal grains, horses, and swine of the surrounding agricultural area. It is the site of industrial establishments producing locomotives and railroad cars, farm implements, textiles, chemicals, vegetable oils, candy, and bricks. The city is a Roman Catholic bishopric, with a cathedral erected during the 12th century. Györ was established as a Magyar stronghold about 900 A.D., on the ruins of the ancient Roman outpost of Arabona. Throughout its history, Györ has served as a gateway to both east and west. Pop. (1968 est.) 80,000.

GYPSIES, wandering close-knit communal people thought to have originally emigrated from India, now dispersed throughout the world and distinguished by their general refusal to settle anywhere permanently. Gypsies usually are swarthy, with dark hair and eyes. Because they move constantly, no current precise count of their total number is available. A recent estimate has put the number between 5,000,000 and 6,000,000.

In referring to themselves, most gypsies use the word *rom* (man). They are known, however, by different names in the various countries through which they have roamed. The English name for them is an altered form of the word Egyptian. The gypsies were once believed to have come from Egypt.

Way of Life. Most gypsies travel about in small groups. Their traditional means of transportation is the horse-drawn wagon, but large covered motor vehicles are replacing the wagons in the more technologically advanced Western countries. In good weather gypsies prefer to camp in the open air rather than in their vehicles. A few gypsies still set up tents, the oldest kind of gypsy dwelling.

A Gypsy woman of North Africa prepares a meal over an open fire as her children wait in their tent-dwelling.
UPI

Gypsy groups have their own form of government. Each group is almost always headed by a man elected by the people for his capacity of judgment and leadership ability. The moral leader or guardian of the group is a wise, often aged, woman who seldom appears in public but whose opinion is always sought on family matters. Gypsy groups also have their own criminal codes and courts. The court, which consists of the elders of the group, deliberates in secret. The most severe penalties for major offenses are banishment and death, and most gypsies, if given the choice between the two punishments, would rather die than be banished from their group.

Although gypsies generally profess to believe in the religions of the various peoples among whom they move, their acceptance of any local religion rarely extends to practices which conflict with their own established beliefs and customs. Thus, while they believe in some kind of a higher being, they continue to observe their ancient forms of nature and moon worship. Death is especially important in their rituals, and they have many taboos relating to death and to the dead; see RELIGION; RITE; TABOO. For example, they never speak the name of a person after his death. Among the numerous gypsy superstitions are a belief in the efficacy of charms and curses and a belief that women should be avoided at certain times. Customs vary from group to group. Among some gypsy groups women bear their children outdoors. Other groups permit near relatives to marry. An almost universal custom among them is their habit of wearing cast-off, ragged garments. Many gypsies also share the same preferences for foods and the same eating habits; hedgehog is considered a special delicacy. They cook most of their meals over an open fire and eat outdoors.

Gypsy men usually work as blacksmiths, coppersmiths, horse traders, and musicians. Increased mechanization, however, is rapidly eliminating the need for such work. Many of the women are still fortune-tellers or make baskets, combs, and mats. Both sexes operate booths at carnivals and fairs. A few gypsy bands support themselves simply by begging necessities from local people who, often poor themselves but fearful of being cursed by the gypsies, give them whatever they can afford.

Language. Gypsy groups speak numerous dialects of Romany, a language which belongs to the Indic branch of the Indo-European languages (q.v.). Most of these dialects contain words adopted from the languages of countries through which the gypsies have wandered, but all present-day Romany dialects preserve to some degree the sound system and grammar of their parent language. Thus, for example, while one group of gypsies might speak a dialect combining some Romany with many words borrowed from Armenian, Bulgarian, English, French, German, Greek, and Persian, another group might speak a relatively pure Romany.

Music and Folklore. Gypsy musicians contributed significantly to the central European musical tradition, particularly from the 15th to the 18th century by developing a special style of instrumental dance music. Gypsy bands, usually led by a violinist, perform compositions which consist mainly of improvised variations on a melody. This musical style allows the band members great freedom in playing any tune, in much the same manner as a jazz band; see JAZZ; MUSIC.

Gypsies have no significant written literature, principally because they never used an alphabet of their own to record their steadily changing language. They do possess, however, a vast body of folk tales consisting of a mixture of elements drawn from the folklore of numerous Asian and European regions through which they have traveled.

History. Why and when the gypsies left their place of origin are not known exactly. They reached Persia about the beginning of the 10th century. There they split into a number of groups, some wandering into Syria, Egypt, and northern Africa, and some wandering into southern and eastern Europe. Groups of gypsies arrived in central and continental western Europe before the middle of the 14th century. They appeared in northern Europe and Russia early in the 16th century.

Gypsies have experienced persecution all over Europe wherever they have wandered, primarily because of their strangeness and different customs. In early times, gypsies were flogged, imprisoned, and executed for crimes such as cannibalism and witchcraft. They were banished from countries in which they refused to settle permanently or to do lawful work; in others they were made to pay a tax for protection.

In recent times, except for the mass extermination of European gypsies in concentration camps by the Germans during World War II, gypsies have not been flagrantly persecuted. Instead, many European countries, and some in the Western Hemisphere, have tried to change the gypsies' way of life by requiring them, among other things, to adopt modern sanitary practices, and to send their children to school. Partly as a result of these measures, some gypsies have taken permanent residences. Most gypsies, however, still cling to their itinerant ways.

GYPSOPHILA. See BABY'S-BREATH.

GYPSUM, common mineral consisting of hydrated calcium sulfate, $CaSO_4 \cdot 2H_2O$. It is a widely distributed form of sedimentary rock, formed by the precipitation of calcium sulfate from sea water, and is frequently associated with other saline deposits, such as halite and anhydrite, as well as with limestone and shale; see SEDIMENTARY ROCKS. Gypsum is produced in volcanic regions by the action of sulfuric acid on calcium-containing minerals, and it is also found in most clays as a product of the action of sulfuric acid on limestone. It occurs in all parts of the world; some of the best workable deposits are in France, Switzerland, and Mexico, and in California, Ohio, Michigan, and Utah in the United States. Alabaster, selenite (qq.v.), and satin spar are varieties of gypsum.

Artificial gypsum is obtained as a by-product in an old method for the manufacture of phosphoric acid. Phosphate rock, the essential constituent of which is tricalcium phosphate, is treated with sulfuric acid, producing phosphoric acid and gypsum. The gypsum is compacted into blocks and used for construction of nonsupporting walls in buildings. By properly controlling the concentration and temperature of sulfuric acid added to phosphate rock, a mixture of monocalcium phosphate, dicalcium phosphate, and gypsum may be obtained. This mixture is a valuable fertilizer, superphosphate.

Gypsum crystallizes in the monoclinic system in white or colorless crystals, massive or foliated in formation. Many specimens of gypsum are colored green, yellow, or black by impurities. It is soft enough to scratch with a fingernail (hardness ranges from 1.5 to 2), and has a specific gravity of 2.3. When heated to 128° C. (262.4° F.), gypsum loses part of its water of hydration and is converted into plaster of Paris, $CaSO_4 \cdot \frac{1}{2}H_2O$. Finely ground plaster of Paris, when moistened with water, sets in a short time into a hard mass of gypsum, the rehydrated crystals forming and interlocking in such a way that there is expansion in volume.

Because of its property of swelling and filling all interstices upon drying, plaster of Paris is used extensively in making casts for statuary, ceramics, dental plates, fine metal parts for preci-

GYPSY MOTH

sion instruments, and surgical splints. Uncalcined gypsum is used as a fertilizer in the form of land plaster for arid, alkaline soil. It is also used as a bed for polishing plate glass and as a basis for paint pigments. Large amounts of gypsum are used as a retarder in Portland cement (q.v.).

GYPSY MOTH, large Old World moth, *Porthetria dispar*, of the family Liparidae, accidentally introduced about 1868 into New England, where the ravenous, orchard-destroying larvae became a serious economic menace. Initially confined to the New England area, the gypsy moth recently invaded other northeastern States. The spread of the insect is attributed to hurricanes which struck the Atlantic seaboard in the 1950's. It is believed that the heavy winds carried debris laden with gypsy-moth eggs southward and westward of their original range.

The gypsy moth is closely related to the browntail moth and the tussock moth, both of which are similarly destructive. The adult female gypsy moth is white with dark wing markings. The wing span is about 2½ in. The female has a heavy body and rarely flies, despite well-developed wings. Throughout her adult life-span, the female gypsy moth remains near the pupal shell from which she emerged. The adult male is olive brown with dark wing markings, and, though a powerful flier, has much smaller wings than the female.

The yellow eggs, which measure a twentieth of an inch in diameter, are deposited in masses numbering from less than 200 to more than 1000, and are covered with buff-colored scales from the abdomen of the adult female. The larvae occasionally appear within a few weeks, but more often they hatch in the following spring. The larvae are yellow, with long hairs, and have four longitudinal rows of colored tubercles. One tubercle from each row appears on each of the larval segments, those on the anterior segments being blue and those behind being red. The caterpillars devour the foliage of numerous trees, especially of oaks and birches.

Because repeated defoliation kills the trees, State authorities in infested areas have instituted intensive control measures. The Department of Agriculture directs its efforts toward preventing the spread of the gypsy moth into other areas. See ENTOMOLOGY, ECONOMIC.

GYRFALCON *or* **GERFALCON.** See FALCON.

GYROCOMPASS. See COMPASS; GYROSCOPE: *Applications of the Gyroscope*; NAVIGATION: *Navigation Instruments.*

GYROSCOPE, any rotating body that exhibits two fundamental properties: gyroscopic inertia, or rigidity in space, and precession, the tilting of the axis at right angles to any force tending to alter the plane of rotation. These properties actually are inherent in all rotating bodies, including the earth itself. The term gyroscope is commonly applied to spherical, wheel-shaped, or disk-shaped bodies that are universally mounted so that they are free to rotate in any direction. Such bodies can be used to demonstrate these properties or to serve the important purpose of enabling man to sense his movements in space. A gyroscope that is constrained from moving around one axis other than the axis of rotation is sometimes referred to as a gyrostat. Actually, in nearly all of its practical applications, the gyroscope is constrained or controlled in this way, and it is customary to add the prefix gyro to the name of the particular application, as, for instance, gyrocompass, gyrostabilizer, gyropilot, and gyrosyn compass.

Gyroscopic Inertia. The rigidity in space of a gyroscope is a consequence of Newton's first law of motion (*see* NEWTON'S LAWS OF MOTION), which states that a body tends to continue in its state of rest or uniform motion unless subject to outside forces. Thus, the wheel of a gyroscope, when started spinning, tends to continue to ro-

The voracious gypsy moth causes much damage to trees as it consumes the leaves.   UPI

GYROSCOPE

Gyroscopic devices. Directional gyroscopes, used to provide flight heading information to aircraft pilots, undergo final inspection in the manufacturing process.
Sperry Rand Corp.

tate in the same plane about the same axis in space. An example of this tendency is a spinning top, which has freedom about two axes in addition to the spinning axis. Another example is a rifle bullet which, because it spins or revolves in flight, exhibits gyroscopic inertia, tending to maintain a straighter line of flight than it would if not rotating. Rigidity in space can best be demonstrated, however, by means of a model gyroscope consisting of a flywheel supported in rings in such a way that the axle of the flywheel can assume any angle in space. When the flywheel is spinning, the model can be moved about, tipped, or turned at the will of the demonstrator; but the flywheel will maintain its original plane of rotation as long as it continues to spin with sufficient velocity to overcome the friction between itself and its supporting bearings.

Gyroscopes constitute an important part of automatic-navigation or inertial-guidance systems in aircraft, spacecraft, guided missiles, rockets, and ships and submarines; *see* Guided Missiles; Rocket; Submarine. In these systems, inertial-guidance instruments comprise gyroscopes and accelerometers that continuously calculate exact speed and direction of the craft in motion. These signals are fed into a computer, which records and compensates for any aberration in the predetermined course. See *Automatic Pilot,* below.

Precession. When a force applied to a gyroscope tends to change the direction of the axis of rotation, the axis will move in a direction at right angles to the direction in which the force is applied. This motion is the resultant of the force produced by the angular momentum of the rotating body and the applied force. A simple example of precession can be seen in the rolling hoop: to cause the hoop to turn a corner, guiding pressure is not applied to the front or rear of the hoop as might be expected, but against the top. This pressure, although applied about a horizontal axis, does not cause the hoop to fall over, but causes it to precess about the vertical axis at right angles to the applied pressure, with the result that it turns and proceeds in a new direction.

Applications of the Gyroscope. By utilizing the characteristic of gyroscopic inertia and applying the force of gravity to cause precession, the gyroscope can be made use of as a directional indicator or compass. Briefly, if we consider a gyroscope as mounted at the equator of the earth, with its spinning axis lying in the east-west plane, the gyro will continue to point along this line as the earth rotates, because of

A miniature gyroscope designed to provide the precise responses required in spacecraft guidance and control systems.
Sperry Rand Corp.

GYROSCOPE

"rigidity in space". For the same reason, the east end will rise (in relation to the earth) although it continues to point the same way in space. By attaching a tube partially filled with mercury to the frame of the gyro assembly in such a way that the tube tilts as the gyro axle tilts, we can take advantage of the effect of gravity about the horizontal axis of the gyro. In other words, the weight of the mercury on the west or low side applies a force about the horizontal axis of the gyro. The gyro resists this force and precesses about the vertical axis toward the meridian. In the gyrocompass the controlling forces are applied automatically in just the right direction and proportion to cause the gyro axle to seek and hold the true meridian, that is, to point north and south.

Gyrocompasses are used in naval vessels and merchant fleets all over the world. They are free from the vagaries of the magnetic compass; they indicate true, geographic north rather than magnetic north, and they have sufficient directive force to make practicable the operation of accessory equipment such as course recorders, gyropilots, and repeater compasses. The marine gyropilot has no gyroscope, but picks up electrically any divergence from the set course reference supplied by the gyrocompass; these signals are amplified and applied to the steering engine of the ship to cause the rudder to return the ship to its proper course. See COMPASS: *Gyrocompass.*

Automatic Pilot. The automatic pilot, or autopilot, detects variations from the selected flight plan of an airplane and supplies corrective signals to the ailerons, elevator, and rudder; *see* AIRPLANE: *Flight Control.* A vertical gyroscope detects changes in pitch or roll, and a directional gyroscope detects changes in heading. The altitude is sensed by a barometric sensor. The speed with which these changes occur on each axis is determined by rate gyroscopes or accelerometers. This combination of displacement (how much) and rate (how fast) provides a very precise indication of the response needed. The gyroscopes transmit electrical signals to an electronic computer, which combines and amplifies them. The computer then transmits corrective signals to servomotors attached to the control surfaces of the aircraft, which move to produce the desired response; *see* SERVOMECHANISM. An autopilot controller attached to the computer enables the pilot manually to insert maneuvers, such as turns, climbs, and dives, which require a coordinated movement of the control surfaces. At the discretion of the pilot, an assortment of navigation and radio aids can be coupled to the autopilot for automatic navigation. These include inertial navigation systems, Doppler-radar-navigation systems, and radio navigation beacons. Beams used in instrument-landing-systems (I.L.S.), installed at airport runways, can also be coupled to the autopilot. In poor visibility, the I.L.S. used with the autopilot directs the aircraft automatically to the desired glide path and aligns it with the runway. See NAVIGATION: *Electronic Navigation.*

Flight instruments such as the artificial horizon, the directional gyro, the gyrosyn compass, and the turn-and-bank indicator employ single gyroscopes. The artificial horizon spins with its axis vertical and supplies the pilot with a pitch-and-bank reference in the form of a gyro-actuated horizon bar observed in relation to a miniature airplane on the dial of the instrument. The directional gyro spins about a horizontal axis. This is one of the few gyroscopic instruments that functions on the principle of rigidity in space alone, that is, like a free, unconstrained gyroscope. For this reason it is subject to wander or drift, and must be checked, and reset if necessary, at frequent intervals. The gyrosyn compass, unlike the directional gyro, is north seeking. It is in effect a gyro-stabilized magnetic compass. The turn-and-bank indicator is a primary flight instrument used in every airplane. This instrument employs the precessional forces of the gyroscope to actuate an indicator that shows the pilot his rate of turn.

During World War II, a successful gunsight was developed for antiaircraft guns in naval vessels. Two gyroscopes are used, one for tracking in azimuth, the other for elevation. As the gun pointer swings his gun to keep the target in the sight, the gyros precess and control the sighting mechanism in such a way that the gun is automatically set ahead with the proper amount of lead for the projectile to intercept the target.

A supersensitive gyroscope, many times more accurate than conventional instruments, was developed in the mid-1950's for use in automatic flight of supersonic aircraft and guided missiles; it is capable of detecting very slow motion through angles as small as $.00003°$.

H, eighth letter in the English and Latin alphabets. Originally derived from the Semitic ⌷, *cheth,* which was adopted into the Pheonician alphabet as ⌷, the letter was introduced into Greek with the name *hēta* and the sound of an aspirate (*see* PHONETICS). It disappeared later in the Greek of Asia Minor, leaving the name *ēta.* In the later Semitic, Western Greek, and Latin alphabets it continued to represent an aspirate, as it does usually in modern English. In vernacular Latin the aspiration was dropped, probably at an early date. As a result, h is normally silent in the Romance languages (q.v.), as it is in many English words, such as honor. It is silent also in several English dialects and is pronounced erroneously or dropped in the Cockney dialect of London. The letter h combines into digraphs with other consonants to form various consonant sounds, such as *gh* in lau*gh, ph* in telegra*ph, rh* as in *rh*yme, the two *th* sounds in *th*en and *th*in, *sh* in *sh*ould, soft *ch* as in *ch*ill, hard *ch* in *ch*orus, and *wh* in *wh*ere.

In music, German notation employs H as a symbol for B natural. This usage dates back to a time when a rounded capital B was used to indicate B flat and a square B, ⌷, to indicate B natural. The German use of H is a corruption of the latter form.

In medieval Latin, H was employed as the symbol for 200 in the Roman numeral system.

The letter, usually in the form of a qualifying noun, also denotes an object having the shape of a capital H, as in H beam.

As an abbreviation, H is used to denote, in chemistry, the element hydrogen; in physics, the henry, the magnetic unit of flux intensity; in spectroscopy, a line in the spectrum produced by calcium; and in terrestrial magnetism, the horizontal component of the earth's magnetism. The lowercase h is used in the metric system as an abbreviation for hecto- (hundred), and it also stands for hour, height, and hardening. The lowercase italicized form is the symbol for altitude and for Planck's constant (q.v.) in physics. For H-hour, *see* D-DAY. M.P.

HAAKON, name of seven kings of Norway, the most important of which include the following. *See also* NORWAY: *History.*

Haakon I, called HAAKON THE GOOD (914?–61), King (935–61), the illegitimate son of King Harold I (*see under* HAROLD). Haakon, who was raised in the Christian religion by Athelstan (q.v.), King of England, dethroned his half brother Eric Bloodaxe (d. 954) with the help of Athelstan. Haakon introduced Christianity into Norway, alienating many of his countrymen. He was succeeded by his nephew Harold II.

Haakon III Sverresson (d. 1204), King (1202–04), the son of King Sverre (1152–1202). During his brief reign he solved the inherited issue of investiture (q.v.) of the clergy and recalled the self-exiled bishops to Norway. He was succeeded by his cousin Inge II (1204–63).

Haakon IV Haakonsson, called HAAKON THE OLD (1204–63), King (1217–63), the illegitimate son of King Haakon III. During his reign he won for Norway Iceland and Greenland (1262) and part of Scotland (1263). He was succeeded by his son Magnus VI.

Haakon VII (1872–1957), King (1905–57), the second son of Frederick VIII, King of Denmark (*see under* FREDERICK), born Carl in Charlottenlund, Denmark. He was chosen king of Norway by the Storting, or parliament, a choice reaffirmed by a plebiscite. The Norwegian crown had become vacant when the union between Norway and Sweden was dissolved; the Swedish throne was retained by Oscar II (q.v.), King of Sweden. During World War II, after the Germans invaded Norway in 1940, Haakon led the resistance for two months, then went to Great Britain to head the Norwegian government-in-exile. He returned to Norway in 1945. He was succeeded by his son Olaf V (*see under* OLAF).

115

HAARLEM

HAARLEM, formerly HARLEM, city in the Netherlands, and capital of North Holland Province, on the Spaarne R. near the North Sea, 12 miles w. of Amsterdam. The chief industries in Haarlem are printing and typecasting, brewing, bleaching, and dyeing, and the manufacture of chocolates, cotton goods, paint, and railway cars. In addition, Haarlem is the center of a prosperous trade in bulbs, notably tulip and hyacinth. A notable building in the city is Saint Bavo's Church, or the Groote Kerk, built in the 15th century, and containing an organ with 5000 pipes, one of the largest instruments of its kind in the world. In front of the church stands a statue of Laurens Janszoon Coster (fl. 1440), to whom the Dutch ascribe the invention of printing. The town hall (13th century), formerly the residence of the counts of Holland, contains canvases by the celebrated Dutch painter Frans Hals (q.v.) and a valuable collection of early printed works. Other buildings of note are the Frans Hals Museum, the Dutch Society of Sciences, and the Pavilion (1788), a château in Italian style containing an industrial art museum.

Haarlem took a prominent part in the revolt of the Netherlands against Spanish rule. In 1572 the city was besieged by a Spanish army of 30,000 men, and after a resistance of seven months, was compelled to capitulate. Four years later, William I (q.v.), known as William the Silent, Prince of Orange, delivered Haarlem from Spain and incorporated the city into the United Netherlands; see NETHERLANDS, THE: *History*. The New York City section of Harlem (q.v.) was named after Haarlem by early Dutch settlers. Pop. (1968) 172,941.

HABAKKUK, book of the Old Testament (*see* BIBLE), in the King James Version, HABAKKUK. In some English versions of the Bible used by Roman Catholics it is entitled Habacuc. It is one of the twelve prophetic books of the Old Testament known, primarily because they are all short, as the Minor Prophets (see BIBLE, CANON OF THE). The book of Habakkuk consists of three chapters. The first and second chapters are considered by most scholars to be the work of the Hebrew prophet Habakkuk (q.v.). The third chapter is thought by many scholars to be the work of another, probably later, unknown author, a theory strongly supported by the total

The Great Market in Haarlem. Netherlands Information Service

omission of or reference to this chapter in the Dead Sea Scroll of the Habakkuk Commentary (see DEAD SEA SCROLLS).

The book divides into three distinct sections. The first section (1–2:5) may be read as a dialogue between Habakkuk and God. Habakkuk laments, protests, and questions the suffering of the righteous and the flourishing of the wicked (1:1–4, 12–17, 2:1). God declares that He is raising up a nation, which shall be all-conquering and violent (1:5–11). God reveals, however, that the defeat of that nation "will surely come" (2:3), for "his soul which is lifted up is not upright in him" (2:4). God concludes His revelation by asserting that "the just shall live by his faith" (2:4), a key passage for its role in later Protestant theology, and recalled in the New Testament in Rom. 1:17, Gal. 3:11, and Heb. 10:38; see FAITH. The second section (2:6–20) consists of five denunciations (each one beginning "Woe to" or "Woe unto") directed against an unspecified people. This people, or nation, despoils others, seeks gain for itself in evil ways, builds towns and cities with the blood of the vanquished, degrades neighboring peoples shamelessly, and speaks to wood and stone idols that are dumb. The Chaldeans, mentioned earlier in the book (1:6), usually are taken to be this oppressive nation (see BABYLONIA). The third section (chapter 3), "A Prayer of Habakkuk" (3:1), is a poem descriptive of the triumphant manifestation of God, Who is the joy and salvation of His "anointed" (3:13).

The historical situation reflected in the book of Habakkuk is not easy to determine. If the oppressor nation was the Chaldeans, the words of Habakkuk may reflect events either several years before or immediately after the Chaldeans seized Jerusalem in 597 B.C. (see ISRAEL, KINGDOM OF). The underlying religious message of Habakkuk is that evils cannot endure; each has its appointed time, but ultimately righteousness always prevails.

HABAKKUK (fl. 7th cent. B.C.), eighth of the twelve minor Prophets and author of the first two chapters of the Old Testament book which bears his name; see book of HABAKKUK. Because he is mentioned nowhere in the Old Testament except in the book of Habakkuk, virtually nothing is known about his life. Habakkuk is believed to have lived during the latter part of the 7th century B.C. and to have appeared as a prophet of the tribe of Judah (q.v.), announcing the divine punishment that was to come upon the Israelite nation at the hands of the Babylonians (see BABYLONIA: *History*). His name means "embrace" in Hebrew.

HABANA, LA. See HAVANA.

HABEAS CORPUS (Lat., "[that] you have the body"), in United States and English law, a writ, or order, issued by a court to a person having custody of another, commanding him to produce the detained person in order to determine the legality of the detention. The writ of habeas corpus is of English origin; its original purpose was to liberate illegally detained persons, and it is still a protection against arbitrary imprisonment. The earliest use of the writ as a constitutional remedy against the tyranny of the crown took place in the latter part of the 16th century, when it was applied in behalf of persons committed to prison by the privy council.

Many ways of avoiding the effectiveness of the writ were subsequently developed. In a case in 1627 the judges decided that a sufficient answer to a writ of habeas corpus was that the prisoner was detained by warrant of the privy council. In 1641 Parliament, by legislation that abolished the Star Chamber (see STAR CHAMBER, COURT OF), endeavored to increase the effectiveness of the writ. This law provided that persons who were imprisoned by a court exercising jurisdiction similar to the Star Chamber, or by command of the king or of the privy council, should be granted a writ of habeas corpus without delay; and that the court was to determine within three days after the return of the writ the legality of such imprisonment. The subsequent refusal of judges to issue writs of habeas corpus during vacation periods resulted in the passage by Parliament of the Habeas Corpus Act of 1679. That statute imposed severe penalties on any judge who refused without good cause to issue the writ, and upon any officer or other person who failed to comply with it. After that date the authority of the court was paramount to any order of the sovereign, and the writ became a powerful weapon for the protection of the liberty of the king's subjects. The statute, however, dealt only with imprisonment for criminal offenses, and it was not until 1816 that its benefits were extended to persons detained for other reasons.

Protection against arbitrary imprisonment by the right of habeas corpus is not found in continental Europe. In the democratic countries of Western Europe, however, the codes of criminal procedure require that an arrested person be informed with reasonable promptness of the charges against him and be allowed to seek legal counsel. On the other hand, in many other countries, persons are subjected at times to lengthy periods of imprisonment without being informed of the charges. The writ of habeas cor-

HABEAS CORPUS

pus has been adopted in many Latin-American countries, either by constitutional provision or statutory enactment, but has frequently been nullified in practice during times of political or social upheaval.

United States Law. The use of habeas corpus is established by both Federal and State constitutions. Article I, Section 9 of the Constitution of the United States (q.v.) provides that the privilege of the writ of habeas corpus shall not be suspended except in cases of rebellion or invasion, when the public safety may require it. The constitutions of most States contain similar provisions, and in some States suspension of the writ is forbidden in any case. Massachusetts suspended the privilege of the writ from November, 1786, to July, 1787, on the occasion of Shays' Rebellion (q.v.). The outstanding instance in the U.S. of the suspension of the right of habeas corpus occurred in 1861 during the American Civil War, when President Abraham Lincoln (q.v.) suspended it by Presidential proclamation. In 1863 Congress explicitly empowered Lincoln to suspend the privilege of the writ during the war. In recent years the courts in several States have suspended the privilege when State executives have declared martial law during strikes. See MARTIAL LAW.

In the U.S. the writ was originally limited to cases of illegal imprisonment, but its use was subsequently extended, and it is now also applicable to controversies in divorce and adoption proceedings involving the custody of infants. The basis for such applications of the writ is the assumption that the State has the right, paramount to any parental or other claims, to dispose of children as their best interests require.

Both Federal and State courts issue writs of habeas corpus. Federal courts, however, can issue such writs only under given conditions, as when a prisoner is detained by order of the Federal government or has been committed for trial before a Federal court. Federal courts can also issue writs of habeas corpus when a charge against a prisoner concerns an act done in pursuance of a Federal law or order of a Federal court, or when his detention is alleged to be in violation of the Federal Constitution or of a law or treaty of the U.S. The jurisdiction of the Federal courts in this regard extends to a foreigner, if he has acted under the authority of his own government, so that his guilt or liability must be determined by international law. The State courts may issue the writ in all cases which do not fall exclusively under the jurisdiction of the Federal courts.

HABER, Fritz (1868–1934), German chemist, born in Breslau (now Wrocław, Poland) and educated at the Technische Hochschule, Berlin. After teaching chemistry in Karlsruhe, he was appointed professor of physical chemistry at the University of Berlin in 1911. Subsequently he became director of the Kaiser Wilhelm Institute for Physical Chemistry in Berlin. During World War I Haber was chief of the German chemical warfare service and he directed the chlorine gas attack at the second Battle of Ypres (q.v.). Because of the anti-Semitic policies then prevailing in Germany, Haber resigned his post and went to Switzerland, where he died the following year.

Haber's greatest achievement was his discovery in 1913 of a process for synthesizing ammonia by the direct combination of nitrogen and hydrogen; see NITROGEN FIXATION. The method was adapted to commercial use in the 1930's by German chemist Karl Bosch (q.v.). The Haber–Bosch process is used in the manufacture of explosives and in the production of fertilizers. Haber also made fundamental contributions to the field of electrochemistry (q.v.). He was awarded the 1918 Nobel Prize in chemistry.

HABIMAH, former name of a Hebrew-language theatrical company, resident in Israel. Organized in Moscow in 1917 during the Russian Revolution (q.v.) by members of the Moscow Art Theater, the Habimah was the first Hebrew-language theater. The troupe left the U.S.S.R. in 1926 on an international tour that included the United States and ended in Palestine. Since 1929 the Habimah has been established in Tel Aviv (now Tel Aviv-Jaffa). In 1948 the company made another international tour, appearing in New York City in its traditional production of *The Dybbuk*, a Hebrew translation by the Russian-born Hebrew poet Chaim Nachman Bialik (q.v.) of a Yiddish folk play by S. Ansky (1863–1920). The company changed its name in 1958 to Israel National Theater. See DRAMA: *National Drama: Other National Drama*; YIDDISH LITERATURE.

HABIT, in psychology, fixed tendency acquired by an organism during its lifetime. Formerly, academic and philosophical psychologists drew a broad distinction between habit, which is acquired after birth, and instinct and reflex (qq.v.), which are congenital. With the development of the dynamic point of view in psychology and the dramatic presentation of the conditioned-reflex mechanisms by the Russian physiologist Ivan Petrovich Pavlov (q.v.) in the early part of the 20th century, psychologists have tended to limit use of the term "habit", replacing it in specific applications by more exact terminology. In describing what they once termed "the accident habit", for example, they have come to speak of accident proneness. Medical psychologists have tended to replace the term "habit spasm," an involuntary twitching of a part of the body, by the term "tic". Such phenomena as tics and stuttering (see STAMMERING), sometimes described as habits, are now regarded as neuroses or as symptoms of neuroses. See MENTAL DISORDERS: *Neuroses*.

HABSBURG. See HAPSBURG.

HACHIOJI, city of Japan, in Tokyo Prefecture, on central Honshu Island, 23 miles w. of Tokyo. A rail and trade center for the surrounding agricultural area, Hachioji is also an important center of the silk industry. Pop. (1965) 208,000.

HACKENSACK, city in New Jersey, and county seat of Bergen Co., on the w. bank of the Hackensack R., 12 miles N. of Jersey City. Hackensack has railroad service and maintains a municipal airport. Although the city is principally a residential community, it is the site of factories manufacturing chemicals, paperboard, metal products, glass, and clothing. Hackensack was first settled by the Dutch about 1640, and Huguenots (q.v.) settled there in 1678. It was occupied alternately by the British and Americans during the American Revolution. Hackensack was incorporated as a village in 1868 and as a city in 1921. Pop. (1960) 30,521; (1970) 35,911.

HACKMATACK. See LARCH.

HADASSAH, THE WOMEN'S ZIONIST ORGANIZATION OF AMERICA, organization founded in 1912 by Henrietta Szold (q.v.), American social worker and Zionist leader; see ZIONISM. It supports a comprehensive program of medical care and research, preventive medicine, and health education, in Israel, based at the Hadassah-Hebrew University Medical Center in Jerusalem. Hadassah began sponsoring medical services in Palestine in 1913, and the first of its several hospitals was opened in Jerusalem in 1918. In 1939 a comprehensive medical center, the first in Palestine, was opened on Mt. Scopus, where it operated until 1948 when hostilities forced transfer of operations to scattered sites in Israel. The current medical center was opened in 1961.

Hadassah Israel Education Services maintains two high schools and a two-year community college, the first such educational institution in Israel. Hadassah is also the United States agency for Youth Aliyah, a child-welfare movement, which since 1934 has brought more than 135,000 Jewish children from approximately eighty countries to live and study in Israel.

In the U.S. Hadassah conducts a community action program whereby members volunteer their services in their own communities to schools, homes for the elderly, health clinics, and other local agencies. Hadassah also sponsors programs of religious and general education in Jewish life. Its membership totals about 320,000 organized in 1300 chapters and groups on the mainland and in Hawaii and Puerto Rico, with national headquarters in New York City.

HADDINGTON. See EAST LOTHIAN.

HADDOCK, marine fish, *Melanogrammus aeglifinus*, of the Cod family Gadidae, differing from the cod in its smaller mouth, longer anterior dorsal fin, and in the black line which runs along its side. It is about 2 ft. long and has a

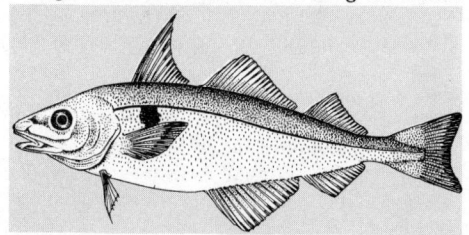

Haddock, Melanogrammus aeglifinus

brown back and silvery underside; a black spot is located on each side, behind the gills. It is abundant in the North Atlantic Ocean from Iceland to Cape Hatteras. The haddock is an important food fish; it is frequently sold smoked, when it is known as finnan haddie, or dried.

HADEN, Sir Francis Seymour (1818–1910), British etcher and surgeon, born in London, England, and educated at the universities of London, Paris, and Grenoble. Although he was a successful surgeon, Haden is best known as an artist. His most important works are his etchings, chiefly landscapes, notable for their rich patterns of light and shade. He was greatly influenced by the etchings of the Dutch painter Rembrandt (q.v.) and did much to familiarize the public with Rembrandt's art in published works. Haden founded the Royal Society of Painter-Etchers and Engravers in 1880. The chief collections of his etchings are in the British Museum, London, and in the New York City Public Library. He was knighted in 1894.

HADES, in Greek mythology, god of the dead. He was the son of the Titans Cronus and Rhea, and the brother of Zeus and Poseidon (qq.v.). When the three brothers divided up the universe after they had deposed their father Cronus, Hades was awarded the underworld. There, with his queen Persephone (q.v.) whom he had abducted from the world above, he ruled the kingdom of the dead. Although he was a grim and pitiless god, unappeased by either prayer or sacrifice, he was not evil. In fact, he was known also as Pluto (q.v.), lord of riches, since both crops and precious metals were believed to come from his kingdom below ground.

The underworld itself was often called Hades. It was divided into two regions: Erebus, where the dead pass as soon as they die, and Tartarus (q.v.), the deeper region, where the Titans had been imprisoned. It was a dim and unhappy place, inhabited by vague forms and shadows, and guarded by the three-headed, dragon-tailed dog, Cerebus (q.v.). Sinister rivers separated the underworld from the world above, and the aged boatman Charon (q.v.) ferried the souls of the dead across these waters. Somewhere in the darkness of the underworld Hades' palace was located. It was represented as a many-gated, dark and gloomy place, thronged with guests, and set in the midst of shadowy fields and an apparition-haunted landscape. In later legends, the underworld is described as the place where the good are rewarded and the wicked punished.

HADFIELD, Sir Robert Abbott (1858–1940), British metallurgist, born near Sheffield, England, and educated at Sheffield Collegiate School. The son of a steel manufacturer, Hadfield studied chemistry and metallurgy in college and later developed many important metallurgical processes. He is best known for his invention in 1882 of a method for manufacturing manganese steel, the first steel alloy to be both hard and ductile. He was knighted in 1908, became a fellow of the Royal Society in 1909, and was created a baronet in 1917. One of his books, *Metallurgy and Its Influence on Modern Progress* (1926), is a standard reference work.

HADHRAMAUT or **HADRAMAUT,** coastal district forming most of the E. half of the Peoples Democratic Republic of Yemen, extending about 400 mi. along the Gulf of Aden to Muscat and Oman on the E. In addition to the coastal plain, about 30 mi. wide, Hadhramaut contains an interior plateau. Although Hadhramaut is for the most part barren, a number of valleys yield a luxuriant vegetation. The main crops are dates, millet, wheat, coffee, and tobacco. Mukalla is the largest town. Exports include tobacco, coffee, and salt; the chief imports are cotton goods, coal, fuel oil, and foodstuffs. Archeological researches disclose that Hadhramaut, called Hazarmaveth in the Bible, was the site of a highly developed civilization in ancient times. Between 1934 and 1967, Hadhramaut successively formed part of the Aden Protectorate and the Federation of South Arabia, under the control of Great Britain. Area, about 60,000 sq.mi. Pop. (est.) 150,000.

HADLEY, Arthur Twining (1856–1930), American economist and educator, born in New Haven, Conn., and educated at Yale University and the University of Berlin. He taught at Yale, starting as a tutor in 1879 and becoming a professor of political science in 1886. He was commissioner of labor statistics for the State of Connecticut between 1885 and 1887. He published *Railroad Transportation, Its History and Its Laws* (1885), which established his reputation as an economist and an expert on railroads. His most important work was *Economics: an Account of the Relations between Private Property and Public Welfare* (1896), in which he argued that public morality rather than governmental control is needed to solve economic problems. From 1899 to 1921 Hadley was president of Yale. During his term of office the university prospered and many new buildings were dedicated. After his retirement from Yale, Hadley became director of a number of railroads.

HADLEY, Henry Kimball (1871–1937), American composer and conductor, born in Somerville, Mass. He received his early musical training from his father and later entered the New England Conservatory, at which he studied with the American composer George Whitefield Chadwick (1854–1931). At the age of twenty-two Hadley toured the United States as conductor of the Schirmer-Mapleson Opera Company. In 1909, after several years spent studying and composing in Europe, he became the conductor of the Seattle Symphony Orchestra. From 1911 to 1916 he conducted the San Francisco Symphony Orchestra. He was appointed associate conductor of the New York Philharmonic-Symphony Society in 1920 and formed the Manhattan Symphony Orchestra in 1929. Among his best-known works are an orchestral rhapsody, *The Culprit Fay* (1909); the symphony *The Four Seasons* (1901); and the opera *Cleopatra's Night* (1918), first produced by the Metropolitan Opera Company, New York City, in 1920.

HADRIAN, in full PUBLIUS AELIUS HADRIANUS (76–138 A.D.), Emperor of Rome, born in Italica near Seville, Spain, and educated at Rome. Under his uncle, the emperor Trajan (q.v.), Hadrian filled high offices of state. When Trajan died Hadrian was proclaimed emperor by the army, and his appointment was ratified by the Roman senate. The Roman Empire at the time was in an extremely critical state as a result of barbarian invasions and the revolts of subject peoples. Hadrian, realizing the necessity of consolidation, resolved to limit the boundaries of the Roman Empire and established the series of defensive fortifications (*limites*) that historically marked the end of Roman territorial expansion. The emperor strengthened his position at Rome by liberality toward the people, by generous support of poor children, and by a considerate attitude toward the senate. During his first year in office, Hadrian traveled to the provinces of Asia Minor. Subsequently, in two extended tours, he visited nearly every Roman province, traveling as far north as Britannia and as far east as Syria. Everywhere he went, he set local political, military, and economic affairs in order and consolidated loyalty to Rome. In 128 A.D., he assumed the title *pater patriae* ("father of the country"). In 134–35 he revisited Judea to put down an insurrection of the Jewish revolutionary leader Simon Bar Cocheba (q.v.). Hadrian spent the last years of his life partly at Rome and partly at Tibur, the site of his palatial villa. He was followed as emperor by his appointed successor Titus Aurelius Fulvus Boionius Arrius who ruled as Antoninus Pius (q.v.).

HADRIAN'S WALL, ancient Roman stone and masonry wall, 74 mi. long, about 20 ft. high, and about 8 ft. thick, traversing Great Britain from Solway Firth to the estuary of the Tyne R. Constructed about 121–26 A.D. by order of Hadrian (q.v.), Emperor of Rome, to protect the northern boundary of Roman Britain against the invasions of hostile tribes, the wall linked a series of heavily garrisoned forts and fortified sentry posts. It served also to demarcate the frontier of Roman civil jursidiction. A military road ran along the south side of the fortifications. A few sections of the wall are still standing.

HADROSAURUS, genus of dinosaurs in the order Ornithischia, found fossil in Cretaceous rocks of the Laramie Epoch in Wyoming. These large dinosaurs, which reached 35 ft. in length, were characterized by a flattened bill, resembling that of a duck, with which they grasped the marsh grass and other vegetation comprising their food. The bill, unlike that of a duck, contained many small teeth. Their hides were thick, but not covered by armor. Their heads were large, and their tails were thick and heavy. The hadrosaurs moved about swampy pools on their thick, three-toed hind limbs; their forelimbs, which were five-toed, were small and weak.

HAECKEL, Ernst Heinrich (1834–1919), German biologist and philosopher, born in Potsdam. He studied medicine and natural science at the universities of Berlin, Würzburg, and Vienna. After 1861 he taught comparative anatomy and zoology at the University of Jena, where a chair in zoology was created for him in

Emperor Hadrian (bust in the Vatican Museum).
Bettmann Archive

Ernst Haeckel

HAFIZ

1865. Haeckel made many expeditions for scientific study and gathered material for a great number of monographs on descriptive and systematic zoology, including *Calcareous Sponges* (1872), *Siphonophora* (1869), and *Radiolaria* (1887). He was the first German biologist who fully supported the theory of evolution (q.v.) proposed by the British naturalist Charles Robert Darwin (*see under* DARWIN). Haeckel, by means of his many books and lectures, helped popularize the Darwinian theory in Germany. In his *General Morphology* (1866) and *Natural History of Creation* (1868) Haeckel attempted to work out the practical applications of organic evolution. He formulated the biogenetic law (q.v.), a theory that each organism, in its growth, exactly repeats each stage of development previously experienced in the evolution of the species. Haeckel also made the first attempt to apply the doctrine of organic evolution to the whole field of morphology (q.v.) and proposed a classification of the various orders of animals based on their evolutionary relationships. *See* CLASSIFICATION; TAXONOMY.

Haeckel attempted to apply the doctrine of evolution to philosophy and religion in *Die Welträtsel* ("The Riddle of the Universe", 1899). Among Haeckel's other books are *Die Systematische Phylogenie* ("Systematic Phylogeny", 1894) and *Der Kampf um den Entwickelungsgedanken* ("The Struggle for the Idea of Evolution", 1905).

HAFIZ, name used by SHAMS UD-DIN MOHAMMED (1320?-89), Persian poet, born in Shiraz (now in Iran). "Hafiz" is a title of respect for one who has memorized the Koran (q.v.), and although the poet was nominally a follower of the ascetic Islamic philosophy of Sufism (q.v.), in his poetry he constantly satirized the hypocrisy of its religious leaders. Hafiz enjoyed the patronage of several rulers of Shiraz and many of his poems celebrate the gay life of the court. His work, collected under the title of *Divan*, contains more than 500 poems, most of them written in the form of ghazels, a traditional Persian form of highly structured rhyming couplets. The qualities for which Hafiz is most admired are his love of the common man and his scorn of hypocrisy in both laymen and religious leaders. His poetry has been translated into several Western languages. The first complete English translation appeared in 1891.

HAFNIUM, sometimes called CELTIUM, element with at.no. 72, at.wt. 178.49, b.p. over 3000° C. (5432° F.), m.p. about 2220° C. (4028° F.), sp.gr. 13.1, and symbol Hf. It was discovered in Copenhagen in 1923 by the Hungarian chemist Georg von Hevesy (q.v.) and the Dutch physicist Dirk Coster (1889–   ). On the basis of a prediction by Danish physicist Niels Bohr (q.v.) that element 72 would resemble zirconium in structure, they looked for the element in zirconium ores. Hafnium is found in nearly all ores of zirconium, and is forty-seventh in order of abundance of the elements in the crust of the earth. It resembles zirconium so closely in chemical properties and crystal structure that separation of the two elements is extremely difficult. Separation is accomplished most efficiently by means of the ion-exchange (q.v.) technique. Hafnium is used in the manufacture of tungsten filaments. Because of its resistance to high temperatures, it is used in combination with zirconium as a structural material in nuclear-power plants.

HAG, common name for a cyclostome, the hagfish (q.v.), or for a bird, the hagdon or shearwater (q.v.).

HAGAR, in the Old Testament, concubine of the patriarch Abraham and mother of Ishmael (qq.v.). Hagar was the handmaid of Abraham's wife, Sarah, who because she was barren, gave Hagar to her husband in the hope of producing heirs. When Hagar conceived a child, however, Sarah became jealous and regretted her decision. To escape Sarah's persecution, Hagar was forced to flee into the desert. Reassured by an angel, she returned to bear Abraham a son, Ishmael (Gen. 16). Eventually Sarah conceived and bore a child, who was named Isaac (q.v.). After Isaac's birth, Sarah persuaded Abraham to drive Ishmael and his mother away. They wandered into the desert, where an angel appeared to them and prophesied greatness for Ishmael (Gen. 21:1-21).

The story of Hagar has been interpreted in various ways. According to some scholars, Hagar personifies a tribe that at one time had been closely related to some of the Hebrew clans. Rivalry resulted in a separation, which is pictured as a dismissal of the inferior by the superior clan.

The story of Hagar is introduced in the New Testament and in rabbinical literature. She is allegorically contrasted with Sarah by Saint Paul (q.v.), who represents Hagar, the bondwoman, as the earthly Jerusalem and Sarah, the free woman, as the heavenly Jerusalem. Paul also similarly contrasts Ishmael and Isaac (Gal. 4:22-31). A Jewish tradition identifies Hagar with Abraham's second wife, Keturah (Gen. 25:1), and another makes her the daughter of an Egyptian pharaoh.

In Islamic tradition, Hagar is Abraham's true wife, and Ishmael, the favorite son. Ishmael is identified as the progenitor of the Arabs.

HAGDON. *See* SHEARWATER.

HAGEN, city of West Germany, in North Rhine-Westphalia State, on the Ennepe R., 10 miles S. of Dortmund. Hagen has large iron and steel works. Among other important industries are cotton printing, sugar refining, brewing, distilling, and the manufacture of railroad cars, chemicals, tobacco products, and paper. Alabaster and limestone are quarried nearby. Hagen was included in the British zone of occupation after World War II, during which more than a third of the city was destroyed by Allied air bombardments. Pop. (1968) 200,266.

HAGEN, Uta Thyra (1919–), American actress, born in Göttingen, Germany, and educated at the University of Wisconsin and the Royal Academy of Dramatic Art in London. She made her professional debut in New York at the age of nineteen in the role of Nina in Chekhov's *The Seagull*, with Alfred Lunt and Lynn Fontanne. In 1943, in *Othello*, she played the role of Desdemona opposite Paul Robeson, who played the title role. For her role in *The Country Girl* she received the Antoinette ("Tony") Perry award, the Donaldson award, and the New York Drama Critics Circle award as the best actress of the 1950–51 season. In 1962 she appeared in the role of the tempestuous wife, Martha, in the play *Who's Afraid of Virginia Woolf?* by the American dramatist Edward Franklin Albee (q.v.). For her role she again won the Tony and New York Drama Critics Circle awards as that season's best actress. Beginning in 1947 she taught acting in New York City at the Herbert Berghof Studio, a school of acting she helped to found.

HAGEN, Walter (1892–1969), American professional golf player, born in Rochester, N.Y. Among the numerous championships he won are the United States Open (1914 and 1919), the Professional Golfers' Association championship (1921, 1924, 1925, 1926, and 1927); and the British Open (1922, 1924, 1928, and 1929). One of his noteworthy feats was his defeat of the great American golfer Robert Tyre Jones (q.v.) in a challenge match in Florida in 1926. Hagen was prominent in the early Ryder Cup matches, a competition between American and British professional golfers. He served as captain of the American team in 1927, 1929, 1931, and 1933, and as honorary captain in 1937 and 1947. He retired from active competition in 1940 and in 1956 published his autobiography, *The Walter Hagen Story*.

HAGERSTOWN, city in Maryland, and county seat of Washington Co., on Antietam Creek, 6 miles N. of its confluence with the Potomac R., and 72 miles N.W. of Baltimore. Hagerstown is served by railroad and maintains a municipal airport. The city is the center of a fertile agricultural area and is especially noted for the facture of pipe-organs, sandblasting and dust-control equipment, aircraft, transportation equipment, textiles, and wood products. Hagerstown is the site of the annual Washington County Fair. The Antietam National Battlefield Site and Antietam National Cemetery are located 11 miles S. of Hagerstown; *see* ANTIETAM, BATTLE OF. The site of the present city was first settled about 1737 by the German immigrant Jonathan Hager. In 1762 it was laid out as Elizabeth Town, named for his wife. The site was incorporated as Hagerstown in 1814. Pop. (1960) 36,660; (1970) 35,862.

HAGFISH, common name for any of several eel-like, parasitic, marine cyclostomes in the order Myxinoidea, the most primitive of the craniate vertebrates. The hagfishes, which attain a maximum length of almost 3 ft., are extremely slimy, boneless animals, with vestigial eyes, a single large nostril, and a circular sucking mouth surrounded by four pairs of tentacles. The roof of the mouth contains a single tooth; the muscular tongue has two rows of strong, pointed, horny teeth which are periodically shed and reformed. The voracious hagfish attaches itself to the body of a fish by means of its mouth and tentacles, and files through the skin and flesh with its rasping tongue. It subsists solely on the blood and flesh of fish, and can consume several times its own weight in a few hours. While attached to its prey it breathes through two external gill openings situated on each side of its body. The hagfish is found in all temperate seas. The best-known hagfish is the bright-red *Myxine glutinosa*, about 15 in. long, found in the North Atlantic Ocean. The common Pacific species belong to the genus *Eptatretus*. *See* CYCLOSTOMATA; compare LAMPREY.

HAGGADA *or* **AGGADA** (Heb. *haggādāh*, from *higgīdh* "to relate"), in Judaism, the body of nonlegal rabbinical lore, comprising legends, anecdotes, and parables, which exemplifies the religious and ethical principles of the traditional law compiled in the Talmud and Midrash (qq.v.) during the first centuries of the Christian era. The Haggada is a complement to the Halakah (q.v.), or legal sections of rabbinical literature. The Haggada and Halakah were set down concurrently. Although there are innumerable numbers of Haggadic passages in the Talmud, the great bulk of Haggadic lore was assembled in separate compilations known as Midrashim,

HAGGAI

An illuminated Haggada that was compiled in Spain during the 13th century and is now in the collection of The Jewish Theological Seminary of America, New York City. New York Times

that is, homiletic interpretations of the Old Testament. For the most part, the oldest Midrashim reflect Halakah rather than Haggada. The greatest of the Haggadic Midrashim is the *Midrash Rabbah,* or Great Midrash, a verse by verse interpretation of the entire Pentateuch (q.v.) and also of the five scrolls (Esther, Ruth, Lamentations, Ecclesiastes, and Song of Songs) which are read on the various Jewish holidays. The Haggada is the primary source of knowledge of the theology of the ancient rabbinic Judaism. The term Haggada denotes also the prayer book used at the seder, or ritual dinner observed at Pesach (q.v.) or Passover. This prayer book, besides many Psalms, reproduces extracts from the traditional Haggada chosen for their special relevance to the holiday. S.Sa.

HAGGAI, book of the Old Testament (*see* BIBLE), in the King James Version, HAGGAI. In some English versions of the Bible used by Roman Catholics it is entitled Aggeus. It is one of twelve short prophetic books of the Old Testament known, because of their brevity, as the Minor Prophets (*see* BIBLE, CANON OF THE). Scholars consider that the book was written by an unknown disciple of the Hebrew prophet Haggai (q.v.). This generally accepted view is based mainly upon the impersonality of the third-person references to Haggai and the descriptions of him as "the prophet".

Haggai's prophecy was uttered in 520 B.C., a year of blight, drought, and general dissatisfaction for the exiles who had recently returned to Jerusalem from Babylon (*see* BABYLONIAN CAPTIVITY). The prophet attributes these misfortunes to the failure of the people to finish rebuilding the Temple (*see* TEMPLE: *Temple at Jerusalem*). He declares that the Lord is punishing them for decorating their own houses before completing the house of the Lord, and he urges Zerubbabel, governor of Judah (q.v.), and Joshua, the high priest, to rally the people to their primary task (chapter 1). Work begins again within a month (1:14–2:1), but the people soon must be encouraged again. Haggai rallies them the second time by prophesying that the spirit of the Lord will remain with them, that He will bring silver and gold from all nations, and that He will fill the new Temple with His glory (2:1–9).

The book concludes with two prophecies uttered later in the same year. The first (2:10–19) questions the priests concerning clean and unclean Temple rituals, condemns certain people, possibly the Samaritans (q.v.), for their impure ways, and promises fruitfulness now that the second Temple has been founded. The second prophecy (2:20–23) predicts a day of the Lord, at which time all the heathen nations will be overthrown.

Haggai is valuable historically because of the picture it gives of the immediate postexilic period, described chiefly by the longer books of Ezra and Nehemiah (qq.v.). In the entire Old Testament, Haggai and the short book of Zechariah (q.v.) cast the only other light on this important but somewhat obscure period. The religious importance of Haggai lies in its emphasis on the rebuilding of the Temple and on the reinstituting of correct Temple rituals, without which the older beliefs and practices of Judaism (q.v.) might have been lost.

HAGGAI (fl. 6th cent. B.C.), Biblical figure, tenth of the twelve Minor Prophets, and principal figure of the Old Testament book of Haggai (q.v.). He was born in Babylon during the Babylonian Captivity (q.v.) of the Israelites, and was among the first of those who returned to Jerusalem after Cyrus the Great (q.v.), King of Persia, conquered Babylon in 539. Haggai prophesied in the year 520, and died shortly thereafter.

HAGGARD, Sir Henry Rider (1856–1925), British novelist, colonial administrator, and agriculturist, born in West Bradenham Hall, Norfolk, England, and educated at Ipswich grammar school. At the age of nineteen he went to Natal, now part of the Republic of South Africa, and later served in the Transvaal (q.v.) as a master of the high court. When the Transvaal was granted autonomy in 1881, Haggard returned to London. He was admitted to the bar at Lincoln's Inn in 1884, but did not practice law, devoting most of his time to agriculture, on his estate in Norfolk, and to writing novels. His *King Solomon's Mines* (1885) was an immediate success; its story, suggested by the ruins at Zimbabwe (q.v.) in Rhodesia dealt with the adventures of an English explorer among remote tribes. The characters who appeared in the book were featured in several others, including *She* (1887), *Allan Quatermain* (1887), and *Ayesha, or the Return of She* (1905). In addition to writing more than forty novels, Haggard was an advisor to the British government on agriculture. His books on farming include *Rural England* (2 vol., 1902), and *The Poor and the Land* (1905). He was knighted in 1912. An autobiography, *The Days of My Life*, was published posthumously in 1926.

HAGGIS, ancient Scottish dish consisting of oatmeal, onions, seasonings, and the chopped liver, heart, lungs, and suet of a sheep or, less commonly, of a calf, and cooked in the stomach of the animal. The national dish of Scotland, haggis is served on November 30, Saint Andrew's day, and on the birthday of the Scottish poet Robert Burns (q.v.).

HAGIA SOPHIA. See ISTANBUL; SAINT SOPHIA.

HAGIOGRAPHA. See BIBLE, CANON OF THE: *The Old Testament.*

HAGUE, THE (Du. *'s Gravenhage* or *Den Haag*), administrative center of the Netherlands, and capital of South Holland Province, 3 miles E. of the North Sea, and 33 miles S.W. of Amsterdam. In addition to railroad facilities, the city, the third largest in population in the country, is served by a branch of the canal between Rotterdam and Amsterdam. The Hague is the official residence of the court and diplomatic groups and the seat of the states general, the ministry, the council of state, and the high court of the Netherlands. The general government buildings are situated in the center of the city around the Vyver, a small artificial lake. The royal palace dates from the 16th century, and was enlarged early in the 19th century. An equestrian statue of William I (q.v.), known as William the Silent, Prince of Orange, stands in front of the building. The Binnenhof (inner court) and Buitenhof (outer court), comprising a group of government structures dating in part from the 13th century, include the palace of the states general, the Treveshall, the courts of justice, and the Ridderzaal (Hall of the Knights), built in 1252, in which the states of the Netherlands repudiated the sovereignty of Philip II (q.v.), King of Spain, on July 26, 1581; *see* NETHERLANDS, THE: *History.* Ancient towers and gateways surround the group. Nearby is the Mauritshuis, completed in 1644, containing a renowned gallery of Dutch paintings, including several by the 17th-century Dutch painter Rembrandt (q.v.). Among the other notable buildings in The Hague are the Royal Library, founded in 1798, which contains early illuminated manuscripts and a collection of medals, coins, and antique gems; the town hall, dating from 1565; the municipal museum; the provincial government building; and the Palace of Peace, which was dedicated in 1913, and which houses the International Court of Justice (q.v.) and an extensive international law library. A monument in memory of the Dutch philosopher Baruch Spinoza (q.v.) stands opposite the house in which he died in 1677. His tomb, together with the tombs of the Dutch statesmen

Government buildings along the Vyver, an artificial lake in The Hague. A statue of Jan De Witt, 17th-century Dutch statesman, is in the foreground.

Netherlands Information Service

Cornelis De Witt and Jan De Witt (*see under* DE WITT), is contained in the Nieuwe Kerk (New Church), a building dating from the early 17th century. The Groote Kerk (Great Church) of Saint James, built in the 15th and 16th centuries, is another of the notable buildings in the city.

Canals intersect The Hague and lindens shade several of the avenues. The city is known for the beauty of its suburbs, and is connected with the seaside resort of Scheveningen by a broad, tree-lined highway. A forested park, called the Haagsche Bosch (The Wood), surrounds a 17th-century royal villa, the Huis ten Bosch (The House in the Wood). The villa is richly decorated and contains valuable collections of art.

The Hague is mainly residential, and commerce and industry are comparatively unimportant. The principal industries are lithographing, printing, distilling, copper and lead smelting, and the manufacture of iron castings, furniture, and jewelry.

History. Originally a hunting seat of the counts of Holland, the Hague became a princely residence in 1250 and subsequently developed into the administrative center of Holland, serving as the seat of the states general in the 16th century. In the 17th and 18th centuries The Hague was the diplomatic capital of Europe. The Triple Alliance (q.v.), of England, Sweden, and the Netherlands against France (1688), and the Triple Alliance of England, France, and Holland (1717) for the preservation of the Peace of Utrecht, were among the European agreements concluded there during that period. Between May 18 and July 29, 1899, the city was the site of the Hague Peace Conference, held in the Orange Hall of the Huis ten Bosch; *see* HAGUE CONFERENCES. One of the results of the conference was the establishment of the International Court of Arbitration, or the Hague Tribunal, with its seat at The Hague. To house this court the Palace of Peace was erected; Andrew Carnegie (q.v.), the American industrialist and philanthropist, contributed $1,500,000 toward the expenses of its construction. After World War I the Permanent Court of International Justice, created by the League of Nations (q.v.), and often called the World Court (q.v.), sat in the Palace of Peace. The present occupant, the International Court of Justice (q.v.), is based upon the Permanent Court and was created by the United Nations (q.v.) at the San Francisco Conference in 1945. The greater part of The Hague was undamaged by the German invasion and occupation of the Netherlands during World War II. Pop. (1968) 563,614.

HAGUE CONFERENCES, term generally applied to two international peace conferences, one of which took place near the end of the 19th and the other at the beginning of the 20th century at The Hague.

The first conference was called on the initiative of Czar Nicholas II (q.v.), Emperor of Russia for the purpose of discussion and possible agreement among the principal nations of the world concerning the problems of maintaining universal peace, reducing armaments, and ameliorating the conditions of warfare. Twenty-six countries accepted the invitation to the conference issued by the minister of foreign affairs of the Netherlands and, on May 18, 1899, 101 delegates, including jurists, diplomats, and high army and naval officers, held their first meeting, at a 17th-century villa in The Hague, the Huis ten Bosch (The House in the Wood). The last meeting took place on July 29, 1899. The chairman of the American delegation was Andrew Dickson White, ambassador to Germany; among the members of the delegation were Alfred Thayer Mahan, the naval officer and noted historian, and Seth Low (qq.v.), president of Columbia University.

The delegates to the first conference entered into three formal conventions or treaties. The first and most important treaty set up permanent machinery for the optional arbitration of controversial issues between nations (see ARBITRATION, INTERNATIONAL); this machinery took the form of the Permanent Court of Arbitration (q.v.), popularly known as the Hague Court or Hague Tribunal. The second and third conventions revised some of the customs and laws of warfare to eliminate unnecessary suffering during a war on the part of all concerned, whether combatants, noncombatants, or neutrals. These two conventions were supplemented by three declarations, to stay in force five years, forbidding the use of poison gas, expanding (or dumdum) bullets, and bombardment from the air by the use of balloons or by other means.

The conference is considered to have been one of the most significant international conferences of modern times if only because it was the first multilateral international conference on general issues since the Congress of Vienna in 1815, and because it set up the Permanent Court of Arbitration. The conference failed to limit armament, however, or provide for compulsory arbitration of international disputes. The great nations refused to adopt compulsory arbitration because it would have infringed on national sovereignty.

The idea of holding the Second International Peace Conference was first promulgated by United States Secretary of State John Milton Hay (q.v.), in 1904, and it was called three years later on the direct initiative of the Russian government. The conference took place at The Hague from June 15 to Oct. 18, 1907, and was attended by representatives from forty-four countries. The second conference resulted in thirteen conventions, which were concerned principally with clarifying and amplifying the understandings which had been arrived at in the first conference. In particular, new principles were established in regard to various aspects of warfare, including the rights and duties of neutrals, naval bombardment, the laying of automatic submarine contact mines, and the conditions under which merchant ships might be converted into warships; see PRIVATEER. The second conference recommended that a third conference be held within eight years. The government of the Netherlands actually began preparations for such a conference, to be held in 1915 or 1916; the outbreak of World War I, however, put an end to the preparations. After 1919, and until the formation of the United Nations (q.v.) in 1945, the functions of the Hague conferences were largely carried on by the League of Nations (q.v.). See also DISARMAMENT; WAR.

HAGUE TRIBUNAL. See PERMANENT COURT OF ARBITRATION.

HAHN, Otto (1879–1968), German physical chemist, born in Frankfort-am-Main, and educated at the universities of Marburg and Munich. In 1911 he became a member of the Kaiser Wilhelm Institute for Physical Chemistry in Berlin and served as director of the institute from 1928 to 1945, when it was taken into Allied custody after World War II. Hahn's greatest contributions were in the field of radioactivity. In 1918 he discovered, with the Austrian physicist Lise Meitner (q.v.), the element protoactinium (q.v.). Hahn, with his co-workers, Lise Meitner and the German chemist Fritz Strassmann (1902–), continued the research started by the Italian physicist Enrico Fermi (q.v.) in bombarding uranium with neutrons. Until 1939 scientists believed that elements with atomic numbers higher than 92 (known as transuranic elements) were formed when uranium (q.v.) was bombarded with neutrons. In 1938, however, Hahn and Strassmann, while looking for transuranic elements in a sample of uranium that had been irradiated with neutrons, found traces of the element barium. This discovery, announced in 1939, was irrefutable evidence, confirmed by calculations of the energies involved in the reaction, that the uranium had undergone fission, splitting into smaller fragments consisting of lighter elements in the periodic table; see NU-

HAHNEMANN

CLEAR ENERGY; PERIODIC LAW. Hahn was awarded the 1944 Nobel Prize in chemistry for his work in nuclear fission.

During World War II, Hahn was one of the German scientists who worked on the problem of utilizing atomic energy for military purposes. When his laboratories at the Kaiser Wilhelm Institute were bombed, he and his staff were evacuated to a small village in southern Germany, where he was later found by the American scientific mission headed by the American physicist Samuel Abraham Goudsmit (1902–) and interned. After a short internment in Great Britain, Hahn returned to Germany and settled in Göttingen, West Germany; there he became president of the Max Planck Society for Advancement of Science in 1946 and served in that position until 1960. His works include *Applied Radiochemistry* (1936). It was proposed in 1970 that the newly synthesized element Number 105 be named hahnium in honor of Hahn.

HAHNEMANN, (Christian Friedrich) Samuel (1755–1843), German physician, born in Meissen, and educated at the universities of Leipzig, Vienna, and Erlangen. He practiced medicine in various cities, finally settling in Leipzig. In 1790, while translating an English medical text into German, he noticed that the symptoms of disease that were cured by the use of quinine (q.v.) were the same as those produced in a healthy person who had taken quinine. This observation led Hahnemann to formulate the "law of similars", stating that a disease can be cured by those drugs that produce symptoms of the same disease in a healthy person. In 1800 Hahnemann asserted further that drugs were more effective when used in small doses and that the greater the dilution of the medicine, the more potent is its effect. He called his new treatment homeopathy (q.v.), in opposition to the general practice of medicine, which he called allopathy, and he organized a school of homeopathy in Leipzig. Hahnemann administered a large number of drugs to healthy subjects, including himself, and studied the symptoms produced; he was thus one of the first investigators of pharmacology to put that science on a systematic, experimental basis. Hahnemann's beliefs were met with hostility in Leipzig, particularly by the apothecaries, and he was forced to leave the city in 1821. He lived in Köthen until 1835, then moved to Paris, France, where he practiced and had a large following until his death. Hahnemann's chief work is *Organon der Rationellen Heilkunde* (1810; Eng. trans., *Organon of the Rational Art of Healing*, 1913).

HAHNIUM. *See* ELEMENTS, CHEMICAL.

HAIDA, group of Indian tribes native to the Queen Charlotte Islands, British Columbia, Canada. Their languages constitute the Skittagetan linguistic family, which is related to the Athapascan and Tlingit stocks, and is itself a member of a proposed larger family, the Na-dene (q.v.). The Haida represent one of the most advanced Indian cultures of the North Pacific region. Skillful carvers, they produce miniature totems, utensils made of black slate, large wooden family totems, and decorated canoes. The Haida use canoes for both traveling and fishing, and the economic organization of the tribes, which is largely maritime, centers around them. Contact with the civilization of white men has decimated their numbers. From a peak population of considerably more than 8000 (the number recorded in the first census in 1841) and a territory that extended, in raids, as far south as the mouth of the Columbia R., they have been reduced to a group of about 500 people.

HAIFA (anc. *Sycaminum*), city and chief seaport of Israel, on the Wadi Kishon (a dry river), at the foot of Mt. Carmel, about 55 miles N. of Tel Aviv-Jaffa. Railroads and highways connect Haifa with other parts of Israel. Oil from the Negev is refined in Haifa. Industrial establishments in the city include plants for the production of heavy machinery, the assembly of automobiles, production of cement, chemicals, and textiles. The Israel Institute of Technology, a school for higher learning, is located in Haifa. The city was known as Sycaminum in Biblical times and as Caiphas during the time of the Crusades in the 11th and 12th centuries; *see* CRUSADES. In the 12th century a castle, built on the site by Crusaders, was destroyed by Saladin (q.v.), Sultan of Egypt and Syria. The city remained relatively unimportant until the 20th century, when a railroad was built connecting it with Damascus, Syria. It became a leading port of Israel after the establishment of that country in 1948. Pop. (1969 est.) 212,200.

HAIG, Douglas, 1st Earl Haig (1861–1928), British soldier, born in Edinburgh, Scotland, and educated at the University of Oxford and the Royal Military College at Sandhurst. He joined the British army in 1885, serving in the Sudan in 1897, in the South African War (q.v.) from 1899 to 1902, and later in India where he was promoted to the rank of major general in 1904. After serving for a short time as director of the War Office in London, he returned to India in 1909 as chief of the general staff, becoming lieutenant general in the following year. He was ordered home in 1911 to command troops stationed at the military academy at Aldershot.

At the outbreak of World War I (q.v.) in 1914, Haig was given command of the 1st Army Corps of the British Expeditionary Force (B.E.F.) in France and Belgium. Later in the year he was promoted to the rank of full general and took command of one of the two armies of the newly expanded B.E.F., under the supreme command of General John Denton Pinkstone French (q.v.). Heavy losses at Loos-en-Gohelle in 1915 increased discontent with French's direction of the war and resulted in the appointment of Haig as commander in chief of the B.E.F. in 1915. Although he directed the British forces in France for the duration of the war, Haig's handling of the major campaigns, particularly at Sommes in 1916 and at Passendale in 1917, were harshly criticized by Prime Minister Lloyd George (q.v.).

After the war Haig assumed the post of commander in chief of the home forces supervising the demobilization of the British troops. When that position was abolished in 1921, he devoted his energies to the welfare of ex-servicemen. He was one of the founders and first president of the British Legion, formed to unite the many small associations of ex-servicemen in the country. He was created Earl Haig in 1919, and Baron Haig of Bemersyde in 1921.

HAIKU, verse form in Japanese literature consisting of three unrhymed lines containing, respectively, five, seven, and five syllables.

The ideal haiku presents two vivid images, one usually indicating a general or long-enduring condition, the other a momentary perception. The meaning or conclusion to be drawn from the images is not stated explicitly, but is left for the reader to elicit for himself. The most famous haiku, by the Japanese poet Bashō, born Matsuo Munefusa (1644–94), illustrates the perfect form:

furu ike ya	"This ancient pond here:
kawazu tobikomu	A frog jumps into the pond:
mizu no oto	Sound of the water."

As a separate form, haiku evolved from one portion of the *renga*, or linked verse, of 14th-century Japanese poetry; see JAPANESE LITERATURE: *Kamakura-Muromachi Period*. The form was adopted extensively during the 15th century by monks of the Zen (q.v.) sect of Buddhism. The monk Yamazaki Sokan (1465–1553) is traditionally the first poet to have used the form separately and is known as the father of haiku. In the 18th century the poets Tanaguchi Buson (1716–84) and Kobayashi Issa (1763–1828) wrote haiku that Japanese critics consider nearly as perfect as those of Bashō. Masuoka Shiki (1867–1902), who emphasized naturalness, brought new life to the form late in the 19th century. Under his influence, thousands of people began to write haiku, and by the middle of the 20th century hundreds of thousands of Japanese were writing haiku on a high level of competence and hundreds of Japanese magazines were devoted to the form.

The compression and suggestiveness of the haiku form, which demands the use of sharp objective images, influenced the 20th-century Anglo-American poetic movement known as imagism (q.v.). Some imagists imitated the verse form, but the most successful adaptions of haiku poems are short, free-verse epigrams contrasting two vivid images, especially those by the American poet Ezra Pound (q.v.). In the late 1950's, when many American artists began to be interested in Zen Buddhism and its art forms, a number of American poets experimented again with haiku.

HAIL, form of precipitation consisting of roughly spherical pellets of ice and snow usually combined in alternating layers. True hailstorms occur only at the beginning of thunderstorms and never when the ground temperature is below freezing. Raindrops or snow pellets formed in cumulonimbus clouds are swept vertically in the turbulent air currents characteristic of thunderstorms. The hailstone grows by the repeated collisions of these particles with supercooled water, that is, water which is colder than its freezing point yet remains in liquid form. This water is suspended in the cloud through which the particle is traveling. When the particles of hail become too heavy to be supported by the air currents, they fall to earth. Particles of hail range in diameter from $\frac{1}{16}$ in. to 5 in.; large particles, called hailstones, are sometimes very destructive. Often several hailstones freeze together into a large, shapeless, heavy mass of ice and snow. The so-called hail that occurs in the winter consists of frozen raindrops; see SLEET.

HAILE SELASSIE, original name TAFFARI MAKONNEN or TAFARI MAKONNEN (1892–   ), Emperor of Ethiopia, born in Harar, and privately educated. In 1916, when his cousin Zauditu (1876–1930) became empress of Ethiopia, Taffari was made regent, heir to the throne, and ras, or prince. In 1928 Taffari was declared negus, or king. Upon the death of the empress two years later, he was crowned emperor of Ethiopia and changed his name to Haile Selassie. In 1931 he granted a limited constitution to his subjects establishing a parliament and a court system.

HAIL MARY

The Italians invaded Ethiopia in 1935. After his capital, Addis Ababa (q.v.), fell to the Italians in May, 1936, Haile Selassie left the country and went to Geneva, Switzerland, to appeal to the League of Nations (q.v.) for help. The League did not support Ethiopia and Haile Selassie was forced to live in exile in Great Britain. In 1941, during the British offensive in east Africa in World War II, the Italian forces in Ethiopia were defeated and the British restored Haile Selassie to the throne. See WORLD WAR II: *The War in Africa*.

As emperor, Haile Selassie encouraged education and foreign investments in Ethiopia and attempted to westernize the country. He abolished slavery in 1942, built schools and colleges, reorganized the government and the armed forces, and rebuilt Addis Ababa as a modern city. In 1955 he promulgated a new constitution, which extended suffrage to the entire adult population and gave the parliament more powers.

Since World War II Haile Selassie has been a leader in the movement toward political and economic union of African states. Largely through his efforts the Organization of African Unity (q.v.) was founded in Addis Ababa in 1963. See ETHIOPIA: *History*.

HAIL MARY. See AVE MARIA.

Emperor Haile Selassie of Ethiopia with President Richard M. Nixon during an official visit to the U.S. in 1969.
UPI

HAINAN, island of the People's Republic of China, part of Kwangtung Province, in the South China Sea S. of Luichow Peninsula. Kiungchow Strait, about 15 mi. wide, separates the peninsula from the island, which adjoins the Gulf of Tonkin on the E. Between its N. and S. extremities, Hainan has a length of about 160 mi. and an extreme width of about 90 mi. The S. half is traversed by a series of mountain chains, the highest of which has a maximum elevation of about 6000 ft. The region has numerous extinct volcanoes, but many of the slopes and valleys are covered with dense tropical vegetation. The N. portion of the island, except for occasional mountainous outcroppings, consists of level plains. Hainan contains rich mineral deposits, including gold, tin, iron, lead, and silver, but the economy is predominantly agrarian. Among the leading crops are rice, rubber, coconuts, sugar, betel nuts, and pineapples. Large numbers of hogs, cattle, and ducks are raised.

People of Chinese origin comprise about two thirds of the population of Hainan. Several aboriginal tribes, locally designated the Maiu and Lois, inhabit the more remote areas of the mountainous region. The Maiu tribes originated on the Chinese mainland; the Lois show marked physical similarities to the Igorot (q.v.) tribe of the Philippines and speak the same language. A Chinese possession since 111 B.C., Hainan was occupied by the Japanese in February, 1939, during the Sino-Japanese War. The island was liberated in 1945 by the Chinese Nationalists, and in 1950 it passed to the Chinese Communists. Kiungchow is the administrative center, and the chief seaport is Hoihow. Area, about 13,000 sq.mi., pop., about 3,000,000.

HAIPHONG, second largest city and chief seaport of North Vietnam, on the delta of the Red R., about 20 mi. from the Gulf of Tonkin, and about 60 miles E. of Hanoi. The port has modern facilities for handling waterborne freight and is visited by ships from France, Great Britain, Japan, and Communist countries. Haiphong is linked to Hanoi by rail and to Hanoi and other inland points by roads and waterways. Industrial enterprises, including zinc and coal mines, are located near or in the city. Certain industrial and transportation facilities in and near the city were damaged from bombings carried out during the Vietnam conflict; see VIETNAM, WAR IN. Pop. (1960) 369,248.

HAIR, collective term for slender, threadlike outgrowths of the epidermis of mammals (see SKIN), forming the characteristic covering of those animals. No animals other than mammals have true hair, and all mammals have hair. Even such apparently hairless mammals as rhinoceroses, elephants, and armadillos have hairs around the snout, at the tip of the tail, and behind each scale, respectively. Whales and manatees have hair only in the embryonic state. When the individual hairs are fine and closely spaced, the coat of hair is called fur; when soft and kinked and matted together the coat is called wool. Coarse, stiff hairs are called bristles; when they are also pointed, as in the hedgehog and the porcupine, they are called spines (or, popularly, quills). The term hair is sometimes extended to include any similar structure, especially the "hairs" forming the pubescence of certain plants.

Individual hairs are composed chiefly of the horny scleroprotein known as keratin, and contain neither blood vessels nor nerves. They usually contain pigment (except in the case of albinos), but sometimes also contain interstitial air bubbles that give the hair a silvery color. The shaft of the hair consists of modified epithelial cells arranged in columns surrounding a central medulla (or core), and covered with thin, flat scales. The root of each hair is contained in a tubular pit in the epidermis, called the hair follicle. The hair grows from the bottom of the follicle and is nourished by the blood vessels in a papilla that extends into the follicle and, for a short distance, into the root of the hair. A minute muscle, the *arrector pili,* is attached to each hair follicle; under the control of the autonomic nervous system the muscle contracts to make the hair "stand on end". Most mammals other than man possess tactile hairs, usually growing from the upper lip and eyebrows, with their roots set in erectile tissue richly supplied with sensory nerves.

In man the development of the hair begins in the embryo, and, by the sixth month, the fetus is covered by a growth of fine hair, the lanugo. In the first few months of infancy the lanugo is shed, and is replaced by hair, characteristically coarse over the cranium and the eyebrows and fine and downy over the rest of the body. At puberty coarse hair develops in the armpits and over the pubic region in both sexes; in males the hair over the upper lip and the lower jaw begins to grow coarse to form the beard. The rate of growth of the hair varies with the age of the person and with the length of the hair. When a hair is short, its rate of growth averages about ¾ in. per month; by the time the hair is a foot long, the rate of growth is reduced by one half. The fastest growth is found in women from sixteen to twenty-four years of age.

In anthropology the form of the hair is one of the most important and reliable characteristics of race. The nearly black hair of Negro, Papuan, and Melanesian is characterized as woolly. It grows from a curved follicle, which imparts a spiral twist, and is flat or tapelike in cross section. The hair of the Chinese, Japanese, Eskimo, and American Indian is straight, coarse, long, and almost always black. It grows from a straight follicle; it is round in cross section, and has an easily distinguished medulla. The hair of Ainu, European, Hindu, and Semite is wavy, and is intermediate between the straight and the woolly types. It grows from a straight follicle, but has a slight tendency to curl; it is oval in cross section and among individuals exhibits a wide range of color, from light blond to black. See RACES OF MANKIND.

Hair Diseases. Disorders of the hair shaft or hair follicle cause abnormal growth or abnormal or premature falling of the hair. Certain abnormal conditions such as dull or dry hair are caused by physical or chemical agents. Too frequent use, for instance, of permanent-waving chemicals or of shampoos or lotions, especially those containing alcohol or free alkalies, often cause such conditions. The cause of excessive hairiness is obscure, but in several cases it has been traced to tumor of the adrenal cortex, or to disorders of the pituitary gland, the thyroid gland, and the ovary. Premature graying of the hair is associated with anxiety, shock, and deficiency diseases (see VITAMIN), and in certain

HAIRDRESSING

cases with hereditary factors. Alopecia, or baldness, is also due principally to hereditary factors. Certain forms of baldness may, however, be due to other causes: alopecia prematura, in which the hair of a young person falls out without preliminary graying, may also be caused by seborrhea (q.v.); alopecia areata, in which the hair falls out in irregular patches, is believed by doctors to be caused by inflammation, nerve disorders, or local infections. Diffuse falling of the hair, ordinarily a normal phenomenon, may reach abnormal proportions after a fever higher than 103° F. (39.4° C.), during a debilitating disease, or as a result of surgical shock.

Infections of the hair follicle also cause a variety of hair diseases. Tinea favosa, or favus, is caused by the fungus *Achorion schoenleinii;* it is characterized by the formation around the mouths of the follicles of small crusts, which frequently resemble a honeycomb. Tinea trichophytina, or ringworm (q.v.), is caused by fungi of the genus *Trichophyton.* These diseases have been treated successfully by epilation (removal of the hair from the affected follicles), cleansing with soaps or oils to remove encrustation, and application of fungicides. Treatment with X rays has also been successful in some cases.

Hairy parts, particularly of the head and pubis, are subject to troublesome infestations by minute insects and mites. *See, for example,* CHIGGER; LOUSE.

HAIRDRESSING, process employed in lending greater beauty to the hair of the head. The process includes a specific arrangement of the hair and may also include cutting, curling, perfuming, bleaching, dyeing, powdering, or waxing of the hair, and the addition of false hair, such as a wig or fall, a headdress, or other adornment.

Ancient and Medieval Styles. Hairdressing has been practiced from prehistoric times and among all peoples from the most primitive to the most highly civilized. Statuary and bas-reliefs of the ancient Assyrians, Persians, and Egyptians show that these people subjected the hair of head and beard to decorative processes, including curling, anointing, and dyeing. They also adorned the hair with ribbons and with ornaments of gold and silver. In the above-mentioned countries, wigs were commonly used to conceal baldness. In ancient Egypt, feminine hairdressing, as revealed by sculptures and mural paintings, was extremely elaborate. Three styles of feminine hairdressing prevailed: the hair was divided into numerous locks or tresses, each thickly plaited; into numerous long parallel braids grouped into two masses, the smaller falling in front of the shoulder, the larger, behind; or into two broad and flat braids, one on each side of the head, the back hair being cut short.

Among the early Hebrews a head of thick hair was held in esteem; a bald man was subject to suspicion of leprosy. In later times the Jews regarded long hair on a male as evidence of effeminacy. During the time of the ancient Jewish kingdoms, Jewish women wore their hair long, sometimes curling or plaiting it. After the Exile in the 1st century A.D., Jewish women cropped their hair at marriage and wore sheitels, or wigs, a custom that is still practiced by orthodox women.

Among the ancient Greeks, boys generally wore the hair long but cut it short when they reached the age of eighteen. The men wore it short and curled in small ringlets. In Sparta, however, the boys wore their hair short and the men wore it long. Greek women dressed their hair elaborately. They parted it in the center of the crown, brought it down over the temples, and carried the two divisions toward the back, finally fastening them over the point where the part began, or tying them into a tuft or knot on the back of the head. The tied mass of hair was usually enclosed by a hood or net. Curling of hair was so general in Athens that it gave rise in that city to a new industry. The first professional hairdressers in history flourished in Athens. After the 4th century B.C., styles in male hairdressing showed a growing tendency toward simplicity, while the coiffures of women became more and more elaborate. The early Romans wore their hair long, but after about 300 B.C. short hair prevailed. Roman women of the period of the Republic wore their hair in a simple and natural style, and those of the Roman Empire adopted elaborate forms of headdress. When a woman did not have sufficient hair of her own for the number of curls and plaits desired, she added false hair, usually blonde, taken from captive members of the Germanic tribes with which Rome was at constant war. About the 8th century, the tonsure, a form of hairdressing in which a part of the head was shaved, was adopted by monastic orders of the Roman Catholic Church to indicate the dedication of the priests to the service of God.

The early Britons wore their hair and beards long, but after the Roman conquest of England in the 1st century A.D., the Britons adopted the Roman custom of shaving off the beard and cutting the hair short. The Saxons (q.v.), who ruled England in the 9th, 10th, and part of the 11th centuries, wore their hair long and parted at the front of the head. The Danes, who ruled England from 1016 to 1042, generally wore their hair

Hair styles. Above, left: Ancient Greek hair style shown on preclassical statue. Above, right: Italian Renaissance style with varying lengths of tresses. Below: Elaborately ornamented 18th-century French hair styles.

Bettmann Archive

HAIRDRESSING

long. After the Norman invasion of England in 1066, the style of wearing the hair very long was adopted by both women and men, including members of the clergy and soldiers. Both these classes had, in general, previously worn their hair short. During the Plantagenet (q.v.) period (1154–1399), the hair was worn somewhat shorter. From the 13th to the 16th century it was worn cut short but was kept bushy at the sides, cut close over the forehead, and curled just below the ears. From the 13th to the 15th century, women's hair was usually worn in a covering of gold network known as a caul. The hair was sometimes curled and ornamented with jewelry. During the early 15th century, women's hair either hung down the back in curls or was confined within a jeweled caul or tightly covered by a headdress such as a turban. In the late 15th century, a profusion of hair, with heavy sidelocks, was considered fashionable. During the reign of Henry VIII (q.v.) from 1509 to 1547, it became the fashion for men to part their hair in the center and comb it straight down the sides of the head. With the accession of Queen Elizabeth I (q.v.) in 1558, came the introduction of large and elaborate coiffures for women that were the forerunners of the gigantic coiffures worn in England and on the Continent during the 18th century. From about the 17th century, hairdressing in England closely followed fashions on the Continent and is thus referred to in the account of European hairdressing below.

From the earliest period to the 14th century, hairdressing customs differed at different times among the various peoples of central and western Europe. Among the early Celts and Germans, with the exception of the Saxons, short hair was worn only by slaves or as a sign of disgrace by those convicted of violating some tribal law. Both Celts and Germans wore the hair long and tied behind the head. By the end of the 8th century the long-haired style gener-

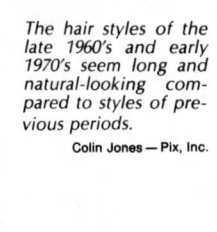

The hair styles of the late 1960's and early 1970's seem long and natural-looking compared to styles of previous periods.

Colin Jones — Pix, Inc.

ally prevailing among Germanic tribes had changed in the particular tribe known as the Franks (q.v.). In the 9th century their king Charlemagne (q.v.) and his immediate successors wore their hair short. The Saxons, on the contrary, who had been wearing their hair short, about the 9th century began to wear it over the shoulders or tied up and fastened with a pin. In France and elsewhere in Europe in the 11th century and later, the custom prevailed of forming the hair into one or two cues. These were bound by ribbons and placed over the shoulders from the back.

The Era of Coiffures. Elaborate coiffures for both men and women came into vogue in Europe at the end of the 14th century. The method of hairdressing shown in portraits of King Henry IV (q.v.) of France and of his minister of finance, Maximilien de Béthune, Duc de Sully (q.v.) is typical of the style in which men of the upper classes dressed their hair during the late 16th and the early 17th century. The beard was combed out and elaborately curled and by the use of a gum was made to extend out from both sides of the lower lip into a stiff, fanlike shape. The moustache was curled and, also by means of a glutinous substance, was held rigidly up and away from the mouth. The hair of the head was combed straight back from the forehead. In the early portion of the reign of Louis XIV (q.v.), from 1643 to 1715 in France, and during the reign of Charles I (q.v.), from 1625 to 1649 in England, the hair of men, worn long, was perfumed and, to prevent it from being blown about by the wind, was tied with ribbons into long and heavy locks. Wigs came into fashion in France in the 17th century. Introduced by Louis XIII (q.v.), who wore an elaborately curled wig to conceal his baldness, the custom was continued by Louis XIV (q.v.), who wore a towering wig to make himself appear tall. From royalty the fashion spread to courtiers and other members of the French nobility, and from France to other parts of Europe and also to America. Charles II (q.v.), King of England, adopted the fashion during his period of exile in France and brought it to England with him when he was restored to the English throne in 1660.

In the last two thirds of the 17th century and in the first part of the 18th, hairdressing styles for women were simple. About the middle of the 18th century, however, French feminine coiffures which were the models followed in the rest of Europe and in England, grew more and more elaborate. In the reign (1715–74) of Louis XV (q.v.) they became lofty constructions of curls stiffened with wire, cloth, or other materials. On top of the huge pile of hair was placed a cap or hat decorated with flowers or plumes. In the reign (1774–92) of Louis XVI (q.v.), the style became even more extravagant. The extreme was perhaps reached by a hairdresser of the late 18th century who devised the *coiffure à la frégate,* a high vertical structure of hair held in place by gigantic combs and adorned with jewels, the whole crowned by the model of a warship of the period.

Modern Styles. The French Revolution (q.v.) brought about simplicity in hairdressing styles for both men and women. After the beginning of the 19th century, men in Europe and America generally wore their hair short. In the first part of the 19th century, women arranged their hair in a series of ringlets which they permitted to fall to the sides of the head, and which they gathered around the back of the head with a ribbon. Later in the century, elaborate hairdressing styles for women came into vogue again; their chief feature was the use of the chignon. During World War I it became fashionable for women to wear their hair cut short, and shorter hairstyles have prevailed since. Particularly after World War II, increasing numbers of women patronized professional hairdressers regularly. Hair coloring became widely accepted. During the second half of the 20th century, hairstyles for women became more varied than they had ever been, ranging from very short to long, and from natural, unset styles to carefully curled or artificially fluffed ones. Although most men continued to wear relatively short hair, including closely cropped "crew cuts", longer hair became the vogue with many young men during the late 1960's.

HAIRSTREAK, common name for any butterfly in the genus *Thecla* of the family Lycaenidae, which contains the copper butterflies (q.v.) and the blues. The hairstreaks, which have wing spans of from 1 to 2 in., have characteristic hairlike markings on the undersides of their wings and, in most of the common forms, fine, hairlike tails on the hind wings. Their caterpillars feed on the leaves, flowers, buds, and stems of plants.

More than fifty species of hairstreaks are found in North America. The common hairstreak, *T. melinus,* found throughout the United States, is ¾ in. long with a wing span of 1½ in. Above it is dark gray, bordered with black, white, and orange; below it is lighter gray, streaked with orange and marked with black oblongs, with an orange patch at the rear angle of each back wing. The front wings are smooth bordered; the rear wings are wavy bordered

HAIRWORM

with a thin tail at the rear of each. The caterpillars, which are greenish-gray, feed on hop seeds, hopvines, and bush clover, as well as on many weeds.

HAIRWORM, or HAIR EEL or HORSEHAIR WORM or HORSEHAIR SNAKE, common names for any brown, elongated, threadlike worm of the class Nematomorpha or of the order Mermithoidea of the class Nematoda, both in the phylum Aschelminthes. These common names were originated by superstitious people who believed that horsehairs turned into these living worms when dropped into water. Hairworms when young live as parasites within the bodies of insects; later they leave their host near water and become nonparasitic, aquatic adults, several inches in length. Fully mature hairworms sometimes reach a yard in length.

The Nematomorpha resemble Nematodes (q.v.) in certain aspects of their life cycle but are now generally recognized as a separate class, distinct from the class Nematoda. Their nervous system consists of an anterior mass of nerve tissue and one ventral cord. The body cavity is lined with epithelium and swells, at the posterior end, into an excretory cloaca into which, in both sexes, the paired genital ducts open. The class Nematomorpha is divisible into two orders: Gordioidea and Nectonematoidea. The female gordiid lays masses of eggs on plants or on rocks underwater. The larvae hatched from the eggs have special boring organs with which they puncture the skin of an insect living near the water. Larvae of *Gordius robustus,* the best-known species, are parasitic on crickets and grasshoppers and mature within their host; larvae of the genus *Parachordodes* bore into midges; if the midges are eaten by beetles, the threadworms mature in the bodies of the beetles. When adult, the hairworms bore out of their host and enter fresh water. Hairworms in Gordioidea are also called "Gordian worms" because they are often found in knotted clusters reminiscent of the Gordian knot.

The order Nectonematoidea contains the single genus *Nectonema,* which is pelagic in marine waters as an adult and parasitic in hermit crabs and true crabs during the larval stages.

Hairworms of Mermithoidea are Nematodes, often found 2 or 3 ft. below the ground in wet soil as well as in fresh water, and commonly appearing above the ground in large numbers after a rain. Unlike other Nematodes the middle portions of their body cavities are solid, fat-containing organs from which the gonads, and the female eggs, draw nourishment. A well-known species is *Mermis nigrescens.*

HAITI, independent republic of the West Indies, occupying the w. third of the island of Hispaniola (q.v.). A boundary extending 193 mi. from N. to S. separates Haiti from the Dominican Republic. The country is situated between about lat. 18° N. and lat. 19°80′ N. and long. 73° W. and long. 75° W. The total land area is 10,714 sq.mi.

THE LAND

Haiti is crescent shaped and is characterized physiographically by mountain chains and isolated mountain passes, interspersed with valleys. Pic La Selle, the highest peak, rises to an altitude of 8793 ft. above sea level. The coasts are elevated, for the most part, and greatly indented, forming many natural harbors. The numerous rivers, most of which are short, swift, and unnavigable, have their sources in the mountains. The largest river, the Artibonite, is navigable for about 100 mi. The country also has several large lakes. Haiti has no active volcanoes, but destructive earthquakes are frequent.

Climate. The temperature along the coasts ranges between 70° and 94° F., with a variation from winter to summer of not more than 10°. The mountains are considerably cooler; the average temperature is about 77° F. Rainy seasons occur from April to June and October to November.

Natural Resources. The country has a good supply of natural resources, which are primarily agricultural. Valuable forests of cedar, oak, mahogany, and pine cover the mountain slopes and river banks. Substantial mineral deposits exist, but have not been fully exploited.

Plants and Animals. Haiti has luxuriant tropical flora. Numerous fruits include guava, orange, grapefruit, mulberry, lime, breadfruit, and mango.

No large wild animals or poisonous snakes are native to Haiti, but crocodiles and iguanas are plentiful.

Geese, flamingos, pelicans, wild ducks, egrets, and snipe have their habitat along the shores. Other birds are the hawk, white owl, kingfisher, woodpecker, pigeon, and dove.

Waterpower. Hydroelectric power is provided by three plants, one on the Artibonite R., one at Cap-Haïtien, and a plant inaugurated in 1971 at Peligre. In 1970 some 88,000,000 kw hours of hydroelectric power were generated.

THE PEOPLE

About 90 percent of the population of Haiti are Negro descendants of African slaves; the remainder are mulattoes of French and African descent, and Caucasians of European backgrounds. Although the official language is

HAITI

INDEX TO MAP OF HAITI

Departments

L'Artibonite	C 2
Nord	C 2
Nord-Ouest	B 2
Ouest	C 3
Sud	B 3

Cities and Towns

Anse-à-Veau	B 3
Anse-d'Hainault	A 3
Aquin	B 3
Archaie	C 3
Bainet	C 3
Belladère	D 3
Camp-Perrin	B 3
Cap-Haïtien	C 2
Cayes-Jacmel	C 3
Chardonnière	A 3
Corail	B 3
Coteaux	A 3
Croix-des-Bouquets	C 3
Dame-Marie	A 3
Dérac	D 2
Dessalines	C 2
Fort-Liberté	D 2
Gonaïves	C 2
Grand-Rivière-du-Nord	C 2
Grand-Goâve	C 3
Gros-Morne	C 2
Hinche	D 2
Jacmel	C 3
Jean-Rabel	B 2
Jérémie	B 3
Kenscoff	C 3
Lascahobas	D 3
Le Borgne	C 2
Léogane	C 3
Les Anglais	A 3
Les Cayes	B 3
Limbé	C 2
Limonade	C 2
Maissade	C 2
Marigot	C 3
Miragoâne	B 3
Mirebalais	C 3
Moron	A 3
Ouanaminthe	D 2
Pétionville	C 3
Petite-Rivière-de-l'Artibonite	B 2
Petit-Goâve	C 3
Pignon	C 2
Pilate	C 2
Plaisance	C 2
Port-à-Piment	A 3
Port-au-Prince (cap.)	C 3
Port-de-Paix	B 1
Port-Margot	C 2
Saint Louis-du-Nord	C 2
Saint-Louis-du-Sud	B 3
Saint-Marc	C 2
Saint-Michel-de-l'Atalaye	C 2
Saint-Raphaël	C 2
Saltrou	C 3
Thomonde	C 3
Tiburon	A 3
Trou-du-Nord	D 2
Verrettes	C 2

Physical Features

Artibonite (river)	C 2
Baradères (bay)	B 3
Cheval Blanc (pt.)	B 2
Dame-Marie (cape)	A 3
Fantasque (pt.)	C 3
Gonâve (gulf)	B 2
Gonâve (isl.)	B 3
Grande Cayemite (isl.)	B 3
Gravois (pt.)	A 4
Irois (cape)	A 3
Jamaica (channel)	A 3
La Selle (peak)	C 3
Léogane (channel)	B 3
Macaya (peak)	B 3
Manzanillo (bay)	D 2
Massif de la Selle (mts.)	C 3
Noires (mts.)	C 2
Saint-Marc (channel)	C 3
Saumâtre (lake)	C 3
Tortue (channel)	C 2
Tortue (isl.)	C 1
Trois Rivières (river)	C 2
Vache (isl.)	B 3
Windward (passage)	B 2

French, the Creole dialect is more widely spoken. The principal religion is Roman Catholicism; many Haitians, however, practice a form of animism known as voodoo (qq.v.). The country has a primarily agrarian society.

Population. The population of Haiti (census 1970) was 4,205,755. The United Nations estimated the overall population density at 455 per sq.mi. in 1970. About 85 percent of the population lives in rural areas.

Political Divisions and Principal Cities. Haiti is divided into 9 departments, 26 arrondissements, and 300 communes. The capital, Port-au-Prince (pop., late 1960's est., 500,000), is the commercial center as well as a free port. Cap-Haïtien (pop., 30,000) is the only other city. The towns such as Les Cayes and Gonaïves all have populations under 15,000.

Education. Free, compulsory education is provided by law; the literacy rate, however, is only 15 percent. The country does not have adequate facilities, and many children do not attend any type of educational institution. In the early 1970's some 300 urban elementary and secondary schools had an annual enrollment of about 202,000 students.

The University of Haiti at Port-au-Prince comprises the faculties of dentistry, law, science and medicine; enrollment in the late 1960's amounted to some 1500 students annually. Other institutions of higher learning include a polytechnic school at Port-au-Prince and two law schools, one at Cap-Haïtien, the other at Cayes.

Culture. The development of an active tourist trade between 1945 and 1961 helped to alter radically the rigid cultural stratification of Hai-

HAITI

tian life. Until then the division between the French elite and the peasants was nearly complete.

The predominantly Negro population today is developing a native Haitian culture that is gaining recognition both inside Haiti within the upper classes and in other countries. A Creole theater has been established where Creole plays and plays translated into Creole are performed. Concerts of native music and dances are held frequently. The changes reflect a general trend toward wider acceptance of and pride in the Creole traditions, language, and religion. *See* LATIN-AMERICAN MUSIC; SPANISH-AMERICAN LITERATURE.

LIBRARIES AND MUSEUMS. The country has several fine libraries. The collections of the Brothers of Saint Louis de Gonzage, the National Archives, and the Bibliothèque Nationale each contain rare works dating from the colonial period. Also devoted to Haitian history is the National Museum, the two sections of which are located in Port-au-Prince and Cap-Haïtien.

THE ECONOMY

During the 1960's, political instability had kept the economy stagnant and prevented the effective development of either the industrial or agricultural sectors. With the return of political stability in the early 1970's, tourism, which had been in decline, increased gradually, especially from the United States. Revenue is derived principally from customs duties and export taxes. Several foreign firms mine bauxite and copper. Recent annual budget figures show in revenues about $29,600,000, and about the same amount in expenditures.

Agriculture. About 80 percent of the total labor force (2,500,000) are farmers. Land is overworked, and soil erosion is a problem. Only one third of the country is arable. Most farms are small (3 acres), family-owned units, on which the farmer raises his own food and a few other crops for cash sale. Coffee is the principal crop. Other important crops are sugarcane, cocoa, sisal, cotton, and tobacco. In the early 1970's some 36,000 tons of coffee, 67,000 tons of sugarcane, 2000 tons of cocoa, and 16,000 tons of sisal were harvested annually. Livestock is raised on small farms, and meat requirements are met by local production.

Forest, Fishing, and Mining Industries. About 8000 sq.mi. of Haiti are forested. Many regions have been deforested in the search for fuel, and reforestation plans are under way. In the early 1970's more than 1,300,000 cu.ft. of roundwood were produced annually. Mining is limited to copper and bauxite production. About 697,000 tons of bauxite and about 144,000 tons of copper were mined in 1970.

Manufacturing. Haitian industry is concentrated in the processing of agricultural products. The country has two textile mills, several sisal mills, coffee mills, a sugar refinery, and factories for the production of cement, plastics, paints, pharmaceuticals, and soap. The so-called *petite industrie*, or handicraft industry, turns out such products as wood carvings and masks.

Currency, Banking, and Trade. The unit of currency is the gourde (5 gourdes equal U.S.$1; 1972), consisting of 100 centimes. The Banque Nationale de la République d'Haiti is the sole bank of issue and government depository.

The principal exports are coffee, sugar, sisal, and handicrafts. Cotton goods and foodstuffs are the principal imports. In the late 1960's the total value of exports was some $32,000,000 annually; imports were valued at about the same amount.

Transportation. Haiti has about 400 mi. of all-weather highways and about 1500 mi. of secondary roads. Domestic air service is provided by a government-operated airline; the country is also served by several international airlines. The Haitian air force operates an airline connecting Port-au-Prince with other Haitian towns.

Communications. In the late 1960's Haiti had some 4500 telephones, 83,000 radio sets, and 11,000 television receivers. Port-au-Prince has six daily newspapers; the circulation, combined with that of one weekly newspaper in Cap-Haïtien, was 14,000. Major cities and towns of Haiti, as well as foreign countries, are connected by the state-owned telegraph system.

Labor. The government exercises a strong influence on all trade unions. In 1962 a new labor code was passed declaring the closed shop illegal, and providing for compulsory collective bargaining, arbitration, and contracts in those businesses in which two thirds of the employees are organized.

GOVERNMENT

Haiti is governed by the constitution of 1964, expressly written to allow the president to retain his appointment for life.

Central Government. Executive power is vested in the president. The new constitution gives the president the power to dissolve the legislature and govern by decree in cases of emergency.

HEALTH AND WELFARE. The government maintains limited health and social-welfare programs. The national lottery is the main source of welfare funds; UNESCO provides extensive aid for children.

HAITI

At the request of the government, various international health organizations are conducting programs within Haiti to combat malaria, yaws, and tuberculosis.

Legislature. The unicameral legislature has fifty-eight members, who serve terms of six years and are elected by popular vote.

Local Government. The departments are headed by prefects appointed by the central government. An elected mayor administers each commune. The administration of local government is limited.

Judiciary. The judiciary comprises a Court of Cassation and lesser courts of appeal, civil courts, and justices of the peace. The president appoints all judges, and holds the right to pardon.

Defense. The Haitian armed forces comprise an army, an air corps, and a coast guard; total strength is about 6000. The commander in chief is the president. He also heads a paramilitary civilian militia comprised of an active reserve of some 10,000 armed government partisans. A secret police (*Tonton Macoute* or "bogeymen") is also maintained.

HISTORY

Since the time of its discovery the island has been known as Hispaniola (q.v.). The earliest historical incidents of note surround the Haitian Negro general and liberator Toussaint L'Ouverture (q.v.), who helped free (1793) the slaves, led French republican forces in forcing (1798) the British to withdraw, and by 1801 ruled the entire island. Toussaint strongly resisted efforts by Napoleon I (q.v.), Emperor of France, to reestablish slavery; he was defeated (1802) by French forces and later died a prisoner in France.

The island of Hispaniola was declared independent of French colonial rule in 1804 by the Negro general Jean Jacques Dessalines (q.v.). The name was changed to Haiti and Dessalines assumed the title of emperor. In 1806 Dessalines was assassinated, and for some years thereafter the northern part of Haiti was held by Henri Christophe (q.v.). In the southern part of the island a republic was established by the mulatto Alexandre Sabès Pétion (q.v.). Upon the death of Christophe in 1820, Jean Pierre Boyer (q.v.), the successor to Pétion, consolidated his power throughout the whole island. In 1844 the eastern part of the island declared its independence as the Republic of Santo Domingo, now the Dominican Republic.

The subsequent history of Haiti was characterized by a series of bitter internecine struggles for political ascendancy between the Negroes and the mulattoes. In 1849 a Negro, Faustin Élie Soulouque (1785–1867), proclaimed himself emperor as Faustin I, and for ten years ruled in a despotic manner. At the beginning of 1859, the

President François Duvalier (left) of Haiti and Governor Nelson A. Rockefeller of New York wave to the crowd gathered outside the national palace in Port-au-Prince during a 1969 visit. UPI

A camera-shy woman on her way to market in Port-au-Prince, capital of Haiti. UPI

mulatto Nicholas Fabre Geffrard (1806–79) restored republican government; he remained in office until 1867.

Disorder persisted, however, leading finally in 1915 to intervention by the United States. Under American occupation, order was restored to Haiti, and Philippe Sudre Dartiguenave held the presidency from 1915 to 1922. Early in 1916, the United States Senate ratified a treaty with Haiti by which the U.S., for a period of ten years, agreed to render economic and political assistance to put the government on a firm footing.

An insurrection against U.S. authority was put down in 1920. The assistance treaty, upon its expiration, was extended for another decade. Despite widespread improvements achieved under the American occupation, Haitian hostility to outside interference manifested itself in periodic uprisings. During the following four years the U.S. and Haiti negotiated the eventual withdrawal of American aid. The nineteen-year American military occupation of Haiti was terminated on Aug. 15, 1934, when U.S. marines were finally withdrawn. Throughout the next three years, Haiti experienced the economic repercussions of the worldwide depression. In 1937 President Sténio Joseph Vincent (1874–1959) charged that several thousand migrant Haitian workers who had crossed the border of the Dominican Republic in search of employment had been massacred by Dominican troops. The accusation was denied by Rafael Leonidas Trujillo Molina (q.v.), the Dominican dictator. The dispute was settled in 1938 when the Dominican Republic agreed to indemnify Haiti.

In 1939 President Vincent took steps to maintain himself in office beyond the expiration of his second term and to augment his semidictatorial powers. Confronted with strong local opposition and U.S. disapproval, Vincent announced that he would not seek reelection. The Haitian legislature thereupon elected former minister to the U.S. Élie Lescot (1883–   ) to the presidency. Following the Japanese attack on Pearl Harbor (q.v.) in December, 1941, President Lescot, with unanimous approval of the legislature, declared war on Japan on Dec. 8 and on Germany and Italy on Dec. 12. Early in 1942 Haiti permitted U.S. antisubmarine aircraft to make use of the Port-au-Prince landing field. In 1943 the Haitian-American Agricultural Development Corporation (SHADA) made progress in cultivating sisal, lemon grass, the cacao plant, and the rubber-yielding *Cryptostegia* vine. On April 20, 1944, President Lescot's term of office was extended by the Haitian legislature for seven years.

Haiti signed the charter of the United Nations on June 26, 1945, becoming one of the original fifty-one members of that association. Growing political disturbances in Haiti led, on Jan. 11, 1946, to the military ouster of President Lescot, who fled to Miami, Florida. On Aug. 16 Dumarsais Estimé (1900–   ) was elected president.

Haiti signed the Inter-American Treaty of Reciprocal Assistance (*see* Rio Treaty) in September, 1947, and the charter of the Organization of American States (O.A.S.) in April, 1948. During 1949 Haitian revolutionaries, with encouragement from the Dominican government, precipitated a domestic crisis and provoked Estimé to declare a state of siege on Nov. 15. In May, 1950, the Haitian president was forced to resign and a military junta ruled the country until elections were held on Oct. 8. Paul E. Magloire (1907–   ), a soldier and member of the junta, won the presidency by a large majority.

During 1951 the Magloire government encouraged foreign investment to strengthen the national economy, and settled differences with the Dominican Republic. In 1956 a controversy developed over the extent of President Magloire's term of office; on Dec. 12 Magloire relinquished all power. A period of political upheaval followed until September, 1957, when François ("Papa Doc") Duvalier (q.v.), a member of the Estimé government, was elected president.

The Duvalier Regime. Fear of his political rivals led Duvalier to declare several of them outlaws. At his bidding, the legislature imposed a state of siege on May 2, 1958, and on July 31 authorized him to rule by decree. In this period Duvalier organized the *Tonton Macoute*, an armed force under his personal control, to intimidate opposition. Duvalier dissolved the bicameral legislature on April 8, 1961, and announced the formation of a new unicameral legislature. All of the candidates for the new body, elected on April 30, were Duvalier followers. On Sept. 15 the legislature granted him extensive economic powers. United States aid was suspended in 1961, to demonstrate disapproval of Duvalier's policies.

On April 19, 1963, a military plot against Duvalier was uncovered and smashed. Haitian police invaded the Dominican embassy to seize government foes but withdrew when Dominican President Juan Bosch (1909–) threatened to use armed force against them. The refusal of the Haitian government to permit the embassy refugees to leave the country safely led to a buildup of Dominican troops on the Haitian border. The troops withdrew on May 13, but Haitian exiles in the Dominican Republic made several unsuccessful invasions of Haiti in August in the hope of triggering a popular uprising. A hurricane on Oct. 4 and a landslide on Nov. 10 caused about 5500 deaths and extensive property damage in Haiti.

A life term as president for Duvalier and a new red and black flag (to symbolize the link between Haiti and Africa) were authorized by a new constitution proclaimed by the legislature on June 21, 1964. Haitian exiles operating out of the Dominican Republic continued to make invasion attempts, and rebel groups within the country remained active, despite the oppressive tyranny of Duvalier and the *Tonton Macoute*. In the first ten years of his rule the president executed some 2000 political enemies and drove others into exile. The preoccupation of the regime with its own security was reflected in the fact that in recent years defense expenditures represented about 25 percent of the budget.

In January, 1971, the legislature amended the constitution to permit Duvalier to name his son, Jean-Claude Duvalier (1951–), as his successor. The young Duvalier became president after his father's death on April 21, 1971.

In the early 1970's efforts were undertaken to improve the economy of Haiti, with the aid of loans totaling almost $12,000,000 made by the Inter-American Development Bank in 1972.

HAJJ *or* **HADJ.** See Islam: *Religious Duties: Pilgrimage.*

HAKE, common name for any of several soft-rayed, marine, acanthopterygian fishes in the Cod family (Gadidae) and in the family Merlucciidae which was formerly included in the Cod family. Fish of both families are carnivorous.

The hake in Gadidae, which are also called codlings, are found on both sides of the North Atlantic Ocean, and are characterized by stringy, narrow pelvic fins attached to the throat and trailing in the water. This feature has led to the English name forkbeard for the common European species, *Urophycis blennoides*, also known as hake's dame. The squirrel hake, *Phycis chuss,* is the common American species and is about 2 ft. long. This fish, and the white hake, *P. tenuis,* are sought by fishermen for their oil and for their air bladders, used in the manufacture of isinglass.

The Merlucciidae, or true hake, are found on both sides of the Atlantic Ocean, in the Mediterranean Sea, and in the Pacific Ocean, off the United States, Chile, and New Zealand. The common European hake, *Merluccius merluccius,* is a slender fish, reaching 4 ft. in length, and has a long, pointed snout. Unlike the silver hake, or whiting, *M. bilinearis,* found most commonly between Cape Cod, Mass., and Cape Sable, Nova Scotia, it is not valued as food.

The name hake is also applied to the kingfish, or northern whiting, *Menticirrhus saxatilis*.

HAKKA (Chin., "guest" or "stranger"), term applied to a migratory people of southern China. Their origin has not been proved; they may be descended from the Burmese or Thais, or from the aboriginal inhabitants of northern China. The Hakka have always been persecuted by the natives of the regions in which they have settled. They differ from the Chinese in dress and customs, and speak a distinct dialect, related to those of southern China. The Hakka are a thrifty, industrious people, engaging chiefly in agriculture, and working as quarrymen, stonemasons, porters, and barbers. When for a period they have been free from persecution, as under the Han dynasty (202 B.C.–220 A.D.), several

HAKLUYT

Hakka have attained high public office. During the Tang dynasty (7th to 9th centuries) they settled in the mountains of Fukien Province and during the 13th century they fought in the Chinese imperial army against the invading armies of the Mongol military leader Kublai Khan (q.v.). They were again persecuted, after the 14th century, under the Ming dynasty, and moved to Kwangtung Province. One of the best known of the Hakka is Hung Hsiu-ch'üan (1812–64), leader of the Taiping Rebellion (q.v.).

HAKLUYT, Richard (1552?–1616), English geographer, born in London, and educated for the ministry at the University of Oxford, where he became interested in geography and exploration. His first book, *Divers Voyages Touching the Discovery of America and the Islands Adjacent* (1582), describes English exploration in the New World. This work brought him fame, and he was appointed chaplain to Sir Edward Stafford (1552–1605), English ambassador to France, with instructions to collect information on Spanish and French voyages to America. His best-known work is *Principal Navigations, Voyages, and Discoveries of the English Nation* (1589; rev. and expanded, 3 vol., 1598–1600). A compilation of the accounts of sea captains and explorers, it includes facts but also some dubious information about sea monsters and regions still unexplored.

After 1603 Hakluyt was influential in promoting English colonization in the New World as a member of the London Company (q.v.). The Hakluyt Society, founded in his honor in England in 1842, publishes books of discovery, exploration, and travel.

HAKODATE, city and seaport of Japan, on the S.E. coast of Hokkaido Island, on a rocky promontory in Tsugaru Strait, about 420 miles N. of Tokyo. The harbor, opened in 1859 to foreign trade, is one of the finest in the world, spacious and easily accessible. For many years Hakodate was used by Russia as a winter port. Although it has lost its former rank in international shipping and trade, Hakodate is still important in Japanese interisland communication. Fishing is one of the chief industries. Exports from the city include fish products, sulfur, rice, and timber. Pop. (1965) 252,000.

HALAKAH, or HALACHA (Heb., "path" or "way"), in Judaism, the body of traditional law that is based on rabbinical interpretation and supplements the scriptural law contained in the Pentateuch (q.v.), the Law of Moses. Transmitted by word of mouth by the highest rabbinical authorities, these supplementary laws were first written down in the Talmud (q.v.), during the first five centuries of the Christian era, and in the Midrash (q.v.), or scriptural exegesis. The Halakah is the purely legal content of these works, the illustrations and amplifications of the ethical, political, and religious principles involved in the laws being set down in the Haggada (q.v.). After the completion of the Talmud, the Halakah continued to develop, as it was applied to new situations by rabbinic authorities. The Haggada also continued to develop, in the form of compilations, commentaries, and mystical and moral literature.

HALBERSTADT, city of East Germany, in Magdeburg District, 56 miles N.W. of Halle, and 29 miles S.W. of Magdeburg. The chief industries in the city are the processing of foods, tanning, and the manufacture of paper, rubber, machinery, gloves, and cigars. The earliest record of Halberstadt dates from 820. In the 10th century the city was made a bishopric of the Holy Roman Empire (q.v.), and in 1813 it was annexed by Prussia. Among its famous buildings is a Gothic cathedral, built in the 13th and 14th centuries, that contains many valuable medieval objects of art. The Liebfrauenkirche, or Church of Our Lady, which dates from the 12th and 13th centuries, contains fine reliefs and mural frescoes. Many of the old private residences in Halberstadt are decorated with wood carvings. Following World War II the city was included within the Soviet zone of occupation. Pop. (1960 est.) 44,894.

HALDANE, name of a distinguished British family originating in Scotland, of whom the most famous members are the following:

Richard Burdon Haldane, Viscount Haldane of Cloan (1856–1928), philosopher and statesman, born in Edinburgh, Scotland, and educated at the universities of Edinburgh and Göttingen. He was elected a Liberal member of the British Parliament in 1885, and became secretary of state for war in 1905. As war secretary Haldane completely reorganized the British army and established a training program for reserve officers and a scientific research department. After 1909, Haldane served the British government in several offices as an advisor on education; his recommendations resulted in the establishment of provincial universities and evening college courses, in government subsidies for education, as well as in other measures designed to make higher education more widely available. Haldane was created viscount in 1911 and served as lord chancellor from 1912 to 1915. Because of his known admiration for German philosophy and his earlier attempts to prevent war with Germany, he was excluded from holding high

Richard Burton Haldane — Bettmann Archive

government posts during World War I for political reasons. The war, however, proved the value of his earlier army reforms. In 1924 he was lord chancellor to the first British Labour government. As a philosopher, Haldane examined the doctrine of the German philosopher Georg Wilhelm Friedrich Hegel (q.v.) in the light of modern scientific discoveries. Haldane's books include *The Reign of Relativity* (1921) and *The Philosophy of Humanism* (1922). His *Autobiography* was posthumously published in 1929.

John Scott Haldane (1860–1936), physiologist, younger brother of Richard, born in Edinburgh, Scotland, and educated at the universities of Edinburgh and Jena. After teaching physiology at the universities of Dundee and Oxford, Haldane in 1913 became director of a mining research laboratory that was, after 1921, affiliated with the University of Birmingham. In connection with mining and industrial diseases caused by poor ventilation, he conducted extensive research into respiration. Among his most important contributions to physiology were his discovery that breathing is regulated by the concentration of carbon dioxide in the respiratory center of the brain, and his development of methods and equipment for determining the amounts of oxygen and carbon dioxide in the blood. Haldane founded and became joint editor of the *Journal of Hygiene*. Among his writings are *Mechanism, Life and Personality* (1913), *Respiration* (1922), *Materialism* (1932), and *The Philosophy of a Biologist* (1935).

J(ohn) B(urdon) S(anderson) Haldane (1892–1964), biologist, son of the preceding, born in Oxford, England, and educated at Eton College and New College, University of Oxford. After teaching at Oxford and at the University of Cambridge, Haldane was appointed professor of genetics (1933) and, later, of biometry (1937) at University College, University of London. In 1957 he became research professor at the Indian Statistical Institute, Calcutta, and in 1961 he retired to continue his research at Bhubaneswar, Orissa, India. Haldane was elected Fellow of the Royal Academy in 1932 and an honorary member of the Academy of Sciences of the U.S.S.R. in 1940. He was a research consultant for the British admiralty from 1940 to 1944. Well known for genetic discoveries, he measured the rate of mutation (q.v.) in human genes. Haldane wrote books for the general public as well as for biologists. His writings include *The Inequality of Man* (1932), *The Causes of Evolution* (1933), *The Marxist Philosophy and the Sciences* (1938), *New Paths in Genetics* (1941), *What Is Life?* (1948), *Everything Has a History* (1951), and numerous scientific papers.

HALE, Edward Everett (1822–1909), American writer and clergyman, born in Boston, Mass. and educated at Harvard University. He was pastor of the Church of the Unity, Worcester, Mass., from 1846 to 1856, and of the South Congregational Church, Boston, from 1856 to 1901. From 1903 until his death he served as chaplain of the United States Senate. Hale is known for his fictional writings and for his abolitionist sympathies during the period immediately preceding the American Civil War; his best-known work, the patriotic short story "The Man Without a Country" (1863, published in *The Atlantic Monthly*), is believed to have encouraged supporters of the Union cause. Hale wrote almost seventy books and was editor of the magazines *Old and New* and *Lend a Hand*. He was also a member of the National Academy of Arts and Letters. His writings include the novel *Ten Times One Is Ten* (1870), which led to the formation of many charitable organizations; the novel *In His Name* (1873); *A New England Boyhood* (1893), reminiscences of New England life; *If Jesus Came to Boston* (1894), an attempt, in fiction, to reconcile religion with rapidly changing social conditions; and *Memories of a Hundred Years* (2 vol., 1902).

HALE, George Ellery (1868–1938), American astronomer, born in Chicago, Ill., and educated at the Massachusetts Institute of Technology. While Hale was still in college, his father built a small observatory near Chicago, called the Kenwood Observatory, where Hale did original research and in 1889 invented the spectrohelio-

HALE, JOHN PARKER

graph (q.v.). In 1892 Hale was appointed associate professor of astrophysics at the University of Chicago and in 1895 he organized the Yerkes Observatory (q.v.), of which he served as director until 1904. In 1904 he organized the Mount Wilson Observatory (q.v.), which he directed until 1923. Hale was active in many scientific organizations, among them the National Research Council (q.v.). He was a foreign member of the Institute of France and the Royal Society of London. Hale conceived and helped to design the largest telescope in the world. The instrument, a reflector with a 200-in. mirror, was installed at Mount Palomar Observatory (q.v.) in 1948 and named the Hale Telescope in his honor. His writings include *The Study of Stellar Evolution* (1908), *The Depths of the Universe* (1924), and *Beyond the Milky Way* (1926).

HALE, John Parker (1806–73), American statesman, born in Rochester, N.H., and educated at Bowdoin College. He studied law and was admitted to the bar in 1830. His political career began in 1832 when, as a Jacksonian Democrat, he was elected to the New Hampshire legislature. From 1843 to 1845 he was a member of the United States House of Representatives; during this period his vigor in the antislavery cause eventually brought about his expulsion from the regular Democratic Party. In 1845 he led a powerful and successful personal campaign to help other candidates in his native State, and the New Hampshire legislature came under the control of Whigs and independent Democrats. As an independent Democrat, he was a United States Senator from 1847 to 1853, the first antislavery man to be elected to that body; during his term he was responsible for the legislation that abolished flogging in the navy. In 1852 he campaigned unsuccessfully for President as the candidate of the Free-Soil Party (q.v.). Later, as a member of the Republican Party, he served in the Senate from 1855 to 1865, and during the American Civil War consistently supported the policies of President Abraham Lincoln (q.v.). In 1863 Hale was accused of corruption in connection with his work for the Navy and, although a Senatorial investigation acquitted him of having committed any crime, his reputation was damaged and he was not nominated for another term. From 1865 to 1869 he served as U.S. minister to Spain.

HALE, Sir Matthew (1609–76), English jurist and statesman, born in Alderley, Gloucestershire, and educated at Magdalen College, University of Oxford, and Lincoln's Inn. He was called to the bar in 1637 and acted as defense counsel at the trials of many Royalists during the Great Rebellion (q.v.). Hale had a long public career, including service as a justice of Common Pleas in 1654 and as a member of Parliament from 1654 to 1660. In 1660 Charles II (q.v.), King of England, knighted Hale and appointed him chief baron of the exchequer; from 1671 to 1676 Hale was chief justice of the King's Bench, then the highest judicial office in England.

Although Hale, as a member of Parliament, shared in the Parliamentary triumph over the crown during the Great Rebellion, he was sympathetic to the Royalists and he labored to bring about a settlement between the two factions. Eventually he took an active part in the restoration of the monarchy under Charles II (q.v.), King of England. *See* ENGLAND: *History.*

Hale's private studies included investigations in classical law, history, the sciences, and theology. He exercised considerable influence on subsequent legal thought, and his best-known work, *The History and Analysis of the Common Law of England* (published posthumously in 1713), furnished the British jurist Sir William Blackstone (q.v.) with a basis for his *Commentaries.*

HALE, Nathan (1755–76), hero of the American Revolution, born in Coventry, Conn., and educated at Yale College (now Yale University). He taught school from 1773 until shortly after the outbreak of the American Revolution (q.v.) in 1775, when he became a lieutenant in the Continental Army. The following year he was promoted to captain. While stationed near New York City under the command of the American officer Major Thomas Knowlton (1740–76), Hale volunteered, in early September, 1776, to perform spy duty behind the British lines on Long Island. Disguised as a schoolmaster, he secured vital military information, but on Sept. 21, before he could return to safe territory, he was captured. The next morning he was hanged in New York City by the British as a spy. His last words are supposed to have been: "I only regret that I have but one life to lose for my country." A statue of Hale by the American sculptor Frederick William MacMonnies (q.v.) stands in City Hall Park, New York City.

HALEAKALA NATIONAL PARK, volcanic area on the island of Maui, 26 miles S.E. of Kahului, Hawaii. Haleakala, "house of the sun", includes Red Hill (10,023 ft.), the Puu Ulaula Observatory, and the Haleakala crater. The latter, the largest inactive volcanic crater in the world, is 2000 ft. deep, 7.5 mi. long, 2.4 mi. wide, and 20 mi. in circumference. Colorful cinder cones abound in the crater, which can be reached on foot or by horse. Several tourist cabins are located nearby.

The execution of Nathan Hale (depicted in a 19th-century woodcut). Granger Collection

Birds are plentiful in the area, as are endemic plants, notably the silversword *(ahinahina)*. From 1916 until 1961 Haleakala and Hawaii Volcanoes National Park (q.v.) were united as Hawaii National Park. Haleakala National Park covers 27,282.78 acres. It is administered by the National Park Service (q.v.).

HALES, Stephen (1677–1761), British physiologist, born in Bekesbourne, England and educated at Corpus Christi College, University of Cambridge. Although he was curate of Teddington, England, after 1709 and remained an active clergyman all his life, Hales is best known as a physiologist, chemist, and inventor. His investigations are reported in his famous work, *Statickal Essays*, which was published in two volumes. The first, *Vegetable Staticks* (1727), deals with the physiology of plants; because of it, Hales is recognized as the founder of the science of plant physiology. The second volume, *Haemastaticks* (1733), embodies his research on the mechanics of blood flow. By means of animal experimentation, Hales was able to show that the circulating blood exerts pressure; see BIOPHYSICS. Hales also investigated reflex actions and demonstrated that they depended on the existence of the spinal cord. His other research dealt with the behavior of gases, methods of ventilating ships and large buildings, the technique of determining ocean depths, and the processes of food preservation. In addition to his other works, Hales wrote anonymously *A Friendly Admonition to the Drinkers of Brandy and Other Distilled Spirit* (1734).

HA-LEVI, Judah. See JUDAH HA-LEVI.

HALÉVY, originally LÉVY, name of a distinguished French family of men of letters, of whom the most prominent are the following:

Jacques Fromental Élie Halévy (1799–1862), composer, born in Paris. He received his musical education at the Paris Conservatory, and studied counterpoint, fugue, and composition with the Italian composer Maria Luigi Carlo Zenobio Salvatore Cherubini (q.v.). In 1819 he won the Prix de Rome with his cantata *Herminie*. He later was professor of harmony and of composition at the Paris Conservatoire. His first popular success was the satirical opera *Le Dilettante d'Avignon* ("The Amateur of Avignon" 1829). It was, however, the grand opera *La Juive* ("The Jewess"), produced at the Paris Opéra in 1835, that established Halévy as a major operatic composer. This success was followed by another in the same year, the comic opera *L'Éclair* ("Lightning"). Halévy wrote more than thirty operas, and although many of them were hurriedly written and marred by poor libretti and careless workmanship, his best works revealed talent for soaring melody, vivid dramatic characterization, and theatrical effectiveness.

HALFBEAK

Ludovic Halévy (1834–1908), playwright and novelist, nephew of Jacques, born in Paris. He held various minor posts in the French civil service from 1852 to 1865, and during this period began to write for the theater. His first success, a libretto for *Orphée aux Enfers* ("Orpheus in the Underworld"), with music by the French composer Jacques Offenbach (q.v.), was performed in 1858. After 1860 he frequently collaborated with the French playwright Henri Meilhac (1831–97) on drawing-room comedies, such as the farce *Froufrou* (1869), and on comic operas, such as *La Belle Hélène* ("Beautiful Helen", 1864) and *La Périchole* (1868), for which Offenbach wrote the music. Halévy's best-known libretto was written for the opera *Carmen* by the French composer Georges Bizet (q.v.). Halévy's novels, most of which were sympathetic depictions of the life of the lower middle class, included *L'Abbé Constantin* ("Father Constantine", 1882). He was elected to the French Academy in 1884.

Élie Halévy (1870–1937), historian, son of Ludovic, born in Étretat and educated at the École Normale Supérieure, Paris. He obtained a professorship at the École Libre des Sciences Politiques in 1898. His writings, which dealt chiefly with historical and philosophical subjects, included *La Formation du Radicalisme Philosophique* (3 vol., 1901–04; Eng. trans., *The Growth of Philosophic Radicalism*, 1934), a study of English utilitarian and radical philosophers, and *Histoire du Peuple Anglais au XIXe Siècle* (6 vol., 1912–48; Eng. trans., *A History of the English People in the Nineteenth Century*, 6 vol., 2nd ed., 1949–52), a carefully documented study of the political, economic, and religious evolution of British institutions and ideas.

HALFBEAK, common name for the small tropical fish in the family Hemiramphidae, closely related to the flying fish (q.v.) and in general form resembling the garfish, but having the lower jaw prolonged far beyond the upper jaw, which is short and weak. Halfbeaks are found near the surface in both salt and fresh water. They subsist on algae. The common species, *Hyporhamphus unifasciatus*, found off America from Maine to Argentina, is about 13 in. in length, of which almost 3 in. is lower jaw. It often leaps out of the water, obtaining the necessary leverage by placing the tip of its lower jaw under a floating object. Other species, especially those in the genus *Euleptorhamphus*, found off Bikini Atoll in the Pacific Ocean, fly by spreading their fins after a leap. Many flying fish have a jaw structure similar to the halfbeak when young and they are sometimes considered descended from primitive halfbeaks. In Thailand halfbeaks of the genus *Dermogenys* are cultivated for fish fights, and are second only to the fighting fish in endurance. Fish of this genus utilize their beaks while fighting and engage in active "swordplay", but they rarely draw blood. The fight continues until one or both of the participants are too exhausted to continue. Halfbeaks are called gars (see GAR) in the United States and garfish in Australia and New Zealand.

HALF-LIFE, length of time in which half the atoms in a radioactive substance disintegrate. The half-life of a reaction is directly proportional to the amount of the substance decaying. For example, the half-life of one isotope of plutonium (q.v.) is 24,360 years. An ounce of plutonium-239 will be reduced to one-half ounce after 24,360 years, and after another 24,360 years one half of the half-ounce, or one quarter of an ounce, will be left. The decay proceeds indefinitely. The half-life of the radioactive isotope (see ISOTOPE; TRACERS) of carbon with atomic mass 14 is 5570 years; that of phosphorus-32 is 14.3 days; of nitrogen-13, ten minutes; and of polonium-212, three ten-millionths of a second. See RADIOACTIVITY.

HALFTONE. See PHOTOENGRAVING.

HALIBUT, common name for either of two species of flatfish (q.v.) in the genus *Hippoglossus*, related to the flounder. Halibut are longer, thicker, and heavier than any of the other flatfish, and differ somewhat in development. The upper, dark-brown side of the halibut corresponds to the right side of its embryo to which the left eye has migrated during development. The white underside corresponds to the left side. The dorsal and ventral fins also migrate so that they are situated at the new top and bottom of the adult fish. Unlike other flatfish, the result of the young halibut's development is a completely symmetrical fish.

The maximum size of the female is 9 ft. in length and 700 lb. in weight; the male reaches a maximum weight of about 40 lb. The flesh of the halibut is excellent food and the oil of its liver is even richer in vitamins A and D than cod-liver oil. Halibut are active and voracious, feeding principally on fishes and the larger crustaceans. They are sexually mature at twelve years of age and live for more than thirty years. Their age may be determined by the organic deposits in their ear bones (otoliths) which are laid down in seasonal rings. A female twelve years of age deposits 200,000 to 500,000 eggs at a time; one twenty years of age deposits 2,750,000 eggs; and older females produce even more. The eggs are laid in water at a depth of 900 ft.

HALIFAX

Pacific Halibut, Hippoglossus stenolepis

and drift with the currents at the same level until the birth of the young. The fish live in shallow water until sexual maturity, when they go down to depths of several thousand feet in search of food. Halibut are found in cold portions of the northern Atlantic and Pacific Oceans, and halibut fishing is a major industry in Canada and the northern United States. In 1924 these two countries established the International Fisheries Commission for the Study of the Pacific Halibut, *Hippoglossus stenolepis,* the more important of the two species, found along western North America from northern Alaska to Oregon, and off Hokkaido, Japan. The Atlantic halibut, *H. hippoglossus,* is found off Newfoundland southward to Massachusetts, and off Greenland, Iceland, the British Isles, and Scandinavia.

HALICARNASSUS (mod. *Bodrum*), city of ancient Caria (q.v.), in what is now Turkey, on the Ceramic Gulf, now the Gulf of Kos. The city was founded by the Dorians (q.v.) and was conquered by the Persians in the 5th century B.C. Later, having freed itself from Persian rule, the city became the capital of the independent province of Caria, and the seat of the Carian kings, the most famous of whom was Mausolus (377–353 B.C.). In his memory was erected, about 325 B.C., a tomb called the Mausoleum (q.v.), one of the Seven Wonders of the Ancient World; *see* SEVEN WONDERS OF THE WORLD. The Greek historians Herodotus and Dionysius of Halicarnassus (qq.v.) were born here. During the 15th century, Halicarnassus was fortified by the Knights of Saint John of Jerusalem (q.v.), who named it Petronion in honor of Saint Peter. Ruins of the ancient city are found at Bodrum.

HALIFAX, title in the British peerage with the rank of baron, viscount, earl, or marquis, created for several prominent members of the Savile, Montagu, and Wood families. A notable holder of the title was the statesman Sir George Savile (q.v.), created Marquis of Halifax in 1682. The statesman and financier Charles Montagu (q.v.) was created Baron Halifax in 1700 and earl of Halifax in 1714; he died without issue and the earldom was recreated in 1715 for his nephew George Montagu (d. 1739). Upon George's death his son, George Montagu Dunk (1716–71), became 2nd Earl of Halifax; as president of the board of trade from 1748 to 1761, Dunk helped to found the colony of Nova Scotia (q.v.), in Canada, the chief town of which was named Halifax after him. The political leader Charles Wood (1800–85) was created viscount Halifax in 1866. He served under Victoria (q.v.), Queen of Great Britain, as chancellor of the exchequer (1846), first lord of the admiralty (1855), secretary of state for India (1859–66), and lord privy seal (1870–74). His grandson was the statesman Edward Frederick Lindley Wood, Earl of Halifax (q.v.), who succeeded his father as 3rd viscount and was created earl in 1944.

HALIFAX, city and seaport in Canada and capital of Nova Scotia Province, on a peninsula which extends into Halifax Harbor, an inlet of the Atlantic Ocean, about 200 miles s.w. of Sydney. The city is on a hill overlooking the harbor, formerly Chebucto Bay, which is composed of two large basins, the harbor proper and Bedford Basin. The landlocked harbor has an area of 13 sq.mi. and a minimum depth of 30 ft. Founded in 1749 as a British naval base intended to rival the French port of Louisburg, Halifax has retained its naval importance and is now commercially important as well. A naval dockyard covering an area of 14 acres extends along 2700 ft. of the waterfront. The city is a port of call for some thirty-six steamship lines, connecting the city with American and European ports. Harbor and dockage equipment include storage plants and facilities for the transshipment of goods. Halifax is an important Atlantic railroad terminus and is

HALIFAX

served by an airport. Goods manufactured or processed in the city, principally for export, include sugar, oil, wood products, skates, confections, spices, paint, varnish, cordage, paper boxes, clothing, nuts and bolts, fish, and fish products. Other exports include lumber, flour, and agricultural products. Machine shops, shipyards, and insulating and steam-packing works are located in the city.

Dalhousie University, founded in 1818, the government house, the provincial parliament, and the Citadel, one of the older forts in the city, are among the public buildings. On Dec. 6, 1917, during World War I, a great part of the city was destroyed and hundreds of lives were lost when a munitions ship exploded after colliding with another ship in the harbor. Halifax is an archiepiscopal see for the Roman Catholic Church and an episcopal see for the Anglican Church. Pop. (1966) 86,792; (1971) 122,035.

HALIFAX, Great Britain, municipal, parliamentary, and county borough of West Riding, Yorkshire, England, about 5 miles s.w. of Bradford. In the 15th century Halifax became a center for the cloth trade and in the 17th century was granted two markets and two fairs. It was incorporated in 1848 and became a county borough in 1888. Among notable buildings of the borough are the Heath Grammar School, founded in 1585; the Piece Hall, built in 1799 for the display and sale of piece goods; and the Rose and Crown Inn, on Black Lane, where the British novelist Daniel Defoe (q.v.) is reputed to have written parts of his novel *Robinson Crusoe*. The manufacture of cotton, woolen, and worsted goods and of carpets, iron, steel, and machinery are the most important industries in Halifax. Pop. (1969 est.) 93,570.

HALIFAX, Edward Frederick Lindley Wood, Earl of (1881–1959), British statesman, born at Powderham Castle in Devonshire, England, and educated at the University of Oxford. He was a member of the Conservative Party in the House of Commons from 1910 to 1925. After holding a number of minor posts in the government, he became viceroy of India in 1926. In India he sought to quell the widespread dissent against British government by a policy of cooperation with Indian Nationalist leaders, particularly Mohandas Karamchand Gandhi (q.v.). In 1931 Halifax returned to England, succeeded his father as 3rd viscount Halifax in 1934, and became Conservative Party leader in the House of Lords in 1935. He was appointed secretary of state for foreign affairs early in 1938 and played an important role in the negotiation of the Munich Pact (q.v.). From 1941 to 1946 he was ambassador to the United States. He was created earl of Halifax in 1944. The following year he served as a member of the British delegation to the United Nations Charter Conference, held at San Francisco, Calif. A number of his important addresses were collected and published under the title *Speeches on Foreign Policy* (1940) and *American Speeches* (1947); his autobiography, *Fullness of Days*, was published in 1957.

HALITE or ROCK SALT, mineral form of common salt, with the chemical composition sodium chloride, NaCl. Halite is a common mineral, formed by the drying of enclosed bodies of salt water; subsequently the beds so formed have often been buried by the rock strata formed from other sedimentary deposits. Beds of halite range in thickness from a few feet up to one hundred feet, and have been found at great depths beneath the surface of the earth. This mineral is often found associated with gypsum, sylvite, anhydrite, calcite, clay, and sand. Halite is widely disseminated over the world; in the United States notable deposits are found in New York, Michigan, Ohio, Kansas, New Mexico, and Utah.

Halite crystallizes in the isometric system, usually in the form of cubes, and shows perfect cubic cleavage. It is colorless and transparent when pure, but is often tinted yellow, red, blue, or purple by impurities. It has a hardness of 2½ and a specific gravity of 2.16.

Since World War II, U.S. production of rock salt has grown from about 3,000,000 tons per year to more than 14,000,000 tons annually in the early 1970's. For uses of the mineral, *see* SALT, in common usage.

HALL, Asaph (1829–1907), American astronomer, born in Goshen, Conn., and educated at the University of Michigan. In 1862 he was appointed an aid in mathematics at the United States Naval Observatory in Washington, D.C., and a year later he was promoted to professor, a position he held until he retired in 1891. From 1895 until 1901 he was professor of astronomy at Harvard University. Hall is best known for his discovery, in 1877, of the two moons of the planet Mars (q.v.), Phobos (Gr. "fear") and Deimos (Gr. "terror").

HALL, Charles Martin (1863–1914), American chemist and inventor, born in Thompson, Ohio, and educated at Oberlin College. As a student Hall became interested in the production of aluminum (q.v.) which was then very expensive because of inefficient methods of extraction from its ores. In 1886, eight months after his graduation, Hall developed the first practical process for extraction of aluminum by means of electrolysis; see ELECTROCHEMISTRY. In 1888 the Pittsburgh Reduction Company (later the Aluminum Company of America) was founded for the purpose of producing aluminum by the Hall process. Hall became vice-president of the company in 1890.

The process of aluminum manufacture today is essentially identical with the process developed by Hall; a similar process was developed independently by a French chemist Paul Héroult (1863–1914), probably a few months later.

The Hall process made aluminum available for the first time in commercially usable quantities at a price that was competitive with steel and other metals.

HALL, Granville Stanley (1844–1924), American psychologist and educator, born in Ashfield, Mass., and educated at Williams College, Union Theological Seminary, Harvard University, and in Germany. After teaching philosophy and later psychology at various American colleges, Hall was appointed professor of psychology and pedagogics at Johns Hopkins University in 1883. In 1889 Hall was named president of the newly founded Clark University (q.v.) in Worcester, Mass. Under his guidance considerable work was done in educational research at the university during its first twenty years. Hall contributed to numerous educational journals, and was instrumental in the development of the new science of educational psychology. His work in that field shows the influence of the American philosopher William James (see under JAMES), with whom Hall had studied at Harvard. In 1887 Hall founded the American Journal of Psychology; he resigned the presidency of Clark University in 1919, but continued writing until his death. Hall's books include Adolescence (2 vol., 1904); Jesus the Christ, in the Light of Psychology (2 vol., 1917); Senescence, the Last Half of Life (1922); and Life and Confessions of a Psychologist (1923).

HALL, James (1793–1868), American writer and jurist, born in Philadelphia, Pa., and privately educated. After serving in the War of 1812 he was admitted to the bar in 1818 and settled in Shawneetown, Ill., in 1820. There he established a law practice and became editor of the Illinois Gazette, a newspaper. He became a judge of the Circuit Court and, in 1828, was appointed State treasurer. At Vandalia, then the State capital, he edited the Illinois Intelligencer and, in 1830, established the Illinois Monthly Magazine, the first literary periodical west of Ohio. After 1833 Hall worked in Cincinnati, Ohio, as an editor and, later, as a bank official. Hall is known chiefly for his books about life in the West. His works include Legends of the West (1832); Sketches of History, Life, and Manners in the West (2 vol., 1834–35); and, with the American government official Thomas Loraine McKenney (1785–1859), a History of the Indian Tribes of North America (3 vol., 1836–44).

HALL, James Norman. See NORDHOFF, CHARLES BERNARD.

HALLAM, name of a family of British men of letters, of whom the most distinguished are the following:

Henry Hallam (1777–1859), historian, born in Windsor, Berkshire, England, and educated at the University of Cambridge. He practiced law until 1812, when he inherited large estates from his father and obtained a government post as commissioner of stamps. He devoted the rest of his life to historical research and writing. Although Hallam's Whig (q.v.) political bias often colored his historical judgment, his work is notable for factual accuracy and for his thorough research into original source materials. His major works are A View of the State of Europe During the Middle Ages (1818), The Constitutional History of England From the Accession of Henry VII to the Death of George II (1827), and Introduction to the Literature of Europe in the 15th, 16th, and 17th Centuries (4 vol., 1837–39).

Arthur Henry Hallam (1811–33), poet and essayist, the son of Henry, born in London, England, and educated at the University of Cambridge. As a student Hallam showed great literary promise, which unfortunately remained unfulfilled because of his early death. He is commemorated in the elegy In Memoriam (1850) by the British poet and friend of his student days, Alfred, Lord Tennyson (q.v.). Hallam's writings were collected posthumously by his father and published in 1834.

HALLANDALE, city of Florida, in Broward Co., on the Atlantic coast, about 15 miles N. of Miami. Hallandale has a vegetable-packing industry, and is the site of the Gulf Stream Race Track. Pop. (1960) 10,483; (1970) 23,849.

HALLE, or HALLE AN DER SAALE, city in East Germany, and capital of Halle District, on the Saale R., about 20 miles N.W. of Leipzig. The principal product of Halle is salt, which is obtained from salt springs on an island in the Saale R. Other important industries include brewing, sugar refining, printing, the making of machinery, and processing of foodstuffs. Halle is the site of the University of Halle, founded in 1694 by Frederick, Elector of Brandenburg, later Frederick I (q.v.), King of Prussia. The university has long been noted as a center of Protestant theology. Among the noteworthy buildings in Halle

HALLE, ADAM DE LA

are the medieval town hall, the 12th-century Sankt Moritzkirche, and the 16th-century Marienkirche. A statue of the composer George Frederick Handel (q.v.), born in Halle, stands in the main square of the city.

In the 9th century Halle was a fortress. It early became known for its valuable saltworks, and received a charter as a town in 981. During the 13th and 14th centuries Halle was a free city of the Hanseatic League (q.v.). After the Peace of Westphalia in 1648, Halle became part of the electorate of Brandenburg. Following World War II the city was incorporated into the Soviet zone of occupation. Pop. (1968) 262,749.

HALLE, Adam de la. See ADAM DE LA HALLE.

HALLÉ, Sir Charles (1819–95), originally KARL HALLE, German-British pianist and conductor, born in Hagen, Westphalia. He revealed his musical talents at a very early age and studied music in Darmstadt, Germany, and in Paris. Hallé began to give chamber concerts in Paris but moved to Manchester, England, during the French Revolution of 1848. He worked there as a music teacher, pianist, and conductor until 1857 when he formed what was to become the famous Hallé orchestra. He remained the conductor of the orchestra for the rest of his life and became a devoted popularizer of the music of the French composer Louis Hector Berlioz (q.v.). In 1893 Hallé helped found the Royal College of music in Manchester.

HALLECK, Fitz-Greene (1790–1867), American poet and satirist, born in Guilford, Conn., and educated in local schools. In collaboration with the American poet Joseph Rodman Drake (1795–1820), he wrote the satirical sketches *The Croaker Papers,* which were published in the New York *Evening Post* in 1819. Halleck commemorated the death of Drake in his best-known poem, "Green Be the Turf Above Thee". His books of verse include *Fanny* (1819), *Alnwick Castle, with Other Poems* (1827), and *Poetical Works* (1847).

HALLECK, Henry Wager (1815–72), American army officer, born in Westernville, N.Y., and educated at Union College, and the United States Military Academy at West Point. He was an expert in military fortifications. In 1846 he wrote *Elements of Military Art and Science,* which was used during the American Civil War as a training manual for volunteer officers.

Halleck served on the West coast during the Mexican War. He resigned from the army in 1854 and had a successful career as a lawyer and industrialist until the outbreak of the Civil War, when he reentered the army with the rank of major general. He commanded the Department of Missouri and planned the Western campaign of 1862. In July, 1862, he was appointed general in chief of the armies of the United States, and held that post until 1864 when he was superseded by General Ulysses Simpson Grant (q.v.). Halleck served as chief of staff of the army until 1865. He filled that administrative post with great success, although historians are generally agreed that he was overly cautious as a field commander. After the war Halleck remained in the army, serving at San Francisco and, after 1869, at Louisville, Ky. His writings include *Bitumen: Its Varieties, Properties, and Uses* (1841), *A Collection of Mining Laws of Spain and Mexico* (1859), and *International Law* (1861).

HALLEL (Heb., "praise"), in Jewish ritual, selection from the Psalms (q.v.), chanted as part of the liturgy during certain festivals. The more frequently used selection includes Ps. 113–118 and is known as the Egyptian Hallel, presumably because Ps. 114 begins, "When Israel went out of Egypt . . ."; it is sung in synagogues on the first two days of Pesach, on Shabuoth, on Sukkoth (qq.v.), and on each morning of the eight days of Hanukkah (q.v.). An abridged version is sung on the last six days of Pesach and at the new moon. The Egyptian Hallel is also sung at the close of the seder, the domestic Pesach service, and is, presumably, the hymn that was sung by Jesus and his disciples at the end of the Last Supper (Mark 14:26). A second Hallel, the Great Hallel, consists of Ps. 136 alone; it is sung at Pesach and during Sukkoth and recited every Sabbath. Originally, the Hallel consisted of either Ps. 113 or Ps. 114; the psalms now included in the ritual are later additions, made about 160 A.D.

HALLELUJAH or **ALLELUIA** (Heb. halălūyāh, "praise (ye) the Lord"), interjection used in hymns and liturgies of the Orthodox Church, the Roman Catholic Church, and the Church of England (qq.v.). The Roman Catholic Church omits the Hallelujah from the liturgy of the dead and from the services from Septuagesima, the third Sunday before Lent (q.v.), until the Easter Vigil Mass. Composers of religious and semireligious music have made much use of it; one notable example is the "Hallelujah Chorus" in the oratorio *Messiah* by the German composer George Frederick Handel (q.v.).

HALLER, Albrecht von (1708–77), Swiss physiologist, botanist, physician, and poet, born in Bern, and educated at the universities of Tübingen and Leiden. After completing his medical training Haller conducted extensive botanical and anatomical research, which gained him a professorship in medicine, anatomy, surgery, and botany at the University of Göttingen in 1736. While at Göttingen, he wrote extensively on a variety of subjects for the monthly journal of the university. Haller resigned his chair in 1753 and returned to Bern, where he held various municipal and state positions, and where he wrote many of his major works.

Haller made many scientific discoveries, among them the distinction between sensitive and irritable tissues. He demonstrated that irritability, which is the ability to contract when touched, is a property of all living tissue, whereas sensitivity is limited to tissues supplied with nerves.

Haller published many scientific works, including *Elementa Physiologiae Corporis Humani* ("Elements of the Physiology of the Human Body", 8 vol., 1757–66), considered the first modern treatise on physiology. His literary works include the poem "Die Alpen" ("The Alps", 1729), a landmark in German descriptive poetry, and three philosophic romances, *Usong* (1771), *Alfred* (1773), and *Fabius and Cato* (1774), which express his views on various forms of government.

HALLEY, Edmund (1656–1742), British astronomer, born in London, England, and educated at the University of Oxford. In 1676 he went to the island of Saint Helena (q.v.) to observe and catalogue the fixed stars of the Southern Hemisphere. As a reward for this work, he was made a fellow of the Royal Society in 1678. Halley was intrigued by the theories of the British physicist Sir Isaac Newton (q.v.) and encouraged him to write the *Principia*, which Halley then published in 1687 at his own expense. Halley made a series of sea voyages from 1698 to 1701 to study the variations of the compass from true north, and to chart the tides in the English Channel. He was made astronomer royal in 1721, and began an eighteen-year study of the complete revolution of the moon through its ascending and descending nodes.

Halley's most important scientific treatise was *Astronomiae Cometicae Synopsis* ("Synopsis on Cometary Astronomy"), begun in 1682 and published in 1705. In this work, Halley applied Newton's laws of motion (q.v.) to all available data on comets, and then mathematically demonstrated that comets move in elliptical orbits around the sun. His accurate prediction of the return in 1758 of a comet (now known as Halley's comet) validated his theory that comets are part of the solar system. *See* COMET.

HALL OF FAME FOR GREAT AMERICANS, structure on the campus of New York University, in New York City, erected in 1900 for the purpose of honoring Americans who have made signal contributions to the welfare or culture of the United States. A semicircular, open-air colonnade 630 ft. in length, with a massive substructure, the hall was designed by the American architect Stanford White (q.v.). Bronze portrait busts, carved by distinguished American sculptors, line the colonnade.

Elections to the Hall of Fame are held every three years and are conducted by a committee of about one hundred prominent Americans representative of the fifty States. Candidates may be nominated by any citizen of the U.S. The candidates must have been dead at least twenty-five years and must have been citizens of the U.S., either through birth or naturalization. Agreement of three fifths of the committee is necessary for election. The original plan provided for a total selection of 150 men and women.

Edmund Halley

PERSONS ELECTED TO THE HALL OF FAME FOR GREAT AMERICANS

John Adams (U.S. President)
John Quincy Adams (U.S. President)
Jane Addams (social worker)
Louis Agassiz (naturalist)
Susan Brownell Anthony (reformer)
John James Audubon (naturalist, artist)
George Bancroft (historian, statesman)
Henry Ward Beecher (clergyman)
Alexander Graham Bell (physicist, inventor)
Daniel Boone (pioneer)
Edwin Thomas Booth (actor)
Phillips Brooks (clergyman, author)
William Cullen Bryant (poet, journalist)
William Ellery Channing (clergyman)
Rufus Choate (lawyer)
Henry Clay (statesman)
Samuel Langhorne Clemens (author)
Grover Cleveland (U.S. President)
James Fenimore Cooper (author)
Peter Cooper (manufacturer, philanthropist)
Charlotte Saunders Cushman (actress)
James Buchanan Eads (inventor, engineer)

Continued on page 152

HALLOWEEN

HALL OF FAME — Continued

Thomas Alva Edison (inventor)
Jonathan Edwards (clergyman, theologian)
Ralph Waldo Emerson (author)
David Glasgow Farragut (naval officer)
Stephen Collins Foster (songwriter)
Benjamin Franklin (author, diplomat)
Robert Fulton (engineer, inventor)
J(osiah) Willard Gibbs (mathematical physicist)
William Crawford Gorgas (army surgeon, sanitation expert)
Ulysses Simpson Grant (U.S. President)
Asa Gray (botanist)
Alexander Hamilton (statesman)
Nathaniel Hawthorne (author)
Joseph Henry (physicist)
Patrick Henry (orator, patriot)
Oliver Wendell Holmes (author)
Oliver Wendell Holmes, Jr. (jurist)
Mark Hopkins (theologian, educator)
Elias Howe (inventor)
Washington Irving (author)
Andrew Jackson (U.S. President)
Thomas Jonathan ("Stonewall") Jackson (soldier)
Thomas Jefferson (U.S. President)
John Paul Jones (naval officer)
James Kent (jurist)
Sidney Lanier (poet)
Robert E (Edward) Lee (soldier)
Abraham Lincoln (U.S. President)
Henry Wadsworth Longfellow (poet)
James Russell Lowell (author, diplomat)
Mary Lyon (educator)
Edward Alexander MacDowell (musician)
James Madison (U.S. President)
Horace Mann (educator)
John Marshall (jurist, statesman)
Matthew Fontaine Maury (naval officer, oceanographer)
Maria Mitchell (astronomer)
James Monroe (U.S. President)
Samuel Finley Breese Morse (inventor, artist)
William Thomas Green Morton (dentist)
John Lothrop Motley (historian)
Simon Newcomb (astronomer, economist)
Thomas Paine (philosopher, author)
Alice Freeman Palmer (educator)
Francis Parkman (historian)
George Peabody (businessman, philanthropist)
William Penn (founder of the colony of Pennsylvania)
Edgar Allan Poe (author)
Walter Reed (army surgeon, bacteriologist)
Theodore Roosevelt (U.S. President)
Augustus Saint-Gaudens (sculptor)
William Tecumseh Sherman (soldier)
Joseph Story (jurist)
Harriet Beecher Stowe (author, abolitionist)
Gilbert Charles Stuart (portrait painter)
Sylvanus Thayer (soldier)
Henry David Thoreau (author, naturalist)
Booker Taliaferro Washington (educator)
George Washington (U.S. President)
Daniel Webster (statesman, orator)
George Westinghouse (inventor, industrialist)
James Abbott McNeill Whistler (artist)
Walt Whitman (poet)
Eli Whitney (inventor)
John Greenleaf Whittier (poet)
Emma Willard (educator)
Frances Elizabeth Willard (educator, reformer)
Roger Williams (founder of the colony of Rhode Island)
Woodrow Wilson (U.S. President)
Orville Wright (inventor)
Wilbur Wright (inventor)

See separate articles for all persons listed.

HALLOWEEN or **ALLHALLOWS EVE,** name applied to the evening of October 31, preceding the Christian feast of Hallowmas, Allhallows, or All Saints' Day (q.v.). The observances connected with Halloween are believed to have originated among the ancient Druids, who believed that on that evening, Saman, the lord of the dead, called forth hosts of evil spirits. The Druids customarily lit great fires on Halloween, apparently for the purpose of warding off these spirits; see DRUIDISM. Among the ancient Celts, Halloween was the last evening of the year, and it was regarded as a propitious time for examining the portents of the future. The Celts also believed that the spirits of the dead revisited their earthly homes on that evening; see CELTIC PEOPLES AND LANGUAGES. After the Romans conquered Britain, they added to Halloween features of the Roman harvest festival held on November 1 in honor of Pomona, goddess of the fruits of trees; see ROMAN RELIGION AND MYTHOLOGY.

The Celtic tradition of lighting fires on Halloween survived until modern times in Scotland and Wales, and the concept of ghosts and witches is still common to all Halloween observances. Traces of the Roman harvest festival survive in the custom, prevalent in both the United States and Great Britain, of playing games involving fruit, such as ducking for apples in a tub of water. Of similar origin is the decorative use of jack-o'-lanterns, or hollowed-out pumpkins that are carved to resemble grotesque faces and lit by candles placed inside.

HALLSTATT CULTURE, culture characteristic of the first stage of the Iron Age in central and western Europe and the Balkans. It received its name from the Austrian village of Hallstatt, in Upper Austria Province, about 140 miles S.W. of Vienna. In Hallstatt a necropolis containing more than 2000 graves and a great number of artifacts was excavated between 1846 and 1899. The period covered by the Hallstatt Epoch extends from about 1000 to 400 B.C.

Hallstatt was an early salt-mining community with mine shafts reaching to 1300 ft. by the end of the Bronze Age. The Hallstatt culture was characterized by elaborate funeral rites, involving, at different stages of the epoch, both cremation and inhumation. In general the age was marked by an increasing use of iron and an increasing skill in iron work, though occasionally older, Bronze-Age materials and techniques reappeared. Hallstatt art has endured mostly in the form of iron and bronze work and pottery, used as grave furniture, and decorated in symmetrical, repetitive, geometric patterns. In the few instances when artists took forms from nature, they distorted them into standardized geometrical shapes. See ARCHEOLOGY: *Current Research: The Urban Revolution.*

HALLUCINATION, error of any of the five senses of perception, as when one perceives a nonexistent object or feels a sensation without external stimulus. In normal persons hallucinations occur in the twilight state between sleeping and awakening, in delirium, in delirium tremens (qq.v.), and in exhaustion. Hallucinations may be induced under hypnosis (q.v.) and are generally visual, involving humans, animals, or insects; those of smell and taste usually occur only in brain disease. Persistent hallucinations are characteristic of schizophrenia; see MENTAL DISORDERS: *Psychoses—Schizophrenia*. In auditory hallucination, a schizophrenic psychosis triggered by abstinence from or overindulgence in alcohol, the victim believes that he hears accusing voices, to which he reacts by calling the authorities, barricading himself, or occasionally by committing suicide. Hallucination is distinguished from illusion (q.v.), a misperception of actual experience.

Hallucinations are common following self-administration of certain drugs, notably mescaline (see PEYOTE), marijuana (q.v.), and lysergic acid diethylamide (LSD). The effects of mescaline and marijuana evaporate shortly after administration ceases, but those of LSD often persist. See DRUGS, ADDICTION TO; PSYCHEDELIC DRUGS.

HALO, phenomenon of light refraction caused by ice crystals in the atmosphere between the observer and the sun or moon. The commonest form of halo is a circle of colored light surrounding the disk of the sun or moon. Light from the sun or moon is bent by the atmospheric ice crystals at a 22° angle toward the observer. Thus, the halo is a circle whose radius is 22° from the center of the disk. Sometimes a secondary halo caused by the refraction from ice crystals is seen outside the primary halo at a distance of 46° from the center of the sun or moon. Colored images resembling the disk of the sun may also be seen. Called parhelia, or sun dogs, they sometimes can be seen spaced 22° from the sun in a vertical or horizontal direction.

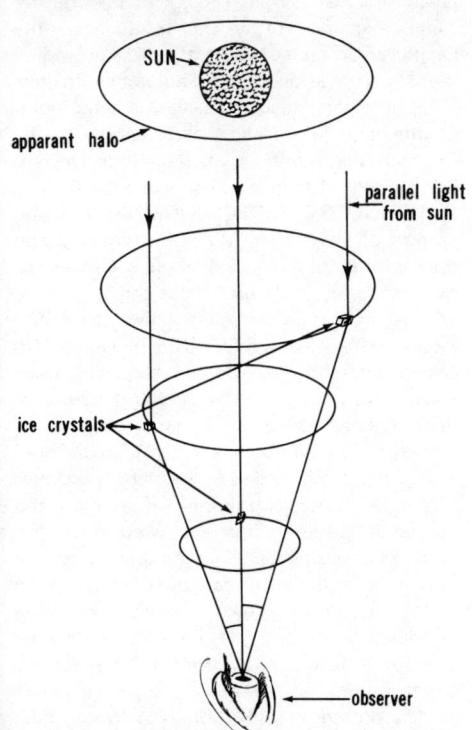

Halos are larger in diameter than the coronas seen around the sun or moon in hazy weather. Coronas are caused by the diffraction (q.v.) of light by water particles in the atmosphere. A corona is similar to a rainbow (q.v.) and a fogbow. Fogbows occur when sunlight strikes a fog bank (see FOG), producing a colored arc about 40° from the center of the disk of the sun. *See* METEOROLOGY; OPTICS.

HALOGENS (Gr. *hals*, "salt"; *genes*, "born"), in chemistry, group of five closely related elements, fluorine, chlorine, bromine, iodine, and astatine. The name halogen, or salt-former, refers to the property of each of the halogens to form with sodium a salt similar to common salt (sodium chloride). The halogens are all chemically active. Each member of the group has a valence of minus one and combines with metals to form halides as well as with metals and nonmetals to complex ions. See individual articles on the elements.

HALS, Frans (1580–1666), Dutch painter, born in Antwerp, Belgium, and probably trained by the Dutch painter Karel van Mander (1548–1606). Hals is regarded as one of the greatest masters of the art of portraiture. He spent all of his adult life in Haarlem, the Netherlands, finding patronage with the wealthy middle-class merchants and burghers of his time. Throughout his life he received important commissions for group portraits of the officers and corporations of Haarlem, and at the end of his life he was granted a small pension by the city.

In all of his portraits Hals achieved an air of complete spontaneity: his subjects give the impression of being caught in a fleeting, but characteristic, pose and expression. The gay mood of the early 1624 work "The Laughing Cavalier" (Wallace Collection, London), his apparently momentary smile and stance, demonstrate Hals' ability to present the immediacy of a sketch by the use of rapid, spontaneous brushstrokes. The broad brushstroke is characteristic of his work and adds a robust and lively quality to his portraits, particularly to the genre or character pieces he painted from 1620 to 1640 (see GENRE PAINTING). One of the most famous, the portrait of the gypsy tavern girl "La Bohémienne" (Louvre Museum, Paris), completed in 1630, owes its gaiety and brightness to two other painting techniques Hals employed: fully illuminating the figures with direct light, and blending the brilliant colors directly on the canvas.

Although his portraits appear spontaneous and uncalculated, Hals was an expert technician

"Portrait of a Man" (1640–45) by Frans Hals.
National Gallery of Art — Widener Collection

and his studies are always skillfully composed. His talent is particularly evident in his eight group portraits of the burgher guards and corporations of Haarlem, all of which are now in the Frans Hals Museum of that city. In all these group portraits Hals demonstrates his ability to catch each man in a characteristic pose, thus giving the group an air of informality and naturalness; each individual is clearly portrayed, yet all are linked in a pattern that is well balanced in line and color. As his style matured, Hals replaced the bright colors of his earlier canvases with a more monochrome color treatment. In his last group portrait, "The Lady Regents of the Saint Elizabeth Hospital", completed in 1664, he limited his palette to somber shades of black and gray, relying on broader and more vigorous brushstrokes to accentuate light and color value. This work is considered his masterpiece because the style lends a greater austerity and depth to the study, while it simultaneously fuses the group into a natural and harmonious pattern. In this portrait study, Hals achieves a new dignity and feeling for the character of the subjects that is absent from his earlier works, yet retains a spontaneous effect by the dexterity and facility of his brushwork.

The reputation of Hals was revived during the 19th century by the impressionist painters who admired his brilliant lighting effects and the freedom of his brushwork; see IMPRESSIONISM. Approximately one third of the paintings of Hals are in American museums.

See DUTCH PAINTING: *The Dutch Masters.*

HALSEY, William Frederick (1882–1959), American naval officer, born in Elizabeth, N.J., and educated at the United States Naval Academy at Annapolis, Md. During World War I, he commanded a destroyer patrol force and was awarded the Navy Cross. He was made rear admiral in 1938, vice admiral in 1940, and admiral in 1942. Halsey played a major role in the Pacific campaigns of World War II. In January, 1942, he directed carrier raids against the Japanese on Marshall and Gilbert islands, for which he was awarded the Distinguished Service Medal. In October of the same year he was given command of the Allied naval forces in the South Pacific, and in November, as tactical commander of the Solomon Islands campaign, defeated the Japanese at Guadalcanal (q.v.). In 1944 he became commander of the U.S. Third Fleet in the Pacific, and directed the naval attacks preceding the Allied invasion of the Philippines. In July, 1945, he commanded the seaborne aerial bombardment of Japan, and was promoted to the five-star rank of admiral of the fleet in December. He retired from active service in 1947.

HÄLSINGBORG, or HELSINGBORG, city and seaport of Sweden, in Malmöhus Province, on the Öresund, or the Sound, about 300 miles s.w. of Stockholm, opposite Helsingør, Denmark, with which it is connected by railway ferry. The modern city was established in the early 15th century near the site of the old town, which was known as a trade center as early as the 9th century. A ruined fortress is all that remains of the old town. The city belonged to Denmark until 1658, when it was ceded to Sweden. The Danes recaptured it several times, however, and it did not come under permanent Swedish control until 1710. Hälsingborg is an important port and one of the leading manufacturing centers in the country. It is located near the only coalfield in Sweden and near large clay deposits. Among the principal industrial establishments are sugar and copper refineries, breweries, superphosphate works, potteries, and rubber factories. Pop. (1968) 81,451.

HALTOM CITY, village of Texas, in Tarrant Co., adjoining Fort Worth, 5 miles N.E. of the downtown area. Pop. (1960) 23,133; (1970) 28,127.

HALYS. See KIZILIRMAK.

HAM. See MEAT.

HAM, in the Old Testament book of Genesis (q.v.), the second of the three sons of Noah (q.v.) who repopulated the earth after the deluge (q.v.) or flood. According to the genealogy presented in Genesis, Ham fathered four sons, the progenitors of the southern peoples of the earth. Cush became the ancestor of the Ethiopians; Mizraim of the Egyptians; Canaan of the Canaanites, the pre-Israelite inhabitants of Palestine; and Phut of an African people inhabiting Libya (Gen. 10:1, 6–20). Egypt is referred to several times in the Psalms (q.v.) as the "land of Ham" (Ps. 78:51; 105:23, 27; 106:22), evidently because of the genealogy in Genesis. The name of the Egyptian deity, Ammon, may well have been derived from the same source. Philologists and ethnologists recognize a distinct North African family of peoples and tongues that they term Hamitic, classifying it as coordinate with the Aryan and Semitic families. See HAMITES.

HAMA (Biblical, *Hamath*), city of Syria, on both banks of the Orontes R., about 120 miles N.E. of Damascus. The principal products of the city and the surrounding region are grain and wool, silk, and cotton textiles. An ancient city, Hama was once an important center of the Hittites (q.v.) and is frequently mentioned in the Bible as Hamath. Pop. (1967 est.) 148,176.

HAMADAN, city in Iran, and capital of Hamadan Governorate, in a fertile region, about 180 miles S.W. of Tehran. The city is known for the manufacture of rugs, leather trunks, and copperware. It is the center of the Iranian shellac and leather trade, and is commercially important because of its position on the principal route between Baghdad and Tehran. The city of Hamadan has a number of bazaars and several mosques. Also in the city are two tombs of special interest, one claimed to be that of the Biblical Mordecai and Esther (see ESTHER), and the other that of the Arabian philosopher-physician Avicenna (q.v.). The city is believed to occupy the site of the city of Ecbatana, capital of the ancient Medes; see MEDIA. During World War I Hamadan was the scene of fighting between Russian and Turko-German forces. The Russians captured the city in 1915, were expelled by the Turks in 1916, but regained control in the following year. The Iranian government later regained possession of Hamadan and other Iranian towns held by Russia. British troops occupied Hamadan for a time in the spring of 1918. Pop. (1966) 124,167.

HAMADRYAD. See DRYAD.

HAMAMATSU, city of Japan, in Shizuoka Prefecture, on the island of Honshu, near the Philippine Sea, 42 miles S.W. of Shizuoka, and midway between Tokyo and Kyoto. The city is an important road hub and is on the Tokaido rail line. Manufactures include textiles, chemicals, hats, electrical equipment, musical instruments, and plastic and wood products. Several resorts are in the vicinity. Hamamatsu was a military base during World War II. Pop. (1965) 392,632.

HAMAN, or AMAN, in the Old Testament book of Esther, an Amalekite (see AMALEKITES), who was the influential chief minister of the Persian king Ahasuerus (q.v.). See ESTHER.

HAMATH. See HAMA.

HAMBORN. See DUISBURG.

HAMBURG, State and city of West Germany, bounded on the N.W., N., and N.E. by the State of Schleswig-Holstein, and on the S.E., S., and S.W. by the State of Lower Saxony (qq.v.). The State and the city of Hamburg have been coextensive since 1937. The city-state is on the N. branch of the Elbe River (q.v.) at its confluence with the Alster R., about 75 mi. inland from the mouth of the Elbe and about 178 miles N.W. of Berlin. It consists mainly of narrow strips of land contiguous to the lower reaches of the Elbe.

Hamburg consists of an old section, situated on the E. side of the Alster R., a new section (*Neustadt*) on the W. side, and several suburbs. The old section, which contains the heart of the commercial district, is crossed by numerous canals. Among the outstanding features of Hamburg are the many bridges spanning the canals; the Inner Alster and Outer Alster, artificial lakes created by a dam at the mouth of the Alster; the ancient ramparts, converted into a system of gardens and promenades around the old section of the city-state; and the *Hopfenmarkt*, the principal public square. Noteworthy historic buildings include Town Hall, an elaborate structure in the German Renaissance style, completed in 1897; the Church of Saint Peter, parts of which date from the 12th century; the churches of Saint Catharine and Saint Jacob, both medieval structures; the Church of Saint Michael, a building in the Renaissance style with a lofty spire (about 440 ft.), completed in 1762; and the Church of Saint Nicholas, a Gothic structure with a spire 482 ft. in height, one of the highest in the world. Hamburg has a number of educational and cultural institutions, including the University of Hamburg (founded in 1919), a nautical school, a school of marine ar-

The Inner Alster, an artificial lake in the old section of Hamburg. The Lombards Bridges (right), built atop the ancient city ramparts, separate the Inner and Outer Alsters.
German Information Center

chitecture, an opera house and several theaters, several museums, botanical and zoological gardens, and a municipal library.

Hamburg is the principal seaport, chief commercial center, and second largest city of West Germany. In addition to vast accommodations for receiving and discharging transoceanic passengers and freight, the distribution facilities at the port include rail and inland-waterway connections with all major points in the interior of Germany.

Hamburg is also an important manufacturing and industrial center. Shipbuilding and related industries flourished prior to and during World War II. Many of these enterprises were extensively damaged by Allied air raids, but they have been revived. Other leading industries of Hamburg include oil refining, food processing, and the manufacture of chemicals, machinery, and household products. The city-state also has a fishing fleet and is a publishing and printing center. Hamburg has some rural areas, in which crops of cereals, potatoes, and vegetables are raised and dairy products are produced.

Government. Since 1952 the city-state has been governed by a thirteen-member senate, elected by a house of burgesses, which consists of 120 popularly elected members. The city-state is divided into seven local administrative districts.

History. Hamburg was founded as *Hammaburg*, a fortress established by Charlemagne (q.v.), Holy Roman Emperor, about 808 as a defense outpost against neighboring pagan tribes. Extending his campaign to convert the pagans to Christianity, Charlemagne founded a church in the vicinity of the fortress in 811. The church quickly became the center of Christian civilization in northern Europe and, as such, was subject to frequent attacks by hostile natives. Hamburg was designated an archbishopric in 834. In 847, two years after the town was sacked by Norsemen (q.v.), the seat of the archbishopric was transferred to Bremen (q.v.).

Despite destructive raids by the Danes and Slavs, Hamburg endured and, in 1189, received a charter from Frederick I (q.v.), Holy Roman Emperor. The charter, an award for services rendered during the Third Crusade, granted the town important commercial privileges. Defensive alliances concluded with Lübeck (q.v.) in 1241 and with Bremen in 1249 led to the formation of the Hanseatic League (q.v.), a federation

HAMILTON

of north German States. By decree of Maximilian I (q.v.), Holy Roman Emperor, Hamburg became a free city of the Holy Roman Empire (q.v.) in 1510. By 1529 Hamburg had accepted the Reformation (q.v.), and had become a haven for Lutheran, Calvinist, and Jewish refugees of Europe. During the Thirty Years' War (q.v.) the commercial prosperity of the city declined disastrously. A brief revival, initiated by the establishment of trade ties with the United States in 1783, was terminated by the Napoleonic Wars (q.v.). The forces of Napoleon I (q.v.), Emperor of France, occupied the city in 1811.

Reestablished as a free city after the downfall of Napoleon, Hamburg became a member of the Germanic Confederation in 1815. Hamburg recovered swiftly from the effects of the French occupation and continued to expand despite a destructive fire in 1842. The city was a member of the North German Confederation (q.v.) from 1867 to 1871, when it became a constituent State of the German Empire. A popular uprising in Hamburg in November, 1918, on the eve of the German surrender in World War I, heralded the overthrow of the German Empire and the formation of a republican government. The former Prussian towns of Altona, Harburg, and Wandsbek, and a number of rural districts were incorporated into Hamburg on April 1, 1938.

A submarine base and center of the German war effort during World War II, Hamburg was the target of frequent Allied air raids. British troops occupied the city-state in May, 1945. In 1949 Hamburg became a State of West Germany.

Area, 288 sq.mi.; pop. (1968 est.) 1,822,837.

HAMDEN, town of Connecticut, in New Haven, Co., 5 miles N. of the city of New Haven. Hamden was the site of the arms factory of the American inventor Eli Whitney (q.v.). The town still manufactures firearms as well as electrical equipment, wire and wire products. Hamden was settled about 1664 and incorporated in 1786. Pop. (1960) 41,056; (1970) 49,357.

HAMELN, city of West Germany, in Lower Saxony State, on Weser R., about 30 miles S.W. of Hannover. The city, located in a farming and cattle-raising area, is a river port and transportation center. The chief manufactures are blankets, furniture, and rugs. The city is the scene of the legendary appearance of the Pied Piper, who was asked to rid Hameln of rats during a plague in 1284. Historic buildings include the so-called Ratcatcher's House, built in 1602–03, on which are frescoes depicting the legend. Originally an outpost of the Saxons (q.v.), Hameln was made a city around 1200. In 1426 it became a member of the Hanseatic League (q.v.). After changing hands several times the city passed to Prussia before World War II. Pop. (1967 est.) 47,600.

HAMILCAR BARCA, or HAMILCAR BARCAS (270?–228 B.C.), Carthaginian general, appointed commander of the Carthaginian forces in Sicily during the First Punic War between Carthage and Rome; see PUNIC WARS. In 247 B.C. after establishing himself in the mountains near Panormus (now Palermo), Hamilcar made frequent raids on the southwest Italian coast. His actions forced the Romans to withdraw many of their troops from the port city of Lilybaeum (now Marsala), thereby freeing an important Carthaginian supply route. The defeat of the Carthaginian fleet in 241 B.C. terminated the war, and Hamilcar negotiated the peace in which Carthage was forced to cede Sicily and pay heavy financial indemnities. When the Carthaginian government refused to pay the mercenaries that he had engaged for the Sicilian campaign, his troops, joined by a number of Libyan slaves, revolted. Hamilcar was summoned to suppress the uprising, and he succeeded in defeating the rebels in 238 B.C. Appointed commander in chief of the army in 237 B.C., Hamilcar began the reconquest of Spain, planning to build a new empire from which he could launch a major attack on Rome. He spent nine years in Spain, organizing the conquered tribes into an army that was of great help to his son, the Carthaginian general Hannibal (q.v.), during the Second Punic War.

HAMILTON, township of New Jersey, in Mercer Co., between Crosswicks and Assunpink creeks, adjoining Trenton on the E. Hamilton Square, Yardville, and Mercerville are the largest of the many communities included within the township. Other communities are Groveville, East Trenton, and White Horse, the site of an American Revolution tavern. The suburban residential areas adjoining Trenton make up much of Hamilton; the N.E. part of the township has farms. Manufacturing plants in the suburban area produce building materials, rubber goods, pottery, and radiators. Hamilton is the site of the State Fair Grounds. Pop. (1960) 65,035; (1970) 79,609.

HAMILTON, city in Ohio, and county seat of Butler Co., on the Great Miami R., 25 miles N. of Cincinnati. It is served by railroad and maintains a municipal airport. The city is an important manufacturing center and the trading center of a rich farming and stock-raising area. Industrial establishments in Hamilton include paper mills, foundries, machine shops, and factories manu-

HAMILTON

facturing bank vaults and safes, heavy machine tools, motors, and auto parts. The city is the site of several business colleges. Hamilton is commemorated in *A Boy's Town* by the American author William Dean Howells (q.v.), who lived in the city as a boy. The city grew up around Fort Hamilton, a stockade built on the site in 1791 by General Arthur St. Clair (1736?–1818), first governor of the Northwest Territory (q.v.). The town was laid out in 1794 and named Fairfield. In 1796 the fort was abandoned, and the town was renamed Hamilton, becoming the county seat in 1803. It was incorporated as a village in 1810 and as a city in 1857. Pop. (1960) 72,354; (1970) 67,865.

HAMILTON, city of Canada, in Ontario Province, and county seat of Wentworth Co., at the W. extremity of Lake Ontario, 40 miles S.W. of Toronto. The city is served by railroad and by Great Lakes and oceangoing vessels and maintains a municipal airport. Hamilton Harbor is landlocked, and is one of the largest and best equipped harbors on the Great Lakes. With its abundant water power, derived from nearby falls, and natural gas obtained from fields in the vicinity, Hamilton has become one of the most important manufacturing centers in Canada. It has more than 500 manufacturing plants, including the largest agricultural-implement factory in the British Commonwealth. The major industry is the manufacture of iron and steel. Other basic industries include the production of wire, heavy machinery, electrical equipment, textiles, and automobiles. Hamilton is also the center of a noted fruit-growing area. It is the site of McMaster University, founded in 1887, and its affiliate, Hamilton College. The city is an episcopal see of the Anglican Church and of the Roman Catholic Church. Dundurn Castle, in Hamilton, contains a museum of local history. The city maintains a park system covering approximately 2000 acres, which includes bathing beaches, golf courses, and botanical and rock gardens. Hamilton was permanently settled in 1778, and incorporated as a city in 1846. Pop. (1966) 298,121; (1971) 309,173.

HAMILTON, Great Britain, burgh in Lanark County, Scotland, on the Clyde R. about 1 mi. from its confluence with the Avon R., 11 miles S.E. of Glasgow. The principal industries are the manufacture of electrical equipment, carpets, and knitwear. Among the prominent structures of the town are the burgh buildings, with a clock tower 130 ft. high; and the county buildings, executed in the Greek Revival style. Hamilton is the origin of the title belonging to the premier peer of Scotland, the duke of Hamilton and Brandon. Two miles N. of the town is the famous Bothwell Bridge, where the Covenanters (q.v.) were defeated in 1679 by the forces of Charles II (q.v.), King of England, Scotland, and Ireland. Pop. (1969 est.) 46,397.

HAMILTON, city in New Zealand, and administrative center of Waikato County, in Auckland District, on the Waikato R., 70 miles S.E. of Auckland. It is the largest inland city in New Zealand and the commercial center for a large area of North Island. In the surrounding region, dairying, lumbering, grass farming, and the raising of sheep, cattle, and pigs are important. The Ruakura Animal Research Station, nearby to the E., is internationally known. Parks lie along the river and at Lake Hamilton. Hamilton was settled by militiamen during the Maori uprisings of the 1860's. Pop. (1970) 70,000.

HAMILTON, town on the main island of Bermuda, and capital of the British colony of Bermuda. The town has an excellent landlocked harbor, Great Sound, and enjoys a flourishing tourist trade. Hamilton was founded in 1790. Pop. (1968 est.) 3000.

HAMILTON, former name of a river in Labrador. See CHURCHILL.

HAMILTON, Alexander (1755–1804), American statesman, born on the West Indian island of Nevis, the son of James Hamilton, a Scottish trader, and of Rachel Fawcett (Faucette) Levine. In 1769, after the death of his mother and the bankruptcy of his father, he entered the countinghouse of Nicholas Cruger at Saint Croix, where he exhibited such ability that in two years he was entrusted with the entire charge of the business. With the aid of funds advanced by friends to further his education, from 1772 to 1774 he studied at a grammar school at Elizabethtown, N.J., and then entered King's College (now Columbia University).

Revolutionary Involvement. Hamilton's advocacy of the American cause began at a public meeting in the "fields" (now City Hall Park) in New York City, with a brilliant, well-reasoned speech urging the calling of a general congress of the colonies. He also wrote two pamphlets anonymously, *A Full Vindication of the Measures of Congress from the Calumnies of Their Enemies* (1774) and *The Farmer Refuted* (1775), in answer to Loyalist pamphlets signed "Westchester Farmer". His pamphlets were at first attributed to such leaders as John Jay (q.v.) and Robert R. Livingston (*see under* LIVINGSTON); when his authorship became known, they brought Hamilton wide recognition. See AMERICAN REVOLUTION.

On the outbreak of the war, Hamilton be-

HAMILTON

came a captain of artillery and served with distinction in the battles of Long Island, White Plains, Trenton, and Princeton (see individual articles on these battles). His courage and ability won him the notice of General Nathanael Greene (q.v.), who introduced Hamilton to George Washington (q.v.) with a recommendation for advancement. In March, 1777, Washington made Hamilton his aide-de-camp and confidential secretary. He acquired great influence with Washington, as both friend and adviser,

Alexander Hamilton — Bettmann Archive

but he was ambitious for military glory, and took advantage of a rebuke from the general to resign his post in 1781. He remained in the army, however, and, taking command of a regiment of infantry, distinguished himself at Yorktown; see YORKTOWN: *Siege of.*

Lawyer and Statesman. In 1780 he married Elizabeth Schuyler, daughter of General Philip John Schuyler (q.v.), a member of an influential family in New York. At the close of the revolution Hamilton left the army and studied law at Albany. He served a term in Congress in 1782–83, and then returned to the practice of law, becoming one of the most eminent lawyers in New York City.

In 1786 he took a leading part in the Annapolis Convention, called to consider the problems of interstate commerce and other matters not covered by the Articles of Confederation (q.v.), and drafted the resolution that led to the assembling of the Constitutional Convention at Philadelphia in the following year; see CONSTITUTION OF THE UNITED STATES. At the Constitutional Convention, Hamilton presented his plan of a strongly centralized federal government, even though his two fellow delegates from New York were Anti-Federalists who outvoted him on every measure. His plan involved representation based on wealth and property, and absolute veto power vested in the executive; the aristocratic principles of the plan were rejected by the convention, but the forms were largely adopted. Although he was unable to obtain the form of government he desired, Hamilton turned his energy and ability to securing ratification of the constitution adopted by the convention. He conceived and started the series of essays that were published in the New York *Independent Journal,* and that were subsequently collected and published under the title of *The Federalist* (q.v.). Fifty-one of the eighty-five essays were written by Hamilton, and constitute the works by which he is best known.

Secretary of the Treasury. Shortly after the establishment of the new government in 1789 with Washington as President, Hamilton was appointed secretary of the treasury. Finding public credit in disrepute, official accounts of the state treasury deficient, and the national economy in a generally unhealthy condition, Hamilton instituted a series of reforms and wrote reports that have strongly influenced the administration of the national government since that time. His reports on public credit raised materially the low concept of national honor of the time, and were instrumental in securing the passage of measures for the funding of the public debt. In a report favoring the establishment of a national bank, he advanced the principle of the "implied powers" of the Federal government under the Constitution, which later greatly influenced the decisions of the Supreme Court of the United States (q.v.). His report on manufactures was notable as one of the first departures from the economic theories of the Scottish economic theorist and philosopher Adam Smith (q.v.), and as the genesis of the American protective policy; it advocated the establishment of a protective tariff and bounties to be paid in the encouragement of manufactures from the surplus funds derived from the tariff; see TARIFFS, UNITED STATES. Hamilton was also largely responsible for the organization of the entire administrative structure of the government, and his reports on subjects beyond his immediate responsibilities illustrate his versatility and ability as a statesman.

HAMILTON, ANDREW

Final Writings and Rivalry With Burr. In 1795 Hamilton, after declining appointment as chief justice of the Supreme Court, returned to law in New York City. He continued his activities in political matters, however, and with a series of essays signed "Camillus" defended Jay's Treaty (q.v.) as the best that could be obtained. Washington respected his ability and judgment and consulted him often. In 1798, at Washington's insistence, Hamilton was appointed major general, second in command of the army organized when war with France seemed imminent. Hamilton was the leader of the Federalist Party (q.v.); he supported John Adams (q.v.) for the presidency, but after the election of the latter they became political opponents, and Adams expelled Hamilton's friends from the cabinet and other offices.

In the election of 1800, which was thrown into the House of Representatives because Thomas Jefferson and Aaron Burr (qq.v.) had received equal numbers of electoral votes (*see* ELECTORAL COLLEGE), Hamilton exerted his great influence in favor of Jefferson, who had always been his chief political opponent (*see* DEMOCRATIC PARTY), rather than favor Burr, whom he considered to be a man of dangerous ambitions. In 1804 Hamilton was instrumental in the defeat of Burr as candidate for governor of New York State. After his defeat Burr forced a quarrel on Hamilton and challenged him to a duel. Although he strongly disapproved of dueling, Hamilton felt obliged to accept the challenge, and they met at Weehawken, N.J., on the spot where Hamilton's eldest son had been killed in a duel three years before. Hamilton was mortally wounded and died the next day.

His country house, now known as the Hamilton Grange National Memorial, is in New York City.

HAMILTON, Andrew (1676?–1741), American colonial lawyer, born in Scotland. He came to America about 1700, settling first in Virginia and later in Philadelphia, where he practiced law. He was appointed attorney general of Pennsylvania in 1717, served as a member of the provincial assembly from 1727 to 1739, and was responsible for choosing the site and general design of the Pennsylvania State House, later Independence Hall (q.v.). He is best known for his defense in 1734, of the American publisher John Peter Zenger (q.v.) against a charge of seditious libel. Hamilton delivered an eloquent defense, based on the theory that publication of the truth does not constitute libel, and won an acquittal that established the precedent for freedom of the press in the American colonies.

HAMILTON, Edith (1867–1963), American writer and educator, born in Dresden, Germany, of American parents, and educated at Bryn Mawr College, and the universities of Leipzig and Munich. She organized the Bryn Mawr School in Baltimore, Md., and served as its headmistress from 1896 to 1922. Her first book, *The Greek Way,* was published in 1930. This was followed by *The Roman Way* (1932), *Mythology* (1942), and *Echoes of Greece* (1957). She also translated several ancient Greek plays into English and wrote many articles for periodicals. In 1957, in recognition of her efforts to further the culture of ancient Greece, the Greek government made her an honorary citizen of Athens.

HAMILTON, Sir Ian Standish Monteith (1853–1947), British soldier, born of British parents on the island of Kérkira, Greece (then the British protectorate of Corfu), and educated at Wellington College and the Royal Military College, Sandhurst. He entered the army in 1872, saw his first action in 1879 in Afghanistan, and was wounded two years later while fighting in South Africa. He later participated in British expeditions to the Sudan and to Burma. In 1899 Hamilton commanded a brigade in the South African War (q.v.), and in the same year he was promoted to the rank of major general. He later became chief of staff to the British secretary for war, Horatio Herbert Kitchener (q.v.). During the Russo-Japanese War (q.v.), Hamilton accompanied Japanese troops as a British observer. In 1907 he was promoted to the rank of general; he spent the first months of World War I as commander of the Central Force, an army responsible for the defense of Great Britain. In 1915 he was given command of an Anglo-French force which had been formed to attack the Turkish army as part of the Gallipoli and Dardanelles Campaign (q.v.). After his failure to land troops successfully, Hamilton was relieved of his command. He retired from the army in 1920 and thereafter spent much of his time writing. His books include *Gallipoli Diary* (2 vol., 1920) and *History of the Great War. Military Operations, Gallipoli* (2 vol., 1929–32).

HAMILTON, Lady (1761?–1815), British court beauty, mistress of the British naval hero Horatio Nelson (q.v.), born Emma Lyon, of poor parents in Great Neston, England. At about the age of twenty she became the mistress of a minor English nobleman and member of Parliament, Charles Greville (1749–1809), and under his tutelage studied dancing, singing, and acting. In 1784 Greville, who had fallen into debt, agreed to send Emma to his uncle, Sir William Hamilton (1730–1803), the British ambassador to the court of Naples, who desired her as his mistress; in return, Hamilton paid off Greville's debts. In Naples, Emma became the favorite of the court, confidante of Queen Maria Carolina (1752–1814), and the chief liaison agent between the queen and the ambassador. In 1791 she visited England with Hamilton, and during their stay they were married.

Her first meeting with Lord Nelson took place two years later in Naples; in 1798 she rendered assistance to him by obtaining supplies needed for his campaign on the Nile; see NILE, BATTLE OF THE. In 1800 the ambassador, Lady Hamilton, and Nelson returned to England together, and in the following year she bore Nelson a daughter, Horatia Nelson Thompson (1801–1881). Upon her husband's death in 1803, Lady Hamilton received a lifetime annuity of £800; soon afterward she went to live with Nelson. Two years later, when Nelson was killed at the Battle of Trafalgar, she received his Merton estates and an annuity of £500. Despite these bequests, her extravagant habits and penchant for gambling soon left her penniless. She was imprisoned for debt in 1813; regaining her freedom after one year, she went to Calais, France, where she died seven or eight months later.

"Lady Hamilton as Nature", a portrait by the 18th-century British artist George Romney. Frick Collection

HAMILTON, Sir William Rowan (1805–65), British mathematician and astronomer, born in Dublin, Ireland, and educated at Trinity College, Dublin. Hamilton was a distinguished student and in 1827, while still an undergraduate, he was appointed professor of astronomy at Trinity College. The next year he was made Astronomer Royal for Ireland, and in 1835 he was knighted. Hamilton spent the rest of his life working at Trinity College and in the observatory at Dunsink, near Dublin. Hamilton is known chiefly for his work in vector analysis and in optics (qq.v.). In the field of dynamics he introduced Hamiltonian functions, which express the sum of the kinetic and potential energies of a dynamic system; they are of importance in the development of modern dynamics and for the study of quantum mechanics (q.v.).

HAMILTON COLLEGE, institution of higher learning for men, chartered in 1812, and located in Clinton, N.Y. The college evolved from an academy established in 1793 for the education of Indian youths. Areas of concentration are anthropology, art, biology, chemistry, economics, English literature, geology, government, Greek, history, Latin, mathematics, music, philosophy, religion, physics, psychology, and modern languages. The bachelor of arts degree is awarded. In 1968 the college library housed more than 275,000 bound volumes. Student enrollment in 1968 was 853, the faculty numbered 87, and the endowment was about $18,227,000.

In 1965 Kirkland College for girls was founded by Hamilton College. The campus is located on land adjacent to the Hamilton campus and the first freshman class of 165 students was admitted in September, 1968. The two colleges share facilities, services, and activities.

HAMITE, group of Caucasian peoples, originally of northern and northeastern Africa and the Canary Islands. Anthropologists are in dispute about the precise ethnological definition of the Hamite; they generally define the group as comprising the Berber (q.v.) of North Africa; the Fula and Tuareg (qq.v.) of the Sudan; the Tibbu, also of the Sudan; the ancient Egyptians; the major Ethiopian peoples; and the Guanche, an extinct people of the Canary Islands.

The typical Hamite is relatively tall and has dark-brown skin and curly black hair. Some Hamite, such as the Berber, occasionally have blond characteristics, the result, probably, of invasion by northern nations; others, south of the Sahara, show the effect of mixture with Negroid peoples. Some ethnologists have attempted to link the Hamite with the Mediterranean peoples, thus tracing their origin to Europe.

The Hamite are in the main agricultural peoples. They are credited with originating the oldest extant writing in the world, the hieroglyphic inscriptions (see HIEROGLYPHICS) of the ancient

HAMITIC LANGUAGES

Egyptians, and were the earliest engineers and architects in massive stone. *See also* SEMITES.

HAMITIC LANGUAGES, name long used for a supposed family of languages in North Africa, including ancient Egyptian, which in the form of Coptic or "Neo-Egyptian" survived until the 17th century A.D.; the Berber (q.v.) languages of northern and northwestern Africa; the Cushitic languages found largely in Ethiopia and Somali, including Galla and Somali (qq.v.); and, in the opinion of some, the Chadic languages of the Lake Chad (*see* CHAD, LAKE) area, the major member of which is Hausa (q.v.). These languages are, in turn, related to the Semitic languages (q.v.). A larger linguistic family called Hamito-Semitic has been suggested. Recent scholarship has shown, however, that the so-called Hamitic languages do not constitute a unity parallel to the Semitic; rather, all the language groups in question are coordinate branches of one family. This family is widely known today as Afro-Asiatic (*see* AFRICAN LANGUAGES), although some writers refer to it as Erythraic. W.E.W.

HAMLET, verse tragedy in five acts by the English dramatist William Shakespeare (q.v.), first acted before 1602 and first printed in 1603. The authorized text of the play as it was performed by Shakespeare's company was printed in 1604, and the work was included in the edition of Shakespeare's plays known as the First Folio (1623).

The source from which Shakespeare drew the material for the tragedy was an earlier play, no longer extant, reputedly written sometime before 1589 by the English dramatist Thomas Kyd (q.v.). The Hamlet story makes its first literary appearance in the *Gesta Danorum* or *Historia Danica* (about 1200; Eng. trans., *The First Nine Books of the Danish History,* 1894) by the Danish historian Saxo Grammaticus (q.v.), who drew upon tradition and the lost Scandinavian sagas. Saxo's narrative was adapted by the French writer François de Belleforest (1530–83) as one of his *Histoires Tragiques* ("Tragic Histories", 1576). In this form it was available to contemporary English writers. According to the Danish historian, Hamlet, called Amleth, was the son of Horvendill, King of Jutland, and his queen Gerutha. Horvendill was killed by his brother Feng, who then married Gerutha; to save his own life, Amleth pretended to be insane. Amleth's mother, overcome by her son's reproaches, later helped him to kill Feng.

In Shakespeare's *Hamlet* the character of the protagonist is of commanding interest. The first scene of the play shows Hamlet's despair over the death of a loved father and the hasty mar-

John Barrymore as Hamlet in 1925. Bettmann Archive

riage of Gertrude, his mother and Claudius, his uncle. Hamlet's extraordinary sensitivity is shown by the extent of the transformation he has undergone; the former Hamlet is described by other characters as the epitome of all courtly virtues, and the signs of his frank and generous nature appear in his rare moments of gaiety and spontaneity. Commanded by the ghost of his murdered father to punish his uncle, Hamlet sets out to prove his uncle's guilt and to find a means of exercising justice.

Critics have sought to convert Hamlet's failure to act swiftly into an intricate problem of character, but at every crucial point Shakespeare provides an explicit reason for the prince's delay. Hamlet's penetrating thoughts are given urgency and immediacy through the frequent use of long soliloquies; and the play as a whole is generally interpreted as an immensely subtle treatment of the crisis occasioned in a thoughtful nature by the need for incisive action.

Hamlet has always been the most popular of Shakespeare's tragedies, and it is universally regarded as one of the greatest works in all dramatic literature. The role of Hamlet has been played by the most distinguished British and American actors, including Edmund Kean (see under KEAN), David Garrick, Sir Henry Irving, Edwin Thomas Booth (qq.v.), John Barrymore (see under BARRYMORE), Sir John Gielgud, Maurice Evans, and Sir Laurence Olivier (qq.v.). Several operas have been based on the play, and in 1948 a notable motion picture version was directed by Olivier, who also played the title role.

HAMLIN, Hannibal (1809–91), fifteenth Vice-President of the United States, born in Paris Hill, Maine. Hamlin studied law in Portland, Maine, and was admitted to the bar in 1833. He was active in Maine politics, serving for several terms as a Democratic member of the State legislature. From 1843 to 1847 he was a member of the United States House of Representatives, and from 1848 to 1856 served as United States Senator from Maine. His antislavery convictions made him instrumental in securing (1846) passage in the House of the Wilmot Proviso (q.v.), which stipulated that slavery should never exist in certain territories Congress was then proposing to purchase from Mexico. In 1856 Hamlin joined the Republican Party (q.v.), which had been formed two years earlier as an antislavery party; the same year he was elected governor of Maine. In 1857 he resigned to run for the United States Senate, in which he again served until 1861. From 1861 to 1865 Hamlin was Vice-President in the first administration of President Abraham Lincoln (q.v.), and was one of Lincoln's important advisers during the Civil War; see CIVIL WAR, THE AMERICAN. From 1869 to 1881 Hamlin was again a member of the U.S. Senate, and from 1881 to 1882 he served as U.S. minister to Spain.

HAMM, city of West Germany, in North Rhine-Westphalia State, on the Lippe R., 19 miles N.E. of Dortmund and 22 miles S.E. of Münster. Hamm, founded in 1226, was a member of the Hanseatic League (q.v.). Hamm is principally a railroad junction and industrial center, with wire and cable mills, machine works, chemical plants, leather factories, and breweries. Coal mines and thermal baths are located nearby. Hamm was one of the most heavily bombed German cities during World War II. Pop. (1960 est.) 68,400.

HAMMARSKJÖLD, Dag Hjalmar Agne Carl (1905–61), Swedish statesman and United Nations official, born in Jönköping, and educated at the universities of Uppsala and Stockholm.

Dag Hammarskjöld   Karsh, Ottawa

He served as undersecretary of the department of finance of the Swedish government and as a member of the economic advisory board from 1936 to 1946, when he entered the diplomatic service as finance specialist in the foreign office. In 1947 he participated in the organizing conference of the European Recovery Program (q.v.) and in 1948–49 was vice-chairman of the executive committee of the Organization for European Economic Cooperation. Named Swedish deputy foreign minister and cabinet minister

HAMMERFEST

without portfolio in 1951, Hammarskjöld was a member and chief of the Swedish delegation to the U.N. in 1952 and early 1953. On April 7, 1953, he was elected secretary-general of the U.N.; he served in that post until his death in a plane crash in Africa in September, 1961, while on a mission concerning a separatist movement in the Republic of the Congo (now the Republic of Zaire).

Hammarskjöld developed the powers and scope of his office in many ways without formal amendment of the provisions of the U.N. Charter relating to his official functions. As a U.N. emissary he traveled widely on missions of great political delicacy and significance, and his frequent successes, both as mediator and as negotiator, won him acclaim as a statesman. He was posthumously awarded the Nobel Peace Prize for 1961. Hammarskjöld's book of meditations, *Markings* (1964), revealed his deeply personal religious and ethical philosophy.

HAMMERFEST, northernmost town of Europe, in Norway, on the island of Kvaløy, in Finnmark County, about 1000 miles N.E. of Oslo. The area is known for the fact that the sun remains above the horizon all day and all night, from mid-May to July 29, and is not seen from Nov. 18 to Jan. 23. Hammerfest is the rendezvous of the fishing and whaling fleets that operate in the Kara Sea and in the waters along the coasts of the Svalbard (Spitsbergen) archipelago. Smoked and salted fish, eiderdown, cod-liver oil, fox skins, and reindeer skins are exported from the town. Pop. (1960) 5604.

HAMMERHEAD or **HAMMERHEAD SHARK,** common name for any shark in the genus *Sphyrna,* characterized by a flattened projection on either side of the crown. The eyes are situated at each end of the rudderlike projections, which enable the shark to maneuver skillfully when chasing its prey. The hammerhead is voracious, feeds on fish and squid, and reaches a length of 16 ft.; it has been known to attack man. It is found in all warm seas and comes as far north along the Atlantic coast of the United States as Massachusetts. The female hammerhead incubates its eggs within its body cavity. Five species are known.

HAMMERSTEIN, name of an American theatrical family, of whom the most distinguished members are the following:

Oscar Hammerstein (1847?–1919), German-American inventor, author, composer, and operatic impresario, born in Stettin, (now Szczecin, Poland). At the age of sixteen he came to the United States and settled in New York City, where he obtained employment in a cigar factory. He invented a cigar-making machine and a number of other devices; from them and from later real estate investments, he derived a large fortune. He wrote several plays, for which he also composed the music. In 1870 he leased the old Stadt (later the Windsor) Theatre, which he managed. Ten years later, he built the Harlem Opera House, which was followed successively with the building of the Columbus Theatre, the Harlem Music Hall, the Murray Hill Theatre, the

Oscar Hammerstein   Musical Courier

first Manhattan Opera House, and the Olympia, Victoria, Republic, and Harris theaters.

In 1906 he built the second Manhattan Opera House, where his productions gave such serious competition to the Metropolitan Opera Company (q.v.) that in 1910 the Hammerstein interests were purchased by the Metropolitan with the understanding that Hammerstein would not produce opera in New York City for ten years. He left immediately for England, and in 1911 he built the Kingsway Opera House in London. That enterprise was a failure, however, and Hammerstein returned to New York to build the American Opera House (1912), in which he intended to produce operas. He was prevented from doing so by the intervention of the courts, which forced him to keep his agreement with the Metropolitan Opera Company. Hammerstein renamed his opera house the Lexington Theater and turned to producing other forms of entertainment.

164

HAMMOND

Hammerstein did much to overcome the inertia of the American public toward opera. His casts were always brilliant and at different times included the Australian soprano Nellie Melba, the Italian coloratura soprano Luisa Tetrazzini, the American soprano Mary Garden, and the Irish tenor John McCormack (qq.v.). Among the celebrated operas that Hammerstein introduced into the American repertory are *Salome* by the German composer Richard Strauss, *Louise* by the French composer Gustave Charpentier, and *Pélleas et Mélisande* by the French composer Claude Debussy (qq.v.).

Oscar Hammerstein, 2nd (1895–1960), songwriter and librettist, grandson of Oscar, born in New York City, and educated at the Hamilton Institute and Columbia University Law School. He displayed considerable talent, both as a lyricist and an actor, in amateur theatrical productions at Columbia. After working in a law office for a year, he decided to make the theater his career. Although his initial employment was as a stagehand, he began to write books and lyrics for musical shows in 1919. In *Wildflower* (1923), his first success, he introduced a theatrical form that he called the musical play, a serious drama set to music and, unlike musical comedy, employing realistic dialogue. All of his subsequent successes were in the same genre. In 1927 he adapted *Show Boat* (1926), a novel by the American writer Edna Ferber (q.v.), for the musical stage in association with the American composer Jerome Kern (q.v.). The production earned high praise. Hammerstein's *Rose Marie*, with music by the American composer Rudolf Friml (q.v.), was produced in 1924. With the Hungarian-born American composer Sigmund Romberg (q.v.), Hammerstein wrote *Desert Song* (1926) and *New Moon* (1928). Hammerstein achieved his greatest successes in collaboration with the American composer Richard Rodgers (q.v.). Their first work, *Oklahoma* (1943; Pulitzer Prize, 1944), an adaptation of the play, *Green Grow the Lilacs* (1931), by the American dramatist Lynn Riggs (1899–1954), won extraordinary critical and popular acclaim. Even more successful was *South Pacific* (1949; Pulitzer Prize, 1950), generally regarded as one of the best musical plays ever written. Also in collaboration with Rodgers, Hammerstein wrote *Carousel* (1945), *Allegro* (1947), *The King and I* (1951), *Me and Juliet* (1953), *Pipe Dream* (1955), and *The Sound of Music* (1959). Hammerstein wrote the words for many popular songs, most of which were introduced in his musical plays, including "Indian Love Call" (1924), "Ol' Man River" (1927), "The Last Time I Saw Paris" (1940), "People Will Say We're in Love" (1943), and "Some Enchanted Evening" (1949).

HAMMETT, (Samuel) Dashiell (1894–1961), American detective-story writer, born in Saint Marys County, Md. He left school at the age of thirteen and traveled in many parts of the United States, holding a variety of positions. During World War I he served as an ambulance driver in France. For eight years after the war he was a private detective; the experience gained during this period furnished much of the material that he later used in his novels. The first two of these, *Red Harvest* (1929) and *The Dain Curse* (1929) met with immediate popularity, and with the publication of *The Maltese Falcon* (1930) Hammett was recognized as the forerunner of a new so-called tough school of detective fiction.

He is noted especially for realism and unconventional directness of character delineation and dialogue; for the impact of his plot narration, often involving detailed description of acts of sadistic brutality; and for sophisticated cynicism in social attitudes. *The Glass Key* (1931) was written in a similar vein, but in *The Thin Man* (1932) Hammett introduced a note of gaiety and humor into his previously grim writing.

Many of his novels were later made into highly popular radio programs and motion pictures, and he spent some years writing screenplays in Hollywood. In World War II, he enlisted in the United States Army as a private and served in Alaska. During the late 1940's and early 1950's, allegations of pro-Communist activity were leveled against Hammett, and in 1951 he served a six-month prison sentence for contempt of court. *See* MYSTERY STORY: *The Realistic Detective Novel.*

HAMMOND, city of Indiana, in Lake Co., on the Grand and Little Calumet rivers, about 20 miles S.E. of the center of Chicago, Ill. It is served by railroad and is connected with Lake Michigan by a canal. Hammond is an important commercial and manufacturing center of the surrounding Calumet district, one of the richest industrial regions in the world. In addition to extensive railroad-repair shops, industrial establishments in Hammond include printing and bookbinding plants, and large plants producing fabricated steel, railroad cars and equipment, soap and soap products, surgical equipment and supplies, chemicals, punch presses, industrial and tire chains, and agricultural machinery. The city is also the site of iron and brass foundries, feed mills, and factories manufacturing candy, metal toys, and clothing. It was first settled by George Henry Hammond (1838–86), a pioneer in the use of refrigerated railroad cars, who es-

HAMMOND

tablished a meat-packing plant there in 1868. The town, originally called State Line in reference to its situation at the Indiana-Illinois boundary, was renamed Hammond in 1873. It became a city in 1883. Pop. (1960) 111,698; (1970) 107,790.

HAMMOND, city of Louisiana, in Tangipahoa Parish, about 41 miles E. of Baton Rouge. Manufactures include building materials, wood products, and clothing. It is the site of Southeastern Louisiana College, founded in 1925. A State agricultural experiment station is here. Pop. (1960) 10,563; (1970) 12,487.

HAMMOND, James Bartlett (1839–1913), American inventor, born in Boston, Mass., and educated at the University of Vermont, Union Theological Seminary, and the University of Halle, Germany. He served as a war correspondent for the New York *Tribune* during the American Civil War and later edited religious texts. In 1880 he patented one of the first practical typewriters, which he began to manufacture in 1884. The machine, which was a commercial success, employed an interchangeable type wheel carrying a full font of type. Because the wheel, could be replaced, a variety of different typefaces could be used with one typewriter (q.v.).

HAMMOND, John Hays (1855–1936), American mining engineer and financier, born in San Francisco, Calif., and educated at the Sheffield Scientific School of Yale University and at the Royal School of Mines in Freiberg, Germany. In 1880 Hammond took part in a United States Geological Survey of California gold fields; in 1893 he went to South Africa, where he managed mining interests for the British industrialist Cecil John Rhodes (q.v.). Hammond participated in the abortive Jameson Raid (*see* JAMESON, SIR LEANDER STARR), against the Boer government (*see* TRANSVAAL) and was imprisoned and sentenced to death in 1896; he was released on payment of a fine of $125,000. In 1899 Hammond returned to the U.S. where he served as an engineering consultant for several railroads and for the Guggenheim (q.v.) family, for whom he worked until his retirement in 1907. Hammond was also professor of mechanical engineering at Yale from 1902 to 1909. After his retirement he campaigned in the 1908 election for President William Howard Taft (q.v.), and subsequently Hammond held several advisory posts in the American government. *The Autobiography of John Hays Hammond* (2 vol.) was published in 1935.

His son, John Hays Hammond (1888–1965), invented a radio-controlled torpedo for coast defense, incendiary projectiles, and radio-telegraphic devices.

HAMMURABI or **HAMMURAPI** or **KHAMURABI** (fl. 18th cent. B.C.), King of Babylonia, and the greatest ruler in the first Babylonian dynasty. He extended the boundaries of his empire northward from the Persian Gulf through the Tigris and Euphrates (qq.v.) river valleys, and

Head of Hammurabi, a Babylonian sculpture of the 18th century B.C.   William Rockhill Nelson Gallery of Art, Atkins Museum of Fine Arts, Kansas City, Mo.

westward to the coast of the Mediterranean Sea; *see* BABYLONIA: *History.* After consolidating his gains under a central government at Babylon (q.v.), he devoted his energies to protecting his frontiers and fostering the internal prosperity of the empire. Throughout his forty-year reign he personally supervised navigation, irrigation, agriculture, tax collection, and the erection of many temples and other beautiful buildings. Although he was a successful military leader and administrator, Hammurabi is chiefly remembered for his codification of the laws governing all classes and aspects of Babylonian life; *see* HAMMURABI, CODE OF.

HAMMURABI, CODE OF, collection of the laws and edicts of the Babylonian king Hammurabi (q.v.), and the earliest legal code (q.v.) known in its entirety. A copy of the code, engraved on a block of black diorite nearly 8 ft. high, was unearthed by a team of French archeologists at Susa, Iraq, formerly ancient Elam (q.v.), during the winter of 1901–02. The block, broken in three pieces, has been restored and is now in the Louvre in Paris.

Composition of the Code. The divine origin of the written law is emphasized by a bas-relief in which the king is depicted receiving the code from the sun god, Shamash. The quality most usually associated with this god is justice. The code is set down in horizontal columns of cuneiform (q.v.) writing: sixteen columns of text on the obverse side and twenty-eight on the reverse. The text begins with a prologue that explains the extensive restoration of the temples and religious cults of Babylonia and Assyria (qq.v.). The code itself, composed of twenty-eight paragraphs, seems to be a series of amendments to the common law of Babylonia, rather than a strict legal code. It begins with direction for legal procedure and the statement of penalties for unjust accusations, false testimony, and injustice done by judges; then follow laws concerning property rights, loans, deposits, debts, domestic property, and family rights. The sections covering personal injury indicate that penalties were imposed for injuries sustained through unsuccessful operations by physicians, and for damages caused by neglect in various trades. Rates are fixed in the code for various forms of service in most branches of trade and commerce.

A Humane Civil Law. The Code of Hammurabi contains no laws having to do with religion. The basis of criminal law is that of equal retaliation, comparable to the Semitic law of "an eye for an eye". The law offers protection to all classes of Babylonian society; it seeks to protect the weak and the poor, including women, children, and slaves, against injustice at the hands of the rich and powerful.

The code is particularly humane for the time in which it was promulgated; it attests to the law and justice of Hammurabi's rule. It ends with an epilogue glorifying the mighty works of peace executed by Hammurabi and explicitly states that he had been called by the gods "to cause justice to prevail in the land, to destroy the wicked and the evil". He describes the laws in his compilation as enabling "the land to enjoy stable government and good rule", and he states that he had inscribed his words upon a pillar in order "that the strong may not oppress the weak, that justice may be dealt the orphan and the widow". He counsels the downtrodden in these ringing words: "Let any oppressed man who has a cause come into the presence of my statue as king of justice, and have the inscription on my stele read out, and hear my precious words, that my stele may make the case clear to him; may he understand his cause, and may his heart be set at ease"!

See BABYLONIA: *History*; BABYLONIAN ART.

HAMPDEN, John (1594–1643), English statesman and political leader, born in London, and educated at Magdalen College, University of Oxford. In 1621 he was elected to the House of Commons, in which he shortly became associated with the antiroyalist faction led by the English politician Sir John Eliot (q.v.). Hampden opposed the general loan which Charles I (q.v.), King of England, authorized in 1626 without Parliamentary sanction. In retaliation the government imprisoned Hampden during part of the following year. His opposition to the king's usurpation of the prerogatives of Parliament reached a dramatic climax when, in 1637, Hampden refused to pay the ship money, a tax levied by Charles I for support of the royal navy. Brought to trial for that offense, Hampden eloquently defended his position, but the case was decided against him. He was one of the five Parliamentary leaders whom, in January, 1642, the king attempted to imprison, an act that precipitated the Great Rebellion (q.v.). After the outbreak of hostilities Hampden served on the Committee of Public Safety and raised a regiment of infantry in Buckinghamshire, his home county. During the rebellion he was mortally wounded in a battle at Chalgrove Field, near Oxford.

HAMPDEN, Walter, stage name of WALTER HAMPDEN DOUGHERTY (1879–1955), American actor, born in Brooklyn, N.Y., and educated at Harvard University and the Brooklyn Polytechnic Institute. He made his theatrical debut at Brighton, England, in 1901, and from 1904 to 1907 was leading man at the Adelphi Theatre, London. In the latter year he returned to the United States, where he subsequently performed in a wide variety of roles. Notable plays in which he appeared include *Hamlet* (1905), *A Doll's House* (1907), *The Tempest* (1916), *Cyrano de Bergerac* (1923), *Richelieu* (1929), *The Admirable Crichton* (1931), *Ethan Frome* (1938), *Arsenic and Old Lace* (1942), and *Henry VIII* (1946). His interpretations of Hamlet and Cyrano, both of which he played over a number of years, are generally regarded as his greatest roles. He also appeared in motion pictures. From 1927 to 1954 Hampden held the presidency of The Players, the highest honor accorded an American actor.

HAMPSHIRE, Great Britain, county of England, formerly known as SOUTHAMPTON, bounded on the N.W. by Wiltshire, on the N. by Berkshire, on the E. by Surrey and West Sussex, on the S. by the

HAMPTON

English Channel, and on the w. by Dorsetshire. The Isle of Wight, off the coast of Hampshire, is part of the county; see WIGHT, ISLE OF. The county, known popularly as Hants, has an undulating terrain crossed by rolling chalk hills called downs (q.v.). In the s.w. is New Forest, a wooded area that was at one time a royal hunting ground. Hampshire is drained by the Avon, Itchen, Test, and Wey rivers. Agriculture, especially the growing of grain, and the raising of sheep and dairy cattle are the chief occupations. Winchester is the county seat. Bournemouth, Portsmouth, and Southampton (qq.v.) are the industrial centers and principal cities. Hampshire was called Southampton until 1959 when the name was officially changed. Area, excluding the Isle of Wight, 1503 sq.mi.; pop. (1969 est.) 1,511,900.

HAMPTON, independent city in Virginia, on the northern side of Hampton Roads, and opposite Norfolk, with which it is connected by a bridge-tunnel. Industries include the packing, canning, and shipping of meat and fish; sawmilling; and the manufacture of instruments, metal products, radios, electrical equipment, and aircraft parts. Within the city limits are Langley Air Force Base and a National Aeronautics and Space Administration Research Center.

Hampton is the site of Hampton Institute (q.v.), Saint John's Church, built in 1610 and restored in 1728, and the Syms-Eaton Museum, site of the oldest free school in the United States. Fort Monroe at Old Point Comfort was held by Union forces throughout the American Civil War. The fort now contains the Casemate Museum. One of the earliest English settlements was established in the area in 1609. The townsite was settled in 1610 and incorporated in 1852. It was originally called Kecoughtan for the Indian village there. The port was established in 1705. In 1813 during the War of 1812 (q.v.), the Battle of Hampton ensued from the British attempt to capture nearby Portsmouth, and in 1862, during the Civil War, the famous battle of the ironclads *Merrimac* and *Monitor* took place offshore; see CIVIL WAR, THE AMERICAN. Hampton was part of Elizabeth City County from 1634 to 1952, when it was made an independent city comprising the entire county. Pop. (1960) 89,258; (1970) 120,779.

HAMPTON, Wade (1818–1902), American army officer and statesman, born in Charleston, S.C., grandson and namesake of a landowner who at his death in 1835, was reputed to be the richest planter in America. Hampton studied law at the University of South Carolina, but did not enter practice, devoting his time to the management of his extensive estates. He was a member of the South Carolina legislature from 1852 to 1861. At the outbreak of the Civil War, he raised and equipped at his own expense a force known as the Hampton Legion, which participated in the first Battle of Bull Run and in the Peninsular Campaign (q.v.); see BULL RUN, BATTLE OF. Hampton was commissioned a brigadier general in the Confederate army in 1862 and major general in 1863. He was of great assistance in the raids of the Confederate cavalryman James Ewell Brown Stuart (q.v.), and after Stuart's death assumed command of the entire cavalry corps. He was promoted to the rank of lieutenant general in 1865. Hampton was elected governor of South Carolina in 1876 and reelected in 1878. He served in the United States Senate from 1879 to 1891. From 1893 to 1897 Hampton was the Federal commissioner of railroads. *See also* CIVIL WAR, THE AMERICAN.

HAMPTON COURT, palace built in 1515 by order of the English prelate Cardinal Thomas Wolsey (q.v.) near the village of Hampton, Middlesex, England, 15 mi. from the center of London. The cardinal presented the palace to Henry VIII (q.v.), King of England, in 1526; it was used as a royal residence until the reign of George II (q.v.), King of Great Britain. Since this time the palace has been occupied by needy persons recommended by the reigning monarch. Two of the five original quadrangles of the building remain. The edifice, which contains 1000 rooms, is built of red brick with stone facings and is one of the outstanding examples of Tudor architecture. In Hampton Court, Edward VI (q.v.) was born and his mother, Jane Seymour (*see under* SEYMOUR), died a few days later. Charles I (q.v.), King of England, was a prisoner there in 1647. The picture gallery, the royal apartments, the park, and the gardens covering 44 acres are open to the public and constitute a prime attraction for tourists.

HAMPTON INSTITUTE, coeducational institution of higher learning, founded in 1868 in Hampton, Va., by the American Missionary Association, for the purpose of educating Negroes and Indians; see FREEDMEN'S BUREAU. In 1870 the institute received a charter from the State. Hampton Institute is a private corporation, administered by an interdenominational board of twenty-five trustees. The instruction comprises courses in liberal arts, business, home economics, nursing, teaching, and technology. The degrees of bachelor and master are conferred. The most noted graduate is the educator Booker Taliaferro Washington (q.v.). In 1968 the Collis P. Huntington Memorial Library housed more

HAMSTER

than 103,000 bound volumes, including a collection on Negro history. In 1968 enrollment at Hampton Institute totaled 2377, the faculty numbered about 213, and the endowment of the institute was approximately $32,000,000.

HAMPTON NATIONAL HISTORIC SITE, noted mansion in Maryland, about 8 miles N. of Baltimore, consisting of "Hampton", the home of the Ridgely family. The elegance of the mansion, a fine example of American Georgian architecture built from 1783 to 1790, was enhanced by the formal gardens and other improvements added by Charles Carnan Ridgely (1760–1829), who was governor of Maryland from 1816 to 1819. "Hampton" has been largely restored. The mansion, outbuildings, and grounds, covering 45.42 acres, were established as a national historic site in 1948. It is administered by the National Park Service (q.v.).

HAMPTON ROADS, channel off the coast of Virginia through which the estuaries of the James, the Nansemond, and the Elizabeth rivers of Virginia flow into Chesapeake Bay. It extends between Old Point Comfort in the N. and Sewall Point in the s., and is an important commercial waterway of the eastern United States, broad, deep, and ice-free throughout the year. The cities situated on its shores, Norfolk, Portsmouth, and Newport News, all in Va., are leading ports and, together with the neighboring communities, comprise the Port of Hampton Roads, created in 1926. Fort Monroe guards the entrance from Chesapeake Bay. Hampton Roads is one of the principal rendezvous of the United States Navy, which maintains a vast naval base and supply stations at Norfolk.

Hampton Roads is noted also as the site of two historic naval engagements of the Civil War; see CIVIL WAR, THE AMERICAN. On March 8, 1862, the frigate *Congress*, the sloop of war *Cumberland*, the steam frigates *Minnesota* and *Roanoke*, and the ship *Saint Lawrence* were in the channel, when the *Merrimac*, an ironclad Confederate craft, attended by several small escorts, steamed into Hampton Roads from Norfolk and attacked the Federal fleet, destroying the *Congress* and the *Cumberland* before retiring. Federal losses during the engagement amounted to 286 persons, and the Confederates lost about a dozen men in the encounter. On the following day the famous contest between the Federal *Monitor* and the *Merrimac* took place (qq.v.).

HAMPTON ROADS CONFERENCE, informal conference held in Hampton Roads (q.v.), Va., on Feb. 3, 1865, in an attempt to bring the Civil War (*see* CIVIL WAR, THE AMERICAN) to an end. The meeting took place on board a steamer, the *River Queen*, between President Abraham Lincoln and Secretary of State William Henry Seward (qq.v.), representing the United States, and Vice-President Alexander Hamilton Stephens (q.v.), Assistant Secretary of War John Archibald Campbell (1811–89), and Senator Robert Mercer Taliaferro Hunter (1809–87), representing the Confederate States. No agreement was arrived at after a four-hour talk, and the Confederate representatives returned to Richmond.

HAMPTONS, THE, residential area of New York State, in Suffolk Co., extending about 35 miles w. from the easternmost part of Long Island, along the Atlantic Ocean. The area is comprised of the towns of East Hampton (pop., 1960, 8827; 1970, 10,980) and Southampton (pop., 1960, 26,861; 1970, 35,980), which include the villages of East Hampton, Southampton, and Westhampton Beach, and the unincorporated communities of Bridgehampton, Hampton Beach, and Westhampton.

HAMSTER, common name of any of fourteen small, Old World species of rodents in the tribe Cricetini, characterized by large cheek pouches for the transport of food, thick fur, and a short tail. One species attains a length of 1 ft. Hamsters are voracious animals, and they do much damage to crops. They live in many-chambered burrows 4 to 5 ft. below the surface of the ground in cultivated fields. One of the chambers in the burrow is used as a storage room for

Golden hamster, Mesocricetus auratus Orville Andrews — National Audubon Society

HAMSUN

grain in the summer and fall. In winter the hamster hibernates; its sleep is not continuous and it often wakes to feed on its stores. The female bears several litters a year and may produce as many as eighteen young in one litter. The young are weaned when about two or three weeks of age and shortly thereafter leave the parents and construct their own burrows. The fur of some hamsters, notably the unusually colored, black-bellied hamster, *Cricetus cricetus,* is used for the lining of coats, and the flesh is sometimes eaten.

Hamsters range over Eurasia, and especially over the steppes, plains, and deserts of Central Asia. The golden hamster, *Mesocricetus auratus,* is the species widely used in medical research and kept as children's pets. They are currently valuable in investigations of malignant growths, especially mouth cancers. In 1956 it was discovered that hamsters can be infected with the common cold; see COLD, COMMON. This discovery is of great significance to cold-virus research, in that the hamster is the first small laboratory animal found to be susceptible to colds.

HAMSUN, Knut, pen name of KNUT PEDERSEN (1859–1952), Norwegian writer, born in Lom. As a youth he worked as a clerk, salesman, shoemaker's apprentice, coal trimmer, and schoolteacher. At the age of twenty, with no previous formal education, he enrolled at the University of Christiania (now Oslo), planning to become a journalist. Soon he gave up this attempt and emigrated to the United States, where he spent two years working at various occupations and writing chiefly in Minnesota and Wisconsin. In 1884 Hamsun returned to Norway and in 1886 again went to the U.S., where he worked for two years. In 1888 he returned to Norway, and thereafter gave his full time to writing.

Hamsun rose to the front rank of Scandinavian writers with the novel *Sult* (1890; Eng. trans., *Hunger,* 1899), a work dealing with the psychological effects of starvation. It was followed by a number of other novels, about ten in all, including *Pan* (1894; Eng. trans., 1920), *Under Høstsjaernen* (1906; Eng. trans., *Under the Autumn Star,* 1922), and *En Vandrer Spiller med Sordin* (1909; Eng. trans., *A Wanderer Plays on Muted Strings,* 1922). In this period Hamsun's main characters were negative types who posed as severe critics of civilization. Highly individualized and impulsive, and hating organized society, they generally escaped to remote places to avoid responsibility.

A group of later novels reveal Hamsun as a socially minded author. The novels *Børn av Tiden* (1913; Eng. trans., *Children of the Age,* 1924) and *Markens Grøde* (1917; Eng. trans., *Growth of the Soil,* 1920) took up various problems of society as a whole. *Growth of the Soil,* considered Hamsun's greatest novel, deals with peasant life. Hamsun received the 1920 Nobel Prize for literature. In his later novels, however, including *Landstrykere* (1927; Eng. trans., *Vagabonds* 1930), Hamsun returned to the depiction of the rootless, wandering individual of modern society.

Hamsun had strong antidemocratic views throughout his life. He was an admirer of Prussian militarism in World War I. In World War II he openly expressed his sympathy with the National Socialist government of the German dictator Adolf Hitler (q.v.), and was the only Norwegian writer of first rank who publicly welcomed the German invasion of Norway in April, 1940. In 1946 he was tried for collaboration, but because of his age his sentence consisted only of a fine.

HAMTRAMCK, city of Michigan, in Wayne Co., surrounded by Detroit with the exception of the N.W. portion, which adjoins the city of Highland Park. Hamtramck is an industrial center, noted for the manufacture of automobiles and automobile accessories. Other important industries in the city are oil refining, and the manufacture of paints and varnishes, pottery, electrical supplies, alloy and metal products, and tools and dies. Most of the population is of Polish extraction. Hamtramck, incorporated as a village in 1901 and as a city in 1922, is named for Colonel John Francis Hamtramck, the first American commander of the fort at Detroit after the British forces evacuated it in 1796. Pop. (1960) 34,137; (1970) 27,245.

HAN, Chinese dynasty, founded by Liu Pang (247–195 B.C.), a soldier of fortune who became duke of P'ei, later prince of Han, and subsequently (about 202 B.C.) the acknowledged emperor of the country. The capital was at Changan (now Sian in Shensi Province), but later about 25 A.D., in the reign of the fifteenth Han emperor, it was moved to Loyang in Honan Province; hence the chronological division of the dynasty into Western (Earlier or Former) Han and Eastern (Later) Han. The end of the dynasty as rulers of all China came in 220 A.D. when the empire broke up into three kingdoms of which the western one is known as the Minor Han (221–64 A.D.). In all, fourteen emperors ruled during the Earlier Han, twelve during the Later Han, and two during the Minor Han. For the achievements of the Han dynasty, *see* CHINA, PEOPLE'S REPUBLIC OF: *History.*

John Hancock, a portrait painted in 1765, by the American artist John Singleton Copley.
Museum of Fine Arts, Boston

HANCOCK, John (1737–93), American patriot and statesman, born in Braintree, Mass. (now part of Quincy), and educated at Harvard College (now Harvard University). After his graduation, in 1754, he joined the mercantile firm of his uncle and guardian, the colonial businessman Thomas Hancock (1703–64). In 1764 he inherited the business and a substantial fortune. He was elected to the Massachusetts legislature two years later.

The famous signature of John Hancock Culver Service

Hancock first became embroiled with the British government in 1768, when customs officials seized his sloop *Liberty* because he had unloaded a cargo of Madeira wine without paying import duties. His vigorous defense in the ensuing lawsuits won him wide popularity among the anti-British elements in Massachusetts. After the Boston Massacre (q.v.) of 1770, he served on the committee that demanded the removal of British troops from Boston. He was prominently identified with the colonial cause thereafter, working closely with the Revolutionary patriot Samuel Adams (q.v.) in the leadership of the Whig, or Patriot, party in Massachusetts. The fateful British expedition to Lexington and Concord, on April 18–19, 1775, had as one of its major objectives the capture of Hancock. He was specifically excluded, along with Adams, in the general amnesty offered to the Revolutionary leaders by the British two months later.

From 1775 to 1780 Hancock was a member of the Continental Congress (q.v.), serving as presiding officer during the first two years. By virtue of this office, he was the first to sign the Declaration of Independence (q.v.). He was the first governor of the State of Massachusetts, holding that office from 1780 to 1785 and from 1789 until his death. Although he was initially opposed to the Federal Constitution, he later supported it and served as president of the Massachusetts convention which approved the document in 1788.

HANCOCK, Winfield Scott (1824–86) American soldier and politician, born near Lansdale, Pa., and educated at the United States Military Academy, West Point, N.Y. He entered the army in 1844 as a second lieutenant. During the Mexi-

HANCOCK

can War (q.v.) he commanded a company and became a first lieutenant; by the time of the Civil War he had risen to the rank of captain.

In 1861 Hancock was given the rank of brigadier general of United States Volunteers and assigned to command a brigade in the Army of the Potomac. He first led his troops in action at the Battle of Williamsburg, Va., on May 5, 1862, and was prominent at the Battle of Antietam. He also fought at the Battle of Fredericksburg, the Battle of Chancellorsville, and the Battle of Gettysburg. At Gettysburg, Hancock was in sole command until the arrival of General George Gordon Meade (q.v.) and, in command of the left flank and later of the center of the Union troops, he was largely responsible for stemming the main Confederate attacks. During the course of the battle he was wounded. In 1864 Hancock was especially conspicuous at the Battle of the Wilderness, at Spotsylvania Court House, and at the Battle of Cold Harbor; in that year he was made a brigadier general of the regular army. See separate articles under the names of the battles mentioned.

In 1866, after the war, Hancock became a major general, commanding the Department of Missouri and participating in campaigns against the Indians there. He was then transferred to the South to supervise the rehabilitation of the States of Louisiana and Texas. The moderation of his measures was opposed in Washington, and in 1867 he was relieved at his own request and assigned to command the Military Division of the Atlantic, with headquarters at Governors Island, N.Y., where he remained for most of the years until his death.

Hancock was active in the Democratic Party, and carried on his political and military careers simultaneously. In 1880 he was the Democratic nominee for President, campaigning for election while on military duty, but was narrowly defeated by the Republican candidate, James Abram Garfield (q.v.).

HAND, terminal portion of the arms or anterior limbs of man and the other members of the order Primates (q.v.), especially adapted for grasping. The grasping appendages of other mammals and lower forms of animals are sometimes called hands in order to distinguish them from the feet of the hind limbs, but true hands appear only in the primates. Superficially the hand consists of a broad palm attached to the forearm by a joint called the wrist. At one side and at the outer edge of the palm are five digits, the thumb and four fingers. The thumb in man is so articulated that it can be opposed or brought opposite to the fingers and thus be employed for grasping small objects. The fingers themselves can be folded forward over the palm for the holding of objects. The chief difference between the hands of man and those of the other primates is that the thumbs of the latter cannot be opposed to the fingers.

The human hand has twenty-seven bones: the eight bones of the carpus or wrist, arranged in two rows of four; the five bones of the metacarpus or palm, one to each digit; and the fourteen digital bones or phalanges, two in the thumb and three in each finger. The carpal bones fit into a shallow socket formed by the bones of the forearm.

The movements of the human hand are accomplished by two sets of muscles and tendons: the flexors, for bending the fingers and thumb,

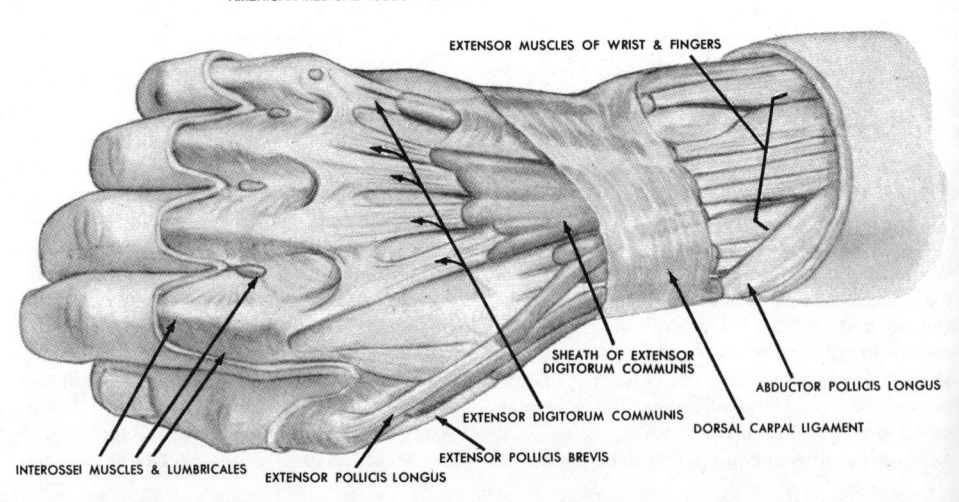

Diagram of the hand and wrist.
TODAY'S HEALTH published by
AMERICAN MEDICAL ASSOCIATION

HANDBALL

and the extensors, for straightening out the digits. The flexor muscles are located on the underside of the forearm and are attached by tendons to the phalanges of the fingers. The extensor muscles are on the back of the forearm and are similarly connected. The human thumb has two separate flexor muscles that move the thumb in opposition and make grasping possible. The articulation of the human hand is more complex and delicate than that of comparable organs in any other animals. Because of this articulation, man is the only animal able to use and manipulate a wide variety of tools and implements.

HAND, (Billings) Learned (1872–1961), American jurist, born in Albany, N.Y., and educated in law at Harvard University. After practicing law in Albany and New York City, he was appointed a judge of the United States District Court for the Southern District of New York in 1909. He was appointed to the United States Circuit Court of Appeals for the Second Circuit in 1924 and was its presiding judge from 1939 until his retirement in 1951. During his active life Hand wrote more than 2000 legal opinions, many of which were of far-reaching judicial influence, including those on questions of copyright, monopoly, and constitutional law. *The Spirit of Liberty*, a collection of his papers and addresses, was published in 1953.

His cousin, Augustus Noble Hand (1869–1954), also was a renowned jurist, who served with him on the appeals court from 1927 to 1953.

HANDBALL, competitive game of ball in which a ball is hit with the hand against a wall alternately by opposing players. Singles handball is played between two opponents; doubles, another common form, is played by two teams of partners. The modern version of the sport is thought to have been introduced into the United States by Irish immigrants in the 19th century. Now played outdoors at parks and beaches and indoors at clubs and gymnasiums, handball is one of the most popular sports in the nation.

Handball Courts. Handball may be played on a one-wall, a three-wall, or a four-wall court. The one-wall court involves only a front wall, 20 ft. wide by 16 ft. high. The remaining court boundaries are two sidelines, each 34 ft. long, and a connecting back line, 20 ft. wide. A line known as the short line is drawn straight across the floor 16 ft. from the front wall; this line separates the front and back courts. Service markers, 9 ft. in back of the short line, extend 6 in. in from each of the sidelines. The area between the short line and the service markers is called the service zone and is where a player must stand when putting the ball into play. The sidelines should extend 3 ft. behind the back line; this area, known as the apron, is necessary, as in tennis, to retrieve shots that bounce within the boundary lines very near the sides or back of the court.

The three-wall court consists of a front wall, 20 ft. wide by 20 ft. high, and two side walls, each jutting perpendicularly off opposite ends of the front wall and running back a distance of from 40 to 44 ft. The short line is 20 ft. from the front wall, and the service line is 15 ft. from the front wall. The service zone lies between the service line and the short line, 18 in. from the side walls. Some three-wall courts exhibit variations such as tapered-down walls, modified side walls coming back only 20 or 25 ft., and in some cases, a partial ceiling.

The four-wall court, actually a five-wall court, involves a front and a back wall, two side walls, and a ceiling. The walls have been standardized to 20 ft. wide and 20 ft. high at the front, 40 ft. wide and 20 ft. high at the sides, and a minimum of 12 ft. high at the back. The lower back wall allows spectators to view the game. Court ceilings have recessed lighting to eliminate any possibility of accidental interference on ball bounces. The short line, the service line, and the service zone are located exactly as on a three-wall court. The small rectangular area formed at each side of the service zone is called a service box; in doubles, the partner of the server stands in the box during the serve.

Glass-walled courts were introduced in 1945. Today many courts have back and side walls made of glass, thus allowing galleries for spectators.

Equipment and Special Terms. The ball used in the game is made of soft, black rubber. The ball is hollow-centered, its total weight usually being 2.3. oz. It is $1\frac{7}{8}$ in. in diameter, with a $\frac{1}{32}$ in. allowable variation. The rebound from a 70-in. drop must be 42 to 48 in. at a temperature of 68° F.

Handball players wear form-fitting gloves, usually made out of soft leather. The gloves serve to protect the hands and to prevent moisture on the hands from making the ball slippery. Players also wear shoes with good traction to prevent them from slipping or falling as they run about the court.

Like most sports, the language of handball includes some special terms. A hinder is an interference with the flight of the ball. When a hinder is called, the play goes over, that is, it is

HANDBALL

repeated. A handout is the transfer of the serve to the opposing team. A short occurs when a served ball fails to rebound from the front wall behind the short line. Hitting the ball on the fly means playing the ball before it strikes the floor.

Playing Rules and Penalties. The purpose of the game is to hit the ball against a wall with either hand in such a way that the opponent or opponents cannot return the ball, that is, drive it back against a wall, before it has hit the floor twice. The open palm or the clenched fist may be used in hitting the ball. A point is awarded to the server if the ball is missed by the receiver; points can be scored only by the server. If during the volley the server misses a return, his opponent, rather than gaining a point, becomes the server. The achievement of 21 points wins a game. Usually the best of three games wins a match.

The play begins with the serve of the ball by a player standing in the service zone. In serving, the player drops the ball to the floor and on its rebound strikes it with one hand so that it hits the front wall and rebounds on the court behind the short line; in four-wall games the ball may hit one side wall en route before hitting the floor or being played on the fly by the receiver. On the first serve the receiver may choose to return a short serve. If a server hits two consecutive shorts, however, he loses the serve.

The volley commences after the legal serve is made. The receiver must return the ball to the front wall off one bounce, or on the fly, without allowing the ball to touch the floor a second time. The receiver can return the ball straight to the front wall or use any combination of walls or ceiling. In turn, the server must do the same, and the volley ensues until one player is unable to make the return.

Handball rules assure the players both ample view of the ball and freedom in making shots. Referees are instructed to call a hinder when the view or maneuverability of a player is obstructed. In such a hinder call the play goes over. If, in the opinion of the referee, the player moves into the way of the receiving or shooting of the ball and could have moved sufficiently to allow such freedom, then an avoidable hinder is called, resulting in a handout or point, as the case may be. If the player is hit by a shot by his opponent in any part of the court before the ball legally reaches the front wall, it is also a hinder and play goes over. If on the serve the server hits himself with the ball on the fly, it is a handout. If, in doubles, a player hits his partner on the fly while serving, it is a hinder and play goes over. If the ball is hit on the wrist or forearm, it is a handout or point, as the case may be.

Important Skills. Basically, the skills of handball may be broken down into mastery of the many types of shots, close control of the rebound, and strong, skillful use of either hand. The ball can be stroked overhand, sidearm, or underhand. In the sidearm stroke, the player should be low, parallel to the floor, to achieve the most effective shot. The development of the offhand shot, that is the weaker left-hand stroke of a right-handed player, is important. It is advantageous, too, to control or direct the ball to the offhand of the opponent, thus forcing his weaker return.

United States Handball Association. In 1950 the United States Handball Association (U.S.H.A.) was formed by a Chicago home builder, Bob Kendler, to promote the game, improve tournament conditions, and standardize court sizes and rules. In 1970 the association, with headquarters in Skokie, Ill., had about 12,000 members throughout the world.

HANDEDNESS. See AMBIDEXTERITY; LEFT-HANDEDNESS; RIGHT-HANDEDNESS.

HANDEL, George Frederick (1685–1759), German-born British composer, born in Halle, where he was given instruction by a local musician in playing the organ, harpsichord, violin, oboe, and probably other instruments, and in composition. In keeping with the custom of his day, he familiarized himself with the music of contemporary German and Italian composers by copying their scores.

George Frederick Handel — Musical America

After studying law in 1702 at the University of Halle, Handel went to Hamburg as a violinist in the orchestra of the Hamburg Opera, an institution that favored the works of Italian composers. Handel's first opera, *Almira,* was produced here in 1705. From 1706 to 1710 Handel traveled to Italy, enjoying the patronage of wealthy Italians. His opera *Rodrigo* was produced in Florence in 1708, and *Agrippina* had an enormous success in Venice in 1709. He returned to Germany as music director to the Elector of Hannover, who later became George I (q.v.), King of Great Britain.

In 1710 Handel traveled to London, where in 1711 he produced *Rinaldo,* the first of more than forty operas that he eventually wrote for London audiences. In 1712 he left his post in Hanover for a second trip to London and remained in England for the rest of his life. From 1720 to 1728 he composed works for the newly organized Italian opera theater, the Royal Academy of Music, and from 1729 to 1737 he assumed administrative and artistic control of the theater. During the 1730's, however, Italian opera began to decline in popularity in London, and Handel turned attention to another genre, the English oratorio (q.v.), which was less expensive to produce than opera and which appealed to the middle classes, who had always felt excluded from the court-oriented Italian opera. The composer wrote more than a dozen oratorios, including his best-known work, *Messiah* (1742). Beginning in 1739 he organized annual seasons of oratorio performances during Lent, at which he improvised on the organ. Handel became a British subject in 1726. He was buried with public honors in Westminster Abbey.

Although Handel wrote a great deal of instrumental music and many Italian operas, his greatest achievement was the creation of the English oratorio. In the composition of his oratorios he borrowed many features from Italian opera, particularly the format of three acts and the use of virtuoso arias. In modern performances of Handel's oratorios, some of the music is usually omitted, producing two acts rather than three. The oratorio arias, however, are cast in various forms rather than in the standard three-part *da capo* form that prevailed in Italian opera; *see* ARIA; OPERA. In his choruses, where his oratorio style reached its highest expression, Handel used counterpoint (q.v.) to emphasize the drama. Although he often wrote long melodies with broad contours, he usually divided them into short phrases that facilitate the breathing and tone production of the singers. At climactic moments he drew all voice parts into a middle singing range for maximum volume and intensity. At the same time, Handel was careful to set the texts of his oratorios so that all words could be clearly understood. His approach to choral writing served as a model for later British composers.

HANDWRITING ANALYSIS. *See* GRAPHOLOGY.

HANDY, W(illiam) C(hristopher) (1873–1958), American composer, cornetist, and bandmaster, born in Florence, Ala. He was educated in the public schools, and by his father and paternal grandfather, both of whom were clergymen. He began his musical career as a cornet soloist and bandmaster with minstrel shows; one of his earliest engagements was with the World's Columbian Exposition in Chicago in 1893. From 1900 to 1902 he was a music teacher at the Agricultural and Mechanical College in Huntsville, Ala. Handy turned to composition in 1907; his first published song was "Memphis Blues" (1912). Among his other popular songs are "Saint Louis Blues" (1914), "Beale Street Blues" (1917), and "Loveless Love" (1921). During his career Handy founded a music-publishing house and edited and wrote a number of books, including the autobiographical *Father of the Blues* (1941). Originally, the blues were a type of Negro folk song little known outside the southern United States. Handy's songs brought the blues to international attention. *See also* BLUES; MINSTREL SHOW.

HANFORD, city in California, and county seat of Kings Co., in the San Joaquin Valley, about 29 miles S.E. of Fresno. The city is a processing, and shipping center. Hanford has light manufacturing. Pop. (1960) 10,133; (1970) 15,179.

HANFORD, Federal reservation in the State of Washington, in Benton County. It covers 650 sq.mi., along the Columbia R., about 25 miles E. of Yakima. The reservation was established in 1942 for use by the United States Atomic Energy Commission and has the largest plutonium production facility in the world. A New Production Reactor (N.P.R.) completed in 1963 uses heat from plutonium production to generate steam for an 800,000-kw electric plant. The Hanford reservation also is used as a "graveyard" for the burial of radioactive waste materials.

HANGCHOW, city in the People's Republic of China, and the capital and chief commercial city of Chekiang Province, on Hangchow Bay, at the mouth of the Tsientang R., about 100 miles s.w. of Shanghai. The Grand Canal, for many centuries the principal artery of trade between N. China and the Yangtze delta region, terminates at the city. Because of the shallowness of Hangchow Bay, Hangchow is not accessible to oceangoing vessels; most of the foreign trade of the city is routed through Shanghai. Trade with inland points is facilitated by means of the Fuchun R., the Grand Canal, and a network of subsidiary canals. The city is an important point on the railroad from Shanghai to Vietnam. It is a manufacturing center, producing tapestries, cotton textiles, silk fabrics, and processed rice. One of the most ancient cities of China, Hangchow is surrounded by massive walls with a circumference of 12 mi. The city had just passed its zenith when it was visited late in the 13th century by the Italian traveler Marco Polo (q.v.), who characterized it as the most beautiful city in the world. Despite many vicissitudes, particularly the large-scale destruction during the Taiping Rebellion (q.v.) in 1861, Hangchow retains ornate Buddhist temples, memorial halls, shrines, monasteries, and gardens. Pop. (1957 est.) 784,000.

HANGING, method of capital punishment (q.v.), by suspending the condemned person by the neck, usually with a noosed rope or cord, from a frame with a crosspiece commonly known as a gallows. Hanging is the official means of execution in several countries, and in six States of the United States.

Death through hanging may result from compression of the windpipe, obstruction of blood flow, and rupture of nerve structures in the neck; all may be factors in a death by hanging, especially when death is not instantaneous. Death is instantly fatal in a hanging in which the spinal cord is damaged or severed through the fracture or dislocation of the first three cervical vertebrae; see SPINAL COLUMN.

Originally, hanging was not a method of capital punishment, but of inflicting indignity upon the dead body of a criminal. The practice of hanging an already executed murderer in chains upon a gibbet, a simple gallows consisting of one upright post with a crosspiece at the top, continued in Great Britain well into the 19th century. As far back as the days of the Roman Empire, however, Germanic tribes used hanging as a method of execution, and from them the measure was adopted by the Anglo-Saxon peoples. Hanging was first adopted in England in 1214, when a nobleman's son was hanged for piracy. In time, hanging displaced more barbarous methods of capital punishment. Compare LYNCHING.

HANGING GARDENS OF BABYLON. See BABYLON; SEVEN WONDERS OF THE WORLD: *Seven Wonders of the Ancient World.*

HAN KIANG *or* **HAN,** river of the People's Republic of China, one of the chief tributaries of the Yangtze R., and a main artery of trade of central China. From its source in the s.w. portion of Shensi Province, the Han flows generally s.e. across Hupei Province, emptying into the Yangtze at Wuhan. The Han Kiang, about 900 mi. in length, is navigable by river steamers for about 300 mi. above Wuhan and by smaller craft throughout most of its course. Several commercial cities, including Fancheng, are on the banks of the Han Kiang.

HANKOW, former city of the People's Republic of China, in Hupei Province, on the N. bank of the Yangtze R., about 500 mi. from its mouth and at its confluence with the Han R. The cities of Hanyang and Wuchang (q.v.), which, together with Hankow, have been known since 1950 by the composite name of Wuhan (q.v.), lie on opposite banks of the Han and the Yangtze. Hankow, at the head of navigation of the Yangtze, is accessible to oceangoing vessels; this circumstance, the navigability of the Yangtze by river steamers as far inland as Ichang, 200 mi. farther e., and the navigability of the Han for 300 mi. above its junction with the Yangtze, make Hankow the chief commercial city of central China. Its commercial importance is enhanced by its location on the railway from Peking to Canton. Among the principal cargoes handled at Hankow are timber, hides, cotton, tea, and silk. Hankow is one of the leading manufacturing centers of central China, producing steel, textiles, flour, soap, cement, processed rice, vegetable oils, and a wide variety of other commodities. Hankow was heavily damaged by flooding in 1931 and by invading Japanese forces in 1938.

HANNA, Marcus Alonzo, known as MARK HANNA (1837–1904), American politician and businessman, born in New Lisbon (now Lisbon), Ohio. After one year at Western Reserve College (now Western Reserve University), he entered his father's wholesale-grocery business. He was singularly successful in this and other enterprises, including the coal-and-iron business, the operation of railway and steamship lines, and banking.

Beginning in 1880, Hanna became increasingly active in the Republican Party (q.v.). At the Republican National Convention of 1888 he managed the unsuccessful bid of United States Senator John Sherman (q.v.) for the Presidential nomination. In 1896, Hanna did secure the Presidential nomination for another protégé, Governor William McKinley (q.v.) of Ohio, at the Republican national convention. As chairman of the Republican National Committee Hanna managed the subsequent campaign, raising a huge war chest to win the election for McKinley.

In 1897 Hanna was appointed to fill an unexpired term in the United States Senate by the governor of Ohio. He was elected to a full term in the Senate the following year. One of the most influential advisers of President McKinley, Hanna advocated and secured a lasting alliance between the Republican Party and corporate business interests. After the assassination of McKinley in 1901, Hanna acted as adviser to the new President, Theodore Roosevelt (q.v.), and helped him to settle the anthracite coal strike of 1902.

HANNAH, or ANNA, in the Old Testament (1 Sam. 1–2), mother of the prophet Samuel (q.v.), whom she dedicated to God.

HANNIBAL, city of Missouri, in Marion and Ralls counties, on the Mississippi R., 120 miles N. of Saint Louis. It is served by railroad and by river steamers and barges; an airport is 4 miles N.W. of the city. The Mark Twain Memorial Bridge to Illinois spans the Mississippi at Hannibal. The principal industries in Hannibal are the processing of food and beverages and the manufacture of shoes, stamped-metal foundry products, machinery, cement, and concrete blocks. In addition, Hannibal has railroad repair shops, woodworking shops, and printing facilities. In the vicinity of the city are deposits of shale and limestone. The site of Hannibal-La Grange Junior College (Baptist), established in 1858, Hannibal is noted also as the boyhood home of the American author Mark Twain (see CLEMENS, SAMUEL LANGHORNE), who lived here between 1839 and 1853. A statue of him stands in Riverview Park, overlooking the river, and the house in which he lived is maintained by the city as a memorial. *The Adventures of Tom Sawyer* and *The Adventures of Huckleberry Finn,* two of Mark Twain's most celebrated works, have their setting in Hannibal. Hannibal was first settled in 1818, and was incorporated as a city in 1845. Pop. (1960) 20,028; (1970) 18,609.

HANNIBAL (247–183 B.C.), Carthaginian general, son of Hamilcar Barca (q.v.). At the age of nine Hannibal accompanied his father on the Carthaginian expedition to conquer Spain. Before starting, the boy vowed eternal hatred for Rome, the bitter rival of Carthage (q.v.). From his eighteenth to his twenty-fifth year, Hannibal was the chief agent in carrying out the plans by which his brother-in-law Hasdrubal (q.v.) extended and consolidated the Carthaginian dominion on the Iberian Peninsula. When Hasdrubal was assassinated in 221 B.C., the army chose Hannibal as commander in chief. In two years he subjugated all Spain between the Tagus and Iberus (Ebro) rivers, with the exception of the Roman dependency of Saguntum (Sagunto), which was taken after a siege of eight months. The Romans branded this attack a violation of the existing treaty between Rome and Carthage and demanded that Carthage surrender Hannibal to them. On the refusal of the Carthaginians to do so, the Romans declared war on Carthage in 218 B.C., thus precipitating the Second Punic War (see PUNIC WARS).

Crossing the Alps. The march on Rome began in 218 B.C. Hannibal left New Carthage (now Cartagena), Spain, with an army of about 40,000, including cavalry and a considerable number of elephants carrying baggage and later used in battle. He crossed the Pyrenees and the Rhône R., and traversed the Alps in fifteen days, beset by snowstorms, landslides, and the attacks of hostile mountain tribes. After recruiting additional men among the friendly Insubres, a Gallic people of northern Italy, to compensate for the loss of about 15,000 men during the long march, Hannibal subjugated the Taurini, a tribe hostile to the Insubres, and forced into alliance with himself all the Ligurian and Celtic tribes on the upper course of the Po R. Then, late in the year, he vanquished the Romans under Publius Cornelius Scipio Africanus (see under SCIPIO) in the battles of Ticino and Trebbia. In the following year, 217 B.C., Hannibal inflicted a crushing defeat upon the Roman consul Gaius Flaminius (q.v.) at Lake Trasimenus. After his victory Hannibal crossed the Apennines and invaded the Roman provinces of Picenum and Apulia, recrossing thence to the fertile Campania, which he ravaged.

The Roman general Quintus Fabius Maximus Verrucosus (see FABIUS), sent from Rome to oppose Hannibal, adopted a highly cautious strategy. Avoiding any decisive encounter with the Carthaginian troops, he nevertheless succeeded in keeping Hannibal at bay, thus giving the Romans the opportunity to recover from their military reverses. Hannibal wintered at Gerontium, and in the spring of 216 B.C. took up a position at Cannae (q.v.) on the Aufidus (Ofanto) R. There he almost completely annihilated a Roman army of more than 50,000 men under the consuls Lucius Aemilius Paulus (d. 216 B.C.), who was killed in the battle, and Gaius Terentius Varro (d. after 200 B.C.), who escaped with the remnant. Carthaginian losses were about 6700 men.

After the Battle of Cannae, the character of the war underwent a change. Hannibal needed reinforcements, which the Carthaginian government refused to furnish, and he also lacked

Hannibal and his army crossing the Rhône River on the march to Rome.

siege weapons. He marched on Neapolis (Naples), but failed to take the city. The gates of wealthy Capua (q.v.), one of the Italian cities which had fallen to Hannibal in consequence of his victory at Cannae, were opened to him, however, and there he passed the winter of 216–215 B.C. In 211 B.C. Hannibal attempted to take Rome, but the Romans successfully maintained their fortified positions. The Romans then retook Capua. The loss of this second city of Italy cost Hannibal the allegiance of many of his Italian allies, and put an end to his hopes of further replenishing his army from their ranks. After four years of inconclusive fighting, Hannibal turned for aid to his brother Hasdrubal, who forthwith marched from Spain. Hasdrubal, however, was surprised, defeated, and slain by the Roman consul Gaius Claudius Nero (fl. 216–201 B.C.) in the Battle of the Metaurus (Metauro) R. **Roman Victory.** In 202 B.C., after fifteen years, and with the military fortunes of Carthage rapidly declining, Hannibal was recalled to Africa to direct the defense of his country against a Roman invasion under Scipio Africanus the Elder. When he met Scipio at Zama, North Africa, his raw troops fled, many deserting to the Romans, and his veterans were cut down. Carthage capitulated to Rome, and the Second Punic War finally came to an end.

After a peace had been concluded with the Romans in 201 B.C., Hannibal immediately set about making preparations for a resumption of the struggle. He amended the Carthaginian constitution, reduced corruption in the government, and placed the finances of the city on a sounder basis. The Romans, however, charged him with working to break the peace, and he was obliged to flee Carthage, taking refuge at the court of Antiochus III, King of Syria (*see under* ANTIOCHUS). With Antiochus he fought against the Romans, but when the Syrian monarch was defeated at Magnesia (Manisa) in 190 B.C. and signed a treaty with Rome pledging to surrender Hannibal, the latter escaped to Prusias II, King of Bithynia (r. 192–148 B.C.), in northern Asia Minor. When Rome once more demanded the surrender of Hannibal, he committed suicide by taking poison.

See CARTHAGE; ROME, HISTORY OF.

HANNO (fl. 5th cent. B.C.), Carthaginian navigator who undertook a voyage of exploration along the west coast of Africa. He probably sailed as far as present-day Sierra Leone. When he returned to Carthage, he inscribed an account of his travels on a tablet which he deposited in the temple of the Phoenician god Moloch (q.v.). The original narrative was composed in the Phoenician language; a translation exists written in Greek and entitled *Periplu* ("Voyage").

HANNO, known as HANNO THE GREAT (fl. late 3rd cent. B.C.), Carthaginian politician and general. As the leader of the pro-Roman aristocratic party, Hanno was the chief opponent of Hamilcar Barca (q.v.), a famous Carthaginian general of the First Punic War against Rome; see PUNIC WARS. In 240 B.C., after the war, Hanno incited a rebellion among Hamilcar's troops by withholding their pay. Called on to quell the mutiny, Hanno failed. The insurrection, growing in strength, developed into a serious threat to Carthage (q.v.), and Hanno was replaced by Hamilcar, who ended the rebellion in 237 B.C.

Hanno continued to advocate peace with Rome, and during the Second Punic War opposed entrusting the chief command to Hannibal (q.v.), Hamilcar's son. In 202 B.C., after the defeat of Hannibal by the Romans at Zama, North Africa, Hanno was one of the commissioners sent to the Roman general Scipio Africanus the Elder (see under SCIPIO).

HANNOVER, or HANOVER, historic region in West Germany, now part of Lower Saxony State. Hannover was successively an electorate and a kingdom of Germany and later a province of Prussia. After Nov. 1, 1946, it became a part of the administrative region of Lower Saxony in the British occupation zone of Germany. The province of Hannover covered an area of 14,953 sq.mi. and had a population of about 3,500,000. It extended from the Harz Mts. on the S. to the North Sea on the N., and from the Netherlands on the W. to Prussian Saxony, Brandenburg, and Brunswick on the E. The city of Hannover (q.v.), now the capital of Lower Saxony, was the administrative center of the former province. Other important cities of Hannover Province were Osnabrück, Hildesheim, Wilhelmshaven, Harburg-Wilhelmsburg, Lüneburg, Göttingen, and Emden.

Rich mineral deposits, including coal, copper, lead, silver, and iron, are found in the region, which is noted also for its dairy industry. Among the leading industries in this area of Lower Saxony are shipbuilding, ironmaking, brewing, and the manufacture of machinery, cutlery, cotton and linen textiles, and tobacco products. The principal agricultural products include rye, flax, potatoes, hops, tobacco, and sugar beets.

History. Hannover was established as a kingdom in 1815 by the Congress of Vienna; see VIENNA, CONGRESS OF. It had been officially known prior to that time as the electorate of Brunswick-Lüneburg. The electorate, which was formed in 1692 from the territories of the ducal family of Brunswick (q.v.), gradually acquired, in popular usage, the name of its capital city, Hannover. Ernest Augustus, the first Elector of Hannover (1629–98), married Sophia Dorothea (1666–1726), granddaughter of James I (q.v.), King of England. In 1714 their son, George Louis, Elector of Hannover, became George I (q.v.), King of Great Britain. For nearly 125 years thereafter, both Hannover and Great Britain were ruled by the same sovereign. The electorate was involved in the War of the Austrian Succession (see SUCCESSION WARS) as an ally of Austria, in the Seven Years' War (q.v.) on the side of Prussia, and in the Napoleonic Wars (q.v.) as part of the anti-French coalition of European powers. In 1803 the electorate was occupied by the French. Napoleon I (q.v.), Emperor of France, incorporated part of it into the new Kingdom of Westphalia in 1807. In 1810 the remainder of the electorate was added to Westphalia, but later that year Napoleon withdrew a portion of the territory and united it with France. The electorate was restored to George III (q.v.), King of Great Britain, shortly after the expulsion of the French armies in November, 1813.

For an extended period following its transformation into a kingdom by the Congress of Vienna, Hannover was the scene of bitter political strife between liberal political groupings and the monarchy. Several revolutionary uprisings in 1831 were quelled, but continuing liberal pressure forced the promulgation of a liberal constitution in 1833. Hannoverian succession was limited to males; in 1837 William IV (q.v.), King of Great Britain, died without legal heirs. Thus the crown of Hannover passed not to Victoria (q.v.), Queen of Great Britain, but to William's brother Ernest Augustus, Duke of Cumberland (1771–1851). The reign of this ruler, who immediately abrogated the constitution of 1833, was marked by a renewal of the revolutionary movement, and in 1848 Ernest Augustus was compelled to liberalize the government. During the reign from 1851–66 of Ernest's son George V, King of Hannover (see under GEORGE), the kingdom was allied in 1866 with Austria against Prussia in the Seven Weeks' War (q.v.). By the terms of the Treaty of Prague, which ended the war, Hannover was annexed and made into a province by the Prussian kingdom. The province was occupied by British troops following the collapse of Germany in World War II. On Nov. 1, 1946, with the formal liquidation of the State of Prussia, Hannover was merged with the former States of Brunswick, Oldenburg, and part of Schaumburg-Lippe to form the new State of Lower Saxony. See GERMANY: *History.*

HANNOVER, or HANOVER, city in West Germany, and capital of Lower Saxony State, on the

HANNOVER

Leine R., about 78 miles S.E. of Bremen, and about 158 miles W. of Berlin. A railroad junction point, Hannover is one of the major commercial centers of N.W. Germany. It has an extensive trade in coal, timber, grain, hides, wine, horses, and local manufactures. The leading industrial products of the city are machinery, hardware, asphalt, glass, furniture, pianos, processed foods, chemicals, oilcloth, and tobacco products. Printing establishments, railroad-repair shops, breweries, and distilleries are also located in Hannover. Altstadt, the old section of the city, has many medieval features, including narrow streets, gabled houses with overhanging balconies, and the Markt Kirche, a brick structure dating from the 14th century. The oldest ecclesiastical edifice in Hannover is the Kreuzkirche, constructed about 1300. Among other notable structures are the former Rathaus (city hall), built in Gothic style between 1439 and 1455; the former royal palace, completed in 1640 and now an art museum; and the landscaped gardens of Herrenhausen, formerly the summer residence of the royal family of Hannover. The city has a number of outstanding historical museums, libraries and technological institutes, as well as other cultural and educational institutions.

Hannover first assumed importance in 1241, when Otto, 1st Duke of Brunswick-Lüneburg, later Hannover (1204–52), granted it a municipal charter. The town became a member of the Hanseatic League (q.v.) in 1481. In 1636 the Brunswick-Lüneburg family established residence in Hannover. Although serving as the seat of government of the electorate and, later, of the kingdom, Hannover grew slowly. The commercial and industrial development of the town began after the annexation of the kingdom by Prussia in 1866. During World War II Hannover was a frequent target of Allied air raids. The city was captured by United States forces in April, 1945. Pop. (1968 est.) 521,904.

HANOI, largest city and capital of North Vietnam, on the Red R., about 80 mi. inland from the Gulf of Tonkin, and about 60 miles W. of Haiphong. An important transportation center, Hanoi has a large airport and is a railroad hub for lines extending from the port of Haiphong to Muong Khuong on the border with China, and to Nam Dinh and other cities in the country. The trading center of a rich agricultural area, Hanoi has industrial establishments engaged in rice milling and in the production of textiles, bricks and tiles, china, leather goods, soap, and chemicals. Handicraft products include embroidery, jewelry, and wood and copper articles. Points of interest include Petit Lac, a scenic lake with an island on which is built a pagoda of the Great Buddha; the University of Hanoi; a large

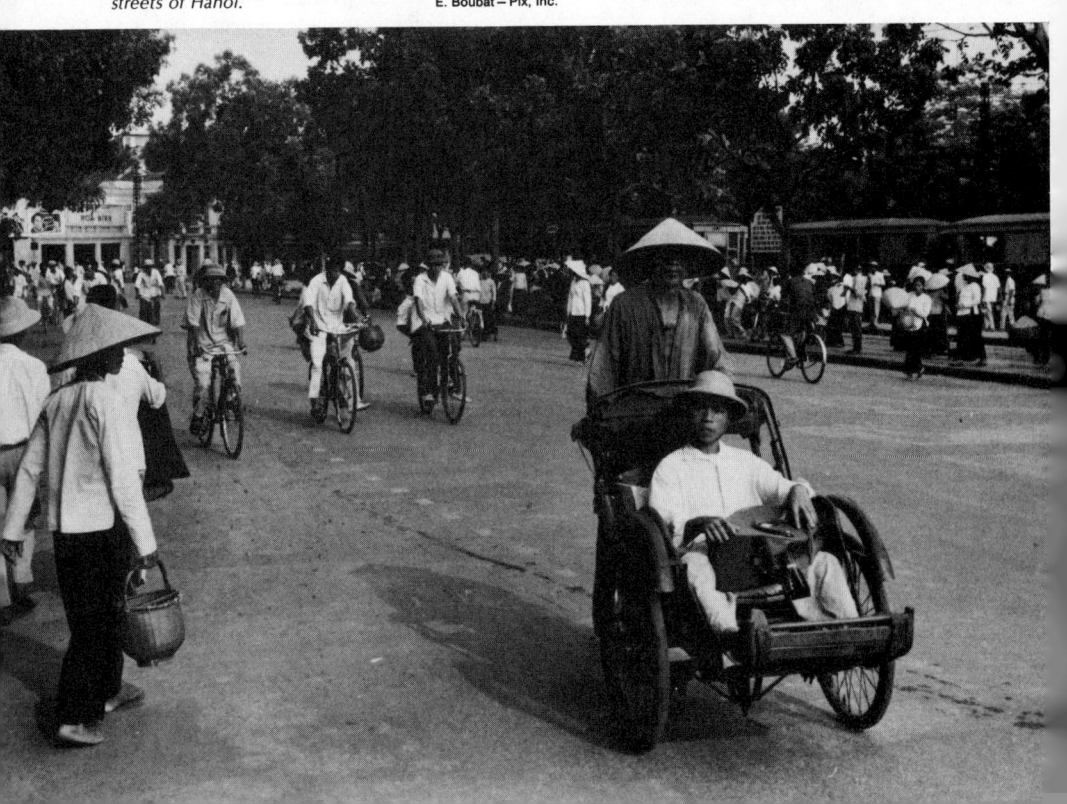

Bicycles are the common mode of transportation in the streets of Hanoi. E. Boubat – Pix, Inc.

Asian library; and the Museum of the Far East, which houses collections of fine art and archeological treasures.

Long a strategically important Annamese town (see ANNAM), Hanoi was made the capital of French Indochina in 1887. It was occupied by Japanese troops during World War II. Following the restoration of French control in Indochina, Hanoi figured prominently in the ensuing hostilities (1946–54) between the Communist-led Viet Minh and the French Union forces; see INDOCHINA: *History.* In accordance with the terms of the truce agreement signed in July, 1954, France evacuated Hanoi in October, and the city was occupied by Viet Minh forces. A Communist government was established in North Vietnam with Hanoi as the capital. During the war in North and South Vietnam Hanoi was bombed by American planes. The bombings caused damage to the city, especially to fuel depots and the railway in Hanoi and suburbs; see VIETNAM, WAR IN. Pop. (1968 est.) 643,576.

HANOVER. See HANNOVER.

HANSEATIC LEAGUE *or* **HANSE TOWNS** (from OHG. *hansa,* "league"), synonymous designations applied to a federation of northern German towns organized during the 13th century for the protection and enhancement of mutual commercial interests. At the peak of its ascendancy, the league was a potent force in the politics of Europe. The federation developed as a result of conditions peculiar to medieval Europe, including the gradual emergence of free cities and merchant guilds (see GUILD); the disintegration of centralized authority within Germany; the expansion of German colonization, influence, and trade in the region east of the Elbe R.; the consequent stimulation of north German trade with England and the continental ports on the English Channel; and the prevalence of pirates and highwaymen along the main arteries of trade.

As early as the beginning of the 13th century, German merchants who had settled on the Baltic island of Gotland (q.v.) created a mercantile association, consisting of Cologne (q.v.) and twenty-nine other towns. The Gotland association secured important trading privileges abroad, notably in England, Flanders, and Russia. In 1241, while the Gotland association was in the ascendancy, the town of Lübeck, a rival commercial center, completed with Hamburg (qq.v.) a treaty providing for joint control of the route between the Baltic and North seas. This alliance, which was strengthened by another agreement some years later, gave the signatories a powerful position in the commerce of northwestern Europe. In consequence of these developments, the sphere of influence of the Gotland association gradually diminished. The Lübeck-Hamburg union was immeasurably strengthened in 1252, when highly advantageous commercial treaties were arranged with Flanders (q.v.). Thereafter, Bruges (q.v.), the chief city of Flanders and a leading mercantile center of Europe, figured significantly in the development of the league. Rostock and Wismar concluded an alliance with Lübeck in 1259 for common action against bandits and pirates. Less than a decade later, the merchants of Lübeck and Hamburg acquired the right to establish trading organizations in London, where Cologne merchants had previously enjoyed a monopoly. About the same time, the mercantile interests of Lübeck and Hamburg obtained full or partial control of trade between Germany and the coastal towns of eastern England. Attracted by the mounting influence and prosperity of the Lübeck-Hamburg union, various other northern German towns, notably Bremen and Danzig (now Gdańsk, Poland), became affiliated with the organization. Other mercantile leagues of German towns, grouped on a regional basis, gradually accepted the hegemony of Lübeck and its allies. Among these regional leagues was one comprised of certain towns of Westphalia, the Rhineland, and the Low Countries; another consisted of the trading centers in the duchy of Saxony and the mark of Brandenburg, in what is now East Germany; a third was made up of Prussian and Livonian (Latvian and Estonian) towns. The federation, officially designated as the Hansa in 1343, soon included more than eighty-five towns.

Political Power. The League took its first major political action in 1362, when it declared war on Denmark in retaliation against the seizure of Visby, on the island of Gotland. Eventual victory over Denmark, which was compelled in 1370 to grant indemnities, strategic territories, and other concessions, tremendously increased the power and prestige of the league. Shortly thereafter, Richard II (q.v.), King of England, confirmed the preferential commercial treaties that his government had made with the Hansa towns. The following century was a period of great prosperity for the association. It created new centers of trade and civilization in northern Europe, integrated the commerce of the region, contributed to the development of agriculture and the industrial arts, perfected a system of weights and measures, and constructed canals and highways. Intimidated by the naval establishment of the league, many sovereigns of Europe sought alliances with the organization. The league was democratically ruled by a diet (q.v.), composed of delegates from the member towns, but at no time did it succeed in creating a centralized governmental structure. This circumstance, the source of frequent internal dissension, contributed eventually to its disintegration. The process of disintegration, which began toward the close of the 15th century, was accelerated by a variety of other factors, primarily the rise and consolidation of sovereign states in other parts of Europe, the discoveries of America and a new route to India, and the growth of Dutch and English sea power. Increasing friction between the league and England culminated, in 1589, in the English seizure of sixty-one Hanseatic vessels. The outbreak of the Thirty Years' War (q.v.) in 1618 was another severe blow to the tottering organization. By 1630 the league consisted of only Lübeck, Bremen, and Hamburg. This attenuated union endured for thirty-nine years, but the three cities retained nominal political independence and the traditional designation of Hansa towns until the revocation of these privileges in 1934 by the government of the German dictator Adolf Hitler (q.v.).

HANSEN, Armauer Gerhard Henrik (1841–1912), Norwegian physician, born in Bergen, and known for his discovery of the bacillus of leprosy (q.v.), technically called, after him, Hansen's disease. Hansen began his studies of leprosy at the Bergen Leper Hospital, at which he was assistant medical officer. Having demonstrated that the disease can be contagious, Hansen was given financial backing by the Medical Society of Christiania (now Oslo) to enable him to continue his investigations. The bacillus of the disease was discovered by him in 1874, and was named Hansen's bacillus. He was instrumental in having the Norwegian government take measures to reduce the incidence of the disease in the country and his policy of isolation of lepers is thought to have had the same general effect throughout Europe.

HANSEN'S DISEASE. *See* LEPROSY.

HANSE TOWNS. *See* HANSEATIC LEAGUE.

HANSON, Howard (1896–   ), American composer and educator, born in Wahoo, Nebr., and educated at the University of Nebraska, the Institute of Musical Art in New York City, and Northwestern University. The first musician to be awarded a fellowship of the American Academy of Arts and Letters, he studied in Rome from 1921 to 1924. Upon his return to the United States, he served as director of the Eastman School of Music in Rochester, N.Y., until 1964, when he became director of the Institute of American Music at the University of Rochester. Besides composing works in the Romantic tradition, Hanson did much to foster interest in American music by organizing concerts and festivals featuring contemporary American composers. His best-known works are the *Nordic Symphony* (1922), the *Romantic Symphony* (1930), and the opera *Merry Mount* (1933). His Symphony No. 4 (1943) won a Pulitzer Prize in 1944 and a George Foster Peabody Award in 1946. Hanson is the author of *Harmonic Materials of Modern Music* (1960).

HANTAN, city of China, coextensive with Hantan special district, in Hopei Province, 150 miles N.E. of Chengchow, and 250 miles S.W. of Peking. Hantan is on the Peking-Wuhan Railway and is the center of an important cotton-growing region. Corn, millet, and kaoliang sorghum are also grown in the area. The city expanded greatly after the development of the cotton-milling industry in the 1950's. Pop. (1958 est.) 380,000.

HANUKKAH, *or* CHANUKAH (Heb., "dedication"), annual festival of the Jews celebrated on eight successive days beginning on the 25th day of Kislev, the third month of the Jewish calendar, corresponding, approximately, to December in the Gregorian calendar. Also known as the Festival of Lights, Feast of Dedication, and Feast of the Maccabees, Hanukkah commemorates the rededication of the Temple of Jerusalem (*see* TEMPLE: *Temple at Jerusalem*) by Judas Maccabee (*see under* MACCABEES) in 165 B.C., after the Temple had been profaned by Antiochus IV Epiphanes (*see under* ANTIOCHUS), King of Syria and overlord of Palestine.

In 168 B.C., on a date corresponding approximately to Dec. 25 in the Gregorian calendar, the Temple was dedicated to the worship of Zeus Olympius (*see* ZEUS) by order of Antiochus. An altar to Zeus was set up on the high altar. When Judas Maccabee recaptured Jerusalem three years later, he had the Temple purged and a new altar put up in place of the desecrated one. The Temple was then rededicated to God with festivities that lasted eight days. According to Talmudic tradition, only one cruse of pure olive oil, sealed by the high priest and necessary for the rededicatory ritual, could be found, but that small quantity burned miraculously for eight days. A principal feature of the present-day celebration, commemorating this miracle, is the lighting of candles, one the first night, two the second, and so on until a special eight-branched candelabrum is completely filled. The story of Hanukkah is told in the Apocrypha

The traditional lighting of candles during the Jewish festival of Hanukkah commemorates the rededication of the Temple of Jerusalem in 165 B.C. UPI

books of the Old Testament (*see* BIBLE: *The Apocrypha*) entitled Maccabees (see books of the MACCABEES). S.L.

HANYANG. *See* WUHAN.

HAPSBURG, *or* (Ger.) HABSBURG, name of a noble and royal German family which, at various periods in European history, was the ruling house of Germany, as a separate kingdom as well as a part of the Holy Roman Empire, and of Austria, Bohemia, Hungary, Spain, and many smaller European realms.

The founder of the family, as far as can be ascertained, was Guntram the Rich (fl. 10th cent.), a German count. The name of the family is derived from a family seat, the castle of Habsburg, or Habichtsburg ("Hawk's Castle"), built in 1028 on the Aare R. in what is now Aargau Canton, Switzerland. Werner I (d. 1096) was the first descendant of Guntram to call himself Count of Habsburg. The countship descended in a direct line to Albert the Rich, Count of Zürich (d. 1199), a great-grandson of Werner I. By the time of Albert, the family held large estates in Switzerland, Alsace, and parts of Germany, some of them acquired through the already traditional method of making advantageous marriages. Albert himself added extensive domains in Switzerland; and his successor, Rudolf the Old (d. 1232), acquired the countships of Laufenburg and Aargau, also in Switzerland. Albert the Wise (d. 1239) and Rudolf the Younger, the sons of Rudolf the Old, divided the family possessions. Rudolf, who received Laufenburg, founded the house of Hapsburg-Laufenburg, which became extinct in the direct male line in 1415; most of the family possessions reverted to the elder branch, known as the Hapsburg-Hapsburg line. This branch, comprising the descendants of Albert the Wise, gave the house of Hapsburg its historical fame, beginning with Albert's son, Rudolf I, Holy Roman Emperor and King of Germany. The direct male Hapsburg line became extinct in 1740 with the death of Charles VI, Holy Roman Emperor; the family thenceforth descended in the female line, beginning with Charles' daughter, Maria Theresa, Archduchess of Austria, who, by her marriage to Francis Stephen, Duke of Lorraine, later Francis I, Holy Roman Emperor, founded the House of Hapsburg-Lorraine, the imperial house of Austria-Hungary; *see* PRAGMATIC SANCTION. Among the more famous members of the Hapsburg-Lorraine line, other than Austrian rulers, are Marie Antoinette, daughter of Francis I and Maria Theresa and wife of Louis XVI, King of France; Marie Louise (1791–1847), second wife of Napoleon I, Emperor of France, and daughter of Francis II, Holy Roman Emperor; and Maximilian I, Emperor of Mexico.

Austria. During the first centuries that the duchy of Austria existed as an entity, it was nominally at the disposal of the Holy Roman

183

HAPSBURG

The tombstone of Rudolf I of Hapsburg, in the Cathedral of Speyer, Germany. Granger Collection

Empire. In 1276 Emperor Rudolf I forced Ottokar II, King of Bohemia (1230–1278), to relinquish his Austrian conquests and killed him at the Battle of the Marchfeld. Five years later, Rudolf invested his sons, Albert and Rudolf, with princely titles and with the duchy jointly. Under Frederick III, Holy Roman Emperor, in 1453 the domain became an archduchy. The succession was made hereditary in the Hapsburg line, and, after 1740, in the Hapsburg-Lorraine dynasty, the last monarch of which was Charles I, Emperor of Austria.

Bohemia and Hungary. In 1526 Ferdinand I, Holy Roman Emperor, was elected king of Bohemia and Hungary, which he claimed by right of his marriage to Anna, sister of Louis II, King of Bohemia and Hungary (1506–26). From 1526 the thrones of these two countries became hereditary possessions of the Hapsburg archduchy of Austria, which in 1804 became the Empire of Austria.

Germany. Beginning in 1438 with Albert II, Holy Roman Emperor and King of Germany, all Holy Roman emperors and German kings except Charles VII (r. 1724–45) and Francis I (r. 1745–65) were Hapsburgs, those ruling from 1765 to the end of the empire in 1806 were of the House of Hapsburg-Lorraine. See HOLY ROMAN EMPIRE.

Spain. Philip I, King of Castile, son of the Holy Roman emperor Maximilian I, married Juana (1479–1555), daughter of Ferdinand V and Isabella I, joint rulers of Spain. On the death of Isabella in 1504, Philip became nominal joint ruler of Castile with Juana, although Ferdinand was the actual ruler. The Spanish Hapsburgs included Charles V, Holy Roman Emperor, and the Spanish kings Philip II, Philip III, Philip IV, and Charles II. Charles II willed the throne to Philip V, first Bourbon King of Spain.

Other Possessions. Hapsburg dominions, either as part of large monarchies or as independent territories, have included Naples, Sicily, Sardinia, Milan, Mantua, Parma, and Piacenza, in Italy; Franche-Comté and Burgundy, in France; and the Netherlands.

See separate articles for those persons mentioned whose birth and death dates are not given.

HARA, Takashi (1854–1921), Japanese statesman, born in Morioka. He studied law and was a journalist before he entered the Japanese diplomatic service in 1886 as chargé d'affaires in Paris. Between 1886 and 1906 he held important diplomatic and political posts and was also editor in chief successively of two Osaka newspapers. In 1900 he became the principal organizer of the Seiyukai or liberal party. He became the leader of the party in 1914. He served as minister for home affairs in a number of cabinets and in 1918 became prime minister, the first commoner to hold the office. His administration was conservative in policy, opposing universal suffrage, labor unions, and other Western political ideas. His cabinet was formed on the model of cabinets of Western Europe, being drawn from members of his own party.

HARA-KIRI, or HARI-KARI (Jap., "belly-cutting"), Japanese practice of ceremonious suicide by disembowelment, a method originally restricted by custom to noblemen and later adopted by all classes. The term is also used to signify any suicide performed for the sake of personal honor. Hara-kiri originated in feudal Japan (see JAPAN: *History*), when it was used by samurai (q.v.), or warrior noblemen, to avoid the dishonor of capture by their enemies. It later became virtually an indirect method of execution, whereby a noble, upon receiving a message from the mikado (q.v.), or emperor, that his death was essential to imperial welfare, performed hara-kiri, following a rigidly prescribed ritual.

In most cases of so-called obligatory hara-kiri, a richly ornamented dagger accompanied the imperial message, to be used as the suicide weapon. A specified number of days was allotted to the offender for his preparations for the ceremony. A red-carpeted dais was constructed in the home of the offending noble, or in a temple. At the beginning of the final ceremony, the nobleman, dressed in ceremonial costume and attended by a group of friends and officials, took his place on the dais. Assuming a kneeling position, he prayed, took the dagger from the representative of the emperor, and publicly avowed his guilt; then, stripping to the waist, he plunged the dagger into the left side of his abdomen, drawing it slowly across to the right side and making a slight upward cut. At the final moment a friend or kinsman beheaded the dying nobleman. Subsequently, the bloodstained dagger was customarily sent to the emperor as proof of the death of the nobleman by hara-kiri. If the offender committed voluntary hara-kiri, that is, acted on his own guilty conscience rather than by order of the emperor, his honor was considered restored and his entire estate went to his family. If hara-kiri had been ordered by the emperor, half of the property of the suicide was confiscated by the state.

As practiced by persons of all classes, hara-kiri frequently served as an ultimate gesture of devotion to a superior who had died, or as a form of protest against some act or policy of the government. The practice eventually became so widespread that for centuries an estimated total of 1500 deaths occurred annually by this method; more than half of these were entirely voluntary acts.

Hara-kiri as an obligatory form of execution was abolished in 1868. Incidences of it as a form of voluntary suicide are rare in modern times. Many Japanese soldiers in recent wars, including World War II, resorted to hara-kiri to escape the ignominy of defeat or capture.

See BUSHIDO; SUICIDE.

HARALD, kings of Norway. See HAROLD.

HARAR, city in Ethiopia, and capital of Harar Province, about 225 miles E. of Addis Ababa and 30 miles S.E. of Dire Dawa, at an elevation of 6000 ft. The city lies in a fertile coffee-growing district; other products of the area are cotton, fruit, and grains. The city also has a flourishing livestock market. Harar, a major city of Ethiopia, is surrounded by a high wall, and contains the palace of the governor, an Abyssinian church, and a number of mosques. Harar was founded by Arabs in the 7th century A.D., and in the 16th century was the capital of an independent Muslim State. It was conquered by Ethiopia in 1887. Pop. (1967 est.) 42,771.

HARBIN, city of the People's Republic of China, in Heilungkiang Province, on the Sungari R., about 220 miles N.E. of Mukden. The second-largest city (after Mukden) of Manchuria (q.v.), Harbin is a flourishing commercial center, in the heart of a rich agricultural region. The city is served by railway lines providing direct connections with all major points in N.E. Asia, by inland water carriers operating on the Sungari and its affluents, and by air. In addition to being the center of an extensive trade in grain, soybeans, sugar, tobacco, lumber, furs, leather, and woolen goods, Harbin is the site of large railway-repair shops and numerous manufacturing industries, as well as flour mills and other food-processing plants. The commercial importance of Harbin dates from the completion (1901) of the Chinese Eastern Railway, an extension of the Trans-Siberian Railway. Following the subjugation (1931-32) of Manchuria by Japan and the establishment of the puppet state of Manchukuo, Harbin became the capital of the newly organized province of Pinkiang. The city remained under the control of Japan until the end of World War II. In April, 1946, during the civil war between the Chinese Nationalists and Communists, Harbin was captured by Communist forces. Pop. (1965 est.) 1,600,000.

HARBOR, naturally or artificially protected basin on an ocean, lake, or river where ships may be anchored or docked without danger from waves or high winds. In the strictest sense the term harbor is confined to the water area of

HARBOR

a port, but in general usage it includes the protective breakwaters and jetties and the piers and docks that surround the harbor proper; see BREAKWATER; DOCK. According to their use, harbors may be divided into three types: harbors of refuge, commercial harbors, and naval harbors. A harbor of refuge is a harbor created solely as a temporary haven for ships in storms. Commercial harbors are equipped with docking or other facilities for the loading and unloading of cargo and, usually, with installations for the refueling and repair of ships. Naval harbors contain, in addition to the facilities of the commercial harbor, buildings and equipment for the storage and handling of munitions. A number of large and important harbors such as those of San Francisco and New York City in the United States and Southampton, England are both commercial and naval harbors.

Harbors may also be classified into three types according to the ways in which they are protected. Natural harbors have the protection of natural bays, peninsulas, headlands, or offshore islands. Improved harbors are those in which the natural features that afford shelter have been augmented with breakwaters and other works. Artificial harbors are entirely protected by man-made structures.

Natural Harbors. Most of the important natural harbors have been improved to some extent by dredging channels that permit ships of deep draft to use them. This is the case in New York Harbor, one of the finest natural harbors in the world. Before 1885 the 24-ft.-deep natural channel through the sandbanks at the mouth of the harbor was entirely adequate for the vessels that used the port. As larger vessels were constructed, however, it became necessary to deepen the channel and ultimately to cut an artificial channel, the Ambrose Channel, to the northeast of the natural one. Both channels now are maintained at a depth of 40 ft. by regular dredging. Among the other important natural harbors of the world are those of San Francisco

An aerial view of New York Bay, one of the busiest natural harbors in the world.   Port of New York Authority

and Boston in the U.S.; Southampton and Falmouth in England; Rio de Janeiro, Brazil; Kingston, Jamaica; Sydney, Australia; Hong Kong; and Bombay, India. During World War II the United States Navy made extensive use of the natural harbor facilities afforded by such large Pacific atolls, or coral islands, as Kwajalein; see CORAL REEFS AND CORAL ISLANDS.

Improved Harbors. Constructed in all parts of the world, improved harbors are designed to suit the natural topography of the locations. One type of improved harbor has been made by providing a channel entrance to an inland bay or lagoon by means of jetties. The harbors of Charleston, S.C., and Galveston, Texas, are of this type, as are those of Venice, Italy, and Durban, Republic of South Africa. Many bay and lagoon harbors suffer from the sanding or silting of the entrance channel between the jetties, so that constant dredging becomes a necessity. In some cases the natural building up of a sandbar at the entrance to the harbor has necessitated the complete abandonment of the harbor.

In open bays, or in bays in which the mouth is directly open to prevailing winds and storms, protection can often be given by constructing a single breakwater to guard the harbor mouth. The harbor of Los Angeles, Calif., is of this type, with a single breakwater stretching out from the land to protect the opening to the inner harbor.

Artificial Harbors. On coastlines having no natural shelter, harbors are made by surrounding an area of water with a series of breakwaters to form an artificial bay. The plans of such harbors vary widely but all have at least two breakwaters with the harbor entrance between them. One of the largest completely artificial harbors is that of Buffalo, N.Y., on Lake Erie. Other important harbors of this type include Marseille, France; Port Said, Arab Republic of Egypt; Casablanca, Morocco; Naples, Italy; and Trieste on the Adriatic Sea.

History. The earliest artificial harbor works known are those built on the island of Crete by the Minoans in about 2000 B.C.; archeologists do not entirely agree on this date. In the 13th century B.C. the Phoenicians created the harbors of Tyre (q.v.) and Sidon (see SAIDA) by building moles, or breakwaters. Under Roman rule many harbors were constructed around the Mediterranean Sea, some of which, such as Taranto and Brindisi in Italy, are still used.

In the centuries following the fall of the Roman Empire no harbors were made, but the art of harbor engineering was revived in the Middle Ages when sea commerce had become an important source of revenue to the Italian republics. The harbors of Venice and Genoa were begun in this period, and in both ports some of the original works still survive. France followed the example of Italy, embanking, protecting, and deepening the mouths of rivers to make such harbors as those of Le Havre, Dieppe, and Dunkirk. The first harbors in Great Britain were those built at Hartlepool, England, in 1250 and at Arbroath, Scotland, in 1394. In the 16th and 17th centuries many harbors were protected with piers and jetties.

In America little was done to improve natural anchorages until the 18th century, when the colonial government made improvements to the more important northeastern harbors such as Boston, New York, and Philadelphia. Under the United States Constitution all harbor rights are vested in the Federal government, and the design, construction, and maintenance of harbors are the responsibilities of the United States Army Corps of Engineers. In many cases cities and States pay for harbor improvements with their own funds, but the work is supervised by the Federal government.

Federal funds for harbor work are appropriated by Congress in an annual or biennial river and harbor bill. The first regular appropriation made for harbor improvement was $30,000 voted by Congress in 1892 for building public piers in Philadelphia. In the early 1970's the appropriation for river and harbor work amounted to about $1,280,000,000 annually.

HARBORD, James Guthrie (1866–1947), American army officer and business executive, born in Bloomington, Ill., and educated at Kansas State Agricultural College. He enlisted in the United States Army in 1889 and was commissioned in 1891. In the Spanish-American War he held the temporary rank of major in the cavalry, and from 1903 to 1914 served in the Philippine Constabulary with the temporary rank of colonel. He served under the American general John Joseph Pershing (q.v.) on the Mexican border, and was Pershing's chief of staff in Europe from 1917 to 1918 in World War I. Later in 1918 Harbord commanded a brigade at Château-Thierry (see MARNE, BATTLE OF THE) and then a division in the Soissons offensive. He was promoted to major general in 1919, and from 1921 to 1922 he was deputy chief of staff of the U.S. Army. He left active duty in 1922, and retired with the rank of lieutenant general. He was president of the Radio Corporation of America from 1923 to 1930, and thereafter chairman of the board until a month before his death.

HARDANGER FJORD, fjord of the Hardanger Mts. (Hardanger Fjeld) region, Hordaland

HARDECANUTE

County, s.w. Norway, extending 114 mi. from the sea (70 mi. from the fringe of islands at its mouth) and attaining a maximum depth of about 2100 ft. Many smaller fjords branch off the main inlet, which is itself separated into numerous parts, each having a different name. Waterfalls cascade from the slopes of the mountains which line the fjord. In the areas bordering the Hardanger Fjord are fertile valleys and many small villages. The Hardanger inhabitants preserve traditional customs, dress, and dialect. Both the Hardanger Fjord and Fjeld are popular with vacationists and tourists.

HARDECANUTE, or HARDICANUTE or HARTHACNUT (1019?–42), King of Denmark (1035–42) and King of England (1040–42), last of the Danish kings of England, the son of King Canute (q.v.) and Emma of Normandy (d. 1052), born probably in Denmark. He was heir to the English realm, but when Canute died in 1035 Hardecanute was in Denmark. His illegitimate half brother, Harold Harefoot, later Harold I (q.v.), King of England, who was then in England, took control of that country and was accepted as king by the English witenagemot (q.v.) in 1037. The ensuing struggle between the two brothers was ended by the death of Harold in 1040. Hardecanute, officially chosen as king by the witenagemot, was unpopular with his subjects and left the control of the realm to his mother and the powerful Godwin, Earl of the West Saxons (d. 1053). Hardecanute was succeeded in Denmark by Magnus I, King of Norway (see under MAGNUS), and in England by his half brother Edward the Confessor (see under EDWARD).

HARDEN, Sir Arthur (1865–1940), British chemist, born in Manchester, England, and educated at Owens College (now the Victoria University of Manchester) and the University of Erlangen, Germany. Harden was professor of biochemistry (q.v.) at the University of London and head of the biochemical department of the Lister Institute, also in London. He was known for his researches in enzymes (q.v.), particularly in alcoholic fermentation (q.v.), and shared the 1929 Nobel Prize for chemistry with the Swedish chemist Hans von Euler-Chelpin (q.v.). Harden was editor of the *Biochemical Journal* after 1912 and the author of *Alcoholic Fermentation* (1911), as well as several textbooks on chemistry.

HARDENBERG, Baron Friedrich von, pen name NOVALIS (1772–1801), German poet and novelist, born in Mansfeld, and educated at the universities of Jena, Leipzig, and Wittenberg. He was one of the founders of the Romantic movement in German literature; see GERMAN LITERATURE: *The Classical and Romantic Period*. He is particularly noted for his lyric poetry and prose, which are characterized by deep religious mysticism. His best-known work is his book of lyric poetry *Hymnen an die Nacht* (1800; Eng. trans., *Hymns to the Night,* 1889), which expresses his bereavement over the death of his fiancée. Among his other poems are *Geistliche Lieder* (1799; Eng. trans., *Devotional Songs,* 1802). Novalis was also the author of the unfinished novel *Heinrich von Ofterdingen* (1802), generally considered his best work, which has appeared in several English translations. See also ROMANTICISM.

HARDENBERG, Prince Karl August von (1750–1822), Prussian statesman, born in Hannover, and educated at the universities of Leipzig and Göttingen. He was in the civil service of various German states before becoming a Prussian minister of state in 1792. In 1795 he was the Prussian delegate at Basel, Switzerland, where he negotiated the Treaty of Basel ending Prussian participation in the French Revolution (q.v.). Hardenberg was foreign minister of Prussia from 1804 to 1806, and chancellor from 1810 to 1817. In the latter office he gave effect to liberal social, economic, and educational policies, and played a prominent part in the War of Liberation (1813–14) fought by most of the German states against France during the Napoleonic Wars (q.v.). With the title of prince, awarded for his contributions during the war, Hardenberg was the chief representative of Prussia at the Congress of Vienna (1814–15; see VIENNA, CONGRESS OF) and at the conferences in Paris after the second abdication of Napoleon I (q.v.), Emperor of France, in 1815. At both Vienna and Paris, Hardenberg was outmaneuvered by the Austrian statesman Prince Klemens von Metternich (q.v.), who in the general postwar settlement in Europe secured for Austria a more advantageous position in German affairs than Hardenberg could obtain for Prussia.

HARDHEAD. See STEELHEAD.

HARDING, Chester (1792–1866), American painter, born in Conway, Mass. Originally a cabinetmaker, then successively a soldier in the War of 1812, a house painter, a tavernkeeper, and a sign painter, he became a self-taught portrait painter. In 1823 he went to London, England, where his art proved very popular. After his return to the United States he worked in Saint Louis, Philadelphia, and Boston, and in 1831 settled in Springfield, Mass., painting portraits of American statesmen, including John Randolph (1829, National Gallery of Art, Washington, D.C.). Other works are in the collections

Warren Gamaliel Harding making a speech at his home in Marion, Ohio, during the 1920 Presidential campaign.
UPI

of the Metropolitan Museum of Art, in New York City, and in the Corcoran Gallery of Art, Washington, D.C. His autobiography was published in 1890.

HARDING, Warren Gamaliel (1865–1923), twenty-ninth President of the United States, born on a farm in Morrow County, Ohio. He spent most of his life in Marion, Ohio, where he published a newspaper and was active in a variety of business ventures. A tall and distinctly handsome man, warm and congenial, he had a gift for florid oratory that carried him to the State senate in 1898 and to the lieutenant governorship in 1902. After one term in that office, Harding continued to serve the Republican Party (q.v.). He was friendly to the city bosses, loyal to President William Howard Taft (q.v.), and an outspoken opponent of former President Theodore Roosevelt (q.v.). In 1914 he was elected to the United States Senate, where he was known as a friendly, preeminently likable man of plain tastes and conventional judgments. He favored protective tariffs (see TARIFFS, UNITED STATES) and the tax interests of big business. In foreign affairs he supported participation in World War I but opposed the League of Nations (q.v.).

When the Republican National Convention of 1920 became locked in a bitter battle between the "Old Guard" party regulars and the "insurgent" or "progressive" reformers, Harding presented himself as an available compromise. His record of bland conservatism satisfied the Old Guard while his image as a small-town businessman pleased at least some of the progressives. As an acceptable second choice to most delegates, he received the Presidential nomination, with Governor Calvin Coolidge (q.v.) of Massachusetts as Vice-Presidential candidate. Harding received 16,143,407 votes, defeating his Democratic opponent, James Middleton Cox (q.v.), by 7,013,079 votes.

President Harding personified the mood of postwar relaxation that the American people had so eagerly awaited. His speeches called for a return to "normalcy", and he was inclined to follow the inclinations of the Congress. His clemency on Christmas Day, 1921, to a number of radicals who were serving prison sentences for opposition to the war impressed most citizens as both generous and courageous. His appointment of the statesman Herbert Clark Hoover and the financier Andrew William Mellon (qq.v.) to his cabinet inspired general confidence, especially among financial and business circles, but some of his other appointments were less successful. After Harding's death investigators discovered that his secretary of the

HARDNESS

interior, Albert Bacon Fall (q.v.), had taken personal profits from the naval oil reserves at Teapot Dome, Wyo. Several other such scandals tarnished the President's reputation, although no evidence was found that Harding himself had profited from these manipulations.

The Congressional elections of 1922 were a severe setback for the President and his party. Not long thereafter, Harding began a long and exhausting transcontinental tour. Returning from Alaska to Seattle, Wash., he seemed unnerved by fatigue and by the knowledge that his friends had betrayed his trust. In a condition of deep anxiety and nervous depression, he suffered a heart attack, then contracted pneumonia and died suddenly on Aug. 2, 1923, in the Palace Hotel in San Francisco, Calif.   N.H.C.

HARDNESS, ability of a solid substance to resist surface deformation or abrasion. Various interpretations, depending on the usage, are applied to the term. In mineralogy, hardness is defined as the resistance of the smooth surface of a mineral to scratching. A soft surface is scratched more easily than a hard surface; thus a hard mineral, such as diamond, will scratch a soft mineral, such as graphite, and the hard mineral will not be scratched by the soft. The relative hardness of minerals is determined according to the Mohs' scale of hardness. In the Mohs' scale, named for the German mineralogist Karl Friedrich Mohs (1773–1839) who devised it, ten common minerals are arranged in order of increasing hardness and are assigned numbers: 1, Talc; 2, Gypsum; 3, Calcite; 4, Fluorite; 5, Apatite; 6, Orthoclase (feldspar); 7, Quartz; 8, Topaz; 9, Corundum; and 10, Diamond. The hardness of a mineral specimen is obtained by determining which mineral in the Mohs' scale will scratch the specimen. Thus, galena, which has a hardness of 2.5, can scratch gypsum and can be scratched by calcite. Although hardness is not synonymous with durability, the hardness of a mineral determines to a great extent its durability; precious gems are harder than quartz and are not scratched and dulled by the finely divided particles of quartz present in dust.

In metallurgy and engineering, hardness is determined by impressing a small ball or cone of a hard material on the surface to be tested, and measuring the size of the indentation. Hard metals are indented less than soft metals. This test to determine the hardness of metal surfaces is known as the Brinell test, named after the Swedish engineer Johann August Brinell (1849–1925) who invented the Brinell machine for measuring the hardness of metals and alloys.

Hardness is related to the strength, durability, and toughness of solid substances, and in common usage the term is often extended to include those properties.

HARDY, Thomas (1840–1928), British novelist and poet, born in Dorsetshire, England, and educated in the local schools and later privately. His father, a builder, apprenticed him early to a local ecclesiastical architect engaged in restoring old churches. After 1862 Thomas worked for an architect in London. Despite his success as an architect, he began writing poetry in 1859 and gave increasing time to it. He turned to

Thomas Hardy   Bettmann Archive

prose to support himself, but his first novel, *The Poor Man and the Lady*, written in 1868, was never published.

Early Writings. Hardy published three novels, *Desperate Remedies* (1871), *Under the Greenwood Tree* (1872), and *A Pair of Blue Eyes* (1873), before *Far from the Madding Crowd* (1874). In this work he portrayed Dorsetshire as the imaginary county of Wessex. The novel is, however, not invested with the tragic gloom of his later novels. Some lesser works followed, including *The Woodlanders* (1887) and two volumes of short stories *Wessex Tales* (1888) and *Life's Little Ironies* (1894).

Along with *Far from the Madding Crowd,* his best novels are *The Return of the Native* (1878), which is his most closely knit narrative, *The Mayor of Casterbridge* (1886), *Tess of the D'Urbervilles* (1891), and *Jude the Obscure* (1895). All are pervaded by a belief in a universe dominated by the inevitability of the biology of the

British naturalist Charles Darwin (see under DARWIN) and the physics of the British philosopher and mathematician Sir Isaac Newton (q.v.). Occasionally the determined fate of man is altered by chance, but when the human will challenges necessity, the former loses. Through intense, vivid descriptions of the heath, the fields, the seasons, and the weather, Wessex attains a physical presence in the novels, and acts as a mirror of the psychological conditions and the fortunes of the characters. These fortunes Hardy views with irony and sadness. The British critic Gilbert Keith Chesterton (q.v.) wrote that Hardy "became a sort of village atheist brooding and blaspheming over the village idiot". In Victorian England, Hardy did indeed seem a blasphemer, particularly in *Jude,* which treated sexual attraction as a natural force unopposable by human will. Criticism of *Jude* was so harsh that Hardy announced he was "cured" of novel writing.

Later Works: Poetry and Drama. At the age of fifty-five Hardy returned to writing poetry, a form he had previously abandoned. *Wessex Poems* (1898) and *Poems of the Past and Present* (1901) contained poems he had written earlier. In *The Dynasts* written between 1903 and 1908 Hardy created what some consider his most successful poetry. An unstageable epic drama in 19 acts and 130 scenes, it deals with the role of Great Britain during the Napoleonic Wars. Hardy's vision is the same as in his novels: history and the actors, who are wracked by feeling, are nevertheless dominated by necessity. Hardy's short poems, both lyric and visionary, were published as *Time's Laughing Stocks* (1909), *Satires of Circumstances* (1914), *Moments of Vision* (1917), *Late Lyrics and Earlier* (1922), *Human Shows, Far Fantasies* (1925), and *Winter Words* (1928). Hardy's techniques of rhythm and his diction are the two aspects of his poetry most often cited. Among his most successful shorter poems are "Channel Firing, April 1914"; "Wessex Heights"; "In Tenebris, I"; "God's Funeral"; and "Nature's Questioning".

HARE. See RABBITS AND HARES.

HARE, Maude Cuney. See NEGROES IN THE UNITED STATES: *History: New Leaders.*

HAREBELL. See CAMPANULA.

HARELIP *or* **SPLIT LIP** *or* **CLEFT LIP,** deformity of the upper or lower lip of a human being, called harelip because it resembles the notched upper lip of a hare or rabbit. Harelip, a birth defect, is caused by failure in the embryological development of the lips and is often associated with other deformities, especially cleft palate (q.v.). Harelip of the upper lip usually appears on the left or right side, or on both sides (unilateral or bilateral harelip). On the lower lip, however, harelip usually appears in the center. Harelip can be treated with plastic surgery, preferably in early childhood. See BIRTH DEFECTS.

HARGHESSA, or HARGEISA, town in Somalia, and capital of Harghessa Province, in the Ogo Highland, 90 miles S.W. of Berbera. The town is located in a stock-raising area and trades in wool, hides, and skins. A summer capital of the former British Somaliland, Harghessa was the official capital from 1941 to 1960, when the protectorate merged with Italian Somalia to form the republic. Pop. (1966) 53,000.

HARGREAVES, James (d. 1778), British inventor and industrialist, born probably in Blackburn, England. In 1760 he invented, or aided in inventing, a carding machine. The spinning jenny, which Hargreaves is credited with inventing in 1764 and which he named after his daughter, made possible the automatic production of cotton thread. A spinning mill was erected by Hargreaves in Nottingham in 1768, but he did not patent his machine until 1770. The patent was declared invalid by the courts because he had sold some of the machines before patenting them. Nevertheless, Hargreaves achieved moderate success as a yarn manufacturer in competition with other users of the jenny. In spite of opposition by hand workers, spinning became a factory industry and an important part of the factory system in England. See FACTORIES AND THE FACTORY SYSTEM; SPINNING.

HARI-KARI. See HARA-KIRI.

HARI RUD (anc. *Arius*), river of Asia, in Afghanistan, Iran, and the Turkmen S.S.R., rising in the Koh-i-Baba range W. of Kabul, Afghanistan, and flowing W. to the Iranian border, thence N., forming successively the boundary between Afghanistan and Iran and that between the Turkmen S.S.R. and Iran, and finally disappearing in the steppe region S. of the Kara-Kum Desert in the Turkmen S.S.R. In Afghanistan, between the towns of Obeh and Kuhsan, the waters of the river are used to irrigate the Herat region, noted for its fertility. Where the river courses through Soviet territory, it is known as the Tedzhen. The total length of the Hari Rud is about 650 mi.

HARKINS, William Draper (1873–1951), American chemist, born in Titusville, Pa., and educated at Stanford University and the University of Chicago. He was professor of chemistry at the University of Montana (1900–12), and did advanced research in 1909 at the Institute for Physical Chemistry in Karlsruhe, Germany, under the German chemist Fritz Haber (q.v.). Harkins became assistant professor of chemistry at the University of Chicago in 1912, and associ-

HARKNESS

ate professor from 1914 to 1917. He was also professor of physical chemistry from 1907, and director of rubber research from 1942.

Harkins is best known for his work on the stability of atomic nuclei, nuclear chemistry, and for his prediction of the existence of the neutron (q.v.) and heavy hydrogen; see DEUTERIUM. He also did considerable research in solar and stellar heat, the chemistry and physics of surfaces, and isotopic weights. Harkins based his so-called packing-fraction concept, which refers to the minute amount of energy consumed when, for example, four hydrogen atoms are converted into a helium nucleus, on the mass-energy equation ($E = mc^2$) of the German-American physicist Albert Einstein (q.v.). This conversion was to form the basis of nuclear fusion and led to the development of the hydrogen bomb; see NUCLEAR WEAPONS.

HARKNESS, Edward Stephen (1874–1940), American philanthropist, born in Cleveland, Ohio, and educated at Yale University. He inherited a large fortune from his father, Stephen Vanderburg Harkness (1818–1888), a partner of John Davison Rockefeller (see under ROCKEFELLER). Although a prominent financier and railroad director, Harkness gained prominence as a philanthropist. He made donations to many educational institutions and organizations, for social and charitable work, in both America and Europe. Among the institutions to which he contributed were the Metropolitan Museum of Art and the New York Public Library, for which he also acted as trustee; Harvard and Yale universities; and the Columbia-Presbyterian Medical Center in New York City.

Harkness made his most memorable donations in the field of medicine for research, treatment, and education. In 1918, when his mother, Anna M. Harkness (1838?–1926), established a foundation known as the Commonwealth Fund, his liberal contribution formed the major part of the endowment. The assets of the foundation are used for medical research and education, medical and public-health services in rural areas, and mental-health services. It also publishes books relating to the activities it supports, and grants fellowships to British and Commonwealth students and civil servants for postgraduate work in the United States.

HARLAN, name of two American jurists who were grandfather and grandson.

John Marshall Harlan (1833–1911), born in Boyle County, Ky., and educated at Centre College and at Transylvania University (now Transylvania College), where he studied law. During the American Civil War, from 1861 to 1863, he served as a colonel in the Union Army. In 1863 he was elected attorney general of Kentucky, a position he held for four years. He took an active part in politics and was an unsuccessful Republican candidate for the governorship of Kentucky in 1871 and 1875. In 1877 he was appointed to the Supreme Court of the United States by President Rutherford Burchard Hayes (q.v.). Harlan held the office for thirty-four years, and became known as a justice of marked independence and a defender of civil rights, particularly the rights of Negroes and people in the unincorporated territories of the U.S.

John Marshall Harlan (1899–1971), born in Chicago, Ill., and educated at Princeton University, the University of Oxford and New York University Law School. He was admitted to the New York bar in 1924. The following year he was named an assistant to the U.S. attorney for the Southern District of New York. He was appointed special assistant attorney general of the State of New York in 1928. From 1930 to 1943 Harlan engaged in the private practice of law. During World War II he was chief of the Operations Analysis Section of the 8th Air Force. He resumed private practice after the war. As chief counsel of the New York State Crime Commission between 1951 and 1953, he exposed racketeering and corruption on the New York waterfront. Harlan was appointed a judge of the Second United States Circuit Court of Appeals in 1954.

From 1955 to 1971, upon the nomination of President Dwight David Eisenhower (q.v.), he served as an associate justice of the Supreme Court of the United States (q.v.). Harlan frequently dissented from the liberal decisions of the majority of the Court. He thus exercised a restraining influence on the recent general trend of the interpretation of the law by the Court. Harlan is noted for his technical proficiency in legal matters. He is well known for clarifying fine legal points and for explaining the reasoning that prompted his decisions.

HARLEIAN COLLECTION. See BRITISH MUSEUM; HARLEY, ROBERT, 1ST EARL OF OXFORD; LIBRARY.

HARLEM, former village, now a residential and business district of the borough of Manhattan, New York City. The name is generally applied to that part of the borough lying between the East and Harlem rivers and Eighth Avenue north of 106th Street. The section is known as the unofficial capital of the Negro population of the United States, although many Latin-Americans, principally from Puerto Rico, also reside in the area. The principal business thoroughfare of Harlem is 125th Street, running E. and w., and its widest street is Seventh Avenue, which cuts through the district from N. to S. Housing conditions in most areas of Harlem are notoriously bad, and the community contains extensive slum areas. In recent years a number of housing developments have been erected for low-income residents of Harlem.

The first settlement of Harlem occurred in 1636, on the site of the present-day Mount Morris Park. In 1658 the village was named New Haarlem by Peter Stuyvesant (q.v.), the Dutch colonial administrator, after Haarlem (q.v.), the Netherlands. New Haarlem retained its character as a Dutch village and a pastoral community for almost two centuries, while the other early Dutch settlement of New Amsterdam became, as New York City, the most important commercial center in the U.S. About 1830 Harlem began to develop as a suburb of New York City, and with the arrival of the elevated rapid transit lines in 1880 it reached its peak as a fashionable residential area. The district began its development as a Negro population center during World War I, when many thousands of Negroes came to New York City from the South and the West Indies in search of industrial employment. See also NEGROES IN THE UNITED STATES.

The old village of Harlem was described by the American author Washington Irving (q.v.) in his *Knickerbocker's History of New York.*

HARLEM RENAISSANCE. See NEGROES IN THE UNITED STATES: *History: The Harlem Renaissance;* NEGRO LITERATURE, AMERICAN.

HARLEQUIN, or ARLECCHINO or ARLEQUIN (Old Fr. *hellequin,* "demon" or "goblin"), conventional character in the Italian commedia dell'arte (q.v.) of the 16th to 18th centuries and of modern pantomime (q.v.). Harlequin first appeared in 12th-century French folk literature as an invisible, prankish goblin and, as Alichino, was one of the demons mentioned in the *Inferno* section of *The Divine Comedy* (q.v.) by the Italian poet Dante Alighieri (q.v.). In the commedia dell'arte, Harlequin was a clownish, black-masked servant who courted the forward girl Columbine and who was intended to ridicule the supposedly clownish citizens of Bergamo, Italy. From this original character two characters of modern pantomime have arisen: Pierrot, the blundering, pathetic figure of French pantomime; and Harlequin, the shaven-headed, motley dressed clown, represented in pantomime in many countries. Harlequin's original demonlike character is preserved in the wooden sword he always carries, which, like a magic wand, enables him to perform miraculous feats. The word harlequin has become practically synonymous, in modern usage, with clown or with a motley combination of colors.

HARLEQUIN SNAKE. See CORAL SNAKE.

HARLEY, Robert, 1st Earl of Oxford (1661–1724), English statesman, born in London. He entered Parliament as a Whig member in 1689 and remained in the House of Commons until his elevation to the nobility in 1711. In 1701 he became speaker of the house, and three years later, through the influence of John Churchill (q.v.), 1st Duke of Marlborough, was made a secretary of state for the northern part of the country. Although Harley was at this time ostensibly a supporter of the Whig ministry, he began to influence Queen Anne (q.v.) against two of her principal ministers, Sidney Godolphin (1645–1712) and Marlborough. In 1707 they became suspicious of his activities, and early the next year forced him out of the government.

As a critic of the ministry for the costliness of the war with France (*see* SPANISH SUCCESSION, WAR OF THE), Harley gained great popularity. He was successful in influencing public opinion by employing the English writers Daniel Defoe and, later, Jonathan Swift (qq.v.) as political propagandists. In 1710, when Marlborough and his party lost favor with the queen, Harley was appointed chancellor of the exchequer. He tried unsuccessfully to form a coalition ministry of both parties, but in 1711 his popularity was entirely restored after a refugee from France attempted to assassinate him. Harley was created earl of Oxford and appointed lord treasurer.

He reformed the finances of the country, and in 1713 forced the Peace of Utrecht (*see* UTRECHT, PEACE OF) through the House of Lords by the creation of twelve new peers. He soon lost his influence with the queen, and the next year was replaced in office by a former friend, the statesman Henry St. John, 1st Viscount Bolingbroke (q.v.). Harley retired from public life, but in 1715, after the death of Queen Anne, the new king of Great Britain, George I (q.v.), imprisoned him in the Tower of London (q.v.) on suspicion of plotting for the return of the Stuart dynasty. He was released in 1717, and the charges against him were dismissed. Harley, assisted by his son Edward Harley (1689–1741), spent his last years collecting books and manuscripts. The so-called Harleian Collection was purchased by the government in 1753 for £10,000 and given to the British Museum (q.v.), which was founded that year. The collection consisted of 7639 volumes and 14,236 original rolls, charters, deeds, and other legal documents.

HARLINGEN, city of Texas, in Cameron Co., about 25 miles N.W. of Brownsville. The city is the shipping point for the surrounding irrigated agricultural area in which citrus fruits, cotton, and vegetables are grown. Harlingen has rail and air service and is linked with the Intracoastal Waterway. Industries in the city include the processing of cotton and food, and plants producing chemicals, machinery, and metal products. Harlingen was founded about 1900. Pop. (1960) 41,207; (1970) 33,503.

HARMENSEN, Jacob. See ARMINIUS, JACOBUS.

HARMODIUS AND ARISTOGITON, two Athenian youths of the 6th century B.C., renowned for their great friendship. Hipparchus (about 555–514 B.C.), the younger brother of and coruler with the tyrant Hippias (q.v.), tried to supplant Aristogiton in this friendship. Failing to do so, he subjected the sister of Harmodius to public insult. Thereupon the friends formed a plot to murder both Hipparchus and Hippias on the day of the Panathenaea (q.v.), the most important festival of ancient Athens. They attacked and slew Hipparchus but failed to kill Hippias. Harmodius was at once killed by the guards of the tyrant, and Aristogiton was tortured and executed. Within four years, Hippias was expelled by the Athenians, who subsequently honored Harmodius and Aristogiton as martyrs to the cause of liberty. See also PISISTRATUS.

HARMONIA, in Greek mythology, daughter of Ares, god of war, and Aphrodite, goddess of love, and wife of Cadmus, founder of Thebes (qq.v.). At Harmonia's wedding, which was attended by the gods, Aphrodite gave her a beautiful necklace made by Hephaestus (q.v.), god of metalwork. Although the gift brought her good fortune, it brought only death and misery to her family. In their old age Harmonia and Cadmus were transformed into serpents.

HARMONICA, either of two musical instruments.

Glass Harmonica. This instrument was invented in the early 1760's by the American scientist and statesman Benjamin Franklin (q.v.), who based his work on the much simpler musical glasses invented by the Irish musician Richard Pockrich (1690?–1759) in 1743. In the Franklin version, a series of glass basins, graduated in size to produce distinct tones, is fixed on a horizontal spindle which is made to revolve by means of a treadle. The spindle is arranged in a trough of water so that the glasses are kept wet. The sound is produced by touching the fingers to the wet edges. This instrument was popular in the late 18th and the early 19th centuries. It formed the basis for several pieces by such notable composers as Wolfgang Amadeus Mozart and Ludwig van Beethoven (qq.v.).

Mouth Organ, invented independently in

A woodcut illustration of a mouth organ.
Bettmann Archive

Germany and England during the 1820's, the mouth organ is a small, oblong box fitted with a row of air channels, each leading to a small metal reed. Alternating tones of the scale are produced by blowing or suction. The instrument is universally popular as a children's toy, and in the United States it is often used in the popular-music styles known as country and western. The American harmonica virtuoso Larry Adler (1914–   ) and others have used the instrument in recitals and with symphony orchestras.

HARMONICS, series of subsidiary vibrations that accompany a primary or fundamental vibration, as in the vibrations of a stringed instrument or the oscillations of a tuned electrical circuit. The frequencies of harmonic vibrations are integral multiples of the frequency of the fundamental vibration: if the fundamental has a frequency of 100 cycles per sec., the second harmonic has a frequency of 200, the third of 300, and the fourth of 400. Harmonics in music are a class of overtones that bear simple mathematical relationships, such as 1:2, 1:3, or 1:4, to the fundamental.

A stretched string when plucked with a pick or set into vibration with a violin bow will vibrate in several ways. Its fundamental vibration will be that of the whole length of the string vibrating as a unit, but the string will also vibrate in halves, thirds, quarters, and so on, producing the various harmonics, most of which are

HARMONY

beyond the range of hearing of the human ear. Since the mid-18th century, string-instrument players have played harmonics that are produced when the strings are not allowed to vibrate as a whole, but are made to vibrate in thirds, quarters, and so on. This technique enables the player to produce a thin, reed-like sound, and to extend the upper range of his instrument beyond its natural limit.

Most musical tones and electrical oscillations consist not of one fundamental frequency alone, but of a combination of the fundamental with varying amounts of the harmonics related to the fundamental. The presence and amplitude of the various harmonics determine the quality of the sound and the wave form of the electrical oscillation. A number of devices such as the phonodeik and the cathode ray oscilloscope can be used to obtain a graphic picture of such complex vibrations or oscillations, and their components can be calculated mathematically by means of Fourier series, developed by the French mathematician Baron Jean Baptiste Joseph Fourier (q.v.). See ELECTRONICS; FREQUENCY; PITCH; SOUND; VIBRATION.

HARMONISTS, 19th-century Protestant sect (see PROTESTANTISM), founded in Germany by the German religious reformer George Rapp (q.v.). Members of the group moved to the United States in 1803 and established the town of Harmony, Pa., which they soon made into a prosperous agricultural and industrial center. The Harmonists, also called Rappists, Harmonites, and Economites, practiced a cult derived from quietism (q.v.). Its tenets included severe asceticism, celibacy (qq.v.), and community ownership of property (q.v.). The sect later migrated westward and established (1815) New Harmony (q.v.), Ind. In 1825 they returned to Pennsylvania to found their final home, Economy (now Ambridge). Eventually the community fell into financial decline, and in 1906 it dissolved. See also COMMUNISM: *American Experiments.*

HARMONIUM. See ORGAN: *Reed Organs.*

HARMONY, basic element in music, occurring when two or more pitches (see PITCH) are sounded successively, as in a melody (q.v.), or simultaneously, as in a chord (q.v.). The development of harmony has produced three distinct types of music, each of which flourished during a particular historical period.

Monophonic Music. The music of ancient Greece and of the early Middle Ages was basically monophonic; that is, musical compositions consisted of a single melody without accompaniment. Chant (q.v.) is an example of monophonic music that continues to be performed.

In such music some of the pitches used seem stable or final. They appear frequently at the beginning and the end of a phrase or a section of a chant. The most stable usually appear at the end of the entire composition (as well as elsewhere). The unstable pitches appear within phrases, suspended between the stable pitches. Often the pitches in a piece of monophonic music can be arranged in a continuous ascending row with the most stable pitch at the bottom. The row thus formed is called a mode (q.v.). During the Middle Ages the pitches of most music could be arranged into one of seven basic modes, two of which were retained in later times and are now called the major and minor scales. See SCALE.

By the 9th century some musicians had begun to add a second voice part to chant melodies. With this development a new factor was added to the element of harmony: the vertical relationship between two pitches sounded simultaneously. Again, some vertical combinations, called intervals (see INTERVAL), seemed stable or final and appeared at important structural points in a composition. Other intervals sounded unstable and were used only on weak beats between stable intervals. Because personal harmonic sensitivity has appeared to change over the centuries, however, the intervals considered stable by medieval musicians often sound incomplete to modern ears.

Polyphonic Music. During the 12th century compositions began to consist of two or more relatively independent melodic lines constructed so that they would sound well together, producing polyphonic music. At first most composers were concerned only with the vertical relationship between an upper voice part and the lowest one. From about 1400, however, composers began to take note of the entire vertical sound and to value successions of vertical sounds that flowed smoothly from one to another. The kind of smoothness that was desirable could only be achieved within the modes now called major and minor. The other modes fell into disuse during the 17th century. In focusing their energies on only two modes (which themselves are closely related), composers gradually became aware of many subtle tensions among the pitches of these modes and among combinations of pitches, or chords. Some pitches seemed unable to stand alone and needed to move, or resolve, toward others. Similarly, some chords could not stand alone but needed to resolve toward others. The entire set of such relationships came to be known as tonality (q.v.).

195

Homophonic Music. Music in the 18th century became increasingly homophonic, in that compositions consisted basically of a succession of chords accompanying a single melody. Composers gained full control of the many subtle harmonic relationships within the system called tonality. The first book on this subject, *Traité de l'Harmonie* (Fr., "Treatise on Harmony"), was written in 1722 by the French composer Jean Philippe Rameau (q.v.). Tonality reached its apex near the end of the 18th century in the music of the Viennese Classic School. See MUSIC: *The Preclassic and Classic Periods.*

By the early 19th century tonality was the harmonic language of all composers, who now turned their ingenuity to expanding and using it in an original and striking manner. They circumvented the normal tensions in tonality by inserting chords for their color, or effect, alone, and they prolonged tensions by delaying the normal resolutions of chords. By the end of the 19th century, such composers as the German Richard Wagner (q.v.) were writing passages with little or no feeling of tonality. Composers had also begun to look to the music of Eastern countries, to ancient European folk music, to medieval and Renaissance music, and elsewhere for novel ways of coloring tonality. They used enough tonal resolutions, however, to keep music within the 18th-century harmonic tradition.

Atonality. A sharp break with the 18th-century tradition occurred in the early 20th century when some composers began to experiment with atonal music. Here, no system, modal or tonal, determined the choice of pitches. The Viennese composer Arnold Schönberg (q.v.) was among the first to write atonal music; he was also the founder of a method of writing music, called the twelve-tone system (q.v.). Although much music written in the 20th century is still largely tonal, many composers have now abandoned all harmonic systems. They have begun to rely on their own sensitivity to sound, on what sounds appropriate in any given situation. See MUSIC: *The 20th Century.*

HARMSWORTH, Alfred Charles William, Viscount Northcliffe (1865–1922), British publisher, born in Chapelizod, near Dublin, Ireland, and largely self-educated. From 1880 to 1886 he was a free-lance reporter, and in 1887 he established a general publishing house in London. With his brother Harold Sidney Harmsworth (1868–1940), he founded in 1888 *Answers,* a popular weekly periodical. This periodical and others formed the basis of the Amalgamated Press, later the largest periodical-publishing enterprise in the world.

In 1894 Alfred Harmsworth purchased the nearly bankrupt London *Evening News,* and within one year he reorganized it into a profitable investment. Two years later he founded the immediately successful London *Daily Mail,* a halfpenny newspaper in which he introduced women's columns, serial stories, and other features. The London *Daily Mirror,* launched in 1903 as a penny paper for women, was at first a financial failure, but Harmsworth converted it into a halfpenny illustrated paper, and it quickly became a success. In 1903 he was made a baronet, and two years later he was elevated to the peerage as Baron Northcliffe. He acquired control of *The Times* (London) in 1908, reorganized and enlarged it, and in 1914, by lowering the price, he brought about a tremendous rise in circulation. He introduced a number of reforms into newspaper management, notably a five-day week and higher salaries for editorial employees, and a profit-sharing system for key members of his staff.

During World War I, Northcliffe editorially urged the vigorous prosecution of the war. His attacks on the government of Prime Minister Herbert Henry Asquith (q.v.) were partially responsible for the formation in 1916 of the coalition government of Prime Minister David Lloyd George (q.v.). In 1917, after serving as chairman of the British war mission to the United States, Northcliffe was created a viscount. The following year he became director of propaganda in enemy countries. After the war, his chief editorial efforts were devoted to the settlement of the Irish opposition to British rule; see IRELAND, REPUBLIC OF: *History: The Irish Revolution.*

HARNACK, Adolf von (1851–1930), German Protestant theologian, born in Dorpat (now Tartu, Estonian S.S.R.), and educated at the universities of Dorpat and Leipzig. He was appointed professor extraordinary of church history at the University of Leipzig in 1876, and later held professorships at the universities of Giessen, Marburg, and Berlin. He served as president of the Evangelical Congress from 1902 to 1912, and as director of the Prussian National Library from 1905 to 1921. Harnack exerted a profound influence on modern Protestant theology. He advocated free criticism of Church dogma and sought to dissociate Christianity from early Greek philosophical influences. His writings include *Lehrbuch der Dogmengeschichte* (4 vol., 1886–90; Eng. trans., *History of Dogma,* 7 vol., 1894–99), *Das Wesen des Christentums* (1900; Eng. trans., *What Is Christianity?,* 1901), and *Briefsammlung des Apostel Paul* ("Collected Epistles of the Apostle Paul", 1926).

HARNESS RACING

HARNESS RACING, form of horse racing in which each competing horse pulls a lightweight, two-wheeled cart, called a sulky or racing bike, which is manned by a skilled driver. Two kinds of races are usual, one for trotting horses and one for pacing horses. These two types of horses belong to the same breed, but they are trained to employ different gaits, or running styles. The fastest trotters and pacers can cover a mile in less than two minutes, although they cannot equal the speed of a galloping racehorse ridden by a jockey.

The world center of harness-racing activity is the United States, where some 30,000,000 persons annually witness the competitions. The governing body is the United States Trotting Association, which has jurisdiction over harness racing in the U.S. and in the Maritime Provinces of Canada. The sport is also popular in France and other European countries, and in Australia and New Zealand.

Types of Horses and Equipment. Pacers and trotters are standardbreds, bred mostly from thoroughbred horses of the type ridden by jockeys in flat racing, but standardbred horses also have a small admixture of blood inherited from sturdy farm or work horses. As a result, standardbred horses are stronger and more tractable than the high-strung thoroughbred saddle horses. The typical harness-racing horse is smaller than a flat-racing thoroughbred, standing about 14 to 16 hands (4 ft. 8 in. to 5 ft. 4 in.) high and weighing between 900 and 1150 lb. Most male standardbred horses are descended from Hambletonian, a 19th-century stallion.

Trotters and pacers differ from each other in the way they coordinate the movements of their legs; see HORSES: *Gaits.* The trotter is a diagonally gaited horse, that is, it moves its left front leg and right hind leg in unison in a smooth, high-stepping motion. The pacer is a laterally gaited horse, moving its right front leg and right hind leg in unison in a swaying, side-to-side motion. Pacers are somewhat swifter than trotters; the mile record for pacers is 1 min. 53⅗ sec., compared with 1 min. 54⅘ sec. for trotters. By contrast, the mile record for a galloping saddle horse ridden by a jockey is 1 min. 32⅕ sec. (these records are for oval tracks). Some harness-racing horses, notably the American horse Calumet Evelyn, have competed with equal proficiency as pacers and as trotters.

A harness-racing sulky consists of a lightweight wooden or duralumin (an aluminum-copper-magnesium alloy) frame mounted on ball-bearing bicycle wheels. Wooden sulkies weigh about 39 lb.; some all-duralumin sulkies weigh only 7 lb. Drivers may be of either sex, and may be amateur or professional. Most of the drivers participating in major races, however, are full-time professionals. Some tracks require that drivers weigh more than an established minimum, and others impose no weight requirements.

Harness-racing tracks are usually oval. In the U.S., about thirty-two of the forty-eight tracks conducting extended pari-mutuel betting meets are half-mile tracks; five are mile tracks; and the others are odd fractions of a mile in circumference. The non-commercial tracks in the U.S. are usually half-mile ovals. The tracks built exclusively for harness racing have a harder, faster surface than have the tracks used for flat racing. About 315 noncommercial tracks are used for harness racing in the U.S. At these tracks, State and county fair racing meets are held; few of these are betting meets. The seating capacity of harness-racing tracks varies widely. One popular track, Roosevelt Raceway in Westbury, N.Y., has a grandstand capacity of 20,000 persons, and as many as 54,000 have attended the track in a single day.

Pari-mutuel Betting. Under the system, now in use almost universally in the U.S., the betting odds are computed from the relation between the amount wagered on a horse and the total amount wagered on the race, less a percentage deducted by the State for taxes. As in flat racing, wagers are made on the horses to finish first, second, or third. Odds are computed automatically by a device known as a totalizator, and are electronically flashed on screens or on closed-circuit television sets.

Harness races are decided by single trials, known as dashes, which predominate at commercial tracks; or they are decided by a series of trials, called heats, generally run at fair meets and in some stake races, usually with large sums of prize money at stake. Originally, horses were required to finish first in three heats out of five to become winners; now, however, a two-out-of-three system is common.

For purposes of competition, horses are grouped into different classes according to age, previous performance, previous earnings, or sale value ("claiming price"). Harness races at all pari-mutuel tracks, and at most others as well, are conducted with the aid of a mobile starting gate. This utilizes long horizontal rails, mounted on a slowly moving automobile and extending across the width of the track. The horses draw up to the starting gate and, if they are aligned evenly along the arms of the gate as it crosses the starting line, the race is declared officially

A close winner in a heat of the Hambletonian, one of the most lucrative of all trotting races. UPI

under way. The gate is then quickly folded as the automobile speeds off the track.

The leading meets are conducted by associations belonging to the Grand Circuit, founded in 1873. Its membership varies frequently. Any track electing to sponsor a Grand Circuit harness meet becomes a member and is represented on the Board of Stewards, which decides meet dates and establishes general regulations.

History. Harness racing as an organized activity is an American innovation dating from the early 19th century. In the early races, the horses usually carried riders and did not draw vehicles. Sulkies came into use in the 1830's and 1840's. The first known speed record was an unofficial mark set in 1806 by the American trotter Yankee: 2 min. 59 sec. for one mile under saddle. Subsequently, improved breeding and training methods led to much faster performances, notably that of the trotter Lady Suffolk in 1845: 2 min. 29½ sec. for the mile.

During the first half of the 19th century, most of the fast American horses were descendants of Messenger, an English thoroughbred brought to the U.S. in 1788. Hambletonian, descended from Messenger and foaled in 1849, became the greatest stud horse in harness-racing history. The most important of all harness-racing stake events for trotters was named for Hambletonian. This event, first held at Syracuse, N.Y., in 1926, was run at Goshen, N.Y., 1930–42; at Yonkers, N.Y., in 1943; at Goshen again, 1944–56, and at Du Quoin, Ill., since 1957.

Hambletonian raced infrequently but sired 1335 foals between 1851 and 1874. Adios, active in the 1940's and 1950's, is considered the greatest sire of pacers. His progeny hold records in all age groups at one-mile tracks. Among others, Adios sired Bullet Hanover, Adios Harry, and Adios Butler, all outstanding pacers in the 1950's and 1960's.

Goldsmith Maid (1857–85) is considered the most remarkable trotting horse of that early era. She raced only once before the age of eight, but after that she set many records. She made her fastest time at the age of nineteen and was still racing a year later. Goldsmith Maid earned a total of $364,200, a world record at the time. The American trotter to win the most money, $885,095, was Su Mac Lad (1956–65). Cardigan Bay (1959–68), a pacer bred in New Zealand but racing principally in the U.S., won $1,000,671 and thus became the first harness horse to earn more than $1,000,000.

Among the leading drivers in the 1930's and 1940's was Ben White, who won the Hambletonian four times, and Sep Palin, who handled a great trotter, Greyhound. In the 1950's and

HAROLD (England)

1960's, the leading drivers were Stanley Dancer, Billy Haughton, Frank Ervin, John Simpson, Sr., Del Cameron, Harry Pownall, Joe O'Brien, Lucien Fontaine, and Del Insko. Many drivers are also trainers; some are owners and trainers; a few are women. Some drivers are amateurs who own their own horses and compete at fairs; they are called gentlemen drivers.

Following the introduction of night racing in 1940 at Roosevelt Raceway in Westbury, N.Y., harness racing enjoyed a nationwide increase in popularity. Crowds attending races grew very large, especially at night meets, and many new tracks were built.

The United States Trotting Association (U.S.T.A.), a corporation organized in 1938 by leading horsemen led by E. Roland Harriman (1895–   ), was established primarily to eliminate the confusion resulting from the fact that the various sectional organizations in control of harness racing had so many different rules. The chief functions of the association are to improve the breed of horses used in harness racing; to establish rules for standardbreds, their registration and the investigation of their pedigrees; to establish rules for the conduct of the sport and provide penalties for infraction of rules; and to sanction race meetings and issue licenses to track officials, owners, and drivers. The association has a board of directors consisting of three members from each of its eleven regional districts, and each district also has its own board of directors. The U.S.T.A. publishes an official year book which contains statistics on all phases of harness racing and breeding, including a roster of all racers who have been timed in 2 min. 5 sec. or less for the mile.

The term standardbred, used to describe all trotters and pacers, was made official in 1879 by the National Association of Trotting Horse Breeders.

In States that sanction pari-mutuel betting, the State harness-racing commissions cooperate with the U.S.T.A., but the laws of each State govern the betting and the general conduct of the sport.

In 1951 a museum, the Hall of Fame of the Trotter, was established at Goshen, N.Y. Records of famous events in harness racing are kept there and memorabilia are on display in an original stable setting that depicts the history of the sport.

Three of the major stake races in each division have been designated triple-crown events, comparable to the Kentucky Derby, the Preakness, and the Belmont Stakes in flat racing. By winning all three of these events, a horse becomes the holder of the triple crown. In trotting, the triple-crown events are the Hambletonian, the Kentucky Futurity, held at Lexington, Ky., and the Yonkers Futurity, held at Yonkers, N.Y. In pacing, the three events are the Little Brown Jug at Delaware, Ohio, the Messenger Stake at Roosevelt Raceway, and the Cane Futurity at Yonkers. In 1968, for the first time, the triple crown was won in each division. Nevele Pride, trained and driven by Stanley Dancer, won the Hambletonian, the Kentucky Futurity, and the Yonkers Futurity for the trotting triple crown. Rum Customer, driven by Billy Haughton, won the Little Brown Jug, the Messenger Stake, and the Cane Futurity for the pacing triple crown.

Nevele Pride was retired in 1969 and sold for breeding purposes to a syndicate for $3,000,000, a record price for harness racers. The four-year-old colt held ten world records. The most important of these was the mark of 1 min. $54\frac{4}{5}$ sec. for a race over a one-mile track. In setting this record in August, 1969, Nevele Pride bettered the record, set by Greyhound, that had stood for 31 years.

In 1969, according to the U.S. Trotting Association, a total of $1,819,965,781 was wagered at 66 member tracks in the U.S. Purses totaled $80,683,497. The total attendance for the year at all pari-mutuel tracks that reported official attendance figures was 24,695,063. The U.S. Trotting Association, with headquarters in Columbus, Ohio, had 31,561 members in 1969.

See also HORSE RACING, FLAT.

HAROLD I, known as HAROLD HAREFOOT (d. 1040), King of England (1035–40), illegitimate son of Canute II (q.v.), King of Denmark, Norway and England. Upon his father's death, Harold claimed the English crown, despite Canute's designation of Hardecanute (q.v.), Harold's legitimate half brother, as the successor. The English witenagemot (q.v.) settled the rival claims by giving Mercia and Northumbria to Harold, and Wessex to Hardecanute. Hardecanute remained in Denmark, however, and Wessex gave its allegiance to Harold, who became king of all England in 1037. His reign was oppressive and was marked by continual struggle with Hardecanute.

HAROLD II (1022?–66), King of England (Jan. 6, 1066–Oct. 14, 1066), last of the Saxon rulers. The second son of Godwin, Earl of Wessex (d. 1053), Harold was made Earl of East Anglia in 1045. In 1051 Godwin lost the favor of Edward the Confessor, Saxon King of England (*see under* EDWARD), and was exiled with his sons, but in 1052 the lands and titles of the family

HAROLD (Norway)

were restored in order to strengthen the security of the country. In 1053 Harold succeeded his father as earl of Wessex, becoming chief minister to the king and the most powerful man in the realm. Through his efforts, the warlike Welsh were subdued in 1063. A revolt against Harold's brother Tostig, Earl of Northumbria (d. 1066), caused Harold to banish Tostig, an action which restored the peace but made a bitter enemy.

Probably in 1064, Harold was shipwrecked off the coast of Normandy and captured by William, Duke of Normandy, later William I (q.v.), King of England. In order to secure his release, he was forced to swear that he would support William's claim to the crown of England. When King Edward was dying, he recommended that the throne be awarded to Harold, whom the witenagemot (q.v.) elected and crowned. William immediately asserted his claim, which was supported by the dispossessed Tostig and Harold III (see under HAROLD) of Norway. Tostig and his Norwegian ally invaded Yorkshire and, after several military successes, were routed by the English forces at Stamford Bridge on Sept. 25, 1066. Three days later, William landed in Sussex with his army, forcing Harold to rush southward to meet him. The armies engaged at Senlac Hill on Oct. 14; see HASTINGS, BATTLE OF. The defeat and death of Harold made William, thereafter called the Conqueror, ruler of England.

HAROLD or **HARALD,** name of three kings of Norway.

Harold I (Norw. *Haarfager*), called HAROLD THE FAIRHAIRED (850?–933), King (860–930), the first ruler to unite all Norway into a single dominion. He succeeded his father, Halfden the Swarthy (d. 863), as ruler of several small kingdoms in southern Norway. According to a Norse saga, Harold's beloved, Gyda, the daughter of a neighboring king, refused to wed him unless he should become king of all Norway. He therefore waged continual war against the other petty rulers until in 872 he defeated a general confederacy of Norwegian chieftains in a naval battle at Hafrsfjord and became lord of the entire kingdom. As a result of his conquest many of the lesser kings left Norway and founded Viking colonies on the heretofore uninhabited islands of the Orkneys, Hebrides, Shetlands, and Faeroes. These Vikings, or Northmen (q.v.), harried the Norwegian coast so effectively that Harold was forced to send an expedition against them. The success of the expedition caused a second large migration; many Vikings fled to Iceland, which became an independent Viking commonwealth (see ICELAND: *History*), and others founded Normandy (q.v.) on the coast of France. Harold established a strong kingdom, but his later reign was disturbed by strife between his sons. When he became old, the king abdicated in favor of his favorite son, Eric Bloodaxe (d. 936), who ruled from 930 to 934, when he was deposed by his half-brother Haakon I (see under HAAKON).

Harold II (Norw. *Graafeld*), called HAROLD GRAYFELL (930?–70?), King (961–70), the son of Eric Bloodaxe. Harold and his brothers ruled Norway until 970, when Earl Haakon (937?–95), a feudal vassal, killed Harold and seized control of the kingdom.

Harold III (Norw. *Haardraade*), called HAROLD HARD RULER (1015–66), King (1047–66), a descendant of Harold I. Harold participated in the battle of Stiklestad in 1030, fighting beside his half brother, Olaf II (q.v.), King of Norway, against Norwegian rebels aided by Denmark. When Olaf was killed, Harold was forced to flee. During the course of his travels, in the next fourteen years, Harold visited several Russian cities and, in 1033, entered the service of Zoe, Empress of the Byzantine Empire (r. 1028–50), becoming head of the Varangian guards. His exploits in the Mediteranean are described in many Norse sagas. Harold returned to Norway in 1046 and his nephew, Magnus I, called the Good, (see under MAGNUS), who was then king, gave him half the kingdom in return for half the treasure Harold had amassed in the East. Upon the death of Magnus, a year later, Harold became sole ruler. He warred against the Danes until 1064. In 1066 he joined with Tostig, Earl of Northumbria (d. 1066), in warfare against Tostig's brother, Harold II (q.v.), King of England, at the battle of Stamford Bridge in England. Harold III was killed on Sept. 25, 1066.

See NORWAY: *History*.

HAROUN-AL-RASCHID. See HARUN AL-RASHID.

HARP, stringed musical instrument, usually triangular in shape, played by plucking with the fingers of both hands. The strings are stretched between two sides of the frame, one of which contains a sounding board and the other, the wrest pins by which the strings are tuned.

The typical modern harp is a double-action instrument with forty-six strings (six and one-half octaves, with seven strings to the octave), the bass strings made of covered wire and the treble strings usually of gut. The strings are vertical, stretching from a straight body containing the sounding board upward to a curved neck. The third side of the triangle forms the pillar, or forepillar, which is vertical and rests on the

HARP

A blind harper (portrayed in a detail from an ancient Egyptian stone relief).
Bettmann Archive

pedal box. The harpist sits with the body between his legs and tilts the harp toward himself, enabling him to pluck the strings. Each of the seven pedals in the pedal box controls one string in each octave. When the pedal is depressed one notch, each string it controls is raised one half step (for example, from C flat to C natural); when it is depressed two notches, each is raised one whole step.

The harp can play any note or combination of notes on the diatonic scale; combinations are usually played in the form of an arpeggio (q.v.) rather than a chord. Unusual effects can be produced by plucking a number of strings at one time and by playing extended arpeggios over several octaves. Because of its rich, resonant tone, the harp came into use as an orchestral instrument during the 19th century.

The harp is among the oldest musical instruments; it was in use in Mesopotamia as early as 3000 B.C., and in Egypt by 1200 B.C. In ancient Greece and Rome harps were less popular than related instruments such as the lyre (q.v.). The harp of medieval Europe came from Ireland, where it is traditionally the national instrument. The distinctive features of the true Irish harp, called the clarsach, were a large soundbox carved from a single block of wood, a pillar that curved inward, and heavy brass strings. The medieval harp of continental Europe, ranging in size from seven to seventeen strings, had a thin frame and gut strings, producing a more delicate sound than the clarsach.

The modern harp was originated in 1720 with the introduction of foot pedals that stopped, or tuned, the strings by semitones. This device left the player's hand free to pluck the strings while playing accidentals (sharped or flatted notes), which previously had been produced by retuning the strings or by stopping them by hand during a performance. In 1810 the French manufacturer Sèbastien Érard (1752–1831) introduced a

Harpers Ferry, situated at the junction of the Potomac (foreground) and Shenandoah rivers.

double-action harp in which the foot pedal can raise the pitch of each string one or two semitones.

HARPER, William Rainey (1856–1906), American educator and Hebraist, born in New Concord, Ohio, and educated at Muskingum College, New Concord, and Yale University, from which he received the Ph.D. degree at the age of nineteen. He was appointed professor of Hebrew in the Baptist Union Theological Seminary, Chicago, in 1880, and in 1886 he became professor of Semitic languages at Yale. In 1891 he was appointed first president of the newly formed University of Chicago, and made great contributions to the growth and development of that university. He was the author of many books on the Bible and education, including *The Prophetic Element in the Old Testament* (1905) and *The Trend in Higher Education* (1905).

HARPERS FERRY, town of West Virginia, in Jefferson Co., at the confluence of the Potomac and Shenandoah rivers, 55 miles N.W. of Washington, D.C. Maryland, Virginia, and West Virginia are separated at this point by the two rivers. The town, in the Blue Ridge Mts., overlooks a picturesque gorge of the Potomac. Harpers Ferry was first settled about 1734 by the American pioneer Robert Harper (1713–82), who established a ferry across the Potomac at that point. In 1796 a United States arsenal and armory were established at Harpers Ferry, and many of the rifles used in the War of 1812 were manufactured there. The town became famous after the raid of John Brown (q.v.), who seized the arsenal on Oct. 16, 1859.

The town was also a military objective of considerable importance during the American Civil War, because of its strategic situation at the lower end of the Shenandoah Valley; see CIVIL WAR, THE AMERICAN. On April 18, 1861, the day after the secession of Virginia, the Federal garrison of forty-five men abandoned the post and set fire to the arsenal upon learning of the approach of a superior force of Virginians. It was held by Confederate troops until June 15, when it was again occupied by Federal troops. General Robert E. Lee (*see under* LEE), advancing northward in command of Confederate forces, found his lines of communication in the Shenandoah Valley obstructed by the garrison at Harpers Ferry, and sent General Thomas Jonathan Jackson (q.v.) to capture the Federal force. After a bombardment of two days, Harpers Ferry was surrendered on Sept. 15, 1862. Colonel Dixon S. Miles, in command of the garrison, was mortally wounded during the attack, and the total Federal loss in killed and wounded was 217, with 12,250 being taken prisoner. The Confederate loss in killed and wounded was 288. After being held alternately by the Confederate and Federal

An upright harpsichord manufactured and hand-decorated in Italy in the 17th century. Metropolitan Museum of Art

armies, Harpers Ferry was permanently occupied by Federal troops in 1863 following the Battle of Gettysburg (q.v.). Harpers Ferry National Historical Park, commemorating historical events in the area, covers 1530 acres in West Virginia and Maryland; it was established in 1963. Pop. (1960) 572; (1970) 423.

HARPER WOODS, city of Michigan, in Wayne Co., about 4 miles N. of Grosse Pointe. Harper Woods was incorporated in 1951. Pop. (1960) 19,995; (1970) 20,186.

HARPIES, in Greek mythology, foul creatures with the heads of old women, and bodies, wings, beaks, and claws of birds. They could fly with the speed of the wind, and their feathers, which could not be pierced, served them as armor. The Harpies frequently snatched up mortals and carried them off to the underworld, always leaving behind a sickening odor.

One of the many perils to be overcome by the Argonauts in their quest for the Golden Fleece (qq.v.) was an encounter with these dread, half-human creatures, who were slowly starving a pathetic old man by befouling his food before he could eat it. The Argonauts were on the point of killing the dreadful creatures when Iris (q.v.), goddess of the rainbow, intervened. At her request they merely drove the Harpies away. The Trojan prince Aeneas (q.v.) also came upon the Harpies during his adventures, but he and his crew put out to sea to escape them.

HARPSICHORD (It. *cembalo*), stringed keyboard musical instrument developed in Europe during the 14th or 15th century and widely used from the 16th to the early 19th century. Harpsichords have been made in a variety of sizes and shapes, ranging from a small box that rests on a table to a large instrument that resembles a modern piano (q.v.). The strings of the harpsichord are not struck by hammers as in a piano, but are plucked by mechanical plectra, producing a soft, incisive tone quality that adds clarity to the execution of melodic lines. The instrument is particularly effective in contrapuntal music, in which several melodic lines unfold simultaneously; *see* COUNTERPOINT.

HARQUEBUS

The harpsichord was superseded by the piano early in the 19th century, but came back into use during the 20th century in performances of music of the 16th, 17th, and 18th centuries and in many 20th-century compositions. Beginning in the late 1950's it was also adopted by many composers and performers of popular music.

HARQUEBUS or **ARQUEBUS**, also called HACKBUT or HAGBUT, primitive portable firearm used in the 15th and 16th centuries. It originally consisted of a heavy barrel and a straight stock, and was so heavy and cumbersome that it required a support for firing. Later improvements included provision of a longer, bent stock, which permitted firing from the shoulder. The original firing mechanism, a matchlock operated by a trigger, was later replaced by a wheel lock. Toward the end of the 16th century the harquebus was superseded by the musket. See also SMALL ARMS.

HARRIER. 1. The name applies to a small species of hunting dog closely resembling the English foxhound (q.v.), although proportionally having a larger head. About 20 in. high and weighing about 45 lb., the harrier is used for hunting hares and other small game. **2.** The name given to any of various species of slender, long-legged, blue-gray or brown hawk (q.v.), especially the genus *Circus*, having high-angled wings. These hawks nest in high grass and fly low over marshes in search of rodents, reptiles, and insects. The only North American species of harrier is the marsh hawk, *C. hudsonius,* found in swampy regions from northern Canada to northern United States in summer, and as far south as Central America in winter. The similar hen harrier, *C. cyaneus,* is found in northern Europe and Asia.

HARRIMAN, name of an American family prominent in the development and management of railroads, and in finance, government, and diplomacy.

Edward Henry Harriman (1848–1909), railroad magnate, born in Hempstead, N.Y. At the age of fourteen he became an office boy in a Wall Street firm and seven years later bought a seat on the New York Stock Exchange. In 1883 he became a director of the Illinois Central Railroad, and in 1897 formed a syndicate which acquired the bankrupt Union Pacific. He eliminated competition by gaining control of many other lines, including the Central and Southern Pacific railroads. His unsuccessful attempt to wrest control of the Chicago, Burlington & Quincy Railroad, and later the Northern Pacific from James Jerome Hill (q.v.) resulted in a panic on the New York Stock Exchange in 1901. In an effort to settle the dispute, Harriman joined forces with Hill and John Pierpont Morgan (see under MORGAN) to form a holding company, the Northern Securities Company; a 1904 decision by the Supreme Court of the United States held the company in violation of antitrust laws, and it was dissolved. An investigation of Harriman's holdings by the Interstate Commerce Commission in 1906–07 exposed nothing illegal. See RAILROADS: *United States Railroads.*

W(illiam) Averell Harriman (1891–   ), financier, government official, and diplomat, son of Edward, born in New York City, and educated at Yale University. After heading various railroad, shipping, and banking enterprises, he entered government service in 1934 and was thereafter closely associated with the New Deal (q.v.) and the Democratic Party. During World War II he was Lend-Lease (q.v.) administrator from 1941 to 1943, when he became ambassador of the United States to the Soviet Union. He served as ambassador to Great Britain (1946), U.S. secretary of commerce (1946–48), director (1951–53) of the Mutual Security Agency, governor of New York State (1955–58), assistant secretary of state for Far Eastern affairs (1961–63), and undersecretary of state for political affairs (1963–64). In 1968 he served in Paris as head of the U.S. delegation conducting preliminary peace talks with representatives of North Vietnam, with the aim of achieving a negotiated settlement of the Vietnamese conflict (see VIETNAM, WAR IN). He is the author of *America and Russia in a Changing World: A Half Century of Personal Observation* (1971).

HARRIS, Frank (1854–1931), British-American author, critic, and editor, born in Galway, Ireland. He left school in 1870 and went to the United States, of which he later became a citizen. He studied law at the University of Kansas, and in 1875 was admitted to the Kansas bar. He later returned to Europe and studied at universities on the continent before settling in London; there, at various times, he edited the London *Evening News* and the periodicals *Fortnightly Review* and *Saturday Review.* In 1913 he again journeyed to the U.S., and during World War I was editor of *Pearson's Magazine.* Shortly after the end of World War I he went to Nice, France, where he resided until his death. His fictional writings include *The Bomb* (1908), a novel based on the Haymarket Square Riot (q.v.) in Chicago, Ill.; and the short-story collections *Elder Conklin* (1894) and *Montes the Matador* (1900). In *Contemporary Portraits* (1927), he presented short, vivid sketches of the many political and literary figures whom he knew. His full-length biogra-

HARRISBURG

phies, including *Oscar Wilde, His Life and Confessions* (1916) and *The Life of George Bernard Shaw* (1931), and his autobiography *My Life and Loves* (3 vol. 1923–27), are marked by outspoken frankness.

HARRIS, Joel Chandler (1848–1908), American writer, famous as the creator of the "Uncle Remus" tales, born in Eatonton, Ga. He served on the staff of the Atlanta *Constitution* from 1876 through 1900. During that period he attained wide reputation as a writer of Negro dialect. His whimsical, imaginative stories, based on Negro legends and centering about the figure of Uncle Remus, an aged, philosophical, Negro storyteller, were among the first writings of American Negro folk literature; see NEGRO FOLKLORE, AMERICAN. The collections containing these stories include *Uncle Remus, His Songs and Sayings* (1880), *Nights with Uncle Remus* (1883), *Uncle Remus and His Friends* (1892), and *Uncle Remus and Brer Rabbit* (1906).

Harris also wrote a number of works depicting Southern life, among them the short-story collections *Mingo, and Other Sketches in Black and White* (1884) and *Tales of the Home Folks in Peace and War* (1898), and the novels *Sister Jane: Her Friends and Acquaintances* (1896) and *Gabriel Tolliver: A Story of Reconstruction* (1902).

HARRIS, Roy (1898–   ), American composer and educator, born in Lincoln County, Okla. After studying composition with Arthur Bliss (q.v.) and others, he went to Paris in 1926 to study with Nadia Boulanger (q.v.). He returned in 1929 to begin an extended teaching career, including posts at Westminster Choir School in Princeton, N.J. (1933–38), at Cornell University (1941–42), at Colorado College, Colorado Springs (1942–48), and at Utah State University (beginning in 1948). Harris has written many instrumental works, including the symphonic overture *When Johnny Comes Marching Home* (1935) and *Folk-Song Symphony* (1940), the orchestral work *Kentucky Spring* (1949), Symphony No. 7 (1951), the cantata *Francis of Assisi* (1961), string quartets, string and piano quintets, and choral works.

HARRIS, Townsend (1804–78), American merchant and diplomat, born in Sandy Hill (now Hudson Falls), N.Y. Although his own formal education had ended when he was thirteen, he was elected to the New York City Board of Education in 1846 and served as president for two years. His campaign for the establishment of a free city college led to the founding in 1847 of the Free Academy, now called City College, part of The City University of New York.

Harris was appointed the first United States consul general to Japan in 1855 and the first U.S. minister to Japan in 1859. He won the confidence of the Japanese and in 1858 arranged a commercial treaty that secured for Americans the rights of trade, residence, missionary operations, and teaching in Japan.

HARRISBURG, city and capital of Pennsylvania, and county seat of Dauphin Co., on the E. bank of the Susquehanna R., 105 miles w. of

Aerial view of Harrisburg.　　　　　　　　　　Ewing Galloway

HARRISON

Philadelphia. Four bridges span the river, which is a mile wide at Harrisburg but is not navigable. The city is a political, commercial, and industrial center, with extensive rail and air service. It is surrounded by a mining and agricultural area producing coal, iron ore, livestock, poultry, general farm crops, and dairy products. Several thousand persons are employed in the Harrisburg railroad shops. Among other industrial establishments in the city are printing and publishing firms, meat-packing plants, iron and steel plants, and factories producing processed foods, lumber products, rails, machinery, textiles, knit and leather goods, clothing, chemicals, candy, and tobacco products.

Capitol Park, in the heart of the city, is the site of the principal State buildings, including the Pennsylvania State Capitol (1906), the dome of which, rising to 272 ft., was designed after that of Saint Peter's Basilica in Rome. The marble staircase in the capitol was modeled after that of the Paris Opera, and the building is noted also for its bronze doors, mural decorations, and stained-glass windows. The Pennsylvania State Museum, also in Capitol Park, exhibits the original Penn Charter, granted to the founder of the colony William Penn (q.v.) in 1681, as well as manuscripts of Pennsylvanian composers and authors. The Pennsylvania Farm Show Building in the northern section of the city covers 13 acres under one roof. Harrisburg has a total park area of 1100 acres, including River Park, which extends 5 mi. along the river. The municipal bathing beach and baseball park occupy an island, reached by two bridges, in the middle of the Susquehanna.

Harrisburg was first settled about 1715 by John Harris (d. 1748), who established a trading post on the site and operated a ferry across the river. The settlement was known as Harris's Ferry until 1785, when John Harris, Jr. (1726–91), laid out a town and named it Harrisburg. It became the county seat of the newly created Dauphin Co. in the same year. In 1791 Harrisburg was incorporated as a borough, and in 1812 it was made the capital of the State. The city of Harrisburg was chartered in 1860. Pop. (1960) 79,697; (1970) 68,061.

HARRISON, town of New Jersey, in Hudson Co., on the Passaic R., about 2 miles N.E. of central Newark. Manufactures include steel products, chemicals, and metal products. Pop. (1960) 11,743; (1970) 11,811.

HARRISON, Benjamin (1726?–91), American patriot and statesman, born in Charles City County, Va. He was a member of the Virginia legislature from 1749 to 1775, from 1777 to 1781, and from 1784 to 1791. As representative from Virginia to the Continental Congress (q.v.) from 1774 to 1777, he helped lay the groundwork for the departments of State, War, and the Navy. He was one of the signers of the Declaration of Independence (q.v.) and presided over the debates preceding its adoption. From 1782 to 1784 he served as governor of Virginia. In 1788 he was a member of the Virginia convention which ratified the Federal Constitution. He was the father of William Henry Harrison, and the great-grandfather of Benjamin Harrison (qq.v.), Presidents of the United States.

HARRISON, Benjamin (1833–1901), twenty-third President of the United States and grandson of William Henry Harrison (q.v.), the ninth President, born on his grandfather's estate in North Bend, near Cincinnati, Ohio. He graduated from Miami University in Oxford, Ohio, in 1852 and made his home in Indianapolis, Ind., where he became a prominent lawyer and leader of the Republican Party (q.v.). Harrison's record as a Union army officer and his moderate views as a United States Senator from 1881 to 1887, won him the Presidential nomination in 1888. Following a quiet campaign, the principal issue of which was support for protective tariffs (see TARIFFS, UNITED STATES), Harrison received 5,447,129 popular votes, 90,628 fewer than his Democratic opponent, President Grover Cleveland (q.v.), but his strength in the key States carried him to victory; see ELECTORAL COLLEGE.

As President, Harrison played a passive role in matters of patronage and reform of the civil service (q.v.), and because of this he failed to influence the warring factions of his party. During his administration, however, Congress passed the Sherman Antitrust Act (q.v.), which reflected a growing public anxiety over huge combinations of business interests. It also passed the so-called McKinley Tariff in 1890, which raised duties on manufactured goods to the highest levels yet reached. The Sherman Silver Purchase Act, which required the government to buy most of the silver mined in the country, and which was generally considered a reward to silver-producing Western Republicans who supported the tariffs, was also enacted during his administration; see MONEY: *The Monetary System of the United States*. The public resentment against the tariff, which caused prices to rise sharply, and displeasure with the Republican monetary policy, was influential in the election of 1892. Harrison lost both the popular and the electoral vote to Grover Cleveland and returned to his law practice in Indiana.

N.H.C.

HARRISON, William Henry (1773–1841), ninth President of the United States, son of the statesman Benjamin Harrison and grandfather of the twenty-third President, Benjamin Harrison (qq.v.), born in Berkeley, Va. After studying medicine briefly in Philadelphia, he joined the United States Army in 1791. He served in the Northwest Territory (q.v.) as an aide to General Anthony Wayne (q.v.) in campaigns against the Indians. In 1798 Harrison was appointed secretary of the Northwest Territory, and in the following year he represented the territory as its first delegate to Congress. As the first governor of Indiana Territory, Harrison defeated an Indian attack at a battle on the Tippecanoe R. on Nov. 7, 1811; see TIPPECANOE, BATTLE OF. Subsequently appointed commander of the Army of the Northwest, he embarked on a campaign to oust the British and Indians from Detroit. The British burned Detroit and attempted to withdraw, but on Oct. 5, 1813, Harrison overtook them on the banks of the Thames R. in Ontario. He captured the entire British force, and his victory ended the Indian confederacy and gave the Americans firm control of the northwestern frontier.

After the War of 1812 (q.v.) Harrison served as a Whig in the United States House of Representatives (1816–19), in the Ohio State Senate (1819–21), and in the United States Senate (1825–28). In 1828 President John Quincy Adams (q.v.) appointed him minister to Columbia, but he was recalled by President Andrew Jackson (q.v.) in the following year. Nominated for President by the Anti-Masonic Party (q.v.), he ran unsuccessfully against the Democratic candidate, Martin Van Buren (q.v.) in 1836. His impressive showing, however, led to his renomination for the Presidency by the Whig Party (q.v.) in 1840, with John Tyler (q.v.) of Virginia as the Vice-Presidential candidate. The Whigs, still a coalition of groups rather than a cohesive political party, took no clear stand on important issues but waged a bizarre campaign in which they ridiculed Van Buren and glorified Harrison as a simple log-cabin frontiersman. His victories over the Indians were recalled in the slogan "Tippecanoe and Tyler, too". In the election Harrison received 1,274,624 votes and Van Buren 1,127,781 votes. Harrison appointed Daniel Webster (q.v.) as secretary of state and planned to follow a program suggested by Senator Henry Clay (q.v.) of Kentucky. One month after his inauguration, however, the sixty-eight-year-old President, exhausted by the campaign and by the hordes of office-seekers who sought his favor, contracted a severe cold and died of pneumonia. He was the first President to die in office. N.W.P.

HARRISONBURG, independent city of Virginia, in Rockingham Co., about 35 miles N.E. of Charlottesville, in the Shenandoah Valley. The city is a processing center for the area, and has varied manufacturing. It is the site of the Madison College, founded in 1908, and of the Eastern Mennonite College, founded in 1917. The George Washington National Forest Headquarters is here. Nearby are limestone caverns. Pop. (1960) 11,916; (1970) 14,605.

HARROGATE, Great Britain, municipal borough in West Riding, Yorkshire, England, 18 miles N. of Leeds. Harrogate is made up of two townships, Low Harrogate and High Harrogate, which are connected by a series of residences. High Harrogate is situated in the uplands, where the climate is bracing; Low Harrogate lies in a protected position and has a mild winter climate. More than eighty mineral springs, some of which were discovered in the 16th century, attract tourists to Harrogate, which for nearly

HARROW SCHOOL

three centuries has been the chief inland vacation and health resort of N. England. The borough was incorporated in 1884. Pop. (1969 est.) 62,680.

HARROW SCHOOL, institution of secondary and higher education of England, on a 300-acre site in Harrow on the Hill, now a part of Greater London. The school was founded in 1571 by John Lyon (1514?–92), a prosperous yeoman, under a charter granted by Elizabeth I (q.v.), Queen of England. In 1590 Lyon drew up the statutes of the institution, providing for the education of thirty poor boys of Harrow parish, and left two thirds of his fortune to the school when he died. In 1611, pupils were admitted to the first completed building, which is still in use today. Some fifty years later, when the school was in financial difficulties, a clause in the statutes permitting the enrollment of "foreign" (or nonparish), paying scholars was invoked; Harrow's rise to its present eminent academic position dates from this enlargement of the institution. The governing body of the school, under the Public Schools Act of 1868, consists of fifteen members, selected by the universities of Cambridge, London, and Oxford, the Royal Society of London for Improving Natural Knowledge (qq.v.), the lord chancellor of Great Britain, and the assistant masters of Harrow. The course of instruction was originally exclusively classical, but studies are currently offered in classics, history, geography, economics, modern languages (including Spanish and Russian), mathematics, science, and agriculture. Among the distinguished graduates of the school are the English statesmen Sir Robert Peel and Lord Palmerston (qq.v.), and the British statesman Sir Winston Leonard Spencer Churchill (*see under* CHURCHILL), as well as the British novelist Anthony Trollope (*see under* TROLLOPE), the Irish dramatist Richard Brinsley Sheridan, and the British poet George Gordon Byron (qq.v.). Harrow School has about 680 pupils.

HART. *See* DEER.

HART, Albert Bushnell (1854–1943), American historian and educator, born in Clarksville, Pa., and educated at Harvard University and the University of Freiburg. He taught history and government at Harvard from 1883 until 1926, when he retired. From 1904 to 1908 Hart edited the historical series *The American Nation* (28 vol., 1903–18), to which he contributed two volumes, *Slavery and Abolition* (1906), and *National Ideals Historically Traced* (1907). His other writings include *The Monroe Doctrine: an Interpretation* (1917), and *George Washington* (1927).

HART, Moss (1904–61), American playwright and stage director, born in New York City. His first successful play, *Once in a Lifetime*, was produced in 1930 after he had rewritten it in collaboration with the American playwright George S. Kaufman (q.v.). Through 1940 Kaufman and Hart together produced a series of comedies notable for witty dialogue and well-drawn, somewhat exaggerated characters. Among these works are *You Can't Take It with You* (1936; Pulitzer Prize, 1937), which celebrates a family of amiable eccentrics, and *The Man Who Came to Dinner* (1939), a thinly veiled caricature of the American writer and raconteur Alexander Woollcott (q.v.). Hart was the sole author of the libretto for the musical comedy *Lady in the Dark* (1941), which he also directed, and his serious drama *Christopher Blake* (1946) won critical acclaim. He wrote the screenplay for the film *Gentleman's Agreement* (1947), and served as director of the Broadway musical comedy *Camelot* (1960). Hart's account of his early years in the theater, *Act One*, appeared in 1959.

HARTE, Francis Brett, known as BRET HARTE (1836–1902), American writer, born in Albany, N.Y. In 1854 he went to California, where he worked as a schoolteacher, an express messenger, and a printer. In 1860 he became a typesetter for the *Golden Era*, a San Francisco newspaper, to which he contributed a highly successful series of parodies satirizing the works of well-known contemporary writers.

In 1868 he helped establish and became editor of a literary publication, the *Overland Monthly*. Many of Harte's best-known stories, including "The Luck of Roaring Camp" and "The Outcasts of Poker Flat", were published in the *Monthly,* as was his comic poem "Plain Language from Truthful James".

These works, which have come to be regarded as classics of American regional literature, are notable for descriptions of the lusty, humorous, and sometimes violent life typical of the mining camps and towns of California in the second half of the 19th century. A collection of his stories, published in 1870 under the title *The Luck of Roaring Camp and Other Sketches,* was greeted with acclaim throughout the United States.

Harte subsequently went to New York City, where he was commissioned to write for the *Atlantic Monthly,* but the quality of his contributions was far below the standard of his earlier writings. The ensuing decline in his popularity, coupled with his extravagant mode of living, soon left him almost penniless. Friends obtained

Red hartebeest, Alcelaphus caama
Dick Wolff – South African Tourist Corp.

an appointment for him as U.S. consul at Krefeld, Germany, in 1878; two years later he was transferred to Glasgow, Scotland, where he remained until 1885. He continued to write while serving in these positions, and his later stories "An Ingénue of the Sierras" and "A Protégée of Jack Hamlin's", both written in 1893, are considered by some critics to be superior to his early works.

HARTEBEEST, common name for any of several antelope in the genus *Alcelaphus*, characterized by a long, narrow head, shoulders higher than the hindquarters, and a cowlike tail. The ringed horns, curved like the arm of a lyre, which are present in both sexes, do not grow directly out of the sides of the head but arise from a short central horn. Most species are about 4 ft. high at the shoulder, and are brownish gray in color, with black markings on the face, and a white or yellow patch on the rump. Hartebeests are keen-sighted, fleet-footed beasts which can outdistance greyhounds and the fastest horses. They feed on grass and inhabit open plains or dry desert regions, being capable of going without water for several weeks at a time. Their flesh is good to eat. Two species are known, found only in Africa.

HARTFORD, city and capital of Connecticut, and county seat of Hartford Co., at the head of navigation on the Connecticut R., 38 miles N. of Long Island Sound, about 35 miles N.E. of New Haven, and 100 miles N.E. of New York City, and 120 miles S.W. of Boston, Mass. Hartford is served by rail and by major airlines.

The principal public building in Hartford is the State Capitol, on Capitol Hill overlooking Bushnell Park. Built of Connecticut marble, it was completed in 1878. Facing the Capitol on the S. are the State Office Building and the State Library and Supreme Court Building. Memorial Hall, in the latter building, houses a portrait of President George Washington by the American painter Gilbert Stuart (qq.v.) and the Connecticut royal charter of 1662. The Old State House (1796), a National Historic Landmark, which was designed by the American architect Charles Bulfinch (*see under* BULFINCH), is now a museum containing historical collections. A notable ecclesiastical building is the First Church of Christ (Congregational), organized in 1632. Opposite the church is the Travelers Insurance Company building, with a tower rising to 527 ft.

Among the cultural institutions of Hartford are the Wadsworth Atheneum, housing the public library and the quarters of the Connecticut Historical Society; the Colt Memorial Museum, with a collection of early firearms; and the Avery and Morgan memorials, museums of art. The numerous educational institutions include the colleges of law, insurance, and social

The Phoenix Mutual Life Insurance Company's impressive building on Constitution Plaza in Hartford. Ewing Galloway

work of the University of Connecticut (see CONNECTICUT, UNIVERSITY OF), the Hartford Seminary Foundation (Protestant), the Hartford (junior) College for Women, the Hartford State Technical Institute, the Hartford College of Law, and the Hartford College of Insurance. The University of Hartford is in West Hartford.

Commerce and Industry. Hartford is an important commercial and manufacturing center, and is especially noted as an insurance center. In addition to insurance the principal industries are the manufacture of fabricated metals, aircraft, and machinery, and the processing of food. Hartford has an extensive wholesale and retail trade, with a trading area embracing about half of Connecticut. It is also an important market for agricultural products, particularly tobacco.

About 2 miles E. of Hartford, also on the Connecticut R., is the town of East Hartford. The chief products of the town are airplane engines and processed tobacco. East Hartford was founded in 1633 and incorporated in 1783. Pop. (1970) 57,583.

On the Connecticut R., 3 miles S. of Hartford, is the town of Wethersfield. Settled in 1634, it was the scene of an Indian massacre three years later. The town has many 18th-century buildings. Wethersfield was incorporated in 1637. Pop. (1970) 26,662.

Adjoining Hartford on the W. is the town of West Hartford, a residential suburb and a shipping point for tobacco, dairy products, and garden truck. In the town are the American School for the Deaf (founded in 1817) and Saint Joseph College (1925) for women. Settled in 1679, West Hartford was part of Hartford until 1854, when it was incorporated separately. Pop. (1970) 68,031.

History. In 1633, within the limits of the present city, the Dutch built a trading post called the House of Hope; the site is still known as Dutch Point. The first English settlers came to the area from New Towne (now Cambridge), Mass., in 1635–36. Peter Stuyvesant (q.v.), governor of New Netherland, and commissioners from the English settlements signed a treaty at Hartford on Sept. 19, 1650, by which boundary disputes were adjusted. In 1662 a royal charter was granted the Connecticut colony, and Hartford became the capital. In 1687 Sir Edmund Andros (q.v.), governor of the New England colonies, went to Hartford to demand the surrender of the royal charter, but was thwarted in his purpose; see CHARTER OAK. From 1701 to 1875 Hartford and New Haven were joint capitals of Connecticut. Hartford was incorporated as a city in

1784. The development of Hartford was marked by the building in the city of the first woolen mill in New England in 1788 and by the writing of the first insurance policies in 1794. In 1814–15 the city was the site of the Hartford Convention.

Hartford was at one time an important literary and publishing center. One of the oldest newspapers in the United States, the Hartford *Courant,* founded in 1764, is still published. The lexicographer Noah Webster (q.v.), who was born in 1758 in what is now West Hartford, published his *Grammatical Institute of the English Language* (3 vol., 1783–85) in Hartford. Between the late 1780's and the early 1800's, the city was the home of many of the Hartford Wits, also known as the Connecticut Wits, a group of Federalist writers who published a series of political parodies and satires. Hartford was also the residence of the writers Harriet Beecher Stowe and Samuel Langhorne Clemens (Mark Twain) and of the poet Wallace Stevens (qq.v.).

Population. The population of Hartford in 1960 was 162,178; in 1970 it was 158,017.

HARTFORD CONVENTION, in United States history, the political assembly representing the Federalist Party (q.v.) of the New England States, which met at Hartford, Conn., on Dec. 14, 1814, and adjourned on Jan. 5, 1815. The delegates to the convention numbered twenty-six, of whom twelve came from Massachusetts, seven from Connecticut, four from Rhode Island (all appointed by the legislatures of their respective States), two from counties in New Hampshire, and one from Windham County, Vt. The convention was called in consequence of the opposition of the New England Federalists to the War of 1812 (q.v.) between the U.S. and Great Britain. The New Englanders were unsympathetic to the war because of its crippling effect upon their fishing industry and foreign commerce. The object of the convention was to devise means of security and defense against foreign nations, and also to safeguard the privileges of the individual States against alleged encroachments of the Federal government. Because the meetings of the convention took place behind closed doors, and because the members were pledged to absolute secrecy, a rumor spread to the effect that the New England States were contemplating secession from the Union. Subsequent investigation failed to disclose any basis for the report, which nevertheless irreparably damaged the reputation of the Federalist Party, already in disfavor because of its pro-British, aristocratic tendencies.

The recommendations of the convention, stated in the form of proposed amendments to the Federal Constitution, (see CONSTITUTION OF THE UNITED STATES) were that taxation and representation in each State should be proportionate to the number of its free inhabitants; that no new State should be admitted to the Union except upon a two-thirds vote in both houses of Congress; that Congress (see CONGRESS OF THE UNITED STATES) should not have the power to impose more than a sixty-day embargo on ships owned by citizens of the U.S.; that Congress should not prohibit foreign commerce or declare offensive war except by a two-thirds vote; that no person thereafter naturalized should be entitled to sit in Congress or to hold any civil office in the Federal government; that the Presidency should not exceed one term; and that the President should never be chosen twice successively from the same State. The delegates further resolved that if their recommendations should not be heeded, and if the defense of their respective States should still be neglected, a further convention should be held, vested "with such powers and instructions as the exigency of a crisis so momentous may require". The legislatures of Massachusetts and Connecticut approved the proposed Constitutional amendments and dispatched commissioners to Washington, D.C., to urge their adoption. The war, however, was practically over before the convention finished its business, and the American victory at New Orleans (see NEW ORLEANS, BATTLE OF) on Jan. 8, 1815, increased the popularity of the government and hastened the downfall of the Federalist Party, which did not survive the Presidential election of 1816. See STATES' RIGHTS.

HARTLEY, David (1705–57), British philosopher, born in Armley (now part of Leeds), Yorkshire, England, and educated at Jesus College, University of Cambridge. He studied at first for the church, but dissented on some points in the official creed of the Church of England, and took up the study of medicine. He practiced as a physician successively in Newark, Bury Saint Edmunds, London, and Bath, where he died.

Hartley's major work, *Observations on Man, His Frame, His Duty, and His Expectations* (2 vol., 1749), was the first attempt to explain all the phenomena of the mind by a theory of association; see ASSOCIATION OF IDEAS. Although thinkers before him, among them the British philosophers John Locke and David Hume (qq.v.), had used the principle of association to explain many of the more developed mental contents and processes, Hartley carried their ideas to a new point of comprehensiveness. Like them he considered the mind to be a *ta-*

bula rasa—that is, a blank—prior to the experience of sensation, but he extended the laws of mental growth through contiguous associations to include not only such phenomena as memory (which others had done), but also imagination, reason, and the emotions. He argued that developed or adult emotions were the products of elementary feelings uniting, passing into new connections, and giving rise to complex emotions, under the general law of contiguity.

Another of Hartley's major theories dealt with the physical nature of sensation, and was drawn from the *Opticks* (1704) by the English scientist Sir Isaac Newton (q.v.). Hartley argued that any sensation of the external world sets up a vibratory motion in the nerve affected, producing corresponding vibrations in the cerebral substance; he assumed that impulses directed from the brain to the muscles proceed in the same manner.

HARTLEY, Marsden (1877–1943), American painter, born in Lewiston, Maine. He studied at the Cleveland School of Art and later the Chase School and the National Academy of Design in New York City. In 1901 he returned to Maine, where he painted a series of impressionistic landscapes; *see* IMPRESSIONISM. In 1912 he went to Europe for the first time, becoming associated for a time with the *blaue reiter* ("blue rider") group of German expressionist painters; *see* EXPRESSIONISM. From this movement and from the cubism (q.v.) of the French painter Paul Cézanne (q.v.), Hartley evolved the highly personal style of his later works. For many years he wandered about Europe and the United States, finally settling in Maine in the 1930's. There he found subjects, mountains and rocks and people, appropriate to his harshly colored, boldly outlined landscapes and genre scenes. A fine example of his work, "Lobster Fishermen" (1941), is in the Metropolitan Museum of Art in New York City.

HARTLINE, Haldan Keffer (1903–), American biophysicist, born in Bloomsburg, Pa., and educated at Lafayette College and Johns Hopkins University and the universities of Leipzig and Munich in Germany. Between 1940 and 1953 he taught biophysics at Cornell University, the University of Pennsylvania, and Johns Hopkins University. In 1953 he joined the faculty of the Rockefeller Institute for Medical Research (now Rockefeller University) in New York City. Hartline shared the 1967 Nobel Prize in medicine and physiology with the Swedish neurophysiologist Ragnar Granit and the American biochemist George Ward (qq.v.) for their individual research into the physiology of vision. Hartline demonstrated through his studies the manner in which the eye differentiates between form and movement.

HARTMANN VON AUE (fl. 1190–1210), German poet. All that is known about his life comes from his works, where it appears that he was a member of the lesser Swabian nobility, that he served at the court of a Swabian nobleman named "von Aue", and that he participated in a crusade organized in 1197 by Henry VI (q.v.), Holy Roman Emperor and King of Germany. One of the great German epic poets, Hartmann wrote four long influential works. The poems *Erec* and *Iwein* are based on narratives by the 12th-century French poet Chrétien de Troyes (q.v.), and are the earliest German works to adapt the legends of the Arthurian cycle (q.v.). His *Gregorius* is about the conflict between the values of chivalry (q.v.) and those of Christianity. *Der Arme Heinrich* ("Poor Heinrich"), considered his greatest poem, tells the story of a famous knight whose pride is punished with leprosy, and who is healed by the devotion of a young girl.

HARTSHORN. *See* AMMONIA.

HART'S-TONGUE FERN, common name of a herb, *Phyllites scolopendrium*, belonging to the Fern family Polypodiaceae. The hart's-tongue, unlike typical ferns, has long, dark-green, strap-shaped undivided fronds, dotted with parallel rows of sporangium clusters. It is common in temperate regions of Eurasia, and is found in Mexico and a few isolated localities in the eastern United States, in ravines and under limestone cliffs.

HARUN AL-RASHID (766–809), fifth caliph (q.v.) of the Abbassid dynasty of Baghdad, ruler from 786 to 809. His name is translated as "Aaron the Upright". He was the son of the third Abbassid caliph, Al-Mahdi (r. 775–85), and succeeded to the throne on the death of his brother Al-Hadi (r. 785–86). The period of his reign marked a notable development of culture. Until 803 administrative power was entrusted to Yahya ibn-Khalid (d. about 803), the grand vizier, or councilor of state, and head of the illustrious family of the Barmecides. Baghdad, the capital of Harun's realm, became the most flourishing city of the period. Tribute was paid to the caliph by many rulers, and splendid edifices were erected in his honor at enormous cost. He is said to have exchanged gifts with Charlemagne (q.v.), Holy Roman Emperor. Harun was a generous patron of learning, poetry, and music, and his court was visited by the most eminent Muslims of the age. He was celebrated in countless songs and stories, and is perhaps best known to the West as the caliph whose court is described in the *Arabian Nights* (q.v.).

From 791 to 809 Harun's empire was at war with the Byzantine Empire, and in 807 Harun's forces occupied the Byzantine province of Cyprus. Toward the end of his reign Harun was influenced to depose the Barmecides, and in 803 he imprisoned the grand vizier. Harun died while on his way to put down an insurrection in the eastern part of his empire.

HARVARD, John (1607–38), English clergyman, born in London, and educated at the University of Cambridge. In 1637 he emigrated to New England and settled in Charlestown (now part of Boston), Mass., where, although never formally ordained, he was active as a minister for a short time. Upon his death he left the college at New Towne (later Cambridge), Mass., half his fortune and his library of 400 books. The Massachusetts General Court named the institution Harvard College in his honor in 1639. *See* HARVARD UNIVERSITY.

HARVARD COLLEGE OBSERVATORY, astronomical observatory originally founded in Cambridge, Mass., in 1839 and reestablished from 1843 to 1847 by public subscription. It is a part of the department of astronomy of Harvard University (q.v.). The principal optical telescopes are a 61-in. reflector and a 16-in. reflector at the Agassiz Station in Harvard, Mass. At the same location are an 84-ft. radio telescope and a 24-ft. radio telescope. The observatory also maintains a radio astronomy station in Fort Davis, Texas.

The observatory in Cambridge is especially concerned with research in theoretical astrophysics and laboratory spectroscopy, as well as the design and construction of instrumentation for orbiting solar observatories. A branch station has been located in Bloemfontein, South Africa, since 1891.

HARVARD UNIVERSITY, privately controlled nonsectarian institution of higher learning, the oldest university in the United States situated chiefly in Cambridge, Mass. The institution was founded in 1636 by the General Court of the Massachusetts Bay Colony (*see* MASSACHUSETTS: *History*) and opened for instruction in 1638. In 1639 the college was named for the English clergyman John Harvard (q.v.), its first benefactor. It was incorporated in 1650 and chartered as a university in 1780.

Harvard College, the oldest division of the university, offers undergraduate courses in the liberal arts leading to the B.A. degree; classes are open also to undergraduate and graduate students of Radcliffe College (q.v.), an affiliated institution for women.

Distinctive features of undergraduate life at Harvard are the House Plan, which encourages social and intellectual exchange between students and teachers, the General Education program, and the tutorial system. During the first year at Harvard College students live in halls within Harvard Yard, a walled enclosure containing residence halls, classroom buildings, libraries, and other university structures; thereafter they reside outside the yard in eight large residences, known as houses, which are named in honor of illustrious alumni or, in the case of the eighth, for Josiah Quincy (q.v.), a former president (1829–45) of Harvard College. Each house accommodates about 350 undergraduates, who are chosen as a representative cross section of the student body, and a group of faculty members who serve as tutors. Every undergraduate receives individual instruction from a tutor, usually in his own house. Each house has a library, dining hall, common room, dormitories, and athletic teams that engage in intramural competition; the houses sponsor music, drama, and art study groups.

Schools of the University. The university has ten graduate schools. The various schools were founded in the following order: medicine (1782), divinity (1816), law (1817), dental medicine (1867), arts and sciences (1872), business administration (1908), education (1920), public health (1922), and design (1936). The John Fitzgerald Kennedy School of Government, established in 1966, is the successor to the Graduate School of Public Administration, which had been founded in 1935. Engineering courses are provided in Harvard College and in the graduate school of arts and sciences by a division of engineering and applied physics. All the graduate schools except the schools of business administration and divinity are open to both men and women. Harvard cooperates in the Harvard-Radcliffe Management Training Program for Women. Women also attend summer sessions in the arts and sciences and in education. The professional schools confer appropriate degrees; the graduate school of arts and sciences confers the degree of master in most fields and the doctorate of philosophy.

Institutes of special studies at the university include the Harvard-Yenching Institute for Far Eastern Studies, the Russian Research Center, the Center for Middle Eastern Studies, the Center for International Affairs, the Center for International Legal Studies, and the Defense Studies Program. The university sponsors fellowship programs for mature practitioners in the professions of journalism, public administration, trade

The Harvard campus. Above: Massachusetts Hall, built in 1720, the oldest Harvard building, now houses the offices of the university president and staff. Left: The Carpenter Center for the Visual Arts, one of the most recent buildings of the university, was designed by Le Corbusier, the French architect.
Harvard University News Office

HARVARD UNIVERSITY

unionism, advanced management, conservation, and elementary- and secondary-school teaching. It cooperates closely with the Andover Newton Theological School; Boston University (q.v.) School of Theology; Episcopal Theological School; the School of Religion and the Fletcher School of Law and Diplomacy, both of Tufts College; and the Massachusetts Institute of Technology (q.v.). Astronomical observatories are maintained in Colorado, Massachusetts, and New Mexico in the U.S. and in South Africa (see HARVARD COLLEGE OBSERVATORY). At Harvard, Mass., there is an important station for radio astronomy. In addition, Harvard owns and operates the Arnold Arboretum in Boston and two large forests totaling 6000 acres in Petersham, Mass., and Cornwall, N.Y.

Harvard Library, Museums, and Press. The Harvard library, which in 1971 had more than 8,279,000 volumes, is the largest and oldest university library in the U.S and is exceeded in size by few libraries in the world. The central collection, housed in the Harry Elkins Widener Memorial Library, is utilized widely for advanced studies and scholarly research. The Houghton Library has collections of rare books and manuscripts. Undergraduates rely principally on the large Lamont Library and the separate house libraries. The university possesses, in addition, fifty special libraries and nearly a score of departmental libraries. Its collections relating to Hebrew culture, Celtic literature, the fine arts, the Italian Risorgimento, linguistics, Portuguese language and literature, the theater, business history, law, and medicine are especially noteworthy.

Museums maintained by the university in the Cambridge-Boston area include the Museum of Comparative Zoology (1859), the Gray Herbarium (1864), the Peabody Museum of Archaeology and Ethnology (1866), the Arnold Arboretum (1872), the Semitic Museum (1889), the William Hayes Fogg Museum of Art (1895), and the Busch Reisinger Museum of Scandinavian and Germanic Culture (1902). The university supports various scientific research laboratories, including the Computation Laboratory (1946), in which mechanical methods of mathematical calculation are investigated. With the Massachusetts Institute of Technology, the university dedicated the 6,000,000,000 electron-volt Cambridge Electron Accelerator in 1962.

The Harvard University Press, founded in 1913, publishes works of scholarly and general interest. Among the numerous periodicals issued by groups associated with the university are the *Harvard Business Review* and the *Harvard Law Review*. The best-known undergraduate publications are the *Lampoon,* a humorous magazine; the *Advocate,* a literary periodical; and the *Crimson,* a daily newspaper. The university is active in educational radio and television through its membership in the Lowell Institute Cooperative Broadcasting Council of Boston, Mass.

Development. Harvard occupies about 4000 acres in the Cambridge-Boston area. Home football games and other athletic events are contested in Harvard Stadium, which has a seating capacity in excess of 38,000, and on Soldiers' Field, a large area adjoining the stadium.

The university is governed by a self-perpetuating corporation, known as the President and Fellows of Harvard College. The oldest corporation in America, it comprises the president, a treasurer, and five fellows. Its decisions are in large part subject to the revisory power of a thirty-member board of overseers elected by the alumni.

Harvard College conferred its first B.A. degree in 1642. At first the university was supported jointly by the Congregational Church (see CONGREGATIONALISM) and the government of Massachusetts, but the college gradually acquired private financial resources and a considerable degree of autonomy. By 1865 the university was fully autonomous.

During the latter half of the 19th century Harvard experienced a period of unprecedented growth, which began under the presidency (1869–1909) of the American educator Charles William Eliot (q.v.). Eliot firmly established the elective system for undergraduates, organized the graduate school of arts and sciences, and strengthened and improved the other graduate schools. Eliot's successor, Abbott Lawrence Lowell (see under LOWELL), served from 1909 to 1933. His achievements included the introduction of the tutorial system and the House Plan and expansion of the university plant. James Bryant Conant (q.v.), president from 1933 to 1953, greatly broadened the geographical base from which the student body was drawn, introduced a rigorous system for selecting permanent faculty members, and built the Graduate Center for housing advanced students. Conant was succeeded in June, 1953, by Nathan Marsh Pusey (q.v.), former president of Lawrence College in Appleton, Wis. During the first several years of his tenure Pusey rallied increased support for the divinity school, encouraged increased challenge and more opportunity for independent work in the college, and launched (1957) "A Program for Harvard College", an

HARVEST FISH

$82,500,000 fund-raising campaign to finance expansion of the physical plant and otherwise strengthen support of the liberal arts at Harvard. In 1971 Derek Curtis Bok (1930–), dean of the Harvard Law School, was appointed to succeed Pusey as president.

Notable Americans in many professions have attended Harvard College during the past three centuries, among them Increase and Cotton Mather; Ralph Waldo Emerson; Henry David Thoreau; Henry and William James; James Russell Lowell; Oliver Wendell Holmes, the man of letters, and his son Oliver Wendell Holmes, the jurist; Robert Frost; T(homas) S(tearns) Eliot; and five U.S. presidents, namely, John Adams, John Quincy Adams, Theodore Roosevelt, Franklin Delano Roosevelt, and John Fitzgerald Kennedy (qq.v.). A sixth U.S. President, Rutherford Birchard Hayes (q.v.), was a graduate of the Harvard law school.

In 1971 enrollment totaled 16,370 full-time students, including 1200 in Radcliffe College; faculty members numbered 5170. The university endowment was approximately $733,000,000.

HARVARD UNIVERSITY, DEPT. OF PUBLIC RELATIONS

HARVEST FISH, common name of several marine acanthopterygian fishes in the family Stromateidae, especially *Palometa simillima* and the butterfish, *Poronotus tricanthus*. Both fish are short, *P. simillima* averaging 10 in. in length, and the butterfish, 12 in. Their bodies are flattened from side to side and are deep from top to bottom. They lack pelvic fins as adults. Jellyfishes constitute their chief food. Harvest fishes are found in the Atlantic Ocean from Cape Cod to Brazil and are valued as food. The species *P. simillima* is the only northern representative on the American Pacific coast, where although not a pompano (q.v.), it is called the California pompano. The butterfish is known under many other names, including dollarfish, lafayette, sheepshead, and starfish.

HARVEST FLY. See CICADA.

HARVESTMEN or **HARVEST SPIDERS.** See DADDY LONGLEGS.

HARVEST MITE, or HARVEST BUG, common name for the chigger (q.v.).

HARVEST MOON, full moon at harvest time in the North Temperate Zone, or more exactly, the full moon occurring nearest to the autumnal equinox (*see* ECLIPTIC) September 23. At this season the moon rises at a point opposite to the sun, or close to the exact eastern point of the horizon. Moreover, the moon rises at this season only a few minutes later each night, affording on several successive evenings an attractive moonrise close to sunset time and strong moonlight almost all night. The continuance of the moonlight after sunset is useful to farmers in northern latitudes, who are then harvesting their crops. The full moon following the harvest moon, which exhibits the same phenomena in a lesser degree, is called the hunter's moon.

HARVEY, city of Illinois, in Cook Co., on the Little Calumet R., 20 miles s. of the center of Chicago, of which it is a residential and manufacturing suburb. The principal industries in the city are the manufacture of automobile components, stoves, foundry equipment, diesel engines, cement, aluminumware, and road, mining, and oil-well machinery. Thornton Junior College (1927) is located in Harvey. Founded in 1890, Harvey was incorporated as a village in 1891 and as a city in 1895. Pop. (1960) 29,071; (1970) 34,636.

HARVEY, George Brinton McClellan (1864–1928), American journalist and publisher, born in Peacham, Vt., and educated at Peacham Academy. He became managing editor of the New York *World* in 1891. From 1893 to 1898 he made a fortune in the construction and administration of electric railways. In 1899 he purchased a monthly periodical, *The North American Review*, and was its editor until 1926. He also was president of the publishing firm of Harper & Brothers (now Harper & Row) from 1900 to 1915 and editor of *Harper's Weekly* from 1901 to 1913. A leading supporter of President Woodrow Wilson (q.v.), he turned against him after Wilson asked him not to voice his support in his periodicals, which were suspected of representing the views of certain financial interests. In 1918 Harvey founded the *North American Review's War Weekly* (later *Harvey's Weekly*), in which he attacked Wilson's policies, particularly the proposal that the United States enter the League of Nations (q.v.). Harvey later was a prominent supporter of President Warren Gamaliel Harding (q.v.) and was his ambassador to Great Britain from 1921 to 1923.

HARVEY, William (1578–1657), English physician and anatomist, born in Folkestone, Kent, and educated at the universities of Cambridge and Padua. He was admitted as a fellow of the Royal College of Physicians in 1607. In 1609 he became physician of Saint Bartholomew's Hospital, and in 1615 he was made professor of anatomy and surgery at the College of Physicians. Harvey perfected his theory of the circulation of the blood (q.v.) in 1616, publishing his findings in Latin in 1628, *Exercitatio Anatomica de Motu Cordis et Sanguinis in Animalibus* (briefly, "On the Circulation of the Blood"). In this book Harvey explained his discovery of the

HARZ MOUNTAINS

William Harvey (center) demonstrates the circulation of the blood to King Charles I of England.
Bettmann Archive

work of the heart in receiving blood from the veins and propelling it through the arteries. His reasoning prepared the way for the Italian anatomist Marcello Malpighi (q.v.), who demonstrated the existence of the capillaries, the final link in the circulation of the blood between the arteries and the veins.

Harvey acted as physician to two English kings, James I and Charles I (qq.v.). Under the sponsorship of Charles, he conducted researches on embryology (q.v.), publishing his results in his book *Exercitationes de Generatione Animaliam . . . ad Timoribus Uteri et de Conceptione* (briefly, "On the Generation of Animals", 1651). In this work Harvey discussed his investigations concerning the formation of the embryo and disproved the old idea of spontaneous generation (q.v.). Harvey stated the dictum *omne vivum ex ovo*, "all life comes from the egg", a finding on which much of the modern science of embryology is based. A complete English translation of Harvey's writings was published in 1847.

HARVEYIZED STEEL. *See* Armor.

HARZ MOUNTAINS, northernmost mountain range of Germany, extending over an area of 784 sq.mi. between the Elbe and Weser rivers. The N.W. part of the system is called the Upper Harz (average elevation 2100 ft. above sea level) and the S.E. part, the Lower Harz (average elevation 1000 ft. above sea level); the loftiest peak in the range is Brocken (q.v.), rising to a height of 3747 ft. above sea level in the Upper Harz. Abundant forests and pasture lands cover the slopes of both parts of the range, and fertile plateaus are located in the Lower Harz. Ever since the 10th century, mining has been carried on in the Harz Mts., which contain veins of silver, lead, gold, copper, iron, sulfur, alum, and arsenic. The quarrying of marble, granite, and alabaster, the manufacture of coarse lace, and the breeding of native songbirds, chiefly canaries, are also important occupations. Pagan traditions have survived in the Harz region longer than in any other part of Germany, and have given rise to a number of weird and romantic legends, many of which have been incorporated into German literature. The Walpurgis Night legend (*see* Walburga, Saint), centering on the Brocken, forms a

HASDRUBAL

part of the poetic drama *Faust*, by the German dramatist Johann Wolfgang von Goethe (q.v.).

HASDRUBAL, name of two Carthaginian generals who achieved historic importance.

Hasdrubal (d. 221 B.C.), succeeded his father-in-law Hamilcar Barca (q.v.) as commander of the Carthaginian forces in Spain in 228 B.C. He expanded the Carthaginian holdings in the new province by diplomatic methods, founding a new capital at New Carthage (now Cartagena), and negotiating a treaty with Rome that fixed the boundaries of the province. He was assassinated.

Hasdrubal (d. 207 B.C.), son of Hamilcar Barca. In 218 B.C. at the beginning of the Second Punic War between Carthage and Rome (*see* PUNIC WARS), he succeeded his brother Hannibal (q.v.) as commander of the Carthaginian armies in Spain. Hasdrubal successfully countered Roman attacks on Spain until 208 B.C. when he was forced to retreat into Gaul (q.v.). Two years later he led his troops across the Alps into Italy to bring reinforcements to Hannibal. He encountered the Roman army at the Metaurus R. (now Metauro R.) in central Italy, and was defeated and killed. His failure to reach Hannibal with the necessary reinforcements was a decisive factor in the outcome of the war.

HASHIMITE *or* **HASHEMITE,** the name of two Arabian dynasties.

The descendants of Hashim, of the tribe of Koreish, traditionally the custodians of the sacred Muslim shrine, the Kaaba, at Mecca. The Hashimites included the founders of Islam, notably the Prophet Muhammad; his paternal uncle Abbas, progenitor of the Abbasid dynasty of caliphs (*see* CALIPH), which ruled Islam from 750 to 1258; and his son-in-law, the Caliph Ali. The modern Arabian dynasty, by tradition descended from Muhammad, was founded in 1916 by Husein ibn-Ali, King of the Hejaz (1856–1931), in Arabia. Sons of Husein ibn-Ali were Ali ibn-Husein, King of the Hejaz (1878–1935), who was forced to resign in 1925 by ibn-Saud, King of Saudi Arabia; Abdullah ibn-Husein, King of Jordan; and Faisal I, King of Iraq. Hussein I, King of Jordan, is a grandson of Abdullah ibn-Husein. Faisal II, last King of Iraq, was a grandson of Faisal I. *See* ARABIA: *History*; IRAQ: *History*; JORDAN, HASHEMITE KINGDOM OF: *History*.

See also separate articles for those individuals whose birth and death dates are not given.

HASHISH *or* **HASHEESH.** *See* CANNABIS; DRUGS, ADDICTION TO.

HASIDIM *or* **CHASIDIM** (Heb., "the saintly ones"), in ancient Jewish history, especially pious persons. From passages in the Psalter (*see* PSALMS), the books of Maccabees (q.v.), and the Talmud (q.v.), it seems evident that the term was used for those who distinguished themselves by loyalty to Jewish law and by charitable deeds. They opposed the Hellenizing efforts (*see* HELLENIST) of Antiochus IV, King of Syria (*see under* ANTIOCHUS), clinging closely to the teachings and practices of Judaism and often suffering death rather than transgress them.

In modern times the name Hasidim is applied to a mystical sect established in Poland about 1750 by the religious leader Israel the Baal Shem-Tob (q.v.) and after his death led by Dov Ber of Mezricz (d. 1773). The followers of the Baal Shem-Tob were characterized by belief in miracles, participation in enthusiastic prayer services, devotion to the ideal of brotherly love, and emphasis on emotional piety as opposed to strictly disciplined study and ritual. The sect grew rapidly, numbering about 50,000 in 1770.

The established rabbinical leaders denounced the sect bitterly. Although it is true that some of the Hasidic spiritual leaders became corrupt, the sect remains an influence today, both on

An Hasidic Jew wearing a hat, called a shtreimel, *and a long coat, called a* bekesheh.   Israel Information Services

King Hassan II of Morocco makes an address as King Faisal of Saudi Arabia listens.
UPI

Jewish life and, through the work of the Jewish religious philosopher Martin Buber (q.v.), on Christianity. A number of Hasidic communities exist in Israel and the United States, the members being distinguished by modesty of appearance among the women and by traditional garb and hair styles among the men and boys.

N.N.G.

HASMONAEAN. See MACCABEES, family.

HASSAM, Childe (1859–1935), American painter and etcher, born in Dorchester, Mass., and educated at the Boston Art School and the École des Beaux-Art in Paris. Hassam was the chief American exponent of impressionism (q.v.). His primary objective both in his paintings and in his etchings was to represent the effects of sunlight in city scenes and in landscapes of rural New England. He won several awards for his work and was elected to the National Academy of Design in 1906. His works include "July 14 Rue Daunon" (1910), and "Church at Gloucester" (1918), both in the Metropolitan Museum of Art, New York City.

HASSAN II, in full MOULAY HASSAN (1930–), King of Morocco (1961–), born in Rabat. Hassan received his education in Rabat and qualified for the licentiate in law through the extension division of the University of Bordeaux in Rabat. He succeeded his father, Muhammad V (1913–61), to the throne in February, 1961.

Muhammad and his family were exiled by the French from 1953 to 1955, during the Moroccan independence movement which ended in success when the French granted independence in 1956. The following year Hassan was invested as crown prince and made commander in chief of the Moroccan army. He was minister of defense and vice-premier from 1960 until his ascension to the throne. As king, Hassan instituted many social and economic reforms and sought greater unity with the other Arab countries of North Africa. His relatively conservative regime, however, aroused hostility among some leftist Arab countries, such as Algeria and Libya. In 1971 and 1972 Hassan survived two assassination attempts by the Moroccan military, but he was unable to gain political support to install a civilian government.

HASSEL, Odd (1897–), Norwegian chemist, born in Oslo and educated at the universities of Oslo and Berlin. He was appointed professor of physical chemistry at Oslo in 1934, a post he held until his retirement in 1964. Hassel shared the 1969 Nobel Prize in chemistry with the British organic chemist Derek H. R. Barton (q.v.) for their independent research in the 1950's, leading to a new concept of conformation analysis in chemistry through study of the three-dimensional geometric configurations of molecules.

HASTIE

HASTIE, William Henry. See Negroes in the United States: *The Negro and the New Deal: The Civil Rights Movement*; Virgin Islands of the United States: *History*.

HASTINGS, city in Nebraska, and county seat of Adams Co., 100 miles w. of Lincoln. Hastings has rail and air service, and is the shipping point and trading center of an extensive agricultural area of s. Nebraska and n. Kansas. Grain and livestock are the principal products shipped. The chief industries in Hastings are meat packing and the manufacture of creamery products, flour, agricultural implements, air-conditioning equipment, foundry products, brick and tile, grain bins and tanks, millwork products, automotive and airplane parts, irrigation pumps, and fertilizers. Hastings is the site of Hastings College (Presbyterian), established in 1882. The municipal museum, called the House of Yesterday, contains an extensive collection of Great Plains memorabilia. Hastings was settled in 1872 and incorporated as a city in 1874. Pop. (1960) 21,412; (1970) 23,580.

HASTINGS, Great Britain, municipal, county, and parliamentary borough of Sussex, England, on the English Channel, about 62 miles s.e. of London. The borough is a popular summer resort, with large bathing facilities and a boulevard, 3 mi. in length, fronting the English Channel. Other features of Hastings are the Marina promenade, a number of public parks and gardens, and the ruins of an 11th-century Norman castle. Hastings was a flourishing community during the Anglo-Saxon period of English history and received mention in 928, during the reign of Athelstan (q.v.), as the site of a royal mint. In the reign (1042–66) of the Saxon king Edward the Confessor (*see under* Edward), the town was enfranchised as one of the Cinque Ports (q.v.). The Duke of Normandy, later William I (q.v.), King of England, led his invading army ashore in the vicinity of Hastings on Sept. 28, 1066. The subsequent battle, in which William conquered Harold II (q.v.), the last Saxon King of England, occurred about 6½ mi. inland from the town; *see* Hastings, Battle of. After 1377, when it was raided and burned by the French, Hastings declined in importance as a seaport. The town was heavily damaged by German air raids in World War II. Pop. (1969 est.) 69,020.

HASTINGS, Thomas (1860–1929), American architect, born in New York City, and educated at the École des Beaux-Arts in Paris. In 1886 he formed a partnership with the American architect John Merven Carrère (q.v.) who shared his belief in the importance of the classical traditions of Europe to modern American architecture. With Carrère, Hastings designed a number of notable public buildings, mostly in classic Greek and Roman and Italian Renaissance styles. Among them are the New York Public Library in that city and the Senate Office Building in Washington, D.C.

HASTINGS, Warren (1732–1818), British statesman and colonial administrator, born in Churchill, Oxfordshire, England. At the age of eighteen he went to India as a clerk in the service of the English East India Company (q.v.), but he soon revealed his administrative talent and was advanced through the ranks of the company, serving on administrative councils that governed the cities of Calcutta and Madras. By 1772 he had been appointed to the most important post in India, the governorship of Bengal. As governor Hastings instituted a series of judicial and financial reforms, including the establishment of a series of civil courts and the imposition of a uniform duty on all imports. In 1773 Parliament limited the authority of the East India Company, and the British government appointed Hastings the first governor-general of India, with a governing council of four members. Although he was blocked by the council at every turn, during his tenure Hastings was able to initiate extensive judicial and civil-service reforms. From 1778 to 1782 he successfully defended the dominions of the East India Company from attacks by the native Indian rulers, who had aligned themselves with the French. His victory secured British influence in India, but in order to defray the expenses of the war Hastings was forced to confiscate the property and financial resources of some local rulers who refused to contribute for the war expenses.

Many liberals in England feared his growing power and in 1784 Parliament passed a bill abolishing the political autonomy of the East India Company in India. Hastings felt he could not work under the divided authority of the company and the crown, and he resigned as governor-general. After his return to Great Britain he became the victim of a long political struggle between Parliament and the East India Company for control of the government of India. In 1788 he was brought to trial by a Parliamentary group, led by his personal enemy and former colleague on the governor-general council, the British politician Sir Philip Francis (1740–1818). Hastings was charged with high crimes and misdemeanors, accusations based largely on his confiscation of property and money while in office. The trial, at which the British statesman Edmund Burke (q.v.) delivered a celebrated oration for the prosecution, lasted seven years; in 1795 Hastings was completely exonerated, but his fortune had been depleted by the cost of his defense. Hastings spent the rest of his life in retirement in England; after 1804 he accepted a pension by the East India Company. He is regarded as one of the founders of the British Empire in India.

HASTINGS, BATTLE OF, in English history, decisive military engagement fought on Oct. 14, 1066, between a national army led by Harold II, Saxon King of England, and an invasion force led by William, Duke of Normandy, later William I (qq.v.), King of England. William was a claimant of the English throne, which he maintained had been promised to him previously by his cousin, Edward the Confessor, King of England (*see under* EDWARD). William challenged the election of Harold as king on Edward's death, and with the blessing of Pope Alexander II (r. 1061–73) prepared to invade England. The invading army, which included infantry armed with crossbows and contingents of heavily armed cavalry, landed on the English coast near Hastings on Sept. 28, 1066. After a forced march from Yorkshire, where Harold had just defeated and slain his rebellious brother Tostig, Earl of Northumbria (d. 1066), in the Battle of Stamford Bridge, the English army, numbering about 7000 men, occupied a height (later called Senlac Hill) on the Hastings-London highway about 6½ miles N.W. of Hastings. The royal force was composed exclusively of infantry, armed with spears, swords, and battle-axes.

The initial Norman attack, launched at 9:00 A.M. on Oct. 14, failed to dislodge the English, who met the barrage of enemy arrows with interlocked shields. The English axmen turned back a Norman cavalry charge, whereupon a section of the Norman infantry turned and fled. At this juncture, several units of the English army broke ranks, contrary to Harold's orders, and pursued the retreating Normans. Other Norman troops quickly surrounded and annihilated these units. Taking advantage of the lack of discipline among the English soldiers, William ordered a feigned retreat. The stratagem led to the entrapment of another large body of English troops. Severely weakened by these reverses and demoralized by the mortal wounding of Harold by an arrow, the English were forced to abandon their strategic position on the crest of Senlac Hill. Only small remnants of the defending army survived the subsequent onslaughts of the Norman cavalry. The victory of William at Hastings paved the way for Norman subjugation of all England. See ENGLAND: *History*.

HAT, headdress or covering for the head, of a particular shape or design, and especially such a covering having a crown and a brim. Like all types of headdress, the hat may serve several purposes; it may be used chiefly as an ornament, or to protect the head against climate, or to indicate the office, military rank, or political or religious affiliation of the wearer. A variant of the hat, the cap, differs by not having a brim or by having a brim that only partially encircles the crown, resembling a visor.

Hats of the Past. The origin of hats is unknown, but some knowledge of their early uses can be derived from extant sculpture and painting. In the ancient empire of Assyria (q.v.) the hat served as a mark of occupation or office: musicians wore hats resembling the lower half of the body of a fish, the crown being shaped like the tail; cooks wore tiaralike caps. The men of ancient Greece and Rome wore three principal types of hats: the *causia*, a felt hat with a high crown and broad brim slightly rolled; the *petasos*, worn chiefly by travelers, a broad-brimmed hat of felt, with a low crown and tied under the chin or behind the ears; and the *pileus*, a simple cap of felt, often resembling a skullcap that is, a close-fitting, lightweight cap without a brim. The use of hats was far less extensive in ancient times than it is today. Greek and Roman women generally wore no hats, covering the hair with a veil. They supplemented this in cold or wet weather with a square-shaped hood made of linen in the summer and of wool in the winter.

Anglo-Saxon, or Old English, men wore close-fitting, conical-shaped caps made of animal skins with the hair left on the hide and the shaggy side turned outward. The caps of members of the wealthy class were ornamented. Anglo-Saxon women wore long veils, which were sometimes kept in place by a gold circlet or headband.

In medieval Europe, caps or hoods of a simple design were in vogue for head covering until the late Middle Ages, when hats became extravagant and eccentric in shape and proportions. Thus the ordinary hat of the 11th century, which had a folded brim and a crown that fell to one side, in the 14th century had loose folds that reached to the shoulder; by the 15th century it had developed folds that fell to the knee, ending in a long, thin point. The close-fitting, helmet-shaped cap of the 12th century was succeeded in the 13th by a hat with a high crown, peaked front, and turnup back, and in the 15th by a high hat that was often brimless. Toward the end of the 15th century, flat hats with low

HAT

crowns and brims, sometimes with a bunch of plumes placed in front and curving backward, came into vogue. They were usually worn over a scarlet skullcap and tilted to one side. Women's hats of the period were particularly extravagant. They were elaborate, towering structures ending in such objects as cornucopias and baskets. An especially eccentric piece of millinery was a creation with a high receding crown that was flanked by huge horns.

In the 16th century the fashion changed to flatter headgear. Men in general wore hats with broad, serrated brims; women wore caps of velvet or gold brocade; and the upper classes had hats shaped like the tam-o'-shanter, which were decorated with feathers and worn tilted. During the reign of Elizabeth I (q.v.), Queen of England, men's hats were narrow, with a turndown, curved brim and a full crown circled with a gold band or with a feather worn on the right. Also in vogue for men were small, tight-fitting, round hats with rolled brims and with feathers in front. Women wore hats that had a brim curved in over the brow, hats with full-gathered crowns, and tall hats with feathers at the side.

Through the 17th century, the size and shape of hats changed frequently. Through the reign of James I (q.v.), King of England, men's hats featured broad brims and high crowns ornamented at the back and sides with feathers; the brim was often fastened up on the right side with a jewel. In the time of his successor, Charles I (q.v.), men's hats had slightly lower crowns and curved brims with feathers falling over them to side or back. During the civil wars that were fought through the mid-century, political and religious differences were marked by hats: the Puritans (q.v.) wore steeple hats, which were high and narrow and devoid of ornaments, whereas a Cavalier (q.v.) wore a hat with a low, broad crown and a feather stuck to one side. The Quaker hat, a plain hat with a round, low crown and a broad brim, dates from the origin of the Quaker sect (see FRIENDS, SOCIETY OF) in the middle of the 17th century. After the Restoration in England in 1660, the fashionable wore hats with a high crown decorated by a band and a bow in the front; the hats featured flat, waved, or curved brims and feathers on either side or all around. The three-cornered hat, made by turning up the brim at both sides and in front, came into vogue in the second half of the 17th century and remained in style until the beginning of the 19th century, when it was replaced by the top hat.

Contemporary Men's Headwear. In the modern period the design and manufacture of flamboyant hats for men have diminished and basic styles seem to continue through longer periods of time. The principal types of men's hats that originated or came into general use in the 19th century and are still in vogue today are the felt hat, the silk hat, and the straw hat.

Felt (q.v.) hats are made principally of fur. Some, however, are made of a mixture of fur and wool, and others of wool alone. Two principal kinds exist: the soft felt hat, and the stiff or hard felt hat, known as the derby in the United States and the bowler in Great Britain. The latter has a dome-shaped crown and a narrow brim. The soft felt hat, which was introduced into the U.S. in 1851 by the Hungarian patriot and statesman Lajos Kossuth (q.v.), who visited the country in that year, was for a time known as the Kossuth hat.

The second surviving type, the silk hat, worn usually on formal occasions, has a high, straight crown made of calico and covered by a glossy plush of silk. It was developed in the Italian city of Florence about the middle of the 18th century, but did not come into general use until the first half of the 19th century.

Straw hats, the third type, are made from straw braids that come from Italy, China, and Japan. Italian straw braid, the two principal types of which are called the leghorn and the Milan braid, is particularly valued. Stiff straw hats having a flat crown and straight brim are popularly called boaters or skimmers. The principal type of light hat for summer wear in the U.S., in addition to the straw hat, is the Panama hat, made chiefly in Ecuador and Colombia from shreds of the immature leaf of the tree *carludovica palmata*.

Modern Millinery. Today, hats for women are made of a variety of materials, including felt, straw, velvet, plastic, and natural and synthetic fabrics, and are often decorated with ribbons, veiling, feathers, artificial flowers, and other ornaments. Bright colors are frequently used, matching or contrasting with a particular garment. Women's hats vary in size and shape according to current styles in costume and according to the taste of the individual wearer.

Popular for centuries with women as well as men is the beret, a soft, flat, visorless cap usually made of wool. The beret worn by the Basque peasants in France is the most widely known of this type. Another popular basic design is the calotte, a close-fitting skullcap that, by adding trimmings or material, can be made into a variety of shapes.

In past years, trends in hat fashions were established by designers in Paris, France. The re-

HAT

An elaborate hat style was popular in the 15th century.
French Embassy Press & Information Division

vival of the sou'wester, a hat with a wide slanting brim that is longer in the back and has optional ear flaps and ties, was initiated by the French fashion designer Christian Dior (q.v.). The Spanish couturier Christóbal Balenciaga (1895–1972), also working in Paris, popularized the big mushroom brim. Recently the influence of Paris milliners has diminished somewhat and New York now ranks with Paris as the two top fashion-setting cities. Currently popular American designers in the hat industry are the French-born Lily Daché and the American designer Sally Victor.

The Hat Industry. The transition from making hats by hand to machine manufacture in the U.S. occurred in the 1850's when the first efficient felt-hat-manufacturing machine was developed. Factories were built up throughout the New England States, establishing that area as the leading center for hat production. By 1875 the hat industry became a thriving, although small-scale, business. Traveling salesmen, known as drummers, representing their jobbing, or wholesale, houses, sold hats to small, individually owned hat shops all over the country. About 1890 the industry began mass production; manufacturing standards were established, wages were standardized, and modern methods were initiated. The industry continued to expand and by 1950 was almost completely converted into machine manufacture.

Today, specially developed machines have reduced the production of hats to a continuous belt operation. One of the initial phases in the process is forming, which occurs when an operator measures out the appropriate material for one hat and feeds it into a forming machine. The formed cone is then squeezed through rollers in sizing machines. In the next step it is dyed, after which blocking, or shaping, takes place. Finishers mold the hat into its final shape, and trimmers bind or hem the brim, sew in linings, and add whatever embellishment is required to finish the product.

Most aspects of the hat industry in the U.S.,

The simplicity and comfort of hats worn during the late 1960's contrast sharply with the historic example shown above left.
UPI

HATCH ACT

such as manufacture, sales, labor, and design, are divided into two segments: millinery, or women's hats, and hats for men. The extensive geographical and industrial scope of the industry has allowed only infrequent and general correlations of pertinent statistics. During a typical year in the late 1960's, the millinery industry was estimated to average $350,000,000 in retail gross sales, with approximately 60,000,000 hats produced. The total labor force included some 10,000 workers, with an added 2000 holding such positions as managers, designers, and salesmen. Leading centers of production were New York City and Framingham, Mass. The wholesale income grossed by men's hats averaged about $114,000,000 annually during the same period. Major manufacturing centers for men's hats were Winchester, Tenn.; Garland and Corsicana, Texas; Philadelphia, Sunbury, and Allentown, Pa.; and Saint Joseph, Mo.

HATCH ACT, popular designation of the Political Activity Act, passed by Congress in 1939 and amended in 1940, forbidding Federal employees to engage in certain types of political activity and placing ceilings on campaign expenditures. The act is so called after its author, Senator Carl Atwood Hatch (1889–1963) of New Mexico. An earlier (1887) Hatch Act, named for Representative William Henry Hatch (1833–96) of Missouri, provided for direct Federal aid for the study of scientific agriculture.

Among its provisions the Hatch Act prohibited such practices as threatening, intimidating, or coercing voters in national elections; made it illegal for administrators in U.S. civil service to interfere with the nomination and election of candidates to Federal office; proscribed the practices of promising and withholding certain kinds of employment and unemployment relief as a reward or punishment for political activity; and prohibited the solicitation of political contributions from relief recipients.

The Hatch Act was amended in 1940 to put a $5000 ceiling on annual individual contributions to campaigns for any one candidate for election to Federal office, and to limit the contributions received and expended by political committees to $3,000,000 a year. The purchase of goods or advertising, the proceeds of which would benefit candidates for election to Federal office, was prohibited. All provisions of the act relating to Federal employees were extended to State employees engaged in any function financed by Federal funds. Later, New York State enacted legislation that put into effect many of the provisions of the Hatch Act. See ELECTORAL REFORM: *Electoral Reform in the United States.*

HATHAWAY, Anne (1557?–1623), wife of William Shakespeare (q.v.), born near Stratford-on-Avon, England. She married Shakespeare in 1582 and became the mother of his three children. During his London career, she appears to have remained in Stratford-on-Avon. Her cottage at Shottery, near Stratford-on-Avon, has been preserved as a historic site.

HATHOR. See EGYPTIAN RELIGION.

HATSHEPSUT or **HATSHEPSET** or **HATASU** (fl. about 1500 B.C.), Egyptian Queen of the XVIII Dynasty; see EGYPT, ARAB REPUBLIC OF: *History: The New Kingdom.* She was the daughter of Thutmose I (*see under* THUTMOSE), and became the wife of her half-brother Thutmose III, with whom she ruled after the ouster of their father. During their reign, which lasted until her death (except 1496–1493 B.C.), she was supreme in Egypt. She built the sumptuous temple at Deir el-Bahri near Thebes, approached by a lane of sphinxes and surrounded by obelisks. The temple, rebuilt over a period of many years by European archeologists, contains many evidences of the reign of Queen Hatshepsut, notably, a vivid mural representation of the Egyptian expedition to Punt, an ancient district in east-central Africa.

HATTERAS, CAPE. See CAPE HATTERAS.

HATTIESBURG, city in Mississippi, and county seat of Forrest Co., at the confluence of the Leaf and Bowie rivers, 70 miles N. of Gulfport. Hattiesburg has rail and air service. Situated in a fertile agricultural area, the city is an important commercial and manufacturing center. Among the varied products manufactured or processed in Hattiesburg are clothing, lumber, naval stores, fertilizers, boilers, castings, piping, roofing, and paper and rubber products. The city is the site of the University of Southern Mississippi, established in 1910. Hattiesburg was founded in 1881 and soon became a lumbering center. It was incorporated as a town in 1884 and as a city in 1899. Pop. (1960) 34,989; (1970) 38,277.

HAUGESUND, city and seaport of Norway, in Rogaland County, on the Karmsund, an arm of the North Sea, 35 miles N.W. of Stavanger. The city extends over the small islands of Risøy, which has a modern harbor, and Hasseløy. In 1965 Haugesund annexed Torvastad, on the island of Karmøy, with which it is connected by a bridge over the Karmsund. The city is a major fishing and processing center for herring, mackerel, and lobsters; other industries include shipbuilding, ironworking, canning, and textile manufacturing. Haugesund has an art gallery and a city museum. Nearby to the N. is Haraldshaugen, reputedly the burial place of Harold (*see under* HAROLD), the 10th-century king who united Norway. Pop. (1965 est.) 27,488.

HAUPTMANN, Gerhart (1862–1946), German dramatist, novelist, and poet, born in Bad Salzbrunn (now Szczawno Zdroj, Poland). After spending a short time studying sculpture in Breslau (now Wrocław, Poland) and Jena, he turned to writing. Hauptmann was greatly influenced by the works of the Norwegian playwright Henrik Ibsen (q.v.), and, after experimenting with various literary forms, he also adopted the drama as his prime medium of expression. In his first play, *Vor Sonnenaufgang* (1889; Eng. trans., *Before Dawn,* 1909), Hauptmann shares Ibsen's concern for social problems by realistically portraying the problems of the working class. The play traces the moral disintegration of a group of peasant families who have become suddenly wealthy because of the discovery of coal on their land. In its concern for the environmental and hereditary factors that shape the life of the individual, the play is the first example of naturalistic drama in Germany; *see* NATURALISM, in literature. Hauptmann continued to show a deep concern for the life of the lower classes. The fate of a group of Silesian weavers is depicted in his greatest work, *Die Weber* (1892; Eng. trans., *The Weavers,* 1899). In this drama of social protest, Hauptmann introduces a new literary vehicle: he portrays conflict by making the class of peasants, rather than an individual, the protagonist of the play.

Hauptmann soon abandoned the purely naturalistic drama. In *Hanneles Himmelfahrt* (1893; Eng. trans., *Hannele,* 1894), he combines naturalistic elements with a more romantic and highly symbolic verse form. This trend toward Romanticism (q.v.) is fully realized in his 1896 verse play, *Die versunkene Glocke* (Eng. trans., *The Sunken Bell,* 1898), an almost mystical symbolic fantasy of the struggles of an artist. In the same year Hauptmann turned again to the realistic drama, but instead of emphasizing social issues he traces the effects of moral corruption in the individual; *see* REALISM, in literature. In *Fuhrmann Henschel* (1898; Eng. trans., *Drayman Henschel,* 1913), and in a later play, *Rose Bernd* (1903; Eng. trans., 1913), Hauptmann traces the tragic theme of an individual who is destined to be destroyed by his own innate human shortcomings and moral weakness. Hauptmann gives his fullest treatment to the problem of fate and free will (q.v.) in a series of plays based on the ancient Greek legend of the doomed House of Atreus, cursed by the gods (*see* ATREUS, HOUSE OF), *Die Atriden-Tetralogie* (1941–45; "The Teralogy of the Atrids").

Hauptmann did not confine himself to one genre. The most famous of his less serious plays is *Der Biberpelz* (1893; Eng. trans. *The Beaver Coat,* 1912), a comedy satirizing the Prussian officials of imperial Germany. He also wrote a number of novels, notably, *Der Ketzer von Soana* (1918; Eng. trans. *The Heretic of Soana,* 1923), and epic poems.

Although Hauptmann continued to write until his death, he is chiefly remembered for his naturalistic plays of the late 19th and early 20th centuries. He was awarded the 1912 Nobel Prize in literature. *See* GERMAN LITERATURE: *After 1871: Naturalism.*

HAUSA, name of an African people of northwestern Nigeria and southwestern Niger. The Hausa are a racially diverse, but culturally fairly homogeneous, tribe numbering about 10,000,000 to 15,000,000 people.

Historically organized into a group of feudal city-states, the Hausa were conquered from the 14th century on by a succession of West African kingdoms, among them, Mali, Songhai, Bornu, and Fula (qq.v.). They occasionally attained enough power and unity, however, to throw off foreign domination and to engage in local conquest and slave raiding themselves. In the opening years of the 20th century, with the Hausa on the verge of overthrowing the Fula, the British invaded northern Nigeria and instituted their policy of indirect rule. Under the British the Fula were supported in their political supremacy and the Hausa-Fula ruling coalition, still dominant in northern Nigeria, was confirmed; *see* AFRICA: *History: West African Kingdoms.* The beginnings of this coalition were, however, much earlier, because the Fula governed by simply assuming the highest hereditary positions in the well-organized Hausa political system. Large numbers of the ruling Fula have now become culturally and linguistically Hausa.

Although the earliest Hausas were animists (*see* ANIMISM), an Africanized Islam (q.v.) is now the dominant religion among all but several thousand pagan Hausa, called Maguzawa. Hausa culture manifests a greater degree of specialization and diversification than that of most of the surrounding peoples. Subsistance agriculture is the primary occupation of most, but other skills such as tanning, dyeing, weaving, and metalworking are also highly developed. Hausas have long been famous for wide-ranging itinerant trading, and wealthy merchants share the highest social positions with the politically powerful and the learned.

The Hausa language is the largest and best-known member of the Chadic subfamily of the

HAUTBOY

Afro-Asiatic family of languages; see AFRICAN LANGUAGES. Hausa has borrowed freely from other languages, especially Arabic, and is adapting well to the demands of contemporary cultural change. It has become a common language for millions of non-Hausa west Africans, and sizable Hausa-speaking communities exist in each major city of west and north Africa as well as along the trans-Saharan trade and pilgrimage routes. An extensive literature and several periodicals in Romanized script have been produced since the beginning of British rule; see AFRICAN LITERATURE. An Arabic-based writing system, developed prior to British conquest, is still in limited use.

HAUTBOY, Anglicization of the French word for oboe, *hautbois* (literally, "high wood"). See OBOE.

HAVANA (Sp. *La Habana*), city, capital, and chief seaport of Cuba, and the largest city in the West Indies. The city is on the w. side of the Bay of Havana, on the N. coast of the island about 90 miles s. of Key West, Fla. The Bay of Havana is one of the safest harbors in the world; a narrow strait affords entrance to the bay, which is navigable by ocean-going vessels. The E. side of the outer entrance is dominated by Morro Castle, a 16th-century fortress. Castillo de la Punta, another old fortress, is on the w. side of the strait. Numerous docks, warehouses, and related facilities occupy considerable frontage along the inner harbor, and a substantial part of the imports and exports of the island are handled through Havana. Sugar refining and tobacco processing are the principal industries. Other industries include distilling, food processing, and the manufacture of textiles. Havana is the most important rail, highway and air terminus in Cuba, although in the late 1960's international air service to Cuba was limited to connections with Mexico, Spain, and certain Communist-bloc nations.

Havana is one of the oldest and most picturesque cities of the Western Hemisphere. Before the Cuban revolutionary Fidel Castro (q.v.) assumed power in 1959, it was a popular winter resort, particularly for United States tourists. The buildings of Havana are constructed largely of white coral limestone. The original portion of the city, located near the inner entrance of the harbor, contains narrow, crooked streets, old houses with overhanging balconies, and various historic landmarks. Beyond the older section, Havana is essentially modern, with numerous

The Capitol in Havana   Burton Holmes — Ewing Galloway

magnificent residences, imposing public buildings and ecclesiastical edifices, beautiful parks and plazas, and broad, tree-lined boulevards. Many of the larger private homes have been turned into government offices, student residences, or other public facilities by the Castro regime. Among the boulevards are the Paseo de Martí, better known as the Prado, the Avenida del Puerto, the Malecón, the Alameda de Paula, and the Avenida de las Misiónes. Several of the drives, notably the Avenida del Puerto, extend along the edge of the bay. Notable buildings include the national Capitol, a white limestone structure similar in design to the United States Capitol, the Capitanía, administrative headquarters of the captain of the port, the presidential palace, and the University of Havana. Besides Morro Castle, the outstanding historic landmarks are the former convent of Santa Clara, constructed in 1644; El Castillo de la Real Fuerza (called La Fuerza), a fortress built between 1565 and 1583 and once the headquarters of the Spanish colonial governors; the Cathedral of the Immaculate Conception, dating from 1656; the city post office, originally the Church of San Francisco, which dates from 1575; the Castillo del Principe, another old fortress, now used as the city jail; and the City Hall, a former palace of the colonial governors, completed in 1792 and generally regarded as the best example of Spanish colonial architecture in Cuba. Among the principal public parks of Havana are the Plaza de la Fraternidad, the Parque Central, and the Parque de Colón. The city has a number of notable educational and cultural institutions, including, besides the University of Havana, the former Catholic University of Saint Thomas of Villanova, now the Makerenko Institute for teachers, the Municipal Conservatory of Music, the National Museum, and the National Library.

History. Founded in 1515 on the site of the modern town of Batabaño by the Spanish administrator Diego Rodríguez de Silva y Velásquez (q.v.), Havana was transferred to its present location in 1519. The excellent harbor and strategic location of the settlement made it the chief Spanish naval station in the New World, the port at which Spanish treasure ships assembled before the voyage back to Spain. As a result, during the late 16th and early 17th centuries Havana was often under siege by English, Dutch, and French pirates. By the time of the French and Indian War (q.v.) the city had been heavily fortified and enclosed within a wall, but in August, 1762, Havana was captured by a British fleet. In the following year the city was restored to Spain in exchange for Spanish holdings in present-day Florida, and, under easier trade restrictions from the mother country, Havana prospered as a commercial center. In February, 1898, the battleship U.S.S. *Maine* was accidentally blown up in Havana harbor, and during the ensuing Spanish-American War (q.v.) the port was blockaded by the U.S. fleet. Under the U.S. military administration, which assumed control of Havana after defeating Spain, Havana again flourished commercially. In addition, sanitary conditions were improved (*see* GORGAS, WILLIAM CRAWFORD) and many areas of the city were rebuilt and modernized. For the history of Havana after 1898, *see* CUBA: *History.* Pop. (1966 est.) 990,000.

HAVANA, UNIVERSITY OF, institution of higher learning, located in Havana, Cuba. The university is under the jurisdiction of the ministry of education and is financed by the national government. Authorized by a papal bull in 1721, the university was established in 1728 by the Dominican convent of San Juan de Létran. The university was secularized and expanded in 1842. The constitution of 1940 guaranteed legal and financial autonomy. The university consists of the faculties of science, humanities, medicine, agriculture and veterinary medicine, and engineering. A course of study lasting four to seven years leads either to the *licentiatura* or to a professional diploma and represents the equivalent of American baccalaureate-degree work. Postgraduate studies in a number of fields lead to the *doctorado,* the equivalent of an American degree of master, after about two more years of study. The university libraries contain more than 383,000 bound volumes. In 1968–69 the student body numbered about 24,000 and the faculty, about 3145.

HAVASUPAI, American Indian tribe of northwestern Arizona, linguistically of the Yuman (q.v.) stock. The Havasupai are essentially a nomadic tribe, spending the spring and summer months in Cataract Canyon, a branch of the Grand Canyon (q.v.), and the fall and winter on the plateau above it.

Although a small tribe, said to comprise only 185 members, the Havasupai have a singular freedom from culture contacts. Living at the bottom of a canyon isolated from the outside world by barriers of rock, and almost entirely self-supporting, they have preserved their indigenous culture to a greater degree than any other tribe in the Southwest, and their basket weaving, language, and customs have been the objects of considerable study.

HAVDALAH. *See* PRAYER, JEWISH.

HAVERFORD

HAVERFORD, township of Pennsylvania, in Delaware Co., between Cobbs and Darby creeks, 7 miles N.W. of downtown Philadelphia, of which it is a residential suburb. Manufactures include machine parts, chemicals, electronic equipment, glass products, and chewing gum. Haverford is composed of chiefly residential communities, including Llanerch, Manoa, South Ardmore, Oakmont, Brookline, Bon Air, and Penfield. It is often considered a single urban unit and referred to as Havertown, to distinguish it from the adjoining unincorporated village of Haverford, in Lower Merion township, Montgomery County. Haverford College (1833) lies partly in the township. Pop. (1960) 54,019; (1970) 55,132.

HAVERHILL, city of Massachusetts, in Essex Co., at the head of navigation of the Merrimack R., 3 miles S. of the New Hampshire boundary and 33 miles N. of Boston. Haverhill is served by a railroad, and is an important manufacturing, shipping, and trading center of an extensive dairying and agricultural area embracing part of N. Massachusetts and S. New Hampshire. Haverhill, the site of a tannery as early as 1642, has long been a leading shoe-manufacturing center. Other important industries are the manufacture of leather goods, hats, boxboard, and communications equipment. The city is the site of Bradford Junior College for women, founded in 1803 as Bradford Academy. The birthplace of the American poet John Greenleaf Whittier (q.v.) is maintained as a public shrine. The house, built in 1688, was described by Whittier in his rural idyll *Snow-Bound*. The John Ward House (1641) stands on the grounds of the Haverhill Historical Society.

Prior to the arrival of the first English settlers from Ipswich, Mass., in 1640, an Indian village known as Pentucket, "The Place by the Winding River", stood on the site of Haverhill. The present name, for Haverhill in England, was adopted in 1645. As a frontier town in colonial days, Haverhill was long harassed by Indian raids. Hannah Dustin (1657–1730?), a mother of eight captured during one such attack in 1697, escaped after scalping nine of her captors; a monument to her is opposite the city hall. In 1708 a French and Indian force killed sixteen of the inhabitants. Haverhill was incorporated as a town in 1641 and as a city in 1869. Pop. (1960) 43,346; (1970) 46,120.

HAVERSTRAW, village of New York, in Rockland Co., on Haverstraw Bay, an expansion of the Hudson R., 32 miles N. of New York City. The village lies at the foot of Little Tor and High Tor, the latter hill rising to a height of 832 ft. The principal industries in Haverstraw are traprock quarrying and the manufacture of clothing.

A stone marker indicates the site of the meeting between the American soldier and traitor Benedict Arnold and the British major John André (qq.v.) on the night of Sept. 22, 1780, to plan the surrender of the American garrison at West Point (q.v.). The region around Haverstraw abounds in additional landmarks of the American Revolution. Haverstraw was first settled by Dutch colonists about the middle of the 17th century and was incorporated as the village of Warren in 1854. The present name was adopted in 1873. Pop. (1960) 5771; (1970) 8198.

HAVRE, city in Montana, and county seat of Hill Co., on the Milk R., near Fresno Reservoir about 103 miles N.E. of Great Falls. Havre has light manufacturing. It is the site of Northern Montana College, founded in 1913. Nearby is a State agricultural experiment station. Pop. (1960) 10,740; (1970) 10,558.

HAVRE, LE. See LE HAVRE.

HAWAII, Pacific State of the United States. The State consists primarily of the Hawaiian Islands, an archipelago of the North Pacific Ocean, and includes also Palmyra Island and several other islets unrelated geographically to the archipelago. Situated near the geographic center of the North Pacific Ocean, the Hawaiian Islands lie within the area bounded by 28°25' N. lat. on the N., by 154°48' W. long. on the E., by 18°55' N. lat. on the S., and by 178°25' W. long. on the W. The archipelago is composed of some twenty islets and islands, of which eight are inhabited. In the order of size, the inhabited islands are Hawaii, Maui, Oahu, Kauai, Molokai, Lanai, Niihau, and Kahoolawe.

Area (47th State in rank)	6450 sq.mi.
Land	6425 sq.mi.
Inland water	25 sq.mi.
Population	(1970, 40th in rank) 768,561
	(1960, 43rd in rank) 632,772
	(1950) 499,794
Altitude	sea level to 13,796 ft
Capital and largest city	Honolulu (1970) 324,871
Entered Union (50th State)	Aug. 21, 1959
Nickname	The Aloha State
Motto	Ua Mau Ke Ea O Ka Aina I Ka Pono
(The Life of the Land Is Perpetuated in Righteousness)
Song (not official)	"Hawaii Ponoi"
Tree	Kukui
Flower	hibiscus
Bird	nene (Hawaiian goose)

THE LAND

All of the larger islands of the archipelago are mountainous and of volcanic origin. Hawaii, the largest (4021 sq.mi.) and southernmost of the islands, is the top of a gigantic submerged mountain. It contains four volcanic peaks: Mauna Kea (q.v.), now extinct, the highest peak (13,796 ft) in the islands; the dormant Hualalai; Mauna Loa (13,680 ft.), an active volcano; and Kilauea (q.v.

A catamaran, modern version of the ancient outrigger canoe, arrives at Waikiki Beach. Diamond Head, a famous promontory, rises in the distance.
Hawaii Visitors Bureau

which has the largest active crater in the world. Maui (720 sq.mi.), the second-largest island, is a flat isthmus connecting two mountains; in the E. is Haleakala (q.v.), the largest extinct crater known to man; and in the W. is Puu Kukui (5790 ft.). Oahu, although ranking third in size (589 sq.mi.), is the most important island of Hawaii. It was once two great volcanoes, which erosion has reduced to mountain ranges: the Koolau (highest point, 3105 ft.) along the N.E. coast, and the Waianae Range (highest point, Kaala, 4030 ft.) along the S.W. The central plateau between the mountains is fertile and cultivated. Kauai (551 sq.mi.) is a mountainous island with two peaks, Kawaikini and Waialeale, in the center. Kauai has several short streams and thus is the only island among the Hawaiian group that can be said to have rivers.

Climate. The inhabited islands of Hawaii lie within the tropical zone, but the climate is tempered by the prevailing N.E. trade winds. The mean annual temperature in the vicinity of Honolulu is 74.9° F., with extremes of about 71.5° F. in January and about 78.3° F. in August.

Climate	Honolulu
Normal temperatures (in °F.)	
January maximum	79.1
January minimum	65.8
July maximum	84.6
July minimum	73.0
Annual	75.9
Normal precipitation (in inches)	
Wettest month	3.76
Driest month	0.33
Annual	21.89

Temperatures as high as 98° F. and as low as 25° F. are frequently recorded in the islands, the lower temperatures occurring at extreme elevations. Wide variations of climatic conditions, especially rainfall, result from the mountainous terrain. Maximum precipitation occurs on the windward slopes of the islands. Rainfall totaling 200 in. annually is common in these regions, and

HAWAII

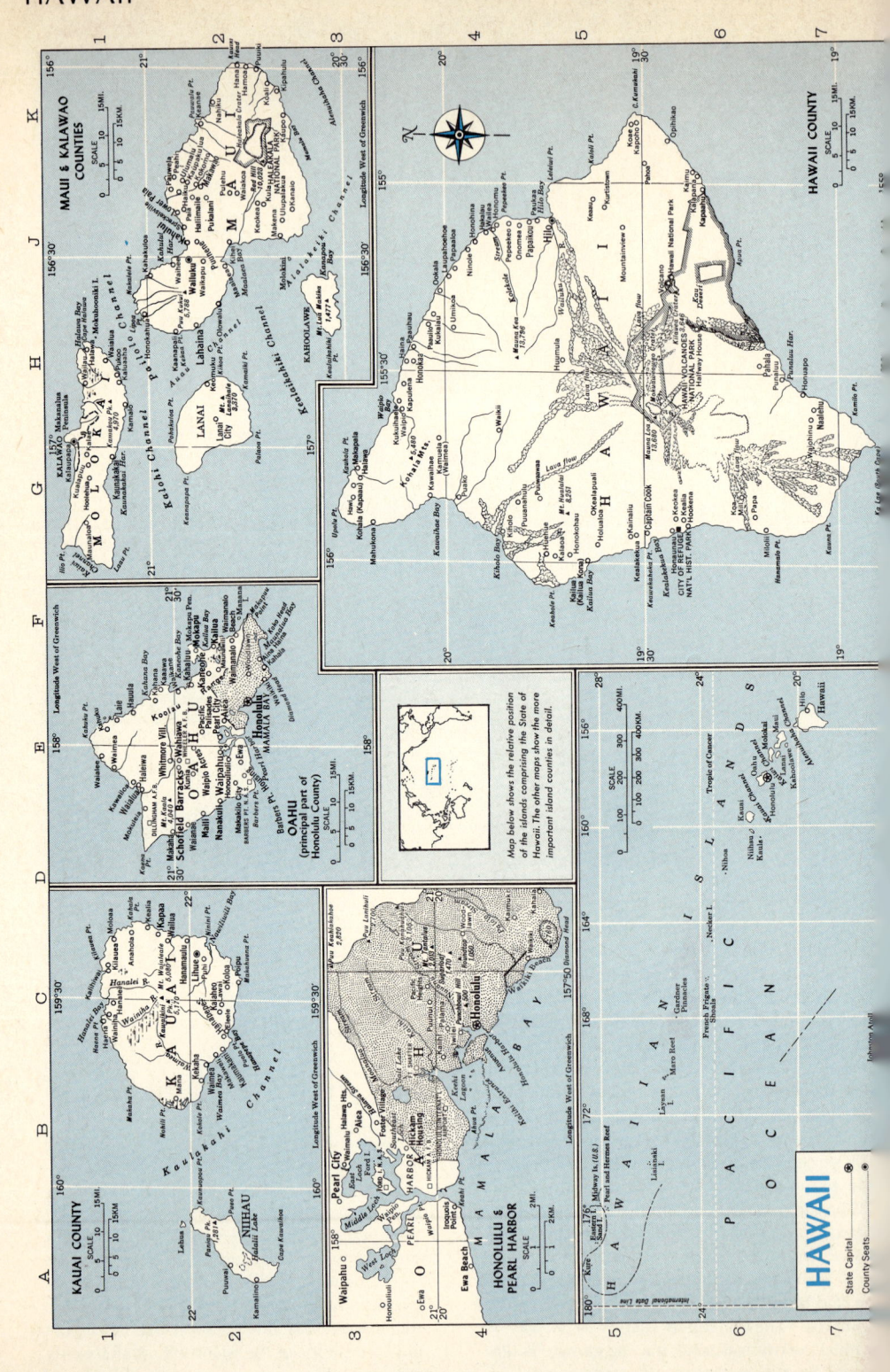

HAWAII

INDEX TO MAP OF HAWAII

Cities and Towns

Aiea	B 3
Aina Haina	F 2
Anahola	C 1
Barbers Pt. Housing	B 3
Captain Cook	G 5
Eleele	C 2
Ewa	A 4
Ewa Beach	A 4
Foster Village	B 3
Haena	C 1
Haiku	H 3
Hakalau	J 7
Halawa	G 3
Halawa Heights	B 3
Haleiwa	E 1
Halfway House	H 6
Haliimaile	H 2
Hana	C 1
Hanalei	C 2
Hanamaulu	E 1
Hanapepe	E 1
Hauula	H 1
Hawaii National Park	G 5
Hawi	G 3
Hickam Housing	B 4
Hilo ⊙	J 7
Holualoa	G 5
Honaunau	G 6
Honohina	H 4
Honokaa	H 1
Honokohau	G 5
Honolulu ⊙	C 4
Honomu	J 5
Hoolehua	G 1
Iroquois Point	A 4
Kaaawa	F 1
Kaanapali	J 1
Kahakuloa	E 2
Kahaluu	J 2
Kahuku	G 1
Kahului	J 2
Kailua	F 2
Kailua (Kailua Kona)	F 5
Kainaliu	G 1
Kalae	G 5
Kalaheo	D 5
Kalaoa	J 6
Kalapana ⊙	C 1
Kalaupapa ⊙	C 1
Kalihiwai	C 1
Kaluaaha	H 7

Kamalo	H 1
Kamuela	G 3
Kaneohe	F 2
Kapaa	D 1
Kapaau (Kohala)	C 3
Kapoho	K 5
Kapulena	H 4
Kaumakani	E 2
Kaunakakai	H 6
Kaupakulua	G 4
Kawaihae	E 1
Keaau (Olaa)	J 7
Keaau	J 5
Kealakekua	G 5
Kealia	B 3
Keanae	G 6
Kekaha	E 1
Keokea	K 2
Keokea	H 2
Kihei	C 1
Kilauea	C 2
Kipahulu	K 2
Koae	K 5
Koali	K 2
Kohala (Kapaau)	G 3
Kokomo	K 2
Koloa	C 2
Kualapuu	G 1
Kukaiau	H 4
Kukuihaele	H 3
Kula	J 2
Kunia	E 2
Kurtistown	J 5
Lahaina	E 1
Laie	H 2
Lanai City	A 1
Laupahoehoe	F 1
Lawai	C 2
Lihue ⊙	J 7
Lower Paia	J 7
Maalaea	E 2
Mahukona	D 2
Maili	D 2
Makaha	D 2
Makakilo City	G 3
Makapala	K 2
Makawao	G 2
Makaweli	G 5
Maunaloa	G 6
Mililani	E 2
Milolii	D 1
Mokapu	D 1
Mokuleia	A 3
Moloaa	E 2
Mountainview	J 5
Naalehu	H 7

Nanakuli	D 2
Ninole	J 4
Olowalu	H 2
Onomea	J 4
Ookala	H 4
Paauilo	H 4
Pacific Palisades	E 2
Pahala	H 6
Pahoa	J 5
Paia	J 2
Papaaloa	J 5
Papaikou	J 5
Paukaa	K 1
Pauwela	B 3
Peahi	J 2
Pearl City	B 4
Pepeekeo	K 2
Poipu	C 2
Puhi	H 1
Pukalani	J 7
Pukoo	G 4
Pulehu	K 2
Punaluu	K 5
Puuanahulu	G 3
Puuiki	K 2
Puunene	G 5
Puuwaawaa	A 2
Puuwai	G 1
Schofield Barracks	H 4
Spreckelsville	J 5
Ulupalakua	J 3
Volcano	E 2
Wahiawa	J 7
Waiakoa	E 1
Waialee	J 7
Waialua	D 2
Waianae	J 4
Wahee	D 2
Waikapu	H 4
Waikiki	C 4
Wailau	H 1
Wailea	J 7
Wailua ⊙	D 2
Wailuku	B 3
Waimanalo Beach	F 2
Waimea	B 3
Waimea (Kamuela)	G 3
Wainiha	C 1
Waiohinu	G 7
Waipahu	B 4
Waipio Acres	E 3
Whitmore Village	E 1

Physical Features

Ahua (point)	B 4
Alalakeiki (channel)	J 3
Alenuihaha (channel)	E 7
Anuenue (isl.)	C 4
Apua (point)	J 6
Auau (channel)	H 2
Barbers (point)	E 2
Barbers Point Naval Air Station	E 2
City of Refuge Nat'l Hist. Park	G 6
Diamond (head)	C 5
Dillingham A.F.B.	D 1
East Loch (inlet)	B 3
Ford (isl.)	B 3
Ford Island Naval Air Station	B 3
Fort Shafter	C 6
French Frigate (shoal)	C 6
Gardner Pinnacles (isl.)	C 6
Haena (point)	C 1
Halalii (lake)	A 2
Halawa (point)	H 1
Halawa (cape)	H 1
Halawa (stream)	B 3
Haleakala (crater)	K 2
Haleakala Nat'l Park	K 2
Hanalei (bay)	C 1
Hanalei (river)	G 4
Hanamalo (point)	F 7
Hawaii (isl.)	H 5
Hawaii Volcanoes Nat'l Park	H 6
Hickam A.F.B.	B 4
Hilo (bay)	J 5
Honolulu (harbor)	C 4
Honolulu Int'l Airport	B 4
Hualalai (mt.)	G 5
Ilio (point)	G 1
Ka Lae (South) (cape)	G 7
Kaala (mt.)	E 1
Kaena (point)	D 1
Kahana (bay)	B 1
Kahoolawe (isl.)	E 1
Kahului (harbor)	H 3
Kailua (bay)	F 2
Kailua (bay)	B 4
Kaiwi (channel)	F 2
Kalihi (stream)	F 5
Kalihi Entrance (strait)	E 6
Kalohi (channel)	C 3

Kaloli (point)	B 4
Kamaiki (point)	G 1
Kamakou (mt.)	H 2
Kamilo (point)	J 3
Kanapou (bay)	J 7
Kaneohe (bay)	J 6
Kau (desert)	E 6
Kauai (channel)	C 1
Kauhola (point)	G 3
Kauiki (head)	K 2
Kaula (isl.)	D 6
Kaulakahi (channel)	G 7
Kauna (point)	G 2
Kaunakakai (harbor)	B 2
Kaunuopou (point)	A 2
Kawaihae (bay)	C 1
Kawaihoa (cape)	F 5
Keahole (point)	H 3
Kealaikahiki (channel)	F 6
Kealaikahiki (point)	B 4
Kealakekua (bay)	H 2
Keanapapa (point)	F 5
Keawekaheka (point)	B 4
Kechi (lagoon)	F 2
Kekaa (point)	F 4
Kiholo (bay)	B 5
Kikoa (point)	H 2
Kilauea (crater)	A 2
Kilauea (point)	C 1
Kohala (mts.)	G 4
Koko (head)	B 2
Kokole (point)	F 2
Kolekole (mt. range)	J 4
Koolau (mt. range)	E 2
Kumukahi (cape)	K 5
Kure (isl.)	A 5
Laau (point)	G 1
Lanai (isl.)	H 2
Lanaihae (mt.)	B 5
Laysan (isl.)	G 5
Lehua (isl.)	G 1
Leleiwi (point)	K 5
Lipoa (point)	H 1
Lisianski (isl.)	B 5
Lua Makika (mt.)	J 3
Maalaea (bay)	D 1
Makaha (point)	D 1
Makahuena (pen.)	B 1
Makanalua (pen.)	E 1
Makapu (point)	F 2
Mamala (bay)	B 2
Mamalu (bay)	B 4
Manana (isl.)	K 3
Maro (reef)	C 6
Maui (isl.)	B 4
Mauna Kea (mt.)	H 4

Mauna Loa (mt.)	G 5
Maunalua (bay)	F 2
Middle Loch (inlet)	A 3
Mokapu (pen.)	B 3
Moanalua (stream)	F 2
Mokuaweoweo (crater)	H 6
Mokuhoonlki (isl.)	G 1
Molokai (isl.)	J 7
Molokini (isl.)	J 2
Nakalele (point)	D 2
Nawiliwili (bay)	D 6
Necker (isl.)	A 2
Niihau (isl.)	B 1
Ninini (point)	C 4
Nohili (point)	H 1
Nuuanu (stream)	C 4
Oahu (isl.)	E 2
Pailolo (channel)	H 1
Palaoa (point)	D 4
Palolo (stream)	B 1
Paniau (mt.)	C 4
Pauwalu (point)	K 2
Pauwela (point)	A 2
Pearl (harbor)	K 1
Pearl and Hermes (reef)	A 3
Pepeekeo (point)	B 5
Pohakuloa (point)	H 2
Pueo (point)	A 2
Punchbowl (hill)	H 7
Punaluu (harbor)	C 2
Puolo (point)	C 2
Puu Keahiakahoe (mt.)	D 3
Puu Konahuanui (mt.)	D 3
Puu Kukui (mt.)	J 7
Puu Lanihuli (mt.)	D 3
Red Hill (mt.)	K 4
Roundtop (mt.)	C 4
Salt (lake)	H 2
Shafter, Fort	B 3
South (Ka Lae) (cape)	G 7
Southeast Loch (inlet)	B 3
Sugarloaf (hill)	C 4
Tantalus (mt.)	D 4
Upolu (point)	G 3
Waialeale (mt.)	C 1
Waikiki (beach)	C 4
Wailuku (river)	J 5
Waimanalo (beach)	F 2
Waimea (bay)	B 2
Waimea (river)	C 1
Wainiha (river)	C 1
Waipio (pen.)	A 3
Waipio (point)	A 3
West Loch (inlet)	A 3
Wheeler A.F.B.	E 1

⊙ County seat.

231

Powerful waves strike the shore of Molokai, an island still almost entirely in its natural state.
Canadian Pacific Airlines

the mean annual rainfall near the summit of Mt. Waialeale (5170 ft.), on Kauai Island, is 444 in., one of the highest recorded averages in the world. Precipitation on the leeward sides of the mountains is generally low. In the vicinity of Honolulu, for example, the mean annual rainfall is about 28.5 inches.

Plants and Animals. The Hawaiian Islands have extremely varied flora, including more than 900 species of flowering plants, about 140 species of ferns, and many other indigenous varieties of plant life. Imported species, highly cultivated for food or industrial purposes, include sugarcane, pineapple, taro, banana, yam, breadfruit, coconut, papaya, olona, tobacco, sisal, candlenut, mango, citrus fruits, and coffee.

The only native land mammal of the islands is a species of bat. The Hawaiian monk seal is a marine species found only in the islands. Bird life is abundant. Several species of lizards comprise the reptilian fauna. Land and freshwater gastropods are exceptionally varied and numerous. The coastal waters teem with fish, of which there are more than 600 species.

Parks and Other Places of Interest. Hawaii has three national parks: Haleakala National Park, on Maui; and Hawaii Volcanoes National Park and City of Refuge National Historical Park (qq.v.), both on Hawaii. The National Memorial Cemetery of the Pacific, in Punchbowl Crater, Oahu, is the resting place of 14,000 dead of World War II and Korea. Other places of interest in Hawaii include Pearl Harbor (q.v.), on Oahu, the U.S. naval base attacked by the Japanese on Dec. 7, 1941, bringing the U.S. into World War II. Also on Oahu are the world-famous Waikiki Beach, and Diamond Head, an extinct crater overlooking Honolulu. On Molokai is the leper colony where the Belgian missionary Father Damien (q.v.) devoted his life to caring for the patients. On Kauai is Waimea Canyon, called by Hawaiians the "little Grand Canyon".

Sports. Hawaii offers excellent saltwater fishing in the waters around the islands; species include marlin, bonito, dolphin, swordfish, and tuna. Four species of freshwater fish—rainbow trout, largemouth and smallmouth bass, and bluegill sunfish—have been introduced into the streams, estuaries, and reservoirs. Game animals hunted are Axis deer, feral sheep, feral goat, feral pig, and numerous game birds, including

Hawaii. Plate 1. Lava fountains, typical of volcanic activity in Hawaii, enhance the natural beauty of the islands. Above: A 1955 fountain eruption of Kilauea, on the island of Hawaii. Below: Lava fountains from Kilauea in 1969, a year in which the erupting lava built a new volcanic shield 300 ft. high.   National Parks Service

U.S. Geological Survey

Statue of King Kamehameha I, founder of a Hawaiian dynasty that endured for about a century, until 1872. The monument is a tourist attraction in the civic center of Honolulu.

Hawaii. Plate

Hawaiian girl, adorned with flowers, displays some of the tropical fruits that abound in the islands.

Pictures Plate 2, United Air Lines

HAWAII

pheasant, quail, dove, and partridge. Although Mauna Loa presents few challenges to the experienced mountain climber, it is perhaps the most unusual climb in the national park system for the tourist-hiker; the trail winds 18 mi. through lava fields to the summit of the volcano.

THE PEOPLE

According to the 1970 decennial census, the population of Hawaii was 768,561, an increase of 21.5 percent over the 1960 population. The urban segment comprised 638,683 persons, 83.1 percent of the total, compared with 76.5 percent in 1960. The rural segment comprised 129,878 persons, 16.9 percent of the total, compared with 23.5 percent in 1960. Ethnically, the 1970 population was distributed as follows: white persons, 298,160; nonwhites, 470,401, including 217,307 Japanese, 93,915 Filipinos, 52,039 Chinese, 7573 Negroes, and about 100,000 others. The percentage of native-born residents was about 90.2; of foreign-born, 9.8. The major countries of origin of the foreign-born were Japan, China, and Canada. The 1970 population density averaged 119.6 per sq.mi., compared with 98.5 in 1960.

The chief cities are Honolulu, on Oahu Island, the capital, largest city, and principal port; and Hilo, on Hawaii Island, the second-largest city, center of the flower industry.

Education. The public-school system of Hawaii was established in 1840. Education is free and compulsory for all children between the ages of six and sixteen.

ELEMENTARY AND SECONDARY SCHOOLS. In 1970 public elementary schools numbered about 145 and public secondary schools about 50. Enrollment in 1971 was about 130,000 in elementary and about 53,000 in secondary schools. Teachers in the public-school system in 1972 numbered more than 4750 in elementary and about 3300 in secondary schools. In 1970 private institutions numbered more than 65 elementary and more than 25 secondary schools; enrollment in 1971 was about 17,000 elementary and 1100 secondary students. Teachers in private schools numbered about 1200 in the late 1960's.

UNIVERSITIES AND COLLEGES. In the early 1970's Hawaii had a university and college enrollment of about 37,000. The University of Hawaii, which is State-supported, administers the Center for Cultural and Technical Interchange between East and West, founded in 1960 as an international training facility and college. The State also maintains five public two-year community colleges. Private institutions include Chaminade College, Honolulu Christian College, the Church College of Hawaii, and Maunaolu College, as well as several business and technical schools.

LIBRARIES AND MUSEUMS. The Library of Hawaii, in Honolulu, has about 400,000 volumes. Cultural institutions include the Thomas A. Jaggar Memorial Museum, on the island of Hawaii, with natural history exhibits; the Lyman House Memorial Museum, on Hilo, displaying missionary relics; and, in Honolulu, the Bishop Museum, with collections of Pacific arts and artifacts and a center for ethnological research; the Honolulu Academy of Arts; and the Queen Emma Museum, featuring memorabilia of the Hawaiian monarchy and housed in the queen's summer palace. Of special interest is Ulu Mau Village, in Honolulu, a restoration of a chief's village. Honolulu supports a symphony orchestra and a community theater.

THE ECONOMY

The economy of Hawaii differs from that of other States. More than 63 percent of all personal income is derived from private nonfarm sources, almost 34 percent from governmental sources (including social security and military benefits), and a little more than 3 percent from agriculture. In the mid-1960's the largest amount of wage income derived from any one source was paid by the military. Lesser amounts of wages were paid, in descending order, by other national and local governmental sources, wholesale and retail trade, and services. More than 27 percent of nonfarm workers are employed by government. The number of tourists visiting Hawaii each year increased by 493 percent between 1957 and 1967. The annual tourist expenditure in the State is about $460,000,000.

Manufacturing. According to the most recent Census of Manufactures (1967), production workers in Hawaii totaled 19,000; the largest groups were employed in food-processing plants and in printing and publishing. Almost three quarters were employed in the Standard Metropolitan Statistical Area (q.v.) of Honolulu, and most of these worked in the city of Honolulu. The value added by manufacture (see VALUE) in the largest industries totaled $186,000,000 for food and kindred products, $27,000,000 for printing and publishing, and $18,400,000 for stone, clay, and glass products. In the rapidly growing construction industry, the value of completed construction soared from $134,000,000 in 1957 to $442,000,000 in 1968. According to the most recent published figures, the value added by all manufacture in Hawaii in 1969 was $351,000,000.

Agriculture. The agriculture of Hawaii is diversified, with concentration on sugarcane, pine-

235

Dole Photo

Agriculture in Hawaii. Above: An aerial view of a pineapple plantation. The fields are terraced and contour-planted in an effort to combat soil erosion. Below: A diesel engine hauls cane on a huge sugar plantation. Modern equipment and methods have contributed to the growth of the Hawaiian sugar industry.

Marking Hawaiian history. Right: The waves along Waikiki Beach attract surfers from all over the globe. Below: The airmail stamp issued in Honolulu on Aug. 21, 1959 commemorates the admission of Hawaii into the Union. Bottom: Iolani Palace, home of the 19th-century native rulers and the original State capitol, is now a museum.

UPI

Hawaii Visitors Bureau UPI

HAWAII

apple, cattle, and dairy products, in order of value. The principal field crops are sugarcane and pineapple. In the late-1960's, according to latest available statistics, Hawaii ranked first among the States in production of sugarcane for sugar and seed. Among minor crops, macadamia nuts are growing in quantity and commercial importance. Farms numbered about 4600 in 1970, totaling some 2,340,000 acres and averaging 509 acres each. Cash income from crops, livestock, and government payments in 1968 was $215,762,000.

Fishing. The major catch of the Hawaiian fisheries is tuna. The catch varies from year to year; in 1970, a high point, it reached 11,000,000 lb. (tuna catch, 8,500,000 lb.) and a value of $4,000,000.

Mining. The principal minerals produced in Hawaii, in order of value, are stone, cement, sand and gravel, and pumice. In the early 1970's, according to the latest available statistics, mineral production was valued at $29,000,000 annually, representing less than 1 percent of all U.S. mineral production. In quantity of production, the State ranked fourth in pumice. The major deposits of the raw materials for cement are located in Honolulu County; of stone and pumice, in Hawaii County; and of sand and gravel in Maui County.

Forestry. The forest land of Hawaii consists predominantly of hardwoods. Primarily under private ownership, the forest land comprises some 1,000,000 acres. It produces a net annual cut of sawtimber of about 11,000,000 bd.ft.

Transportation. The first railroad in Hawaii was the Oahu Railway & Land Co., inaugurated on Nov. 16, 1889, and since abandoned. The only railroad in the State is the Kahului R.R., with 25 mi. of track. Rural and municipal roads totaled 3529 mi. in 1970. Highways of the Federally aided Interstate Highway System totaled 52 mi. in 1970; Federally aided primary and secondary roads totaled 1118. Airports numbered about 58 in 1971, and 7 airlines provided trunk and interisland service in the late 1960's. Among 7 major seaports are Seward and Honolulu.

Communications. The first newspaper in Hawaii was a small religious paper, founded in 1834; the first secular paper was the *Sandwich Island Gazette,* founded in 1836. The State in 1971 had five daily newspapers and two Sunday papers. Among the leading papers were the Honolulu *Star-Bulletin* and *Advertiser.* Of twenty-eight AM and four FM (one educational) radio stations, the earliest was KGU, founded in 1922 in Honolulu. Four television stations were in operation.

GOVERNMENT

Hawaii is governed under the constitution of 1950, as amended. Executive authority is vested in a governor and lieutenant governor, elected for four-year terms; an attorney general, appointed by the governor; and other appointed officials. Legislative authority is exercised by the Senate, with twenty-five members elected for four-year terms; and the House of Representatives, with fifty-one members elected for two-year terms. The legislature meets annually. The judicial system includes a five-member supreme court, circuit courts, and district courts. The State has four counties.

Hawaii is represented in the United States Congress by two Senators and two Representatives.

Voting Qualifications. Suffrage is extended generally to U.S. citizens eighteen years of age who have resided one year in the State and three months in the election district.

HISTORY

Hawaii was originally settled by Polynesians, who probably migrated from southeastern Asia around the 6th century in large seagoing canoes. In later centuries a feudal system of land ownership akin to that of medieval Europe arose, under which lands on the islands as well as fishing rights in the coastal waters were owned by chiefs, who allotted smaller portions to commoners to till for them and took part of the produce. A system of taboos (*see* TABOO) regulated relations between commoners and chiefs. Interisland warfare was frequent.

The British explorer James Cook (q.v.) was the first European recorded to have visited the archipelago. Cook, who landed at Kauai on January 18, 1778, named the group the Sandwich Islands, in honor of the Earl of Sandwich. At that time, political sovereignty in the islands was divided among four native monarchs. Between 1782 and 1810, Kamehameha I (1739?–1819), the king of Hawaii, extended his rule over the other islands. The dynasty established by Kamehameha, a wise, capable ruler, endured until 1872. In the interim, the Hawaiian kingdom came increasingly under the influence of Western civilization, particularly after the arrival, beginning in 1820, of missionaries from New England. Among other things, the missionaries devised a written form for the Polynesian language, taught many of the islanders to read and write, and converted large numbers of them to Christianity. Constitutional rule was adopted in the kingdom in 1840, and twelve years later the royal government was liberalized. For more than two decades after the death of Kamehameha V (1830–

Hawaii. Plate 3. *Views of the island of Oahu. Above: Sunset on the beach at Waikiki, outside of Honolulu. Below: The 760-ft. Diamond Head, an extinct volcano and famous Hawaiian landmark, dominates the horizon behind a luxury hotel outside the capital.*

United Air Lines

Hawaii. Plate 4. Nuuanu Pali, a 1200-ft. high pass on the island of Oahu. Cutting through the Nuuanu Valley, perhaps the most beautiful area of the islands, the pass faces sheer rocks often 2000 ft. high.

United Air Lines

HAWAII VOLCANOES NATIONAL PARK

72), the last of the dynasty, the kingdom was torn by political strife, a result of royalist attempts to usurp constitutional rule. The constitutional movement, supported mainly by foreigners who favored annexation of the kingdom by the United States, effected the deposition of Queen Liliuokalani (1838–1917) on January 17, 1893, and the organization of a provisional government. The American diplomat James Henderson Blount (1837–1903) was appointed special commissioner to the islands by President Grover Cleveland (q.v.) in 1893. After investigating the crisis Blount reported against the provisional government. Failing to secure approval of the annexation project from President Cleveland, the constitutionalists, led by Sanford Ballard Dole (q.v.), proclaimed on July 4, 1894, establishment of the Hawaiian Republic. The movement for annexation continued, and on July 6, 1898, the Congress of the United States approved the necessary legislation. On June 14, 1900, the islands were formally constituted as the Territory of Hawaii.

Steps Toward Statehood. A protracted movement for admission of the territory as a State was endorsed by the Hawaiian electorate by a vote of 46,174 to 22,428 in the elections of 1940. Subsequently, a bill authorizing the admission of the territories of Alaska and Hawaii as the 49th and 50th States of the U.S., respectively, was introduced into the United States Congress. The bill received the approval of the House of Representatives in 1947 and again in 1950, but the Senate failed to take action. Delegates from the various islands convened (April, 1950) in a Statehood convention and drafted a State constitution. This document was approved later in 1950 by the territorial legislature and electorate.

The United States Senate approved a bill for Hawaiian and Alaskan Statehood in 1954, but the Congress took no further action on the bill. In 1955 the bill was reintroduced in the Congress, but was rejected by the House. In March, 1959, the Congress approved the legislation granting Statehood to Hawaii. President Dwight D. Eisenhower (q.v.) issued the formal proclamation of Statehood on Aug. 21. Hawaii participated in its first Presidential election in 1960 and gave a slim majority of its votes to the Democratic candidate, John F. Kennedy (q.v.). Hawaii voted Democratic in 1964 and 1968; in 1968 Hubert Horatio Humphrey (q.v.) received 141,325 votes and the Republican candidate, Richard Milhous Nixon (q.v.), 91,425 votes. In 1972 Hawaii gave President Nixon 167,414 votes, and the Democratic candidate, Senator George S. McGovern (1922–   ) of South Dakota, 100,617.

HAWAII, largest island of the Hawaiian Islands, forming a county and two thirds of the total area of the State of Hawaii (q.v.), in the Pacific Ocean, about 2150 miles s.w. of San Francisco, Calif. The island is the southernmost and most easterly of the Hawaiian archipelago and is separated from Maui and Kahoolawe islands by the Alenuihaha Channel, a strait about 30 mi. wide. The island is triangular in shape and has a coastline of about 300 mi. Like the other islands of the Hawaiian chain, Hawaii was formed by volcanic action and is extremely mountainous. The dominant feature of the terrain is a series of volcanoes, linked by lava ridges that range from 3000 to 7000 ft. in height. The highest of the volcanoes is Mauna Kea (q.v.), 13,823 ft. above sea level, and now inactive. South of Mauna Kea is Mauna Loa, the most massive mountain in the world. Its height is 13,680 ft. Kilauea (q.v.), a volcano projecting from the side of Mauna Loa, is frequently active. A notable eruption of Kilauea, which is included with Mauna Loa in the Hawaii Volcanoes National Park (q.v.), occurred in 1959. Earthquake tremors are frequently felt in Hawaii, and seismic sea waves caused great damage in 1946 and 1960. The island has considerable scenic beauty, an equable climate, extensive transportation facilities, including a railway along the N.E. coast and motor highways, and numerous vacation resorts. Coffee, cane sugar, and pineapples are the leading products. Hilo (q.v.) is the administrative center, largest town, and principal seaport of the island. Area, 4030 sq.mi.; pop. (1960) 61,332; (1970) 63,468.

HAWAII VOLCANOES NATIONAL PARK, park on the island of Hawaii, in the State of Hawaii, which includes two active volcanoes, Mauna Loa and Kilauea (q.v.). The first, rising 13,680 ft. above sea level, is the largest volcano in mass in the world. Its summit crater, Mokuaweoweo, is more than 3 sq.mi. in extent, with walls rising to 600 ft. This crater is no longer active, but during the frequent eruptions of Mauna Loa the lava flows from newer craters on the sides of the mountain. One of the most voluminous flows in historic times lasted twenty-three days in 1950. The highly fluid lava, liberated through a fissure 13 mi. long, traveled to the sea at an average speed of 5.8 miles per hour and was sufficient in quantity to pave a four-lane highway extending four and one-half times around the earth. Kilauea (4090 ft. above sea level) projects from the slopes of Mauna Loa; its crater is the largest active volcanic crater in the world, covering 4.14 sq.mi. Within its 500-ft. walls is the vast inner pit, Halemaumau, some-

HAWK

times called the "House of Everlasting Fire". Kilauea's activity is confined to this inner pit. In 1959 a spectacular eruption produced fountains of molten lava up to 1900 ft. in height, by far the highest ever witnessed in Hawaii, and probably in the world. From 1916 until 1961 Hawaii Volcanoes National Park and Haleakala National Park (q.v.) on Maui Island constituted Hawaii National Park. Hawaii Volcanoes National Park covers 220,344.84 acres. It is administered by the National Park Service (q.v.). *See* VOLCANO.

HAWK, common name for certain birds of prey of the Hawk family Acciptridae, which also includes the eagles and kites. The hawk has a strong, curved beak, long legs with large, powerful claws, and a long tail. Contrary to popular belief, few hawks feed on poultry; although two or three species regularly eat birds, most subsist chiefly on small rodents, reptiles, and insects. The hawk is keen-sighted and most species have a loud, piercing cry. It builds bulky, loosely constructed nests of twigs and bark at the top of a high tree or on a rocky ledge. Two to six eggs are laid in a clutch.

The hawk was formerly grouped in the same family as the falcon (q.v.) from which it differs in having broad, rounded wings. In falconry (q.v.), or hawking, the falcon is known as noble hawk and the true hawk as ignoble or short-winged hawk. Many American species of falcon are today popularly called hawks because of past confusion between members of the Hawk and Falcon families. Nine genera in the Hawk family are found in North America, including buteo, eagle, harrier, and kite (qq.v.), as well as the birds commonly called hawks.

Two well-known American hawks are the sharp-shinned hawk or bird hawk, *Accipter striatus,* and Cooper's hawk, *A. cooperii,* both found throughout North America. These two hawks are unusual in that their diet consists chiefly of birds. The sharp-shinned hawk is about 1 ft. long. Above it is blue-gray; below, white, streaked with gray, black, and light orange. The tail is square-tipped. Cooper's hawk, also known as the quail or swift hawk, is similar in coloring when young to the sharp-shinned hawk; when adult it differs in having a black crown. It is from 14 to 20 in. long and has a rounded tail. Cooper's hawk eats chickens, grouse, ducks, and pigeons. The Mexican black hawk, *Buteogallus anthracinus,* is found from southern Arizona and Texas to northern South America. It is about 22½ in. long and is grayish black.

The common European hawk is the sparrow hawk, *Accipter nisus,* which is about 14 in. long

Hawks used in falconry are cast at small game such as rabbits and hares. UPI

and resembles the sharp-shinned hawk in coloring. The American sparrow hawk, *Falco sparverius,* also known as the American kestrel, is not a hawk but a falcon. It is the commonest falcon in the United States. It is about 10 in. long, and is chestnut above and tan below. The crown is red; the sides of its head are bluish. The wings of the sparrow hawk are bluish gray streaked with white. Another American falcon is the peregrine, *F. peregrinus anatum,* a subspecies of the European peregrine falcon. It is about 17 in. long, and is leaden blue above and tan below. The pigeon hawk, *F. columbarius,* is another falcon widely distributed in the U.S. It is about 11 in. long, and is bluish above and brown below.

HAWKING. *See* FALCONRY.

HAWKINS *or* **HAWKYNS,** name of an English family of seamen and merchants, of whom the most prominent are the following:

Sir John Hawkins (1532–95), admiral and privateer, born in Plymouth. In 1562, 1564, and 1567, he carried cargoes of slaves from the West African coast of the West Indies. This slave trade was a violation of Spanish laws, and in 1568, as Hawkins was preparing to return to England, he was attacked by the Spanish fleet in the harbor off Veracruz (now Veracruz Llave, Mexico). Hawkins managed to escape with two ships, but the attack convinced him that war with Spain was inevitable. In 1570 he pretended to betray Elizabeth I (q.v.), Queen of England, to the Spanish in order to gain information about the proposed Spanish invasion of England. He entered Parliament in 1571, and later served as treasurer and comptroller of the navy. He used his position to prepare the English navy for war with Spain; making a number of important improvements in ship construction and rigging, and increasing the size of the English fleet. In 1588 he served as rear admiral in command of the *Victory* during the defeat of the Armada (q.v.) of Spain, and was knighted for his service. In 1590 he made an unsuccessful voyage to the Azores in search of the Spanish silver fleet. He died on an expedition to the West Indies.

Sir Richard Hawkins (1562–1622), naval hero, the only son of Sir John, born in Plymouth. He served as a captain during the expedition of the English navigator Sir Francis Drake (q.v.) to the West Indies in 1585, and commanded the royal ship *Swallow* during the defeat of the Spanish Armada in 1588. In 1593 he began a voyage around the world with the intention of preying on the Spanish colonies in South America. After plundering the town of Valparaíso, Chile, he was captured by two Spanish ships and was imprisoned, first in Lima, Peru, and then, in 1597, in Spain. He was ransomed in 1602 and returned to England, where he was knighted in 1603. In 1604 he was elected to Parliament and in the same year he became vice admiral of Devonshire.

HAWKINS, Sir Anthony Hope, pen name ANTHONY HOPE (1863–1933), British novelist and playwright, born in London, England, and educated at the University of Cambridge. He practiced law from 1887 to 1894, when he turned to writing. He published several plays and over twenty novels throughout his career, but his fame rests on his first work, *The Prisoner of Zenda* (1894), and its sequel, *Rupert of Hentzau* (1898). Both works are light novels of adventure, intrigue, and romance set in a mythical European kingdom, and are typical of the literature popular before World War I. *The Prisoner of Zenda* was first adapted successfully for the stage in 1896 and is still performed. The novel has also been filmed several times; the most recent version was released in 1952. Hawkins was knighted in 1918 for his services in the British ministry of information during World War I.

HAWKINS, Coleman ("Bean"). See JAZZ: Modern Jazz.

HAWKMOTH or **HUMMINGBIRD MOTH** or **SPHINX MOTH,** common name for any of the large moths of the family Sphingidae, which are world-wide in distribution. The hawkmoth has a thick body, pointed at the hind end; its forewings are long, narrow, and pointed, and its hind wings are short. It averages about 1½ in. long with a wingspread of 4 to 5 in. It is a powerful and graceful flyer, and usually flies at twilight. The adults feed on nectar. The larvae, 3 to 4 in. long when fully grown, are hairless and usually have a horny projection on the last abdominal segment. They habitually assume a sphinxlike position when at rest by raising the anterior segments of their body. The larvae are leaf eaters and feed upon a large variety of herbs, vines, and trees. The larvae pupate on the ground or a few inches underground; the cocoon often has a hollow extension to accommodate the developing tongue. The larvae of several species are capable of producing squeaking sounds. A number of wasps use the hawkmoth larva to provision their young by stinging and thus paralyzing the larva, after which the female wasp lays her eggs on the larva. The eggs hatch and the immature wasp feeds on the live larva.

HAWKSBILL TURTLE or **TORTOISESHELL TURTLE,** common name for a small, carnivorous sea turtle, *Eretmochelys imbricata,* the most valuable of all the turtles. It is characterized by a hooked, beaklike upper jaw and by two pairs of large prefrontal shields on the top of the head between the eyes. Natural, commercial tortoiseshell is obtained only from these shields, which are black or dark brown in color, richly splashed with yellow. The shields are removed from the back of the turtle by the application of heat, often while the animal is still alive. The turtle usually survives such treatment and regenerates new shields which, however, are of low quality and are unfit for commercial use. Tortoiseshell turtles reach a maximum length of about 3 ft. and subsist on fish, mollusks, crustaceans, and various sea plants. They are found in all warm seas, and in the southwestern Pacific are called carets. See TURTLES AND TORTOISES.

HAWKWEED, common name of plants of the genus *Hieracium,* belonging to the Chicory family. The genus comprises about seventeen species of ray-flowered, perennial herbs, most of which are native to North America and Eurasia. The orange hawkweed, or devil's paintbrush, *H. aurantiacum,* which has basal leaves and small orange-red flowers on long, hairy stems, is a common weed in fields of the N.E. United States. It grows to a height between 8 and 30 in. The king devil, *H. pratense,* is a yellow-flowered hawkweed, having bristly basal leaves and smooth upper leaves. It grows in the same area as the orange hawkweed, ranging from 1 to 3 ft. tall. The rattlesnake weed, *H. venosum*, is a yellow-flowered species of the eastern U.S., having thin, often purple-veined leaves and growing from 1 to 3 ft. in height.

HAWKYNS. See HAWKINS, family.

HAWORTH, Sir Walter Norman (1883–1950), British chemist, born in Lancashire, England, and educated at the universities of Manchester and Göttingen. He was professor of chemistry at the University of Durham from 1920 to 1925 and after 1925, professor of chemistry at the University of Birmingham, where he was made vice principal in 1947. Haworth did outstanding research in carbohydrates and vitamins. For this work he shared the 1937 Nobel Prize in chemistry with the Russian-Swiss chemist Paul Karrer (q.v.). He was knighted in 1947.

HAWTHORN, small tree of the genus *Crataegus,* belonging to the Rose family, Rosaceae. The hawthorn, which is native to temperate regions, is widely cultivated as an ornamental, particularly in hedges. It has dense, sharply thorned branches; single, irregularly toothed leaves that turn to brilliant colors in autumn; tiny, red fruits that persist throughout the winter; and fragrant, white flowers borne in clusters. The best-known species is the English hawthorn, *C. oxyacantha,* known also as the mayflower. The numerous garden varieties of this species have white, pink, or red double flowers. Other species, native to the United States, include the Washington hawthorn, *C. phaenopyrum,* found in the South, and the cockspur hawthorn, *C. crus-galli,* an eastern species with shiny leaves and long thorns. The genus includes more than 90 species in the Old World and more than 800 in North America. Many of the latter are believed to be natural hybrids.

HAWTHORNE, suburban city of California, in Los Angeles Co., 11 miles s.w. of Los Angeles. Manufactures include chemicals, aircraft, missile and satellite equipment, toys, electrical and electronic equipment, plastic and rubber products, business machines, and carpets. The area has truck farms and produces oil. Developed early in the 20th century, Hawthorne was incorporated in 1922. Pop. (1970) 53,304.

HAWTHORNE, Nathaniel (1804–64), American novelist, born in Salem, Mass., and educated at Bowdoin College. In 1825 after graduating from college he returned to his Salem home, living in semiseclusion and writing for publication. His work received little public recognition, however, and Hawthorne attempted to destroy all copies of his first novel *Fanshawe* (1828), an unsuccessful work that he had published at his own expense. During this period he also contributed articles and a large number of short stories to magazines and other periodicals. Several of the short stories were published in the volume *Twice-Told Tales* (1837), which, although not a financial success, established Hawthorne as a leading writer. These early works are largely historical sketches and symbolic and allegorical tales, dealing with moral conflicts and the effects of Puritanism (*see* PURITANS) on colonial New England.

Hawthorne was unable to earn a living by literary work and in 1839 he took the job of weigher in the Boston customhouse. Two years later he returned to writing and produced a series of sketches of New England history for children, *Grandfather's Chair: A History for Youth* (1841). The same year he joined the communal society at Brook Farm (q.v.) near Boston, hoping to be able to live comfortably enough to marry

Nathaniel Hawthorne, a daguerreotype by the American photographer Mathew B. Brady. Granger Collection

and still have time to devote to his writing. The demands of the farm were too great, however; Hawthorne was unable to continue his writing while doing farm chores and after six months he withdrew from the community. In 1842 he married Sophia Amelia Peabody (1809–71) of Salem, and settled in Concord, Mass., in a house called the Old Manse. During the four years he lived in Concord, Hawthorne wrote a number of tales that were later collected and published as *Mosses from an Old Manse* (1846). Included in the volume were "Roger Malvin's Burial", "Rappaccini's Daughter", and "Young Goodman Brown", tales in which Hawthorne's preoccupation with the effects of pride, guilt, sin, and secrecy are combined with a continued emphasis on symbolism and allegory.

The Scarlet Letter and Later Works. In order to survive Hawthorne returned to government service in 1846 as surveyor of the Salem customhouse. After three years he was dismissed because of a change in political administration, but he had already begun writing *The Scarlet Letter* (1850), a novel that was to bring him international fame as a writer. Regarded as his masterpiece and as one of the classics of American literature, *The Scarlet Letter* reveals both Hawthorne's superb craftsmanship and the powerful psychological insight with which he was able to probe guilt and anxiety in the human soul.

In 1850 Hawthorne moved to Lenox, Mass., where he enjoyed the friendship of his admirer the American novelist Herman Melville (q.v.). At Lenox he wrote another novel, *The House of the Seven Gables* (1851), in which he traces the decadence of Puritanism in an old New England family, and two collections of stories, *A Wonder Book for Girls and Boys* (1852) and *Tanglewood Tales for Girls and Boys* (1853), retelling classical legends for children. During a short stay in West Newton, Mass., he produced *The Snow-Image and Other Twice-Told Tales* (1852), which show his continuing preoccupation with the themes of guilt and pride, and *The Blithedale Romance* (1852), a novel inspired by his life at Brook Farm.

In 1852 Hawthorne returned to Concord, where he wrote a campaign biography of his college friend Franklin Pierce (q.v.). After his election to the Presidency, Pierce rewarded Hawthorne with the consulship at Liverpool, England, a post he held until 1857. In 1858 and 1859 Hawthorne lived in Italy, collecting material for his heavily symbolic novel *The Marble Faun* (1860).

In 1860, on the eve of the American Civil War, Hawthorne returned to the United States. His isolation from current partisan politics is indicated in his dedication of his last book, *Our Old Home* (1863) to the former President, Pierce, who was highly unpopular because of his support of the Southern slave owners. Hawthorne died while traveling with Pierce in 1864 and was buried at Concord. His posthumously published works include the unfinished novels *Septimius Felton* (1872), *The Dolliver Romance* (1876), *Dr. Grimshawe's Secret* (1883), and *The Ancestral Footsteps* (1883), and his *American Notebooks* (1868), *English Notebooks* (1870), and *French and Italian Notebooks* (1871).

In all his works Hawthorne is concerned with ethical problems. With modern psychological insight he probes the secret motivations in human behavior, and the guilt and anxiety that he believed resulted from all sins against mankind, especially those of pride. In his preoccupation with sin he follows the tradition of his Puritan ancestors, but in his concept of the consequences of sin, as either punishment due to lack of humility and overwhelming pride, or regeneration by love and atonement, he deviates radically from the idea of predestination (q.v.) held by his forebears. Hawthorne's emphasis on allegory and symbolism often makes his characters seem shadowy and unreal, but his best characters reveal the emotional and intellectual ambivalence he felt to be inseparable from the Puritan heritage of America.

HAY, term applied to forage plants, such as certain grasses and legumes, used to make cured fodder for livestock. Curing may be done in the field, by barn finishing, or by artificial dehydration.

Hay that is to be field cured is cut in the morning as soon as the dew has evaporated. The hay is raked into rows, called windrows, as soon as the leaves begin to wilt. Windrows are turned with pitchforks the following day to allow the hay to dry uniformly. When the weather is favorable, field-cured hay is ready for storage in the afternoon of the day following cutting. The hay is then stored indoors in a haymow, or piled in a large outdoor heap, called a haycock. Properly cured field hay contains between 20 and 25 percent of moisture.

Barn-finished hay is incompletely dried in the field and then placed in a mow, where drying is completed by forcing natural or heated air through the hay.

In artificial dehydration, hay is taken from the field as soon as it is cut, or after it has wilted. The hay is then chopped to a suitable size and passed through a hot-air chamber which rapidly evaporates the moisture.

HAY

Proper curing is necessary for efficient preservation of hay. If hay is not dried soon after harvesting, fermentation processes reduce the quantity of carbohydrates and carotene; see CARBOHYDRATE; VITAMIN: *Vitamin A*. Excessive drying, on the other hand, results in loss of protein (q.v.).

The area devoted to the growing of hay in the United States in the mid-1960's totaled more than 65,000,000 acres; the annual yield averaged about 116,000,000 tons. For information on hay grasses and legumes, see GRASSES; LEGUME.

HAY, river of Canada, rising in the Rocky Mts. in N.E. British Columbia, and flowing N.E. through Alberta, emptying into Great Slave Lake in Mackenzie District, Northwest Territories. The Hay has a total course of about 360 mi., and is navigable for 140 mi. from its mouth. In its upper course, the flow of the river is swift, forming falls and rapids, the most notable of which are the Alexandra Falls, which have a drop of about 250 ft.

HAY, John Milton (1838–1905), American statesman and writer, born in Salem, Ind., and educated at Brown University. In 1858 he entered the law office of his uncle in Springfield, Ill. He was brought to Washington, D.C., in 1861 to serve as assistant to his friend John Nicolay (1831–1901), who was private secretary to President Abraham Lincoln (q.v.). He continued to serve the President in this capacity in the critical period of the American Civil War (q.v.) and it was during this period that he and Nicolay collected the material for the two monumental works on which they later collaborated: *Abraham Lincoln: A History* (10 vol., 1890), a critical biography that is still highly regarded today; and *Abraham Lincoln: Complete Works* (2 vol., 1894).

From 1865 to 1870 Hay held minor posts in the United States legations in Paris, Vienna, and Madrid. After his return to the U.S. he served on the editorial board of the New York *Tribune*, publishing sketches of his experiences in Spain, *Castilian Days* (1871), and a collection of poems in the dialect of the Illinois frontier, *Pike County Ballads* (1871). Except for the period 1879 to 1880 during which he served as assistant secretary of state, Hay devoted the next several years to writing, publishing (in addition to the works on Lincoln) a novel satirizing the labor-union movement in the U.S., *The Bread-Winners* (1884).

After serving (1897–98) as ambassador to Great Britain, Hay served until his death as secretary of state to Presidents William McKinley and Theodore Roosevelt (qq.v.). During this period the U.S. began to play an increasing role in international affairs, and Hay did much to protect U.S. interests especially in the Far East. He directed the peace negotiations at the close of the Spanish-American War (q.v.), securing U.S. influence in the Pacific by the annexation of the Philippines. In 1899 he initiated the Open Door (q.v.) policy in China, which guaranteed equal trade opportunities for all countries. He defined the U.S. policy even more emphatically in 1900 following the outbreak of the Boxer Rebellion (q.v.), declaring that the U.S. would continue to uphold both the territorial and administrative integrity of China and the policy of free trade. In 1903 Hay arranged for arbitration of a dispute between the U.S. and Great Britain over the boundary between Alaska and Canada. In the same year he successfully negotiated the Hay-Pauncefote Treaty (q.v.), which opened the way to American construction and management of the Panama Canal (q.v.).

HAYDN, (Franz) Joseph (1732–1809), Austrian composer, born in Rohrau, Lower Austria Province. He was educated first by an uncle, and then at the choir school of the Cathedral of Saint Stephen in Vienna, where he remained until 1749. For the next ten years he supported himself by giving music lessons and further educated himself in music. By 1760 Haydn had written his first symphony and several string quartets.

Early Recognition. In 1761, after holding two short-time positions, he entered the service of the wealthy Hungarian family of Esterházy (q.v.) as assistant music director, becoming musical director in 1766. His performances in the family palace, Esterháza, attracted the attention of the aristocrats and artists who gathered there, and by 1780 Haydn was well known throughout the courts of Europe. His musical development, marked by continual experimentation with new styles and techniques, can be traced through the 80 symphonies, 43 string quartets, most of his 23 operas, and numerous arias, songs, and liturgical works composed during his residence at Esterháza.

Haydn made two successful tours to England, in 1791–92 and 1793–94, composing and conducting twelve symphonies, all of which were enthusiastically received. The works, often called the London symphonies, are regarded as Haydn's crowning achievement. They include such famous compositions as the Symphony No. 94 in G major ("Surprise"), Symphony No. 101 in D major ("Clock"), and Symphony No. 103 in E flat major ("Drum Roll"). Conceived on a grander scale than any Haydn had yet attempted, these symphonies reveal most clearly

Joseph Haydn

the profound effect of his friendship with the young Austrian composer Wolfgang Amadeus Mozart (q.v.). The two men had established a friendship in 1781 that significantly influenced the works of both. This influence is shown in Haydn's music by an expanded harmonic range and by a rhythmic intensity not found in his earlier compositions.

After his London success Haydn returned to his positition with the Esterházy family, which had reduced the extent of its musical activities, requiring from Haydn only a yearly mass for the name day of the princess. During his last years, however, Haydn composed some of his finest chamber music and his two great oratorios, *The Creation* (1798) and *The Seasons* (1801), notable for their effective use of solo voices.

Haydn's Achievements. Haydn has been called the father of modern orchestral music. Using structural principles of the sonata form he greatly enhanced the expressive power of its various sections; see SONATA: *Sonata Form.* In the symphony (q.v.), he added a new movement, in the form of a minuet (q.v.), between the second and last movements. His expansion of the orchestra (q.v.), which in his London ensembles numbered as many as forty players, enabled him to experiment with varied techniques of orchestration (q.v.), giving the percussion added importance and using pedal tones in the bassoon or horns. Among his innovations in harmony (q.v.) were numerous compositions in such rarely used keys as C sharp, F sharp, and B major, and the introduction of modulations to keys a third away from one another.

Noted for his chamber music (q.v.), Haydn increased the intricacy of its musical structure, especially in the string quartet, where he composed extensive thematic developments for each instrument. All of his compositions, moreover, are marked by the clarity of form and the lucidity of thematic development that characterize classicism (q.v.) in music, as opposed to the ornate counterpoint (q.v.) of the baroque style, which Haydn's music largely replaced. Despite the apparent simplicity of many of his works, with their melodies often taken from folk songs and their simple and robust quality, Haydn greatly influenced subsequent composers. His structural innovations and the originality of his musical thought produced music of enduring vitality and variety. His many works include 104 symphonies, 85 string quartets, 52 piano sonatas, 4 oratorios, 14 masses, and other liturgical works, in addition to many overtures and vocal and chamber works.

See MUSIC: *History.*

HAYES, Bob, in full ROBERT LEE HAYES (1942–), American runner and football player, born in Jacksonville, Fla. In 1963, while a student at Florida Agricultural and Mechanical University, Hayes set a world record of 9.1 sec. for the 100-yd. dash. As a member of the United States team at the 1964 Olympic Games, he won the 100-meter dash by 3 yd., and equaled the world record of 10 sec. In another Olympic race, running as anchor man on the U.S. 400-meter relay team, he helped set a world record for that event. In 1965 Hayes became a professional football player with the Dallas (Texas) Cowboys of the National Football League.

HAYES, Helen (1900–), American actress, born Helen Hayes Brown in Washington, D.C. She made her theatrical debut at the age of five in Washington, where she became a popular child actress in a series of performances with a stock company. She first appeared in New York City in 1908 in a musical comedy called *Old Dutch.* With the exception of two years (1912–14) during which she attended school in Washington, Miss Hayes worked as an actress for more than sixty years. Among the milestones in her career were appearances on Broadway in *Dear Brutus* (1918), by the British playwright Sir James M. Barrie (q.v.); *Clarence* (1919), adapted from a novel by the American novelist Booth Tarkington (q.v.); *What Every Woman Knows* (1926), also by Barrie; *Mary of Scotland* (1933), by the American playwright Maxwell Anderson (q.v.); *Victoria Regina* (1935), by the British au-

HAYES, PATRICK JOSEPH

thor Laurence Housman (q.v.), perhaps her most famous role; *The Wisteria Trees* (1950), adapted by the American theatrical director Joshua Logan (q.v.) from the play *The Cherry Orchard* by the Russian dramatist Anton Chekhov (q.v.); and *Time Remembered* (1958), written by the French playwright Jean Anouilh (q.v.). In the theatrical seasons of 1966–67 and 1967–68 Miss Hayes performed with the Association of Producing Artists-Phoenix Theatre repertory company both in New York City and on tour. In addition to playing scores of roles on radio and television, she was seen in the motion pictures, including *Arrowsmith* (1931); *The Sin of Madelon Claudet* (1931), for which she received an award as the best actress of the year from the Academy of Motion Picture Arts and Sciences; *A Farewell to Arms* (1932); *Vanessa* (1935); and *Anastasia* (1956). Miss Hayes married the American playwright Charles MacArthur (1895–1956) in 1928. In 1955, to celebrate her fiftieth anniversary on the stage, the Fulton Theatre in New York City was renamed the Helen Hayes Theatre. Miss Hayes is the author of the autobiographies, *A Gift of Joy* (1965), written in collaboration with the American editor and critic Lewis Funke (1912–   ), and *On Reflection* (1968) with the American writer Sanford Dody (1918–   ).

HAYES, Patrick Joseph, Cardinal (1867–1938), American Roman Catholic prelate, born in New York City, and educated at Manhattan College and the Catholic University of America (qq.v.). He was ordained to the priesthood in 1892, and he became chancellor in 1903, and auxiliary bishop in 1914, of the archdiocese of New York. At the outbreak of World War I he was named bishop of the armed forces, an international diocese comprised of all Roman Catholics in the United States Army and Navy. A leading figure in the Catholic war effort, he was one of the four episcopal members of the executive committee of the National Catholic War Council. As archbishop in 1919, and as cardinal in 1924, Hayes did much to reorganize and administer the Catholic charities in New York City. In the 1930's he was an active foe of the newly formed American Birth Control League and of the proposed child labor (q.v.) amendment, which he regarded as a dangerous encroachment on parental rights by the Federal government.

HAYES, Roland (1887–   ), American tenor, born in Curryville, Ga., and educated at Fisk University. His American debut in 1915 was followed by a series of concert tours in both the United States and Europe that included a command performance before George V (q.v.), King of Great Britain, in 1921. Although Hayes was an outstanding performer of art songs, he was noted for his interpretation of Negro spirituals and is credited with making them well known on the concert stage. In 1925 he received the Spingarn medal, awarded annually for high achievement by an American of African descent. Hayes continued to perform until 1962 when, on his seventy-fifth birthday, he gave a special farewell concert at Carnegie Hall in New York City. He was a member of the music faculty at Boston University, and the editor of an edition of spirituals, *My Songs: Aframerican Religious Folksongs* (1948).

HAYES, Rutherford Birchard (1822–1893), nineteenth President of the United States, born in Delaware, Ohio. He attended Kenyon College and the Harvard Law School before beginning the practice of law in Cincinnati, where he

Rutherford B. Hayes — New York Historical Society

joined the newly formed Republican Party (q.v.). After serving with distinction in the American Civil War, he was elected to the United States House of Representatives and served from 1865 to 1867. He won the governorship of Ohio in 1867, and his election to that office for a third term in 1875 brought him national prominence.

An accomplished administrator, Hayes was highly regarded both by the supporters of President Ulysses Simpson Grant (q.v.) and by the reform-minded liberal elements of the party. He used his extraordinary political skill to obtain the nomination for President in 1876. In the election he received 4,036,572 popular votes and his Democratic opponent Governor Samuel Jones Tilden (q.v.) of New York received 4,284,020 popular votes. The returns, however, were disputed in three States. After much controversy, Congress appointed an electoral commission (see ELECTORAL COMMISSION OF 1877) which, by a majority of only one vote, awarded the disputed electoral votes to Hayes.

Early in his term, Hayes brought the policy of Reconstruction (q.v.) to an end by withdrawing Federal occupation troops from the former Confederate States. This move was designed to build and encourage a strong Republican Party in the South. Hayes saw it as a means of restoring the Union. He also hoped that it would protect the civil rights of the freed slaves; see CIVIL RIGHTS AND CIVIL LIBERTIES. In other matters the President supported the reform of the civil service (q.v.) and opposed inflationary policies during the depression of the 1870's. Having announced in 1876 that he desired only one term as President, he returned to Ohio at the expiration of his tenure of office, continuing to work for such causes as the education of the freed slaves in the South. N.H.C.

HAY FEVER, or POLLINOSIS, form of seasonal rhinitis (q.v.) caused by allergy to pollens. Its symptoms are intense seizures of sneezing (q.v.); inflammation of nose and eye membranes; itching of soft palate, pharynx, and ears; wheezing; and gastric disturbance. It is permanent and troublesome, but not dangerous to life. Because it is the same type of allergy associated with infantile eczema, atopic dermatitis, bronchial asthma, and some food allergies, about 30 percent of untreated susceptible persons may acquire one or more of these disabilities, especially asthma. Persons with a family history of hay fever may inherit a tendency to react, not to specific allergens, but to those to which they are exposed. Perhaps 8 to 10 percent of the United States population is variably affected.

Hay fever occurs annually at the same season. It is a reaction to inhalation of airborne pollens to which an individual is sensitive. In the spring, these pollens are released by trees; in the summer, by grasses, fungi, and grain rusts; and in the fall, by ragweeds. Goldenrod, rose, and other pollens distributed by insects generally are not irritants. Symptoms are worse in the morning and on dry and windy days, but are relieved during heavy rain.

A doctor may determine the sensitizing agent or agents by scratching the skin of the patient and applying various pollens. The pollens to which the patient is allergic will produce a wheal-and-flare reaction in him. Injection of pollen extract, a more sensitive test giving more positive indications, requires safeguards against possible reaction affecting the whole body. Because hay fever involves an antigen-antibody reaction in which body histamine is released to irritate blood vessels and glands, some antihistaminic agents may furnish relief. Conjunctival symptoms are relieved by specific eye drops. Air conditioning and pollen filters may help.

Long-term therapy involves a series of injections of pollen extracts before the pollen season begins; repeated annually, these relieve 75 percent of cases. Treatment continued throughout the year may even have better results. Good results are reported from one or two injections a year of pollen extract in mineral oil, which releases the extract gradually. Because the oil is not eliminated, however, it may produce chronic local inflammation.

Nonseasonal allergic rhinitis, that often affects the same persons and produces the same symptoms as hay fever, is caused by such inhaled antigens as house dust, feathers, and animal danders. It may also be caused by allergic reactions to nose and sinus bacteria, but seldom to foods or drugs. Nasal drops that might cause constriction of the blood vessels and psychosomatic factors may bring about attacks. The presence of polyps in the nose and, at the same time, chronic sinusitis often indicate bacterial allergy. If neglected, perennial allergic rhinitis may lead to asthma and increased susceptibility to sinus infections. Treatment consists of elimination of the offending agents; prednisone, prednisolone, and corticotropin are the drugs of choice. See ALLERGY; ASTHMA, BRONCHIAL; HISTAMINE.

HAYMARKET SQUARE RIOT, riot which took place on May 4, 1886, in Haymarket Square, Chicago. A strike was taking place at the McCormick reaper works in Chicago, and on the previous day several men had been killed by the police during a riot at the plant. The May 4 meeting was called at the Haymarket as a protest against police violence by a group of mainly German-born anarchist workers (see ANARCHISM) living in Chicago. The police attempted to disperse the Haymarket meeting, and in the ensuing riot a bomb was thrown which killed seven policemen and wounded twenty-seven. Eight anarchists attending the meeting were arrested and charged with being accessories to the crime, on the basis that they had publicly and on frequent occasions advocated such violence.

HAYNE

The eight were tried and found guilty of the bomb throwing; seven were sentenced to death and one to imprisonment. Eventually four were hanged, one committed suicide, the sentence of two was commuted to life imprisonment, and one was sentenced to a fifteen-year term. In 1893 the three who were in prison were pardoned by the governor of Illinois, John Peter Altgeld (q.v.), on several grounds, of which the most important was that no evidence had been presented at the trial actually connecting the defendants with the throwing of the bomb.

HAYNE, Robert Young (1791–1839), American politician, born in Colleton District (now Charleston Co.), S.C. He studied law in Charleston, and was admitted to the bar in 1812. In 1822, after serving four years in the South Carolina legislature (1814–19) and two years as attorney general (1819–22), he was elected to the United States Senate. As an advocate of free trade, Haynes vigorously opposed the Federal protective tariff laws of 1824 and 1828; see TARIFFS, UNITED STATES.

By about 1830 Hayne had become the Southern spokesman for the doctrine of States' rights (q.v.), a position which he defended in that year in a series of debates with Senator Daniel Webster (q.v.) of Massachusetts. Basing his argument on the nullification (q.v.) doctrine that had been formulated in 1828 by Vice-President John Caldwell Calhoun (q.v.), Hayne argued that the States could, at their discretion, nullify or refuse to enforce a Federal law. Although Webster, who argued for the supremacy of the Federal government, was the acknowledged victor of the debate, the Senate argument over States' rights and free trade continued. When the Congress passed an even more restrictive tariff in 1832, Hayne resigned his seat to give Calhoun a place on the Senate floor. Hayne continued to be active in politics, however, and was elected governor of South Carolina in 1832. As governor he upheld the nullification doctrine and played a leading role in the South Carolina convention that nullified the 1832 Federal tariff law. When President Andrew Jackson (q.v.) threatened to use force to ensure compliance with the tariff law, Hayne replied by issuing an order raising 10,000 troops to defend the nullification edict. Civil war was avoided, however, when both leaders accepted the compromise tariff bill introduced by Senator Henry Clay (q.v.) of Kentucky. Hayne served one term as governor of his State and one year as mayor of Charleston. He spent his last years trying to establish a railroad line between Charleston and Cincinnati, Ohio.

HAYNES, Elwood (1857–1925), American inventor, born in Portland, Ind., and educated at Worcester Polytechnic Institute and Johns Hopkins University. In 1894 he designed and constructed one of the first successful American automobiles, now on exhibition at the Smithsonian Institution in Washington, D.C. He also built the first rotary-valve gas engine in 1903. Haynes developed a number of special chromium steels, including Stellite (1910), an alloy of chromium, cobalt, and tungsten, which is used for high-speed cutting tools, and a type of stainless steel, which he patented in 1919.

HAYNES, John (1594–1654), American colonial administrator born in Essex, England. In 1633 he joined the Puritan emigration to America, settling in Newe Towne (now Cambridge), Massachusetts Bay Colony. As governor of the colony (1635–36), he banished the clergyman and later founder of the Rhode Island colony, Roger Williams (q.v.), a move that he later regretted. In 1637 Haynes settled in Hartford, Conn., and helped frame a new governing code for the colony, known as the Fundamental Orders of Connecticut. He was elected governor in 1639, and was reelected under the provisions of the code in alternate years until his death.

HAY-PAUNCEFOTE TREATY, agreement negotiated in 1901 between the United States and Great Britain, providing for the construction and regulation of a canal across the Isthmus of Panama; it was signed by John Hay (q.v.), then U.S. secretary of state, and Lord Julian Pauncefote (1828–1902), then British ambassador to the U.S. The treaty superseded the Clayton-Bulwer Treaty (q.v.) of 1850 as the definitive statement of Anglo-American policy concerning an Atlantic-Pacific canal.

The Spanish-American War (q.v.) of 1898 created an American interest in South and Central America. American public opinion began to demand abrogation of the 1850 treaty, which permitted neither the U.S. nor Great Britain to act alone in regard to the canal. Although several attempts had been made by European companies to construct the canal, the U.S. decided that such an enterprise should be wholly American. Great Britain was amenable, provided that the neutrality of a canal zone would be maintained.

Conversations between Hay and Pauncefote, in 1900, resulted in a draft treaty giving the U.S. complete direction of the construction project, establishing permanent neutrality of the zone and a ban on fortifications, and inviting other nations to join in guarantees of neutrality. The United States Senate, refusing to ratify the original draft, amended it to permit the U.S. to take any measures for its own defense in the canal zone, and deleted the clause concerning other nations. Great Britain opposed these amendments, and conversations were resumed. A revised draft was presented to the Senate in 1901 and ratified shortly after its presentation. By the terms of the ratified treaty, the U.S. was given full control of the construction and management of the canal; the U.S. was named sole guarantor of the neutrality of the canal and was permitted to build fortifications; and the canal was opened to ships of any nation under equal terms, although the U.S. could forbid passage in time of war. In 1911 Great Britain claimed that the U.S. had contravened the last clause by passing the Panama Canal Act, exempting American coastal shipping from paying canal tolls; President Woodrow Wilson (q.v.), agreeing with the British view, persuaded Congress to repeal the act in 1914. *See* PANAMA CANAL.

HAYS, city in Kansas, and county seat of Ellis Co., about 132 miles N.W. of Wichita. Hays is a marketing center for the agricultural and oil-producing area. It is the site of Fort Hays Kansas State College, established in 1901. Pop. (1960) 11,947; (1970) 15,396.

HAYS, Will H(arrison) (1879–1954), American politician and motion-picture executive, born in Sullivan, Ind., and educated at Wabash College. He practiced law in Indiana, and was active in the administration of the Republican Party in the State. He served as chairman of the Republican National Committee from 1918 to 1920, and as postmaster general under President Warren Gamaliel Harding (q.v.) in 1921–22. Hays resigned from politics to become president of the Motion Picture Producers and Distributors of America, Inc. in 1922. He successfully removed the threat of government and civic censorship of motion pictures by instituting a motion-picture moral code in 1934. The code, which was sanctioned by all the leading men in the industry, provided for industry regulation of both production and advertising. He retired in 1945.

HAYWARD, city of California, in Alameda Co., on San Francisco Bay, 15 miles S.E. of Oakland, connected with the San Francisco Peninsula by the San Mateo Bridge. It is known for the raising of poultry, pigeons, rabbits, and flowers; other industries include bus assembly, fruit and vegetable canning, and the manufacture of steel and beryllium products, aircraft and auto parts, glass products, construction equipment, sporting goods, and salt. The city is the site of California State College at Hayward (1957) and of Chabot College (1961). Founded in 1854 by Guillermo Castro, owner of the vast Rancho Lorenzo, Hayward was named for William Hayward, who had settled in the area in 1852. The city was incorporated in 1876. Pop. (1960) 72,700; (1970) 93,058.

HAYWOOD, William Dudley, known as BIG BILL HAYWOOD (1869–1928), American labor leader, born in Salt Lake City, Utah. By the age of nineteen he was the secretary-treasurer of an independent union of metal miners known as the Western Federation of Miners. In 1904 he led the members in a strike at Cripple Creek, Colo., the first in a series of labor disputes that attracted national attention and that brought accusations against Haywood of inciting the workers to violence. In 1905 he presided at the foundation of the Industrial Workers of the World (q.v.), a militant labor organization dedicated to the idea of class struggle and to the socialist political philosophy known as syndicalism (q.v.). In 1906 Haywood and other leaders of the organization were accused of being implicated in the murder of the former governor of Idaho, Frank R. Steunenberg (1861–1905). Haywood was defended by the famous criminal lawyer Clarence Seward Darrow (q.v.), and was acquitted in 1907. Haywood continued to engage in union activities, however, notably in the 1912 strikes of textile workers in Lawrence, Mass., and in Patterson, N.J. He was removed from his position on the national committee of the Socialist Party in 1913 for advocating violence in labor disputes. When the United States entered World War I Haywood was arrested on charges of sedition and for his antimilitarist activities. He was tried in 1918, but later released on bail pending a new trial. He fled to the Soviet Union, where he remained until his death. His autobiography, *Bill Haywood's Book*, was posthumously published in 1929.

HAZELNUT, common name applied to trees and shrubs of the genus *Corylus,* belonging to the Birch family Betulaceae. Hazelnut trees are found throughout the temperate regions of North America and Eurasia. Each plant has separate male flowers borne in catkins and female flowers borne in clusters. The fruit, called the filbert or hazelnut, is an ovoid nut. Two species of hazelnut, *C. americana,* the common hazelnut, and *C. cornuta,* the beaked hazelnut, are native to the United States. Nuts of these native species are small, and so the plants, which grow to a height of about 9 ft., are not cultivated. The European filbert, *C. avellana pontica,* the cobnut, *C. avellana grandis,* the giant filbert, *C. maxima,* and several hybrids among them furnish the bulk of commercially grown filberts, and are raised extensively in Europe and the U.S.

They often attain a height of 30 ft. The thick-shelled nut is highly prized for the sweet flavor of the meat. When pressed, filberts yield a bland fixed oil equivalent in quantity to approximately half their weight. Several varieties of hazelnut, especially *C. maxima purpurea,* are grown for decorative purposes.

HAZEL PARK, city of Michigan, in Oakland Co., adjoining Detroit and 10 miles N. of the downtown area. Manufactures include precision machinery, bearings, duplicating and construction equipment, and screws. The Hazel Park Race Track is situated here. Hazel Park was incorporated in 1941. Pop. (1960) 25,631; (1970) 23,784.

HAZLETON, city of Pennsylvania, in Luzerne Co., 30 miles S. of Wilkes-Barre. Hazleton, lying at an altitude of 1800 ft. above sea level, is the highest city in the State. It is in the heart of the anthracite region, and is an important coal-mining center. Other industries in the city include the manufacture of iron and steel products, pumps, chemical filters, electronic equipment, knit goods, and clothing. Hazleton is the site of a branch of Pennsylvania State University. Coal was first discovered in the region in 1818, and Hazleton was founded in 1820. It was incorporated as a borough in 1856 and as a city in 1891. Pop. (1960) 32,056; (1970) 30,426.

HAZLITT, William (1778–1830), British essayist and critic, born in Maidstone, Kent, England. He spent a short time at the Unitarian theological seminary at Hackney, but soon abandoned the ministry to study painting and philosophy. In 1812 he became drama critic for the London *Morning Chronicle* and a frequent contributor to several periodicals. His first book, *The Round Table* (1817), was a collection of essays from his articles in the *Examiner,* a weekly newspaper owned by his friend the British essayist Leigh Hunt (q.v.). Hazlitt soon began to publish other collections of his magazine and newspaper essays. Two of his most famous collections, *Table Talk* (1821–22) and *The Plain Speaker* (1826), cover a variety of subjects ranging from art and philosophy to politics and athletics. These works helped to establish Hazlitt's reputation as the most versatile critic of his day. He was close friends with several of the literary figures of his time, including Samuel Taylor Coleridge, William Wordsworth, and Charles Lamb (qq.v.). *The Spirits of the Age* (1825), a work that is regarded as his critical masterpiece, contains valuable biographical sketches of these writers and of other intellectual leaders of his time.

Hazlitt lectured extensively on the English drama, particularly on the plays of the Elizabethan period. He collected his lectures and some of his articles in a series of books, *Characters of Shakespeare's Plays* (1817), *Lectures on the English Poets* (1818), *Views of the English Stage* (1818), *Essays on the English Comic Writers* (1819), and *Dramatic Literature of the Age of Elizabeth* (1821). With these works Hazlitt established himself as one of the foremost literary critics of the Romantic period (*see* ROMANTICISM), and as a master of the informal essay.

William Hazlitt   Bettmann Archive

Throughout his life he was a firm believer in the principles of liberty that inspired the French Revolution (q.v.). His admiration for Napoleon I (q.v.), Emperor of France, led him to write a *Life of Napoleon* (4 vol., 1828–30). Hazlitt is regarded as one of the greatest masters of English prose; his smooth, colorful style greatly influenced both his contemporaries and many subsequent writers.

H.D. *See* DOOLITTLE, HILDA.

HEADACHE, or CEPHALAGIA, deep-seated pain in any part of the head except the face. Although widespread, often accompanying fever or eyestrain, perhaps less than 1 percent of cases have any serious clinical basis. This small group includes headaches caused by severe injury to, and bleeding (q.v.) inside, the head; encephalitis and meningitis (qq.v.); and serious disease of the nose, teeth, and ears. Less commonly, it follows surgical procedures. Still rarer are imaginary headaches that have no connection with a pain mechanism.

HEALTH

Headaches are classified according to the region of the head at which they appear: occipital, in the back of the head; parietal, under the crown; frontal, under the brow; and temporal, under the temples. Location is not generally of diagnostic significance. One exception is unilateral headache, occurring regularly on one side of the head, which may denote migraine (q.v.) or brain tumors or abscesses.

Most headaches fall into two categories, both arising in an environment of frustration, anger, resentment, and anxiety that leads to emotional upset and weariness: (1) those caused by continuous contraction of face, scalp, and neck muscles; and (2) those attributable to painful swelling of the arteries of the brain and head. Muscle-contraction headaches arise from tightening of or pressure on the muscles of the head, jaws, neck, and upper back, causing tenderness, limitation of motion, and a feeling of bandlike tightness. Arterial or vascular headaches are caused by painful swelling of the arteries of the brain and may appear in the temples or forehead, at the back of the head or neck, or at the back of the upper jaw, and are sometimes felt in the shoulder. Rising blood pressure is seldom a cause; in fact, many hypertensives never suffer headaches; see HYPERTENSION.

Muscle-contraction headaches are best treated by massage, warm baths, and psychological counseling to help the sufferer adjust to difficult life situations. Aspirin, phenobarbital, and codeine help relieve the pain. Vascular headaches may require administration of carefully regulated doses of drugs that reduce constriction. Cure is aimed at discovering and eliminating the underlying causes.

See NEURALGIA.

HEALTH, condition associated with a sense of physical and mental well-being, in which all body structures and organs are anatomically and physiologically normal. In order to be productive and to find his life experience rewarding, gratifying, and fulfilling, the individual must be healthy. Health is also important to society in general; if a society is to flourish, its members must be fit and able to work efficiently and productively.

The factors essential to the maintenance of health include regular and sufficient rest, a well-balanced diet, regular habits of elimination, clothing suitable to the climate and occupation, a healthful environment in which to live and work, and personal hygiene, which comprises cleanliness, dental care, good posture, and emotional balance.

Preventative Medicine. With a new sense of the importance of good health, society has become increasingly concerned with preventive medicine, which seeks to forestall the development of illness and to maintain a constant state of health. One aspect of preventive medicine involves the early detection of disease. In their early phases, many diseases cause few or no symptoms but, if unchecked, may progress slowly and unsuspectingly. For this reason, annual medical and dental checkups are encouraged by all medical authorities.

The recommended frequency of checkups varies with age and sex. The infant should be examined every few weeks. After the age of three, examinations may be reduced to two a year. Checkups are required before the child begins school; many schools and colleges now provide annual examinations. Adult men should have a complete physical examination at least once a year, and women should be examined twice a year after the age of thirty.

Preventive medicine also involves awareness of situations that may lead to the development of illness. Increasingly, efforts are being made to alert the public to pernicious influences that may constitute health hazards. An example is the growing awareness of the ill effects of smoking, as it has become established that the incidence of heart, lung, and some other diseases is significantly higher among smokers than among persons who do not smoke.

Preventive medicine is also concerned with diet. It is known that certain diets are deficient or lacking in essential food elements, vitamins, and minerals; see FOOD: *Composition*; NUTRITION, HUMAN; TRACE ELEMENTS; VITAMIN. Many schools offer courses to acquaint students with the importance of proper nutrition in the maintenance of health. Apart from the problems of appearance created by obesity (q.v.), awareness of the dangers of overweight has led to emphasis on its control in order to reduce the likelihood of such associated disorders as diabetes mellitus, arthritis, hypertension (qq.v.), and heart disease (*see* HEART: *Diseases of the Heart*). The relationship of dietary fats, particularly saturated fat, to the development of hardening of the arteries, or arteriosclerosis, and coronary heart disease has received much attention; *see* ARTERY: *Diseases of the Arteries*; FATS AND FIXED OILS.

Other Factors Affecting Health. Physical fitness in the maintenance of health has also been emphasized in recent years; more and more, physicians advise their patients to include a regular program of exercise as part of the daily schedule.

HEALTH

Environmental pollution is receiving national attention as the public becomes aware of the dangers to health of breathing polluted air or consuming polluted water; see AIR POLLUTION; WATER POLLUTION. The hazards of exposure to excessive radiation have also become a matter of concern. In the field of drugs and chemicals, increasing pressures have been brought upon the pharmaceutical industry and the government to ensure that medications put on the market are both safe and effective; see FOOD AND DRUG ADMINISTRATION. Awareness of the importance of maintaining health is also seen in the public concern about automobile safety, alcoholism (q.v.), abuse of narcotic and hallucinogenic drugs (see DRUGS, ADDICTION TO; NARCOTICS) and the use of toxic materials such as pesticides; see AGRICULTURAL CHEMISTRY.

See also DISEASE; NADER, RALPH; PUBLIC HEALTH.

HEALTH, BOARDS OF. See PUBLIC HEALTH.

HEALTH, EDUCATION, AND WELFARE, DEPARTMENT OF, Executive Department (q.v.) of the Federal government of the United States, created by Congress on April 11, 1953. The department is administered by a secretary, who is appointed by the President with the approval of the Senate. The secretary is assisted by an undersecretary and eight assistant secretaries.

All functions of the Federal Security Agency (q.v.) were transferred to the department when it was established; many additional functions have been added by subsequent legislation. The function of the department is the promotion of

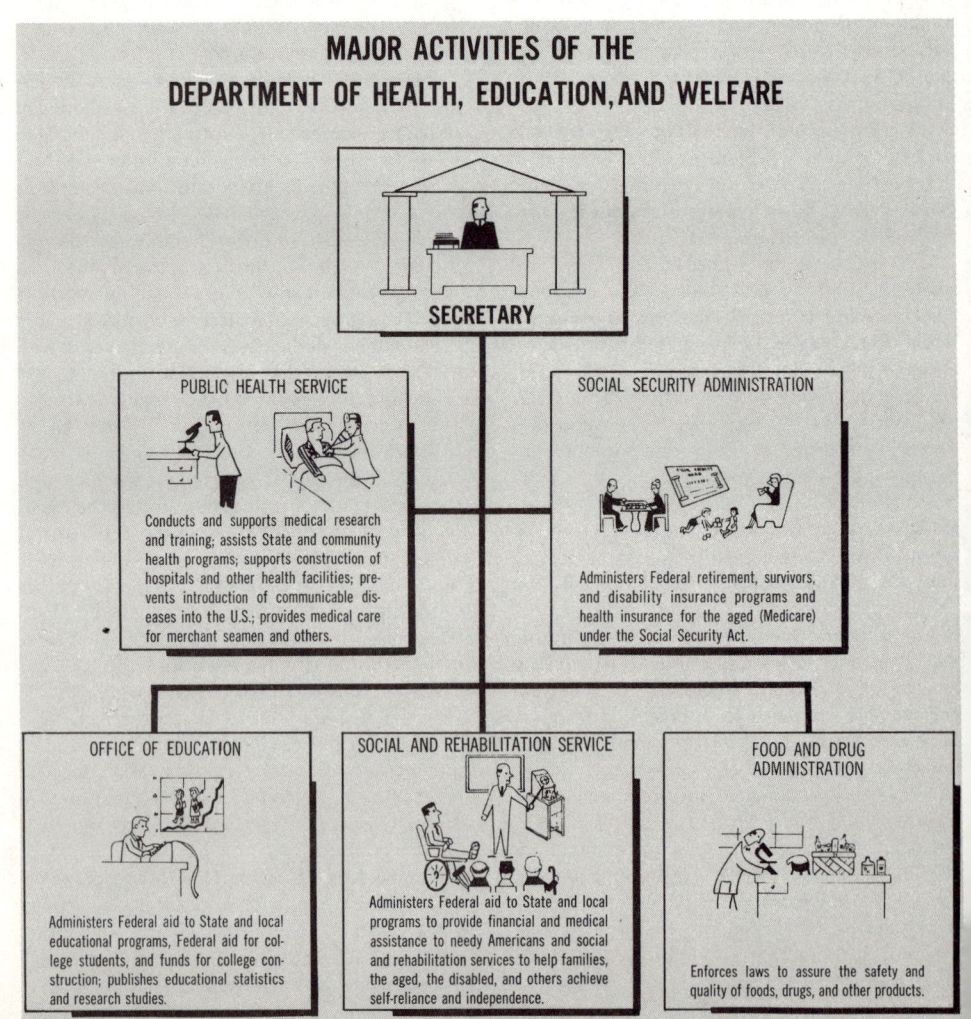

Chart showing the major operating agencies and services under the direction of the Department of Health, Education, and Welfare. Graphics Institute

MAJOR ACTIVITIES OF THE DEPARTMENT OF HEALTH, EDUCATION, AND WELFARE

SECRETARY

PUBLIC HEALTH SERVICE
Conducts and supports medical research and training; assists State and community health programs; supports construction of hospitals and other health facilities; prevents introduction of communicable diseases into the U.S.; provides medical care for merchant seamen and others.

SOCIAL SECURITY ADMINISTRATION
Administers Federal retirement, survivors, and disability insurance programs and health insurance for the aged (Medicare) under the Social Security Act.

OFFICE OF EDUCATION
Administers Federal aid to State and local educational programs, Federal aid for college students, and funds for college construction; publishes educational statistics and research studies.

SOCIAL AND REHABILITATION SERVICE
Administers Federal aid to State and local programs to provide financial and medical assistance to needy Americans and social and rehabilitation services to help families, the aged, the disabled, and others achieve self-reliance and independence.

FOOD AND DRUG ADMINISTRATION
Enforces laws to assure the safety and quality of foods, drugs, and other products.

HEALTH INSURANCE

the general welfare in the fields of health, education, and social and economic opportunity. The department administers more than 250 programs covering a broad range of areas. These programs include Social Security (q.v.); Medicare and Medicaid (q.v.); financial aid for college students; Federal assistance for State and local programs for disadvantaged children in elementary and secondary schools; construction funds for hospitals, medical schools, and colleges and universities; grants for State and local programs to support needy persons and protect the health and welfare of children; vocational rehabilitation of the disabled; programs for older Americans; medical research; air-pollution control; and supervision of compliance with civil-rights legislation by schools, hospitals, and other facilities receiving Federal financial assistance from the department.

The seven major operating agencies of the department are the Environmental Health Service, the Food and Drug Administration, the Health Services and Mental Health Administration, the National Institutes of Health, the Social Security Administration, the Office of Education, and the Social and Rehabilitation Service (qq.v.). The four first-named agencies constitute the reorganized Public Health Service.

The department also administers the Office of Child Development, the Office of Equal Opportunity, the Office of New Careers, and the President's Council on Physical Fitness and Sports (see PHYSICAL FITNESS). Among its other responsibilities are the American Printing House for the Blind, which distributes educational materials for the blind free of charge to public institutions; Gallaudet College, which provides college education for the deaf; and Howard University (q.v.).

HEALTH INSURANCE, insurance designed to meet the costs of sickness and disability. In many countries health insurance is a function of government; see NATIONAL HEALTH INSURANCE. Although the United States government provides health-insurance protection to the aged and to certain other persons, in general such insurance is voluntary, purchased privately, and is underwritten by nongovernment insuring organizations.

Three main categories of health-insurance protection are offered by various U.S. private and government plans: medical-care insurance, loss-of-income insurance, and accidental-death and -dismemberment insurance. Medical-care insurance covers the costs of hospitalization, surgical procedures, and general medical care. Loss-of-income insurance (called also disability insurance) provides cash payments as compensation for loss of income resulting from sickness and disability. Accidental-death and -dismemberment insurance pays a lump sum to a policyholder or his beneficiaries when loss of life or loss of some bodily function, organ, or member occurs accidentally. For a discussion of benefits payable to employees injured at work, see WORKMEN'S COMPENSATION.

Voluntary health insurance became firmly established in the U.S. during the 1930's, when many insurers began to offer a wide variety of medical-care insurance plans. In the late 1960's, it was estimated that 162,853,000 persons in the U.S. had hospital insurance, 150,396,000 had surgical insurance, and 122,570,000 were covered for doctors' visits and other routine medical expenses. In addition, more than 62,226,000 persons were protected by major medical insurance, which meets the cost of serious or prolonged illness, 57,912,000 persons had some form of voluntary loss-of-income insurance, and 30,408,000 were protected by group accidental-death and -dismemberment certificates.

Medical Care Insurance. A common type of medical-care insurance covers hospitalization costs in part or in full. It is taken out voluntarily in the U.S., and is provided by nonprofit hospital-service corporations, such as Blue Cross, or by insurance companies. Blue Cross plans operate independently of each other, each arranging contracts with certain hospitals in its area of jurisdiction. Under these contracts the hospitals furnish specified services to Blue Cross members and are reimbursed directly by the local plan. Although costs and benefits vary, members can transfer from one plan to another.

Most people enroll in group Blue Cross plans at their jobs, but nearly all plans offer individual membership to those unable to do so. A typical Blue Cross plan allows semiprivate accomodations in member hospitals for a specified number of days each year, in addition to nursing care and other needed hospital services such as laboratory examinations, use of the operating room, and medication. A subscriber confined in a non-member hospital pays the difference between the hospital's costs and the Blue Cross allowance; if hospitalized while traveling outside the Blue Cross area, he is entitled to hospital services. A subscriber occupying a private room generally pays the difference between this charge and that provided for in his contract. Blue Cross benefits for maternity cases are available after a specified waiting period, usually ten months.

In the late 1960's, more than 67,000,000 people

HEALTH INSURANCE

were enrolled in Blue Cross, excluding those covered by Medicare and other public-service programs. Seventy-six plans were in operation in the U.S., one in Puerto Rico, four in Canada, and one in Jamaica.

Hospital cash-indemnity insurance provides cash payment for each day that the policyholder is hospitalized up to the maximum number of days specified in the policy. Provision usually is made for meeting the cost of ancillary hospital services as well. Dependents and maternity benefits may be included at extra cost. Hospital cash-indemnity insurance may be purchased individually or through a group. Under a group plan, the master contract covering all subscribers is issued to the employer, union, or welfare-plan trustees. A minimum number of employees must subscribe in order to qualify for group coverage. In addition to this minimum, a group plan may require an additional percentage of eligible employees in order to prevent "adverse selection", that is, participation by poor risks only.

Insurance for surgical expenses and for payment of physicians' fees is also available through Blue Shield plans, which are often operated in conjunction with Blue Cross. Like Blue Cross, the plans are arranged by contract between group or individual subscribers and the local Blue Shield plan. Coverage is for medical, surgical, and various ancillary services, which are paid for in full to members whose incomes are below a specified level. In the late 1960's seventy-two Blue Shield plans were in operation in the U.S., one in Puerto Rico, and nine in Canada, with a total membership of about 59,679,000, excluding Medicare.

Other plans include the Health Insurance Plan of Greater New York (HIP). Unlimited care is available at the medical-group center, at the member's home, or in the hospital. The HIP subscriber must select his physician from among those in the group serving his area. Another plan, Group Health Insurance (G.H.I.), pays in full all bills of participating doctors, in accordance with an agreed payment schedule. Nonparticipating physicians are paid the scheduled allowances but may charge additional amounts, which the patient must pay. Care under the G.H.I. plan, subject to certain limitations, includes visits to a doctor's office, a doctor's visits to the home, and surgery in hospitals. The medical-expense policies offered by insurance companies indemnify the insured for his expenses; benefits vary widely.

Surgical-expense contracts offered by insurance companies state maximum amounts payable for specific operations. Surgical-expense protection frequently can be purchased in combination with hospital-expense coverage or loss-of-income policies. Both individual and group contracts are available.

All of the medical-care plans described above are provided by private enterprise on a voluntary basis. Recent health-insurance developments in the U.S. are the government programs called Medicare and Medicaid (q.v.). By agreement with the United States Social Security Administration, Blue Cross plans administer Medicare hospital-insurance benefits, and Blue Shield organizations in many areas handle the financial aspects of the Medicare medical-insurance program.

Under the Medicaid program, the Federal government matches funds appropriated by States to provide medical care to all persons eligible for payments under Federal-State public-assistance programs, to the blind and otherwise handicapped persons with marginal incomes, and to children of low-income families.

Loss-of-Income Insurance. This type of insurance, also called disability insurance, protects against loss of income resulting from nonoccupational sickness or accident. Such a policy specifies payment during a limited period of a weekly amount equal to a percentage of the average salary but not exceeding a maximum amount, for twenty-six weeks.

Loss-of-income policies may be purchased from insurance companies by groups or individuals. Comparable protection is afforded by paid sick-leave plans of private firms and government agencies, and by union-administered plans and employee mutual-benefit associations.

Several States require weekly cash payments to employees disabled by an injury that did not result from their work. In New York State the weekly benefit amount is one half of the employee's average weekly wage, with a minimum benefit of $20 per week (or the full weekly wage if it is less than $20) and a maximum of $65. Benefits are payable to a maximum of twenty-six weeks in any fifty-two consecutive weeks or for any single disability. No benefits are payable for periods during which unemployment insurance or workmen's compensation (q.v.) benefits are paid.

Accidental-Death and -Dismemberment Insurance. This insurance, providing lump-sum benefit payments to the policyholder or his beneficiaries in case of accidental loss of life or of some bodily function, organ, or member, can be obtained by individual or group contract. It

HEARING AIDS

is often combined with other health insurance, but the benefits are payable only if the disability results from an accident. Limited types of accidental-death and -dismemberment policies are available, such as automobile-accident policies limited to highway accidents, travel-accident policies limited to common carriers, and trip-ticket policies limited to one trip on a commercial airplane or other common carrier.

HEALTH SERVICES AND MENTAL HEALTH ADMINISTRATION (H.S.M.H.A.), agency of the United States Department of Health, Education, and Welfare (q.v.), established in 1968. Part of the Public Health Service, the H.S.M.H.A. attempts to improve the physical and mental health services available to the people of the U.S. and to foster the development of comprehensive health-care systems. It provides direct health services to certain segments of the population. The major efforts of the administration, however, are aimed at expanding the role of the Federal government in the organization and delivery of health services at the community level, through programs of comprehensive health planning, regional medical plans, community mental health centers, and health services research and development.

In 1969 the H.S.M.H.A. was delegated responsibility for administering the Maternal and Child Health programs, formerly assigned to the Children's Bureau, and the new Center for Family Planning Services. With the licensing of a new live-virus vaccine to prevent German measles (q.v.), or rubella, a large-scale campaign was instituted to ensure that all children between the ages of one and twelve are inoculated, thereby reducing the risk of spreading the disease to pregnant women; see BIRTH DEFECTS: *Environmental Factors*.

The National Institute of Mental Health, an H.S.M.H.A. component, conducts and supports programs designed to sustain mental health, prevent mental illness, and treat and rehabilitate those who are mentally ill. The institute has been conducting a vigorous information campaign on the dangers of drug abuse.

See also DRUGS, ADDICTION TO; MENTAL DISORDERS; MENTAL HEALTH; PSYCHEDELIC DRUGS.

HEARING, one of the five special senses (q.v.), by which sound waves are perceived by man and animals; see SOUND. The most important function of hearing in birds and animals is for communication, as a signal of danger, and in mating. The human sense of hearing has reached a stage of exceptional refinement with the development of the arts of speech and music. In mammals hearing is accomplished by the organ of Corti, located within the inner ear, in a spiral canal known as the cochlea; see EAR. The organ of Corti, which consists of hair cells and fiber cells containing the end organs of the cochlear nerves, reproduces sound waves and transmits impulses to the brain (q.v.) via the auditory nerve. In lower vertebrates this is achieved through the sensory receptors of the lagena, the corresponding organ that is the terminus of the cochlea. See AUDITION; NERVOUS SYSTEM: *Anatomy and Function*.

HEARING AIDS, electronic devices that amplify sounds for persons with hearing impairments. Hearing aids have the same basic components as any public-address system, but all components are miniature, and the amplified sound is delivered to the ear of the hearing-aid user only. The microphone, amplifier (consisting of transistors and integrated electronic circuits), miniature receiver, and battery of a hearing aid are enclosed either in a chassis or shell which is worn behind the ear, or in the stem or

A deaf child is amazed to hear the sound of his own voice with the aid of a hearing device.   Wide World

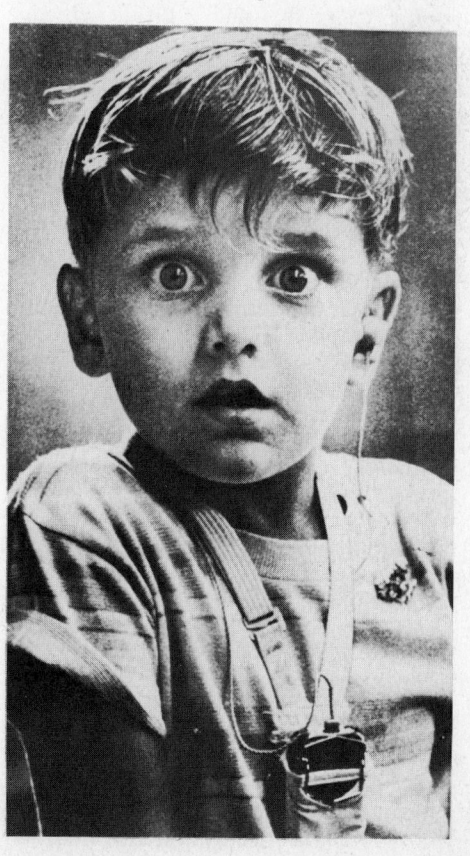

257

temple portion of eyeglasses. A small tube directs the amplified sound from the receiver into the ear canal of the wearer. A unit small enough to fit into the ear canal with only a small protruding part has been developed. Devices as small as these can be used by many persons with mild or moderate hearing losses. Individuals with more severe hearing impairments require more amplification and therefore a more powerful amplifier, usually encased in a chassis smaller than a package of cigarettes, which can be carried easily in a shirt pocket or in a special holder on the chest. A cord connects the amplifier to the receiver in the ear of the wearer. If the hearing loss is caused by malformation of the ear canal or impaired function of the middle ear (see EAR) a different type of receiver may be used; for example, a small vibrator may be clamped against the mastoid bone behind the ear by means of a headband; the sound is conducted by the vibrator through the bones of the head to the inner ear.

HEARN, Lafcadio, full name PATRICIO LAFCADIO TESSIMA CARLOW HEARN (1850–1904), Anglo-Japanese writer of Irish-Greek descent, born on the Greek island of Levkás, and educated in England and France. He emigrated to the United States at the age of nineteen, working as a journalist, first in Cincinnati, Ohio, and later (1887) in New Orleans, La. He supplemented his earnings by translating strange stories from various countries; two of his most important collections are *Strange Leaves from Strange Literature* (1884), tales from exotic literature, and *Some Chinese Ghosts* (1887), a group of Oriental legends. Hearn spent two years (1887–89) on the island of Martinique, publishing a record of his experiences there in *Two Years in the French West Indies* (1889). He went to Japan in 1890 and taught for awhile in the local school at Matsue. He described the feudal customs he observed there in his *Glimpses of Unfamiliar Japan* (1894). In 1895 he became a Japanese citizen under the name Yakumo Koizumi. From 1896 to 1903 as a professor of English literature at the University of Tokyo, he wrote twelve books explaining the life, customs, and folklore of Japan. The most successful of these works were *Out of the East* (1895), *In Ghostly Japan* (1899), *Kwaidan* (1904), and *Japan: An Attempt at Interpretation* (1904), the summation of his observations on Japanese culture.

HEARSAY EVIDENCE. See EVIDENCE.

HEARST, William Randolph (1863–1951), American publisher, born in San Francisco, Calif. He was the son of the American industrialist and politician George Hearst (1820–91) and the philanthropist Phoebe Apperson Hearst (1842–1919), and he attended Harvard University. His father, who as a member of the Democratic Party served in the United States Senate from 1886 to 1891, acquired the San Francisco *Examiner* in 1880. In 1887 he made his twenty-three-year-old son owner and editor of the *Examiner*. Borrowing from other publishers sensational journalistic methods of the type later

William Randolph Hearst   New York Journal-American Photo

called yellow journalism, Hearst and the paper prospered. In 1895 he purchased the New York *Morning Journal* and in 1896 began publication of the *Evening Journal*. By the middle of that year, the combined daily circulation of these two newspapers had reached the then unprecedented figure of 1,500,000.

An avid politician, Hearst was elected to the United States House of Representatives as a Democratic Party member from New York City in 1903 and 1905. In 1904 he sought but failed to win the Presidential nomination of his party. He was defeated in campaigns for the mayoralty of New York City in 1905 and 1909 and for the governorship of New York State in 1906. Later he unsuccessfully attempted several times to win another nomination for the governorship.

Meanwhile Hearst was steadily expanding his journalistic domain, until in 1927 he controlled a chain of twenty-five newspapers, published in most of the major cities of the United States. In the same period he developed the International News Service, a press agency which supplied his papers with news and photographs from all parts of the world; feature articles, comics, and columns of opinion and gossip were syndicated or distributed from his headquarters to all papers of his chain for simultaneous publication. As Hearst acquired newspapers, he also entered the field of magazine publishing. Eventually his magazine properties included *Hearst's International-Cosmopolitan, Good Housekeeping, Harper's Bazaar, Town and Country,* and several periodicals published in Great Britain.

The economic depression of the 1930's caused Hearst to reduce the number of his newspaper holdings to seventeen. Of these, the largest, in circulation, were the New York *Daily Mirror,* the New York *Journal-American,* the Chicago *Herald-American,* the Los Angeles *Examiner,* and the Boston *Sunday Advertiser.* In addition, he published the *American Weekly,* distributed to all of the Hearst Sunday papers and to several others as well.

Newsreels and Controversial Policies. Hearst, recognizing the value of the motion picture, began producing newsreels about 1911. Eventually he controlled both Hearst-Metrotone News, one of the largest newsreel companies, and Hearst Cosmopolitan Film Corporation, producer of feature films. His other activities encompassed industrial investments in South America and Africa, and the collecting of fine and decorative art for his estate at San Simeon. Since 1958 a California State park, San Simeon includes not only the castlelike main house, but a zoo, an airport, a private theater, and guest houses that are reassembled French châteaus.

Through his extensive publishing and motion-picture enterprises, Hearst was able to exert a vast influence on American public opinion. Late in the 19th century, reports, some written by Hearst himself, on Spanish atrocities in Cuba aroused the public until the United States declared war against Spain; *see* SPANISH-AMERICAN WAR. Although he was an early supporter of President Franklin Delano Roosevelt, he later became an ardent critic of the economic policies of the Roosevelt administration and of that of President Harry S. Truman (qq.v.).

The nature of the policies advocated by Hearst's publications made him one of the most controversial figures of his time. He was denounced by many for his isolationist policy and for his extreme nationalism. He was praised by others as an ardent patriot, who was devoted to what he considered the best interests of his country.

Today the Hearst publishing enterprise and its policies are continued under the direction of the editor in chief, his son William Randolph Hearst, Jr. (1908–).

See JOURNALISM; NEWSPAPERS; PERIODICALS.

HEART, in anatomy, the hollow muscular organ that receives blood from the veins and propels it into and through the arteries. In man the heart of an individual is about the size of his closed fist, and makes up $\frac{5}{8}$ to $\frac{2}{3}$ of 1 percent of his total weight. It is situated behind the lower part of the breastbone, extending more to the left of the midline than to the right. It is roughly conical in shape, with the base directed upward and to the right and slightly backward; the apex touches the chest wall between the fifth and sixth ribs. The heart is held in place principally by its attachment to the great arteries and veins, and by its confinement in the pericardium, a double-walled sac with one layer enveloping the heart and the other attached to the breastbone, the diaphragm, and the membranes of the thorax.

Within the adult heart are two parallel, independent systems, each consisting of an auricle, or atrium, and a ventricle; from their anatomical positions these systems are often designated the right heart and the left heart respectively.

Structure and Function. Blood from the body returns through two large veins, the superior and inferior venae cavae, to the right atrium; in addition the blood which has supplied the heart muscle is drained directly into the right atrium through the coronary sinus. Return of venous blood to the right atrium takes place during the entire heart cycle, and to the right ventricle only during the part of the cycle called diastole, or relaxation, when both right heart cavities constitute a common chamber; near the end of diastole, contraction of the right atrium completes the blood filling of the right ventricle. The rhythmic contractions of the right ventricle expel the blood through the pulmonary arteries into the capillaries of the lung, where the blood receives oxygen (*see* RESPIRATION). The lung capillaries then empty into the pulmonary veins which in turn empty into the left atrium. Pulmonary venous return to the left atrium and left ventricle proceeds in the same manner as and simultaneously with the venous return to the right heart cavities. Contraction of the left ventricle rhythmically propels the blood into the aorta and from there to all arteries of the body, including the coronary arteries which supply the heart muscle.

The blood forced from the ventricles during systole, or contraction, is prevented from returning during diastole by valves at the openings of the aortic and pulmonary arteries. These

HEART

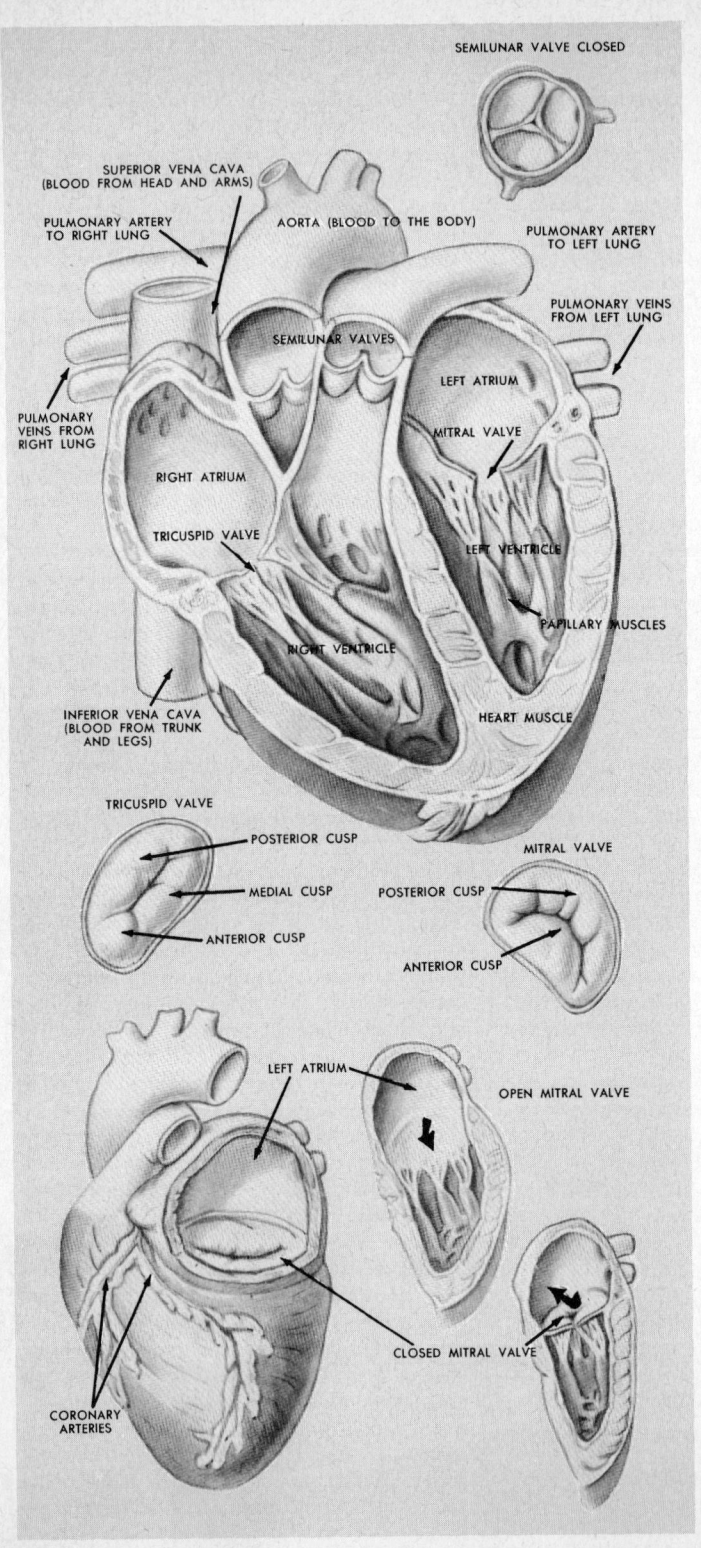

The human heart. A fist-sized bundle of muscle tissue, the heart functions as a double pump. One side of the heart pumps blood through the pulmonary, or lung, circuit; the other squeezes blood through a system of arteries, capillaries, and veins that reach every part of the body. Blood is returned to the heart by the superior and the inferior vena cava and enters the atrium, or chamber, on the upper right side of the heart. It is drawn into the right ventricle below by a partial vacuum when the lower chamber relaxes after a beat. On the next contraction of the heart muscle, the blood is squeezed into the pulmonary arteries which carry it to the right and the left lungs. The blood receives a fresh supply of oxygen in the lungs and is pushed back into the heart by way of the pulmonary veins, entering at the left atrium. The blood is first drawn into the left ventricle and then pumped out again through the aorta, the major artery, which connects with smaller arteries and capillaries reaching all parts of the body. A system of valves, the tricuspid, mitral, and semilunar, direct the flow of blood in the right direction and prevent a backflow of the vital fluid.

TODAY'S HEALTH, published by the AMERICAN MEDICAL ASSOCIATION

valves consist of three semilunar (half-moon-shaped) flaps of membrane, which are curved in the direction of blood flow and which open readily on pressure in that direction; when the original pressure subsides, back pressure forces the edges of the flaps together. The tricuspid valve, situated between the right atrium and ventricle, is composed of three triangular flaps of membrane, and the bicuspid or mitral valve, between the left atrium and ventricle, has two such flaps. The bases of the flaps in both these valves are attached in a groove at the junction of the atrium and ventricle, and the free edge is anchored by tendinous cords, known as the chordae tendinae, to the muscles of the heart wall. The flaps remain open until the ventricle fills with blood. When the ventricle begins to contract, the valve is closed by pressure. The chordae tendinae prevent inversion of the flaps during this period of systolic pressure.

The rate of heartbeat is controlled by the autonomic nervous system (q.v.), being accelerated by the sympathetic system and depressed by the parasympathetic system. Nervous impulses originate rhythmically in a special nervous node, the sinus, or sinoatrial node, located in the right atrium near the superior vena cava. The impulses travel along a slender bundle of neuromuscular fibers, called the bundle of His, or the atrioventricular bundle, which, after a relay at the atrioventricular node, branches into two bundles, one for each of the ventricles. Through these specialized fibers the nervous impulse stimulates, at rapid speed and in known orderly sequence, contraction of the heart-muscle fibers themselves.

Although the nerves and certain drugs (*see* STIMULANT) influence the rate of the heartbeat, heart muscle is inherently contractile and will continue beating at a regular rate even when all connection with the nervous system is severed. Tissue from a chicken heart has been kept alive and beating in a flask for many years.

In the embryo the heart develops from the fusion of the two ventral aortas, forming a single pulsating organ. Separation into right and left heart takes place later with the formation of an interauricular and an interventricular septum (partition). The separation is not completed, however, until the lungs begin their function at birth. Before birth the blood is oxygenated in the placenta and returns to the right auricle through the inferior vena cava; it is then directed by the Eustachian valve through the foramen ovale, a persistent opening in the interauricular septum. After birth the Eustachian valve degenerates to a rudiment and the foramen ovale normally closes, but the opening may persist in varying degree even in the adult in about one fifth of the population.

The heart produces two sounds in each cycle of the beat. The first is rather dull and is caused by vibration of the auriculoventricular valves and by the contraction of the ventricular muscle fibers; the second is sharp and is caused by the sudden closing of the aortic and pulmonary valves. In disease these sounds may be replaced or accompanied by murmurs caused by turbulent blood rushing through abnormal valves or openings; detection of such murmurs is of great importance in diagnosis. *See also* CIRCULATION OF THE BLOOD; CIRCULATORY SYSTEM.

Heart Diseases. Disorders of the heart arise from congenital defects, structural or functional changes, infection of the heart tissues, and from the effects of infections elsewhere in the body, high blood pressure, drugs, and prolonged overexertion.

Congenital heart defects include persistence of fetal connections between the arterial and venous circulations, such as the ductus arteriosus, a vessel normally connecting the pulmonary artery and the aorta only until birth. Other important developmental anomalies involve the partition separating the four cardiac cavities and the large vessels issuing from them. In newborn "blue babies", the pulmonary artery is narrowed and the ventricles are connected by an abnormal opening; in this condition, called cyanosis, the skin has a bluish tinge because the blood receives insufficient oxygen. Formerly the expectation of life for such infants was extremely limited; modern surgical developments, however, give blue babies a much better chance of survival.

Rheumatic heart disease is one of the most serious forms of heart disease of childhood and adolescence. It is often secondary to focal infections of such structures as the tonsils or sinuses, and follows attacks of rheumatic fever (q.v.). The damage to the heart generally involves the entire heart and its membranes; in mild cases inflammation of the pericardium and heart muscle causes only temporary damage, but generally the damage to the lining of the heart and to the valves persists, especially after recurrent attacks.

Myocarditis (q.v.) is inflammation or degeneration of the heart muscle. Although it is often caused by various diseases such as syphilis, goiter, endocarditis, or hypertension (qq.v.), myocarditis may appear as a primary disease in adults or as a degenerative disease of old age. It may be associated with dilation (enlargement

HEART

due to weakness of the heart muscle) or with hypertrophy (overgrowth of the muscle tissue).

Other important diseases of the heart include diseases of the coronary arteries which supply blood to the cardiac muscle. These are of two main types, coronary arteriosclerosis, which is a common cause of angina pectoris (q.v.), and coronary infarction, which leads to death of the muscle in the region of a vessel obstructed by a blood clot; coronary thrombosis occurs when a blood clot forms and attaches itself within one of the two coronary arteries (q.v.). See ARTERY: *Diseases of the Arteries.*

Minor variations in the heart rhythm usually have little pathological significance. The heart rate responds to the demands of the body over such a wide range that such variations are generally within normal limits. Respiratory arrhythmia (variation of the heartbeat with inspiration and expiration) is a normal phenomenon, and extra systoles (occasional irregularities in the heart rhythm) may have no significance. Paroxysmal tachycardia (recurrent periods of extremely fast heartbeat) causes no damage in a normal heart, but if the heart is diseased, the heart muscle may become weaker, and congestion of the lungs and the large veins may follow. Complete heartbeat irregularity, known as auricular fibrillation, is usually a serious symptom associated with such diseases as rheumatic infection, exophthalmic goiter, chronic myocarditis, and coronary arteriosclerosis.

Increasingly common among older persons is cor pulmonale, or pulmonary heart disease, which usually is the result of a lung ailment, such as emphysema (q.v.), or a disease affecting circulation to the lungs, such as arteriosclerosis of the pulmonary artery, marked by enlargement of the right ventricle, wheezing, coughing, and chest pain.

Diagnosis. An important diagnostic tool is the electrocardiograph, an instrument for recording the electrical currents produced by the heart muscle during various phases of contraction. The efficiency of the heart as a pump may be measured accurately by the use of cardiac catheterization. In this technique a tube is introduced through a vein or an artery or both, into the right or left or both heart cavities, the pulmonary artery, and the aorta. This process permits deterioration of the rate of blood flow and recording of blood pressure in intracardiac and large vessels. By means of this technique abnormal communications between right and left heart cavities may be detected. In another diagnostic technique called angiocardiography, or cinefluoroscopy, photographic recordings are obtained of the heart cavities and of the pathways and contours of the pulmonary vessels and the aorta with its branches; the technique involves injecting a substance opaque to X rays into a vein. Another instrument, the ballistocardiograph, known popularly as the swinging bed, records the body motion caused by ejection of blood from the heart. These three new methods of diagnosis have been the source of considerable progress in the study of heart disease.

Surgery. Outstanding surgical techniques have been devised for repairing many types of congenital and acquired heart defects. In the treatment of coronary thrombosis, anticoagulant drugs such as heparin (q.v.) and dicumarol are effective in preventing the formation of blood clots in the circulation. Although improved therapeutic measures have lengthened considerably the life expectancy of heart patients, diseases of the heart lead all others as cause of death in the United States.

More than 15,000 persons now wear artificial pacemakers, which give timed electrical shocks to make the heart muscles contract; over 20,000 persons suffering from cardiac diseases have been fitted with artificial heart valves. Other artificial heart devices include the Kantrowitz-Avco auxiliary ventricle made of silicone rubber and plastic, developed in the U.S. by Adrian Kantrowitz (1918–), a surgeon, and Arthur Kantrowitz (1913–), a physicist. The American surgeon Michael Ellis DeBakey (q.v.) developed an air-driven booster pump that diverts blood from the left auricle to the aorta. It is used to relieve a weakened heart of much of the work of pumping blood through the system. Dr. Adrian Kantrowitz also designed a temporary balloon pump that is inserted into the aorta to control blood pressure and relieve the work load of the heart.

Heart Transplants. In 1967 a human heart was transplanted into the body of another person. The South African surgeon Christiaan Neethling Barnard (q.v.) performed the first such operation, and similar operations were performed shortly afterward by Adrian Kantrowitz in Brooklyn, N.Y., and by Norman Edward Shumway (1923–) in Palo Alto, Calif. Within the year more than eighty heart-transplant operations were performed, most notably by the American surgeon Denton Cooley (q.v.). The first patients survived for only brief periods because of various complications, but with improved techniques many later patients recovered satisfactorily. A major hazard to the success of a heart transplant is the natural tendency of the human body to reject tissues from another

Heart. Plate 1. A graphic illustration of the development of coronary thrombosis in the coronary artery of a hamster. The artery in the magnified photograph (above), supplying blood to the heart muscle, shows signs of obstruction by a thrombus, or plug. The plug develops with the abnormal thickening and hardening of the arterial walls, as in this case, or as a result of a blood clot. The vital blood vessel narrows gradually until it is blocked completely (below).

Laboratory photographs by Dr. Roman Vishniac

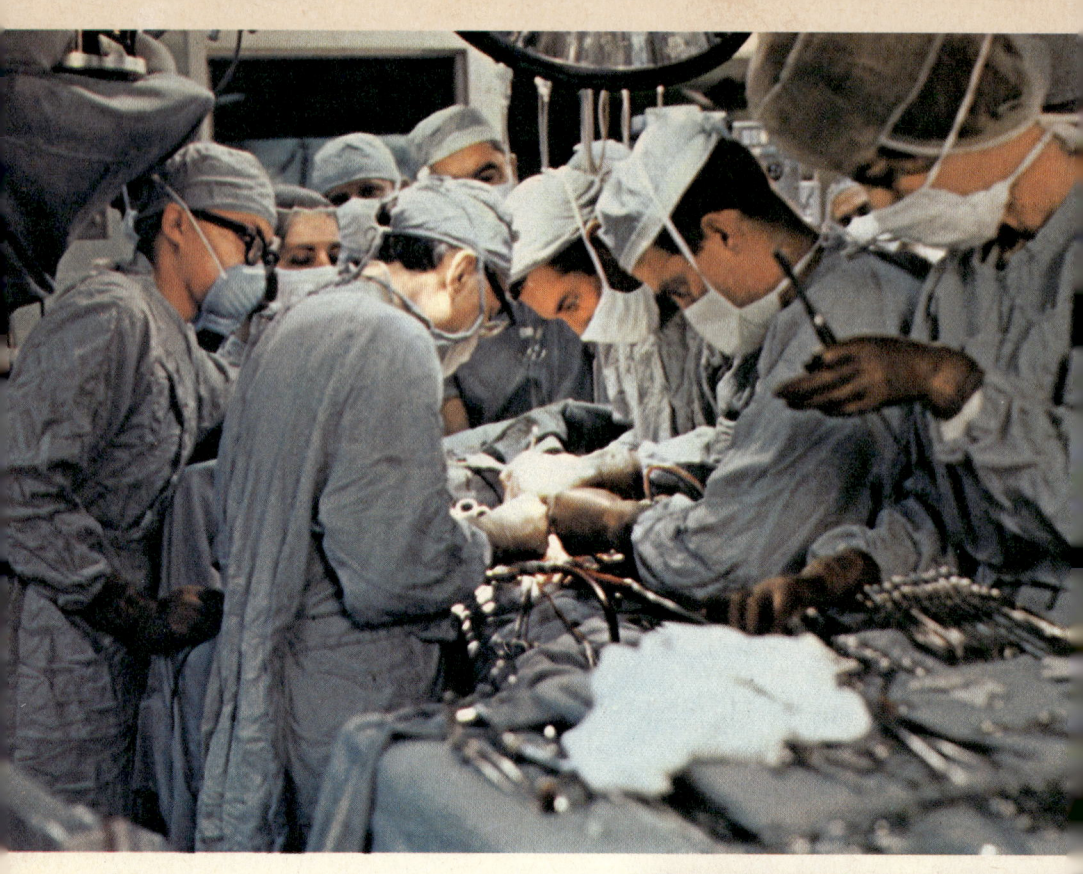

Heart. Plate 2. Above: A surgical team performs a heart-transplant operation. Below: A close-up view of the heart and lung tissue of the patient during the early stages of cardiac surgery. Below, right: A biventricular artificial heart made entirely from synthetic materials. Conceived by Dr. Michael E. DeBakey of Baylor College of Medicine in Houston, Texas, and developed in cooperation with Dr. C. William Hall and Dr. W. W. Akers, of Southwest Research Institute, San Antonio, and Rice University, Houston, respectively, the device, which is being tested, is made of impervious Dacron fiber imbedded in Silastic material.

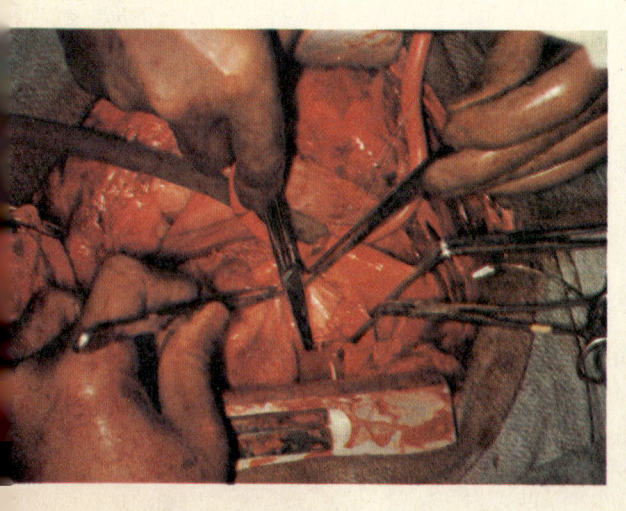

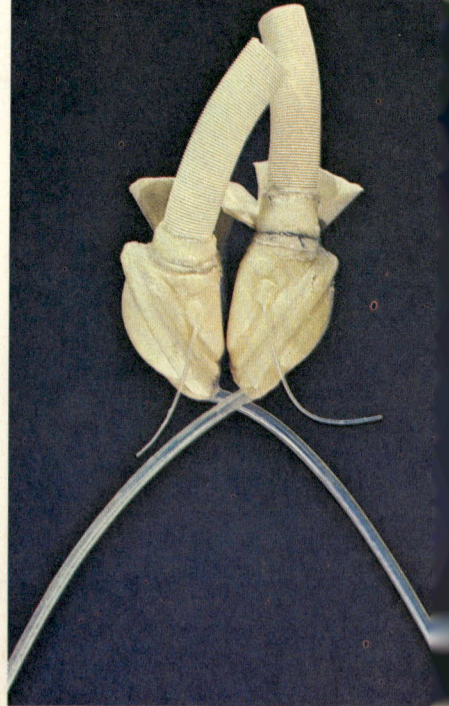

HEAT

individual; the process is similar to the immune reaction experienced in blood transfusions, Rh-factor complications, and allergies. See IMMUNITY. In the transplant procedure, the heart of the recently deceased donor is connected to a heart-lung machine, which consists of two pumps that squeeze blood through plastic tubes, simulating the heart, and an artificial lung in which the blood is spread out in a film to allow it to collect oxygen from the atmosphere. The machine, attached to blood vessels of the body, pumps blood from the veins into the artificial lung and then pumps the oxygenated blood back into the arteries. During a heart transplant, use of this machine prevents damage to the heart until it is placed in the body of the recipient. The heart recipient is also maintained on a heart-lung machine until the transplant is completed; the natural heartbeat is restored by electric shock.

HEARTS, game of cards, usually played by three or four persons, in which each player attempts to lose as many tricks as possible in order to lose all his cards in the heart suit. The game is played with a standard deck of fifty-two cards, with cards of low value first being discarded if necessary to give each player an equal number of cards. The cards are then dealt in succession, one at a time, to the players. The first player to the left of the dealer plays any card he likes, the rest of the players following suit. The highest card of the suit led wins the trick (ace is high), and the winner leads the next trick. If a player cannot follow suit, he may play any card he pleases, and thus has an opportunity to get rid of his hearts. When all the tricks have been played, each player counts the number of hearts he has taken in and, in the usual method of scoring, scores one point for each heart; after several hands have been played, the person with the lowest number of points wins the game.

Many variations of the game have been devised. In one, the queen of spades is given the value of thirteen in the settling of the score. In another, a player may attempt to take in all thirteen hearts in the deck. If he succeeds, he gains a bonus by losing points; if he fails, the game is scored in the usual way.

HEARTSEASE. See SELFHEAL; VIOLET.

HEAT, in physics, transfer of energy from one part of a substance to another, or from one body to another by virtue of a difference in temperature (q.v.); see ENERGY. Heat is energy in transit and it always flows from a substance at a higher temperature to the substance at a lower temperature, raising the temperature of the latter, and lowering that of the former substance, provided the volume of the bodies remains constant. Heat does not flow from a lower to a higher temperature unless another form of energy transfer, work (q.v.), is also present. See also POWER.

Until the beginning of the 19th century, the effect of heat on the temperature of a body was explained by postulating the existence of an invisible substance or form of matter termed caloric. According to the caloric theory of heat, a body at a high temperature contained more caloric than one at a low temperature, losing some caloric to the other body on contact and increasing its temperature, while lowering its own temperature. Though the caloric theory successfully explained some phenomena of heat transfer, experimental evidence was presented in 1798 by the American-born British physicist Benjamin Thompson (q.v.), later known as Count Rumford, and Sir Humphrey Davy (q.v.) in 1799, which suggested that heat, like work, was a form of energy in transit. Between 1840 and 1849 the British physicist James Prescott Joule (q.v.), in a series of very accurate experiments, provided conclusive evidence which showed that heat was a form of energy in transit and that it could cause the same changes in a body as work.

Temperature. The sensation of warmth or coldness of a substance on contact is determined by the property known as temperature. Although it is easy to compare the relative temperatures of two substances by the sense of touch, it is impossible to evaluate the absolute magnitude of the temperatures by subjective reactions. Adding heat to a substance, however, not only raises its temperature, causing it to impart a more acute sensation of warmth, but also produces alterations in several physical properties, which may be measured with precision. As the temperature varies, a substance expands or contracts, its electrical resistivity (see RESISTANCE) changes, and in the gaseous form, it exerts varying pressure. The variation in a standard property usually serves as a basis for an accurate numerical temperature scale (see below).

Temperature depends upon the average kinetic energy of the molecules of a substance, and according to kinetic theory (q.v.), energy may exist in rotational, vibrational, and translational motions of the particles of a substance. Temperature, however, depends only on the translational molecular motion. Theoretically, the molecules of a substance would exhibit no activity at the temperature termed absolute zero (q.v.); see MOLECULE.

HEAT

Temperature Scales. By international agreement at the Congress on Weights and Measures held in Paris, France, in 1887, it was decided that the variation in pressure of a constant volume of hydrogen (q.v.) should serve as a universal standard for the measurement of temperature changes. The fixed points on the temperature scale chosen at the congress were the freezing point and the boiling point (qq.v.) of pure water saturated with air at a pressure of one atmosphere (q.v.). The number ascribed to each fixed point varies, however, on different scales adopted by various countries.

Five different temperature scales are in use today, the Celsius scale, known also as the centigrade scale, the Fahrenheit scale, the Kelvin scale, the Rankine scale, and the international thermodynamic temperature scale; see THERMODYNAMICS; THERMOMETER. The centigrade scale, with a freezing point of 0° C., and a boiling point of 100° C., is widely used throughout the world, particularly for scientific work, although it was superseded officially in 1950 by the international temperature scale. In the Fahrenheit scale, used in English-speaking countries for purposes other than scientific work, and based on the mercury thermometer, the freezing point of water is defined as 32° F., and the boiling point as 212° F.; see MERCURY. In the Kelvin scale, the most commonly used thermodynamic temperature scale, zero is defined as the absolute zero of temperature, that is, −273.15° C., or −459.67° F. Another scale employing absolute zero as its lowest point is the Rankine scale, in which each degree of temperature is equivalent to one degree on the Fahrenheit scale. The freezing point of water on the Rankine scale is 492° R. and the boiling point is 672° R.

In 1933 scientists of thirty-one nations adopted a new international temperature scale with additional fixed temperature points, based on the Kelvin scale and thermodynamic principles. The international scale is based on the property of electrical resistivity, with platinum wire as the standard for temperature between −190° C. and 660° C. Above 660° C., to the melting point of gold, 1063° C., a standard thermocouple, which is a device that measures temperature by the amount of voltage produced between two wires of different metals, is used; beyond this point temperatures are measured by the so-called optical pyrometer, which uses the intensity of light (q.v.) of a wavelength emitted by a hot body for the purpose.

In 1954, the triple point of water, that is, the point at which the three phases of water, vapor, liquid, and ice, are in equilibrium (q.v.), was adopted by international agreement as 273.16° K. The triple point can be determined with greater precision than the freezing point, and thus provides a more satisfactory fixed point for the absolute thermodynamic scale. In cryogenics, or low-temperature research, temperatures as low as 0.003° K. have been produced by the demagnetization of paramagnetic materials; see CRYOGENICS. Momentary high temperatures, estimated to be greater than 100,000,000° K. have been achieved by nuclear explosions; see NUCLEAR WEAPONS.

Heat Units. Heat is measured in terms of the calorie (q.v.), defined as the amount of heat necessary to raise the temperature of 1 g of water at a pressure of one atmosphere from 15° C. to 16° C. This unit is sometimes called the small or gram calorie to distinguish it from the large calorie, or kilocalorie, equal to 1000 calories, which is used in nutrition studies. In mechanical-engineering practice in the United States and Great Britain, heat is measured in British thermal units (B.T.U.); see BRITISH THERMAL UNIT. One B.T.U. is the quantity of heat required to raise the temperature of 1 lb. of water 1° F., and is equal to 252 calories. Mechanical energy can be converted into heat by friction (q.v.), and the mechanical work necessary to produce one calorie is known as the mechanical equivalent of heat. It is equal to 4.1855×10^7 ergs per caloric or 778 ft.-lb. per B.T.U. According to the law of conservation of energy, all the mechanical energy expended to produce heat by friction appears as energy in the objects on which the work is performed. This fact was first conclusively proven in a classic experiment performed by Joule who heated water in a closed vessel by means of rotating paddle wheels and found that the rise in water temperature was proportional to the work expended in turning the wheels.

If heat is converted into mechanical energy, as in an internal-combustion engine (q.v.), the law of conservation of energy also applies. In any engine, however, some energy is always lost or dissipated in the form of heat because no engine is perfectly efficient. See HORSEPOWER.

Latent Heat. A number of physical changes are associated with the change of temperature of a substance. Almost all substances expand in volume when heated and contract when cooled. The behavior of water between 0° C. and 4° C. (32° F. and 39° F.) constitutes an important exception to this rule. The phase of a substance refers to its occurrence as either a solid, liquid, or gas, and phase changes in pure substances occur at definite temperatures and pressures; see PHASE RULE. The processes of changing from

HEATH

solid to gas, solid to liquid, and liquid to vapor (q.v.) are referred to as sublimation, melting, and vaporization respectively. If the pressure is constant, these processes occur at constant temperature. The amount of heat required to produce a change of phase is called latent heat, and hence, latent heats of sublimation, melting, and vaporization exist; see DISTILLATION; EVAPORATION. If water is boiled in an open vessel at one atmosphere pressure, the temperature does not rise above 100° C. (212° F.), no matter how much heat is added. The heat that is absorbed without changing the temperature of the water is the latent heat; it is not lost but is expended in changing the water to steam and is then stored as energy in the steam; it is again released when the steam is condensed to form water; see CONDENSATION. Similarly, a mixture of water and ice in a glass will not change its temperature if heated until all of the ice is melted. The latent heat absorbed is used up in overcoming the forces holding the particles of ice together, and is stored as energy in the water. To melt 1 g of ice, 79.7 calories are needed, and to convert 1 g of water to steam at 100° C., 541 calories are needed.

Specific Heat. The heat capacity, or the measure of the amount of heat required to raise the temperature of a unit mass of a substance one degree, is known as specific heat. If the heating process occurs while the substance is maintained at a constant volume or is subjected to a constant pressure, the measure is referred to as the specific heat at constant volume or at constant pressure. The latter is always larger than, or at least equal to, the former for each substance. Because 1 calorie causes a rise of 1° C. in 1 g of water, the specific heat of water is 1 calorie/g/°C. In the case of water, and other approximately incompressible substances, it is not necessary to distinguish between the constant-volume and constant-pressure specific heats, as they are approximately equal. Generally, the two specific heats of a substance depend upon the temperature.

Transfer of Heat. The physical methods by which energy in the form of heat can be transferred between bodies are conduction and radiation (q.v.). A third method, which also involves the motion of matter, is called convection (q.v.). Conduction requires physical contact between the bodies or portions of bodies exchanging heat, but radiation does not require contact or the presence of any matter between the bodies. Convection occurs when a liquid or gas is in contact with a solid body at a different temperature and is always accompanied by the motion of the liquid or gas. The science dealing with the transfer of heat between bodies is called heat transfer (q.v.).   R.S.T.

HEATH, common name applied to the plant family Ericaceae and to two ericaceous genera, *Calluna* and *Erica,* which are also called heather. The common heath or heather, also called broom or ling, is *C. vulgaris,* native to northern and western Europe and now also found in New England and the maritime provinces of Canada.

Branch of heather, Calluna vulgaris *(right), and the bell-shaped flower (left).*

It is the principal vegetation of low waste areas near seacoasts of both continents. This plant is a small, evergreen shrub which usually grows only a few inches tall but may exceed 3 ft. in height when growing in sheltered places. It has purple stems bearing small, crowded leaves and feathery spikes or racemes of small, white or pink, bell-shaped flowers. The stems are used in making brooms, baskets, and brushes. The flowers,

HEATH

which have a pleasant odor, are often made into sachets.

The genus *Erica* contains about 500 species, the majority of which are native to the western portions of South Africa, although many species grow in the Mediterranean region, and a few extend into northern Europe. Two species, *E. cinerea*, which grows to a height of 18in. and bears rose-purple flowers, and *E. tetralix*, which may grow to a height of 2 ft. and bears rose-red flowers, are naturalized on Nantucket Island, Massachusetts. No members of the genus are native to the United States. The Scotch or purple heath, *E. cinerea*, is an abundant northwestern European species which produces large amounts of nectar in its nectaries. Its capsular fruits are eaten by grouse and other moorland birds. Other common species of the British Isles are *E. tetralix*, the cross-leaved heath, and *E. vagans*, the Cornish heath. The white heath, tree heath, bruyère, or brier, *E. arborea*, which grows in the western Mediterranean region, has thick, heavy, woody underground roots called brierroot, used in making brier pipes. The Irish heath, *Daboecia cantabrica*, is a close relative of the true heaths.

Several heaths are cultivated in gardens of the U.S. The most popular and hardy form for northern gardens is *C. vulgaris*, but many of the more attractive South African species of *Erica* are grown in California.

HEATH, Edward Richard George (1916–), British politician, born in Broadstairs, England, and educated at the University of Oxford. After service (1940–46) in the British army in World War II, Heath was (1946–47) an administrator in the ministry of civil aviation. He resigned to join a London banking firm. Elected (1950) to the House of Commons as Conservative Party (q.v.) member for Bexley, a suburb of London, Heath became assistant party whip (1952) and then chief party whip (1955). He also served as minister of labor (1959–60), lord privy seal (1960–63), and president of the board of trade (1963–64). When the Conservative Party won an upset victory in the elections of June, 1970, Queen Elizabeth II (q.v.) commissioned Heath to form a government. As prime minister, he announced that his party would lead Great Britain into the European Economic Community (q.v.), reduce taxes, and strengthen the economy and the British presence overseas.

HEATHER, popular name for plants of the genera *Calluna* and *Erica*, also called heath (q.v.).

HEATH HEN. *See* PRAIRIE CHICKEN.

HEATING, VENTILATING, AND AIR CONDITIONING, name applied to the related processes designed to regulate atmospheric conditions within buildings for comfort or for industrial purposes. The term "heating" implies essentially the combustion of a fuel to raise the temperature in a given space to a more satisfactory level than that of the atmosphere. Ventilation, either separately or in combination with the heating or air-conditioning system, controls both the supply and exhaust of air within given areas in order to provide sufficient oxygen to the occupants and to eliminate annoying odors. Air conditioning designates control of the indoor environment throughout the year to create and maintain desirable conditions of temperature, humidity, and air circulation and purity for the occupants of that space or for the industrial materials that are handled or stored there.

HEATING

The heating process may be direct, as from a fireplace or stove in an individual room, or indirect, as in a central system in which steam, heated water, or heated air passing through pipes or other ducts transports thermal energy to all the rooms of a building.

Fireplaces. The earliest heating system was the open fire with which primitive men warmed their dwellings. Subsequently, stoves and braziers of various types were developed by the ancient Romans. Such devices still are employed in various parts of the world. The fireplace was developed in the colder regions of Europe as a method of heating rooms by means of an open fire. The first fireplaces were hearths, recessed into the walls of buildings, with short flues that communicated with the open air. Fireplaces with chimneys sufficiently high above the roof of the building to provide adequate draft for the fire were introduced during the 12th century.

Ordinary fireplaces consist of a hearth enclosed on three sides with brick and surmounted by a completely enclosed chimney or flue that carries away the smoke and other combustion products of the fire. On the hearth is either a metal grate, raised on legs, or a pair of metal supports called firedogs or andirons. Grates are used for such fuels as coal, coke, or charcoal, and andirons, for wood. These devices promote combustion by permitting the circulation of air under the fuel.

The useful heat given off by a fireplace consists of direct radiation from the burning fuel and of indirect radiation from the hot side and back walls. From 85 to 90 percent of the heat from the burning fuel is lost in the combustion gases that go up the chimney. Fireplaces are included in modern houses mainly for esthetic reasons rather than thermal efficiency. To improve heating efficiency, however, some mod

HEATING, VENTILATING, AND AIR CONDITIONING

ern fireplaces are built with an arrangement of interior ducts in which cold air from the room is warmed and then recirculated through the room.

Stoves. The stove, an enclosure of metal or ceramic materials in which fuel is burned, is an improvement over the fireplace because it is in contact with the air of the room and by convection delivers heat to the air passing over it. An efficient stove delivers about 75 percent of the energy of the burning fuel. In some rural areas in the United States and in many other parts of the world stoves are employed extensively for heating houses. The fuels burned in stoves include wood, coal, coke, peat, gas, kerosene, and fuel oils.

Central Heating. Central-heating systems, in which one centrally located heating unit is used to warm several rooms or an entire house, were developed in the 19th century. A type of centralized heating, utilizing hot water, was used to a limited extent in Great Britain about 1816, but the first successful central system, introduced in 1835, used warm air. This system subsequently came into extensive use in the U.S. Steam heating was developed about 1850.

Present-day central-heating systems provide heat from a central furnace for a single building or a group of buildings. In large systems steam or hot water usually is employed for distribution of the heat. The central-heating systems of dwellings, schools, and institutions generally are privately maintained; in a complex of closely grouped buildings central-heating service may be provided by a public utility. The term "district heating" is applied to systems in which a large number of buildings are supplied with steam from central boiler rooms operated by a public utility.

WARM-AIR SYSTEMS. The simplest warm-air heating system consists of a firebox and waste-gas passage set within a sheet-metal casing, and ducts leading to the various rooms. To insure natural circulation of the warm air, which tends to rise, the furnace usually is situated below the first floor of the house. Cold air, either from within the house or from outdoors, is admitted between the firebox and the casing and is heated by contact with the hot surfaces of the furnace. Frequently the furnace is arranged so

A large industrial heater designed to serve a steam-turbine generator unit.   Westinghouse

HEATING, VENTILATING, AND AIR CONDITIONING

that the warm air passes over a water pan in the furnace for humidification before circulating through the house. As the air is heated, it passes through the ducts to individual grills or registers in each room of the upper floors. The grills or registers can be opened or closed to control the temperature of the rooms.

The chief problem in this type of system is to obtain adequate air circulation. Unless the warm-air ducts are comparatively large in diameter, slanted upward from the furnace, and are properly insulated to prevent heat losses, the system may not heat a house adequately.

In a forced-circulation system a fan or blower is placed in the furnace casing; such a system insures the circulation of a large amount of air even under unfavorable conditions. Dust filters may be included in the system to insure the cleanliness of the air. When combined with cooling, humidifying, and dehumidifying units, forced-circulation systems may be used effectively for heating and cooling. Forced-circulation warm-air systems are presently the most popular for residential installations.

HOT-WATER SYSTEMS. In the first hot-water heating systems the waters of natural hot springs reputedly were used as a source of heat. Modern systems of this type employ a boiler (q.v.), in which water is heated to a temperature of from 140° to 180° F. (60° to 83° C.). The water is then circulated by means of pipes to radiators located in the various rooms. Circulation of the hot water can be accomplished by natural methods, but forced circulation utilizing a pump is far more efficient because it provides flexibility and control.

There are one- and two-pipe systems in use. In the one-pipe system water is admitted to each radiator from the supply side of the main pipe, circulates through the radiator, and flows back into the same pipe. The disadvantage of this arrangement is that the water becomes increasingly cool as it flows away from the furnace, and hence the radiators farthest from the furnace must be larger than those nearer the furnace in order to deliver the same amount of heat. In the two-pipe system all radiators are supplied with hot water at the same temperature from a single supply pipe and the water from all the radiators flows back to the furnace through a common return pipe. The two-pipe system is more efficient and easier to control than is the one-pipe system. In both systems an expansion tank is required to compensate for variations in the volume of water in the system as it is heated and cooled. Closed expansion tanks contain about 50 percent air, which compresses and expands to compensate for volume changes in the water.

STEAM SYSTEMS. Steam-heating systems closely resemble hot-water systems except that steam rather than hot water is circulated through the pipes to the radiators. The steam condenses in the radiators, giving up its latent heat; see HEAT: *Latent Heat.* Both one-pipe and two-pipe arrangements are employed for circulating the steam and for returning to the boiler the water formed by condensation.

There are three main types of steam systems, namely air-vent systems, vapor systems, and vacuum, or mechanical-pump, systems. A subatmospheric type is less commonly used.

The one-pipe air-vent system is an arrangement in which the force of gravity causes the condensate to flow from the radiator to the boiler in the same pipe through which steam reaches the radiator. This type is the least expensive to install, but the pipes must be large to accommodate both the steam and the condensate. Air vents on each radiator permit air to be forced out of the radiator by the steam during the warm-up period and occasionally during operation.

The vapor type is a two-pipe system in which steam passes into the radiator through an inlet valve and air and condensate are delivered to the return pipe by means of a steam trap on the radiator. The condensate is returned to the boiler and the air is discharged either through one central air vent in the basement or, in larger installations, through a vent for each zone heated by the system. If the system is constructed with tight joints the rate at which air reenters the system is so reduced that minimal pressure is required to propel the steam. A vapor system, though more expensive to install than the one-pipe system, is more economical of fuel because it can be operated on the low-firing cycle of the furnace.

Vacuum systems resemble vapor systems in that each radiator is equipped with an inlet valve and a steam trap, but differ in having a vacuum pump installed in the return piping. With the pump a partial vacuum is maintained in the system so that the steam, air, and condensate circulate more readily. The condensate and air return to a central point from which the condensate is pumped back into the boiler and the air is expelled into the atmosphere. With a full vacuum system the condensate does not have to be returned by gravity, so that radiators can be situated either above or below the boiler.

Heating Equipment. Various types of equipment are necessary in heating.

HEATING, VENTILATING, AND AIR CONDITIONING

RADIATORS AND CONVECTORS. The devices generally employed to transfer heat from the heating system to the area to be warmed are known commonly as radiators and convectors. Ordinary radiators consist of a series of cast-iron grids or coils having a comparatively large total surface area. The convector consists of a network of finned steel or nonferrous-metal tubes. These units are placed in enclosures designed to permit air circulation; thus heat is provided largely by convection rather than by radiation. Stores, warehouses, and factories frequently are equipped with so-called unit heaters in which an electric fan or blower forces a blast of air through heating coils.

RADIANT, OR PANEL, HEATING. Although in all forms of direct heating heat is provided in part by radiation, the term "radiant heating" is applied popularly to systems in which floors, walls, or ceilings are used as the radiating units. Steam or hot-water pipes are placed in the walls or floors during construction of the building. If electricity is used for heating, the panels containing heating elements are mounted on the wall or ceiling of the room. Radiant heating provides uniform heat and has a comparatively low cost of operation. Efficiency is high because radiant heat raises the inside-surface temperature, thereby providing comfort at a lower room-air temperature than other systems.

FURNACES. Furnaces for heating systems conventionally are fired with such fuels as oil, gas, or coal. As the fuel burns it heats metal surfaces that in turn transfer the heat to water, steam, or air according to the system used. If the furnace uses coal as a fuel and is hand fired, the firebox contains a grate. Furnaces fired by automatic stokers contain chain grates, feed screws, or other devices for conveying the coal to the fire and for removing the ashes from the fire. When oil or gas is used as fuel, the firebox contains special burners that are operated automatically by a remote thermostatic control. In most modern furnaces, the entire unit, both firebox and boiler, is enclosed in an insulated casing. *See also* FURNACE.

Special Heating Systems. In recent years attempts have been made to devise new heating systems that would require less fuel or possess other advantages over conventional systems. The most important of these experimental systems are solar heating and heat pumps.

During each hour of sunlight about 0.9 kilowatt of solar energy falls on each square yard of the earth's surface. This energy has been harnessed both experimentally and practically to heat hot water for domestic uses and even to produce power, particularly in tropical regions; *see* SOLAR POWER.

The amount of energy available from the sun is more than sufficient to heat buildings, but the chief problem in designing a solar-heating system is to store the heat of the sun so that there is an adequate reserve for nights and cloudy days, especially in areas with severe winters. In one of several methods of heat storage incorporated into experimental houses, a series of metal plates, protected by glass, is arranged at the top of the house, perpendicular to the rays of the sun during the winter months. Air warmed by circulating around these plates is then drawn into so-called storage bins containing cans of Glauber's salt, which melts at approximately 90° F. (33° C.). The warm air melts the chemical, storing heat in the form of latent heat of fusion. At night and on sunless days, cool air circulating in the storage bins is warmed as the chemical releases its latent heat, and the warmed air is circulated through the house. The only power used in this heating system is the comparatively small amount used to operate the electric blowers that circulate the air. Tests showed that this solar system is entirely adequate to heat a house during winter months in New England and that the heat-storage capacity is sufficient to keep the house warm during ten successive sunless days.

The principle of the heat pump is that of a mechanical refrigerating system in reverse; *see* REFRIGERATION. Air or water from an outside source is pumped into the system and cooled by the heat-absorption action of a refrigerant. The refrigerant is then compressed, and the heat released by the condenser is used to warm the air within the house. One great advantage of the heat-pump system is that during the summer months the cycle can be reversed and the system can be used to cool the air within the house. Such a system burns no fuel and only a pump, a compressor, and a blower are required. Successful heat-pump systems have been installed in a number of large and small buildings, both for commercial and for domestic heating.

Portable Heating Units. Houses lacking central-heating systems are equipped with various types of portable and semiportable heating devices, many of which can be moved from room to room as needed. The most common types are kerosene stoves and electric heaters. The usual kerosene stove is made of sheet metal and contains one or more wick burners that heat metal flues within the stove. Kerosene stoves heat both by radiation and by convection, drawing in cool air through vents in the

271

HEATING, VENTILATING, AND AIR CONDITIONING

bottom of the stove and emitting heated air from top vents. Known generally as space heaters, large stoves of this general pattern can provide adequate heat for several rooms. The simplest electric heaters are radiant heaters having a resistance-heating unit in front of a reflector, which concentrates the radiant heat into a narrow beam. Some radiant heaters include a fan, which circulates air around the heating unit, thus warming by convection as well as by radiation. Another recently developed type of electric heater consists of a plate of heat-resistant glass in which resistance wires are embedded. The entire plate is warmed by the wires and gives off radiant heat. Because the heater has no incandescent wires, it is safer than the older type.

Electric-steam radiators are used to supplement other heating systems. These radiators are miniature steam-heating systems in which an electrical-heating unit generates enough steam to warm a small conventional radiator partially filled with water. No pipe connections are necessary and the units can be moved from place to place and plugged into any light socket.

VENTILATION

Buildings in which people live and work must be ventilated to replenish oxygen, to dilute the concentration of carbon dioxide and water vapor, and to minimize unpleasant odors. A certain amount of air movement or ventilation ordinarily is provided by air leakage through small crevices in the building's walls, especially around windows and doors. A wind blowing against the side of a house creates an excess of pressure on the windward side and a low-pressure area on the leeward side; the air pulled through the cracks by the difference in pressure provides natural ventilation. Chimney flues and other openings in a building promote ventilation also by drawing off warm air from the interior of the building. Such haphazard methods are adequate for residences but not for public buildings, such as stores and theaters, which accommodate large numbers of people.

Engineers estimate that for adequate ventilation the air in a room should be changed completely from one and a half to three times each hour or that about 10 to 30 cu.ft. of outside air per minute should be supplied for each occupant. Providing this amount of ventilation usually requires the use of mechanical devices to augment the natural flow of air.

Simple ventilation devices include fans or blowers that are arranged either to exhaust the stale air from the building or to force fresh air into the building, or both. Ventilating systems may be combined with heaters, dust filters, humidifying and dehumidifying apparatus, and cooling devices. In such installations outside air often is circulated with a certain amount of redistributed air from within the building, particularly if the air inside has been heated or cooled.

AIR CONDITIONING

Theoretically, an air-conditioning system consists of centralized equipment that provides an atmosphere with controlled temperature, humidity, and purity at all times regardless of weather conditions. In popular usage, however, the term "air conditioning" often is applied improperly to air cooling. Many so-called air-conditioning units consist merely of blower-equipped refrigerating units that simply provide only a flow of cool, filtered air.

A number of manufacturing processes, such as those used in the production of paper, textiles, and printed matter, require air conditioning for the control of conditions during manufacture. Air conditioning of this kind usually is based on adjusting the humidity of the circulated air. When dry air is required, it is usually dehumidified by cooling or by dehydration. In the latter process it is passed through chambers containing adsorptive chemicals such as silica gel. Air is humidified by circulation through water baths or sprays. When air must be completely free of dust, as is necessary in the manufacture of certain drugs and medical supplies, the air-conditioning system is designed to include some type of filter. The air is passed through water sprays or through a labyrinth of oil-covered plates in some filters; in others, dust is removed electrostatically by means of precipitators. See COTTRELL PRECIPITATOR.

Centralized air-conditioning systems, providing fully controlled heating, cooling, and ventilation, as required, are employed widely in theaters, stores, restaurants, and other public buildings. Such systems, being complex, generally must be installed when the building is constructed. In older buildings, single apartments or suites of offices may be equipped with a refrigerating unit, blowers, air ducts, and a plenum chamber in which air from the interior of the building is mixed with outside air. Such installations are used for cooling and dehumidification during the summer months, and the regular heating system is used during the winter. A smaller apparatus for cooling single rooms consists of a refrigerating unit and blower in a compact cabinet that can be mounted in a window.

The design of an air-conditioning system depends upon several factors, including the type of structure in which the system is to be placed,

The size and complexity of an industrial air conditioner (above) contrasts with the compact room air conditioner used for offices and homes (below).

Carrier Corporation

HEAT, MECHANICAL EQUIVALENT OF

the amount of space to be cooled, the number of occupants, and the nature of their activity. A room or building with large windows exposed to the sun, or an indoor office space with many heat-producing lights, requires a system with a larger cooling capacity than an almost windowless room in which cool fluorescent lighting is used. The circulation of air must be greater in a space in which the occupants are allowed to smoke than in a space, of equal capacity, in which smoking is prohibited. In homes or apartments most of the cooled or heated air can be recirculated without discomfort to the occupants; but in laboratories or factories, employing processes that generate noxious fumes, no air can be recirculated and a constant supply of cooled or heated fresh air must be supplied.

Small air-conditioning units, which provide only ventilation, filtering, and air cooling, are rated commonly in terms of tons, British thermal units (B.T.U.) per hour, and horsepower. A ton of cooling capacity is the amount of cooling furnished by the melting of 1 ton of ice in 1 hr., and is equivalent to 12,000 B.T.U.'s (A B.T.U. is the amount of heat removed from 1 lb. of water when its temperature is lowered by 1° F.; see HEAT.) The only accurate measurement of the cooling power of air-conditioning units is a B.T.U. rating. The horsepower rating is misleading because it represents the power of the motor rather than the cooling capacity of the unit. Air conditioners with the same horsepower ratings may differ as much as 4000 B.T.U.'s in cooling power. B.H.J.

HEAT, MECHANICAL EQUIVALENT OF, or JOULE'S EQUIVALENT, in physics and engineering, the quantitative relationship (in unit values) between heat and mechanical work (qq.v.). The British physicist James Prescott Joule (q.v.) first established the relationship in 1840, and this led to the formulation of the first law of thermodynamics (q.v.). For the exact value of the mechanical equivalent of heat see HEAT: *Heat Units.* See also HORSEPOWER.

HEAT PUMP. See HEATING, VENTILATING, AND AIR CONDITIONING: *Special Heating Systems.*

HEATSTROKE, term loosely applied to three distinct conditions. If it occurs indoors in a superheated environment, it is termed heatstroke; when it is caused by exposure to sun, it is called sunstroke. It is caused by disturbance of the heat-regulating centers of the central nervous system (q.v.), and the body cannot eliminate enough heat by sweat and body water from the lungs. The consequent accumulation of body heat results in salt and water imbalance and may cause circulatory collapse. A victim of heatstroke may experience headache, tingling, numbness, dizziness, and mental confusion. Heatstroke is associated with a drying-out of the skin as sweating stops, an alarmingly fast respiration, pulse rate, and blood pressure that may lead to convulsions and coma. If the victim also suffers from alcoholism, high blood pressure, arteriosclerosis, or chronic kidney disease, the attack is likely to be worse. Unconsciousness comes suddenly.

Untreated heatstroke is usually fatal; even a third of treated cases may die if the body temperature rises above 108° F., and death is more likely if it goes above 110° F. High fever (q.v.) over a long period of time may cause shock, irreversible brain damage, pulmonary edema, or heart or kidney failure. The first thing to do is to lower the body heat by soaking the patient in cold or iced water until the temperature drops to 102° F. Cooling by wrapping the patient in wet sheets is an acceptable substitute. Vigorous massage of soft tissues and extremities is required to force cooled blood to overheated organs. If the temperature rises again it can be treated in the same way. A week may be required to restore the sweating function and maintain normal body temperature. Bed rest is essential.

Heat exhaustion is less dramatic and threatening, but may progress to heatstroke if not treated. Although it exhibits many of the same symptoms, it is distinguished from heatstroke by a decrease in blood pressure and pulse, no elevation of temperature, and continued perspiration. It is caused by depletion of salt and water by excessive sweating and treated by removal from the heated environment, bed rest, and gradual replacement of salt and water by mouth. Heat collapse or syncope, a lesser manifestation, causes sudden, temporary unconsciousness and is self-limiting. It is cured by allowing the patient to rest in a horizontal position. People forced to work in high temperatures may avoid heat exhaustion by ingesting additional amounts of water and salt.

Heat cramps involves painful contractions of abdominal muscles as well as cramps and twitching of muscles in the extremities after drinking much water and after the body is depleted of salt by perspiration. Body temperature and heart and circulatory functions, however, remain normal. Heat cramps are common in those who do hard labor under extreme heat, but they respond promptly to intake of salt.

Persons exposed to excessive heat can protect themselves from these dangers by proper ventilation of working and sleeping quarters and by wearing thin, loose clothing. A rich diet and stimulants should be avoided, and intake of salt and water should be increased. Persons who work in superheated industrial environments or engage in military maneuvers, as in desert warfare, may undergo a two-week period of acclimatization to lower pulse, respiration, and body temperatures, resulting in dilution and increase in volume of sweat.

HEAT TRANSFER, in physics, process by which energy in the form of heat is exchanged between bodies or parts of the same body at different temperatures; *see* ENERGY; HEAT; TEMPERATURE. Heat is generally transferred by convection, radiation (qq.v.), and conduction. Though these three processes can occur simultaneously, it is not unusual for one mechanism to overshadow the other two mechanisms. Heat, for example, is transferred by conduction through the brick wall of a house, the surfaces of high-speed aircraft are heated by convection, and the earth receives heat from the sun by radiation.

Conduction. This is the only method of heat transfer in opaque solids. If the temperature at one end of a metal rod is raised by heating, heat is conducted to the colder end, but the exact mechanism of heat conduction in solids is not entirely understood. It is believed, however, to be partially due to the motion of free electrons in the solid matter, which transport energy if a temperature difference is applied. This theory helps to explain why good electrical conductors also tend to be good heat conductors; *see* CONDUCTOR, ELECTRICAL. Though the phenomenon of heat conduction had been observed for centuries, it was not until 1882 that the French mathematician Jean Baptiste Joseph Fourier (q.v.) gave it precise mathematical expression in what is now regarded as Fourier's law of heat conduction. This physical law states that the rate at which heat is conducted through a body per unit cross-sectional area is proportional to the negative of the temperature gradient existing in the body.

The proportionality factor is called the thermal conductivity of the material. Materials such as gold, silver, and copper have high thermal conductivities and conduct heat readily, but materials such as glass and asbestos have values of thermal conductivity hundreds and thousands of times smaller, conduct heat poorly, and are referred to as insulators; *see* INSULATION. In engineering applications it is frequently necessary to establish the rate at which heat will be conducted through a solid if a known temperature difference exists across the solid. Sophisticated mathematical techniques are required to establish this, especially if the process varies with time, the phenomenon being known as transient-heat conduction. With the aid of analog and digital computers these problems are now being solved for bodies of complex geometry (q.v.); *see* COMPUTER; DATA PROCESSING.

Convection. Conduction occurs not only within a body but also between two bodies if they are brought into contact, and if one of the substances is a liquid or a gas, then fluid motion will almost certainly occur. This process of conduction between a solid surface and a moving liquid or gas is called convection. The motion of the fluid may be natural or forced. If a liquid or gas is heated, its mass (q.v.) per unit volume generally decreases. If the liquid or gas is in a gravitational field, the hotter, lighter fluid rises while the colder, heavier fluid sinks. This kind of motion, due solely to nonuniformity of fluid temperature in the presence of a gravitational field, is called natural convection; *see* GRAVITATION. Forced convection is achieved by subjecting the fluid to a pressure gradient and thereby forcing motion to occur according to the law of fluid mechanics (q.v.). Convection heat transfer, which is a combination of the processes of conduction and fluid motion, is even more difficult to analyze mathematically than pure heat conduction. Because of its widespread occurrence and importance to engineering, however, convection has been the subject of a considerable amount of experimental research.

The ordinary household radiator is a device for transferring heat to the colder room air by conduction and convection from hot water or steam. Because heat transfer by radiation is relatively quite small, these devices are more appropriately referred to as convectors, a term now gaining widespread acceptance especially if they are of the finned variety. Fins are thin metal protrusions from the tubes containing the hot fluid, which are added to enhance the overall effectiveness of the convection process.

Radiation. This process is fundamentally different from both conduction and convection in that the substances exchanging heat need not be in contact with each other. In fact they can be separated by a vacuum (q.v.). Radiation is a term generally applied to all kinds of electromagnetic-wave phenomena; *see* ELECTROMAGNETIC RADIATION. The true nature of radiation and its transport mechanism have not been completely established. Some radiation phenomena can be described in terms of wave theory (*see* WAVE MOTION), and others can be explained in terms of quantum theory (q.v.). Neither theory, however, completely explains all experimental

HEAT TRANSFER

observations. The German-born American physicist Albert Einstein (q.v.) conclusively demonstrated in 1905 the quantized behavior of radiant energy in his classical photoelectric experiments. Prior to Einstein's experiments the quantized nature of radiant energy had been postulated, and the German physicist Max Planck (q.v.) in 1900 used quantum theory and the mathematical formalism of statistical mechanics to derive a fundamental law of radiation; see MATHEMATICS; MECHANICS; STATISTICS. The mathematical expression of this law, called Planck's distribution, relates the intensity or strength of radiant energy emitted by a body to the temperature of the body and the wavelength of radiation. This is the maximum amount of radiant energy that can be emitted by a body at a particular temperature. Only ideal or so-called black bodies emit such radiation according to Planck's law. Real bodies emit at a somewhat reduced intensity. The contribution of all frequencies to the radiant energy emitted by a body is called the emissive power of the body, the amount of energy emitted by a unit surface area of a body per unit of time. As can be shown from Planck's law the emissive power of a surface is proportional to the fourth power of the absolute temperature. The proportionality factor is called the Stefan-Boltzmann constant after two Austrian physicists Joseph Stefan (1835–93) and Ludwig Eduard Boltzmann (q.v.) who in 1879 and 1884 respectively discovered the fourth power relationship for the emissive power. According to Planck's law all substances emit radiant energy merely by virtue of having a positive absolute temperature. The higher the temperature, the greater the amount of energy emitted. In addition to emitting, all substances are capable of absorbing radiation. Thus, although an ice cube is continuously emitting radiant energy, it will melt if an incandescent lamp is focused on it because it will be absorbing a greater amount of heat than it is emitting.

Opaque surfaces can absorb or reflect incident radiation. Generally, dull, rough surfaces absorb more heat than bright, polished surfaces, and bright surfaces reflect more radiant energy than dull surfaces. In addition, good absorbers are also good emitters and good reflectors, or poor absorbers are poor emitters. Thus, cooking utensils generally have dull bottoms for good absorption and polished sides for minimum emission to maximize the net heat transfer into the contents of the pot. Some substances, such as gases and glass, are capable of transmitting large amounts of radiation. It is experimentally observed that the absorbing, reflecting, and transmitting properties of a substance depend upon the wavelength of the incident radiation. Glass, for example, transmits large amounts of short wavelength (ultraviolet) radiation, but is a poor transmitter of long wavelength (infrared) radiation; see INFRARED; ULTRAVIOLET RADIATION. A consequence of Planck's distribution is that the wavelength at which the maximum amount of radiant energy is emitted by a body decreases as the temperature increases. Wien's displacement law, named after the German physicist Wilhelm Wien (q.v.), is a mathematical expression of this observation and states that the wavelength of maximum energy, expressed in microns (millionths of a meter), multiplied by the Kelvin temperature of the body is equal to a constant, 2878. Most of the energy radiated by the sun, therefore, is characterized by small wavelengths. This fact, together with the transmitting properties of glass mentioned above, explains the greenhouse effect. Radiant energy from the sun is transmitted through the glass and enters the greenhouse. The energy emitted by the contents of the greenhouse, however, which emit primarily at infrared wavelengths, is not transmitted out through the glass. Thus, although the air temperature outside the greenhouse may be low, the temperature inside the greenhouse will be much higher because there is a sizable net heat transfer into it.

In addition to heat transfer processes that result in raising or lowering temperatures of the participating bodies, heat transfer can also produce phase changes such as the melting of ice or the boiling of water. In engineering, heat-transfer processes are usually designed to take advantage of these phenomena. In the case of space capsules reentering the atmosphere of the earth at very high speed, a heat shield that melts in a prescribed manner by the process called ablation is provided to prevent overheating of the interior of the capsule. Essentially, the frictional heating produced by the atmosphere is used to melt the heat shield and not to raise the temperature of the capsule; see FRICTION.

R.S.T.

HEAVEN, in Christian theology, place where the Deity, although present throughout infinite space, gives a more immediate manifestation of His glory to the souls of just men, who, being made perfect, enjoy there the bliss of intuitive contemplation of the Godhead, the beatific vision. Heaven is the abode of the blessed angels who minister to the Most High in perpetual praise and adoration; see ANGEL.

Among primitive peoples the concept of life

after death was substantially that of a shadowy continuation of life on earth. Even in that concept, however, the principle of the necessity for vindication of divine justice was manifested. This principle is illustrated in the distinction between Elysium and Tartarus (qq.v.) in the Greek and Roman religions and in the various depths of *Sheol* (*see* HELL) of the Jewish Scriptures. Later Jewish mystics regarded the heavens as contained in the seven spheres of the firmament and found in the Persian doctrine of resurrection a hope of release from *Sheol* to a new life on earth or in the heavens; *see* ZOROASTRIANISM.

The Greek philosopher Aristotle (q.v.) declared that all (polytheistic) religions united in placing the abode of the gods in the most elevated place in the universe. Such regions were, in classical times, considered as closed to ordinary mortals. The Islands of the Blessed, sometimes identified with Elysium, were reached only by heroes, demigods, and favorites of the gods. The heaven of later polytheistic religions was conceived of as a place where mortals might continue the pleasures of earthly life, as in the Valhalla (q.v.) of the Germans and Scandinavians and the happy hunting ground of the American Indians.

The general belief of Christians is that, since the Resurrection of Christ, the souls of the just who are free from sin are admitted immediately after death into heaven, where their chief joy consists in an unclouded vision of God. Their bliss is eternal, but at the general Resurrection the souls are to be reunited to their perfected bodies to enjoy an existence like that of the angels of light (Luke 20:36). *See also* MILLENNIUM.

Islam, in the Koran (qq.v.), adopts the concept of the seven heavens of the firmament, differing in degrees of glory from the seventh, the abode of the Most High, downward to the first, or most earthly, paradise (q.v.). Although the Koran portrays the happiness of heaven as the unrestricted and inexhaustible partaking of the joys of physical sense, many writers consider this portrayal to be purely allegorical.

Nirvana, the heaven of Buddhism (q.v.), is a state of extinction of all desire and of union with Brahma (q.v.), achieved by perfecting the soul in the course of its successive transmigrations; *see* TRANSMIGRATION.

HEAVISIDE LAYER. *See* IONOSPHERE.

HEAVY HYDROGEN. *See* DEUTERIUM.

HEAVY WATER, term applied to water in which the hydrogen of the water molecule consists entirely of deuterium (q.v.), the heavy hydrogen isotope (q.v.) of mass number 2. Heavy water, known also as deuterium oxide, is designated by the symbol D_2O. Ordinary rain water contains about one molecule of deuterium oxide for every 5000 molecules of water.

The term heavy water might also be extended to include tritium oxide, that is, water in which the hydrogen consists of the heavy hydrogen isotope of mass number 3, called tritium (q.v.). Heavy water is used principally as a coolant in nuclear reactors; *see* NUCLEAR ENERGY; NUCLEAR POWER.

HEBBEL, Friedrich (1813–63), German playwright, born in Wesselburen, Schleswig-Holstein, then a Danish province. He was self-educated, but also attended lectures on law, literature, and philosophy at the University of Heidelberg. As a young man Hebbel lectured and wrote in Hamburg, Heidelberg, and Munich, but he received little recognition or financial success until 1845, when he moved to Vienna. In 1849 he married the Austrian actress Christina Enghausen (1817–1910), who appeared in many of his plays.

Among Hebbel's earlier plays are the prose drama *Judith* (1840; Eng. trans., 1914) and the prose tragedy *Maria Magdalena* (1844; Eng. trans., *Mary Magdalene,* 1913), which in its realism was the forerunner of the problem plays of the Norwegian dramatist Henrik Ibsen (q.v.); *see* REALISM. Hebbel's reputation, however, rests chiefly on the dramas he wrote after 1845, including the blank-verse tragedy *Herodes und Mariamne* (1848; Eng. trans., *Herod and Mariamne,* 1912), the prose tragedy *Agnes Bernauer* (1851; Eng. trans., 1909), the verse tragedy *Gyges und sein Ring* (1854; Eng. trans., *Gyges and His Ring,* 1914), and the trilogy *Die Niebelungen* (1862; Eng. trans., *The Nibelungs,* 1903).

HEBE, in Greek mythology, the goddess of youth, the daughter of Zeus and Hera (qq.v.). Hebe served for a long time as cupbearer to the gods, serving them their nectar and ambrosia. She was replaced in this office by the Trojan prince Ganymede (q.v.). According to one story, she resigned as cupbearer to the gods upon her marriage to the hero Hercules (q.v.), who had just been defied. In another, she was dismissed from her position because of a fall she suffered while in attendance on the gods.

HEBER, Reginald (1783–1826), British prelate and hymn writer, born in Malpas, England, and educated at Brasenose College, University of Oxford. In 1804 he became a fellow of All Souls' College, Oxford, and three years later was ordained to the Anglican ministry. In 1815 he was appointed lecturer at Oxford and in 1822 preacher at Lincoln's Inn, London. In the latter

HEBREW LANGUAGE

year he became bishop of Calcutta, India. His writings include *Poetical Works* (1812; complete edition, 1841) and the prose works *A Life of Bishop Jeremy Taylor* (1822), *Journey Through India* (2 vol., 1828), and two posthumously published volumes of sermons (1829, 1830). He is chiefly known for his hymns, including "From Greenland's Icy Mountains"; "Brightest and Best"; "God, that Madest Earth and Heaven"; and "Holy, Holy, Holy, Lord God Almighty".

HEBREW LANGUAGE, Semitic language originally adopted by the *'ibhri,* or Israelites (*see* HEBREWS), when they took possession of the land of Canaan (q.v.) west of the Jordan R. in Palestine (q.v.). The language has also been called the speech of Canaan, and Judean, after the kingdom of Judah (q.v.). Modern Hebrew is the official language of Israel (q.v.), where the Hebrew-speaking population is estimated at 1,100,000.

Biblical Hebrew (*see* BIBLE: *The Old Testament*) dates, as a living language, from the 12th century to the 2nd century B.C., at the latest. The territory of Phoenicia (q.v.) adjoined Canaan, and it is probable that Hebrew in its earliest form was almost identical to Phoenician; however, of the closely related Hebrew and Phoenician language (q.v.) groups Hebrew is decidedly the more important. The bulk of the Old Testament is written in Hebrew; Hebrew literature also contains the division of the Talmud known as the Mishnah (qq.v.), which contains the codification of the rabbinical laws. This section of Hebrew literature was edited about 200 A.D., at a time when Hebrew had long ceased to be the speech of the Jews. After 586 B.C., when Judah was conquered by Babylonia (q.v.), the Jews in Palestine came to use Aramaic (*see* ARAM) in both speech and secular writings. Jews outside of Palestine spoke in the language of the countries in which they had settled. Hebrew was preserved, however, as the language of ritual and sacred writing, and underwent periodic literary revivals.

Biblical Hebrew. The original Biblical Hebrew alphabet (*see* ALPHABET) consisted only of consonants; vowel signs and pronunciation currently accepted for Biblical Hebrew were created by scholars known as Masoretes (*see* MASORA) after the 5th century A.D. These scholars standardized various dialectal differences.

The vocabulary of Biblical Hebrew is small. Concrete adjectives are used for abstract nouns. The paucity of particles, which connect and relate ideas, and the limitation to two verb tenses (perfect and imperfect) cause an ambiguity regarding time concepts; various syntactic devices were employed to clarify relations of time (*see* SYNTAX). A past action was indicated by the first in a series of verbs being in the perfect tense and all following verbs in the imperfect; for present or future action the first verb is in the imperfect tense and all subsequent ones in the perfect.

Post-Biblical Hebrew. Mishnaic Hebrew was more adaptable to practical use than Biblical Hebrew. The vocabulary and syntactic innovations were strongly Aramaic, and about 300 words were borrowed from Greek and Latin. New senses, or meanings, and forms were given to Biblical Hebrew words, and the expressions of time were clarified. Hebrew vocabulary was further augmented in the Middle Ages by the Arabic influence on philosophic writing and through translations of Arabic philosophical and scientific works.

Modern Hebrew. When the Jews moved to Palestine Hebrew was revived as a spoken language. Modern Hebrew, *Ivrit,* was declared the official language of Israel in 1948. The alphabet has twenty-two characters; the vocabulary is based on Biblical Hebrew, and the syntax on Mishnaic Hebrew. Long vowels are generally expressed in writing by unpronounced consonant sounds. Scriptures, children's books, and poetry use the Masoretic points, which are dots or dashes. Pronunciation is modeled on Ladino, the language of the Sephardic Jews who live mainly in Turkey, Greece, and Bulgaria. A great number of new words, particularly scientific terms, were needed in order to adapt the ancient written language to contemporary use; the Lithuanian-born scholar Elieser Ben-Yahuda (1858–1922) single-handedly coined 4000 new words from Biblical Hebrew roots. The national languages of Israeli immigrants, and Yiddish, the language of the Ashkenazi, or eastern European Jews, have also influenced modern Hebrew.

See also JEWISH LITERATURE; SEMITIC LANGUAGES; YIDDISH LANGUAGE.

HEBREW LITERATURE. See JEWISH LITERATURE.
HEBREW MUSIC. See JEWISH MUSIC.
HEBREWS, name given to a group of tribes of Semitic stock that, according to tradition, migrated from Mesopotamia (q.v.) to Palestine. Some scholars, however, trace their origin to the Wilderness, rather than Mesopotamia. The Hebrews moved to Egypt, where they were enslaved. When released from bondage in Egypt under the law-giver Moses (q.v.), they journeyed through the Wilderness, and thereafter, under Joshua (q.v.), they conquered and settled Palestine; *see* PALESTINE: *History.* The term Hebrew is applied in the Bible to Abraham (Gen.

14:13). Etymologically, "Hebrews" seems to mean "those who pass from place to place" or "nomads", a designation applied to them by the Amorites (q.v.). It is assumed generally by scholars, though denied by some, that the Hebrews are the people called Habiru or Habiri in the tablets found at Tell el-Amarna, Egypt; written about 1400 B.C., these were found in 1887. This assumption coincides with Biblical tradition; the Amarna correspondence, however, makes no reference to the origin or ethnic character of the Habiru. In Gen. 40:15, Joseph (q.v.) explains to the Egyptians that he had been kidnapped from "the land of the Hebrews"; in Exod. 2:6, the daughter of Pharaoh recognizes Moses as "one of the Hebrews' children". The implication of these sources is that in early times the Israelites were known to foreigners as Hebrews. In later times the Israelites applied the name to themselves, as in Jonah 1:9; see also JEWS. See HEBREW LANGUAGE. S.Sa.

HEBREWS, book of the New Testament (see BIBLE), in the King James Version, THE EPISTLE OF PAUL THE APOSTLE TO THE HEBREWS. The authorship of this Epistle has been a subject of controversy since earliest Christian times, during which it was ascribed to various persons other than Saint Paul (q.v.); for instance, to one of the Apostolic Fathers (q.v.), or to an unknown scribe who supposedly had recorded Paul's oral teachings. In both the Eastern Church (see ORTHODOX CHURCH) and the ancient Greco-Egyptian city of Alexandria (q.v.), it came to be regarded as the work of Paul, either directly or through a translator. This opinion was adopted by Saint Augustine (q.v.) and, later, by the Roman Catholic Church.

Modern scholars are almost unanimous in holding that the Epistle was not written by Paul. Basing their view entirely on internal evidence, that is, on the text alone, they point to (among other proofs) certain characteristically different uses of language and writing styles. The Greek used in this book, for example, is purer than that of any other New Testament writing. The writer always cites the Septuagint, instead of a Hebrew version of the Old Testament; and he reasons from the Greek renderings of the Hebrew originals; see BIBLE: *Manuscripts, Versions, Editions, and Translations.* The writing style is rhythmic and the form carefully planned and systematic, as opposed to the abruptness and sudden transitions that are characteristic of the Pauline writings.

The Epistle contains no specific address and begins without the usual greeting. It is assumed to have been intended for and read first by a congregation (or congregations) composed largely of converts from Judaism (q.v.). These converts apparently had second thoughts, most likely because of the increasing general persecution of Christians in the Roman Empire during the latter part of the 1st century; see CHRISTIAN CHURCH, HISTORY OF THE.

The Epistle is mainly a theological treatise in its first and longest part (1:1–10:18), the essential argument of which is the superiority of Christianity over Judaism. The briefer, concluding part (10:19–13:25) offers a "word of exhortation" (13:22) to Christians to persevere in the faith. Three major points are elaborated in support of the theological position. Christ as the Son of God absolutely excels the Hebrew lawgiver Moses (q.v.), the prophets, and angels (see ANGEL; PROPHECY); for these were lower ministers between God and man, whereas God has made Christ "captain of . . . salvation perfect through suffering" (2:10). Christ is the "great high priest" (4:14); His priesthood is "for ever" (5:6), and "being made perfect" (5:9), it thus supersedes "the Levitical priesthood" (7:11) in every way. Christ as the Son and as the high priest are considered one in the third point. As high priest, Christ sacrifices Himself, offering "once for all" (10:10) His own body in exchange for man's eternal salvation; whereas the Levites (q.v.) stand "daily ministering and offering oftentimes the same sacrifices, which can never take away sins" (10:11).

A date before 70 A.D., the year in which the Temple was destroyed by the Romans, is most often suggested for the writing of Hebrews, particularly because no distinguishable Jewish Christian community remained after the fall of Jerusalem; see Jews: *Subject Judea;* TEMPLE: *Temple at Jerusalem.* Some modern scholars, however, believing Hebrews to be concerned chiefly with problems typical of the immediate post-Apostolic age, suggest a date closer to the end of the 1st century A.D.; see APOSTLE. The book has borne its present title since 200 A.D.: why and how it acquired that title are still subjects for scholarly conjecture.

HEBREW UNION COLLEGE-JEWISH INSTITUTE OF RELIGION, theological seminary for the education of rabbis, located in Cincinnati, Ohio, with branches in Los Angeles, Calif., New York, N.Y., and Jerusalem, Israel. The seminary is sponsored by the Union of the American Hebrew Congregations and the Reform Jewish Community of America. Women students are admitted to certain classes. Hebrew Union College, the first rabbinical school in the United States, was founded in 1874 in Cincinnati and

HEBREW UNIVERSITY

opened for instruction in 1875. In 1950 it was merged with the Jewish Institute of Religion, a seminary founded in New York City in 1922. The college confers baccalaureate and graduate degrees in Hebrew letters, divinity, philosophy, sacred music, and education. The Hebrew Union College Biblical and Archaeological School, opened in 1963, also confers graduate degrees. In 1968 the library at Cincinnati, distinguished for its collection of Judaica, housed more than 200,000 bound volumes; an additional 150,000 are in the libraries of the three branches. In 1968 total enrollment was 252, the faculty numbered 39, and the endowment was about $6,510,000.

HEBREW UNIVERSITY, THE, autonomous coeducational institution of higher learning, located in Jerusalem, Israel. The university is administered by a board of governors, although seventy percent of its funds are provided by the national government. The university was founded on Mt. Scopus in 1925 and transferred to the Jewish sector of Jerusalem in 1948 after the partition of the city. A new campus was begun in 1954 at Giv'at Ram in the western section of the New City of Jerusalem. The university has the following faculties: humanities, science, medicine, dentistry, law, agriculture, and social science. Schools of pharmacy, education, social work, and a graduate library school are also part of the university. The degrees of bachelor, master, and doctor of philosophy are awarded. These degrees are about the equivalent of American degrees. The library contains more than 2,000,000 bound volumes, including the world's finest collection of Judaica. In 1968–69 the student enrollment was about 12,200; the academic staff numbered about 1570.

HEBRIDES *or* **WESTERN ISLANDS,** archipelago of about 500 islands in the Atlantic Ocean, off the W. coast of Scotland. The islands are divided into two groups, the Outer Hebrides and the Inner Hebrides, by the North Minch and Little Minch straits and the Sea of the Hebrides. The Hebrides are administrated by Ross and Cromarty, Inverness, and Argyll counties. The chief islands of the Outer Hebrides, which extend about 130 mi. from N. to S., are Lewis-with-Harris, North Uist, South Uist, and Barra. The distance from the N. to the S. extremity of the Outer Hebrides is about 130 mi. The largest of the Inner Hebrides is Skye (q.v.), and the other

A view of Tobormory on the Isle of Mull, part of the Inner Hebrides. UPI

An ancient stone relief found in Thessaly depicting Hecate.
Bettmann Archive

important islands of the group are Mull, Islay, Jura, Tiree, and Coll. Less than 100 of the Hebrides are populated, and most of the inhabitants live on Lewis with Harris, Skye, and Islay. The population as a whole is declining through emigration, especially to Canada. The climate of the Hebrides is comparatively mild. The archipelago has a rocky terrain, which is broken by many bogs, moors, lakes, and valleys. The only forests of importance are on Lewis with Harris, Skye, Mull, and Jura islands. Less than 250,000 acres of the total area is arable. Fishing, the raising of livestock, and tourism during the summer months are the principal occupations. Other economic activities include the growing of oats and potatoes, distilling, quarrying, and the production of woolen textiles, especially Harris tweed. Regular boat and air connections are maintained between the mainland and the principal islands. The largest town is Stornoway (pop. 1961, 5248), on Lewis with Harris.

In ancient times the archipelago was known as the Hebudae or the Ebudae. In 563 A.D., the Irish missionary Saint Columba (q.v.) established a Celtic monastery on the tiny island of Iona in the Inner Hebrides. During the 8th century the islands were invaded by the Norsemen (q.v.), and Norway retained control of the Hebrides until 1266, when the archipelago was transferred to Scotland. During the next few centuries, Scottish chieftains, primarily the leaders of the clans MacDougall and MacDonald, ruled the islands. The royal house of Scotland gradually reduced the influence of the chieftains and gained full authority over the Hebrides in 1748. The Scottish novelist Sir Walter Scott (q.v.), whose *The Lord of the Isles* (1815) dealt with the Hebrides, and several other Scottish and British authors have written vivid portrayals of the islands. Total area, 2900 sq.mi. Pop. (1961) 61,795.

HEBRON, city of Jordan and, according to some authorities, one of the oldest communities in the world, situated in a mountainous region, about 20 miles S.W. of Jerusalem. Among the interesting features of Hebron are the narrow winding streets, the flat-roofed stone houses, the native bazaars, and the mosque of El-Haram. The mosque is built around the supposed sepulcher of the Old Testament patriarch Abraham (q.v.) and his family. Hebron has a number of small-scale industrial establishments, which produce cotton goods, leather water containers, and glass bracelets, rings, and lamps.

Frequently mentioned in the Bible, Hebron was closely identified with Abraham. The town was captured by the Hebrew leader Joshua (q.v.). In later years David (q.v.), King of Judah and Israel, made Hebron his capital, and it was here that Absalom (q.v.), son of David, began his revolt against his father. Hebron was destroyed by the Romans during the reign of the emperor Vespasian (q.v.), restored by early Muslims, and captured by the Christians during the Crusades. In 1187 the town again became a Muslim possession under Saladin (q.v.). British troops occupied Hebron in December, 1917, during World War I. By the provisions of the United Nations Palestine partition plan in 1947, Hebron was part of the Palestinian territory awarded to Jordan. In June, 1967, following the Six-Day War between Israel and the neighboring Arab countries, Hebron was occupied by Israel. See PALESTINE: *History;* JORDAN, HASHEMITE KINGDOM OF: *History.* Pop. (1967 est.) 43,000.

HECATE, in Greek mythology, goddess of darkness, and the daughter of the Titans (q.v.) Perses and Asteria. Unlike Artemis (q.v.), who represented the moonlight and splendor of the night, Hecate represented its darkness and its terrors. On moonless nights she was believed to roam the earth with a pack of ghostly, howling dogs. She was the goddess of sorcery and witchcraft, and was especially worshipped by magicians and witches, who sacrificed black lambs and black dogs to her. As goddess of the cross-

281

roads, Hecate and her pack of dogs were believed to haunt these remote spots, which seemed evil and ghostly places to travelers. In art Hecate is represented with either three bodies or three heads, and with hissing serpents entwined about her neck.

HECHT, Ben (1894–1964), American writer, born in New York City. At the age of sixteen, he became a reporter for the Chicago *Journal*; he then worked on the Chicago *Daily News* until 1923. In that year he founded the Chicago *Literary Times*, a periodical that for the next two years expressed the iconoclastic views of a group of artists and writers living in Chicago after World War I. His first novel, *Eric Dorn* (1921), was followed by some 24 other books, about 250 short stories, and 20 plays. His plays were collaborations with, most notably, the American playwright Charles MacArthur (1895–1956), with whom he coauthored several of his most successful plays, including *The Front Page* (1928), *Twentieth Century* (1933), and *Ladies and Gentlemen* (1939). He also wrote or collaborated on some 60 screenplays, including *Scarface* (1932), *Nothing Sacred* (1937), and *Wuthering Heights* (1939). With MacArthur he wrote and produced two outstanding films, *Crime Without Passion* and *The Scoundrel*, in 1934. Two of his last books were his autobiography, *A Child of the Century* (1954) and a biography of Charles MacArthur, *Charlie* (1957). His work is known for its original dramatic qualities, flamboyance, and wit.

HECKER, Isaac Thomas (1819–88), American Roman Catholic priest, born in New York City, brought up as a Protestant. In 1843 he was a member of the cooperative community of Brook Farm (q.v.), Mass., and also lived for a time at Walden (q.v.) with the writer Henry David Thoreau (q.v.). In 1844 Hecker was converted to the Roman Catholic faith and was ordained a priest of the Redemptorist order (*see* REDEMPTORISTS), in England, in 1849. Returning to the United States, he conducted missions to Catholics from 1851 until 1857; to proselytize non-Catholics, he wrote *Questions of the Soul* (1855) and *Aspirations of Nature* (1857). In 1858, with several colleagues, Hecker founded the Society of Missionary Priests of Saint Paul the Apostle, known as Paulist Fathers, or Paulists (q.v.). He became the congregation's first superior and served until his death. In 1865 he founded the periodical *Catholic World* and in 1866 the Catholic Publication Society, predecessor to the Paulist Press.

HECKSCHER, August (1848–1941), American industrialist and philanthropist, born in Hamburg, Germany. He came to the United States in 1868. Beginning as a coal-mine laborer, he eventually became one of the foremost industrialists in the nation and the director of several financial and industrial corporations. Heckscher donated millions of dollars for the construction of social service buildings in New York City, including the endowment of several parks and summer camps for the benefit of tenement dwellers. He was chairman of the Heckscher Foundation for Children (q.v.), which he founded in 1921. His grandson, August Heckscher (1913–) was a director of the Twentieth Century Fund, commissioner of parks, City of New York, and a Fellow of the Academy of Arts and Sciences. Heckscher also occasionally served as cultural advisor to the late John F. Kennedy during his presidency.

HECTOR, in Greek mythology, the eldest son of King Priam and Queen Hecuba of Troy, and husband of Andromache (qq.v.). In the epic poem the *Iliad* (q.v.) by the Greek poet Homer (q.v.), Hector is the greatest of the Trojan warriors. As commander of the Trojan forces, he was instrumental in holding off the Greek army for nine years, and finally was able to force the Greeks back to their ships. During the battle, however, Hector killed Patroclus, the inseparable friend of Achilles (qq.v.), the greatest of the Greek warriors. Achilles had withdrawn from the fighting because of a quarrel with King Agamemnon (q.v.), the leader of the Greek forces, but in order to avenge the death of his friend he returned to the battlefield. Grief-stricken and frenzied, Achilles pursued Hector three times around the walls of Troy, killed him, and then tied his lifeless body to his chariot and dragged it around the walls and back to Patroclus' funeral pyre. Learning that the Greeks were withholding burial rites from his son, Hector's father, the sorrowing Priam, with the aid of the god Hermes (q.v.), went to Achilles and begged him to relinquish Hector's corpse. Moved by the sorrow of the aged king, Achilles agreed to yield the body of Hector and declared a truce to permit the Trojans to honor their dead hero with a suitable burial. A description of the funeral honors paid to Hector concludes the *Iliad*. In contrast to the fierce Achilles, Hector represents the chivalrous warrior. *See* TROJAN WAR.

HECUBA, in Greek mythology, wife of Priam, king of Troy, to whom she bore Hector, Paris, Cassandra (qq.v.), and sixteen other children. Following the fall of Troy and the death of Priam, the aging Hecuba was taken prisoner by the Greeks. During the siege of Troy, her youngest son Polydorus had been entrusted to the care of the king of Thrace. On the way to Greece, where she was being taken by her captors, Hecuba discovered that Polydorus had been murdered on the Thracian shore. In revenge, she put out the eyes of the king and murdered his two sons. According to legend Hecuba met death in one of three ways: in despair at her capture she leapt into the Hellespont (now the Dardanelles); she was killed for abusing her captors; or she was metamorphosed into a dog.

HEDGEHOG, or HEDGEPIG or URCHIN, common name for any spiny, Old World mammal in the genus *Erinaceus* of the family Erinaceidae. Although superficially similar in appearance to the porcupine, it is more closely related to the mole and shrew; see INSECTIVORA. The hedgehog, which is found in Europe, Asia, and Africa, is characterized by a coat of long, stiff, pointed spines on its back. The fur on its underside is soft. Hedgehogs average 10 in. long and are somber-hued, varying in color from light tan in some species to black in others. They have pointed snouts, small eyes, short legs, and vestigial tails. When endangered, the hedgehog rolls itself into a ball by the action of several powerful, superficial (integumentary) muscles which arise from the head and neck on each side and loop around the rump. In this position its spines project in all directions. Hedgehogs conceal themselves in hedgerows during the daytime and emerge at night to hunt the insects which constitute their chief food; they also eat worms, frogs, snakes, mice, and birds' eggs. European hedgehogs hibernate during the wintertime but their torpor is not deep and they occasionally awaken and emerge from their nest of dry leaves to hunt food. Members of this genus apparently breed throughout the year in the tropical part of their range but the European hedgehog has a definite breeding season. In July or August the European hedgehog gives birth to four to eight young, which are blind and almost naked except for tiny soft white spines that harden in two or three days.

HEDIN, Sven Anders (1865–1952), Swedish explorer and geographer, born in Stockholm, and educated at the universities of Uppsala, Berlin, and Halle. During his first major Asian expedition, he crossed the Pamirs (q.v.), charted the Chinese lake Lop Nor, and finally arrived at Peking. He then journeyed to Tibet by way of Mongolia, Siberia, and the Gobi desert. Hedin explored Tibet and Sinkiang, discovered the sources of the Brahmaputra, Indus, and Sutlej rivers, and, in 1906, discovered and named the Trans-Himalayas. Accounts of these travels appeared in *Scientific Results of a Journey in Central Asia, 1899–1902* (8 vol., 1904–08), *Trans-Himalaya* (3 vol., 1909–12), and *Southern Tibet* (12 vol., 1917 –22). In 1927 Hedin led an expedition of Chinese and Swedish scientists into central Asia. In addition to his scientific books, he wrote *Through Asia* (1898), *The Conquest of Tibet* (1935), *My Life as an Explorer* (1926), and many other popular accounts of his travels.

HEDONISM (Gr. *hēdonē*, "pleasure"), in philosophy, the doctrine that pleasure is the sole or chief good in life and that the pursuit of it is the ideal aim of conduct. Two important hedonistic theories were expounded in ancient Greece. The Cyrenaics (q.v.), or egoistic hedonists, espoused a doctrine in which gratification of one's immediate personal desires, without re-

African hedgehog, *Erinaceus frontalis*
New York Zoological Society

gard for other persons, was considered the supreme end of man's existence. Knowledge, according to the Cyrenaics, is rooted in the fleeting sensations of the moment, and it is therefore futile to attempt the formulation of a system of moral values in which the desirability of present pleasures is weighed against the pain they may cause in the future. Unlike the egoistic hedonists, the Epicureans, or rational hedonists, contended that true pleasure is attainable only by reason. They stressed the virtues of self-control and prudence in all things. See EPICUREANISM.

The doctrines of hedonism as expounded and developed in antiquity survived practically without change until modern times. In the 18th and 19th centuries such British philosophers as Jeremy Bentham (q.v.), James Mill, and John Stuart Mill (see under MILL) propounded the doctrine of universalistic hedonism, better known as utilitarianism (q.v.). According to this theory, the ultimate criterion of human behavior is the good of society, and the guiding principle of individual moral conduct is held to be allegiance to that which procures and promotes the welfare of the greatest number of people.

HEERLEN, city of the Netherlands, in Limburg Province, 15 miles N.E. of Maastricht and about 5 miles W. of the West German border. The city is an industrial center in the coal-mining region of the S.E. Netherlands. Pop. (1968) 76,389.

HEGEL, Georg Wilhelm Friedrich (1770–1831), German philosopher, born in Stuttgart. He was educated at home and in the grammar school of Stuttgart until he was eighteen years old. He then studied theology at the University of Tübingen, graduating in 1793. His university career was unremarkable, and his teachers thought him particularly deficient in knowledge of philosophy. For several years after leaving the university he held positions as a tutor, during which time he studied economics and government, and attempted to fathom the true meaning of Christianity. In 1801, after receiving a small legacy from his father, he obtained a position as Privatdocent, or lecturer, at the University of Jena. He had already outlined the general framework of his system of philosophy, but had published no works of importance. His first important treatise, *Phänomenologie des Geistes* (Eng. trans., *The Phenomenology of the Mind,* 1931), was published in 1807. In 1808 he became rector of the gymnasium of Nuremberg, a post he held until 1816. He married in 1811, and his greatest work, *Wissenschaft der Logik* (Eng. trans., *The Science of Logic,* 2 vol., 1929), began to appear in 1812 and was completed with the publication of the third volume in 1816. From 1816 to 1818 Hegel was professor of philosophy at the University of Heidelberg, and from 1818 to his death he held a chair of philosophy at the University of Berlin.

A Spiritual Absolute. Hegel's belief is that the fundamental reality, the Absolute (q.v.), is spiritual rather than physical in nature. This all-embracing reality, according to Hegel, is rational,

Georg Wilhelm Friedrich Hegel German Information Center

and only the rational is real. According to his system, the only approach to reality is by means of logic. Anything that can be proved by logical means to be self-consistent in rational and real. Hegel also adopted an individual logical method, known as the dialectic (q.v.), in his search for the Absolute. This method consists of contrasting a statement, or thesis, with its opposite, or antithesis, and uniting them to form a synthesis, a statement containing the essence of both the thesis and antithesis. By this type of reasoning he believed that the natural error of all finite statements can be ultimately eliminated and the Absolute Idea realized. To Hegel, this Absolute Idea consists of pure thought thinking about pure thought: "This unity is consequently the absolute and all truth, the Idea which thinks itself".

The Progress of History. Hegel saw the progress of world history as parallel to dialectic reasoning. He described history as a progress from Pure Being, which he identified with China, to the Absolute Idea, which he tended to identify with the Prussian State. "The history of the world is the discipline of the uncontrolled natural will, bringing it into obedience to a universal principle and conferring subjective freedom. The East knew, and to the present day knows, that one is free; the Greek and Roman world, that some are free; the German world knows that all are free". Nevertheless Hegel felt that America was the land of the future and that the Absolute would reveal itself "perhaps in a contest between North and South America". The idea of contrast, of strife between the opposites, colored all Hegel's thinking and led him to believe in the necessity for war and even the necessity for clearly defined classes within a state. In his view the state was the worldly organization which most closely approached reality, and the individual citizens of the state approached reality only through their participation in the state.

Pure Hegelianism had a profound though short-lived effect on European philosophers, and its influence was still felt in Great Britain until about the beginning of the 20th century. Indirectly Hegel's works have had an even more far-reaching effect, because, to a certain degree, they served as the philosophical foundation of Marxian dialectical materialism and of the worship of the state by 20th-century communists and fascists; see COMMUNISM; FASCISM.

HEGIRA or **HEJIRA** (Ar. *hijrah*, "flight"), specifically, flight, in 622 A.D. of the prophet Muhammad (q.v.) from Mecca to Yahrib (now Medina), both in what is now Saudi Arabia; by extension, the term is applied to any similar flight or emigration. Caliph Omar I (q.v.) selected the year of the Hegira as the first year of the Muslim era. Hence, 622 A.D. became 1 A.H. (*anno hegirae*) in the Muslim calendar, which Omar systematized in 639.

HEIDEGGER, Martin (1899–   ), German philosopher, born in Messkirch. After receiving his doctoral degree from the University of Freiburg in 1914, he was appointed professor of philosophy at the University of Marburg in 1923. In 1928 he returned to his alma mater as professor of philosophy. In 1933 Heidegger was named rector of the university, but returned to teaching the following year. *Existenz-philosophie*, or philosophy of existence, was first expounded by Heidegger in *Sein und Zeit* (1927; Eng. trans., *Being and Time*, 1962). In this book Heidegger argues that because the life of man is finite and ends in death, man must assume the responsibility for achieving meaningful results in his lifetime. He contends that this realization does not lead to despair, but to an increased humanity and a greater concern and experience with the present. Because of his marked influence on the French philosopher Jean-Paul Sartre (q.v.) and on French existentialism (q.v.), Heidegger has been termed an existentialist philosopher, a designation he firmly rejects. Some of his other works are *Was ist Metaphysik?* (1929; Eng. trans., *What Is Metaphysics?*, 1949); *Vom Wesen der Wahrheit* (1943; Eng. trans., *On the Essence of Truth*, 1949), *Was ist Philosophie?* (1956; Eng. trans., *What Is Philosophy?*, 1958), and *Vom Wesen des Grundes* (1969; Eng. trans., *The Essence of Reasons*, 1970).

See also PHILOSOPHY: *Modern Philosophy: Analytical Philosophy*.

HEIDELBERG, city of Australia, in Victoria State, between the Yarra R. and Darebin Creek, 7 miles N.E. of Melbourne. Heidelberg is a commercial center adjoining a sheep-raising and agricultural area. The Yarra Bend National Park is nearby to the s. Pop. (1966) 63,810.

HEIDELBERG, city of West Germany, in Baden-Württemberg State, on the s. bank of the Neckar R., 11 miles S.E. of Mannheim. The city occupies a long, narrow site between the river and a parallel range of thickly wooded hills. Heidelberg is an important railway junction. Among the local manufactures are beer, cigars, electrical appliances, hand luggage, metal products, printing presses, and pianos. The chief source of income is the tourist trade.

On the summit of Jettenbühl (640 ft.), which dominates the eastern portion of the city, is Heidelberg Castle, one of the most impressive historic landmarks of Germany. Dating from the 13th century, the structure, now largely in ruins, preserves numerous examples of medieval, Renaissance, and baroque (qq.v.) German architecture. One wing, an addition in the Renaissance style called the Friedrichsbau, was restored early in the 20th century. Of particular interest are the four granite columns located in the castle courtyard, which were once part of a castle belonging to Charlemagne (q.v.), Holy Roman Emperor. The cellar of Heidelberg Castle contains the famed Heidelberg Tun, a wine vat with a capacity of 49,000 gal. Noteworthy ecclesiastical edifices of Heidelberg are the 15th-century church of Saint Peter, on the door of which the Bohemian theologian and martyr Jerome of Prague (q.v.) nailed his celebrated theses in criticism of the papacy; and the Church of the Holy Ghost, also dating from the 15th century. To a considerable extent, the world renown of the city derives from the University of Heidelberg; see HEIDELBERG, UNIVERSITY OF.

The community developed around Heidel-

HEIDELBERG, UNIVERSITY OF

berg Castle and was, until 1721, the capital of the Palatinate (q.v.). During the Reformation, Heidelberg was one of the chief strongholds of German Protestantism (qq.v.). French troops sacked the town during the Thirty Years' War (q.v.). In 1689 and 1693, Heidelberg was further damaged by invading French troops. Following World War II Heidelberg was assigned to the United States zone of occupation. Pop. (1968 est.) 121,466.

HEIDELBERG, UNIVERSITY OF, officially RU-PRECHT-KARL-UNIVERSITÄT, oldest German university, located in Heidelberg, West Germany. The university is an autonomous institution under the jurisdiction of the ministry of education and is financed by the State of Baden-Württemburg. The university was founded in Heidelberg, then in the Palatinate, in 1386 by Rupert I, Elector of the Palatinate (d.1390). The real work of organization was done by the first rector of the university, the religious scholar Marsilius von Inghen (1330?–96), who established it as a Catholic institution. In the middle of the 16th century, during the Reformation, a reorganization in which the great Protestant scholar Melanchthon (q.v.) played a prominent part, changed Heidelberg into a Protestant university. The institution prospered until the period (1618–48) of the Thirty Years' War (q.v.) between Catholics and Protestants; in 1622 the Catholic commander in chief Johan Tserclaes, Count of Tilly (q.v.), captured the town and took possession of the university. Its noted collection of manuscripts, the Bibliotheca Palatina, was sent to the Vatican, Rome. In 1626 the university suspended operation, and in 1652 it was reorganized as a secular institution. During the next century and a half its work went on under great difficulties, mainly caused by the wars in which the Palatinate engaged with France. Stability did not return to the university until 1803, when the Palatinate ceded the town of Heidelberg to the Grand Duchy of Baden and Charles Frederick, Grand Duke of Baden (1728–1811), took the university under his patronage. In the 19th and 20th centuries the university was a renowned center of learning and attracted many foreign students, including Americans. The institution currently has faculties of Protestant theology, law, medicine, philosophy, and natural sciences and mathematics, as well as more than eighty institutes, clinics, and seminars associated with the various faculties. Courses of study lead to a *Diplom* or the degree of *Doktor*. These courses, usually lasting four years, are roughly equivalent to work for an American degree of master. The library contains 1,500,000 bound volumes. In 1969–70 students numbered about 11,300, including 1500 foreign students.

HEIDENSTAM, Verner von (1859–1940), Swedish poet and novelist, born on his father's estate in Orebro County. After ill health forced him to interrupt his study of art, he traveled for several years in southern Europe and the Orient. His first book of poetry, *Vallfart och Vandringsår* ("Pilgrimage and Wanderyears", 1888), was based on his travel experiences. Heidenstam was noted for his colorful style and for the lyricism of his language, and was an important member of the group that revolted during the 1880's against realism in Swedish literature. In the epic poem *Hans Alienus* (1892), he described a search for beauty through various countries and periods of time. In his collections of verse, *Dikter* ("Poems", 1895) and *Nya Dikter* ("New Poems", 1915), he revealed a naturalistic point of view; see NATURALISM. Heidenstam is considered one of the most important Swedish poets of his time.

Heidenstam's use of Swedish historical backgrounds in his novels supported his theory that the modern Swedish literary renaissance should be based on the national culture. Among his outstanding works of historical fiction are *Karolinerna* (1897–98; Eng. trans., *The Charles Men*, 1920), *Heliga Birgittas pilgrimsfärd* ("Saint Birgitta's Pilgrimage", 1901), and *Folkungaträdet* (2 vol., 1905–07; Eng. trans., *The Tree of the Folkungs*, 1925). He was awarded the 1916 Nobel Prize in literature.

HEIFETZ, Jascha (1901–   ), Russian-American violinist, born in Vilna (now the Lithuanian S.S.R.). He entered the Vilna music school at the age of four and graduated four years later, having made his concert debut at about the age of seven. After graduation he entered the music conservatory at Saint Petersburg (now Leningrad), at which he studied with the Hungarian-American musician Leopold Auer (q.v.). Heifetz appeared in the United States for the first time in 1917 and was hailed by critics as one of the most important violinists of all time. He became an American citizen in 1925. Heifetz has made many world tours, receiving high acclaim for his technique and the lyrical quality of his violin tone.

HEINE, Heinrich (1797–1856), German poet, literary critic, and essayist, born in Düsseldorf, of Jewish parents. He attended private and public schools in Düsseldorf until 1815. While staying with his uncle Salomon Heine, a Hamburg banker, Heine fell in love with his daughter Amelie, but she did not return his love. This early experience is the source for the motifs of yearning, disappointment, and romantic irony in his poetry. After failing in a business venture financed by his uncle, he yielded to the urging of his benefactor and began (1819) to study law at the University of Bonn. The following year he transferred to the University of Göttingen. The law could not hold his interest, which became increasingly fixed on poetry. Discontented with the pedantic atmosphere of Göttingen, he moved to Berlin in 1821. There he came into contact with the German philosopher Georg Wilhelm Friedrich Hegel (q.v.), who profoundly influenced his philosophic outlook. He also became acquainted with such eminent German romanticists as Adelbert von Chamisso, Friedrich Heinrich Karl de La Motte-Fouque (qq.v.), Karl August Varnhagen von Ense (1785–1858), and particularly Varnhagen's wife, Rahel Levin (1771–1833), whose brilliant salon he frequented. See GERMAN LITERATURE: *The Classical and Romantic Period.*

Early Poetry and Prose. Heine remained in Berlin until 1823, writing poetry. In 1822 his first volume of verse, *Gedichte* (Eng. trans., *Poems,* 1884), was published; it attracted attention because of the delicacy and lyrical beauty of the poems. From 1824 to 1825 he again studied law at Göttingen. Because the profession of law was prohibited to Jews in Germany at that time, Heine became a Christian in 1825 in order to obtain a law degree. Although he qualified, he never actually practiced law. In 1826 *Die Harzreise* (Eng. trans., *The Harz Journey,* 1887), a prose account of a trip he had taken to the Harz Mts. in 1824, was published. This work, with its wit, gaiety, and grace of style, won success immediately and established Heine's literary reputation. In 1827 his *Buch der Lieder* (Eng. trans., *Book of Songs,* 1884), the collection of lyric poems for which he is best known, was published.

Heine lived in England and Italy as well as in various parts of Germany from 1827 to 1831. During that period he wrote the three volumes of travel sketches that, with *Die Harzreise,* make up the four volumes of his *Reisebilder* (1826–31; Eng. trans., *Travel Pictures,* 1887). He also wrote a number of prose works in which he displayed sympathy with the democratic ideas of the French Revolution (q.v.) and bitterly satirized the despotic feudal regimes of the various kingdoms and duchies of Germany. He celebrated the French Revolution in his poem "Die Grenadiere" ("The Grenadiers") and called Napoleon I (q.v.), Emperor of France, "the revolution personified". Heine became a prominent member of a literary group known as Young Germany, which attacked the German romantic school for having come under monarchial and ecclesiastical domination. He hoped to obtain a professorship of German literature in Munich or elsewhere in Germany, but his political ideas brought him into the disfavor of the established German governments; Prussia banned both

Drawing of Heinrich Heine by his friend Marc Charles Gabriel Gleyre (1806–74). Bettmann Archive

Heine and the third volume of *Reisebilder.* Seeking a more congenial political and literary atmosphere and filled with enthusiasm for the revolution of 1830 in France, which overthrew the senior Bourbon dynasty (*see* BOURBON), Heine left for Paris in 1831. Except for two brief visits to his native land, he spent the rest of his life there.

Final Works. In Paris Heine was a correspondent for several German newspapers and a friend of writers such as Honoré de Balzac and George Sand and of composers such as Louis Hector Berlioz and Frédéric François Chopin (qq.v.). In 1835 the writings of the Young Germany group were banned in most of Germany, and Heine's income was considerably reduced. Subsequently he lived chiefly on a subsidy from his uncle, supplemented for a time by a pension from the French government. In 1841 he married his mistress, a French shopgirl whom he loved deeply. Four years later he contracted a spinal disease that confined him to this "mattress grave", as he called it, from 1848 to the day of his death. Nevertheless some of his most notable works date from the last years of his life.

Heine's personality was composed of sharply conflicting elements: a pagan joy of life and a Hebraic feeling for ethical values; a love of romanticism and a hatred for the German romantic writers of his time because of their subservience to reactionary political and religious forces; a German patriotism and a humanitarianism that embraced the entire world; a nominal Christianity and a lifelong attachment to Judaism. These conflicts created in Heine the spirit of disillusionment, of mockery, and of biting satire that characterizes so much of his writing. As a German lyric poet he is considered second only to Johann Wolfgang von Goethe (q.v.); his prose is the best written in German in his time.

HEIR, in popular usage, any person succeeding to an estate (q.v.), whether of real property or of personal property, either by will (q.v.) or by intestacy. In English common law (q.v.), an heir (or heir at law) is one who succeeds only to real property, by intestacy and not by will. In the statutory law of many States of the United States, the word "heir" still has this meaning. In most States it is generally construed to mean a successor by intestacy to both real and personal property. The various State statutes specify in detail the person or persons who will succeed to a decedent's estate if he has not left a will; see DESCENT. In Scotland the heir at law also inherits some or all of the movable property of the dead person. In England the term "heir apparent" is applied to a child who will be heir on the death of his parent; the term "heir presumptive" is applied to a person who will be heir barring the birth of a closer relative of the person from whom he expects to inherit.

HEISENBERG, Werner (1901–), German physicist, born in Würzburg, and educated at the University of Munich. In 1923 he became an assistant to the German-British physicist Max Born (q.v.) at the University of Göttingen, and from 1924 to 1927 held a Rockefeller Foundation grant to work with the Danish physicist Niels Henrik David Bohr (q.v.) at the University of Copenhagen. In 1927 Heisenberg was appointed professor of theoretical physics at the University of Leipzig. Subsequently he served as professor at the universities of Berlin (1941–45), Göttingen (1946–58), and Munich (from 1958). In 1941 he became director of the Kaiser Wilhelm Institute for Physics (renamed in 1946 the Max Planck Institute of Physics).

Heisenberg was in charge of scientific research in connection with the atomic-bomb project in Germany during World War II. Under his leadership, attempts were made to construct a pile in which the chain reaction would proceed so rapidly that it would produce an explosion, but these attempts were never realized. He was interned in England for a time at the end of the war.

Heisenberg, one of the foremost theoretical physicists in the world, made his great contributions in the theory of atomic structure. Starting in 1925 he developed a new theory of quantum mechanics, called matrix mechanics, in which the mathematical formulation was based on the frequencies and amplitudes of the radiations absorbed and emitted by the atom, and on the energy levels of the atomic system; see QUANTUM MECHANICS: *Matrix Mechanics*. The uncertainty principle (q.v.) formulated by Heisenberg played an important role in the development of quantum mechanics and also in the trend of modern philosophical thinking. Heisenberg was awarded the 1932 Nobel Prize in physics. Among his many writings are *The Physical Principles of the Quantum Theory* (1930), *Cosmic Radiation* (1946), *Physics and Philosophy* (1958), and *Introduction to the Unified Theory of Elementary Particles* (1967).

HEJAZ or **HEDJAZ.** See ARABIA: *History*; SAUDI ARABIA: *The Land*.

HEKLA, volcano of S.W. Iceland, about 20 mi. from the Atlantic Ocean and 70 miles E. of Reykjavík (q.v.). The mountain has a circumference of 12 mi. at the base and is surmounted by three snow-covered peaks, the tallest of which is 4747 ft. above sea level. The volcano has erupted more than twenty times since the 11th century, most disastrously in 1766; the most recent eruption was on May 6, 1970.

HEL or **HELA,** in Norse mythology, the goddess of the dead. She dwelt beneath one of the three roots of the sacred ash tree, Ygdrasil, and was the daughter of Loki (q.v.), the spirit of mischief or evil, by the giantess Angerbotha (Angerboda). Odin (q.v.), the All-Father, hurled Hel into Niflheim, the realm of cold and darkness, itself also known as Hel, over which he gave her sovereign authority.

HELENA, city in Arkansas, and county seat of Phillips Co., on the Mississippi R., about 100 miles S.E. of Little Rock. Helena is a port city and a rail center and has varied manufacturing. On July 4, 1863, during the American Civil War, Confederate forces attacked Union troops holding the town in an unsuccessful attempt to divert Union troops from the siege of Vicksburg (q.v.). Pop. (1960) 11,500; (1970) 10,415.

HELENA, city and capital of Montana, and county seat of Lewis and Clark Co., at the E. foot of the Continental Divide about 50 miles N.E. of

The State Capitol of Montana in Helena.
Ewing Galloway

Butte, and 75 miles s.w. of Great Falls. Helena has rail and air service. It lies at an altitude of approximately 4000 ft. above sea level, overlooking an irrigated agricultural and stock-raising area known as the Prickly Pear Valley or Helena Valley, and is surrounded by a productive mining region. The numerous mines in the vicinity yield gold, silver, lead, and zinc. Since 1935 gold has been obtained also from formerly unworkable gravel deposits by the use of huge dredges. In addition to mining and smelting, the principal industries in the city are the manufacture of paint, brick and tile, cement blocks, fabricated steel, and machine-shop and foundry products. The most prominent buildings in Helena are the State Capitol, erected in 1899, which contains the collection of the Historical Society of Montana, and Saint Helena Cathedral (Roman Catholic), opened in 1924, a partial replica of the Cathedral of Milan, Italy. Helena is the site of Carroll College (Roman Catholic), established in 1910.

History. Helena was founded in 1864, following the discovery of gold in Last Chance Gulch, the city's main street. By 1868 an estimated $16,000,000 in gold had been obtained from Last Chance Gulch, and the town that had sprung up around it had a population of 7500. Helena became the capital of the Territory of Montana in 1875 and was incorporated as a city in 1881. At about that period, the development of the city was slowed by the exhaustion of the early mines; but the arrival of the Northern Pacific Railroad in 1883 and the growth of the silver-mining industry brought renewed prosperity. Helena became the State capital in 1889. Following earthquakes in 1935, buildings in the city were improved and strengthened against similar future occurrences. Pop. (1960) 20,227; (1970) 22,730.

HELENA, Saint (d. about 330), wife of the Roman emperor Constantius I (*see under* CONSTANTIUS), and mother of Constantine I (q.v.), Emperor of Rome. She was probably born in Drepanum, later called Helenopolis in her honor, in the ancient Roman province of Bithynia. Constantius divorced her, because of her nonpatrician origin, when he was named caesar, or successor to the throne of the Roman Empire, in 293. She devoted the rest of her life to religious pilgrimages, visiting Jerusalem about 325 and founding there the Church of the Holy Sepulchre and the Church of the Nativity. According to some legends she was the discoverer of the True Cross in Palestine. Her feast day is August 18.

HELEN OF TROY

Ancient Greek sculpture of the abduction of Helen of Troy by Paris, which sparked the Trojan War.
Bettmann Archive

HELEN OF TROY, in Greek mythology, the most beautiful woman in Greece, daughter of the god Zeus and of Leda (qq.v.), wife of King Tyndareus of Sparta. While still a child, she was abducted by the hero Theseus (q.v.), who hoped in time to marry her, but she was rescued by her brothers, Castor and Pollux (q.v.). Later, her fatal beauty was the direct cause of the Trojan War (q.v.).

The story of the ten-year conflict began when the three goddesses Hera, Athena, and Aphrodite asked the Trojan prince Paris (q.v.) to pick the most beautiful among them. After each of the goddesses had attempted to influence his decision, Paris awarded the golden apple to Aphrodite, who had promised him the love of a woman of surpassing beauty.

Soon afterwards Paris sailed to Greece, where he was hospitably received by Helen and her husband Menelaus (q.v.), King of Sparta. Unfortunately, Helen as the fairest of her sex, was the prize destined for Paris. Although she was living happily with Menelaus, she fell under the influence of Aphrodite and allowed Paris to persuade her to elope with him, and he carried her off to Troy. Menelaus then called upon the Grecian chieftains to help him rescue his wife, and with few exceptions they responded to his call. During nine years of indecisive conflict, Helen sat at her loom in the Trojan palace weaving a web of her own sad story. Then Paris and Menelaus decided to meet in single combat between the opposing armies, and Helen was summoned to view the duel. As she approached the tower, where the aged king Priam (q.v.) and his chieftains sat, her beauty was still so matchless and her sorrow so great that no one could feel for her anything but compassion. Although the Greeks claimed the victory in the battle between the two warriors, Aphrodite helped Paris escape from the enraged Menelaus by enveloping him in a cloud and taking him safely to Helen's chamber, where Helen came to comfort him.

After the fall of Troy, Menelaus was reunited with his wife, and they soon left Troy for their native Greece. They had, however, incurred the displeasure of the gods, and were therefore driven by storms from shore to shore in the Mediterranean, stopping in Cyprus, Phoenicia, and Egypt. Arriving at length in Sparta, they resumed their reign and lived the rest of their days in royal splendor. They had one daughter, Hermione (q.v.).

HELGOLAND (Eng. *Heligoland*), island of West Germany in the North Sea about 40 miles N.W. of Cuxhaven. The island, about 1 mi. long and less than ⅓ mi. wide, is mainly a rocky eminence, known as the Oberland, with a maximum elevation of about 200 ft. Steep cliffs surround the Oberland on all sides. A narrow spit of sand, called the Unterland, extends along the S.E. base of the uplift. The major portion of the island community, a fishing and resort village, is on the Oberland. Helgoland is a free port.

A former possession of Denmark, Helgoland was seized by Great Britain in 1807. Great Britain ceded the island to Germany in 1890, whereupon it became a part of the Prussian province of Schleswig-Holstein (q.v.). In the period preceding World War I, the German government established on the island a comprehensive system of fortifications, including gun emplacements and submarine pens. British and German naval units fought a sharp naval engagement off Helgoland on Aug. 28, 1914, shortly after the outbreak of World War I; *see* HELGOLAND BIGHT, BATTLE OF. As provided by the terms of the Treaty of Versailles, the fortifications on Helgoland were demolished following World War I; *see* VERSAILLES, TREATY OF. The island was subsequently refortified by the government of the dictator Adolf Hitler (q.v.), and served as a major German submarine base during World War II.

In May, 1945, after the collapse of Germany, the fortress was surrendered to the armed forces of Great Britain. British naval personnel razed the fortifications on Helgoland on April 18, 1947, by the detonation of 3500 tons of explosives that blasted away part of the cliffs. Helgoland became part of West Germany in 1952. Pop. (1967) 2705.

HELGOLAND BIGHT, BATTLE OF, naval engagement of World War I, fought between British and German naval forces on Aug. 28, 1914. Confined to Helgoland Bight (now Helgoland Bay), an arm of the North Sea to the east and south of the island of Helgoland (q.v.), the action began as a raiding operation by British submarines and destroyers, supported by a flotilla of light cruisers, against German patrol vessels. The fighting during the initial phase of the battle was attended by considerable confusion mainly because of a low-hanging fog. After suffering several early reverses, including the loss of a destroyer, the Germans concentrated six light cruisers in the battle area. By 11:00 A.M., the German cruiser force had secured tactical superiority over the British raiders. The British, at this juncture, directed an appeal for help to Rear Admiral David Beatty (q.v.), commander of four heavy battle cruisers in reserve positions about 50 miles N.W. of Helgoland. Although the British succeeded in destroying the German cruiser *Mainz* before the arrival of Beatty, the Germans retained their tactical advantage, threatening the isolated British force with annihilation. The detachment commanded by Beatty reached the battle area at 12:30 P.M., and two German cruisers, the *Cöln* and the *Ariadne*, were sunk in quick succession. The remnants of the German force escaped. Besides the destruction of four vessels, German losses included serious damage to other fleet units and more than 1200 casualties. Through their victory, accomplished at the cost of damage to four vessels and seventy-five casualties, the British substantially advanced the Allied naval strategy of blockading the German coast.

HELIANTHUS. *See* SUNFLOWER.

HELICOPTER, heavier-than-air craft that derives its lift not from fixed wings like those of conventional airplanes, but from a power-driven rotor or rotors, revolving on a vertical axis above the fuselage. Helicopters can rise or descend vertically, can hover, and can move forward, backward, or sideways. The helicopter was the first type of heavier-than-air craft capable of vertical flight. It differs from the autogiro (q.v.), another form of rotating-wing aircraft, in that its rotor gives both lift and propulsion.

The rotor of a helicopter usually has two, three, or four blades radiating symmetrically from a central hub. The rotor is driven by an engine, usually in the fuselage, through gears, which reduce the speed of rotation to less than the speed of the engine. An important feature of helicopter design is the development of devices to counteract the torque, or the reaction force developed when the rotation of the rotor in one direction tends to turn the fuselage in the opposite direction. The most common form of antitorque device is a small vertical propeller, similar to an airplane propeller, mounted at the tail of the helicopter in such a position as to push the tail to one side. Other types of helicopters use paired rotors turning in opposite directions, which automatically neutralize each other's torque. In some helicopters the paired rotors are mounted one above the other on a single axle; and in others they are placed on struts on either side of the fuselage or at the

HELICOPTER

front and back of the fuselage. Small, ram-jet engines (*see* AIRPLANE: *Propulsion*) mounted on the tips of the rotor blades have been used to provide power in experimental helicopters and to eliminate torque.

When a helicopter is rising vertically from the ground or descending vertically, the lift on all the rotor blades is the same, because they are all moving through the air at the same speed. However, when the craft is moving forward (or in any horizontal direction), the lift on some blades is greater than that on others. During each cycle the speed of the blades through the air varies, depending upon whether the direction of the rotation is the same as or opposite to that of the motion of the helicopter. The airspeed of the blade is equal to its speed of rotation plus the forward speed of the helicopter during one half of the cycle and minus the forward speed during the other half. Hence, if the blades were fixed in a horizontal position the amount of lift provided by the blade would vary during the cycle because lift increases with airspeed, and the helicopter would tilt to one side. To avoid this type of instability, most single-rotored helicopters have flapping blades. The blades are hinged close to the hub in such a manner that the blade rises when moving at greater airspeed to reduce the lift and drops when moving at lower airspeed to increase the lift. Thus, the effect of the varying airspeed as a result of blade rotation is nullified.

A helicopter can be flown in any direction, forward, backward, or sidewise, by tilting the rotor in the desired direction. Tilting the rotor changes its lift from purely vertical to a combination of vertical and horizontal. To turn a helicopter, the rotor is first tilted in the direction of the turn and then the thrust of the tail propeller is altered to turn the fuselage in the desired direction. Ascent and descent in helicopters are controlled by increasing or decreasing the speed of the rotor, the pitch of the rotor blades, or both. In the event of a power failure, the rotor of a helicopter is disengaged and will autorotate like the rotor of an autogiro, maintaining enough lift to permit the craft to descend to a safe landing.

Uses. The helicopter has two principal advantages: the ability to fly slowly or to hover; and the ability to take off and land in a restricted space. Airports for helicopters are called heliports. One of the most important nonmilitary uses of the helicopter is in searching for and rescuing lost persons, particularly in the sea and in mountainous regions. A helicopter can provide rescue for a man from a life raft, a small forest clearing, a mountainous ledge, or other hazardous places. If the land space is large enough, the helicopter can alight and take a person aboard. If the area is too small for a landing, the man can climb a rope ladder to the hovering helicopter, or he can be lifted with a winch, cable, and basket. A helicopter can provide quick, safe transportation to hospitals and other such institutions. The craft can also operate from the decks of small vessels at sea and can land and take off from a rooftop in the center of a congested city. Because a helicopter can hover and fly as slowly as desired, it provides an efficient means for the inspection of pipelines and power lines from the air. Many helicopters are employed in this work. Like conventional aircraft, the helicopter can be flown by instruments at night or in bad weather. It has the further advantage of greater safety because of its maneuverability and controllable speed. Helicopters are used successfully for fire patrols in forest areas, for dusting crops with insecticides, for aerial prospecting, for aerial planting of seed for reforestation and erosion control, for passenger transportation, and for postal service in large cities, even bringing the mail directly from the airport to the roof of the post office. Helicopters range in size from the single-passenger type, to large, multiengine craft carrying fifty or more passengers.

Special helicopters have also been designed for the lifting of heavy equipment. These so-called flying cranes have been used to locate power-transmission towers and pipelines in inaccessible areas and to salvage military equipment in war zones. Economically, the principal limitation of the helicopter is its low maximum forward speed (about 200 m.p.h.), and the accompanying high cost per passenger-mile. Commercial service helicopters are therefore currently limited to flight distances of 100 mi. or less.

History. It is reported that the ancient Chinese had a hand-spun toy sometimes called a "flying top" that rose upward when revolved rapidly. It is probable, however, that the first man to envisage the possibility of a man-lifting helicopter and actually to experiment with models of his designs was the 15th-century Italian artist, engineer, and architect Leonardo da Vinci (q.v.), who made drawings showing an aircraft with a helical rotor around 1500. Da Vinci planned to use muscular power to revolve the rotor, though such power would never have been sufficient to operate a helicopter of that type successfully.

Among experimenters who worked in the first quarter of the 20th century were the Frenchmen

Sikorsky Aircraft

Military helicopters. Above: The crane version of the CH-54A, used by U.S. forces in Vietnam, can carry loads up to 10 tons. Below: Simplicity of construction characterizes the U.S. Air Force XH-20 helicopter, designed for a wide variety of short-range military operations.

McDonnell Aircraft Corp.

HELICOPTER

Maurice Leger, Louis Charles Bréguet (1880–1955), Étienne Oehmichen, and Paul Cornu (1881–1944); the Hungarian-American Theodore von Kármán (q.v.); Raoul Pescara in Spain; Jacob Christian Ellehammer in Denmark; Igor I. Sikorsky (q.v.) in Russia, and J. Newton Williams and Emile Berliner (q.v.) and his son Henry Berliner in the U.S. The Russian-born George DeBothezat and his co-worker Ivan Jerome developed their four-rotored craft for the U.S. Army Air Service. Corradino d'Ascanio in Italy, Oscar von Asboth of Hungary, and others attacked the many problems of vertical lift with varying success. The Berliner helicopter was probably the first craft supported by its powered rotors to make a controlled flight. The distance was only about 100 yd., and the altitude about 15 ft., but the helicopter was being maneuvered at the will of the pilot, Henry Berliner. The invention of the hinged, flapping rotor blade by the Spaniard Juan de la Cierva (q.v.) made possible the development of practical helicopters.

The first truly successful helicopter was a twin-rotor machine designed by the German engineer Henrich Focke (1890–   ), which was flown in 1936. In 1939 the aeronautical engineer Igor Sikorsky, now a naturalized American, flew a practical single-rotor craft, the VS-300. Its successor, the XR-4, made the first cross-country flight, from Stratford, Conn., to near Dayton, Ohio, about 760 mi., May 13–17, 1942.

In 1967 two Sikorsky HH-3 helicopters made the first transatlantic flight, from New York to Paris, using aerial refueling. The Lockheed AH-56A and Piasecki Pathfinder-3 were the first models to attain speeds in excess of 250 m.p.h. Two models of the Kaman Huskie reached altitudes of 25,000 ft. The Piasecki Pathfinder-1 had the greatest range, 1565 mi. The fastest European helicopter, the Soviet Ka-11, has a speed of 227 m.p.h. The Polish Mi-2 has a range of 1150 mi. The Soviet Mi-10 flying crane is capable of lifting a 33,000-lb. load to a height of 7000 ft. The Soviet Mi-6 carries 3000 gallons of water for aerial firefighting. Approximately 2000 helicopters were used by U.S. forces in the Vietnam conflict to evacuate the wounded, to transport personnel and cargo, to observe enemy activities, and to draw ground fire from the Vietcong. The Sikorsky CH-54A can carry 10 tons of cargo or 67 battle-equipped soldiers. The CH-53 model is equipped with three 7.62 mm guns that fire up to 4000 rounds of ammunition per minute. The Bell Huey Cobra is designed with a front-seat cockpit for the gunner, with remotely operated turret. It flies at 200 m.p.h. and can move vertically at 5800 ft. per minute.

The economic use of the helicopter in commercial transportation for flight distances up to about 250 mi. has not yet been proved. In this field, the helicopter has to compete with vertical takeoff-landing (V.T.O.L.) and short takeoff-landing (S.T.O.L.) aircraft. Some helicopters now in design stage, such as the Sikorsky S65-200, have supplementary stub-wings and forward-facing propellers in addition to a main and a tail rotor. If successful, these helicopters would be able to carry eighty-five passengers at cruising speeds of up to 265 m.p.h. See also AIRPLANE.
L.A.B.

HELIGOLAND. See HELGOLAND.

HELIODORUS (3rd cent. A.D.), Greek writer, born in Emesa (now Homs), Syria. He was the author of the *Aethiopica*, a Greek romance that influenced the work of later authors, notably the Spanish novelist Miguel de Cervantes Saavedra, the Italian poet Torquato Tasso, and the French dramatist Jean Baptiste Racine (qq.v.).

HELIOPOLIS (Lat., fr. Gr. *Hēliou polis*, "city of the sun"), city of ancient Egypt, the center of sun worship during the pre-Christian Egyptian civilization. The ruins of Heliopolis are 5 miles E. of the Nile R. at the apex of the Nile delta, and about 6 miles N.E. of Cairo. Heliopolis was originally the center of worship of the god Tem, deity of the setting sun, later regarded as a form of the sun god Ra. In Egyptian theological literature, the city was known as Per-Ra ("City of Ra"), of which the Greek name is a translation. In the Bible, the city is referred to as On, Aven, and Beth-Shemesh. Although the history of Heliopolis goes as far back as about 2900 B.C., the city reached its greatest development during the New Kingdom, beginning about 1580 B.C., when Ra, later called Amon-Ra, came to be regarded as the chief god of the Egyptian pantheon; see EGYPTIAN RELIGION. Under Ramses II (*see under* RAMSES), during the 13th century B.C., the temple of Heliopolis reached the height of its influence, with almost 13,000 priests and slaves serving in it. Most of the religious literature of ancient Egypt was written by the priests of Heliopolis, who were renowned for their learning, and the temple was the repository for royal records. The city declined under later dynasties, and the Ptolemies (*see* PTOLEMY) almost disregarded it. When Rome occupied Egypt, the obelisks of Heliopolis were removed (*see* CLEOPATRA'S NEEDLES), and the walls of its buildings used as construction materials for other cities.

HELIOPOLIS, city of the Arab Republic of Egypt, in Cairo Governorate, 15 miles N.E. of downtown Cairo. Modern Heliopolis is a planned city; the first buildings were constructed in 1905. The city has a racetrack and other sports facilities and is the site of the international airport of Cairo. Heliopolis is named for the nearby ancient ruined city, which was an important cultural center until the advent of Christianity, capital of the New Kingdom, and a center for the worship of the sun god Ra. The modern city is sometimes called New Cairo and Heliopolis Oasis. Pop. (1960) 124,774.

HELIOPOLIS, ancient name for Ba'albek (q.v.).

HELIOS, in Greek mythology, the ancient sun god, son of the Titans (q.v.) Hyperion and Thea, and brother of Selene (q.v.), goddess of the moon and Eos, goddess of the dawn. Helios was believed to ride his golden chariot across the heavens daily, giving light to gods and men. At evening he sank into the western ocean, from which he was carried in a golden cup back to his palace in the east. Helios alone could control the fierce horses that drew his fiery chariot. When his son, Phaëthon (q.v.), persuaded Helios to let him drive the chariot across the sky, Phaëthon was killed.

Helios was widely worshiped throughout the Grecian world, but his principal cult was at Rhodes. One of the Seven Wonders of the World (q.v.), the Colossus of Rhodes, was a representation of Helios. He is often identified with the later Greek god of the sun Apollo (q.v.).

HELIOTROPE, or TURNSOLE, common name of plants of the genus *Heliotropium,* belonging to the Borage family Boraginaceae. The genus contains more than 200 species which grow in the temperate zones of both hemispheres. Heliotropes are annual herbs with smooth-edged, alternate leaves. The flower is small and has a five-parted calyx, a salver-shaped, five-lobed corolla bearing five stamens, and a deeply four-lobed ovary. The fruits are nutlets. Common heliotrope, *H. europaeum,* is a native of Europe, naturalized in waste areas of the eastern United States. It has a hairy stem, bearing oval leaves. The white flowers are borne on spikes which are coiled in the bud. Seaside heliotrope, *H. curassivicum,* is a smooth-stemmed plant native to waste places in the northeastern U.S. It has lance-shaped leaves and white or pale-blue flowers. Peruvian heliotrope, *H. arborescens,* is the common cultivated heliotrope, grown in gardens all over the U.S.; it can grow to a height of 8 ft. The white to deep-purple flowers have a heavy, vanillalike scent. Essential oils from the

Peruvian heliotrope, Heliotropium arborescens
A. W. Ambler – National Audubon Society

HELIOTROPE

petals of this species are used in making perfumes. The Peruvian heliotrope has a somewhat woody base and can be trained to a treelike shape by continued pruning of side branches. Two plants also sometimes called heliotrope, although not within the same family, are the garden heliotrope, *Valeriana officinalis,* of the Valerian family, Valerianaceae and the winter heliotrope, *Petasites fragrans,* of the Composite family Compositae.

HELIOTROPE, gem mineral more commonly known as bloodstone (q.v.).

HELIOTROPISM. See Tropism.

HELIUM (Gr. *helios,* "sun"), element with at.no. 2, at.wt. 4.003, b.p. $-268.94°$ C. ($-452.09°$ F.), m.p. solidifies under 26 atmospheres pressure below $-272.2°$ C. ($-457.9°$ F.), sp.gr. 0.1785, and symbol He. Helium is one of the chemically inert gases (q.v.), has monatomic molecules, is colorless and odorless, and is the lightest of all gases except hydrogen. The French astronomer Pierre Janssen (1824–1907) discovered helium in the spectrum of the corona of the sun during an eclipse in 1868. Shortly afterward it was identified as an element and named by the British chemist Sir Edward Frankland and the British astronomer Sir Joseph Norman Lockyer (qq.v.). The gas was first isolated from terrestrial sources by the British chemist Sir William Ramsay (q.v.) in 1895. In 1907 British physicist Sir Ernest Rutherford (q.v.) showed that alpha particles are the nuclei of helium atoms. Later investigation confirmed his evidence.

Properties. At sea level, helium occurs in the atmosphere in the proportion of 5.4 parts per 1,000,000. The proportion increases slightly at higher altitudes. About 1 part per 1,000,000 of atmospheric helium consists of the lighter helium isotope of mass 3, called helium-3. Helium-3 is now thought to be a product of the decay of tritium (q.v.), a radioactive hydrogen isotope of mass 3. The common helium isotope, helium-4, probably comes from radioactive alpha emitters in rocks. Natural gas is the major commercial source of helium. It is recovered from natural gas in Kansas; in Saskatchewan, Canada; and in the U.S.S.R. Annual U.S. production of helium in the late 1960's amounted to more than 4,500,000,000 cu.ft. By far the largest users of helium are agencies of the U.S. government.

Helium is the most difficult of all gases to liquefy and is impossible to solidify at normal atmospheric pressures. These properties make liquid helium extremely useful as a refrigerant and for experimental work in producing and measuring temperatures close to absolute zero (q.v.; see also Cryogenics). Liquid helium may be cooled almost to absolute zero at normal pressure by rapid removal of the vapors above the liquid. At a temperature slightly above absolute zero, it is transformed into helium II, also called superfluid helium, a liquid with unique physical properties. It has no freezing point, and its viscosity is apparently zero; it passes readily through minute cracks and pores and will even creep up the sides and over the lip of a container. The conductivity of helium II is nearly 1,000,000 times that of ordinary liquids. Helium-3, which has an even lower boiling point than ordinary helium, exhibits markedly different properties when liquefied.

Uses. Because it is noncombustible, helium is preferred to hydrogen as the lifting gas in lighter-than-air balloons; it has 92 percent of the lifting power of hydrogen although it weighs twice as much. Helium is used to pressurize and stiffen the structure of rockets before takeoff and to pressurize the tanks of liquid hydrogen or other fuel in order to force fuel into the rocket engines. It is useful for this application because it remains a gas even at the low temperature of liquid hydrogen. A potential use of helium is as a heat-transfer medium in nuclear reactors because it remains chemically inert and nonradioactive under the conditions that exist within the reactors.

Helium is used in inert-gas-arc welding for light metals such as aluminum and magnesium alloys which might otherwise oxidize; the helium protects heated parts from attack by air. Argon is also used for this purpose but gives a cooler arc and results in less penetrating welds. (see Welding: *Arc Welding.*) Helium is used in place of nitrogen as part of the synthetic atmosphere breathed by deep-sea divers, caisson workers, and others, because it reduces susceptibility to bends (q.v.). This synthetic atmosphere is also used in medicine to relieve sufferers of respiratory difficulties because helium moves more easily than nitrogen through constricted respiratory passages.

Helium is transported as a gas in small quantities, compressed in heavy steel cylinders. Larger amounts of helium may be shipped as a liquid in insulated containers, thus saving shipping costs because the containers for the liquid are smaller and weigh less than the cylinders used to hold an equal amount of gas.

HELL, in theology, any place of punishment and privation for the souls (see Soul) of men after death. More strictly, the term is applied to the place of eternal punishment of the damned, whether angels (see Angel) or men. The doctrine of the existence of hell is derived from the principle of the necessity for vindication of divine justice, combined with the human experience that evildoers do not always appear to be punished adequately in their lifetime.

Among the early Teutons the term "hell" signified a place under the earth to which the souls of all mortals, good or bad, were consigned after death; it thus denoted a conception similar to that of the Hebrew *Sheol.* Among the early Jews, as in other Semitic nations, existence in *Sheol* was regarded as a shadowy continuation of earthly life where "the wicked ceased from troubling and the weary were at rest". Later the dictum of the prophet Isaiah (q.v.; Isa. 14) that the king of Babylon "shall be brought down . . . to the uttermost depths of Sheol" gave rise to the concept of various depths of *Sheol,* with corresponding degrees of reward and punishment.

Early Christian writers used the term "hell" to designate (1) the Limbo (q.v.) of infants, where the unbaptized enjoy a natural bliss, but are denied the supernatural bliss of the vision of God (see HEAVEN); (2) the Limbo of the fathers, in which the souls of the just who died before the advent of Christ awaited their redemption, and which is mentioned in the Apostles' Creed, "He [Christ] descended into hell" (see CREEDS); (3) a place of purgation from minor offenses leading inevitably to Heaven (see PURGATORY); and (4) the place of punishment of Satan and the other fallen angels and of all mortals who die unrepentant of serious sin. The last of these interpretations has the greatest acceptance today.

The duration of the punishments of Hell has been a subject of controversy since early Christian times. The writer and theologian Origen (q.v.) and his school taught that the purpose of these punishments was purgatorial, and that they were proportionate to the guilt of the individual. Origen held that, in time, the purifying effect would be accomplished in all, even devils; that punishment would ultimately cease; and that all in Hell eventually would be restored to happiness. This doctrine was condemned by the second Council of Constantinople (see CONSTANTINOPLE, COUNCILS OF), in 553, and a belief in the eternity of the punishments in Hell became characteristic of both the Orthodox Church and the Roman Catholic Church (qq.v.). It also passed into the creeds of the churches of the Reformation (q.v.), but the doctrine of Hell was rejected by many of the more radical thinkers of the Renaissance (q.v.), especially in the Baptist and Unitarian churches; see BAPTIST; UNITARIANISM.

In modern times the belief in physical punishment after death has been abandoned by certain Protestants, and the endless duration of this punishment has been rejected by many. The question as to the nature of the punishments of Hell is equally controversial. Opinions range from that holding the pains of Hell to be no more than the remorse of conscience (q.v.) to the orthodox belief that the "pain of loss" (the consciousness of having forfeited the vision of God and the happiness of heaven) is combined with the "pain of sense" (actual physical torment).

HELLAS (Gr., "land of the Hellenes"), name that came to be applied to ancient Greece, together with the Greek islands and colonies, after the great migrations of Hellenic peoples, beginning about 1100 B.C. Modern Greece, in accordance with the classical tradition, is also known as Hellas or Ellas. See GREECE: *History.*

HELLBENDER, or GIANT SALAMANDER, large amphibian, *Cryptobranchus alleganiensis,* in the order Urodela. It is sometimes called "alligator", "water dog", or "mud puppy". Unlike the true mud puppy (q.v.), which it resembles, its gills are internal and the skin on the sides of its body is wrinkled. The hellbender reaches a length of 2 ft. and is gray or dark brown in color. Its head and body are flattened and the tail is laterally compressed to facilitate swimming. Hellbenders are common in the Ohio R. and its tributaries. They live on the gravelly bottom of the river and subsist on worms, insects, and small crustaceans. They are often caught by fishermen. The female hellbender lays about four hundred eggs under a stone in August or September and eats many of them in the six-week period before they hatch. The male often guards the eggs but is also occasionally cannibalistic.

The closest relative to the hellbender is the giant salamander, *Megalobatrachus japonicus,* of China and Japan, which reaches a length of 5 ft., and is eaten in the Orient.

HELLEBORE, common name of plants in the genus *Helleborus* of the Buttercup family, Ranunculaceae. Hellebores are native to Eurasia. The flowers have five large, petallike sepals, eight to ten inconspicuous tubular petals, many stamens, and three to ten pistils. Green hellebore or Christmas flower, *H. viridis,* produces yellow flowers in late winter or early spring outdoors. It is occasionally used in gardens and has become naturalized in the eastern United States. The more common Christmas rose, *H. niger,* bears large white flowers outdoors in midwinter to early spring, depending on location. The name Christmas rose is somewhat misleading since the plant is neither a rose nor does

HELLEN

it normally bloom at Christmas. Since classical Greek times, the Christmas rose has had a reputation for being poisonous, but few cases are on record.

The false hellebores belong to the genus *Veratrum* of the Lily family, Liliaceae. Eastern false hellebore, *V. viride,* is a conspicuous perennial herb of wet open woods and meadows throughout much of the country. It has numerous large leaves which are narrow at both ends

Hellebore and false hellebore. Left: The green hellebore, Helleborus viridis. *Right: Eastern false hellebore,* Veratrum viride.

and are accordion-pleated lengthwise. Western false hellebore, *V. californicum,* of high spring range country is similar in appearance. The rootstocks of these plants and of the related European white hellebore, *V. album,* are known to contain a number of alkaloids. Extracts have been used in various ways in medicine and as an insecticide. In man, the alkaloids act to reduce blood pressure. Recently, it has been discovered that the vegetation of false hellebores can produce birth abnormalities in sheep and other animals if eaten by the dam at a particular time in pregnancy. The susceptible period is less than one day. The common deformity produced, known as cyclopia, is malformation of the face resulting in a single median eye or two eyeballs in a single central socket. The stockmen term such animals monkey-face lambs.

HELLEN, ancestor of the Hellenes or Greeks. He was the son of Pyrrha and Deucalion (q.v.), who were spared because of their piety in a devastating flood that destroyed all creation. Hellen was believed to be the father of the principal nations of Greece. From his sons Aeolus (q.v.) and Dorus sprang the Aeolians and the Dorians (qq.v.), and from his son Xuthus came the Acheans and the Ionians (qq.v.).

HELLENISM. See GREECE: *History: Ancient Greece: Hellenistic Period.*

HELLENIST (Gr. *Hellenistes;* fr. *hellenizein,* "to speak or make Greek"), term designating a person, not of Greek blood, who adopts or imitates the Greek way of life. The term was especially applied to the Jewish people who adopted the Greek culture and language following the Macedonian conquest of the Middle East in 338 B.C.; see GREECE: *History: Ancient Greece: Hellenistic Period.* In countries outside Palestine, especially Egypt, Cyrenaica, and Syria, the Jewish people came into close contact with Greek thought and literature, and eventually came to speak Greek as their native tongue, using it even in the synagogues. Within Palestine itself the Hellenistic influences were strong, particularly during the rule of the Selucid king Antiochus IV (*see under* ANTIOCHUS). When, however, he attempted to impose worship of the Greek gods, the Jews revolted under the leadership of Judas Maccabaeus (*see* MACCABEES) and established an independent Jewish state relatively free of Hellenism. In Acts 6:1 and 11:20, the Apostle Paul (q.v.) contrasts Hellenists ("Grecians") with Hebrews, Jews who resisted Hellenistic influences.

HELLESPONT or HELLESPONTUS. See DARDANELLES.

HELL GATE, narrow part of the East R., between Manhattan Island and the borough of Queens, New York City, enclosing Ward's Island on the E. and W. The channel separating Ward's and Randall's islands is called Little Hell Gate.

Hell Gate was long a notorious danger to navigation because of its tortuous course, powerful tidal currents, and jagged rocks. As early as 1851 an attempt was made to clear away the obstructions, and on Oct. 10, 1885, the channel was finally freed by blasting. The channel derives its name from the Dutch *Helle Gat* ("Beautiful Pass"). It is spanned by the Hell Gate railroad bridge (1917) and by the Triborough Bridge for motor vehicles and pedestrians (1936).

HELLMAN, Lillian (1905–), American playwright, born in New Orleans, La., and educated at New York University and Columbia University. She worked as a book reviewer and play reader before beginning her career as a playwright. Her plays are distinguished for the forcefulness of their subject matter, for character development, and for expert construction. Among them are *The Children's Hour* (1934), in which a malicious child's lies ruin the lives of two schoolteachers; *The Little Foxes* (1939), in which the members of a Southern family struggle unscrupulously with one another for the family wealth; and *The Watch on the Rhine* (1941), in which a leader of the anti-National Socialist underground visiting the United States is forced to kill a National Socialist agent. Her other plays include *The Searching Wind* (1944); *Another Part of the Forest* (1946); *The Autumn Garden* (1951); *The Lark* (1955), a story of Joan of Arc (q.v.), adapted from the play *L'Alouette* by the French dramatist Jean Anouilh (q.v.); and *Candide* (1956), a comic operetta based on the satire of the same name by the French author Voltaire (q.v.). *Toys in the Attic* (1960) received the Drama Critics Award for that year. She was awarded the 1970 National Book Award in arts and letters for the autobiography, *An Unfinished Woman: A Memoir* (1969). Lillian Hellman was elected a member of the American Academy of Arts and Letters (q.v.) in 1962.

HELMAND (anc. *Etymander*), river of Afghanistan, rising in the Koh-i-Baba mountain range, w. of Kabul, and flowing generally s.w. until it enters Seistan, the border district between Afghanistan and Iran, there turning N. and forming the boundary between the two countries until it disappears in the swamps of Seistan. In its early course the river is a mountain stream. About 40 miles N. of the town of Girishk, it descends to level terrain. Below its junction with the Arghandab R. near the village of Kala Bist, 30 miles s. of Girishk, the Helmand attains a maximum width of 900 to 1200 ft. and a maximum depth of 12 ft. The length of the river is about 700 mi.

HELMET, protective covering for the head, usually made of metal, leather, or plastic, used in warfare, certain occupations, and sports. Military helmets have been used from the earliest times, and have been made in many different forms. The simplest form, a close-fitting skullcap, apparently made of iron, leather, and bronze, appears on Assyrian monumental reliefs. The oldest-known elaborations of this form were used by the Greeks, Etruscans, and late Romans, and included protective devices for the neck and face, and plumes or carved figures which surmounted the crown.

From the beginning of the 15th century until around 1650, types of helmets proliferated throughout Europe. Certain important types, diverse in size and shape and more or less elaborately decorated, were called the salade, the armet, the burgonet, and the morion (*see* ARMOR). As the use of firearms in warfare became more general, helmets lost their utility, especially as protection for the face. Modern military helmets, such as those worn in World Wars I and II, afford no protection for the face; they are usually steel coverings designed for maximum protection of the head against shrapnel and ricocheted bullets.

The basin-shaped type used by British and United States forces in World War I was soon widely adopted in construction industries, with strong lightweight plastic later often substituted for steel. Specialized helmets of leather or plastic are used in such sports as football, lacrosse, and automobile racing. In many States of the U.S., helmets must be worn by all motorcyclists.

HELMET CRAB. *See* KING CRAB.

HELMHOLTZ, Hermann Ludwig Ferdinand von (1821–94), German physiologist and physicist, born in Potsdam. He studied medicine and natural science in Berlin and served as a surgeon in the Prussian army from 1843 to 1848. From 1849 to 1871 he was professor of physiology successively at the universities of Königsberg (now Kaliningrad, Russian S.F.S.R.), Bonn, and Heidelberg. From 1871 until his death he was professor of physics at the University of Berlin and also served, after 1888, as director of the physicotechnical institute at Charlottenburg.

Helmholtz was one of the great scientists of the 19th century. His reputation was securely established in 1847 when he wrote a treatise in which he gave the earliest general account of the principle of the conservation of energy. Throughout the rest of his career he made important contributions, both of a theoretical and a practical nature, in many diversified fields of science, including physiology, optics, acoustics, chemistry, mathematics, magnetism, electricity, and mechanics.

HELMONT

His investigations in the field of physiological optics led to his invention of the ophthalmoscope (an instrument used to view the interior of the eye), a clarified explanation of the mechanisms of sight, and the development of a theory of color vision, based on the work of the British physicist Thomas Young (q.v.). Helmholtz's *Physiological Optics* (1856–66) was the definitive study of the physiology and physics of vision. He also studied the physiology of hearing, accurately explaining the mechanism of the ear. His work with musical sounds resulted in the discovery that the tonal quality of a musical sound is created by the overtones or harmonics (q.v.) associated with the tone. His investigations into the functions of sound and hearing led to the publication of his *Sensations of Tone* (1862), which formed the basis of the scientific study of acoustics.

In the study of electricity and magnetism Helmholtz contributed to the understanding of electrodynamics, investigated the motion of electricity in conductors, and developed the theory of the electromagnetic properties of light. His last researches were of a purely theoretical nature.

See PHYSICS.

HELMONT, Jan Baptista van (1557?–1644?), Flemish physician and chemist, born in Brussels (now in Belgium), and educated at the University of Louvain. A curious mixture of mystic, alchemist, careful observer of nature, and experimenter, Helmont was the first to postulate the existence of gases distinct from air; he claimed the word "gas" as his own coinage. He believed that the prime elements of the universe are air and water, and proved to his satisfaction that plants are composed only of water by planting a willow of known weight in soil of known weight and weighing the willow and the soil five years later. The willow had gained 169 lb. and the soil had lost practically no weight, and he ascribed the gain in weight of the willow to its having taken up water (for the modern explanation of this experiment, see PHOTOSYNTHESIS). His hypothesis of a mystic system of supernatural bodies that control the body had no scientific validity; but he accurately applied chemical principles to physiology, believing that nutrition resulted from the conversion of dead food to living tissue through the action of ferments, and suggesting that alkalies be used to correct excess acidity of the digestive juices. His works were published posthumously in 1648 as *Ortus Medicinae, vel Opera et Opuscula Omnia* ("The Fount of Medicine, or Complete Works").

HELODERMA. See BEADED LIZARD.

HÉLOÏSE. See ABELARD, PETER.

HELOTS, in ancient Greece, bondsmen or serfs of the Spartans. They were probably the original inhabitants of Sparta (q.v.), who were enslaved by the Dorian conquerors of that territory; see DORIANS. The helots represented the lowest of the four classes of Spartans, and had virtually no civil or political rights. They were entirely the property of the state, which assigned them to work on the land of individual Spartans. For their masters, the helots were required to provide a certain fixed amount of produce each year, retaining for themselves only whatever they produced in excess of that amount. The helots could be freed or sold only by the state. In wartime they were used as soldiers, or as oarsmen in the galleys. Because they were a large and discontented class, the helots were viewed by the ruling Spartans with suspicion and fear. During the Peloponnesian War (see GREECE: *History: Ancient Greece*) about 2000 helots who had been freed for services to the state were secretly murdered, to forestall plotting against their rulers.

HELPER, Hinton Rowan (1829–1909), American writer, born in Davis County, N.C. In 1850 he joined the California gold rush (see FORTY-NINERS), and as a result of his experiences wrote his first book, *The Land of Gold* (1855). He then made a thorough study of Negro slavery in America, and in 1857 published *The Impending Crisis of the South: How to Meet It*. Helper opposed slavery not for moral or humanitarian reasons, but because of his concern with the poor whites and small farmers of the South. His book incensed Southern Democrats, and gratified Northern Republicans, who distributed 100,000 copies during the 1860 Presidential election campaign. In 1861 President Abraham Lincoln (q.v.) appointed Helper United States consul at Buenos Aires, Argentina. After five years he returned to the U.S. and resumed writing. He produced three violently racist books attacking the Negro: *Nojoque* (1867), *Negroes in Negroland* (1868), and *Noonday Exigencies* (1871). Helper spent the later years of his life trying to promote a railway between Hudson Bay and the Strait of Magellan, about which he wrote *The Three Americas Railway* (1881). This project failed and, poverty-stricken and embittered, he committed suicide.

HELSINGØR (Eng. *Elsinore*), town and seaport of Denmark, in Frederiksborg County, Sjaelland (Zealand), on the E. coast of the island, 28 miles N. of Copenhagen. Helsingør, with Kronborg Castle E. of the town, is famous as the locale of the tragedy *Hamlet* (q.v.), by William Shake-

HELSINKI

The Lutheran Suurkirkko or Great Church overlooks Senate Square in Helsinki. Consulate General of Finland

speare (q.v.). The castle, built during the 16th century, is now used chiefly as a maritime museum. Among the principal industries of the town are glass manufacture, the weaving of fishing nets and coarse cloth, shipbuilding, marine engineering, and iron founding. Helsingør has a fine harbor, equipped with dry docks for the repair of ships. A railway ferry joins Helsingør with Hälsingborg, Sweden, across the Øresund. Pop. (1960) 26,658.

HELSINKI (Sw. *Helsingfors*), largest city, capital, and chief seaport of Finland, and capital of Uusimaa Province, on a small peninsula extending into the Gulf of Finland, about 100 miles S.E. of Turku. Small islands fringe the peninsula, and the entrance to Helsinki harbor is protected by the fortifications of Suomenlinna (Sw. *Sveaborg*), covering seven of the islands.

Helsinki is laid out with spacious streets interspersed with many gardens and parks. Architecturally, Helsinki is a mixture of old and modern styles, with the old senate house and the Suurkirkko, or Great Church, representing the older buildings, and the railroad station, designed in 1918 by the Finnish architect Gottlieb Eliel Saarinen (*see under* SAARINEN) as a notable example of modern architecture. Helsinki is the cultural and commercial, as well as the political, center of Finland. The University of Helsinki has been situated in the city since 1828, when it was moved from Turku, where it was founded in 1640. The National Museum of Finland, the opera, and several theaters, playing in both Finnish and Swedish, are located in the capital.

The principal manufactures of Helsinki include paper, textiles, liquors, china, chemicals, and metal goods; agricultural and dairy products and lumber and wood products are exported in considerable quantity. A major part of the commercial activity is centered on the harbor, in which separate facilities are maintained for passengers and small shipments, for bulk shipments of lumber and wood products, and for handling large incoming cargoes of coal and grain. The port can accommodate any vessel, but it is icebound from January to May, except for a channel that is kept clear by an icebreaker. Helsinki is also an international airline center.

Helsinki was founded by Gustavus I Vasa, King of Sweden (*see under* GUSTAVUS) in 1550 on a site some miles inland from its present location, to which it was removed in 1640. In 1713, during the Northern War (1700–21) between Russia and Sweden, the city was destroyed by a retreating Swedish force; the present fortifications were begun in 1729. Finland was incorpo-

HELVETIA

rated into the Russian Empire in 1809; and Helsinki was made the administrative capital of the Grand Duchy of Finland in 1812; since 1917 the city has been the capital of the Finnish Republic (see FINLAND). In 1952, Helsinki was the site of the Olympic Games. Pop. (1968 est.) 532,310.

HELVETIA, ancient Latin name for Switzerland, meaning "the territory of the Helvetii". The term is still applied in poetry, and is used to inscribe the currency and postage stamps of Switzerland.

HELVETIC REPUBLIC, Swiss republic established by France in 1798 which endured until 1803. See SWITZERLAND: *History*.

HELVETII, Latin designation for an ancient Celtic people who, at the time of the Gallic wars of the Roman soldier and statesman Gaius Julius Caesar (q.v.), inhabited what is now the western portion of Switzerland. Specifically, the territory of the Helvetii was bounded by the Jura mountain range on the west, the Rhône R. on the south, and the Rhine R. on the north and east. The Helvetii had their own completely democratic political administration, their chief town being Aventicum (modern Avenches). According to Caesar's *Commentaries* they were the bravest of the Gallic peoples.

In 107 B.C., influenced by reports of gold and plunder available in southern Gaul and Rome, the Helvetii crossed the Jura Mts. and defeated a Roman army. Five years later they joined the Cimbri (q.v.) in an attempted invasion of Italy, but were repulsed. In 58 B.C., under the pressure of German invasions, all the Helvetii, numbering almost 370,000, began a mass migration to what is now southern France. Caesar, then proconsul in Gaul, pursued them with an army and inflicted an overwhelming defeat at Bibracte, near modern Autun in central France, more than two thirds of the Helvetii were annihilated. The remainder returned to their homeland, becoming subject to the rule of Rome. See GAUL; SWITZERLAND: *History*.

HELVÉTIUS, Claude Adrien (1715–71), French philosopher, born in Paris. He was appointed farmer general, a post that involved the collection of the royal income, in 1738, but subsequently resigned because of the corruption of his colleagues in office, and purchased the office of *maître d'hôtel*, or steward, to his patroness Queen Maria Leczczyńska (1703–68), wife of Louis XV (q.v.), King of France. He then devoted his time to literary efforts and his most famous work, *De l'Esprit*, was published in 1758 (Eng. trans., *Essays on the Mind,* 1807). In this work Helvétius, whose personal life was a model of virtue, carried the theory of hedonism (q.v.) to an extreme of selfish sensuality, declaring that all human faculties, including judgment, the power of comparison, and even memory, are mere attributes of physical sensation; that the only motive of human activity is self-interest; and that no choice exists between good and evil or right and wrong, because even self-sacrifice is a mere choice between competitive pleasures. Helvétius' work was condemned as an affront to public morals by the theological faculty of the Sorbonne, Paris, and was publicly burned in 1759. *De l'Homme, de Ses Facultés Intellectuelles et de Son Éducation* (1772; Eng. trans., *A Treatise on Man: His Intellectual Faculties and His Education,* 1777), an attempt to refute the doctrines of the French philosopher Jean Jacques Rousseau (q.v.), was also publicly burned.

HELWÂN, city of the Arab Republic of Egypt, in Cairo Governorate, 2 miles E. of the Nile R. and 15 miles S.E. of Cairo. Since 1958 iron and steel have been produced in a modern industrial area. Helwân is a noted resort, with medicinal springs, hotels, and a golf course. It is the site of the Institute of Technology, an observatory, and a meteorological station. Pop. (1960) 94,385.

HEMATITE, common mineral and the most abundant ore of iron, composed of ferric oxide, Fe_2O_3. It is widely distributed over the world, occurring in rocks of all ages. In the United States hematite comprises about 50 percent of all the iron ore mined. The chief iron-ore districts in the United States, and probably the most important hematite regions in the world, are located along the shores of Lake Superior in Michigan, Wisconsin, and Minnesota. Extensive deposits are also found in the Appalachian region extending from New York to Alabama, with particularly noteworthy deposits in eastern Tennessee and northern Alabama.

Hematite occurs in rhombohedral crystals, called specular iron in massive formations, and in earthy forms, called red ocher. The crystals are translucent, range in color from dark gray to black, and have a brilliant metallic luster; the earthy varieties are lusterless and red. The hardness ranges from 5.5 to 6.5 and the specific gravity from 4.2 to 5.25.

In addition to being the principal ore of iron, hematite is a constituent of a number of abrasives and pigments.

HEMEL HEMPSTEAD, Great Britain, municipal borough in Hertfordshire, England, on the Gade R., 6 miles W. of Saint Albans and 22 miles N.W. of the center of London, of which it is a suburb. A community of 21,000 in 1947, Hemel Hempstead was chosen for development as one of the "new towns" and now has paper and textile mills, tanneries, and agricultural-machinery plants. Remains of a Roman village are located in the borough. Mentioned in writings as early as 705, the borough was rural until after its planned development. Pop. (1969 est.) 66,200.

HEMICHORDATA or **HEMICHORDA**, phylum of the animal kingdom, previously considered a subphylum of the phylum Chordata, containing several species of wormlike marine creatures, characterized by a stiff structure akin to a notochord in their head regions. The hemichordates have no common names because they are not popularly known. They are important in biological study because they represent the closest link between invertebrates and vertebrates. These animals show such typical vertebrate characteristics as a dorsal anterior nerve ganglion and gill clefts in all species, at least embryologically. Unlike vertebrates, hemichordates have no tail in either their adult or their embryological stages. Externally their bodies are divided into three segments, a head or proboscis segment, a collar segment, and a comparatively long trunk segment.

The phylum Hemichordata contains two classes, Enteropneusta and Pterobranchia. Enteropneusta contains a number of species which burrow in sand and mud of beaches, ingesting the mud into the mouth, which is situated near the junction of the head and collar segments, and straining minute forms of life from it. Sexes are separate in this order. The larvae are free-swimming at first, but later sink to the mud and gradually become transformed into adults. A common species on the Atlantic coast of the United States is *Saccoglossus kowalevskii*, which reaches a length of 8 in. Other common species in this class belong to the genus *Balanoglossus* (q.v.). Pterobranchia is a class of minute, deep-sea, sessile hemichordates which contains three genera: *Atubaria, Cephalodiscus,* and *Rhabdopleura*. These animals live in cylinders which are secreted by cells of the head region. They are unusual in having cilia-bearing arms on the collar which gather food. They breed by budding. The buds of *Cephalodiscus* leave the parent and form new individuals while those of *Rhabdopleura* remain with the parent and form colonies. Compare Ascidiacea.

HEMICRANIA. See Migraine.

HEMIMORPHITE, or CALAMINE, mineral and zinc ore, of formula $Zn_4Si_2O_7(OH)_2 \cdot H_2O$. Hemimorphite crystallizes in the orthorhombic system (see Crystal: *Crystallography*); it has hardness 5 and sp.gr. 3.4; and its crystals are white or pale colored, with a vitreous (glassy) luster. It often resembles smithsonite, a zinc carbonate, with which it is frequently found in nature. British mineralogists reverse the assignment of the names hemimorphite and smithsonite. Deposits of hemimorphite occur in England, the United States, and the U.S.S.R.

HEMINGWAY, Ernest (1899–1961), American novelist and short-story writer, born in Oak Park, Ill., and educated at Oak Park High School. He became a reporter for the Kansas City *Star*, but left this job within a few months to serve as a volunteer ambulance driver in Italy during World War I. He later transferred to the Italian infantry and was severely wounded. After the war he was a correspondent for the Toronto *Star* and then settled in Paris, France. While in Paris, Hemingway was encouraged in creative work by the American expatriate writers Ezra Pound and Gertrude Stein (qq.v.). After 1927 Hemingway spent long periods of time in Key West, Fla., Spain, and Africa. During the Spanish Civil War (see Spain: *History: Civil War*), he returned to Spain as a newspaper correspondent. In World War II he was again a correspondent and later was a reporter for the United States First Army; although he was not a soldier, he participated in several battles. After the war he settled near Havana, Cuba, and about 1958 moved to Ketchum, Idaho.

Hemingway was an avid fisherman, hunter, and bullfight enthusiast and he drew heavily on his experiences in writing. His adventurous life brought him close to death several times: in the Spanish Civil War when shells burst into his hotel room; in World War II when he was struck by a taxi during a blackout; and in 1954 when his airplane crashed in Africa. His death is regarded as a suicide.

A Writer of the "Lost Generation". One of the foremost authors between the two World Wars, Hemingway in his early works depicted the life of two types of people. One type consisted of men and women deprived, by World War I, of faith in the moral values in which they had believed, and who lived with cynical disregard for anything but their own emotional needs. The other type were men of simple character and primitive emotions, such as prizefighters and bullfighters. Hemingway wrote of their courageous and usually futile battles against circumstances. His earliest works include the collections of short stories *Three Stories and Ten Poems* (1923), his first work; *In Our Time* (1924), tales reflecting his youth; *Men Without Women* (1927), a volume that included "The Killers" remarkable for the description of impending

HEMINGWAY

Ernest Hemingway, a noted sportsman as well as a writer, on a hunting trip in Sun Valley, Idaho.
Wide World

doom; and *Winner Take Nothing* (1933), stories characterizing unfortunates in Europe. The novel which established his reputation, *The Sun Also Rises* (1926), is the story of a group of morally irresponsible Americans and Britons living in France and Spain, members of the so-called "lost generation" of the post-World War I period. In 1929 he published his second important novel, *A Farewell to Arms,* the story of a deeply moving love affair in wartime Italy between an American officer in the Italian ambulance service and a British nurse. The story ends with her death in childbirth. The novel was followed by two non-fiction works, *Death in the Afternoon* (1932), prose pieces mainly about bullfighting; and *Green Hills of Africa* (1935), accounts of big-game hunting.

Social Concern. Originally using themes of helplessness and defeat, Hemingway in the late 1930's expressed concern for social problems. His novel *To Have and Have Not* (1937) and his play *The Fifth Column,* published in *The Fifth Column and the First Forty-Nine Stories* (1938), strongly condemned economic and political injustices. Two of his best short stories, "The Short Happy Life of Francis Macomber" and "The Snows of Kilimanjaro", were part of the latter work. In the novel, *For Whom the Bell Tolls* (1940), dealing with the Spanish Civil War, he shows that the loss of liberty anywhere in the world is a warning that liberty is endangered everywhere. During the next decade his only literary efforts were *Men At War: The Best War Stories of All Time* (1942), which he edited, and the novel *Across the River and into the Trees* (1950). In 1952 Hemingway published *The Old Man and the Sea,* a powerful novelette about an aged Cuban fisherman, for which he won the 1953 Pulitzer Prize for fiction. In 1954 Hemingway was awarded the Nobel Prize in literature. The last work published in his lifetime was *Collected Poems* (1960). His posthumously published books include *A Movable Feast* (1964), an account of his early years in Paris; *By Line: Ernest Hemingway* (1967), selected newspaper articles and dispatches; *Ernest Hemingway, Cub Reporter: Kansas City Star Stories* (1970); and *Islands in the Stream* (1970), a sea novel. Other works representing 3000 manuscript pages remain to be published.

Hemingway's style is characterized by crispness, laconic dialogue, and emotional understatement. His writings and his personal life exerted a profound influence on the American writers of his time. Many of his writings are regarded as classics of American literature and some of his stories have been made into motion pictures.

See AMERICAN LITERATURE: *20th Century.*

HEMIPTERA. See BUG.

HEMLOCK, common name of two different genera of poisonous herbs of the Carrot family, Umbelliferae. Poison hemlock, *Conium maculatum,* is the plant which was used to put the Greek philosopher Socrates (q.v.) to death. Its lacy, carrotlike foliage, growing from a long, white, carrotlike taproot, appears in early spring and is followed by reduced leaves later in the summer. The small white flowers are grouped in flat-topped umbels. One aid in recognizing poison hemlock is the fact that the leaf stalks are usually conspicuously spotted with purple. Poison hemlock grows as a luxuriant weed of roadsides, and in unimproved fields and waste areas throughout the United States and southern Canada. It is easily mistaken for the even more common wild carrot, which is not poisonous. All parts of the poison hemlock contain alkaloids which affect the nervous system, producing symptoms of trembling, incoordination, loss of sensation, and eventual paralysis of respiration.

Water hemlock, *Cicuta maculata,* is related botanically to poison hemlock, but toxicologically it is entirely different. The roots, and, to a much lesser extent, the foliage, contain a complex unsaturated alcohol which brings on symptoms of convulsions in man and animals. The amount of root that must be eaten to cause death is very small; consequently, water hemlock is one of the most dangerous of all poisonous plants in North America. Water hemlock grows in swamps, along streams, and in other moist locations. The foliage, which arises in early spring in a cluster from the roots, is divided and redivided into leaflets with regularly pointed and notched edges. A central vein runs the length of each leaflet. From it, secondary veins run toward the edge, ending in or near the notches of the leaf rather than in the points; this is unusual and helps in distinguishing water hemlock from other similar plants. Two other characteristics that help in identification are the roots and the structure of the stem where it joins the roots. The roots consist of clusters (rarely only one) of 1- to 2-in.-long, dahlialike tubers (larger in some western species), which have a mousy or pungent odor when fresh.

J.M.K.

Poison hemlock, Conium maculatum Robert H. Wright — National Audubon Society

HEMLOCK, common name for coniferous trees of the genus *Tsuga* belonging to the Pine family, Pinaceae. The genus includes about ten species, four of which are native to temperate North America, and the remainder to eastern Asia. They are tall, straight evergreens with slender branches bearing scattered, two-ranked leaves and pendulous cones.

The eastern hemlock, *T. canadensis,* grows in hilly forests in northeastern United States and eastern Canada. It is a tall tree, usually 60 to 100 ft. in height, with light, spreading, delicate foliage. The leaves are dark green with longitudinal white lines on the lower surfaces. The wood of eastern hemlock is used extensively as construction lumber, and tannins (q.v.) produced by the bark were at one time used for tanning leather. The Carolina hemlock, *T. caroliniana,* is a somewhat smaller tree, rarely as tall as 70 ft., which grows in the mountains of Virginia, the Carolinas, and Georgia. The mountain hemlock, *T. mertensiana,* is another relatively small species, 20 to 90 ft. tall, which grows along the Pacific coast from Alaska to California. The western hemlock, *T. heterophylla,* is the tallest species in the genus, sometimes reaching a height of 200 ft. It grows along the Pacific coast from southeastern Alaska to central California. Like the eastern hemlock, it is an important softwood timber tree. About 90 percent of the hemlock used for lumber is western hemlock, and most of the remainder is eastern hemlock.

Small specimens of eastern and Carolina hemlock are used extensively as ornamental trees. Two Asian species, the Japanese hemlock, *T. diversifolia,* and Siebold's hemlock, *T. sieboldi,* are cultivated in northern U.S. The North American yew, which belongs to an unrelated coniferous genus, is sometimes called ground hemlock; see YEW.

HEMOGLOBIN, most prevalent of the special blood pigments that transport oxygen; it is present in all but most primitive animals. It participates in the process by which blood carries to the cells their required nutrients and transports their waste products to the excretory organs; see CELL; EXCRETION. Hemoglobin also carries from the lungs or gills, where the blood is oxygenated, the oxygen required by body cells. When saturated with oxygen, it is called oxyhemoglobin. After hemoglobin releases oxygen to the body tissues, it reverses its function to pick up carbon dioxide, the principal product of tissue respiration, for transport to the lungs, where it is expired. In this form, it is known as carboxyhemoglobin. See BLOOD; RESPIRATION.

Hemoglobin is contained entirely in the erythrocytes, or red blood cells, comprising perhaps 35 percent of their weight. An additional small percentage is composed of the structural elements of hemoglobin and a large number of hormones, enzymes (qq.v.), and vitamins (see VITAMIN). The balance is water. To combine properly with oxygen, erythrocytes must contain adequate hemoglobin; this in turn depends on the amount of iron in the body. The organism derives its store of iron by absorption from the gastrointestinal tract (see DIGESTION); except in hemorrhage (see BLEEDING). The organism conserves and constantly reuses the supply of iron. A deficiency of hemoglobin caused by a lack of iron leads to simple anemia (q.v.).

A quantity of 100 milliliters of blood carries 12 to 17 grams of hemoglobin which carries more than 20 times its volume of oxygen. Hemoglobin combines so firmly with carbon monoxide (q.v.) that it can no longer combine with oxygen, causing asphyxiation (see ASPHYXIA). After a life of perhaps 120 days, erythrocytes are destroyed in the spleen (q.v.) or in the course of circulation, their hemoglobin is broken into its constituents, including iron, which enters new blood cells formed in the bone marrow. When blood vessels rupture, the red cells are released and escape into tissue, where they are broken down. The hemoglobin is converted into a number of bile pigments, the color of which is responsible for the appearance of bruises.

In the late 1960's blood-research scientists discovered three so-called initiation factors necessary for the production of new proteins in the body cells. These factors made it possible for the researchers to make hemoglobin in test-tube systems outside the human body. C.V.M.

HÉMON, Louis (1880–1913), French novelist, born in Brest. After studying for a diplomatic career, he went to Canada in 1911 and worked as a farm laborer near Lake Saint John, Québec, while gathering material for his major work, *Maria Chapdelaine* (1914; Eng. trans., 1921). Shortly after sending this vivid, realistic novel of French-Canadian pioneer life to the French newspaper *Le Temps,* Hemón was killed by a train near Chapleau, Ontario. The tremendous success of *Maria Chapdelaine,* first published as a serial, inspired the publication of three of Hemón's earlier novels and a travel journal.

HEMOPHILIA, disease characterized by an abnormal tendency to bleed profusely from the slightest wound and caused by insufficiency or absence of a blood protein that participates in the complex chemical reactions involved in blood clotting; see BLOOD: *Coagulation.* It may occur spontaneously, following severe exertion, or as the result of a simple cut. Before the advent of modern therapy, the chance of survival to adulthood was poor.

Half of all cases have an identifiable history of the disease; in other instances, it may be attributable to a spontaneous mutation of genes; see HEREDITY: *Mutation.* Inheritance is controlled by a recessive sex-linked factor carried by the mother. Of the children of a normal male and a carrier female, half the boys will be hemophiliacs and half the girls will be carriers; of the children of a hemophiliac male and a normal female, all the girls will be carriers and all the boys will be normal. Such males cannot transmit the disability; women carriers are themselves free of the disease. The classic case of transmission involves Victoria (q.v.), Queen of Great Britain, whose daughters carried the disease to the Spanish and Russian royal houses.

The application of globulin or fibrin foam may help coagulation in local hemorrhages. In unavoidable surgery, the use of an electrocautery to seal the blood vessels and injections of antihemophilic globulin derived from animal and human plasma may be life-saving. Blood transfusions are not always effective, since the essential factor rapidly disappears during circulation.

See HEREDITY: *Sex-Linkage.*

HEMORRHAGE. See BLEEDING.

HEMORRHOIDS or **PILES,** small swellings, occurring in or around the rectum or at the anus caused by enlargement of the superficial veins. Those arising at the end of the rectum and protruding beyond the anus are called external hemorrhoids; those developing inside the rectum are internal hemorrhoids. The internal type occasionally prolapses, or protrudes from the anus, causing discomfort by strangulation; to relieve the pain, the prolapsed hemorrhoid must be replaced within the anal sphincter muscle. Occasionally, the two types may merge to form a continuous so-called mixed hemorrhoid.

Hemorrhoids may cause no symptoms. Sometimes they itch, or cause pain in the rectum. They often bleed. Symptoms are most likely to occur after defecation, particularly after passing a hard stool. Continued bleeding, even if slight, over a long period may cause anemia. Occasionally a clot will form inside a hemorrhoid, producing severe pain. This is known as a thrombosed hemorrhoid.

A common ailment among adults, hemorrhoids often are associated with habitual constipation and with pregnancy. Anxiety and other mental stress may be contributory factors. The treatment includes palliative measures, such as the use of suppositories, astringent ointments, medication to keep the stool soft, hot sitz baths, and a diet low in residue. Bothersome piles may be desensitized by an ether spray, opened, and relieved. In advanced cases, hemorrhoids may be destroyed by the injection of various solutions, such as carbolic acid in oil, or removed by surgical procedures.

HEMP, common name of an Asian annual herb, *Cannabis sativa,* which produces strong pliable fibers; the name is also used for the fibers themselves. This species is often called true hemp or Indian hemp. It is cultivated in Eurasia, the United States, and Chile. A hemp plant may be as small as 3 ft. or as high as 15 ft., depending on the climate and the kind of soil in which it grows. The male plants bear flowers in axillary racemes and die soon after pollination has taken place; female plants bear flowers in short, crowded spikes and die after the seed matures. Plants of both sexes are used for fiber.

Hemp stems are hollow and have a fibrous inner bark. The fibers from this bark are used to make a great variety of textile products, including coarse fabrics, ropes, sailcloth, and packing cloth. Soft fibers, used for making clothing fabrics in Asia, are obtained from hemp harvested at the time of pollination; strong, coarse fibers are obtained from mature plants. The fibers are removed and processed by methods similar to those used in processing flax (q.v.). The stalks are allowed to decompose partially; they are then dried, broken, and shaken to separate the woody stalks from the fibers.

The seed of hemp, or hempseed, is commonly used as birdseed. Hempseed also yields a fixed oil (*see* FATS AND FIXED OILS) called oil of hemp, used in manufacture of soap and oil paints. A resin, called charas, produced by female flower heads and seeds of hemp, is used as a constituent of narcotic smoking mixtures in India. Flowers and leaves of hemp are used by the Arabs to produce the narcotics bhang, hashish, and marijuana (q.v.); these substances are used as narcotics under the name *Cannabis* (q.v.). See DRUGS, ADDICTION TO.

Unrelated plants that are commonly called hemp include bowstring hemp, henequen, manila hemp (qq.v.), and sisal (*see* AGAVE). Sunn hemp is obtained from *Crotalaria* (q.v.), an herb native to India. A palm which grows in eastern Asia, *Chaemerops excelsa*, is called hemp palm because fibers obtained from its leaves are used for cordage. See FIBER.

HEMPFIELD, township of Pennsylvania, in Westmoreland Co., 25 miles S.E. of downtown Pittsburgh. Coal is mined in the W. part of the township; manufactured products include electrical equipment, aluminum products, glass, and plant-nursery products. The township consists of villages scattered over a wide area; the largest of these are Grapeville, Luxor, Hannastown, New Stanton, Wendel, and Edna. Hannastown, settled in 1774, was the center of western Pennsylvania at the time of the revolution, but no traces of the early settlement remain. Pop. (1960) 29,704; (1970) 39,196.

HEMPSTEAD, town of New York, in Nassau Co., about 20 mi. by rail E. of New York City. A residential suburb and retail center, it is the site of Hofstra University, founded in 1935. The Town of Hempstead (pop. 1970, 800,684) includes 21 incorporated villages, among them Freeport, Garden City, Lynbrook, and Rockville Centre, and 23 unincorporated communities. The Presbyterian Society of Hempstead, organized in 1644, is the oldest in the United States. The village of Hempstead, center of the town, was settled in 1644 and incorporated in 1853; pop. (1960) 34,641; (1970) 39,411.

HEN. See FOWL.

HENBANE, common name for an Old World herb, *Hyoscyamus niger,* of the Nightshade family, Solanaceae. Henbane has been introduced into North America and is now naturalized in widely scattered locations across the northern

Henbane, Hyoscyamus niger

United States and southern Canada. The plant is coarse, hairy, and evil-smelling, and bears alternate, bluntly lobed leaves. The flowers are bell-shaped, displaying a dull yellow, five-pointed tube streaked with purple and surrounded by a green, five-pointed calyx that continues to grow and encloses the fruit as it matures. Henbane leaves and seeds contain tropane alkaloids, especially hyoscyamine, hyoscine (scopolamine), and atropine, and have been used in medicine since classical times. This plant should be considered potentially poisonous, if eaten.   J.M.K.

HENCH, Philip Showalter (1896–1965), American physician, born and educated in Pittsburgh,

HENDERSON

Pa. His lifelong association with the Mayo Clinic began in 1921, and he became head of the department of rheumatic diseases in 1926. Hench was the first to use cortisone (q.v.) in the treatment of arthritis (q.v.). He shared the 1950 Nobel Prize in medicine and physiology with the American biochemist Edward Calvin Kendall and the Swiss chemist Tadeus Reichstein (qq.v.).

HENDERSON, city in Kentucky, and county seat of Henderson Co., on the Ohio R., about 110 miles s.w. of Louisville. The city has varied manufacturing. The Audubon Memorial State Park is nearby. The American naturalist John James Audubon (q.v.) lived in Henderson from 1810 to 1819. Pop. (1960) 16,892; (1970) 22,976.

HENDERSON, city in North Carolina, and county seat of Vance Co., about 40 miles N.E. of Raleigh, near the s. tip of the John H. Kerr Reservoir. The major crop in the area is tobacco, of which Henderson is a distribution point; livestock is raised and dairy farming is carried on. Manufactures include chemicals, textiles, and glass containers. Henderson was founded in 1840. Pop. (1960) 12,740; (1970) 13,896.

HENDERSON, Arthur (1863–1935), British statesman and Labour Party leader, born in Glasgow, Scotland. In early life he worked as an iron molder and trade-union leader. Henderson entered Parliament in 1903. He was one of the founders of the Labour Party, and served as party chairman (1908–10, 1914–17) and as secretary (1911–34). During his political career, Henderson held several important cabinet posts, including home secretary (1924) and foreign secretary (1929–31). He became president of the World Disarmament Conference in 1932, and was awarded the 1934 Nobel Peace Prize.

HENDERSON, Richard (1735–85), American jurist and colonizer, born in Hanover County, Va., and educated privately in law. In 1768 he was appointed an associate justice of the superior court of North Carolina. He retired from the court in 1773 to pursue his interest in colonizing the western frontier. In 1774 he organized the Louisa Company, known after January, 1775, as the Transylvania Company, to colonize much of what is now Kentucky and Tennessee. The American frontiersman Daniel Boone (q.v.) acted as advance agent for the company, negotiating Indian treaties and founding the town of Boonesborough (now Boonesboro, Ky.). Henderson moved to Boonesborough, but his title was challenged by both Virginia and North Carolina, and the American Revolution further interrupted his plans. He later participated in the settlement of western Tennessee and was a member of the North Carolina legislature and council of state. *See* KENTUCKY: *History.*

HENDRICKS, Thomas Andrews (1819–85), American political leader, born near Zanesville, Ohio. He studied law and was admitted to the bar in 1843. Hendricks became active in Democratic Party politics and was elected to the Indiana State legislature in 1848. He served in the United States House of Representatives (1851–55) and in the United States Senate (1863–69). In 1872 Hendricks was elected governor of Indiana. He was the unsuccessful Vice-Presidential candidate in 1876; he was elected Vice-President in 1884, but served under President Grover Cleveland (q.v.) for only eight months before his death.

HENEQUEN, common name applied to *Agave fourcroydes,* and to the fibers produced by its leaves; see AGAVE. Henequen fiber, which is the chief material for manufacturing binder twine, is grown primarily in Cuba and Yucatán, Mexico. Henequen has spiny, sword-shaped leaves. In harvesting, mature leaves are severed at the base and the spines are removed with large knives. The leaves are scraped by machines that separate the pulpy tissues from the fiber. The fiber is finished by brushing and drying, and is then baled for market. The finished yellow-white fibers, sometimes called Mexican sisal, are strong and flexible; *see* HEMP.

HENGELO, city of the Netherlands, in Overijssel Province, 5 miles N.W. of Enschede. Among the principal industrial establishments of Hengelo are textile factories, dyehouses, machine shops, and breweries. Pop. (1968) 69,094.

HENGIST AND HORSA, two brothers who are said to have led a Germanic invasion of Britain in 449. According to the 8th-century British historian Saint Bede (q.v.) and the *Anglo-Saxon Chronicle* (q.v.), the brothers were asked to help the Britons defend themselves against the Picts (q.v.). When the Picts were defeated, Hengist and Horsa settled in Kent; they revolted against the Britons and Horsa was killed.

HENGYANG, city of the People's Republic of China, in Hunan Province, on the Siang R. at the mouth of the Lei R., 90 miles s.w. of Changsha. A major road hub on the Wuhan-Canton Railway, the city is also a river port and at the head of navigation on the Siang R. Hengyang was made an independent municipality in 1943. During World War II a United States air base was located here. Pop. (1958 est.) 240,000.

HENLEY, William Ernest (1849–1903), British writer and editor, born in Gloucester, England, and educated at the Crypt School, where the headmaster, poet Thomas Edward Brown (q.v.)

befriended and inspired him. Although crippled early in life by osteomyelitis, an inflammatory disease of bone, Henley was remarkably courageous, spirited, and prolific as a writer. His most famous poems are "England, My England" and "Invictus", which concludes with the well-known lines, "I am the master of my fate;/I am the captain of my soul." Henley's books of poetry include *A Book of Verses* (1888) and *In Hospital* (1903). *Views and Reviews,* essays on art and literature, appeared in 1890. Henley collaborated with his friend the British author Robert Louis Stevenson (q.v.) on four plays, and Stevenson modeled the character Long John Silver in *Treasure Island* after him. Henley also collaborated with J. S. Farmer on the *Dictionary of Slang and Its Aanalogues* (1894–1904). He contributed articles to many periodicals, and as a critic and editor he helped popularize the work of the British writer Rudyard Kipling and the Irish poet William Butler Yeats (qq.v.).

HENLEY REGATTA, annual program of rowing races at Henley-on-Thames, 20 miles S.E. of Oxford, England, called in full the Henley Royal Regatta, and usually held in July. It was first staged in 1839 and has been held annually ever since, except in time of war. It has become the major amateur rowing event in Great Britain and perhaps the best known in the world. Most of the events cover a distance of 2310 yd., and every event is open to amateur rowers from any country. Boats ranging from eight-oared sculls to single sculls are included in the contests. The first American victory in the regatta, for the eight-oared event, was won in 1914 by the Harvard Athletic Association Boat Club. John Brendan Kelly, Jr. (1927–   ), of Philadelphia, Pa., brother of Princess Grace of Monaco (1929–   ), won the single sculls event in 1947 and again in 1949. *See* ROWING.

HENNA, common name of a small shrub, *Lawsonia inermis,* belonging to the Loosestrife family, Lythraceae, and of the dye obtained from its leaves. The shrub, which is also called alkanna and mignonette tree, grows in moist places in northern Africa and southern Asia. It bears small, fragrant, white or rose flowers in clusters. The orange-red dye produced by its leaves is used extensively in the United States as a rinse to impart a reddish color to hair. Women of Muslim countries use the dye to stain the nails and tips of their fingers and parts of their feet; men of these countries use the dye to color their beards. The dye is also used to stain leather and hides and to color the hoofs and manes of horses. Mummies of ancient Egypt have been found wrapped in henna-dyed cloth.

HENNEPIN, Louis (1640?–1701), Flemish Roman Catholic monk and explorer in America, born in Ath (now in Belgium). He entered the Franciscan order at an early age. After serving as chaplain in the army of Louis II, Prince of Condé (*see under* CONDÉ), he went to Québec, Canada, in 1675. In 1676 and 1677 he worked as a missionary among the Iroquois Indians, and in 1678 he accompanied the French explorer Robert Cavelier, Sieur de La Salle (*see* LA SALLE), on an expedition through the Great Lakes to the Illinois R., on the banks of which they built Fort Crève Coeur, near the site of the present Peoria. From there Father Hennepin was sent by La Salle on a voyage to explore the upper Mississippi R., which he did by canoe, ascending the river as far as the Falls of Saint Anthony, now the site of Minneapolis, Minn. He reached the falls in July, 1680, and after giving them their name, proceeded further through the present State of Minnesota. He was captured by Sioux Indians, with whom he lived until his rescue, in June, 1681, by Daniel Greysolon Duluth (1636–1710), leader of a French exploring party from the Lake Superior region. Father Hennepin returned to Québec and then sailed for France. In 1683 he published *Description de la Louisiane* (Eng. trans., *A Description of Louisiana,* 1938), an account of his travels. He later wrote *Nouveau Voyage* (1696) and *Nouvelle Découverte d'un Très Grand Pays Situé dans L'Amérique* (1697). These two books, combined, appeared in English in 1698 under the title *A New Discovery of a Vast Country in America.* His assertion that he had preceded La Salle to the mouth of the Mississippi was soon discredited.

HENRI, Robert (1865–1929), American painter and teacher, born in Cincinnati, Ohio, and educated at the Pennsylvania Academy of Fine Arts, and the Académie Julian and the École des Beaux-Arts in Paris. In 1891, he began to paint and teach in Philadelphia. There he met the painters John Sloan, William James Glackens, and George Benjamin Luks (qq.v.), and inspired them to paint American life with vigorous, dramatic realism. They moved to New York City, where, with Henri as their guiding spirit, they joined other painters to form The Eight, or the so-called Ashcan school. The Eight broke with academic tradition, especially in their portrayals of the squalor of city life, and were active in the 1913 Armory Show, which introduced modern European art to America. Henri taught at the Art Students League and other schools in New York City, championed juryless exhibitions, and traveled extensively, painting indigenous people, especially appealing children. *The Art Spirit,* a

HENRIETTA MARIA

book compiled from Henri's lectures, was published in 1923 and is still read. As a painter, Henri is best known for his warm, vibrant portraits, which are included in the collections of the Metropolitan Museum of Art in New York City, the Art Institute of Chicago, and other leading museums.

HENRIETTA MARIA (1609–69), Queen Consort of England, the wife of King Charles I and mother of Charles II (qq.v.). She was the daughter of Henry IV (q.v.) of France and Marie de Médicis (q.v.). Henrietta Maria's brother Louis XIII (q.v.), King of France, consented in 1624 to her marriage to Charles, then prince of Wales, on condition that the English laws directed against Roman Catholics be revised; the marriage took place, but the laws were not revised. Because Henrietta Maria engaged in political intrigue to aid the Catholic cause, the queen greatly increased the unpopularity of her husband. In 1642, after the outbreak of the Great Rebellion (q.v.), she went to the Continent to secure money and troops to assist the Royalists. The following year she returned with money and joined Charles at Oxford. The situation grew worse for the Royalists, however, and in 1644 Henrietta Maria fled to France. She continued to solicit aid for Charles until his execution in 1649. After the Restoration (q.v.) of Charles II in 1660 she was awarded a Parliamentary grant and permission to live in England, where she resided until 1665 when she returned to France.

HENRY, name of a number of European rulers. Brief accounts of less important monarchs are included in this article under the names of the countries that they ruled. The most important monarchs are described in separate biographical sketches, to which the reader is referred.

The English name Henry appears in German as *Heinrich,* in French as *Henri,* in Italian as *Enrico,* in Polish as *Henryk,* in Portuguese as *Henrique,* and in Spanish as *Enrique.*

CASTILE AND LEÓN

Henry I (1204–17), King of Castile (1214–17), the son and successor of King Alfonso VIII (*see under* ALFONSO).

Henry II (1333–79). See HENRY II, King of Castile and León.

Henry III (1379–1406), King of Castile and León (1390–1406) and son and successor of King John I (*see under* JOHN). Although at the beginning of his reign the country was plagued with continual disorder and violent anti-Semitism, Henry was soon able to placate the nobility and restore royal authority. The conquest of the Canary Islands (q.v.) began under his sponsorship in 1402.

ENGLAND

Henry I (1068–1135). See HENRY I, King of England.

Henry II (1133–89). See HENRY II, King of England.

Henry III (1207–72). See HENRY III, King of England.

Henry IV (1367–1413). See HENRY IV, King of England.

Henry V (1387–1422). See HENRY V, King of England.

Henry VI (1421–71). See HENRY VI, King of England.

Henry VII (1457–1509). See HENRY VII, King of England.

Henry VIII (1491–1547). See HENRY VIII, King of England.

FRANCE

Henry I (1008–60). See HENRY I, King of France.

Henry II (1519–59). See HENRY II, King of France. Henry VI (q.v.), King of England, although crowned (1431) in France as Henry II, never ruled there and is not numbered among the French kings.

Henry III (1551–89). See HENRY III, King of France.

Henry IV (1533–1610). See HENRY IV, King of France.

GERMANY

The title King of Germany was borne by several Holy Roman emperors named Henry; see below; *see also* separate article, HOLY ROMAN EMPIRE.

HOLY ROMAN EMPIRE

Henry I (876?–936). See HENRY I, King of Germany.

Henry II (973–1024). See HENRY II, Holy Roman Emperor.

Henry III (1017–56). See HENRY III, Holy Roman Emperor.

Henry IV (1050–1106). See HENRY IV, Holy Roman Emperor.

Henry V (1081–1125). See HENRY V, Holy Roman Emperor.

Henry VI (1165–97). See HENRY VI, Holy Roman Emperor.

Henry VII (about 1275–1313). See HENRY VII, Holy Roman Emperor.

NAVARRE

Henry I, called HENRY THE FAT (1210?–74), King of Navarre (1270–74). The marriage of his daughter in 1284 to Philip, later Philip IV (q.v.), King of France, brought Navarre under the control of the French monarchy.

Henry III (1553–1610). See HENRY IV, King of France.

HENRY (England)

POLAND
Henry (1551–89). See HENRY III, King of France.

PORTUGAL
Henry (1512–80). See HENRY, King of Portugal.

SARDINIA
Henry (1225?–72). Although his father, Frederick II (q.v.), Holy Roman Emperor, granted him the title King of Sardinia in 1243, Henry never ruled. He spent most of his time after the coronation in Italy, where he became involved in the struggle between the Guelphs and Ghibellines (q.v.). Henry supported the Ghibellines, a political faction that wanted the Holy Roman Empire (q.v.), rather than the papacy, to be the dominant influence in Italy. Henry was captured by the Guelphs in 1249 and remained imprisoned until his death.

SICILY
Henry (1165–97). See HENRY VI, Holy Roman Emperor.

HENRY II (1333?–79), King of Castile and León (1369–79), born in Seville. He was the illegitimate son of Alfonso XI, King of Castile and León (see under ALFONSO), who made him count of Trastamara. After the accession of Alfonso's legitimate son Pedro el Cruel (q.v.) to the throne of Castile and León in 1350, Henry fled to France. With an army of mercenaries financed by the kings of France and Aragon, Henry invaded Castile and León in 1366 and drove Pedro from the throne. Edward (q.v.), Prince of Wales, intervened for Pedro, however, and defeated Henry at Nájera in 1367. In 1369 Henry defeated and killed Pedro, becoming king. During his reign he continued his alliance with Charles V (q.v.), King of France, in the wars against England. He was succeeded by his son John I (see under JOHN).

HENRY I (1068–1135), called HENRY BEAUCLERC (Fr. "Scholar"), King of England (1100–35), fourth son of William I (q.v.), King of England, born in Selby. Because his father, who died in 1087, left him no land, Henry made several unsuccessful attempts to gain territories on the Continent. When William II (q.v.), King of England, died in 1100, Henry took advantage of the absence of his older brother, Robert II, Duke of Normandy (1054–1134), to seize the royal treasury and have himself elected king by the nobles. Henry subsequently secured his position with the nobles and with the Church by issuing a charter of liberties that acknowledged the feudal rights of the nobles and the rights of the Church. In 1101 Robert invaded England, but Henry persuaded him to withdraw by promising him a pension and military aid on the Continent. In 1102 Henry put down a revolt of nobles, who subsequently took refuge in Normandy, where they were aided by Robert. By defeating Robert at Tinchebray, France, in 1106, Henry won Normandy. During the rest of his reign, however, he constantly had to put down uprisings that threatened his rule in Normandy. The conflict between Henry and the archbishop of Canterbury, Anselm (see ANSELM OF CANTERBURY, SAINT), over the question of lay investiture (the appointment of church officials by the king), was settled in 1107 by a compromise that left the king with substantial control in the matter.

Because he had no surviving male heir, Henry was forced to designate his daughter Matilda (1102–67) as his heiress. In the latter part of his life he was concerned with securing her succession to the throne.

HENRY II (1133–89), King of England (1154–89), first monarch of the house of Anjou, or Plantagenet (q.v.) and grandson of Henry I (q.v.), King of England. In 1151 he was made Duke of Normandy. The following year, on the death of his father, he inherited the Angevin territories in France. By his marriage in 1152 to Eleanor of Aquitaine (q.v.), Henry added Aquitaine, Guienne, and lands in southern France to his possessions. Henry claimed the English kingship through his mother, Matilda (1102–67). She had been designated the heiress of Henry I but had been deprived of the succession by Stephen (q.v.), King of England and nephew of Henry I. In 1153 Henry defeated Stephen's armies in England and compelled the king to choose him as his successor; on the death of Stephen in the following year, Henry became king. During the first few years of his reign Henry quelled the disorders that had developed during Stephen's reign, regained the northern counties of England, which had previously been ceded to Scotland, and conquered North Wales. In 1171–72 he conquered southeastern Ireland also.

During his reign, Henry carried on a quarrel with Thomas à Becket (see BECKET, THOMAS À, SAINT), Archbishop of Canterbury, concerning ecclesiastical courts. The dispute began in 1164 over the question of trying ecclesiastics accused of crime. By the Constitutions of Clarendon (see CLARENDON, CONSTITUTIONS OF), the supreme authority was vested in the royal rather than the ecclesiastical courts. Becket refused to approve the constitution and was so persecuted that he fled to France. Fearing papal interdiction, Henry effected a reconciliation with the archbishop. After returning to England in 1170, Becket was murdered by four knights who were loyal to Henry but were not acting on his orders. Henry

HENRY (England)

was, nevertheless, held responsible, and as a result he had to concede on the question of ecclesiastical authority and perform penance at the shrine of the archbishop.

From the beginning of his reign, Henry was involved in conflict with Louis VII, King of France, and later with Louis' successor, Philip II (qq.v.), over the French provinces that Henry claimed. A succession of rebellions against Henry headed by his sons and furthered by Philip II and by Eleanor, began in 1173 and continued until Henry's death. Henry was succeeded by his son Richard I (q.v.), called Richard Lion-Hearted.

HENRY III (1207–72), King of England (1216–72), member of the house of Anjou, or Plantagenet (q.v.), and son of John (q.v.), King of England. Henry succeeded to the throne at the age of nine, on the death of his father. During his minority the kingdom was ruled by a regent, but after 1221 the English statesman Hubert de Burgh (see under BURGH), was the chief power in the government. During the regency the French, who occupied much of eastern England, were expelled, and rebellious barons were subdued.

Henry was declared of age in 1227. In 1232 he dismissed Hubert de Burgh from his court and commenced ruling without the aid of ministers. Henry displeased the barons by permitting the pope to extract large amounts of money from the English people, by filling government and church offices with foreign favorites, and by squandering money on Continental wars, especially in France. In order to secure the throne of Sicily for one of his sons, Henry agreed to pay the pope a large sum. When the king requested money from the barons to pay his debt, they refused and in 1258 forced him to agree to the Provisions of Oxford, whereby he agreed to share his power with a council of barons. Henry soon repudiated his oath, however, with papal approval. After a brief period of war, the matter was referred to the arbitration of Louis IX (q.v.), King of France, who decided in Henry's favor. Simon de Montfort (q.v.), Earl of Leicester, accordingly led the barons into war; see BARON'S WAR. In 1264 Simon defeated Henry at Lewes and took him prisoner. In 1265 Henry's son and heir, Edward, later Edward I (q.v.), King of England, led the royal troops to victory over the barons at Evesham, about 25 mi. south of Birmingham. Simon de Montfort was killed in the battle, and the barons agreed to a compromise with Edward and his party in 1267. From that time on Edward ruled England, and when Henry died, he succeeded him as king.

HENRY IV (1367–1413), King of England (1399–1413), first Lancastrian king (see LANCASTER, HOUSE OF), son of John of Gaunt (q.v.), Duke of Lancaster. He was well known as Henry of Lancaster, and also as Henry of Bolingbroke. From 1387 until 1390 he was a leader of the party that opposed his cousin Richard II (q.v.), King of England. Henry subsequently fought with the Teutonic Knights (q.v.) against the Lithuanians

Henry IV, King of England Bettmann Archive

and made a pilgrimage to Jerusalem. After his return to England he allied himself with the king. Because of a quarrel with Thomas Mowbray, 1st Duke of Norfolk (see under NORFOLK), in 1398, Henry was exiled for six years by Richard, who promised that Henry would not be deprived of his inheritance. When Henry's father died, however, Richard confiscated the Lancastrian estates willed to Henry. Consequently, Henry raised an army, invaded England, and captured Richard, who later abdicated. Henry was elected king by Parliament in 1399. In 1400 he suppressed a revolt of nobles who supported Richard. The same year the Scots and the Welsh, aided by the French, began a rebellion against the English crown. The Scots were defeated at Humbleton Hill in 1402, but the Welsh continued the rebellion for seven years under the leadership of the Welsh chief Owen Glendower (q.v.). In 1403 the Percy family (see PERCY, SIR HENRY) rebelled against Henry because they were dissatisfied with the rewards for service he had bestowed upon them; they were defeated in the Battle of Shrewsbury in the same year.

HENRY (England)

Wars and rebellions persisted after that date but diminished in number. During his reign Henry IV persecuted the religious sect known as the Lollards (q.v.). He was succeeded by his son, Henry V (q.v.).

HENRY V (1387–1422), King of England (1413–22), member of the house of Lancaster and son of Henry IV (q.v.), King of England. In 1403 Henry led the royal army in the defeat of the rebellious Percy family (see PERCY, SIR HENRY) at Shrewsbury. He also commanded the English forces that put down the revolt led by the Welsh chief Owen Glendower (q.v.). In 1410–11, when his father was incapacitated by illness, Henry headed the royal council, but was removed after a political quarrel with his father. On succeeding to the throne in 1413 Henry V restored Sir Henry Percy's son to his lands and titles; he also honorably reburied at Westminster Abbey the remains of Richard II (q.v.), who had died in prison during Henry IV's reign. The new king continued his father's policy in persecuting the religious sect known as the Lollards (q.v.) and executed their leader, Sir John Oldcastle (q.v.), in 1417.

In 1415 Henry warred against France, winning in that same year the Battle of Agincourt; see AGINCOURT, BATTLE OF. Two years later he invaded and conquered Normandy, and in 1419 he captured Rouen. He concluded a peace treaty at Troyes in 1420 with Charles VI (q.v.), King of France, obtaining Charles' daughter, Catherine of Valois (q.v.), in marriage and securing the regency of France and the promise of succession to the French throne on the death of Charles. When Henry returned to England in 1421, leaving his brother Thomas, Duke of Clarence (see under CLARENCE), as governor of Normandy, the French rose in opposition to English rule and defeated the duke. Henry returned to France for a third campaign, but he became ill and died. He was, at the time of his death, the most influential ruler in western Europe. He was succeeded by his son Henry VI (q.v.).

HENRY VI (1421–71), King of England (1422–61; 1470–71), last king of the house of Lancaster, and son of Henry V, King of England and Queen Catherine of Valois (qq.v.), born in Windsor. While still an infant he succeeded his father to the throne of England and, under the terms of the Treaty of Troyes, succeeded his grandfather, Charles VI (q.v.), King of France, to the French throne. During Henry's minority, his uncles John of Lancaster (q.v.), Duke of Bedford, and Humphrey, Duke of Gloucester (1391–1447), acted as regents. Henry's kingship in France was contested by his uncle (see CHARLES VII, King of France). In 1429 the French heroine Joan of Arc (q.v.) led her troops to victory over the English at Orléans, France, and Charles was subsequently crowned king. English power in France declined further in 1435 when the Duke of Bedford, Henry's regent in France, died, and Philip the Good (q.v.), Duke of Burgundy, deserted his English allies, making a separate peace with Charles. Charles captured Paris in 1436, Normandy in 1450, and Guienne in 1451. By the time the fighting ended in 1453 the only French territory that remained in English hands was Calais. See HUNDRED YEARS' WAR.

Heavy taxation and other governmental abuses in England led in 1450 to a rebellion by the men of Kent under the English rebel leader Jack Cade (q.v.). Henry was further opposed by a faction of nobles, who supported Richard, Duke of York (see under YORK, HOUSE OF), the next in line of succession to the throne. The Wars of the Roses (see ROSES, WARS OF THE) between the houses of Lancaster and York began in 1455. After intermittent fighting Henry was captured by the Yorkists at Northampton and was compelled to acknowledge Richard rather than his own infant son as successor. In 1460 Richard was killed by Henry's forces at Wakefield. Richard's son subsequently became leader of the Yorkists, proclaimed himself Edward IV (q.v.), King of England, and won the Battle of Towton, ending Henry's reign.

Henry and his queen consort, Margaret of Anjou (q.v.), escaped to Scotland, where they remained until 1464. In that year he returned to take part in a rebellion against Edward. Henry was captured in 1465 and imprisoned in the Tower of London (q.v.). Margaret subsequently secured the aid of Richard Neville, Earl of Warwick (see under NEVILLE), who in 1470 drove Edward from the kingdom. Henry, however, had suffered attacks of insanity all his life and was now completely incapacitated. But he became nominal ruler again, until he was dethroned and returned to the tower by Edward in 1471. Henry died soon afterward, probably murdered by Edward's order.

HENRY VII, often called HENRY TUDOR (1457–1509), King of England (1485–1509), first ruler of the house of Tudor, born in Pembrokeshire, Wales. He was the son of Edmund Tudor, Earl of Richmond (1430?–56), and Margaret Beaufort, Countess of Richmond and Derby (q.v.), a direct descendant of John of Gaunt (q.v.), Duke of Lancaster. After the Yorkist Edward IV, King of England, seized the throne from the Lancastrian Henry VI (qq.v.), King of England, in 1471, Henry Tudor, a Lancastrian,

HENRY (England)

took refuge in Brittany. He became head of the house of Lancaster on the death of Henry VI in the same year. In 1483, taking advantage of the indignation aroused against Richard III (q.v.), King of England, whose nephews, Edward V (q.v.) and Richard, Duke of York (1472–83), were murdered in the Tower of London (q.v.), presumably by order of Richard III, Henry crossed over to Wales, where he gathered an army of supporters. In 1485, at Bosworth Field in England (see BOSWORTH FIELD, BATTLE OF), he met and defeated Richard III, who was killed during the battle. Henry Tudor was subsequently crowned Henry VII in London. In the following year he married the Yorkist heiress, Elizabeth (1465–1503), eldest daughter of Edward IV, uniting the houses of York and Lancaster and ending the Wars of the Roses (see ROSES, WARS OF).

After his accession Henry had to contend with several Yorkist uprisings, notably one led by the English impostor Lambert Simnel (fl. 1486–1525), who claimed to be Edward, Earl of Warwick (1475–99), the last Yorkist claimant to the throne. The real earl of Warwick was actually imprisoned by Henry in the Tower of London at the time. Another revolt was led by the Walloon impostor Perkin Warbeck (1474?–99), who claimed to be Richard, Duke of York (1472–83), the younger of the murdered sons of Edward IV. Although both impostors had strong backing in England and abroad, their forces were defeated by Henry. In 1494 Henry sent the English statesman Sir Edward Poynings (1459–1521) to Ireland to reestablish English control in that country. Henry managed to maintain peaceful relations with Austria, Spain, and France throughout most of his years as king. The reorganization in 1487 of the Star Chamber (see STAR CHAMBER, COURT OF) was one of several means by which Henry strengthened the royal power over the nobles.

HENRY VIII (1491–1547), King of England (1509–47), son of Henry VII (q.v.), King of England. On the death of his father, Henry succeeded to the throne and married his brother's widow Catherine of Aragon (q.v.), having been betrothed to her through a papal dispensation secured in 1503. This union was the first of Henry's six marriages, which were affected by the political and religious conditions of the time and by the monarch's increasingly despotic personality. At the beginning of his reign Henry's good looks and hearty personality, his fondness for sport and the hunt, and his military prowess, endeared him to his subjects. A monarch of the period known as the Renaissance (q.v.), he entertained numerous scholars and artists, including the German painter Hans Holbein (q.v.), who painted several famous portraits of the king and members of his court.

A Question of Divorce. In 1511 Henry joined in the Holy League against France (see FRANCE: History: The Valois Dynasty) and in 1513 led the English forces through a victorious campaign in northern France. Deserted by his allies, Henry arranged a marriage in 1514 between his sister Mary (1496–1533) and Louis XII (q.v.), King of France, with whom he formed an alliance. The successor of Louis, Francis I (q.v.), met Henry at a magnificently staged meeting on the Field of the Cloth of Gold (q.v.) in 1520, but no significant political decisions resulted from this meeting. In 1525 riots broke out in England in protest against an attempt by Henry to levy taxes for military purposes, and he withdrew from major military activity in Europe.

In 1527 Henry announced his desire to divorce his wife, on the grounds that the papal dispensation making the marriage possible was invalid. The chief reason for the divorce was that Catherine had failed to produce a male heir. Her only surviving child was Mary, later Mary I (q.v.), Queen of England. In addition, Henry was in love with Anne Boleyn (q.v.), a young and beautiful lady-in-waiting of the queen. Several obstacles, however, stood in the way of the divorce. Charles V (q.v.), Holy Roman Emperor, Catherine's nephew, strongly opposed the divorce, and Pope Clement VII (see under CLEMENT), whom Charles had made a prisoner, could not invalidate the marriage without displeasing his captor. In 1528 the pope was persuaded to appoint the English cardinal and statesman Thomas Wolsey (q.v.) and Lorenzo Campeggio (1474?–1539), a papal legate, to try the case in an English legatine court. In 1529, however, the pope summoned the case to Rome. When prospect of securing a papal annulment seemed hopeless, Henry dismissed Wolsey and appointed Sir Thomas More (q.v.) chancellor and Thomas Cromwell (q.v.) his chief adviser. Both men favored ecclesiastical reform within the Church.

The Break with the Papacy. Henry then proceeded to dissolve one by one the ties to the papacy. With the aid of parliamentary legislation Henry first secured control of the clergy, compelling that group in 1532 to acknowledge him as head of the English church. In the following year Henry secretly married Anne Boleyn, who was crowned queen after Henry's obedient archbishop of Canterbury, Thomas Cranmer (q.v.), declared the marriage with Catherine void and that with Anne valid. An act

HENRY (England)

Henry VIII, a portrait by the court painter Hans Holbein the Younger.

of succession affirmed the declaration of the archbishop and established Anne's progeny as heirs to the throne.

Although Henry was immediately excommunicated he repudiated papal jurisdiction in 1534 and made himself the supreme ecclesiastical authority in England. The English people were required to affirm under oath Henry's supremacy and the act of succession. Sir Thomas More and the English cardinal John Fisher (1459–1535), were executed for refusing to accept the religious supremacy of the English monarch. Henry dissolved the monastic communities, and gave much of their property to the nobles in exchange for their support.

Charging Anne Boleyn with incest and adultery, Henry had her executed in 1536. A few days after Anne's death, Henry married Jane Seymour (*see under* SEYMOUR), who died in 1537 after bearing Henry's only son, Edward, later Edward VI (q.v.). A marriage was arranged in 1540 with Anne of Cleves (1515–57) in order to form a tie between England and the Protestant princes of Germany. Because Anne was unattractive and because Henry found the political alliance no longer to his advantage, he divorced her after several months, and married Catherine Howard (q.v.) in the same year. Catherine Howard was executed in 1542 for having been unchaste prior to marriage and having committed adultery. In the following year Henry married his sixth wife, Catherine Parr (q.v.), who survived him.

Between 1542 and 1546 Henry was involved in war with Scotland and France. His troops defeated the Scots at Solway Moss in 1542. They captured Boulogne-sur-Mer from the French in 1544, and when peace was made in 1546 Henry received an idemnity from France.

HENRY (France)

Effects of Henry's Reign. Although he altered the church, Henry did not wish to introduce Protestant doctrine. Those who refused to accept Church of England (q.v.) teachings as well as those who rejected Henry's authority over the church were executed. The licensing of an English translation of the Bible, the issuance of Cranmer's litany, and the translation into English of certain parts of the traditional service were the only important religious changes made during Henry's reign. He profoundly influenced the character of the English monarchy, however, and intensified the authoritarian elements characteristic of the Tudor (q.v.) dynasty to which he belonged. The great strength of government developed by Henry was used powerfully in the reign of Elizabeth I (q.v.), Queen of England, his daughter by Anne Boleyn. See also ENGLAND: History.

HENRY I (about 1008–60), King of France (1031–60), son of Robert II (q.v.), King of France. From the beginning of his reign he was occupied in putting down rebellions led by members of his family and other French nobles. Between 1035 and 1047 he assisted his nephew William, Duke of Normandy, later William I (q.v.), King of England, in establishing William's authority over rebellious Norman nobles. Henry later grew jealous of William's power and waged unsuccessful war against him in 1054 and 1058. Henry was succeeded by his son Philip I (see under PHILIP).

HENRY II (1519–59), King of France (1547–59), second son of Francis I (q.v.), King of France, born in Saint-Germain-en-Laye. He married the Florentine noblewoman Catherine de Médicis (q.v.) in 1533 and when his father died in 1547, Henry succeeded to the throne. He was largely influenced during his reign by his mistress, Diane de Poitiers (1499–1566), Duchesse de Valentinois, and by Duc Anne de Montmorency, Constable of France, (1493–1567). An ardent Roman Catholic, Henry persecuted the Protestants in the later years of his reign; see HUGUENOTS. He continued the war waged by his father against Charles V (q.v.), Holy Roman Emperor, seizing from Charles in 1552 the bishoprics of Metz, Toul, and Verdun. Engaging in war with England in 1557–58, Henry won back Calais and Guînes, the last English possessions in France. From 1556 to 1559 Henry waged war in Italy against Philip II (q.v.), King of Spain. The French troops were defeated and all French possessions in Italy were lost. The wars with Philip were terminated in 1559 by the Treaty of Cateau-Cambrésis; see CATEAU-CAMBRÉSIS, TREATY OF. Henry was succeeded by his son Francis II (q.v.).

HENRY III (1551–89), King of France (1574–1589), third son of Henry II (q.v.), King of France, born in Fontainebleau. Henry took part in the victories over the Huguenots (q.v.) at Jarnac and at Moncontour in 1569. In 1572 he aided his mother, Catherine de Medicis (q.v.), in planning the Massacre of Saint Bartholomew's Day (see SAINT BARTHOLOMEW'S DAY, MASSACRE OF). He was elected king of Poland in 1573, but after one year returned from Poland to France to become the French ruler on the death of his brother Charles IX (q.v.), King of France. The wars between the Roman Catholics and Protestants continued throughout Henry's reign, and he took advantage of the strife to increase his power. In 1576 he issued the Edict of Beaulieu, which accorded more privileges to the Huguenots. Displeased with the edict, the Catholics, under the leadership of Henri I de Lorraine, Duc de Guise (see under GUISE), formed the Holy League, and renewed war with the Huguenots. The war ended in 1577 with the Peace of Bergerac. The League was revived in 1584, however, when Henry's younger brother died, leaving the Huguenot Henry of Navarre, later Henry IV (q.v.), King of France, heir to the throne of the childless king. In the following year the king excluded Henry of Navarre from the succession and repealed all the privileges granted to the Huguenots, causing Henry of Navarre to begin the so-called War of the Three Henrys against the league and the king. After the termination of the war in 1587 Henry III found his power rivaled by that of Henri de Lorraine. In 1588, on the Day of Barricades, the citizenry of Paris, under the leadership of Henri de Lorraine, revolted against the king, forcing him to flee the city. The king subsequently had Henri de Lorraine and his brother, Louis II de Lorraine (1555–88), assassinated and allied himself with Henry of Navarre, whom he declared to be his successor. The two Henrys then became joint leaders of a Huguenot army. While attempting to regain Paris in August, 1589, Henry III was fatally wounded by Jacques Clément (1567?–89), a Dominican friar.

HENRY IV, often called HENRY OF NAVARRE (1553–1610), as Henry III, King of Navarre (1572–1610), and as Henry IV, King of France, (1589–1610), the first of the Bourbon line. He was born in Pau, France, the son of Anthony of Bourbon, Duke of Vendôme (d. 1562), and Jeanne d'Albret, Queen of Navarre (1528–72). Henry was raised as a Calvinist (see CALVINISM). As a member of the Huguenot army, he participated in the religious wars between 1568 and 1570; see HUGUENOTS. After the death of the

Henry IV of France, statue on the Pont Neuf, Paris.
UPI

French Huguenot chief Louis I de Bourbon, Prince de Condé (see under CONDÉ), in 1569, Henry was declared titular leader of the Huguenots, with the French admiral Gaspard de Coligny (q.v.) actually in command. In 1572 Jeanne d'Albret died and Henry became king of Navarre. Over the protests of both Protestants and Roman Catholics, Henry married Margaret of Valois, sister of Charles IX (qq.v.), King of France, the same year. The Massacre of Saint Bartholomew's Day (see SAINT BARTHOLOMEW'S DAY, MASSACRE OF) took place within a week after the marriage, and Henry was forced to espouse Catholicism to save his life. For four years following that event he remained at the French court, a virtual prisoner. When he finally escaped in 1576, he joined the Protestants in Gascony, where he repudiated his conversion and resumed command of the Huguenot army.

On the death of François, Duc d'Alençon (1554–84), Henry became heir presumptive to the French throne. Because the Catholics renewed their protest against Henry of Navarre's becoming the royal heir, Henry III (q.v.), King of France, proclaimed Henry of Navarre ineligible to succeed to the throne. The dispute over the succession to the French throne led to the outbreak of the War of the Three Henrys, so-called

HENRY (Germany)

because it involved the French Catholic chief Henri I de Lorraine, Duc de Guise (see under GUISE), Henry III, and Henry of Navarre. The war ended in 1587 with the Protestant victory at Courtras. In the next year, after the murder of Henri de Guise and his brother the French cardinal Louis II de Lorraine (1555–88) by the royal guard, an understanding was arranged between Henry III and Henry of Navarre. Both Henrys subsequently proceeded, as joint leaders of the Huguenot army, to lay siege to Paris.

Henry III was assassinated in 1589, and Henry of Navarre succeeded to the throne as Henry IV. His right to the throne, however, was contested by the Catholics, and to secure his claim he waged war against them. Henry was victorious at Arques in 1589 and at Ivry-la-Bataille in 1590, but Spain intervened on the side of the Catholics and defeated his plans until he professed himself a Catholic in 1593. The declaration of conversion caused the major cities of the kingdom to surrender, with Paris capitulating in 1594. The war, however, continued until 1596. Peace was concluded with Spain at Vervins two years later. In 1598 Henry signed the Edict of Nantes (q.v.), which secured for the Protestants liberty of conscience and guaranteed the administration of impartial justice.

Henry's first marriage had been annulled by the pope in 1599. In 1600 the king married the Italian noblewoman Marie de Médicis (q.v.). The rest of his reign was devoted to recovery from the damage of civil war. Henry, a popular ruler, encouraged agriculture, commerce, and industry, and this resulted in a new prosperity for all classes. Under his aegis the financial system of France became more stable. At the time of his death Henry was preparing to make war on the Hapsburg rulers of Austria and Spain. Henry was assassinated by a religious fanatic, François Ravaillac (1578–1610).

HENRY I, called HENRY THE FOWLER (876?–936), King of Germany (919–36), the first of the Saxon line of German kings. In 912 Henry succeeded his father as Duke of Saxony. Following the death of Conrad I, King of Germany (see under CONRAD), in 918, Henry was chosen king by the Franconian and Saxon nobles. In 926 Henry secured a nine-year truce from warfare with the Magyars; see HUNGARY: *History: Ancient and Medieval History*. During that period he transformed many of the small towns of Germany into fortified cities, containing trained troops of mounted warriors. His military preparations were successfully tested at the defeat of the Wends (q.v.) in 929. When the Magyars invaded Thuringia in 933, Henry defeated them

HENRY (Holy Roman Empire)

decisively. He defeated the Danes in the following year and seized territory from them. Henry was the first to create a united Germany (see GERMANY: *History*), and although he never received the imperial crown, he is generally recognized as one of the Holy Roman Emperors; see HOLY ROMAN EMPIRE. He was succeeded by his son Otto I (see under OTTO).

HENRY II, called HENRY THE SAINT (973–1024), Holy Roman Emperor (1002–24), last of the Saxon emperors, born in Abbach, Bavaria. When Henry's cousin Otto III, Holy Roman Emperor (see under OTTO), died without heir, Henry was elected to succeed him. From 1004 until 1018 he carried on intermittent warfare with Boleslav I, King of Poland (see under BOLESLAV), regaining Bohemia, one of the German territories taken by Poland. In 1004 Henry invaded Italy and was crowned king of the Lombards. Returning to Germany, he persuaded Rudolf III, King of Burgundy (r. 993–1032), to agree that Burgundy should be united with Germany upon Rudolf's death. In 1014 Henry went to Rome, where he was crowned emperor by Pope Benedict VIII (see under BENEDICT). In 1021, at the request of Pope Benedict, Henry undertook a third expedition to Italy, restoring order and establishing his authority there. Famed for his piety, Henry was active in church reform and established a number of monasteries and schools. He was canonized in 1146. Henry was succeeded as emperor by Conrad II (see under CONRAD).

HENRY III, called HENRY THE BLACK (1017–56), Holy Roman Emperor (1039–56). In 1039 he succeeded his father, Conrad II, Holy Roman Emperor (see under CONRAD). When in 1041 the Bohemians invaded the lands of Henry's vassals, the Poles, Henry brought them to submission, compelling the duke of Bohemia to recognize his suzerainty. Between 1043 and 1045 Henry campaigned successfully to restore the deposed Hungarian king to his throne and for a short time afterward controlled Hungary. Henry was greatly concerned with church reform and went to Rome in 1046 to settle the conflict caused by three rival claimants to the papacy. Setting aside the three antipopes, he appointed a German bishop, who, as Pope Clement II (r. 1046–47), crowned Henry holy Roman emperor. During the rest of his reign Henry appointed three succeeding popes, all Germans. Returning to Germany, he contended with domestic rebellions. Henry supported the church's attempts to check clerical abuses, and strengthened the power of the papacy which proved disadvantageous for his son, Henry IV (q.v.), Holy Roman Emperor.

HENRY IV (1050–1106), Holy Roman Emperor (1056–1106), born in Goslar, Germany. When Henry was six years old he succeeded his father, Henry III (q.v.), Holy Roman Emperor. During most of his minority, his mother ruled in his name. After Henry came of age in 1065 he crushed a rebellion in Saxony. About that time there began the struggle between pope and emperor for temporal power in the empire; see HOLY ROMAN EMPIRE. Despite a papal decree prohibiting appointment of Church officials by the

Henry IV, Holy Roman Emperor (from a 12th-century German manuscript). Granger Collection

emperor, Henry appointed prelates in various parts of Italy in 1075. On being reprimanded by Pope Gregory VII (see under GREGORY), Henry convoked a German council at Worms in 1076 to depose the pope. This act resulted in the excommunication of the emperor, with the consequent release of his subjects from allegiance to him. The nobles formed a coalition, threatening not to recognize Henry unless he secured absolution by February, 1077. By dressing as a penitent and standing barefoot in the snow for three days outside the castle of Canossa (q.v.), where Pope Gregory was staying, Henry obtained readmission to the communion of the Church.

The German nobles, however, elected Rudolf,

HENRY (Holy Roman Empire)

Duke of Swabia (d. 1080), to replace Henry. This election caused a civil war. In 1080 the pope recognized the kingship of Rudolf and again excommunicated Henry. Henry again declared Pope Gregory deposed and had the Italian archbishop Guibert of Ravenna (1030?–1100) elected in his stead as Pope Clement III. Rudolf was killed in 1080, and Henry regained control of Germany. He then led his forces into Italy and in 1084 captured Rome, where he was crowned emperor by Clement III. A Norman army, led by the Norman adventurer Robert Guiscard (q.v.), came to the aid of Pope Gregory, however, and drove Henry from Rome. Henry returned to Germany and there participated in a long series of civil wars, in which his sons eventually turned against him. In 1105 he was taken prisoner by his son Henry, later Henry V (q.v.), Holy Roman Emperor, and forced to abdicate. Escaping in the next year, Henry IV solicited aid from various sources, including England, Denmark, and France. He died at Liège, Belgium, while gathering an army.

HENRY V (1081–1125), Holy Roman Emperor (1106–25), born in Goslar, Germany. In 1104 Henry rebelled against his father, Henry IV (q.v.), Holy Roman Emperor, captured him, and forced him to abdicate. The young Henry became undisputed ruler on the death of his father in 1106.

In 1110 Henry agreed to respect the decree of Pope Paschal II (*see under* PASCHAL) against lay investiture, that is, the appointment of Church officials by the king, providing the pope would crown him and that the Church would surrender all its secular property and rights within the empire. Because Henry's demand raised such a furor among the clergy when it was announced to them on the day of coronation, Paschal refused to crown Henry, who thereupon departed from Rome, taking the pope prisoner. To gain his freedom, the pope allowed Henry the power of investiture and crowned him emperor, but in 1112 he retracted his concessions. From 1114 to 1121 many of the German princes rebelled against Henry. Although northern Germany was in revolt in 1116, Henry invaded Italy to seize the territories left to the papacy by Matilda, Countess of Tuscany (1046–1115). After driving Pope Paschal from Rome, Henry had himself recrowned in 1117 by Maurice Bourdin, Archbishop of Braga (d. 1125), whom he set up as antipope Gregory VIII after the death of Paschal in 1118. Henry was accordingly excommunicated by Paschal's successor, Pope Gelasius II (r. 1118–19).

On returning to Germany Henry concluded peace with his former domestic enemies at the diet of Würzburg in 1121. By the Concordat of Worms in 1122 he established a compromise on investiture with the papacy, abandoning the antipope Gregory VIII, and being reinstated in the communion of the Church. In the last year of his reign the emperor, in alliance with his father-in-law, Henry I (q.v.), King of England, led an unsuccessful expedition against Louis VI (q.v.), King of France. Henry V was succeeded by Lothair II (*see under* LOTHAIR).

HENRY VI (1165–97), Holy Roman Emperor (1191–97), and King of Sicily (1194–97), born in Nijmegen (in present-day Netherlands). When his father, Frederick I (q.v.), Holy Roman Emperor, departed in 1189 on the Third Crusade, Henry became regent for him. In 1190 Henry put down a rebellion of nobles led by Henry the Lion (q.v.), Duke of Saxony. In the following year, after the death of Frederick I, Henry was crowned Holy Roman Emperor at Rome. Claiming the crown of Sicily through his wife, Henry then advanced against Tancred, King of Sicily (d. 1194). Henry failed to take Naples and was forced to return to Germany, where he found German nobles, led by Henry the Lion, in revolt. In 1192 the emperor captured and held for ransom Richard I (q.v.), King of England, brother-in-law of Henry the Lion. In return for the release of Richard in 1194, the emperor was able to bring Henry the Lion to terms and thus restore peace in Germany. In the same year Tancred died, and Henry gathered a large army and invaded Italy. With little difficulty he conquered Sicily and was crowned king. Henry tried unsuccessfully in 1196 to make the imperial crown hereditary in the Hohenstaufen family. He did, however, succeed in securing the eventual succession of his son Frederick as Frederick II (q.v.), Holy Roman Emperor. Henry was succeeded by Otto IV (*see under* OTTO).

HENRY VII, known as HENRY OF LUXEMBURG (about 1275–1313), Holy Roman Emperor (1308–13), first of the line of Luxemburg, born in Buonconvento, Italy. On the death of Albert I, Holy Roman Emperor (*see under* ALBERT), in 1308, Henry was elected to succeed him. In 1310 Henry entered Italy; he was crowned king of the Lombards the following year and Holy Roman Emperor in 1312. While in Italy he attempted to end the strife between the Guelphs and Ghibellines (q.v.). Declaring himself to be impartial, he secured the homage of both factions; but the Guelphs soon rebelled, and Henry was forced to side with the Ghibellines. Allied with Frederick II (q.v.), King of Sicily, in 1313 Henry was preparing an attack on

HENRY (Portugal)

the Guelph leader Robert, Duke of Anjou and King of Naples (1275–1343), when he died. He was succeeded by Louis IV (q.v.), Holy Roman Emperor.

HENRY (1512–80), King of Portugal (1578–80), son of Emanuel (q.v.), King of Portugal. Henry was educated for the priesthood and at the age of about twenty-seven was consecrated bishop of Évora and appointed Grand Inquisitor of Portugal. Under his direction the Inquisition (q.v.) became a powerful force in Portugal, and Henry was made a cardinal in about 1545. He acted as regent for his nephew Sebastian, King of Portugal (1554–78) during the minority of the young king. In 1578 Henry succeeded to the throne when Sebastian disappeared during a battle with the Moors. Henry left no heir and Portugal became a Spanish possession after his death.

HENRY, called HENRY THE NAVIGATOR (1394–1460), Prince of Portugal, noted as the patron of navigation and exploration, born in Oporto. He was the third son of John I (q.v.), King of Portugal. Henry participated in the capture of Ceuta in North Africa from the Moors in 1415. Subsequently he made his residence at Sagres, Portugal, near Cape Saint Vincent, and there established an observatory and the first school for navigators in Europe. Henry not only greatly developed the science of navigation, but also made improvements in the art of shipbuilding. The caravel, a sailing ship, was designed at Sagres; see SHIPS AND SHIPBUILDING: *Ships of the Middle Ages: Early European Types.* He made no voyages himself, but under his direction many important expeditions were undertaken along the west coast of Africa. Henry's navigators reached Madeira in 1420, sailed around Cape Bojador in 1434, sailed to Cape Blanc in 1441, rounded Cape Verde in 1445, and reached the mouth of the Gambia River in present-day Gambia about 1446. The influence Henry had upon navigation continued after his death and resulted in the circumnavigation of Africa and the opening of a new trade route to the East.

HENRY THE LION, or (Ger.) HEINRICH DER LÖWE (1129–95), Duke of Saxony (1139–80), and Duke of Bavaria (1156–80), the son of Henry the Proud, Duke of Bavaria and Saxony (1108–39), born in Ravensburg. At the age of ten he succeeded his father to the duchy of Saxony, which his mother and grandmother administered for him until 1146. In 1147 Henry demanded that the Diet of Frankfort restore to him the duchy of Bavaria, which had been taken from his father. Upon being refused, Henry began an unsuccessful war against Conrad III, King of Germany (see under CONRAD). After Conrad's death, however, Henry's duchy was restored to him by Frederick I (q.v.), Holy Roman Emperor. Henry subsequently aided Frederick in wars in Poland and Italy between 1157 and 1159. Possessing both German and Italian territories that extended from the North and Baltic seas to the shores of the Adriatic Sea, Henry was a formidable figure in the Holy Roman Empire. To curb his power a league of nobles, archbishops, and bishops was formed in 1166. In two years of warfare against the league, however, Henry was triumphant. In 1168 Henry took as his second wife, Matilda (1156–89), the daughter of Henry II (q.v.), King of England. In 1172–73 he made a pilgrimage to Jerusalem. By refusing to aid Frederick I in an Italian expedition, Henry instigated a quarrel (1175–76) between himself and the emperor. As a result, Henry was placed under the ban of the empire. He was deprived of most of his possessions in 1180 and twice forced into exile, in 1182 and 1189, spending most of his time in England. When he returned to Germany shortly after the second exile, Henry took part in a rebellion of German nobles against Henry VI (q.v.), Holy Roman Emperor. He made peace with the emperor, however, at Fulda in 1190. Henry was a capable ruler, one of his greatest accomplishments being the colonization of northern Germany.

HENRY, Joseph (1797–1878), American physicist, born in Albany, N.Y., and educated at Albany Academy. He was appointed professor of mathematics and natural philosophy at Albany Academy in 1826 and professor of natural philosophy at Princeton University in 1832. The foremost American physicist of his day, Henry did his most important work in electromagnetism. He discovered the principle of electromagnetic induction (see INDUCTION) a few years before the British physicist Michael Faraday (q.v.) announced his discovery of electromagnetically induced currents, but Faraday published his findings first and is credited with the discovery. The discovery of the phenomenon of self-inductance, which Henry announced in 1832 is, however, attributed to him, and the unit of inductance is named the henry in his honor.

Henry experimented with and improved the electromagnet, which had been invented in 1823 by the British inventor William Sturgeon (1783–1850). By 1829 he developed electromagnets of great lifting power and efficiency and essentially of the same form used later in dynamos and motors (see DYNAMOELECTRIC MACHINERY). He also developed electromagnets that were capable of magnetizing iron at a distance from the source of current and in 1831 he constructed the first practical electromagnetic telegraph. Henry also devised and constructed one of the first electric motors. In 1842 he recognized the oscillatory nature of an electric discharge.

In 1846 Henry was elected secretary and director of the newly formed Smithsonian Institution (q.v.) and served in those positions until his death. Under his direction, the institution stimulated activity in many fields of science. He organized meteorological studies at the Smithsonian and was the first to use the telegraph to transmit weather reports, to indicate daily atmospheric conditions on a map, and to make weather forecasts from meteorological data. The successful meteorological work of the Smithsonian Institution led to the creation of the United States Weather Bureau (see WEATHER SERVICE, NATIONAL). Henry was a founder of the American Association for the Advancement of Science and president of the National Academy of Sciences (qq.v.) from 1868 to 1878.

HENRY, O. See PORTER, WILLIAM SYDNEY.

HENRY, Patrick (1736–99), American orator and statesman, born in Hanover County, Va., and largely self-educated. From 1751 until 1760 he was first a storekeeper and then a farmer. Failing at both occupations, he undertook the study of law and in 1760 was admitted to the Virginia bar.

By 1763 he had become a prominent lawyer in Virginia. In 1765 he became a member of the colonial legislature of Virginia, the House of Burgesses, where he introduced seven resolutions against the Stamp Act (q.v.), concluding his speech with: "Caesar had his Brutus, Charles the First his Cromwell, and George the Third—may profit by their example". In answer to the cries of treason from conservative members, Henry replied, "If this be treason, make the most of it." Five of his resolutions were carried by a small majority, and all seven were printed in the colonial newspapers as the "Virginia Resolves." Reelected to the House of Burgesses in 1769, Henry joined with the radical faction, which was ready to precipitate an open break with Great Britain. When the House of Burgesses was dissolved in 1774, Henry became a member of the revolutionary convention of Virginia. Speaking before the convention in 1775, he urged the adoption of a resolution to establish a state of

Patrick Henry (from a 19th-century engraving). Granger Collection

defense in Virginia with a speech that is famous for these words: "I know not what course others may take, but as for me, give me liberty or give me death!"

Henry was subsequently made chairman of a committee to prepare a defense plan for Virginia during the American Revolution (q.v.). Between 1774 and 1776 he was a delegate to the first and second Continental Congresses (see CONTINENTAL CONGRESS). In 1776 Henry assisted in drafting the Virginia Constitution and from 1776 until 1779 and again from 1784 until 1786 served as governor of the State. During his first gubernatorial term he sent the American soldier and frontiersman George Rogers Clark (see under CLARK) on a military expedition to the Northwest. As a delegate to the Virginia convention for the ratification of the Constitution of the United States (q.v.) in 1788, Henry opposed the document on the ground that it threatened the rights of States and individuals. Largely through his efforts, the provisions known as the Bill of Rights (q.v.) were adopted as the first ten amendments to the Constitution. Henry was offered many governmental posts, but declined them, continuing his law practice. In 1799 he was elected to the Virginia legislature but died before taking his seat.

HENRY'S LAW, law concerning the nature of solubility of gases in liquids, formulated by the British chemist William Henry (1774–1836). It states that when the temperature is kept constant, the weight of a gas that dissolves in a liquid is proportional to the pressure exerted by the gas on the liquid. For example, at a pressure of 1 atmosphere and a temperature of 20° C., 0.0434 grams of oxygen dissolve in 1 liter of water; at a pressure of 10 atmospheres and a temperature of 20° C., 0.434 grams (or 10 times 0.0434) of oxygen dissolve in 1 liter of water. It has been observed that Henry's law does not apply to gases that are extremely soluble in water, such as hydrogen chloride or ammonia.

HENSON, Matthew A. See PEARY, ROBERT EDWIN.

HENYANG. See HENGYANG.

HENZADA, city of Burma, in Irrawaddy Division, on the Irrawaddy R., 75 miles N.W. of Rangoon. It is a river port, linked with Bassein and Rangoon by steamer and with Bassein and Kyangin by rail. Rice and tobacco are grown in the vicinity, and timber, chiefly teakwood, is obtained in the mountains nearby. Woodcarving is an important local handicraft. Henzada was a part of the kingdom of Pegu and was annexed by Burma in 1753. Pop. (1953) 61,972.

HEPARIN, one of the many natural anticlotting substances of the blood, stored in a variety of body tissues, but most abundant in the liver. It is obtained for medical use from the livers or lungs of domestic animals, and was thus first prepared by the American physiologist William Henry Howell (1860–1945) in 1918. Research on survivors of the atomic bomb at Hiroshima indicates that radiation causes an overproduction of body heparin and creates a tendency to hemorrhage.

Injected heparin is valuable because it interferes directly with the clotting process and is almost immediately effective. Heparin is useful in the treatment of frostbite and bacterial endocarditis and in preventing clot formation during blood transfusion. It is also used in the treatment of stroke patients suffering from embolism, the sudden obstruction of an artery or vein by a blood clot deposited by circulation. While it does not dissolve established clots, it prevents their growth and slows the formation of new clots.

Because heparin disappears from the blood in a matter of hours, it is often given in conjunction with another anticoagulant, coumarin, which interferes with production of prothrombin, a substance required for blood clotting.

HEPATICA (Gr. *hepatikos,* "liver"), genus of perennial herbs, commonly called liverleaf, belonging to the family Ranunculaceae. Hepaticas have thick, heart-shaped, evergreen leaves, each with three lobes, somewhat reminiscent of the three lobes of the human liver. They grow in open woodlands and bloom in early spring. Hepaticas can be transplanted to gardens from the wild state or propagated by seeds or division of roots. The two North American species are distinguished from each other by the shape of the leaves: *H. triloba* has rounded lobes and *H. acutiloba* has pointed lobes. Both species bear delicate purple, blue, pink, or white flowers. A European species, *H. angulosa,* frequently cultivated in gardens of the United States, has toothed leaves and pale-blue flowers. Hepaticas are attacked by the late spore stages of a rust fungus, *Tranzschelia punctata.* Since earlier spore stages of this rust attack stone fruit such as almond, cherry, plum, peach, and apricot, hepatica is often for this reason eradicated from the neighborhood of orchards. See RUST.

HEPATICAE, scientific name of a class of the phylum Bryophyta (q.v.) comprising simple, mosslike plants commonly called liverworts. Liverworts grow in shaded, moist places all over the world; some liverworts are floating plants, but most are found in deep forests. The typical

HEPATITIS

Male gametophytes (top), female gametophytes (bottom) of Hepaticae plants of the order Marchantia.

liverwort is a flat, leaflike growth called a thallus. It obtains minerals and moisture from the soil by means of rootlike hairs called rhizoids. Reproduction is accomplished by the union of gametes produced by sex organs called antheridia (male) and archegonia (female) and by spores produced in structures called sporangia.

Botanists divide the liverworts into three distinct orders: (1) Marchantiales, or thallose liverworts; (2) Jungermanniales, or leafy liverworts; and (3) Anthocerotales, including hornworts. The Marchantiales consist of plants having simple, disklike bodies. Most Jungermanniales have leafy thalli, resembling those of the mosses. Anthocerotales have simple thalli that produce long, hornlike sporangia.

HEPATITIS, acute infection, primarily of the liver, occurring in two forms caused by related but distinct filterable viruses.

Infectious Hepatitis. This disease has caused rural and urban epidemics for thousands of years. The virus, which can be ingested orally or injected on improperly sterilized hypodermic needles, has an incubation period of from two to six weeks, and often appears in areas of poor sanitation and overcrowding where milk and drinking water are contaminated. It is common in army camps and in institutions where small children are crowded together; outbreaks have been caused by eating shellfish taken in water contaminated by sewage. The virus is present in the blood for only one or two weeks, but can be recovered from the feces for as long as eighteen months after infection. It produces specific antibodies in the blood that confer immunity only to infectious hepatitis. Travelers to areas of infection may be protected by injections of pooled gamma globulin (q.v.), which will either avert or reduce attacks for a period of six months. The onset of infectious hepatitis is gradual, accompanied variably by fever, poor appetite, nausea, vomiting, diarrhea, and pain in the upper right abdomen. The disease occurs most frequently in young people.

Serum Hepatitis Another form of the disease, has been recognized only since World War II, when it was revealed in the course of investigating the cause of 50,000 cases of jaundice that occurred about three months following inoculations with yellow fever vaccine containing human serum. Study of the serum revealed the presence of an infectious agent differing from the virus known to cause infectious hepatitis. Serum hepatitis can be transmitted only by injection. It has an incubation period of from six weeks to six months and is readily transmitted in contaminated vaccines, pooled plasma, and fibrinogen. Many cases follow transfusions of blood taken from symptom-free donors who have no history of liver disease or jaundice; virus may be recovered from the blood of such asymptomatic carriers for periods of at least five years. Antibodies to this virus confer immunity only to the serum form of the disease; gamma globulin is of doubtful value. Improperly sterilized hypodermic needles and syringes, surgical and dental instruments, razors, and tattoo needles are prime sources of infection. It is often acquired by drug addicts who share hypodermic syringes. The illnesses caused by the two viruses are virtually identical and both cause the same type of degeneration in the liver. With the onset of jaundice, the patient may feel better. The period of illness is variable in both diseases and may last from as little as a week to as much as eight weeks. Jaundice usually reaches its maximum within two weeks and thereafter gradually clears. Convalescence takes weeks; complete recovery may require from four to six months.

Perhaps one percent of cases in young people and ten percent in the elderly may sustain serious liver damage. A very few may go on to develop cirrhosis or chronic liver disease, and perhaps one percent progress to fulminant hepatitis, in which the liver is virtually destroyed.

No specific treatment exists beyond bed rest and a diet high in calories, protein, and carbohydrate supplemented by vitamins. In the acutely ill, corticosteroids may minimize symptoms of liver damage without improving the underlying disease. *See* JAUNDICE; LIVER.

HEPBURN

HEPBURN, Katharine (1909–), American actress, born in Hartford, Conn., and educated at Bryn Mawr College. She made her theatrical debut in *The Czarina* in 1928. She scored a notable success on Broadway four years later in the role of Antiope in *The Warrior's Husband*.

Katharine Hepburn   UPI

Shortly afterward she accepted a contract to act in motion pictures, although in succeeding years she alternated between stage and screen appearances. Among the theatrical productions in which she has appeared are *The Lake* (1933); *Jane Eyre* (1936); *The Philadelphia Story* (1939), in which she gave one of her finest performances in the role of Tracy Lord; *Without Love* (1942), and *Coco* (1969), a musical based on the life of the French couturiere Gabrielle Chanel (q.v.). Miss Hepburn also starred in the film version of *The Philadelphia Story* (1939), for which she won the 1940 New York Film Critics award for the best performance by an actress. Among other motion pictures in which she was starred are *A Bill of Divorcement* (1933); *Morning Glory* (1933), for which she received the best-actress award for that year from the Academy of Motion Picture Arts and Sciences; *Mary of Scotland* (1936); *Stage Door* (1937); *Dragon Seed* (1944); *The African Queen* (1952); *Summertime* (1953); *The Rainmaker* (1956); *Long Day's Journey into Night* (1962); *Guess Who's Coming to Dinner* (1967), for which she won another Academy award; and *The Lion in Winter* (1968), for which she shared the best-actress award.

HEPHAESTUS, in Greek mythology, god of fire and metalwork, the son of the god Zeus and the goddess Hera (qq.v.), or sometimes the son of Hera alone. In contrast to the other gods, Hephaestus was lame and awkward. Shortly after his birth, he was cast out of heaven, either by Hera, who was repelled by his deformity, or by Zeus, because Hephaestus had sided with Hera against him. In most legends, however, he was soon honored again on Olympus, and was married to Aphrodite (q.v.), goddess of love, or to Aglaia, one of the three Graces (q.v.). As the artisan among the gods, Hephaestus made their armor, weapons, and jewelry. His workshop was believed to lie under Mt. Etna, a volcano in Sicily. Hephaestus is often identified with the Roman god of fire Vulcan (q.v.).

HEPPLEWHITE, George (d. 1786), English cabinetmaker. He learned the art of furniture making in Lancaster, subsequently setting up a shop

Classic Hepplewhite chair, with shield-shaped back and slender, tapered legs.   Metropolitan Museum of Art

for his trade in the parish of Saint Giles, Cripplegate, London. Hepplewhite is regarded as one of the best English designers and furniture makers. His work is characterized by a classic simplicity and delicacy. Hepplewhite chairs are particularly distinguished for their comparatively small size; the shield or heart shape of their backs; their slender legs, often tapering to a spade foot; and their painted or inlaid ornamentation. Many of Hepplewhite's best designs are contained in the posthumously published volume *Cabinet-maker and Upholsterer's Guide* (1788). See CHAIR: *Modern Chairs*; FURNITURE: *18th-Century England*; INTERIOR DECORATION: *The Eighteenth Century.*

HERA, in Greek mythology, queen of the gods, the daughter of the Titans Cronus and Rhea, and the sister and wife of the god Zeus (qq.v.). Hera was the goddess of marriage and the protector of married women. She was the mother of Ares, god of war, Hephaestus, god of fire, Hebe (qq.v.), goddess of youth, and Ilithyia, goddess of childbirth. Hera was a jealous wife, and often persecuted Zeus' mistresses and children. She never forgot an injury, and was known for her vindictive nature. Angry with the Trojan prince Paris for preferring Aphrodite (qq.v.), goddess of love, to herself, Hera aided the Greeks in the Trojan War (q.v.) and was not appeased until Troy (q.v.) was finally destroyed. Hera is often identified with the Roman goddess Juno (q.v.).

HERACLES or **HERAKLES.** See HERCULES, Greek hero.

HERACLITUS (about 540–475 B.C.), Greek philosopher, born in Ephesus in Asia Minor. Because of the loneliness of his life and the obscurity and misanthropy of his philosophy, he was called the "dark philosopher" or "weeping philosopher".

Heraclitus was in a sense one of the founders of Greek metaphysics (q.v.), although his ideas stem from those of the Ionian School of Greek philosophy; see GREEK PHILOSOPHY: *The Ionian School.* He postulated fire as the primal substance or principle that, through condensation and rarefaction, creates the phenomena of the sensible world. Heraclitus added to the "being" of his predecessors the concept of "becoming" or flux, which he took to be a basic reality underlying all things, even the most apparently stable. In ethics, he introduced a new social emphasis, holding virtue to consist in a subordination of the individual to the laws of a universal, reasonable harmony. Although his thought was strongly tinged with elements of popular theology, he attacked the concepts and ceremonies of the popular religion of his day.

Only one work, *On Nature,* is definitely attributable to Heraclitus. Numerous fragments of this work were preserved by later writers, and collected editions of all of his surviving fragments may be found in several modern editions.

HERACLIUS (about 575–641), Byzantine Emperor (610–41), son of the imperial governor of North Africa, born in Cappadocia. In 610 he joined his father in leading a revolt against the reigning emperor, the tyrannical Phocas (d. 610), sailed from Carthage, seized Constantinople (now İstanbul, Turkey), and ascended the throne. In this period the Byzantine Empire (q.v.) was seriously threatened by the invasion of the Asian Avars (q.v.), who swept across southern Russia and into the Balkans, which they raided in conjunction with the infiltration of Slavic tribes from the north. Simultaneously, the empire was attacked, both in Asia Minor and in Egypt, by Persia. Constantinople was besieged jointly by the Persians and the Avars in 619 and again in 626.

To face the double danger Heraclius accelerated the militarization of the empire. The former political system, consisting of separate civilian and military administrations, was replaced by one incorporating provinces, called themes, in which the military commanders also wielded civilian authority. The Avars were gradually pushed back from the capital toward central Europe, where they settled. A series of great campaigns against Persia began in 622 and assumed the character of a crusade, because their goal was the rescue of a cross (q.v.), presumed to be the Holy Cross, that had been carried off by the Persians after their sack of Jerusalem in 614. By 628 the imperial armies reached the vicinity of the Persian capital of Ctesiphon (now in Iraq), enemy resistance collapsed, and Heraclius solemnly restored the cross to Jerusalem in the spring of 630. To parallel his administrative reorganization of the empire, Heraclius attempted religious reforms. He sought to mediate between the orthodox party and the Monophysites (q.v.) of the eastern provinces by imposing the Monothelite doctrine (*see* MONOTHELITES) on the empire, but he pleased neither party thereby and aroused serious disturbances.

Heraclius' outstanding military victories may have strengthened the empire in the long run, but the constant wars and religious dissension left it unable to stem a new Muslim threat that was rising in Arabia. Before the end of his reign Syria, Palestine, and Egypt fell to Islam (q.v.).

HERALDRY, originally, all of the numerous duties and functions of a herald or officer at arms, including the devising and granting of armorial bearings, or coats of arms. The term now usually refers to the branch of knowledge dealing with the history and description of armorial bearings.

HERALDRY

Symbolic and ornamental figures similar to those used in heraldry have been used as tribal or national emblems and standards since ancient times. The ancient Thracians used the sow; the Romans, the eagle; the Saxons, the white horse; the French, first the lion and later the fleur-de-lis. The practice of carrying personal armorial devices on shields and banners began during feudal times, when it was necessary for a knight, with his face covered by the visor of his helmet, to be recognized at a distance; see FEUDALISM. True arms, however, are hereditary rather than personal emblems. Such insignia were depicted on shields carried in the Third Crusade (see CRUSADES) in the 12th century; in the following century the practice was introduced of embroidering the family insignia on the surcoat worn over the coat of mail, giving rise to the term "coat of arms". In England armorial insignia were assumed by knights as they pleased until early in the 15th century, when King Henry V (q.v.) restrained the practice. In 1483 King Edward IV (q.v.) established the Heralds' College to supervise armorial bearings. In addition to individuals, organizations entitled to coats of arms are families, kingdoms, lordships, towns, episcopal sees, abbeys, and corporations.

The entire display of a person's arms is called an achievement of arms. It includes the escutcheon or shield, the helm or helmet, the crest, the motto, the mantle, the supporters, and the torse or wreath, all described below. Of these parts the escutcheon is most important.

The term escutcheon is derived from the French *écusson*, which signified a shield with arms portrayed upon it, as distinguished from a plain shield. It is usually in the shape of a conventionalized shield, except in the oval-shaped arms of churchmen and in the lozenge-shaped arms of ladies. To facilitate description, heralds divided the shield from top to bottom into three areas: chief, fess, and base; and from right to left (of the wearer of the shield) into dexter, middle or pale, and sinister. The shield bears various charges, or figures, represented in different tinctures.

The term tincture includes the representation of metals, colors, and furs. The two metals in common use are or (gold) and argent (silver). They are represented in painting by yellow and white, respectively; in black and white drawings or engravings, gold is represented by white stippled with fine black dots and silver by plain white. The principal colors are gules or red, azure or blue, sable or black, vert or green, and purpure or purple. A charge emblazoned in the natural color of the object represented is said to be proper. The furs are ermine, representing ermine tails, and vair. Colors and furs are also represented in drawings by conventional hatchings and figures.

Charges. Every figure depicted on an escutcheon is called a charge. Charges are classified by heralds as honorable ordinaries, subordinaries, and common charges. No sharp distinction exists between honorable ordinaries and subordinaries or between subordinaries and common charges.

HONORABLE ORDINARIES. These are simple geometrical figures delineated by straight lines or by partition lines of irregular forms. The straight lines include the pale, a perpendicular stripe; the fess, a horizontal bar across the middle of the escutcheon; the bar, one of two or more horizontal lines; the bend, a diagonal band; and the chevron, two diagonal stripes meeting at an angle with the point up. Various crosses are important honorable ordinaries. The irregular partition lines have specific patterns, known as engrailed, invected, wavy or undy, nebuly, indented, dancetty, raguly, dovetailed, embattled or crenélé, and potented. In some of the oldest escutcheons an honorable ordinary constitutes the only charge.

FIELD. The field of an escutcheon may be of two or more tinctures, divided by one or more partition lines. A shield divided vertically is parted, or party per, pale, and a shield divided vertically and horizontally is called party per cross, or quarterly. If one of the divisions is also quartered, the original division is called a grand quarter. A shield parted per saltire (divided into four parts by two crossed diagonal lines) and per cross is called a gyronny of eight, and each segment is called a gyron. When the shield is completely divided into a number of equal parts by lines in the direction of a pale, bend, bar, or chevron, it is said to be paly, bendy, barry, or chevronny, and the number of divisions is specified, as, for example, a paly of six or and sable. A field divided by vertical and horizontal lines is called checky, and one divided by intersecting diagonal lines is called lozengy or fusilly (see lozenge, below). A field strewed with an indefinite number of small charges so as to produce a pattern is said to be semé of that charge. Fretty describes a field covered with an open network of diagonal interlaced ribbons.

SUBORDINARIES. The bordure, or border, is often considered as an honorable ordinary. It consists of a band encircling the shield, and often bears small charges. The orle is a narrower border that does not touch the edges of the shield. The di-

HERALDRY

minutive of the orle is the tressure, which is usually double and is often embellished with fleurs-de-lis.

The quarter consists of the dexter chief quarter of the shield. If the figure occupies less than a full fourth of the shield, it is called a canton, and if quarter or canton is parted per bend (diagonally) each triangle is called a gyron.

Flanches consist of the dexter and sinister flanks of the shield, cut off by curved lines. The diminutives are flasques and voiders.

The lozenge is a diamond-shaped figure with four equal sides. When a lozenge is voided, that is, represented only in outline with the tincture of the field showing inside, it is called a mascle; when it is pierced with a round opening it is called a rustre. A charge similar to the lozenge, but much narrower in relation to its height, is known as a fusil.

A small shield charged upon the escutcheon is called inescutcheon; it may be charged or plain. A billet is a small rectangular charge that is about twice as high as it is wide.

Among the charges considered by some to be subordinaries and by others to be common charges are the pall and roundle. The pall is a Y-shaped charge, representing the insignium conferred by the pope upon the archbishops. Roundles are circular charges, which are distinguished by different names according to their tinctures: when they are of gold, they are called bezants; of silver, plates; of red, torteaux; of blue, hurts; of purple, golps; of green, pommes; and of black, pellets or ogresses. A voided roundle is an annulet.

COMMON CHARGES. Common charges are conventional representations of familiar objects which sometimes portray the history or character of the individual or family. More often, they are a pun on the family name (canting arms). One of the most important of such charges is the lion. An early armorial representation of the lion is on the seal (about 1164) of Philip I, Duke of Flanders. Later it was adopted by the rulers of England, Scotland, Norway, Denmark, Wales, and other European states. The earliest position of the heraldic lion was rampant, that is, erect and facing right and with only one foot on the ground. Salient is similar to rampant, except that both hind feet are on the ground. A beast of prey walking to the right is passant, and a beast of the chase, as a stag, is trippant. A crouching beast is couchant if the head is raised, and dormant if the head is resting on the forepaws. No specification is made when the head is shown in profile looking forward, but when looking toward the observer it is called gardant, and looking backward, regardant. Two lions rampant placed face to face are called combatant, and back to back, addossé. Lions, as well as other animals, are often crowned or gorged (collared) with a torse or coronet. Animals used as heraldic charges include the bear, bull, boar, deer, goat, dog, fox, horse, and hedgehog, and occasionally the elephant, camel, mole, ape, cat, and mouse. Common birds are the eagle and the falcon. Mythical beasts such as the griffin, unicorn, dragon, and basilisk are also used.

Many charges represent articles connected with the occupation or position of the individual, as swords, bows and arrows, helmets, battle-axes, and lance heads for knights, and miters and crosiers for bishops and abbots. The sun surrounded by rays is said to be in his splendor, and is usually depicted as having a human face. The moon is represented by a crescent with cusps pointing upward; if the cusps point toward dexter, it is called an increscent, if toward sinister, a decrescent. The five-pointed star is seldom used, as it is indistinguishable from the mullet, or spur rowel, except that the latter is sometimes pierced. The conventional star, the estoile, is shown with six wavy rays.

External Ornaments. In addition to the escutcheon, the achievement of arms may include the helm, the crest, the motto, the mantle, the supporters, and the wreath or coronet.

The helm, the natural accompaniment of the shield in representing a warrior, was added to arms before the beginning of the 14th century. After the end of the 16th century, its form and position were modified in English heraldry to indicate the rank of the bearer; thus, helmets of knights and princes are portrayed full faced, and those of peers and gentlemen, in profile.

The crest is the most ancient of armorial bearings. It was worn by the warrior chiefs of Greek and Roman antiquity, and served not only as a mark of rank but also as a conspicuous emblem in battle, around which soldiers might rally. In heraldry the crest is represented attached to the top of the helmet; its base is surrounded by a wreath, a circlet of twisted ribbons tinctured of the principal metal and color of the shield.

The motto, originally the war cry of the bearer, is now a phrase or sentence containing an allusion to the family, the arms, or the crest. It is placed in a scroll either above the crest or below the shield.

The mantle originally was a piece of cloth that protected the helmet from the heat of the sun. It became more decorative and was usually shown in the principal colors of the shield.

The supporters are figures, usually people or

HERALDRY

Heraldry of colonial America. Above: The achievement of arms, or coat of arms, of the Ohio Company, founded by London merchants and Virginia planters and chartered in 1749. Right: The component parts of the arms of the Ohio Company. Granger Collection

animals, placed on each side of the shield. They were originally mere decoration, but later came to indicate the head of a family of distinction.

The wreath, coronet, and miter are adjuncts of the arms of persons entitled to wear them. Any collar or badge of an order to which the bearer may have a right is also properly portrayed in his achievement. The collar surrounds the shield; badges hang from it.

Blazonry. In tournaments of the Middle Ages, whenever an unknown knight arrived, it was the duty of the herald to blasen (blow) a trumpet for attention, and then describe to the assemblage the bearings on the escutcheon of the knight. From this practice the term blazonry came to designate the accurate and specific description of a coat of arms.

In describing an achievement of arms, the name of the person, domain, or institution bearing the arms is given first. The blazoning of the escutcheon is then given, describing first the field, with specification of its tinctures and the shape and direction of its partition lines. The description of the charges follows, starting with the principal charge, which is assumed to be in the center of the shield unless otherwise specified. In general, ordinaries are given first, except for chief, canton, and bordure, which are described last. For example: France, ancient, azure, semé of fleurs-de-lis, or; Erskine, argent, a pale, sable; Gainsborough, or fretty gules, a canton, ermine.

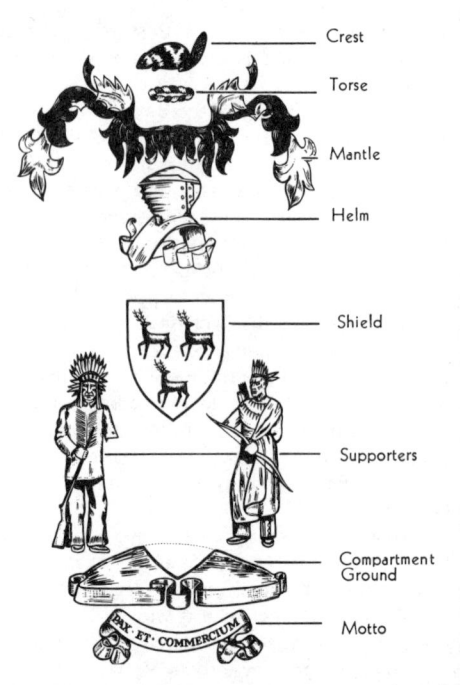

When two identical charges are mentioned, they are placed in pale, that is, in a vertical line, unless otherwise specified; three are placed in pile, two above and one below. An ordinary may debruise (overlie and partly hide) a charge of the field; in such case the charge is mentioned first. By heraldic convention, repetition is avoided: when a tincture recurs in a description, the phrase "of the first" or "of the second" (tincture mentioned) or "of the field" is substituted; to avoid repetition of a number, the phrase "as many" is used. For example: Anglesey, sable, on a cross engrailed between four eagles displayed, argent, five lions passant gardant, of the field; Leith, or, a cross crosslet fitchy, sable, between three crescents in chief (in the upper part of the field), and as many lozenges in base, gules.

DIFFERENCING. From the earliest days of heraldry, only the head of a family had the right to inherit unchanged the entire paternal arms. In the early times junior branches of the family differenced their arms by changing certain tinctures, or by substituting charges, as three mullets for three billets. In modern times younger sons wear the paternal arms with a difference, or mark of cadency. The difference of the eldest son is the label, a narrow bar with pendants, usually three, borne in chief. It covers any other charges, as it is considered a temporary mark, sewed over the shield, rather than charged upon it. The differences of the second and younger sons are, respectively, crescent, mullet, martlet (a bird), annulet, fleur-de-lis, rose, cross moline (a cross with the ends of the arms split and curled back), and octofoil.

MARSHALING OF ARMS. The proper arrangement of arms in an escutcheon is called marshaling of arms. In early heraldry it was the practice to display no more than one coat of arms on an escutcheon. If, however, the wife was an heiress (that is, without brothers and therefore entitled to inherit the paternal arms), the arms of husband and wife were sometimes displayed side by side on separate escutcheons. This practice was followed by dimidiation, in which both shields were parted per pale, and the dexter half of one was joined to the sinister half of the other. Dimidiation was followed, in turn, by impaling, in which both coats were shown entire in the halves of a shield parted per pale.

The blazoning of different coats on a shield divided both horizontally and vertically is called quartering; the first quartering known is that of Castile and León about 1270. The divisions of the shield are called quarters and are numbered horizontally from dexter chief to sinister base. Sovereigns quarter their shields to show dominion, sometimes showing more than twenty coats in a single escutcheon. The commonest reason for quartering, however, is to indicate descent from heiresses who have married into the family. In the case of a single quartering, the paternal arms are shown in the first and fourth quarters; the maternal arms in the second and third. The third and fourth quarters may, after several generations, be occupied by the arms of a second and third heiress. When the coat of the heiress is already quartered, it is placed entire in the appropriate quarter, which is then called a grand quarter. Although the arms of certain European families may show as many as thirty coats marshaled into a single escutcheon, the practice in British heraldry is to select only the most important. H.N.

HERAT, city in Afghanistan, and capital of Herat Province, on the Hari Rud, about 425 miles w. of Kabul. Herat is thought to have been founded in the 3rd century B.C. by Alexander III (q.v.), King of Macedonia, known as Alexander the Great. In the 7th century A.D. the city was captured by the Muslims. The Mongol conqueror Tamerlane (q.v.) made it his capital in 1381. During his reign it became a center of Persian art and learning. The Afghans captured Herat in 1749. Principal architectural features of the city are the old city walls and gates, Islamic tombs, and the Great Mosque. The city is a trading center for the grain, fruit, vegetables, and sheep of the surrounding agricultural area. Pop. (1965 est.) 62,000.

HERB, in botany, term applied to any seed plant that does not develop permanent woody tissue aboveground, but the aboveground parts of which die at the end of each season. The term is applied by pharmacists to any plant or plant part that has medicinal properties. Herb parts that are used as food or seasoning are called culinary herbs or potherbs. Compare SHRUBS; TREE.

HERBARIUM, collection of dried plants, or specimens of plants, which are systematically arranged, usually either geographically or alphabetically. The purpose of an herbarium is to preserve plants which cannot be kept in the fresh state, to serve as a reference collection for botanical comparison and research. Plant specimens are pressed and dried between sheets of smooth, heavy paper by means of adhesive strips. Loose bits of plant material, such as fruits and seeds, are placed in an envelope attached to the herbarium sheet. Each sheet is carefully labeled with the name of the plant and its habitat, the date and place of collection, the name of the collector, and other pertinent data.

HERBART, Johann Friedrich (1776–1841), German philosopher and educator, born in Oldenburg, and educated at the University at Jena. After leaving Jena he tutored for several years in Switzerland, where he became interested in the work of the Swiss educational reformer Johann Heinrich Pestalozzi (q.v.). In 1805 Herbart was appointed professor of philosophy at the University of Göttingen. Herbart went to Königsberg (now Kaliningrad, U.S.S.R.) in 1809 to fill a similar post. In 1833 he returned to Göttingen, where he remained until his death.

Herbart's system of philosophy stems from the analysis of experience. The system includes logic, metaphysics, and aesthetics as coordinate elements. He rejected all concepts of separate mental faculties, postulating instead that all mental phenomena result from interaction of elementary ideas. In applying his philosophy to education, Herbart believed that educational methods and systems should be based on psychology and ethics: psychology to furnish necessary knowledge of the mind, and ethics to be used as a basis for determining the social ends of education. Among Herbart's principal works is *Lehrbuch zur Psychologie* (1816; Eng. trans., *A Textbook in Psychology,* 1894).

HERBERT, name of a prominent family of English noblemen, including the earls of Pembroke and Montgomery, the earls and marquises of Powis, the earls of Carnarvon and the barons

HERBERT

Herbert of Cherbury. Among the more important members of the family are the following.

William Herbert, 3rd Earl of Pembroke (1580–1630), statesman and patron of letters, born in Wilton, and educated at the University of Oxford. He was a prominent figure at the court of James I (q.v.), King of England, and he was chamberlain of the royal household from 1615 to 1625, and lord steward from 1626 until his death. After 1617 Herbert was chancellor of the University of Oxford; Pembroke College was renamed for him in 1624. He invested in the great exploration and trading companies of his day and used a great part of his wealth to support many of the artists of his time, including the English playwrights Ben Jonson and Philip Massinger (qq.v.). Herbert is sometimes identified with the "Mr. W.H." to whom William Shakespeare inscribed his *Sonnets,* and the edition of Shakespeare's plays known as the *First Folio* (1623) is dedicated to Herbert and his brother Philip, 4th Earl of Pembroke and 1st Earl of Montgomery (1584–1650).

Edward Herbert, 1st Baron Herbert of Cherbury (1583–1648), philosopher and diplomat, born in Wales, and educated at the University of Oxford. He was English ambassador to France from 1619 to 1624 and was created Baron Herbert of Cherbury in 1629. His most important philosophical work, *De veritate* (1624; Eng. trans., *Of Truth,* 1937), was the first purely metaphysical treatise to be written by an Englishman. In this work Herbert argues that the universality of man's belief in the existence of God and the necessity of worship and repentance is indicative of an *a priori* truth that has been apprehended by reason. This antiempirical theory of knowledge is one of the earliest formulations of the philosophy of deism (q.v.), and it earned Herbert the appellation "father of English deism". Herbert also wrote a book of poems and an autobiography, which were discovered and published in 1764 by the British writer Horace Walpole (*see under* WALPOLE).

George Herbert (1593–1633), poet and clergyman, brother of Edward, born in Wales, and educated at the University of Cambridge. He was made a fellow of the university in 1616 and served as public orator from 1619 to 1627. He gave up his secular ambitions, however, and took holy orders in the Church of England (q.v.) in 1630. He spent the rest of his life as rector in Bemerton. Herbert is best known for his poetry, which was published posthumously under the title *The Temple: Sacred Poems and Private Ejaculations* (1633). His poems are characterized by a precision of language, a metrical versatility, and an ingenious use of imagery or conceits that was favored by the metaphysical school of English poets such as John Donne (q.v.). Many of Herbert's poems are of a religious nature, often revealing his own spiritual struggles and the solace he found in the priesthood. He also wrote a book of principles for the guidance of rural clergymen, *A Priest to the Temple, or the Country Parson* (1652). Herbert is the subject of a sympathetic biography by the English essayist Izaak Walton (q.v.).

George Edward Stanhope Molyneux Herbert, 5th Earl of Carnarvon (1866–1923), Egyptologist, born near Newbury, and educated at Eton College and the University of Cambridge. He traveled widely as a young man, and in 1903 he went to Egypt for the first time. Four years later, he and the British archaeologist Howard Carter (q.v.) began excavations at the ancient city of Thebes (q.v.). They gave an account of their findings in *Five Years' Exploration at Thebes* (1912). Their work was interrupted by World War I, but they returned to Egypt after the war. On Nov. 4, 1922, while digging in the Valley of the Kings, they discovered the tomb of King Tutankhamen (q.v.) of the XVIII Dynasty. On Feb. 17, 1923, they opened the tomb, which revealed a significant collection of Egyptian art in addition to the mummy of the monarch. Carnarvon died two months later. *See* EGYPTIAN ARCHAEOLOGY: *History.*

HERBERT, Victor (1859–1924), Irish-American cellist, conductor, and composer, born in Dublin. He studied at the Stuttgart Conservatory in Germany, and was a private pupil of German cellist Bernhard Cossmann (1822–1910). After touring France, Italy, and Germany as first cellist with several orchestras, Herbert returned to Stuttgart to study theory and composition. In 1886 he went to New York City and obtained the position of first cellist in the orchestra of the Metropolitan Opera House, where his wife had been engaged to sing German opera. In 1898 he became conductor of the Pittsburgh Symphony Orchestra, but retired from that position in 1904 to devote himself to composition.

Herbert wrote more than forty highly popular operettas, of which some of the best known are *The Fortune Teller* (1898), *Babes in Toyland* (1903), *The Red Mill* (1906), and *Naughty Marietta* (1910). Among the enduringly popular songs from these operettas are "Kiss Me Again", "Gypsy Love Song", "Italian Street Song", and "A Kiss in the Dark". Herbert also composed a cello concerto, a number of orchestral rhapsodies and symphonic poems, and two grand operas, *Natoma* (produced in Philadelphia

HERCULES

Victor Herbert — Library of Congress

1911) and *Madeleine* (produced in New York City, 1914), which did not, however, attain the popularity of his operettas. Herbert helped to organize the American Society of Composers, Authors and Publishers (q.v.) known as ASCAP.

HERBERT HOOVER NATIONAL HISTORIC SITE. See HOOVER, HERBERT CLARK; NATIONAL PARK SERVICE.

HERBLOCK. See BLOCK, HERBERT LAWRENCE.

HERCEGOVINA. See BOSNIA AND HERCEGOVINA.

HERCULANEUM, ruined city of ancient Italy, at the base of the volcano Vesuvius, about 5 miles E. of Naples. According to legend the city was founded by the mythical Greek hero Hercules (q.v.) for whom it is named. Herculaneum was severely damaged in the year 63 by a violent earthquake, and in 79 it was buried, together with the city of Pompeii (q.v.), by lava, ashes, and mud more than 50 ft. thick during an eruption of Vesuvius (q.v.).

The remains of the buried city were first discovered in 1706. Systematic excavations of the ruins began in 1738, and have proceeded intermittently since that time. The excavations have shown that Herculaneum was a popular resort area for wealthy Romans. Many of the richly adorned villas and the theater that have been uncovered have yielded fine marble and bronze sculptures, paintings, and an extensive library of papyrus roles. These treasures, together with many other objects such as vases and domestic implements, are displayed in the National Museum in Naples.

HERCULES, large constellation of the Northern Hemisphere, lying between Lyra and Corona Borealis (qq.v.). Hercules is best seen during the summer. It is represented by the figure of the Greek hero Hercules (q.v.) in a kneeling position. The stars of the constellation are of third magnitude or dimmer. Hercules contains a globular cluster, called Messier 13, of more than 50,000 stars, about 34,000 light years from the earth, which can be seen by the naked eye. The direction of motion of the solar system is toward Hercules.

HERCULES, in Greek mythology, Roman name of the Greek hero Heracles, noted for his strength and courage, and for his many legendary exploits. He was the son of the god Zeus (q.v.) and Alcmena, wife of the Theban general Amphitryon (q.v.). Hera (q.v.), the jealous wife of Zeus, was determined to kill her unfaithful husband's offspring, and shortly after Hercules' birth she sent two great serpents to destroy him. Hercules, although still a baby, strangled the snakes. As a young man Hercules killed a lion with his bare hands. As a trophy of his adventure, he wore the skin of the lion as a cloak and its head as a helmet. The hero next conquered a tribe that had been exacting tribute from Thebes. As a reward, he was given the hand of the Theban princess Megara, by whom he had three children. Hera, still relentless in her hatred of Hercules, sent a fit of madness upon him during which he killed his wife and children. In horror and remorse at his deed Hercules would have slain himself, but he was told by the oracle at Delphi (q.v.) that he should purge himself by becoming the servant of his cousin Eurystheus, King of Mycenae. Eurystheus, urged on by Hera, devised as a penance the twelve difficult tasks, the "Labors of Hercules".

The Twelve Labors. The first task was to kill the lion of Nemea, a beast that could not be wounded by any weapon. Hercules stunned the lion with his club first and then strangled it. He then killed the Hydra that lived in a swamp in Lerna. This monster had nine heads: one head was immortal; when one of the others was chopped off, two grew back in its place. Hercules seared each mortal neck with a burning torch to prevent reproduction of two heads; he buried the immortal head under a rock. He then dipped his arrows into the Hydra's blood to make them poisonous. Hercules' next labor was to capture alive a stag with golden horns and bronze hoofs that was sacred to Artemis (q.v.), goddess of the hunt, and the fourth labor was to capture a great boar that had its lair on Mt. Erymanthus. Hercules then had to clean up in one

"Hercules Slaying the Hydra" (1460), by the 15th-century Florentine artist Antonio Pollaiuolo. Alinari

day the thirty years of accumulated filth left by thousands of cattle in the Augean stables (q.v.). He diverted the streams of two rivers, causing them to flow through the stables. Hercules next drove off a huge flock of man-eating birds with bronze beaks, claws, and wings that lived near Lake Stymphalus. To fulfill the seventh labor Hercules brought to Eurystheus a mad bull that Poseidon (q.v.), god of the sea, had sent to terrorize Crete. To bring back the man-eating mares of Diomedes, King of Thrace, Hercules killed Diomedes, then drove the mares to Mycenae. Hippolyta (q.v.), Queen of the Amazons (q.v.), was willing to help Hercules with his ninth labor. As Hippolyta was about to give Hercules her girdle, which Eurystheus wanted for his daughter, Hera made Hippolyta's forces believe Hercules was trying to abduct the queen. Hercules killed Hippolyta, thinking she was responsible for the ensuing attack, and escaped from the Amazons with the girdle. On his way to the island of Erythia to capture the oxen of the three-headed monster Geryon, Hercules set up two great rocks (the mountains Gibraltar and Ceuta, which now flank the Strait of Gibraltar) as a memorial of his journey. After Hercules had brought back the oxen he was sent to fetch the golden apples of the Hesperides (q.v.). Because Hercules did not know where these apples were, he sought help from Atlas (q.v.), father of the Hesperides. Atlas agreed to help him if Hercules would support the world on his shoulders while Atlas got the apples. The old man did not wish to resume his burden, but Hercules tricked Atlas into taking the world back. The twelfth and most difficult labor of Hercules was to bring back the three-headed dog Cerberus (q.v.) from the lower world. Hades (q.v.), god of the dead, gave Hercules permission to take the beast if he used no weapons. Hercules captured Cerberus, brought him to Mycenae, and then carried him back to Hades.

Death of the Hero. Hercules later married Deianira, whom he won from Antaeus, son of the sea-god Poseidon. When the centaur Nessus attacked Deianira, Hercules wounded him with an arrow that he had poisoned in the blood of the Hydra. The dying centaur told Deianira to take some of his blood, which he said was a powerful love charm, but was really a poison. Believing that Hercules had fallen in love with the princess Iole, Deianira later sent him a tunic dipped in the blood. When he put it on, the pain caused by the poison was so great that he killed himself on a funeral pyre. After death he was brought by the gods to Olympus and married to Hebe (q.v.), goddess of youth.

Hercules was worshiped both as a god and as a mortal hero. He is usually represented as strong and muscular, clad in a lion skin and carrying a club. The most famous statue of Hercules, the Farnese Hercules, is in the Museo Nazionale in Naples, Italy.

HERCULES'-CLUB, common name of several small trees and shrubs that bear branches or fruits having a real or fancied resemblance to clubs. The name is most often applied to members of the genus *Zanihoxylum*, sometimes called prickly ash because of their prickly leafstalks. Southern prickly ash, or the toothache tree, *Z. clava-herculis*, is a small, prickly tree that grows in the southeastern United States and the West Indies. It bears small, white flowers in cymes. The angelica tree, *Aralia spinosa* is also called Hercules'-club.

HERCULES, PILLARS OF. See Pillars of Hercules.

HERDER, Johann Gottfried von (1744–1803), German philosopher and literary critic, born in Mohrungen (now Morag, Poland), and educated at the University of Königsberg (now in Kaliningrad, U.S.S.R.), at which he studied under the German philosopher Immanuel Kant (q.v.). In his first important work, *Fragmente über die Neuere Deutsche Literatur* ("Fragments on Modern German Literature", 1767), Herder advocated the emancipation of German literature from all foreign influences. He soon became the leader of the *Sturm und Drang* literary movement that sought to free German writing from the influence of French classicism; see German Literature: *The Classical and Romantic Period*. Herder developed the idea of a *Volkgeist* or national character, basing his argument on the folk languages and folk customs of various nations, and stressing the differences rather than the similarities between them. His teachings were a source of inspiration to many German writers, especially to the young man who became the leader of the German Romantic school, Johann Wolfgang von Goethe (q.v.).

From 1784 to 1791 Herder published a four-volume study, *Ideen zur Philosophie der Geschichte der Menschheit* (Eng. trans., *Outlines of a Philosophy of the History of Man,* 1800). Although Herder failed to complete his study, the treatise embodies most of his ideas and remains his chief contribution to philosophy. He also published a collection of popular poetry and folk songs, *Stimmen der Völker in Liedern* ("Voices of the People in Songs", 2 vol., 1778–79), and *Vom Geist der Hebräischen Poesie* ("On the Spirit of Hebrew Poetry", 2 vol., 1778–79), in which he puts forth his historical interpretation of the Bible.

HEREDIA, city in Costa Rica, and capital of Heredia Province, on the central plateau, 6 miles N.W. of San José. It is situated on the Pan American Highway and on the Costa Rican Railway. Heredia, the center of an important coffee-growing region, processes coffee, trades in livestock, and manufactures soap and matches. It is the site of a teachers' college and 18th-century churches. Founded in 1571, Heredia is one of the oldest cities in the area, but it has declined in importance with the growth of San José. Pop. (1965 est.) 20,523.

HEREDIA, José María de (1842–1905), French poet, born near Santiago de Cuba, Cuba, and educated in Havana and Paris. Although Spanish by birth, Heredia remained in France after 1861, writing poetry that was greatly influenced by the Parnassians (q.v.), a school of French poets who advocated impersonality and a concentration on form in their works. Heredia published several poems in the 1866 edition of the Parnassian journal, *Le Parnasse Contemporain,* choosing the sonnet as his medium of expression. In 1893, he published *Les Trophées* (Eng. trans., *Trophies,* 1963), a collection of 118 sonnets and a few other poems divided into five groups, four devoted to the history of the world from Hellenistic times to the Renaissance, and the last on nature and the dream. In these poems, Heredia presents dramatic moments with objectivity, avoiding all personal comment and all philosophical implications. His technical brilliance made him the acknowledged master of the French sonnet, and he was elected to the French Academy in 1894. After 1901 he was librarian at the Bibliothèque de l'Arsenal in Paris.

HEREDITY, transmission of physical and mental traits from parents to offspring. Traits that are determined by heredity may be modified by environmental influences during the lifetime of an organism, but these modifications are not passed on to succeeding generations. The scien-

HEREDITY

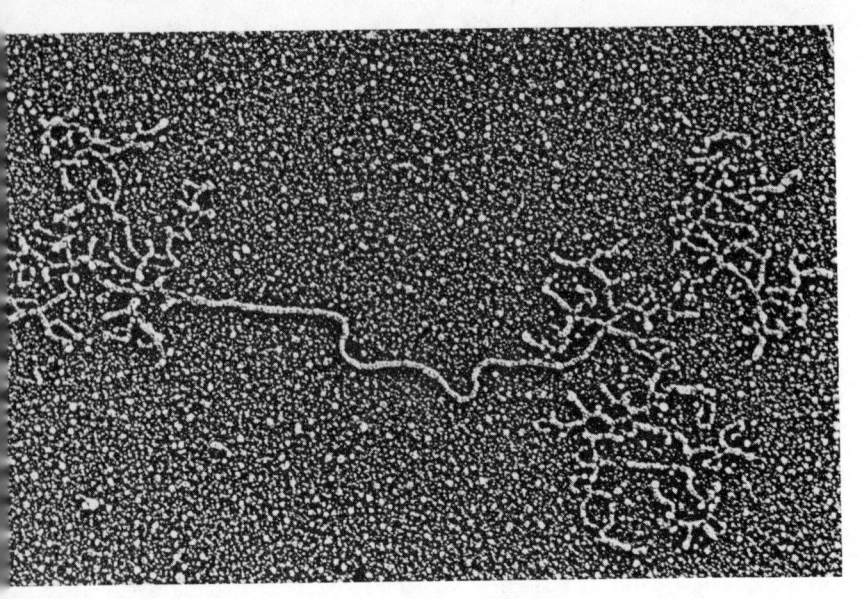

Electron microscope picture of a single gene, magnified 79,300 times. The web-like forms at each end are other sections of genetic material. UPI

tific study of heredity is known as genetics, a name coined by the British biologist William Bateson (q.v.). Animals and plants that reproduce sexually almost always produce offspring that are similar to the parents and to one another in major characteristics, such as number of legs or kind of fruit, but somewhat dissimilar in particular characteristics, such as size of flowers.

Physical Basis of Heredity. All higher organisms are aggregations of small cells which are visible under a high-powered microscope. Every living cell (q.v.) is the result of the division of a preexisting cell. All the cells of a human being, for example, result from successive divisions of a single cell, called the zygote, which was formed at conception by the union of an egg cell with a sperm cell; see FERTILIZATION. The zygote is identical in the structure of its hereditary material with the cells produced by its successive divisions to form the cells of the body. Each cell consists of a layer of material called the cytoplasm surrounding a centrally located body called the nucleus. Each nucleus contains a fixed number of minute, threadlike objects called chromosomes (q.v.). Chromosomes vary in size and shape, but pairs of similar chromosomes are usually present in the normal nucleus. For example, every normal cell in the human body, according to recent evidence, contains twenty-three pairs of chromosomes, whereas every normal fruit-fly cell contains four pairs. Each chromosome contains many small, discrete particles called genes. Each gene is located at a particular place on a particular chromosome and has the potentiality of expressing a hereditary trait in one or more ways.

The process of growth and development by which a single-celled zygote becomes a many-celled adult (see EMBRYOLOGY) is accomplished by a type of cell splitting called mitosis; in mitotic division each chromosome divides into two equal parts. The two parts travel to opposite ends of the cell, and when division is complete, each of the resulting cells has the same number of chromosomes and the same genes as the original cell; see CELL: *Cell Division.*

Higher organisms such as man, which reproduce sexually, are formed from the union of sex cells called gametes (q.v.). Gametes are produced by cells located in organs called gonads (q.v.). The female gonads, called the ovaries (see OVARY), produce gamets called ova or eggs, and the male gonads, or testes, produce gametes called spermatozoa or sperms. Gametes are produced by a special type of division of gonad cells, called meiosis, which differs from mitotic division in one significant respect: in meiosis one chromosome derived from each pair of chromosomes is transmitted to each of the resulting gametes, so gametes contain exactly one half the number of chromosomes found in the other cells of the body. When two gametes unite in fertilization, the resulting cell, the zygote, contains the same number of chromosomes as do the body cells of the parent. For example, ordinary body cells of man contain 46 chromosomes, gametes contain 23 chromosomes, and zygotes contain 46 chromosomes. See also REPRODUCTIVE SYSTEM.

HEREDITY

The union of gametes brings together two sets of genes, one from each parent. When, in herbs, for instance, a gamete from a red-flowered four o'clock, carrying a gene *R*, for red, unites with another gamete carrying *R*, the offspring is *RR* (red). When a gamete from a white-flowered four o'clock, carrying a gene *W*, for white, unites with another gamete carrying *W*, the offspring is *WW* (white). When a gamete from a red-flowered four o'clock unites with a gamete from a white-flowered four o'clock, the offspring will contain both genes, *RW*, producing a pink-flowered plant. The pink-flowered plant cannot produce gametes carrying genes for pink, however, because pink is the result of the interaction of genes *R* and *W*. Genes, such as *R* and *W*, which are located at the same position on paired chromosomes, are called alleles. When an organism has a pair of similar alleles for a given trait, such as a four o'clock having the constitution *RR* or *WW*, it is said to be homozygous for that trait; when it has dissimilar alleles, such as *RW*, it is said to be heterozygous for that trait.

Dominance. In the above example, the effects of *R* and *W* were equal in determining the flower color of four o'clocks. Most pairs of alleles are unequal in effect, so that one of the alleles is expressed whenever it is present, regardless of the presence of the other allele. The allele that is always expressed is called the dominant allele, and the allele that is expressed only when the dominant is absent is called the recessive allele. For convenience, alleles are usually designated by a single letter; the dominant allele is represented by a capital letter and the recessive allele by a small letter. Thus red is *R* and white is *r*. For example, when a purebreeding red-flowered garden pea, *RR*, is crossed with a purebreeding white-flowered garden pea, *rr*, the offspring are all red-flowered, *Rr*. The parental red-flowered plants look exactly like the red-flowered offspring, but do not have the same genetic constitution. The expressed characteristic of the plant (such as red flowers) is called the phenotype and the actual genetic constitution (such as *RR* or *Rr*) is called the genotype. When heterozygous plants, *Rr*, are crossed with one another, the offspring are produced in an approximate ratio of three red plants to one white plant. Half the gametes produced by the heterozygous plant are *R* and the other half are *r*. When these gametes are dispersed at random, they unite according to the laws of chance. The action of the gametes may be expressed mathematically as $(\frac{1}{2}R + \frac{1}{2}r)^2$, which yields offspring in the ratio $\frac{1}{4}RR + \frac{1}{2}Rr + \frac{1}{4}rr$. The *RR* and *Rr* plants, which together constitute three quarters of the offspring, produce red flowers, and the *rr* plants, which constitute one quarter of the offspring, produce white flowers.

Most characteristics of organisms are dependent on the influence of more than one gene, but as long as the genes involved are on different chromosomes, the independent behavior of each gene is exactly the same as in the case of flower color in garden peas; see CHROMOSOME. Thus, when two hypothetical dominant genes, *A* and *B*, are present as heterozygotes, along with their recessive alleles, *a* and *b*, the plant *AaBb* will produce the following gametes: ¼ *AB*, ¼ *Ab*, ¼ *aB*, ¼ *ab*. This proportion of gametes, uniting at random, would give the following offspring: 1/16 *AABB*, 2/16 *AABb*, 1/16 *AAbb*, 2/16 *AaBB*, 4/16 *AaBb*, 2/16 *Aabb*, 1/16 *aaBB*, 2/16 *aaBb*, 1/16 *aabb*. The phenotypes resulting from these genotypes are: 9/16 expressing characters *A* and *B*, 3/16 expressing *A* but not *B*, 3/16 expressing *B* but not *A*, and 1/16 expressing neither *A* nor *B*. This proportion of phenotypes, called the 9:3:3:1 ratio, is common among crosses involving two pairs of genes located on different chromosomes in the same organism.

Linkage. When two genes occur on the same chromosome they are said to be linked, and are expected to behave as a unit as long as the chromosome remains a unit. Thus, when genes *C* and *D* occur on the same chromosome, a pair of chromosomes in a heterozygous organism can be designated (*CD*) (*cd*). Gametes formed by the organism would contain either (*CD*) or (*cd*). In a cross between (*CD*) (*cd*) and (*cd*) (*cd*), with each chromosome behaving as a unit, the expected offspring are: 50 percent (*CD*) (*cd*), showing both dominant characters *C* and *D*, and 50 percent (*cd*) (*cd*), showing neither *C* nor *D*; no *Cdcd* or *cDcd* are formed. Instances of this kind are occasionally found when the two genes are very close to one another on the chromosome. When the genes are farther apart, linkage is not complete, but partial. If linkage is partial, intermediate results would be obtained, such as 45 percent (*CD*) (*cd*), 45 percent (*cd*) (*cd*), 5 percent (*Cd*) (*cd*), and 5 percent (*cD*) (*cd*). Geneticists have found that most genes on a single chromosome are only partially linked, and that the weakness of the linkage is proportional to the distance between the genes. The breaking of such a linkage, called crossing over, is caused by exchange of material between two chromosomes of a pair. The results of this process of chromosome exchange can be seen under a microscope during meiosis. At that stage,

335

HEREDITY

crossing over occurs almost invariably (with a few exceptions, such as during production of fruit-fly spermatozoa); but if two genes are close together, a break is unlikely between them, and linkage might be nearly complete. By statistical analysis of the percentage of crossing over in such crosses the distance between genes may be measured, and the location of genes on chromosomes may be determined in this manner.

Gene Action. The action of genes is seldom a simple relationship in which a single gene controls a single trait. Many genes are known to affect more than one trait. For example, a gene which produces white eyes in the fruit fly, a common laboratory insect (see DROSOPHILA), also produces effects on fertility, color of testes, and shape of sperm sacs. Many characteristics, such as flower color in the sweet pea, require the simultaneous action of several or many genes for expression. Purple-flowered varieties require the action of a dominant gene *P* to produce purple pigment, but no pigment is produced if another dominant gene *C* is not also present. A sweet pea having *C* and *P* will therefore produce purple flowers, but sweet peas having *C* without *P*, *P* without *C*, or neither *C* nor *P* will produce white flowers.

Some genes that affect a single trait when separate will interact to produce a very different trait when they are together. The comb shape of certain domestic poultry, for example, is determined by two pairs of genes. When the dominant gene *R* only (instead of the recessive *r*) is present, a fowl has a low, regular "rose" comb; when the dominant gene *P* only (instead of the recessive *p*) is present, a fowl has a higher, three-ridged "pea" comb; when both *R* and *P* are present, a fowl has a "walnut" comb, which resembles a walnut in shape; and when neither *R* nor *P* is present (but only *r* or *p*, instead), a fowl has a single, erect blade, called a "single" comb.

Several genes, called inhibiting genes, are known to prevent the expression of other genes. White Leghorn poultry, for example, are homozygous for a gene, *C*, for color, but are also homozygous for an inhibiting gene, *I*, which prevents the expression of color; the White Leghorn genotype is *CCII*. White Wyandotte poultry, on the other hand, do not carry this inhibitor, but they also lack the dominant gene *C* for color; the White Wyandotte genotype is *ccii*. Hybrids between White Wyandottes and White Leghorns, having the genotype *CcIi*, are white; the offspring of these heterozygotes, however, are 13/16 white and 3/16 colored. Only the *CCii*

and *Ccii* offspring (which possess *C* but lack *I*) are colored.

Lethal Genes. Genes that cause the death of the organisms which carry them are known as lethals. Approximately one quarter of the offspring resulting from crosses between yellow house mice die in an embryonic stage. The three quarters that survive are produced in a ratio of two yellow to one dark. The result is explained by the fact that yellows that can live are heterozygous for yellow fur color, having the genotype *Yy*. In a mating between two yellows, the offspring expected are ¼*YY* (which die): ½*Yy* : ¼*yy*. *Y* is therefore a dominant gene which is lethal when homozygous; yellow mice that survive are *Yy*, and dark mice are *yy*.

Quantitative Inheritance. Hereditary traits which are expressed as variations in quantity or extent, such as weight, size, or degree of pigmentation, are usually dependent on many genes. In many of these instances, the number of allele-pairs which contain at least one dominant gene determines the extent of expression of the trait. The height of a plant, for example, might be determined by a series of four genes, *A*, *B*, *C*, and *D*, and might average 10 in. in height when the genotype is *aabbccdd*. Each allele pair which contains a dominant might increase the average height by 4 in., and so a plant which was *AABBccdd* would be 18 in. tall, and a plant *AABBCCDD* would be 26 in. tall. Actually the results would seldom be so regular. Dominance is often incomplete in such instances, so that plant *AaBbCcDd* may be shorter than plant *AABBCCDD*. Inheritance of quantitative characteristics that depends on several genes is called multiple-factor inheritance. Many kinds of hybrid plants attain unprecedented weights and sizes in the first hybrid generation, but return to their old characteristics during subsequent generations. The theory of multiple-factor inheritance explains this phenomenon of "hybrid vigor" by supposing that the increase in the first hybrid generation is caused by a combination of dominant alleles that did not exist in either of the parent strains. For example, if the hypothetical plant mentioned above had the genotype *AABBccdd*, it would average 18in. in height. Another strain, *aabbCCDD*, would also average 18 in. in height. Either strain, regardless of the number of generations inbred, would maintain the same average height. When a cross is made between *AABBccdd* and *aabbCCDD*, the hybrid is *AaBbCcDd*, which would average 26 in. in height. In the following generation, however, the possible gametes vary genetically from *ABCD* to *abcd* and all genotypes from

Heredity. Plate 1. Molecular deoxyribonucleic acid (DNA), the master genetic chemical, shown in a photomicrograph by Dr. Roman Vishniac.

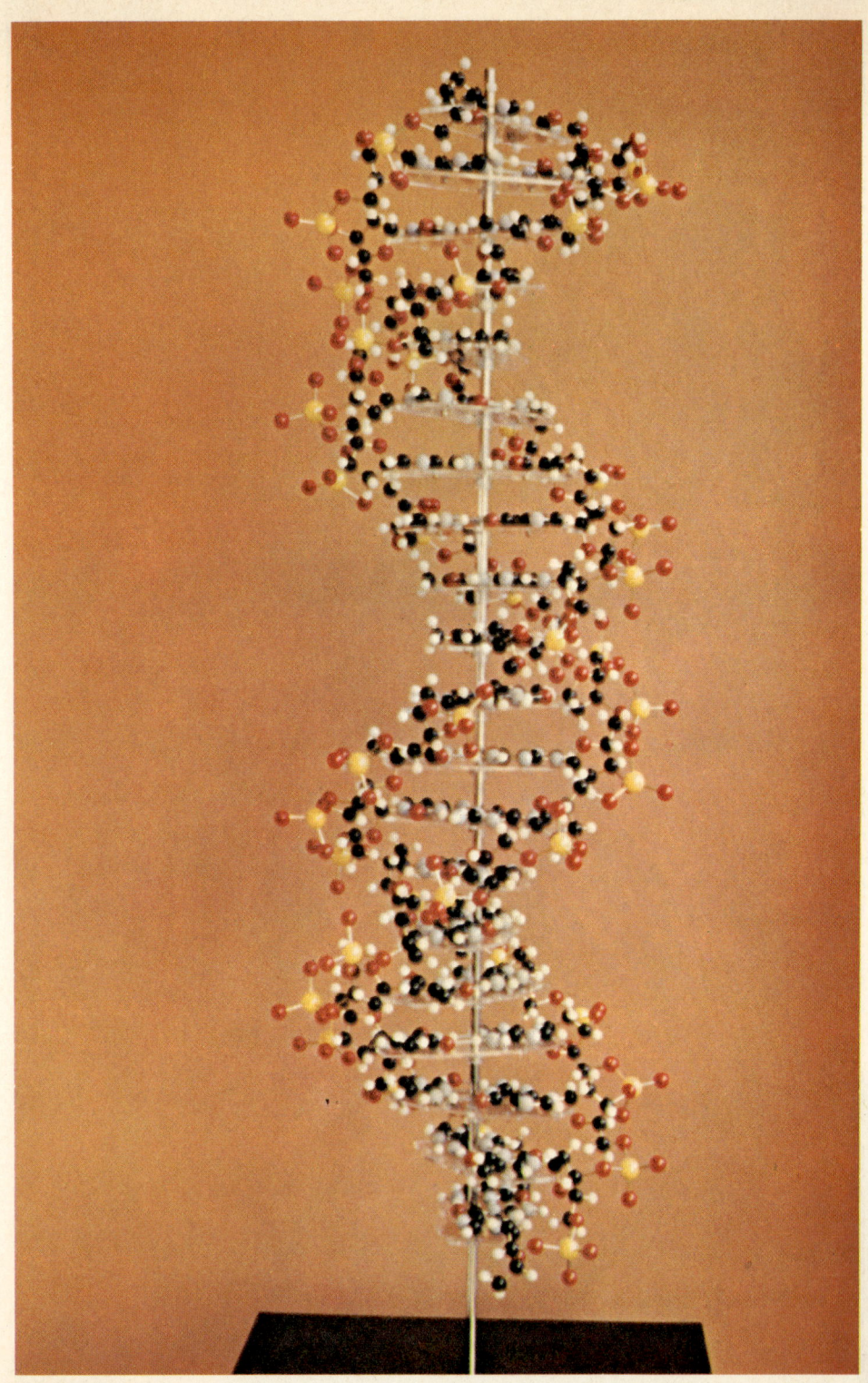

Heredity. Plate 2. *A model of the structure of the DNA molecule, the colored blocks indicating the spatial groupings of the atoms within the molecule. The red blocks represent hydrogen atoms; the blue, oxygen; the black, carbon; the green, nitrogen; and the yellow, sulfur.*

Pfizer Inc.

HEREDITY

AABBCCDD to *aabbccdd* would result. The amount of variation in height would therefore range from 10 to 26 in., but only a minority would exceed 18 in. in height. When multiple-factor traits are bred to a state of complete homozygosity, as in *AABBCCDD,* they will continue to breed true at the high level, if self-fertilized or inbred. Homozygosity cannot be obtained for most traits, however, because several members of a multiple-factor complex will usually be linked genes, which are difficult to obtain in the necessary rearranged form.

Chromosome Action in Heredity. Some genetic variation is controlled by the behavior of chromosomes as discrete units, rather than merely as carriers of genes. Sex, for example, is usually determined by the action of a single pair of chromosomes; gene-controlled abnormalities of the endocrine system may alter the expression of secondary sexual characteristics, but cannot completely reverse sex. Body cells in man contain 46 chromosomes. In the human female, these chromosomes consist of 23 pairs, the members of which are much alike, but in the male there are 22 similar pairs and 1 pair consisting of two chromosomes that are dissimilar in size and structure. The 22 pairs of chromosomes which are alike in both male and female are called autosomes. The remaining pair of chromosomes, in both sexes, are called the sex chromosomes or heterochromosomes. The sex chromosomes in the female are identical in appearance, and are called X chromosome; one of the sex chromosomes in the male is an X chromosome, but the other is shorter and is called the Y chromosome. When gametes are formed, each egg produced by the female, who is XX, contains an X chromosome, but the sperms produced by the male, who is XY, can contain either an X or Y chromosome. Male offspring result from the union of an egg (bearing an X chromosome) with a sperm that bears a Y chromosome. Female offspring result from the union of an egg with a sperm that bears an X chromosome.

Modifications of this mechanism occur in plants and lower animals. Moths, for example, have males with the two sex chromosomes alike (ZZ) and females with the two sex chromosomes different (ZW). Poultry have ZZ males, and females, designated Z-, that lack one sex chromosome.

Sex-Linkage. The human Y chromosome is approximately one third as long as the human X chromosome. As a result, many of the genes on the X are not present on the Y. Hereditary characteristics carried by genes located on the portion of the X that has no corresponding portion on the Y are sex-linked. The disease called hemophilia (q.v.) in humans is caused by a sex-linked recessive gene, *h*. A female with *HH* or *Hh* is normal; a female with *hh* carries hemophilia, but this genotype tends to be lethal. When a male carries *h* on his X chromosome, there is no allele present on the Y to offset it, and so hemophilia is expressed. Such a hemophilic male has the genotype *h-*, as far as gene *h* is concerned; a normal male has the genotype *H-*. When a normal male marries a female who is heterozygous for expression of gene *h*, the offspring of the marriage are *HH* and *Hh* (girls), *H-* (normal boys), and *h-* (hemophilic boys). The characteristic is not expressed in *Hh* girls because of the presence of the dominant normal gene, *H*. *Hh* women are called carriers, because they transmit hemophilia to half their sons. Queen Victoria (q.v.) of England, who was an ancestor of many hemophilic members of European royalty, had the genotype *Hh*. Several other abnormal conditions, such as red-green color blindness, hereditary myopia, night blindness, and ichthyosis (a skin disease), have been identified as sex-linked traits in man.

Chromosome Alterations. Chromosomes occasionally alter in form. A section of a chromosome may become detached from the main body and later reunite with it. When the portion has turned in the opposite direction before uniting, it is called an inversion; when it reunites with the main body at a different position than it previously occupied, it is called a translocation. Occasionally a portion will reunite with the other chromosome of the pair. The chromosome to which it originally belonged is said to have a deficiency, and the chromosome to which it is later attached, and which has the portion in question represented twice, is said to have a duplication. These chromosomal rearrangements often have a visible hereditary effect.

A characteristic in Drosophila, called Bar because bar-shaped eyes are produced instead of normal oval eyes, was originally considered a gene effect by geneticists, but later researchers discovered that the characteristic was caused by a duplication on the chromosome that carries the characteristic. Another characteristic in Drosophila, called Notch-wing, is caused by a deficiency on the X chromosome. When a female having one normal and one deficient X chromosome is crossed with a male having normal X and Y chromosomes, those of the male offspring that inherit the deficient X chromosome from the female parent die.

HEREDITY

Mutation. The transmission of existing hereditary traits usually follows the definite patterns described above, but the evolutionary history of every organism indicates that new traits that cannot be explained by these rules occasionally arise. Biologists have assigned the term mutation to changes in genetic structure which produce new characteristics. The term is generally used to include both gene changes and changes in chromosome structure and number.

Gene mutations are changes, probably chemical, that alter the expression of characteristics by genes. Mutations that occur naturally are called spontaneous mutations. Gene mutations can be induced artificially by use of X rays and other forms of radiation, sudden temperature shocks, and certain chemicals, notably mustard gas.

Most genes have been found, by statistical surveys of large populations, to be quite stable; rates of mutation are very low. The rate of mutation from *H* to *h* in human hemophilia, for example, is about 1 mutation per 100,000 germ cells. The rate of mutation in several Drosophila genes is of a similar magnitude, ranging from 1 per 50,000 to 1 per several hundred thousand germ cells. Mutation is not ordinarily the loss of a gene, but a change in its structure, as a gene which has mutated can usually mutate back to its original form. A single gene may mutate in several ways; the resultant alleles created by these mutations are called multiple alleles. For example, a gene that takes part normally in the production of red eyes in Drosophila can mutate to produce white eyes or any of at least eighteen other color variations. Mutability of genes may be influenced by the presence of other genes that affect the spontaneous-mutation rate. The mechanisms that cause such modifications of mutability are not known.

The majority of gene mutations are harmful to the organisms which carry them. They are, however, usually recessive and so are not expressed as visible characteristics unless two recessive genes are brought together in a mating to produce homozygous recessive offspring. This result is most likely to occur in inbreeding, the mating of closely related organisms which may have inherited the same recessive gene from a common ancestor. Mutations rarely occur simultaneously in more than one gene of an organism; this fact indicates that even when genes are caused to mutate by the effects of change in environmental conditions, the change does not affect all genes equally. Even two members of the same gene pair usually mutate independently; if a mutation of *R* to *r* occurs in a cell of genetic constitution *RR*, the resulting cell is usually *Rr*. It is apparent from these facts that gene mutation can never produce new species within a short period of time; a large complex of useful gene mutations must be accumulated over a long period of time under the influence of the environmental conditions that occasioned their multiplication in order to produce a species of organism distinct from the original one.

Spontaneous changes in chromosomes, called chromosome mutations, include (1) changes that take place within chromosomes, such as

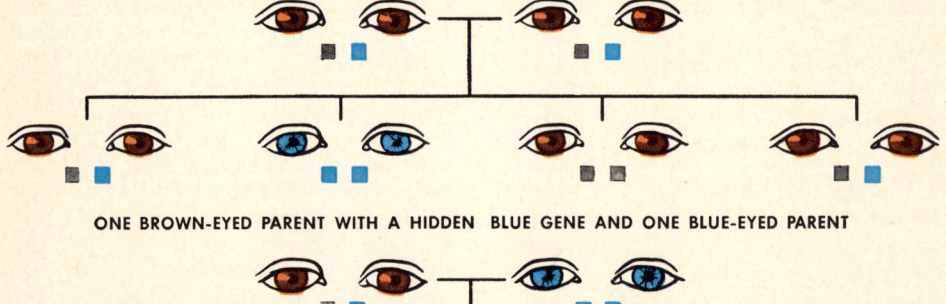

Eye color is a hereditary factor controlled by genes. Brown eye genes are dominant, blue eye genes are recessive. The chart indicates the percentage of offspring having brown eyes when one or both parents have brown eye genes. TODAY'S HEALTH, published by the AMERICAN MEDICAL ASSOCIATION

deficiencies, duplications, inversions, and translocations; and (2) changes in the number of chromosomes. The normal number of chromosomes in nongametic cells of higher plants and animals is called the diploid or 2n number. Gametes, having half this number of chromosomes, are said to be haploid or 1n. When a 2n gamete-producing cell in plants fails to divide in the usual manner to produce 1n gametes, it may produce 2n gametes. When 2n gametes unite, a 4n (tetraploid) zygote is produced, but when a 2n gamete unites with a normal (1n) gamete, a 3n (triploid) zygote is produced. Continued doubling of chromosomes results only in plants that are even multiples, such as 6n (hexaploid), and 8n (octoploid). Hybridization between successive levels results in odd multiples, for example, 4n × 6n = 5n (pentaploid). All organisms having chromosome numbers higher than 2n are called polyploid, and the process which produces them is called polyploidy. Polyploidy is the only known process under which new species arise in a single generation. It is largely confined to hermaphroditic organisms, such as most flowering plants and a few invertebrate animals. The principles of polyploidy are useful in the artificial evolution of new species by plant breeders; natural evolution of new species of flowering plants has been caused in some measure by polyploidy. Existing species of wheat, for example, have 14, 28, or 42 chromosomes; the 14-chromosome species are diploid, the 28-chromosome species are tetraploid, and the 42-chromosome species are hexaploid. Similarly, the violet genus includes species which have 12, 18, 24, 30, 36, 42, 48, 54, or 96 chromosomes. Plant polyploids are characteristically larger, thicker, and more sturdy in form than their diploid ancestors.

Human Heredity. The inheritance of physical characteristics in man is one of the most important, but least developed, aspects of genetics. Investigators of human heredity have no opportunity to direct the sequence of matings from generation to generation, so information on human pedigrees is obtained from relatively unsatisfactory observation of small family groups. Furthermore, the length of a human generation is between twenty and forty years, contrasted with two weeks, the approximate length of a *Drosophila* generation. Most human characteristics are transmitted by multiple-factor inheritance; identification of separate genes is almost impossible without performing breeding experiments. Despite these barriers to scientific investigation, the modes of transmission of several known traits have been determined.

The inheritance of blood groups has been investigated extensively. A,B,O blood groups are determined by a set of three main alleles, only two of which are present in any one human being. The A,B,O series has four major blood groups: O, A, B, and AB. The genotypes that correspond to these blood groups are:

Blood Group	Genotypes
O	oo
A	AA or Ao
B	BB or Bo
AB	AB

Gene *o* is recessive to genes *A* and *B*, but genes *A* and *B* are equally dominant, and so the genotype *AB* expresses both genes equally. Knowledge of inheritance of blood groups has become useful as a possible means of exonerating men who are accused of fathering illegitimate children. The following table indicates the method of exclusion:

If the baby is	and the mother is	the father cannot be
O	O, A, or B	AB
AB	A	A or O
AB	B	B or O
AB	AB	O
A	B or O	B or O
B	A or O	A or O

The inheritance of several other series of alleles, affecting the composition of proteins in the blood and causing differences in the population, has been definitely established. See BLOOD: *Blood Types*.

A few other human characteristics, such as red hair, are controlled by recessive genes, but most genetically identified traits are rather rare abnormalities. Red-green color blindness and myopia are controlled by sex-linked recessive genes similar to the gene that causes hemophilia (q.v.). Migraine, certain types of hereditary deafness, albinism, and certain types of feeble-mindedness and anemia are caused by recessive genes.

Cytological Inheritance. Not all hereditary characteristics are determined by the particular genes in the chromosomes or even by the larger characteristics of the chromosomes an individual possesses. Certain snails, such as *Limnaea peregra,* show a peculiar type of delayed inheritance. *Limnaea* shells may coil to right or left, depending on given genes, but it is the genes of the mother, not those of the offspring itself, which determine the direction of coiling. The variegated (white-spotted) leaves of several plants, such as *Pelargonium,* are determined by hereditary factors that are carried not in the chromosome, but in the cytoplasm of leaf cells. In these plants the inheritance of leaf color de-

HEREDITY

pends on reproduction of small cytoplasmic plastids. When a plastid in a young leaf cell mutates from green to colorless, all the plastids which are formed from successive divisions of the original plastid may remain colorless. Large areas of leaves occupied by such colorless plastids are white. In recent years evidence has been accumulating that the cytoplasm of many lower organisms contains plasmogenes, self-reproducing units occurring outside the chromosome.

History. Early theories of heredity were based on pure speculation. The ancient Greek philosopher Aristotle (q.v.) and the preformationists of the 17th century, for example, thought that the gamete produced by one of the parents contained a miniature offspring, similar to the parent in all respects except size. The theory of preformation collapsed when the cellular nature of organisms and of gametes was established by observation; see CELL. Scientists realized that gametes do not contain small replicas of the characteristics they transmit, but merely act as agents for the transmission of substances that determine these characteristics. Speculation on the mechanism of hereditary transmission continued during the 18th and 19th centuries, mostly without the support of experimental evidence. The French naturalist Jean Baptiste de Lamarck (q.v.) proposed that changes caused in an organism by environmental influences are passed on to the offspring; see LAMARCKISM. The British naturalist Charles Robert Darwin (see under DARWIN) felt that heredity is partially determined by environmental influences. Although he did not insist that environment was the sole determining factor, he suggested, in his theory of pangenesis, that each cell of the body continually emits minute particles, called gemmules, that travel throughout the body and finally reach the gonads, where they enter the gametes. According to this theory, all parts of the body contribute influences that are transmitted to succeeding generations. Pangenesis is essentially similar to Lamarckism, and both theories are easily discredited; humans who have lost a leg, for example, do not produce offspring who lack a leg. The last of the major speculative theories of heredity was proposed by the German zoologist, August Weismann (q.v.), in 1892. He believed that changes in the germ plasm caused by external influences are transmitted from one generation to the next, but that changes imposed on the body by external influences rarely affect the germ plasm. Weismann assumed that the primary constituents in germ plasm were minute particles, similar to the present-day conception of genes, which he called "biophores".

Modern study of genetics began in 1900, when several plant breeders independently discovered a technical paper written by an Austrian monk, Gregor Johann Mendel (q.v.). The paper, published in 1866, described a lengthy series of experiments with garden peas that Mendel had completed in 1865. Mendel discovered that hereditary characteristics behave as if they were determined by particles which are present in pairs in ordinary body cells, but present singly in gametes. He stated that such pairs segregate in the production of the gametes and rejoin at random in fertilization; see MENDEL'S LAW. The results obtained by Mendel were substantiated through repetition of his experiments by many biologists. During the early years of the 20th century, geneticists found that Mendel's law can be applied to hereditary transmission in practically all plants and animals. Following these discoveries, the American geneticist Thomas Hunt Morgan (q.v.) and his coworkers, working with Drosophila, discovered that sex-linked traits are carried on X chromosomes, that genes are arranged in linear order on all chromosomes, and that genes on a single chromosome behave as a single unit. By performance of literally thousands of linkage experiments involving millions of flies, geneticists have prepared accurate "maps" of the location of about 1000 genes on the four chromosomes of this insect. Drosophila has become the most popular subject for hereditary experimentation because it has a short breeding cycle, has only four chromosome pairs, is easy to breed, and has exceptionally large chromosomes in its salivary glands.

During the period when Mendel's results were being substantiated, a Dutch botanist, Hugo Marie De Vries (q.v.), proposed that spontaneous changes in genotype observed in evening primroses were due to gene changes that he named mutations. Later geneticists found that variations in evening primrose were actually due to chromosomal behavior, but the principles of De Vries' theory stimulated experimentation to determine the cause of other mutations. Morgan and his coworkers were responsible for discovering a large number of naturally occurring mutations in Drosophila, and knowledge of the nature of mutation has been broadened further by the work of the American geneticist Hermann Joseph Muller (q.v.) on artificially induced mutations in the same insect.

Beginning in the late 1930's great strides were made in the development of hybrid plants.

HEREDITY

Many hybrid plants that have desirable traits are sterile, because of the inability of the gamete-producing organs to bring forth functional gametes. This inability results from the dissimilarity between the chromosomes contributed by the two strains used to produce the hybrid. When chromosomes are doubled to form a tetraploid, however, two sets of chromosomes from each parental strain are available as partners for the chromosome-pairing process of meiosis. The provision of suitable partners makes possible the formation of functional gametes having one set of chromosomes from each strain. Geneticists have found that tetraploidy can be induced by means of such chemical compounds as colchicine (q.v.) and podophyllin (see MAY-APPLE). Agriculturists and horticulturists soon developed many fertile hybrid plants by using these compounds. Temperature shocks, which have been found to produce doubling of chromosome number, may account for spontaneous chromosome doubling under natural conditions of extreme heat or cold.

In the field of pure genetical research, much basic information has been accumulated through use of sac fungi, such as *Neurospora* and *Penicillium*, as experimental plants. Sac fungi grow rapidly and have a high mutation rate. The mutants, many of which have abnormal metabolism, can be isolated easily in culture media similar to those used for bacteria. The mutations apparently block the ability of the organisms to produce individual enzymes necessary for normal metabolism. With a given enzyme altered or absent, the mutant, called a "nutritional deficient", is unable to synthesize a particular substance necessary to its life, and so requires the presence of this substance in its food supply; the normal organism thrives without the same substance. Led mainly by the American biologist George Wells Beadle (q.v.), the study of chemical processes in nutritional deficients as compared with normal fungi has thrown much light on the manner in which constituents of protoplasm are synthesized.

The years following World War II brought remarkable findings in the genetics of bacteria and viruses. It has now been demonstrated that some bacteria, and even some of the viruses, called bacteriophages, which infest bacteria, undergo a process of union akin to sexual reproduction. The mechanism of hereditary transmission was found to parallel that in higher organisms. Spontaneous mutants arise in random fashion, as in higher forms, and not as adaptations to conditions in the culture medium. Nutritionally deficient mutants have been produced in the bacteria by irradiation and chemical treatment. Methods have been developed for garnering mutant bacteria that lack the ability to synthesize one particular substance or another. The techniques involve inducing mutations of all kinds in the biological material and then transferring it to a culture medium lacking the particular substance for which a deficiency mutant is desired. At the same time penicillin, which kills only growing organisms, is added to the medium. Unable to grow in the deficient medium, the mutants of the desired type survive the normal organisms and other mutants, all of which are destroyed by the penicillin. Thus, specific mutants can be isolated and are then transferred to a medium in which they can thrive.

Considerable progress has been made in the study of the chemical nature of chromosomes and genes. Evidence indicates that nucleic acids (q.v.) are the fundamental hereditary substances of cells. Nucleic acids are found in the cell nucleus. In experiments with bacteria and bacterial viruses, deoxyribonucleic acid (DNA), a major constituent of chromosomes, has been identified as genetic material. When DNA was extracted from one strain of bacteria, it was found to transmit its hereditary characteristics to a related strain treated with the extract. Furthermore, the transformed bacteria passed on the newly acquired traits to the next generations. In similar research with plant viruses, ribonucleic acid (RNA), which is found chiefly in the cytoplasm of cells, was demonstrated to be capable of performing a genetic function. Both DNA and RNA have now been synthesized in the laboratory and recently a complete yeast gene consisting of 77 nucleotides was synthesized by Nobel Prize winning geneticist Dr. H. Gobind Khorana (q.v.).

As a result of these investigations, the concept of the gene has changed considerably. Although still defined as the unit of heredity, it is no longer pictured as a discrete, independent particle of chromosome structure. Geneticists had calculated that the gene was probably not larger than 1/20th micron (1 micron = 1/1000 of a millimeter), too small to be seen even with a high-powered optical microscope, but within the range of the electron microscope. The rope-like strands of the chromosome can be greatly magnified in electron-microscope photographs. In such photographs, the individual strands appear to comprise numerous fibrils, each with a diameter much smaller than that ascribed to genes. *See also* EUGENICS; EVOLUTION; NATURAL SELECTION; PLANT BREEDING.   S.C.

HEREFORD CATTLE, breed of beef cattle, originating in Herefordshire in southwestern England. The Hereford strain has proved especially successful in the United States since its introduction into Kentucky in 1817. Herefords are not the most common nor the most profitable breed on the western ranges. Herefords are red with white faces and markings; they have short legs, straight backs, great strength and thickness of loin, and heavy layers of flesh. Polled Herefords are a hornless breed developed in 1901 by selective breeding. *See also* CATTLE.

HEREFORDSHIRE, or HEREFORD, Great Britain, county of s.w. England, drained by the Wye, the Frome, and the Teme rivers. The Black Mts. are in the s.w. part of the county, and an undulating lowland plain lies between the Welsh Uplands and the Malvern Hills on the E. Industries other than agriculture are insignificant; more than four fifths of the area is devoted to pastureland, orchards, and fields of hops. The county is noted for its livestock; the famous breed of Hereford cattle (q.v.) was developed here. Herefordshire was the site of border warfare between the English and the Welsh during the Middle Ages. Numerous fortifications built during that period have been preserved; the most famous, known as Offa's Dyke, was built in the 8th century. Area, 842 sq.mi.; pop. (1969 est.) 142,060.

HERESY, any religious doctrine opposed to the dogma of a particular church, especially a doctrine held by a person professing faith in the teachings of that church. The term originally meant a belief that one arrived at by oneself (Gr. *hairesis,* "choosing for oneself"), and is used to denote sectarianism in the Acts of the Apostles and in the Epistles of Saint Paul (q.v.). In later Christian writings, the term is used in the opprobrious sense of a belief held in opposition to the teaching of the Church.

With the establishment of Christianity in the Roman Empire, heresy came to be considered a crime against the state, punishable by civil law. Heresy was also generally outlawed in countries with an established or state-supported church until the time of the Reformation (q.v.), when the Protestant principles of private interpretation of the Scriptures and denial of ecclesiastical authority in all matters of belief were adopted.

See separate articles on important heresies and heresiarchs, such as ALBIGENSES; ARIUS; GNOSTICISM; ICONOCLASM; MONARCHIANISM; MONOPHYSITES; MONOTHELITES; WALDENSES.

HERKIMER, Nicholas (1728–77), American Revolutionary general, born in a German settlement near Herkimer, N.Y. After serving in the French and Indian War (q.v.) he was appointed a brigadier general in the New York militia. In August, 1777, he led his troops to the relief of Fort Stanwix, which was under attack by British troops under the command of the British officer Barry St. Leger (1737–89). His company was ambushed at Oriskany, N.Y., and during the ensuing battle, which was one of the bloodiest of the war (*see* ORISKANY, BATTLE OF), Herkimer was mortally wounded. The county and the village of Herkimer, N.Y. were named in his honor.

HERMAPHRODITISM, in biology, presence in one individual, plant or animal, of both male and female gonads or organs of sex cell production; *see* REPRODUCTION. The term is derived from the legend of Hermaphroditus (q.v.).

Hermaphroditism occurs in the great majority of flowering plants: monoclinous plants have hermaphrodite or perfect flowers (q.v.), each of which has both male and female elements (stamens and carpels), and monoecious plants have flowers containing only male elements and others containing only female elements, both occurring on the same plant. Only a few flowering plants are dioecious, that is, carrying male and female organs on different plants. Most hermaphroditic plants produce male and female elements at different times to ensure cross-pollination; however, a few, such as the violet and the evening primrose, are habitually self-pollinated; *see* POLLINATION.

Hermaphroditism habitually occurs in many invertebrate animals, in the hagfish and tunicate, and in the sea bass of the genus *Serranus*. It occurs occasionally in other fishes, in frogs, toads, and certain newts among the amphibians, but rarely in higher forms of animal life. Hermaphrodite animals are rarely self-fertilizing; in most cases the spermatozoa and ova mature at different times (successive hermaphroditism) or the male and female external organs are located so that self-fertilization is impossible. Among the invertebrates, sponges, coelenterates, some mollusks, and earthworms are regularly hermaphroditic. Flatworms have a complete set of male and female gonads in each segment and regularly fertilize themselves.

The females of many species of both plants and animals regularly or occasionally reproduce independently of males; this phenomenon, called parthenogenesis, is, however, entirely different in nature from hermaphroditism.

True functional hermaphroditism is rare or absent in higher animals. One occasionally sees animals called hermaphrodites that appear intermediate in form between males and females, but such animals are usually sterile, and, when fertile, probably never produce both fertile eggs and fertile sperm. Such organisms are often called intersexes or sex-intergrades; intersexes in the fruit fly have been shown to arise from inheritance of an abnormal ratio of maleness (autosomes) to femaleness (X chromosomes); see HEREDITY. Cases of intersexual individuals, called pseudohermaphrodites, have been observed in human medical practice; they may be produced by inherited factors, but often show functional disturbance of the endocrine glands, especially of the pituitary or adrenal glands, and do not possess two sets of functioning sex organs. Because of the complete homology between male and female sex organs, it may be difficult to tell whether a human hermaphrodite is a female with overdeveloped clitoris or a male with underdeveloped penis, cleft scrotum, and nondescendant testes. Recently, many human beings have undergone surgical or hormone treatment to modify their nonfunctioning sex characteristics and emphasize the sex indicated by those that are functional.

HERMAPHRODITUS, in Greek mythology, a youth who was transformed by the gods into a being half male and half female, after a nymph, whose love he rejected, prayed to be forever united with him.

HERMES, in Greek mythology, messenger of the gods, the son of the god Zeus (q.v.) and of Maia, the daughter of the Titan Atlas (q.v.). As the special servant and courier of Zeus, Hermes had winged sandals and a winged hat, and bore a golden Caduceus, or magic wand, entwined with snakes and surmounted by wings. He conducted the souls of the dead to the underworld, and was believed to possess magical powers over sleep and dreams. Hermes was also the god of commerce, and the protector of traders and herds. As the deity of athletes he protected gymnasiums and stadiums, and was believed to be responsible for both good luck and wealth. Despite his virtuous characteristics, Hermes was also a dangerous foe, a trickster, and a thief. On the day of his birth he stole the cattle of his brother, the sun-god Apollo (q.v.), obscuring their trail by making the herd walk backward. When confronted by Apollo, Hermes denied the theft. The brothers were finally reconciled when Hermes gave Apollo his newly invented lyre. Hermes was represented in early Greek art as a mature, bearded man; in classical art he became an athletic youth, nude and beardless.

HERMIONE, in Greek mythology, daughter of Helen of Troy and Menelaus (qq.v.), King of Sparta. Although she was betrothed to Orestes (q.v.), King of Mycenae, after the Trojan War (q.v.) Hermione married Neoptolemus (q.v.), the son of the Greek hero Achilles (q.v.). Orestes later killed Neoptolemus and became Hermione's second husband.

HERMIT CRAB *or* **ROBBER CRAB,** common name for any of the marine decapod crabs in the family Paguridae and for several terrestrial crabs in the family Parapaguridae. They are found on, or just off, the coasts of Europe and the Americas. Hermit crabs are armorless animals, the largest of which are found along the Pacific coast and attain a length of from about 12 to 18 in. They insert their abdomens into gastropod mollusk shells that they carry about with them for protection. The abdomens of the crabs are soft and asymmetrical, flexed and twisted to fit into the whorls of the borrowed shells. Their abdominal appendages are especially modified for keeping the shell firmly supported on the body.

Hermit crabs are often forced to seek new shells because they have outgrown their old ones; they change their housing whenever chancing upon another shell into which they can fit. Most hermit crabs are marine. The few terrestrial forms are tropical and belong to the same family as the coconut crab (q.v.). The

Hermes, a Roman copy of a Greek sculpture of the 4th century B.C.

HERMIT THRUSH

common American species of hermit crab is *Pagurus longicarpus*.

HERMIT THRUSH, common name for a small North American thrush, *Hylocichla guttata*, usually found in evergreen forests. The hermit thrush lives in Canada and the northern United States during the summer and spends the winter in the southern States. It is about 7 in. long, brown above and white below, with the breast and throat spotted with black. The hermit thrush characteristically cocks its chestnut red tail and droops it slowly when alarmed. The bird is noted for its beautiful, flutelike song.

HERMON, MOUNT (Ar. *Jebel esh Sheikh*, "mountain of the chief" or *Jebel eth Thelj*, "snowy mountain"), mountain of the Jebel esh Sharqi (Anti-Lebanon) range, in southern Syria, near the Syrian-Lebanese border. The highest of its three summits reaches a height of 9232 ft. above sea level. The mountain is noted for its majestic beauty and has been the inspiration for much imagery in Hebrew poetry. Remains of ancient temples, one probably dedicated to the Semitic deity Baal (q.v.) and several bearing Greek inscriptions, are located on its slopes. Mount Hermon is believed to have been the site of the Transfiguration of Christ. See TRANSFIGURATION, FEAST OF THE.

HERMONTHIS. See EL KARNAK.

HERMOSILLO, city in Mexico, capital of Sonora State, on the Sonora R., at the mouth of the San Miguel R., 170 miles S. of Nogales and about 1000 miles N.W. of Mexico City. Situated on the Pacific Highway and the west-coast railroad, Hermosillo is the trade center of an agricultural area that produces a great variety of tropical fruits, as well as cotton, wheat, sugarcane, corn, and beans.

The mining area located to the E. produces gold, silver, copper, and molybdenum. Industries in the city include metal casting, food processing, and the manufacture of cement, shoes, beer, and handicrafts. Hermosillo is the site of the state museum and the University of Sonora. The city is connected by road with the fishing resort of Bahía Kino, 65 miles to the W. on the Gulf of California. Hermosillo is on the site of an Indian settlement called Pitic; the modern city was founded in the middle of the 18th century. During the War of the Reform and conflicts with the French in the mid-19th century, several skirmishes took place in Hermosillo. Pop. (1969 est.) 196,500.

HERNE, town of West Germany, in North Rine-Westphalia State, about 40 miles N.E. of Cologne. Herne is the industrial center of the Ruhr coal district, and the main port on the Rhine-Herne and Dortmund-Ems canals. Coal mining in the vicinity was begun in 1856. Pop. (1968 est.) 101,955.

HERNIA, *or* RUPTURE, the protrusion of an organ or part of an organ or other structure through the wall of the cavity that normally contains it. Hernias are qualified by the name of the part that protrudes or the area through which protrusion occurs. Thus, an inguinal hernia, perhaps the most common form, is one that passes through the abdominal wall in the groin area. A diaphragmatic or hiatus hernia is one in which part of the stomach or a loop of the intestine herniates upward through an opening in the diaphragm into the chest cavity. An umbilical hernia is one in which the bowel or the membranous apron overlying it, known as the omentum, protrudes through the abdominal wall under the skin at the navel. Many hernias are caused by a congenital weakness of the sustaining tissue or incomplete closure of passages that should have closed during fetal life, but have remained open. Other hernias may be caused by accidents or by the weakening of a normally solid area by an incision; the most common example of this is a hernia that develops in an abdominal scar following surgery. Such hernias are often called incisional or ventral hernias.

Hernias often develop in an area of weakness following an unusual stress or strain. Frequently, an inguinal hernia may be observed in a man who has recently lifted a heavy object or experienced a severe bout of coughing. Inguinal hernias are more likely to occur in men than in women because the spermatic cord passes through the abdominal wall in the inguinal region, leaving a site of natural weakness prone to hernia formation.

The symptoms of a hernia vary considerably. Such a visible external hernia as the inguinal type usually causes no distress; hernias that

Hermit thrush, Hylocichla guttata
American Museum of Natural History

occur within the abdominal cavity sometimes cause intense pain. Generally, hernias will reduce or slide back, either spontaneously or when mild pressure is exerted upon them. These are said to be reducible hernias. Occasionally, hernias are trapped and cannot slide back, in which case they often become painful; these are said to be irreducible or incarcerated. Unless reduced by surgery, an incarcerated hernia may become strangulated, in which case the blood supply to the organ trapped within the hernia is interrupted, and the tissue in the hernial sac rapidly becomes gangrenous. When a hernia is easily reducible, it is sometimes treated by external support in the form of a truss, which keeps it in place.

In children, an important site of hernia is through the incompletely closed fontanels of the skull (q.v.). The membranes enclosing the brain may protrude through the fontanel and, in severe cases, some of the brain substance may be contained in the hernial sac. Such a condition is known as meningocele, and is very serious. Meningoceles may also form along the spinal column. Various other organs of the body may also herniate, producing such conditions as cystocele, hernia of the bladder, and gastrocele, hernia of the stomach.

HERO, in Greek mythology, priestess of Aphrodite (q.v.), goddess of love, at Sestos, a town on the Hellespont (now Dardanelles). Hero was loved by Leander, a youth who lived at Abydos, a town on the Asian side of the channel. They could not marry because Hero was bound by a vow of chastity, and so every night Leander swam from Asia to Europe, guided by a lamp in Hero's tower. One stormy night a high wind extinguished the beacon and Leander was drowned. His body was washed ashore beneath Hero's tower, and in her grief, she threw herself into the sea.

HEROD, name of a dynasty, rulers of Roman Palestine in the last century B.C. and the 1st century A.D. The most important members of the dynasty are the following.

Herod the Great (73?–4 B.C.), King of Judea (37–4 B.C.), the second son of Antipater, Procurator of Judea (d. 43 B.C.). Antipater's death marked the beginning of a period of intrigue and warfare. Herod's Roman-backed rule in Judea was contested by Antigonus II (*see under* ANTIGONUS), last scion of the Hasmonaean dynasty (*see* MACCABEES), who was supported by the Parthians (*see* PARTHIA). When the Parthians invaded Palestine and Antigonus ascended the throne, Herod escaped to Rome. There, in 39 B.C., he was proclaimed king of Judea by the Roman senate. Not until 37 B.C., however, did Herod succeed in putting down the forces opposed to him. With Roman aid he broke the Hasmonaean power and had Antigonus executed. He then sought to consolidate his position with the Jews by marrying a princess of the Hasmonaean line, who became his second wife, Mariamne (d. 29 B.C.).

The first years of Herod's reign were troubled by hostility between two Jewish sects, the Sadducees and Pharisees (qq.v.), and by the enmity of surviving members of the Hasmonaean house, who secured a friend in Cleopatra, Queen of Egypt (*see under* CLEOPATRA). Herod ultimately prevailed against his adversaries mainly because of the defeat of Cleopatra and Marcus Antonius (q.v.) at the hands of the Roman statesman Gaius Octavius, later the Emperor Augustus (q.v.). Despite the fact that Herod had supported Marcus Antonius in his power struggle with Octavius, the latter was convinced that Herod would continue to rule according to the dictates of Rome; Octavius consequently confirmed Herod as king of Judea in 31 B.C. Thereafter Herod's political enemies were suppressed.

The years from 25 B.C. to 13 B.C. were for the most part prosperous. During this period Herod devoted himself to a great number of architectural projects, including the construction at Jerusalem, Jericho, and Caesarea of theaters, amphitheaters, and hippodromes for the Grecian games inaugurated in honor of Augustus. To protect the Judean frontier against Arab incursions, he built or rehabilitated a chain of fortresses, which were later to prove of great value to the Jews in their insurrection against Rome. He began the rebuilding of the Temple (*see* TEMPLE: *Temple at Jerusalem*) with close regard for the religious scruples of the people. The final years of Herod's reign were embittered by the ceaseless and complicated political intrigues within his palace. During this period Jesus Christ (q.v.) was born. On his last visit to Rome Herod obtained imperial consent to dispose of his kingdom as he saw fit. A few hours before Herod died he made a will, in which he gave Judea, including Samaria and Idumaea, to his son Herod Archelaus (d. before 18 A.D.), with the title of king; Galilee and Perea to another son, Herod Antipas (see below), with the title of tetrarch; and Gaulanitis, Auranitis, Trachonitis, Batanea, and Panias to a third son, Herod Philip (d. 34 A.D.). This will was confirmed by Emperor Augustus, and despite disorders on the part of the people, who desired to be rid of Herodian rule, was put into effect.

HEROD

Herod Antipas (fl. 1st. cent. A.D.), son of Herod the Great. He was tetrarch of Galilee and Perea from 4 B.C. to 39 A.D. Although comparatively little is known of his reign, he appears to have governed ably. Antipas possessed the cunning of his father but lacked his diplomacy and talent for war. He divorced his first wife, daughter of Aretas IV (r. 9 B.C.–40 A.D.), King of the Nabataeans, and married Herodias (14? B.C.–after 41 A.D.), wife of his half brother Herod Philip (d. 34 A.D.), thus precipitating a war with Aretas in which Antipas was defeated. Herod was censured for his marriage by John the Baptist (q.v.), whose execution Antipas was enticed into ordering (Mark 6:14–29) by the machinations of Herodias through her daughter, Salome (q.v.). Later, at the urging of his ambitious wife, Antipas went to Rome and demanded of Emperor Caligula (q.v.) that he be granted the title of king. Instead, Caligula deposed and banished him to Lugdunum (Lyon) in Gaul. Antipas is the Herod most frequently mentioned in the New Testament; it was to him that Jesus Christ was sent by Pontius Pilate (q.v.), procurator of Judea (Luke 23:7–15).

Herod Agrippa I (about 10 B.C.–44 A.D.), last king of Judea (41–44 A.D.), the son of Aristobulus II and Berenice (q.v.) the daughter of Salome. Agrippa spent his youth at the court of the Roman Emperor Tiberius (q.v.), but his spendthrift habits left him heavily in debt and he was forced to retire to Palestine. In the closing years of Tiberius' reign Agrippa returned to Rome and was appointed companion to the emperor's grandson, Gaius Caesar (later Roman Emperor Caligula). When Caligula acceded to the throne in 37 A.D., he granted Agrippa the tetrarchy of Herod Philip (d. 34 A.D.), Agrippa's uncle, and the Syrian territory of Lysanias, Tetrarch of Abilene (fl. 1st cent. A.D.). With these lands, Agrippa was given the title of king, the Roman senate adding the honorary rank of praetor. In 40 A.D. he obtained the fortified tetrarchy of Herod Antipas (see above), and in the following year the new Roman emperor, Tiberius Claudius Drusus Nero Germanicus (*see under* CLAUDIUS), gave Agrippa the additional territory of Judea and Samaria. He was thus finally in possession of the whole region over which his grandfather, Herod the Great, had ruled. To preserve peace, Herod Agrippa adopted a pro-Jewish policy. His extreme personal piety and official support of Jewish interests endeared him to the people but earned him the strong disfavor of both the Roman civil population and the Roman troops in his domains.

Herod Agrippa I is mentioned in the New Testament as a persecutor of the early Christians. According to Acts 12, it was he who had Saint James the Greater (*see under* JAMES) put to death and Saint Peter (q.v.) imprisoned.

Herod Agrippa II (27–100? A.D.), King of Chalcis in Lebanon from 48 A.D., and king of various territories in northern Palestine from 53 A.D., the son and successor of Herod Agrippa I. He received his early education at the court of Emperor Tiberius Claudius Drusus Nero Germanicus in Rome. Because Agrippa was extremely young at the time of his father's death in 44 A.D., Claudius was persuaded not to give him the succession. The whole of Palestine thus passed under direct Roman rule. In 53 A.D., however, Agrippa received the former tetrarchy of Herod Philip (d. 34 A.D.), and in 56 A.D. Roman Emperor Nero (q.v.) augmented Agrippa's territory with the cities of Tiberius and Julias in Galilee and Tarichaea in Perea, with surrounding lands and villages. Agrippa was influential among the Jews, and during his reign attempted to remedy the conflict between them and Rome (*see* JEWS: *Subject Judea*). At the outbreak of the Jewish revolt (66–73 A.D.), Agrippa remained loyal to Rome. He was rewarded for his allegiance at the end of the war by a northward extension of his territory, and in 75 A.D. he was honored with the rank of praetor. It was before Herod Agrippa II that Saint Paul (q.v.) was brought in Caesarea, on the eve of his deportation to Rome, as related in the New Testament (Acts 26). At Agrippa's death, the Herodian dynasty lost its prominence in the history of the Middle East.

HERODES ATTICUS, Tiberius Claudius (101–77 A.D.), Greek scholar, rhetorician, and patron of learning, born in Marathón. He restored several ruined cities in Greece and built several public works, including the Odeum (music hall) in Athens, the stadium at Delphi (q.v.), and the baths at Thermopylae (q.v.). He came to Rome to become the teacher of Marcus Annius Verus, later the Roman emperor Marcus Aurelius (q.v.).

HERODOTUS (484? B.C.–425 B.C.), Greek historian, known as the father of history, born in Halicarnassus (now Bodrum, Turkey). He is believed to have been exiled from Halicarnassus about 457 B.C. for conspiring against Persian rule. He probably went directly to Sámos, from which he traveled throughout Asia Minor, Babylonia, Egypt, and Greece. The direction and extent of his travels are not precisely known, but they provided him with valuable firsthand knowledge of practically the entire ancient world. About 447 B.C. he went to Athens, then the center and focus of culture in the Greek world, where he won the admiration of the most illustrious men of Greece, including the great Athenian statesman Pericles (q.v.). In 443 B.C. Herodotus settled in the Athenian colony of Thurii in southern Italy. He devoted the rest of his life to the completion of his great work, entitled *History*.

The *History* has been divided by later authors into nine parts, the last of which deals with the history of the armed conflicts between Greece and Persia (q.v.) in the early 5th century B.C.; see

Herodotus

GREECE: History: Ancient Greece. The earlier books deal with the customs, legends, history, and traditions of the countries of the ancient world, derived in part from the work of predecessors, but widely supplemented with knowledge gained from his own travels. The *History* is the first known creative work to be written in prose. Both ancient and modern critics have paid tribute to the grandeur of design and to the lucid and delightfully anecdotal style that characterize the work.

HEROIN, name of a narcotic, also known as diacetylmorphine, formula $C_{21}H_{23}NO_5$, which is derived from morphine (q.v.). Heroin is a white crystalline powder with a bitter taste; it is slightly soluble in water, more soluble in alcohol and chloroform. Originally created as a substitute for morphine that would have less tendency to cause addiction, heroin has proved to be more habit-forming than morphine. It is four to eight times more powerful than morphine and is the drug preferred by most addicts. The importation, manufacture, and possession of heroin are prohibited in the United States, and the World Health Organization (q.v.) has recommended that all countries forbid its use, but worldwide illicit trade in heroin persists.

Two morphine antagonists, nalorphine and levallorphan, are used in treating acute heroin poisoning, but they are not effective in curing heroin addiction. Methadone, a narcotic subject to control by the Bureau of Narcotics and Dangerous Drugs, has been used to a limited extent to end heroin craving in addicts in order to help rehabilitate them; see NARCOTICS AND DANGEROUS DRUGS, BUREAU OF.

See also DRUGS, ADDICTION TO; NARCOTICS.

HERON, common name for any tall, gaunt wading bird in the family Ardeidae of the stork order, found in swamps and marshes and on mudbanks in all warm parts of the world. Included among the herons are several groups of birds more commonly known as bitterns, boatbills, and egrets (qq.v.); see also NIGHT HERON.

Herons have elongated necks, legs, and bills; they resemble cranes but are smaller; see CRANE. They fly with their necks bent in an S shape, with their heads supported between their shoulders. Their bills average 8 in. in length and are sharp-edged and pointed. Herons have four, long-clawed toes on each foot, three of which are directed forward, and the fourth backward. The claw on the middle of the forward toes has a rough, comblike inner margin that is used by the heron in preening its soft plumage. Herons often have a headdress of feathers, some of which during the breeding season grow into long, hanging plumes. The birds mate and nest in large groups known as heronries. Most species construct their loose, flat, platform-style nests high in the branches of a swamp tree. Notable exceptions are the bitterns, that place their nests among reeds on the ground. Two to six pale-blue eggs are laid in a clutch. Herons feed on aquatic animal life. Most species do not stalk their prey but, waiting in shallow water or on land, spear it with their long bills.

Eleven genera of herons are found in North America. One of the best known is the great blue heron, *Ardea herodias,* that is widely distributed in North America and winters as far south as northern South America. This bird is about 3 ft. long and has a wing span of about 6 ft. Above it is a bluish gray; below, white streaked with black. Its crown is white with a black crest; the sides of its head are black and its face is slate blue. Its legs and feet are black.

Great blue heron, Ardea herodias
Allan D. Cruickshank — National Audubon Society

During the mating season two feathers of this bird's crest become long and threadlike. Another well-known American species is the green heron, *Butorides virescens,* with a similar range. The bird is about 14 in. long, and is shiny green above and reddish brown below. The great white heron, *A. occidentalis,* is a large, completely white heron, about 3½ ft. long, found in Florida, Mexico, and the West Indies. Common to the Louisiana bayous is the Louisiana heron, *Hydranassa tricolor,* that is approximately 2 ft. in length. It is bluish gray above, with a white rump, and is white below; its crest is light brown in color. This bird often flies north as far as New England at the end of the mating season. The little blue heron, *Florida caerulea,* is common in the southeastern United States. It is about 2 ft. long, and is slate blue above and reddish brown on the head and neck.

The common European heron, *A. cinerea,* is about 3 ft. long and is similar in coloring to the great blue heron. It was formerly hunted with peregrine falcons (q.v.). The African heron or giant heron, *A. goliath,* that stands 5 ft. high, is the tallest member of the family.

HERO OF ALEXANDRIA, *or* HERON OF ALEXANDRIA (fl. 3rd century or as early as the 1st century A.D.), Greek mathematician and scientist. About eighteen Greek writers were named Hero, or Heron, making identification difficult, but he appears to have been of Egyptian birth, to have done his work in Alexandria, Egypt, and to have written at least thirteen works on mechanics, mathematics, and physics. He developed various mechanical devices, including the *aelopile,* a rotary steam engine; *Hero's Fountain,* a pneumatic apparatus in which a vertical jet of water is produced and sustained by air pressure; and the *dioptra,* a primitive theodolite, a surveying instrument. He is best known, however, as a mathematician. In geometry and geodesy he handled problems of mensuration more successfully than anyone of his time. He also devised a method of approximating the square roots and cube roots of numbers that are not perfect squares or cubes. The formula attributed to him, however, for finding the area of a triangle in terms of its sides was devised before his time.

HEROPHILUS (fl. 300 B.C.), Alexandrian physician, born in Chalcedon (now Kadiköy, Turkey). He is known as "the father of scientific anatomy" because he was the first to base his conclusions on dissection of the human body. He studied the brain, recognizing it as the center of the nervous system. He distinguished the motor from the sensory nerves, and accurately described the eye, brain, liver, and pancreas, and the salivary and genital organs. He was first to recognize that the arteries contain blood, not air. His works, which include commentaries on Hippocrates and a treatise on anatomy, were lost. *See* GREEK LITERATURE: *The Hellenistic Period.*

HERPES (Gr. *herpein*, "to creep"), name applied to several types of skin eruptions characterized by formation of blisters, often developing in a creeping or spreading fashion. The term embraces primarily two distinct disorders, herpes simplex and herpes zoster, both caused by viruses.

Herpes Simplex. Also known as cold sores or fever blisters, this is an eruption of blisters that often occur during the course of or after one of a variety of diseases associated with fever, most commonly colds, influenza, and pneumonia. They usually appear around the mouth and on the lips (herpes labialis), about the nose, face, and ears, in the mouth and pharynx, and occasionally where skin and mucous membrane come together, as in the genital area. Sometimes accompanied by headache and fever, the condition usually begins with a mild itching, followed by the development of clusters of blisters that break and crust to form scabs that eventually dry up. The process may last one to three weeks. In many cases new clusters of blisters appear as others heal.

Occasionally, the virus invades the central nervous system to cause a form of encephalitis or benign meningitis. A very rare form, presumably contracted from the mother, is fatal in the newborn. Susceptible persons may suffer attacks during pregnancy, menstruation, or emotional strain, or after injury, exertion, or exposure to sun or heat. Except for dressings and lotions to relieve pain, itching, or inflammation, there is no established therapy. The disease, which may recur, is not serious and runs a benign course to recovery.

Herpes Zoster. Known as shingles, this is a related but different disease caused by a virus that attacks a sensory nerve. The skin over the nerve generally breaks out in blisters a few days after the onset of the disorder, which is accompanied by pain and frequent numbness or hypersensitivity along the course of the nerve. The blisters are at first clear, but become cloudy within a few days and form crusts that dry up after five or ten days. The agent that causes the disease is thought to be either the virus that causes chicken pox or a closely related one. In children, chicken pox is often followed by attacks of shingles.

The skin manifestation of the disease is not serious, but the pain caused by the inflammation of the underlying nerve can be severe, lasting for weeks; recovery may be followed by persistence of neuralgia in the area of the involved nerve. Normally, medication relieves pain, and the disease subsides spontaneously. More severe cases may be treated with such steroids as cortisone. In persistent pain, the involved nerve is blocked by drugs, treated by radiation, or cut.

An occasional serious complication common to both diseases is the formation of lesions at the margins of the cornea of the eye that, in healing, may join to form ulcers that scar the cornea.

HERPETOLOGY, branch of zoology concerned with study of the amphibia and reptile (qq.v.). Research deals with taxonomy, or orderly scientific classification, distribution, and life history of species and is often concentrated in areas where reptiles are of economic importance, as in the use of skins for leather, of eggs for food, and of gland extracts for perfumes. Many herpetologists concentrate on one species, such as the alligator, crocodile, lizard, or snake, on turtles and tortoises (qq.v.), or on the study of fossil remains of extinct species of reptiles; *see* PALEONTOLOGY.

HERRICK, Robert (1591–1674), English poet, born in London, and educated at the University of Cambridge. In 1629 he became vicar of Dean

Robert Herrick, a print by the contemporary English engraver William Marshall.   Bettmann Archive

HERRING

Prior in Devonshire, but in 1647, during the Great Rebellion (q.v.), he was deprived of his position because of his royalist sympathies. Following the restoration of Charles II (q.v.), King of England, Herrick was reinstated at Dean Prior, where he resided from 1662 until his death. His chief work is the volume *Hesperides, or the Works both Human and Divine of Robert Herrick, Esq.* (1648). Within the same book, but under a separate title page bearing the date 1647, was printed a group of religious poems, *His Noble Numbers.* The entire collection contains over 1200 short poems, ranging in form from epistles, eclogues, and epigrams to love poems. The themes are pastoral, dealing mostly with English country life and village customs. Herrick was greatly influenced by classical Roman poetry. His work is noted for its diversity of form and for its style, melody, and feeling. Many of his poems, such as "To the Virgins to Make Much of Time", "Corinna's Going a-Maying", and "Delight in Disorder", were anthologized and several were set to music. See CAVALIER POETS.

HERRING, common name for any marine, teleost fish in the large family Clupeidae, economically the most important group of fish to North America and western Europe. The family contains approximately 175 species, including the menhaden, the pilchard (the young of which are common sardines), and the shad (qq.v.). They are abundant throughout the North Atlantic Ocean, in the North and Baltic seas, and in the North Pacific Ocean. Most of the clupeids are about 1 ft. long when mature; the largest species, the shad, reaches 30 in. in length. They are characterized by a single short dorsal fin in the middle of the upper margin of the body, and by an anal fin similarly located below. The head is scaleless, and the slender body is covered with thin, cycloid scales in which rings of organic material, rich in guanine (see GUANO), are laid down each season. By counting these rings, scientists can determine the age of clupeids, which live as long as twenty years. Clupeids swim near the surface of the water in huge schools, and feed on plankton.

Spawning activity is quite varied among the clupeids. Some, such as the American shad, *Alosa sapidissima,* migrate into rivers and spawn in fresh water. Others, such as the Pacific American sardine, *Sardinops caerulea,* spawn offshore in spring and summer and have eggs that float at the surface. The Pacific herring, *Clupea pallasi,* and the Atlantic herring, *C. harengus,* spawn in shallow bays and deposit their eggs on seaweeds and shells.

North Sea herring mature at three to four years of age, Baltic Sea herring at five to eight, and herring found farther north in the Bering Sea mature even later. Herring of southerly seas die at an earlier age than those inhabiting more northerly regions; consequently those found in the north grow to a larger size.

The term herring, when unqualified, usually refers to the Atlantic herring, *C. harengus.* This fish, abundant in the Atlantic Ocean and found along the coast of the United States north of South Carolina, grows to a length of 1 ft. and is bluish-green above, silvery below. The young, and the young of the European sprat, *C. sprattus,* are often called whitebait, and are considered table delicacies. The Pacific herring, *C. pallasi,* found from Alaska to Mexico, is a similar fish. The fall herring, *Pomolobus mediocris,* so called because it spawns in the fall, is found south of Cape Cod; it is sometimes called Hickory shad. The blueback, *P. aestivalis,* also known as the summer or glut herring, is unusual because it ascends into fresh water to spawn. Another common herring is the branch or spring herring, or alewife (q.v.), *P. pseudoharengus.*

The name herring is also applied to several freshwater fish, such as the lake herring, or cisco, of the Great Lakes, and the rainbow herring, a smelt (q.v.). The chimera, an ocean fish, is sometimes called "king of the herrings".

The fishing, processing, and marketing of different species of the Herring family is a major industry in the U.S., Great Britain, Norway, Denmark, the Netherlands, Germany, France, and Portugal. Besides fresh and salted herring, the products of this industry on the market include red herring, which has been smoked until it is hardened; kippered herring, which is slightly salted and partially smoked; so-called bloaters, which are large herring, heavily salted and partially smoked; and canned sardines. The total annual catch of herring in the U.S. in the late 1960's averaged more than 1,000,000 lb., worth between $3,000,000 and $4,000,000. See FISHERIES.

HERRING GULL, common name for a large gull (q.v.), *Larus argentatus,* abundant on both sides of the North Atlantic Ocean, in inland waters of North America, and in the North Pacific Ocean from Japan to the Bering Straits. The adult herring gull, which is about 22 in. long, is silvery gray above and white below. The bill is yellow, with a bright red patch near the tip of the lower mandible; its wings are tipped with black and streaked with white; and the legs and feet are flesh pink. Young herring gulls are dark brown, streaked with gray. Herring gulls commonly follow ships out of harbor to pick up gar-

Herring gulls, Larus argentatus
Gordon Smith— National Audubon Society

bage. They normally subsist on marine organisms, but also eat carrion, turnips, potatoes, and grain. At high tide they float on the surface of the water, and when the tide ebbs they congregate on the shores. The cry of the herring gull is loud, high-pitched, and wailing. Herring gulls breed in the spring in large communities off the coasts or on freshwater islands of the northeastern United States and south central Alaska, and also in British Columbia, northern North Dakota, and central Wisconsin. They winter from southern Alaska south to lower California and Mexico, and from the Gulf of Saint Lawrence and the Great Lakes south to Cuba, Yucatán, and the coasts of Alabama and Texas.   K.A.C.

HERRIOT, Édouard (1872–1957), French statesman and man of letters, born in Troyes, and educated at the École Normale Supérieure in Paris. He entered politics in 1904 as a member of the municipal council of Lyon and in the same year was elected mayor of Lyon, an office he held continuously from 1905, except for three years during World War II.

Herriot was one of the most eminent and active French political leaders of his time and a leader of the Radical Socialist Party. From 1919 he was a member of the Chamber of Deputies; he was premier of France in 1924–25, for a short time in 1926, and again in 1932; and president of the Chamber of Deputies from 1936 to 1940. He refused to collaborate with the Germans after their conquest of France in 1940 or with the government that had been set up in Vichy under Marshal Henri Philippe Pétain (q.v.). Herriot was arrested in 1942 and kept interned in France and Germany until 1945, when he was liberated by Soviet troops. He was a deputy to the Constituent Assembly that wrote the constitution for the Fourth Republic (*see* FRANCE: *History: The Fourth Republic*) in 1946. The same year he was elected a deputy to the first National Assembly to meet under the new constitution. In 1947 he was elected leader or speaker of the National Assembly and held that office until 1953.

As early as 1905 Herriot had won a literary reputation. Among his best works are a biography, *La Vie de Beethoven* (1929, Eng. trans., *Life and Times of Beethoven,* 1935), and a political study, *Les États-Unis de l'Europe* (1930, Eng. trans., *The United States of Europe,* 1930), in which he advocates a confederation of European countries. He was elected to the French Academy in 1946.

HERSCHEL, family of British astronomers, including the following.

Sir William Herschel, originally FRIEDRICH WILHELM HERSCHEL (1738–1822), born in Hannover, Germany. At the age of nineteen he went to England, working as a music teacher and organist, but devoting all his spare time to the study of astronomy and mathematics. Unable to procure adequate instruments, he constructed and constantly improved his own telescopes. In 1774 with the aid of his sister, Caroline (1750–1848), he began a comprehensive and systematic survey of the heavens. In 1781 he discovered a new planet, which he named Georgium Sidus in honor

353

of George III (q.v.), King of Great Britain, but which is now universally called Uranus (q.v.). A year later he was appointed private astronomer to the king, a position that enabled him to devote all his time to his astronomical pursuits. He erected a telescope at Slough with a 48-inch mirror and a focal length of 40 ft. Using this instrument, he discovered two satellites of Uranus and the sixth and seventh satellites of Saturn (q.v.). He studied the rotation period of many planets and the motion of double stars (q.v.), and also catalogued more than 800 double stars. He studied nebulae, contributing new information on their constitution and increasing the number of observed nebulae from about 100 to 2500. Herschel was elected to the Royal Society in 1781, and was knighted in 1816. He is considered the founder of sidereal astronomy.

John Frederick William Herschel (1792–1871), son of William, born in Slough, England, and educated at the University of Cambridge. He reexamined the double stars and nebulae observed by his father and added many more to the elder Herschel's catalogues. To complete the survey of the heavens undertaken by his father, he led an expedition to the Cape of Good Hope in 1834 to study the stars of the Southern Hemisphere, and published the results in 1847. He became president of the Royal Astronomical Society in 1848. He was also a distinguished chemist, and was the first to apply the terms positive and negative to photographic images. Herschel was knighted in 1831, and was created baron in 1850.

HERSEY, John (Richard) (1914–), American author and journalist, born in Tientsin, China, and educated at Yale University and the University of Cambridge. He joined the staff of the weekly newsmagazine *Time* in 1937, and during World War II he served as a *Time* correspondent in both the Pacific and European theaters of operations. Subsequently he was a senior editor of *Life* and editor of the magazine '47 and '48. Hersey is the author of *Men on Bataan* (1942) and *Into the Valley* (1943), vivid accounts of the war in the Pacific; *A Bell for Adano* (1944; Pulitzer Prize, 1945), a novel about the Allied occupation of Italy; *Hiroshima* (1946), a graphic report on the atomic bombing of that Japanese city; *The Wall* (1950), a novel about the World War II Jewish community of Warsaw, Poland; *A Single Pebble* (1956), a novel set in modern China; *Too Far To Walk* (1966), a modern version of the Faust legend; *The Algiers Motel Incident* (1968), a nonfiction treatment of the riots that occurred in Detroit, Mich., in 1967; and *Letter to the Alumni* (1970), correspondence about the gap between the younger and older generations.

HERSHEY, Alfred Day (1908–), American biologist, born in Owosso, Mich., and educated at Michigan State College. From 1934 until 1950 he taught at Washington University, Saint Louis, Mo. In 1950 he joined the genetics research unit of Carnegie Institution in Cold Spring Harbor, Long Island, N.Y. In 1962 he was named director of the unit. Hershey shared the 1969 Nobel Prize in medicine and physiology with the German-American biologist Max Delbrück and the American biologist Salvador E. Luria (qq.v.) for their studies in molecular biology. Hershey proved through the use of radioisotopes that deoxyribonucleic acid (DNA), the basic substance of heredity, enters bacteria to act as the genetic transmitter of a virus. See HEREDITY; NUCLEIC ACIDS.

HERSHEY, Lewis B(laine) (1893–), American army officer, born near Angola, Ind. He received a B.S. degree from Tri-State College, Angola, in 1912. Hershey's military career began in 1911, when he enlisted in the Indiana National Guard. In 1917 he was ordered to active duty, receiving his commission as captain a year later. Hershey was commissioned a permanent captain of field artillery in 1920. Thereafter he rose through the grades until 1956, when he achieved the rank of lieutenant general. From 1936 until 1940 Hershey was assigned to the Joint Army and Navy Selective Service Committee, developing plans for the drafting of manpower. Hershey became director of the Selective Service System in 1941; see SELECTIVE SERVICE. Except for a brief period of retirement in 1946 he served in that capacity until 1970, when he was appointed adviser to the President on manpower mobilization. In the same year he was promoted to the rank of general.

HERTFORDSHIRE, or HERTFORD or HERTS, Great Britain, county of s.w. England, traversed in the N.W. by an extension of the Chiltern Hills. The Lea is the principal river of this chiefly agricultural county. Much of the land is devoted to pasture for dairy cattle, but wheat, hay, and vegetables are also important crops. The s. part of the county is a residential and industrial center, and much of it is included in the greater-London area. Saint Albans is the largest and most important city in the county; Hertford is the county seat. Many important battles during the English civil wars in the latter half of the 15th century were fought in Hertfordshire. Area, 631 sq.mi.; pop. (1969 est.) 903,390.

HERTOGENBOSCH, 'S. See 'S HERTOGENBOSCH.
HERTZ, Gustav (1887–), German physicist, born in Hamburg, and educated at the universi

ties of Göttingen, Munich, and Berlin. In conjunction with the German-born American physicist James Franck (q.v.), Hertz studied the effect of the impact of electrons on atoms. As a result of these experiments, which were the first demonstration of the quantum theory (q.v.) of the German physicist Max Planck (q.v.), Hertz and Franck were awarded the 1925 Nobel Prize in physics. Hertz served as professor of experimental physics, first at the University of Halle from 1925 to 1927 and then at the Berlin Technische Hochschule from 1928 until 1935, when he resigned to become director of the Siemens Research Laboratory in Berlin. In 1945 he went to the U.S.S.R. to continue his work in atomic research, and was awarded the Stalin Prize in 1951. From 1955 until his retirement in 1960 Hertz served as professor of physics at the University of Leipzig in East Germany.

HERTZ, Heinrich Rudolph (1857–94), German physicist, born in Hamburg, and educated at the University of Berlin, where he was an assistant to the German scientist Hermann Ludwig Ferdinand von Helmholtz (q.v.). From 1883 to 1885 Hertz was a lecturer on theoretical physics at the University in Kiel, from 1885 to 1889 a professor of physics at the technical school in Karlsruhe, and after 1889 a professor of physics at the university in Bonn. On the basis of a series of experiments with electricity that he conducted from 1886 to 1889, Hertz clarified and expanded the electromagnetic theory of light that had been put forth by the British physicist James Clerk Maxwell (q.v.) in 1884. Using the spark of an induction coil, Hertz proved that electricity can be transmitted in electromagnetic waves, which travel at the speed of light and which possess many other properties of light, such as similar wavelength patterns and reflections, refraction, and polarization properties. His experiments with these electromagnetic waves (renamed Hertzian waves in his honor) led to the development of the wireless telegraph and the radio. The unit of frequency that is measured in cycles per second was renamed the hertz; it is commonly abbreviated Hz. See ELECTROMAGNETIC RADIATIONS.

HERTZOG, James Barry Munnik (1866–1942), South African political and military leader, born in Wellington, and educated in Stellenbosch and Amsterdam. Appointed a judge in the Orange Free State in 1895, Hertzog soon became the leader of the anti-British, pro-nationalist group known as the Boers (q.v.). During the South African War (q.v.) he served as a leader of the Boer forces, and signed a peace treaty in 1902 only after the British agreed to recognize Dutch as an official language in the defeated republics. From 1907 to 1910, as attorney general and director of education in the Orange River Colony (temporarily the designation for the Orange Free State) he strove to keep anti-British feeling alive. Using frank racist appeals, and uncompromisingly rejecting government proposals for the development of the Union of South Africa within the framework of the British Empire, Hertzog succeeded in forming a coalition between the Labor Party and his own Nationalist Party (founded 1924), which advocated complete independence from Great Britain. The coalition party gained a majority in the Parliament of the Union in 1924, and Hertzog was elected prime minister. He held this post until 1939 when, following the outbreak of World War II, he opposed joining Britain in a declaration of war against Germany, and advocated neutrality. He was voted down by parliament, however, and was forced to resign his ministry in favor of the man he had succeeded as prime minister in 1924, the pro-British statesman Jan Christiaan Smuts (q.v.). For the remaining three years of his life Hertzog was a leader of the movement within South Africa for a negotiated separate peace with Germany; in 1940 he declared himself a supporter of National Socialism (q.v.).

HERULI, warlike Teutonic tribe, probably expelled from Scandinavia before the middle of the 3rd century. They are first mentioned by medieval historians as allies of the Goths (q.v.) on marauding expeditions around the coasts of the Black and Aegean seas about 260. Little is heard of them until the early 6th century when the Heruli kingdom in the Elbe R. basin was vanquished and dissolved by the Lombards (q.v.). The Heruli were dispersed; some members migrated to Scandinavia, and others entered the Roman army. After the middle of the 6th century the name completely disappeared.

HERZBERG, Gerhard (1904–), Canadian physicist, born in Hamburg, Germany, and educated at the Institute of Technology, Darmstadt, and at the universities of Göttingen, and Bristol, England. He taught at Darmstadt (1930–35) and at the universities of Saskatchewan (1935–45) and Chicago (1945–48). In 1955 he became director of the Division of Pure Physics of the National Research Council of Canada, where he had been a staff member since 1948; in 1969 he was named distinguished research scientist of the council.

A naturalized Canadian citizen, Herzberg performed research upon atomic spectroscopy and the structures of diatomic and polyatomic molecules; his spectral studies were valuable in the identification of molecules in the atmospheres of the planets and in outer space. Herzberg was awarded the 1971 Nobel Prize in chemistry for his research in the electronic structure and geometry of molecules in general, and of free radicals in particular. Herzberg's work has earned for his laboratory a worldwide reputation as a leading center of molecular spectroscopy; see SPECTRUM: *Spectroscopes*. His more than 200 publications, dealing primarily with spectroscopy and quantum mechanics (q.v.), include the monumental *Molecular Spectra and Molecular Structure* (3 vol., 1939–66).

HERZEGOVINA. See BOSNIA AND HERCEGOVINA.

HERZL, Theodor (1860–1904), Jewish writer and journalist, founder of modern political Zionism (q.v.), born in Budapest, Hungary. Although he had studied law in Vienna, Austria, Herzl devoted himself to a literary career. He was soon a well-known playwright and essayist, and in 1891 he was appointed Paris correspondent for the Vienna *Neue Freie Presse* ("New Free Press"). The violent anti-Semitism (q.v.) that erupted in France in 1894 as a result of the court-martial of the Jewish army officer Alfred Dreyfus (*see* DREYFUS AFFAIR) deeply affected Herzl. Until that time he had believed that gradual assimilation of the Jews with the Christian peoples of Europe was the best solution to anti-Semitism, but the repercussions of the court-martial convinced him that the problem could be solved only if the Jews became a separate national group with sovereignty over their own territory. In 1896 Herzl published a pamphlet, *Der Judenstaat* (Eng. trans., *The Jewish State,* 1896), advocating the establishment of a Jewish state. Although this solution to the problem of anti-Semitism had been previously suggested by other Jewish leaders, Herzl was the first to call for immediate political, internationally recognized action. To help implement his plan he called for a Zionist congress in 1897, which met in Basel, Switzerland. As a result of the congress, Palestine was chosen as the site for the future Jewish state because of its associations with Jewish history. A World Zionist Organization was also established to help lay the economic foundation for the proposed state.

Because Palestine was then in Turkish hands, Herzl attempted to negotiate with Abdul-Hamid II, Sultan of Turkey (1842–1918), who was sympathetic to the Zionist cause. These negotiations proved fruitless, however, as did Herzl's interviews with other rulers, statesmen, and financiers. Although he died before he could see his dream of a Jewish homeland fulfilled, Herzl is regarded as one of the greatest influences in the movement that led to the creation of the State of Israel (q.v.) in 1948. In 1949 his remains were transferred to a mountain west of Jerusalem that was named Mt. Herzl; it is also the site of a memorial to the Jewish victims of World War II. Herzl wrote a novel, *Alt Neuland* (1902; Eng. trans., *Old-New Land,* 1941) which describes a utopian Jewish state in Palestine, and a diary (3 vol., 1922; Eng. trans., *The Complete Diaries of Theodor Herzl,* 5 vol., 1961). N.N.G.

HESBURGH, Theodore Martin (1917–), American clergyman and educator, born in Syracuse, N.Y., and educated at the University of Notre Dame, Holy Cross College, and Catholic University of America. He was ordained a priest in 1943 and two years later he began his association with Notre Dame. From 1945 to 1947 he served as veterans' chaplain; thereafter he became assistant professor of religion, and quickly rose to departmental chairman. In 1949 he was appointed executive vice-president of the university, and three years later university president. In addition to his duties at Notre Dame, Hesburgh became a member of the United States Commission on Civil Rights in 1957 and was chairman of the commission from 1969 to 1972. He is the author of *Theology of Catholic Action* (1945), *God and the World of Man* (1950), and *Patterns for Educational Growth* (1958).

Theodor Herzl — Zionist Organization of America

HESIOD (8th cent. B.C.), Greek poet, born in Ascra, Boeotia (now Palaioppanagia, Greece). After the death of his father, Hesiod left Ascra and settled in Naupaktos. There, as in his youth, he tended sheep and led the life of a farmer.

Except for what Hesiod reveals of himself in his poetry, little is definitely known of his life. Modern scholars place him in the Homeric age of Greek literature (q.v.). His first poem "Works and Days" is the earliest example of didactic poetry, that is, poetry meant to be instructive rather than entertaining. The work embodies Hesiod's experiences as a Boeotian farmer, and is interspersed with many episodes of allegory and fable. In a simple, moralizing style Hesiod stresses the importance of hard work and righteousness. He gives practical advice on how to live, giving hints and rules on husbandry and charting a religious calendar of the months with propitious and unpropitious days for certain farming tasks. The main theme of the work is the moral decay of mankind; Hesiod traces the history of the world through five stages, from the age of gold to his own age of iron, which he believed evil.

Hesiod is also credited with writing the "Theogony" ("Genealogy of the Gods"), a poem in which the large and amorphous body of Greek myths is systematized and expanded to include the newer divinities unknown in the Homeric poems. The "Theogony" recounts the creation of the world out of chaos, the birth of the gods, and descriptions of their adventures. The closing portion of the poem contains a list of the daughters of Zeus (q.v.), the father of the gods, and mortal women. It forms the introduction to a lost poem, the "Catalogue of Women", which in the few fragments that survive, traces the exploits of heroes born to mortal women.

Of other works by Hesiod only titles and fragments remain, and even these, most scholars believe, were probably written by Hesiod's imitators, who as a group were called the Hesiodic school. In this group are the didactic poem "Maxims of Cheiron", the genealogical poem "Aegimius", and the mythical poems "Marriage of Ceyx" and "Descent of Theseus to Hades". Although generally regarded as inferior to the Greek poet Homer (q.v.) in power of language, imaginative grasp, and grandeur of conception, Hesiod occupies a unique place in Greek literature for his moral precepts and his sententious, colloquial style.

HESPERIDES, in Greek mythology, the daughters of the Titan Atlas (q.v.) or of Hesper, the evening star. Aided by a dragon, the Hesperides guarded a tree, with branches and leaves of gold, that bore golden apples. The tree had been given to the goddess Hera (q.v.) on her wedding day by Gaea (q.v.), Mother Earth. One of the twelve labors imposed upon the hero Hercules (q.v.) was to bring back the golden apples of the Hesperides.

HESS, Dame Myra (1890–1965), British pianist, born in London, England. She began her training at the Guildhall School of Music and Drama, and in 1902 won a scholarship to the Royal Academy of Music, where she studied for five years. She was an immediate success at her debut in 1907, at which she played the *Concerto in G* by the German composer Ludwig van Beethoven (q.v.), with the orchestra under the British conductor, Sir Thomas Beecham (q.v.). She subsequently made concert tours throughout Europe and (after 1922) the United States. In London she helped to establish the Myra Hess scholarship for young pianists. Myra Hess had an unusually large repertoire, and was particularly noted for her playing of the works of the Italian composer Domenico Scarlatti, the German composer Johann Sebastian Bach, and the Austrian composer Wolfgang Amadeus Mozart (qq.v.). She was made a dame of the British Empire in 1941.

HESS, Rudolf (1894–   ), German National Socialist leader, born in Alexandria, Egypt (now the Arab Republic of Egypt). He went to Germany at the age of fourteen, and upon the outbreak of World War I enlisted in the German army. He first met the German dictator Adolf Hitler (q.v.) shortly thereafter, when both were serving in the same regiment. In 1921 he joined the Nationalist Socialist Party which had just been formed by Hitler and his associates; see NATIONAL SOCIALISM. He participated in the Nazi attempt to overthrow the Bavarian government in 1923, and was imprisoned with Hitler at Landsberg. While serving his sentence, he took down, at Hitler's dictation, a large part of the work which later became famous as *Mein Kampf*.

Hess ably abetted Hitler in the struggle that carried the National Socialists to power in Germany in January, 1933. In April of that year he was appointed Hitler's deputy in charge of the party organization. In 1934 he was elevated to the rank of minister and appointed a member of Hitler's cabinet. Hitler named him third deputy of the Reich in 1939, placing him directly below the Nazi leader Hermann Göring (q.v.) in line of succession to absolute power.

Two years later, when World War II was reaching its height, Hess made a solo airplane flight to Scotland; upon his immediate arrest as a prisoner of war he announced that he had flown to Great Britain to persuade the British government to cease hostilities and join Germany in an assault on the Soviet Union. At the war crimes trials held at Nuremberg in 1945–46, he was convicted as a major war criminal and sentenced to life imprisonment in Spandau Prison in Berlin. *See* WAR-CRIMES TRIALS: *Nuremberg Trials.*

HESS, Victor Franz (1883–1964), Austrian physicist, born in Waldstein, and educated at the universities of Graz and Vienna. After lecturing and teaching in various universities in Austria from 1907 to 1921, he came to the United States and became director of research for a radium corporation in New York City and consultant to the United States Bureau of Mines. He returned to Austria and became professor of physics at the universities of Graz and Innsbruck from 1925 to 1931 and 1931 to 1937 respectively. From 1938 to 1956 he was professor of physics at Fordham University, New York City. He was one of the earliest workers in the field of cosmic rays. As early as 1911 he measured cosmic-ray activity at altitudes as great as 30,000 ft. He shared the 1936 Nobel Prize in physics with the American physicist Carl David Anderson (q.v.). Hess is the author of *Conductivity of the Atmosphere* (1928) and *Cosmic Rays and Their Biological Effects* (1949).

HESS, Walter Rudolf (1881–   ), Swiss physiologist, born in Frauenfeld, and educated at the universities of Lausanne, Bern, Berlin, Kiel, and Zürich. He served as professor of physiology and as director of the Physiological Institute at the University of Zürich from 1917 until his retirement in 1951. Hess is best known for his studies on the functioning of the nervous system. He shared the 1949 Nobel Prize in medicine and physiology with the Portuguese neurologist Antonio Caetano Moniz (q.v.).

HESSE (Ger. *Hessen*), State of West Germany, bounded on the N. by the States of North Rhine-Westphalia and Lower Saxony, on the E. by East Germany, on the S. by the States of Bavaria and Baden-Württemberg, and on the W. by the State of Rhineland-Palatinate. Wiesbaden is the capital; other major cities are Frankfurt, Kassel, Darmstadt, and Offenbach (qq.v.). Hesse is a heavily forested upland, broken by hills and mountain ranges. The Taunus (q.v.) and the Vogelsberg mountains cut central Hesse, and the Odenwald and Spessart ranges cross the S. part of the State. The Rhine River (q.v.) and its tributaries, the Lahn R. and the Main River (q.v.), drain the W. part of the State, and the Eder, Fulda, and Weser (q.v.) flow through the N.E. Area, 7931 sq.mi.; pop. (1967 est.) 5,262,729.

Farming is the main economic activity. In addition to wine grapes, the chief agricultural products are cereals, potatoes, fruit, tobacco, and flax. Dairying is also important, and forests are extensive. The State has small deposits of iron, manganese, salt, and lignite. Industry, which is concentrated in the S.W., consists of chemical, machinery, and vehicle manufacturing. Textiles and electrical and scientific equipment are also produced.

The State is governed by a cabinet headed by a minister-president. The cabinet is responsible to a popularly elected diet.

History. The people of Hesse were converted to Christianity in the late 7th century and incorporated into the Frankish empire; *see* FRANKS. In the 12th century the region was part of the landgraviate of Thuringia (q.v.). Hesse was established as a separate landgraviate in 1247 by Duchess Sophia (d. 1284), niece of the Thuringian ruler Henry Raspe (1202?–47). Her son, called Henry the Child (1244–1308), became the first male landgrave of Hesse in 1263. During the 16th century the rulers and people of the landgraviate played an important part in the Reformation (q.v.). Landgrave Philip the Magnanimous (1504–67) founded Marburg University, a Protestant institution, in 1527.

Following Philip's death, the landgraviate was divided among his four sons. Two branches of the family subsequently became extinct, and their holdings were absorbed by the surviving lines, the houses of Hesse-Darmstadt, descended from George I (1547–96), and Hesse-Kassel, started by William IV (1532–92). Important landgraves of Hesse-Kassel include Frederick I (q.v.), King of Sweden, and Frederick II (1720–85), the ruler who furnished Hessian troops to the British during the American Revolution.

In 1803 Hesse-Kassel was constituted an electorate, and in 1806 Hesse-Darmstadt was elevated to a grand duchy. In 1866, after siding with Austria in the Seven Weeks' War (q.v.), Hesse-Kassel was annexed by Prussia; Hesse-Darmstadt was forced to cede Hesse-Homburg, a landgraviate that had been established out of its territory in 1622. The Prussians merged Hesse-Kassel, Nassau, parts of Hesse-Darmstadt, and Frankfurt (q.v.) into the new province of Hesse-Nassau in 1867.

Hesse-Darmstadt remained a grand duchy until after World War I, when it became a State in the Weimar Republic. After World War II the area was made part of the American occupation zone. Subsequently, most of Hesse-Nassau was

HESSIAN FLY

Hermann Hesse — Wide World

merged with Hesse-Darmstadt. In 1946 the merged territories were established as the State of Hesse.

HESSE, Hermann (1877–1962), German-born Swiss novelist and poet, born in Calw, Swabia. He attended several schools but abandoned each in order to educate himself through reading and to be free to write. In 1911 he made a trip to India to study Indian mysticism. Hesse's early novels, among which are *Peter Camenzind* (1904; Eng. trans., 1961), *Unterm Rad* (1905; Eng. trans., *The Prodigy*, 1957), and *Nachbarn* ("Neighbors", 1908), are characterized by musical prose, sensitive scenic description, and an atmosphere of nostalgic melancholy. Among his later novels, which show his deep insight into human nature and profound wisdom, *Demian* (1919; Eng. trans., 1923), a psychoanalytical novel; *Siddhartha* (1923; Eng. trans., 1951), the story of a search for spiritual happiness; *Der Steppenwolf* (1927; Eng. trans., 1929), a novel violently criticizing the spiritually barren modern world; *Narziss und Goldmund* (1930; Eng. trans., *Death and the Lover*, 1932), a tale contrasting spiritual and mundane life; *Das Glasperlenspiel* (1943; Eng. trans., *Magister Ludi*, 1949), and *Goldmund* (1959). Hesse's verse is collected in *Gesammelte Dichtungen* ("Collected Poetry", 6 vol., 1952) and prose writings in *Beschwörungen*

("Exorcisms", 1955). In 1970 the first English translation of *Poems* was published; the volume contains thirty-one poems on homesickness.

By the time Hesse received the Nobel Prize in literature in 1946, only three of his works had been translated into English.

HESSIAN FLY, small, mosquitolike, nematocerous fly, *Mayetiola destructor,* of the family Cecidomyiidae. In the larval state it is more destructive to wheat in the United States than any other insect pest, and also damages rye and barley crops. In a recent year, damage attributed to the Hessian fly was estimated at $100,000,000, and losses due to the ravages of the pest averaged slightly more than 1 percent of the wheat crop. The fly first appeared in the U.S. on Long Island, New York, toward the end of the 18th century. It takes its common name from the belief held by Americans at that time that it was imported in the bedding straw sent to the Hessian mercenary troops from their native land. At present the Hessian fly is widely distributed in the wheat-growing regions of the U.S., and is also found in Canada, Europe, northern Africa, western Asia, and New Zealand.

Two, or occasionally three, generations of Hessian flies appear yearly. The adult first appears in March in the southern States, in May in Michigan. It is about $\frac{1}{10}$ in. long, dark brown to black, with long, beaded antennae and sparsely veined wings. The female lays its cylindrical, pink eggs, about $\frac{1}{50}$ in. in length, on the leaves of wheat plants. The adult flies live from several days to two weeks, their life being longest in warm, humid weather. The eggs hatch in about

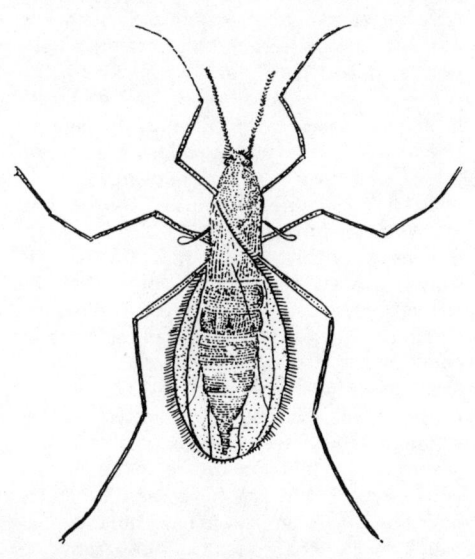

Hessian fly, Mayetiola destructor

359

three weeks, and the pink larvae, which turn white in three or four days, move down the plant to the roots or to the space between the leaf base and the stem. They then bore into the stem and suck the sap, weakening the plant until the upper portions break off. The larvae, which grow to about ¼ in., pupate toward the end of June or beginning of July; the larval skin hardens, turns brown, and encloses the developing insect in a shell similar in appearance to the outer coat of a flaxseed, from which comes the common term "flaxseed stage" for the pupal period. The new adults emerge in late August or early September, mate, and lay their eggs. The larvae of this generation usually pupate in late October and remain in the "flaxseed stage" until the following spring, but occasionally, during a mild winter, they continue to develop and produce a third generation.

Control measures against blights caused by the Hessian fly include rotation of crops so that wheat is not grown in the same soil for two successive years; delayed seeding of a future crop until the autumn brood of flies has disappeared; and planting of wheat varieties resistant to the Hessian fly.

HESSIAN TROOPS, popularly called HESSIANS, German mercenaries hired by the British government to serve against the colonials in the American Revolution (q.v.). *See also* HESSE: *History.*

HESTIA, in Greek mythology, virgin goddess of the hearth, the eldest daughter of the Titans Cronus and Rhea (qq.v.). She was believed to preside at all sacrificial altar fires, and prayers were offered to her both before and after meals. Although she appears in very few myths, she was worshiped widely and most cities had a common hearth where her sacred fire burned. In Rome Hestia was worshiped as the goddess Vesta, and her fire was attended by six virgin priestesses known as vestal virgins (q.v.).

HEVELIUS, Johannes *or* **HEWEL, Johannes** *or* **HÖWELCKE, Johannes** (1611–87), Polish astronomer, born in Danzig (now Gdańsk). He studied law at the University of Leiden, the Netherlands, and, after traveling in Europe, settled in Danzig in 1634. There he became a town councilor and worked as a brewer. His chief interest was astronomy, and in 1641 he began to construct an observatory in his home. His studies of the surface of the moon and his discovery of the libration of the moon in longitude, recorded in *Selenographia* ("Lunar Topography", 1647), are said to have laid the foundation for the study of lunar topography. He also observed sunspots, catalogued many stars, discovered four comets, studied the phases of Saturn, and was one of the first to observe the transit of Mercury (q.v.).

HEVESY, Georg von (1885–1966), Hungarian physicist, born in Budapest, and educated there and in Germany. He taught in Germany from 1926 to 1930, and lectured in the United States at Cornell University from 1930 to 1934. From 1934 to 1943 he worked at the University of Copenhagen under the Danish physicist Niels Bohr (q.v.). He was appointed associate professor at the University of Stockholm institute of organic chemistry in 1943.

Hevesy worked on the separation of isotopes (*see* ISOTOPE) and their use as tracers in chemical and biological research in 1923. He was largely responsible for the discovery in 1923 of the element hafnium (q.v.). He received the 1943 Nobel Prize in chemistry for his work in radioactivity and the 1959 United Nations Atoms for Peace Award. His works include *Manual of Radioactivity* (2nd ed. 1932), and *Chemical Analysis with X-Rays and Its Application* (1931).

HEXATEUCH, term used to describe the first six books of the Bible: Genesis, Exodus, Leviticus, Numbers, Deuteronomy, and Joshua. These books are considered as a literary whole because they describe the history of the Jews from the Creation through the reconquest of Palestine. The terms Pentateuch (q.v.), describing the first five, and Octateuch, describing the first eight books of the Bible, were used in antiquity; Hexateuch is a term coined by more modern students of the Scriptures. *See* BIBLE.

HEYERDAHL, Thor (1914–), Norwegian anthropologist and explorer, born in Larvik, Norway, and educated at the University of Oslo. In 1947, to prove the theory that prehistoric Indians of the Americas had migrated to islands of the Pacific, Heyerdahl, with a crew of five, voyaged 4300 mi. from Callao, Peru, to the Tuamotu Islands of Polynesia on a balsa raft. Named *Kon-Tiki*, the raft was modeled on boats such as ancient Peruvians might have constructed. The historic voyage lasted 101 days. In 1954, also to establish migration by ancient South Americans, Heyerdahl led a Norwegian archeological expedition to the Galápagos Islands; and an expedition to Easter Island and the East Pacific in 1955–56. In 1969, to prove that ancient Egyptians could have reached America 4000 years ago, he attempted to cross the Atlantic in a papyrus boat, *Ra I*, but foundered after traveling 2800 mi. in fifty-six days. The following year he set sail from Morocco in *Ra II* and successfully landed at Bridgetown, Barbados, in fifty-seven days. He is the author of *Kon-Tiki* (1948), *Aku-Aku, The*

Secret of Easter Island (1958), *Sea Route to Polynesia* (1968), and *Expedition Ra* (1970). His film of the Kon-Tiki expedition won an Academy of Motion Picture Arts and Sciences award in 1951.

HEYMANS, Corneille (1892–1968), Belgian physiologist, born in Ghent, and educated at the universities of Ghent and Viënna, and at Western Reserve Medical School (now part of Case Western Reserve University). Heymans began his career as a physician and lecturer in the early 1920's. In 1930 he was appointed professor of pharmacodynamics at the University of Ghent, and during World War II, from 1940 to 1944, served as head of the medical department of the Belgian Relief Commission. For his studies in the physiology and pharmacology of respiration and circulation, together with his detection of the importance of the sinus aorta mechanism in respiration, Heymans won the 1938 Nobel Prize in medicine and physiology. He is the author of *Le Sinus Carotidien* (Eng. trans., "The Carotid Sinus", 1933).

HEYROVSKY, Yaroslav (1890–1967), Czechoslovakian chemist, born in Prague, and educated at the universities of Prague and London. He remained in England until the end of World War I, returning to Prague, where he taught chemistry at Charles University, from 1920 to 1954. Heyrovsky won the 1959 Nobel Prize in chemistry for his invention in the 1920's of polarography, a process by which the chemical composition of oxidizable substances can be determined.

HEYSE, Paul von (1830–1914), German novelist, poet, and dramatist, born in Berlin, and educated at the University of Berlin. For most of his career he was under the patronage of the Bavarian kings Maximilian II (1811–64) and Ludwig II (1845–86). Heyse was noted for the realism and structural perfection of his writings. The most famous of his prose novelettes is *L'Arrabiata* (1855; Eng. trans., *The Fury*, 1855); others are *Das Mädchen von Treppi* (1858; Eng. trans., *The Maiden of Treppi*, 1874) and *Andrea Delfin* (1859; Eng. trans., 1864). His novels include *Kinder der Welt* (1873; Eng. trans., *Children of the World*, 1882). He wrote numerous poems and about sixty plays. He also did translations from English, Spanish, and particularly Italian, literature. Heyse was an opponent of the naturalistic and impressionistic movements in German literature of the last quarter of the 19th century; the counterattacks upon him by members of these schools caused him to lose considerable literary prestige in Germany. Heyse was awarded the 1910 Nobel Prize in literature, the first German writer to receive this honor.

HEYWARD, DuBose (1885–1940), American writer, born in Charleston, S.C. His native city was the background for several colorful novels about Negro life in Southern city slums. In his first novel *Porgy* (1925), set on the Charleston waterfront, he made effective use of the Gullah Negro dialect of South Carolina. His other novels are *Angel* (1926), *Mamba's Daughters* (1929), *Peter Ashley* (1932), *Lost Morning* (1936), and *Star Spangled Virgin* (1939). In collaboration with his wife, Dorothy Heyward (1890–1961), he wrote a dramatization of his novel *Porgy*, which was produced under that name in New York City in 1927 and won the Pulitzer Prize. The play was made into a folk opera entitled *Porgy and Bess* (1935) by the American composer George Gershwin (q.v.). Also in collaboration with his wife, Heyward dramatized *Mamba's Daughters*, which was produced in New York City in 1939. Heyward was the author of a volume of verse, *Skylines and Horizons* (1924).

HEYWOOD, John (1497?–1580?), English dramatist and epigrammatist, probably born in Hertfordshire. He was a friend of the statesman Sir Thomas More (q.v.), through whom he was introduced to the courts of the Engish rulers Edward VI and Mary I (qq.v.), at which he became a favorite. Shortly after the accession (1558) of Elizabeth I (q.v.) to the English throne, Heywood left England for Mechelen, Belgium, where he spent the rest of his life.

Heywood wrote several short dramatic pieces, known as interludes, to be performed at court, including *The Four P's* (printed 1569), *The Play of the Wether* (1533), and *The Play of Love* (1533). These interludes are regarded as the precursors of English comedy. Heywood was also the author of the well-known *Epigrammes* (1562), a collection of more than 600 epigrams and proverbs. He also may have written the two interludes *The Pardoner and the Frere* and *Johan Johan* (both printed anonymously, 1533). His other works include a number of ballads, among them a long allegorical poem entitled *The Spider and the Flie* (1556), which represented Roman Catholics as the flies, Protestants as the spiders, and Queen Mary as the maid destroying the spiders.

HEYWOOD, Thomas (1574?–1641), English dramatist and writer, born in Lincolnshire, and educated at the University of Cambridge. According to his own testimony he wrote more than 220 plays for the English stage. He exhibited a remarkable talent for quick dramatic construction and for fanciful situations, and was most successful in the writing of domestic dramas. His chief plays include the comedies *The*

HEZEKIAH

Royal King and the Loyal Subject (performed about 1602), and *The Wise Woman of Hogsdon* (performed about 1604); the tragedies *A Woman Killed with Kindness* (performed, 1603), and *The English Traveller* (printed, 1633); and the chronicle histories *Edward IV* (2 parts; 1599) and *If You Know Not Me, You Know Nobody* (2 parts; 1605–06). Heywood was the author of several poems, including "Troia Britannica" ("England's Troy", 1609) and "The Hierarchy of the Blessed Angel" (1635); compilations and translations; and *An Apology for Actors* (1612).

HEZEKIAH (Heb. *Hizqīyāh*, "Jehovah strengthens"; Gr., *Ezekias*), King of Judah (715?–687 B.C.), son and successor of Ahaz (q.v.). The most important event of his reign was the Assyrian invasion of Judah in 701 B.C. Four years before the invasion, when Sennacherib (q.v.) acceded to the Assyrian throne, Hezekiah had joined an Egyptian coalition formed to defy the power of Assyria. The coalition was defeated, however, in 701 B.C. by Sennacherib, who reestablished Assyrian authority and forced Hezekiah to pay a heavy tribute (2 Kings 18:13–16). In a second expedition against Judah, about 690 B.C., the Assyrians were routed, before they could attack, by a disaster, described in the Old Testament as a visitation of an angel that destroyed 185,000 men (2 Kings 19:35); this disaster was pictured by the Greek historian Herodotus (q.v.) as a plague of field mice. Modern scholars believe it to have been an outbreak of plague (q.v.). Hezekiah is noted as a great religious reformer; he was probably influenced by the prophet Isaiah (q.v.), who lived during his reign.

HIALEAH, city of Florida, in Dade Co., at the edge of the Everglades, less than 10 miles N.W. of Miami. Part of the Miami winter-resort area, it is noted for its horse-racing track, Hialeah Park. Just south of Hialeah is Miami International Airport. Pop. (1960) 66,972; (1970) 102,297.

HIAWATHA, legendary chieftain of the Iroquois (q.v.) Indians, said to have lived about 1570. He is credited with having brought about the union of the Five Nations (q.v.) of the Iroquois for their mutual protection against the aggressive and stronger Algonquin (q.v.) Indians. According to legend, Hiawatha employed miraculous powers to protect his people from the evil forces of nature. He also instructed the Iroquois in the arts of medicine, agriculture, and navigation. He was the inspiration for the famous poem, *The Song of Hiawatha*, by the American poet Henry Wadsworth Longfellow (q.v.).

HIBBING, village of Minnesota, in Saint Louis Co., 75 miles N.W. of Duluth. It lies in the heart of the Arrowhead resort country, noted for its lakes and forests, and is surrounded by the Mesabi Iron Range. Within the area is the largest open-pit mine in the world. Iron ore in commercial quantities was first discovered in the vicinity of the present village in 1891. Hibbing was laid out in 1893 and incorporated in the same year. Pop. (1960) 17,731; (1970) 16,104.

HIBBS, Ben (1901–), American editor and journalist, born in Fontana, Kan., and educated at the University of Kansas. Having worked on newspapers in Colorado and Kansas, Hibbs in 1929 became associate editor of the *Country Gentlemen* magazine published by the Curtis Publishing Company. Promoted to editor in 1940, he modernized the magazine's style and raised its circulation to an all-time high. In 1940 he was named editor of the *Saturday Evening Post,* Curtis' most prestigious magazine. He proceeded to revise the *Post*'s format by including more color layouts and shorter stories; he also changed the *Post*'s editorial views on national and international issues, bringing them more into line with contemporary opinion. Hibbs left Curtis in 1962, and in the following year he became senior editor of *The Reader's Digest* magazine.

HIBERNATION, relatively dormant condition resembling sleep in which many animals pass the winter. Any animal that remains inactive for many weeks with a body temperature lower than normal may be said to be in hibernation, but physiological changes that occur during dormancy differ greatly among different animals. A highly adaptive hibernator, such as a ground squirrel, will at the appropriate season retreat underground, reduce its body temperature drastically within a few hours, and become dormant, even though the temperature outside the burrow may be well above freezing. It emerges quickly from hibernation as a burst of metabolic energy warms the body to operating level in a similarly short time. During hibernation the squirrel's metabolic rate may be 10 percent below normal, its heart may beat only 10 or 20 times a minute (instead of from 200 to 300), and it may breathe only 4 times a minute (instead of from 100 to 200).

Less highly adaptive hibernators, such as reptiles, reduce their activity more gradually until conditions are too cold for activity; conversely, they require the increasing warmth of spring to return them to full activity.

Amphibians and reptiles generally hibernate where temperatures do not drop below freezing; some insects secrete an organic chemical compound called glycerol, which acts like a

A ground squirrel in hibernation continues his sleep, unaware that he has been picked up and photographed.
C. G. Hampson—
National Audubon Society

kind of antifreeze in the blood and allows them to tolerate temperatures far below freezing. No birds are able to enter a state of prolonged hibernation. Those that lack sufficient insulation to survive long, cold winters migrate to warmer climates. Aestivation, a condition of torpidity or dormancy similar to hibernation, is induced by heat and dryness. Many snails, for example, aestivate in unfavorable hot, dry seasons, when food and moisture are scarce.

HIBERNIA or **IERNE,** name by which Ireland was known to the classical writers of Greece and Rome. The Greek form was first used by the philosopher Aristotle (q.v.), who mentions two islands in the Atlantic Ocean beyond the Pillars of Hercules (q.v.) that were called Albion (Great Britain) and Ierne. The most important of all classical writers on Hibernia was the 2nd-century A.D. Alexandrian geographer Ptolemy (q.v.) who gave a more or less accurate description of the country, including the names of the principal rivers, promontories, seaports, and inland towns.

HIBISCUS, genus of plants, commonly called rose mallows, belonging to the Malvaceae family. The genus is native to warm, temperate regions of the Northern Hemisphere. The hibiscus flower is characterized by a five-pointed calyx that is surrounded by a set of colored bracts growing just beneath it, giving the appearance of a double calyx. The large, showy flowers have five petals, a column of fused stamens with kidney-shaped anthers, and several pistils. The fruit is a many-seeded, five-celled pod.

Shrubs of *Hibiscus* are extensively cultivated throughout the North Temperate Zone. Rose of Sharon or shrubby althea, *H. syriacus,* is a tall Asiatic shrub with smooth leaves. Cultivated varieties have open, bell-shaped flowers in colors ranging from white to yellow, rose, red, and purple. The Chinese hibiscus or China rose, *H. chinesis,* a shrub or tree that grows as tall as 30 ft., is the official flower of Hawaii. It produces huge, showy flowers. Chinese hibiscus is cultivated in the continental United States. The musk mallow, *H. abelmoschus,* is an annual herb growing as tall as 6 ft. It bears large yellow flowers with crimson centers, and is widely cultivated in Florida and the West Indies.

Musk mallow, Hibiscus abelmoschus
Robert Lamb—
National Audubon Society

HICCUP

Several species of *Hibiscus* grow in the wild state in North America. The swamp rose mallow, *H. moscheutos,* is a tall perennial herb with ovate leaves and white flowers with rose-colored centers. It grows along salt marshes of the eastern U.S. Rose of Sharon frequently escapes cultivation, forming thickets along roadsides and in wet waste places.

Okra (q.v.) is the fruit of a plant of the closely related *H. esculentus,* widely cultivated in the southeastern U.S. and the West Indies.

HICCUP or HICCOUGH, paroxysmal, involuntary contraction of the diaphragm (q.v.), which occurs in conjunction with contractions of the larynx and closure of the glottis, arresting the outflow of air. Mild cases of hiccups generally occur spontaneously, lasting only a few minutes, and are commonly induced by minor stomach upsets. Hiccups of a severe character are usually associated with heart attacks, pneumonia, or post-operative abdominal conditions, or tumors or infections in the thoracic cavity. They may also occur from disorders under the diaphragm, particularly when the diaphragm is pushed up, as by distension of the stomach, pancreatitis, or peritonitis. Occasionally severe hiccups occur during pregnancy, and they may also accompany such metabolic disorders as uremia or kidney failure and liver failure. Very occasionally, hiccups may be ascribed to psychogenic factors.

Mild cases of hiccups usually disappear without treatment or simply by breathing in and out of a paper bag, which causes the inspiration of a higher concentration of carbon dioxide than is found in normal air. More severe forms can sometimes be treated by stimulation of certain areas in the back of the nose where it joins the pharynx. Where other methods fail, gastric lavage and injections of chlorpromazine may be effective.

Prolonged cases of hiccups may lead to exhaustion and inability to eat or rest. Because the contractions of the diaphragm that cause hiccups find their origin in abnormal stimulation of one of the phrenic nerves, it may be necessary to paralyze one or both of these by electric stimulation or anesthesia, or in extreme cases to sever them surgically.

HICKOK, James Butler, known as WILD BILL HICKOK (1837–76), American frontiersman and law enforcement officer, born in Troy Grove, Ill. At the age of eighteen he moved to Kansas Territory and at nineteen he was elected constable of Monticello Township. After serving for several years as a stagecoach driver, he became a scout for the Union army during the American Civil War. In 1866 he was appointed deputy United States marshal at Fort Riley, Kans., and in this capacity he participated in many battles with the Indians and served as a scout under various American military leaders. In 1869 he became marshal of Hays City (now Hays) and for nine months in 1871 he was marshal of Abilene. These Kansas towns, then turbulent way stations for cattlemen, were pacified by Hickok's courage and skill as a marksman. In 1872 and 1873 he toured the Eastern part of the U.S. as a member of the wild west show of William F. Cody (q.v.). Hickok was shot to death in a saloon in Deadwood, Dakota Territory; he is the subject of many frontier legends.

HICKORY, common name for trees of the genus *Carya,* belonging to the Walnut family. The genus comprises about ten species native to North America and eastern and southeastern Asia. It includes some of the most valuable timber and nut-producing species in the United States. Hickory trees have tough, hard wood and bear large, pinnately compound leaves. The staminate flowers are in three-branched catkins.

The most valuable nut-producing hickory is *C. illinoensis,* the pecan (q.v.). The shagbark, *C. ovata,* produces most of the nuts marketed as hickory nuts. It is a tall tree, from about 70 to 90 ft., that grows in the eastern U.S. Shagbark nuts are light brown, globular, and thin-shelled. Big shellbark or king nut, *C. laciniosa,* that grows from about 80 to 100 ft. tall, is native to Ohio and Mississippi Valley regions of the U.S. Shellbark nuts are reddish brown and have thick shells. Mockernut or black hickory, *C. tomentosa,* that grows to a height of about 80 ft., is native to the eastern U.S. It bears light brown nuts that have very thick shells. The pignut (q.v.), *C. glabra,* produces nuts that are palatable when young but bitter when mature. The bitternut or swamp hickory, *C. cordiformis,* reaches a height of about 40 to 60 ft. and produces white, thin-shelled, bitter nuts. It is native to rich, wet woods throughout the eastern U.S.

HICKORY, city of North Carolina, in Burke and Catawba counties, about 34 miles N.W. of Gastonia. The city manufactures textiles, furniture, and foundry products. Nearby dams provide hydroelectric power. It is the site of Lenoir-Rhyne College, established in 1891. Pop. (1960) 19,328; (1970) 20,569.

HICKS, Elias (1748–1830), American Quaker minister, born in Hempstead, Long Island, N.Y. He became a widely known preacher by the time he was twenty-seven. His vigorous preaching during his tours of the United States and Canada (after 1775), his attacks on slavery, and

HIEROGLYPHICS

his inclination toward Unitarianism (q.v.) in religious doctrine gained him a wide following. In 1827-28, opposition to his preaching caused the Society of Friends to split into two sects, the Orthodox and the Liberal, or Hicksite. See FRIENDS, SOCIETY OF.

HICKSITES. See HICKS, ELIAS.

HICKSVILLE, unincorporated suburban village of New York, in Nassau Co., on Long Island, part of Oyster Bay town, about 20 miles E. of New York City. Hicksville is in an area growing truck-farm crops and producing electrical and electronic equipment, glass products, truck bodies, plastic products, aircraft parts, instruments, cement, machinery, paper and metal products, apparel, and fertilizer. The area was settled in 1648. Pop. (1960) 50,405; (1970) 48,075.

HIDALGO Y COSTILLA, Miguel (1753–1811), Mexican priest and revolutionist, educated at Valladolid (now Morelia, Mexico). In 1778 he was ordained a priest and in 1803 was given charge of the parish of Dolores, in Guanajuato. He worked to improve the economic condition of his poor parishioners, mostly Indians, by teaching them to cultivate vineyards and operate small industries such as brickmaking. In 1809 Hidalgo joined a secret society dedicated to freeing Mexico from the oppression of the Spanish colonial government. On Sept. 16, 1810, Hidalgo, carrying a banner depicting Our Lady of Guadalupe, patron saint of Mexico, proclaimed a crusade and was joined by hundreds of his parishioners and by thousands of Mexican natives. He captured the towns of Guanajuato and Guadalajara in October. Although he had the advantage, Hidalgo failed to march on Mexico City. On Jan. 11, 1811, his army was completely routed near Guadalajara by a small force of Spanish soldiers. Hidalgo fled north, but he was captured and shot. After the establishment of the Mexican republic in 1824, the priest was regarded almost as a saint. The State of Hidalgo was named for him, and the town of Dolores became Dolores Hidalgo. The day on which he proclaimed his revolt (Sept. 16) is celebrated as the Mexican Independence Day. See MEXICO: *History.*

HIDATSA, known as the MINNETAREE or MINITARI, also called the GROS VENTRE (Fr., "big belly"), Indian tribe of Siouan (q.v.) stock, who ranged in the area now comprising the State of North Dakota. The name Hidatsa came into usage about the middle of the 19th century and was derived from the name of a tribal village. Today the Hidatsa reside on the Fort Berthold Indian Reservation in North Dakota.

HIDDENITE. See SPODUMENE.

HIERATIC WRITING. See HIEROGLYPHICS.

HIERO *or* **HIERON,** the name of two rulers of ancient Syracuse (q.v.).

Hiero I (d. 466 B.C.), Tyrant (478–466 B.C.), successor to his brother Gelon (q.v.). Hiero, known for his military craft, had, before his accession to power, distinguished himself at the battle of Himera (q.v.) in 480 B.C. As tyrant he made Syracuse the greatest city in Sicily and founded in 475 B.C. the city of Aetna. His victory over the Etruscans at Cumae, on the Italian coast, in 474 B.C. preserved the independence of the Greek colonists in Italy. In 472 B.C. the Syracusan army defeated Thrasydaeus (d. 472 B.C.), ruler of Akragas (modern Agrigento; q.v.), and Hiero became supreme ruler of the island. The tyrant was known as a cruel ruler, but he was noted for his patronage of poets and philosophers, including such great writers as Pindar and Aeschylus (qq.v.).

Hiero II (308–215 B.C.), Tyrant (about 265–215 B.C.). He fought under Pyrrhus (q.v.), King of Epirus, against the Roman invaders of Sicily (278–275 B.C.), and after the departure of Pyrrhus in 275 B.C. was chosen commander of the Syracusan army. Hiero's military successes against the Mamertines in 270 B.C. resulted in his election as tyrant by the grateful citizens of Syracuse. In 264 B.C. Hiero allied himself with the Carthaginians in besieging the Mamertines at Messana (Messina), but the Romans defeated the Syracusan army. A year later Hiero concluded a treaty with Rome, and he remained a Roman ally thereafter. During the Punic Wars (q.v.) Hiero assisted his allies with money and troops and was awarded great honors by the Romans. Later historians described him as a wise and just ruler.

HIEROGLYPHICS, characters in a system of writing that consist of representations of objects rather than purely conventional signs. The term is also applied to the system of writing using such characters, and especially to the writing of the Maya (q.v.), early Indians of Mexico, and of the ancient Egyptians; see EGYPTIAN LANGUAGE AND LITERATURE. The writings of other North American Indians were pictorial, but did not amount to a hieroglyphic system; the writings of ancient Babylonia (*see* CUNEIFORM) and China were originally picture writings, but at an early date they were simplified and conventionalized to the extent of losing their hieroglyphic character.

The hieroglyphic writing of ancient Egypt was already well developed by about 3400 B.C. It consisted of pictograms, signs representing objects

HIEROGLYPHICS

or associated ideas, and phonoglyphs, signs representing the sounds of the words for the object depicted. In the Egyptian language, as in other north African and Middle East tongues, the essential meaning of a word was represented by its root, the consonant framework, stripped of prefixes, suffixes, and vowels. Thus the hieroglyph for ear, representing the root *sdm*, was used not only for "hear" but also for "to paint the eyes", with the root *śdm*. In order to specify the meaning intended, which was not always clear from the context, the symbols for each word included one or more determinatives. Thus the hieroglyph for man acted as a determinative to indicate that the hieroglyph associated with it represented the name of a man. A book (a roll of papyrus) was the determinative signifying that an abstract meaning was intended, and a book with an ear represented "hearing". Other common determinatives included those for motion, force, buildings, inhabited places, and foreign countries.

Two forms of hieroglyphic writing were in common use, the epigraphic, or monumental, hieroglyphics, which were carved or painted on stone or wood with precise detail, and the hieratic, or cursive, form, written on papyrus with a blunt reed pen. Monumental hieroglyphics were carved in vertical columns read from top to bottom, or in horizontal lines, from right to

Hieroglyphics on the lid of an Egyptian sarcophagus record a prayer for the dead man, whose soul is represented by a human-headed falcon with outspread wings.
Louvre

left. Occasionally, on balanced tablets flanking a central figure, one tablet contained hieroglyphics carved from right to left, and the other from left to right. The hieratic form, conventionally inscribed from right to left, was in use as early as the I Dynasty, and had become common by 2500 B.C. Although the hieratic form was intended as a precise transcription of hieroglyphics sign by sign, it was gradually modified until in time little resemblance remained.

About the 6th century B.C. another form of script, the demotic, came into common use, and the hieratic, which had previously been used for all purposes, was restricted to the transcription of religious writings. Demotic was a more cursive and conventionalized development from the hieratic script, and, like the other forms of hieroglyphics, was written from right to left. It remained in use until the 5th century A.D. After that time knowledge of hieroglyphic writing was lost, and was not rediscovered until the decipherment of the Rosetta Stone (q.v.) in the 19th century; see EGYPTIAN ARCHEOLOGY; EGYPTIAN LANGUAGE AND LITERATURE; WRITING.

HIERONYMUS, Saint Eusebius. See JEROME, SAINT.

HIGGINSON, Thomas Wentworth Storrow (1823–1911), American writer, clergyman, and soldier, born in Cambridge, Mass., and educated at Harvard University and the Harvard Divinity School. From 1847 to 1850 he was a Unitarian pastor in Newburyport, Mass., but in the latter year, moved by intense abolitionist conviction, he resigned his pastorate to run unsuccessfully for Congress. Holding a pastorate in Worcester, Mass. (1852–61), he was active in antislavery agitation, particularly in Kansas. At the outbreak of the American Civil War, Higginson enlisted as a captain in a regiment of Massachusetts volunteers; from 1862 until 1864, when he was discharged because of a wound received in 1863, he served as colonel in command of the first Negro regiment in the United States Army.

At the close of the war he turned to literature, distinguishing himself as a prolific man of letters and an advocate of the political rights of women. He became a confidante and mentor of the American poet Emily Dickinson (q.v.), who referred to him as her "Dear Preceptor". After her death he edited her *Poems* (2 vol., 1890–91) with the American author Mabel Loomis Todd (1858–1932). Among his other numerous works is *Army Life in a Black Regiment* (1870), a vivid account of his Civil War experiences.

HIGH CHURCH. See CHURCH OF ENGLAND.

HIGH COMMISSION, COURT OF, former ecclesiastical tribunal of England, established in 1549 to punish heresy, schism, and other offenses against the peace and dignity of the Church. The court was condemned by the English Bill of Rights (q.v.) in 1689. See ECCLESIASTICAL COURTS.

HIGH FIDELITY, technique of recording, broadcasting, and reproducing sound to match as closely as possible the characteristics of the original sound. The term is used also to designate the equipment used to amplify and reinforce the sound, and to the sound produced in this manner. Designed for the enjoyment of the listener, a high-fidelity system used in the home does not reproduce the full crescendo of a symphony orchestra, because such a sound level would be impractical in a living room. To achieve high-fidelity reproduction the sound must be virtually without distortion and must include the full frequency range of human hearing, from about 20 Hz to 20 kilohertz; see FREQUENCY; SOUND.

DEVELOPMENT

After the advent of sound recording (q.v.) in 1877, many inventors attempted to achieve high-quality reproduction. The rise of radio (q.v.) broadcasting in the 1920's stimulated improvements in microphones, amplifiers, loudspeakers, and phonographs and resulted in greatly improved transmission of the rich overtones of musical instruments. By 1940 most of the techniques essential for high fidelity had been discovered. The development in the late 1930's of frequency modulation (q.v.), the radio-transmission system known popularly as FM, offered a means of high-fidelity broadcasting and reception. Many listeners who were dissatisfied with commercial radio broadcasting at that time acquired FM receivers, and many hobbyists assembled their own systems. Not until after 1948, when the long-playing (LP) microgroove record became available, did high fidelity attract widespread attention. The long-playing records not only supplied music for about 25 min. on each side, but also greatly extended the sound range. Commercial phonographs and radios, however, were not capable of reproducing the full frequency range provided by these records. As a result of public demands for better sound-producing equipment, the production of high-fidelity systems became a major industry in the 1950's.

High fidelity for the home system begins with the recording or transmission of the original sounds, usually musical. Successful high-fidelity recording and broadcasting require carefully designed, expensive, precision equipment.

Because many factors, besides equipment,

HIGH FIDELITY

determine the way sound is heard, a high-fidelity system must be adjusted to meet various requirements. The human ear, for example, is an imperfect instrument, differing in each person. All listeners are not satisfied by the same quality of sound reproduction. Furthermore, the sensitivity of the ear varies with high and low notes. Another consideration is that rooms in which the music is heard and even recording studios may not have the good acoustics (q.v.) required for high-fidelity sound. The proportions of the listener's room are very important. Draperies, rugs, and stuffed furniture tend to deaden sound; hard, reflecting surfaces may cause unpleasant reverberations. A good high-fidelity system is flexible enough to cope with these variable listening conditions.

COMPONENTS

A high-fidelity system consists of the following components: the turntable and tone arm, the amplifier, the speakers, and the control unit. Supplementary components include the tuner and the tape recorder. The turntable and tone arm translate the vibrations on a phonograph record into electrical voltage variations, that are strengthened by the amplifier; the speakers transform the amplified voltage variations into sound; and the control unit coordinates these elements, making individual adjustments possible. The tuner and the tape recorder provide additional sources of sound. The most modern high-fidelity components often carry out more than one function. An example would be a combined tuner-preamplifier-amplifier unit.

The Turntable and Tone Arm. (For the basic operating principles of these elements, see PHONOGRAPH.) In modern high-fidelity systems these components are carefully designed and constructed so that they will provide accurate reproduction without extraneous noise. The turntable is rotated by a motor that turns at a constant speed, thus avoiding distortions called wow and rumble. Wow consists of a slow variation in pitch caused by variation in the speed of the turntable, and rumble is a low-frequency tremor caused by defects in the turntable. Both of these defects are more likely to occur in automatic record changers, which are used for uninterrupted listening to many records, than in the precise turntable used in well-designed music systems.

The tone arm and the cartridge form one of the most critical parts of the high-fidelity installation. The finely balanced tone arm holds a cartridge, which in turn holds a stylus, preferably tipped with long-wearing diamond. To reproduce recorded sound accurately and with minimum wear on the record, the cartridge must provide maximum compliance, that is, an easy lateral and vertical motion of the stylus. The stylus, moreover, must contact the record at a precise angle and with the proper pressure.

The Amplifier. The amplifier converts the relatively weak electrical impulses received from the tone arm into power sufficient to drive the speakers. The amount of power that an amplifier can produce is rated in watts. Depending on the requirements of the speaker system, an amplifier may deliver from 10 to 125 watts of electrical power. The amplifier is controlled, as a rule, by a device called the preamplifier, which amplifies minute sound-signal voltages too small for the amplifier to handle. Preamplifiers boost the bass and attenuate the treble to compensate for the poor bass and strong treble response of phonograph records. Most amplifiers are equipped with the so-called solid-state circuits for maximum power and ease of maintenance; see TRANSISTOR.

The Speaker System. An electromechanical device that produces audible sound from the amplified audio voltages, the speaker system usually uses separate speakers to handle high and low sounds; see LOUDSPEAKER. A crossover, or dividing network, leads the sound signal from the amplifier and sends correct portions of it to each speaker or driver. Large speakers, called woofers, reproduce low-frequency sound; high-frequency tones emerge from tweeters, small speakers often placed above the woofers. A woofer and a tweeter are usually mounted together in a screened enclosure. At least two such enclosures are required for stereophonic sound.

The Control Unit. As the nerve center of the high-fidelity system, the control unit performs a number of critical functions. For example, the surface noises of old records are attenuated by means of a device called the scratch filter; another device, the rumble filter, cuts down low-pitched noises, such as vibration from the phonograph motor; the loudness control compensates for the inability of the ear to hear high and low notes as clearly as it hears the middle range, by increasing the relative level of treble and bass tones, when the record is played at a reduced volume. The control unit also adjusts sound signals from the record player, the tape recorder, or the tuner.

The Tuner. The AM/FM tuner allows the listener to receive broadcasts from stations in the broadest band of the radio spectrum, from 500 to 1650 kilohertz (AM), 88 to 108 megahertz (FM). From the broadcast signals reaching the

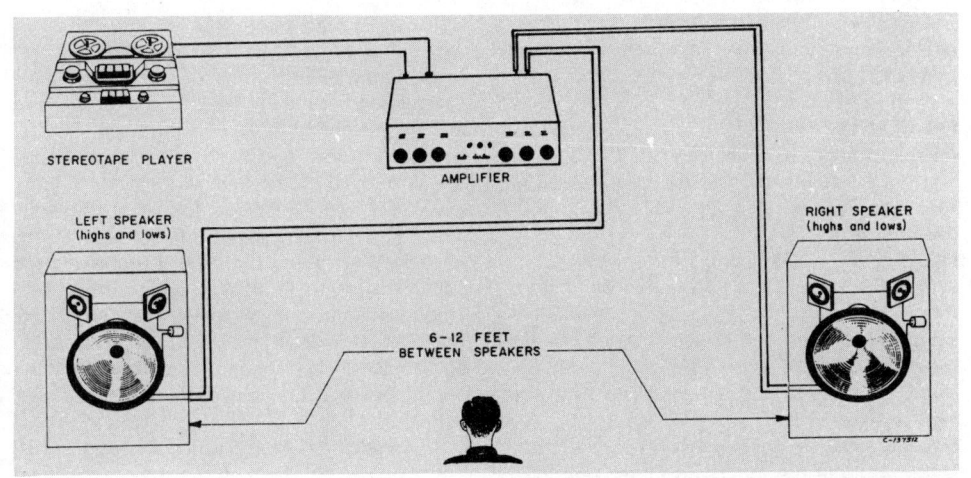

HIGHLAND FLING

In stereophonic recordings, sound is recorded through two separate channels. Stereophonic sound is produced by playing these recordings on dual-channel equipment capable of receiving and amplifying the sound impulses separately and directing them to separate loudspeaker systems. Radio Corp. of America

antenna, the tuner selects the frequency of the desired station to the exclusion of other stations in the broadcast range. It then extracts the audio voltage representing the program being transmitted and amplifies this voltage to activate the speakers of the high-fidelity system.

The Tape Recorder. This device records and reproduces sound magnetically on tape, which usually consists of thin plastic coated with a magnetic oxide. With the tape recorder, an audio enthusiast can record sound on tape, play the recording, and then erase the tape for reuse. Record manufacturers also supply prerecorded tapes, either on reels or in small packages known as cassettes. Tape can supply hours of recording time, and because it is virtually immune to the damage that eventually mars phonograph records, its life is practically unlimited.

STEREOPHONIC SOUND

Stereophonic sound represents an increasingly successful attempt to recreate in a pair of ears the conditions that would exist near an actual sound source, such as an orchestra. The sound is picked up separately from the left and the right hand sides of an orchestra, and through the use of two or more carefully placed speakers, sound from a stereophonic recording is directed toward the listener in such a way that he seems to hear music from the left, from the right, and from the center. More important, he becomes aware of a veil of sound that seems to have depth and solidity, as well as directionality.

In the early 1970's, a new system of recording and reproduction, known as quadriphonic or quadrasonic sound, was introduced in the United States. It was essentially similar to the two-channel sound system, except it involved a four-channel recording and a four-speaker reproduction system. *See* SOUND RECORDING.

Stereophonic radio broadcasts can be received on an FM tuner through a process called multiplexing, which consists of the simultaneous transmission of two broadcast signals on a single FM wave. At the source of the broadcast, two microphones pick up the sound, which is then fed along separated channels to the FM station transmitter. At this point a modulation process produces two signals on a single channel. Received by the listener's tuner, these different signals from the left-hand and right-hand microphones are separated, drawn through a dual amplifier, and fed into separate speakers for reconversion into stereophonic sound.

M.C.

HIGHLAND, town of Indiana, in Lake Co., 6 miles s.w. of Gary. The area has many truck farms and gardens. Highland was settled by Dutch immigrants in 1850; it was incorporated in 1910. Pop. (1960) 16,284; (1970) 24,947.

HIGHLANDERS, various regiments of the British army, originally recruited in the Highlands (q.v.) of Scotland. Among the most famous of the Highland regiments are the First Battalion Royal Highlanders, founded in 1729, commonly called the Black Watch (q.v.), and the Gordon Highlanders, founded in 1787 by George Gordon, 5th Duke of Gordon (1770–1836). The term also refers to the inhabitants of the Scottish Highlands.

HIGHLAND FLING, folk dance of Scotland, danced by natives of the Scottish Highlands. One or more persons take part in the dance, which was originally a victory dance after battle.

369

HIGHLAND PARK

The expression "fling" comes from the characteristic step of the dance in which the dancer hops and turns on one foot and beats his ankle with the other foot.

HIGHLAND PARK, city of Illinois, in Lake Co., on Lake Michigan, 25 miles N. of Chicago, of which it is a residential suburb. It was settled in 1834 and incorporated in 1867. Pop. (1960) 25,532; (1970) 32,263.

HIGHLAND PARK, city of Michigan, in Wayne Co., completely surrounded by Detroit. It is a manufacturing center, and a residential suburb of Detroit. The principal industries are the manufacture of automobiles, boats, and marine and industrial engines. Highland Park was incorporated in 1918. Pop. (1970) 35,444.

HIGHLANDS, mountainous portion of Scotland, including the Inner and Outer Hebrides, extending N. and W. of the Grampians (q.v.). The region has no political or civil boundary, and is separated only by a vague line of demarcation from the division called the Lowlands. The Highlanders were distinguished from the Lowlanders for centuries by race and language, particularly by the persistence of the Gaelic language among them. They have long been a popular subject for poetry and fiction, being most memorably treated in the poems and novels of Sir Walter Scott (q.v.). The most important industries of the Highlands are fishing and sheep raising. The chief cities are Aberdeen and Inverness (qq.v.).

HIGH POINT, city of North Carolina, in Guilford and Randolph counties, in the Piedmont region, 19 miles S.E. of Winston-Salem and 99 miles N.W. of Raleigh. It is served by railroad, and by major airlines. The leading industries of the city are furniture and hosiery manufacturing; other industrial products include paint, chemicals, and machinery. High Point is the site of the semiannual Southern Furniture Exposition. High Point College (Methodist), in the city, was established in 1924.

High Point was settled in 1853 and received its name as a result of being the highest point on the original survey for the old North Carolina Railroad between Goldsboro and Charlotte. It was incorporated in 1859, and the first furniture factory was established there in 1888, marking the beginning of the city's industrial growth. Pop. (1960) 62,063; (1970) 63,204.

HIGH PRIEST, in a religious hierarchy, head of a priesthood. The term is particularly used for the head of the Jewish priesthood in ancient Israel. Until the Deuteronomic reform (see DEUTERONOMY) in the 7th century B.C., the Jews had no absolute central religious authority. The institution of high priest was ancient, however, beginning, according to the Pentateuch (q.v.), with Aaron, elder brother of the prophet and lawgiver Moses (qq.v.). The office is recorded as having descended to Aaron's third son, Eleazar, and thenceforward in the line of Eleazar (Exod. 28, Num. 3:32). In the time of the second Temple (see TEMPLE: *Temple at Jerusalem*) the high priest came to be considered the head of the theocracy (q.v.) and the official representative of the nation to its Persian rulers. The priesthood was kept in the family of Aaron until the subjugation of Israel by the Greeks and, later, the Romans, when foreign rulers began to confer the office as they pleased. See JEWS: *Subject Judea.*

The regulations for the office are set down in Lev. 8, 9, and 21. The high priest was permitted to marry only an Israelite virgin, and he was forbidden any impure contact that might defile him. His functions consisted principally of the administration of the Temple and the Jewish religion. Only he could enter, once a year, on Yom Kippur (q.v.), the innermost sanctuary of the Temple, known as the Holy of Holies; there the sacred Ark of the Covenant (q.v.) was kept. He was also custodian of the Urim and Thummim (q.v.). He wore vestments of great splendor, except when entering the Holy of Holies, at which time he wore a simple white robe. He proclaimed divine revelations, having the exclusive privilege of consulting God directly. Although the high priest had no official judicial power, appeal to him could be made in any matter, and no important decision affecting national policy could be taken without his consent.

The Roman religion also required a high priest, who was called the Pontifex Maximus (Lat., "greatest bridgemaker"); see ROMAN RELIGION AND MYTHOLOGY. In Mormonism, all the priests of the Melchizedek, or higher, priesthood are called high priests; see REORGANIZED CHURCH OF JESUS CHRIST OF LATTER-DAY SAINTS.

HIGH SCHOOL. See EDUCATION IN THE UNITED STATES; EDUCATION, SECONDARY.

HIGH SEAS, in international law, the open sea, including the whole extent of the sea not the exclusive property of any particular country. Traditionally, every country bordering on the sea has exclusive sovereignty over that sea for a distance of 3 mi. (a marine league) from its shores, and the sea beyond the territorial limits is open or common to all countries. Many countries, however, claim control over wider areas for certain purposes, such as protection of fisheries.

Within the territorial limits of 3 mi., the courts

of the nations contiguous to the sea has jurisdiction; beyond the 3-mi. limit international law prevails. A number of treaties with other countries, negotiated by the United States during the Prohibition (q.v.) era of the 1920's, gave the U.S. the right to board vessels, suspected of transporting intoxicating liquors illegally, outside the 3-mi. limit as far as 12 mi. from the shores of the U.S.

See also SEARCH, RIGHT OF; SEAS, FREEDOM OF THE; TERRITORIAL WATERS.

HIGHWAY. See ROAD.

HIIUMAA or **DAGÖ,** island of the Soviet Union, in the Baltic Sea, 14 mi. off the w. coast of the Estonian S.S.R., s.w. of the entrance to the Gulf of Finland and N. of the Island of Saaremaa. In 1561 Hiiumaa was acquired by Sweden and in 1710 by Russia, which ceded it to Estonia in 1919. Along with the rest of Estonia, Hiiumaa was incorporated into the Soviet Union in 1940. The principal industry of the island is fishing. Many of the inhabitants are Swedish. Area, 371 sq.mi.

HIJACKING, in law in England and the United States, a type of robbery (q.v.) defined as the forcible taking of property from the person of another on a public road or highway, and regarded as a compound larceny (q.v.). Such an offense on land is also known as highway robbery. In 16th-century England, such robbery was made a felony (q.v.) without so-called benefit of clergy. In the U.S. hijacking applies most often to the theft of goods in transit by truck. A notable historical example of the practice was the common seizure of illicit liquor by rival gangs during the era of prohibition (q.v.).

In the air, hijacking, also called sky-jacking or air piracy, is defined as the forcible commandeering of an aircraft while in flight. In the U.S., under a 1961 Federal law, it is an offense punishable by not less than twenty years or by death. As a form of piracy (q.v.), hijacking is also punishable under international law and is justiciable, that is, liable to trial by a court of justice, anywhere. See AIR LAW.

HILARION, Saint (290?–371), Palestinian monk and hermit, born near Gaza, and educated in Alexandria, Egypt, where he became a convert to Christianity. He visited Saint Anthony (q.v.) in the Egyptian desert and, on his return to Palestine, Hilarion became the first monk and hermit in that country. He lived as an anchorite in the desert marshes near Gaza for a number of years and attracted many disciples by his piety and by the miraculous cures attributed to him. In order to achieve solitude once again Hilarion went to Egypt in 360, but his retreat was discovered by his followers. He set out again in search of solitude, traveling first to Sicily, and finally to Cyprus, where he died. Most of the knowledge about Hilarion's life is taken from the writings of Saint Jerome (q.v.). His traditional feast day, no longer included in the Roman Catholic calendar, is Oct. 21; see SAINT.

HILARY, Saint (315?–367?), Christian prelate and doctor of the Church, born in Poitiers, France. Of pagan parentage, Hilary was a convert to Christianity. About 353 he was elected bishop of Poitiers, and immediately began a rigorous suppression of the heresy of Arianism (see ARIUS) in his diocese. Although his Arian opponents secured his banishment to Phrygian in 356, Hilary attended the synod of Seleucia (q.v.) in 359, where he delivered a scholarly and vigorous defense of orthodoxy. He returned to Poitiers in 361 and continued until his death to attack Arianism. His feast day is Jan. 13.

HILBERT, David (1862–1943), German mathematician, born in Königsberg (now Kaliningrad, U.S.S.R.). He was educated at the University of Königsberg and taught at that institution from 1893 to 1895. From 1895 to 1930, when he retired, Hilbert was professor of mathematics at the University of Göttingen. He made a thorough examination of Euclidean geometry and established the science of axiomatics as he attempted more rigorous definitions of some of Euclid's intuitive premises; see AXIOM. Hilbert's system of axioms was published in his book *Grundlagen der Geometrie* (1899; Eng. trans., *Foundations of Geometry,* 1902); see GEOMETRY. He also worked on relativity (q.v.) and the theory of relative fields, on the theory of numbers (q.v.), and on integral equations (see CALCULUS: *Integral Calculus*). His studies on mathematical logic are considered major contributions to the field. See MATHEMATICS: *History*.

HILDA, Saint or **HILD, Saint** (614–80), English abbess, born in Northumbria. Converted to Christianity about 627 by the Roman missionary Saint Paulinus (d. 644), she ruled the monastery of Whitby from 657 until her death. During her rule Whitby was a gathering place for important ecclesiastics and scholars; the Old English poet Caedmon (q.v.) lived there. Her feast is Nov. 17.

HILDEGARD, Saint (1098?–1179), German abbess, born in Böckelheim, and educated at the Benedictine convent of Disenberg of which she became abbess in 1136. She later founded the convent of Rupertsberg, near Bingen. Saint Hildegard is renowned for her mystical experiences, which she recorded between 1141 and 1150. They were first published in 1513. Her traditional feast day is Sept. 17.

HILDESHEIM

HILDESHEIM, town of West Germany, in Lower Saxony State, at the base of the Harz Mts., 17 miles S.E. of Hannover. It is chiefly industrial, manufacturing agricultural tools, bricks, paper, stoves, machines, cigars, textiles, and beer, and processing foodstuffs, sugar, and leather. In 822 it became the seat of a bishopric and in the early 11th century the bishop of Hildesheim, Saint Bernward (d. 1022), made the city an important center of Romanesque architecture. After becoming a free city of the Holy Roman Empire in the 13th century, Hildesheim was accorded municipal rights (1249) and in that same period entered the Hanseatic League (q.v.). In succeeding years the bishops of the town enlarged their territory by warfare. The bishopric of Hildesheim was secularized in 1803 and twelve years later incorporated into the kingdom of Hannover (q.v.). During World War II, Hildesheim was severely bombed. Among the landmarks that were heavily damaged or destroyed were the Roman Catholic cathedral, the church of Saint Michael, which dated from the 11th century, the town hall, and the building that formerly served as the butchers' guildhall. Pop. (1960) 96,296.

HILL, Ambrose Powell (1825–65), American soldier, born in Culpeper, Va., and educated at the United States Military Academy at West Point, N.Y. He served in the Mexican War and Seminole War (qq.v.) and from 1855 to 1860 with the United States Coast Survey. In 1861, just prior to the outbreak of the American Civil War, Hill resigned from the army to become a colonel in the Confederate service. He fought with distinction in many major campaigns and in 1863 he was made a lieutenant general, commanding one of the three corps of the army of General Robert E. Lee (see under LEE); in that year his troops led the attack which began the Battle of Gettysburg (see GETTYSBURG, BATTLE OF). Hill was killed in action during the fighting around Petersburg, Va.

HILL, Archibald Vivian (1886–   ), British physiologist, born in Bristol, England, and educated at Trinity College, University of Cambridge. From 1920 to 1923 he was professor of physiology at the University of Manchester, and from 1923 to 1925 he held the same position at University College, London. From 1926 to 1951 he served as research professor of the Royal Society and as secretary of the Royal Society from 1935 to 1945. Hill contributed valuable research in physiology and biophysics. For his work on the production of lactic acid associated with the expenditure of energy in muscular activity, he shared the 1922 Nobel Prize in medicine and physiology with the German physiologist Otto Meyerhof (q.v.).

HILL, James Jerome (1838–1916), American railway promoter and financier, born near Rockwood, Ontario, Canada. He left his home in 1856 for a business career in Saint Paul, Minn., and became involved in many mercantile ventures there, including the organization of a river steamboat line to Winnipeg, Canada, and the formation of a fuel company to supply coal to the railroads. In 1878 Hill purchased, with his associates, the Saint Paul and Pacific Railroad. He gradually gained control of a number of smaller lines which he amalgamated into an integrated railway system extending north to the Canadian border and westward to Seattle. In 1890 Hill consolidated all of his railway holdings into one corporate entity, the Great Northern Railway Company. He battled with the railway magnate Edward Henry Harriman (see under HARRIMAN) for control of the Chicago, Burlington & Quincy Railroad, later joining forces with him and John Pierpont Morgan (see under MORGAN) in the formation of the Northern Securities Company. He was president of the Great Northern until 1907 when he retired to become chairman of the board of directors. Hill also played an important part in the organization and funding of the Canadian Pacific Railway, but resigned in 1883 when the line became competitive with his own ventures. His other varied operations, which eventually included stock-market manipulations, mining, and banking, caused him to become known as the "Empire Builder". See RAILROADS: *United States Railroads.*

HILLA, city in Iraq, and capital of Hilla Province, 60 miles s. of Baghdad. Hilla is a road junction and trade center on the Baghdad-Basra railway. It is situated in the center of a large irrigated area that grows dates, barley, rice, wheat, millet, sesame, and beans. The city was built in 1101, partly with bricks taken from the nearby ancient ruins of Babylon. Two other important Mesopotamian ruined cities, Kush and Borsippa (or Birs Nimrod), are nearby. Hilla was an administrative center of the Ottoman Empire in the 18th and 19th centuries. The name is often spelled Hillah, Al Hilla, or Al Hillah. Pop. (1965) 84,717.

HILLARY, Sir Edmund Percival (1919–   ), New Zealand explorer and mountain climber, born in Auckland. During World War II he served in the Royal New Zealand Air Force as a navigator in the South Pacific. An experienced skier and mountaineer, he participated in expeditions to the Himalaya mountains in 1951 and 1952. He joined the British Mt. Everest Expedi-

Edmund Hillary shares a light moment with his fellow New Zealander Wallace George Lowe during the 1953 expedition that reached the summit of Mt. Everest.
UPI

tion of 1953 as one of the chief climbers. Together with the Nepalese Sherpa mountain guide, Tenzing Norkay (q.v.), he reached the summit on May 29, 1953. Later that year Hillary was knighted by Elizabeth II (q.v.), Queen of Great Britain, for his achievement. Beginning in late 1956 he headed the New Zealand party of the British Commonwealth Transantarctic Expedition, an expedition organized in connection with the International Geophysical Year (1957–58). He subsequently led several expeditions in the Everest region. He wrote *Schoolhouse in the Clouds* (1964).

HILLEL, called HILLEL THE ELDER (about 60 B.C.–about 10 A.D.), Jewish rabbi and teacher, the first scholar to systematize the interpretation of scriptural Law, born, according to the Talmud (q.v.), in Babylonia. He received his advanced training in Jerusalem and became an authority on the Law. About 30 B.C. he was elected head of a religious council in Jerusalem. Hillel's emphasis on adherence to ethical norms, personal piety, humility, and loving concern for one's fellows anticipated the moral teachings of Christ. His motto was: "What is hateful to you, do not do to your neighbor". Hillel founded a liberal school of scriptural interpretation, in opposition to the rigid school of Shammai (fl. 1st. cent. A.D.), another scholar. The conflict ultimately was decided in favor of Hillel. For many generations the religious leaders of the Jewish community in Palestine were descendants of Hillel; *see* GAMALIEL.   N.N.G.

HILLMAN, Sidney (1887–1946), American labor leader, born in Zagare (now in the Lithuanian S.S.R.). He came to the United States at the age of twenty, and became a labor-union organizer in the clothing industry in Chicago. He was elected president of the Amalgamated Clothing Workers of America in 1915, and led the strikes

Sidney Hillman   Blackstone Studios

that resulted in the establishment of the 48-hour workweek in New York City in 1916, and the 44-hour workweek in 1919. Subsequently, he attained nationwide prominence as a leader of the American Federation of Labor (q.v.). In 1935 he was one of the leaders of the group of unions that disaffiliated from the A.F.L. to form the Congress of Industrial Organizations (q.v.). He later became a vice-president of the C.I.O. and in 1939 was elected chairman of the executive council of the Textile Workers' Union of America.

HILLQUIT, Morris. see SOCIALIST PARTY.

HILLSIDE, township of New Jersey, in Union Co., adjoining Newark and Elizabeth on the w. The principal industrial establishments in the township are machinery, metal products, and rubber, asbestos, cork, and paper goods. Pop. (1960) 22,304; (1970) 21,636.

HILO, city and seaport of Hawaii, and county seat of Hawaii Co., on the N.E. coast of Hawaii Island, about 225 miles S.E. of Honolulu. The crescent-shaped harbor of Hilo is one of the best within the State, but is often subject to severe tidal waves. The tropical forests surrounding the city and the volcanoes of Mauna Loa and Mauna Kea (qq.v.) rising up behind Hilo add to the beauty of the city, which is an important tourist center. Fruit canning is the principal industry. Pop. (1960) 25,966; (1970) 26,353.

HILVERSUM, city of the Netherlands, in North Holland Province, 16 miles S.E. of Amsterdam. Hilversum is a residential suburb and a summer resort. Several important Dutch radio stations are in the city. Among the important manufactured products of Hilversum are carpets and woolens. Pop. (1966 est.) 103,076.

HIMALAYA, or HIMALAYAS (Skr., "abode of snow"), mountain system of S. central Asia, containing the highest peaks in the world, and consisting of several parallel and converging ranges. The mass of the Himalaya proper extends S.E. and E. from the Indus R. in the w. to the Brahmaputra R. in the E., a distance of about 1500 mi. through West Pakistan Province, Pakistan; Jammu and Kashmir State, India; Tibet; Nepal; Sikkim; and Bhutan. In the N. it descends to the elevated plateau of Tibet, and in the S. to the lowland drained by the Ganges and the Indus rivers; the average width is about 100 mi. to 150 mi. The mean elevation of the range is from 16,000 ft. to 18,000 ft. above sea level, but many peaks rise to more than 25,000 ft. above sea level. Among them are Annapurna and Dhaulagiri (qq.v.) in Nepal; Mt. Everest (q.v.) on the Nepal-Tibet border; Cho Oyo in N.E. Nepal; Kanchenjunga (q.v.) on the Nepal-Sikkim border; Godwin-Austen, or K^2, in Jammu and Kashmir; and Nanda Devi in Uttar Pradesh State, India.

The Himalayan mountain system is divided into three parallel zones extending the entire length of the system. The zones are comprised of the Great Himalayas in the N., which include the main ranges and highest peaks and rise above the snow line to an average elevation of about 20,000 ft.; the Lesser Himalayas to the S., which, at an average elevation of about 12,000 ft. to 15,000 ft., are the intricate middle ranges of the chain; and the Outer Himalayas, which lie between the Lesser Himalayas and the plains, at an average height of 2000 ft. to 5000 ft. At the S. base of the Outer Himalayas three distinct regions separate the true mountains from the plains of Hindustan. These regions are comprised of a belt of detritus, or rocky fragments; a wooded belt stretching along a great part of the range; and a swampy lowland belt N. of the Ganges R., called the Terai.

Precipitation and Temperature. Snow occurs at elevations as low as 2500 ft. above sea level, and snow falls every winter at altitudes over 6000 ft. The snow line in the Great Himalayas lies at about 16,200 ft. on the s. face of the range, and at about 17,400 ft. on the N.; the snow line is higher on the N. apparently because of the dry atmosphere of Tibet. The high main range of the Himalaya forms a vast screen that intercepts and condenses nearly all the moisture carried by the S.W. monsoons (q.v.), which blow from the Indian Ocean from May to October; this moisture is deposited on the s. face of the mountains. At the Indian village of Cherrapunji, for example, which is about 4200 ft. above sea level, the mean annual rainfall is about 430 in. The rainfall varies, however, at different locations and altitudes; a low of about 30 in. of rain per year falls in the region where the Indus issues from the mountains, and in Tibet, which is an arid zone beyond the N. barrier of the range, the average annual rainfall is well below 10 in.

The altitude of the Himalaya affects temperature as well as precipitation. The climate of the S. side varies from subtropical at the base and in the valleys, through temperate at an elevation of about 7000 ft. (the height of most of the Himalayan hill stations or government posts), to frigid at about 12,000 ft. to 15,000 ft. Above the snow line, frost and intense cold prevail throughout the year. In Tibet, conditions are quite different from those on the S. side. Even at 15,000 ft. frost is permanent here only from November to May, while at 12,000 ft. the temperature rises in the summer months to a mean of about 60° F. The daily range of Tibetan temperature is very wide;

A caravan at rest in the barren terrain of the Great Himalayas, between Tibet and Nepal.   United Nations

differences of 50° or even 60° are common, and the temperatures of the dry surface soil vary even more widely.

Glaciers are found in every part of the Himalayan system above the snow line. Although for the most part the glaciers appear to be in retreat, some in the Kanchenjunga group descend to about 13,000 ft. and some in Kumaun to about 12,000 ft., while a few isolated glaciers in Kashmir come as low as 8000 ft. A number of the glaciers are 15 mi. long, and a few have been mapped that are 30 mi. and longer.

The passes through the Himalaya, which often lie along or across these glaciers, are the highest in the world, with an average height of about 10,000 ft. The highest pass used for traffic is the Parang Pass in India, at 18,000 ft. above sea level. All passes over 16,000 ft. are closed by snow from November to May. Small glacial lakes are abundant along the passes and at the heads of the gorges; the chief lakes of the system, however, lie at comparatively low altitudes; they are Naini Tal (altitude 6500 ft.) in Kumaun and Wular Lake (altitude 5200 ft.) in the Vale of Kashmir.

The Geologic Structure. The Himalaya consists chiefly of gneiss, mixed with mica schist in the N. and bands of granite and syenite (qq.v.) in the S. While the upheaval of the system probably commenced early in geologic time, the principal uplift occurred in the middle or late Tertiary Period; *see* GEOLOGY SYSTEMATIC. The chains developed from N. to S. in a series of stages. During each stage mountains were pushed forward along great east-west fault (q.v.) lines over the beds at their S. bases. The sub-Himalayan ridges S. of the main chains resulted from the repeated crumpling and folding of these beds. Even today the system has not reached a state of equilibrium; the frequency of earthquakes along the main fault lines, especially in the central range, indicates that the Himalaya is still evolving.

The Brahmaputra and Indus river systems have their chief sources in the seasonal melting of the Himalayan snows and are in flood at the hottest season of the year, when the moisture they supply is most needed. On the mountains, trees and cultivated grains ordinarily do not grow above an elevation of about 11,800 ft., and shrubs, above about 15,200 ft., although a few flowering plants are found at elevations as high as 19,500 ft. Tea is cultivated along the entire S. face of the mountain system, with the best grades produced at 2000 ft. to 3000 ft.

The Fauna and Flora. Animal and plant life overlaps with that of the Indian peninsula along the outer ranges. For the most part, however, the animals of the main ranges, particularly on the Tibetan side, have an affinity with creatures found to the N. Birds and insects abound throughout the year even above the snow line; tigers and apes are found up to 11,000 ft., and leopards up to 13,000 ft. On the higher passes and peaks, only animals that have adapted to the rigors of intense cold and strong winds can endure; they include the Tibetan ox, or yak (q.v.); a harelike animal called the pika; and several breeds of hairy dogs, which have been domesticated and are used to drive herds over passes as high as 18,000 ft. There have been reports, mainly by the Sherpa, a Tibetan mountain people, of an upright-walking creature with apelike features and a body covered with light brown hair, which has appeared in the high Himalaya. Attempts to verify the existence of the so-called Abominable Snowman, or Yeti (rock dweller), as the Sherpa often call it, have proved fruitless, and the creature is probably mythical.

The great height of the Himalaya and the apparent impossibility of reaching the summits stimulated the ancient Hindus to attribute to the peaks supernatural properties that were associated with the history of some of their deities. In the Puranas (q.v.), the religious works of the Brahmanic Hindus, a Himalayan mountain called Kailas, in S.W. Tibet, is personified in the form of a goddess. Kailas is thought to be the abode of the Hindu god Siva (q.v.) and is the destination of pilgrims journeying to win his favors; see INDIAN MYTHOLOGY: *Gods of the Epic Period.*

HIMEJI, city of Japan in Hyogo Prefecture, on S. Honshu Island, about 30 miles N.W. of Kobe. Himeji has good railroad facilities and is a commercial and industrial center. Among the products manufactured in the city are cotton textiles, leather goods, iron and steel, and chemicals. Notable attractions include a 10th-century Buddhist temple and the remains of a 14th-century feudal castle. Pop. (1967 est.) 386,000.

HIMERA, ancient city of Italy, on the N. coast of Sicily, not far from the modern city of Palermo. Founded in 648 B.C. by colonists from Messina and exiles from Syracuse, Himera achieved great power. In 480 B.C. Carthage sent an expedition to Himera. The Carthaginian forces were defeated by a force of Syracusan Greeks under the command of Gelon (q.v.), Tyrant of Syracuse. The city thus came under the protection of Syracuse and seems to have prospered during the remainder of the 5th century. In 408 B.C. Carthage again attacked Himera and demolished the city. In the following year the citizens moved to a new city, Thermae Himeraeae (modern Termini Imerese), which was held by Carthage until it was taken by the Romans during the First Punic War; see PUNIC WARS.

HIMES, Chester Bomar (1909–), American writer, born in Jefferson City, Mo., and educated at Ohio State University. His early novels are stories of racial protest; his later work often treats the Negro and his problems satirically. Recognition came to Himes with *If He Hollers Let Him Go* (1945), a bitter, violent novel of racial injustice.

In the 1950's Himes became a resident of Europe. He then began to write a series of detective novels, featuring two Negro detectives in Harlem named Grave Digger Jones and Coffin Ed Johnson. The series includes *Cotton Comes to Harlem* (1968), which was made into a motion picture in 1970, and *Blind Man With a Pistol* (1969). Himes has also written many short stories.

HIMMLER, Heinrich (1900–45), German National Socialist official, the head of the Gestapo (q.v.). He joined the National Socialist Party (*see* NATIONAL SOCIALISM) in 1925, and from 1926 to 1930 was its director of propaganda. In 1929 he became chief of the *Schutzstaffel* (known as the SS, or Black Shirts) an elite military force of the party. As head of the Gestapo from 1936 to 1945, he carried out a ruthless program for the extermination of Jews and the suppression of all opposition to the regime of the German dictator Adolf Hitler (q.v.). Hitler appointed him minister of the interior in 1943, and in 1944 Himmler became director of home-front operations and chief of the German armed forces operating within the borders of Germany. In April, 1945, he was captured by the British army. He was scheduled to stand trial with the other German leaders as a major war criminal, but committed suicide shortly after his arrest.

HIMYARITES, ancient Semitic tribe that originated in the extreme southwest of Arabia. Evidence of ancient culture and fragments of South Arabic inscriptions judged to be Himyaritic have been found that date before 700 B.C. The earliest inscription in which the Himyarite kingdom is specifically mentioned, however, dates from around 115 B.C. At that time control of the commercially important region of Sheba passed from the Sabaeans (q.v.) to the Himyarites, who, according to the Roman statesman Pliny (q.v.), by the 1st century B.C. had become preeminent among South Arabian peoples. From this point, however, it is difficult to dissociate their history from that of the Sabaeans. Dynastic rule established in the early Christian centuries was interrupted after 335 A.D. by Abyssinian invasion. Local control was reestablished toward the end of the 4th century. The ruler of the Himyarites at this time adopted Judaism (q.v.) as his religion, thus creating a Jewish-Sabaean kingdom. Early 6th-century persecution of Christians in the area occasioned a further Abyssinian attack. In 525 the kingdom again fell under Abyssinian control. Although throughout this period references to Himyarites suggest that they remained a strong element in the population of the area, most Arab writers of the time used the terms "Himyarite" and "South Arabian" synonymously. In modern times the Himyarite language is still spoken in a small area of the People's Democratic Republic of Yemen (q.v.); it provides a link in the development of Semitic languages (q.v.) from ancient times. J.H.T.

HINDEMITH, Paul (1895–1963), German-American composer, born in Hanau. He studied with the German composers Arnold Ludwig Mendelssohn (1855–1933) and Bernhard Sekles (1872–1934) at the Hock Conservatorium in Frankfurt. At the age of thirteen, while at the conservatory, he played in dance bands and at theaters and cinemas for his livelihood. From 1915 to 1923 he was concertmaster and then conductor of the Frankfurt Opera orchestra. In 1921, with the Hungarian-born Turkish musician Licco Amar (1891–1959) he organized the famous Amar-Hindemith Quartet, in which he played the viola. During the 1920's Hindemith gained recognition as a major composer. In 1927 he became professor of musical composition at the Berlin Hochschule für Musik, a post he held for ten years. In 1934 his work was banned by the government of German dictator Adolf Hitler (q.v.) because of its extreme modernism, and shortly afterward he complied with a request from the Turkish government to reorganize the musical studies program in Turkey. He came to the United States in 1940, and was professor of music theory at Yale University until 1953 when he joined the faculty of the University of Zürich. He had become an American citizen in 1946.

Hindemith was one of the most important figures in 20th-century music. Although some of his earlier compositions tended toward atonality, the bulk of his work is tonal, especially that written after 1935, when his Violin Sonata in E was published. Hindemith wrote operas, including *Morder, Hoffnung der Frauen* (1921) and *Cardillac* (1926). The opera *Mathis der Maler* (1938) is based on the life of the German painter Matthias Grünewald (q.v.); a symphony drawn from themes of the opera is one of Hindemith's best-known orchestral works. He also wrote symphonies, sonatas, concertos, chamber music, and vocal pieces. He was an advocate of *Gebrauchsmusik* ("music for use"), through which he sought to establish closer contacts between the composer and the public by creating work to be performed by school groups and amateurs; one such work was his children's opera, *Wir bauen eine Stadt* (*We Build a Town*, 1931). *Ludus Tonalis* (1943), a set of twelve fugues for all keys, is a group of musical studies through which a pianist may develop his skill and through which the composer demonstrated his theories of counterpoint and tonal organization. Books written by Hindemith include *The Craft of Musical Composition* (1941), *A Concentrated Course in Traditional Harmony* (1943), and *A Composer's World* (1952), his memoirs.

Paul Hindemith UPI

HINDENBURG, Paul von, in full PAUL LUDWIG HANS ANTON VON BENECKENDORFF UND VON HINDENBURG (1847–1934), German general and president. He was born in Posen (now Poznán, Poland), and educated at the cadet school in Berlin. He entered the Prussian army in 1866 and during the next five years took part in the Seven Weeks' War and the Franco-German War (qq.v.). He served forty years in the army of the newly proclaimed (1871) German

HINDENBURG

Paul von Hindenburg — Bettmann Archive

Empire, advancing to general in 1905, and retiring in 1911.

In August, 1914, on the outbreak of World War I (q.v.), he accepted the command of the German eighth army on the Russian border. He and his chief of staff General Erich Friedrich Wilhelm Ludendorff (q.v.) led the Germans to an overwhelming victory over numerically superior Russian troops at Tannenberg (q.v.). Hindenburg was promoted to field marshal and in 1916 he succeeded General Erich von Falkenhayn (q.v.) as chief of the German general staff, and, with Ludendorff, became responsible for the direction of all German forces. In March, 1917, Hindenburg established the German armies in western Europe in a system of trenches across northern France known as the "Hindenburg Line", which the Allied armies did not break until October, 1918.

After World War I Hindenburg retired from the army for a second time in 1919. In 1920 he published his memoirs, *Out of My Life,* in which he claimed the defeat of the German army in World War I had been caused by the domestic revolution which had overthrown the German Empire and established a republic in November, 1918. In 1925 Hindenburg was elected the second president of the republic, and although he sought German unity, he promoted the interests of the Junkers, the Prussian landed aristocracy. In 1932 he defeated the National Socialist Party candidate and later German dictator Adolf Hitler (q.v.) for the presidency, but on Jan. 30, 1933, Hindenburg appointed Hitler chancellor. Hitler gained control of the Reichstag, or the lower legislative chamber, which voted him dictatorial powers on March 25, 1933. Thereafter, Hindenburg was only a figurehead in the German government. See GERMANY: *History: World War I.*

HINDI, Indo-European language which, with component dialects, is spoken by 40 to 45 percent of the population of India. The Indian constitution designates Hindi, written in the Devanagari, a Sanskrit-based script as the official language of the nation. The two main dialects of Hindi are Eastern Hindi and Western Hindi. Eastern Hindi possesses an extensive and important literature which reached its peak in a simple vigorous poetry produced near the beginning of the 17th century; since that time it has been the language most used in northern Indian epic poetry. The most important literary dialect of Eastern Hindi is Awadhi. Western Hindi comprises four main dialects: Kanauji, Braj Bhrasha, Bundeli, and a vernacular Hindustani spoken around Delhi. The first two, like Awadhi, have been literary tongues of northern India. The Hindustani (q.v.) language developed from an obscure dialect of Western Hindi; High Hindi, in turn, was developed from Hindustani. See INDIAN LANGUAGES.

HINDUISM, generic designation for the complex of theological, metaphysical, philosophical, ethical, cultural, and social institutions comprising the predominant religious system of India; see INDIAN RELIGIONS. The fundamental features of Hinduism are reverence for the sacred scriptures known as the Vedas (*see* VEDA); scrupulous observance of various regulations concerning diet, marriage, and burial; and conscientious performance of specified rites, sacraments, and divine invocations. The caste system (*see* CASTE), for centuries a basic institution of Hinduism, is being progressively liberalized in consequence of the reforms initiated by the Indian nationalist leader Mohandas Karamchand Gandhi (q.v.).

HINDUISM

Hinduism often is used synonymously with Brahmanism (q.v.), although the latter term is more correctly restricted to the orthodox faith of the Brahmans (see BRAHMAN), which is closer to older Vedic beliefs than are the later forms of worship constituting modern popular Hinduism.

Written Sources. The term dharma (Skr., "that which is established", from *dharayati,* "he holds, carries, keeps"; a term embracing law, duty, morality, and piety) shows the scope of Hinduism. The chief written sources of Hinduism are the great epic poems the *Ramayana* and *Mahabharata* (qq.v.), and particularly the section of the latter work known as the *Bhagavad-Gita* (q.v.). To these may be added the writings of Vedanta (q.v.); the Puranas (q.v.) and other sectarian treatises such as the sutras (collections of brief aphorisms, precepts, and so forth, usually in verse) of the ancient rishis, or divinely inspired sages, Sandilya and Narada; and speculative and exegetical dissertations by the founders of various Hindu sects.

The Epic Period. This period, starting about the 3rd century B.C., was marked by the development of two main creeds, popular and philosophical. The popular creed centered on various mythological figures. Two relatively minor gods of the Vedic pantheon, Vishnu (q.v.) and Rudra, emerged from the ritualism of Brahmanism as preeminent in popular Hinduism, and Rudra eventually became identified with and supplanted by the god Siva (q.v.). Other gods of the Vedic pantheon, as well as prominent local deities and legendary heroes, were grouped around these two major divinities. In the *Ra-*

Having been brought into the Aryan fold at puberty with the investment of the sacred thread, the devout Brahman reaffirms his dedication once a year by changing his old thread for a new one.

Camera Press — Pix, Inc.

HINDUISM

A religious festival is celebrated by Hindus in Madras, India. United Nations

mayana the ascendancy of Vishnu is an accomplished fact; in the *Mahabharata,* however, the rival claims of Siva are recognizable. A third divinity, Brahma (q.v.), received less emphasis than Vishnu or Siva, but may be regarded as related to the abstract philosophical and metaphysical entity *brahman* (Skr., "prayer"), which designated the power of prayer in Vedic religion and later became the symbol of the supreme principle of the universe.

The philosophical creed of Hinduism in the epic period promulgated the idea that the mystical realization of the identity of the Atman, or innermost essence of the individual soul, with *brahman,* or the supreme soul, may be facilitated through a system of physical and psychic control such as Yoga (q.v.). Systematic meditation, disciplined action involving work for the sake of work and ritual dedication of the fruits of one's labor to the divinity, and complete devotional abandonment to God are other means of achieving this realization and merging of the individual soul in the divine soul; *see* RELIGION: *The Ways of Liberation.* The concept of the reunion of the individual soul with the supreme soul, a doctrine basic to the majority of Indian speculative philosophies, is founded on the assumption that the individual soul must become absolved of all impurity before it can again be merged with the perfect being from which it emanated. Because the individual soul usually is unable to achieve this purification in the short span of one human lifetime, it must pass through as many successive incarnations as are required to eliminate all the evils that keep it from absorption into the supreme soul; *see* TRANSMIGRATION. This cycle of births and deaths is called samsara (and is frequently symbolized in Hindu art and literature by a rotating wheel). When the soul has atoned for all the consequences of deeds done in former incarnations (its Karma, which inexorably determines the nature of future incarnations, until the soul is purified), samsara is annihilated and release and liberation (moksha) attained.

The Puranic Period. The second stage in developing Hinduism, extending from about the 6th to the 16th centuries A.D., is known as the Puranic period. The name is derived from the Puranas, a class of sacred scriptures in verse. With the Tantras, religious writings containing mystical teachings (for example, that the power, or energy, of a Vedic divinity may be manifested in and through various aspects of his consort) and ritual instructions concerned with magic, the Puranas succeeded and supplanted epic Hinduism after the 6th century. The philosophical creed of Puranic Hinduism was enriched by the *Advaita* Vedanta (q.v.), a system of idealistic monism (q.v.) that was elaborated by the Hindu

HINDUISM

scholar, Sankara, or Shankaracharya (788?–838?), from his Upanishadic commentaries (*see* UPANISHADS). According to Sankara, the phenomenal world is an illusion (in Skr., *maya*) rooted in beginningless ignorance (literal translation of the Skr. word *avidya*). The only true reality, Sankara maintains, is Brahman, or absolute being, with which the purified soul is identical. The *Advaita Vedanta* thus opposes an unconditioned, incogitable (inconceivable) Brahman to the qualified, anthropomorphic Brahman of some later Upanishads. The later concept, in which Brahman is personfied as the creator of the universe, is held to be a concession to the unenlightened masses. For the enlightened soul, the ritualism of popular worship has no importance. Sankara's doctrine found much support, but because it tended to subvert established religious authority, it also had numerous adversaries.

With respect to the popular creed, the Puranic period of Hinduism was one of general decline. The Puranic pantheon was nominally the same as that of the epic period; but whereas the epic period was characterized on the whole by harmonious relations among the major deities, the Puranic period exhibited them in a state of discord indicating the destruction of the original concepts personified by the epic gods. The legends of the epic period relating to these gods became, in the Puranic period, amplified and distorted according to the sectarian tendencies of the masses; and the divine character of the gods as disclosed in the *Ramayana* and *Mahabharata* was increasingly alloyed with mundane involvements. Popular worship, whether preserving a semblance of decorum, as with the devotees of Vishnu, or surrendering itself to unbridled license, as with some zealous adherents of Siva and his consort in her various aspects (*see* KALI, for example), shows little or no connection with the Vedic scriptures by which it purports to be inspired. This popular creed of the Puranic period constitutes the Hinduism of the great mass of worshipers of present-day India. *See also* BUDDHISM; JAINISM; SANSKRIT LITERATURE.

At Hardwar, India, Hindus await their turns to bathe in a sacred pool through which the waters of the holy Ganges River flow. UPI

HINDU KUSH

HINDU KUSH, major mountain system of central Asia, extending generally in a southwesterly direction for more than 500 mi., from the plateau region of the Pamir (q.v.) on the borders of Afghanistan; West Pakistan Province, Pakistan; and the Soviet Union. The system lies largely in N.E. Afghanistan between lat. 34° N. and lat. 36° N. and long. 68° E. and long. 74° 30′ E. Outlying ranges, principally the Paropamisus and the Safed Koh, extend the Hindu Kush system across Afghanistan almost to the border with Iran. The system, consisting of granites and schists, or crystalline rocks, probably was uplifted in the Tertiary Period. The system is in part marked by overthrusts of Cretaceous limestones upon Cenozoic shales and clays. See GEOLOGY, SYSTEMATIC.

In the first 100-mi. section w. of the Pamir, the Hindu Kush extends southward. In this section the system has a comparatively wide, plateaulike summit, dotted with small glacial lakes, and passes ranging in height from 12,500 to 17,500 ft. above sea level. The system then turns to the S.W., gains in elevation, and the plateau summit breaks into peaks, the highest of which is Tirich Mir, 25,263 ft. above sea level, in Pakistan. Many other peaks in this section rise more than 20,000 ft. and the system is broken by such passes as the Baroghil, the Dorah, and the Khawak. The Hindu Kush is also the source of many rivers; the most notable are the Amu-Dar'ya R. on the N. slopes, and the Helmand, the Kabul, and the Kunar rivers and several tributaries of the Indus R. on the S. slopes.

The Khawak Pass was used by the Macedonian conqueror Alexander the Great (see ALEXANDER III) and the Mongol emperor Tamerlane (q.v.) in their invasions of India. Today the only road through the Hindu Kush is a highway in the Shikari Pass between the Afghan cities of Kabul and Mazar-i-Sherif.

HINDU MUSIC. See INDIAN MUSIC.

HINDUSTAN (Per. *Hindostan*, "land of the Hindus"), generally, area of the Ganges Plain in N. India or all of N. India from the State of Assam to that of Punjab where Hindi (q.v.), the official language of India, is spoken. Hindustan has also been applied at times to mean the entire Indian subcontinent, and sometimes, especially since the partition of the subcontinent into India and Pakistan in 1947, solely to the Republic of India.
See INDIA, REPUBLIC OF.

HINDUSTANI, name given by Europeans to a mixed language dialect used throughout India for trade and communication between different language groups. Originally derived from the Sanskritic dialect group called Prakrit, Hindustani developed a distinctive character during the Mogul Empire (1526–1761), when Hindi-speaking officials absorbed into their speech Arabic and Persian elements from their Mogul rulers. See INDO-IRANIAN LANGUAGES; SANSKRIT.

The most important subdialect of Hindustani is called Urdu. Along with Bengali, Urdu is the official language of Pakistan and is one of the official languages of India, as well as the standard form of speech used by Muslims in both countries. Urdu is written in Persian-Arabic script and contains more Persian words and grammatical constructions than any other of the subdialects of Hindustani. An artificial subdialect developed in modern times, especially for use by Hindus, is called High Hindi (not to be confused with the Hindi language); in formulating this subdialect, the inventors deliberately avoided a Persianized vocabulary and introduced many elements from Sanskrit (q.v.). Like Urdu, High Hindi is intelligible only to those educated in the language and is not understood by people speaking the standard form of Hindustani. Persons speaking Urdu or High Hindi, however, can understand the standard form of Hindustani, the most widely understood of all the Indian languages and dialects. The standard form of Hindustani may be transcribed today in both Persian-Arabic and Devanagari, or Sanskrit-based scripts.

Hindustani is an analytic language, like all other modern Indian languages, and like Persian and English. Words generally are conjugated and declined by postpositions, affixes, and periphrases. There are two genders, two numbers, two voices, and nine tenses in common use.

In modern times Hindustani has absorbed many European words, mainly nouns. Portuguese was the earliest Western language in contact with Hindustani; French and Dutch elements subsequently appeared, but the effect of all three was relatively slight. English, on the other hand, is of the greatest importance in modern Hindustani. Some words borrowed from English have already appeared in the literature of the language; the bulk of modern technical vocabulary also is being borrowed from the English language. See INDIAN LANGUAGES.

HINES, Earl (1905–   ), American jazz pianist, born in Duquesne, Pa., and popularly known as "Fatha" Hines. During his high-school days in Pittsburgh, Hines played piano in night clubs. In 1922 he went to Chicago and six years later organized his first band. During the 1930's his band was heard by network radio audiences on his own nightly broadcast. Many famous jazz musicians played with the Hines band, including the American saxophonist Charles ("Bird") Parker (1920–55) and the trumpet player John ("Dizzy") Gillespie (1917–   ). In 1947 the Hines band was disbanded and for the next four years he played piano with the band of the jazz trumpeter Louis Armstrong (q.v.); thereafter Hines joined a number of smaller musical groups. His piano style is characterized by intricate rhythms and dynamic use of octaves.

HINGHAM, town of Massachusetts, in Plymouth Co., on Hingham Bay, 12 mi. S.E. of Boston, of which it is a residential suburb. A fishing center prior to the American Civil War, today Hingham is important as a summer resort. Among the places of interest in the town are a two-story building, the Old Ordinary, part of which dates from 1650, and which now contains the collection of the Hingham Historical Society; the Old Ship Church, built in 1681, one of the oldest places of worship in New England, and the gravesite of the American Revolutionary general Benjamin Lincoln (1733–1810). Hingham was settled about 1633 and incorporated in 1635. It was named for Hingham, England, the original home of the first settlers. Pop. (1960) 15,378; (1970) 18,845.

HINNY. See MULE.

HINSHELWOOD, Sir Cyril Norman (1897–1967), British chemist, born in London, England, and educated at the University of Oxford. In 1937, after serving as fellow at Balliol and Trinity colleges, he was appointed professor of chemistry at Oxford. Hinshelwood conducted notable researches on the mechanisms of chemical reactions and made important discoveries concerning molecular chain reactions in combustion processes. For this work he shared the 1956 Nobel Prize in chemistry with the Russian chemist Nikolai N. Semenov (q.v.). He was knighted in 1948 and served as president of the Royal Society from 1955 to 1960.

HIP, or HAUNCH, either of the projecting portions on either side of the body of an animal between the lowest of its ribs and its thigh. The hip is made up of the hipbone, or innominate bone (a part of the pelvis), and of the skin, fat, muscles, and membranes overlying it. The hips of man and the higher primates, which walk erect, are wider than those of quadrupeds; the hips of female animals are wider than those of males.

The hip in fishes is represented by a small pelvic girdle which supports the pelvic fins; in frogs the hind limbs are attached to one central hipbone rather than to two lateral hipbones. Pythons and boas (family Boidae) are the only snakes with hipbones. The hips of crocodiles and of birds are proportionately much longer than those of man.

In all legged animals the weight carried by the hips and the support of at least a portion of the body are transferred to the legs at the hip joint, where the thighbone (femur) joins with the hipbone. In man and in the higher primates the hip joint passes all the weight of the body to the legs; in lower primates that walk on all fours and in quadrupeds the hip joint passes only the weight of the hind portion of the body. In all animals, proper functioning of the hip joint is necessary for maintaining balance and for absorbing shocks when the animal is running, climbing, or jumping.

The Hip Joint of Man. The hip is a ball-and-socket joint; the ball is the spherical head of the thighbone, and the socket is a region on the side of the hipbone known as the *acetabulum* (Lat., "vinegar cup"). The bottom of the socket is solid bone in man, but in birds, crocodiles, and duckbills it is perforate. Friction between the bones of the joint is reduced by a coating of cartilage and by a lubricating agent known as synovial fluid. A thick, Y-shaped ligament from the acetabulum attaches to the neck of the thighbone and serves to maintain the person erect; the center of gravity of the human body is located behind the hip joint, tending to throw the body backward. With the aid of various muscles from the pelvis and thigh, the thighbone is able to rotate and move in any direction, the extent of its movement being limited only by certain supporting ligaments.

The hip and hip joint are subject to a variety of disorders and injuries. Congenital disorders of the hip are occasionally seen in children. Among the most important of these is congenital dislocation of the hip, where the end of the femur, which normally fits into the acetabulum, is not properly developed and does not lie in its proper relationship to the acetabulum. Injuries to the hip joint are common. Severe trauma in athletes often causes the head of the femur to be torn out of its normal position in the acetabulum by the force of the injury, causing dislocation. In older people, injuries, even relatively minor ones, may cause a fracture of the neck of the femur, the small portion that lies just below the head. In addition, the hip joint is subject to tuberculosis and to a variety of inflammations and degenerative changes in arthritis (qq.v.). See BONE; FRACTURE; JOINTS; SKELETON.

HIPPARCHUS (fl. 2nd cent. B.C.), Greek astronomer, born in Nicaea, Bithynia (now İznik in Turkey). Because he was extremely accurate in his research, he is considered the most impor-

HIPPIAS

tant astronomer of his time. A record of his research was preserved in the *Almagest*, the scientific treatise by the Alexandrian astronomer Ptolemy (q.v.), who was greatly influenced by Hipparchus. By comparing his celestial studies with those of earlier astronomers, Hipparchus discovered the precession of the equinoxes; see ECLIPTIC. His calculation of the tropical year, the length of the year measured by the sun, was within $6\frac{1}{2}$ min. of modern measurements. Hipparchus devised a method of locating geographic positions by means of latitudes and longitudes. He catalogued, charted, and calculated the brightness of perhaps as many as 1000 stars. Hipparchus also compiled a table of trigonometric chords that became the basis for modern trigonometry. See ASTRONOMY: *Greek Astronomy*; TRIGONOMETRY: *History*.

HIPPIAS (d. about 490 B.C.), tyrant of Athens, one of the Pisistratidae. After 527 B.C., he and his coruler and younger brother, Hipparchus (about 555–514 B.C.), continued the policies of their father, Pisistratus (q.v.), but did not enjoy the older man's popularity with the Athenians. Hipparchus was killed by Harmodius and Aristogiton (q.v.), and Hippias reigned alone until forced from power in 510 B.C. and exiled. He subsequently lived at the Persian court and served as an adviser with the Persians at Marathon (q.v.).

HIPPOCRATES (460?–377? B.C.), Greek physician. Little is known of his personal life, but it is believed that Hippocrates was born on the island of Kos, Greece, traveled widely, returned to Kos to practice and teach medicine, and died at Lárisa, Greece. He probably wrote only six of the more than seventy works ascribed to him in the *Hippocratic Collection*, but his teaching influenced the writing of the others. He rejected the belief current during his time that evil powers cause illness, and he theorized that an imbalance in the four humors, or bodily fluids, was responsible for disease. He established a link between disease and environment and was unique in practicing preventive medicine through the application of hygienic and dietary measures, resorting to more drastic methods only when necessary. The scientific clarity of the case histories he recorded and his high ethical standards made him the most celebrated physician of his time, and he is still called "the father of medicine".

See DISEASE; GREEK LITERATURE; HIPPOCRATIC OATH; MEDICINE: *Greek*.

HIPPOCRATIC OATH, oath in the *Hippocratic Collection*, which has been taken for more than 2000 years by physicians entering the practice of medicine. Many contemporary medical schools impose an abbreviated version of the Hippocratic Oath as an admonition and an affirmation to which their graduating classes assent. At one time the oath was ascribed to the ancient Greek physician Hippocrates (q.v.), but modern research has shown that the oath may have been composed as late as the 3rd century A.D. A version of the oath, approved by the American Medical Association (q.v.), is as follows:

> "You do solemnly swear, each man by whatever he holds most sacred
> That you will be loyal to the Profession of Medicine and just and generous to its members
> That you will lead your lives and practice your art in uprightness and honor
> That into whatsoever house you shall enter, it shall be for the good of the sick to the utmost of your power, your holding yourselves far aloof from wrong, from corruption, from the tempting of others to vice
> That you will exercise your art solely for the cure of your patients, and will give no drug, perform no operation, for a criminal purpose, even if solicited; far less suggest it
> That whatsoever you shall see or hear of the lives of men which is not fitting to be spoken, you will keep inviolably secret
> These things do you swear. Let each man bow the head in sign of acquiescence
> And now, if you will be true to this, your oath, may prosperity and good repute be ever yours; the opposite, if you shall prove yourselves forsworn."

HIPPOLYTA, in Greek mythology, Queen of the Amazons (q.v.), and daughter of Ares (q.v.), god of war. She was slain by the hero Hercules

Hippocrates — Bettmann Archive

(q.v.) when he took from her, as one of his labors, the girdle given to her by her father. According to another legend she became the wife of the Greek hero Theseus, by whom she had a son Hippolytus (qq.v.).

HIPPOLYTUS, in Greek mythology, son of the Theban hero Theseus and his wife Hippolyta, queen of the Amazons (qq.v.), or sometimes the son of her sister Antiope. Hippolytus was an excellent hunter and charioteer, and a devoted servant of Artemis (q.v.), goddess of the hunt. Hippolytus spurned all women and when his stepmother Phaedra fell in love with him he rejected her advances. In despair at his refusal, Phaedra committed suicide, leaving a letter accusing Hippolytus of having attempted to ravish her. Theseus, believing his son guilty, invoked his father Poseidon (q.v.), god of the sea, to destroy Hippolytus. As the young man drove his chariot along the shore, Poseidon sent a sea monster that frightened his horses; they ran away dashing the chariot to pieces. Mortally wounded, Hippolytus was carried to his father, who had in the meantime learned from Artemis that his son was innocent. As Hippolytus died, the grief-stricken father and son were reconciled.

HIPPOPOTAMUS, or RIVER HORSE, common name of either of two species of artiodactylous mammals comprising the family Hippopotamidae, found only in Africa. The hippopotamuses are heavy-bodied, short-legged, short-tailed animals, resembling pigs more than horses. They have large heads, with small eyes, small ears, and nostrils surrounded by sparse, bristly hairs and equipped with special flaps which close down when the animal goes under water. The eyes and the ears are located on the top of the head. The mouth is huge and contains long, pointed incisor and canine teeth; the common adult hippopotamus has tusklike canine teeth in the lower jaw. They are about 24 in. long, weigh almost 6 lb., and are valued as ivory. The bare skin becomes 2 in. thick, and is used in the making of leather whips, known as "sjamboks". The feet are four-toed. The meat of the hippopotamus is edible and soup is made from the hide.

The common brown or gray hippopotamus, *Hippopotamus amphibius,* once widely distributed throughout Africa and now found south of lat. 17° N., is one of the largest four-footed animals. It reaches a length of 14 ft. and weight of over 4 tons; because of its short legs it stands no higher than 5 ft. at the shoulder. Its stomach is over 10 ft. long. This animal is semiaquatic, spending most of the day with only its eyes,

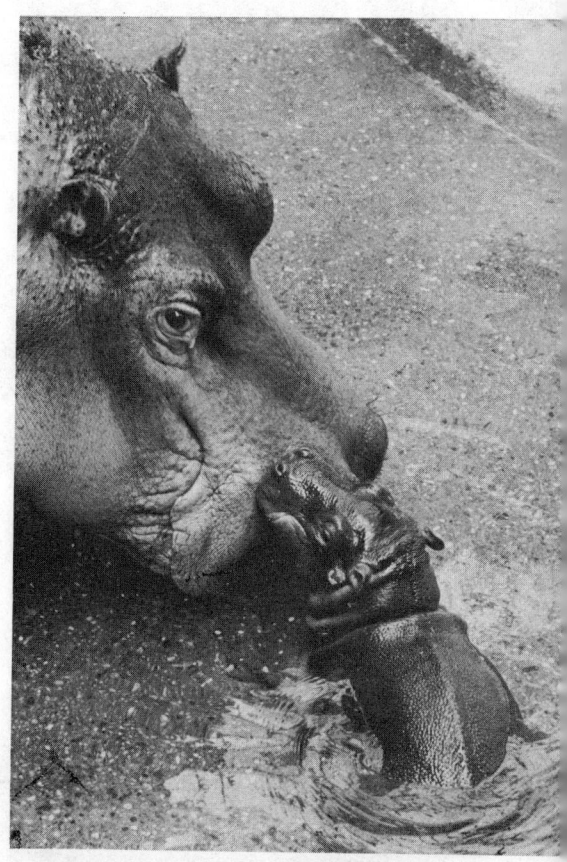

Hippopotamus, Hippopotamus amphibius, *mother and calf.*
UPI

ears, and nostrils above the surface of a river, and capable of remaining under water for as long as 25 min. During the day it feeds on aquatic vegetation, and often swims more than 25 mi. in search of food, emerging at night to feed on land plants; it is fond of sugar cane and corn, and sometimes enters plantations, where it does more damage by trampling the plants than it does by feeding. Hippopotamuses have occasionally been seen in mountain rivers at heights of over 5000 ft. above sea level, and at temperatures near freezing. Common hippopotamuses travel in herds of about forty animals. The cow bears one young at a time, and fights ferociously if the calf is attacked. Old bulls, like old elephants, sometimes go berserk and attack other hippopotamuses or men. The species is widely hunted; natives kill it by harpooning, or in pitfalls, or by fencing it in and starving it to death.

The pigmy hippopotamus, *Choeropsis liberiensis,* is about half the size of the common hip-

Pygmy hippopotamus, Choeropsis liberiensis.
Jeanne White — National Audubon Society

popotamus. It is found only in w. Africa, especially in Liberia. It is black on top, with a greenish sheen; below it is yellowish green. It is less aquatic than the common hippopotamus, and is found in cool forests and in marshlands. Pigmy hippopotamuses almost always travel in pairs, rarely forming a herd.

Remains of many fossil hippopotamuses have been found in European and Indian deposits of the Pliocene Epoch and Quaternary Period (qq.v.); fossils found in England seem to be of the same species as the present-day common hippopotamus.

HIROHITO (1901–), Emperor of Japan (1926–). He was born in Tokyo and educated in Japan. In 1921 he visited Europe and became the first Japanese prince to leave his native land. He returned to Japan to serve as regent from 1921 to 1926 during the illness of his father Emperor Yoshihito (1879–1926). On Dec. 25, 1926,

Emperor Hirohito
Consulate General of Japan

HIROSHIGE

Hirohito succeeded to the throne as the 124th emperor in direct lineage. He designated his reign *Showa* ("enlightened peace"). He married in 1924, and the Japanese heir, Crown Prince Akihito (q.v.), was born in 1933.

For the first nineteen years of his reign Hirohito allowed a militaristic party to determine the policy of the Japanese government. This policy led to the seizure of Mukden (q.v.) in 1931, the establishment of the Japanese puppet state of Manchukuo in 1934 (see MANCHURIA: *History*), and the Sino-Japanese War with China from 1937 to 1945 (see CHINA: *History*). In September, 1940, Japan signed a military alliance with the Axis Powers (q.v.), Germany and Italy. In October, 1941, General Hideki Tojo (q.v.), a former war minister, became premier; and without the emperor's interference Tojo masterminded the Japanese attack, Dec. 7, 1941, on the United States (see PEARL HARBOR), precipitating a U.S. declaration of war the following day. Toward the end of the war Hirohito sought peace, and on Aug. 14, 1945 (Japanese time), after atomic bombs had been dropped on Hiroshima and Nagasaki (qq.v.) he broadcast the unconditional surrender of Japan to the Allies. *See* WORLD WAR II: *Decisive Phases of the War Against Japan.*

Hirohito cooperated with the Allied occupation forces headed by General Douglas MacArthur (q.v.) of the U.S. in converting Japan into a democratic nation. On Jan. 1, 1946, Hirohito publicly denied his divinity, ascribed to the emperor by the Shinto (q.v.) religion. He approved the 1947 constitution which created a constitutional monarchy in Japan, and which limited his role largely to a ceremonial one. Hirohito had been implicated in the Japanese war plans, but in the postwar trials of the International Military Tribunal of the Far East (*see* WAR-CRIMES TRIALS: *Tokyo and Other Trials*), he was exonerated of culpability, largely because of the testimony of General Tojo; *see* JAPAN: *History*.

In October, 1971, Hirohito, accompanied by the empress, visited western European countries on a good-will tour. He also met with President Richard M. Nixon in Alaska, at the beginning of the journey.

HIROSHIGE, Ando (1797–1858), Japanese artist and designer of wood-block prints, born in Yedo (now Tokyo). He was the last important figure of the Japanese ukiyoye school, the group of artists who produced painting and color prints of ordinary life. He was noted for his large landscapes in color, particularly for the series "Fifty-three Views Along the Takaido" (1849). In this series he created a variety of atmospheric effects, such as moonlight, snow, mist, and rain by means of color and sharp delicate lines. Hiroshige also executed two series of prints depicting scenes of Tokyo and the volcano Fuji. He was popular in Japan and was also an important influence on impressionism (q.v.) in France

"One of the Stations of the Kiso Kaido" (1835), from a series of more than sixty prints depicting scenes along a highway on Honshu, Japan, by Ando Hiroshige.
Metropolitan Museum of Art — Bequest of Joseph Pulitzer

The Japanese city of Hiroshima as it appeared, almost totally destroyed, shortly after the dropping of the first atomic bomb. U.S. Army

and on the work of the American painter James Abbott McNeill Whistler (q.v.). Collections of his prints are in the Metropolitan Museum of Art, New York City, the Museum of Fine Arts, Boston, Mass., and in other museums.

HIROSHIMA, city in Japan, and capital of Hiroshima Prefecture, on the S.E. coast of the island of Honshu, at the head of Hiroshima Bay. The city was founded in 1594 on six islands in the Ota R. delta. Hiroshima grew rapidly as a commercial city, and after 1868 it was developed as a military center. On Aug. 6, 1945, during World War II, the first atomic bomb to be used against an enemy position was dropped on the city; *see* NUCLEAR ENERGY: *Atomic Bomb.* The Supreme Allied Headquarters reported that 129,558 persons were killed, injured, or missing, and 176,987 made homeless by the bombing. (In 1940 the population of Hiroshima had been 343,698.) The blast also destroyed more than 4 sq.mi. or about 60 percent of the city. In 1949 the Japanese dedicated Hiroshima as an international shrine of peace. Every Aug. 6, since 1947, thousands participate in interfaith services in the Peace Memorial Park built on the site where the bomb exploded.

After the war the city was largely rebuilt and commercial activities were resumed. Textile manufacturing, shipbuilding, engineering, food processing, and the brewing of sake are the main industries. The surrounding area, although mountainous, has fertile valleys where raw silk, rice, and wheat are cultivated. Pop. (1965) 504,245.

HIRSCH, Emil Gustav (1851–1923), American rabbi, born in Luxembourg. He came to the United States as a young man and was educated at the University of Pennsylvania and later at the universities of Berlin and Leipzig. He was appointed rabbi of the Sinai Congregation, Chicago, in 1880, and became widely known as a leader of the Jewish Reform movement; *see* JUDAISM: *Modern Judaism.* He was the first American rabbi to discard the observance of Saturday as the Jewish Sabbath (q.v.), and to hold services in the synagogue on Sunday. Among the publications that he edited at various times are the *Reformer,* published in New York City, and the *Reform Advocate,* published in Chicago. From 1892 until his death, he was professor of rabbinical literature and philosophy at the University of Chicago.

HIRSCH, Baron Moritz, known also by the French form of his name, MAURICE DE HIRSCH (1831–96), German financier and philanthropist, born in Munich, and educated at Brussels. In 1855 he entered the employ of the international banking firm of Bischoffsheim and Goldschmidt, and accumulated a large fortune through investments in railways, copper mines, and other enterprises. He later became a contributor to philanthropic organizations established to help Jews in Europe. Hirsch was one of the principal supporters of the Alliance Israélite Universelle, and founded the Jewish Colonization Society for the resettlement of Russian Jews in agricultural communities outside Russia. To the latter organization he contributed more than $50,000,000. In 1891 he established the Baron de Hirsch Fund in New York City for the benefit of Jews entering the United States.

HISPANIOLA, island of the West Indies, in the Caribbean Sea, lying E. of Cuba and w. of Puerto Rico. Politically, Hispaniola is divided into the separate governments of Haiti occupying the w. third of the island, and the Dominican Republic (qq.v.). It was named La Isla Española by the Genoese-born navigator Christopher Columbus (q.v.) who discovered it on Dec. 6, 1492.

The aboriginal inhabitants of Hispaniola were Arawakan (q.v.) Indians, engaged principally in farming and fishing. They eventually became extinct as a result of exploitation by the early Spanish colonists. Negro slaves were later imported to take the place of the Indian laborers. In time the Spanish migrated from Hispaniola to South America, and for about a century the island was virtually deserted. In 1697, by the Peace of Ryswick that concluded the war between Louis XIV (q.v.), King of France and the Grand Alliance (q.v.), a portion of Hispaniola that had been occupied by French adventurers was formally ceded to France and became known as Saint-Dominique. The remaining Spanish section was called Santo Domingo. The French fostered the production of coffee, sugar, and cotton, and developed a flourishing trade. Intermarriage between the French colonists and the Negroes produced a group known as mulattoes, most of whom were free and became owners of property. In 1789 they were granted political rights by the French national assembly in Paris. The French landlords and planters of Hispaniola, called colons, objected vigorously to political recognition of the mulattoes, and a bitter struggle developed between the two groups. The colons appealed to the British for assistance, whereupon British and Spanish forces occupied a portion of the island.

Pierre Dominique Toussaint L'Ouverture (*see* TOUSSAINT L'OUVERTURE), a Negro who had gained his freedom in the emancipation of the Hispaniolan slaves decreed by the new French republican government in 1793, espoused the cause of France, and drove the British and Spanish invaders from the island. Spain relinquished Santo Domingo to France in 1795. In recognition of his services Toussaint was elevated to the office of governor of Hispaniola. After a victorious war against the mulattoes, who had opposed his authority, he proclaimed himself master of the island. Napoléon Bonaparte, later Napoleon I (q.v.), Emperor of France, sent his brother-in-law, General Charles Victor Emmanuel Leclerc (1772–1802), to replace Toussaint as governor. Although he put up a determined resistance, Toussaint was finally captured and sent to France, where he died in prison.

After Leclerc's death, his successor was defeated by General Jean Jacques Dessalines (q.v.), a Negro, who, in 1804, expelled the French, proclaimed the independence of the island, the name of which was changed to Haiti, and assumed the title of emperor. Two years later Dessalines was assassinated by Henri Christophe (q.v.), a Negro and former lieutenant under Toussaint L'Ouverture. Christophe assumed control of the northern part of Haiti, taking the title of king in 1811; the southern part of the island was established as a republic by the mulatto Alexander Sabès Pétion (q.v.). Following the death of Christophe in 1820, the mulatto Jean Pierre Boyer (q.v.), the successor of Pétion, brought the entire island under his control. In 1822 he seized Santo Domingo, which, having come under Spanish rule again in 1808, had claimed independence in 1821. Boyer ruled until overthrown by revolution in 1843. A year later Santo Domingo again declared its independence, forming the Dominican Republic. The island, as a geographic unit, assumed its former name, Hispaniola. Area of the island, about 29,530 sq.mi.

HISS CASE, events comprising the investigation, trial, and conviction, in 1948 through 1950, of the former American public official Alger Hiss (1904–). His conviction for perjury was the result of his testimony before the Committee on Un-American Activities of the United States House of Representatives in 1948 and 1949 and subsequent investigations by the United States Department of Justice. The case was part of a general inquiry into Communist activity in the U.S.; *see* COMMUNISM; UNITED STATES OF AMERICA: *History: The Truman Administration.*

Hiss, who was president of the Carnegie Endowment for International Peace (q.v.) in 1948, had previously served as a lawyer or administrator in the U.S. departments of Agriculture, Justice, and State. He was secretary general of the

HISTAMINE

conference that organized the United Nations (q.v.) in 1945. Hiss's accuser, (Jay David) Whittaker Chambers (1901–61), was an American writer and for several years an editor of the weekly newsmagazine *Time*. Both men were well known and respected by their professional colleagues.

In 1948, however, Chambers testified before the House Committee that he had been a Communist in the 1920's and 1930's and a courier in transmitting secret information to Soviet agents. He charged that Hiss, also a Communist, had turned classified documents over to Chambers for transmittal to the U.S.S.R. Hiss denied the charges and challenged Chambers to repeat them when he was open to prosecution for libel. Chambers repeated the accusations on a radio broadcast and in a newspaper interview, and Hiss brought two suits for slander against him. In defense, Chambers produced microfilm copies of documents that were later identified as classified papers belonging to the departments of State, Navy, and War, some apparently annotated by Hiss in his own handwriting. The Department of Justice conducted its own investigation, and Hiss was indicted for perjury. The jury failed to reach a verdict, but Hiss was convicted, after a second trial, in January, 1950. He subsequently served a five-year prison sentence and was released in 1954. Throughout, he maintained his innocence. Both men involved presented their own versions of the case; Chambers in *Witness* (1952), and Hiss in *In the Court of Public Opinion* (1957).

The political circumstances surrounding the investigations of Communism at the time led many public figures to support Hiss, at least in the early stages of the case. Prominent in pressing the case against Hiss was Richard Milhous Nixon (q.v.), later President, then a Republican member of the House Committee.

HISTAMINE, or HISTAMINE PHOSPHATE, synthetic amine (beta-imidazolyl-ethylamine, ergamine, or ergotidime) found in minute quantities in ergot (q.v.) and putrified meat products. Although histamine is produced synthetically for medicinal purposes, it is a normal constituent of almost all animal body cells. It is probably produced by bacterial action in the intestinal tract; the body is able to destroy it by enzymatic action and to neutralize its toxic effects, probably by a secretion of adrenalin. In response to certain stimuli the cells release histamine, which immediately effects a dilation of the blood vessels. This dilation is accompanied by a lowering of blood pressure and an increased permeability of the vessel walls, so that fluids escape into the surrounding tissues. This reaction may result in a general depletion of vascular fluids, causing a condition known as histamine poisoning or histamine shock. Allergic reactions in which histamine is released, resulting in the swelling of body tissue, show similarities to histamine poisoning; the two may be basically allied, and the two conditions are treated similarly.

In the 1930's the Italian pharmacologist Daniel Bovet (q.v.), working at the Pasteur Institute in Paris, discovered that certain chemicals counteracted the effects of histamine in guinea pigs. The first antihistamines were too toxic for use on humans, but by 1942 they had been modified so that they could be used in the treatment of allergies. More than 25 antihistamine drugs are now available.

The reaction time to subcutaneous injections of histamine is used as a test for circulatory deficiency characteristic of diseases such as diabetes. Histamine also causes contraction of involuntary muscles, especially of the genital tract and gastrointestinal canal, with an accompanying secretion by associated glands. Because histamine stimulates the flow of gastric juices, it is used diagnostically in patients with gastric disturbances. The ability of the body to localize infections may be due to the secretion of histamine and the subsequent increased local blood supply and increased permeability of the blood vessels. Histamine is sometimes used in the treatment of chronic rheumatism, arthritis, myositis (muscle inflammation), certain types of dermatitis, and in particular of various types of allergies. The last-named use is based on the hypothesis that such treatment will bring about a gradual desensitization of the body to the toxic effects of histamine, but many biologists doubt the ultimate value of such therapy. *See* ALLERGY; SHOCK.

HISTOLOGY, miscroscopic study of animal and plant tissues, comprising groups of cells differentiated for cooperative performance of a particular biological function; *see* CELL. Histology, the study of the structure and processes of interrelated cells, differs from cytology (q.v.), the study of individual cells. Histology is closely connected with embryology, anatomy, physiology, and pathology (qq.v.), inasmuch as it affords techniques that enable the biologist to study respectively the development of tissues into organs, the functioning of the tissues within an organ, and the changes in tissues during disease. Biopsy (q.v.) gives the scientist valuable information about disease processes, while histological studies after autopsy reveal tissue changes that have led to death.

Histology originated in the 17th century in the work of the Italian anatomist Marcello Malpighi and of the Dutch naturalist Anton van Leeuwenhoek (qq.v.). The science progressed slowly until the 19th century, when the compound microscope began to assume its present form and when the *microtome,* an instrument for slicing thin portions of tissue, was invented by the Czech physiologist Johannes Evangelista Purkinje (q.v.). In 1907 the American biologist Ross Granville Harrison (1870–1959) discovered that living tissues could be cultured, that is, grown outside of the parent organ. This discovery introduced a new era in histology and led to many important discoveries; *see, for example,* ENDERS, JOHN FRANKLIN. Work in this area was facilitated by the development in the first part of the 20th century of the electron microscope and by the introduction in 1968 of the scanning electron microscope, which gives three-dimensional magnifications up to 50,000 diameters. *See* MICROSCOPE: *Electron Microscope.*

Five principal groups of tissues are found in the animal body: epithelium, which is found in all the lining and secreting areas of the body; connective tissues, which include bone, cartilage, and other supporting structures; muscle tissue; nerve tissue; and the fluid tissues, blood and lymph. Tissues are also classified on the basis of their embryological origin; *see* EMBRYOLOGY. See separate articles on most of the tissues mentioned. For plant tissues, *see* PLANT MORPHOLOGY.

HISTORY, systematic study of past events, particularly those affecting nations, institutions, arts, and sciences. Derived from *historia,* a Greek word of the 6th century B.C., the term originally denoted a search for knowledge, involving critical inquiry and analytical research, but not narrative. Not until two centuries later did the student of history come to be called the *historikos* ("reciter of stories") instead of the *historeon* ("seeker after knowledge"). Both meanings are important for modern historians. On the one hand, history is investigative, and in this sense it belongs generically to the sciences. On the other hand, it involves narrations of events, and may therefore be considered a literary medium.

Early Historians. Although the civilizations of Egypt and Mesopotamia (qq.v.) possessed written annals as early as 3000 B.C., they produced no work comparable to modern historical studies; *see* CIVILIZATION. Their records, usually comprising lists of dynasties and royal military exploits, were intended to glorify the ruling monarch. Negative criticism and disparaging facts were omitted; hyperbole abounded; and the worldly actions of the monarch were held to be part of a divine plan. Among ancient Middle Eastern peoples only the Hebrews (q.v.) expanded history beyond an account of military affairs, especially in the first five books of the Old Testament, composed between the 9th and 6th centuries B.C.; *see* BIBLE.

In the Far East, the Chinese interest in chronology dates back at least to the 12th century B.C., and history has for centuries constituted one of the major divisions of Chinese literature (q.v.). The first and greatest shaper of Chinese historical thought was the philosopher Confucius in his *Ch'un ch'iu* ("Spring and Autumn Annals"). Although following a strict chronological order, Confucius deliberately passed ethical judgment on the facts he recorded.

The *Historical Records* of Ssu-ma Ch'ien (145–87 B.C.) was arranged by topics and included such elements of cultural history as monographs on the arts and sciences and biographies of eminent men and women. Yuan Shu's *Complete History* in 1173 A.D. was the first Chinese historical tract to deal with the problem of causality (q.v.). Hu Wei (d. 1714) stressed the importance of primary texts and presented historical problems as scientific hypotheses.

In India the writer Kalhana (fl. 12th cent. A.D.) attempted in his *Kashmir Chronicle* to make an objective study of the remote past of his country. After the Muslim invasion of northern India about 1190, several notable histories were produced. Among them was the *Akbar Namch,* a study of the reign of the Muslim emperor Akbar (q.v.) by Abul Fazl (d. 1602).

Japanese historical study followed Chinese models until the end of the 18th century. The *Six National Histories* (887 A.D.), Chikafusa's *Records of the Emperors* (1324), and Hakuseki's *Commentaries* (1700) show a profound Confucian influence.

In the West the first known historian was the Greek Herodotus, who lived in the 5th century B.C. His history of the Persian wars, despite numerous inaccuracies, greatly expanded the scope of historical inquiry. Herodotus was the first scholar in the West to point out the social, economic, and political factors essential to historical studies. His countryman and near contemporary Thucydides interpreted Greek history in philosophical terms as an illustration of the extremes of human nature. A third notable Greek historian was Xenophon, a general who recorded events that he had observed. Among the leading Roman historians were Gaius Julius Caesar, Livy, and Tacitus; of the three, Tacitus is

HISTORY

Herodotus, often called the "Father of History", a statue by the 20th-century American sculptor Daniel Chester French. Bettmann Archive

significant today because, like Thucydides, he recognized an underlying causal meaning in political and social events.

Religious Influences. Medieval European history was largely subservient to the ideals of the Christian religion. During the 5th century, Saint Augustine, in his philosophical work *De Civitate Dei* ("The City of God", 413–26), developed a systematic defense against pagan charges that Christianity was responsible for the fall of Rome. The *Chronicle* of the 7th-century Spanish ecclesiastic and scholar Isidore of Seville and the historical writings of the Italian mystic Joachim of Floris (1145?–1202?) used history as a basis for prophecy. The first successes of Christianity and subsequent ecclesiastical organization were recorded by the Catholic bishop and historian Saint Gregory of Tours and by the 8th-century English historian known as The Venerable Bede. Even the best of these chronicles, such as the account of business and trade in Florence, Italy, given by the Italian Giovanni Villani, saw worldly events as little more than outward signs of the heavenly order.

Muslim historical writing paralleled that of the medieval Christian West both in form and purpose. Based on the chronicle form, Islamic historical thought achieved its fullest expression with al-Tabari (d. 923), who produced a multi-volume history of Islam (q.v.). Like their Christian counterparts, such historical studies were intended to defend and strengthen religion.

Secular Interpretations. Historical thinking during the Renaissance differed from that of the Middle Ages (qq.v.) in offering natural or secular explanations of historical events. New critical methods, largely modeled on Greco-Roman ideals, gave Renaissance history a skeptical tone. In this spirit such scholars as the 16th-century Italians Francesco Guicciardini and Niccolò Machiavelli and the English statesman Sir Thomas More wrote histories of their respective countries. The 14th-century Arab historian Ibn-Khaldun examined the influence of the physical environment on the development of nations.

During the 17th century, historical scholarship was influenced by the religious struggles that led to the Thirty Years' War (q.v.). The religious opponents, anxious to document the validity of their claims, encouraged the close examination of archives. Thus a comprehensive history of German Protestantism appeared in the *Magdeburg Centuries* (1601) of the theologian Matthias Flacius Illyricus (1520–75), and the Italian Paolo Sarpi (1552–1623) composed a critical study of the Catholic Council of Trent (*see* TRENT, COUNCIL OF).

The historical thought of the 18th century adopted the methods of the physical sciences, which dominated the intellectual activity of the period known as the Age of Enlightenment; *see* ENLIGHTENMENT, AGE OF. Particularly influential was the work of the Italian philosopher Giovanni Battista Vico, perhaps the first thinker to formulate a science of history. His theory of the cyclical recurrence of events formed the basis for many subsequent studies. Most historians of the 18th century described events as a strict sequence of cause and effect, severing their dependence on theology, particularly in such works as *The History of the Decline and Fall of the Roman Empire* (1776–88) by the British historian Edward Gibbon. Other notable historical writers included the French men of letters Voltaire and Montesquieu and the Scottish historians David Hume and William Robertson. Their works often included essays on the arts and sciences as well as historical surveys of China, India, and the Americas in terms of their relevance to the history of Western Europe. With its dogmatic faith in the progress and perfectibility of mankind, however, the Enlightenment became intolerant of previous ages. The typical division of history into ancient, medieval, and modern periods is an invention of Enlightenment bias. Many of the assumptions of the Enlightenment were challenged in the works of the French philosopher Jean Jacques Rousseau and by the violence of the French Revolution (q.v.), which provoked a reaction among such historians as the British statesman Edmund Burke.

Scientific Method. The cult of progress was discarded during the 19th century by the German historians Barthold Georg Niebuhr and Leopold von Ranke. Asserting that each age should be studied for itself and that the historian should be concerned solely with historical facts, they sought to give history the precision of science. An especially rigorous approach was undertaken by the German philosopher Georg Wilhelm Friedrich Hegel, who developed a celebrated theory of history based on his philosophical concept of the absolute idea; see ABSOLUTE. Similarly, Karl Marx, the German political philosopher and founder of modern socialism (q.v.), interpreted history according to the economic conditions in which men live. The historical importance of environmental factors was described by the British historian Henry Thomas Buckle in his attempt to find historical laws analogous to those of natural science.

Political history became increasingly important during the 19th century, notably in the works of the French historians Jacques Nicolas Augustin Thierry and Jules Michelet. The causes and effects of the French Revolution form a principal theme in the historical writing of the critic Hippolyte Adolphe Taine, and in the works of the French statesman François Pierre Guillaume Guizot and Louis Adolphe Thiers. The political writer Alexis Charles Henri Maurice Clérel de Tocqueville analyzed the development of political institutions in the United States and in prerevolutionary France. An historical analysis of the importance of political principles was also offered by the British historians Henry Hallam and Frederick William Maitland, while John Emerich Edward Dalberg-Acton, 1st Baron Acton, emphasized the importance of morality and individual freedom in history, a concern that had also been expressed in the historical writings of Thomas Carlyle and James Anthony Froude. In Germany, however, the historian Heinrich von Treitschke saw in history a means of glorifying the state and supported a policy of German nationalism. The Russian novelist Count Lev Nikolaevich Tolstoi viewed history as an accumulation of accidental events beyond the control of a single individual.

Edward Gibbon, detail from a portrait, dated 1779, by the British artist Sir Joshua Reynolds. Bettmann Archive

Also during the 19th century, history emerged as a fully developed literary art, attracting the attention of such literary figures as the French writer Vicomte Françoise René de Chateaubriand, the German poet Baron Friedrich von Hardenberg, and the British novelist Sir Walter Scott, whose works revived interest in the Middle Ages. The British statesman Thomas Babing-

HISTORY

ton Macaulay wrote history in a fine rhetorical style, as did the Americans George Bancroft and William Hickling Prescott. The works of these writers suffered, however, from the lack of a sound underlying philosophy and from inadequate research. Historical studies of a more scientific nature were produced in the U.S. by Henry Brooks Adams and Francis Parkman and in France by Victor Duruy. Major specialized studies included the widely read *The Influence of Sea Power Upon History* (1890) by the American naval officer Alfred Thayer Mahan and the histories of ancient Rome written by the German classical scholar Theodor Mommsen. The Swiss historian Jakob Burckhardt produced influential studies of the development of art. An analysis of the importance of art in human history was a notable element in the work of the celebrated Italian philosopher Benedetto Croce.

The 20th Century. The search for fundamental principles was continued in recent studies, notably in the work of the German philosopher Oswald Spengler and the British historian Arnold Joseph Toynbee. Emphasizing the comparative study of various civilizations, these scholars sought to formulate a general law for the rise and decline of cultures. Spengler believed that all civilizations must inevitably decline. In contrast, Toynbee asserted that decline is not inevitable and may be overcome by the enlightened efforts of mankind. Others who have rejected a philosophy of historical inevitability are the British scholar Sir Isaiah Berlin (1909–) and the American historian Arthur Meier Schlesinger, Jr.

In more specialized studies, historians of the 20th century have been influenced by such sciences as archeology, anthropology, economics, psychology, and sociology (qq.v.). Among those who emphasized the social and economic aspects of history were the American historians Charles Austin Beard and Vernon Louis Parrington. Famous studies of the social history of the English were produced by the French scholar Elie Halevy and the British historian George Macaulay Trevelyan. The British historian Sir Lewis Namier (1888–1960) applied the techniques of psychoanalysis to history. In Russia and mainland China the dominance of Communism (q.v.) produced a complete revision of history on Marxist lines. Many American historians have embarked on a reevaluation of the history of the U.S. in terms of such matters as racial conflict and economic injustices, which, they feel, were not adequately studied by previous historians. The history of science and technology has also become an important area of inquiry.

Historical research has been greatly assisted by the development of the computer (q.v.), making possible the rapid processing of data from artifacts and documents, and by the establishment of associations and journals devoted to the study of history. Notable 20th-century histo-

Motion picture and television director Alfred Hitchcock spoofs Hamlet, using a rubber mask to represent "poor Yorick". UPI

rians include, in addition to those already mentioned, the German Max Weber and the Americans Henry Steele Commager, Samuel Eliot Morison, Allan Nevins, Arthur Meier Schlesinger, Sr., and Frederick Jackson Turner.

See separate articles on most of the individual scholars mentioned in this article for whom birth and death dates are not given.

HITACHI, city of Japan, in Ibaraki Prefecture, on the E. coast of Honshu Island, about 75 miles N.E. of Tokyo. Situated on the coastal Joban railroad line, Hitachi is chiefly a mining and industrial city in an area producing copper, gold, silver, sulfur, and limestone. Manufactures include electrical goods, motors, wire, cement, and clay products. Pop. (1965) 179,703.

HITCHCOCK, Alfred Joseph (1899–   ), American motion-picture director and producer, born in London, England. Although trained as an engineer at Saint Ignatius College, London, Hitchcock became interested in film production and in 1925 directed his first motion picture. Among his early successes in England were *The 39 Steps* (1935) and *The Lady Vanishes* (1940). In 1939 he moved to the United States, and began directing motion pictures in Hollywood. Among his pictures are *Rebecca* (1940), *Strangers on a Train* (1951), *Rear Window* (1954), *Dial M for Murder* (1954), *Psycho* (1960), *The Birds* (1963), and *Topaz* (1969). In addition to making films, Hitchcock edited several collections of short stories, including *Favorites in Suspense* (1959), *Stories My Mother Never Told Me* (1963), and *Stories that Scared Even Me* (1967). He also produced two television series, "Alfred Hitchcock Presents" (1959–62) and "The Alfred Hitchcock Hour" (1963–65).

HITLER, Adolf (1889–1945), German dictator, born in Braunau, Austria. His father was a minor customs official. As a youth Hitler was interested in art and music. He failed, however, to complete his secondary education, and his application to enter the Vienna Academy of Fine Arts was rejected. From 1906 to 1913 he supported himself in Vienna by painting, selling postal cards, and hanging wallpaper. During this period, he became intensely anti-Semitic and anti-socialistic, adopting and developing a number of beliefs on the supremacy of the state and the racial superiority of the German people. In 1913 he moved to Munich, then the center of German artistic life. On the outbreak of World War I Hitler enlisted in a Bavarian regiment. He was twice decorated for bravery and, late in the war, was hospitalized after being temporarily blinded by poison gas. Shortly after the war he helped organize the German Workers' Party, which soon was renamed the National Socialist German Workers' Party, or, popularly, Nazi Party; see NATIONAL SOCIALISM. He quickly established his ascendancy in the group, and the party became the instrument for the realization of his political objectives.

Rise to Power. An effective demagogic orator, Hitler struck a responsive chord among war veterans embittered by defeat and among nationalists hostile to the democratic Weimar Republic, which they blamed for the humiliations Germany suffered under the Treaty of Versailles; see VERSAILLES, TREATY OF. His party, organized along military lines with its own army of brown-shirted *Sturmabteilungen* (SA, "storm troops") was first active in Bavaria. With the aid of Field Marshal Erich Friedrich Wilhelm Ludendorff (q.v.) and other sympathizers, Hitler, in November, 1923, attempted to seize control of the Bavarian government in Munich in an action known as "the beer-hall putsch". The putsch failed, and Hitler was imprisoned for nine months. During his imprisonment he dictated to his aide Rudolf Hess (q.v.) the work *Mein Kampf* ("My Battle", Eng. trans., 1933), in which he set forth his program for the restoration of Germany to a dominant position in Europe.

During the next few years Hitler and his close associates extended the National Socialist Party organization throughout Germany. With the beginning of a worldwide depression in 1929, the party expanded rapidly. It was supported by some leading German industrialists and other conservative elements who feared an uprising of the working class such as had already led to the domination of communism (q.v.) in Russia. Representation of the party in the Reichstag, the lower legislative house, rose from 7 members in 1928 to 230 in 1932, only 74 short of a majority. It was the largest party in the Reichstag. Hitler was defeated in the presidential election of 1932 by the aged President Paul von Hindenburg (q.v.), and control of the government passed from moderate parties to the conservatives. Chancellors Franz von Papen (q.v.) and Kurt von Schleicher (1882–1934) were unable to cope with the political turmoil and economic crisis. Unemployment increased, and street clashes occurred daily between the National Socialists and Communists.

On Jan. 30, 1933, President von Hindenburg appointed Hitler chancellor of a government in which the National Socialists were still a minority. Hitler proceeded to govern, however, without concern for the non-National Socialist coalition members, winning from the Reichstag extraordinary powers to meet an alleged national emergency. He suppressed opposition parties and began the organization of a totalitarian regime called the Third Reich, or third great German empire; see TOTALITARIANISM. In 1934 a number of National Socialists, critical of the conservative economic policy that Hitler was pursuing in alliance with industrialists and militarists, were executed in the so-called "blood purge". Among the slain was Hitler's close associate Ernst Röhm (q.v.), the leader of the SA. On the death in 1934 of Hindenburg, Hitler combined the offices of president and chancellor in himself and assumed the title *Führer* ("Leader"). His associates and leaders in his government included Joseph Paul Goebbels, a masterful propagandist; Hermann Wilhelm Göring, who built and headed the German air force, the Luftwaffe; and Heinrich Himmler (qq.v.), the head of the secret police known as the Gestapo (q.v.).

Dictatorship. In foreign affairs, Hitler's policy was dedicated to the destruction of the Treaty of Versailles and the transformation of Germany into the chief military power in Europe. These nationalistic objectives provided the rationale for a program of German rearmament, through which Hitler further extended his power by assuming complete economic control of the country. He thereupon suppressed all vestiges of revolutionary sentiment among the workers and strengthened his alliance with the major industrial combines. The Third Reich then repudiated the arms-limitation provision of the treaty at the Geneva Disarmament Conference in 1933 and reintroduced universal military training.

Aggression and World War II. Hitler subsequently played on the weaknesses of the world powers, which attempted to appease his aggressive activity through a series of concessions. In addition, he was tacitly regarded by a number of national leaders as an acceptable bulwark against communism and worldwide uprisings of colonial peoples. He therefore felt free to carry out his conquest of Europe. After reoccupying (March, 1936) the Rhineland zone between France and Germany and annexing Austria (March, 1938), the Sudetenland of northern Czechoslovakia (October, 1938), and the remainder of Czechoslovakia (March, 1939), Germany invaded Poland (Sept. 1, 1939), thus precipitating World War II (q.v.). In June, 1941, Germany invaded the Soviet Union, and Hitler took personal command of the armed forces in December. As supreme military commander, Hitler committed a succession of major strategic errors, both in the Soviet Union and on the western fronts, that negated the effectiveness of

Adolf Hitler greets Field Marshal Hermann Göring at a Nazi Party rally at Nuremberg, in September, 1938.
U.S. Army

the German forces. His campaigns led to the virtually complete destruction of German military and industrial power by the superior forces of the Allies.

Defeat and Death. In 1944, a group of army officers, National Socialist officials, and anti-National Socialist civilians who opposed continuation of the war attempted unsuccessfully to assassinate Hitler. The dictator subsequently tried and brutally executed thousands of his alleged opponents in a movement known as "Operation Thunderstorm". Toward the end of the war he is believed to have suffered a nervous breakdown. He remained in Berlin when Soviet troops entered the city toward the end of April, 1945, and on April 30 committed suicide with his mistress, Eva Braun (1911–45), whom he had married the previous day. Positive identification of his body was impossible, but there is no reason to doubt the fact of his death.

Historical Significance. Hitler's initial successes were based largely on his ability to manipulate human passions in the disordered Germany of his time. Substituting illusory goals of nationalistic hegemony for a positive approach to economic and social problems, he was able to delude many Germans into supporting his programs on a purely emotional basis at the expense of their own economic well-being. He was successful, too, in citing presumed enemies of order, such as Jews, Bolsheviks, and foreign powers, as the cause of German distress. The intensity of his accusations, bordering on hysteria, communicated itself forcefully to his followers. His capacity for self-delusion was boundless, however, and the conviction that he was infallible deafened him to advice that might have saved him from disaster.

Hitler was guilty of crimes without precedent in modern times. His racial dogmas led him to pursue a policy of genocide (q.v.), under which deliberate campaigns of extermination were carried out against various nationalities, especially Poles and Russians, and most notably against Jews, some 6,000,000 of whom were put to death at his command during the war; see ANTI-SEMITISM; CONCENTRATION CAMP.

See GERMANY: *History.*

HITTITE LANGUAGE, Indo-European language of the extinct Hittite civilization, surviving in cuneiform (q.v.) inscriptions on tablets excavated at sites in Asia Minor in the region occupied by ancient Hatti; see HITTITES. Hittite, Luwian, and Palaic form the Anatolian group of Indo-European languages (q.v.). Palaic was spoken in the country called Pala, north of Hatti, and Luwian was spoken in the country called Arzawa, west of Hatti, and in Cilicia, south of Hatti. The Hittites called their language Nesian, after Nesa, the first town that they settled, near the site of present-day Kayşeri, Turkey. The first important finds in the language were made by expeditions led by the German Assyriologist Hugo Winckler (1863–1913) in 1906–07 (when royal archives containing nearly 10,000 clay tablets were discovered) and in 1911–12. In 1915 the Czech archeologist Bedrich Hrozný (q.v.) announced that he had deciphered the language and that it was Indo-European, and two years later he produced a Hittite grammar, which proved his contention of Indo-European affinity. Hrozný's arguments were sharply criticized at first, but further study proved the validity of his decipherment and theory. Several glossaries and other grammars have been published since, and some Hittite texts are presently available in translation.

Hittite texts, which date back to 1600 B.C., are the oldest written records of any Indo-European language. Linguists are not yet certain whether the Anatolian group broke away from the parent language, Proto-Indo-European, before any other known Indo-European tongue, or whether it was merely one of the earliest to break away. Scholarly research recognizes a much larger number of Indo-European words in the Hittite language than was previously suspected; the source of many other words remains to be identified.

HITTITES (Heb. *Hittim*), extinct people of the ancient Middle East, inhabiting the land of Hatti on the central plateau of what is now Anatolia, Turkey. The Hittites, whose origin is unknown, spoke an Indo-European language; *see* HITTITE LANGUAGE. They invaded the region, which became known as Hatti, about 1900 B.C. and imposed their language, culture, and rule on the earlier inhabitants, a people speaking a non-Indo-European agglutinative language. The first town settled by the Hittites was Nesa, a town situated near present-day Kayşeri, Turkey. Shortly after 1800 B.C. they conquered the town of Hattushash, near the site of present-day Bogazköy. Nothing more is known of Hittite history until, in the 17th century B.C., the so-called Old Hittite Kingdom was founded by the Hittite leader Labarna, or Tabarna, and Hattushash became its capital. Labarna conquered nearly all of Central Anatolia and extended his rule to the sea. His successors extended Hittite conquests into northern Syria. Mursili I, the second ruler after Labarna, conquered Aleppo, Syria, and raided Babylon about 1600 B.C. (according to one system of chronology; 1530 is suggested by an-

HITTITES

other system; see BABYLONIA) Mursili was assassinated, and there followed a period of internal strife and external weakness which ended during the reign of King Telipinu (about 1550 B.C.). In order to ensure the future stability of the kingdom, he issued strict rules pertaining to the royal succession. The law code may also have been compiled under his reign. Of Telipinu's successors only the names are known.

The New Hittite Kingdom. About 1450 B.C. the so-called New Hittite Kingdom was founded. One of its most important members, the royal prince Suppiluliuma, usurped the throne about 1370 B.C., during a period of foreign invasions. He liberated his country and defeated his main enemy, the kingdom of Mitanni in northern Mesopotamia. He led his armies further into Syria, where his conquests were facilitated by a weakening of Egyptian power during the reign of the pharaoh Amenhotep IV, or Ikhnaton (q.v.). Thus the Hittite kingdom under Suppiluliuma became a great empire rivaling the power of Egypt, Babylonia, and Assyria (qq.v.). After the death of Suppiluliuma the Hittites were able on the whole to maintain their empire, though only by constant warfare. During the 14th and 13th centuries B.C. their holdings extended westward to the Aegean Sea, eastward into Armenia, southeastward into upper Mesopotamia, and southward into Syria as far as present-day Lebanon.

During the latter half of the 14th century the Hittites continued to come into frequent conflict with Egypt. The two great powers struggled for control of Syria until about 1300 B.C., when a decisive battle was fought in Kadesh, Syria, between the Hittite king Muwatalli and the Egyptian pharaoh Ramses II (see under RAMSES). Although Ramses claimed a great victory, the Hittites continued to maintain their hold on Syria. The Hittite king Hattusili III concluded a treaty of peace and alliance with Ramses some sixteen years later and subsequently gave him his daughter in marriage. Thereafter, relations between the Hittites and Egyptians remained friendly until the Hittite empire fell shortly after 1200 B.C. to invaders called the Sea Peoples in Egyptian records.

Hittite City-States. The downfall of the empire was followed by confusion and conflict. Subsequently a number of Hittite city-states, the most famous of which was Carchemish, emerged in southeastern Anatolia and northern Syria. These states were peopled by an intermingled ethnic group, called Syro-Hittites, consisting chiefly of the Hittites, of peoples from the former Hittite empire, and the prior inhabitants of the two areas. The Syro-Hittite rulers used the Luwian language, in which hieroglyphics were employed for writing. Some of these city-states were conquered in the 10th century B.C. by the Aramaeans. Even after it was conquered all of Syria still was called Hatti by the Assyrians. Both the city-states that were conquered by the Aramaeans and those that remained independent finally were made provinces of the Assyrian empire under Sargon II (r. 722–705 B.C.) about 715 B.C. See ASSYRIA.

Early Records and Translations. The primary sources of information about the Hittites came from Egyptian records, notably those of the XIX Dynasty, and from certain passages in the Bible. The earliest of these passages, calling the Hittites "Sons of Heth", refer possibly to the period of the Hittite kingdom. Later passages allude to the Syro-Hittites.

In 1906 the royal archives of the Hittites themselves were discovered in excavations at Bogazköy. These discoveries cast doubt upon many items of information gathered from Egyptian sources. For example, certain military engagements were mentioned as victories for the Hittites, whereas the Egyptian records identify the engagements as Hittite defeats. The invaluable importance of the discovery is that the archives made possible the decipherment of the Hittite language and revealed information about previously unknown aspects of the culture, such as political organization, legislation, and the administration of justice, religion, and literature.

Most of the texts found in the archives were written in the Hittite language, but treaties and state letters were written in Akkadian, the international language of the period, and other texts were written in the Hurrian language of southeastern Anatolia and northern Mesopotamia, a language unrelated to any known linguistic group. The Hittites used the cuneiform (q.v.) system of writing taken from the Babylonians, but they employed also a system of hieroglyphs to inscribe a language closely related to Hittite, possibly a Luwian dialect. Although the hieroglyphs were used during the period of the empire, most inscriptions belong to the period after its downfall. The literature of the Hittites was highly developed, particularly in the form of historical records and stories.

Organization and Achievements. The Hittite king acted as the supreme priest, military commander, and chief judge of the land. During the old kingdom he was assisted by the *pankus,* an advisory council of nobles, which later disappeared. The empire was administered by provincial governors acting as deputies of the king.

HITTITES

Stone relief, probably from a temple, indicating the intricacy and stylization of Hittite sculpture of about 1200 B.C. Metropolitan Museum of Art — Rogers Fund

Territories beyond the empire were ruled often as vassal kingdoms with whose rulers formal treaties were concluded.

The most outstanding achievements of the Hittite civilization lay in the fields of legislation and the administration of justice. The law codes of the Hittites reveal a strong Babylonian influence, but their administration of justice was far more lenient than that of the Babylonians. The Hittites rarely resorted to the death penalty or to bodily mutilation, both of which were characteristic of other civilizations of the ancient Middle East. Furthermore, Hittite justice rested in the main on the principle of restitution rather than retribution or vengeance. The penalty for thievery, for example, was restoration of the stolen object and payment of some additional recompense; restitution in kind was gradually replaced by payment of money.

The Hittite economy was basically agricultural. The principal crops raised were wheat and barley, and the chief animals were cattle and sheep. The Hittites had also mineral riches in the form of copper, lead, silver, and iron. Their metallurgical techniques were quite advanced for the time, and they may have been the first people to work iron.

Religion, Art, and Architecture. Knowledge is incomplete, but it is known that the Hittites worshiped a variety of gods. One of the recurrent phrases found in the state documents is an invocation to the "thousand gods of Hatti", deities worshiped apparently throughout Asia Minor before and during the period of Hittite domination. Scholars have traced Sumerian, Babylonian, Assyrian, Hurrian, Luwian, and other foreign influences in the Hittite pantheon. *See* Assyria; Babylonian Religion; Sumer.

In the rock sanctuary of Yazilikana, near Bogazköy, is a remarkable series of reliefs cut into rock. The reliefs depict two long processions of gods and goddesses advancing toward one another. The majority of the gods remain unidentified, but the two deities heading the processions are the storm god, or weather god, and the sun goddess, the chief deities worshiped by the Hittites. Excavations at the sanctuary revealed a temple built in front of one chamber; the other, smaller chamber seems to have been devoted to the cult of a deceased king.

Hittite mythology, like Hittite religion, represents a combination of elements that reflect the diversity of cults within the empire. Of special interest are certain epic poems containing myths, originally Hurrian with Babylonian motifs. These myths deal with several successive generations of gods who ruled the universe, and with a monster who challenged the rule of the last king of the gods. They are similar to Greek myths contained in the *Theogony* by the Greek poet Hesiod (q.v.) and may have been their prototypes. How the myths might have reached Greece is not clear, but it is possible that they were transmitted during the period of Mycenaean ascendancy in Greece (1400–1200 B.C.); see MYCENAE. Mycenaean Greeks are known to have been in western Anatolia during that period and to have carried on trade with Hittite-held Syria. In addition, Hittite records refer to contacts between Hittite rulers and those of the kingdom of Ahhiyawā, which some scholars identify with the country of the Achaeans (q.v.). Whether or not Hittite cultural elements were transmitted abroad, many of them survived in Anatolia until the time of the first Roman penetration into Asia Minor in 190 B.C. Such deities as the Great Mother and the storm god still were worshiped at that time; the latter was called Jupiter Dolichenus by the Romans.

The art and architecture of the Hittites reveal the influence of nearly all the contemporaneous cultures of the ancient Near East, and of Babylonia especially. Nevertheless, the Hittites achieved a certain independence of style which renders their art distinct. Their building materials were generally stone and brick, although they also used columns of wood. Their palaces, temples, and fortifications, often of massive proportions, frequently were adorned by carved reliefs on walls, gates, and entrances. Their sculpture was stylized and often characterized by intricacy of detail. H.G.G.

HIVES, or URTICARIA or NETTLE RASH, allergic disorder of the skin, characterized by sudden evanescent or repeated appearance of wheals, irregular round skin lesions accompanied by inflammation and itching; see ALLERGY. They commonly appear on covered areas of the skin, but rarely on the palms, soles, or scalp. The disease, often appearing in conjunction with hay fever or asthma, is attributed to an allergic reaction, which occurs rapidly after ingestion, inhalation, injection or contact with an offending antigen.

Agents responsible for acute urticaria include many foods, such as fish, shellfish, nuts, and berries. Of the wide variety of drugs that may cause it, the most prominent are penicillin, serums, insulin, and biological preparations that embody protein. Insect bites may be responsible. Chronic urticaria is often attributable to such contactants as wool, metal, furs, or silk; to focal infections of the teeth, tonsils, or sinuses; to infestations of scabies, lice, bedbugs, and worms; or to allergic reactions to light or extremes of temperature. Many chronic cases are caused by emotional stress and in a large number of cases, no other cause can be found.

Itching may be relieved by ointments or lotions such as calamine. In some cases, hives caused by penicillin may be countered by injections of penicillinase. Since the antigen-antibody reaction characteristic of acute urticaria is believed to involve release of body histamine, injections of epinephrine, ephedrine, or an antihistaminic may afford symptomatic relief. Where psychogenic factors are in control, drugs combining an antihistaminic and a tranquilizer may be of benefit. See PSYCHOSOMATIC MEDICINE.

HOARFROST. See FROST.

HOARHOUND. See HOREHOUND.

HOATZIN or **HOACTZIN,** South American bird, *Opisthocomos hoazin,* which constitutes the suborder Opisthocomi of the order Galliformes. The adult bird is about 14 in. long and is generally dark brown with white markings above and chestnut markings below. It resembles a small pheasant, but has a long, erectile crest of loose feathers on its crown. Its wings and legs are short, its feet are large, and its tail is long and wide, broadly bordered with yellow. The bird feeds on the fruit and leaves of several trees found along the banks of the Amazon R. The hoatzin has a very large crop, in which the leaves are stored. The adult gives off a musky, offensive odor causing the natives to call it "stinkbird" and "stinking pheasant". The hoatzin is arboreal; although it occasionally flies in slow and clumsy fashion, it prefers climbing among the branches of trees. The bird is born with functional claws on the second and third digits of the forelimbs. As the wing feathers develop, these claws degenerate.

HOBAN, James (1762?–1831), American architect, born in County Kilkenny, Ireland, and educated at the University of Dublin. He settled first in Charleston, S.C., and in 1792 moved to Washington, D.C. Between 1792 and 1799, he designed and directed the building of the Executive Mansion, later known as the White House (q.v.), which he also rebuilt and improved after its burning by British forces during the War of 1812 (q.v.). Hoban also worked on the design and execution of the Capitol of the United States (q.v.).

HOBART, city of Indiana, in Lake Co., about 6 miles S.E. of Gary. Hobart is in a region of grain, livestock, and dairy products; it manufactures clay products. Nearby is the Indiana Dunes National Lakeshore. Settled in 1849, Hobart was incorporated in 1921. Pop. (1960) 18,680; (1970) 21,485.

HOBART, city in Australia, and capital of the State of Tasmania, in Buckingham Co. It is on the S.E. coast of the island, on the w. shore of the estuary of the Derwent R., about 375 miles S.E. of Melbourne. Hobart is the largest port of the island. Exports include wool, ores, lumber, grain, hops, and fruit. Among the industrial establishments of Hobart are foundries, tanneries, flour and lumber mills, breweries, and factories producing woolen goods. The University of Tasmania, established in 1890, is located in Hobart. The city was founded as a penal colony in 1804 and named Hobart Town for the British statesman Lord Robert Hobart (1760–1816). Hobart Town became the capital of Tasmania in 1825 and a city in 1857. Pop. (1966) 53,226; with suburbs, 119,415.

HOBART, Garret Augustus (1844–99), American lawyer and statesman, twenty-fourth Vice-President of the United States, born in Long Branch, N.J., and educated at Rutgers College (now Rutgers, the State University). He was admitted to the bar in 1869, and practiced law in Paterson, N.J. Over a period of twenty years, starting in 1871, he was city counsel of Paterson, a member of the New Jersey State Assembly, and vice-president of the State Senate. In 1896 he was elected Vice-President of the United States on the Republican ticket with William McKinley (q.v.). Hobart died before the expiration of his term.

HOBART AND WILLIAM SMITH COLLEGES, privately controlled liberal arts schools, located in Geneva, N.Y. Hobart College, for men, is affiliated with the Protestant Episcopal Church. Chartered in 1822 and known as Geneva College until 1862, Hobart College has shared its campus facilities and faculty with William Smith College, a coordinate school for women, since 1941. Each college, however, has retained its identity and awards its own degrees. The degrees of B.A., B.S., M.A., and M.S. in Ed. are conferred. In 1968 the library serving both colleges housed more than 150,000 bound volumes. Student enrollment in Hobart and William Smith Colleges in 1968 totaled 1530, the combined faculty numbered 122, and the endowment of the colleges was about $2,904,000.

HOBBEMA, Meindert (1638–1709), Dutch painter, born in Amsterdam. Hobbema is second only to his teacher, Jacob van Ruisdale (q.v.), as a Dutch landscape painter. His favorite subject matter was the wooded countryside; his scenes include villages, farmhouses, tree-shaded streams, and, especially, water mills. Hobbema's large, luminous compositions feature masterly draftsmanship and painstaking detail; his palette tends to be subdued. Most of his work was completed before 1668, when he married and, with the help of his wife, received a municipal appointment. His works are found in leading American and European museums, and his masterpiece, "Avenue, Middleharnis" (1689), hangs in the National Gallery in London.

HOBBES, Thomas (1588–1679), English philosopher, born in Malmesbury, and educated at Magdalen Hall, University of Oxford. In 1608 he became the tutor of William Cavendish (d. 1626), later earl of Devonshire; in the following years he made several tours through France and Italy with his pupil and, later, with the son of the latter. During his travels Hobbes met and talked with several advanced thinkers of the time, including the Italian physicist Galileo Galilei and the French philosophers René Descartes

Thomas Hobbes

and Pierre Gassendi (qq.v.). In 1637, while in England, Hobbes became interested in the constitutional struggle between King Charles I (q.v.) and Parliament. He set to work on "a little treatise in English" in defense of the royal prerogative. This work was privately circulated in 1640 under the title *The Elements of Law, Natural and Politic* (published 1650). Hobbes feared that Parliament might have him arrested because of his book, and he fled to Paris; he remained in voluntary exile there for eleven years.

In 1642 he finished *De Cive,* a statement of his theory of government. From 1646 to 1648 he was mathematics tutor to the prince of Wales, later King Charles II (q.v.), who was living in exile in Paris. Hobbes' best-known work, *Leviathan, Or the Matter, Form and Power of a Commonwealth Ecclesiastical and Civil* (1651), is a forceful exposition of his doctrine of sovereignty. The work was interpreted by the followers of the exiled prince as a justification of the Commonwealth and aroused the suspicions of the French authorities by its attack on the papacy. Again fearful of arrest, Hobbes returned to England.

In 1660, when the Commonwealth ended and his former pupil acceded to the throne, Hobbes again came into favor. In 1666, however, the House of Commons passed a bill including the *Leviathan* among books to be investigated on charges of atheistic tendencies. The measure caused Hobbes to burn many of his papers, and to delay publication of three of his works: *Behemoth: The History of the Causes of Civil Wars of England*; *Dialogues Between a Philosopher and a Student of the Common Laws of England*; and a metrical *Historia Ecclesiastica*. At the age of eighty-four, Hobbes wrote an autobiography in Latin verse; within the next three years he translated into English verse the *Iliad* and the *Odyssey* (qq.v.) of the Greek epic poet Homer (q.v.).

Hobbes' philosophy represents a reaction against the liberty of conscience of the Reformation (q.v.), which, he contended, brought anarchy. It effected the breach of English philosophy with scholasticism (q.v.), and he laid the foundations of modern scientific sociology by its attempt to apply to man, as both maker and matter of society, the principles of physical science that govern the material world. Hobbes developed his politics and ethics from a naturalistic basis; he held that all men fear each other, and for this reason must submit to the absolute supremacy of the state in both secular and religious matters. See ETHICS: *Ethics after the Reformation*; INDIVIDUALISM; POLITICAL THEORY; SOCIAL CONTRACT.

HOBBS, city of New Mexico, in Lea Co., on the High Plateau, or Llano Estacado (Staked Plains) section, 95 miles S.E. of Roswell. The surrounding area has irrigated fruit orchards and truck farms and also grows grain and raises cattle and sheep. The chief industries of Hobbs include refining of oil from wells in the area, cotton ginning, food canning and processing, dairying, and the manufacture of chemicals, plastics, tools, cement, and oil-field equipment. Hobbs was founded in 1907 and developed rapidly after the discovery of oil in 1927. Pop. (1960) 26,275; (1970) 26,025.

HOBOKEN, city of New Jersey, in Hudson Co., on the Hudson R., immediately s. of Jersey City, and opposite midtown Manhattan Island, with which it is connected by several tunnels. It is served by railroad and by oceangoing ships. Harbor facilities of Hoboken include extensive dry docks and piers of major steamship companies. Among the industries of Hoboken are shipbuilding, printing, food processing, and the manufacture of paper boxes and containers, chemicals, varnishes, furniture, and machinery. The city is the site of Stevens Institute of Technology, opened in 1871 and named after John Stevens (q.v.), the founder of Hoboken.

The Indians called the region of the present city Hobocan Hackingh, "the land of the tobacco pipe", because of the pipes made there from local stone. Dutch settlers purchased the land in 1630. In 1784 it was acquired by John Stevens, who laid out a town on the site in 1804. During the early part of the 19th century Hoboken was a noted resort and contained the villas of many prominent New Yorkers. It was the site of the first modern game of baseball. Hoboken was incorporated as a city in 1855. Pop. (1960) 48,441; (1970) 45,380.

HOBSON'S CHOICE, expression used to denominate a choice without alternative. The term refers to the practice of an English liveryman, Thomas Hobson (1544?–1631), who required persons who hired a horse to take the one standing nearest the stable door.

HO CHI MINH, assumed name of NGUYEN TAT THANH (1890–1969), President of the Democratic Republic of Vietnam (North Vietnam), born in Kimlien, French Indochina (now in South Vietnam). He took the name Ho Chi Minh, meaning "The Enlightener", in 1940; the name is frequently used in its short form, Ho.

As early as 1923, Ho opposed French colonial rule in Indochina (q.v.) and believed that only Communism (q.v.) could liberate the nations of Southeast Asia from foreign domination. (*See also* NATIONALISM). Ho was led to Communism through his interest in the French Socialist Party, which he had joined on his arrival in Paris in 1918. Between 1919, when he helped found the Communist Party in France, and 1930, when he founded the Communist Party of Indochina, Ho spent a great deal of time in the Soviet Union studying Marxism (*see* MARX, KARL). During this period he also served as an expert on Asian affairs for the Communist parties in Europe, and traveled throughout China and Southeast Asia organizing guerrilla forces in the nationalist-Communist cause, particularly among Vietnamese exiles. After being imprisoned by the British in Hong Kong in 1931 for subversive activities, and under ban of death by the French should he ever return to Vietnam, Ho fled again to the Soviet Union. By 1938, however, he had returned to Asia, this time as a member of the Eighth

Route Army of the Chinese Communist leader Mao Tse-tung (q.v.). In 1940 he reentered his homeland, which at that time was controlled by the Japanese. Taking advantage of the Japanese involvement in World War II (q.v.), Ho organized the nationalists and Communists into the Vietminh, or Independent Front, a 10,000-man guerrilla force that in 1945 forced the Japanese out of Vietnam. The Democratic Republic of Vietnam was proclaimed, with Ho as president. The French did not relinquish their claim to Vietnam, however, and full independence was not achieved until 1954 when the Vietminh guerrillas defeated the French forces at Dien Bien Phu, the last military stronghold of the French in Indochina. Vietnam was then divided at the 17th parallel into the Democratic Republic of Vietnam, or North Vietnam, and the Republic of Vietnam, or South Vietnam, by an international agreement signed in Geneva, Switzerland, in 1954; see VIETNAM: *History*. When North and South Vietnam could not agree on elections leading to reunification of the two states as specified in the Geneva accords, which South Vietnam had not signed, Ho encouraged the Communist guerrillas in South Vietnam (known as the National Liberation Front, or the VietCong) against the regime; see VIETNAM, WAR IN.

Throughout his presidency, which lasted until his death, Ho was able to maintain friendly relations with both the Soviet Union and Communist China, the two major Communist powers that, in the 1960's, had developed radically opposed ideological positions. A four-volume collection of Ho Chi Minh's writings and speeches was published in Hanoi from 1960 to 1962; excerpts from this work have been published in English as *Ho Chi Minh on Revolution* (1967). His *Selected Articles and Speeches* were posthumously published in English in 1970.

See also ASIA: *History: Postwar Turmoil and the 1950's*.

HOCKEY, game in which two opposing teams of players attempt to drive a ball, puck, or other small object through the goal of the opponent by means of sticks that are curved or hooked at one end. Various forms of hockey were well known among the ancient Greeks and Persians. Similar games were played in Europe during the Middle Ages. The game was called *hoquet* in France and was adopted by the English, who altered the name to hockey. Early forms of hockey were played on open fields and were similar to the game now called field hockey. Ice hockey probably arose in Europe during the 18th century, but its present form originated in Canada during the 19th century.

North Vietnamese President Ho Chi Minh is shown arriving on a visit to Budapest, Hungary, in 1957. At right is Istvan Dobi, then president of the Hungarian Presidium.
UPI

Field Hockey. Modern field hockey, as a formalized game, began about 1875 in England. Since then the game has become popular in Europe, India (where it is the national game), Pakistan, and Australia. In the United States, however, field hockey is played almost exclusively by women. The game is played on a field 90 to 100 yd. long and 50 to 60 yd. wide. Each team is composed of 11 players; usually 5 of these are forwards, 2 are fullbacks, 3 are halfbacks, and 1 is a goalkeeper, but the formation may be changed by the captain. The game is divided into two periods of 35 min. each. The teams change goals at the end of the first half. A goal is located at the center of each goal line; each goal consists of two upright posts, 7 ft. high, joined at the tips by a horizontal crossbar 4 yd. wide. A net is attached to the crossbar, the uprights, and the ground behind the goal. The ball is about 9 in. circumference with a cork center wound with twine and a white leather cover. It weighs not over 5¾ oz. Each player carries a stick about 3 ft. long and not exceeding 28 oz. in weight, curved at one end and flattened on the left side (the striking side). Officials at a field-hockey game include 2 umpires, 2 linesmen, and 2 scorekeepers.

The ball is put in play in mid-field through a

Players of the Boston Bruins and New York Rangers chase the puck in a professional ice hockey contest in the National Hockey League. UPI

procedure called a bully: one player from each team taps the ground and the opponent's stick three times before hitting at the ball. A point is scored when a player hits the ball into the opponents' goal from the striking circle, a zone in front of the goal that is roughly a semicircle with a radius of 16 yd. (15 yd. for women) but flattened at the top by a 4 yd.-line parallel to the goal line. Games ending with tied scores remain undecided and are not settled by playing overtime.

Ice Hockey. One of the fastest of all games, ice hockey is played on an oval rink 185 to 225 ft. long and 70 to 100 ft. wide. The rink is surrounded by a board wall about 4 ft. high. Two goal nets, each of which is attached to a frame 4 ft. high and 6 ft. wide, are situated 10 ft. from the ends of the rink. The playing area is divided by two blue lines into three zones of equal size. The zone nearest a team's goal is called its defense zone, the central zone is called the neutral zone, and the farthest zone, nearest the opponents' goal, is called the attacking zone. In professional hockey the rink is also divided in half by a red line.

Each team consists of 6 players, including 1 center, 2 forwards, 2 defensemen, and 1 goalkeeper. Each skater carries a wooden stick having a shaft no more than 53 in. long and a blade no more than 14¾ in. long and 3 in. wide, except the goalkeeper, whose blade is 3½ in. wide. A small disk of hard rubber, 3 in. in diameter and 1 in. thick, called a puck, is used instead of a ball. A point is scored when the puck is driven into the opponents' goal.

Play is begun with a face-off, a play in which the referee drops the puck between the opposing centers. The puck is driven or passed with the sticks. Only the goalkeeper may touch the puck with his hands. The puck may be passed from one player to a teammate, but it must precede any offensive player entering the attacking zone. If a player crosses the blue line on the edge of the attacking zone ahead of the puck, the play is offside, and a face-off is held in the neutral zone near the spot where the infraction occurred. The puck cannot be passed across two lines by the defense. (In collegiate hockey the second line is the blue line of the attacking zone; in professional hockey the second line is the red line at mid-rink.) When the puck is shot the length of the rink without touching an opponent's stick, it is called icing and the puck is returned for a face-off near the defenders' goal.

The game is divided into three 20-min. periods, with a change of goals at the end of each period. If the game is tied at the end of the third period, an additional 10-min. period is played; if the tie is not broken at the end of this period, the game ends in a tie. Penalties are given for interference, holding, excessive roughness, or other infractions of the rules. The offending player is sent to a penalty box for 2 min. for minor infractions and 5 min. for major infractions, such as fighting. The penalized player's team may not use a substitute during the player's penalty period, except when the player is given a misconduct penalty (usually 10 min. for arguing with an official or for bad sportsmanship). The chief official of an ice-hockey game is the referee, who is usually assisted by one or two linesmen.

HODEIDA, city of the Yemen Arab Republic, on the Red Sea, about 100 miles N. of Mocha. Hodeida, the principal seaport of Yemen, exports coffee and hides. The city was largely rebuilt after a fire in 1961, and its port facilities improved and enlarged. A highway between Hodeida and San'a, the capital of Yemen, was completed in 1961. Pop. (1968 est.) 45,000.

HODGKIN, Alan Lloyd (1914–), British biophysicist, born in Danbury, Essex, England, and educated at the University of Cambridge. From 1939 to 1945 he worked on radar development for the Air Ministry. He returned to Cambridge, first as a lecturer, then as assistant research director, and in 1952 was made research professor of the Royal Society. Hodgkin shared the 1963 Nobel Prize in medicine and physiology with his colleague the British physiologist Andrew F. Huxley (*see under* HUXLEY) and the Australian physiologist Sir John C. Eccles (q.v.). Hodgkin and Huxley were cited for their formulation of the mathematical equations expressing the electrical events accompanying the discharge of a single nerve cell.

HODGKIN, Dorothy Crowfoot (1910–), British chemist, born in Cairo, Egypt, and educated at Somerville College, University of Oxford. A fellow of Somerville College, she was named a research professor of the Royal Society in 1960. She was awarded the 1964 Nobel Prize in chemistry for determining the structure of biochemical compounds essential in combating pernicious anemia. *See* BLOOD: *Blood Diseases.*

HODGKIN'S DISEASE, disease characterized by usually painless but progressive enlargement of lymph nodes and other lymphoid tissue; *see* LYMPH. It is a neoplastic disease, that is, a condition in which there is a growth of tissue that serves no physiological function. Generally the cervical lymph nodes are the first nodes to be enlarged and present the first symptom. Later many other lymph nodes become involved, and the spleen usually enlarges. The disease usually is limited to persons between ten and thirty years of age and occurs more frequently in males. The cause has remained unknown since the British physician Thomas Hodgkin (1798–1866) first described the condition in 1832. Treatment may be by one or all of several methods, including surgical excision, irradiation, and chemotherapy, particularly the use of nitrogen mustard. Median survival time is about four years. People who are treated and who have only a few lymph nodes involved, however, may live ten or more years. Complete recovery is extremely rare. In 1970 a study by the National Cancer Institute reported evidence of life-prolonging treatment for Hodgkin's disease with the use of a combination of four drugs, including procarbazine hydrochloride, vincristine, prednisolone, and either cyclophosphamide or nitrogen mustard. Because the prognosis is so unpredictable, it is important that treatment is maximized since prolonged relief, or remission, is always possible. *See* CANCER.

HOE, name of a family prominently connected with the manufacture and improvement of the printing press in America.

Robert Hoe (1784–1833), born in Leicestershire, England. He emigrated to the United States in 1803, worked for a time as a master carpenter, and subsequently was an associate in a business which shifted from carpentry to the manufacture of hand printing presses. In 1823 he became sole proprietor of the business. Hoe constructed and introduced the original Hoe press and developed an improved version of the Napier cylinder press. He was apparently the earliest American machinist to use steam as a motive power in his plant.

Richard March Hoe (1812–86), son of Robert, born in New York City. He entered his father's factory at the age of fifteen, and eventually succeeded him as head of the firm. In 1847 he introduced a press using revolving cylinders, called the Hoe rotary or lightning press, which replaced the old flatbed models. In 1871 he began developing the web press, which superseded the former invention, printing on both sides of a sheet. With the addition of apparatus for cutting and folding sheets, the web press became the basis of the modern newspaper press.

Robert Hoe (1839–1909), grandson of Robert, and nephew of Richard, born in New York City. He carried on the improvements in printing presses and processes which had been initiated by his grandfather and uncle. Under his direction were developed the rotary art press for printing fine illustrations, a multicolor press, and a number of improvements in the efficiency and speed of newspaper presses. He was also a collector of art objects and of rare books and manuscripts. He participated in the founding of The Metropolitan Museum of Art (q.v.) in New York City and amassed a personal art collection valued at several million dollars. In 1884 he organized the Grolier Club, a society of bibliophiles, in New York City and was its first president.

HOFEI, city in the People's Republic of China, and capital of Anhwei Province, near Chao Lake, 90 miles s.w. of Nanking. Hofei is a trade center on an important railroad, in an area that produces rice, cotton, wheat, tobacco, and sweet potatoes; it also has cotton- and silk-weaving and lacquer industries. The city was called Lüchow until 1912. Pop. (1958 est.) 360,000.

HOFER, Andreas (1767–1810), Tirolese patriot, born in Saint Leonhard in the Austrian Alps. When the Tirol was transferred to Bavaria, an ally of France, by the Peace of Pressburg of 1805, Hofer became the leader of resistance to Bavarian rule. He raised a force of Tirolese that in 1809 drove out the Bavarian army. In spite of assurances given to Hofer by Holy Roman Emperor Francis II (q.v.), the Tirol was surrendered to the French by the armistice of Znaim, and a force of 40,000 French and Bavarian troops attempted to occupy the territory. Hofer repulsed the invasion and was elected governor of the Tirol. The Treaty of Schönbrunn of October, 1809, however, again ceded the Tirol to Bavaria, and French troops occupied the region. Hofer revolted once more, but he was defeated and took refuge in the mountains. Two months later he was betrayed to the French, who court-martialed and executed him in Mantua, Italy.

HOFFMANN, Ernst Theodor Wilhelm (1776–1822), German writer, illustrator, lawyer, and composer, born in Königsberg (now Kalingrad, U.S.S.R.). As composer he used the name of Ernst Theodor Amadeus Hoffmann, in honor of Wolfgang Amadeus Mozart (q.v.). He studied law but practiced only for a short period. He then concentrated on painting, music criticism, and composition. In 1816 he became councillor of the court of appeals in Berlin. He is best known, however, as a writer. His works of fiction were among the most influential produced by the Romantic movement in German literature; see GERMAN LITERATURE: *The Classical and Romantic Period*; ROMANTICISM. They combine the grotesque and supernatural with powerful psychological realism. In his first book, *Phanta-siestücke in Callots Manier* ("Fantastic Pieces in the Manner of Callot", 4 vol., 1814–15), a collection of music criticism and short stories, also illustrated by him, appear some of his best-known short stories. His other works include the novel *Die Elixiere des Teufels* (1816; Eng. trans., *The Devil's Elixir*, 1824) and the collections of stories *Nachtstücke* ("Night Pieces", 2 vol., 1817) and *Die Serapionsbrüder* (4 vol., 1819–21; Eng. trans., *The Serapion Brethren*, 1886–92). Hoffmann also composed the opera *Undine* (1816), to a libretto by Baron Friedrich Heinrich Karl de La Motte-Fouqué (q.v.). He is best known as the author of the fantastic tales on which the French composer Jacques Offenbach (q.v.) based his opera *Les Contes d'Hoffmann* ("Tales of Hoffmann", 1881).

HOFFMAN, Malvina (1887–1966), American sculptor, born in New York City. She studied with the French sculptor François Auguste René Rodin (q.v.), and in 1911 achieved international fame with her "Russian Bacchanale", one of several sculpture groups inspired by the Russian ballerina Anna Pavlova (q.v.), her close friend. In 1920 she carved a large monument, "The Sacrifice", in memory of Harvard University students who died in World War I. She is best known for 101 bronzes comprising "Races of Man", a work commissioned by the Field Museum of Chicago and completed in 1932. Her "Pavlova Gavotte" is in the Detroit Institute of Arts, Mich., and a bust of the Polish statesman and pianist Ignace Jan Paderewski (q.v.) is in the American Academy at Rome. Her work is also represented in The Metropolitan Museum, New York City, and in the Carnegie Institute, Pittsburgh, Pa.

HOFFMAN, Paul Gray (1891–   ), American businessman and government official, born in Chicago, Ill., and educated at the University of Chicago. In 1911 he joined the sales staff of the Studebaker Corporation, of which he became president in 1935. He also served as chairman of the Automotive Safety Foundation from 1941 to 1948 and member of the Advisory Committee on Foreign Aid under President Harry S. Truman (q.v.). From 1948 to 1950 he was head of the Economic Cooperation Administration, the Federal agency responsible for the supervision of the European Recovery Program (q.v.). Hoffman served as trustee of the Ford Foundation (q.v.) from 1951 to 1953 and as a U.S. delegate to the General Assembly of the United Nations in 1956–57. He was managing director of the U.N. Special Fund from 1959 to 1966, when he became administrator of the newly formed U.N. Development Program (q.v.), which incorporated the Special Fund. His writings include

Peace Can Be Won (1951) and *World Without Want* (1962).

HOFMANN, August Wilhelm von (1818–92), German chemist, born in Giessen, and educated at the University of Giessen. From 1845 to 1864 he was director of the newly established Royal College of Chemistry in London. The following year he accepted a professorship in chemistry at the University of Berlin. He founded the German Chemical Society in 1868.

Hofmann was one of the great organic chemists of his time. He worked with coal–tar products, from which he isolated benzene and aniline, and which he used in the synthesis of artificial dyes that formed the basis for a new industry; *see* DYESTUFFS. He studied and clarified the chemistry of amines, and the method he discovered for converting amides to amines is now called the Hofmann reaction. He also discovered many organic chemicals, including allyl alcohol and formaldehyde. He was knighted in 1888.

See CHEMISTRY: *Organic Chemistry*.

HOFMANN, Hans (1880–1966), German-born American painter and teacher, born in Weissenberg. He studied painting in Munich for six years before moving to Paris in 1904, where he was influenced by the revolutionary fauvist (q.v.) and cubist movements (*see* CUBISM). Leaving Paris in 1914, he returned to Munich and opened a school of modern art.

In 1933 Hofmann came to the United States, becoming a citizen in 1941. His style gradually developed into abstract expressionism, showing cubist forms heightened by brilliant colors; as a teacher, initially in California and later in New York City, he was one of the most influential figures in this art form. His oil painting "Veluti in Speculum" (1962) is part of the collection of the Metropolitan Museum of Art in New York City.

HOFMANN, Josef Casimir (1876–1957), Polish-American concert pianist and composer, born in Kraków. At the age of sixteen he became a pupil of the Russian pianist and composer Anton Rubinstein (q.v.). He made his first public appearance as a pianist at the age of six and began a long career of concert tours throughout Europe and America. He made his American debut at the Metropolitan Opera House in 1887.

In 1926 he became director and teacher at the Curtis Institute of Music in Philadelphia, Pa., with which he was associated until 1938. Under the pen name Michael Dvorsky he composed a symphony and many works for the piano.

HOFMANNSTHAL, Hugo von (1874–1929), Austrian poet and playwright, born in Vienna, and educated at the University of Vienna. His early lyric and dramatic poetry contributed to the establishment of the Romantic school of poetry and drama in Austria. Among his works are the dramas in verse *Gestern* ("Yesterday", 1891), *Der Tod des Tizian* (1892; Eng. trans., *The Death of Titian*, 1913), and *Jedermann* (1911; Eng.

"Rising Sun" (1958), by Hans Hofmann
Kootz Gallery

trans., *The Play of Everyman,* 1917). He is also noted as the librettist of operas by the German composer Richard Strauss (q.v.), including *Elektra* (1903; Eng. trans., *Electra,* 1908), *Der Rosenkavalier* (1911; Eng. trans., *The Knight of the Rose,* 1912), and *Ariadne auf Naxos* (1912; Eng. trans., *Ariadne on Naxos,* 1913).

See also AUSTRIAN LITERATURE: *The 20th Century;* GERMAN LITERATURE: *Modern Poetry.*

HOFSTADTER, Robert (1915–), American physicist, born in New York City. Hofstadter received his Ph.D. degree from Princeton University in 1938. He joined the faculty of Stanford University in 1950. Using the linear accelerator at the Stanford Linear Accelerator Center and a scattering machine of his own design, Hofstadter was able to measure with great precision the size and shape of the proton and neutron (qq.v.). Both were found to consist of a dense, pointlike core of mesons surrounded by two intermingling layers of meson clouds; see MESON. In the proton, the combined electrical charges of the meson clouds resulted in a net positive charge; the neutron, which has one negatively charged cloud cancelling out one positively charged cloud, carries a neutral charge. Hofstadter shared the 1961 Nobel Prize in physics with Rudolf Ludwig Mossbauer (q.v.).

HOFUF, city of Saudi Arabia, in the Eastern Province, situated in the largest oasis in the country, 180 miles N.E. of Riyadh and about 80 miles S.W. of the Persian Gulf port of Dammam. Hofuf, a walled city and a trade center, is connected by rail and road with Riyadh and Dammam. Manufactures include cloth, copper and brass products, and swords and daggers. The oasis, watered by many springs, grows dates, fruit, rice, wheat, and barley. The Osmaniya oil field is nearby to the S.W. Originally called Hasa, the city was headquarters of the 10th-century Qarmathian terrorist movement; see ARABIA: *History.* It was capital of Hasa Province until the 1960's, when the provincial name was changed and Dammam became the capital. The city's name is also spelled Hufuf. Pop. (1962) 83,000.

HOG, mature specimen of the domestic swine, a member of the family Suidae, which is extensively raised in almost every part of the world as a food animal. Young swine are usually called pigs, but in common usage the three terms, swine, hog, and pig, are often used interchangeably. Hogs are cloven-hoofed animals with heavy, round bodies and short legs. Their skins are thick and partially covered with coarse bristles. The head of the hog has a comparatively long, flexible snout containing the nostrils and the mouth, which has 44 teeth.

Young hogs are frequently called shoats. The adult male hog is usually called a boar and the female adult hog a sow. A female under 15 months of age at the time of farrowing her first litter is known as a gilt. A castrated male is called a barrow. The exact genesis of the domestic hog is not known, but zoologists believe that the animal is a cross between the wild boar of Europe, *Sus scrofa,* and the Asiatic wild boar, *S. vittatus; see* BOAR. The economic value of the hog is considerable. The fresh flesh, known as pork, is a staple meat, and is also smoked or otherwise cured and eaten as ham and bacon; *see* MEAT. Lard, the fat of the hog, is one of the most important edible fats. Hog intestines are used as sausage casings, and other portions of the animal including the head and feet, are regarded as delicacies. The hide of the hog, when tanned, becomes the handsome and durable leather known as pigskin, used extensively in the manufacture of luggage and gloves; pigskin is also used to make the American football, for which it is virtually a synonym. The stiff bristles from the hide are made into paint brushes.

Wild boars were first domesticated by the Chinese in approximately 2900 B.C. In Europe they were probably domesticated independently at a somewhat later date. Archeologists believe that these animals were first domesticated as scavengers, and only later came to be regarded as food animals. Hogs are omnivorous and can live on vegetable and animal garbage. Another reason for the popularity of the hog as a farm animal is that it reproduces more rapidly and matures earlier than any of the other common meat-producing animals.

Breeds. A large number of breeds of hogs have been developed in various parts of the world to meet local conditions of climate and pasturage. In the United States eight separate breeds are widely raised: the Berkshire, an English breed with a black body and white face, feet, and tail tip, which matures early but is not very prolific; the Chesterwhite, a pink-skinned, white-bristled breed from Chester County, Pa., which grazes well, is very prolific, and matures early; the Duroc Jersey, another breed of U.S. origin, red in color, hardy, and maturing to a weight of about 700 lb.; the Hampshire, a breed from England with a black body belted with a white band about the body and front legs, remarkable for its ability to thrive on pasture; the Poland China, developed in Warren Co. and Butler Co., Ohio, a black breed with white feet, which in mature boars may reach weights of almost 1000 lb.; the Spotted Poland China, similar to the Poland

HOG

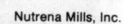

Breeds of hogs raised in the U.S. English breeds: Top, left: Berkshire sow. Center, left: Hampshire boar. American breeds. Bottom, left: Chester White boar, originated in Pennsylvania. Above, right: Poland China boar, known for its great size. Below, right: Chester White sow suckling her young in a prefabricated pen popularly called a pigloo.

China but having numerous white spots on the body; the Tamworth, a red breed of English origin with a maximum of lean meat in its long deep body; and the Yorkshire, an English breed of white hogs which, like the Tamworths, are particularly suited to bacon production. Five other breeds of hogs are found less commonly in the U.S.

Feeding Hogs. In modern farming practice, hogs are not fed on garbage but are given a carefully balanced ration containing proteins, carbohydrates or fats, and minerals. Approximately 400 lb. of balanced feed are needed to add 100 lb. to the weight of a hog. In the U.S., corn is the most important component of hog feeds, but rye, barley, vegetable oils and oil cakes, alfalfa, milk products such as skim milk and dried milk, tankage or slaughterhouse by-products, and fish meal are also employed as components of hog rations. A typical feed mixture for hogs being fattened for slaughter might include 85 lb. of ground corn, 5 lb. of tankage or fish meal, 5 lb. of linseed meal, and 5 lb. of alfalfa hay. Hogs are also fed on forage crops such as alfalfa, clovers, rape, soybeans, and bluegrass.

In the U.S. in the late 1960's, about 80,000,000 hogs were slaughtered annually. The total number of hogs on U.S. farms during the same period averaged over 50,000,000 head each year.

Diseases of Hogs. Like other domestic animals, hogs are subject to a number of diseases, some of which are also dangerous to human beings who may eat meat from infected animals. The most serious disease to which hogs are prone is hog cholera, a highly contagious and fatal disease caused by a filtrable virus. Be-

409

HOG

fore 1905 as much as 13 percent of the hogs in the U.S. succumbed annually to hog cholera. In 1905, however, the Bureau of Animal Industry of the U.S. Department of Agriculture developed an effective serum for this disease. Another serious disease of hogs is swine erysipelas, an illness, characterized by skin outbreaks, fever, and swollen joints, to which human beings are also subject; see ERYSIPELAS. The bacillus causing this disease is known and a serum has been developed which gives immunity (q.v.) for a few weeks. Hogs are also subject to several kinds of enteritis, particularly a form of dysentery (q.v.) commonly called the scours, which affects young pigs. The cause of this disease is not known, but it is apparently partly due to faulty nutrition of the young animals. Brucellosis, caused by the organism *Brucella abortis*, which also affects cattle and man, is less common in hogs than in cows, but is important because the disease can be readily transmitted to men and women who are tending or slaughtering the infected animals; see UNDULANT FEVER. The U.S. Public Health Service (q.v.) estimates that approximately half the cases of human undulant fever in this country are traceable to hogs.

Hogs fed on uncooked garbage are prone to infestation by a number of internal parasites (q.v.), of which the most dangerous are the nematode worms (see NEMATODES) called trichinae, which form cysts in the muscles. Trichinae can be passed on from hogs and other animal hosts to men eating the flesh of the infected animal. Presence of trichinae in the human body can cause the disease called trichinosis (q.v.). Trichinosis may be avoided by thoroughly cooking pork and other hog-flesh foods to kill the parasites. Vesicular exanthema, a highly contagious disease which affects only swine, is also spread through feeding uncooked garbage. The symptoms closely resemble the more dangerous foot-and-mouth disease (q.v.). See DISEASES OF ANIMALS.
K.A.C.

HOGAN, Ben, in full WILLIAM BENJAMIN HOGAN (1912–), American professional golf player, born in Dublin, Texas. He began his golf career in Fort Worth, Texas, and was the leading money winner among American golfers in 1940, 1941, 1942, 1946, and 1948. He won the Professional Golfers' Association championship in 1946 and 1948, the United States Open championship in 1948, 1950, 1951, and 1953, and the British Open championship in 1953.

HOGARTH, William (1697-1764), British painter and engraver, born in London, England. Upon finishing his apprenticeship to a silversmith in 1718, he turned to engraving and first became known in 1726 by his illustrations for the novel *Hudibras* (1726) by the British author Samuel Butler (q.v.). Hogarth began painting about 1728, producing small group scenes such as "The Wanstead Assembly" and "The Politician". By 1735 he established a reputation as a painter of English manners and customs by two

"The Cockpit", an engraving, dated 1759, by William Hogarth.
Metropolitan Museum of Art

410

series of paintings, "A Harlot's Progress" (1731–32) and "The Rake's Progress" (1735). Through the sets of engravings he made from these paintings, however, Hogarth gained wide renown as a brilliant satirist of moral follies. Plagued by the artistic piracy to which his popular etchings were subject, Hogarth secured the passage of a Copyright Act, often called "Hogarth's Act", in 1735.

Two of his most ambitious, although least characteristic works, were the murals "The Good Samaritan" and "The Pool of Bethesda", painted on the staircase of Saint Bartholomew's Hospital in 1735–36. These murals were executed in the "Grand Manner", a highly ornamental style depicting mythological subjects; it was popular in the French and Italian art of the period. In 1745, what many critics claim to be Hogarth's most famous series appeared, "Marriage à la Mode", in a set of six paintings and an equal number of engravings. Hogarth's remarkably exuberant satire, his pungent details of everyday life, and his mastery of complex scenes find perhaps their highest expression in this work. To this period also belong many of Hogarth's portraits. Among his exceptional portraits are the famous "Garrick as Richard III", "The Shrimp Girl", and "Self-Portrait with a Dog".

In 1753 he wrote *The Analysis of Beauty*, in which he tried to establish a fixed standard for principles of aesthetics (q.v.). Four years later he was appointed sergeant painter to George II (q.v.), King of Great Britain. During the last five years of his life, Hogarth was engaged in political feuds with the controversial British political reformer John Wilkes (q.v.), whom he had treated roughly in an engraving. Wilkes retaliated with an attack on Hogarth's "Sigismunda" (1759), which was another attempt at the Italian style. Hogarth's last engraving, "The Bathos", intended as a farewell work, was published in 1764. On his monument is an epitaph written by his friend, the actor David Garrick (q.v.). Many of his important paintings are in London galleries and museums, including the National and the Tate galleries. He is also well represented in the United States in the Frick Collection, the Pierpont Morgan Library, and the Metropolitan Museum of Art, all in New York City; and in other collections.

HOGG, James, known as THE ETTRICK SHEPHERD (1770–1835), Scottish poet, born in Ettrick, Selkirk County. He had no formal education. As a boy he herded sheep and worked on the farm belonging to his father, and from 1790 to 1799 he was a shepherd at Yarrow, where his employer encouraged his gift for composing songs. His first poem, *Donald McDonald,* was published anonymously in 1800. In the following year he visited Edinburgh and arranged for the publication of a collection of his songs, which appeared as *Scottish Pastorals* (1801). In 1802 he met the Scottish poet and novelist Sir Walter Scott (q.v.), who was visiting Ettrick in search of material for his own work. Hogg was sufficiently encouraged by Scott to publish a volume of poems and ballads, *The Mountain Bard* (1807).

Hogg settled in Edinburgh in 1810 and took up writing for a living; in that year the *Forest Minstrel,* an anthology of poems by Hogg and his friends, appeared. With the publication of the volume of ballads, *The Queen's Wake* (1813), his reputation was firmly established.

Hogg became known as the Ettrick Shepherd through the writings of the British author John Wilson (q.v.), who so characterized him in a series of literary dialogues that appeared in *Blackwood's* magazine.

Hogg is regarded as one of the great pastoral poets and songwriters of Scotland. He is particularly known for his poems in the Scottish folk tradition. Others of his works, however, such as *The Poetic Mirror* (1816), a collection of clever parodies, are highly sophisticated. Among his volumes of poetry are *Queen Hynde* (1826) and *The Shepherd's Calendar* (1829). He was also the author of the prose works *The Three Perils of Man* (1822) and *Domestic Manners and Private Life of Sir Walter Scott* (1834), and of a number of tales.

HOGNOSE SNAKE or **HOG-NOSED SNAKE,** common name of short, thick-bodied, harmless North American snakes in the genus *Heterodon* that are characterized by a flattened snout. These snakes are usually black, occasionally with white circular markings down either side of their backs. The average length is about 2 ft. Although harmless, the hognose is widely feared because when under attack it assumes a threatening position, flattening its head, expanding its neck, and opening its mouth and hissing. If these aggressive tactics fail to frighten away the intruder, the hognose pretends to be dead. Because of these tactics the snake is variously known as the puff adder, the hissing adder, and the spreading adder.

The most common species of hognose snakes are *H. platyrhinos,* found throughout the eastern and southern United States, and *H. nasicus,* found in the western plains from Montana to central Mexico.

HOHENSTAUFEN, noble German family, members of which were rulers of the Holy

411

HOHENZOLLERN

Roman Empire, Germany, and Sicily. The name derives from the ancestral castle at Staufen (near Freiburg, Germany). The family began in 1079 with the marriage of Frederick I, Duke of Swabia (d. 1105), to Agnes (d. 1114), daughter of Henry IV (q.v.), Holy Roman Emperor; at the same time Frederick was created Duke of Swabia. The princely line began in 1138 when their son, Conrad III, was elected King of Germany (see under CONRAD). It included the Holy Roman emperors and kings of Germany Frederick I (q.v.), called Frederick Barbarossa, who was also king of Italy, and Henry VI (q.v.), also king of Sicily. Frederick II (q.v.) was Holy Roman Emperor, as well as king of Germany, Sicily, and of Jerusalem. Other Hohenstaufen rulers were Philip, Holy Roman Emperor and King of Germany (see under PHILIP); Conrad IV, King of Germany and of Sicily; and two kings of Sicily, Manfred (1232?–66) and Conradin (1252–68). Enzio (1225?–72), an illegitimate son of Frederick II, assumed the title of king of Sardinia, but was imprisoned; with his death the family line ended. From the accession of Conrad III, the Hohenstaufen family was in constant conflict with another German family, the Guelphs or Welfs; see GUELPHS AND GHIBELLINES. See also GERMANY: History; HOLY ROMAN EMPIRE; ITALY: History: The Papacy Versus the Holy Roman Empire.

HOHENZOLLERN, family of German rulers, originating as a family of counts in Swabia in the 11th or 12th century. The Hohenzollerns ruled Prussia and eventually united and ruled Germany until the end of World War I. Their strong, rigidly disciplined armies gave Prussia a reputation for military excellence.

The Hohenzollerns were named for their ancestral castle, Zollern (later Hohenzollern), located near Hechingen, Swabia. In 1227 the Hohenzollern count Conrad III (1208–61) was made burgrave of Nuremburg by Frederick II (q.v.), Holy Roman Emperor, and the Hohenzollerns of Nuremburg formed a new branch of the family, the Franconian; the original line remained in Swabia. In 1417 Burgrave Frederick II (1372–1440) became elector and margrave of Brandenburg (q.v.). He was succeeded by eleven Hohenzollern electors, the eighth of whom, John Sigismund (1572–1619), became the first duke of Prussia. Frederick William (q.v.), called the Great Elector, expanded and consolidated territory held by Brandenburg, and in 1417 his successor, Frederick III, became Frederick I (q.v.), King of Prussia. During the next century and a half the Prussian throne was held by Frederick William I, who introduced compulsory military service, Frederick II, Frederick William II, Frederick William III, and Frederick William IV (qq.v.). The Prussian King William I (q.v.), became Emperor of Germany in 1871. He was succeeded by Frederick III and William II (qq.v.). Hohenzollern rule ended in 1918 when William II was forced to abdicate.

The Swabian branch of the Hohenzollerns, which ruled the petty principalities of Hohenzollern-Hechingen and Hohenzollern-Sigmaringen, was of little importance in German history. In 1849 Charles Anthony, Prince of Hohenzollern-Sigmaringen (1811–85), ceded his principality to the Prussian king. His son Leopold (1835–1905) was a candidate for the throne of Spain in 1870 (see FRANCO-GERMAN WAR), and his second son became Carol I, King of Rumania (see under CAROL), in 1866. Hohenzollerns retained the throne of Rumania until the abdication of King Michael (1921–) in 1947. The Hohenzollern-Hechingen line of the Swabian branch became extinct in 1869.

See GERMANY: History.

HOIHOW, city of the People's Republic of China, in Kwangtung Province, and capital of the Hainan Administrative District, on the northern coast of the island of Hainan, about 300 miles s.w. of Canton. It is the chief port of the island, with boat connections with Luichow Peninsula. Exports include sugar, livestock, poultry, hemp, betel nuts, and herbs. Important industries are food canning, cotton milling, glassmaking, and tanning. The name is sometimes spelled Hai-k'ou. Pop. (1958 est.) 402,000.

HOKANG, city of the People's Republic of China, in Heilungkiang Province, 40 miles N. of Kiamusze. Hokang is the most important coal-mining center in northeastern Manchuria; its mines extend about 20 miles s. along the rail spur leading to Kiamusze. The surrounding region grows rice, wheat, and kaoliang sorghum. The coal mines were first worked during the Japanese occupation of Manchuria in the 1930's. Hokang was formerly known as Hingshan. Pop. (1958 est.) 200,000.

HOKKAIDO, formerly YEZO or EZO, northernmost and second-largest island of the Japanese archipelago, situated between the Sea of Japan to the w. and the Pacific Ocean to the E. The island is separated from Sakhalin to the N. by La Pérouse Strait, from Honshu to the s. by Tsugara Strait, and from the Kuril Islands to the N.E. by Nemuro Strait. This irregularly shaped island, about 280 mi. wide and 260 mi. long, experiences cool summers and long severe winters because of the prevailing Oyashio Current. Topographically, Hokkaido is characterized by a complexity of mountain systems and volcanic

"View of Fuji from Seven-Ri Beach", one of the series of block prints known as "The Hundred Views of Mount Fuji" (1823–29) by Hokusai.
Metropolitan Museum of Art — Rogers Fund

masses that rise to 7513 ft. above sea level at Daisetsu Mt., the highest point. Heavily forested mountains rise above extensive plains regions of the Ishikari and Tokachi river basins.

Economically the island is the most important stock grazing and dairying area in Japan, producing about 80 percent of its butter and cheese. The Ishikari fields yield about 30 percent of the coal mined in Japan, and deposits of iron and manganese are also found there. Hokkaido is important for its forestry products and the surrounding waters are a rich source of fish. Among the most interesting people on this, the most sparsely populated of the Japanese main islands, are the Ainu (q.v.), an aboriginal group of uncertain ancestry. Hakodate is the chief seaport and Sapporo (qq.v.) is the largest city and administrative center of Hokkaido Prefecture, which is coextensive with the island. Area, including some small adjacent islands, 30,312 sq.mi.; pop. (1966 est.) 5,193,000.

HOKUSAI, also known as KATSUSHIKA HOKUSAI (1760–1849), Japanese painter and wood engraver, born in Yedo (now Tokyo). He is considered one of the outstanding figures of the ukiyoe, or popular, school of print-making. Hokusai entered the studio of his countryman Katsukawa Shunsho (1726–92) in 1775 and there learned the new, popular technique of woodcut print-making. Between 1796 and 1802 he produced a vast number of book illustrations and color prints that drew their inspiration from the traditions, legends, and lives of the Japanese common people. Hokusai's most typical woodblock prints, silkscreens, and landscape paintings, were done between 1830 and 1840. The free curved lines characteristic of his style gradually developed into a series of spirals that imparted the utmost freedom and grace to his work, as in "Raiden, the Spirit of Thunder".

In his late works Hokusai used large, broken strokes and a method of coloring that imparted a more somber mood to his paintings, as in his massive "Group of Workmen Building a Boat". Among his best-known works are the fifteen volumes of "Mangwa" sketches (1812–75), and the series of block prints known as "The Hundred Views of Mount Fuji" (1835). Hokusai is generally more appreciated in the West than in Japan.

HOLBEIN, Hans, the Younger (1497–1543), German painter and master designer of woodcut illustrations, stained-glass embellishment, and jewelry, born in Augsburg. At an early age he began to study painting with his father Hans Holbein, the Elder (1460–1524), and by 1515 he had established himself in Basel, Switzerland, as a book illustrator. He designed many title-page

HOLBEIN

"Anne of Cleves" (1539), by Hans Holbein the Younger.
Archives Photographiques, Paris

woodcuts for book printers and before the end of the same year completed a series of pen-and-ink sketches for an edition of the *Praise of Folly* by the Dutch scholar Desiderius Erasmus (q.v.).

During a trip to Lombardy in Italy in 1518, Holbein encountered the works of the Italian Renaissance painters Andrea Mantegna and Leonardo da Vinci (qq.v.). The impact of these and other artists on Holbein's work can be seen in the Renaissance modeling and composition techniques he adopted in one of his early major portraits, "Erasmus of Rotterdam" (Louvre, Paris), completed in 1523, and in his renowned religious works "Dead Christ" and the "Passion of Christ" (both in the Basel Museum), and the altarpiece "Madonna of Burgomaster Meyer" (Darmstadt, West Germany), all completed between 1519 and 1526. In each of these Holbein shows the greater freedom in draftsmanship and the richness of color that characterize the work of the North Italian masters. In his religious works Holbein integrates this wealth of detail and color with the dignity and severity of characterization appropriate to a religious subject.

In the period 1523 to 1535 Holbein increased his reputation as a book illustrator by a series of fifty-one drawings portraying the medieval allegorical theme, the Dance of Death (*see* DEATH, DANCE OF), and by a number of woodcuts used to illustrate the German translation of the Bible by the German religious reformer Martin Luther (q.v.). Regardless of Holbein's prestige, however, as the austere attitudes of the Reformation (q.v.) permeated Swiss society, the patronage of artists diminished and he was forced to go to England to gain new commissions. Arriving in 1526 with letters of introduction from Erasmus, now his friend and patron, Holbein was engaged to portray several great humanists of the period, including the English statesman Sir Thomas More (q.v.).

Returning to Basel in 1528, Holbein was commissioned to make improvements in an earlier (1521–22) work called "Justice", with which he had decorated the council chamber of the town hall. His additions to this series of frescoes reflect his continuing growth as an artist; the newer, less crowded compositions convey a still greater dramatic impact than his earlier scenes. Unfortunately, none of Holbein's many great frescoes executed here and in England and Germany have survived intact. Their beauty must be judged, instead, from his sketches, which were sometimes preserved, and from copies of the impressive wall paintings made by later artists.

Holbein settled again in England in 1532 and began his career as a master portrait painter. His portrait of the English statesman Thomas Cromwell (q.v.), brought the artist recognition at court, and by 1536 he was established as court painter to King Henry VIII (q.v.). His most significant works, the portraits of Henry VIII and his wife Jane Seymour (*see under* SEYMOUR) were destroyed by fire in 1698. Several of his portraits of other important court figures, including most of the wives of Henry VIII and his son Edward, later King Edward VI (q.v.), are still extant, as are the preliminary studies Holbein made for the works. These drawings, in which Holbein combined chalk, silverpoint, pen, and other media, are among his most admired works; a series of eighty-seven drawings of well-known court figures is a part of the royal collection at Windsor Castle.

Holbein's reputation as a great artist is based on his realistic depictions of individuals and groups in his portrait paintings. His attention to every detail of flesh, hair, dress, and ornamentation and his ability to capture their exact texture neither detract from nor betray the basic character and dignity of his subjects. Holbein also contributed many important drawings for Swiss glass paintings, considered among the finest examples of this great Renaissance art.

HOLBERG, Ludvig (1684–1754), Danish writer, considered the founder of Danish literature (q.v.), born in Bergen, Norway (then ruled by Denmark), and educated at the universities of Copenhagen and Oxford. He became professor of metaphysics at the University of Copenhagen in 1718, professor of public eloquence in 1720, and rector of the university in 1735. In 1747 he was created baron of Holberg.

Holberg wrote a vast body of brilliant dramatic, poetic, and historical works. In doing so, he virtually singlehandedly established Danish as a literary language (see DANISH LANGUAGE). At a time when plays on the Danish stage were given only in German or French and the only literary use of Danish was in hymns and ballads, Holberg wrote more than a dozen plays in his native tongue that were successfully performed. These include the comedies *Den Vaegelsindede* ("The Waverer", 1722) and *Henrik eg Pernille* ("Henrik and Pernille", 1724).

Holberg's poem *Pedar Paars* (1719; Eng. trans. 1962), a satire on contemporary manners, is considered a classic of Danish literature. Other poetical satires are *Metamorphosis* (1726) and *Nicolai Klimii Iter Subterraneum* (1741; Eng. trans., "Journey of Niels Klim to the World Underground", 1960). Holberg wrote a series of scholarly works including a history of Denmark and the philosophical essays, *Moral Reflections* (1744; Eng. trans. 1943). His letters were published in five volumes between 1748 and 1754.

HÖLDERLIN, (Johann Christian) Friedrich (1770–1843), German poet, born in Lauffen-am-Neckar. He studied theology at Tübingen, but did not become a clergyman. The German poet Friedrich von Schiller (q.v.) published some of Hölderlin's early verse in periodicals that he edited, and also obtained for him a position as tutor. In 1804 Hölderlin was appointed librarian to the landgrave of Hessen-Homburg. Hölderlin was subject to periods of mental illness from 1802, and his illness was permanent from 1807, lasting for almost forty years.

Hölderlin's poetry is characterized by the intense subjectivity of the German *Sturm und Drang* period (see GERMAN LITERATURE: *The Classical and Romantic Period*), but at the same time is influenced by the spirit of restraint and balance of Greek classicism. His work forms a bridge between the German classical and Romantic schools. Hölderlin used no rhyme but wrote in a flexible poetic form known later as free verse. He is known principally for his lyrics, including "An die Hoffnung" ("On Hope") and "Der Blinde Sanger" ("The Blind Singer"), and such larger works as the epistolary novel *Hyperion* (2 vol., 1797–99; Eng. trans., 1927) and the fine unfinished tragedy *Der Tod des Empedokles* ("The Death of Empedocles", 1798–99). He also did brilliant German translations of the works of the Greek classical tragedian Sophocles (q.v.).

HOLDING COMPANY. See BUSINESS.

HOLGUÍN, city of Cuba, in Oriente Province, about 20 miles S.W. of the Atlantic Ocean port Gibara, and 65 miles N.W. of Santiago de Cuba. Holguín was founded in the 16th century. It is the trading center for the sugar cane, coffee, tobacco, corn, and cattle of the surrounding area. Pop. (1960) 226,779.

HOLIDAY, day set apart as a religious anniversary, or for the commemoration of some extraordinary event or distinguished person, or for some reason of public policy. Holidays are characterized by a partial or total cessation of work and of normal business activities and are generally accompanied by public and private ceremonies.

Originally, in ancient times, holidays were predominantly religious in character; the word "holiday" derives from "holy day". Subsequently, holidays commemorating historical occasions or distinguished persons outnumbered religious holy days. Today the outstanding holiday of the Christian, Muslim, and Hebrew peoples is one of religious observance, taking place on Sunday, Friday, and Saturday, respectively; see SABBATH.

In the United States, Sunday is not only a religious holiday but is also the only common-law holiday. Other legal holidays are designated by legislative enactment or by executive proclamation. Congress and the President designate the legal holidays for the District of Columbia and the Federal territories but are without power to declare national holidays. Independence Day and other holidays are observed on a national scale as a result of action by the States. In the case of Thanksgiving Day the President proclaims the calendar date and requests national observance, and the States thereupon usually enact the necessary legislation. Federal statutes frequently specify certain days as holidays for purposes related to the legislation.

For the principal legal holidays, in addition to Sunday, observed in the U.S., its territories, and its possessions, see chart on the next page.

Under a 1968 Federal law the following changes have been made in dates of holiday observances, effective in 1971: Washington's Birthday will fall on the third Monday in February; Memorial Day, on the last Monday in May; Columbus Day, on the second Monday in October; and Veterans Day, on the fourth Monday in October.

HOLIDAY

New Year's Day*	January 1
Lincoln's Birthday	February 12
Washington's Birthday	February 22[1]
Good Friday	Friday immediately preceding Easter
Memorial Day or Decoration Day	May 30[1]
Independence Day*	July 4
Labor Day*	first Monday of the month of September
Columbus Day	October 12[1]
Election Day	first Tuesday after the first Monday of the month of November
Veterans Day, formerly Armistice Day	November 11[1] observed as Victory Day in Tennessee
Thanksgiving Day*	fourth or last Thursday of the month of November
Christmas Day*	December 25

* Observed in all States.   [1] Original dates.

In many States the anniversary of the admission of the State to the Union is celebrated as a legal holiday, usually called Admission Day. A number of States commemorate other important events in their history; in Vermont the Battle of Bennington (q.v.), fought in the American Revolution, is commemorated annually on August 16; in Louisiana the Battle of New Orleans (q.v.) of the War of 1812 (q.v.) is commemorated on January 8. Throughout the U.S., the birthdays of great men, other than those noted above, are also celebrated on legal holidays set apart for that purpose. The following days are usually observed but are not legal holidays.

American Indian Day	fourth Friday in September
Armed Forces Day	third Saturday in May
Father's Day	third Sunday in June
Flag Day	June 14
Halloween	October 31
Mother's Day	second Sunday in May
St. Patrick's Day	March 17
St. Valentine's Day	February 14

See also FESTIVALS AND FEASTS.

HOLIDAY, Billie. See JAZZ: *Early Jazz: Big Band Jazz.*

HOLINESS CHURCHES, fundamentalist Protestant bodies that developed from Methodism (q.v.) and hold as their distinguishing feature the doctrine that holiness, or sanctification of the individual, occurs by a second act of grace (q.v.) that follows justification and is supplementary to it; see also FUNDAMENTALISM. The experience of holiness is also referred to as the second blessing. The National Holiness Movement came into being shortly after the Civil War in the United States. Originally a protest movement within Methodism, it opposed the Methodist falling away from the emphasis on sanctification that John Wesley (*see under* WESLEY), the founder of Methodism, had developed. He had stressed original sin (q.v.) and justification by faith, and added that the individual may be assured of forgiveness by a direct experience of the spirit, called sanctification, which he regarded as the step leading to Christian perfection.

Although the main body of the Holiness movement holds that sanctification is a second work of grace, some groups of the Pentecostal movement, an outgrowth of the Holiness churches, maintain that sanctification is essentially the dedication of the believer that begins with his regeneration. Moreover, sanctification must be evidenced by the occurrence of certain spiritual phenomena, such as "speaking in tongues". See PENTECOSTAL CHURCHES.

The major representatives of the Holiness movement (excluding Pentecostal denominations) are the Church of the Nazarene (q.v.) and the Church of God (Anderson, Ind.). The Church of God (Anderson, Ind.) originated about 1880 as a movement within existing churches to promote Christian unity. The founders were interested in relieving the church at large of what they believed was over-ecclesiasticism and restrictive organization, and in reaffirming the New Testament as the true standard of faith and life. In addition to the holiness principle, they believe in, among other doctrines, the divine inspiration of the Scriptures, forgiveness of sin through the death of Christ and the repentance of the sinner, a nonmillennial concept of the return of Christ, and external reward or punishment as a result of the final judgment. In the late 1960's this church had about 145,000 members in the U.S.

In addition, there are about twenty-five smaller Holiness denominations; among the largest is The Christian and Missionary Alliance with about 69,000 United States members in 1969.

HOLINSHED, Raphael *or* **HOLLINGSHEAD, Raphael** (about 1525–about 1580), English chronicler, probably born in Cheshire. He went to London about 1560 and was employed by the royal printer, Reginald Wolfe (d. 1573), to assist in the compilation of a universal history. After Wolfe's death, Holinshed continued the work, publishing it in an abridged form as the *Chronicles of England, Scotland, and Ireland* (2 vol.; 1578). He was assisted in the task by English social historian William Harrison (1534–93), among others. A revised edition of the *Chronicles,* published posthumously in 1587, contained passages offensive to Elizabeth I (q.v.), Queen of England, who ordered the work expurgated. An edition in six volumes was published in London in 1807 and 1808 with the excised passages restored. The fame of the *Chronicles* rests upon their use as source material by William Shakespeare (q.v.), in his historical plays, as well as in *King Lear, Macbeth,* and *Cymbeline.*

HOLLAND, barony of the British peerage. *See under* Fox, family.

416

HOLLAND, city of Michigan, in Allegan and Ottawa counties, on Lake Macatawa, an inlet of Lake Michigan, 20 miles s.w. of Grand Rapids. The surrounding agricultural area produces fruit, sugar beets, poultry, and dairy products. The principal industries in the city are the manufacture of furniture, shoes, chemicals, machinery, boats, furnaces, and metal products. Numerous vacation resorts are located nearby, and the tulip gardens in the parks and residential sections of Holland attract many visitors to its annual tulip festival. The city is the site of Hope College (1851) and Western Theological Seminary (1866), both of the Dutch Reformed Church. The Netherlands Museum contains Dutch historical relics. Holland was settled in 1847 by a group of dissident religious refugees from the Netherlands. It was chartered as a city in 1867. Pop. (1960) 24,777; (1970) 26,337.

HOLLAND. See NETHERLANDS, THE.

HOLLAND, Clifford Milburn (1883–1924), American civil engineer, born in Somerset, Mass., and educated at Harvard University. From 1914 to 1919, as tunnel engineer of the Public Service Commission of New York, he was in charge of construction of the double subway tunnels under the East R. In 1919 he was appointed chief engineer of the New York State and New Jersey Interstate Bridge and Tunnel commissions. He directed construction of the vehicular tunnel under the Hudson River connecting lower Manhattan and New Jersey, which shortly after his death was named the Holland Tunnel in his honor. See TUNNEL.

HOLLAND, John Philip (1840–1914), Irish-American inventor, born in Liscannor, County Clare, Ireland, and educated at the Christian Brothers' School in Limerick. From 1858 to 1872 he taught in Ireland, and in the following year emigrated to the United States settling in Paterson, N.J. Holland was ardently devoted to the cause of Irish independence. In the hope of challenging the naval supremacy of Great Britain he directed his attention to the submarine (q.v.) as an offensive weapon. His first design, offered to the United States Navy in 1875, was rejected as impracticable, but he continued his experiments with the aid of a subsidy from the Fenians (q.v.), and in 1881 launched his submarine the *Fenian Ram* on the Hudson R. A defective power system rendered this craft useless for extended naval operations. In 1895 Holland received his first contract from the U.S. Navy for the development of a usable submarine. Working in conjunction with naval officers, he eventually completed the *Holland,* a submarine with internal-combustion engines for surface power and an electric motor for undersea power, which was launched in Elizabeth, N.J., in 1898. The *Holland* and several other submarines constructed by him were purchased by the U.S. government.

HOLLANDIA. See DJAJAPURA.

HOLLEY, Robert W(illiam) (1922–), American biochemist, born in Urbana, Ill. He received a B.A. degree from the University of Illinois in 1942 and a Ph.D. from Cornell University, Ithaca, N.Y., in 1947. He was a member of the Cornell University Medical School team that first synthesized penicillin (q.v.). Holley's academic career has included post-doctoral work at Washington State University, as well as at the New York State Agricultural Station of Cornell University, at California Institute of Technology and at the soil, plant, and nutrition laboratory of the United States Department of Agriculture at Cornell. In 1968 he joined the Salk Institute for Biological studies, La Jolla, Calif., as a permanent resident fellow. Holley, the first scientist to determine the sequence of sub-units that exist within a nucleic acid, shared the 1968 Nobel Prize in medicine and physiology with the Indian chemist Har Gobind Khorana and American biochemist Marshall Warren Nirenberg (qq.v.). The three scientists independently studied the genetic code, arriving at an explanation of how the four blocks within the genes of a cell arrange the amino acids into chains and thus determine the cell function. See NUCLEIC ACIDS.

HOLLY, common name of the family Aquifoliaceae, containing about 300 species, and of its typical genus, *Ilex* (q.v.). The Holly family consists of trees and shrubs usually having separate staminate and separate pistillate flowers that are small in size, four- to eight-parted in structure, and white or greenish in color. The fruit are usually red drupes, containing two to eight one-seeded stones; see FRUIT: *Types of Fruit.* English

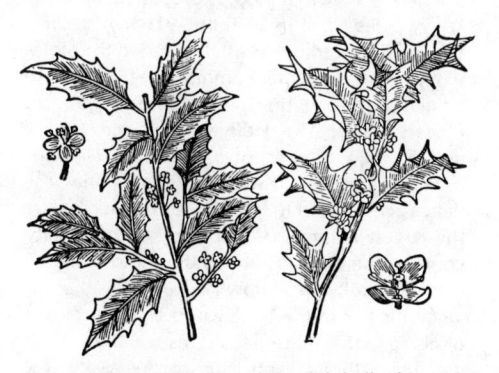

Leaves and fruit of holly. Left: English holly, Ilex aquifolium. *Right: American holly,* Ilex opaca.

HOLLYHOCK

holly, *I. aquifolium,* is a small tree with spiny, evergreen leaves and bright-red fruit. The common American holly, *I. opaca,* is similar to English holly, but has duller, less spiny leaves. It is native to the eastern United States, where it has been harvested so extensively that several States enforce protective laws. Both species of holly are widely cultivated for ornamental purposes and are particularly associated with Christmas (q.v.) tradition. Leaves of a South American species, *I. paraguariensis,* have stimulant properties similar to tea leaves and are used to make an aromatic beverage called maté (q.v.).

HOLLYHOCK, common name of a biennial or perennial herb, *Althaea rosea,* belonging to the Mallow (q.v.) family, Malvacea. It is native to China and is cultivated in gardens of Europe and the United States. Hollyhocks are tall and erect, usually growing 5 to 9 ft. in height. The single stems and the undersides of the heart-shaped, wrinkled leaves are hairy. The large, striking flowers usually bloom in late summer.

Hollyhocks are grown from seed or root cuttings. Most have single blossoms, but newer garden varieties are double-flowered. The most common colors of the flowers are white, yellow, salmon, rose, red, violet, and purple; a few varieties are almost black.

HOLLYWOOD, city of Florida, in Broward Co., on the Atlantic Coast, 17 miles N. of Miami. It is a residential city and a popular winter resort, with 8 mi. of ocean beach. The city has two yacht basins connected with the Intracoastal Waterway, and a fine deep-water harbor. The industries of Hollywood include shipping, canning, citrus fruit packing, and the manufacture of furniture. It was incorporated in 1925. Pop. (1960) 35,237; (1970) 106,873.

HOLLYWOOD, unincorporated community of California, in Los Angeles Co., in the N.W. part of the city of Los Angeles. Hollywood was incorporated as a city in 1903 and became a part of Los Angeles (q.v.) in 1910. In 1911 the first motion-picture studio was established in the Hollywood area, and the community became the center of the motion-picture industry of the United States. The Hollywood community is also a major center of radio and television broadcasting. It is the site of many fine residences, parks, and theaters. Griffith Park, one of the largest natural parks located within a city, contains the Griffith Observatory and Planetarium. The Hollywood Bowl, occupying a natural amphitheater in the Hollywood Hills, is the site of an annual summer music festival and of numerous cultural events. Sunset Boulevard, the main thoroughfare of Hollywood, and Vine Street contain many well-known restaurants, night clubs, and broadcasting studios.

HOLMAN, Nat(haniel) (1896–   ), American basketball coach and player, born in New York City. From 1921 until 1928 he was an outstanding performer with the Original Celtics, a professional basketball team. At the City College of New York (now part of the City University of New York), Holman served as basketball coach from 1919 to 1959. Under his leadership City College teams won 421 games and lost 190. In the 1949–50 season Holman's team won both the National Collegiate Athletic Association (N.C.A.A.) championship and the National Invitation Tournament (N.I.T.). In 1951, however, it was disclosed that key players on this championship team had accepted bribes and deliberately held down the total number of points scored in several games. Holman was suspended during the investigation that followed; he was absolved of blame and returned to his coaching duties.

HOLMES, father and son, members of a distinguished American family.

Oliver Wendell Holmes (1809–94), man of letters and physician, born in Cambridge, Mass., and educated at Phillips Andover Academy and Harvard College (now Harvard University). After several years of medical study and research in Europe, he received a medical degree from the Harvard Medical School in 1836 and began to practice medicine in Boston. From 1838 until 1840 he was professor of anatomy at Dartmouth College, and from 1847 to 1882 professor of anatomy and physiology at the Harvard Medical School. His essay *The Contagiousness of Puerperal Fever* (1843) advanced aseptic techniques in obstetrics and later in surgery; see PUERPERAL FEVER.

Holmes lived in Boston for most of his life, and his name was intimately associated with the city and the New England region. His fame as a writer of light, witty verse and as a raconteur was purely local until 1857. In that year the American poet James Russell Lowell (q.v.) established the *Atlantic Monthly* magazine, for which Holmes began writing a series of twelve papers, *The Autocrat of the Breakfast Table.* These essays, which were published in book form in 1858, achieved immediate popularity for their witty, lively expression of ideas, as well as for their characteristic New England flavor. Holmes soon achieved recognition, both in the United States and Great Britain, as a brilliant writer. He was one of the so-called Boston Brahmins, a circle of intellectually and socially cultivated Bostonians, and belonged to a group of distin-

HOLMES

Oliver Wendell Holmes (1841–1935), jurist, son of Oliver Wendell, born in Boston, Mass., and educated at Harvard College. He served three years in the American Civil War, fighting with the Union army at Ball's Bluff, Antietam, and Fredericksburg, and attaining the rank of captain. In 1867 he was admitted to the bar, and began to practice law in Boston. He edited the *American Law Review* from 1870 until 1873. In 1880 he was a lecturer on common law at the Lowell Institute in Boston. His Lowell lectures, collected as *The Common Law* (1881), became internationally renowned.

Holmes became professor of law at Harvard Law School in 1882, but resigned in the same year to accept an appointment as associate justice of the Massachusetts Supreme Court. He served until 1899 and as chief justice till 1902. In 1902 he was appointed associate justice of the Supreme Court of the United States (q.v.) by President Theodore Roosevelt, and he held the position until his retirement in 1932.

As a member of the Court Holmes was distinguished for his great legal learning, sound judgment, humor, and power of expression. He became famous for his liberal interpretations of the U.S. Constitution and was known as the "Great Dissenter" because of his disagreement with the views prevalent among his colleagues on the Court. He was later supported in his minority opinions by Justice Louis Dembitz Brandeis (q.v.). His *Collected Legal Papers* were published in 1920, and *The Dissenting Opinions of Mr. Justice Holmes* was issued in 1929.

Oliver Wendell Holmes   Brown Brothers

Supreme Court Justice Oliver Wendell Holmes   UPI

guished men of letters including Ralph Waldo Emerson, John Greenleaf Whittier, Louis Agassiz (qq.v.), and Lowell. The essays were followed in the next year by *The Professor at the Breakfast Table* (published in book form, 1860) and *The Poet at the Breakfast Table* (1872). A similar collection, *Over the Teacups*, published when Holmes was eighty years old, shows the same wit and vitality.

Although he was less successful as a novelist, his first novel, *Elsie Venner* (1861), achieved some measure of success. In this depiction of the New England character, Holmes attacked the stern Calvinistic dogmas of earlier days.

Holmes was the author of numerous volumes of poetry, and many of his poems became well known, including "Old Ironsides" (1830), "The Chambered Nautilus", "The Deacon's Masterpiece; or, The Wonderful One-Hoss Shay" (1858), "The Last Leaf", and the hymn "Lord of all being! throned afar". Other writings by Holmes include the essays *Pages from an Old Volume of Life* (1883) and biographies of John Lothrop Motley (1879) and Ralph Waldo Emerson (1885).

Holmes is represented in the Hall of Fame for Great Americans (q.v.).

HOLMES, SHERLOCK

HOLMES, Sherlock. See Doyle, Sir Arthur Conan; Mystery Story: *Detective Fiction: The Detective Story.*

HOLMIUM, element, one of the rare earths (q.v.), with at.no. 67, at.wt. 164.93, b.p. about 2600° C. (4712° F.), m.p. about 1500° C. (2732° F.), sp.gr. 8.80, and symbol Ho. It was discovered by the Swedish chemist Per Teodor Cleve (1840–1905) in 1879. Holmium is one of the least abundant of the rare-earth metals, ranking forty-third in order of abundance of the elements in the crust of the earth. It occurs in gadolinite and other minerals containing rare earths. Holmium oxide, Ho_2O_3, a grayish-white powder, and a few salts, such as the sulfate, have been prepared. The element has been used in electronic devices and as a catalyst.

HOLOGRAPHIC WILL. See Will.

HOLOGRAPHY. See Photography: *Historical Development: 20th Century.*

HOLOTHURIOIDEA, class of the phylum Echinodermata (q.v.) that contains the sea cucumbers, or sea slugs, cucumber- or sausage-shaped animals comprising more than 500 species. Holothurians are found in marine water all over the world, and range in size from several inches to 3½ ft. in length; some of the larger species are considered delicacies in the Orient, and are used in the preparation of soups.

Holothurians differ from other echinoderms in being bilaterally rather than radially symmetrical. This bilateral symmetry is believed to be a secondary adaptation, however. Their bodies are rubbery, without bony skeletons, and contain a few scattered ossicles (calcareous supporting elements). Like other echinoderms, most holothurians have projecting tube feet all over their bodies, especially concentrated about their mouths, which contain parts of the circulatory system and are used as well in locomotion; the tube feet about the mouths of holothurians are modified into tentacles that contain receptors for the sense of smell. These tentacles are also used to push food into the mouth. Most holothurians breathe by means of internal respiratory trees, ramifying organs leading from the cloaca into the body cavity. Contractions of the cloaca force water into the respiratory trees, which empty the water into the body cavity where it mixes with the body fluids and supplies oxygen to them. Some species have Cuvierian organs, cloacal enlargements of the respiratory trees which, when the animal is in danger, are extruded from the body and form sticky masses of threads in which any threatening animal may be entangled. Holothurians feed on minute invertebrates that they filter from the sea water, or find in the sand of the ocean bottom or sweep from the sea water with their oral tentacles.

The commonest holothurians belong to the orders Dendrochirota and Aspidochirota. Dendrochirota is widely distributed in shallow waters, and is characterized by branching tentacles. A well-known species in this order is *Thyone briareus,* a brown sea cucumber, about 5 in. long and 1½ in. thick, found off the Atlantic coast; others include several in the genus *Cucumaria,* the most important being *C. frondosa,* about 2 in. long, which is common in waters off America and Europe. Aspidochirota is found in shallow tropical waters and is characterized by tentacles slightly branched at the tip, forming a shieldlike end plate. *Holothuria* is the typical genus of this order.

Elasipoda is a deep-sea order that contains the genus *Pelagothuria,* the only holothurian

Holstein cow
U.S. Dept. of Agriculture

adapted to a free-swimming adult life. Malpadonia and Apoda are burrowing orders, the latter being slender, wormlike animals without tube feet.

HOLSTEIN-FRIESIAN CATTLE or **HOLSTEIN CATTLE,** breed of dairy cattle which originated in North Holland and Friesland many centuries ago. Holstein-Friesians are the largest of the dairy cattle. They are black and white with irregular markings; a red-and-white variety has been evolved. The cows have very large udders and produce more milk than any other breed. A yield of 9000 lb. of milk per year is considered average production, but better cows produce about 15,000 lb. of milk per year and a few cows have produced between 20,000 and 30,000 lb. in a single year. Although the milk from Holstein-Friesians contains less butterfat than that of other dairy cattle, the breed is the most common among American dairymen because of its ability to produce copious amounts of milk. See AGRICULTURE: *Animal Husbandry*; CATTLE.

HOLY ALLIANCE, league formed after the fall of Napoleon I (q.v.), Emperor of France, at the instance of Alexander I (q.v.), Emperor of Russia, by the sovereigns of Russia, Austria, and Prussia, all of whom agreed to act according to the principles of Christian charity. The document was drawn up by Alexander, and was signed at Paris in September, 1815, by Francis II (q.v.), Holy Roman Emperor, who was also Francis I, Emperor of Austria; by Frederick William III (q.v.), King of Prussia; and by Alexander. In addition to the original signatories, Naples, Sardinia, France, and Spain acceded to the provisions of the alliance, and it received the commendation, although not the signature, of the British prince regent of Great Britain, later George IV (q.v.), King of Great Britain. Prince Klemens von Metternich (q.v.), Austrian minister of foreign affairs, used the alliance as an instrument to further his reactionary policies. The importance of the alliance lay not in the ineffectual agreement itself but in its becoming a symbol of absolutist policies.

HOLY COMMUNION. See LORD'S SUPPER.

HOLY GHOST or **HOLY SPIRIT,** in Christian theology, the third person of the Trinity (q.v.), coincident with the Father and the Son. Jesus Christ referred to the Holy Ghost as "the Comforter, . . . whom the Father will send in my name, he shall teach you all things, and bring all things to your remembrance, whatsoever I have said unto you" (John 14:26). In orthodox belief the Holy Ghost is God, but distinct from the Father and the Son in the same manner as the Son is distinct from the Father. The work of the Holy Ghost is the sanctification and regeneration of the souls of all mankind.

HOLY GRAIL. See GRAIL, THE HOLY.

HOLY LAND, Palestine (q.v.), especially in reference to the places and events recorded in the Bible. See BIBLE SCHOLARSHIP; PALESTINIAN ARCHEOLOGY.

HOLY OF HOLIES. See TABERNACLE.

HOLYOKE, city of Massachusetts, in Hampden Co., on the W. bank of the Connecticut R., 7 miles N. of Springfield. The city is a leading paper-manufacturing center, especially noted for the manufacture of fine writing paper. Other industries are printing and the manufacture of textiles, machinery, and transformers. The Holyoke Museum of Natural History and Art includes exhibits of wildlife and Indian artifacts. The city lies at the foot of Mt. Tom (1202 ft.) which provides facilities for skiing and is part of Mt. Tom State Park. The site of the present city was settled in the early 18th century, and was at first a part of Springfield and then of West Springfield. Its importance as a manufacturing center dates from the completion in 1849 of a dam across the Connecticut R., providing water power for factories. The town was separated from West Springfield and incorporated in 1850; in 1873 it was chartered as a city. Pop. (1960) 52,689; (1970) 50,112.

HOLY ROMAN EMPIRE, designation applied to an amorphous political entity of Western Europe, originated by Pope Leo III (*see under* LEO) in 800 A.D., and in nominal existence until 1806. In its initial stages, the organization was styled Empire of the West. It became known as the Holy Empire in 1157 and as the Holy Roman Empire in 1254.

Establishment. The Holy Roman Empire represented, as the original styling implies, an attempt to revive the Western Roman Empire, which had collapsed in 476; see ROME, HISTORY OF. Throughout the turbulent period, sometimes called the Dark Ages (see MIDDLE AGES) that followed the removal of the last emperor, Romulus Augustulus (q.v.), from the Western throne by the barbarian Odoacer (434?–93), the traditional concept of a temporal realm coextensive with the spiritual dominions of the Church had been kept alive by the popes in Rome. The Byzantine Empire (q.v.), the eastern division of imperial Rome, retained, during part of the period, nominal sovereignty over the territories formerly under the control of the Western Empire, and many of the Germanic tribes that had seized these territories gave formal recognition to the overlordship of the Byzantine rulers. Partly because of this circumstance and for other rea-

HOLY ROMAN EMPIRE

sons, including dependence on Byzantine protection agaist the Lombards (q.v.), the popes also recognized the sovereignty of the Eastern Empire for an extended period after the enforced abdication of Romulus Augustulus.

Growing Tensions. With the coalescence of the Germanic tribes into independent Christian kingdoms during the 6th and 7th centuries, the political authority of the Byzantine emperors became practically nonexistent in the West. The spiritual influence of the western division of the Church expanded simultaneously, in particular during the pontificate (590–604) of Gregory I (see under GREGORY). As the political prestige of the Byzantine Empire declined, the papacy grew increasingly resentful of interference by secular and ecclesiastical authorities at Constantinople (now İstanbul, Turkey) in the affairs and practices of the Western Church. The consequent feud between the two divisions of the Church attained critical proportions during the reign (717–41) of the Byzantine emperor Leo III (680?–741), who sought to abolish the use of images in Christian ceremonies. Papal resistance to Leo's decrees culminated (730–32) in a rupture with Constantinople. After severance of its ties with the Byzantine Empire, the papacy nourished dreams of a revivified Western Empire.

The Imperial Orb, a part of the collection of crown jewels of the Holy Roman Empire.
Kunsthistorisches Museum, Vienna

Some of the popes weighed the possibility of launching such an enterprise and assuming the leadership of the projected state. In the absence of the prerequisite organizational apparatus and confronted with a hostile Lombardy, the Church hierarchy, abandoning the idea of a joint spiritual and temporal realm, seems to have decided to confer imperial status on the then dominant western European power, the kingdom of the Franks (q.v.). Several of the Frankish rulers had already demonstrated their fidelity to the Church (see CHARLES MARTEL), and Charlemagne (q.v.), who ascended the Frankish throne in 768, had displayed ample qualifications for the exalted office, notably by the conquest of Lombardy in 773 and by the expansion of his dominions to imperial proportions.

The Western Empire. On December 25, 800, Pope Leo III crowned Charlemagne Emperor of the West, establishing both a precedent and a political structure that were destined to figure decisively in the affairs of central Europe. The precedent, establishment of the papal prerogative in the selection and coronation of the emperors of the West, endured for nearly 700 years. In its primary stage, the resurrected Western Empire endured as an effective political entity for less than twenty-five years after the death of Charlemagne in 814. The reign of his son and successor Louis I (q.v.) was marked by intensive feudal and fratricidal strife that climaxed in 843 in the partition of the Empire. For an account of the growth, vicissitudes, and final dissolution of the Frankish realm, see FRANCE: *History*.

Despite the dissension within the newly created Western Empire, the popes maintained the imperial organization, except for an interlude extending from 877 to 881, for more than a century after the death of Louis I, conferring the title mainly on rulers of the dynasty of the Carolingians (q.v.). The emperors exercised little authority beyond the confines of their personal dominions, however. After the reign (915–24) of the Lombard ruler Berengar I (d. 924), who was crowned emperor by Pope John X (see under JOHN), the imperial throne remained vacant for nearly four decades. The East Frankish Kingdom, or Germany, capably led by Henry I (q.v.) and Otto I (see under OTTO), emerged as the strongest power in Europe during this period. Besides being a capable and ambitious sovereign, Otto I was an ardent friend of the Roman Catholic Church, as revealed by his appointment of clerics to high office, by his missionary activities east of the Elbe R., and finally by his military campaigns, at the behest of Pope John XII (see under JOHN), against Berengar II, King of Italy (d.

HOLY ROMAN EMPIRE

HOLY ROMAN EMPERORS

Name	Dynasty	Reign
Charlemagne	Carolingian	800–14
Louis I	"	814–40
Lothair I	"	840–55
Louis II	"	855–75
Charles II	"	875–77
Charles III	"	881–87
Arnulf, King of Germany (crowned emperor 896)	"	887–99
Louis III, King of Germany*	"	899–911
Conrad of Franconia, King of Germany*	"	911–18
Henry I, King of Germany*	Saxon	919–36
Otto I (crowned 962)	"	936–73
Otto II	"	973–83
Otto III	"	983–1002
Henry II (crowned 1014)	"	1002–24
Conrad II (crowned 1027)	Franconian	1024–39
Henry III (crowned 1046)	"	1039–56
Henry IV (crowned 1084)	"	1056–1106
Henry V (crowned 1111)	"	1106–25
Lothair II (crowned 1133)	Saxon	1125–37
Conrad III*	Hohenstaufen	1138–52
Frederick I (crowned 1155)	"	1152–90
Henry VI (crowned 1191)	"	1190–97
Philip of Swabia*	"	1198–1208
Otto IV** (crowned 1209)	Guelph	1198–1215
Frederick II (crowned 1220)	Hohenstaufen	1215–50
Conrad IV*	"	1250–54
(The Great Interregnum, 1254–73)		
Rudolf I	Hapsburg	1273–91
Adolf I*	Nassau	1292–98
Albert I*	Austria	1298–1308
Henry VII (crowned emperor 1312)	Luxemburg	1308–13
Louis IV**	Wittelsbach	1314–47
Frederick of Austria**	Austria	1314–22
Charles IV (crowned 1355)	Luxemburg	1347–78
Wenceslaus	Bohemia	1378–1400
Rupert of the Palatinate*	Wittelsbach	1400–10
Sigismund (crowned 1433)	Luxemburg	1411–37
Albert II*	Hapsburg	1438–39
Frederick III*** (crowned 1452)	"	1440–93
Maximilian I*	"	1493–1519
Charles V**** (crowned 1520)	"	1519–56
Ferdinand I	"	1556–64
Maximilian II	"	1564–76
Rudolf II	"	1576–1612
Matthias	"	1612–19
Ferdinand II	"	1619–37
Ferdinand III	"	1637–57
Leopold I	"	1658–1705
Joseph I	"	1705–11
Charles VI	"	1711–40
Charles VII	Wittelsbach	1742–45
Francis I	Hapsburg-Lorraine	1745–65
Joseph II	" "	1765–90
Leopold II	" "	1790–92
Francis II	" "	1792–1806

* Not crowned as emperor.
** Rival king of Germany.
*** Last Holy Roman Emperor crowned by the pope at Rome.
**** Last Holy Roman Emperor crowned by the pope (at Bologna).

966). In 962, in recognition of Otto's services, John XII awarded him the imperial crown and title.

A Union of Germanic States. The Empire of the West, at first an unstable union of Germany and Italy and later a loose union of Germanic states, remained in almost continuous existence for more than 800 years. During the Italo-German phase, the empire played a significant role in central European politics and ecclesiastical affairs. A central feature of the history of this period was the mortal struggle between the popes and the emperors for control of the Church. With the Concordat of Worms (1122), an agreement between Emperor Henry V (q.v.) and Pope Callistus II (q.v.), the emperor relinquished the right of spiritual investiture (q.v.), or installation into ecclesiastical office. All of the emperors were German kings, and because imperial duties and ambitions inevitably required their full attention, German interests were neglected. As one result, Germany, which might have been transformed into a strong centralized state, degenerated into a multiplicity of minor states. The agreement at Worms had removed one source of friction between church and state, but through the 12th century the struggle for political ascendancy continued. In 1157 Frederick I (q.v.), called Frederick Barbarossa, one of the greatest of emperors, first used the designation Holy Empire, ostensibly to increase the sanctity of the crown. Frederick, attempting to restore and perpetuate the ancient Roman Empire, tried to suppress both the restless nobles of Germany and the self-governing cities of Italy. His interventions in the latter country were opposed by the Lombard League (q.v.) and severely strained his relations with the papacy. Pope Adrian IV (*see under* ADRIAN) insisted that Frederick held the empire as a papal fief, but the emperor, who had the support of the German bishops, maintained that his title to it came from God alone; *see also* FEUDALISM. During the almost two decades of sporadic warfare in Italy that followed, Frederick was defeated at Legnano (1176) by the cities of the Lombard League, and the cities thus established their independence from further imperial authority. Emperor Henry VI (q.v.), who claimed the throne of Sicily through marriage, twice invaded Italy and the second time (1194) made Sicily his in fact. Emperor Frederick II (q.v.) renewed imperial efforts to vanquish the Italian cities and the papacy in the 13th century, but he was unsuccessful. For accounts of these and related events, *see* GERMANY: *History;* GUELPHS AND GHIBELLINES; ITALY: *History.*

423

HOLY ROMAN EMPIRE

The Holy Roman Empire had little real importance in European political and religious developments after the Great Interregnum (1254–73). The death of Frederick II in 1250 left the imperial throne vacant, and two rival candidates attempted to win support for their claims. Frederick's son, Conrad IV (see under CONRAD), and William of Holland (see under WILLIAM) first contended for the throne. In 1257 another imperial election was followed by the crowning at Aachen of the English Richard, Earl of Cornwall (1209–72), who was, however, unable to win control of the empire. In effect, this signalized papal victory in the protracted struggle with the empire. Beginning in 1273 with Rudolph I (q.v.), the first of the Hapsburg (q.v.) dynasty, various German kings laid claim to the imperial title and, in several instances, these claims were recognized by the popes. The office was little more than honorary, however, and inasmuch as the empire comprised a loose confederation of sovereign states and principalities, imperial authority was nominal. Louis IV (q.v.), who assumed the title in 1314, successfully challenged the power of the papacy and for a brief period restored the prestige of the empire. In 1356 Charles IV (see under CHARLES) promulgated the Golden Bull (q.v.), which prescribes the form and procedure of imperial election and enhanced the importance of the electors; see ELECTORS, GERMAN IMPERIAL. During the reign of Charles V (q.v.), the empire encompassed territories as extensive as those of Charlemagne. But dynastic rather than ecclesiastical principles composed the chief cohesive element in the imperial structure of Charles V. The medieval concept of a temporal state coextensive and in harmony with the spiritual dominions of the Church survived solely as a theory. As the Protestant Reformation (see REFORMATION) gained headway, even the theory lost practical meaning. The unity of the empire was weakened in 1555 after the Religious Peace of Augsburg (see AUGSBURG) permitted each free city and state of Germany to exercise choice between the adoption of Lutheranism or Catholicism. With the Peace of Westphalia (see WESTPHALIA, PEACE OF) in 1648, which ended the Thirty Years' War (q.v.), the empire lost all remaining sovereignty over its constituent states and France became the leading power in Europe. In its final phase the Holy Roman Empire served mainly as a vehicle for the imperial pretensions of the Hapsburgs, but it performed certain useful functions, including the maintenance of a measure of unity among its component states (see DIET). The later emperors, all rulers of Austria (q.v.) and concerned mainly with aggrandizement of their personal dominions, were mere figureheads. Futile armed intervention against the French Revolution (q.v.) constituted the last important venture of the empire in European politics. Because of well-founded fears that Napoleon I (q.v.), Emperor of France, intended to annex the imperial title, Francis II (q.v.), the last of the emperors, formally dissolved the empire on Aug. 6, 1806, and established the Empire of Austria.

More recently, the concept of the Third Reich (1934–45) held by the German dictator Adolf Hitler (q.v.) was an idealization of the empire's continuity with the First Reich (962–1806) and the Second Reich (1871–1918).

HOLYROOD PALACE, former residence of the Scottish rulers, located in Edinburgh. It occupies the site of the Augustinian Abbey of the Holy Rood erected in 1128 by David I (q.v.), King of Scotland. The sole remains of the abbey are the ruins of the church, which remained a sanctuary until the late 19th century. The palace was built by James IV (q.v.), King of Scotland, destroyed by fire in 1650, and rebuilt by Charles II (q.v.), King of England, between 1671 and 1679. David Rizzio, secretary to Mary, Queen of Scots (qq.v.), was murdered there in 1566. The palace is now open to the public, except when the reigning British monarch is in residence.

HOLY SPIRIT. See HOLY GHOST.

HOLY THURSDAY. See ASCENSION DAY; MAUNDY THURSDAY.

HOLY WATER, water blessed by a bishop or priest, and prescribed for use in the liturgies of some Christian churches. Because water is a natural cleansing agent, the use of holy water is representative of internal purification. Under the Mosaic Law of Judaism (q.v.) sprinkling the hands and face with water before entering the sanctuary was prescribed for all persons who were ritually unclean. From this Jewish practice is derived the present custom of dipping one's fingers in holy water and blessing oneself with it when entering a church.

HOLY WEEK, in Christian liturgy, the week immediately preceding Easter, beginning with Palm Sunday and including Maundy Thursday and Good Friday (qq.v.). The ceremonies of Holy Week commemorate the Passion and death of Jesus Christ. The week was originally called Passion Week (q.v.), but that designation is now given to the week preceding Palm Sunday.

HOMAGE. See FEUDALISM: *Feudal Obligations*.

HOME, earldom in the British peerage. See DOUGLAS, family.

HOME ECONOMICS, art and science of home management, the subject of courses taught at various educational levels in the schools of the United States. The courses usually include the study of nutrition, cookery, clothing and textiles, home furnishing and management, domestic finance, child care and development, hygiene, and handicrafts. Home economics was introduced as a formal subject in American education about 1870, when it became a recognized course in the curriculum of State agricultural colleges. Early in the 1900's Federal funds were made available to secondary schools and universities for home economics programs, and courses are now taught in elementary and high schools, colleges, and vocational schools. University courses in home economics provide professional training in food technology and nutrition, institution administration, child development and family life, and interior design. The Bureau of Human Nutrition and Home Economics (founded 1932), a part of the United States Agricultural Research Service since 1953, conducts research on agricultural products used in everyday living and on economic problems of housing and consumption.

HOMEOPATHY, system of medical practice based on the principle that diseases can be cured by drugs which produce in a healthy person the same pathological effects that are symptomatic of the disease. This doctrine of similarity was first formulated by the German physician Samuel Hahnemann (q.v.) in 1796. Homeopaths also believe that small doses of a drug are more efficacious in curing a disease than large doses. For example, a very small amount of opium, which induces an extreme tendency to sleep, accompanied by profuse perspiration and delirium, cures a fever accompanied by the same symptoms.

Homeopathy was introduced into the United States in 1825. The American Institute of Homeopathy, the national society of homeopathic physicians, was founded in 1844.

HOMER (between 1200 B.C. and 850 B.C.), Greek poet, presumed author of the two great ancient Greek epic poems, the *Iliad* and the *Odyssey* (qq.v.). According to tradition, Homer was a divinely inspired poet, although blind, old, and poor, who made his living as an itinerant bard, or singer. No definite record of his life exists; the cities of Argos, Athens, Chios, Colophon, Rhodes, Salamis, and Smyrna have been claimed as his birthplace. Scholars believe that he came from Asia Minor, possibly Chios or Smyrna.

Our knowledge of the *Iliad* and *Odyssey* dates from the late 6th century B.C. In Athens at that time both poems were recited every four years at the Panathenaea (q.v.) by professional rhapsodists, who seem to have followed a written text. Critical study of the epics was undertaken during the Alexandrian period, beginning about 325 B.C. and culminating with the critic Aristarchus of Samothrace (220?–150? B.C.), who prepared the versions upon which modern texts are based.

The poems do not describe events contemporary with the time of their composition; instead, they draw upon traditional material handed

Homer, a Hellenistic bust in marble.

down from the Greek prehistoric period. The narrative of the siege and destruction of the city of Troy presented in the *Iliad* is related to an actual siege that took place about 1200 B.C.; see TROJAN HORSE; TROJAN WAR; TROY. Both the *Iliad* and the *Odyssey* are in the style of ancient oral poetry. The emphasis is placed on the major theme, on the flow of narrative, and especially on dramatic action; details are generic rather than particular. The language is rich, simple, and dignified, but the Homeric idiom is not identical with the speech of any particular place or time. Rather, it is a traditional dialect, mainly Ionic, with a sprinkling of Aeolic forms, as well as an element of very old Greek; see GREEK LANGUAGE: *Ancient Greek*. For the most part, it is molded by the form of the dactylic hexameter. The hexameter of the poems is perfected, indicating that this metrical form, dating from an earlier period of Greek literature, was then the recognized medium for epic poetry; see GREEK LITERATURE: *The Early Period*.

HOMER

Homer's characters, Achilles, Hector, Nestor, Helen of Troy, Andromache, Penelope (qq.v.), and Odysseus (see ULYSSES), have remained vivid personalities throughout the centuries. The Homeric portrayals of the gods, Zeus, Apollo, Hera, Poseidon, and Athena (qq.v.), have become the ideal types for all subsequent representations of those deities in poetry, painting, and sculpture. The Homeric epics were esteemed by the ancient Greeks as highly as the Bible and Shakespeare later were by other peoples; cultured Greeks knew the *Iliad* by heart. Even at the height of the Attic drama (see GREEK LITERATURE: *The Attic Period*), the *Iliad* and the *Odyssey* were still recited to great audiences. In modern times these two poems have influenced almost every school of Western poetry and literature.

Homeric Question. One of the most prominent literary controversies of the 19th century centered about the uncertainty of Homer's authorship of the *Iliad* and the *Odyssey*. The Homeric Question, as the controversy was called, became an issue after the German scholar Friedrich August Wolf (q.v.) published his *Prolegomena ad Homerum* ("Introduction to Homer", 1795) in which he expounded the theory that the two poems represented the works of several poets that had been put together by an editor of a later period. Wolf's ideas were extremely influential, although many poets and scholars, including the German poet and dramatist Johann Wolfgang von Goethe (q.v.), insisted that works displaying such unity of plot and consistency of characters as did the Homeric epics could have been written only by a single great poet. The controversy continued throughout the 19th century; most scholars accepted the theory that each of the two poems was an editorial conflation based either on various earlier folk epics or, according to the German philologist Ulrich von Wilamowitz-Moellendorff (1848–1931), on a lost original *Iliad* and *Odyssey*.

With the greater archeological knowledge of ancient Greece and Asia Minor gained during the late 19th and early 20th centuries and with more careful study of the Homeric texts by philologists and other scholars, the arguments of Wolf and his successors were gradually refuted. The scholarly consensus in the 20th century is that the *Iliad* and the *Odyssey* are the works of a single poet and that the present versions are relatively faithful representations of the originals, despite the fact that some changes in the texts have been made over the course of perhaps 2000 years. This opinion was borne out by the discovery that a form of Greek was written as early as 1400 B.C. in a Minoan script; see MINOAN CULTURE. Some disagreement still exists between scholars who hold, as did the ancients, that both poems were written by a single poet and those who contend that the *Odyssey* was written somewhat later by an imitator of the poet who wrote the *Iliad*. Modern scholars continue to agree with Wolf and his supporters that the epics employ many incidents, characters, and stock epithets that might previously have been embodied in heroic folk songs. They assume, however, that the poet or poets used these materials only as the basis for poetry that is otherwise completely original.

In addition to the *Iliad* and the *Odyssey*, there existed in ancient Greece a large body of epic poetry dealing with the sack of Troy and other aspects of the Trojan War. These so-called Homeric poems are not attributed to Homer; they are the work of poets of a later day who drew on a traditional body of legend. Only fragments of these epics survive. See EPIC POETRY.

HOMER, Winslow (1836–1910), American painter and illustrator, born in Boston, Mass. Beginning as the apprentice of a lithographer in 1855, he became a well-known illustrator for *Harper's Weekly* and other periodicals, to which he contributed from 1858 to 1876. He was an American Civil War correspondent for *Harper's* from 1862 to 1864, and this experience supplied him with themes for early pictures, such as "Prisoners from the Front" (1866, The Metropolitan Museum of Art, New York City). Another important oil painting among his earlier works is "Croquet" (1866), a work of bold realism and striking color. He painted some Negro genre pieces and other scenes of Southern life in Virginia between 1876 and 1880. In 1881–82, he stayed on the northeast coast of England, which inspired him to paint sea subjects. Finally, in 1884, he settled on the coast of Maine, where he began his series of large marines.

Homer's main themes, both in watercolor and oil, were the sea and the forest, and woodsmen and fishermen, all painted with fidelity and power. After trips to Florida and Bermuda, he painted a series of watercolors in which he captured the intensely bright tropical atmosphere with simple, vivid washes of color. "Hurricane, Bahamas" (1898), a dramatic watercolor at The Metropolitan Museum of Art in New York City, is one of his best-known works. Homer's paintings hang in several American museums, including the Chicago Art Institute, Museum of Fine Arts, Boston, and the National Gallery, Washington, D.C. See WATERCOLOR PAINTING: *History*.

HOME RULE. See IRELAND: *History: The Union*; IRELAND, REPUBLIC OF: *History: The Irish Revolution*; NORTHERN IRELAND: *History.*

HOMESTEAD, borough of Pennsylvania, in Allegheny Co., on the Monongahela R., 7 miles S.E. of the center of Pittsburgh. Homestead comprises an important industrial unit, but most of the huge steel mills for which the borough was noted are now included in the adjacent borough of Munhall. The production of steel is the major industry in the area; other industries include oil refineries and the manufacture of heavy mill machinery, cans, steel-fabricated vehicles, and cement blocks and bricks.

Homestead was laid out in 1871 as Amity Homestead and was incorporated and renamed in 1880. In 1881 the Homestead Steel Works was acquired by Carnegie, Phipps and Co., of which the American industrialist and philanthropist Andrew Carnegie (q.v.) was the principal owner. A dispute between the company and its employees in 1892 resulted in one of the most violent labor strikes in the history of the United States. The Homestead strike was carried on by the Amalgamated Association of Iron and Steel Workers and lasted more than four months. On July 6, during the course of the strike, a riot occurred in which several men were killed and wounded, and on July 12 the State militia was called out by the governor and the borough was put under martial law. The strike, which ended in a victory for the company, was an important factor in checking unionism among steel workers for almost forty years; see STRIKE. Pop. (1960) 7502; (1970) 6309.

HOMESTEAD LAWS, in United States history, collective name for a series of Federal enactments allowing settlers without capital to acquire homesteads. Although sentiment supporting the idea of free land for homesteaders existed from the early days of the U.S., the law was not passed until the American Civil War had begun. The South was antagonistic to the free land movement because it feared homesteaders would be against slavery. When the Republican Party (q.v.) was formed in 1854 it absorbed the free-land sentiment of the Free-Soil Party (q.v.). The secession of the Southern States left the way open for enactment of "the complete and satisfactory homestead measure" called for in a Republican pre-election declaration of 1860. The homestead law was enacted by Congress in 1862. It provided that anyone who was either the head of a family, twenty-one years old, or a veteran of fourteen days of active service, and who was a citizen or had filed a declaration of intent to become a citizen, could acquire a tract of land in the public domain not exceeding 160 acres (a quarter section). The

"Snap the Whip", painting (1872), by Winslow Homer.
Metropolitan Museum of Art—
Gift of Christian A. Zabriskie

HOMESTEAD STRIKE

public domain, or federally owned land (see PUBLIC LANDS) included land in all States except the original thirteen and Maine, Vermont, West Virginia, Kentucky, Tennessee, and Texas. To acquire title to the land, the homesteader was obliged to settle on or cultivate the homestead for five years. The law expressly declared that no land so acquired could be levied against by creditors for the satisfaction of debts contracted prior to the issuance of the land grant. Other Federal homestead laws, subsequently enacted, were essentially modifications of the act of 1862. The Federal homestead laws are important in U.S. history chiefly because they provided an incentive, in the form of easily obtainable land, for the settlement of the West. Largely because the supply of public land suitable for homesteading was exhausted, remaining public lands were withdrawn from homesteading in 1935. Occasionally since then, small areas in Alaska have been opened to veterans for homesteading.

One of the first homesteads established under the 1862 law is the site of Homestead National Monument of America, about 4½ miles N.W. of Beatrice, Nebr. The site was settled by Daniel Freeman and his family on Jan. 1, 1863, when the law went into effect.

HOMESTEAD STRIKE. See HOMESTEAD, PA.

HOME STUDY. See CORRESPONDENCE EDUCATION.

HOMEWOOD, city of Alabama, in Jefferson Co., adjoining Birmingham on the S.E. and 4 mi. from the city center. It borders on Shades Creek on the eastern slopes of Red Mt. The city manufactures wood products and building materials. It is the site of Samford University, the former Howard College (Baptist; 1842). The city was incorporated as Edgewood in 1921 and renamed in 1926. Pop. (1960) 20,289; (1970) 21,245.

HOMEWOOD, village of Illinois, in Cook Co., about 20 miles s. of central Chicago. Homewood has light manufacturing. Nearby is the Washington Park Race Track. Originally known as Hartford, the village received its present name in 1893. Pop. (1960) 13,371; (1970) 18,871.

HOMICIDE, in criminal law, killing of a human being by the act, procurement, or negligence (q.v.) of another. Homicide is a generic term, comprehending not only the crimes of murder and manslaughter, but also the taking of a human life under circumstances justifying the act or in a sense excusing its commission. Thus, the killing of an enemy on the battlefield as an act of war is considered justifiable homicide, and killing, without malice, to save one's own life or the lives of one's dependents, is termed excusable homicide; see also SELF-DEFENSE. The penalties for unlawful homicide vary from State to State and range from the death sentence to various terms of imprisonment. See MANSLAUGHTER; MURDER.

HOMILY, informal sermon on a portion of the Bible, designed to explain the literal meaning and the spiritual or moral significance of the text. The practice of reading the Scripture during public religious services and explaining its lessons in popular form prevailed among the Jews even in ancient times and was adopted by the early Christian churches. Many collections of homilies were made in ancient times, and much of the literature of the Middle Ages is homiletic.

The *Books of Homilies* are two collections of sermons, published in 1547 and 1563, respectively, and later combined, that are frequently consulted in controversies concerning the doctrines of the Church of England (q.v.).

HOMING PIGEON, pigeon (q.v.) that is specially bred and trained to return swiftly to its home. The exact means by which homing pigeons can travel as far as 1000 mi. in order to return home is not known, but it may be related to sensitivity to earth radiations and memory for landmarks.

The ancient Egyptians domesticated pigeons some 5000 years ago. In ancient Greece, the birds carried news of the Olympian games (q.v.). When telegraph service between Brussels and Berlin was temporarily interrupted in 1849, homers were used to carry the messages. In the 20th century, a pigeon trained by the United States Army Signal Corps traveled about 2300 mi. to its home loft. Homing pigeons are also used extensively in researching the means by which birds navigate when homing and migrating over long distances.

The training of a young homing pigeon includes teaching him how to enter his loft and familiarizing him with the area surrounding the loft. He is taken farther and farther away from home, each time being released so that he may find his way back.

Pigeon racing became popular in the 19th century. Pigeons used for races are given a training period to familiarize them with the territory over which the race will be held. Then they are released simultaneously at a central location; the time each pigeon enters its home loft is recorded. Homing pigeons are sometimes called carrier pigeons and homers. See ANIMAL PSYCHOLOGY: *Intelligence*; NAVIGATION.

HOMOGENIZATION. See MILK.

HOMO SAPIENS. See MAN; MAN, ANCIENT.

An equestrian statue of Francisco Morazán, national hero of Honduras, stands before the cathedral in Tegucigalpa, the capital of Honduras. United Fruit Company

HOMS (anc. *Emesa*), city of Syria, on the Orontes R., 85 miles N. of Damascus. It was noted in antiquity for its temple to the sun god, in which the Roman emperor Heliogabalus (q.v.), a native of Homs, was at one time a priest. The town was made a Roman colony under Emperor Caracalla (q.v.) in the early part of the 3rd century. Rebelling Syrian forces under Zenobia (q.v.), Queen of Palmyra, were defeated there by the Roman army of Emperor Aurelianus (q.v.) in 273. In 636 the town was captured by the Arabs. The chief industry of the city is the manufacture of silk. Pop. (1960) 148,386.

HONDO. *See* HONSHU.

HONDURAS, republic in Central America, bounded on the N. and E. by the Caribbean Sea, on the s. by Nicaragua, on the s.w. by the Pacific Ocean and El Salvador, and on the w. by Guatemala. The country lies between about lat. 13° N. and lat. 16° N. and long. 83° W. and long. 89°20′ W. Honduras is one of the largest Central American republics, with an area of 45,000 sq.mi.

THE LAND

Except for two coastal strips, one extending 400 mi. along the Caribbean Sea and the other 40 mi. on the Pacific Ocean, Honduras is a plateau, consisting of broad, fertile plains broken by deep valleys, and mountains rising to elevations of 10,000 ft. in the volcanic ranges on the Nicaraguan frontier. The watershed between the rivers on the Atlantic and the Pacific sides is far to the s., and most of the drainage is to the Atlantic Ocean. Navigable Atlantic rivers include the

HONDURAS

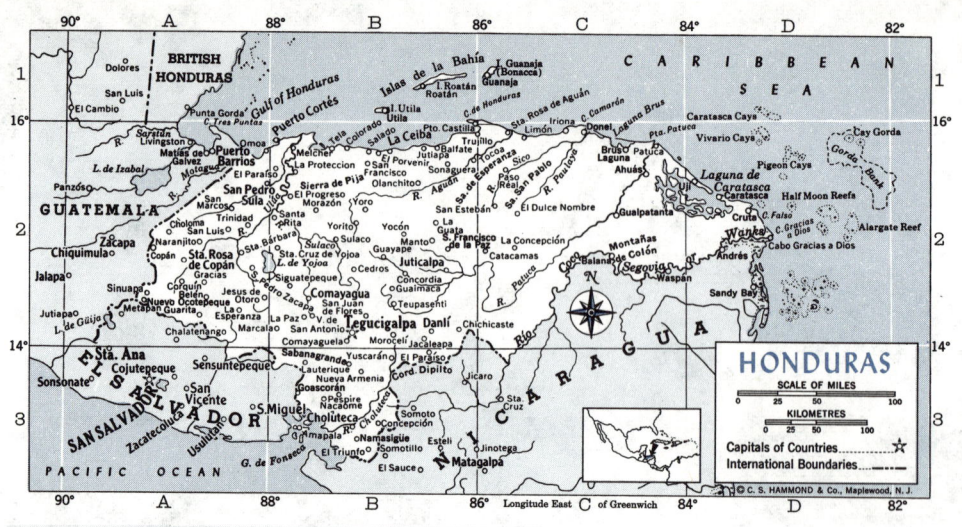

INDEX TO MAP OF HONDURAS

Cities and Towns

Ahuás ....C 2	Jesús de Otoro ......A 2	San Pedro Sula ......A 2	Camarón (cape) ......C 1
Amapala ....B 3	Jutiapa ....B 2	San Pedro Zacapa ....A 2	Caratasca (cays) .....D 1
Balfate ....B 2	Juticalpa ....B 2	Santa Bárbara ....A 2	Caratasca (lagoon) ...D 2
Belén ....A 2	La Ceiba ....B 2	Santa Cruz de Yojoa ..B 2	Choluteca (riv.) ......B 3
Brus Laguna ....C 2	La Concepción ......C 2	Santa Rita ....A 2	Coco (riv.) ....C 2
Catacamas ....C 2	La Esperanza ....A 2	Santa Rosa de Aguán ..C 2	Colón (mts.) ....C 2
Cedros ....B 2	La Guata ....B 2	Santa Rosa de Copán ..A 2	Esperanza (mts.) .....A 2
Choloma ....A 2	La Paz ....B 2	Siguatepeque ....B 2	Falso (cape) ....D 2
Choluteca ....B 3	Lauterique ....B 3	Sinuapa ....A 2	Fonseca (gulf) ....B 3
Colorado ....B 2	Limón ....C 2	Sonaguera ....B 2	Gorda (bank) ....D 2
Comayagua ....B 2	Manto ....B 2	Sulaco ....B 2	Gorda (cay) ....D 2
Comayagüela ....B 2	Marcala ....A 2	Tegucigalpa (cap.) ....B 2	Gracias a Dios (cape) .D 2
Concepción de María .B 3	Morazón ....B 2	Tela ....B 2	Guanaja (isl.) ....C 1
Concordia ....B 2	Morocelí ....B 2	Teupasenti ....B 2	Half Moon (reefs) ....D 2
Copán ....A 2	Nacaome ....B 3	Tocoa ....C 2	Honduras (cape) .....C 1
Corquín ....A 2	Namasigüe ....B 3	Trinidad ....A 2	Honduras (gulf) ......B 1
Danlí ....B 2	Naranjito ....A 2	Trujillo ....B 2	Patuca (pt.) ....C 2
El Paraíso, Copán ....A 2	Nueva Armenia ......B 3	Utila ....B 1	Patuca (river) ....C 2
El Paraíso, El Paraíso .B 3	Nuevo Ocotepeque ..A 2	Villa de San Antonio ..B 2	Paulaya (riv.) ....C 2
El Porvenir ....B 2	Olanchito ....B 2	Yocón ....A 2	Pigeon (cays) ....D 2
El Progreso ....B 2	Omoa ....A 2	Yorito ....B 2	Pija (mts.) ....B 2
El Triunfo ....B 3	Pespire ....B 3	Yoro ....B 2	Roatán (isl.) ....B 1
Goascorán ....B 3	Puerto Castilla ....B 2	Yuscarán ....B 3	San Pablo (mts.) .....B 2
Gracias ....A 2	Puerto Cortés ....B 2		Segovia (Coco) (riv.) .C 2
Guaimaca ....B 2	Roatán ....B 1	**Physical Features**	Sico (riv.) ....C 2
Guanaja ....C 1	Sabanagrande ....B 3		Sulaco (riv.) ....B 2
Guerita ....A 2	San Esteban ....B 2	Aguán (riv.) ....B 2	Ulúa (riv.) ....B 2
Guayape ....B 2	San Francisco ....B 2	Alargate (reef) ....D 2	Utila (isl.) ....B 1
Iriona ....C 1	San Francisco de la Paz .B 2	Bahía (isls.) ....B 1	Vivario (cays) ....D 2
Jacaleapa ....B 2	San Juan de Flores ....B 2	Bonacca (Guanaja)	Wanks (Coco) (riv.) ..D 2
	San Luis ....A 2	(isl.) ....C 1	Yojoa (lake) ....B 2
	San Marcos ....A 2	Brus (lagoon) ....C 1	

Ulúa, which drains approximately a third of the country, and the Segovia, or Coco. Mountain ranges traverse Honduras irregularly in a N.W. and S.E. direction. Forests, covering about 45 percent of the land, yield valuable hardwoods and softwoods. Fertile pasture lands provide the basis for increasingly productive dairy farming and livestock raising. Valuable mineral deposits are also present.

Climate. The climate is generally temperate in the uplands of the interior, with a mean annual temperature of 79° F. The low-lying coastal regions, however, are warmer, and the humidity is oppressive; the mean annual temperature here averages 88° F. The dry season prevails from November to May; the average annual rainfall is about 33 in. in the S. and about 100 in. along the N. coast.

Plants and Animals. Forests of oak and pine cover the cooler highlands, and savanna grasses cover the drier parts of the country.

Honduras has a wide variety of wildlife. Bears, deer, monkeys, wolves, and coyotes are numerous. The cat family includes jaguar, puma, ocelot, and lynx. There is a wide variety of reptiles, and marine and bird life abounds.

THE PEOPLE

About 85 to 90 percent of the population is mestizo (persons of Spanish and Indian blood), the remainder being American Indians, Negroes,

430

HONDURAS

and Europeans. The society is primarily rural.

Population. The population of Honduras (census 1961) was 1,884,765; the United Nations estimated (1970) 2,582,000. The overall population density is about 60 persons per sq.mi. (U.N. est. 1970), with the greatest concentrations in the small towns and villages in the N. coastal and central areas.

Political Divisions and Principal Cities. The country is divided into eighteen departments and a Distrito Central (central district), which are subdivided into municipalities and localities.

The capital and largest city is Tegucigalpa (pop., 1969 est., 218,510), located in the south-central region. The principal city and commercial center in the N. is San Pedro Sula (96,341). Puerto Cortés (22,296) and La Ceiba (35,222) are the chief Caribbean ports. Amapala (3568) is the only usable port on the Pacific.

Language and Religion. Although Spanish is the official language, some English is spoken in the N. The Indians have retained their native dialects.

Religious freedom is guaranteed by the constitution. Most of the people are Roman Catholics; Protestants number about 36,000.

Education. Education is free and compulsory for children between the ages of seven and fifteen. The literacy rate is about 58 percent and is increasing.

In the late 1960's some 345,000 pupils were enrolled in about 4100 primary schools, and some 27,500 students in about 100 secondary, normal, and technical schools.

UNIVERSITIES AND COLLEGES. The National University of Honduras, with faculties in Tegucigalpa and a general studies center at San Pedro Sula, is the major institution of higher learning. Preparatory institutions offer courses in nursing, administration, accounting, and journalism. Annual university enrollment numbers about 2500 students.

Culture. The interaction of both Indian and Spanish strains in Honduran cultural history is clearly visible in the architecture. Many colonial buildings show strong Indian influences combined with baroque, Renaissance, and Moorish styles imported by the Spanish.

With the exception of a few isolated Indian settlements where ancient languages and customs have been preserved, Honduras is primarily a Spanish culture today. The marimba is the most popular instrument and forms the core of many bands. Native folklore, folk music, and dances are limited, and artistic activity is concentrated around the School of Fine Arts in Comayagua, the old capital. *See* LATIN-AMERICAN MUSIC; SPANISH-AMERICAN LITERATURE.

ARCHEOLOGY. In N.W. Honduras lies Copán, a ceremonial center of the Old Empire of the Maya (q.v.), and one of the most important archeological sites in the Western Hemisphere. The Old Empire flourished from about 300 A.D. until 950, approximately the time when Copán seems to have been suddenly abandoned.

The discovery and study of Copán did not begin until the 19th century. Since then several countries and institutions have contributed to the excavation of this remarkable site. Field work has uncovered a stairway with hieroglyphs carved on the risers, pyramids, ceremonial courts, and sculpted stone stelae.

THE ECONOMY

Agriculture is the mainstay of the economy. Government plans are underway to promote and expand the industrial sector, diversify agriculture, improve transportation facilities, and develop hydroelectric projects. Annual electricity production in the early 1970's amounted to some 310,000,000 kw hours. Recent annual budget figures show in revenues some $82,900,000 and about $118,500,000 in expenditures.

Agriculture. About 23 percent of the total land area is under cultivation. Bananas are the chief crop; in the late 1960's some 153,000 tons were harvested annually. Other important crops include sugarcane (735,000 tons), coffee (38,000), rice (30,000), and cotton (12,000).

The livestock population numbers some 2,000,000 cattle and 650,000 pigs. Chickens are raised for local consumption.

Forest and Mining Industries. A reforestation program was started in 1951, but has been hampered by such factors as primitive lumbering methods and poor transportation facilities. Valuable woods include pine, mahogany, ebony, walnut, and rosewood.

Deposits of silver, zinc, and lead are exploited. Other resources, largely unworked, include iron, coal, copper, and antimony. In the mid-1960's some 6500 tons of lead, 8000 tons of zinc, and 114 tons of silver were mined annually.

Manufacturing. Since the mid-1950's Honduran industry has grown significantly, and it is receiving aid from the Central American Common Market (*see* INTER-AMERICAN COOPERATION). Cement, cotton, sugar, and wood products are produced in quantities large enough for export. Textiles, detergents, chemicals, light metals, and food products are manufactured primarily for local consumption. The chief industrial areas

HONDURAS

A laborer stacks bananas, one of the most important crops of Honduras. United Fruit Company

are near the capital and the cities of San Pedro Sula and Puerto Cortés.

Currency and Banking. The unit of currency is the lempira (2 lempiras equal U.S.$1; 1972). The bank of issue is the Banco Central de Honduras. The Municipal Bank and the National Development Bank, both government-controlled, provide credit for developmental projects.

Commerce and Trade. Bananas are the chief export, valued at some $83,500,000 annually in the late 1960's. Other important exports include coffee, wood, and timber. The total value of exports in 1969 was estimated at $169,000,000. Recently imports have risen rapidly, reaching an annual value of some $165,000,000 in the late 1960's. The largest increases are in raw materials and capital goods. The United States is the principal trading partner; imports from the U.S. average about 48 percent of the annual total, and 45 percent of all exports go to the U.S.

Transportation. The three railroads of Honduras are employed principally in the transportation of bananas and run for a total of about 650 mi. along the northern coast. The mountainous character of the country has made aviation an important means of communication. About 35 local airports, 2 international airports, and many small fields are in use. The total length of roads is 3200 mi., of which about 500 mi. were paved in the late 1960's. The Inter-American Highway (100 mi. in Honduras) links the country with the highway systems of Nicaragua, Guatemala, and El Salvador. Lake Yojoa and a number of rivers are navigable by small vessels.

Communications. Some 370 postal service stations, 110 telephone-telegraph offices, and 225 telegraph offices are owned and operated by the government. Fruit and mining companies own about 690 mi. of telephone lines and 1700 telephones. The country also has about 100 radio stations and 2 television stations, and about 147,000 radio receivers and 22,000 television sets.

HONDURAS

Labor. The total labor force numbers some 600,000, of whom almost 70 percent is engaged in agriculture. Labor union organization is not significant, and membership comprises only about 5 percent of the working force.

GOVERNMENT

Honduras declared its independence from the United Provinces of Central America in 1838 and is governed as a republic under the constitution adopted in 1965.

Central Government. Executive power is vested in the president, who is elected by direct and universal vote for a six-year term; he is ineligible to succeed himself immediately. The president appoints public officials and officers of the armed forces, of which he is commander in chief, and is assisted by a cabinet which he appoints. All literate citizens of eighteen years and older are eligible to vote.

HEALTH AND WELFARE. In recent years public health services were made more accessible through the increase in the number of mobile health units and through the development of community participation in health programs. Effective programs have resulted in malaria control, improved sewage, and increased medical personnel. Malnutrition, inadequate housing, and infant diseases, however, still pose grave problems.

The constitution provides social security programs for workers and their families. Funds are collected from employers, employees, and the government. In the mid-1960's less than 5 percent of the labor force was participating in the program.

Legislature. Legislative power is vested in the unicameral Congress of Deputies. The fifty-eight members are popularly elected on a proportional basis to terms of six years.

Political Parties. The two strongest parties are the dominant Nationalist Party and the opposition Liberal Party. Two Communist parties, although prohibited by the constitution, continue to operate covertly in Honduras. The Francisco Morazán Movement (M.F.M.), an organization influenced by the Cuban leader Fidel Castro, (q.v.) also exists.

Local Government. Each department is administered by a governor appointed by the president. Municipalities are governed by popularly elected councils; localities are governed by a mayor and a small administrative body. The Distrito Central is governed by a special law.

Judiciary. The Supreme Court is composed of seven judges elected by congress for six-year terms. The judiciary also comprises courts of appeal, courts of first instance, and local judges.

Defense. All male citizens between the ages of 18 and 55 are subject to military service. The armed forces comprise an army, navy, air force, and a special security force. Under the terms of the Washington Central American Conventions of 1923, the regular army is limited to 2500 men.

HISTORY

The coast of Honduras was discovered by Christopher Columbus (q.v.) in 1502. The first settlement was made in 1524 by Cristóbal de Olid (1492?–1524), a lieutenant of the Spanish explorer Hernando Cortés (q.v.). Olid founded the town of Triunfo de la Cruz, but was induced by reports of rich gold and silver mines to establish an independent government. In 1525 Cortés reached the colony, reasserted his own authority, and founded the town of Natividad de Nuestra Señora on Caballos Bay. A royal governor was appointed to administer the province, which was made a part of the captaincy general of Guatemala in 1539.

A Century of Internal Conflict. In 1821 Honduras revolted against Spanish rule and was annexed to the Mexican Empire. Two years later the country joined the United Provinces of Central America, a federation that lasted until 1838. The countries within the federation were racked by political dissension; the church Conservatives and anticlerical Liberals each wanted the federation to promote its ideas. In 1829 the victorious Liberals imposed their leader, Francisco Morazán (1799–1842), as president of the federation. Morazán, the national hero of Honduras, played a leading role in the unsuccessful effort to keep Central America united.

In 1838 Honduras declared itself independent. Three years later Francisco Ferrera, a Conservative, was inaugurated as the first constitutional president. For nearly seventy-five years thereafter Honduras was involved in internal strife and conflicts with neighboring countries that sought to install puppet presidents because of the strategic geographical position of Honduras.

The 20th Century. In World War I, following the example of the United States, Honduras declared war upon Germany, but did not actively engage in the fighting. The republic subsequently signed the Treaty of Versailles and became a member of the League of Nations. The years between 1918 and 1940 were marked by civil uprisings and economic depression. The economy was even more severely affected following the outbreak of World War II. Honduras, pursuing its policy of cooperation with the U.S., declared war on Japan, Germany, and Italy, the result of which was a curtailment of demand for Honduran exports. The U.S. subsequently

HONDURAS

furnished financial and technical assistance.

Honduras signed the Charter of the United Nations on June 26, 1945, becoming one of the fifty-one original member states of the U.N. In 1947 Honduras became a signatory of the Treaty of Rio de Janeiro; *see* Rio Treaty. Four years later Honduras signed the charter of the Organization of Central American States.

After President Tiburcio Carías Andino (1876–1969) stated he would retire from public life, he was succeeded by Juan Manuel Gálvez (1887–1972), of the Nationalist Party, in the elections of 1948. In November, 1949, the government granted several agricultural development concessions to a subsidiary of United Fruit Co. Widespread criticism of this move led, in 1950, to official reprisals against dissidents, particularly against members of the Liberal Party. Disagreement within the Nationalist Party in 1953 culminated in the emergence of two factions, one headed by Gálvez and the other by Carías. The Liberal Party, championing civil rights and agrarian reforms, broadened its following during the year.

In the election held in October, 1954, no one candidate obtained an absolute majority. In the political crisis that ensued, the acting president, Julio Lozano Díaz, under provisions of the constitution, assumed dictatorial power as chief of state. In elections held in October, 1956, Lozano's followers won all of the seats in congress. Thereupon, a three-man military junta, headed by General Roque J. Rodríquez (1902–), overthrew the Lozano government, declared the election void, and formed a new cabinet representative of all parties. In 1957 a newly selected constituent assembly chose as president Ramón Villeda Morales (1909–71), head of the Liberal Party.

In 1957 Honduras and the other Central Amer-

One of the many elaborately carved stone pillars, excellent examples of pre-Columbian art, that are found at the Mayan site of Copán in northwestern Honduras.
Banco Central de Honduras

ican countries, except Panama, signed a treaty establishing the Central American Economic Union to extend free-trade practices among its members. In 1960 the congress ratified adherence to the Central American Common Market (C.A.C.M.), a trading bloc formed to encourage production and free movement of goods by tariff reduction and economic cooperation.

Several military insurrections against the Villeda regime culminated in its overthrow on Oct. 3, 1963, ten days before the scheduled national election. The military government that seized power outlined a schedule for a return to representative government. A constituent assembly, elected in February, 1965, and controlled by the Nationalist Party, approved a new constitution and elected as president Colonel Oswaldo López Arellano (1921–). López took an active interest in upgrading the Honduran economy and secured loans from international agencies and foreign investments in Honduran industry.

Following charges and countercharges between Honduras and El Salvador over treatment of Salvadorans residing in Honduras, the two countries fought a brief, undeclared war in the summer of 1969. Salvadoran troops pushed several miles into Honduras before a cease-fire was obtained by a peace commission of the O.A.S.

In 1970 the economy, disrupted by the hostilities, began a slow recovery, with the aid of foreign investment and loans from international agencies. The withdrawal of Honduras from the C.A.C.M. in mid-1971 altered trade patterns among the member countries and adversely affected Honduran imports. Bilateral trade agreements were later signed, however, with Costa Rica, Guatemala, and Nicaragua.

President López, barred by the constitution from a third consecutive term, was succeeded in June, 1971, by Ramon Ernesto Cruz (1903–), who headed a coalition government between his National Party and the Liberal Party. In 1972, El Salvador announced its decision to reopen its border with Honduras, closed since the 1969 hostilities, and the political and economic outlook showed signs of increasing stability.

HONDURAS, BRITISH. See BRITISH HONDURAS.

HONEGGER, Arthur (1892–1955), French composer, born in Le Havre, of Swiss parentage. He studied at the Zürich Conservatory from 1909 to 1911. In 1912 he entered the Paris Conservatory, at which he studied harmony, counterpoint, fugue (qq.v.), and composition under the French composers André Gédalge (1856–1927) and Charles Marie Widor (q.v.) and orchestration under Paul Marie Théodore Vincent d'Indy (q.v.). He was a member of *les Six* ("the Six"), a group of French modernists who reacted against the music of their immediate predecessors; *see* SIX, LES. Beginning as a composer of the impressionist school (*see* IMPRESSIONISM, in music) Honegger gradually evolved a personal style characterized by dissonance, strong rhythms, and an emphasis on counterpoint. His ability to describe realistically in music various aspects of contemporary life is exemplified in his two orchestral compositions *Pacific 231* (1923, a musical description of a steam engine) and *Rugby* (1928). His other works include the oratorio *Le Roi David* ("David the King", 1925), the opera *Judith* (1925), and a number of symphonies and ballets. He is regarded as one of the most important composers of the French school of the first half of the 20th century.

HONEY, sweet, thick, liquid substance manufactured by bees to feed their larvae and for subsistence in winter. The nectar (q.v.) of flowers is ingested by worker bees, and converted to honey in special sacs in their esophagi. It is stored and aged in combs in their hives. Bee honey is an important constituent of the diet of many animals, such as bears and badgers, and is put to many uses by man. Other insects, such as the honey ant and various aphids, manufacture a honeylike substance from flowers, from the honeydew of plants, or from the sweet secretions elaborated by other insects; this substance is of little economic importance.

Bee honey is composed chiefly of fructose, glucose, and water, in varying proportions; it also contains several enzymes and essential oils. The color and flavor depend on the age of the honey and on the source of the nectar. Light-colored honeys are usually of higher quality than darker honeys; white honey is derived from the Californian white sage, *Salvia apiana*. Other high-grade honeys are made by bees from orange blossoms, clover, and alfalfa. A well-known, poorer-grade honey is a dark variety elaborated from buckwheat.

Honey has a fuel value of about 1520 calories per pound, and a specific gravity of 1.45 to 1.49 at ordinary room temperature (68° F. or 20° C.). It readily picks up moisture from the air, and is consequently used as a moistening agent for tobacco and in baking. Glucose crystallizes out of honey on standing at room temperature, leaving an uncrystallized layer of dissolved fructose. Honey to be marketed is usually heated by special processes to about 150° F. (65.6° C.) to dissolve the crystals and is then poured into containers sealed against crystallization.

HONEY BADGER

The fructose layer in crystallized honey ferments readily at temperatures of 60° F. (15.6° C.) or over; see FERMENTATION. Fermented honey is used in the production of honey wine or mead (q.v.).

Honey is marketed in the original comb as "comb honey", or centrifuged out of the comb and sold as "extracted honey". "Chunk honey" consists of pieces of comb honey suspended in extracted liquid honey. See HONEYBEE.

HONEY BADGER. See RATEL.

HONEYBEE, social, honey-producing bee of the genus *Apis,* recognized economically as the most valuable of all insects. This reputation commonly rests on its production of honey and beeswax. The honeybee's greatest usefulness, however, is actually in the pollination of an endless number of crops, including fruits, nuts, vegetables, and forage crops, and of many uncultivated plants which prevent erosion (q.v.) by keeping topsoil from being carried into the ocean. See BEE: *Honeybees.*

SOCIAL ORGANIZATION

The honeybee is a social insect which can survive only as a member of a community. The honeybee community is known variously as a colony, nest, or hive.

Castes. The honeybee community consists of three structurally different forms, the queen, the drone, and the worker, constituting castes with different functions in the colony. Each caste possesses its own special instincts geared to the needs of the colony.

THE QUEEN. The queen is the only sexually normal female in the community, and thus is the mother of all drones and workers. Her capacity for laying eggs is outstanding; her daily output often exceeds 1500 eggs, the weight of which is equivalent to that of her own body. Lacking all maternal instincts, the queen has little to do with the management or rearing of her offspring.

Anatomically the queen is strikingly different from her sons, the drones, or her daughters, the worker bees. Her body is long with a much larger abdomen than a worker bee. Her mandibles, or jaws, contain sharp cutting teeth, whereas her offspring have toothless jaws. The queen has a curved, smooth sting which she can use repeatedly without endangering her own life. In contrast, the worker honeybees are armed with straight, barbed stings, so that when a worker stings, the barbed, needle-sharp organ remains firmly anchored in the flesh of its victim. In trying to withdraw the sting the bee literally tears away part of its abdomen, and it dies shortly thereafter. The queen bee lacks the working tools possessed by worker bees, such as pollen baskets, beeswax-secreting glands, and a well-developed honey sac. Her food consists almost entirely of a secretion, called royal jelly, which is produced by the hypopharyngeal glands situated in the head of the worker bee. The average life-span of the queen is one to three years.

THE WORKER BEE. The worker bees at all times far outnumber the drones. During the spring in a Temperate Zone colony the number of worker bees ranges from 8000 to 15,000, and by early summer the number may total more than 80,000. Although lacking the ability to mate and reproduce, the workers possess all the other maternal instincts lacking in the queen bee. They secrete wax, build the honeycomb, gather nectar, pollen, and water, convert the nectar into honey, and clean and, when necessary, guard the hive.

Pollen is the principal source of protein, fat, minerals, and vitamins, the food elements essential for the growth and development of all three castes. Adult bees can subsist on honey or sugar, a pure carbohydrate diet. Besides gathering and storing food for all the members of the community, the workers are responsible for defending the colony and for maintaining the brood nest at 93° F., the optimum temperature required for hatching the eggs and rearing the young. When the hive becomes too hot they collectively ventilate it by fanning their wings. During cool weather they cluster tightly about the nursery and generate heat. The eggs, one of which is laid in each cell, hatch in three days. The larvae are fed royal jelly for the next two days and then pollen and nectar or honey. Each of the hundreds of larvae in a hive must be fed many times a day.

For the first three weeks of their adult life the workers confine their labors to building the honeycomb, cleaning and polishing the cells, feeding the young and the queen, controlling the temperature, evaporating the water from the nectar until it assumes the consistency of thick honey, and many other miscellaneous tasks. At the end of this period they learn to fly, and thereafter they function as field bees and defenders of the colony. The workers that develop early in the season live an extremely busy life which, from egg to death, lasts usually about six weeks. Worker bees reared late in the fall live much longer, usually until spring, as there is little to do in the winter except to eat and keep warm. Honeybees do not hibernate as do other species of bees.

THE DRONE BEE. The drone bee constitutes the reproductive caste. He is stingless and defense-

HONEYBEE

The queen pauses in her egg-laying as worker bees feed and clean her.
Walt Disney Productions, from the film *Secrets of Life*

less, has no pollen baskets or wax glands, and cannot secrete royal jelly. His one function is to mate with the queen. After mating, which always takes place on the wing in the open air, the drone dies immediately. Early investigators of the mating habits of the honeybee invariably concluded that the queen mates only once in her life. Recent scientific studies have established, however, the fact that she usually mates with as many as six or more drones in the course of a few days. The motile sperms, or germ cells, of the drones find their way into a small, saclike organ, called the spermatheca, in the queen's abdomen. The sperms remain viable in this sac during the life of the queen.

Drones are prevalent in colonies of bees in the spring and summer months. As fall approaches they are driven out of the hives by the workers, and left to perish.

Activities. The queen, workers, and drones operate as a team for the welfare of the colony as a whole. The queen is able to control the sex of her offspring. When an egg passes from the ovary to the oviduct, it may or may not be fertilized with sperm from the spermatheca. A fertilized egg develops into a female honeybee, either worker or queen, and the unfertilized egg into a male honeybee, or drone.

The queen lays the eggs which will develop into queens in specially constructed cells, in which the egg adheres to the ceiling. Royal jelly, which has a pastelike consistency, is supplied to the cells in sufficient quantities to prevent the larvae from falling and to feed them.

The worker bees are raised in much smaller, horizontally arranged cells. Inasmuch as the future workers receive royal jelly only during the first two days, the sharp contrast of the anatomy and functions of the queens with those of the workers can be accounted for only by the difference in the type of food consumed during the larval period. The development of the queen from egg to adult requires sixteen days, that of the worker, twenty-one days, and that of the drone, twenty-four days.

A young honeybee emerges from the brood cell. Walt Disney Productions, from the film *Secrets of Life*

The field honeybees bring in nectar from myriads of flowers. On entering the hive with a full honey sac, which is an enlargement of the esophagus, the field bee regurgitates the contents into the mouth of a young worker, called the house, or nurse, bee, which deposits the nectar in a cell and carries out the tasks necessary to convert the nectar to honey. When the honey is fully ripened or thickened, the cell is sealed with an airtight wax capping. Both old and young workers are required to store the winter supplies of honey.

Pollen is carried into the hive on the hind legs of the field bees and placed directly in the cells. The pollen of a given load is derived largely from one floral source, which accounts for the honeybee's outstanding role as pollinator. If it flew from one species to another it would not be effective in the transfer of pollen, but by confining its visitation on a given trip to the blossoms of a single species it serves the function of cross-pollination required in many varieties of plants.

Community Life. The perfection and orderly development of a community of bees provides a fascinating study in social organization. Just as in a city of 50,000 human beings in which all civic efforts are coordinated for the general welfare, so in a community of honeybees the general welfare requires systematic procedures involving a division of labor. Different tasks are performed by various age groups. The youngest adults start their life's work usually as cell cleaners and polishers. Comb building, feeding hundreds of immature bees, caring for the queen, generating heat and fanning, guarding the entrance to the hive, carrying out the dead, and, finally, bringing in nectar, pollen, and water constitute the tasks of more mature workers. There appears to be no central government in a bee colony. The queen definitely is not the ruler, although the life of the colony centers upon her presence and fecundity. The so-called spirit of the hive, which pervades the colony and guides its destiny, is determined by the biological structure of the individuals.

Communication. A well-perfected system of communication exists among the honeybees. In studies of bees begun in the early 1900's, the Austrian zoologist Karl von Frisch (1886–   ) determined many of the details of their means of communication. In a classic paper published in 1923 Von Frisch described how after a field bee discovers a new source of food, such as a

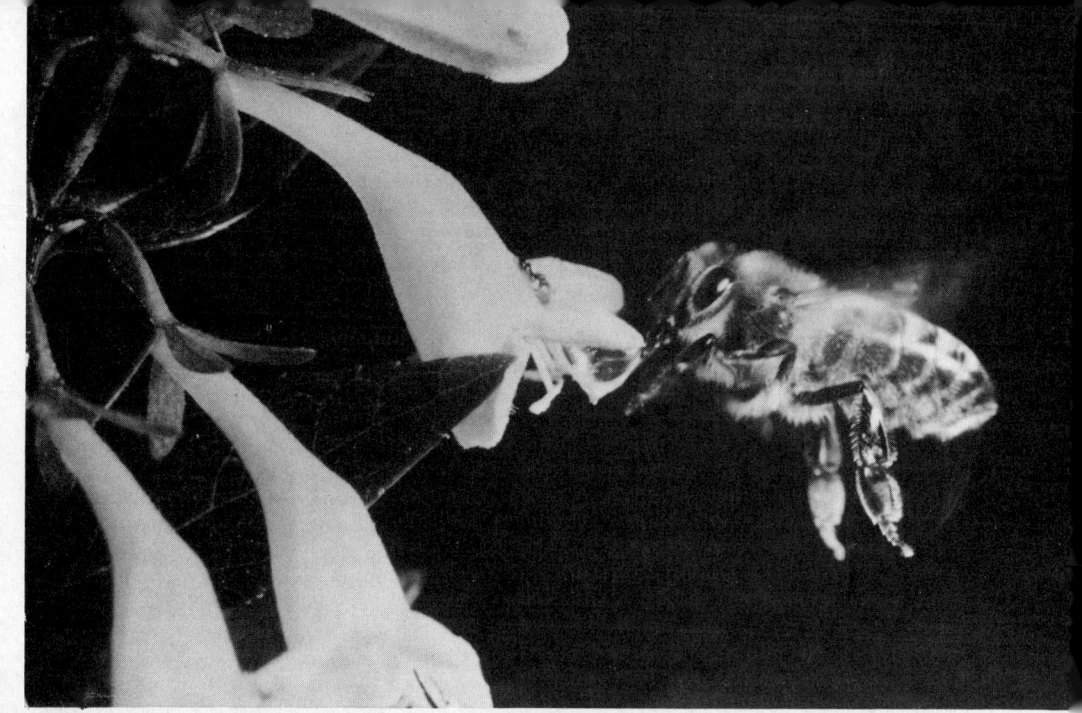

Above: A worker bee extracts honey from a blossom. Below: Queen bees engage in mortal combat to determine which will rule the hive.

Walt Disney Productions, from the film *Secrets of Life*

HONEYBEE

field in bloom, she fills her honey sac with nectar, returns to the hive, and performs a vigorous but highly standardized dance. If the new source of food is within 100 yards of the hive, the bee performs a circular dance, first moving about an inch or more, and then circling in the opposite direction. Numerous bees in the hive closely follow the dancer, imitating her movements. During this ceremony the other workers scent the fragrance of the flowers from which the dancer collected the nectar. Having learned that food is only a few yards away and what it smells like, the other bees leave the hive and fly in widening circles until they find the source.

If the new source of nectar or pollen is from several hundred yards to a mile or two away, the discoverer performs a more elaborate dance characterized by intermittent movement across the diameter of the circle, and constant and vigorous wagging of her abdomen. Every movement of this dance seems to have significance. The number of times the bee circles during a given interval informs the other bees how far to fly for the food. Movement across the diameter in a straight run indicates the direction of the food source. If the straight run is upward, the source is directly toward the sun. Should the straight run be downward, it signifies that the bees may reach the food by flying with their backs to the sun. In the event the straight run veers off at an angle to the vertical, the bees must follow a course to the right or left of the sun at the same angle that the straight run deviates from the vertical. Bees under observation in a glass hive demonstrate their instructions so clearly that it is possible for trained observers to understand the directions given by the dancers and thus to locate the indicated sources of food.

PROBLEMS OF SURVIVAL

To produce honey and beeswax the bees must spend their outdoor life among the blossoms. Their delicate bodies are subject to buffeting by bad weather, and they must generate enough heat to keep from freezing when the temperature drops. During the summer the workers must store enough food to last through the winter. A bee starves to death after a single day without food.

Disease. Honeybees are subject also to various diseases and parasites. American and European foulbrood are two widespread contagious bacterial diseases of the brood. A protozoan parasite, *Nosema apis*, and a virus causing paralysis both destroy adult bees. The bee louse, *Braula caeca*, as an adult, clings to the body of a bee. In Great Britain and several other countries, a parasitic mite, *Acarapis woodi*, which lives in the thoracic tracheae of adult bees, causes serious losses among honeybee colonies. The spread of this disease to the United States was prevented by legislation enacted in 1922 regulating the importation of honeybees.

Natural and Chemical Enemies. Numerous insects and birds prey upon honeybees. In addition, honeybees have become the victims of the insecticides applied to protect crops from destructive insects; see INSECTICIDE.

ECONOMIC VALUE

Because of various modern agricultural practices, such as irrigation and drainage, weed control, and, particularly, the widespread use of insecticides, many species of bees native to the U.S., particularly those that nest in the ground, are waging a losing battle to survive. As a consequence the honeybee, which is not native to the U.S., has become the principal U.S. insect pollinator.

Crop Pollination. The importance of the honeybee to agriculture and to man is readily apparent from the fact that more than fifty of the crops cultivated in the U.S. require insect visitation to the flowers for pollination. The crops which are either entirely dependent on insect pollination or produce more abundantly when bees are plentiful at blossoming time include the fruit crops almond, apple, apricot, avocado, blackberry, blueberry and huckleberry, cherry, cranberry, cucumber, dewberry, gooseberry, grape, mango, muskmelon, peach and nectarine, pear, native persimmon, plum and prune, raspberry, strawberry, tung, and watermelon; and seed crops, such as alfalfa, asparagus, broccoli, brussels sprouts, cabbage, carrot, clovers, cotton, cucumber, onion, radish, squash, sweet clover, and turnip.

The pollen of these plants is too heavy and sticky to be wind-borne, in contrast to that of the cereal crops and the grasses, which are wind pollinated and do not require insect pollinators. It is estimated that the value of the pollinating service rendered by honeybees in the U.S. annually is fifteen or twenty times that of the honey and beeswax produced. For example, more than 100,000 colonies of bees are moved annually into Kern Co., California, to pollinate the alfalfa seed crop. The honeybee is the only insect that can be moved about and taken to the fields for the express purpose of pollination.

Beekeeping. Beekeeping is practiced to some degree in almost every county in the U.S. A place where bees are kept for their honey in a colony or colonies is called an apiary. In the late 1960's the colonies of bees in the U.S. were estimated to number almost 5,000,000, and to pro-

HONEYSUCKLE

duce more than 280,000,000 lb. of honey and nearly 5,500,000 lb. of beeswax annually. The number of persons keeping bees, including backlot beekeepers, hobbyists, and commercial producers handling hundreds of colonies, was estimated at 450,000.

See also CLOVER; HONEY; HYMENOPTERA; INSECT; LARVA; NECTAR; POLLINATION.   J.I.H. & K.A.C.

HONEYCOMB MOTH. See BEE MOTH.

HONEYDEW MELON. See MUSKMELON.

HONEY EATER or HONEYSUCKER, common name for any songbird in the family Meliphagidae, now almost completely confined to Australia. The birds have long, forked, tubular tongues with which they scoop nectar and small insects from the inside of flowers. Their bills are long, down-curved, and sharp. They build loose, cup-shaped nests on bushes and in trees; the females lay from two to five eggs, light buff spotted with dark brown.

The best-known honey eater is the metallic green tui or parson bird, *Prosthemadera novaeseelandiae*, of New Zealand, so called because of a white, collarlike fringe of feathers on each side of its throat. Other honey eaters include the bellbirds, *Anthornis melanura* of New Zealand and *Manorina melanophrys* of Australia, and the soldierbird, *Myzomela sanguineolenta*, the wattlebird, *Anthochaera carunculata*, and the friarbird, *Philemon corneculatus*, of Australia.

HONEY GUIDE or INDICATOR, common name for any small, dull-colored bird in the family Indicatoridae of the woodpecker order, found in Africa and Asia, particularly southeast Asia. The bird is about 10 in. long and has a short bill. The female deposits her eggs in the nests of other birds, especially those of the related, hole-nesting barbet (q.v.). A common species is *Indicator indicator*. The honey guide has a fondness for honey, and men are often able to locate beehives by following it.

HONEY LOCUST, common name of North American leguminous trees of the genus *Gleditsia*, belonging to the Senna family. The common honey locust, *G. triacanthos*, averages about 70 to 80 ft. in height, with some growing as tall as 140 ft. It has heavily fragrant flowers, pinnately compound leaves made up of small leaflets, and branches covered with sharp, stiff thorns about 3 to 4 in. in length. The fruit of the honey locust consists of twisted, brown or black leathery pods, or legumes, often 12 to 18 in. long, containing several flat, black seeds separated by a sweet pulp; see LEGUME. Native to the deep woods of the southeast and central United States, the honey locust is planted extensively in parks. A thornless variety, *G. tricanthos inermis*, is planted as a street tree.

The water locust, *G. aquatica*, is a smaller tree, 25 to 35 ft. tall, which grows in swamps of the southern U.S. Its leaves and flowers are similar to those of the common honey locust, but it has slender thorns which are usually unforked, shorter leaflets.

Several other leguminous trees and shrubs are sometimes called honey locust, including mesquite (q.v.), black locust, and clammy locust; see LOCUST.

HONEYSUCKLE, common name of plants of the genus *Lonicera*. The genus contains about 175 species, all native to the temperate regions of the Northern Hemisphere. Honeysuckles are vines or shrubs with opposite leaves. The flowers of many species are showy and fragrant, and consist of a five-toothed calyx, a funnel-shaped,

Japanese honeysuckle, Lonicera japonica
W. J. Jahoda —
National Audubon Society

HONG KONG

five-lobed, tubular corolla, five stamens inserted on the corolla lobes, and a single pistil. The fruit is a berry.

A common honeysuckle, in England also called woodbine and eglantine, is *L. periclymenum,* a native of Europe cultivated in the United States. It is a popular climber, with very fragrant, light-yellow flowers. The American honeysuckle, *L. dioica,* is similar but with smaller flowers. The perfoliate honeysuckle, *L. caprifolium,* has remarkable upper leaves; pairs of opposite leaves unite to form a single leaf through which the stem passes. This twiner is a native of southern Europe, extensively cultivated in the eastern U.S. as an early-flowering variety. The trumpet honeysuckle, *L. sempervirens,* is a native of the southeastern U.S., having large, fragrant, scarlet flowers. The Japanese honeysuckle, *L. japonica,* is a creeping vine used popularly as a ground cover on slopes. In woodland areas it often becomes a serious pest by overrunning and crowding out other vegetation. Several other Asiatic species are erect shrubs. The Tartarian honeysuckle, *L. tartarica,* native to the Soviet Union and Siberia, bears pink or white flowers which give rise to dark-red berries. The fragrant honeysuckle, *L. fragrantissima,* is a large Asiatic shrub with leathery leaves and cream-colored flowers. Bush honeysuckle is in the related genus *Diervilla.*

HONG KONG, British crown colony in E. Asia comprising the island of Hong Kong (about 29 sq.mi.), Kowloon Peninsula (about 3 sq.mi.), and the New Territories (about 365 sq.mi.) on the mainland, including the waters of the Deep Bay and Mirs Bay and a number of smaller islands. It lies between about lat. 22°26′ N. and lat. 22°49′ N. and long. 113°53′ E. and long. 114°42′ E. Hong Kong Island, located at the mouth of the Canton or Pearl R., about 90 miles S.E. of Canton, extends about 11 mi. from E. to W. and is 2 to 5 mi. wide. It is separated from the mainland by the narrow Leimun Pass. Considerable areas have been reclaimed at Wanchai, Kowloon Bay, and North Point.

Physical Characteristics and Climate. Most of Hong Kong consists of many rugged and irregular islands. Hong Kong is covered with tropical and subtropical trees, and most animals are domestic. The soils are generally acidic and agricultural resources are of minor importance. The chief mineral is iron.

Although within the tropics, Hong Kong has a subtropical climate because of the S.W. monsoon, a moist, warm, equatorial wind which brings a rainy season between May and August. The mean annual temperature is 72° F., with a range from 59° F. in February to 82° F. in July. Typhoons frequently cause great destruction.

People and Principal Cities. The population is almost 98 percent Chinese (including 1,000,000 refugees from Communist China), with some British, Indians, Portuguese, and Americans. The population of Hong Kong (census 1966) was 3,176,400; the United Nations estimated (1970) 4,089,000. The overall population density is about 9995 per sq.mi. (U.N. est. 1969).

Buddhism, the main religion, reflects the dominance of Chinese culture; *see* CHINA, PEOPLE'S REPUBLIC OF: *Culture.* Nevertheless, as a port inhabited and visited by many nationalities, Hong Kong is subject to diverse influences, especially that of the British.

The capital and chief city of Hong Kong colony is Victoria, usually called Hong Kong, which extends some 5 mi. along the N. shore of the island of Hong Kong. The only other city of major importance is Kowloon.

Language and Education. English is the official language, but primarily Cantonese is spoken. Education in Hong Kong is neither free nor compulsory; all education, however, is under the jurisdiction of the Ministry of Education. Hong Kong has four types of schools: government schools, grant schools, government-subsidized schools, and private schools. Other institutions of learning include two teachers' colleges and a training college. In the late 1960's the University of Hong Kong, established in 1912, had some 2200 students and the Chinese University of Hong Kong, formed in 1963, had about 1800 students.

Agriculture and Fishing. Because of the land shortage, Hong Kong imports about half its food supply. Rice is the primary crop. Agriculture, for the most part in the New Territories, is of minor importance; fish is the chief primary product of Hong Kong. Fishing is the occupation of the large segment of Hong Kong's population that dwells on junks or sampans.

Labor and Manufacturing. The rapid influx of a large skilled-labor force since World War II caused industry to replace agriculture as the most important sector in the economy by 1958. In the late 1960's about 77 percent of the exports were manufactured goods, and more than 10,000 factories were employing about 600,000 persons. Textiles are the major industry, employing about 42 percent of the labor force. Important heavy industries include shipbuilding, shipbreaking, and iron foundries. The footwear, synthetics, electrical, electronics, and wool industries are also important, as well as a large handicrafts industry.

HONG KONG

Currency, Banking, and Transportation. The unit of currency is the Hong Kong dollar (1 Hong Kong dollar equals U.S.$0.165; 1970). Of the seventy-three licensed banks in Hong Kong, three issue notes, and many banks are Chinese-owned.

The colony of Hong Kong had about 620 mi. of roads in the late 1960's. With over 110,000 vehicles, Hong Kong has one of the highest vehicle densities in the world. Hong Kong Island is served by an international airport, buses, electric streetcars, and cable cars.

Commerce and Trade. Hong Kong is primarily important because its excellent natural harbor, covering about 17 sq.mi., is the only satisfactory seaport between Shanghai and Indochina. It is a gateway between West and East and a clearing point for commerce throughout s. China and the w Pacific. Import duties are levied only on hydrocarbon oils, toiletries, tobacco, alcoholic beverages, and non-British automotive vehicles. Export and import controls are minimal. Hong Kong maintains direct shipping connections with virtually every major maritime nation in the world. In the late 1960's annual exports totaled about $2,500,000,000 and imports over $2,000,000,000. Major trade partners are the United States, Great Britain, mainland China, and Japan.

Government. Hong Kong is governed with guidance from the Colonial and Foreign Offices at London. Paramount military and civil authority is vested in an appointed British governor representing the crown. An executive council and a legislative council assist him in formulating policy and local laws.

History. Before the British occupation, Hong Kong had a small fishing community and was a haven for pirates and opium smugglers. Britain first utilized the island as a naval base during the Opium War (q.v.) with China. By the Treaty of Nanking in 1842, ending the Opium War, Hong Kong was ceded to the British in perpetuity. After the second Opium War in 1860, Great Britain acquired Kowloon and Stonecutters Island, and in 1898 obtained the New Territories under a 99-year lease.

Hong Kong became a refuge for political exiles from the mainland of China following the establishment of the Chinese Republic in 1911. Ensuing Chinese nationalism was marked by antagonism toward all foreign countries, and a

View of Victoria, capital of Hong Kong. UPI

HONG KONG

Chinese boycott from 1925 to 1927 denied British shipping access to the ports of southern China.

When Japan seized Manchuria in 1932 and the Sino-Japanese War broke out in 1937, China turned to Great Britain and other European countries for its military supplies, and the diplomatic relations between the British in Hong Kong and the Chinese became more friendly. Throughout 1937 hundreds of thousands of Chinese, displaced by Japanese invasion of their country, sought refuge in Hong Kong. Meanwhile, Great Britain began strengthening and expanding the defenses of the colony against possible Japanese attack.

The outbreak of World War II in September, 1939, further dislocated the economic life of Hong Kong, already seriously affected by the Sino-Japanese conflict. The threat of Japanese aggression against Hong Kong was steadily growing. Japanese aircraft bombed Kowloon on Dec. 8, 1941, and ground forces dislodged British troops from Kowloon and the New Territories and the British surrendered on Dec. 25. The Japanese occupied Hong Kong and converted it into a military bastion and supply station for their projected campaigns in east Asia. Their operations were largely hampered, however, by United States submarines and bombing planes. The British reoccupied Hong Kong following the unconditional surrender of Japan on Aug. 14, 1945.

Hong Kong after World War II. Hong Kong swiftly regained its status as a major Far Eastern trade center. Numerous economic dislocations resulted, however, from the Nationalist-Communist civil war in China. Hundreds of thousands of Chinese took refuge in the colony before and after the Communist victory in 1949. Following the U.S.-imposed ban on trade with Communist China in 1950, the commercial activity of Hong Kong declined. The colony had to use its own resources to develop new industries as sources of revenue.

Thousands of newly arrived Chinese from the mainland provided labor and money for the rapid growth of light manufacturing industry during the 1950's and 1960's. In this period, also, the liberal tax policies of the government attracted foreign investment. The resultant economic boom transformed the colony into one of the wealthiest and most productive areas in the Far East. Communist-led riots raged throughout the spring and summer of 1967 and temporarily threatened the political stability of the colony and its relations with Communist China, which gave propaganda support to the demonstrators. By the end of the decade peace and order had been restored.

HONOLULU, city and capital of Hawaii, and county seat of Honolulu Co., which is coextensive with Oahu Island and certain other islands of the Hawaiian chain, about 2090 miles s.w. of San Francisco, Calif. The city proper occupies a magnificent site on the s. coast of Oahu and extends inland to the Koolau Mts., a range with an extreme elevation of about 3100 ft. above sea level. An extinct volcanic crater, known as the Punchbowl, is within the environs of the city, and Diamond Head, a headland 761 ft. above sea level, dominates the E. approach to the harbor. Honolulu harbor, almost completely enclosed by a natural breakwater of coral reefs, has extensive shipping facilities. At the crossroads of transpacific routes, the port is visited regularly by passenger liners and cargo carriers from all parts of the world. The port is also the terminus of an interisland steamship line, a regular point of call of several transpacific airlines, and the center of transpacific cable and wireless services. Honolulu is governed under the mayoral system.

Because of its equable climate (mean annual temperature, about 75° F.) and low annual precipitation, Honolulu is a favorite resort city. Among the chief points of interest are the State capitol, formerly the residence of the Hawaiian royal family, and the surrounding civic center; and Waikiki, an internationally famous beach and pleasure resort. The public parks and gardens contain a profusion of exotic tropical flora. Cultural institutions in the city include the University of Hawaii, and the Bernice Pauahi Bishop Museum, noted for its collections of zoological, ethnographical, and historical materials related to the Hawaiian Islands. Pearl Harbor (q.v.), a huge naval base and the object of the surprise Japanese attack (Dec. 7, 1941) that brought the United States into World War II, is 7 miles w. of the city proper. About 20 miles w. is Schofield Barracks, the principal United States Army post in the State.

Commerce and Industry. Among the principal exports shipped from Honolulu are sugar, canned pineapple fruit and juice, molasses, coffee, and canned fish. Imports include automobiles, petroleum, machinery, chemicals, textiles, paper and wood products, rice, flour, and other foodstuffs. The leading industries of the city are canning, sugar refining, and the manufacture of food-processing machinery, apparel, and various products for the domestic market.

History. The site of Honolulu was discovered by Europeans in 1794 and used as a harbor. In

1845 it became the capital of the kingdom of Hawaii, of the U.S. territory in 1898, and of the State in 1959. The city has grown rapidly in the 20th century as a tourist center and modern residential area. See HAWAII: History.

Population. Between 1910 and 1950 the population of Honolulu increased from 52,283 to 248,034. In 1960 it was 294,194; in 1970 it was 324,871.

HONORABLE ARTILLERY COMPANY. See ARTILLERY COMPANY, ANCIENT AND HONORABLE.

HONSHU or **HONDO,** largest island (sometimes referred to as the mainland) of Japan, bounded on the N. by Tsugaru Strait, which separates it from Hokkaido I., on the E. by the Pacific Ocean, on the S. by the Inland Sea and the Strait of Shimonoseki, which separates it from Shikoku and Kyushu islands, and on the W. by the Sea of Japan. The island is approximately 800 mi. long, ranging in width from 30 mi. to 150 mi. in the central region. Like all of the islands of Japan, Honshu is extremely mountainous. In the central mountain mass, often called the Japanese Alps, occur the loftiest peaks of Japan.

Diamond Head provides an unchanging background to the modern, growing skyline of Honolulu. UPI

Mount Fuji (q.v.), the highest summit of the country, has an elevation of 12,389 ft. above sea level. Mount Asama (q.v.), the largest active volcano of Japan, is about 85 miles N.W. of Tokyo. The Fuji region is often subject to severe earthquakes. The Tone, Shinano, and Kino rivers, among the largest of Japan, are situated on Honshu, and the island also contains numerous lakes that are noted as summer-resort areas.

Extending over approximately eight degrees of latitude, Honshu has wide regional variations of climate. Severe winters, with considerable snow, are common W. of the central uplift and in the N. portion of the island. The Japanese Current brings milder winters to the E. coastal regions in the central island area. Under the influence of the S.W. monsoon, the summers are usually moist and hot, with extreme temperatures as high as 95° F. Typhoons, usually occurring in September and October, bring heavy rains that often cause serious floods. Considerably more than half of the population of Japan resides in the lowlands of Honshu. Besides Tokyo, the leading cities of the island include Osaka, Nagoya, Kyoto, Yokohama, Kobe, and Hiroshima. Area, including that of nearly 200 offshore islands, 88,745 sq.mi. See JAPAN.

HOOCH, Pieter de or **HOOGH, Pieter de** (1629–after 1677), Dutch painter, born in Rotterdam. From 1654 he was a member of the Guild of Saint Luke at Delft, and there painted his finest works, illustrating domestic scenes from Dutch burgher life. He was noted for his paintings of distinctive interiors, in which the typical effect is strong sunlight falling into a room and illuminating a standing figure, such as a maidservant, or a family group seated at a table. In these works, enhanced by sharp patterns of golden light, De Hooch captured the simple, expressive gestures of people occupied with their daily chores. In the painting of genre interiors De Hooch ranks second only to his great Dutch contemporary, Jan Vermeer (q.v.).

De Hooch worked in Amsterdam during his later years. Although his subject matter was similar to that of his earlier period, De Hooch's works of this period are generally considered less noteworthy than his superb Delft productions. He is represented in the principal museums of the world, including the Louvre, Paris; the Rijksmuseum, Amsterdam; the National Gallery of Art, Washington, D.C.; and the Metropolitan Museum of Art, New York City. See DUTCH PAINTING; GENRE PAINTING.

HOOD, John Bell (1831–79), American army officer, born in Owingsville, Ky. He graduated from the United States Military Academy at West Point, N.Y., in 1853, and held a commission in the U.S. Army until the outbreak of the American Civil War, when he resigned and joined the Confederate army. He was promoted to the rank of brigadier general in 1862, and for his able leadership, particularly at the Battle of

"A Boy Bringing Pomegranates", painted (1644–65) by Pieter de Hooch.
Wallace Collection, London

Gaines' Mill, the second Battle of Bull Run, and the Battle of Antietam, was commissioned major general. He fought at Gettysburg and Chickamauga, and in 1864 served as lieutenant general under General Joseph Eggleston Johnston (q.v.). Just before the siege of Atlanta, Hood replaced Johnston in command of the Army of Tennessee in the defense of the city against the army of the Union general William Tecumseh Sherman (q.v.). Hood was defeated and forced to retreat from Atlanta, and after his loss of the battles of Franklin and Nashville in Tennessee, he asked to be relieved of his command. After the war he was a commission merchant in New Orleans. See CIVIL WAR, THE AMERICAN. See also articles on the battles noted above.

HOOD, Thomas (1799–1845), British poet and humorist, born in London, England. In his youth he was apprenticed to an engraver and in later life illustrated several of his own works. He served as an editor of the literary *London* magazine from 1821 until 1823 and during this period became part of the British literary group associated with the journal, including Charles Lamb, Thomas De Quincey, and William Hazlitt (qq.v.). Hood's first work, *Odes and Addresses to Great People* (1825), shows the influence of the British poet John Keats (q.v.), and so does his volume of poetry, *The Plea of the Midsummer Fairies* (1827).

Hood was known chiefly as a humorous writer, who was particularly clever (perhaps to the point of excess) in punning. He won this reputation largely through the writings he contributed while editor of the *Comic Annual* between 1830 and 1842. In these writings Hood deftly caricatured both current events and contemporary figures. He also had great talent as a serious poet as demonstrated in the moving poem "The Dream of Eugene Aram, the Murderer" (1831) and such later works as "Song of the Shirt", "Bridge of Sighs", and "Song of the Labourer". These poems revealed Hood's sympathy with the sufferings of the industrial workers of his time, among whom his name was honored.

Because of ill health Hood lived on the Continent from 1835 until 1840. During that period he continued writing and editing the *Annuals*. On his return to England he edited first the *New Monthly Magazine*, and then, in 1844, started *Hood's Magazine*. His other works include the novel *Tylney Hall* (3 vol., 1834); the volume of humorous sketches *Up the Rhine* (1840); the tragicomic poem "Miss Kilmansegg"; and collected miscellaneous pieces *Whimsicalities* (1844).

HOOD, MOUNT, peak in the Cascade Range, located in Clackamas and Hood River counties, Ore., about 45 miles S.E. of Portland. It rises to 11,235 ft. above sea level and is the highest point in Oregon. Mount Hood is a recreational center, attracting skiers and mountain climbers.

HOODOO. See VOODOO.

HOOF-AND-MOUTH DISEASE, alternate name for foot-and-mouth disease (q.v.).

HOOGHLY, or HUGLI, river of India, in West Bengal State. It is the most westerly of the channels by which the Ganges R. (q.v.) reaches the Bay of Bengal. The Hooghly is the principal channel of navigation of the lower Ganges. It is formed near Santipur, about 40 mi. above Calcutta, by the confluence of the Bhagirathi and Jalangi rivers. The Hooghly is navigable by ocean vessels from its mouth to Calcutta, a distance of about 80 mi. Navigability is maintained, however, by constant engineering operations, especially at the mouth of the river, where shoals and a 7-ft. bore that arises during the monsoon season are hazards to ships.

HOOKE, Robert (1635–1703), English scientist, born on the Isle of Wight, and educated at the University of Oxford. He served as assistant to the English physicist Robert Boyle (q.v.) and assisted him in the construction of the air pump. In 1662 Hooke was appointed curator of experiments to the Royal Society and served in this position until his death. He was elected a fellow of the Royal Society in 1663, and was appointed Gresham professor of geometry at Oxford in 1665. After the Great Fire of London in 1666 he was appointed surveyor of London, and designed many buildings, including Montague House and Bethlehem Hospital.

Hooke anticipated some of the most important discoveries and inventions of his time, but failed to carry many of them through to completion. He formulated the theory of planetary motion as a problem in mechanics, and grasped, but did not develop mathematically, the fundamental theory upon which the British physicist, Sir Isaac Newton (q.v.), formulated the law of gravitation (q.v.). Among Hooke's contributions are the correct formulation of the theory of elasticity, the kinetic hypothesis of gases, and the nature of combustion. He was also the first to use the balance spring for the regulation of watches and devised improvements in pendulum clocks.

HOOKER, Joseph (1814–79), American army officer, born in Hadley, Mass., and educated at the United States Military Academy in West Point, N.Y. During the Mexican War (q.v.) he was brevetted lieutenant colonel at Monterrey.

HOOKER, RICHARD

With the outbreak of the American Civil War he was appointed brigadier general of volunteers, and in 1862 he became brigadier general in the Union army. His skillful leadership and personal bravery won for him the nickname "Fighting Joe".

In January, 1863, Hooker was assigned by President Abraham Lincoln (q.v.) to the command of the Army of the Potomac. He rehabilitated and organized this army, but his command on the battlefield failed to show those qualities that had distinguished him as a corps and division commander. The defeat of the Union troops at Chancellorsville was in large measure because of Hooker's vacillation and inability to cope with the surprise actions of the Confederate leadership; see CHANCELLORSVILLE, BATTLE OF. In deference to Lincoln's lack of confidence in him and the pressure of public opinion in the North, Hooker resigned his command of the Army of the Potomac and was given command of the Eleventh and Twelfth Corps. He fought with distinction at Lookout Mountain (see CHATTANOOGA, BATTLE OF), and was brevetted major general. In 1868 he retired from the army with the full rank of major general.

HOOKER, Richard (1554?–1600), English theologian, born in Exeter, and educated at Corpus Christi College, University of Oxford. He took holy orders in 1581, becoming a clergyman in the Church of England (q.v.). Thereafter he lived in London and then at Boscombe and, finally, Bishopsbourne. He is noted for his *Laws of Ecclesiastical Polity* (8 vol., 1594–1662); the definitive edition, edited by the British clergyman and poet John Keble (q.v.), was published in 1836. The immediate purpose of Hooker's work was to demonstrate the advantages of the episcopal form of organization of the Church of England over the presbyterian form (see PRESBYTERIANISM) used by its opponents. The lasting value of the work stems from its recognition that natural law (q.v.) is unchangeable and eternal, but that the law of the state (positive law), including law affecting the form of government, can be altered when change is necessary or expedient.

HOOKER, Thomas (1586?–1647), American Congregationalist clergyman, born in Markfield, near Leicester, England, and educated at the University of Cambridge. He was pastor of several churches from 1620 until 1630, when he was called to appear before the Court of High Commission for nonconformist views; see HIGH COMMISSION, COURT OF; NONCONFORMISTS. He fled to Holland, where he preached for three years, then sailed for New England, settling first in Massachusetts and after 1636 in Connecticut.

He was the leader of the new settlement in Hartford and of the surrounding Connecticut towns and in 1639 had a leading part in framing the Fundamental Orders of Connecticut (see CONNECTICUT: *History*). He was also an early proponent of the New England Confederation (q.v.).

HOOKE'S LAW. See ELASTICITY.

HOOKWORM, any of several parasitic roundworms of the class Nematoda, particularly those of the genera *Ancylostoma, Necator,* and *Uncinaria*. These worms take their name from the hooklike appendages that surround their mouths. As intestinal parasites they are responsible for diseases of man and animals; see HOOKWORM DISEASE; PARASITE.

HOOKWORM DISEASE, disease caused by parasitic invasion of the intestine by hookworms of the species *Necator americanus, Ancylostoma duodenale,* and, occasionally, *A. braziliense* or *A. ceylonicum;* see HOOKWORM. Hookworm disease, which is marked by pronounced anemia, was formerly prevalent in the southern portion of the United States and is still endemic in many tropical and subtropical countries. The disease is occasionally found among miners in temperate regions. The eggs of hookworms are deposited on the earth in the feces of people suffering from the disease. The eggs develop into larvae which subsist on fecal matter and which have a life of several weeks to several months. These larvae are able to penetrate the skin of any person who touches them; infection is most commonly caused by walking bare-footed in contaminated areas or by handling human feces used as fertilizer. Entering the body, the larvae travel through the blood stream to the lungs, and from there, by way of the bronchial tubes and trachea, to the digestive tract. The larvae then attach themselves to the walls of the intestine and develop in about a month into adult worms.

The symptoms of hookworm disease are anemia, abdominal pain, diarrhea, and general debility, caused largely by loss of blood, which the worms drain from the intestinal wall. Anemia may at times be severe. The disease also usually causes apathy and malnutrition and, in children, underdevelopment.

Hookworm disease is prevalent in the Mediterranean countries in Europe, in Japan, northern Australia, and over much of Asia, Africa, and South America. It is conservatively estimated that more than 225,000,000 persons are afflicted with the disease. The rate of infection is extremely high in tropical and subtropical countries, ranging from 37 percent of the popu-

President and Mrs. Herbert C. Hoover pose for a group photograph. UPI

lation in parts of Brazil to 60 percent in Ceylon. The disease can be prevented by sanitary measures including the disposal or disinfection of fecal matter, the avoidance of contaminated areas, and the wearing of shoes. The disease is successfully treated with anthelmintics (drugs which expel the worms from the intestine) plus dosages of iron salts. *See* PARASITE.

HOOPSKIRT. *See* CRINOLINE.

HOOP SNAKE. *See* MUD SNAKE.

HOOVER, Herbert Clark (1874–1964), thirty-first President of the United States, born in West Branch, Iowa, where his father was a blacksmith. After graduating from Stanford University, he traveled throughout the world as a mining engineer and organizer of major business ventures. Independently wealthy and internationally famous by 1914, he served during World War I (q.v.) as director of the Belgian Relief Commission and as the United States Food Administrator. Although he sometimes used the broad powers that were his in this capacity, Hoover preferred to encourage voluntary cooperation, as when he requested housewives to "sign the pledge" for food conservation. During and after the war Hoover's administrative talents and humanitarian energies were credited with saving millions of people throughout the world from pestilence and famine.

In 1921 Hoover was appointed secretary of commerce by President Warren Gamaliel Harding (q.v.). His conservative principles helped to determine the economic policies of the Harding administration and of the subsequent administration of President Calvin Coolidge (q.v.). Highly regarded by all factions of the Republican Party (q.v.), Hoover won the Republican nomination for President in 1928. In his campaign against the Democratic nominee, Governor Alfred Emanuel Smith (q.v.), of New York, he promised continuing economic prosperity and supported prohibition (q.v.). Hoover received 21,391,993 votes and defeated Smith, the first Roman Catholic to seek the high office and an opponent of prohibition, by 6,375,824 votes.

Early in his term as President, Hoover was confronted by the economic effects of the stock-market crash of 1929 and by the severe depression that followed; *see* UNITED STATES OF AMERICA: *History: The Nation between the Two World Wars. See also* BUSINESS CYCLE: *Theories of the Business Cycle.* Repeatedly stating his belief in the "basic soundness of the American system", Hoover opposed massive governmental intervention in the crisis. He called for voluntary, cooperative efforts by business and indus-

449

HOOVER, J. EDGAR

try as a means of reviving the national economy. As the depression deepened, however, he supported such measures as the establishment of the Reconstruction Finance Corporation (q.v.) and a limited program of public works.

Although he was renominated by the Republican Party in 1932, the increasingly severe concern over unemployment in the country, and the widespread resentment at Hoover's seeming insensitivity to the crisis, led to his defeat by his Democratic opponent, Franklin Delano Roosevelt (q.v.). Hoover subsequently served as adviser to Presidents Harry S. Truman and Dwight David Eisenhower (qq.v.), notably as the chairman of two commissions devoted to studies of government reorganization. His books include *American Individualism* (1922), *The Challenge to Liberty* (1934), *Memoirs* (3 vol., 1951–52), and *An American Epic* (4 vol., 1959–64).

In 1965 Congress established the Herbert Hoover National Historic Site; the site, covering 148 acres, contains Hoover's birthplace, boyhood home, and burial place.   N.H.C.

HOOVER, J(ohn) Edgar (1895–1972), American criminologist and government official, director of the Federal Bureau of Investigation (q.v.) since 1924. He was born in Washington, D.C., and studied law at George Washington University. In 1917 he was admitted to the bar, and in the same year he joined the staff of the United States Department of Justice. Two years later he was appointed a special assistant to the U.S. attorney general. In 1921 he was named assistant director of the Bureau of Investigation of the Department of Justice, and in 1924, the bureau's director. In 1935, when the division became the Federal Bureau of Investigation, Hoover was made director of the F.B.I. He subsequently instituted many of the techniques and procedures that made the F.B.I. famous for its efficient apprehension of criminals. During the 1930's he supervised the investigations that led to the capture of many of the most dangerous criminals in the nation, including the bank robber John Dillinger (d. 1934). In World War II the counterespionage and antisabotage operations conducted by the F.B.I. under his direction were successful in preventing interference by German and Japanese agents with the war effort of the United States. After the war, he directed the bureau in an exhaustive series of investigations designed to curb subversive activities both within the Federal government and in private industries and institutions. His writings include *Persons in Hiding* (1938), *Masters of Deceit* (1958), *A Study of Communism* (1962), and *Crime in the United States* (1965).

HOOVER DAM, structure at the border of Nevada and Arizona, situated at Black Canyon on the Colorado R. 25 mi. S.E. of Las Vegas, Nev. A major engineering achievement, the massive dam is 726 ft. high and 1244 ft. long at the crest. The reservoir for the dam is Lake Mead; see LAKE MEAD NATIONAL RECREATION AREA. Construction began in 1931 as part of the Boulder Canyon project and was completed in 1936. Originally named after President Herbert Clark Hoover (q.v.), the dam was later called Boulder Dam, but in 1947 its initial name was restored.

See DAM: *Types of Dams: Arch Dams*.

HOP, common name of vines in the genus *Humulus*, belonging to the Hemp family Urticaceae. Hop plants have rough stems and heart-shaped leaves having three to seven lobes. Small staminate and pistillate flowers are produced on separate plants. Staminate flowers are borne in loose panicles, and pistillate flowers, borne in catkins, develop into achenes. These fruits are borne at the bases of overlapping bracts. The entire conelike catkin of achenes and bracts, the hop of commerce, is covered with a fine yellow powder called lupulin or hop flour. Lupulin, which gives the hop its bitter flavor and aroma, is used as a sedative in medicine. The common hop, *H. lupulus,* is native to Eurasia and is naturalized in northern and western United States, Australia, and Brazil. The American hop, *H. americanus,* is native to temperate North America. Several unrelated plants are commonly called hop, including bryony and black medick (see MEDICK). The so-called hop plant is sweet marjoram (see MARJORAM).

Cultivation. Catkins of common and American hop are extensively cultivated as a source of hops used in brewing (q.v.). Cultivation of common hop is carried on throughout suitably warm areas of Europe, North America, Australia, and New Zealand. In normal times, Germany, England, and the U.S. are leading hop producers. Cultivation of American hop is common only in the Pacific States. The annual hop production in the U.S. is about 50,000,000 lb.

Hop must be grown in areas having an abundant rainfall during the growth period, and abundant sunlight during the fruiting period. Hop is usually grown from cuttings which are planted in rows about 2 yd. apart in late winter or early spring. Only female plants produce fruit, but a few male plants are included in each hop field because fertilized catkins grow larger and more rapidly than unfertilized catkins. Hop plants are trained to, or guided by, strings suspended above the rows. Catkins become aromatic in late summer and are then harvested.

HOPE, Anthony. See HAWKINS, SIR ANTHONY HOPE.

HOPE, Bob (1903–), American comedian, born Leslie Townes Hope in Eltham, England. His parents brought him to Cleveland, Ohio, when he was four years old. After he completed high school Hope made his first appearance on the Broadway stage in 1927 in *The Sidewalks of New York*. Between 1928 and 1932 he traveled the nightclub and small-theater circuit as a stand-up comic. Later in 1932 he returned to the Broadway stage in a starring role in the musical comedy *Ballyhoo*. Hope first performed on radio in 1935 and three years later was given his own radio show on a major network. In 1938 he appeared in his first of some sixty motion pictures, the comedy *The Big Broadcast*, and was immediately hailed as a star. Some of his outstanding films were *The Cat and the Canary* (1939) with the American actress Paulette Goddard (1911–), and *Road to Singapore* (1940), *Road to Zanzibar* (1941), *Road to Utopia* (1946), *Road to Rio* (1947), and *Road to Bali* (1953), all with the American actress Dorothy Lamour (1914–) and the American singer and actor Bing Crosby (q.v.). When the United States entered World War II, Hope broadcast his radio show from U.S. military camps throughout the world and toured extensively, entertaining American servicemen. He has appeared many times on television, often as master of ceremonies, a role in which his sharp wit and mastery in repartee have been especially effective.

HOPEWELL, independent city and seaport of Virginia, in Prince George Co., on the James R. at the mouth of the Appomattox R., 7 miles N.E. of Petersburg. Served by railroad and by coastal steamer, the city is an important manufacturing center, containing industrial establishments that produce rayon textiles and yarn, paper, and lumber products. Fort Lee, a United States Army base in both World Wars, is nearby.

The site of the present city was first settled in 1613 by Sir Thomas Dale (d. 1619), marshal of Virginia, who founded a settlement at City Point, the present port of Hopewell. It became a leading port of entry during the colonial era. Its development as a manufacturing center began with the establishment of a munitions plant there prior to the entry of the United States into World War I. It was incorporated as a city in 1916. Pop. (1960) 17,895; (1970) 23,471.

HOPEWELL VILLAGE NATIONAL HISTORIC SITE, site of historic interest at Hopewell Village, Pa., about 15 miles S.E. of Reading. The site commemorates, in the village buildings and in a restored iron-smelting furnace, the iron industry of early 19th-century America. The Hopewell Village furnace, built in 1770 and worked until 1883, is one of the oldest ironworks remaining in the United States. It is administered by the National Park Service (q.v.).

HOPI, or MOQUI, North American Indian tribe of the Pueblo (q.v.) group, of the Shoshonean linguistic stock; see AMERICAN INDIAN LANGUAGES. They live in a small group of autonomous villages lying on three high mesas of north-central Arizona. Another village of the group is occupied by descendents of members of the originally unrelated Tewa tribe who were driven from their homes by the Spanish in the 17th century. The Tewa later intermarried with the Hopi. These villages, in which the Hopi culture was retained long into the period of Spanish and American dominance, have been objects of intensive study by anthropologists.

The Hopi tribe is the only branch of the Shoshonean linquistic stock that adjusted successfully to pueblo life. In traditions, social organization, and customs the Hopi are almost identical with the other pueblo Indians, and in modern times their pueblo culture is far better preserved than that along the Rio Grande. The Hopis are industrious farmers, and harvest and store large crops of corn, beans, pumpkins, and some fruits, such as peaches. They also weave baskets and blankets, and are skillful potters and carvers. Hopi houses are built of stone roughly cut and laid, and are finished in plaster by the women. Their ceilings are supported by beams and cross poles, and consist of a compressed mixture of brush and clay. The floors are sometimes flagged and the interior walls are generally whitewashed with gypsum and sometimes ornamented in simple geometric bands. In primitive Hopi houses the doorways, which were the only sources of light, were sometimes built in T-shapes. Windows covered with selenite were introduced under Spanish influence, and modern houses generally have glass windows and hinged doors.

Each of the Hopi pueblos has three chiefs, restricted to communal, ceremonial, and military leadership respectively, and holding their positions for life. The tribe is grouped into exogamous clans; that is, the kinship relationship within each clan is so strong that intermarriage between clan members is forbidden. The clans themselves are usually coupled in pairs, and these links are sometimes strong enough to justify larger exogamous groupings. Marriage is monogamous, and the lines of descent are matrilineal; that is, they are marked through the mother.

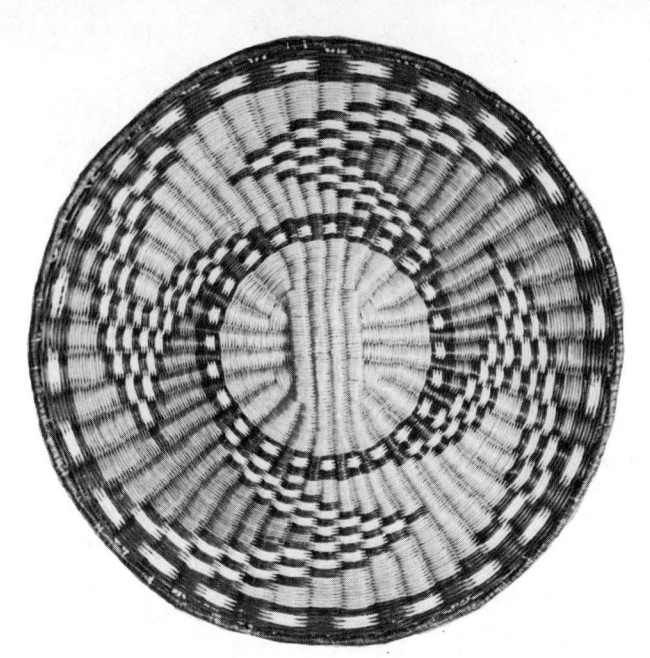

A typical Hopi decorative design in a woven basket-plaque.
Museum of the American Indian — Heye Foundation

Like that of all other pueblo Indians, the Hopi religion is pagan, consists in worship of the forces of nature, and involves propitiating and influencing supernatural powers. Ancestor worship plays an important role in Hopi ceremonies, and some Christian influences can be detected, particularly in the dating of ceremonies and the observance of saints' days. Private rites are held in underground ceremonial chambers called kivas, and public services and dances are commonly performed in the open air. The most important of the Hopi religious ceremonies are the katcina or kachina mysteries (the katcina is the spirit of an ancestor, usually representing a clan, symbolized in ceremonies by a masked and painted dancer or by a carved doll decorated with feathers); the midsummer and midwinter rituals of sun and fire worship; and the celebrated snake dances. In the snake dances, which are actually rain dances, live rattlesnakes, symbolizing the sky god, are held at certain points in the mouths of the dancers. The dances, which are attended by thousands of visitors every summer, are among the most spectacular of all American Indian ceremonies. *See* AMERICAN INDIANS: *Indians of the United States and Canada: Southwest Area.*

HOPKINS, Sir Frederick Gowland (1861–1947), British biochemist, born in Eastbourne, England, and educated at the University of London. From 1905 to 1910 he was a tutor at Emmanuel College, University of Cambridge, and after 1910 he taught physiological chemistry at Trinity College, Cambridge. His research covered many phases of biochemistry. A method for the quantitative determination of uric acid, which he developed, was applied to a variety of physiological and pathological problems. He was the first to prove that lactic acid is a waste product of muscular contraction and succeeded in isolating the amino acid tryptophane from proteins. In 1921 he isolated the tripeptide glutathione from living tissue and showed its importance in the oxidation process in living cells. Hopkins was the first to demonstrate the existence of substances he termed accessory food factors necessary in a balanced diet. Today these and similar substances are known as vitamins. Hopkins was made a fellow of the Royal Society in 1905, and president of that society in 1931. In 1925 he was knighted. He shared the 1929 Nobel Prize in medicine and physiology with the Dutch hygienist Christaan Eijkman (q.v.).

HOPKINS, Gerard Manley (1844–89), British poet and Jesuit, born in Stratford (now part of London, England), educated at the University of Oxford. He became a member of the Roman Catholic Church in 1866 and was ordained a priest in 1877. Hopkins was appointed professor of Greek at the University of Dublin in 1884. He wrote a number of poems that are highly individual in style and that extended the technique of English poetry by a number of innovations. In his poems, Hopkins tried to recapture the uniqueness, or "inscape", of individual objects of the world, both by description, and by intricate techniques of inner rhyme, alliteration, and compound metaphor, all of which yielded a complex type of rhythm the poet termed "sprung rhythm", illustrated, for example in his poem "The Windhover".

None of Hopkins' poems was published during his lifetime, but after his death, his friend, the British poet laureate Robert Seymour Bridges (q.v.), published a selection in an anthology of English 19th-century poetry. A nearly complete edition of Hopkins' poems was published in 1918, and a complete edition in 1930. Among his most characteristic poems, besides "The Windhover", are "Pied Beauty", "Felix Randal", "Duns Scotus' Oxford", and the long religious poem about the martyrdom of a group of German nuns in a shipwreck, "The Wreck of the *Deutschland*".

HOPKINS, Harry Lloyd (1890–1946), American government official, born in Sioux City, Iowa, and educated at Grinnell College. Until 1931 he was engaged in social welfare work. Among the posts he occupied in this field were that of director in New York City for the Association for Improving the Conditions of the Poor, executive secretary of the New York City Board of Child Welfare, divisional director of the Red Cross in New Orleans, and director of the New York Tuberculosis and Health Association.

Hopkins held many important government posts during the economic depression of the 1930's. In 1931 Franklin Delano Roosevelt (q.v.), then governor of New York State, appointed Hopkins director of the State Temporary Relief Administration and chairman the following year. After Roosevelt was inaugurated President in 1933 he appointed Hopkins head of the Federal Emergency Relief Administration; two years later Hopkins was made head of the Works Progress Administration; *see* NEW DEAL. From 1938 to 1940 he was secretary of commerce.

During World War II Hopkins served as administrator of the Lend-Lease (q.v.) program and as a member of the War Production Board and the Pacific War Council. He was also an influential Presidential assistant, and accompanied Roosevelt to the Tehran Conference in 1944 and to the Yalta Conference (qq.v.) in 1945 to consult with Joseph Stalin (q.v.), dictator of the U.S.S.R., and British Prime Minister Sir Winston Leonard Spencer Churchill (q.v.). Roosevelt also sent Hopkins as a personal envoy on a number of important diplomatic missions. On one such mission he laid the groundwork for the Potsdam Conference (q.v.), which was held after the unconditional surrender of Germany.

HOPKINS, Mark (1802–87), American educator, born in Stockbridge, Mass., and educated at Williams College and Berkshire Medical College. He practiced medicine briefly before returning to Williams, where he served as professor of moral philosophy and rhetoric (1830–87) and as college president (1836–72). Hopkins was one of the most influential American educators of his time, especially noted for his ability to encourage individual development and self-realization in his students. A Congregationalist minister as well, ordained (1836), although he never attended a theology school, Hopkins won further renown as a theological and philosophical lecturer; most of his published works were based on his lectures. Hopkins is represented in the Hall of Fame for Great Americans (q.v.).

HOPKINS, Samuel (1721–1803), American theologian, born in Waterbury, Conn., and educated at Yale College. He developed the theology of Jonathan Edwards (q.v.), of whom he was a disciple, into his own system, known as Hopkinsianism. This system sought to reconcile the occurrence of sin with the Calvinist dogma of predestination (q.v.); *see* CALVINISM. Hopkins, a Congregationalist minister, served in Great Barrington, Mass., from 1743 to 1769, when opposition both to his theological opinions and to the dullness of his sermons resulted in his removal. He spent the remainder of his life in Newport, R.I., then a center of the American slave trade, where he courageously denounced slavery, one of the first clergymen to do so.

HOPKINS, Stephen (1707–85), American colonial statesman and jurist, born in Providence, R.I. In 1732 he was elected to the first of twenty-five terms in the Rhode Island general assembly, serving as speaker for seven terms. He was chief justice of the colonial superior court from 1751 to 1754 and again in 1773, and between 1755 and 1767 he served nine terms as colonial governor. Hopkins was a delegate to the Albany Convention (q.v.) in 1754. He also was a member of the Continental Congress from 1774 to 1780 and a signer of the Declaration of Independence (q.v.).

HOPKINSON, Francis (1737–91), American composer, author, and politician, born in Philadelphia, Pa., and educated at the College of Philadelphia (now the University of Pennsylvania). He was the composer of the song "My Days Have Been So Wondrous Free", the first piece of secular music produced in America, and of *The Temple of Minerva*, considered the first American opera. He was also an accomplished harpsichord player.

A lawyer by profession, Hopkinson was active politically. He signed the Declaration of Independence, was a member of the Convention that framed the United States Constitution, and helped to design the first official American flag;

453

HOPKINSVILLE

see FLAG OF THE UNITED STATES. He held various posts in the newly established U.S. government, and from 1779 to 1789 was a judge of admiralty for Pennsylvania. Hopkinson wrote a number of brilliant political satires attacking the British, such as the *Letter Written by a Foreigner on the Character of the English Nation* (1777) and *The Battle of the Kegs* (verse, 1778).

HOPKINSVILLE, city in Kentucky and county seat of Christian Co., 50 miles S.W. of Bowling Green. The city is a leading tobacco and livestock market. Manufactures include lumber, electrical, and dairy products, bricks, shoes, clothing, and textiles. Nearby are the Jefferson Davis Monument State Shrine, containing the birthplace of the Confederate president, and Fort Campbell, a large military base. Hopkinsville was incorporated in 1804. Pop. (1960) 19,465; (1970) 21,250.

HOPPE, William F. (1887–1959), American billiardist, born in Cornwall-on-Hudson, N.Y. Hoppe was regarded by many as the greatest billiard player of all time. Hoppe won the first of fifty-one world billiards titles in 1906 with a victory in 18.1 balkline play. A year later he won the 18.2 balkline title, and he held these two championships intermittently for the next twenty years. He was also world champion of 14.1 balkline (1914), cushion caroms (1933), and 71.2 balkline (1938). However, he was most famous for the twelve three-cushion titles he won between 1936 and 1952 when he retired from tournament play as undefeated champion. Hoppe set many world records, including thirty-three successive victories in 1936, and high grand average score per inning (1.33) in 1950. See BILLIARDS.

HOPPER, DeWolf, in full WILLIAM DEWOLF HOPPER (1858–1935), American actor and singer, born in New York City. He made his debut in 1879, and during the next twenty years he firmly established his reputation as a musi-

"Early Sunday Morning" (1930) by Edward Hopper
Whitney Museum of American Art

cal-comedy star. He was associated with the famous comedy team of Weber and Fields (*see* WEBER, JOSEPH M.), and in 1911 he sang Dick Deadeye in *H.M.S. Pinafore,* the first of twelve Gilbert and Sullivan roles he mastered. Hopper was perhaps most famous for his presentations of the poem *Casey at the Bat,* by Ernest Lawrence Thayer (1863–1940), which he first recited in 1888.

HOPPER, Edward (1882–1967), American painter and etcher, born in Nyack, N.Y. He studied art at the Chase School in New York City. Between 1915 and 1924 he devoted himself to etching and achieved some renown; later, however, he gained wider recognition as a painter. His first one-man show was held at the Museum of Modern Art in New York City in 1933. In 1956 he was elected a member of the American Academy of Arts and Letters.

Hopper is well-known for his paintings of quiet city and small town scenes. By the use of sunlight he gave a homely warmth to commonplace subjects, such as old houses, suburban streets, and seedy hotel rooms. His better-known paintings include "Corner Saloon" (1913), "House by the Railroad" (1925), and "Early Sunday Morning" (1930).

HOPPNER, John (1758–1810), British painter, born in Whitechapel (now part of London). He studied art under the patronage of George III (q.v.), King of Great Britain, and began exhibiting at the Royal Academy in 1778. In 1780 he won the academy's gold medal for his painting, "King Lear". He was appointed portrait painter to the prince of Wales, later, King George IV (q.v.), in 1789 and was elected full academician in 1795.

Hoppner was greatly influenced in his style by the paintings of the British portrait artist Sir Joshua Reynolds (q.v.). To Reynolds' dignified realism Hoppner added boldness of execution, a graceful style, and brilliant tones and colors. Subjects of his principal portraits include the young George IV, Frederick Augustus, Duke of York and Albany, and Arthur Wellesley, 1st Duke of Wellington. His works are exhibited in the National Gallery, Hampton Court, and Saint James's Palace in London. The Metropolitan Museum of Art in New York City owns, among others of his paintings, "Mrs. Baihe", a portrait of the only daughter of Benjamin Franklin (q.v.), the American patriot and scientist.

HORACE, in full QUINTUS HORATIUS FLACCUS (65–8 B.C.), Roman lyric poet and satirist, son of a freedman, born in Venusia (now Venosa, Italy), and educated in Rome and subsequently in Athens, where he studied Greek philosophy and poetry. Soon after the assassination of the Roman general and statesman Gaius Julius Caesar (q.v.) in 44 B.C., he was recruited into the republican army by Marcus Junius Brutus (q.v.), one of the assassins. He was made a military tribune and fought at Philippi (q.v.) in 42 B.C. where the republican army was routed by Mark Antony (see ANTONIUS, MARCUS) and Octavian (see AUGUSTUS). Under the terms of a general amnesty, Horace returned to Rome where he received a government job and began to write poetry.

His verse attracted Vergil (q.v.), then poet laureate, who, about 38 B.C. introduced Horace to the statesman Gaius Cilnius Maecenas (q.v.), a patron of the arts and a friend of Octavian. Maecenas brought Horace into the Roman literary and political circles, and about 33 B.C., he gave Horace an estate in the Sabine Hills where the poet often retired for reflection and writing.
Works of Horace. One of the great Roman poets, Horace's works fall into four categories: satires, epodes, odes, and epistles. Book I of the *Satires* (35 B.C.) and Book II (30 B.C.), both collections of dialogues in hexameter, were an imitation of the Latin satirist Gaius Lucilius (q.v.). The ten satires in Book I and the eight in Book II were tempered by tolerance. The *Epodes*, also issued in 30 B.C., were apparently written earlier for they are an impassioned plea for an end to the civil discord, an end that came with Octavian's victory over Antony at Actium (see ACTIUM, BATTLE OF) in 31 B.C. The seventeen short iambic-couplet poems in the *Epodes* were ad-

Horace

aptations of the Greek lyric style created by the poet Archilochus (q.v.). Horace's chief poetical works were the *Odes*, Books I, II, and III (23 B.C.), adapted from and many directly in imitation of the poets Anacreon, Alcaeus, and Sappho (qq.v.). In the eighty-eight selections of the *Odes*, Horace praises peace, patriotism, love, friendship, country pleasures, and simplicity. Famous for their rhythm, irony, and cultivated urbanity, the *Odes* were often imitated by 18th- and 19th-century English poets; see ENGLISH LITERATURE; ODE.

About 20 B.C., Horace published *Epistles*, Book I, twenty short personal letters in hexameter, giving his observations on society, literature, and philosophy. He is the philosopher of the golden mean, seeking Epicurean (see EPICURUS; EPICUREANISM) pleasures, but always advocating moderation, even in the pursuit of virtue. By this time his reputation was so high that upon the death of Vergil in 19 B.C., Horace succeeded his friend as poet laureate. Two years later he returned to lyric poetry when Augustus commissioned him to write the hymn *Carmen Saeculare* for the secular games in Rome. The dates of Horace's last works, the *Epistles,* Book II, the *Odes,* Book IV, and the *Epistle to the Pisos,* better known as the *Ars Poetica,* are uncertain. The two letters that appear in Book II are both discussions of literary development. *Ars Poetica,* his longest single work, extolled the Greek masters, explained the difficulty and the seriousness of the poetic art, and gave technical advice to would-be poets.

See LATIN LITERATURE: *The Golden Age: The Augustine Period.*

HOREB. See SINAI.

HOREHOUND, or HOARHOUND, common name of *Marrubium vulgare,* a plant belonging to the Mint (q.v.) family Labiatae. Horehound is also the name of an extract made from the dried leaves and flowers of the plant, used in treating coughs and colds. The plant is native to Eurasia and is naturalized in waste places of the N.E. United States. It is an herbaceous perennial growing to a height of about 1 ft. and bearing grayish-white, pubescent (hoary) leaves. The small white flowers, borne in whorled clusters, have a ten-veined, tubular calyx, an asymmetrical corolla, four stamens, and a pistil. The fruit is a nutlet. The leaf surfaces are dotted with small glands that contain an aromatic essential oil. The leaves also contain lignin, tannin (*see* TANNINS), and resins (q.v.). Horehound is used in medicine as a syrup tonic.

Several other mints are commonly called horehound. The black or fetid horehound, *Ballota nigra,* is similar in appearance to *M. vulgare,* but has purple flowers and a foul odor. It is native to Europe and naturalized in the N.E. U.S. The bugleweeds, belonging to the genus *Lycopus,* are sometimes called water horehound.

HORIZON. See ALTITUDE.

HORMONES, substances in animals and in plants which regulate bodily processes such as growth, metabolism, reproduction, and the functioning of various organs. In animals, hormones are secreted directly into the bloodstream by ductless or endocrine glands; *see* ENDOCRINE SYSTEM. A state of dynamic equilibrium is maintained among the various hormones, which are catalytic in action (*see* CATALYSIS), producing their effect in minute concentrations. Their distribution through the bloodstream results in a response which, although slower than that of a nervous reaction, is often maintained over a longer period of time.

Hormones in Animals. The principal organs involved in the production of hormones are the pituitary gland; the thyroid gland; the parathyroids; the adrenal, or suprarenal, bodies; the pancreas (q.v.); the gonads, or male and female reproductive glands; the placenta; and, under certain conditions, the mucous membrane of the small intestine.

The pituitary gland is made up of three parts: the anterior lobe, the intermediate lobe, which is generally thought to be nonfunctional, and the posterior lobe. The anterior lobe is considered the master gland of the endocrine system. It controls the growth of the skeleton, regulates the function of the thyroid, affects the action of the gonads and the adrenals, and produces substances that interact with those excreted by the pancreas, and it may influence the parathyroids. It also secretes the hormone prolactin except when inhibited by the progesterone secreted by the placenta (see below); prolactin stimulates the formation of milk in mature mammary glands. The anterior lobe also secretes the hormone intermedin, which stimulates the functioning of pigment cells. Hormones produced or stored in the posterior lobe increase blood pressure, prevent excessive secretion of urine (pressor-antidiuretic factor), and stimulate contraction in uterine muscle (oxytocic factor). Several of the pituitary hormones are opposed in effect to other hormones, as, for example, the diabetogenic effect that inhibits the performance of insulin. *See* ACTH; PITUITARY GLAND.

The hormone of the thyroid gland (q.v.; *see also* THYROXINE) stimulates general metabolism; it also increases the sensitivity of various organs, especially the central nervous system (q.v.), and has a pronounced effect on the rate of metamorphosis, that is, the change from infantile to adult form. The secretion of the thyroid hormone is controlled primarily by the anterior lobe of the pituitary, but is also affected by the hormones of the ovaries and, in turn, affects the development and function of the ovaries.

The hormone of the parathyroid glands (q.v.) controls the concentration of calcium and phosphate in the blood.

The pancreas secretes at least two hormones, insulin (q.v.) and glucagon, which regulate metabolism of carbohydrates in the body. Insulin, which is a protein (q.v.), was synthesized by American scientists in 1965, and glucagon was synthesized in 1968 by German researchers.

The adrenal glands are divided into two parts, an outer cortex and an inner medulla. Extracts of the cortex contain hormones that control the concentrations of salts and water in the body

HORMONES

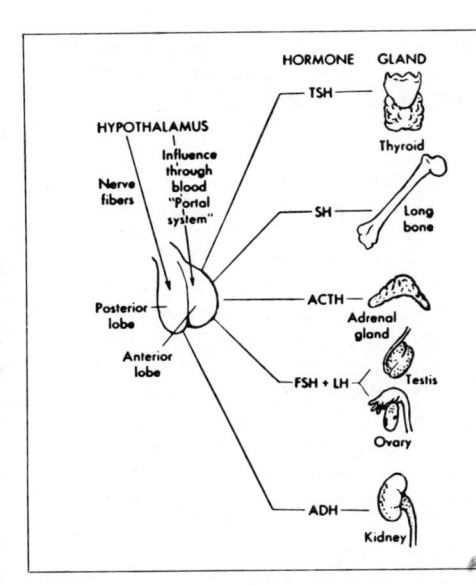

FUNCTIONS

TSH (thyroid-stimulating hormone), or thyrotropic hormone, influences structure and secretory activity of the thyroid. The thyroid controls metabolic rate.

SH (somatotropic hormone), or growth hormone (GH), influences growth of bones, muscles, and viscera. In some way it is related to protein metabolism.

ACTH (adrenocorticotropic hormone), the adrenal cortex controls Na^+, Cl^-, K^+ reabsorption in the kidney. Regulates carbohydrate, protein, and fat metabolism. The adrenal medulla functions in relation to stress reactions.

FSH (follicle-stimulating hormone) is concerned with the ripening of follicles in the female ovary, and activity of the seminiferous tubules in the male. LH (luteinizing hormone) influences secreting cells of the ovaries and testes and maintains their normal activity. Lactogenic hormone maintains secretion of corpus luteum and initiates lactation.

ADH (antidiuretic hormone), or antidiureticpressor hormone, controls water reabsorption in the kidney tubules and in this way helps to regulate the secretion of urine and the water balance of body fluids.

Diagram showing some of the body functions of the hormones secreted by the pituitary body, the small, bean-shaped master endocrine gland situated close to the hypothalamus at the base of the brain.

Macmillan Co.

fluids and are essential for the maintenance of life in an individual; see CORTISONE. The cortical hormones are also necessary for the formation of sugar from proteins and its storage in the liver, and for maintenance of resistance to physical, emotional, and toxic stresses. The cortex also secretes hormones that affect secondary sexual characteristics. The medulla, which is functionally and embryologically independent of the cortex, produces adrenaline (q.v.), or epinephrine, which increases blood sugar and acts to stimulate the circulatory system and the sympathetic nervous system (see AUTONOMIC NERVOUS SYSTEM) and the related hormone noradrenaline. See ADRENAL GLAND.

The gonads, under the influence of the anterior lobe of the pituitary, produce hormones controlling sexual development and the various processes of reproduction. The hormones of the testes control the development of the secondary sexual characteristics of the male; see ANDROGEN; TESTOSTERONE. The hormones of the ovaries are produced primarily in the ovarian follicles. These hormones, called estrogens (see ESTROGEN), are produced by the granulosa cells, and include estradiol, the most important, and estrone, which is related chemically to estradiol and is similar in action but much less potent. Estrogenic hormones interact with those of the anterior lobe of the pituitary to control the cycle of ovulation. During this cycle the corpus luteum is produced, which in turn secretes progesterone (q.v.), and thus controls the cycle of menstruation (q.v.). Progesterone is also formed in large amounts by the placenta during gestation; together with the estrogens, it causes development of the mammary glands and, at the same time, instructs the hypothalamus to inhibit the secretion of prolactin by the pituitary. Various progesterone-like hormones are now used as oral contraceptives to inhibit ovulation and conception. The placenta also secretes a hormone, similar to one produced by the pituitary and called chorionic gonadotropin, which inhibits ovulation. This hormone is present in the blood in substantial quantities and is excreted readily by the kidneys; it is the basis of such tests for pregnancy as the Aschheim-Zondek test (q.v.). *See also* EMBRYOLOGY: *Nutrition and Respiration.*

A special group of hormones is secreted by the mucous membrane of the small intestines at a certain stage of digestion (q.v.). They act to coordinate digestive activities, controlling the motility of the pylorus, duodenum, gall bladder (q.v.), and bile duct. They also stimulate formation of the digestive juices of the small intestines, of liver bile, and of the internal and external secretion of the pancreas. The hormone gastrin is produced by one part of the lining of the stomach and is released into the blood by nerve impulses that are initiated by tasting food or by the presence of food in the stomach. In the stomach, gastrin stimulates the secretion of pepsin, a protein-splitting enzyme, and hydrochloric acid, and stimulates contractions of the stomach wall. Gastrin stimulates secretion of digestive enzymes and insulin by the pancreas, and secretion of bile by the liver.

Deficiency or excess of any one of the hormones upsets the chemical equilibrium that is essential to health, normal growth, and, in extreme cases, to life. The method of treating diseases arising from endocrine disturbances is called organotherapy; it involves the use of preparations of animal organs and synthetic products, and has achieved marked, and at times spectacular, success. See separate articles on such diseases as ADDISON'S DISEASE; CRETINISM; DIABETES MELLITUS; GIGANTISM; GOITER; MYXEDEMA.

In 1967 Dr. Susan Leeman of Brandeis University isolated in cattle a new hormone, sialogen, which stimulates the salivary glands to produce saliva. It is secreted by the hypothalamus at the base of the brain (q.v.). Early in 1971, a team of research scientists at the University of California Medical Center, San Francisco, led by the Chinese-born American biochemist and endocrinologist, Choh Hao Li (1913–   ) announced the successful synthesis of the growth hormone GH. The hormone is responsible in early life for promoting growth, and after adolescence, the continued development and enlargement of all body tissues, and the growth in number and size of body cells.

Hormones in Plants. Plant hormones have been found to play an important part in the physiology of plants. These hormones often possess a chemical structure related to that of animal hormones of similar function; for example, the estrogenic hormones of animals strongly stimulate the flower and seed production of certain plants. A plant hormone that was isolated in the blossoming stage of development was found to prevent plant distortion by inhibiting tumorlike growths. The effect of this hormone on animal tumors has been investigated in cancer research. Plant and insect hormones have been used to control the growth of weeds and of insect pests.

Spraying with certain plant hormones causes weeds to mature just before a cold season, and cold temperatures then kill the weeds. Insect hormones used as pesticides interfere with the metamorphosis of insects so that they do not mature and reproduce.

W.M.S. & P.K.B.

HORN, term applied to one of the hard protuberances, as well as to the modified epidermal tissue or bone (q.v.) of which they are made, that grows from the foreheads or snouts of various ungulate mammals, such as rhinoceroses, deer, giraffes, goats, and cattle. They are generally curved and pointed and serve chiefly as weapons of defense or attack for animals, some of which have both sexes horned. Horns all have in common an essential substance called keratin, a fibrous, generally translucent protein produced in the outer layer of skin; keratin is also a component of beaks, hair, nails, hooves, scales, shells, claws, and feathers.

Horns vary in structure. The horns or antlers of deer, for example, are solid bone. Those of giraffes are also of bone but are covered by skin. The massive single horn of the rhinoceros is a hollow cone of compacted, hairlike structures affixed to underlying bones. The pronghorn of the western United States has a permanent horny core covered by a sheath of horn that is annually shed. Formerly, before the introduction of plastics (q.v.), horn was widely used in making ornamental articles and musical instruments. The term horns is sometimes applied also to analogous appendages in many insects.

See also IVORY.

HORN, usually called FRENCH HORN, musical instrument of the brass group, composed of a slender conical tube, 7 to 18 ft. long, that is coiled in from one to three circles and expands into a widely flared bell. It is played with a small, funnel-shaped mouthpiece, which accounts for its soft, mellow tone.

The horn was developed from the simple, crescent-shaped hunting horn used in France in the late 17th century. This instrument had only one tone and twelve harmonics (q.v.). Greater flexibility was given to the horn about 1750 when the technique of "stopping", using the hand as a mute, was invented. Stopping enabled the musician to bridge gaps in the natural harmonic series; the pitch of the natural open tones could be raised sometimes by a semitone or a tone. Despite this advance, cumbersome crooks and added tubing were necessary for playing in all keys. Only with the invention of valves in the early 19th century did the horn become a fully chromatic instrument. Valves completely revolutionized the horn, because by using them singly or in combination the range of the horn is altered and fresh harmonic series become available. Horns with two or three valves can produce a chromatic scale in three or more octaves.

Most 18th-century orchestras included only one horn, but today two, three, or even four pairs of horns are common. Most compositions were written for horns in the key of F, with a range of about three octaves. The double horn (F and B♭), however, invented at the beginning on the 20th century, is rapidly superseding the single F horn. The double horn has four valves, is shorter and less prone to cracked notes.

HORNBEAM, common name of trees in the genera *Carpinus* and *Ostrya*, belonging to the family Corylacae. Plants of both genera are sometimes called ironwoods. The American hornbeam *C. caroliniana*, also called blue beech or water beech, is a small tree having very hard wood, smooth, gray bark, and birch-like leaves. It bears staminate and pistillate flowers on separate hanging catkins. The fruits are nuts. American hornbeam is native to wet woodlands in the eastern United States. The common hornbeam, *C. betulus*, is a similar plant native to temperate regions of Eurasia. The American hop hornbeam, or leverwood, *O. virginiana*, usually grows in dry soils and has flaky, brown bark, but is similar in other respects to *Carpinus*.

HORNBILL, common name of any large songless bird in the suborder Bucerotes, characterized by a long shell-like, horny bill surmounted by a hollow, brightly colored, horny projection or casque. Hornbills are found in the jungle areas of Africa and southern Asia.

Hornbills are 2 to 5 ft. in length, and are usually black and white in color. They feed on fruit and small animals. The hornbills are noted for their peculiar nesting habits; the female nests in a hollow tree, the opening of which the male plasters over with clay mixed with salivary secretions, leaving only a small opening. While the eggs are being hatched, the male hornbill feeds the female through the opening.

Most hornbills are fruit eaters, except for the African ground hornbill, comprising the family Bucorvus, which is partly terrestrial in its habits, feeding on mice and insects. The largest hornbill, the Asian rhinoceros hornbill, *Buceros rhinoceros*, is well known for its casque, which is turned upward at the anterior end, and looks somewhat like the horn of a rhinoceros. The bird is about 5 ft. long. Another common Asian species is the calao or rufous hornbill, *B. hydrocorax*.

HORNBLENDE (Ger. *horn*, "horn"; *blende*, "dazzling"), silicate, translucent to opaque mineral, typically of general formula $Ca_2Na(Mg,Fe)_4(Al,Fe,Ti)_3Si_6O_{22}(O,OH)_2$, found in metamorphic, igneous, and volcanic rocks; see GEOLOGY: *Petrology*; IGNEOUS ROCKS. Containing considerable iron, aluminum, and some sodium, it has a hardness (q.v.) of 5 to 6 and a sp.gr. of 2.9 to 3.4. Hornblende belongs to the group of minerals known as amphiboles, and is most commonly found in schists (*see* SCHIST) in the form of long, vitreous or silklike prismatic needles dark green, brown, or black in color. It is found in Massachusetts, New Hampshire, and New York, and in Italy, Czechoslovakia, Norway, and Sweden. *See also* TREMOLITE.

HORN, CAPE. *See* CAPE HORN.

Hornbills, of the family Bucerotidae. UPI

HORNED LIZARD

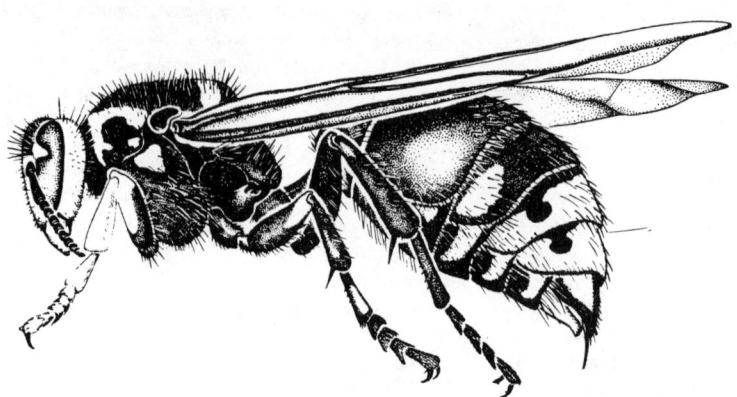

The white-faced wasp, Vespula maculata, is generally known as a hornet.

HORNED LIZARD or **HORNED TOAD,** common name for any short-legged, short-tailed, North American lizard in the genus *Phrynosoma* of the Iguana family, characterized by large spines on the crown and temples, and stiff, erectile, smaller spines along the back. The wide, flattened body is about 3 to 5 in. long, depending on the species. The measurement includes the head but not the tail. Horned lizards inhabit the dry, hot desert regions of w. United States and Mexico. See LIZARD.

HORNELL, city of New York, in Steuben Co., on the Canisteo R., in the Allegheny Mts., about 47 miles N.W. of Elmira. Manufactures include textiles and furniture. West of the city is Stony Brook State Park. Alfred University (1836), well known for its college of ceramics and the Davis Memorial Carillon, containing many bells dating from the 17th and 18th centuries, is nearby. Originally known as Upper Canisteo, the city, which received its present name in 1906, established itself as a railroad-equipment center in the mid-19th century. Pop. (1960) 13,907; (1970) 12,144.

HORNET, name generally applied to any social wasp in the family Vespidae, characterized by a powerful sting and by a large nest constructed of paper that the insects manufacture from partially digested fibers of growing plants. Technically the name hornet is restricted to *Vespa crabro,* a native of Europe, which first appeared in the eastern United States about 1850. This hornet attains a length of more than an inch and is reddish brown streaked with clay yellow. Its nest, which is made of brown paper, is built in the hollows of trees, in crevices in rocks, or in artificial sheltered places, such as between the beams and roof of a barn. It feeds on insects and their larvae and on ripe fruit.

Several wasps in the genus *Vespula* are commonly called hornets. The bald-faced or white-faced wasp, *V. maculata,* widely distributed throughout the U.S., is about 1¼ in. long and is black with white markings on most of its segments and on its face. Its nest, made of gray paper, is large, often more than a foot long, and is usually suspended from a limb of a tree. Yellow jackets, *V. diabolica,* are so called because their bodies are marked with large areas of yellow. Unlike the bald-faced wasp the yellow jackets construct their nests close to or under the ground. A single yellow jacket nest may contain up to 15,000 individuals (*see* INSECT: *Social Insects*). In several species, such as *V. austriaca* and *V. adulterina,* no workers are produced and the female lays its eggs in the nests of other wasps, where the young are fed by so-called foster workers.

HORNEY, Karen (1885–1952), German-American psychiatrist, born Karen Danielson in Hamburg, and educated at the universities of Freiburg and Berlin. She was an instructor at the Institute for Psychoanalysis in Berlin from 1920 to 1932, when she emigrated to the United States. After serving as associate director of the Chicago Institute for Psychoanalysis for two years, she taught at the New York Psychoanalytic Institute from 1934 to 1941. She was appointed dean of the American Institute for Psychoanalysis, which she helped to found, in 1941 and a professor at New York Medical College in 1942.

Horney founded a neo-Freudian school of psychoanalysis based on the conclusion that neuroses are the result of emotional conflicts arising from childhood experiences and later disturbances in interpersonal relationships; see FREUD, SIGMUND. Horney believed that such disturbances are conditioned to a large extent by the society in which an individual lives rather than solely by the instinctual drives postulated by Freud. Among her writings are *The Neurotic*

Personality of Our Time (1936), *New Ways in Psychoanalysis* (1939), *Self-Analysis* (1942), *Our Inner Conflicts* (1945), and *Neurosis and Human Growth* (1950). See PSYCHOANALYSIS: *Psychoanalytic Schools.*

HORN OF PLENTY or **CORNUCOPIA**, in Greek mythology, a horn that supplies anything desired by its owner. In one myth the god Zeus (q.v.), after being raised on the milk of a goat, gave one of the goat's horns to his nurse Amalthaea, telling her that it would provide whatever she wished. In another story the god Hercules (q.v.), during a struggle with the river-god Achelous, captured the horn when Achelous assumed the form of a bull. Often depicted as overflowing with fruits and flowers, the horn of plenty symbolizes abundance.

HORNSBY, Rogers (1896–1963), American professional baseball player, born in Winters, Texas. He began playing professional baseball at the age of eighteen, and in 1915 became second baseman for the Saint Louis Cardinals of the National League. Subsequently he played with the New York Giants, the Boston Braves, and the Chicago Cubs of the National League and the Saint Louis Browns of the American League. As manager of the Cardinals, he guided them to the world championship in 1926. Hornsby is considered one of the greatest right-handed batters baseball has ever known. In his nineteen years in the National League he led the league in batting seven times; he established a modern batting record in 1929 with an average of .424 for the season; and was elected most valuable player in 1925 and 1929. On his retirement from the major leagues, Hornsby had an overall batting average of .358. He was elected to the Baseball Hall of Fame in 1942; see BASEBALL HALL OF FAME AND MUSEUM, NATIONAL.

HORNTAIL, or WOOD WASP, common name for any hymenopterous insect in the family Siricidae, closely related to the sawfly (q.v.). The horntail differs from the sawfly chiefly in having a strong, drilling ovipositor (egg-laying organ) rather than a sawing ovipositor. The insect derives its name from the shape of the ovipositor, which it uses to deposit its eggs in the bark of trees. The larvae are wood borers, living within the tree for as long as two years before they pupate and emerge, leaving a hole about ¼ in. in diameter in the timber. Thus emerging, they often damage stored timber in lumberyards and even injure furniture that has been newly constructed of green wood. The adults are much larger than sawflies; a common species, the pigeon horntail, *Tremex columba,* averages 2¼ in. in length and has a wing span of about 2¼ in.

HOROSCOPE, illustration of the position of the sun, moon, and planets from a given latitude and longitude on earth at a given moment, usually that of birth. The construction of the horoscope is based on the Ptolemaic system (q.v.) in which the earth is stationary and the heavenly bodies move around it in fixed patterns. Astrologers have divided the heavens into twelve sections, each thought to be ruled by a different sign of the zodiac (q.v.) belt through which the sun, moon, and planets move in twelve fixed positions called houses. Once the particular sign and houses have been established, the mythological characteristics of the heavenly bodies, modified by the geometrical relationship between them, are used to foretell events in the life of the individual for whom the horoscope has been drawn. See ASTROLOGY.

HOROWITZ, Vladimir (1904–), Russian-American concert pianist, born in Kiev. He received his musical education at the Kiev Con-

Vladimir Horowitz
UPI

Colts of the domestic horse, Equus caballus.
Standard Oil Co. (N.J.)

servatory, at which he studied under Russian pianist and composer, Felix Blumenfeld (1863–1931). At the age of twenty Horowitz began a series of concert tours of Europe and soon became known as a virtuoso of the highest rank. In 1928 he made his American debut with the New York Philharmonic orchestra, and later made several tours of the United States as well as Europe. Horowitz retired prematurely from the concert stage, because of illness, in the 1950's, and thereafter performed only on rare occasions. One of the foremost virtuosos of all time, Horowitz is particularly notable for his technical brilliance and for his interpretation of Romantic and modern music.

HORSE, mammal of the genus *Equus,* belonging to the family Equidae. The genus contains the domestic horse, *E. caballus,* and three groups of species living in the wild state. One group comprises the zebras, native to Africa; another consists of the asses, including the kiang and onager of Asia and the wild ass of Africa; *see* Ass; Zebra. The third group contains Przhevalski's horse, *E. przhevalskii,* now native to western Mongolia only, but formerly found over a much wider range. The only extant true wild horse, it crosses with the domestic horse and produces fertile progeny. Przhevalski's horse, while not a direct ancestor of *E. caballus,* is believed to be the survivor of a species that contributed to the origin of the domestic horse. Other so-called wild horses in various parts of the world are descendants of domestic horses that have reverted to the wild state.

PREHISTORIC HORSES

The evolution of the horse can be traced through fossil remains to *Eohippus,* a small leaf-browsing mammal of the Eocene Epoch; *see* Geology, Historical. *Eohippus* was about the size of a fox, and had four toes on its forefeet and three on its hind feet. Several species and related genera of *Eohippus* appeared in North America and the Old World during the Eocene; then apparently, the Old World species died out, but the American species gave rise, in the Oligocene Epoch, to the genus *Mesohippus.*

In the Miocene Epoch *Mesohippus* was succeeded by *Hypohippus* and *Anchitherium,* both of which are thought to have colonized the Old World from North America. Other descendants of *Mesohippus* were *Miohippus* and *Merychippus;* the latter genus was the first of the family to have high-crowned teeth, permitting it to feed by grazing on grass rather than by browsing on leaves.

Among the descendants of *Merychippus* in the Pliocene Epoch were *Hipparion,* which apparently spread from North America to the Old World, and *Pliohippus,* which appears to be the progenitor of the genus *Equus,* comprising the modern horses, asses, and zebras.

In each of these developmental stages the animal showed an increase in general size and a reduction in the size of the supplementary toes present in *Eohippus; see* EVOLUTION: *Paleontology.*

During the Pleistocene Epoch the genus *Equus* apparently spread from North America to Eurasia, Africa, and South America. Subsequently the native American horses died out, possibly as the result of an epizootic disease.

Cave dwellings in Europe indicate that horses were plentiful on that continent during the early Stone Age. Dismembered skeletons of horses have been found in and near such dwellings in sufficient number to show that horses were frequently killed and eaten. In Neolithic times, when Europe was largely forested, the number of horses evidently declined. Remains of the Bronze Age include bits and other pieces of harness and clearly demonstrate that horses had become domestic animals in this period.

MODERN HORSES

Mature male horses are called stallions and mature female horses mares. Newborn horses are known as foals, and horses and mares under the age of four are often called colts and fillies, respectively. Most male horses which are not to be used for breeding purposes are castrated or gelded and are then called geldings. Small horses are often called ponies, but properly speaking this term is limited to a few specific diminutive breeds.

Anatomy. The most marked anatomical characteristic of the modern horse is the possession of only a single digit or toe on each of its four feet. This toe, which corresponds to the middle digit of the human hand, is much enlarged and is protected by a horny hoof that surrounds the front and sides of the toe. Vestigial splints corresponding to the second and fourth digits are situated on either side of the foot above the hoof. Fossils of some prehistoric horselike animals had four toes on their forefeet and three toes, with vestigial remains of two more, on their hind feet.

The skull of the horse is long, and the facial bones are twice the length of the cranium. The mandible, or lower jaw, is long and has a broad, flat plate at its lower hind end. The spine is composed of seven cervical, eighteen dorsal, six lumbar, five sacral, and fifteen caudal vertebrae. Horses have forty-four teeth: three incisors, one canine, four premolars, and three molars on each side of each jaw. The incisors, which are used for cropping grass and other herbage, grow in the form of a semicircle. A pronounced gap or diastema exists between the canine teeth and the premolars in which the metal bit used for controlling the horse is placed when the animal is ridden or driven; *see* HORSEMANSHIP. All the teeth have long crowns and comparatively short roots.

The horse, unlike most herbivores, is not a ruminant. It has a simple rather than a complex stomach, and fermentation of fibrous food takes place in a blind pocket or cecum, analogous to the appendix in man, located at the juncture of the small and large intestines. In a large horse the cecum may have a capacity of about 10 gal.

Reproduction. Both male and female horses are sexually mature by the age of two. They are seldom used for breeding purposes, however, before they are three years old. The gestation period is about eleven months, and single births are the rule among horses. Twins are a genuine rarity and only a few births of three or more foals have ever been recorded; *see* REPRODUCTION.

History. Domestic horses were introduced into Babylonia in about 2000 B.C. and into Egypt approximately 300 years later. The animals were brought into Egypt by the Hyksos (q.v.) from northeastern Syria. These Egyptian and Babylonian horses were the forerunners of the swift Arab breeds of the Middle East and northern Africa. Another strain of horses appears to have been domesticated in Europe. Heavily built and slower but more powerful than the Arabians, they are regarded as the early ancestors of the modern draft horses used for plowing and other heavy work. Some authorities also believe that a third ancestral strain found in the British Isles was the prototype of the various breeds of modern ponies.

Throughout most of Europe, from early in the Christian era to about the 17th century, the powerful native horses were used for military mounts, for hauling heavy loads, and as pack animals. During the same period the Arabic world had developed its smaller, fast-galloping breeds, which were introduced into Spain after the Muslim conquest in the 8th century. The horses bred in Spain became famed for their speed and endurance, and many were imported into England and Europe as early as the 12th century. Systematic attempts to improve extant breeds of horses, however, did not take place until the end of the 17th century, when Arab stallions were imported to England and France to breed with mares of native stock.

The first domestic horses introduced into America were of the Arab type, brought by the Spanish conquistadors in the 16th century. Both Hernando Cortes, the Spanish conqueror of Mexico, and the Spanish explorer Hernando de

HORSE

Soto (qq.v.), who discovered the Mississippi R., are believed to have lost or abandoned some of their horses, and these may have been the source of herds of wild horses found in various parts of western North America. Horses left by the Spanish also ran wild on the pampas of South America around the Río de la Plata. The English settlers, especially the early Virginia colonists, imported a large number of horses, primarily for food. In 1646 less than 300 horses existed in all the English colonies of North America.

Types of Horses. In the last 300 years horse breeders have made continuous attempts to improve the various breeds of horses and to develop strains that are particularly suited for specialized tasks. The resultant new breeds include saddle and harness horses especially adapted for racing at the gallop and at a pace trot; hunters; carriage horses; draft horses for pulling heavy loads; polo ponies and cow ponies, small fast horses which can be trained to the complicated maneuvers of roping and the game of polo; and several types of saddle horses. Thoroughbreds are sometimes used as hunters and saddle horses, as are crosses between thoroughbreds and harness horses; see *Breeds* below. The important qualities of a hunter are endurance, fair speed, and the ability to walk, canter, trot, and gallop. Saddle horses are usually higher in the shoulder than draft horses and are commonly trained to use five gaits.

Bold Minstrel, American thoroughbred, clears a jump in an equestrian event. Wide World

HORSE

Gaits. Horses are capable of a variety of gaits. In order of speed the normal gaits are: walk, single-foot, canter, pace, trot, and gallop. The walk is a gait in which the feet are lifted and advanced in the following order: left fore, right hind, right fore, left hind. In an ordinary walk two of the horse's feet are on the ground at all times, and three feet for part of the time. When a horse is walking very slowly all four of his feet may be on the ground at the same time. A horse going at the single-foot lifts and places his feet right hind, right fore, left hind, left fore, and at no time has more than two feet on the ground at once. The canter, pace, trot, and gallop can best be understood by reference to the table below. The table shows which feet are on the ground during the successive stages of these gaits. In the table Lf represents the left fore, Rf the right fore, Lh the left hind, Rh the right hind, and O indicates no feet on the ground.

Canter. Rh, Rh Rf, Rh Rf Lh, Rf Lh, Rf Lh Lf, Lh Lf, Lf, O, Rh.
Pace. Rh, Rh Rf, O, Lh, Lh Lf, O. Rh.
Trot. Rf, Rf Lh, Lh, O, Lf, Lf Rh, Rh, O, Rf.
Gallop. Lh, Rh Lh, Rh, Rh Lf, Lf, Lf Rf, Rf, O, Lh.

Both the single-foot and the pace are sometimes referred to as a rack or amble, and the gallop, which for most horses is the fastest gait, is also sometimes called a run.

Breeds. The Arab or Arabian breed is often divided into three sub-breeds: Turks come from European Turkey and Asia Minor, Arabians from the regions between Damascus and the Euphrates R., and Barbs from the Barbary states of north Africa. Arabians in general are comparatively small horses, standing between 58 and 60 in. at the shoulder (14½ to 15 hands in the terms commonly used by horsemen). They have remarkable powers of endurance and are swift gallopers. All the saddle breeds are derived, in large part, from Arabian stock.

The Thoroughbred was developed in the early 18th century from offspring of three foundation sires, the Byerly Turk, the Darley Arabian, and the Godolphin Barb, and native English mares. It is used primarily for flat-track racing, hunting, and jumping. The American Standardbred, developed in the northeastern United States in colonial times, is a light harness type, and is most often used in trotting races. Biologically, saddle horses are more properly types than breeds, but, due to the popularity of various equestrian sports and activities, registry and breed associations have been established for such important

Newton Viceroy, *a champion stallion of the Clydesdale breed of draft horse.* Anheuser-Busch, Inc.

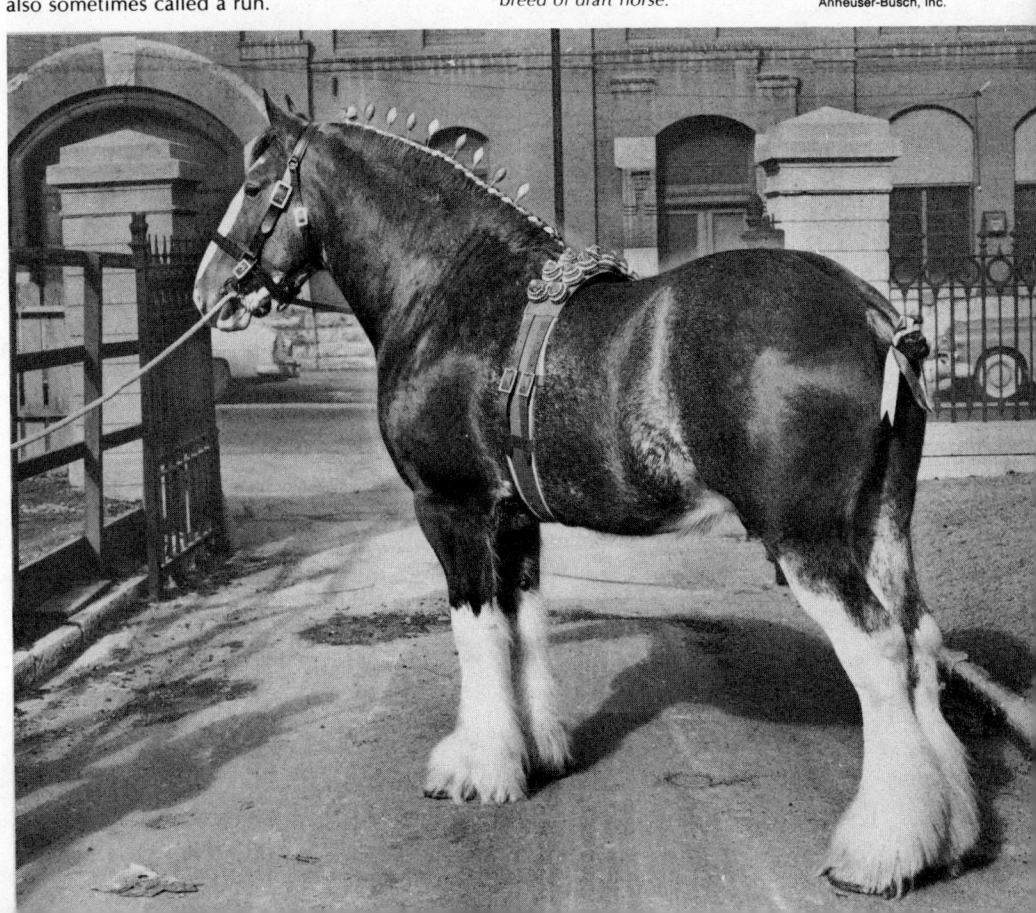

show and racing horses as the American Saddle Horse, the Tennessee Walking Horse, the Morgan, and the quarter horse. Saddle horses are long-legged, and therefore taller and much lighter in weight than draft horses.

The breeds of draft horses are more distinct than those of saddle horses. They include the Belgian, the Shire, the Clydesdale, and the Percheron. The Belgian is one of the largest of horses, reaching a shoulder height of 68 or more inches and weights of as much as 2500 lbs. The English Shire is about the same size and is distinguished by having long hair on its feet up to the fetlock and on the back of the hind legs up to the hock. These breeds represent refinements of the original native horses of their countries of origin. Clydesdales are smaller than either of the above breeds. This breed was founded in Scotland by crossing native horses with Belgian and Shire horses. The Percheron is also a smaller horse, standing about 66 in. at the shoulder. It is a native of the former district of Le Perche in northwestern France and was produced by crossing Arabian horses with the old Flemish breed of which the Belgian is the modern representative.

Several breeds of small horses commonly called ponies are native to Great Britain; among them are the Shetland, the Dales, the Welsh, the Dartmoor, and the New Forest. The smallest of the ponies is the Shetland, which is only about 42 in. in height at the shoulder.

Horses as Food. The flesh of horses closely resembles beef and is often regarded as being more delicate than beef in flavor. Horsemeat is eaten by human beings in most countries of the world where horses exist, but in some areas, such as the U.S. and Great Britain, a prejudice exists against this meat, and some religious groups such as the Jews forbid its use. In many parts of Asia a nourishing drink called kumiss is prepared by fermenting and sometimes distilling mare's milk.

See also HORSEMANSHIP; HORSE RACING.

HORSE BOT. See BOTFLY.

HORSE CHESTNUT. See BUCKEYE.

HORSEFLY, or GADFLY or BREEZE FLY, common name for any of more than 2000 species of brachycerous (having short antennae) flies constituting the family Tabanidae, which is worldwide in distribution. Many of the horseflies are large insects with broad heads, flattened bodies, and large, brilliantly colored, compound eyes. The females have short piercing and sucking mouthparts. They live on the blood of animals. Male horseflies, which do not bite, feed on the nectar of flowers. Female horseflies place their eggs on water plants in summertime. The larvae drop to the moist ground or into water after hatching and feed on small animal life, including insects. They hibernate during winter and spend the spring in the pupal stage. Adults emerge in June.

Many of the larger horseflies in North America belong to the genus *Tabanus,* and are often called greenheads because of their large, bright-green eyes. The small horseflies in the genus *Chrysops* are commonly called deerflies, strawberry flies, or ear flies. Some members of this genus transmit tularemia (q.v.), or deerfly fever, anthrax (q.v.), and other diseases to mammals, including man. See FLY.

HORSE GENTIAN. See FEVERROOT.

HORSEHAIR WORM. See HAIRWORM.

HORSE LATITUDES. See WIND: *The Prevailing Winds.*

HORSE MACKEREL. See TUNA.

HORSEMANSHIP or **EQUITATION,** art of maintaining precise control over a horse while mounted or while driving it from the seat of a vehicle. The term also implies knowledge of the care and feeding of the horse and an understanding of the varieties, uses, and handling of horse equipment, which is known as tack. A number of ancient writings on horsemanship are extant, notably the *High School of Horsemanship* (about 400 B.C.) in which the Greek historian and soldier Xenophon (q.v.) described the perfectly trained horse. Modern horsemanship was greatly influenced by the Spanish Riding School of Vienna, which was founded about 1572.

TACK

The items of equipment essential to effective horsemanship include the halter, bridle, saddle, and stirrups. Tack traditionally is put on the horse from the left, or so-called near side; the right side of the horse is called the off side.

The Halter. The halter is used to control the horse while on foot. It consists of straps around the head of the horse and a ring under the chin to which a lead or tying line may be snapped.

Bridle. The bridle is comprised of the bit, the headstall, and the reins. The bit is a metal bar, constructed in varying degrees of complexity, that fits into the mouth of the horse. The skilled rider exerts control over the horse by means of pressure on the bit. The headstall, to which the bit is attached, is an arrangement of leather straps that is secured about the nose, jaw, and head of the horse. The reins are leather lines attached to the bit on each side of the horse's mouth; they run along each side of the neck to the hands of the rider.

HORSEMANSHIP

Saddle. The saddle is a leather seat that fits over the horse's back, with flaps extending down the sides of the animal. It is held in place by a cinch or girth that encircles the belly of the horse and fastens under each flap. The part of the saddle occupied by the rider is called the seat, the front of which is the pommel and the rear the cantle. Suspended from each side of the saddle by means of adjustable straps are semicircular metal or wooden stirrups, which support the rider's feet.

Although types of saddles vary widely according to their purposes, they consist primarily of two styles: Western, or stock, and English. The English saddle is comparatively light and flat while the stock saddle is heavier with a higher cantle and pommel. The horn, projected from the pommel, serves as anchor for a lariat, which is used when working cattle.

BASIC EQUITATION

The fundamental skills of horsemanship include mounting and dismounting, employing one or more of the various riding styles, or "seats", and using the proper signals for controlling and directing the movements of the horse.

Mounting. Mounting a horse involves several separate acts that are executed in one continuous movement. The rider stands beside the left shoulder of his mount. He faces the horse's hindquarters or the saddle while holding the reins in his left hand, which rests on the horse's neck in front of the pommel. With his right hand he twists the near stirrup toward him, inserts his left foot in it, places his right hand on the cantle, and rises from the ground, transferring his weight to his left foot and both hands. He then removes his right hand from the cantle, swings his right leg up and across the horse's back, and settles lightly into the saddle.

Dismounting. To dismount, the rider again holds the reins in his left hand in front of the pommel. Disengaging his right foot from the stirrup, he swings it backward and across the horse's back, leans against the horse's left side, and transfers his weight to both hands. He then removes his left foot from the stirrup and slides to the ground.

Seat and Hands. The prime consideration with respect to the "seat" is the maintenance of the rider's balance with that of the horse. This is accomplished by the rider sitting directly above his mount's center of balance, which varies according to the function that is performed. A rider must be relaxed and calm in the saddle, as any tension or fear on his part is quickly transmitted to the horse.

Proper use of the hands is a vital factor in good horsemanship. Because any heavy-handedness may injure and eventually spoil the sensitivity of the horse's mouth, light but steady hands on the reins are of utmost importance.

The usual seat for pleasure riding is the forward seat, used on the English saddle. In the forward seat, the rider stays on the horse's back by a maintenance of balance, rather than by gripping the horse with his knees and clinging to the reins. He sits erect in the middle of the saddle with his shoulders back and with the small of his back arched slightly forward. The hands are held low in front of the saddle so that the reins and the rider's arms form straight lines from bit to elbow. One rein is held in each hand, and the horse is made to change direction by a light pulling of the rein on the side toward which the rider wishes it to turn. This procedure is called direct reining. The stirrup supports the foot at the ball, with the heel pressed slightly down, the knees bent, and the lower leg vertical. A properly adjusted stirrup is one that reaches the rider's ankle when the leg hangs freely from the saddle.

For pleasure riding on a Western saddle, the rider sits back against the higher cantle, extends his legs somewhat out from the horse and slightly forward, and places the stirrup at the ball of his foot with the heel pressed down. The stirrups are put at a longer adjustment than for the forward seat on the English saddle, so that the rider's legs are almost in a straight line with his body. Both reins are held in one hand, and the horse is directed by neck reining; that is, by applying the pressure of the rein against the horse's neck on the opposite side of that toward which it is to turn.

Aids. A skilled rider controls his mount by means of various signals, collectively called aids. The natural aids are signals transmitted to the horse by the legs, hands, and voice of the rider and by the shifting of his body weight in the saddle. Natural aids are often supplemented by artificial aids such as spurs and whips, which are used to reinforce learning, not to punish the horse.

To make a horse move forward, the rider squeezes his legs against the sides of the mount. Increasing pressure as well as voice commands are used to quicken the horse's pace. The horse is slowed, stopped, and made to back up by backward pressure on the reins.

Gaits. Most horses have three natural gaits, or series of foot movements: the walk, the trot, and the canter. An extended or faster canter is called a gallop. Each gait requires the rider to assume a slightly different posture. At a walk, he remains

467

HORSEMANSHIP

Gaits. Top: Walk, a slow, four-beat diagonal gait. Center: Left diagonal trot, a cadenced two-beat diagonal gait, the diagonal pair of legs moving simultaneously. Bottom: Right diagonal trot, the rider posting as the horse's right leg moves forward. Opposite page, top: Beginning of canter, a three-beat diagonal gait; the right fore foot leads, then the other fore foot and its diagonal hind foot, and finally the other hind foot. Center: Completion of canter; the left fore and right hind feet are leaving the ground, and the left hind foot will touch, completing the beat. Bottom: The gallop, a four-beat gait in which at certain phases all four feet are off the ground. Drawings in this series by Al Savitt

HORSEMANSHIP

erect in the saddle. In the trot, if he is riding an English saddle, he leans forward slightly and "posts", that is, he moves up and down with the horse's gait; on a Western saddle he presses his buttocks against the cantle and "sits" the trot. In the canter the rider leans slightly forward, shortens his reins, and moves gently with the horse's motion without rising from the saddle. At a gallop he leans even farther forward. *See* HORSE: *Gaits*.

HORSEMANSHIP

Stirrup

English Saddle

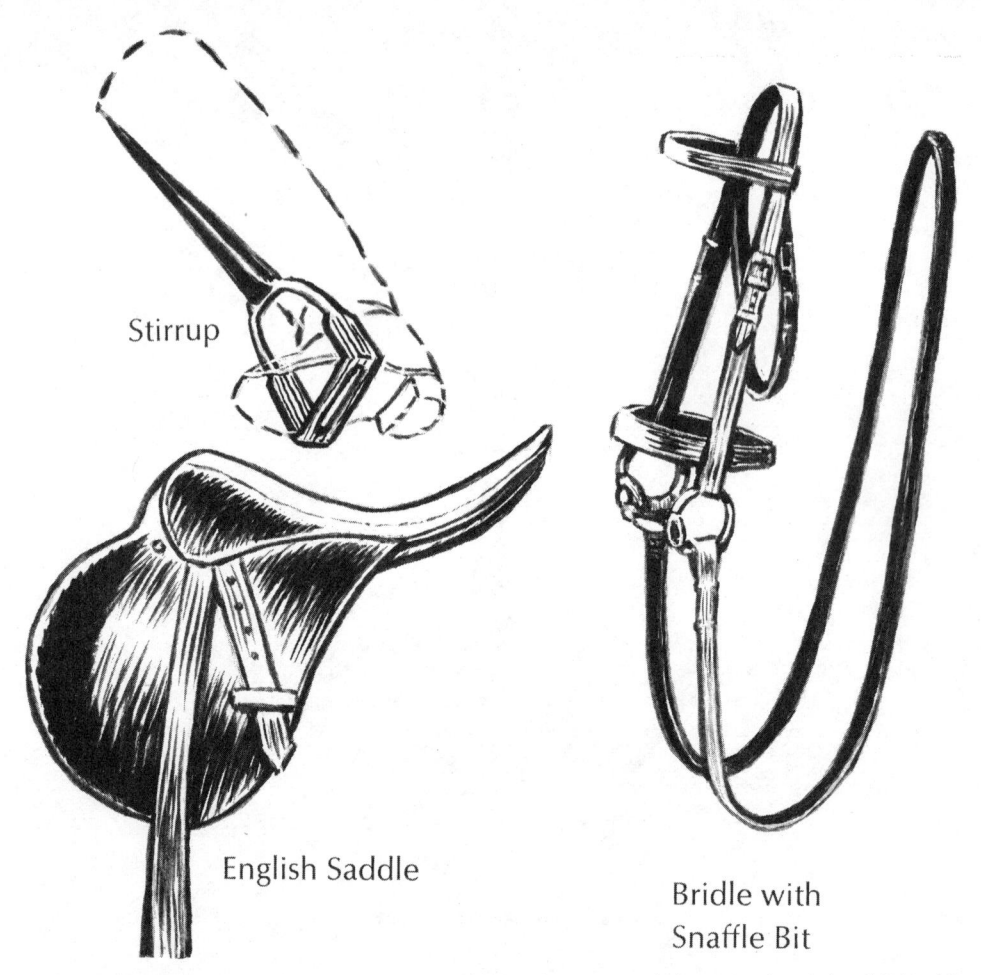

Bridle with Snaffle Bit

Basic riding equipment.

ADVANCED EQUITATION

Many types of advanced equitation are used when jumping, fox hunting, racing, working cow ponies, or showing gaited or so-called high school horses.

Jumping and Hunting. Jumping requires an English forward-seat saddle with knee rolls placed at the front of the saddle flaps for support, slightly shortened stirrups, and a galloping position in the saddle.

In training to jump, the horse is first taught to leap over small barriers while longeing riderless on a longe line (see *Elementary Training*, below). Then the rider mounts and puts the horse over these same barriers, first at a trot and then at a canter. The barriers are then raised, and the rider urges his mount toward each one at a faster pace, using his leg aids to encourage the horse at the takeoff and assisting the horse in keeping its balance in the air by shifting his own body weight.

In fox hunting, knowledge of the rules of the sport and ability to handle the horse over fences and brush in the field are necessary.

Racing. The racing seat of a jockey is an exaggeration of the forward seat. As a racehorse gathers speed and gallops in a straight line, the mount's center of balance moves forward. A jockey therefore crouches forward along the neck of the horse with his legs held high by very short stirrups. The crouching posture affords the added advantages of giving free play to the horse's hind legs, which supply the main impetus of its stride, and of creating less wind resistance than would an upright posture.

Working Cow Pony. By contrast, the cowboy's mount when pursuing cattle often follows an abruptly swerving, zigzag course. The horse's center of balance therefore lies slightly toward the back of its body, since it must remain poised

HORSEMANSHIP

to turn and stop quickly. Consequently, the cowboy sits relatively far back on his mount with legs extended, as in Western pleasure riding. This seat keeps the cowboy in balance with the horse during rapid changes of direction and enables the rider to brace himself against sudden stops. See COWBOYS.

Showing. In riding gaited horses, an English saddle without knee rolls must be used. The gaited horse must be collected or gathered, which means that through the raising of the mount's head and the flexing of the neck and jaw, the horse's hindquarters are brought under him so that he is more balanced, a state that enables him to change gaits with ease. The rider's legs and body are more or less straight up and down, and he uses long stirrups to maintain a centered balance.

In a gaited or pleasure class in a horse show the rider is expected to show the horse at different gaits in both directions around a fenced circular ring. At a trot he must post on the proper diagonal, sitting down on the saddle when the horse's inside front leg hits the ground and rising out of the saddle when the outside front leg is down. The horse must take the proper lead in a canter by presenting the inside front leg first. Most horses have naturally correct leads and alternate them with each change of direction. Others must be made to do so by use of leg and hand aids.

Dressage. The most advanced maneuvers of horsemanship are referred to collectively as *dressage* or *haute école* (high school), which are French terms denoting close control of the horse during complicated actions in which the rider delivers his commands through subtle movements of his hands, legs, and body weight. The purpose of dressage is to refine the coordination of horse and rider to a high degree, and to enable the rider to be complete master of his mount.

ELEMENTARY TRAINING

The training or breaking of a young horse to saddle or harness consists in gradually accustoming the animal to wearing various pieces of tack and then to carrying or pulling a weight. After a halter is put on the colt's head and a lead line is attached, the animal is encouraged to follow the trainer fearlessly, without balking; it then is made to stand quietly during handling or tying. By means of a long rope or "longe line" attached to the halter, the colt is controlled by the trainer from the ground with the help of a whip, and gradually learns to obey voice commands while walking or trotting in a circle; this procedure is known as "longeing."

The next step is to place the bit in the mouth and attach it to the halter until the colt becomes accustomed to the feel of it. Short lines or "side reins" are then run from the bit back to a piece of equipment called a surcingle, a strap encircling the body of the horse, after which longeing again takes place. This procedure sets the colt's head properly with neck arched and mouth on the bit. Then the full bridle is placed on the head, and long reins called "longe lines" are attached to the bit. The animal is again longed in a circle and "driven" from behind, learning obedience to the reins from the trainer on the ground. Finally, a saddle is placed on the colt's back during longeing so that the horse may become accustomed to weight. It is then time for the rider to mount quietly and begin to teach the proper aids and controls from a mounted position. When the colt performs correctly, rewards of carrots and tidbits are recommended.

The forcible breaking of older horses in which a horse, having no previous training, is bridled, saddled, and ridden, is regarded as primitive and unsatisfactory training.

ADVANCED TRAINING

Advanced training, as with advanced equitation, takes many forms. The training of racehorses and cow ponies is a highly specialized art, best accomplished by professional trainers. The horseman who rides for pleasure, however, should have the knowledge necessary to exercise a choice in training his horse to jump, hunt, behave in a show-ring, or learn the basic dressage maneuvers.

Showing. A horse trained for the show-ring must conduct itself in a quiet, collected manner and take the proper leads. In order to teach a horse to slow gait and rack (artificial rather than natural) gaits, the trainer must seesaw the reins from side to side, while simultaneously shifting his weight in the saddle until the horse learns to shift its weight from side to side in a manner similar to a pace, rather than diagonally as in the trot. If the class of showing requires jumping, the horse must change direction as the course specifies and execute each jump in turn.

Dressage. In dressage the horse must master a number of advanced maneuvers such as half and full turns on the proper lead, flying-lead changes at a canter, backing in a straight line, changing direction by sidestepping rather than by turning of the body, and collection and extension of the various gaits. Because these accomplishments are based on the natural movements of the horse, patience, skill, and repetition are the prime teaching factors.

HORSEMANSHIP

DRIVING
In recent years interest in pleasure driving has undergone a revival. Horses or ponies are driven singly or in pairs to carts, buggies, or one of many varieties of carriages. Teams of four are put to large road coaches. Most horses adapt well to driving.

Training. Training first involves driving horses on foot with longe lines. Then they are introduced to the harness, which comprises the bridle, long reins, saddle or back pad, and, around the neck or chest of the horse, a neck or breast collar to which are attached long straps called "traces" that draw the vehicle. The breeching, which fits around the horse's rump, aids in stopping and backing.

The next step involves putting the horse between the shafts of a training cart. The trainer then walks behind the vehicle, controlling the horse by means of the longe lines. When the horse becomes accustomed to pulling the weight of the vehicle, the trainer gets into the cart and drives the horse from the seat. A pacer or trotter is taught to draw a light two-wheeled cart called a racing sulky in much the same manner.

Driver. When the horse has learned to walk, trot, turn, stop, and back with the training cart, it is time to put the animal to a heavier vehicle of the driver's choice. The driver mounts the vehicle from the right side, holding the reins in his right hand and aiding himself up with his left. The reins are transferred to the left hand when the driver sits down. He sits erect with the reins in his left hand, keeping his right hand free to carry the whip and to help manipulate the reins during turns. He urges the horse forward with voice commands and signals with the reins or a touch of the whip.

Proper gaits in driving include a walk, a collected trot, and a faster, or park, trot. The horse is stopped and made to back by the same method as that used in riding.

CARE AND GROOMING
One of the most important adjuncts of horsemanship is the proper care of the mount, which includes its grooming, feeding, medical care, and shoeing. Grooming is a process designed to clean the horse and stimulate its skin. The first step in grooming is to rub, or curry, the horse's body with a rubber comb called a currycomb; the currycomb should be moved in small circles with emphasis on the direction of growth of the hair. The currying process loosens the hair and stimulates the flow of blood through the horse's skin. The horse's body, including its mane and tail, is then curried with a stiff brush, called a dandy brush, which removes loose hair and mud and smooths the horse's coat. Finally, the body and face of the horse are stroked with a soft brush which polishes the coat. Grooming also includes the cleaning of the mount's feet before and after each ride and the periodic removal of excess hair from its tail and mane.

After being ridden, the horse should be rubbed down with a handful of hay or sponged with cool water; it should then be curried, covered with a blanket, and walked until it is dry. If the mount is excessively hot and wet after being ridden, however, the rider should remove its saddle and bridle, cover it with a blanket, allow it to drink a small amount of water, and walk it until it dries off.

The proper feeding of a horse depends on its breed and on the type of work it performs. In general, a saddle horse which weighs about 1200 lbs. and which gets six hours of rigorous exercise daily should be fed three times a day; its meals should consist of 2 or 3 qts. of grain or sweet feed mixed with small amounts of corn and linseed meal. In addition, the horse should be fed bran mash once a week, just prior to its day of rest.

Any medical care given to a horse by its owner should be limited to treatment for minor ailments; more serious illnesses should be treated by a veterinarian. A horse should be treated for intestinal worms once a year, preferably in midwinter.

Proper shoeing is a highly important, although often neglected, aspect of horse care. The horse owner should choose his blacksmith with great care. The type of shoe used depends on such factors as the breed of horse, the type of work it does, and the way it habitually handles its feet.

See HORSE; HORSE RACING; HORSE RACING, FLAT; HORSE SHOWS.

HORSEPOWER, unit of power in the English system for measuring the rate at which an engine or other prime mover can perform mechanical work. It is usually abbreviated h.p., and its electrical equivalent in the United States is 746 watts, and the heat equivalent 2545 British thermal units (B.T.U.). The American horsepower is nearly equal to the English unit, which is defined as the amount of power required to lift 33,000 lb. 1 ft. in 1 min., or 550 ft.-lb. per sec.

The British engineer and inventor James Watt (q.v.) established this value for the horsepower after determining in practical tests that horses could haul coal at the average rate of 22,000 ft.-lb. per min. He then arbitrarily raised this figure by a factor of one half to establish the current value. In the metric system, 1 h.p. is sometimes called *force de cheval* or *cheval-vapeur,* and is defined as 4500 kg–m per min., which is equivalent to 32,549 ft.–lb. per min., or 0.986 of the English horsepower unit.

Three different horsepower values are used to quote the performance of an engine: (1) indicated horsepower is the theoretical efficiency of a reciprocating engine, which is determined from the pressure developed by the cylinders of the engine; (2) brake or shaft horsepower is more commonly used to indicate the practical ability of the engine, or the maximum performance, which is the indicated horsepower minus the power lost through heat, friction (qq.v.), and compression; (3) rated horsepower is the power that an engine or motor can produce efficiently for sustained periods of time.

Electrical motors are capable of surges of power far in excess of their rated horsepower; see DYNAMOELECTRIC MACHINERY. British automobile engines are classified in rated horsepower but their brake horsepower may be four to six times the rated horsepower. The power output of American automobile engines is quoted in brake horsepower, most being rated between 60 and 200 h.p.

HORSE RACING, contest of speed between two or more horses, usually thoroughbreds, which are driven or ridden over a special course. It is one of the most highly organized and commercialized sports. In general, four major types of horse racing are recognized, namely, flat racing, harness racing, steeplechasing, and hurdle racing.

Flat races are contested by saddle horses on a level track or course; see HORSE RACING, FLAT.

Harness races are contested by horses drawing light, two-wheeled carts called sulkies; in this type of race the horses must maintain one of two gaits, a trot or a pace; see HARNESS RACING.

Steeplechases are ridden over a variety of courses having a number of obstacles, such as fences, walls, and ditches, over which the horse must leap; see STEEPLECHASE.

Hurdle races resemble steeplechases, but only fences are used as obstacles.

Both steeplechasing and hurdle racing are popular chiefly in Great Britain, but such races are run occasionally on tracks and over cross-country courses in the United States. The usual steeplechase course is between 2 and 4 mi. long. No records are kept of the speed of steeplechasers or hurdle racers because the courses on which such races are run vary widely.

Besides the major types of horse racing, there are several other forms of contest, including wild-horse races, staged occasionally in rodeos, and quarter-horse races, which are short sprint races for the specially trained work horses used on cattle ranches.

HORSE RACING, FLAT, contest of speed between two or more horses, usually of the type known as thoroughbred (q.v.). The horses, ridden by jockeys, race on specially built tracks over distances ranging usually from 440 yd. to 1½ mi. The sport is called flat racing to differentiate it from the steeplechase (q.v.), which involves jumping over obstacles. For racing purposes, horses customarily are assigned to one of four classes based on their speed. In an effort to equalize the competition between horses of a given class, each animal is assigned a weight handicap based on such factors as its age, its sex, its previous record, and the experience of its jockey. In the southwestern part of the United States, sprint races for the quarter horse, a special breed, are popular; such horses are not recognized as thoroughbreds and compete only against one another.

Racing on horseback has been a popular sport since ancient times and is still a favorite pastime in most countries of the world. In the U.S. in the late 1960's, more than 42,750,000 people wagered about $3,600,000,000 on flat horse races. Other countries in which horse racing is especially popular are Great Britain, France, Italy, Argentina, Australia, Mexico, Canada, Brazil, Cuba, New Zealand, Germany, the Republic of South Africa, and the Soviet Union. Customarily, horse racing is a highly organized and closely controlled sport. The parent body of British racing is the Jockey Club of Great Britain; outstanding American racing bodies include the Jockey Club (which, through its office in New York City, handles the registration of all North American thoroughbreds), the Thoroughbred Racing Association, the National Association of State Racing Commissioners, and the Horsemen's Benevolent and Protective Association.

Horses. All the horses competing in organized flat racing are thoroughbreds, that is, the animals listed in the official national stud books, or registers of their countries. These registers contain the full pedigrees of the horses. Chief among these are the British, American, French, and Italian stud books. The British stud book was begun in 1791 and the American in 1873.

The blood lines of thoroughbreds are carefully traced. All thoroughbreds have as common ancestors one or more of three stallions, namely, the Byerly Turk, the Darley Arabian, and the Godolphin Barb, which were imported into Ireland and England from the Middle East between 1689

HORSE RACING, FLAT

Peytona defeating Fashion *in a famous $20,000 stake race, May 13, 1845, at Union Course; the track was located near Aqueduct Race track at Queens, Long Island, N.Y. (from a Currier & Ives print).*

Parke-Bernet Galleries

and 1724. The three stallions were named after their British owners and the lands of their origin, which were, respectively, Turkey, Syria, and the Barbary coast of north Africa. Because all three horses were swift but lacked endurance, they were mated with strong English mares; the offspring possessed both speed and strength. This method of interbreeding Arabian horses and English mares had been practiced since the 12th century.

The rules of the Jockey Club of Great Britian provide that no horse may be listed in the General Stud Book of the club unless its tap roots can be traced to one of the aforementioned three stallions. To facilitate tracing the lines of descent after much cross-breeding had taken place, three stallions were designated in the 19th century as sires from which the original lines could be followed. These three were Herod, a great-great-grandson, foaled in 1758, of the Byerly Turk; Eclipse (1764), a great-great-grandson of the Darley Arabian; and Matchem (1748), a grandson of the Godolphin Barb. All male lines of thoroughbreds can now be traced to at least one of the three designated sires: Herod, Eclipse, and Matchem.

The quarter horse, produced by mating thoroughbred stallions with domestic mares, is an American racing breed that originated in colonial times in Virginia and the Carolinas. Quarter horses are sturdily built, extremely muscular animals, not so tall as thoroughbreds but capable of running at great speeds for short distances. The typical quarter-horse race is run over a straight course of 2 furlongs, or 440 yd.

The average thoroughbred horse stands between 62 and 65 in. high, is about 8 ft. in length, and weighs between 900 and 1200 lb. when in racing condition. Thoroughbreds usually are in their competitive prime during the ages of three and four, although horses up to nineteen years of age have competed successfully. Both male and female thoroughbreds race in organized competition; some races are for horses of one sex only, but most races are open to entries of either sex. A female horse is known as a filly until its fifth birthday and as a mare thereafter. An unsexed male horse of any age is called a gelding; an ungelded male horse is known until its fifth birthday as a colt and afterward is referred to simply as a horse or a stallion, regardless of its age; when the first of its offspring wins a race, the stallion is thereafter called a sire.

A capable thoroughbred can run a mile in about 1 min. 40 sec. For the mile on an oval track the world record, set in 1968 by the American thoroughbred Dr. Fager, is 1 min. $32\frac{1}{5}$ sec.; over a straight course, the mile record, set in 1963 by the British thoroughbred Soueida, is 1 min. $31\frac{4}{5}$ sec.

In the U.S. each year, about 20,000 horses are raced and about 21,000 foals are registered with the Jockey Club. The purchase price of a thoroughbred suitable for racing or breeding purposes ranges from several thousand to several hundred thousand dollars. The earning power, however, of thoroughbreds during and after their active racing careers is high. Before retiring in 1966 the American champion Kelso, a gelding, won a total of $1,977,896. In 1967 the American thoroughbred Damascus, who in that year won honors as horse of the year and best three-year-old colt, set a record for single-season earnings with a total of $817,941. The highest price ever paid for a thoroughbred was $5,000,000, for the European champion Vaguely Noble, purchased by a syndicate of American breeders in 1968.

In the 1960's, syndicate buying of thoroughbreds became a widespread practice. Each member of such a syndicate bought an interest in a horse, usually between one-quarter and one-tenth share but sometimes even less. By the beginning of 1969, more than thirty of the horses thus syndicated had commanded sums in excess of $1,000,000. Estimated syndicate prices paid for the better-known stallions of this era included $4,800,000 for Buckpasser, $3,200,000 for Dr. Fager, and $2,560,000 for Damascus. High prices were also paid, often by syndicates, at auction sales for yearlings, a brood mare being auctioned for $235,000 in 1966 and a filly for $405,000 in 1968.

Champion stallions are of great value to their owners, not only because they often win considerable amounts of prize money but also because other horse owners and breeders pay substantial sums (called stud fees) for the privilege of mating their own brood mares with these stallions. The expectation is that the offspring (called get) will become champions also.

Tracks. Unlike the courts or playing fields used in many sports, the horse-racing tracks of the world are not uniform in construction or measurements. The race tracks of the two major horse-racing centers, Great Britain and the U.S., differ from each other markedly. For example, American courses have flat, level dirt tracks; British tracks have generally uneven grass or turf surfaces. The more important American tracks are usually 1-mi. ovals; British tracks are laid out in triangular or other shapes. Tracks in the U.S. are almost always surrounded by walls and a fee is charged for admission; in Great Britain many tracks have no walls and admission is free. The U.S. has 106 major tracks and Great Britain has about 70.

In races on American tracks the horses always race in a counter-clockwise direction. On British tracks, some races are counter-clockwise and some are clockwise.

In Great Britain and the U.S. great interest attaches to the running of three classic races (for three-year-olds), which are known in both countries as the Triple Crown. In Great Britain the Triple Crown events are the Epsom Derby, the St. Leger Stakes, and the Two Thousand Guineas races. The American Triple Crown comprises the Kentucky Derby, held at Churchill Downs, Louisville, Ky.; the Preakness Stakes, at Pimlico, near Baltimore, Md.; and the Belmont Stakes, usually run at Belmont Park, Elmont, N.Y. The winning of all three races in either country by a single horse is considered a high mark of achievement. Only eight horses have won the American Triple Crown: these thoroughbreds, together with the years of their victories, are Sir Barton (1919), Gallant Fox (1930), Omaha (1935), War Admiral (1937), Whirlaway (1941), Count Fleet (1943), Assault (1946), and Citation (1948).

Types of Races. Horse races are classified usually as stakes, handicap, allowance, or claiming competitions. The first two classes are for exceptionally fast horses; the others are for slower animals. Most of the major, nationally publicized races are stake or handicap events.

Track officials try to foster close competition within the four classes, notably by the imposition of weight handicaps of varying severity. Metal slugs are placed in the jockey's saddle; in some cases an outstanding horse carries 20 lb. more than its competitors. Most of the races held in the U.S. cover distances ranging from $\frac{3}{4}$ mi. (6 furlongs) to somewhat more than 1 mi. ($8\frac{1}{2}$ furlongs).

Stakes races, or sweepstakes, usually involve horses of the same age. All the horses are assigned the same weight handicap initially, but certain deductions from the handicap may be made later (fillies, for example, carry 5 lb. less

HORSE RACING, FLAT

when competing against colts, and horses ridden by inexperienced jockeys are given a similar advantage). Stakes races are so named from the substantial stake, or entry fee, the owner must pay. The stakes, together with the purse contributed by the track, constitute a pool from which prize money is paid to the winners of the race.

Handicap races are competitions among horses of various ages, usually more than two years. The racing secretary of the track assigns to the entries the weight handicaps he believes will equalize their chances. The horse considered fastest is assigned the highest weight and the slower horses receive proportionately smaller handicaps. The jockey's weight is computed as part of the total weight carried by the horse.

In allowance races the entries are graded on their past records, that is, the amount of money earned previously and the number of races won. Races within the allowance class are graded on a scale from A to F, and horses of approximately the same ability are matched against each other in the appropriate grade.

Claiming races are for horses of presumably inferior speed whose owners wish to sell them. The selling price of the horse is posted before each race, whereupon a buyer may claim the horse at the announced price. The buyer must take possession of the horse after the race is run, regardless of its performance in the race. Experts often purchase at bargain prices claim-

Near the finish line at Belmont Park, Elmont, N.Y., one of the best-known American race tracks.
New York Racing Assn.

HORSE RACING, FLAT

ing horses whose owners underestimate their potential.

Horse races follow a highly organized procedure. Just before the start of a race the jockeys guide their horses into individual stalls within a starting gate located on the starting line. When the horses are evenly aligned in the stalls the starter presses a button, the gates of the stalls swing open, and the horses bolt forward. In Great Britain the horses are started with the aid of a barrier of canvas webbing rather than a starting gate.

As the race proceeds, various track officials follow the action closely through binoculars to detect possible fouls. Motion pictures of the race are made at all major race tracks as an additional means of detecting infractions of racing rules. As the horses cross the finish line, their relative positions are recorded in a still photograph that is inspected by the judges and is later displayed to the spectators. The running time for each race is measured by an electric timer, a device that virtually eliminates subjective error.

Betting. Betting is an important element in the popularity of horse racing. At different times four main types of betting have been in vogue: simple betting between individuals; sweepstakes betting, in which large entry fees, or stakes, are pooled and awarded to the winners; bookmaking, in which a speculator offers odds against each horse and accepts bets against his predictions; and pari-mutuel betting, which is the system used at the major American tracks. The designation "pari-mutuel" is a French phrase translatable as "betting among ourselves". Under the pari-mutuel system, which was developed in France during the 1860's, the betting odds on a given horse are derived from a comparison between the total amount wagered on the horse and the total wagered on all the horses in the race. The odds are computed automatically by a device called a totalizer or totalizator, and they are flashed onto a lighted totalizer board, or "tote board", which is clearly visible to the spectators. When the race begins, betting ends and the totalizer is locked; when the race is over, the machine computes the payoff on the winning horses. Pari-mutuel bettors can wager that a horse will win (come in first), place (come in second), or show (come in third). The highest return on record for a pari-mutuel bet made in the U.S. is $1,885.50 for $2 to win was paid at a Kentucky track in 1912.

Much betting is also done on the basis of combinations, that is, combining bets on more than one horse. Among prevalent combinations are the daily double, the quinella (or quiniella), and the exacta. To win the widely popular daily double, a bettor must predict the winners of two consecutive races at a track (usually the first two races of the day); he buys a combination ticket denoting his choices before either race has begun. To win a quinella, it is necessary to predict the first two horses in a single race, without regard to the order in which they finish. To win an exacta, the bettor must specify the exact order in which the first two horses in a race will finish. The highest return on record for a bet on a daily double is $12,724.80 for $2; the betting took place at Agua Caliente, Mexico, on July 4, 1954.

History. The known history of flat racing on mounted horses dates from the first millennium B.C. Previously, no breed of horse hardy enough to carry human riders for significant distances had been developed, although horse-drawn chariots were in common use. The first formal, mounted horse race known to history took place in Greece about 624 B.C. In Roman times, horse races occasionally were held, although chariot races were much more frequent. After the fall of Rome in the 5th century A.D., horse breeding and racing declined in the West.

In the 6th century A.D., horseback riding was introduced throughout the Middle East by Muslim missionaries, who traveled on horseback as they sought converts. When the Arabs conquered Spain in the 8th century they rode, and were drawn in vehicles by, strong, swift horses of a breed previously unknown in Europe. The fame of the Arabian steeds spread throughout Europe in subsequent centuries. In 1110, Henry I (q.v.), King of England imported an Arabian stallion from Spain; the stallion and other Arabian horses were later mated with strong but slow English mares to breed swift, hardy horses suitable for warfare. Informal races between purebred mounts over straight 4-mi. courses became popular. In 1174, Smithfield Track, the first public race course built since Roman times, was constructed in London. Saddle racing subsequently became a featured sport at most English fairs and a favorite pastime of English royalty and nobility. Among the monarchs who raced purebred mounts was James I (q.v.), who helped to establish racing at Epsom Downs, near the town of Epsom and Ewell, and at Newmarket, a town near Cambridge. Another English monarch, King Charles II (q.v.), who also patronized racing at Newmarket, was known as "the father of the British turf".

In 1665 the first race track in North America was built on Long Island by the English soldier and royal governor of New York, Richard Nicolls

HORSE RACING, FLAT

(q.v.). The first race at the track probably took place in 1666.

The Darley Arabian was brought to Yorkshire from Aleppo, Syria, in 1704. About 1730 the British stallion Bulle Rock, a descendant of the Darley Arabian, arrived in the colony of Virginia. Subsequently, scores of purebred British mares and stallions were imported, raced, and bred. The colonies most actively engaged in racing and breeding were New York, Pennsylvania, Virginia, Maryland, and the Carolinas.

Interest in horse racing continued unabated in the 19th century. Races then were run in three heats over a straight, 4-mi. course. In the late 19th century one-heat races over 4-mi. distances were popular; one-heat races over shorter distances on oval tracks finally became the rule.

In 1894 the Jockey Club, an American organization modeled on the British Jockey Club, was incorporated in New York City. The club was formed to encourage the breeding of thoroughbred horses and the maintenance of high ethical standards in horse racing. Although it did not wield authority comparable to that of the British club, the American Jockey Club exerted a strong, constructive influence on racing and breeding standards throughout the U.S. It drew up a code that became the basis of American racing procedure and conduct, it took over the American Stud Book in 1896, and it subsequently maintained the bureau of registry for all American thoroughbreds.

During the 20th century the popularity of horse racing increased in most parts of the world. In the U.S. a wave of reformist sentiment caused authorities to outlaw bookmaking in many States; most of the same States, however, later legalized pari-mutuel betting, partly because large revenues were easily obtainable through State taxes on the system. Most States with legal pari-mutuel systems also assumed control of local racing activity by creating racing commissions. The existence of these commissions slowly diminished the influence of the Jockey Club.

The American racing scene was dominated in 1919–20 by the sensational performance of the American colt Man o' War. He set American track records and was defeated only once in twenty-one starts. Man o' War was retired to stud in 1921 after amassing $249,465 in winnings.

During the 1930's winter racing, particularly in Florida and California, emerged as a major industry and horse racing became a year-round activity in the U.S. The industry continued to expand during the 1930's and 1940's, creating a need for a centralized national authority. In March, 1942, the Thoroughbred Racing Association of the U.S. was founded in Chicago; the organization, which adopted a stringent code of standards aimed at encouraging a high level of ethics in racing, eventually became the governing body of fifty-six major tracks, including seven in Canada.

HORSERADISH, common name of a tall perennial herb, *Armoracia rusticana*, belonging to the Mustard family. The herb is native to E. Europe and is cultivated all over Europe and the United States. It has very large, lance-shaped leaves, 4 to 12 in. long and often notched. The plant ranges in height from 18 to 30 in. Each of the small, white flowers comprises four sepals, four petals, six stamens, and a two-celled pistil. The fruit is a globe-shaped pod. The pungent roots of horseradish are ground for use as a condiment. If used immediately, ground horseradish root need not be preserved, but bottled horseradish is usually preserved in vinegar. Horseradish is used as a base for other condiments and sauces, in combination with ground beets, mustard, catsup, or thick, bland sauces.

HORSESHOE AND QUOIT PITCHING, two similar games, the essential features of which are the tossing or throwing of a horseshoe or quoit, usually made of iron or steel, at a pin, peg, or stake. The object of the game is to ring the pin or to throw the horseshoe or quoit as close to the pin as possible.

Horseshoe pitching is played on a court 50 ft. long and 10 ft. wide. Iron stakes extending 14 in. above the ground are planted 40 ft. apart. The pitching distance is 40 ft. for men and 30 ft. for women and children; for quoits the distances are 30 ft. and 20 ft. respectively. The horseshoe, an oval-shaped plate of steel or iron with an open end 3½ in. wide, is a maximum of 7⅝ in. long and 7¼ in. wide, and must not weigh more than 40 oz. The game is played by two or four contestants. Each player takes his position at one stake and throws two horseshoes at the other stake. A ringer is made when the thrown horseshoe encloses the stake; it counts three points in scoring. If no player throws a ringer, one point is scored for the shoe closest to the stake. Fifty points wins the game. In the United States the sport is regulated by the National Horseshoe Pitchers Association of America, which was incorporated in 1921. Under its auspices world championships for men and women are held annually.

In the game of quoits, ring-shaped pieces of iron known as quoits are tossed from a line or mark at a pin or peg that is 1 in. high. In the 20th century the use of a rubber quoit has increasingly replaced the metal type, because of accidents from flying pieces of metal as the quoit hits the peg. In the version of the game known as deck quoits, played on shipboard, the quoit is made of rope.

The games of quoits and horseshoe pitching may have originated when soldiers in the Roman army first started to shoe their horses. Both games were brought to colonial America by the English. During the American Revolution period horseshoe pitching was widely played by soldiers of the American army. In the 20th century the game of quoits has practically disappeared in the U.S., while horseshoe pitching has gained in popularity.

HORSESHOE BEND NATIONAL MILITARY PARK, site in east-central Alabama, about 90 miles s. of Birmingham, commemorating the victory on March 24, 1814, of General Andrew Jackson (q.v.) over the Creek Indian Nation; *see* CREEK. Jackson's reputation as an Indian fighter began with his victory at the Battle of Horseshoe Bend. The treaty following the battle ended the Creek War (1813–14) and opened to white settlement about 20,000,000 acres of land in Alabama and Georgia. The park is administered by the National Park Service (q.v.).

HORSESHOE CRAB. *See* KING CRAB.

HORSESHOE FALLS. *See* NIAGARA FALLS (waterfall).

HORSE SHOWS, public exhibitions in which trained horses compete with each other in executing difficult jumps or various intricate maneuvers. The horses are guided by handlers on foot, or they are ridden or driven. The purpose of a horse show is to display purebred horses to breeders, exhibitors, and the generally interested public. Show horses are broadly designated as either breeding-class or performance animals. A breeding-class horse is judged largely on its appearance and movements while being led by a dismounted handler; a performance-class horse is rated largely on its ability to perform such tasks as drawing a manned vehicle or jumping over obstacles while carrying a rider. Performance-class events simulate conditions encountered in hunting, police work, or other pursuits for which the particular horses have been trained.

Horses competing in major shows are assigned to one of the main divisions into which the events of the show are grouped. These divisions include the hunter-and-jumper, light-harness, polo, stock-horse, and draft-horse classifications, which are further subdivided into classes based on such factors as age, size, and ability. In each classification the competing horses are expected to display their mastery of various characteristic skills. For example, in certain events of the hunter-and-jumper category the entries are required to leap across obstacles such as a high wooden rail flanked on either side by two lower rails; in the polo division entries must display ability to wheel, stop short, and perform other maneuvers called for in polo matches; and in the light-harness division, pacers or trotters must draw a four-wheeled wagon equipped for a long road trip.

The criteria by which show judges rate horses include conformation (height, weight, and form of the animal); quality, or degree of refinement in build; substance, or soundness of bone and muscle; condition, or health, training, and fitness; and temperament, or emotional adequacy. In the so-called equitation or horsemanship events the rider is rated for his performance, which includes ring manners and general control of the horse; the mount is not rated in these events.

Horse shows are popular internationally, notably in the United States, Canada, Mexico, Brazil, France, Great Britain, Ireland, Italy, the Netherlands, Sweden, Switzerland, and West Germany. They are usually gala affairs attended by large numbers of people. The outstanding American show is the National Horse Show, which takes place annually at Madison Square Garden, New York City, and features international jumping as one of the special events. Numerous shows are sponsored annually throughout the U.S. by various State fairs and by associations of horse breeders. Other important shows include the Canadian National Exhibition and the Royal Agricultural Winter Fair, held in Toronto, Canada; the Olympia Horse Show, held in London, England; and the Dublin Horse Show, held near Dublin, Republic of Ireland. A special form of horse show, comprising various types of equestrian competition, is a feature of the Olympic Games (q.v.). Rodeos are an informal and, for the most part, American type of horse show; *see* RODEO.

History. The staging of horse shows, in one form or another, dates from ancient times. Chariots and mounted soldiers were a prominent feature of the parades and military reviews of antiquity. Equestrian displays and competitions were featured in the early Olympic Games in Greece and in various public celebrations in ancient Rome. Public displays of horses and horsemanship reached a high point in the Middle Ages. During that period large crowds attended

HORSETAIL

tournaments in which armored knights wielding lances jousted with each other and otherwise exhibited their equestrian skills; these skills became known collectively as *haut école*, a French phrase denoting a high or advanced form of horsemanship. Exhibitions of *haut école* have survived in the performances of the famed Spanish Riding School in Vienna. The style practiced there originated in the *manège*, or covered riding ring, of the 17th century and follows rules laid down at that time. In the exhibitions, extremely intricate and difficult movements are executed by Lippizaners, a breed originally developed as imperial carriage horses. Throughout the Middle Ages and into modern times, country horse fairs, at which prospective buyers could inspect the horses of a given region, were common events.

Horse shows and displays in North America date from the early 18th century, when purebred horses were imported from Great Britain into Virginia and other American colonies. In 1883 the National Horse Show was inaugurated in New York City. About 300 horses, including thoroughbreds, delivery-wagon horses, mounted policemen's steeds, and Shetland ponies, performed or were exhibited at the first shows.

During the 1890's the National Horse Show was patronized by the fashionable, wealthy classes of New York City; it soon became an outstanding social event. In the first decade of the 20th century the number of horse shows given throughout the U.S. increased steadily; this circumstance led in 1917 to the founding of the American Horse Shows Association, the governing body of the sport in the U.S. The National Horse Show was not held in 1943, 1944, and 1945 because of World War II. Since that time the sport has become increasingly popular. In the late 1960's the American Horse Shows Association held approximately 800 annual shows under its jurisdiction.

See Horse; Horsemanship; Horse Racing; Horse Racing, Flat.

HORSETAIL, common name of the genus of perennial, flowerless plants *Equisetum*, the only surviving genus of the subphylum Sphenopsida. During the Carboniferous Period some sphenopsids attained tree size. Present-day sphenopsids are mostly small, siliceous, vascular plants with jointed stems and whorls of microphylls. Sporangia are borne on sporangiophores arranged into a conelike strobilus. Unbranched species of *Equisetum* are popularly referred to as scouring rushes. See Botany: *Classification;* Pteridophyta.

HORTENSIUS, Quintus (114–50 B.C.), Roman lawyer and orator. Soon after his admittance to the bar at the age of nineteen, he won a reputation by successfully defending Nicomedes III, king of the Roman dependency of Bithynia (r. 91–74 B.C.), against the charge of corrupt administration. Hortensius was one of the leaders of the aristocratic party, and rose to become consul in 69. Until the year 70 he was considered unequaled as an orator. In that year, however, he was opposed by the Roman orator and statesman Marcus Tullius Cicero (q.v.), in the case of the Sicilian governor, Gaius Verres (d. 43 B.C.). Hortensius attempted to defend Verres against charges of cruelty and dishonesty in office, but Verres was convicted on the basis of Cicero's first speech. Later, however, Cicero joined the same party as Hortensius, and the two lawyers often worked together in court.

HORTHY, Miklós von Nagybánya (1868–1957), Hungarian admiral and statesman, born in Kenderes, and educated at the Naval Academy of Fiume (now Rijeka, Yugoslavia). During World War I he rose to become admiral of the Austro-Hungarian navy. After the war he returned to Hungary and organized a counter-revolution against the Bolshevist government of Béla Kun (q.v.). Horthy was made commander in chief of the Hungarian armed forces in 1919, and in 1920 the National Assembly elected him regent. As regent, he defeated attempts of Charles I (q.v.), Emperor of Austria and former king of Hungary, to regain the throne, a move in which Horthy was supported by the Hungarian government. Under his regime, Hungary became the first post-World War I nationalist dictatorship in Europe (q.v.), ruthlessly suppressing all political opposition. At the same time, revisionism was made official policy; the peace treaty of Trianon (q.v.) was denounced, and the return of the territories lost after the war was demanded.

Through Horthy's efforts, Hungary joined the Axis Powers (q.v.) in 1940; in 1944, when the tide of World War II turned against the Axis Powers and Horthy attempted to make a separate peace between Hungary and the Allies, Hungary was occupied by German troops, and Horthy was deposed as regent. He disappeared, reportedly as a prisoner of the Germans, until the following year, when he was captured in Bavaria by the United States Army. He was held in protective custody until the end of 1945, and was then released. He did not return to Hungary, but continued to interest himself in Hungarian politics. See Hungary: *History.*